Royal Commission into the poor law

Poor Law Union and Lunacy Inquiry (Ireland)

Royal Commission into the poor law

Poor Law Union and Lunacy Inquiry (Ireland)

ISBN/EAN: 9783741104503

Manufactured in Europe, USA, Canada, Australia, Japa

Cover: Foto ©ninafisch / pixelio.de

Manufactured and distributed by brebook publishing software (www.brebook.com)

Royal Commission into the poor law

Poor Law Union and Lunacy Inquiry (Ireland)

POOR LAW UNION

AND

LUNACY INQUIRY COMMISSION (IRELAND).

REPORT AND EVIDENCE

WITH

APPENDICES.

Presented to both Houses of Parliament by Command of Her Majesty.

DUBLIN:
PRINTED BY ALEXANDER THOM, 87 & 88, ABBEY-STREET,
PRINTER TO THE QUEEN'S MOST EXCELLENT MAJESTY.
FOR HER MAJESTY'S STATIONERY OFFICE.

1879.

[C.—2239.] *Price 8s.*

CONTENTS.

COMMISSIONS.

By the Lords Justices General and General Governors of Ireland.

J. T. BALL, C.

HEDGES EYRE CHATTERTON.

WHEREAS, under the provisions of certain statutes now in force, unions have been formed for the relief of the destitute poor in Ireland, and workhouses have been provided in the said unions for the reception of the sick and destitute poor.

AND WHEREAS it appears unto Us expedient that an inquiry should be held in regard to the number of Poor-Law Unions and Workhouses in Ireland, and to the provision now made for the relief of the sick and destitute poor in workhouses and hospitals, and whether any changes in that respect are necessary or desirable.

Now We, the Lords Justices General and General Governors of Ireland, do hereby nominate and appoint you, Major the Hon. W. LE POER TRENCH, R.E., ANDREW DOYLE, late Local Government Board Inspector in England, and SHARMAN CRAWFORD, late Local Government Board Inspector in Ireland, or any one or more of you to proceed with the utmost despatch, to inquire into and investigate and report on the following subjects:—

1. Whether having due regard to the extent and population of the present Poor Law Unions in Ireland, the necessities of the sick and destitute poor therein, and the proper administration of the Poor Law it would be expedient that any such Poor Law Unions should be dissolved and amalgamated with adjoining Poor Law Unions: and, if so, which of the present Poor Law Unions should be so dissolved, and what portions thereof should be annexed to adjacent Poor Law Unions.

2. Whether having regard to the fact, that each dispensary district should lie wholly within one Poor Law Union, it will be necessary in carrying out the changes that may be recommended under Clause I. to re-arrange any of the present dispensary districts; and, if so, which of the dispensary districts must be so altered, and in what manner should the electoral divisions now comprised therein be dealt with and re-arranged.

3. Whether it would be proper and advisable, in any case or cases to be specified, without making any alteration in the boundaries of the Poor Law Unions, to dispense wholly or in part with existing workhouses, and to provide suitable and convenient accommodation in other adjacent workhouses for the whole, or for any class of the sick or destitute poor of the Poor Law Union the workhouses of which are wholly or in part dispensed with: and, if so, to what particular workhouse or workhouses paupers might be transferred, and under what system, in relation to management, cost of maintenance and other charges such an arrangement might be advantageously and conveniently carried out, and what provision should be made for the conveyance of the aged sick and infirm to and from the workhouses in which they may be relieved.

4. Whether additional workhouse or hospital accommodation is now required in any, and, if so, in what Poor Law Unions, for the adequate relief of the destitute poor, and especially of the sick poor, on account of their great distance from the workhouses of their respective unions.

5. Whether in the event of any Poor Law Union being dissolved, or if any workhouse being dispensed with, wholly or in part, the workhouse of the Poor Law Union so dissolved or the workhouse so dispensed with, or part thereof, might be made available for the reception and treatment of the lunatic poor, or for any other purposes: and

6. Generally to inquire into, and investigate whether any and what changes are required in the existing distribution of destitute poor, and especially children, throughout the workhouses in Ireland.

And We do hereby authorize you, and every one or more of you, by all lawful and proper ways and means, to make full inquiry into the matters aforesaid, in such places in Ireland as to you may seem necessary or convenient. And, for the better enabling you to make the said investigation, We hereby grant unto you, or any one or more of you, full authority for all or any of the purposes aforesaid, to call and examine before you, or any one or more of you, such persons as you shall judge necessary and competent, by whom you may be the better informed on the matters herein submitted for your consideration, and also to call for and examine all such books, documents, papers and records as you shall judge likely to afford you the fullest information on the subject of this Commission, and otherwise to inquire of, and concerning the premises, and every part thereof, by all reasonable ways and means.

And We enjoin that you, or any two of you, upon the examination of the premises do, as soon as can reasonably be, after the date of this Commission, and on or before First day of February, 1878, or such later day as may hereafter be appointed, certify and report to Us, in writing, under your hands and seals respectively, what you shall have done and may find concerning the premises, upon such inquiry and investigation as aforesaid, together with your opinions touching and concerning the several matters hereby referred for your consideration. And We do hereby direct that you, or any one or more of you, may have liberty from time to time to certify your several proceedings to Us, as the same shall be respectively completed and perfected, and for so doing this shall be your warrant.

Given at Her Majesty's Castle of Dublin, this 17th day of July, 1877.

Thomas H. Burke.

By the Lord Lieutenant-General and General Governor of Ireland.

Marlborough.

Whereas it has been represented to us by you, Major the Honorable W. Le Poer Trench, Andrew Doyle, and Sharman Crawford, the Commissioners named in the annexed warrant, bearing date the 17th day of July, 1877, and we are satisfied that it is necessary in order satisfactorily to complete the inquiry, and make the certificate and Report thereby directed, that the time therein appointed for the purposes aforesaid should be extended;

And whereas it appears to us expedient that in addition to the several subjects into which you, the said Commissioners, are directed by the said warrant to inquire, certain further inquiries, hereinafter mentioned, should be made by you;

Now We, John Winston, Duke of Marlborough, Lord Lieutenant-General and General Governor of Ireland, do hereby direct and appoint that the time named in the annexed warrant for completing the inquiry, and making the certificate and Report thereby directed, and doing the several other acts and things in the said warrant appearing shall be extended to, and shall include the 15th day of May, 1878, or such later day as we may hereafter appoint, and we order and declare that the said annexed warrant shall henceforth be of the same force, and have the same effect in all respects as if the 15th* day of May, 1878, had been therein appointed in the premises instead of the 1st day of February, 1878;

And we do hereby further direct and appoint that you, the said Honorable W. Le Poer Trench, Andrew Doyle, and Sharman Crawford, or any one or more of you shall inquire into, and investigate and report on the provisions at present made and existing in Ireland for the care, relief, and treatment of the poor who are lunatic, or idiotic, or imbecile in mind, or who are otherwise suffering from mental disease, and whether it would be expedient, proper, and advisable to make additional and other provision for the care, relief, and treatment of such poor as aforesaid; and if so, in what manner and by what means such additional or other provision should be made, and we do hereby direct and appoint that you, and every one or more of you, for the better enabling you to make the said investigation, shall have the same powers and authorities as are given to you and every one or more of you by the said warrant, in respect of the inquiries thereby directed, and shall include, in the certificate and report which by the said annexed warrant you or any two of you are enjoined to make, what you shall have done and may find concerning the premises upon such inquiry and investigation as aforesaid, together with your opinions touching and concerning the same.

Given at Her Majesty's Castle of Dublin, this 1st day of February, 1878.

By His Grace's Command,

T. H. Burke.

* His Grace was pleased to grant a further extension of the time here assigned to the Commissioners for the completion of their inquiry and Report, to the 15th February, 1879, by letters patent bearing date the 15th August, 1877, and 1st January, 1878, respectively.

LIST OF WITNESSES.

POOR LAW UNION AND LUNACY INQUIRY COMMISSION (IRELAND).

REPORT.

TO HIS GRACE JOHN WINSTON DUKE OF MARLBOROUGH, K.G., LORD LIEUTENANT-GENERAL AND GOVERNOR-GENERAL OF IRELAND.

MAY IT PLEASE YOUR GRACE,

THEIR Excellencies the Lords Justices having been pleased to issue a warrant, bearing date the 17th day of July 1877, authorising and directing us, or any one or more of us, to inquire into and investigate and report upon the following subjects:—

I. Whether it would be expedient that any Poor Law Union in Ireland should be dissolved and amalgamated with the adjoining ones;

II. Whether it would be proper and advisable, without making any alteration in the boundaries of the Poor Law Unions, to dispense wholly or in part with existing workhouses, and to provide suitable and convenient accommodation in adjacent workhouses for the whole or any part of the sick and destitute poor of the Poor Law Unions the workhouses of which are wholly and in part dispensed with;

III. Whether additional workhouse or hospital accommodation is now required in any Poor Law Unions;

IV. Whether in the event of any workhouse being wholly or in part dispensed with the accommodation afforded thereby might be made available for the treatment of the lunatic poor or for any other purpose; and

V. Generally to inquire into and ascertain whether any and what changes are required in the existing distribution of the destitute poor, and especially children, throughout Ireland;

And your Grace, having been pleased by endorsements on the above-mentioned warrant to extend the time for completing the inquiry, and to direct us further to inquire into and investigate and report—

VI. Whether any additional and other provision is required for the better care, relief, and treatment of the poor who are lunatic, idiotic, or imbecile in mind, or otherwise afflicted with mental disease:

We have now the honour to submit for your Grace's consideration the following Report of our proceedings, together with a statement of the conclusions at which we have arrived upon the several matters thus remitted to us for inquiry.

In order to ascertain, in the first instance, the views of the several boards of guardians throughout Ireland upon the subjects referred to us for inquiry, and upon which a few only had adopted any resolution, we addressed to them a list of queries (Appendix A 1), inviting them to state their opinion as to the expediency of dissolving their union, or of dispensing with their workhouse, or of providing additional hospital accommodation. Upon these subjects we have taken care that the fullest opportunity should be afforded to every board of guardians in the country to express their opinion.

We also addressed a similar list of queries to the inspectors of the local government board (Appendix A 2), to whose opinions great weight must be attached on all matters connected with the practical administration of the poor law.

From the clerks of the several boards of guardians we obtained various statistical returns, and other information bearing upon the subjects of our inquiry.

We also addressed communications to the several boards of governors of district lunatic asylums, as well as to the medical superintendents of those establishments. App. C., 6-7.

We reproduce in the Appendix the most material part of the information elicited by these communications.

We afterwards proceeded separately to visit the union workhouses throughout Ireland to make ourselves acquainted with such circumstances in each union as might assist us in the special objects of our inquiry. We also visited the several district lunatic asylums, and conferred with the resident medical superintendents, with a view of obtaining by personal inquiry such information as would enable us to carry out more fully the instructions contained in your Grace's warrant. With a like object we addressed queries to the medical superintendents of the asylums, a copy of which, as well of the replies received, will be found in the Appendix (C 6, p. 229.)

In reply to the inquiry addressed to the guardians, whether they desired that the union which they represented should be dissolved, and the several electoral divisions be annexed to adjacent unions, we received from 104 unions, as will be seen from the return in the Appendix, replies in the negative, and from 11 unions in the affirmative. Before deciding upon holding a formal Inquiry in any union the guardians of which had expressed an opinion in favour of dissolution, we deemed it advisable to confer with the guardians upon the subject. Of the following unions, the guardians, upon reconsideration of the facts submitted to them, rescinded the resolution in favour of dissolution which they had previously passed, viz., Ardee, Baltinglass, Cookstown, Newport, and Portumna, the guardians of the Gortin union deciding not to press their resolution. The unions of Mill-street, Glenamaddy, Belmullet, and Skull only adhered to their original resolutions. In the cases of the two latter unions we did not consider a formal inquiry necessary, for reasons assigned in our letters to those boards, which will be found in the Appendix (pages 97, 100.)

App. A 1, p. 97.

We were thus enabled to obviate the necessity of a formal inquiry in the cases of unions desiring their own dissolution, except in the unions of Mill Street and Glennamaddy.

In the case of Oughterard the guardians applied for the dissolution of the union, but subsequently resolved that in case the dissolution of the union should be found to be impracticable, certain buildings attached to the workhouse might be appropriated as an auxiliary lunatic asylum. Owing to the distance of some electoral divisions from the workhouses of adjoining unions, and the crowded state of the workhouse of the Galway union, the proposed dissolution would be impracticable. At the same time, there are certain electoral divisions in the Oughterard union referred to in the letter of Mr. Wm. Burke, (Appendix A 4, p. 129,) which, in our opinion, might be advantageously transferred to the Ballinrobe union. That, however, is a question for the consideration and decision of the Local Government Board. The objection to such a transfer, that it would involve a great reduction in valuation, a careful inquiry would show is founded upon an error of a very important nature which exists in that and several other unions, the valuation for rateable purposes as we have observed in our reply to a similar application from the guardian of the Belmullet union, being far below the present actual value. To this question of valuation we refer in another part of this Report. Twenty-three unions proposed the dissolution of other unions, allocating the electoral divisions among those adjacent. With regard to these, we selected for the purpose of special inquiry the unions of Cavan, Monaghan, Mill-street, and Ennis. The evidence taken at these inquiries will be found in the Appendix.

Several boards of guardians, although opposed to amalgamation, expressed a desire to extend the limits of their unions by the transfer to them of one or more electoral divisions of adjacent unions. To such applications we uniformly replied that the power of revising the boundaries of unions was vested in the Local Government Board, and the expediency of doing so in any particular case was not within the scope of our inquiry, which was directed specially to ascertain whether it would be expedient to dissolve any union and to amalgamate the electoral divisions comprised in it with adjoining unions.

Although so few boards of guardians have declared themselves in favour of "amalgamation," it would be an error to conclude from that fact that there does not exist amongst a considerable number of ratepayers and of minorities on boards of guardians a strong feeling that such a change would be attended with advantage. The movement in favour of it might be easily revived if the objections to it, as well as the arguments in favour of it, were not fairly stated and fully considered.

The causes which have led to these applications for "amalgamation," or, in other words, for extension of areas of unions, will be made clearer, and the probable consequences of such a change will be better understood, if we refer briefly to the state of things immediately preceding the introduction of a Poor Law into Ireland, to the principle upon which that law was founded, and to the history of its earlier as well as of its later administration.

The period that preceded 1829 was little favourable to the consideration of any measures that affected only the material or physical condition of the poorer classes of the Irish people. Public attention was engrossed by other interests of a wholly different character. Soon after, however, the condition of the labouring population began to excite grave apprehension, a new source of distress, and therefore of danger, being added to those which had prevailed for so long a time. The abolition of the lowest political franchise having extinguished one, and perhaps the strongest, motive for the minute subdivision of land, the consequent consolidation of small holdings came to aggravate the evils that the creation of those small holdings had produced. As Ireland was without any legal provision for the relief of destitution, differing in that respect from every other country in Europe, eviction from his potato plot meant for the peasant and his family "actual starvation." Hence the tenacity with which the occupier of a few roods of land kept hold of them in spite of law and in defiance of the right of property.

Mr. Drummond, writing to the magistrates of Tipperary in 1838, remarks—

"The deficiency of a demand for labour, and the want as yet of any legal provision against utter destitution, leave this humble class, when ejected, without any certain protection against actual starvation. Hence the wholesale expulsion of cottier tenants from their holdings is unfortunately found, with the great body of the people, to establish the strongest feelings—those of self-preservation—on the side even of guilt in vindication of what they falsely assume to be their rights."

Although the voluminous evidence collected at different times by various official inquiries into the causes of distress and crime had shown but too plainly the extent and intensity of suffering amongst the people, and the organized resistance to law that had produced such an amount of agrarian outrage, the Government resolved to institute a fresh inquiry "into the causes and the extent of the distress and crime" then prevailing to perhaps a greater extent than at any former period of the history of the country. Accordingly, in September 1833, a Royal Commission was issued—

"To inquire into the condition of the poorer classes in Ireland, and into the various institutions at present established by law for their relief," and "whether any and what further remedial measures appear to be requisite to ameliorate the condition of the Irish poor or any portion of them."

While these instructions, to which a very wide interpretation was given by the Commissioners, covered the whole ground of the condition of the Irish people, the constitution of the Commission was such as to inspire confidence that the inquiry would be full and impartial. Different creeds, classes, and opinions were fairly represented upon it. The Protestant and Roman Catholic Archbishops of Dublin were associated with men who were assumed to represent the politics of Whig and Tory, the material interests of proprietor and peasant. Whatever opinion may be formed of the conclusions at which the Commission arrived, it is but simple justice to those who conducted the inquiry to say that the mass of evidence collected by them threw more light than did any of the numerous inquiries of preceding years upon the condition of the people, the extent and the assumed causes of the distress that prevailed amongst them. No one upon a candid examination of that report can withhold assent from the statement of the Commissioners that

"No Commission could possibly be entrusted with a wider or more complicated subject for its investigation than ours; few Commissions indeed ever received such wide instructions. Few Commissions have had a greater district over which to extend their examinations. None could have had a larger portion of a community to consult."

Nor certainly could any Commission have collected and presented in an intelligible shape a larger mass of evidence upon such a variety of topics, all bearing upon the matters submitted for inquiry, "the condition of the poorer classes of the people, "and the remedial measures to ameliorate it."

While so much may be fairly said of the labours of the Commission in the collection of evidence, it must be admitted that the impression produced by the conclusions they arrived at was one of profound disappointment. After an inquiry extending over three years, in which voluminous evidence, written and oral, from people of all classes was taken as to the extent of destitution, the modes in which relief was afforded to the destitute, the effects of those modes, the cause of destitution, the rate of agricultural wages, the habits of farm labourers, and the nature and extent of employment in agriculture, whether there might be any measures within the reach of the Legislature which would tend to increase the demand for labour, as to the condition of the manufacturing population and of those engaged in fisheries and mining, the Commissioners made their final report, accompanied by the evidence, several thousand closely printed folio pages, upon which it was founded. They state that—

"There are in Ireland about five agricultural labourers for every two that there are for the same quantity of land in Great Britain; that the agricultural produce of Great Britain is more than four times that of Ireland; that agricultural wages vary from sixpence to a shilling a day; that the average of the country in general is about 8½d., and that the earnings of the labourer come on an average of the whole class to from 2s. to 2s. 6d. a week or thereabouts for the year round; that thus circumstanced, it is impossible for the able-bodied in general to provide against sickness or the temporary absence of employment, or against old age or the destitution of their widows and children in the contingent event of their own premature decease; that a great portion of them are insufficiently provided at any time with the commonest necessaries of life; their habitations are wretched hovels; several of a family sleep together upon straw or upon the bare ground; sometimes with a blanket, sometimes without even so much to cover them; their food commonly consists of dry potatoes, and with those they are at times so scantily provided as to be obliged to stint themselves to one spare meal in the day; there are even instances of persons being driven by hunger to seek sustenance in wild herbs; they sometimes get a herring or a little milk, but they never get meat except at Christmas, Easter, and Shrovetide; some go in search of employment in Great Britain during the harvest, others wander through Ireland with the same view; the wives and the children of many are occasionally obliged to beg; they do so reluctantly, and in general go to a distance from home that they may not be known; mendicancy too is the sole resource of the aged and impotent of the poorer classes in general when children or relatives are unable to support them; to it, therefore, crowds are driven for the means of existence, and the knowledge that such is the fact leads to an indiscriminate giving of alms, which encourages idleness, imposture, and general crime."

Such an account of the condition of the bulk of the people was unhappily not at all exaggerated. Indeed, the character of the published evidence would have justified the Commissioners in giving even a darker colouring to this picture of existing destitution. It might have been supposed then that the evidence would naturally lead to the conclusion that property should be made liable for the relief of the destitution which the neglect or abuse of property had in the main produced. But from that conclusion a majority of the Commissioners drew back.

Although opposed to a Poor Law for Ireland founded upon the principle that destitution alone should give a right to relief, the Report of the Commissioners may be said to have indirectly led to its enactment. In the face of the published evidence Government could not hesitate to accept the obvious conclusion of the Commission that "remedial measures were necessary." The choice of "remedial measures," however, seemed to lie between the suggestions of the Commission, and a legal provision for *all* classes of destitute poor.

It was considered by many, including the most prominent members of the Government, that the "remedial measures" suggested by the Commission were palliatives, not remedies, and that they involved principles of the most dangerous tendency, the application of which in Ireland would have been a legalised subversion, if we may use the phrase, of all social order. A system of outdoor relief, unprotected by any test of destitution, from which the able-bodied, however urgent their distress, were excluded; loans from the public Exchequer for the improvement of private property through the agency of Government Commissioners; the assumption that it is the duty of the State to find profitable employment for the people; a system of emigration, partly voluntary and partly penal, were amongst the most prominent of the "remedial measures" suggested by the Commissioners. The most important portion of the Report, however, was the distinct objection to the application to Ireland of the principle of the English Poor Law.

By the publication of this Report the Government of the day was placed in a position of extreme difficulty. To reject the complicated scheme for the improvement of Ireland that had been submitted to them by the Commissioners, without proposing any measure instead of it, was a course that in the existing state of the country could not, without serious danger, be adopted. But between the scheme of the Commissioners and the adoption of a Poor Law based upon the principle of the English Act, there seemed to be no alternative. Fully sensible of the difficulty and the immense responsibility of such an undertaking, the Government were still encouraged to attempt it by the assured success of the English Act, so recently brought into operation, which, to adopt the phrase of one who afterwards became its ablest administrator, had already "cut up pauperism by the roots." Whether it would be possible to apply the principle of that Act to Ireland was a question upon which neither the Report of the Commissioners nor the evidence taken by them could be accepted as a guide. The Government, therefore, resolved to make special inquiry upon that single question, and intrusted the duty to a man whose experience, sound judgment, and judicial impartiality eminently qualified him for the task. The three well-known Reports of Mr. Nicholls were the result of this inquiry, and became, in fact, the foundation of the Irish Poor Law.

The publication of the Reports of Mr. Nicholls was followed by an intimation that a Bill for the better relief of the Poor of Ireland founded upon the recommendations contained in them would be at once submitted to Parliament. This proposal provoked discussions that were remarkable, even in those days of great public excitement, for the violence and acrimony with which they were conducted. Men representing different interests and influenced by different motives united in opposition to the proposal to give the destitute poor of *all* classes a right to relief at the cost of the property of the country.

That the landowners of Ireland should be opposed to such a measure was, under the circumstances, not unreasonable. The Commissioners by whom all the conditions of the question had been carefully examined had reported:—

"If workhouses were determined upon for Ireland as an actual means of relief they must be established for the purpose of setting vast numbers of unemployed persons to work within them, and of so providing for such persons and their families. We cannot estimate the number of persons in Ireland out of work and in distress during thirty weeks of the year at less than 585,000, nor the number of persons dependent upon them at less than 1,800,000, making in the whole 2,385,000. This, therefore, is about the number for which it would be necessary to provide accommodation in workhouses if all who required relief were there to be relieved, and we consider it morally, indeed physically, impossible so to provide for such a multitude or even to attempt it with safety. The expense of erecting and fitting up the necessary buildings would come to about 4,000,000*l.*, and allowing for the maintenance of each person on 2½*d.* a day, the cost of supporting the whole would be something more than 5,000,000*l.* a year; whereas the gross rental of Ireland (exclusive of towns) is estimated at less than 10,000,000*l.*; the net income of the landlords at less than 6,000,000*l.*, and the public revenue is only about 4,000,000*l.*"

Could the landlords of Ireland in fairness be blamed if they set themselves against a measure that, according to this authoritative statement, would be in effect confiscation of their property?

In support of the proposal it was urged that by giving to the cottier and the holder of con-acre security against absolute destitution, it would tend to loosen the hold upon the land of that large class who, in the struggle for existence, had heretofore clung to it as to a plank for safety. That, however, was a consideration not likely to have much weight with those according to whose code occupation gave a right but little distinguished from ownership. Nor from his own point of view had the small farmer or other employer of labour much reason to favour a proposal that would give the peasant a claim upon the rates to be in part paid by that employer, when wages were found to be insufficient to maintain a family. To these sources of opposition were added others which, though of individuals and not of classes, were hardly less formidable. Sir Robert Peel threw the weight of his great authority and Mr. O'Connell the greater weight of his vast influence into the adverse scale, though to the lasting credit of both they were ultimately found amongst the supporters of the measure.

It is important to bear in mind that the discussions upon the Reports of the Commission and of Mr. Nicholls turned chiefly upon the proposal of the latter to give relief to the destitute of *all* classes. The Commissioners, upon the other hand, would have restricted relief to certain favoured classes. They say,—

"Upon the best consideration which we have been able to give to the whole subject, we think that a legal provision should be made, and rates levied as herein-after mentioned, for the relief and support of incurable as well as curable lunatics, of idiots, epileptic persons, cripples, deaf and dumb, and blind poor, and all who labour under permanent bodily infirmities, such relief and support to be afforded within the walls of public institutions; also for the relief of the sick poor in hospitals, infirmaries, and convalescent establishments, or by extern attendance and a supply of food as well as medicine, where the persons to be relieved are not in a state to be removed from home; also for the purpose of emigration, for the support of penitentiaries to which vagrants may be sent, and for the maintenance of deserted children; also towards the relief of aged and infirm persons, of orphans, of helpless widows with young children, of the families of sick persons, and of casual destitution."

The several suggestions of the Commissioners were discussed and fully considered, each upon its own merits. It was tacitly admitted that not one of them, nor indeed the whole of them together, if adopted, would solve the problem how to deal with the great social difficulty involved in what Mr. Drummond described as "*the lamentably* "*destitute condition of a cottier tenantry possessing no adequate means of continuous* "*support.*" Institutions for the blind and lame and idiotic and insane, hospitals for the sick, penitentiaries for vagrants, asylums for deserted children and for orphans, were all no doubt needful, and it was deplorable that in a civilised country they should be still wanting. Other suggestions of the Commissioners would undoubtedly have introduced into Ireland some of the worst abuses of the unreformed English Poor Law. Whole classes, all who could contrive to get themselves enrolled as "permanently disabled" or "infirm through age;" sick persons and their families; deserted children and orphans; widows with young children,—all these it was proposed to relieve without any test of destitution whatever. The experience of English Poor Law administration had conclusively shown that even within these limits the right of relief without a test of destitution had become the fruitful source of fraud, imposture, and demoralisation. Nor were those whom it was thus proposed to relieve, however entitled to help many of them might be, the class of people whose "great and deep-seated distress" was a source of danger, as it was a discredit to the empire. The proposal of the Commissioners would still leave in a state of destitution "during thirty weeks of the year" between two and three millions, all told, of the labouring population. That was a conclusion that Parliament was not prepared to accept. When the Bill "for the better relief of the Poor of Ireland" was introduced it was seen, with apprehension no doubt by many, but with satisfaction by the majority, that ministers had the courage to ground it upon the simple principle that destitution should give a right to relief. To that rule there should be no exception. The able-bodied labourer unable to obtain work or only at insufficient wages would be as much entitled to relief as would be the most helpless from age, sickness, or infirmity.

It could not be expected that such a proposal would be received by any class without misgiving. That the State should undertake, upon any conditions whatever, such a task as the feeding, clothing, and lodging of a people whose ordinary standard of living was, unhappily, below that of any civilised nation in the world, was pronounced by many as beyond compass by any Government. With great plausibility it was urged that the proffered relief, no matter by what restrictions guarded, would be eagerly accepted by the whole of the destitute population of the country. It would be impossible, so it was contended, to impose upon applications for relief any test that would be at once reasonable and efficient. The condition of a pauper in a workhouse could not, consistently with humane treatment, be rendered so uninviting as to prevent the acceptance of indoor relief by the whole destitute population. But if "the workhouse test" broke down there was nothing to fall back upon. So much was admitted on all hands.

To such objections the answer was in effect:—You are mistaken in supposing that the whole labouring population of Ireland will become paupers. If you throw upon property the burthen of relieving destitution, owner and occupier will have a motive for giving employment that has never yet been applied to either. If you impose such terms upon the receipt of relief as shall make the condition of a pauper less inviting than that of a man who can by any possibility make out the means of existence, there need be no apprehension that relief will be accepted by the bulk of the Irish peasantry.

But, it was urged, how can the State grant such a measure of relief only as shall not make the condition of pauperism more inviting than is the condition of abject poverty to which the mass of the people are reduced? If the State undertake to relieve, it cannot relieve as if it were simply the dispenser of private charity,—voluntarily assisting poverty instead of compulsorily relieving destitution. It must substitute a comfortable dwelling for the miserable hovel of the cottier, warm and decent clothing for rags, a sufficiency at least of nutritive food for the single daily meal of potatoes, too often insufficient in quantity. The mere statement of these conditions was taken to carry proof that the apprehension of the Commissioners would turn out to be but too well founded, and that the whole labouring population would become chargeable as indoor paupers. As a test of destitution the offer of relief in the workhouse might, it was urged, be successful in England. But the condition of society in Ireland being essentially different, such an offer, so far from acting as a test, would be found to be only a temptation and an inducement to pauperism. Besides, was not the existence of destitution but too apparent? Was any "test" necessary to prove it?

The first objection was founded upon a mistaken view of the character of what was called "the workhouse test," and an equally erroneous view, we may be allowed to say, of the character of the Irish people. Upon both points no higher authority can be cited than that of Mr.—afterwards Sir George—Cornwall Lewis. If the reports of Mr. Nicholls were, as we have observed, the foundation of the Irish Poor Law, the reports of Mr. Lewis did more than any discussions, or than any other publications, to allay apprehensions as to the probable effect of the proposed measure, and to satisfy men of all parties that—

1st. No efficient test of destitution could be devised save the offer of relief in the workhouse.

2nd. And that as applied to the poorer classes of Ireland it would be even more effectual than, as a test of destitution, it had been found to be in England.

The "Act for the better relief of the Poor of Ireland" would no doubt have ultimately passed even if "*The remarks on the third Report of the Irish Poor Commissioners*" and the "*Report on the state of the Irish Poor in Great Britain*" had never been published. But it would be difficult to overrate the effect of these reports in allaying the apprehension of the owners of property in Ireland, in giving a right direction to opinion in England, in strengthening the hands of Government, and inspiring with confidence those who might have to organise the administration of the new law. With reference to the first point Mr. Lewis wrote—

"If anything has been proved more decisively than another by the operation of the Poor Law Amendment Act in England, it is that the workhouse is an all-sufficient test of destitution, and that it is the only test, that it succeeds as a mode of relief, and that all other modes fail. * * *

"It is said that the principle on which the workhouse system rests is that it shall be possible to make the condition of the pauper in the workhouse less desirable than that of the independent labourer, and that this cannot be effected in a country where the standard of existence among the labouring population is already the lowest upon which life can be sustained. In England, they affirm, the workhouse system affords a sufficient guarantee against the absorption of property by the paupers, because the condition of the self-supporting labourer can be deteriorated in a public institution; but in Ireland, they contend, this protection would be of no avail, as it is impossible that an Irish labourer could find any change for the worse which should continue to him the barest necessaries of life.

"This argument, it will be observed, proceeds upon the assumption that the effectiveness of the workhouse in deterring applicants for relief is founded on the *physical comforts* enjoyed by its inmates, the chief of which is food. The Irish peasant, doubtless, lives in a cottage which almost always is nearly destitute of furniture, which sometimes has no chimney, and sometimes no window. His body and bed clothes, both for himself and family, are moreover in general scanty and in bad condition. But habit has done much to reconcile him to the defects of his cabin and the poverty of his clothing, and it will probably be admitted by those who most insist on the objection just stated, that if an Irish labourer fared well in respect of his food, he would not, even if his dwelling and clothes remained in their actual state, be inclined to resort to the workhouse as an improvement on the comforts which he would procure by his own industry. The *lowness and scantiness of his diet* therefore, according to this view of the case, form the great obstacle to the introduction of the workhouse system into Ireland, inasmuch as it would be impossible that the workhouse diet could be lower, and not improbable that it would be higher, than dry potatoes all the year round; and it would be quite certain that there would be plenty of this food, and at all the seasons of the year. In England accordingly (say the same reasoners) the workhouse system acts well, because the diet of the self-supporting labourer admits of a deterioration; he can, according to the expression so much clamoured against, be maintained on 'coarser food;' but in Ireland the workhouse system can never act well, or even act at all, because there it is impossible to make any reduction in the scale of the labourer's diet, and consequently the very hinge on which the entire system turns is wanting.

"Now the whole of this reasoning must, it is evident, fall to the ground, if it can be made evident that the *lowering of the diet* is not in fact the keystone of the workhouse system in England, and that the success of this system under the operation of the Poor Law Amendment Act has been owing to a wholly different cause * * *

"The true sanction of the workhouse system is to be looked for in a different quarter. A man struggling with poverty would be content to live in a public institution, on a worse fare than the most rigid parochial economists have ever ventured to introduce into a workhouse, if he was permitted to spend his time *in idleness, to go in and out* of the house at pleasure, and to live in the house with his wife and family. It is the *compulsory labour*, the *discipline*, and the *classification* which are the real objects of the pauper's dislike. The mere physical comforts of a public institution must always be in many respects superior to those attainable by a poor man in his own dwelling. The inmate of a workhouse is certain, whatever may be the quality of his food, of having *enough* of it; he will never, except for punishment, be reduced to *short commons*: this security alone is of considerable importance to a poor man. He is, moreover, certain of always being decently and warmly clad, both by day and night, and this again is a comfort which many independent labourers most frequently want. He never can be exposed to the inconveniences of insufficient houseroom, of neglected repairs, or of want of firing; and consequently is guarded against all suffering from cold weather. Furthermore, he knows that in case of illness he will be regularly attended by a medical man, and will receive all other needful care and assistance. The sum of these benefits is very great; they are inseparable from a maintenance in a public institution, and if a pauper was determined solely by a regard to bodily comforts, there would unquestionably be a sudden and simultaneous rush upon the English workhouses.

"But it is clear that, however important diet may be, there are are other things more important. Of these the chief is *personal liberty*. The inmate of a workhouse is, so long as he remains in the workhouse, a prisoner. He is compelled to perform a daily task of labour; he is subjected to a stated discipline; he rises at a certain hour, he goes to and from his work at certain hours; he has his meals at certain hours; he goes to bed at a certain hour; he is under the control of a superintendent; he does not choose his own food, he is cut off from the outward world; be is even separated from his wife and family when under the same roof as himself. He is a prisoner in every respect, except one, viz., that *he can go out whenever he pleases*, provided that he will undertake to maintain himself. The paupers who have been subjected to the influence of the new workhouses have been fully aware of the true point of pressure, and instead of calling them *starving houses*, or by any like name, have called them *prisons* and *bastilles*. There is doubtless, as has been just mentioned, this one great and essential difference between a prison and a workhouse, that a prison is a place where a man is confined till his sentence has expired, whereas a workhouse is a place where a man is only confined till he will undertake to maintain himself. But although a man may feel that he has it in his power at any moment to dissolve the restraint which binds him, it is not the less unpleasant while it lasts, and in looking forward to the form in which relief, if he asks for it, will be administered, he cannot fail to consider the loss of liberty as its bitterest ingredient." * * * *

"If a workhouse was simply an almshouse, an establishment where poor persons were lodged, clothed, and fed at the public cost, without any restraint of discipline, or forced labour or separation of sexes, does any body suppose that the lowest of the dietaries now in use in any workhouse in England would prevent half the working population from claiming admittance into them? * * * *

"From what has been said, it appears clearly that if there is nothing peculiarly alluring in the food and other comforts of the workhouse, if the fare is about that of an average independent labourer in the district, it may be expected that the *hard labour* of the institution, and the *restraints* used to enforce it, and generally to maintain decency and good order, will deter all applicants for relief who have not a well-founded claim to be supported at the public cost. If the workhouse diet is not much superior to that which an independent labourer enjoys at home, the *forced labour*, the *discipline*, the *separation*, and the *confinement* will be sufficient checks against unfounded applications for relief. Now, in applying this principle to Ireland, it appears that there is nothing in the condition of its labouring population which is inconsistent with the operation of the chief guarantees of the workhouse system. It is true that the low standard of existence among the Irish peasantry enhances the value of the physical comforts inseparable from a public institution to a greater degree than is the case in England. *All* the advantages, therefore, for the introduction of workhouses which exist in England do not exist in Ireland. But the dislike to forced labour and bodily restraint is universal, and may be calculated on with as great certainty among the Irish as among the English peasantry. There is no doubt that relief offered to an Irish peasant by means of a workhouse will be presented in a sufficiently unpalatable form to afford a perfect test of want. So great a value do the Irish labourers in general attach to the blessings of personal liberty, that many persons in Ireland, acquainted with the feelings of the peasantry, have objected to workhouses on the very ground of their unpopularity. This feeling, of the existence of which there can be no doubt, is in fact, so far from its being an obstacle to the introduction of the workhouse system, the surest guarantee of its success; and indeed it is only necessary to suppose the Irish peasant to be endued with the ordinary feelings of human nature, to expect that, rather than work under a taskmaster, and with the temporary loss of personal liberty, he would make any exertions in his power to maintain himself and his family.

"The principle of the workhouse system is simply this: offer everybody relief, but make it so disagreeable that none but those in real want will accept it. This principle is just as applicable to one country as to another. Restraint and confinement are as disagreeable in Ireland as they are elsewhere. It might, as it seems to me, be as well contended that an Irishman does not care for the prison or the gallows, as that he does not care for the workhouse. This argument is indeed an exaggeration of the doctrine that Ireland is not to be governed on the same principle as England.

"From the above remarks, therefore, it may be concluded that there is nothing in the workhouse system itself, and in the means by which it acts, to render it inapplicable to the present circumstances of Ireland."

These passages from Mr. Lewis's reports, in complete accordance with the views of Mr. Nicholls, indicate generally the grounds upon which, after repeated and protracted discussions in successive Parliaments, it was finally determined to enact a Poor Law for Ireland, founded exclusively upon the principle of receiving all applicants for relief into the workhouse. As soon as the Act was passed, Mr. Nicholls, representing the Poor Law Commissioners, with a certain number of Assistant Commissioners, was deputed to take measures to bring it into operation. As the proposal, now the subject of inquiry, to "amalgamate" unions and to dispense with a certain number of workhouses, would be, so far as such a change might be effected, a very material modification of the arrangements then made, it becomes important to ascertain what were the general principles by which the Commissioners were guided in the formation of unions.

Keeping in view that, as outdoor relief was prohibited, the workhouse must be, as Sir Geo. Nicholls expressed it, "the corner stone of the whole system," the first matter that the Commissioners had to consider was the size or extent of the proposed unions. The determination of this question involved very great difficulty, and required the fullest and most careful local inquiries. The interests of the owners of property, often conflicting with each other as well as with the interest of the district in which the property might have to be rated; the convenience of ratepayers who might be called upon to act as guardians; the interest and convenience of the poor who might become chargeable,—all these had to be inquired into and to be examined with the greatest care and minuteness.

The principle that had been adopted in the formation of English unions appeared to the Commissioners to be generally applicable in Ireland. Recognising the expediency of forming "large unions" with a view to economising establishment charges, they fixed as a general rule upon a radius of ten miles from a given centre. To this rule, however, they were, for financial measures,—inability to obtain advances for the building of a sufficient number of workhouses,—unfortunately compelled, as will be seen, to make many exceptions. As in England, the centre should be, for obvious reasons, the market town of a district, "for the people who frequent the " market will find no difficulty in attending at the union workhouse, whether as " guardians, or as applicants for relief, or for any other purpose." Taking that principle for a guide, local interests were to be carefully attended to in the formation of unions. While the boundaries of property were to be observed as far as was compatible with general interest and convenience, the Assistant Commissioners were reminded that—

"It is highly important that all the unions should be formed as compact and complete as possible, for when the country shall have been worked up into unions, each having an organised machinery and a principle of self-government, and with market town as centre, or little capital, it can scarcely be doubted that they will be made available for other purposes, as well as for administration of the Poor Law."

This last suggestion, we may remark in passing, is one that should not be lost sight of, the tendency of legislation being to enlarge the administrative functions of these bodies, imposing upon them duties more varied and important. At no time, indeed, since Irish boards of guardians were constituted can it have been of greater importance than it is now, that they should hold their ground as independent local bodies, ready to accept their place in any wider administrative organisation to which they may be called.

The Commissioners were further of opinion that, if the administration of poor relief was to be efficiently conducted, the machinery of administration must be practically watched over and controlled by the guardians acting as a board. If that were not so, it would too often happen that the decision upon applications for relief would be left to the relieving officer, to the guardians of a particular electoral division, or would be determined by such external influence as the recommendation of ratepayers not unfrequently interested in the result. Now if the attendance of guardians at the weekly or fortnightly meetings was rendered too difficult by the greater remoteness of the place of meeting, the workhouse, one result would be that the decision of cases would by degrees come to be left to the officials, or to a few guardians who might happen to be near residents, the representatives of the remoter divisions ceasing to take any active interest in the business of the union.

Of still greater importance was it that the workhouse of each union should be accessible to the poor of its several electoral divisions. As soon as the unions were formed, and provided with workhouse accommodation, outdoor relief was prohibited. If that rule were not to be set aside, the workhouse should be easily accessible to the class of poor to whom indoor relief should be offered as a test of destitution. Equally important was it in the interest of the aged and infirm, and of the sick poor, that the size of unions should be restricted to such an area as would involve no risk of these classes being either left wholly unrelieved, or of the offer of relief being subject to conditions so hard as in some cases to amount to absolute prohibition.

Another and very important consideration in determining the size of unions was the question of the number of guardians of which a board should consist. Had the principle of union rating been adopted, the separate representation of small areas would have been of less consequence. But as electoral division rating involved divisional representation, it became necessary to limit the number of divisions to be included within the area of each union, so that the number of guardians "would be sufficient for the purpose of deliberation, and yet not so numerous as to impede efficient action." The Commissioners therefore resolved that "the number of elected guardians varying according to circumstances, from 16 to 24, will be best calculated for carrying out the Act."

It was determined that before any union was declared the Assistant Commissioners should make special inquiry into the circumstances of each district, and should furnish such a report as might be regarded—

Firstly.—As a document which would justify the Assistant Commissioner in recommending to the board the union which he proposes.

Secondly.—As comprising all the information necessary to enable the board to judge of and to justify to the Government and to the public, not only the local arrangement and size of the union, but also the proposed workhouse accommodation and establishment of officers.

Thirdly.—As an accurate description of the state of the district in all those particulars that may be affected by the operation of the Act.

The Reports furnished by the Assistant Commissioners in compliance with these instructions, constitute a most valuable body of evidence upon the condition of the several unions to which they relate. To a few of these we shall have occasion to refer in connection with particular applications for "amalgamation." But we may observe generally that they afford very striking evidence of the pains taken in the collection of information, and the care with which the various interests that would be affected were considered,—presenting in these respects a marked contrast to the proceedings of those who now seek to disturb the arrangements then made. In every instance in which it was proposed to form a union a meeting of the inhabitants was called, and the law and the proposed arrangements for carrying it into effect were explained to them by the Assistant Commissioners, who took into consideration any objections that were raised, and any suggestions that were offered, from whatever quarter; and—

"It was not until after this public exposition of the course proposed to be pursued, and a careful and open sifting of testimony for and against it, that the arrangement, for the several unions have been sanctioned."—(Sixth Annual Report of Poor Law Commissioners.)

In accordance with the recommendations of the Assistant Commissioners, thus based in all cases upon very full inquiry, one hundred and thirty unions were formed and came into operation in the course of a very short time after the passing of the Act.

It must not be supposed, however, that 130 unions constituted the full number that, in the opinion of the Commissioners, would be adequate to the requirements of the country. They assented to that number under circumstances stated by Mr. Gulson, one of the Assistant Commissioners who was engaged in laying out the Irish Unions. In his evidence before the Committee of the House of Lords in 1849, Mr. Gulson states that the number of unions originally formed was not so much in accordance with the views of the Commissioners as

"Decided by the means placed at their disposal as regards the cost of the workhouse buildings. It was at first proposed that there should be 80 workhouses; then the number was increased to 100. There was great unwillingness on the part of the Government of that day, however, to find the money; and I recollect, when it was proposed to divide the country into more than 100 unions, great objections were made. It was urged upon us that we might comprise all Ireland in 100 unions, and that the sum required to build 100 workhouses would be all that could conveniently be granted. It was afterwards suggested whether 110 would not be sufficient. At last, however, the number was screwed up to 130. But I quite believe that if we had had the means at our disposal to do exactly that which we thought best, a few of the largest unions in Ireland would at that time have been curtailed in extent. I think some of the members of the Committee will bear me out in that view of the matter, it was with great difficulty that we succeeded in getting the Government of that day to assent even to 130.

"What was the objection?—The cost."

Mr. Gulson is further asked:—

"Was the desire which you say was entertained then to make more unions founded upon the supposition that that number of unions would not be adequate to the fair distribution of relief over very widely extended areas?

"It was; that there were parts of the country in which there might be a difficulty in affording the necessary facilities for relief upon so extended an area.

"Were not those unions found sufficient till the failure of the potato crops?

"I think that in some parts of the west of Ireland the people scarcely knew how to obtain relief; for instance, in the Ballina union, where a man had to come 30 or 35 miles to make his application for relief. I consider that such distances must operate as a bar to that relief which the Act contemplated, and which was intended to be within the reach of every destitute person."

Although the practical working of the law thus introduced was during the first few years more successful and encountered less opposition than might have been anticipated, yet it soon became apparent that, in their anxiety to avoid burthening the ratepayers with heavy establishment charges, but owing chiefly, as we have just shown, to their inability to obtain from the Government the necessary funds, the Commissioners had in several instances constituted Unions comprising areas far too wide for efficient administration. Urgent representations upon the subject came from different quarters, and the facts stated were of such a character as to induce the Government to issue a Royal Commission in March 1848 to inquire and report what alteration might be beneficially made in the number and boundaries of Poor Law Unions and Electoral Divisions. As recent experience had proved—

"That many of the unions were inconveniently large, and that consequently a reduction of their size and the formation of new unions might be assumed to be desirable,"

the Commissioners were instructed to inquire and report—

1. Whether the workhouse is situated at a market town, or other convenient central place, to which the guardians are in the habit of resorting.
2. Whether the size and other geographical circumstances of the union are such as to prevent the guardians and relieving officers from attending the Board without serious interruption to their other duties.
3. Whether the same circumstances prevent the applicants for relief, who desire or who may be required to attend the Board, from doing so without serious inconvenience.

They were required further to report what alterations it would be desirable to make in the boundaries of existing unions, and what new unions it would be desirable to form in order to meet the wants of the country on the points above adverted to.

In conducting their inquiry the Boundary Commissioners adopted a course similar to that which had been taken by the Poor Law Commissioners in forming the then existing unions, the number of which, as we have shown, was far short of their original design. They sought information "from every accessible source," their first step being to "invite all parties interested" to make known the cases of any unions or electoral divisions in which the conditions (1, 2, and 3) above referred to were not fulfilled. A list of queries upon the several subjects of inquiry was addressed to chairmen of boards of guardians, to individual guardians, to the Irish members of both Houses of Parliament, and to numerous individuals of all classes, and were also inserted in the local newspapers. Upon the replies to these queries, and upon information elicited from deputations and private individuals who personally communicated with the Commissioners, the recommendations of the Report are founded. "The replies and statements generally," the Commissioners say, "concurred in repre-" senting many of them as inconveniently large," and they therefore concluded that it would be expedient to form fifty new unions.

To a limited extent this recommendation was adopted, thirty-three unions only having been subsequently declared by the Poor Law Commissioners. Although that important change was not made for several years after the original constitution of unions, yet as the relative advantage of large or small areas was involved in the inquiry, this will be the most convenient place to refer to it.

It is frequently assumed that this addition to the number of unions was made solely in consequence of the great increase of pauperism that was caused by the unprecedented distress of 1846–7 and 8, and it is urged that as that pauperism has so greatly decreased, the unions which it is alleged were declared in consequence of it might be now dissolved and the workhouses closed. This, however, is an erroneous view, and as it underlies much of the feeling to which expression has been given in favour of amalgamation, it calls for notice.

In the first place, it must be observed that in the formation of a considerable number of the Irish unions the Commissioners were compelled to reverse the usual and obvious method of first declaring the union, and then determining, according to its population, the amount of workhouse accommodation to be provided for it. Being restricted to a given expenditure, the Commissioners could only provide a certain number of workhouses, and upon that number in a great measure depended the number of unions. Hence the unwieldy size of many of them, especially in the South and West, and the consequent difficulty of administering the law. Upon the poor this difficulty bore with especial weight, for there was at that time a general disposition to enforce indoor relief in its utmost strictness. The Boundary Commissioners—

"found the opinion universal that the workhouse afforded the only efficient test of destitution; accordingly, in the greater number of the unions of the South and West auxiliary workhouses were resorted to—that is, temporary houses were rented, with temporary staff attached to them; or additions were made to the existing workhouses, with corresponding additional staff; while much injury to the health of the inmates was found to result from the crowded state of the houses. Of the necessity for increased workhouse accommodation, therefore, there could be no doubt, and it only remained to consider whether that necessity was merely temporary, so that accommodation could be most advantageously afforded by temporary means, or whether additional unions with small houses should be interposed among the existing unions. Every analogy and every inference which the better conditioned districts afforded was in favour of the additional unions, and as a main object of these smaller unions was the more vigilant administration of the law with a view to the prevention of abuses, there was every reason to hope that the expense of building and establishment to be incurred by the additional houses would be saved by the greater economy which would be exercised in the administration of relief. We are aware that this opinion has been greatly controverted. * * * But we had to consider the right of the destitute to facile relief, as well as the economy with which relief could be administered; and when we found unions so large that a pauper might be required to travel 30 miles to the workhouse, with the chance of rejection, there could be no hesitation in reducing a distance so prohibitory."

In one case the Commissioners report—

"It was stated to us that a man walked 150 miles before he was ultimately admitted to the house."

More than once, indeed, in the course of our own inquiries, we heard it urged in support of "amalgamation" that the extension of the area would act as an additional check upon applications for relief.

The views of the Commissioners were fully borne out by the communications made to them from the various quarters in which they had sought information. Although the grounds for forming new unions were, in all cases in which they were formed, equally conclusive, and were altogether independent of causes of a temporary nature, we shall refer only to the particular unions in which we were called upon to make special inquiry upon applications for amalgamation. These are Cavan, Monaghan, Ennis, Mill Street, and Glenamaddy. The most convenient course will be to refer first to the considerations that led the Commissioners to interfere with the original arrangements of these and other unions, and to examine in a subsequent part of this Report the reasons that are urged in support of proposals for amalgamation.

The proposal that we had to consider in the case of Cavan was to unite or amalgamate all the electoral divisions of the county into one union.

The history of the formation of the three unions into which the county of Cavan was originally distributed is given in the Report of the Assistant Commissioner, published by the Poor Law Commissioners in 1840. On his arrival in that county, the Assistant Commissioner first directed his attention to obtaining local information respecting the general condition and habits of the people; to what extent and under what form mendicity prevailed; the nature of the relief generally given; by whom afforded, and under what regulations. He made inquiry as to the name and residence of each landed proprietor, or his agent, and the average extent of the several properties within the district. He carefully observed the position, size, and character of the different towns; the nature of their markets, the extent of the district surrounding, and the amount of population frequenting and depending on each. He waited on the principal resident proprietors and agents, and made arrangements for obtaining a return of the extent and position of the several properties in which they were interested, and took a note of any peculiar circumstances affecting them. Having instituted these and such like inquiries, he sketched out and made a rough calculation of the area and population of the three unions into which he proposed to divide the county, taking an imaginary centre for the seat of the workhouse. Upon the basis of this general inquiry, followed up by more minute and very valuable detail in the case of each particular union, the Commissioners declared the unions of Cavan, Cootehill, and Bailieborough.

Notwithstanding the pains thus taken in the formation of these unions, complaints were soon made that the Cavan union was inconveniently large. As soon as the Boundary Commissioners commenced their duties, they instituted inquiries as to the grounds of these complaints. Upon the information afforded to them, they recommended the formation of a fourth Cavan union—that of Bawnboy. This information was elicited by two queries addressed to persons whose position in connection with these unions enabled them to afford the best information upon the subject. They were asked,—

First. Did the size of the union render it inconvenient for guardians and relieving officers to attend?

Secondly. Did the same circumstances render it inconvenient for the poor applying for relief?

The Chairman of the Union, Lord Farnham, replied to the first query,—

"Unquestionably so. I consider the size of the union to be so inconveniently extensive that it is quite impossible for guardians and relieving officers to attend the board without serious interruption to their other duties.

"The distance from which numerous applicants for relief are obliged to come is a matter of very great hardship and inconvenience, and this is particularly felt in those cases in which the guardians are obliged to refuse relief."

Thomas Hartley, Esq., Courtenau:—

"The union being large renders it difficult and laborious for the elected guardians and relieving officers of remote electoral divisions to attend the board.

"The applicants for relief from remote electoral divisions suffer inconvenience when required to attend the board, and particularly in the winter season. From my local knowledge of the union, I think that its area is by far too extensive, and a limitation of its boundaries would be attended with most beneficial effects."

Robert Burrowes, Esq., Stradone:—

"The distance of many of the electoral divisions is such that neither guardians nor relieving officers could attend the board without serious interruption to their other duties.

"The applicants for relief coming from remote divisions suffer the greatest hardships when, from want of room, they are unable to gain admittance to the workhouse, and are obliged to return to their own locality. I think the union might in some directions be curtailed with advantage."

H. T. Kilbee, Esq., Drumkeen, Cavan :—

"The size of the union is altogether too large." [The board at this time had been dissolved, and paid guardians appointed.] "As long as a local board was in existence, the guardians were very remiss in their attendance, but it must be admitted that this neglect was observable generally in the case of those who resided in the nearest as well as in the most remote districts of the union. A mere look, however, at the map of the union will at once show that the guardians of Ballyconnell, Ballymacheugh, and other remote electoral divisions could not have attended at Cavan without serious personal inconvenience. The collectors attended very irregularly, and in fact officers did and would follow the example of negligence generally set by members of the board.

"Paupers could not attend the board from distant electoral divisions without serious personal inconvenience, particularly when old and infirm."

John E. Vernon, Esq., Kilmore House :—

"It would be desirable to withdraw from the union the electoral division of Ballyconnell, annexing it to a union to be formed either at Swanlinbar or Ballyconnell, this union to have for constituent parts those districts of Enniskillen, Mohill, and Cavan unions most distant from their respective workhouses."

From the adjacent unions of Mohill and Enniskillen, the Commissioners received information of a similar character.

Edward H. Trevor and John Gowdy, vice-guardians of Enniskillen Union, state that—

"Tullynamoltra electoral division extends five miles above Bawnboy in the county Cavan, Glen electoral division to the mountains of Glengevlin and Killenagh, to five miles above the Red Lion in same county. All these divisions are distant at least 20 miles from the workhouse, which renders it very inconvenient for the guardians, rate collectors, and relieving officers to attend the board without serious interruption to their other duties. Applicants for relief from these electoral divisions situate in the county of Cavan cannot without serious inconvenience attend the Board: instances have occurred of paupers admitted into the hospital of the workhouse from those divisions with their feet and legs swelled from fatigue and debility, which ultimately resulted in their death."

Edward Archdall, Esq., J. P. :—

"The distance of part of the union from the workhouse makes it impossible for the guardians to attend without serious inconvenience. The electoral divisions of Tullynamoltra Glen and Killenagh should be taken off the Enniskillen union as quite too distant."

Chas. Fausset, Esq., J. P. :—

"The union is so scattered that it must prevent the guardians and relieving officers attending without great inconvenience and serious interruption to their other duties."

William Johnston, Esq., J. P. :—

"The size of the union is too extensive for the guardians and relieving officers to attend to their duties. It prevents applicants for relief at the workhouse, the distance being too far. Several persons would have died last summer, returning from Enniskillen, as they could not be admitted, only for the relief they got from the funds at Swanlinbar and Bawnboy."

Henry J. Archdall, Esq., J. P. :—

"The union is too large, and must cause inconvenience to guardians residing at a distance. I think a poorhouse in vicinity of Swanlinbar or Bawnboy would be an improvement."

Rev. J. L. Porter, Kilskeary :—

"The size and geographical circumstances must undoubtedly prevent the guardians from attending the board.

"The extent and other circumstances prevent the inhabitants from feeling any community of interest, or co-operating with efficiency to manage such an unwieldy monster."

The Earl of Enniskillen :—

"The union is too large. The guardians of the electoral divisions of Tullynamoltra, Glengevlin, Killenagh, and Swanlinbar, (all in the county of Cavan,) have to travel, in the three first divisions at least 15 Irish miles, and in the latter division 10 Irish miles, to get to the poorhouse ; and in the case of the Glengevlin E. D. they have also to cross a mountain between 1,000 and 1,200 feet high. The attendance of guardians from these divisions seldom used to be good."

John Lauder, Esq., Mough House, writing of the Mohill Union :—

"Applicants for relief can attend the board with sufficient convenience, except from those electoral divisions situate north of Ballinamore. With regard to those divisions, I do think the paupers have rather far to go to the Mohill poorhouse."

John Godley, Esq., Killigar :—

"The workhouse is at such a distance from my residence (13 Irish miles) that I found it impossible, when I was a guardian, to attend the meetings of the board with any regularity. Applicants for relief, as well as all persons who may be required to attend the board, must necessarily be much inconvenienced by having to travel such a distance."

Major Haliday and Robt. A. Duncan, vice-guardians:—

"There are several electoral divisions from which the guardians and relieving officers cannot in winter attend the board and transact the business without having to travel at night, or remain in Mohill till the following day. The distances and bad roads entail much inconvenience on the applicants who have to travel so far to attend at the board. A new union could be advantageously formed, taking in a considerable portion of the county of Cavan; the centre of which union should be at Bawnboy, in Cavan, or at Newtown Gore."

Rev. Peter Curran, P.P., Ballinamore:—

"The guardians of seven divisions of the union cannot conveniently attend the board, as being too remote from Mohill, to which they have no recourse. It is not their market town, neither is it assize or sessions town; consequently it cannot be expected that the elected guardians will ever attend the board in Mohill. I have no doubt that hundreds of the poor of those seven divisions have perished for want of poorhouse accommodation."

Francis La Touche, Esq.:—

"The northern or Ballinamore portion of the union is too remote from the workhouse to enable the guardians or applicants for relief to attend conveniently."

Lord Clements:—

"The workhouse is central, and convenient to Mohill Barony, but it is not a place of resort, and is most inconvenient to the guardians of the Barony of Carrigallen, who have not been able to attend the board regularly. With respect to applicants for relief, the inconvenience has been so great during the year 1847 that I have been obliged personally to relieve those that could not be admitted into the house. The journey must be attended with inconvenience to all parties."

Upon such information the Poor Law Boundary Commissioners recommended that certain electoral divisions should be detached from the unions of Cavan, Enniskillen, and Mohill, and, by combining them, to form the union of Bawnboy,—the fourth Cavan union.

We have thought it desirable to reproduce in this case so much of the evidence that determined the Commissioners to form a fourth Cavan union, as, when we come to refer to the evidence given upon the Inquiry held in that union, Your Grace will thus be able to appreciate the consequences that would necessarily follow from acceding to the petition of the Cavan guardians by "amalgamating" all the electoral divisions of the county into one union.

In all the other unions, including those that have passed resolutions in favour of amalgamation, the Boundary Commissioners adopted the same course. They asked the same questions, and received answers generally to the same effect. Mill Street Union was formed upon information that Kanturk was—

"So much too large as to prevent guardians from attending regularly. This applies in a greater degree if possible to applicants for relief,—who, unless they are received into the workhouse, are often obliged either to beg a lodging from some one nearly as poor as themselves, or to sleep on the roadside, subject to the inclemency of the weather,—as, from weakness or illness, it would be impossible for them to walk 10 or 12 miles on a winter's night after six o'clock, having come that distance the same morning, and standing all day, wet, cold, and hungry, at the poorhouse gate, waiting for their cases to be called on."

Several memorials or resolutions numerously and influentially signed were addressed to the Commissioners in favour of the proposal to form a separate union in Mill Street.

It was in consequence of urgent representations of a similar character that the Boundary Commissioners concluded, as we have already stated, to recommend the reduction of the size of several unions by the formation of 50 new ones. This recommendation subsequently received the unanimous approval of a Committee of the House of Lords, by whom in 1849 the whole subject of the working of the Irish Poor Law up to that time was fully investigated. They reported that—

"Additional workhouse accommodation must be provided; and, considering the vast size of some of the present unions, especially in the poorest parts of the country, the Committee concur in the recommendation of the Boundary Commissioners that a considerable number of new unions should be formed, and workhouses attached to them."

Simultaneously with the formation of unions, the Poor Law Commissioners were obliged to provide workhouse accommodation for each. The importance as well as the great difficulty of this task was fully explained by Mr. Nicholls in successive Reports made by him to the Government.

In immediate connection with our present inquiry, it is important to ascertain upon what principle the accommodation of workhouses was originally fixed, and what steps were taken by the Commissioners to give effect to it.

It would appear that the nominal workhouse accommodation was originally determined upon an average estimate of rather less than one and a half per cent. of the population. This certainly would not have been, even if carried out, in excess of the requirements of unions in which out-door relief was absolutely prohibited, and in which distress was so wide-spread and so intense. Although the circumstances of the country have so greatly changed, it will be seen that the change has not affected the amount of available accommodation in workhouses to anything like the extent that is assumed. A brief explanation will make this clear.

In the first place, as will be shown presently, there is a very wide difference, as much as from 40 to 50 per cent., between the nominal and the actual accommodation of nearly all the workhouses. Then, of the accommodation provided, by far the largest proportion was for able-bodied. Comparatively little account was taken of the probable numbers of the aged and infirm, still less of the sick, in fixing the amount of workhouse accommodation. This was not at all from indifference to the wants of these classes. But the workhouse was intended mainly as a test of destitution for the able-bodied, by whom it was anticipated that very much the largest proportion of applications would be made. The infirmaries were originally designed as hospitals for the sick of the workhouse only, and not of the whole union, as they have since become. A separate measure for providing hospital accommodation for the unions was part of the general scheme of the Government, and in contemplation of such provision being made, the infirmaries were constructed. This was explained by Mr. Nicholls in a letter addressed to the Home Secretary in 1844:—

"As regards the infirmary accommodation, I have no doubt of its being sufficient for the sick inmates of the house, for whom alone it was intended; but, owing to the insufficiency of hospital accommodation in many districts, and the inadequate means that exist for affording medical aid to the sick poor, admission to the workhouse has frequently been given rather on account of sickness than on the ground of destitution, and hence the workhouse infirmaries have in some cases been found to be inadequate. But this was not contemplated when the buildings were planned; and subsequently a measure was prepared for increasing and organising medical relief."

The measure proposed by Mr. Nicholls was, however, never carried into effect.

Owing to the great distress that prevailed in 1847–8, the amount of additional workhouse accommodation that became necessary greatly exceeded the original estimate of the Commissioners, as it did the ascertained permanent wants of the country.

"This," say the Commissioners in their Report of 1848–9, "has taken place under the influence of a strong and growing conviction that the abuses incidental to outdoor relief are not to be contended with by any administrative agency when such relief is conducted on a large scale, and that a system of workhouse relief is preferable not alone in ordinary times but in seasons of the severest distress. Thus building after building has been hired in aid of the workhouses originally built, and the entire accommodation which was originally calculated at 100,000, and which during the year 1847–8 was increased to 150,000, has during the present season been extended so as to contain more than 250,000, inmates."

From this brief notice of the formation of unions throughout Ireland, and the very extensive provision made for in-door relief, it will be understood how, upon the occurrence of any considerable diminution of pauperism, the nominal workhouse accommodation would be found to be in excess of the immediate wants of Poor Law Administration. When this became apparent, guardians somewhat hastily concluded that because the Workhouse of a particular union was found to be too large for its requirement, therefore the Workhouse might be dispensed with altogether. At a very early period an attempt was made to give effect to this view, not merely in particular unions but throughout the whole of Ireland.

In the year 1857, a meeting was held in Dublin of representatives of Poor Law Unions, at which a memorial to His Excellency the Lord Lieutenant was adopted, in the course of which it stated:—

"That there is at present a superabundant and very unnecessary amount of indoor accommodation, exceeding by about four times what is required, and this at a period when not only pauperism, but also the population is on the decrease, there being only 53,000 inmates of workhouses in the 163 Unions in Ireland, or one-fifth of the number in 1851, the number then being 250,000."

Referring to this passage the Local Government Board in their 10th Annual Report observe—

"This language appears to be connected with an impression, that establishment charges are in proportion to the extent of the existing accommodation in the workhouses, and that vacant accommodation is, therefore, in itself an evil requiring remedy, by way of abatement."

These passages express clearly the two grounds upon which the amalgamation of Unions has been from time to time, and is now, urged by different boards of guardians.

It is still assumed—

1st. That the workhouse accommodation of Ireland is enormously in excess of the actual or probable want of the country; and

2nd. That by diminishing the number of Unions a considerable saving of establishment charges might be effected.

In replying to the memorial the Local Government Board appear to have admitted, impliedly at least, the correctness of the statement as to the excess of workhouse accommodation, and dealt chiefly with the argument implied in it, that establishment charges are in proportion to workhouse accommodation. It is to be regretted, we think, that the statement as to workhouse accommodation should have been allowed to pass unexamined. It becomes the more necessary that the serious error involved in it should be now corrected, as in a return presented to Parliament in the last session it is authoritatively repeated in a more exaggerated form than it has been yet put forward by the advocates of amalgamation. According to that return the workhouses of Ireland afford accommodation for 147,222 persons, while the number accommodated during the year 1877 was 43,632. If that statement were correct, or even approximately correct, the argument in favour of amalgamation, so far as it rests upon the alleged excess of accommodation, would undoubtedly have considerable weight. But the statement is in all essential respects the reverse of correct.

Commons Parliamentary Paper, No. 200, session 1878.

The gross accommodation of the workhouses in Ireland has been declared upon a principle and upon a scale of measurement that could not fail to mislead and which have in fact misled in every case in which they have been applied.

The rule adopted was simply to ascertain the cubic contents of every sleeping room, or rather of every room that could be made available as a sleeping room, and then, without reference to either height or width, apportion it according to a fixed amount of cubic space for each inmate. No account seems to have been taken of the need of adequate day-room accommodation for the several classes. Infectious wards and probationary wards, though only available, however commodious they may be, for a very limited number, are included in the return at their full capacity of accommodation upon the scale of cubic space; while in some cases buildings that have either ceased to be used or are unfit for use as accommodation for inmates are included.

The accommodation of any public building as a barrack, an hospital, or a workhouse, can be fixed accurately only by a scale of measurement of sleeping wards, in which account shall be taken, not merely of cubic space, but also of superficial space, as well as of the necessity of adequate day-room accommodation. Rooms that are sixteen or seventeen feet high, as are very many of the wards in Irish workhouses, could not contain as dormitories, much less "accommodate," the number of inmates that would be allotted to them upon the usual scale of allowance of cubic space only. In several workhouses we found by actual measurement that wards were certified for a number that allowed less than two feet of wall space for each inmate, 46 persons being allotted to sleep upon a length of ninety feet. That they have been so occupied is no doubt true. In the time of the famine, when, according to the evidence of a medical officer who had experience of that period, "he had to creep in between the people" * * * "on his hands and knees separating the living from the dead," the overcrowding of workhouse wards was unavoidable. But for any such appropriation of wards for ordinary use there can be no justification.

Dr. Moore, Ev. 522, 523.

If the Local Government Board had occasion at the present time to reconsider the accommodation of Irish workhouses, we are satisfied that the limit would be fixed at from 45 to 50 per cent. below the numbers given in the recent Parliamentary Return.

We feel justified in making this statement from having applied the test of a carefully prepared schedule of what we consider should be taken as the *minimum* requirements of space for the accommodation of the several classes in a sufficient number of workhouses varying in dimensions and structural arrangement.

The Local Government Board not considering it expedient to revise those returns, it became necessary for us to make ourselves a careful estimate of the allowance of wall space, floor space, and cubic space that should be provided per head of each class to be accommodated.

We concluded to prepare this schedule, as at an early period of our inquiry it became evident to us that the estimates of accommodation upon the books of the various houses were wholly fallacious and misleading.

This subject recently occupied the attention of the Local Government Board in England, and of the Board of Superintendence in Scotland. It was considered of such importance in connection with the London Metropolitan workhouses, that in 1866 a committee composed of men peculiarly qualified for such an inquiry was appointed by the President of the Poor Law Board to consider and report upon the question. The English Local Government Board have laid down a scale of minimum space requirements, which is, as far as possible, adopted in the construction of new workhouses and in the appropriation of existing buildings.

Availing ourselves of the Report of the Metropolitan Cubic Space Committee, and, taking the regulations adopted in England and Scotland, we have applied them as far in our schedule as the circumstances and the general construction of Irish workhouses would admit, being of opinion that the space necessary for the proper accommodation of workhouse inmates in Great Britain is no more than, under ordinary circumstances, should be provided for the same class in Ireland. This schedule we have submitted to three professional gentlemen,—Sir Dominick Corrigan, Dr. J. T. Banks, and the Deputy Surgeon General, James J. Holloway, whose report upon it will be found in the Appendix. They report that the schedule is one of which they approve, and which in their opinion ought to be adopted. A 9., p. 168.

We reproduce in the Appendix, p. 250, a plan which will illustrate the general arrangement of the most usual type of Irish workhouse. Plate XII.

The front or entrance building forms a structure distinct from the rest of the house; it stands some distance in advance of the main building, and is described by the architect, Mr. Wilkinson, as consisting of—

> "One floor (above the ground) on which the board room and clerk's office are placed; underneath these are the waiting hall, in which applicants for relief are received, and a room for the porter, who has charge of the paupers on their admission, for the purpose of seeing that they are washed, cleaned, and clothed in the workhouse dress, he is therefore placed near the probationary wards."

These wards are almost invariably detached from the main building, so as to secure the body of the house from the risk of infection from persons previous to their being examined by the medical officer and declared free from disease.

The accommodation afforded by these wards has hitherto been included in the returns of permanent available accommodation, but as it is only intended for the use of paupers awaiting the doctor's inspection, until admitted to their several departments, it should not be so included.

The main building is approached through a narrow strip of garden, which separates the boys' yard on the right, from the girls' yard on the left. The centre of the main building contains the master's and matron's apartments, so placed as to be within easy access of all classes; the kitchen, laundry, and stores are close adjoining, so as to be immediately under the master's and matron's inspection. On either side of the officers' apartments are situated the rooms for children: they have separate staircases, which are also used by the master and matron, and which communicate with the schoolrooms on the ground floor. Each of the extreme wings contains on the ground floor a day-room and dormitory for the aged and infirm, the upper floors having been intended to afford dormitory accommodation for the able-bodied.

The dining-hall was constructed to serve three purposes, *e.g.*, that of dining-hall, and chapel, and, by means of a double partition, it was intended, should occasion require it, to be made available for day-rooms for the able-bodied men and women. For this latter purpose it is now generally quite unsuitable, half the building having in most workhouses been permanently converted into and fitted up as a place of worship.

The infirmary is placed at the back of the building, occupying a position distinct from the wards of the house, and sufficiently convenient, it was supposed, for the supply of food from the kitchen offices, without entailing the necessity of a separate establishment. This expectation has not been realized, as each infirmary now has its own kitchen range.

Wards or cells are placed at each end of the infirmary building for idiots, epileptics, and lunatics. To the character of these wards we refer in another part of this Report. The accommodation in the infirmaries as originally provided was very limited, and was intended for the reception and treatment of such acute cases as might occur in the workhouse. These buildings we found to be generally crowded with a large proportion of cases whose only ailment was "old age;" this crowding is the consequence of the very limited accommodation in the main buildings originally appropriated for the class of "aged and infirm." This has been remedied in some few unions by the appropriation to this class of the dormitories on the first and second floors, situated above the original aged and infirm dormitory in each wing, the three wards being directly connected by staircases of easy ascent. This arrangement, where carried out, has been attended with the best results, as, while turning vacant space to a legitimate use, it has materially relieved the pressure on the accommodation in the infirmaries, and it is one which, we think, might be advantageously adopted in any reappropriation of the house accommodation.

The able-bodied are, in very rare instances only, provided with separate day-rooms; the dining-halls not being available for the purpose, separate classification can rarely be maintained.

The fever hospitals are generally detached buildings. We have no remark to make concerning them, except that they appear to be admirably suited to their purpose, and that the accommodation returned as afforded by them appears to have been arrived at on a proper basis. This class of building, however, should not be included in the general estimate of available workhouse accommodation. Infectious wards must always be in reserve, so to speak.

The classes provided for in our schedule are The Sick, under the heads of the ordinary sick of both sexes, with a due proportion of suitable accommodation in separate wards for special purposes, *e.g.*, "lying-in," "ophthalmic," "itch," and "offensive cases"; and The Healthy, under the heads of "The aged and infirm"—(*a.*) Bed-ridden; (*b.*) Those in rooms occupied partially by day and night; "Mothers with infants;" "Able-bodied adults," both sexes; "Children," both sexes.

The Sick.

Ordinary Cases.—The rules laid down by the English Local Government Board place the minimum allowance of space per patient as under:—

Wall space, 6 feet; floor space, 60 feet; cubic space, 600 feet; with day-room accommodation for every second inmate.

The Scotch Board of Superintendence names the minimum as 700 cubic feet.

The Metropolitan Cubic Space Committee recommends 6 feet of wall space and 850 feet of cubic space, the height of the ward contemplated being 12 feet.

The infirmary accommodation is so limited in Ireland that it would be out of the question to attempt to provide day-room accommodation for the patients. We consider, however, that the English scale without the day-room may fairly be adopted as a minimum, with the proviso that no height over 10 feet shall be included in the computation of the cubic space.

Special Cases.—*Lying-in.*—The English Local Government Board fixes the minimum requirements for this class at—wall space, 8 feet; floor space, 80 feet; cubic space, 960 feet. (Rooms 12 feet high.)

The Metropolitan Cubic Space Committee allow 1,200 cubic feet.

The space available in Irish workhouses is so limited that it would be in vain to look for such an allowance of cubic space as the last named; but we think that the English scale may be adopted of 8 feet wall space, 80 feet floor space, and 800 feet cubic space, height up to 10 feet only being included in the computation of the latter.

"Itch" and "ophthalmic" cases we find grouped with "offensive" cases in the report of the Metropolitan Committee, and we think that where accommodation can be provided for these classes it should be on the same scale as that we adopt for the "lying-in" patients.

The Healthy.

Aged and Infirm.—*Bed-ridden.*—To this class the English Local Government Board allots the same minimum space as they give to their infirmary patients.

The Metropolitan Cubic Space Committee gives them 6 feet of wall space and 850 feet of cubic space. (Rooms 12 feet high.)

For this class we think that the minimum requirements should be fixed at the same as those adopted for the ordinary sick, viz., wall space, 6 feet; floor space, 60 feet; cubic space, 600 feet (height up to 10 feet only being included in the computation).

Aged and Infirm.—*In rooms partially occupied by day and night.*—The Metropolitan Cubic Space Committee, after insisting that each sick ward should have the use of a day-room, says, without specifying the height of the wards, that with such provisions "500 cubic feet for each bed will suffice."

Taking 10 feet as our standard height for computation of cubic space, and say 18 feet as about the width of our dormitory (it is rather over the average), to afford this cubic space each bed would require 50 feet of floor space, and say 5 feet 6 inches of wall space.

It appears to us reasonable to adopt these figures, viz., 5 feet 6 inches wall space, 50 feet floor space, and 500 feet cubic space, as the minimum for this class, with a suitable day room.

MOTHERS WITH INFANTS.—The English Local Government Board lays down 5 feet as the minimum of wall space to be required.

Taking the dimensions of their ordinary dormitories as 10 feet in height and 18 feet in width, gives us what we think reasonable to adopt, viz., 5 feet wall space; 45 feet floor space; 450 feet cubic space. For this class a nursery day room should be provided.

ABLE-BODIED ADULTS, BOTH SEXES.—For this class 250 feet of cubic space, without any reference to the height of the dormitory, and without any day-room accommodation, is the scale, if such it can be called, upon which the accommodation in most of the Irish workhouses has been computed.

The Scotch Board of Superintendence gives them a minimum of 4 feet 6 inches wall space, and 400 feet of cubic space. This with dormitories 18 feet wide would give about 40 feet of floor space.

The English Local Government Board provides, 1st, that in their ordinary wards of 18 feet in width and 10 feet in height a minimum of wall space should be afforded of 4 feet; and, 2nd, that in wards not exceeding 16 feet in width, in which two rows of beds are placed, the said beds should be placed with *their sides* to the walls, which would monopolise about 7 feet of wall space, and make the floor space 56 feet and cubic space 560 feet.

The Metropolitan Cubic Space Committee does not appear to have made inquiries under this head, as it merely reported that it had no evidence before it to make it appear that 300 feet was too little.

As the dormitories are in very few instances more that 16 feet in width, we consider that, without going so far as to adopt the 2nd English scale, we shall be fixing upon a very moderate scale in adopting the Scotch of 4 feet 6 inches wall space, and 400 feet cubic space.

The mattresses in most of the workhouses appear to be about 3 feet wide. The above allowance of wall space would leave but 18 inches between the beds, which would appear to us to be little enough.

For this class separate day or work rooms should be provided.

CHILDREN, BOTH SEXES.—The English Local Government Board regulations fix 3 feet 9 inches as the minimum of wall space for each single bed, and 5 feet for each double bed.

The Scotch Board lays down 300 cubic feet as the minimum of cubic space to be required per child, though "in point of fact the allowance given in three of the most important workhouses in Scotland ranges from 400 to nearly 700 feet for children."

For this class we think that the Scotch minimum of 300 cubic feet may be adopted.

The school-rooms can serve as day rooms for this class.

In the old class of house there are attics, which are credited with affording a considerable amount of accommodation. This woodcut will convey an idea of the accom-

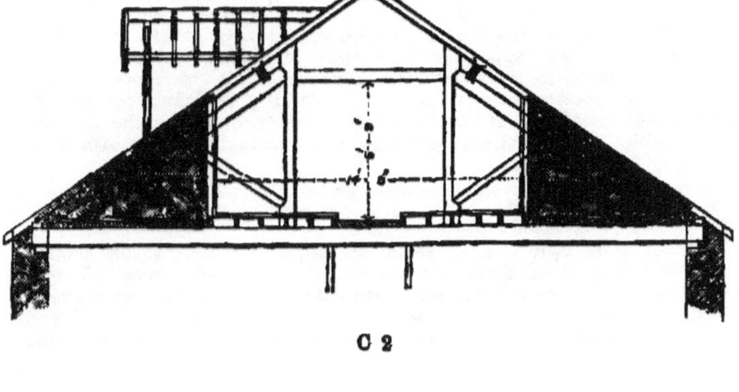

modation afforded. Unless in cases of great urgency, they should not be occupied, as they are unfit for permanent occupation, being wanting in space, and from their situation subject to the extremes of heat and cold. We have generally found them turned to the use for which they would appear to have been originally intended, viz., "stores."

In considering the practical application of the scale of accommodation that we have adopted, it must be observed that in Ireland, as in England, the character of indoor pauperism has within a comparatively short time become totally changed. This was observed many years ago by Dr. Edward Smith in his report to the Local Government Board upon the arrangement of provincial workhouses in England:

"Workhouses," he observes, "which were built after the passing of the present Poor Law are still comparatively new, and yet how great a change has taken place in the condition of the poor, the views of guardians, and the opinion of the public, whether professional or otherwise, during the last 30 years. When the present workhouses were erected, the aged and sick poor were generally allowed out-door relief, and provision in the workhouse was chiefly required for the able-bodied. Now the aged and some of the sick are brought into the workhouse, and the able-bodied inmates have, comparatively speaking, disappeared. Hence it must be manifest that, with so great a change of circumstances, equal changes in the construction and organisation of workhouses are required, and yet the fabric of a workhouse is not of itself changeable, and is not readily remodelled."

A state of things similar to this may be observed in the greater number of Irish workhouses. A considerable portion of the room provided for able-bodied inmates is now unoccupied by that class, while, as a rule, the infirmary accommodation that was originally provided is now found to be insufficient. "Sick," "aged and infirm," and "children" are the classes that now constitute the in-door pauperism of Ireland. The two former are, as we have indicated, far in excess of the accommodation that is specially provided for them.

The character of workhouse classification and the necessity of enforcing it are points that seem to be lost sight of by those boards of guardians who urge amalgamation of Unions upon the ground of there being a great excess of workhouse accommodation. When the guardians of the Cavan Union, for example, found it stated in the return of the Local Government Board that their workhouse could accommodate 1,234 inmates, while the average number in 1877 is only 258, they not unnaturally persisted in contending that they have a great deal of available spare accommodation. But the accommodation of that workhouse has been fixed upon a scale which, as we have pointed out, is altogether misleading. The gross number of all classes that could be accommodated, with proper regard to health and classification, does not in fact, as will be seen by and bye, exceed 613. It will very often happen that, while particular departments of a workhouse may be full or overcrowded, there may be a great deal of spare accommodation in other departments, and this in fact is found to be the case in a very considerable number of Irish workhouses. It may be also observed that the pressure for admission is of those classes for whom there is the least or no spare accommodation. To meet this difficulty the workhouse officials are not unfrequently compelled to disregard the prescribed rules of classification. In the Cavan workhouse, for example, cases that require medical treatment have sometimes been warded in other parts of the house, "until a bed becomes vacant in the hospital," beds having been in the meantime laid down upon the floors of the lobbies. It may be assumed that, no matter what may be the aggregate accommodation of a workhouse, there cannot be said to be spare available accommodation if any department be overcrowded. No doubt this may be to a great extent remedied, and has been in many cases remedied, as we have already observed, by a redistribution of the workhouse wards. We may here observe that a remeasurement of Irish workhouses with a view to fixing not merely the gross number, but the numbers of the several classes to be retained in them, and, what is of equal importance, to reappropriating the wards, appears to us to be imperatively called for. This, we repeat, is the more necessary as the misapprehension that has heretofore prevailed as to the extent of workhouse accommodation is but too likely to be confirmed by the Parliamentary Return to which we have already referred. It is true that in that return attention is called to the following note:

"The orders under seal, from which these figures are taken, were of a prohibitory nature, having been used (? issued) to prevent the workhouse from being overcrowded. In recent years the limited number has not been approached except in a few cases."

The order, however, to be effective for the object indicated, should prohibit any excess, not merely of the gross number, but of a specified number of each class. Although it may be true that "in recent years the limited (gross) number" may not have been approached, yet in a considerable number of cases the number of particular classes—the sick—aged and infirm—that can be properly accommodated has been very much exceeded. If the sealed order is to "prevent the workhouse from being overcrowded," it should prevent any department of it from being overcrowded, and should fix the accommodation of the several classes by wards, the mode now adopted in declaring the accommodation in English workhouses. In the earlier period of our inquiry we were ourselves misled by the official declaration of the accommodation of the workhouses of the Ballymoney and Limavady Unions. Having been instructed by Your Grace to ascertain and report whether, with a view to provide accommodation for lunatics in the Londonderry Asylum District without incurring the expense of enlarging the asylum, a workhouse in the district could be appropriated for the purpose, we selected that of the Coleraine Union as being specially adapted for the purpose. We assumed that the workhouses of Ballymoney and Limavady, to which it would have been necessary to have transferred the paupers of Coleraine, would afford the required accommodation for them. These two workhouses were certified to accommodate 755 and 701 inmates respectively, while the number of inmates in the three houses amounted (in February 1877) to only 533. But coming to deal with this gross accommodation by classes, we find that not only is the total certified number greatly in excess of the available space, being reduced under our Schedule from 1,456 to 668, but that the accommodation for the "sick" and "aged and infirm" was less by one-third than the numbers in the houses on the date named.

Another serious mistake that is made by those who ground their applications for amalgamation upon the supposed excess of accommodation in workhouses, is the assumption that the number of inmates upon a given day represents the extent to which the workhouse is made available for the relief of distress. As well assume that an hospital through which a thousand patients may pass in the course of a year affords relief to only one hundred because one hundred may happen to be the average daily number of patients or the number in it upon a particular day. The extent to which workhouses in Ireland are made available, not merely to test the destitution of the able-bodied, but as hospitals for the sick, places of refuge for the aged and infirm, and schools for the young, is, we apprehend, very imperfectly known or appreciated by the majority of those who so strongly advocate the closing of these establishments.

The "certified" accommodation of the workhouses of Ireland, which as we have shown is far in excess of the actual available accommodation, is for 147,222 inmates. It is true that the average daily number of inmates in 1876, the year in which the guardians of all the Irish unions were invited to co-operate in a movement in favour of amalgamation, was only 43,688. But the total number of persons who had received relief in the workhouses during the year was 182,749. The corresponding numbers in the preceding year, 1875, were—

Average daily number - - - - 45,935
Number relieved during the year - - 213,794

As a further illustration of this view of the question of amalgamation, we reproduce from the Reports of the Local Government Board the statement and comparison for a series of years, from 1859 to 1877 inclusive, of the numbers of the several classes relieved in the workhouses.

Year ended 29th September.	Number of Paupers in Workhouse at the commencement of the Year.	Number of Persons admitted during the Year: Number admitted in Sickness: Suffering from Fever or other contagious Disease	Suffering under other Diseases	Suffering from accidental Injury	Total number admitted in Sickness	Number admitted who were not Sick	Total number admitted during the Year	Number of Births in the Workhouse during the Year	Total number of Persons relieved in the Workhouse during the Year	Number of Deaths in the Workhouse during the Year
1859	36,636	9,953	32,600	2,107	44,630	70,334	114,394	2,376	153,706	8,003
1860	35,206	9,107	36,456	2,025	47,588	85,312	132,900	2,443	170,349	9,677
1861	38,294	9,368	38,378	2,317	49,658	114,830	164,698	2,445	204,423	10,550
1862	41,295	11,163	44,855	2,234	58,264	165,433	223,697	2,815	267,807	12,740
1863	45,181	14,469	44,957	2,431	61,857	178,270	240,127	2,977	298,265	13,296
1864	49,087	15,757	43,027	2,280	61,064	151,157	212,221	2,889	261,147	12,765
1865	44,032	18,410	41,498	2,363	62,291	139,095	201,386	2,751	252,170	12,355
1866	44,657	13,353	38,327	2,863	54,449	130,146	184,387	[illegible]	232,104	11,341
1867	41,378	11,708	43,174	2,431	57,312	153,895	211,207	2,654	268,139	13,162
1868	45,313	11,909	41,534	2,564	55,607	185,236	240,843	2,397	268,953	11,570
1869	47,775	9,976	41,602	2,441	54,019	131,358	135,377	2,410	235,562	11,347
1870	45,018	8,153	39,086	2,510	49,749	133,386	168,135	2,253	230,439	10,697
1871	42,873	8,718	38,313	2,510	49,540	131,492	181,032	2,103	225,310	10,060
1872	40,891	10,249	39,920	2,340	52,509	137,239	189,740	1,953	232,236	11,345
1873	40,834	8,285	43,747	2,422	54,404	152,078	206,482	1,963	249,798	12,254
1874	41,446	8,463	39,368	2,573	50,405	159,800	209,205	1,844	258,195	10,795
1875	42,886	8,015	37,064	2,888	47,967	121,182	169,149	1,759	213,794	11,470
1876	40,506	6,576	36,570	2,385	46,531	95,070	140,601	1,643	182,749	10,668
1877	39,773	6,940	39,660	2,330	49,190	108,235	157,356	1,706	196,831	10,793

It is not easy to understand how the facts disclosed in this table can have been overlooked or disregarded by those who urge the closing of workhouses upon the ground that they are only partially made use of. The figures certainly suggest some considerations which materially affect the question as to the expediency of closing any of the workhouses in which so large a proportion of the indigent poor are relieved, though only temporarily.

It is to be observed that the total number relieved, if relieved at the same time, would be far in excess of the actual accommodation. It is true that the average duration of residence in the workhouse does not exceed three months (in 1876 it was 87 days). But bearing in mind that the persons relieved are of a class that a single adverse season, a short harvest, a scarcity of fuel in a hard winter, might compel to remain in the workhouse for a much longer period, so that the average number of inmates in any given month might be doubled in the month following, it becomes absolutely necessary to reserve a very wide margin of accommodation for such contingencies.

Then if we analyse the in-door pauperism of any given half year—taking for example the half year ended the 29th September 1876—we find that the numbers of able-bodied and their children classified as follows were:—

Adults:—	
Married couples—Males	1,296
Females	1,296
Other males	19,611
Other females	22,252
Children under 15 of able-bodied inmates:—	
Illegitimate	7,369
Other children	12,875

It appears that no fewer than 44,455 classed as "able-bodied" persons were relieved in the workhouses in the course of the summer half year of 1876—a favourable period of a by no means exceptionally bad year. These with the children (20,244) make a total of 64,699 of able-bodied and those dependant upon them. If workhouses are to be really efficient for the purpose of testing destitution there is no pretence for alleging that even the "certified," still less the actual, accommodation for able-bodied is in excess of the reasonable requirements of poor law administration.

But, looking to the character and condition of the humbler classes of the Irish people, the value of a workhouse as a means of testing destitution is but slight compared with its usefulness in giving shelter to the aged and infirm, hospital accommodation to the sick, and education to the young.

A more striking contrast it would be difficult to present than between the condition of the poor people who may be found in the wards appropriated for aged and infirm in an Irish workhouse, and the same class outside its walls. The sleeping rooms in the former are commodious, well ventilated, and warm, generally speaking clean, in many houses scrupulously so, though we found not a few where there was decided room for improvement; the diet is wholesome and sufficient; the bedding is good; the clothing decent and comfortable. The dwellings of the same class outside are too often wretched hovels, unfit for human habitation, yet crowded, without regard to health or decency, by struggling families who are ill fed and in rags. In visiting the workhouses of Ireland we could not fail to mark this most striking and painful contrast.

As hospitals for the treatment of the sick poor the workhouses in Ireland appear to us to merit the confidence with which they seem to be now regarded by all classes. Although many of them even in remote rural districts will bear comparison with similar establishments in any part of the kingdom, they may, as we have pointed out, by re-distribution of rooms, be rendered much more useful than they are. Still the extent of their present usefulness may be estimated from the fact that during the year 1877 no fewer than 49,120 persons were admitted to them for treatment, of whom 6,954 were suffering from fever or other dangerous contagious disease, 39,660 suffering from ordinary diseases, and 2,520 from accidental injury.

Of the educational advantages conferred upon children in Irish workhouses we shall have occasion to speak in another part of this Report. But here we may observe that the general appearance and demeanour of the children in these establishments is most gratifying. Healthy and cheerful looking, generally speaking, clean and tidy in person and dress, and very orderly in conduct, these children offer an excellent example of what may be done by care and attention to improve the younger generation of even the very humblest class of Irish poor.

It thus appears, we think, not only that the first reason urged in favour of shutting up a considerable number of workhouses—that there is a large amount of superfluous accommodation—is greatly exaggerated, but that under no circumstances could they be shut up without inflicting hardship and suffering upon the poor. It is true, indeed, that, connected with a very considerable number of workhouses, there are detached buildings,—hospitals, ranges of sheds school buildings,—that, having been erected to meet an emergency, are no longer required for strictly poor law purposes. As, however, these may be made available in the way that we shall suggest in a subsequent part of this Report, guardians need no longer have even a colourable ground for complaining, if our proposal be adopted, that they are compelled to keep up a large amount of useless unappropriated workhouse accommodation.

Although the statements as to pecuniary saving—the other reason put forward by guardians in support of applications for amalgamation—have been fully and conclusively met by the replies of the Local Government Board to separate applications, it yet seems desirable to inquire generally, and as applied to the whole country, what would be the amount of the saving likely to be effected by amalgamation if carried out as proposed?

In the abstracts of the Union accounts, the charges are made up under the following heads:—

1 In-maintenance and clothing of workhouse inmates.
2. Out-relief in money and kind.
3. Cost of maintenance in deaf and dumb and blind asylums and in extern hospitals.
4. Establishment charges.
5. Collector's poundage.
6. Workhouse burial expenses.
7. Election law and other expenses.
8. Medical charities and vaccination expenses.
9. Expenditure under Sanitary Acts.
10. Expenses under Burial Grounds Act.
11. Expenses under Superannuation Acts.

The only items of expenditure mentioned above which would in any material degree be lessened by amalgamation would be Nos. 4 and 11, viz., the establishment charges and the expenses under Superannuation Act.

The establishment expenses of a Union are included under the following heads:—

1. Salaries and rations of officers.
2. Additional buildings—repairs and improvements.
3. Furniture, utensils, and implements of work.
4. Fuel, light, and other necessaries debited to establishment.
5. Printing, books, stationery, advertising, and postage.
6. Drugs and medical or surgical appliances.
7. Rent and taxes.
8. Farm seeds, labour, &c.

A portion of these expenses is defrayed by Parliamentary grant, viz., the salaries of the officers employed in the education of the children, half the salary of the medical officers, and half the cost of drugs and medical appliances used in workhouses, which so far cease to be a charge upon the rates of the Union.

With regard to the poundage of rate required to meet the establishment charge, it might be supposed that this should always be greater in Unions having a small valuation on which to assess these expenses, but a reference to the return in Appendix will show that such is not the case, the establishment charge in many of the Unions having a large valuation being greatly in excess of other Unions having a much smaller valuation; thus, Cork Union, with a valuation of 338,406*l.*, had to levy 8 1/15*d.* in the £ to defray its establishment charge, whilst in the adjoining Union of Kinsale, with the valuation of 59,327*l.*, the charge was defrayed by a rate of 2¼*d.*; South Dublin, with a valuation of 621,538*l.*, had to pay 5⅓*d.*, whilst Celbridge, with a valuation of 114,578*l.*, got off for 2⅓*d.*; Sligo, with a valuation of 97,864*l.*, paid 3*d.*, whilst Dromore West, with a valuation of 36,868*l.*, paid only 2¼*d.*; and Belfast, with a valuation of 606,436*l.*, paid 4*d.*, whilst Lisburn, with a valuation of 171,300*l.*, paid only 1½*d.* A 7., p. 166.

There are a few cases of Unions, however, where the valuation being exceptionally low, the establishment charge must fall heavily upon the rates; as, for instance, Belmullet, having only a valuation of 10,949*l.*, the charge amounted to 13*d.*; Newport, with a valuation of 13,168*l.*, had to pay 10*d.*; Clifden, with a valuation of 17,870*l.*, 8¾*d.*, and Dunfanaghy, with a valuation of 11,532*l.*, 8½*d.* In these cases, with a few more in the west of Ireland, it would be very desirable, if possible, to reduce the charge; but the great distances from the workhouses to which, even if it were unobjectionable upon other grounds, large numbers of the sick and infirm classes in all the above-mentioned Unions would have to be removed, render it impossible to recommend amalgamation with other Unions.

It is generally assumed that by amalgamation a considerable saving would be effected, not only in establishment charges, but also in the reduction of cost of in-maintenance, the consumption of fuel and other necessaries not being increased in proportion to the
A 8., p. 163. increase of inmates; but the return in Appendix shows that a large number of inmates by no means necessarily leads to a diminished cost in this respect. Thus, in the South Dublin Union, with an average of 2,638 inmates, the average weekly cost amounted to 3*s.* 5*d.*, whilst in the adjoining Union of Celbridge, with an average of 162 inmates, it amounted to 2*s.* 11¼*d.* In Belfast, with an average of 2,043, the cost was 2*s.* 7½*d.*, whilst in Lisburn, with an average of 221 inmates, the cost was only 2*s.* 0¾*d.* per head. Castlederg, with an average of 65, and Stranorlar, with an average of 54 inmates, being among the very lowest of the Unions situate in the province of Ulster.

The same observations apply to the Unions situate in the provinces of Munster and Connaught, showing conclusively that an increased number of inmates does not necessarily lead to a diminution in the cost of workhouse maintenance.

It is to be observed that if amalgamation was considered advisable, the Unions which would be selected for extinction must necessarily be those which are the least in area, and in which the establishment expenses (though forming a high poundage on the rates of the Union) are the smallest in amount, and may be estimated on an average to impose a cost of from 500*l.* to 600*l.* per annum on the Union.

If the whole of this amount were saved to the small Unions by amalgamation, it would undoubtedly afford considerable relief; but such would not be the case, as the saving would be shared by all the amalgamated Unions, and render the amount of saving in each inconsiderable, which we may illustrate by an example.

The Union of Baltinglass applied to be dissolved and amalgamated with the adjoining unions of Naas, Athy, Carlow, and Shillelagh. The average establishment charges paid out of the union funds may be estimated at 1,100*l.* per annum, of which probably a sum not exceeding 800*l.* would be saved, the balance being swallowed up by the increased establishment charges of the other unions and the necessity of keeping up a fever hospital at Baltinglass. The benefit of this saving would not be confined to the Baltinglass Union, but would in somewhat varying proportions be spread over the entire area having a valuation of 507,000*l.*, and would only show an average saving of one third part of a penny in the pound.

It is evident therefore that the anticipation of those Guardians who reckon upon a large pecuniary saving as the result of "amalgamation" would not be realised. There are other consequences, however, that would be certain to result from such a change which are too important to be left unnoticed.

That a very considerable extension of out-door relief would follow from any considerable extension of the area of unions is admitted by those who are in favour as well as by those who are averse to it, and with both, indeed, constitutes one of the avowed reasons for supporting or opposing the scheme In the circular
Mr. Sanderson, Ev. 89. letter in which the guardians of the Cavan Union invite the representatives of the other unions throughout Ireland to co-operate with them in their endeavour to dispense with a certain number of workhouses, they suggest a system of out-door relief "judiciously administered" as a mode of meeting the obvious difficulty of relieving destitution in an area so wide as that contemplated in their proposal of amalgamation. As the system of out-door relief thus recommended for general adoption affords a fair illustration of what might be looked for from its extension, we shall take leave to call your Grace's attention to the evidence upon the subject that was given upon the inquiries at Cavan, Monaghan, Ennis, Millstreet, and Glennamaddy. Before we notice this evidence, however, it may not be inopportune to refer generally to the system of out-door relief, its origin, progress, and extant, which now prevails in several unions in Ireland.

During the discussions that preceded the passing of the Irish Poor Relief Act all parties appear to have been impressed with the necessity of absolutely prohibiting out-door relief. The danger that would arise from any relaxation of the rule was urged by men of the highest authority.

"Out-door relief," Sir George Lewis wrote, "when once established, opens an indefinite career to abuse; the wit of man cannot foresee a tithe of the evils to which, under peculiar circumstances, it may give rise. The united sagacity of the whole human race could not, in the reign of Elizabeth, have predicted the varied and subtle forms of mischief which are developed in the Report of the English Poor Law Commission of Inquiry. There is no branch of legislation of which it is truer than of Poor Laws, that every weak point will be scrutinised. A thousand eyes are constantly, and in every quarter, on the look-out to detect an opening for fraud. The tendency of water to escape through the minutest cranny of a vessel in which it is confined is not greater or more certain than the tendency of the community to obtain relief if they can by any contrivance get it on easy terms. Above all laws a Poor Law ought, therefore, to be fenced round with strong checks and guarantees. Every man's hand will be in the purse of the public almoner if he has not powerful repellents to keep them off. What then are we to think of the prudence of a proposal to introduce an extensive system of relief among perhaps the poorest peasantry in the civilised world, without a protection that has, at any rate, been proved to be sufficient, and is, probably, the only one to be relied on?"

Similar views were urged in Parliament and out of it, and ultimately prevailed, as we have already stated, in the framing of the Act. Relief in the workhouse was the principle upon which that law was grounded, and the principle upon which for some time it was successfully administered. Deep and widespread as was the distress that prevailed in Ireland at that period, the machinery of the Poor Law was found to be adequate to cope with it. The erection of workhouses having been completed with extraordinary rapidity, the Poor Law, within a few years of its enactment, was in active and successful operation. Very great difficulties indeed had to be encountered upon its introduction.

"In their earlier investigations the Assistant Commissioners found that extremely vague and exaggerated notions were entertained of the law itself and its probable effects. Some persons felt the utmost degree of alarm, and considered that it would eventually lead to the destruction of property; others again contended that it would be productive of no effect whatever, that the workhouse would be useless, and that the pauperised classes would remain as at present, dependent upon charitable contributions for support. All, however, appeared to view the approach of the Commissioners with more or less alarm, and to regard the introduction of the new law as a new evil."

To this statement of their earlier difficulties the Commissioners were able to add in the same Report (1839):—

"By unwearied exertion and great patience and perseverance in explaining the objects and intentions of the new law, and by the weight of examples drawn from its application in an amended form in England, the Assistant Commissioners succeeded in removing much of the alarm and misapprehension which at first prevailed, and in obtaining very general co-operation; and we have the great satisfaction of stating that all opposition has now subsided, and that the law, if not universally popular in Ireland, is at least universally acquiesced in."

The unusual distress that began to prevail at a later period taxed to the uttermost all the resources of Poor Law administration. Scarcity of food from the partial failure of the potato crop was aggravated by scarcity of fuel owing to the continued wetness of the season, and great pressure was brought to bear upon the Commissioners to relax the prohibition from giving out-door relief. The Commissioners were fortunately protected by the law, which left them no discretion, else they must have been overborne by the urgent representations of distressed unions. This, they contended, was precisely the contingency in which it was most necessary to adhere inflexibly to a prohibitory rule; and in a circular addressed to boards of guardians, they explained not merely the provision of the law, but the expediency of upholding it. Within a brief period, however, there fell upon the country the greatest calamity that it had yet endured. Ireland was stricken with famine. No Poor Law could bear the strain of such a dispensation, and aid was sought from other sources. It came, as it usually comes in such emergencies in this country, abundantly, from the public treasury as well as from private charity, and was administered, it must be said, lavishly and indiscriminately.

Under the circumstances, that may have been unavoidable. But the immediate result was such as to prove that the direct tendency of any system of out-door relief is to demoralise the people and absorb the property of the country. Every precaution appeared to have been taken to guard against the danger necessarily involved in an undertaking by Government to provide work at wages for all who were or might allege that they were in distress. Under the Labour Rate Act the Board of Works organised a scheme, theoretically unobjectionable, for the administration of the relief funds placed at their disposal. The principle adopted was to give no relief to able-bodied except in return for work; the work to be task-work under an elaborately organised system of supervision. The result is thus described by Sir Charles Trevelyan—a name so honourably associated with the history of that period:

"Thousands upon thousands were pressed upon the officers of the Board of Works in every part of Ireland, and it was impossible for those officers to test the accuracy of the urgent representations that were made to them. The attraction of money wages regularly paid from the public purse, or 'the Queen's pay' as it was popularly called, led to a general abandonment of other descriptions of industry in order to participate in the advantages of the relief works. Landlords competed with each other in getting the names of their tenants placed upon the lists. Farmers dismissed their labourers and sent them to the works; the clergy insisted on the claims of the members of their respective congregations; the fisheries were deserted, and it was often difficult to get a coat patched or a pair of shoes mended, to such an extent had the population of the South and West of Ireland turned out upon the roads. The average number employed in October was 114,000, in November, 285,000; in December, 440,000; and in January 1847, 570,000."

In the following March the number was found to have reached 734,000, representing with their dependants upwards of 3,000,000 of persons. In the same month the expenditure upon relief works, including labour, plant, and cost of staff, was 1,050,772*l.*

We have thus briefly glanced at the history of that period, because the existence of exceptional distress was the ground upon which the Legislature consented to relax the principle of the original Poor Law, by authorising the administration of that out-door relief to which we desire to direct attention.

"The sanction of out-door relief," writes Sir George Nicholls of the Extension Act, "is a most important departure from the principle of the original statute, and was wrung from the Legislature by the distressing circumstances in which the country was placed by the successive failures of the potato crop. With starvation raging, almost universally, around, it was felt that it would be impossible to maintain the restriction of relief to the limits of the workhouse. The concession must, however, be regarded as exceptional, and as being intended to meet an exceptional case; for the necessity of workhouse relief being the established rule, never perhaps, commanded more general assent than at the time when a departure from it was sanctioned."

Before a Committee of the House of Lords, by whom Sir George Nicholls was examined, he gave it as his opinion that

"*The rule of in-door relief should be departed from only so far and in such a way as would secure its resumption with the least difficulty and at the earliest possible period.*"

The discussions that took place in both Houses of Parliament upon the introduction of the Relief Extension Act indicate very plainly that the Government by which it was proposed and the majorities by which it was supported, as well as the minorities by which it was opposed, were fully sensible of the danger involved in such a measure. The assent, given to it reluctantly, was given upon a sort of tacit understanding that it was, as Archbishop Whately observed, "a choice of evils"—a measure to be repealed as soon as the pressing necessity for it might have passed away. The necessity for it has passed away. Not so the mischief that it was certain to produce.

When the Extension Act was proposed the proceedings under the Labour Rate Act were still fresh in the public mind, and it was reasonably feared that all the safeguards of the Poor Law would be borne down by the pressure of imposition as well as of real distress. These apprehensions found very general expression in the debates which preceded the passing of the Act. That they were not exaggerated may be shown from the experience of a single union, the Glenties, in Donegal, as described in evidence before the Parliamentary Committee which, in 1849, inquired into the operation of the Irish Poor Law. A former chairman of that union informed the Committee that out of a population of 43,571 the aggregate number in receipt of relief from about the beginning of January to the 10th of March was 39,000. Two of the guardians by whom relief was administered had been themselves upon the relief works, the chairman of the Board being, according to the report of the inspector, "a retired tinker." The witness continued,—

"After a great deal of persuasion, the Commissioners were got to alter the qualification" (of guardian, raising it from 5*l.* to 10*l.*). "The result was a new board, differently constituted, who elected a very different chairman. In the following year—that is, in March 1849—the number in receipt of relief was brought down from 39,000 to 9,000."

Another witness before the same Committee, the Rev. Daniel Liddy, parish priest of Abbyfeale, is asked—

"What effect has the system that has been worked for the last few years had in your opinion upon the morals of the people?—I think it has had a very deteriorating effect.

"Has the respect for oaths diminished in that district?—It has very much diminished.

"To what do you attribute that?—I attribute it to the desire on the part of the very destitute poor to avail themselves of relief (out-door) by every means they can.

"Has their attention to their religious duties diminished from the same cause?—I regret to say it has."—(1330-1-2-3-4, Commons Report, 1849.)

Speaking of a particular relieving officer the same witness says—

"It came to my knowledge that persons who brought him whiskey were put on the relief list, and really destitute and starving creatures were left off."

A great deal of evidence of a similar character may be found in the Report from which these extracts are taken.

That evidence led the Committee of the House of Lords, before whom it was given, to resolve unanimously that—

"No permanent system for the relief of the poor can be carried out in Ireland, safely and beneficially to receivers or payers, without a return to the principle of the original law,—by a strict application of in-door relief to all classes of paupers, subject only to occasional exceptions, under authority of the Poor Law Commissioners, of the old and impotent, *when it is impossible to find room for them in the workhouse.*"

It is often alleged that, as out-door relief is, under the Extension Act, restricted to certain classes from whom able-bodied are excluded, there is but little fear that the giving of it will be abused. Practically, however, it operates injuriously in two ways. Not only is relief given in undeserving cases, and from unworthy motives, but deserving cases are often dismissed with what, in the evidence, is aptly enough designated "a subsidy to mendicancy." The creation of privileged classes of paupers is also a direct inducement to fraud, the non-qualified class seeking to qualify themselves, or those dependent on them, for relief.

"The able-bodied," as Sir George Lewis put it, "will feign sickness; the old will feign infirmity; parents will expose their children; fathers will abandon their families. There will be all the opportunities for fraud that existed under the old English Poor Law, with an enormously increased inducement * * Moreover," observes the same authority, "the workhouse acts not only in preventing wilful imposture, but also in stimulating to exertion those persons on the confines of health and sickness, of strength and weakness, who do not know their own powers until they are pressed to exert them. In fact, when we speak of a man's means of supporting himself we speak of that which does not admit of being ascertained; that which a man himself does not know until he chooses to exert himself. A man may, in perfect sincerity, underrate his own means of gaining a livelihood; and he may require some external pressure, such as a workhouse, to rouse him from his lethargy, and to put him on his mettle"

But no such advantage is attainable if the workhouse accommodation be insufficient or so remote as not to be easily accessible. In every case in which amalgamation has been proposed it was admitted that the workhouse that might be retained would be not only distant from many parts, but barely sufficient to contain the in-door pauperism of the combined Unions. In most cases indeed the accommodation would be insufficient. But no fact is more clearly established in connection with Poor Law administration than that out-door relief invariably increases, that the demand for it is in fact created and guardians driven to grant it as soon as workhouse accommodation is found to be insufficient. When the late Mr. Edward Senior was examined as to the assumed excess of workhouse accommodation in Ireland, speaking from his experience as an Irish Poor Law Inspector, he observed:—

"If you offer the workhouse to a hundred persons, you will find that probably not five will accept it, but if it were full all the 95 would apply at once for out-door relief, which you would not be justified in refusing."

And that is one of many conclusive reasons for retaining a sufficient margin of spare accommodation in every workhouse in Ireland.

If the principle of "The Extension Act" as a permanent measure be unsound, the progress of out-door relief under it is undoubtedly the most unsatisfactory indication connected with Poor Law administration in Ireland. Year by year, for more than 20 years, it has gone on steadily increasing, having grown from 611 cases in 1857 to 19,601 cases in 1878. The rate of progress is thus exhibited:—

Years.	Cases.	Years.	Cases.
1857	611	1868	9,348
1858	823	1869	9,605
1859	777	1870	11,220
1860	1,133	1871	12,698
1861	2,333	1872	14,608
1862	3,334	1873	16,814
1863	4,623	1874	17,084
1864	5,284	1875	17,085
1865	6,058	1876	17,655
1866	6,156	1877	18,152
1867	8,349	1878	19,601

While the number of "*cases*" relieved has increased from 611 to 18,151, the number of "*persons*" for the same period has increased from 1,096 in 1857 to 32,429 in 1877.

To appreciate the full significance of these remarkable figures they must be read in connection with a corresponding statement of *in-door* pauperism. The following table exhibits the numbers in receipt of relief in the workhouse on the first Saturday of January for each year from 1857 to 1877 :—

Saturday, January 3, 1857	-	55,183		Saturday, January 4, 1868	-	56,063
" " 2, 1858	-	49,308		" " 2, 1869	-	56,934
" " 1, 1859	-	43,599		" " 1, 1870	-	53,687
" " 7, 1860	-	43,218		" " 7, 1871	-	50,815
" " 5, 1861	-	47,352		" " 6, 1872	-	48,738
" " 4, 1862	-	55,168		" " 4, 1873	-	49,856
" " 3, 1863	-	60,038		" " 3, 1874	-	49,193
" " 2, 1864	-	59,867		" " 2, 1875	-	49,805
" " 7, 1865	-	59,498		" " 1, 1876	-	46,214
" " 6, 1866	-	54,435		" " 6, 1877	-	45,762
" " 5, 1867	-	54,930		" " 5, 1878	-	49,365

It thus appears that while the number of persons in receipt of *out-door* relief *increased* from 1,096 in 1857 to 32,429 in 1877, the number in receipt of *in-door* relief, that is, of the really destitute, had *decreased* from 55,183 in 1857 to 45,762 in 1877.

If instead of taking the number in receipt of in-door relief upon a particular day, the first Saturday of January in each year, we take the "average daily number," we find that in 1857 it was 50,665, while in 1877 it had fallen, almost progressively year by year, to 43,052.

Not less striking is the contrast between the expenditure on account of out-door relief as compared with that of in-door relief during the same period.

Within the last twenty years very great improvement has been introduced and sanctioned in the dietaries of Irish workhouses, followed of course by corresponding increase in the cost of maintenance. Notwithstanding this, the increase of expenditure on account of in-door relief is but slight, as will be seen, in proportion to that of out-door relief.

Year ended 29th September.		Population.	In-Maintenance.	Out-door Relief.	Year. ended 29th September.		Population.	In-Maintenance.	Out-door Relief.
			£	£				£	£
1856	-	5,972,851	358,943	2,345	1867	-	5,486,509	418,269	40,075
1857	-	5,919,454	292,685	2,412	1868	-	5,465,914	436,842	44,785
1858	-	5,890,814	266,070	3,135	1869	-	5,449,094	403,255	48,184
1859	-	5,861,711	284,202	3,239	1870	-	5,418,512	381,884	59,181
1860	-	5,820,960	272,682	5,514	1871	-	5,895,007	382,566	69,744
1861	-	5,788,415	327,970	9,675	1872	-	5,372,199	401,840	80,477
1862	-	5,775,588	373,216	14,750	1873	-	5,337,261	446,760	91,154
1863	-	5,718,235	380,737	18,872	1874	-	5,314,844	457,944	93,587
1864	-	5,640,527	366,732	21,173	1875	-	5,309,494	416,172	94,775
1865	-	5,594,589	365,180	25,335	1876	-	5,321,618	390,097	97,403
1866	-	5,522,942	371,368	29,748	1877	-	5,338,906	405,755	102,227

It is true that the annual value of rateable property has increased within the same period from 11,709,934*l*. to 13,512,652*l*., and the pressure may not be so sensibly felt now as undoubtedly it will be, if out-door relief should progress in the same proportion during the next as it has done during the last twenty years.

The Poor Law Commissioners (Ireland), in their Report for 1869, observe—repeating what they had said in 1862—

"The degree of distress existing at any time in Ireland is not to be inferred from the total number in receipt of out-door relief, but that it is accurately indicated by the number receiving relief in the workhouse, the total number on out-door relief at any time being dependent more on the views of the boards of guardians as to the safety and expediency of affording it than on the number of the applicants or the pressure of distress."

In fact in-door relief in Ireland is the strict Poor Law relief of destitution, of the extent of which it is a very accurate gauge. Out-door is, or rather is intended to be, the charitable relief of poverty, the extent of which it is impossible to gauge. The confounding of these—destitution with poverty—legal relief with charity—is at the root, as it has been often observed, of the maladministration of all Poor Laws, acting as an encouragement to imposture, while it robs of its voluntary character whatever assistance may be given from benevolent motives to deserving poor.

It is true that the per-centage of out-door pauperism upon the population is at present low, as is also the proportion of out-door to in-door poor. But that which was so much feared when the Extension Act was proposed is certainly coming to pass.

Out-door relief is now not only freely administered in many unions, but is regarded as being unobjectionable in principle and economical in practice. That it is more acceptable to the poor than is relief in the workhouse, is not unfrequently urged in its favour. But

"Of this we may rest assured," Sir Geo. Lewis wrote in 1863, "that if in Ireland relief is offered in an agreeable shape, and if the giving of it is determined, not by a test of the necessities of each individual, but by the class to which he belongs, the greatest possible extension to relief will be given within the limits of these classes, and that many persons will succeed in passing themselves off as members of such class who do not, in fact, belong to them."

Another authority, Mr. Gulson, who had much and varied experience in England as well as in Ireland, observed before the Committee of the House of Lords in 1849:—

"The application of the strict workhouse test affords, in my opinion, the only possible mode of escape from the confiscation of a large portion of the landed property of Ireland. That is my confident opinion derived from a long experience in the Poor Law administration both in Ireland and in England; for although the present power of expansion possessed by the Commissioners may be small, great pressure may be and has been brought to bear upon this power; and when the barrier is once broken down, the flood of pauperism will inevitably overwhelm the whole property of the locality in which out-door relief is obtainable."

The danger thus indicated was fully recognised by the Government that introduced the Bill; and during the discussion upon it the necessity of adopting it as a measure of only a temporary character was admitted. Indeed, an amendment limiting the period of its duration was adopted, and, though subsequently rescinded upon the motion of Lord Lansdowne, the expediency of reconsidering the measure at some future time was fully recognised by his Lordship, on the part of the Government. But in Poor Law administration, when a vicious principle is once admitted in practice, it becomes almost impossible for the administrators to retrace their steps. What are described as "exceptional cases" come to be, from one cause or other, the rule of administration, until by degrees, almost imperceptible, the worst abuses strike root and become firmly established. Such is the history, as it has been traced step by step, of the maladministration of Poor Laws in England, until finally it reached a height that defied any remedy short of what has been not improperly described as "a social revolution." And even within the limited range of our inquiry upon this subject, the same causes might be observed at work in Irish unions. It will be seen from the evidence at the inquiries at Cavan and Monaghan—with the former of which unions the present movement in favour of amalgamation originated—that the chief supporters of that proposal "approve of out-door relief;" that out-door relief is given in "payment of rent,"—in aid of insufficient earnings,—in such inadequate amounts that the recipients are compelled to subsist upon charity; that it is systematically given upon the requisition of a few ratepayers, and not, after inquiry, upon the report of the relieving officer. The evidence of one of the officers of the Cavan Union as to the system of relief that prevails in that union, and which it is proposed to extend to the whole county, appears to be sufficiently important to reproduce here. Mr. Byrne, an experienced and very intelligent officer, stated that he has been relieving officer for many years of a large district of the Cavan Union; pays from 11*l*. to 14*l*. out-door relief weekly; a shilling a week is the general sum to each pauper. In three out of four cases this shilling a week is given to pay rent; the paupers "wait for him to go up with the money to enable them to pay their rent."

[Margin: Hansard, vol. 92, pp. 430, 795. — Mr. Byrne, Ev. 600–603. Ev. 604, 607. Ev. 608. Ev. 609.]

"Does it happen," he is asked, "to be within your knowledge that upon any occasion relief is given for the payment of rents through the influence of any person or persons interested in the payment of the rent?—It does happen, and the way it is done is this: Persons get up a memorial, and get it signed by others in the locality, in favour of giving out-door relief to a certain person, and that memorial is sent in here; and very often the signatures and the memorial itself are all in the one handwriting. Here is one (produced) I got to-day, and it is all in the one handwriting, and I get hundreds of them in the month; then the guardians consider them, and make their ruling. Ev. 610.

"I need not ask you whether you consider that a judicious administration of out-door relief?—No; as far as I am concerned, my ideas are opposed to that, and I have had thirty years' experience of it. * * * I think 1s. a week is only a kind of penal servitude for these persons—simple starvation—for they cannot live on it. Ev. 611.

"Will you describe to me what class of residences are these which these rents have been required for? —I inspect a number of them as sub-sanitary officer, and the most of them the down rain is coming in. Some of them (the houses) are narrow, say about eight feet to twelve feet, for three or four of a family to live in. They would be, in my opinion, many of them unfit to put animals in. Ev. 612.

"And it is within your knowledge that rents are being paid for such habitations out of the rates,—for habitations, as you say, unfit for human beings?—Yes; to pay the rent, or some of it, for sometimes the rent is over 1s. a week. Ev. 613.

Ev. 614. "Is it within your knowledge, Mr. Byrne, that many of these people receive relief in aid of begging?—I know they are obliged, many of them, to eke out their subsistence by begging through the country, for I have met them going out to beg after I have paid them their weekly shilling.

Ev. 615. "You have met them going out to beg?—Yes; numbers of them. They beg to get a living, and they pay their rent with the out-door relief.

Ev. 616. "They are obliged to beg for their subsistence?—Yes; a good number of them.

Ev. 617. "And you, as a relieving officer, when you attend the Board of Guardians here, don't you tell them of these things?—I am not allowed to express an opinion save and except upon some occasion when it is asked. I have no discretion in the matter. For instance, there have been sixteen cases put on the book to-day for next week, and my opinion has not been asked about one of them. My opinion is never consulted, except by the chairman and vice-chairman. They are the only two gentlemen who consult me. The whole matter is carried by one member of the board proposing that such and such a person should get relief, and by another guardian seconding it, and the body carrying it.

Ev. 618. "It is proposed by guardians interested in the giving of the relief?—Yes; interested through individuals outside.

Ev. 619. "One supporting the other to-day, and getting supported again?—Yes; and, in my opinion, it is a simple act of cruelty to give many of these poor people a shilling a week.

Ev. 620. "There are one or two cases here on one week which I am rather curious to know about. I observe there the name of a blind man upon the list, P. M———, fifty years of age: he gets 1s. a week. Is he living with any friend?—He is getting 1s. 6d., and that 1s. 6d. is well applied. He lives with his sister.

Ev. 621. "The next case to that is the case of H———, 65 years of age. She gets only 1s. a week?—I know her. That woman was put on entirely in despite of the advice I gave in the matter. I would not willingly give her out-door relief at all, because she had two daughters, and each of them has become a prostitute.

Ev. 622. "We need not go into that; but she has been getting out-door relief in despite of your advice?—Yes; and in despite of my efforts for four years. She is not in Cavan. I brought her before the board on one occasion, and had her struck off the list, and then I went away to the seaside, and when I came back I found she was on again in despite of my opinion.

Ev. 623. "Have you any doubts that the effect of giving relief in such a case is that it is most corrupting and demoralizing to the neighbourhood?—I believe it is giving a reward to vice, and makes the virtuous poor in the neighbourhood look upon the system of doing it as unjust and unfair. That was my idea.

Ev. 624. "And altogether you are of opinion that the pauperism of this union might be much diminished if there was a more judicious administration of relief, and that such would not entail the slightest hardship on the poor?—I am; not the slightest hardship to the poor. There are cases in which money should be given where it is not given, and there are cases in which it is given where it is only encouraging idleness by giving it.

Ev. 625. "That is, that you have very frequently met, as relieving officer, cases where, according to your opinion, no relief ought to be given, and you know that it is withheld in cases where, according to your opinion, relief ought to be given?—There are ten or twelve cases I would have had under relief at present, and I believe there is about twenty per cent. of those on out-door relief that should not be on at all.

Ev. 626. "That is your idea, from your knowledge of the district, and from your experience?—Yes; that though these people get on the books here without my knowledge, I make it my business to inquire who they are, and why they got on, and then I make a representation about it to the board. Those who get on to-day, I will see about them before Saturday next.

Ev. 627. "But to-day, when the guardians placed them on through these memorials, you knew nothing about them?—Nothing at all.

Ev. 628. "And you say three-fourths of the memorials that come forward are a counterpart of that one you have produced?—Yes; all in the one handwriting, memorials, signatures, and all. All the names are signed by the one person.

Ev. 629. "These names are put on your book to-day: I want to know are they put on for out-door relief at once, or in order that you should make inquiries about them first?—They are put on my book to-day for out-door relief at once.

Ev. 630. "Have you not reported them to the board previously?—No, when I get these memorials I enter them in the application book without knowing anything about them. The memorials are sent before the board, and the guardians give it to them on the memorials.

Ev. 631. "That is, you get a memorial, and on receipt of it you enter the case in your application and report book, and that application and report book is brought before the board without your knowing anything more about the party?—Nothing more about the party.

Ev. 632. "Do you not investigate the cases before you bring them before the board?—No, I do not. All the names are entered into my book that is brought before the board with the memorials, and on the memorials being read the guardians give the relief. That is the way the thing is done generally.

Ev. 633. "(To Mr. Grier.)—These memorials which have been produced by Byrne here, are they a part of your records?—No.

Ev. 634. "We may take this with us as an illustration of the working of your system?

Ev. 635. "Mr. Grier.—Yes; there are some genuine signatures there. I know them to be genuine signatures.

"To the Board of Guardians, Cavan Union.

"We, the undersigned inhabitants of the townland of Derrylahan, most humbly showeth that Bridget Brady, of said townland, is in a most destitute way, and very much needs relief. Hoping the guardians will be kind enough to consider her situation—

"Luke McCavey.
"Farrell Smyth.
"Patrick Bell.
"James Byers."

"Dated 10th December 187.

"But, in fact, the system of out-door relief here appears to be a system of applications by a certain number of ratepayers, and not by the pauper to the relieving officer, and the case investigated by him? Ev. 636.

"Witness.—I am not consulted at all. Ev. 637.

"Mr. Grier.—Of course the relieving officer sometimes brings cases forward himself Ev. 638.

"But as a rule is it not the fact that the relief is granted in the manner stated by Byrne; that is, the application is made, not by the pauper to the relieving officer, but by a certain number of ratepayers through memorials? Ev. 639.

"Mr. Grier.—Well, latterly it is more the habit to send these memorials to the board.

"How long is it since this system of giving relief upon applications by memorials came into existence?—Within the last two years. Ev. 640.

"Does it prevail now to a considerable extent?—Yes; to be the prevalent way. Ev. 641.

"The relieving officer is, so to speak, put aside, and relief is administered on memorials?— Ev. 642.

"Mr. Grier.—But if the relieving officer considered that the relief ought not to be given, the guardians would not give it. Ev. 643.

"His evidence appears to be that the guardians would not listen to his opinion at all, but that they simply make their rule on reading the memorials?— Ev. 644.

"Mr. Grier.—Oh, sometimes they would listen to him." Ev. 645.

This evidence of the Relieving Officer is confirmed by a guardian, one of the active promoters of what is termed "the Cavan scheme" of amalgamation. We quote from the evidence of Mr. Duignan, the guardian of Killeshandra Electoral Division in the Cavan Union.

"In the town of Killeshandra, where I live, you will get a man and his wife and two or three children. The wife is a grand knitter, and can knit and earn money. The poor man may have no employment, and he makes application to the guardians upon the question of his distress He will get a document signed by six or seven ratepayers of the electoral division, saying he wants out-door relief. He won't get the out-door relief until the ratepayers sign that, and then let the ratepayers pay. Ev. 324.

"Then the relief is given upon the certificate or requisition of the six or seven ratepayers?—Yes; with my own judgment Then I give them 2s. a week—1s. for himself and 1s. for his wife. Of course if he has a family I give them an additional sum. I find that he and his wife can live very comfortably on that 2s. a week. The wife will come and buy thread from your humble servant to knit, and then she gets money for her work; and have we the right to saddle the guardians with the cost of keeping these people altogether, when the wife can earn money that way? Ev. 325.

"I want to know whether the relief is given after examination of the case by the relieving officer, or upon examination of the case by a number of ratepayers?—It is by the wisdom and prudence of the guardians. Ev. 326.

"Well, then, that is what you consider a judicious system of out-door Poor-Law relief—that a number of ratepayers sign a memorial in favour of some persons in their district or electoral division getting relief, and that the guardians are bound to attend to that?—I believe they are, because they (the ratepayers) have to pay the money." Ev. 327.

An argument constantly urged in favour of substituting out-door for in-door relief is that "it is cheaper,"—a pauper will be satisfied to accept a shilling a week out-relief whose maintenance in the workhouse would cost at least three shillings. No more effectual plan could be hit upon for the manufacture of pauperism than by the practical application of such views. Indeed, the danger of their being found to prevail was one of the grounds of objection to the Relief Extension Act, and was urged with great force by the late Lord Clancarty in the speech in which he moved the rejection of the Bill. Hansard, vol. 92, p. 78.

"As the option is given" (he urged) "to guardians to relieve certain classes, if they please, out of the workhouse, and as it is alike notorious that relief can be more cheaply given in individual cases, and most certain that the destitute poor in general will accept the minimum of out-door relief in preference to subjecting themselves to the restraint of the workhouse, the consequence is obvious * * * I see with regret the probability that under the operation of this Act, which thus permits out-door relief, the comparative cheapness of giving it, combined with the willingness of the poor to receive it, may check that which has been found beneficial in the existing law, and the country be betrayed into the general adoption of a practice alike demoralising to the poor and fraught with eventual ruin to property."

A certain way of "betraying the country" into the adoption of this practice would be to extend the areas of unions beyond a reasonable distance from the workhouse, and thus create the necessity of giving out-door relief in a large proportion of cases, and at the same time to furnish a colourable pretext for giving it where no such necessity really existed. In the opinion of the Vice Chairman of the Bailieborough (co. Cavan) union, amalgamation "would be one of the most formidable excuses and one of the greatest arguments ever put into the mouths of the advocates of out-door relief, which must be greatly extended if the workhouses were few and far between."

A very striking illustration of the mischievous effect of any deviation, however slight, from the rule of indoor relief, is furnished by the history of the Newtownards union.

No union in Ireland was formed under more favourable circumstances. In area 93,924 acres, and population 53,873, it was of that reasonable extent that offered facilities for local administration. The Assistant Commissioner by whom the union was formed described it as—

"Rich and highly cultivated, and the buildings and occupations are generally larger than in any union I have yet recommended * * * Both as regards the land and its inhabitants, there is a general appearance of prosperity and comfort, which is strikingly contrasted with the aspect of other parts of Ireland in which I have been officially employed. The farmers here approach much nearer to that highly respectable class, the pride of England, so well known by the appellation of 'English yeomen.' Their houses are clean, substantial, and in good repair: their homesteads well furnished, all presenting visual evidence of prosperity. * * * Great care and attention have for many years been bestowed upon the poor and their relief."

The formation of the mendicity societies through the agency of which relief was administered is then described. Except that these societies were supported by voluntary contributions, the system of relief resembled as nearly as possible that which has attracted some attention recently, and is known as "the Elberfeld system."

"The greatest vigilance," Mr. Gulson wrote, "seems to have been exercised by the visitors appointed for each district, whose business it was personally to visit and inquire into each individual case of necessity, before relief was afforded; and a periodical revision of all cases on the books was carefully entered into by the monthly committees, whose regular and voluntary exertions entitled them to the highest praise, and prove that, where the public interests are concerned, the aid of persons of station and character may be relied upon equally in Ireland as in England."

The subscription upon which the mendicity societies had been maintained having proved insufficient, a rate was agreed to, of 4*d*. per acre upon land, and 6*d*. in the pound on the value of houses. The report of Mr. Gulson thus continues:—

"The means that have been adopted in this district for the relief of the poor, the vigilance exercised, and the success which has attended their efforts, have rendered this locality more free from pauperism, mendicancy, or destitution than any that has yet come within my notice since I have been in Ireland." * * * "I venture to predict that as the district contains so many gentlemen who have for years devoted their attention to the subject, and who understand the true principle of Poor Law, as is shown by their proceedings, the Newtownards union will be a pattern of good management and of beneficial operation."

And apparently so it was for many years Until 1863 there was no outdoor relief, and the expenditure for indoor relief was low. In 1863, however, the door for out-relief was opened, and four cases, "exceptional" of course, were admitted. The next year the number was 12, which in the following year rose to 56. Then follows—

1869	203
1871	326
1873	398
1875	381
1877	391

Thus it has come about that this favoured union has now the distinction of exhibiting the highest rate of pauperism in the province.

Nor are the results of expenditure less deserving of attention. In 1859, when no outdoor relief was given in the union, and the population was 54,093, the expenditure for relief was 1,435*l*. In 1877, when the population had fallen from 54,093 to 48,231, and the number in receipt of outdoor relief exceeded the number in the workhouse, the expenditure on account of relief had risen from 1,435*l*. to 4,448*l*.

An examination of the relief list of this union shows that the system of relief, as in other unions where outdoor relief prevails to any considerable extent, is the distribution of small doles—as a shilling a week,—just sufficient to pauperise without affording substantial assistance. The system we found to be generally at variance with the views of the most experienced guardians, who would gladly welcome a legislative prohibition of what threatens to grow into a very serious evil.

If we look to the effect of a system of outdoor relief in Ireland as illustrated, not by the condition of a particular union, as Newtownards, but by a much wider examination, the result will be found to be still more striking. A comparison of a number of unions in which no outdoor relief is given with an equal number of a similar character and about equal population in which outdoor relief prevails exhibits these remarkable results :—

Union.	Valuation.	Population.	Average Daily Number in receipt of Relief.			Poor Relief Expenditure.			Poundage.	Per-centage of Paupers to Population.		
			Indoor.	Outdoor.	Total.	Indoor.	Outdoor.	Total.	s. d.	Indoor.	Outdoor.	Total.
Dingle	22,837	20,245	153	—	153	1,197	—	1,197	1 0¾	·7	—	·7
Ennistymon	36,896	23,355	252	119	371	2,375	464	2,839	1 8½	1·1	·5	1·6
Bandon	73,598	25,739	186	—	186	1,515	—	1,515	0 5	·7	—	·7
Ennis	74,096	26,530	424	229	653	3,814	685	4,499	1 2¾	1·6	·8	2·4
Listowel	52,258	34,283	109	—	109	877	—	877	0 4	·3	—	·3
Kanturk	77,206	32,796	405	386	791	3,898	766	4,664	1 2¾	1·2	1·1	2·3
Kinsale	58,336	24,894	186	—	186	1,137	—	1,137	0 4¾	·5	—	·5
Clonmel	70,690	24,069	428	279	707	3,690	464	4,154	1 2¼	1·8	1·1	2·9
Scarriff	26,769	13,953	169	—	169	1,556	—	1,556	1 2¼	1·2	—	1·2
Tulla	33,760	13,768	216	101	317	2,060	386	2,406	1 5¼	1·6	·7	2·3
Fermoy	103,383	22,784	295	6	301	2,409	55	2,464	0 5¾	·9	—	·9
Middleton	94,330	30,404	306	440	746	2,242	1,291	4,533	0 11¾	1·0	1·4	2·4

It appears from that statement that the Dingle union, with a population of 20,245, gives no outdoor relief, while in Ennistymon, with a population of 23,355, 32 per cent. of its pauperism is outdoor. The total pauperism of the union that gives no outdoor relief very little exceeds half per cent. : while in the other union the pauperism is 1·6 per cent. or nearly three times as large. Nor is the financial result less remarkable. The poundage in Dingle, where there is no out relief, upon a valuation of 22,881*l.* is 1*s.* 0¾*d.* ; while at Ennistymon, upon the much larger valuation of 36,896*l.*, the poundage for relief is 1*s.* 8½*d.* In Bandon, where no out relief is given, with a population of 25,739, the total pauperism is 186, or ·7 per cent. ; while in Ennis, where considerably more than half the pauperism is outdoor, with a population of 26,530, the number of paupers is 653, or 2·4 per cent. While the poundage in Bandon, upon the valuation of 73,598*l.*, is only 5*d.*, in Ennis, upon a valuation of 74,096*l.*, it is 1*s.* 2¾*d.* The comparison of Listowel with Kanturk is still more remarkable :—out of a population of 34,283 in Listowel there are only 109 persons in receipt of relief, not one receiving outdoor relief ; but in Kanturk, with a smaller population, there are 791 persons receiving relief, of whom 386 are outdoor. The total expenditure in Listowel for the year was 887*l.*, while in Kanturk for the corresponding period the amount was 4,664*l.* ; the poundage in the one case being 4*d.* upon a valuation of 52,258*l.*, and in the other 1*s.* 2¾*d.* upon a valuation of 77,206*l.*,—the per-centage of pauperism being in Listowel ·3, and in Kanturk 2·3. Similar results are shown by a comparison of the pauperism and expenditure of the other six unions in the preceding table. Although there may be differences in the habits and the industrial condition of the population of these contrasted unions, they would, we believe, be wholly insufficient to account for the very remarkable contrast exhibited in the table to which we have referred.

Again, if we take a number of unions in which the system of outdoor relief has been adopted, and compare their condition as to pauperism and expenditure in the year in which outdoor relief was given for the first time with their condition in 1877, the same conclusion will be found to be established from a different point of view. It will be observed that in many unions in which outdoor relief has been introduced there has been a sensible increase of pauperism and expenditure, while in those unions which have adhered to the system of indoor relief there has been a sensible decrease of pauperism in every union, and of expenditure in all save two.

Unions	Pauperism and Expenditure the First Year in which Out-relief was given in the Union.						Pauperism and Expenditure in 1877.				
	Year.	Indoor Paupers	Outdoor Paupers	Total	Per-centage of Pauperism to Population.	Total Relief.	Indoor Paupers	Outdoor Paupers	Total.	Per-centage of Pauperism to Population	Total Relief.
						£					£
Cornfin - -	1871	114	9	123	1·7	589	156	63	219	3·0	1,478
Ennis - -	1869	448	1	449	1·6	3,476	424	229	683	2·4	4,499
Kilrush - -	1861	285	1	286	·7	2,079	334	290	616	1·7	3,782
Cork - -	1862	2,516	85	2,531	1·7	17,617	2,318	1,052	5,370	2·3	24,394
Mallow - -	1865	434	1	435	1·3	2,748	412	451	863	2·7	4,207
Millstreet -	1862	427	18	445	1·2	2,519	308	440	748	2·4	4,588
Killarney - -	1857	864	2	866	·8	2,266	315	431	746	1·6	4,805
Croom - -	1862	221	16	237	1·3	1,982	223	207	430	2·5	2,562
Kilmallock -	1862	676	2	678	1·7	5,124	672	641	1,313	3·7	7,374
Limerick - -	1863	1,892	1	1,893	2·1	12,600	1,296	903	2,299	2·9	14,922
Newcastle -	1861	340	5	345	1·1	2,271	270	247	587	1·8	3,456
Rathkeale -	1857	191	1	192	·6	1,169	204	471	675	3·8	3,761
Carrick-on-Suir -	1859	310	3	313	·9	1,522	275	222	337	1·8	2,780
Cashel - -	1863	544	12	556	1·7	3,383	412	376	768	2·7	5,158
Tipperary -	1863	475	19	494	1·0	3,343	487	461	948	2·2	6,217
Dungarvan -	1863	402	52	454	1·3	2,962	361	184	545	2·3	4,123
Waterford -	1852	1,782	11	1,796	2·6	6,260	969	1,062	2,041	3·5	10,646

UNIONS in which no OUT RELIEF has been given.

	1867.					1877.				
Scariff - - -	197	—	197	1·3	1,407	169	—	169	1·2	1,356
Bandon - - -	205	—	205	·8	1,601	184	—	186	·7	1,515
Kinsale - - -	170	—	170	7	1,398	136	—	136	·5	1,137
Dingle - -	196	—	196	·8	1,400	158	—	158	·7	1,197
Listowel - -	243	—	243	7	1,803	109	—	109	·3	877
Borrisokane - -	145	—	145	1 1	1,038	120	—	120	1·0	1,056
Clogheen - -	235	—	235	1·0	1,868	222	—	222	1·0	2,261

Finally, if we compare the condition in 1867 and 1877 of 40 of the unions in which no outdoor relief has been given with that of a similar number in which the system of outdoor relief prevails, it will be seen that while in the former there has been a *decrease* of 6 per cent. in pauperism, in the latter there has been an *increase* of 44·3 per cent.; and whilst the expenditure in the former has increased only 8·5 per cent., it has increased in the latter 25.5 per cent. Here are the particulars of this comparison.

UNIONS in which no OUTDOOR RELIEF is given.

Unions.	1867.		1877.	
	Total Pauperism.	Total Relief	Total Pauperism.	Total Relief.
		£		£
Ballycastle -	119	924	95	796
Belfast - -	1,786	14,081	3,094	17,971
Armagh - -	326	2,186	286	2,345
Lurgan - -	418	3,958	391	3,337
Ballyshannon -	194	1,109	143	1,016
Dunfanaghy - -	53	318	51	284
Letterkenny - -	125	1,020	98	993
Stranorlar -	74	488	65	390
Kilkeel - -	117	769	64	585
Enniskillen - -	279	1,659	273	1,845
Irvinestown - -	138	839	110	881
Limavady - -	152	860	133	864
Londonderry -	417	2,319	349	2,217
Magherafelt - -	173	1,208	302	1,425
Carrickmacross -	120	917	117	1,157
Clones - -	128	852	76	657
Monaghan - -	180	1,142	134	1,156
Castlederg - -	63	296	66	397
Gortin - -	50	373	84	351
Ballyvaughan -	151	1,189	204	1,454
Scariff - -	197	1,407	169	1,356
Bandon - -	205	1,601	186	1,515
Bantry - -	112	723	115	723
Clonakilty - -	208	1,455	144	1,880
Fermoy -	303	2,139	301	2,464

Unions.	1867.		1877.	
	Total Pauperism	Total Relief	Total Pauperism.	Total Relief.
		£		£
Kinsale - -	170	1,398	136	1,137
Mitchelstown -	244	1,462	220	1,675
Dingle - -	196	1,400	158	1,197
Listowel - -	243	1,803	109	877
Tralee - -	638	4,577	523	4,487
Borrisokane -	145	1,038	120	1,056
Clogheen - -	235	1,868	222	2,261
North Dublin -	2,130	18,477	2,199	20,773
Rathdown -	344	5,148	351	6,731
Parsonstown -	314	2,437	257	2,231
Oldcastle - -	214	1,741	207	1,862
Ballinasloe -	204	1,431	210	2,087
Ballinasloe -	265	3,009	265	2,373
Gort - -	131	1,253	194	1,567
Mount Bellew -	147	1,085	111	924
Oughterard -	139	969	84	788
Manorhamilton -	148	900	114	1,019
Newport -	107	610	98	718
Westport - -	181	1,293	140	1,033
Total - -	12,324	94,548	11,956	103,136

4 5 per cent decrease in pauperism.
9 3 per cent increase in relief

Note.—It is not strictly accurate that "no out-door relief" has been given in these unions, as in 25 of them—owing to the cases being unfit for removal to the workhouse—temporary out relief was given to 174 cases in all, at a total cost of 466*l.* Virtually, however, out-door relief does not prevail in these unions.

UNIONS in which the GUARDIANS give OUTDOOR RELIEF.

Unions	1867. Total Pauperism.	1867. Total Relief	1877. Total Pauperism	1877. Total Relief
		£		£
Ballymena	473	3,036	940	4,736
Ballymoney	350	1,273	391	1,484
Lisburn	285	1,820	351	2,212
Bawnboy	243	1,327	294	1,304
Cavan	284	1,953	530	2,980
Inishowen	207	1,307	396	1,470
Banbridge	310	1,811	463	2,734
Newtownards	510	3,248	745	4,448
Dungannon	245	1,709	350	2,208
Strabane	337	1,935	474	2,757
Killadysert	182	1,219	316	1,997
Kilrush	336	3,094	616	8,753
Kanturk	768	4,340	791	4,664
Mallow	445	3,493	563	4,907
Midleton	443	2,614	748	4,533
Killarney	421	3,576	746	4,805
Kilmallock	805	5,717	1,313	7,374
Newcastle	592	2,838	537	3,459
Rathkeale	452	3,040	673	3,781
Cashel	599	4,803	789	5,133
Clonmel	671	5,102	707	4,154
Nenagh	488	3,831	875	4,135
Tipperary	398	3,874	948	6,117
Dungarvan	516	3,936	545	4,128
Carlow	850	5,185	1,918	6,652

Unions.	1867. Total Pauperism	1867. Total Relief.	1877. Total Pauperism.	1877. Total Relief
		£		£
Athy	330	3,422	711	5,366
Naas	704	4,085	929	5,224
Urlingford	285	1,857	261	1,895
Edenderry	355	1,828	303	2,188
Tullamore	643	4,855	709	4,593
Ballymahon	179	1,339	231	1,538
Longford	446	2,774	508	2,776
Ardee	400	3,674	680	3,336
Dundalk	452	2,807	758	3,865
Dunshaughlin	248	1,787	339	2,642
Kells	236	2,248	437	3,204
Navan	559	3,315	851	4,020
Mountmellick	685	4,109	844	5,723
Mullingar	131	3,399	1,256	5,987
Enniscorthy	642	3,808	843	4,714
New Ross	985	6,895	1,346	5,970
Wexford	730	4,896	1,014	6,092
Tuam	293	3,280	506	3,397
Mohill	216	1,494	289	1,954
Total	19,960	135,558	28,805	170,184

44·3 per cent. increase in pauperism.
25·5 per cent. increase in relief.

The history of the progress of poor relief—indoor and outdoor—in every union in Ireland during a period of 27 years is fully traced in the elaborate statistical statement prepared for our use by our Secretary, and which we consider of sufficient value to be printed in the Appendix to this Report.

We should not feel justified in presenting this subject in so much detail if it were not that it appears to us to be intimately connected with the proposal to extend the areas of unions by "amalgamation." There can, we think, be no question that the proposals that have been made upon the subject would, if adopted, lead to a very great extension of a system, the growth and character of which deserve the most serious consideration of all who are interested in the efficient administration of the Poor Law in Ireland.

We may now revert to the special applications that have been made to us for "amalgamation" of unions.

The first inquiry that we held was at the request of the guardians of the Cavan union. Subsequently, as we have already stated, we held inquiries at Monaghan, Ennis, Mill Street, and Glennamaddy.

In reply to our circular letter, the guardians of the Cavan union state they are—

"of opinion that the workhouse of that union is quite adequate to accommodate the poor of this county, and they recommend that the workhouses at Bailieboro', Bawnboy, and Cootehill be closed." App. A 1, p. 102.

Together with this resolution the guardians communicated to us a copy of a petition to Parliament, in which they repeat that— Mr. Sanderson, Ev. 89.

"The workhouse of this union is large enough to accommodate double the number of paupers receiving relief in the county of Cavan," and they "therefore pray that your honourable House will cause a re-arrangement of Poor Law unions in Ireland, so as very considerably to reduce the number of workhouses by making a central house for each county."

In order to avoid any misunderstanding as to the precise object of that proposal, we inquired from the guardians whether they contemplated the formation of a union which should comprise all the electoral divisions of the county, and were informed in reply that—

"The guardians intended that all the electoral divisions in county Cavan should be attached to one central workhouse for the county." App. A 1, p. 102.

Although it will be seen from the evidence that the guardians, with whom applications for amalgamation have originated, or who put themselves forward to support such applications, do not appear to have any definite idea of what is meant by amalgamation, yet as the formation of county unions is the measure for which the Cavan guardians have petitioned Parliament, and in support of which they seek the co-operation of all the other unions in Ireland, we present on the opposite page a map in illustration of the effect of the proposed change in this particular case. We have already reproduced a portion of the evidence upon which the Commissioners formed the fourth Cavan union—that of Bawnboy. The strongest reason urged in favour of that change was the unwieldy size of the then existing unions, which was found to be attended with much inconvenience to the guardians, as well as much downright cruelty to the poor. It will be seen by reference to the map on the opposite page that the proposed Cavan union—which is coloured red, the existing Cavan union being shaded—comprises portions of the unions of Enniskillen, Bawnboy, Cootehill, Granard, Bailieborough, Oldcastle, and Kells. The electoral divisions that it is proposed to transfer from the Enniskillen union lie at distances from Cavan varying from 28½ miles, the nearest, to 38 miles, the farthest. From Kells it is proposed to transfer an electoral division—Mullagh—which is only six miles from the workhouse of the Kells union, but is 26½ from Cavan. The effect of the proposed change is further shown by the tables of relative distances on the margin of the map.

Although the resolution of the Cavan guardians in favour of the formation of a county union was adopted after repeated consideration of the question, it would yet appear from the evidence that those who supported this scheme had, as we have just observed, no clear or definite idea of what they really intended by it. Mr. Kennedy, the proposer of that resolution, having explained the origin of this proposal,
Mr. Sanderson, Ev. 71. Mr. Samuel Saunderson, an ex-officio guardian, was examined. He "is in favour of amalgamation generally." He has only considered amalgamation "generally," not the Cavan scheme in particular. He is not in favour of amalgamation "by which the other workhouses should be closed altogether." He is in favour of—

Ev. 72. "Uniting the electoral divisions, but not to do away with the powers of other guardians in other divisions * * * Does not think the guardians ever meant that all the sick from all the unions should be brought here; only that the able-bodied should be brought in here and kept at a much lower rate than they are when they are scattered as they are now; that the staff in the other unions may be reduced—say to half. Would not say more than that." * * *

Ev. 74. He supports the Cavan scheme of amalgamation "to a certain degree. The
Ev. 75. guardians did not enter into the particulars of how it should be done." He would
Ev. 85–87. not dissolve or do away with the boards of guardians of the other unions in the county, nor would he do away with the workhouses altogether, as—

Ev. 87, 127. "There must be some provision for the sick and infirm. * * * What I think we wished for was that all the able-bodied (of course we exclude the sick as we mentioned) paupers should be sent in here; that in the places where the houses were closed the guardians were to have their meetings
Ev. 128. and send their paupers in here. * * * The workhouses we propose to do away with, but to have
Ev. 129. hospitals for accident, and infectious cases and for the infirm. * * The persons who would come here would be persons likely to live for a long time—ye still infirm. In certain cases they would come here, and the other unions should be only charged with the actual cost of providing for them here, and of course with a fair proportion of household expenses. That is what we purpose. We should leave all the unions to their own guardians to deal with such matters as out-door relief, their own contracts, &c. We never proposed to take away the responsibility from the other guardians
Ev. 130. We don't propose to dissolve the other boards. * * * All we propose is that we should take
Ev. 133. charge of their able-bodied paupers and all the others who would come here."

Ev. 162. "Is your proposal to retain the several unions as they now exist, and simply to make this house a boarding-house for a certain class of paupers—as I understand that is your proposal?—I suppose it would come very nearly to that.

Ev. 163. "Would it not come absolutely to that?—Well, I suppose so.

Ev. 164. "Don't you see the difference between constituting all the unions one union, and simply retaining the workhouse of this union for a certain class of paupers who could be carried here, while you would be leaving the other workhouses as auxiliary for a class of persons who could not be carried to this house—that is your proposal?—Yes. Of course, we were not prepared with a scheme, and the necessary evidence cut and dry, as to what we propose; but we thought that by all the unions consulting together a great reduction could be made.

Ev. 165. "This scheme has been before the board of guardians of the Cavan union since 1857. It has been more recently fully before the board in 1876 and 1877?—Yes.

Ev. 166. "Yet Mr. Kennedy says he has not had time to enter into a calculation of the expenses. What I want to know is whether you have had time to come to any agreement as to what you mean? Mr. Kennedy thinks that he meant one union for the whole county. You state that you mean four unions for the whole county, with one workhouse for one purpose, and three workhouses for other purposes. Is not that a fair statement of Mr. Kennedy's proposal and yours?—I think Mr. Kennedy and myself agree. You call them workhouses—we call them infirmaries.

Ev. 167. "Mr. Kennedy does not agree with you, inasmuch as he would dissolve the whole of the other unions—Bawnboy, Bailieborough, and Cootehill?—I think if you explain to Mr. Kennedy what you mean by dissolving the other unions, you will find that is not so. I don't think Mr. Kennedy ever meant that all the responsibility should be taken from the other unions.

Ev. 168. "Mr. Kennedy.—No.

Ev. 169. "Then you did not mean a scheme of amalgamation; it is not an amalgamation of unions, but simply an amalgamation of one class of paupers in this workhouse?—Well, yes; but we consider that that is an amalgamation of unions, if we get their paupers here.

"Do you consider it an amalgamation of paupers if you only bring one class of paupers to this workhouse, leaving the other paupers in the other workhouses, and not at all interfering with the

BAILIEBOROUGH.

Electoral Division	Distance from Bailieboro.	Distance from Cavan
Bailieboro	—	23
Carnagarve	3	28
Drumanespic	5½	14½
Killinkere	4½	10½
Skeagh	4½	24½
Errisbane	7	23½
Enniskeen	9½	27½
Kingscourt	7	30½
Lisagoan	5	28
Shercock	6	29½
Tegart	4½	27½
Termon	9½	18

ENNISKILLEN.

Electoral Division	Distance from Enniskillen	Distance from Cavan
Ecly	14	38
Killinagh	16½	33½
Tebane	18½	37½
Tuam	14½	36½
Dowra	21½	34½
Derrylahen	16	34
Drumakeenan	20½	32
Derrynananta	22	36½

GRANARD.

Electoral Division	Distance from Granard	Distance from Cavan
Scrabby	7½	14½
Lough Dawra	6½	14
Drumlumman	6½	14½
Kilcogy	5	17
Kilgolagh	4¾	19

OLDCASTLE.

Electoral Division	Distance from Oldcastle	Distance from Cavan.
Lurgan	8½	14
Ballyjamesduff	6¾	12½
Virginia	6½	4o½
Castlerahan	4	15
Kilbride	4½	17
Munter Connaught	8½	19

Boundaries of existing Unions colored Blue

Proposed Cavan Union colored Red

Workhouse Sites +

Scale of Miles

KELLS.

Electoral Division.	Distance from Kells.	Distance from Cavan.
Mullagh	6	26½

BAWNBOY.

Electoral Division	Distance from Bawnboy.	Distance from Cavan
Ballyconnel	4½	16
Ballymagauran	4	19
Bawnboy	—	20
Benbrack	8½	26½
Bilberry	5½	14½
Carn	7	13
Diamond	9	12
Doogarry	6	13
Kinawley	5	28
Lessanover	4	16
Pedar-a-vol-ore	3½	27
Swanlinbar	6½	30
Templeport	3½	23½
Tircahan	4	25

COOTEHILL.

Electoral Division.	Distance from Cootehill	Distance from Cavan
Ashfield	3½	13½
Cormingtown	9	13½
Cootehill	—	15¾
Corraneary	6	10
Drumcarn	9½	6½
Drung	8¾	8½
Knappagh	6	20¼
Lara, North	8	7½
Lara, South	10½	11½
Rakenny	4½	11½
Tullyvin, East	8½	12½
Tullyvin, West	4½	11½

To Face Page XXXVI

the University of

electoral divisions of the other unions? Is that your idea of amalgamation?—Certainly, we don't confine ourselves, so that we must not interfere with other unions at all, because when it becomes practically worked out, we would find that parts of other unions lie in here, and that they should all come out to form the county union. That is for after consideration.

"Are you prepared to state whether or not you mean to amalgamate, that is, to reconstitute the union by taking in, by absorbing, into the Cavan union the electoral divisions which now constitute the other three unions in the county?—So far as I have stated, most decidedly yes. Ev. 170.

"But what you have stated is that you desire to leave the whole responsibility of their local administration to the other boards of guardians, that is, to leave them as they are now?—Certainly. Ev. 171.

"And simply to make this a boarding-house for their paupers?—Yes. Ev. 172.

"Of a particular class?—Of all the paupers of the county, able-bodied—— Ev. 173.

"Exactly; that this should be constituted a workhouse for a certain class?—Yes. Ev. 174.

"And that there should be four boards of guardians still existing, and that the four unions should be represented by these four boards of guardians?—Yes. Ev. 175.

"That is your idea of amalgamation?—Yes." Ev. 176.

Another guardian of the Cavan union, Mr. Henry Faris, stated that he was the person who first brought forward the proposal for amalgamation in 1857, when the question was first mooted. Referring to Mr. Saunderson's proposal that an hospital should be kept up in each union, Mr. Faris says, Mr. Faris, Ev. 479.

"I don't see the use in having such an hospital at all. It would simply be knocking down one house and building up another." Ev. 481.

. To remedy the want of an hospital Mr. Faris would—

"Get a nice spring car, covered overhead, with a bed inside to hold two or three people, one, say, at Bawnboy, another at Bailieborough, and another at Cootehill, under the care of the relieving officer of those places, and in case there was a pauper to be removed who was sick or infirm, you could hire a donkey or a horse to bring the persons here. It is nonsense," Mr. Faris thinks, "to talk of that sort of removal being injurious to the poor through the closing of the hospitals" He would "give the hospitals up altogether. * * Would only have the one workhouse and no hospitals. Would bring all the poor here (to Cavan), irrespective of distance, convenience, or condition." Ev. 484. Ev. 485–487.

Similar diversity of opinion, indeed absence of any opinion at all, as to what was intended by the proposal to "amalgamate" unions, prevailed amongst those guardians of the Monaghan union who professed themselves supporters of that proposal.

The first witness examined there, Mr. Wm. Woods, a guardian—

"Was not prepared to go into the scheme of amalgamation. * * * The public generally, the ratepayers, are very much in favour of one workhouse for the county; but, as a trial, would be much inclined to retain two of them for the present, as an experiment." Mr. Woods, Ev. 715–717.

Asked if he means that he would amalgamate the whole of the electoral divisions of the county Monaghan into one union, having two workhouses for that one union, he replied—

"I have not studied the matter sufficiently to give a proper answer to that;" although "the subject has been considered at three different meetings of the guardians, he has not formed any definite opinion as to details; * * * but Mr. Kelly, who is the mover of these resolutions, asked a friend of his, Mr. Roberts, who is a guardian in the Clogher electoral divisions situate in the county, to give an explanation." Ev. 720. Ev. 721.

Asked—

"How many electoral divisions there are in the county?—I don't know Ev. 724.

"Have you made any calculations at all?—Not the least. Ev. 725.

"Have you made no calculation of the population which would be comprised in your proposed new union?—No. Ev. 726.

"Or of the rateable valuation?—No, I have not. Ev. 727.

"Nor of the pauperism?—No; I have not gone into the subject at all, so far as calculation is concerned. Ev. 728.

"But does not the whole scheme depend upon calculations?—No doubt; but I thought after we resolved on amalgamation that the Poor Law Board or the Commissioners would make the calculation." Ev. 729.

Mr. Kelly, "the mover of the resolutions," being examined, stated that from his experience of thirty years, and Mr. Kelly, Ev. 756.

"Having given a great deal of consideration to the subject for a long time, what he thought of it was to amalgamate those union workhouses (of Monaghan) into one or two. I say two, but a great number of the ratepayers say that one would do. * * * My meaning is that we have adjoining counties and adjoining unions, and to amalgamate them (the electoral divisions) with the union most convenient—to the house that is nearest to them, as far as possible. Ev. 756. Ev. 760.

"You speak of the amalgamation of workhouse and the amalgamation of adjoining counties; do you mean that all the electoral divisions of the county of Monaghan should be amalgamated into one union, to be called the Monaghan union?—I would say into two unions, and some of the outlying divisions should be amalgamated into other counties or unions, any of them that would suit or fit." Ev. 761.

Ev. 774. Finally this witness sums up his views by the statement—

Ev. 776. "In a bulk way amalgamation would be a saving. Mr. Roberts can give figures for that. * * * Taking it in the lump, and taking the opinion of the ratepayers generally, we are for amalgamation."

Mr. Roberts, the guardian of the Clogher union, referred to by the two preceding witnesses, after some not very intelligible explanations of his plan of amalgamation, finally concluded—

Mr. Roberts, Ev. 821–832. "I would amalgamate all Ireland as a general question. * * * There are 163 unions, and I would make 81 of them."

The proposal of the Cavan guardians which we have been considering, to combine all the electoral divisions of the county into one union, is made upon two grounds:—

1st. That the workhouse accommodation is greatly in excess of the requirements of the union:

2nd. That such amalgamation would effect a considerable saving in establishment charges.

Having already stated in detail and with reference to the whole country the ground upon which we are compelled to dissent from these statements, it remains only to examine them with reference to the particular union to which they are declared to be particularly applicable, and the guardians of which invite adhesion to their views and co-operation in giving effect to them from every other board of guardians in Ireland.

Is it the fact that "the workhouse of the Cavan union is adequate to accommodate the poor of the whole county"? So far from that being so, it will appear that, according to the schedule that we have adopted, or to any other reasonable scale of accommodation, the workhouse is not adequate to the wants of the Cavan union alone.

As in the case of every other workhouse in Ireland, the accommodation of this was fixed upon a scale of cubic capacity only. According to that scale the sleeping or dormitory accommodation for healthy adults and children was fixed by a sealed order of the Commissioners in 1861, as follows: for

Adult Males - - -	285
Boys - - - -	122
Adult Females - - -	303
Girls - - - -	122

or a total for healthy adults and children of 832. In addition, accommodation was provided for 94 ordinary sick, and 134 in the fever hospital. The way in which these numbers were arrived at illustrates the error to which we have already called attention, and may be shown by the case of a single dormitory which is represented by this woodcut.

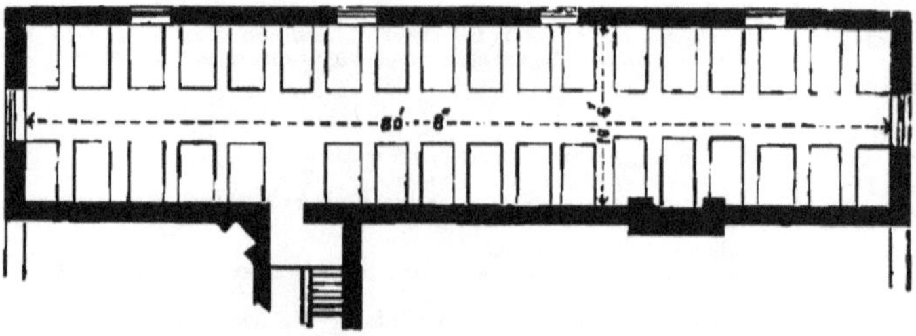

This plan represents a room 80 feet long, and 16 feet 6 inches wide. According to cubic space capacity, two such rooms in the Cavan workhouse, giving 250 feet for each inmate, would accommodate 190 persons, or 95 in each room. But in order to place 95 inmates in a room 80 feet long, and less than 17 feet wide, it would be necessary to place two rows of beds with gangway down the centre, each row consisting of 48 and 47 beds respectively. But if each bed be two feet six inches wide, and reasonable space be allowed between the beds, and deduction be made for space occupied by door and fire-place, it would not be possible to place more than 16 beds on one side and 14 on the other. Thus two rooms which are assumed to provide accommodation for 190, would in fact accommodate only 60, 30 in each. A similar error, though not to the same extent, prevails in the appropriation of the other rooms in this workhouse, of which the actual accommodation as contrasted with the certified accommodation is shown by this table.

	Under sealed orders.		Under Schedule A.
Infirmary:			
Male	47		28
Female	47		33
In Infirmary Building:			
Lunatics and idiots	39	Male	0
		Female	16
Aged and Infirm:			
Male	32		22
Female	32		22
Healthy Adults:			
Male	285		128
Female, single	303		104
Mothers with infants			30
Children:			
Male	122		96
Female	122		96
Separation Ward:			
Number	13		11
Total	1,042	Total	595
Probationary:			
Male	29		7
Female	29		11
Grand totals	1,100		613

It will be observed that in the estimate of general accommodation in this workhouse the "probationary wards" are included as capable of accommodating 58 persons. But in workhouse administration it is essential that probationary or "receiving" wards, as they are usually termed, should be strictly reserved for the purpose for which they are nominally appropriated, and, therefore, in estimating the permanent accommodation available daily of this workhouse they must be altogether left out of account. If with a view to preserve proper classification this rule be adhered to, the sleeping accommodation for adults in health, and for children, cannot be regarded as being in excess of the requirements of the existing Cavan union.

If, however, we pass from the sleeping accommodation of the healthy adult inmates and children to the provision made for the "aged and infirm," we find that so far is it from being true that the accommodation of this workhouse is sufficient for that class of poor in all the unions in the county, that it is, in fact, insufficient for the Cavan union alone. Two wards—one for each sex—are appropriated for that class; each ward certified for 32 inmates; total 64. But upon a day, October 26th, on which the workhouse was visited by a member of this Commission the number of aged and infirm inmates was 69,—five in excess of the certified number. It happens, not unfrequently, that, owing to want of room in the proper wards, aged and infirm are compelled to go upstairs to dormitories of other classes which are, for many reasons, unsuitable to them. Indeed, one of the officers observed of this, he often felt that it "was cruel to those poor people to compel them to go up to these rooms."

In the construction of every workhouse "day rooms" should always be provided in proportion to the sleeping accommodation; but in the construction of Irish workhouses this provision was very inadequately made. This was owing partly to motives of economy, and partly to its being assumed that the able-bodied would be occupied in domestic work or labour of some description. This defect in these establishments is very sensibly felt now that they are occupied by aged and infirm people. It would, therefore, imply a great want of consideration for the reasonable comforts of these classes if, in calculating workhouse accommodation, the necessity of having sufficient day rooms was not taken into account. But in the workhouse of the Cavan union this is altogether insufficient, even for the union as at present constituted. There is only one day room for men and one for women of all classes, and it is so arranged that the wards occupied day and night by the aged and infirm open directly out of it. This is a very objectionable arrangement, and would certainly become still more objectionable if the number of inmates were increased by "amalgamation" with other unions. If the increase took place, as it almost certainly would, in the number of aged and infirm, it would be necessary to convert the day rooms into sleeping rooms for that class, the workhouse being thus left without any day room accommodation whatever for adults of either sex.

The observations that we have already made upon the defects of the infirmary accommodation of Irish workhouses apply with as much force to Cavan as to any of them. Originally designed, as were the infirmaries of all other unions, as an hospital for the workhouse only, it has become the hospital for the union, and, inadequate as it is for that purpose, it is now seriously proposed that it should become by "amalgamation" an hospital for the whole county. It is often, as will be seen by the evidence,
Mary Keany, Ev. 698. overcrowded; the nurse is sometimes obliged to lay down beds upon the floor, to put two patients to sleep in the same bed; children suffering from itch are mixed with other children, "who often take the infection one from the other."

From the other unions the evidence as to workhouse accommodation is to the same effect, and to refer to it would be simply to repeat what we have said with reference to the workhouse of the Cavan union.

Nor is the argument in favour of amalgamation that is founded upon the assumed saving of expenditure of more weight. If we take the establishment charges of each union separately, and compare them with the amounts that would be levied upon a county union as proposed, we find that establishment charges of the existing Cavan union, after deducting the sum that is repaid from the Parliamentary grant, amount to 1,050*l.* 1*s.* 8*d.* The valuation of the union being 112,853*l.*, the net poundage for establishment charges would be $2\frac{1}{4}d.$ in the pound. The same principle of calculation gives a poundage for

The Bailieborough	union of	- - -	$3\frac{3}{4}d.$
" Bawnboy	"	- - -	$3d.$
" Cootehill	"	- - -	$2\frac{1}{8}d.$
" Enniskillen	"	- - -	$2\frac{1}{5}d.$
" Granard	"	- - -	$2\frac{1}{3}d.$
" Oldcastle	"	- - -	$2\frac{8}{11}d.$
" Kells	"	- - -	$2\frac{1}{6}d.$

But the net establishment charges of the proposed county union, including the cost of hospitals in the remote parts of the union, would be 1,811*l.*, and the rateable value being 271,355*l.*, the poundage would be for establishment charges $1\frac{7}{11}d.$

In no union therefore would the possible saving amount to as much as 2*d.* in the pound. Even if the expenditure was not otherwise increased by an addition to outdoor relief, the saving of 2*d.* in the pound would be a very small advantage to set against the hardship to the poor, and the inconvenience to guardians that would be caused by the proposed extension of the area of the Cavan union. This is certainly the view of the boards of guardians of the majority of those unions that would be directly affected by amalgamation. Such a change, if made at all, must be made simply in compliance with the wishes of a bare majority of one union, and in opposition to the strongly expressed wishes of the majority of the other unions that would be involved in the change. At the inquiries held at Cavan, Monaghan, and Ennis, we sought to ascertain the views of the guardians of those unions from which it was proposed to transfer electoral divisions to adjacent unions, as well as of those to which additions would be made. From the unions that would be affected by amalgamation, strong objections were urged to such a course. These objections were subsequently sustained by the evidence of guardians who attended the several inquiries.

The proposal of the guardians of the Cavan union would, by absorbing all the Cavan electoral divisions into the proposed union, affect five other unions in the county. The views of those unions were represented by deputations appointed by the several boards of guardians at the inquiry that we held at Cavan. The objections to the proposal, stated temperately and with clearness, prove conclusively that, if carried, it would be in opposition to the interests and with total disregard to the wishes of the majority of those who would be affected by it. From the Enniskillen union eight electoral divisions would be transferred to the proposed Cavan union. Mr. John

Nixon, deputed by the guardians of the Enniskillen union to represent their views, stated that the proposed transfer—

"Would be a very great hardship on the poor and sick, and on the ratepayers generally. The guardians could not attend here: it would not be possible. We require to leave home the day before to come here, and would get back late at night. Our rates are low, and we are satisfied. The elected guardians are quite unanimous in wishing to remain with Enniskillen, and we come here to protest against any change being made." Mr. Nixon, Ev. 355.

Mr. James Bracken, another ex-officio guardian of the Enniskillen union, stated that—

"At the last meeting of the guardians (Lord Belmore in the chair) he was asked to attend here with Mr. Nixon (the last preceding witness) as a deputation, and to protest against the proposal. That was passed unanimously. He has spoken to several of the elected guardians of these eight divisions, and they think the proposal would be most injurious. Mr. Bracken, Ev. 375.

Cootehill is another union that would be affected by proposals of amalgamation;—not only by the proposal of the Cavan guardians, but by a proposal of the Monaghan guardians, which was the subject of a subsequent inquiry. Upon both occasions the Earl of Dartrey attended to represent the views of the board of guardians of which he is chairman. He repeated at Cavan the opinion that he had already communicated to us as having been unanimously sanctioned by the Cootehill guardians. Owing to the distance of Cootehill from the nearest union with which there is a railway communication (Castleblayney) the guardians of Cootehill— Lord Dartrey, Ev. 385.

"Would practically have no control over the expenditure of their rates, while the management generally of their Poor Law business would be left in the hands of the guardians of the other unions." Ev. 385.

There would be little or no saving, owing to the outlay in conveyance of paupers and travelling expenses of relieving officers, and other officers that must be retained, and—

"It would be financially objectionable to the Cootehill guardians to be aggregated to other unions, where the rates are higher, as is the case in all the surrounding unions. * * * During the past seven years the rates in Cootehill union vary from 6d. to 8½d. in the pound: the average rate over the whole union at present is 8½d. in the pound." Ev. 385.

This low rate is very much attributable to the fact that outdoor relief is discountenanced by the guardians of the Cootehill union. Mr. Philip Smith, an ex-officio guardian of the Cootehill union,—

"Quite agrees with Lord Dartrey that our low rates is owing to the strict look-out the guardians keep in the matter of outdoor relief, by giving it only to persons who are temporarily ill, and who cannot be removed to the workhouse." Mr. Smith, Ev. 393.

Mr. Smith "has not the slightest doubt" that the adoption of the same system would reduce the rates in Cavan as it has done in Cootehill. Ev. 394.

It deserves to be noticed that Cootehill, in which the strict administration of relief has been attended with so much advantage, was, before the introduction of the Poor Law, the most pauperised district in that part of Ireland. Writing of Cootehill in 1839, Mr. Otway, the Assistant Poor Law Commissioner, says,—

"There are no consolidated public funds or institutions for the general relief of the poor. Once a week the shopkeepers of Cootehill dole out a small portion of tobacco, sugar, tea, or whatever commodity is the cheapest and worst in their shop, to each beggar who asks of him, on condition of their not asking again for the remainder of the week. This mode of relief (if it can be so miscalled), or rather this selfish and indolent mode of getting rid of importunity, I need not say, is productive of the most injurious consequences, and aggravates the evil it would pretend to relieve: it impoverishes both the receiver and the giver." * * * "The town, on the 'dole day' as it is called, presents a disgusting and lamentable spectacle, a frightful example of the evils of indiscriminate and voluntary almsgiving. * * * "I feel assured" continues Mr. Otway, "that one-half of the money value of the alms now wasted in unprofitable and indiscriminate charity, wrung in most cases from the pressing necessities of the deserving poor, would be found, if computed, more than equal to any equable rate that it will be necessary to raise for the relief of the really destitute poor in the workhouse under the provisions of the Poor Relief Act."

Yet, no doubt, in those days this system of alms and dole giving was regarded as a "judiciously administered system of outdoor relief." In principle it certainly differs but little from the practice that is spoken of with approval by some of the advocates of amalgamation in the Cavan union, and which they desire to extend from their own union to the whole county.

A third ground of objection to the Cavan proposal stated by Lord Dartrey is that—

"It would be extremely grating to the feelings of the poor to be removed so far from the locality where all their friends reside; and in the case of patients who ought to resort to the fever hospital, the Ev. 385.

distance would be a positive bar to their making use of it, and consequently there would be great danger of the spread of infection through the patients remaining with their families in their own houses."

Granard is another of the unions that would be dismembered by the Cavan proposal of amalgamation. Although two ratepayers attended the Inquiry to express approval of the transfer of "Scrabby" electoral division to Cavan, yet the clerk of the union attended, by direction of the guardians, to communicate the following resolution:—

Mr. Higgins, Ev. 413. "This Board is of opinion, that in place of giving to Cavan union the electoral divisions in that county in the Granard union, the old boundary of the union should be restored."

Ev. 413. This resolution was supported by a statement of great force and clearness, which will be found in the evidence of Mr. Higgins, the clerk of the union.

From Oldcastle, another union that would be affected by the Cavan scheme of amalgamation, we received evidence to the same effect. Mr. Thomas Battersby, vice-chairman of the board of guardians, was deputed by that body to declare that they were "decidedly of opinion" that the proposed scheme of amalgamation "would not be a wise measure, either for us or for Cavan." The Oldcastle board of guardians are "entirely unfavourable" to the proposal. "We get on very well." Mr. Battersby states:—

Mr. Battersby, Ev. 433.

Ev. 436.

Ev. 436. Ev. 437. Ev. 438. Ev. 441. Ev. 444.

"Our union, I believe, is as well managed as most unions, and the people are very well satisfied as far as the management of it goes. We have by far the lowest rate of outdoor pauperism in the county. We give outdoor relief to only 63, while the numbers for other Unions in the county are 475, 807, 700. Our rates are low, our pauperism is low,—which may be ascribed to the fact that we set our faces against giving indiscriminate out-door relief," than which "nothing strikes more at the root of the Poor Law system. This is the blot upon the system. If the union was made very large, so that many of the paupers lived at long distances, it would tend to increase the outdoor relief in the union. The workhouse being more difficult to reach, it would be necessary to give outdoor relief more largely;" and, in his opinion, "nothing is more ruinous under the Poor Law system." Nor, in his opinion, "would it be possible for guardians of outlying divisions to attend meetings in Cavan."

And these are not merely individual opinions, but represent the views of the board of guardians of the Oldcastle union. There is one other union in the county of Cavan that would be affected by the proposed scheme of amalgamation—the Union of Bawnboy.

We have already stated that this union was formed for the purpose of remedying the great inconvenience which was found to result from the extent of the Cavan union. The Cavan guardians, who are in favour of amalgamation, propose, not simply to undo the work of the Boundary Commissioners by reverting to the old formation of the Cavan union, but, by giving a still wider extension to the area of the union, to aggravate the evil then complained of, and for which the formation of the Bawnboy union was adopted as a remedy. Against this proposal the board of guardians of the Bawnboy union unanimously protest. They deputed a number of guardians to attend the Inquiry for the purpose of expressing their opinions. One of the deputation, Mr. Patrick Maguire, in accounting for the absence of the chairman, illustrated one evil that would result from the proposed extension of the Union:—

Mr. Maguire, Ev. 461. "I think," he observed, "the spirit of the Poor Law was that it contemplated the relief of the poor; and this would be very injurious to the poor. For instance, I would mention that our chairman was to have been here to-day, but the stormy character of the weather has detained him, although he has his carriage to come in; and if it detained him, how could the poor be brought a similar distance in an open cart without injury to them?"

As to the reception by the Bawnboy guardians of the Cavan proposal, Mr. Maguire states:—

Ev. 449. "When the petition (of the Cavan guardians) was sent forward to Bawnboy to get the concurrence of the guardians there, they would not entertain it at all. It did not occupy them two minutes. They unanimously rejected it on its being read."

Mr. M'Govern, Ev. 472. Mr. James M'Govern, who attended the Inquiry in compliance with the wish of the guardians, stated that a deputation of five was appointed—

"to protest against the Cavan proposal, on the ground of the very great inconvenience it would entail in the removal of paupers here, and also that it would favour the extension of out door relief. They also stated that it would be an impossibility for the guardians to attend here to the interests of the electoral divisions which they represent, and that in fact they would lose all control over the expenditure of that portion of the union,"

which it was proposed to transfer to Cavan.

Mr. S. Kennedy, Ev. 54 et seq. It thus appears that the five unions having electoral divisions in the county protest against the transfer of them to a county union;—a proposal emanating from a section only of the Cavan guardians, made in absolute and avowed ignorance of its financial bearings, without consideration, as we have already observed, for the convenience of the representatives of remote divisions, in total disregard of the hardships that would be inflicted upon the poor, and simply with a view of relieving themselves, as they imagine, at the expense and in spite of the opposition of their neighbours, from the financial consequences of their own injudicious administration of the law. It is but just to add, however, that one of the guardians who signed the memorial in favour of amalgamation, Mr. James McCann, with creditable candour came forward to state that— Mr. Dingnan, Evidence. Mr. H. Faris, Ev. 487.

"Upon reconsideration, and from the arguments I have heard here to-day, I think that amalgamation would be injurious. . . . I wish, therefore, to express my distinct withdrawal from the petition." Mr. McCann, Ev. 500.

The application of the guardians of the Monaghan union was equally opposed by representatives of the other unions which would be affected by the change. As it was proposed to transfer several electoral divisions from the Cootehill union, the Earl of Dartrey attended the Monaghan Inquiry, as he had done the Cavan Inquiry, to protest on behalf of the Cootehill guardians against the proposal. He stated that at a board meeting attended by 27 guardians, they were unanimous in expressing their decided opposition to amalgamation. They thought it would not serve the interests of the poor, or the interests of the ratepayers. In the first place, they would rather keep the management of their affairs in their own hands. In the next place, the saving would be infinitesimal when you take into consideration the extension that would be given to outdoor relief by dividing the country into large districts. There would in addition be the amount to be paid as compensation to officers who would be discontinued, cost of conveying paupers, and allowance to relieving officers for travelling expenses. The Cootehill guardians were also of opinion that it would be a great hardship upon the poor sending them out of their own districts to be relieved, and that it would be very detrimental to them to have to go long distances to apply for relief. In conclusion Lord Dartrey observed that the proposal if adopted,

"would entail great hardships on the poor, without yielding any corresponding advantage to ratepayers. These are our chief reasons for opposing amalgamation." Lord Dartrey, Ev. 925.

Clones is another union which would be affected by the proposal of the Monaghan guardians. We would direct special attention to the very clear, temperate, and forcible statement in which Mr. Brady, their chairman, stated the objections of the Clones guardians to the dismemberment of their union. Mr. Brady, Ev. 938–962.

It would thus appear that the scheme of amalgamation inquired into at Monaghan was a proposal supported by five and opposed by four guardians of that union, and unanimously opposed by the guardians of the other unions that would be affected by it.

The third Inquiry was at Ennis, upon an application for the extension of the area of the Ennis union by dissolving adjacent unions and annexing portions of them to Ennis. The object of this proposal would appear to be simply to transfer to Ennis a certain amount of rateable property, unaccompanied by a proportionate amount of population or pauperism. Mr. Thomas Greene, vice-chairman of the board of guardians, explained this in reply to a question put to him:—

"I set out by stating that very few paupers would come in from those districts" (which it was proposed to detach from another union). "A great part of the districts are grazing land, not inhabited by the class of paupers that become workhouse inmates. In fact, every one you find there is a farm labourer, and when distress arises, it could be met by outdoor relief instead of indoor." Mr. Greene, Ev. 985.

From the other unions which would be affected by the proposed change, representatives attended the Inquiry to protest against it.

The chairman of the Tulla union (Captain Geo. O'Callaghan)— Capt. O'Callaghan,

"Thinks the feeling of the ratepayers is against amalgamation. If amalgamation will reduce our rates, I am for it. If it be shown there will be no decrease, I prefer things as they are. I think that is the feeling of most people in Tulla union; it is simply a question of pounds, shillings, and pence. * * * The extension of area would decidedly affect the attendance of guardians;" it would "tend very much against their attendance." "Of course there are greater facilities for the poor to attend at Tulla than there would be at Ennis." Ev. 1092. Ev. 1096.

Robert Spaight, Esq., an ex-officio guardian of the Tulla union, stated that—. Mr. Spaight, Ev. 1112.

"Yesterday a resolution was passed at the board, when there was a very large meeting, and the chairman, vice-chairman, and I were asked to attend to protest against amalgamation. We do not think it would be for the interest of the ratepayers. We would be for amalgamation if it would decrease the rates. There are a great many gentlemen here who think that if these workhouses were done away with they would have no rates to pay; but, for the very good reasons stated by Mr. Crawford, we do not think it would be so."

From the Corrofin union, the chairman, Major C. W. Studdert, attended, together with the deputy chairman and deputy vice-chairman, to protest against amalgamation, and communicated to us a very strong resolution of the guardians in that sense. The guardians of this Union are of opinion that—

Major Studdert, Ev. 1116.

"Very great hardship and injury to the sick and destitute poor would result from amalgamation;" and they "feel that the interests of the poor, which they are bound to protect, should not be overlooked through a desire to effect what would appear to be a doubtful saving to the ratepayers."

The resolution of the guardians, which enters somewhat fully into the question of amalgamation, will be found in the Appendix, in the evidence of Major Studdart. Finally, Charles Geo. Mahon, an ex-officio guardian of Killadysert union, stated that he—

Mr. Mahon, Ev. 1138.

"adopted in full every expression used by Captain O'Callaghan and Mr. Spaight. Amalgamation would be a great inconvenience to the poor. Our chairman holds these views."

It should be observed that the accommodation for the sick in the Ennis workhouse is not adequate to the want of that union as at present constituted. An extension of the union would involve the necessity of a considerable extension of infirmary accommodation.

Mr. Howard, Ev. 1140–1203. Mr. Hegarty, Ev. 1205–1220. Mr. Astre, Ev. 1226. Mr. Murphy, Ev. 1238.

The next Inquiry we held was at Mill Street, the guardians of which Union are divided upon the subject. The arguments in favour of amalgamation in this case are very fully and clearly put by the vice-chairman, Mr. John Howard; as are the reasons against, with equal clearness and force, by one of the elected guardians, Mr. Jeremiah Hegarty. Representatives from two unions (Macroom and Kanturk) which would be affected by the proposed amalgamation attended to protest against it, partly upon the ground of the additional expense that would be entailed upon those unions, and partly upon the ground, which we can ourselves confirm, that the workhouses of these unions could not accommodate the poor that would be transferred from Mill Street.

Mr. Clancy, Ev. 1253–1311. Mr. McDonnell, Ev. 1312–1415. Mr. Hughes, Ev. 1460–1471.

The last Inquiry that we held was upon the application for amalgamation received from the guardians of the Glenamaddy union. None of the unions to which it was proposed to transfer electoral divisions were represented at that Inquiry. But the evidence given both by the advocates and opponents of "amalgamation" serves to illustrate the insufficiency of the grounds upon which such a change is proposed, as well as the force of the objections to it. The question appears to have been discussed by the guardians upon several occasions, and finally a resolution in favour of dissolving the union was adopted by a majority of one,—the numbers being seven for and six against.

The only reason urged in favour of dissolving the union, and distributing the electoral divisions amongst neighbouring unions, was that it would lead to a considerable saving in expenditure.

Mr. McDonnell, Ev. 1409. Ev. 1408.

It was not contended, nor could it be so with any show of reason, that there would be a diminution in out-door relief. The chief advocate of amalgamation is of opinion that if amalgamation would tend to the extension of out-door relief, the ratepayers "would not be worse off;" though he is also of opinion that the system of out-door relief that prevails in the union is simply "subsidising mendicancy." He and the guardians who concur in opinion with him think that amalgamation would not entail any hardship upon the poor, though they are all decidedly of opinion that it would be most inexpedient to retain an hospital in Glenamaddy. The following resolution was adopted by them upon the subject:—

Ev. 1252.

"That in the event of this union being amalgamated with the adjoining unions, it will be necessary to discontinue the hospital attached to the workhouse, and have the sick paupers therein removed to the respective unions to which they may be chargeable, and to dispose of the workhouse and grounds for the benefit of the union, and in the event of superannuation being granted to any of our officers that same be borne jointly with unions with which we may amalgamate."

Against that view the guardians who are opposed to the dissolution of the union protest strongly. One of them thinks that "it would be very inhuman to "dispense with the hospital;" "it could not be done away with without very great "injustice and hardship to the poor." Another guardian, "in the interests of the poor, "would very much prefer seeing the union remain as it is." A third thinks "it "would be a great hardship on the poor, and a most inhuman thing, to bring them to "far distant unions while they could be well cared for here."

The argument urged in support of the assumption that amalgamation would lead to a considerable saving of expenditure, scarcely merits serious consideration. It is assumed that the whole of the establishment charges would be saved, and that the saving would amount to 7¾*d.* in the pound on the valuation—the actual poundage for establishment being only 5*d.* It is true that the author of this financial operation, by which 7¾*d.* can be saved out of 5*d.*, qualifies his statement. Being asked whether he had taken into account the proportion which the electoral divisions of the dissolved union would have to pay towards the establishment charges of the unions with which they might be incorporated, frankly replies, "I made out merely what answered my "own purposes, leaving you and the Board to make out the remainder." Again, it was urged that, owing to the alleged difficulty of obtaining contracts, the cost of in maintenance was very high, and would be reduced by amalgamation; while, in fact, the cost of maintenance is found to be lower in the Glenamaddy union than in three out of the four unions with which it is proposed to incorporate its electoral divisions, the proportions being—

Mr. Roberts, Ev. 848.

	s.	*d.*
Glennamaddy - - - - -	3	1¾
Roscommon - - - -	3	7½
Castlerea - - - -	3	8¼
Tuam - - - - -	3	5½
Mount Bellew - - - - -	2	11

By such representations, it would appear, were the majority of the guardians led to apply for the dissolution of the union, without reference to the probable increase of outdoor relief, or to the hardships that would result to the sick poor.

Applying to the proposal of the Glennamaddy guardians the test of the correct poundage of the establishment charges in the union itself, and in the unions with which it was proposed that it should be amalgamated, we find that, so far from a saving of 7¾*d.* in the £ being effected, the saving in establishment charges would not be more than 2⅓*d.* in the electoral divisions it was proposed to transfer to Castlereagh; about 2*d.* in those for transfer to Tuam and Mount Bellew, and less than 1*d.* in those to be added to Roscommon. We do not consider that this small prospective saving would at all compensate for the hardship to the poor which would be occasioned by the dissolution of this union.

Although the number of applications in favour of "amalgamation" deliberately and upon full consideration made by boards of guardians may be counted, if we may adopt the phrase, upon the fingers of one hand, yet proposals to increase the size of some existing unions by the transfer of adjoining electoral divisions have been made by guardians who are averse to "amalgamation." As this is a matter the Local Government Board have authority to deal with, we did not consider that we were called upon to examine, with a view to giving effect to them, the applications made to us. We may observe, however, that, so far as those applications came under our notice, they appear to have been too often suggested merely by a desire to obtain an addition of rateable value, without a proportionate addition of pauperism, from neighbouring unions. It is superfluous to add that such a change is strenuously opposed by those unions which would be injuriously affected by it. Indeed, it is important to bear in mind that not a single proposal for extension of area has come from any union which would not have to be carried out in the teeth of strenuous opposition from the other unions from which one or more electoral divisions would be transferred. Thus, although the guardians of the Abbeyleix Union are prepared to receive any portion of Castlecomer union, the Castlecomer guardians object to an aleration in boundaries, though a memorial in favour of "amalgamation," numerously and influentially signed by ratepayers, was presented to us. Copies of this memorial, and of our reply, will be found in the Appendix. The guardians of the Athlone union consider that their union might be enlarged by taking portions of Parsonstown and Ballymahon unions, and they are of opinion that the necessity for a union of Ballymahon has long since passed away: the guardians of Ballymahon and Parsonstown, however, differ from this view, and object to an alteration of boundaries. The guardians of Carrick-on-Suir union consider that it would be inexpedient to dissolve their union, and are of opinion that a good portion of the Kilmacthomas, Thomastown, Callan, and Clonmel unions might be annexed thereto. The guardians of Kilmacthomas are of opinion that the townlands nearer to Kilmacthomas than to the unions to which they belong might, with advantage, be added to Kilmacthomas: the guardians of Thomastown, Callan, and Clonmel unions object to an alteration of boundaries. The

App. A 3, p. 127.
App. A 1, p. 101.
App. A 1, p. 108.
App. A 1, p. 101.
App. A 1, p. 107.
App. A 1, p. 108.

guardians of the Nenagh union would not object to take part of the Borrisokane union; but the Borrisokane guardians object to an alteration of boundaries. The guardians of the Oldcastle union think that it would not be expedient to dissolve their union, but are of opinion that Delvin union ought to be dissolved, and a portion of it added to Oldcastle: the Delvin guardians, however, are opposed to an alteration of boundaries. The guardians of the Omagh union resolved, "We do not think the Omagh Union should be dissolved, but are strongly of opinion that the smaller unions of Gortin, Castlederg, and Clogher, might be advantageously dissolved:" the Gortin guardians leave the matter in the hands of the Commissioners, but the guardians of Castlederg and Clogher object to any alteration of boundaries. Although it would be impossible to dissolve the Roscrea union, the guardians think that the necessity for Donaghmore union has ceased, and that it should be added to Roscrea; but the Donaghmore guardians are of opinion that it would be inexpedient to dissolve the Donaghmore union, and suggest its extension by adding portions of other unions to it. These references, which we might extend to the majority of unions, indicate not only the view of "amalgamation" that is generally taken by boards of guardians, but also show the impossibility of giving effect to them. Apart from the objections stated to "amalgamation" in particular cases, the difficulty of reconciling the views of guardians, as illustrated by their replies to our queries, would, in our opinion, fully justify any reluctance on the part of the Local Government Board to disturb the existing formation of unions, except for reasons much stronger than those usually urged in support of such a change.

App. A 1, p. 104.
App. A 1, p. 99.
App. A 1, p. 104.

Before leaving the subject of amalgamation, we would observe that in our personal communications with guardians in many parts of the country, we frequently found an erroneous impression prevailing as to the pressure of the poor-rates, "that their pressure (poundage being quoted) was very heavy," and "that some expedient, be it amalgamation or rate-in-aid, should be hit upon to give relief, and to reduce the rates to the level prevailing in more favoured unions." This impression is the natural result of a comparison of charges, *as represented by the poundage;* but a little inquiry generally sufficed to show that the grievance was more imaginary than real, and that it is the consequence of the unequal valuation prevailing in different parts of the country.

To account for this inequality it is only necessary to remember that the tenement valuation of Ireland was commenced about the year 1844, and was not completed until about the year 1860, the province of Ulster being the last valued. Thus it came about that many unions were valued during the "bad times," when the land was stripped of its stock, and when, in the Encumbered Estates Court, it was selling for eleven years purchase.

When it is borne in mind that the poor-rates at that time were unusually high, amounting in some instances to as much as 10*s*. and 15*s*. in the £, and that the Act provided that in estimating the net annual value the amount paid in rates and taxes should be deducted, it will be easily understood that in unions valued during this period of depression, the poundage charge will appear much higher than in unions valued when prices were good and the country prosperous.

We may cite a case—an extreme one no doubt—but still illustrating the unsoundness of any conclusions as to the pressure of taxation which are founded upon consideration of the poundage charge only. The case is that of the electoral division of Kilcummin in the Oughterard union, and a case much quoted during the union rating agitation. In this electoral division the poundage charge for the year 1877–8 stood as high as 4*s*. 3*d*. in the £. The total expenditure, however, only amounted to 84*l*. The area of the electoral division is 14,844 acres, its population (in 1871) was 822, and the valuation on which this poundage was based 160*l*.

The Valuation Acts, though providing by the annual revision for the valuation of new buildings, railways, &c., do not provide for any revision of the valuation of the lands. As it is impossible for a fair judgment to be formed of the pressure of local taxation without the foundation of an equable valuation, and as we believe that misconceptions under this head were among the influences which led to the present inquiry, we feel it right to bring this important subject under Your Grace's consideration.

HOSPITAL ACCOMMODATION.

The question whether additional hospital accommodation is required must be considered in connection with the general system of medical relief now established in Ireland. That system is not, strictly speaking, poor law (medical) relief of destitution, but the administration of "medical charity." It is, in fact, an extension, through "the Medical Charities Act," of the system which prevailed before the introduction of the Poor Law, under which gratuitous medical relief was afforded nominally to the working classes—practically to classes much above them as well—by means of—

Dispensaries, Infirmaries, and Fever Hospitals.

The dispensary system, apart from the question of hospital accommodation, appears to be well adapted to the condition of society in Ireland. Whatever may be its defects, it meets, to an extent not surpassed in any other part of the kingdom, the great want of the humbler classes,—medical aid, always accessible. To describe adequately the advantages, or to ascertain what may be the defects of this system, would require and fully justify an inquiry much more extensive, minute, and technical than we felt called upon or indeed were authorised to undertake. A letter from the Medical Association, which is printed in the Appendix, directing attention to alleged abuses of the dispensary system, merits careful consideration. The indiscriminate distribution of dispensary tickets is not merely an injustice to medical practitioners, but must have a pauperising influence upon a large class of the recipients. To what extent this evil prevails, and how it can be best met, are questions that certainly seem to call for investigation.

If the statements in that letter be well founded, they afford striking evidence of the tenacity with which an abuse once admitted into Poor Law administration retains its hold through every change in the system. The gratuitous medical relief given indiscriminately, which is now a subject of complaint by the Medical Association, was one of the evils complained of before the passing of the Poor Law, and which the Commissioners were desirous of correcting by the reformed dispensary system under the Medical Charities Act.

"In some of the dispensary districts," they say in their Report of 1841, "it appears that all the working classes, including farmers, independent of such a resource, consider themselves entitled to dispensary attendance, and usually obtain it. In other districts persons of respectable station, possessing one or two hundred acres of land, as well as money and other property, obtain gratuitous medical attendance for themselves and families. Some proprietors, it appears, recommend all their tenantry, rich as well as poor, for dispensary relief, including domiciliary attendance. Yet the rules of all these institutions specify that relief shall be given to the poor only. In many cases this rule is adhered to, but in a far greater number it is not enforced." * * * Again they observe, "It was obviously the intention of the legislature, in making provision for the medical relief of the sick poor in Ireland, that those persons only should obtain relief gratuitously who were themselves unable to pay for it. It may be impossible always to discriminate between this class and the one immediately above it, and in a condition to contribute moderately; and under existing circumstances it is perhaps right that the latter class should also be supplied with gratuitous medical relief; but not so with those persons who are obviously in a condition to provide medical aid for themselves and their families. Yet it is certain that in many parts of Ireland numerous individuals obtain the benefit of the infirmaries and the dispensaries, especially of the former, who are well known to be in possession of ample means to pay for any medical attendance of which they may be in need."

Irrespective of the abuse referred to by the Medical Association, the dispensary system appears to be admirably organised for the purpose of affording extern and domiciliary medical assistance to the poor in the several districts. The distribution of the whole country, comprising 163 unions, into 720 dispensary districts, in which are provided 1,092 dispensaries or dispensary stations, with a staff of 806 medical officers, with 42 apothecaries and 226 midwives, would seem upon the whole to afford sufficient means for rendering extern and domiciliary medical assistance to the poor. The extent to which this is done may be seen from this statement, taken from the last annual report of Local Government Board for the year ended 30th September 1877.

Province	Number of New Cases attended and registered during the year.		
	Dispensary Tickets	Visiting Tickets	Total
Ulster - -	110,562	55,997	166,559
Munster - -	139,711	52,220	191,931
Leinster - -	158,194	59,415	217,609
Connaught - -	57,106	16,843	73,949
Total Ireland -	465,573	184,475	650,048

With reference to these figures, the important point for consideration is whether any, and if so what, proportion of the number (184,475) who appear to have been visited during the year at their own homes were prevented, by distance or any other cause that could be remedied, from accepting relief in the infirmaries? Upon the answer to that question will depend whether additional hospital accommodation is required for the general sick.

The existing accommodation for that class consists of the union infirmaries. These institutions are always in connection with workhouses,—a portion, in fact of the workhouse premises. Originally designed for the accommodation of the sick poor who might happen to be in receipt of indoor relief, they have, by legislative changes, come to be the hospitals for all those within each union who claim indoor treatment under the Medical Charities Act. With a view to ascertain whether they were adequate to the wants of the several unions, we addressed queries to the Inspectors of the Local Government Board, as well as to Boards of Guardians. We subsequently inquired whether any additional hospital accommodation was required in the unions. The replies which we received are printed in the Appendix. With few exceptions, to which we shall refer presently, the replies indicate that the hospital accommodation is adequate. That it is so, or rather that it may be rendered so, for the number who apply for admission, may be accepted as generally true. That which we have occasion to observe in another portion of this Report of Lunatic Asylums is equally true of workhouse infirmaries. Intended as hospitals for the sick, they are too often crowded with aged and infirm—chronic cases which can derive little, if any, benefit from medical treatment. That was one of the abuses of the old infirmary system, for the correction of which the Commissioners looked to the operation of workhouse administration.

"When all the workhouses," they wrote in 1841, "shall have come into operation, it is highly probable that a considerable number of the chronic cases which were previously treated in the infirmaries will be absorbed in the workhouses; and it may be presumed that the infirmaries will thus become more useful to the class of patients for which they are chiefly intended, namely, those whose ailments require intern hospital accommodation."

What was true of the county and other infirmaries when that was written, is, as we have just observed, true of the workhouse infirmaries now. A considerable number of beds in them are occupied by cases unsuitable for hospital treatment. By transferring that class of inmates to their own department—the aged and infirm wards of workhouses,—and removing lunatics to auxiliary asylums, as suggested in another part of this Report, the infirmaries of workhouses may be rendered quite adequate to the general wants, as at present ascertained, of their several unions.

There remains the question, already suggested, is additional infirmary accommodation required for any considerable proportion of that large class who are now in receipt of domiciliary medical relief? It may be observed that the number of that class has kept pretty stationary for the last ten years, during which the total number of visiting tickets issued appears to have been :—

Year ended 30th Sept.	Visiting Tickets
1865	202,338
1866	191,285
1867	191,680
1868	183,155
1869	195,797
1870	203,900
1871	193,764
1872	210,859
1873	191,649
1874	186,138
1875	198,662
1876	189,419
1877	184,475

The numbers admitted on account of sickness (exclusive of fever cases) to the workhouse infirmaries appears to have fluctuated as little as have the numbers of patients treated at their own homes. There is, therefore, no *increased* pressure for hospital accommodation for the sick. But the number of cases admitted to workhouse infirmaries is certainly not large, being only 27 per cent. in proportion to those visited at their own homes, the exact numbers being—"visited at their own homes" during the year ended 30th September 1877, 184,475; admitted to the workhouse hospitals during the year, 49,120. Many reasons may be assigned for this disproportion. The majority of the cases may be, probably are, unsuitable for workhouse hospital treatment. The unwillingness of patients to be removed, and the very natural unwillingness of friends to allow them to be removed, is always an obstacle to hospital treatment. Although home-nursing, if unattended with risk to the family, should be encouraged and assisted, the alternative of intern treatment should always be available. Dr. Barrett, one of the Medical Assistant Commissioners, writing in 1839, observes very truly,

"A great deal of the distress among the poorer classes is, beyond a doubt, to be ascribed to the inadequacy of medical relief, *especially to the want of hospital accommodation.* * * * The extern assistance afforded by the dispensary does not relieve the poor man from the expense attending sickness. His capital is consumed in procuring drinks, sustenance, and other necessaries, to alleviate the sufferings of the sick-bed; his clothes and furniture are pledged to supply his wants in the course of a protracted illness, and when at length he recovers he finds himself and his family reduced to beggary."

That is by no means an exaggerated statement of the effect of protracted illness in the cottage of the peasant or labouring man. There is, however, no reason to conclude that if greater facilities than now exist for intern treatment were afforded to the poorer classes they would be much more extensively taken advantage of than they are at present. Although the return published by the Local Government Board in their last Report shows that upwards of 36 per cent. of the inmates of workhouses on the 1st of January 1877 were hospital patients, there is nothing to indicate to what extent the admissions are affected by greater or less distance of the workhouse, or by insufficiency of accommodation. It is sometimes urged that the workhouse infirmary can only be made available for the district immediately surrounding. That was true enough of infirmaries before the passing of the Medical Charities Act. It appears from the Report of the Commissioners in 1840, that of the total number, 18,989, admitted to the 41 infirmaries then established, 10,457 came from a distance within five miles, 4,562 from five to ten miles, and 3,970 from more than ten miles. But the advantage of infirmary treatment was in those days by the regulations of the institution restricted nearly to the narrow area within which subscribers could be found. The infirmary was usually placed in the most populous part of the district. The difficulties of communication were great, while the prejudice against hospital treatment was stronger than, happily, it is found to be at present.

To the question whether the general accommodation for the sick in workhouse infirmaries is sufficient, the replies of the Inspectors of the Local Government Board are, with very few exceptions, in the affirmative. In no case does the deficiency of general infirmary accommodation appear to be very serious. In Waterford—

"There is a deficiency of accommodation for the sick poor *at times*. There are some temporary buildings that ought to be replaced. In winter there has always been pressure." App. A. p. 111.

In Kilmacthomas, Mr. W. Hamilton writes,—

"Last winter there was pressure on this hospital, *but there is plenty of spare accommodation in the union building.*"

In Kilmallock—

"An additional room is required in the lying-in ward." p. 135.

In Kanturk—

"Wards in male hospital, small and confined, and do not present perfect facility for constant supervision." p. 126.

These remarks indicate the general character of such deficiencies as may be observed in the infirmaries for ordinary sick. It is obvious that they can be very easily remedied, especially if additional room be afforded by the removal of lunatics to auxiliaries. The addition of the "idiots' wards" of workhouses to the ordinary infirmary accommodation would render these buildings, adequate to the wants of the several unions.

Upon the whole, we feel justified by the evidence communicated to us to report to Your Grace that the hospital accommodation for the sick, exclusive of fever cases, is generally sufficient, or that, where it is not so, it may be rendered so by reclassification and the removal of lunatics.

There are unions, however, in which additional hospital accommodation appears to be indispensable, and others in which it is strongly recommended by the Inspectors of the Local Government Board. Before we refer to these special cases we would direct the attention of Your Grace to the provision of fever hospitals as distinct from general infirmary accommodation.

In no branch connected with the relief of the poor in Ireland is so marked a contrast presented between the past and the present as in the accommodation provided for fever cases. In 1839, when the subject was inquired into, some counties were found to be without any fever hospital at all; several had only one, although the county Cork had as many as 13; Tipperary 12. For the whole of Ireland there were only 91. In Mayo there was one fever hospital for a population of 366,328; in Clare one hospital to a population of 258,322; in Donegal one to a population of 289,149; Londonderry one to a population of 222,012. In some of these hospitals the conditions of admission were so restricted as to exclude from the benefits of the institution all patients residing at a greater distance than two miles. Nothing could be more deplorable than was the condition of a fever-stricken population under such circumstances. Indeed, in the history of the physical sufferings of the lower classes of the Irish people there is not a more distressing chapter than that which describes the condition to which a considerable proportion of the population was often brought down through want of adequate provision for fever and other dangerous contagious diseases. The evidence taken before Parliamentary Committees and by Royal Commissions, and the statement of professional men, abound with facts confirmatory of this. Some of these statements, indeed, would be hardly credible if not vouched by men of character and position. One of the Medical Assistant Commissioners, writing even so late as 1840, says,—

"Painful instances were stated in the course of my inquiry to have occurred of late, in which persons seized with fever or cholera, or to whom an accident had befallen, were obliged to be abandoned to their fate, left under a hedge or in a ditch or pit by the road-side to perish because there was no place to take them to. If a wandering beggar were taken sick he had no alternative, in several places, but to lie in the open air. Sometimes the poor would build a hut over him."

At present there is at least one fever hospital in every union in Ireland with an average population of less than 35,000 with an average acreage of 128,000.

No greater inducement could be offered to Boards of Guardians to extend and improve the accommodation for fever cases, and to give every facility and encouragement to the poor to avail themselves of it, than the well established fact that fever, apparently ineradicable from a district, has disappeared in consequence of the establishment of an hospital, and the timely removal to it of the fever patient of a family. Dr. Millet, one of the physicians of the Cove Fever Hospital, writes in 1852—

"Eight years ago I raised a subscription, and laid the foundation of our present fever hospital Previously to the erection of this refuge for the poor in fever, its ravages and consequences were heart-rending and deplorable in respect to the poor sufferers, and appalling to the community. Many of these unfortunate beings lodged in huts by the ditches and road sides; since its establishment, typhus *has almost disappeared.*"

Dr. Phelan, writing some years later, states that in 68 fever hospitals there were admitted within the year 20,113 cases, upon which he observes:—

"The removal of these cases to hospitals must have been the means of preventing an equal number, perhaps a much greater, from being attacked with fever, and consequently of saving the lives of at least as many as died in hospital, viz. 957. Their support in hospital preserves a considerable number of families from becoming paupers, for it is a notorious fact that when fever once attacks two or three members of a poor family, pauperism and mendicity are the consequences, as they are obliged to pawn or dispose of their clothes and any little furniture they possess, to obtain food and drink during such illness, when the sick are not sent to hospital."

Dr. Hallaran, physician to the Drangon and Newcastle dispensaries, wrote at the same time:—

"Often several members of the same families get fever, one after the other, by which I have known some families to be utterly ruined, partly from the loss of time and neglect of their business, and partly from the expense which their scanty funds so badly enabled them to bear."

The extraordinary and progressive diminution in the number of fever cases is one of the most satisfactory results of improved medical administration. Making every reasonable allowance for the effect of a great decrease in population, improved condition of the humbler classes, and much greater attention to sanitary arrangements, the result is still such as to justify the opinion that the general establishment of fever hospitals is a main cause to which the diminution of fever and a consequent decrease of pauperism may be ascribed. In the year 1840, before the famine, and not an exceptionally unhealthy year, the number of intern patients relieved in 95 fever hospitals was 41,694. The subjoined table exhibits the decrease during the last 13 years in the number of cases treated in the union fever hospitals of the whole of Ireland. Although the "total" number of cases in each year may appear to be large, it is only by taking the "average daily number" (which is shown in the last column) that a correct estimate can be formed of the actual requirement for fever cases, or of the sufficiency of the present accommodation.

Year ending 29th Sept.	Under Treatment at Commencement of Year.	New Fever Cases during Year.			Total treated during the Year.	Average Daily Number in Workhouse Fever Hospitals
		Admitted from Workhouses.	Admitted direct in Sickness	Total		
1865	1,845	7,252	18,410	25,662	27,507	1,824
1866	1,497	6,072	13,553	19,625	21,122	1,357
1867	1,124	6,660	11,708	18,363	19,487	1,237
1868	1,202	6,467	11,209	17,676	18,878	1,196
1869	1,164	4,955	9,976	14,931	16,095	1,020
1870	872	4,488	8,163	12,641	13,513	916
1871	861	3,281	8,718	11,999	12,860	923
1872	814	3,705	10,249	13,954	14,768	1,089
1873	802	4,134	8,235	12,369	13,171	930
1874	650	3,275	8,469	11,744	12,394	898
1875	809	3,169	8,015	11,184	11,993	801
1876	635	2,476	6,576	9,062	9,687	667
1877	746	2,681	6,940	9,621	10,367	700

A similar reduction is shown in the number of extern patients treated at their own homes by the dispensary medical officers. The total numbers appear to have been—

Year ending 30th September.	Total Number.
1865	26,566
1866	22,287
1867	18,975
1868	17,400
1869	16,882
1870	15,744
1871	15,574
1872	15,604
1873	14,454
1874	14,424
1875	13,280
1876	11,646
1877	11,896

In their last annual report the Local Government Board observe, with reference to the facts shown by the preceding tables,—

"It is worthy of remark that in the year 1866 the Sanitary Act, 29 & 30 Vic. cap. 96. came into operation, and was followed in seven years afterwards by the Public Health Act, 1874."

We may, perhaps, reasonably assume that the "daily average" number of extern patients bears about the same proportion to the "total" number as in the case of intern patients.

If that be so, it certainly affords most satisfactory evidence, not merely of the decline and low rate in the number of fever patients, but of the extent to which intern treatment now prevails through the country. The opinions which have been communicated to us, as well as the returns to which we have just referred, appear to us to fully justify the conclusion that the provision of hospital accommodation for fever and other dangerous contagious diseases is generally adequate to the wants of the population. There can be no doubt, however, that in some exceptional cases additional hospital accommodation is indispensable, and that in other cases it may be desirable to extend it.

In addition to the old county fever hospitals, many of which are disused, though available if required, the unions have been provided with fever hospital accommodation, either in detached buildings or in wards of the infirmary, separated from the other portion, though under the same roof.

In very many of the unions the provision for infectious cases in separate hospitals is out of all proportion to the existing wants, or, it may be reasonably hoped, the probable future wants of the unions in which they have been erected. They were built to meet as far as possible the overwhelming pressure of the famine fever, and in contemplation of a permanent need of such accommodation. We have already explained how great a change has taken place in the number of fever cases as well as in the general sanitary condition of the country. This justifies us in recommending, as we do in another part of this Report, the appropriation of several of these detached hospitals as auxiliaries. Where county fever hospitals may not be available, there would still remain, connected with nearly all the infirmaries, wards that either are or easily can be appropriated for infectious cases.

Although the hospital accommodation in workhouses, both for the general sick and for infectious cases, may be considered to be generally sufficient, or, where it is not, may be easily rendered so, there are cases in which additional accommodation, apart from the workhouses, appears to be indispensable, and other cases in which it is recommended as desirable.

The cases in which additional provision appears to be indispensable are parts of unions so remote from the workhouse, or so difficult of access, as to render the workhouse hospital virtually useless. Of such a character is the case of Innishboffen in the Clifden union, of which Dr. Brodie (the Inspector of the Local Government Board) writes,—

App. A. p. 133.

"The nearest point of the mainland, Claggan, is distant, say, eight miles from the island, and an equal distance from the union workhouse hospital. Often in bad weather all communication between the island and the mainland is interrupted for several consecutive days. *For some years past fever of a bad type has appeared amongst the islanders, and the patients suffering from the disease have to be treated in their miserable cabins.* There is a dispensary officer residing on the island, and if a dispensary building, capable of containing, say, six beds for the reception of patients suffering from fever or other contagious disease, could be procured on the island, it would, I have no doubt, be hailed as a boon both by the medical officer and the poor islanders."

There are other places, remote or difficult of access, where, from want of hospital accommodation, the poor are exposed to much suffering and privation. In every such place, the particulars of which can be communicated to the Local Government Board by the local representative of the department, the establishment of an hospital of the character suggested by Dr. Brodie should be imperative. Among these places may be named the island of Achill, in the Newport union, which is populous and at a great distance from the workhouse hospital; and Dungloe, in the Glenties union, to which attention is called by Mr. R. Hamilton. Tory island, Rathlin, and the island of Bear, also are places which, detached from the mainland, are at times difficult of access.

Mr. Richard Hamilton calls attention, in his letter to us of 4th March, to Moville on Lough Foyle, and Rathmullen on Lough Swilly,—

p. 130.

"Anchorages where vessels constantly lie; there is no accommodation within reasonable reach of either of them to which sailors suffering from disease could be removed."

There are other places, anchorages on different points of the coast, in which, if only as a sanitary precaution, accommodation for a few patients should be always available.

As to the necessity of providing additional hospital accommodation in such places as those to which we have just referred, there can be no doubt. As to the expediency of supplementing workhouse infirmaries by cottage hospitals or wards in connection with dispensaries there is considerable difference of opinion amongst the Inspectors of the Local Government. Mr. William Hamilton, who, in the very interesting letter which we print in the Appendix, has dealt fully with the whole question of medical relief, recommends a very extensive establishment of cottage hospitals in the unions of his district; and it must be allowed that he supports his suggestions by general reasons of great cogency. Upon several incidental questions connected with poor law administration the letter of Mr. Hamilton contains many valuable suggestions. Upon the question of providing cottage hospitals he would appear to be supported to a certain extent by some of his colleagues, though opposed by others. Mr. Richard Hamilton thinks—

"It would be desirable to have a few beds in every village for the treatment of urgent cases of illness."

Mr. R. Bourke states that—

p. 131.

"There are portions of the unions of Limerick and Kilrush where the distance from the workhouse infirmary is so great that some such provision (as a few rooms in connection with or adjacent to existing dispensaries) would be of the utmost importance to the sick poor.

The difficulty and even danger of removing patients to a distance of 15 or 18 miles, some of the electoral divisions being as remote, is urged by Mr. Bourke as a reason for establishing those subsidiary hospitals.

"I am aware," he says, "that medical officers have in some instances declined the responsibility of ordering such removals."

He therefore considers that provision of the kind indicated in our letter "would be of the utmost value" in certain places,—Cappamore in Limerick union, and Carrigaholt in Kilmore union.

Dr. McCabe is of opinion that—

"The provision of one or two rooms in connection with or adjacent to existing dispensaries, for the local treatment of cases of infectious diseases, in preference to the removal of such cases to the hospital of the union workhouse, would contribute to the better administration of medical relief." App. A. p. 132.

And Dr. Roughan is of opinion that cottage hospitals in places where the workhouse is very remote,

"are very much needed." There are "many localities that would derive much convenience from having small hospitals attached to them."

Upon the other hand, Mr. O'Brien, while—

"Fully sensible that the more accessible hospital accommodation is rendered for the sick poor, the better it will in every way be, and the more readily will it be availed of by them" p. 131.

states that there is no necessity whatever for the establishment of cottage hospitals or wards in connection with dispensaries in his district. The workhouse hospitals are,

"Upon the whole, central, convenient, and easily accessible; and there would be considerable expense both in providing a building, however limited, and maintaining it in a condition of efficiency."

Dr. Burke states that in the eighteen unions in his district,

"There is not an instance in which I would recommend the establishment of an hospital in connection with a dispensary." p. 132.

He considers the hospitals of the workhouses sufficient.

Mr. Horsley states that, "except perhaps in one or two cases" in his district, it would not be practicable to establish local "miniature hospitals," as he terms them. The objection that would probably stand in the way of any general establishment of sick wards in connection with or in the neighbourhood of dispensaries are thus clearly summed up by Mr. Horsley:— p. 132.

"1. The difficulty, amounting almost to an impossibility, of obtaining—without building—in the dispensary districts farthest removed from the workhouse hospitals, suitable miniature hospital accommodation near the medical officer's residence.

"2. The difficulty of procuring careful, trustworthy, and efficient nurses for such establishments.

"3. The difficulty of establishing such a system of discipline and supervision as would preclude the relatives and friends of patients from resorting, at all times and hours, to these auxiliary hospitals, ostensibly for the purpose of ascertaining their condition, but oftentimes from less worthy motives; and also the abuse which, I think, would, in remote places, arise by the admission of patients labouring under other than really infectious cases.

"4. The large additional taxation—though this should not be considered when proper medical treatment of the sick absolutely requires it—which would, I fear, infallibly result from carrying into practical effect a system which, in this country, would afford too much scope for the exercise of the jobbing propensities to which the humbler classes are, I am sorry to think, already too prone.

"5. Upon the whole,—although small hospital accommodation might possibly be obtained at the following places, Crookhaven in the Skull Union, Abbeyfeale in the Newcastle Union, and Sneem, in the Kenmare Union—I think that, if really good invalid carriages or ambulances were provided for the conveyance of the sick from all parts of the union to the workhouse hospital, there would be no real necessity for smaller or intercepting establishments."

The advantages of workhouse hospitals, especially for the poor in the remote electoral divisions, greatly depends upon the adoption of this last suggestion of Mr. Horsley, which is also referred to by some of his colleagues. It appears to us to be absolutely necessary that in every union there should be provided and always available for the conveyance of patients "a really good invalid carriage or ambulance." In several unions the means of conveyance of patients is exceedingly defective. Even the "Crimean ambulance," which appears to have been made over to the guardians in many unions, is a heavy clumsy machine, ill adapted for use in Irish unions of great extent. Not merely the providing of a "really good invalid carriage or ambulance," but the keeping of it in a proper state, should be strictly enforced in every union in the country.

Defects more or less serious in the organisation of medical relief in Ireland are complained of in various communications which have been addressed to us. Though not called upon to consider how far these complaints may be well founded, or to discuss suggestions which are offered for remedying alleged abuses or defects, it would be unjust to conclude these observations without recording our opinion that the "medical charities" of Ireland, is, with all its defects of administration, in advance of any similar system yet organised in any country in Europe.

DISTRIBUTION OF PAUPER CHILDREN.

In considering any proposal for the redistribution of indoor juvenile pauperism, attention must be paid to the conditions under which children are admitted to workhouses; whether the great bulk of them are of the fluctuating class passing through the workhouse within the year, and therefore unavailable for any such plan of distribution as district school or boarding out; or whether there is such a proportion of permanently chargeable children, "orphans" or "deserted," as would make it expedient or practicable for guardians to provide for them otherwise than in the workhouses of their respective unions.

In the Appendix we print a return which exhibits very clearly the state of juvenile pauperism, and the conditions unavoidably imposed upon guardians in dealing with it. The results may be thus shown in a tabular form :—

	Orphans and Deserted.		With Parents	
	Under 4 years of age.	Over 4 years of age.	Under 4 years of age.	Over 4 years of age.
In all the houses on December 31st, 1876	1,414	5,217	3,200	4,681
Admitted during the year 1877	1,417	4,363	11,367	14,326
Discharged during the year 1877	1,286	4,255	10,950	13,798
In the houses on December 31st, 1877	1,583	5,325	3,617	5,209
Number of those in the houses on December 31st, 1876, still remaining on December 31st, 1877.	977	3,620	1,272	2,279

Notwithstanding the pains taken by clerks of unions in preparing these returns, it is possible that some slight inaccuracies may still exist in some of them. Any such errors, however, if they exist, would not affect the general results, which have a most important bearing upon the whole question of indoor pauper education, and the practicability of a redistribution of children. The fact to which we would, in the first instance, beg to direct the attention of Your Grace is that the indoor juvenile pauperism of Ireland is essentially fluctuating; that the largest, far the largest, proportion of the children come and go, and are in fact under the authority of their parents, and not of the guardians. This is the really important fact that must be borne in mind in considering the question as to the redistribution of children upon which Your Grace has called upon us to report.

Different schemes for the redistribution of indoor pauper children have been from time to time suggested and partially adopted. The professed object has been to cure certain vices and defects assumed to exist and to be inherent in the present system of workhouse education. To enable us to reply to the question submitted to us by Your Grace we have sought to ascertain—

1. Whether the system of workhouse training is in its results such as to call for interference.

2. Whether, if interference were deemed to be necessary, it would be desirable or practicable to alter the existing system of distribution of children in workhouses.

The evidence which we have received as to the condition and the results of workhouse education is contained in the replies of the Inspectors of the Local Government Board, of guardians and officers of unions, and of the Secretary of the Board of National Education, the whole of which is printed in the Appendix.

With reference merely to the educational or literary results of workhouse schools, the evidence is equally satisfactory and conclusive. Tried by the same tests, applied by the same examiners, workhouse children are found to be quite on a par with and in some subjects in advance of children of ordinary schools. As to this there can apparently be no doubt.

This is a return handed in by Dr. Newell. It shows the actual average earnings, and the *possible* average earnings in each subject in ordinary and workhouse schools, taking into account the varying rates in each class.

—	Workhouse Schools.		Ordinary Schools.	
	Average per Pupil.	Possible Average per Pupil.	Average per Pupil.	Possible Average per Pupil.
	s. d.	s. d.	s. d.	s. d.
Reading - - - -	1 11½	2 2½	1 11¾	2 3
Spelling - - - -	0 9½	1 0	0 9¼	1 0
Writing - - - -	1 1½	1 2½	1 1¾	1 3¼
Arithmetic - - - -	1 3	1 10¼	1 4½	2 0
Grammar - - - -	0 5½	0 10	0 6½	0 11¾
Geography - - - -	0 8½	1 1	0 7¾	1 1¾
Agriculture - - -	1 8	2 2½	1 1¼	2 4
Bookkeeping - - -	1 8	2 7	1 4¼	2 7½
Needlework - - -	1 0¾	1 2½	1 3½	1 4½

Whether the effect upon the future conduct and career of the children is equally satisfactory, is of course a totally different and much more important consideration. Upon few questions connected with Poor Law administration does there exist greater diversity of opinion than upon the best mode of educating pauper children. Nor is there one upon which it would appear to be more difficult to ascertain facts sufficiently authentic and numerous to support any very precise conclusions, still less to justify the definite and unqualified condemnation of the existing system that is so constantly heard. District schools, "boarding out," an extension of out-door relief, are means recommended in turn for correcting alleged evil results from bringing children up in workhouse schools. If we may trust the evidence collected by us, there is but slight ground for attributing to workhouse training any considerable proportion of failures in after life. Indeed, if only reasonable allowance be made for difficulties which are inseparable from the very nature of juvenile pauperism, the workhouse education in Ireland would seem to be not the least creditable part of Poor Law administration.

In order to justify any extensive change in the present system of distributing indoor pauper children, two things should be proved by clear and indisputable evidence. It should be shown, first, that the results of the present system are essentially bad; and next, that the system, if defective, cannot be satisfactorily improved.

Upon the first point we have the opinion of the Inspectors of the Local Government Board, and of guardians and officers of unions. We have also certain facts which, though not conclusive, are yet of considerable value.

The opinions to which we refer do not profess to be founded upon minute inquiry into the history of any considerable number of individual cases. Yet, short of such inquiry, no satisfactory conclusion can be drawn as to the success or failure of the system. Too much weight, therefore, must not be attached to the replies to which we have referred. At best they are only the expression of strong impressions, but impressions of persons who have had exceptional opportunity of observation. The replies of the Inspectors of the Local Government Board do not, we apprehend, profess to be more than this. Nor, when the clerk of one union states,—

"My experience, extending over a period of 30 years, tends to convince me that a workhouse is not a good place to bring up children. With very few exceptions, I have never known those so reared ever turn out well,"—

can such a statement be accepted as more than an opinion, requiring to be tested by careful inquiry into the history of every child who has been reared in that work-house during a given period. Nor can more authority be claimed for the opinion of the clerk of an adjoining union, who says, "for the class of boys in the workhouse a "better system of bringing up could not be found." Still, whatever may be the value of the replies which we print in the Appendix, the tenor of these is unmistakeably favourable. They indicate the existence of a general desire on the part of guardians to do fairly by the children, to provide suitable training for them, and to get them into service under favourable conditions. They also point very clearly to such a defect as the want of systematic industrial training.

Apart from mere statements of opinion, we have a class of facts often referred to as an unerring indication of the result of workhouse training, especially of girls. Short of such an inquiry as was undertaken by the late Mrs. Senior, and has recently been fully made by Inspectors of the Local Government Board in England, and which it would certainly be very desirable to undertake in Ireland, perhaps the best evidence of the result of workhouse training would be found in a return of the number of inmates in a workhouse upon a given day, with a statement of the cause of their chargeability; with also a statement of the total number of mothers of illegitimate children in the workhouse on a given day, and how many of these had been inmates of the workhouse, as children, for a period of three years or upwards. The result of such an Inquiry appears to be singularly creditable to the management of Irish Unions. It will be seen that of those who have been reared in the workhouses, and have returned to them, the large majority are cases of bodily infirmity unconnected with misconduct. The replies to our question,—

"Are there any adult inmates in your workhouse now who were brought up in it as children; if so to what cause is their destitution attributable?"—

show, as we have said, that in the majority of cases the cause of destitution is inability, from bodily infirmity, to earn a livelihood. A certain number of those inmates, however, are mothers of illegitimate children.

It is too often and too readily assumed that because a woman returns under such circumstances to a workhouse in which she has been reared, workhouse training is responsible for her misconduct. But, even if the fact were so, the proportion of such cases to those who have had the advantage of domestic training is strikingly small,—only 360 out of a total of 2,687. Here is a statement of the number of both classes in the workhouses in each county in Ireland on 30th November 1878.

Province.	County.	No. of Mothers of Illegitimate Children who were in the Workhouses on 30th November 1878.		
		Who were themselves Inmates as Children for three years and upwards.	Who were brought up outside the Workhouse.	Total.
Ulster -	Antrim - -	16	200	216
	Armagh - -	6	56	62
	Cavan - -	17	37	54
	Donegal - -	7	62	69
	Down - -	10	100	110
	Fermanagh - -	4	37	41
	Londonderry -	4	78	82
	Monaghan - -	6	24	30
	Tyrone - -	13	95	108
		83	689	772
Munster - -	Clare - -	33	84	117
	Cork - - -	37	220	257
	Kerry - -	12	52	64
	Limerick - -	22	92	114
	Tipperary - -	27	138	165
	Waterford - -	15	81	96
		146	667	813
Leinster -	Carlow - -	4	31	35
	Dublin - -	15	173	188
	Kildare - -	14	53	67
	Kilkenny - -	24	96	120
	King's Co. - -	4	27	31
	Longford - -	4	33	37
	Louth - -	20	18	38
	Meath - -	5	53	58
	Queen's Co. -	4	42	46
	Westmeath - -	5	45	50
	Wexford - -	5	94	99
	Wicklow - -	13	48	61
		117	713	830

Province.	County.	No. of Mothers of Illegitimate Children who were in the Workhouses on 30th November 1878. Who were themselves Inmates as Children for three years and upwards	Who were brought up outside the Workhouse	Total.
Connaught -	Galway - -	14	93	107
	Leitrim - -	3	19	22
	Mayo - -	4	49	53
	Roscommon - -	2	43	45
	Sligo - -	—	45	45
		23	249	272
Ulster - - - -		83	689	772
Munster - - - -		146	667	813
Leinster - - -		117	713	830
Connaught - - -		23	249	272
Total Ireland - -		369	2,318	2,687

We do not think that the results of workhouse training, so far as they can be ascertained, afford any reason for interfering with the existing system of distributing children in unions. In some cases, the system may be advantageously modified, in others the details of management may be improved; but the principle of bringing up the children of each union in the workhouse of the union cannot, we think, be replaced with advantage by any other system. The only attempts to replace it that have been made in Ireland are those under the School Districts Order, and the system known as "boarding out." The former was simply an order directing guardians to send children from one workhouse to another. Except as a measure of economy, or as a means of increasing the efficiency of a school by increasing the number of children in it, this plan of amalgamating schools has nothing whatever to recommend it. The alleged evils of bringing children up in workhouses is continued,—indeed, is probably aggravated, while none of the alleged advantages of "district schools" are secured. The effects of this system of "distributing" children is very fully and clearly stated in the Report of the Inspectors of the Local Government Board, Mr. Bourke, Mr. Richard Hamilton, Mr. Robinson, and Mr. Otway; while the conclusions arrived at by the Local Government Board upon the subject are thus stated in the Tenth Annual Report of that Department :—

"Many poor women with families have left the workhouse, or refused to enter it, although in great need of relief, because they found their children, or some of them, would be sent to a workhouse many miles distant, and preferred begging through the country to relief on these terms." "I am led," writes Mr. Otway, "to believe that the working of the Districts School Order has operated as a new and *most stringent* test; that children have absconded sooner than remain in a workhouse removed from their friends and parents; that parents have taken their own and their children's discharge, rather than allow their children to remain in the workhouse of another union."

The feeling that induces parents to refuse to allow their children to be sent to schools at a distance may be a mischievous and unreasonable prejudice. But it will always—so deeply rooted is it—present an insurmountable obstacle to the benevolent deportation that is often recommended, of pauper children of all classes to district or industrial schools. The only children who could be so removed would be "orphans" and "deserted." The large proportion of the fluctuating class, as well as the reluctance of parents to part with them, renders it indispensable to have schools in workhouses. But the removal of orphans and deserted—the permanent class—would so deteriorate the character of workhouse schools as in a little time to justify the reproach of inefficiency to which they are so often and so unfairly exposed. It would, of course, be very erroneous policy, as well as very unjust to the class of permanent children, to retain them in workhouses simply with a view of maintaining a certain degree of efficiency in the schools at the expense of their future success in life. It does not appear that this is so; nor need it necessarily be so. Even if we put aside as of little value the opinions communicated to us as to the success, generally speaking, of workhouse education, it is very plain, we think, that failure, where there is failure, may be ascribed to causes not inherent in the system, and which admit of remedy.

There is in the majority of Irish workhouses very little of what is so often stigmatised as the "corrupting influence of workhouse association." The indoor pauperism consists of aged and infirm and sick, with a small per-centage of persons of ill-conduct. So far as the children are concerned, classification is well observed; in many workhouses very strictly so indeed. It may be truly said that outdoor children are exposed to more demoralising influences in a single town of a county than are the indoor children in all its workhouses put together. The defect of workhouse education appears to be the want of systematic, well organised industrial training. Too much is sacrificed to merely literary advancement. As there are some unions in which industrial training is carefully attended to, and with the best results, why should it not be insisted upon in all?

Another very serious defect in the treatment of workhouse children is the want of care in getting them into suitable places of service, as well as the want of subsequent supervision. Upon this point the clerk of the Castlecomer union writes to us:—

"I should think that the children brought up in workhouses should, if the workhouses are properly conducted, compare favourably with the children of the labouring classes. Nearly all the children brought up in the workhouse of this union have turned out well. The guardians are most particular as to the persons to whom they hire them out; and too much importance could not be attached to the action of boards of guardians in this respect. When children are hired out to persons who treat them kindly and take an interest in them, they become attached to their employers, and pursue a life of industry. Where children are indiscriminately hired out to whoever may offer them employment, opposite results may reasonably be looked for."

In some unions children are sent out at an early age and to such unsuitable occupations as "herding," at which they are kept for the summer months and then returned to the workhouse. In others mothers are allowed to hire out their children, remaining in the workhouse themselves though receiving the wages of the children. Such abuses where they exist, as well as the want of systematic industrial training, can be easily corrected.

The first step, as it appears to us, towards improvement would be to transfer the inspection of these schools from the National Board of Education to the Local Government Board, as Dr. Newell so strongly recommends. The influence of that department could then be brought more directly to bear upon boards of guardians, and existing defects would be more certainly brought to light, and could be more effectually remedied. There is no reason in the nature of the case why such a report as this—one of the many of the same sort communicated to us—should not be equally applicable to every *rural* workhouse in the country:—

"RATHDOWN.

"1. In male department the industrial training is chiefly agricultural. There is a farm attached to the workhouse where a systematic course of cropping is successfully carried out, most of the operations being performed by the school-boys, who are employed on the farm four hours daily, and who acquire skill and dexterity in the use of agricultural implements. The boys are also trained to make up their beds, scrub their dormitories, &c., and to be as self-reliant as circumstances will permit. Boys of proper age and otherwise suitable are taught in the workhouse the following trades, viz., tailoring, shoemaking, and baking. In female department the industrial training consists in teaching the girls to sew neatly; make, wash, and mend their clothes, knit their stockings, scrub and keep in order their dormitories, &c., and occasionally to weed and pick stones on land.

"2. The agricultural training is conducted under the supervision of the schoolmaster; the trades-boys are under the supervision of proper tradesmen, and the matron and schoolmistress superintend the industrial training of the girls.

"3. The guardians experience no difficulty in getting the children into service, the demand being in excess of the supply.

"4. As a rule, no conditions are imposed on persons taking children to service. No terms of wages are made; the children are to give their services in exchange for food and clothing, the guardians giving an outfit in the first instance.

"5. Children are not apprenticed in this union.

"6. Children are sent to service at ages varying from 11 to 15 years, and in many cases retain their first places for lengthened periods, the question of 'wages' being very often the cause of change.

"7. The practice of sending out children to temporary employment does not prevail in this union.

"8. There are but three adult inmates in this workhouse now who were brought up in it as children, their destitution being due to physical or mental debility.

"Upon the subject of 'the education of children in workhouses,' I beg to tender the following observations to the Commissioners, basing my statements upon over twenty-four years' experience in this union:—

"The schools are in connection with the Board of National Education, and the National School Inspector's reports thereon are almost invariably of a satisfactory character. A Committee of Guardians examine the schools annually in the literary subjects taught, and have always reported favourably. A fair amount of proficiency is attained in the essential branches of reading, writing, and arithmetic, by a considerable proportion of the pupils, and the per-centage of answering at the 'results examinations' will contrast favourably with that attained in ordinary national schools. The religious instruction of the children is carefully attended to by the chaplains. I may add that several of the former pupils of these schools have attained respectable positions in life. Two of them are at present teachers of national schools, one was an officer of this house, one is an hospital assistant, others are clerks, shop assistants, &c.

"Considering the parentage of the greater portion of the children reared in the workhouse, and other adverse circumstances, I feel bound to assert that the literary and industrial training of the workhouse children of this union is successfully carried out.—" Joseph D. Cope, Clerk of Union."

With large urban unions the case is different. For reasons sufficiently intelligible, a school within the walls of such unions as Dublin (North and South), Cork, Belfast, and other large centres of population, must be unavoidably exposed to much deteriorating influence. The great object to aim at in these cases is to keep the children in establishments wholly separated from, but within reasonable distance of, the workhouse. Such schools being within the union would be available for pauper children of all classes, fluctuating as well as permanent. If organised upon the principle now adopted, after much consideration, in other parts of the kingdom, in blocks of cottages, cheaply built and inexpensively managed, in which the daily life of children might be brought to resemble, more nearly than is possible in large associated buildings, the life of the class to which they belong, a great advance would be made upon any existing system of pauper education in Ireland. We may observe that at Cork and Limerick there exist agricultural schools which the National Education Board are about to close, and which would be both conveniently situated and admirably suited for detached schools, with peculiar facilities for systematic industrial training.

In such unions as those to which we have referred, the guardians have already with great liberality provided school buildings to which little exception can be taken, except that they are within the workhouse premises. It would be very unreasonable to expect the guardians in those cases to make other provision for schools at their own expense. But if the school buildings in these workhouses were purchased from the guardians as auxiliary lunatic asylums, in accordance with a recommendation we make in a subsequent part of this Report, we have no doubt they would be willing to appropriate the purchase money to providing separate schools. The school buildings of the South Dublin, Cork, and Belfast workhouses, and a block of buildings in the Limerick workhouse, already partially occupied as an auxiliary asylum, could be admirably adapted as auxiliaries, and would supply what is very much needed in the districts to which we refer.

With separate schools of an industrial character for the larger unions, and improved administration in the workhouse schools of rural unions, there is no reason why the education of pauper children in Ireland should not be as satisfactorily provided for, according to its condition, as any other system of education in any other part of the kingdom.

Although of opinion, for the reasons already stated, that no change can be advantageously made in the distribution of pauper children, except by organising separate schools in certain unions, we think that the system of training children in workhouses admits of considerable improvement. The want of *systematic* industrial training tells most unfavourably upon the future of the workhouse child. That it can be introduced into every workhouse is shown by the experience of those unions in which it has been attended with undoubtedly good results. The first step towards effecting an improvement in this respect would be to transfer the inspection of workhouse schools to the Local Government Board. The necessity of such a change, as well as the advantage that might be expected to result from it, is very forcibly stated by Dr. Newell in his evidence:—

"Do you think that it would be advantageous to the children were their industrial and literary training conducted under one head, as in the English Poor Law Department?—Most advantageous and most desirable. The Inspectors of National Schools feel that their inspection is of little value, because the teachers are not the servants of the Commissioners of National Education, nor, indeed, in any sense amenable to their control, which is indirect, feeble, and frequently nil. Inspection is too often discharged in a perfunctory manner. It should be performed by officers directly connected with the Department of State to which the schools belong,—by officers who could devote their whole time and energies to the schools,—taking cognizance not only of the literary proficiency of the classes, but of the educational, technical, and moral training,—examining the institutions patiently, and not in a hurried manner, once a year,—studying and comparing the methods pursued in schools of this class, and of schools akin to them in other countries; and bringing directly under the notice of the responsible authorities suggestions for their improvement. The Inspectors of National Schools are at present nominally serving two masters. Formerly the Poor Law Inspectors were required to examine these schools."

Of "boarding out" under the orders of the Local Government Board as a means of distributing pauper children, we are not in a position to express an opinion either favourable or the reverse. Very little value can be attached to any reports that are not founded upon careful personal inquiry into the circumstances of every individual case. As we were not prepared to enter upon such an inquiry, and as it can be more properly undertaken by the Local Government Board, we offer no opinion upon a system which in Ireland has so many advocates, but under which children are everywhere liable to be exposed to serious danger.

LUNATIC POOR.

In obedience to your Grace's instruction, we have further inquired whether any additional and other provision is required for the better care, relief, and treatment of the poor who are lunatic, idiotic, or imbecile in mind, or otherwise afflicted with mental disease.

With a view to enable your Grace to determine whether any, and, if so, what legislative or administrative change may be necessary or desirable for the better care of the lunatic poor, we have referred to the evidence and reports of previous inquiries; to the reports of those who are officially responsible for the inspection of asylums and the lunatic wards of workhouses; we have examined separately the accommodation provided for lunatics in all the union workhouses; we have visited the several district lunatic asylums; addressed communications and received replies from the governors and from the medical superintendents of these asylums, and received evidence from Sir Dominick Corrigan, the Inspectors of Lunacy, and some of the medical superintendents of asylums. These communications, with the evidence of witnesses, will be found in the Appendix.

App. C 7, p. 239.
App. C 6, p. 229.

Of the early condition of the lunatic poor of Ireland very little is accurately known. Not until a comparatively recent period did any statistical returns exist to indicate even the gross number, still less the classification of the insane. Calculations of the number have been occasionally made upon the somewhat fanciful hyphothesis that lunacy was in a fixed proportion to a population of which there was not as yet even an accurate census. A provision in the will of Dean Swift, or rather an erroneous construction of it, to the effect that if 140 lunatics could not be found in Ireland to occupy the hospital that was founded by his munificent charity, the vacant beds might be occupied by other persons, is referred to before the Committee on Lunacy Law of 1877, "to show the " expansion of insanity since that time, there being now about 18,000 lunatics in " Ireland." What this reference, if correctly made, might show, would be, not as Dr. Nugent seemed to think, "the expansion of insanity," but the more accurate information that we now possess upon the subject. There was but too much truth, though in a sense quite different from that in which he wrote, in the characteristic couplet in which Swift assigns the reason why

> "He gave the little wealth he had
> To build a house for fools or mad;"

which was

> "To show by one satiric touch
> No nation needed it so much;"—

a lamentable fact, to which his attention had just been called by "The Proposal" of Sir William Fownes. That lunacy prevailed to a very considerable extent at the period referred to may be concluded, not merely from indications in the social history of the country, but from the unerring traces in more recent times of hereditary mental disease.

To whatever extent insanity may have prevailed, the treatment of the insane was most deplorable. How, indeed, could it be otherwise? Legislation had, as yet, made no efficient provision for the care of insanity, the one form of affliction that family affection, however strong, or private charity, however liberal, was powerless to alleviate. A member of the House of Commons, giving evidence before a Select Committee in 1817, stated:—

> "There is nothing so shocking as madness in the cabin of the Irish peasant, where the man is out labouring in the fields for his bread, and the care of the woman of the house is scarcely sufficient for attendance on the children. When a strong man or woman gets the complaint the only way they have to manage is by making a hole in the floor of the cabin, not high enough for the person to stand up in, with a crib over it to prevent his getting up. The hole is about five feet deep, and they give this wretched being his food there, and there he generally dies. Of all human calamities, I know of none equal to this in the country parts of Ireland that I am acquainted with."

That statement was read before the Select Committee of the House of Lords in 1843 to a witness, Dr. Phelan, who had long and varied experience in connection with the management of lunatic asylums, and as Assistant Poor Law Commissioner. He was asked—

> "Have you known cases of very great suffering and great abuse which, without being precisely of the character described, are analogous to it?" His reply was, "I have known cases analogous to it. Since I became an Assistant Commissioner even I have seen cases analogous to it."

As late as 1816, in a Report made by the Surgeon General and Physician General of Ireland, it is stated—

> "Lunatics and idiots have been for many years past promiscuously huddled together in the same apartments, and even placed frequently in the same beds with helpless paupers of sane mind, while a crowd of female lunatics have been dispersed indiscriminately among the pauper wards, to the utter

destruction of all decency and moral feeling throughout the whole establishment. A charity thus constituted, instead of being a benefit, is a real nuisance in the country, and, if it cannot be worked in a better manner, ought, in our humble judgment, to be abandoned altogether."

The late Mr. Baron Leslie Foster, when examined before the Committee of 1817, states—

"I have seen three, and certainly two, lunatics in one bed in the House of Industry. I have seen, I think, not fewer than fifty or sixty persons in one room, of which I believe the majority were insane, and the rest paupers not affected with insanity. I have seen in the same room a lunatic chained in a bed, the other half of which was occupied by a sane pauper."

Until the enactment of the Irish Lunatic Asylums Act, lunatics as such were not provided for by law at all. "They were," says Sir Robert Ferguson, "generally supposed to be sent to gaols;"—"they were sent as persons *supposed* to have committed a crime." When some provision was at length made for the better care of these unhappy beings, the interference of the legislature was a measure of police, not of humanity. Lunacy was treated as a crime, and the lunatic (to use Lord Monteagle's phrase) "as though he was a malefactor;" not merely "supposed" to have committed a crime, but assumed to have been convicted of it. It would be tedious, and unattended with any practical advantage in this inquiry, to trace the history of legislation through the various fruitless enactments that give evidence at once of the existence of a great evil and of inability to cope with it. The result of this earlier legislation may be summed up not unfairly in a sentence:—Grand juries "empowered" to present 100*l.* for the maintenance of lunatic wards and declining to do so; and of the later legislation, in the words of the Lords Committee of 1843, as furnishing "a distressing example of human suffering, of mistaken legislation, and of objectionable practice."

The extent and the character of the evils that were brought to light by successive Parliamentary inquiries led at length to the enactment of the 1 & 2 Geo. 4, which authorized the Lord Lieutenant to form districts; to direct the building of a sufficient number of asylums; to appoint governors of the asylums when built; a board of control and correspondence invested with extensive powers with reference to the building and management of asylums; and, finally, with the concurrence of the Privy Council, to frame rules for the conduct of such asylums. Though amended from time to time, this Act may be considered as being substantially the groundwork of the existing system of Irish lunacy administration. Under its provisions, as amended, asylums have been multiplied; and the present system, with its immense advantages and its great defects, has been introduced and established throughout the whole of Ireland.

Side by side with this system has grown up another, which is, in some respects, as will be seen, hardly less important,—the relief of lunatics in workhouses.

We propose to trace very briefly the history of these two systems of lunacy administration, from their introduction down to the present time, to point out in what respect they appear to us to be defective, and to suggest the changes that, in our opinion, ought to be made in them.

From the passing of the 1 & 2 Geo. 4. down to the passing of the Irish Poor Law, the whole of the lunatic poor were relieved in 10 district asylums, the Cork House of Industry, and the several county gaols. As the Cork House of Industry was subsequently merged in a district asylum, and other provision was made for the lunatics who were confined in gaols, we shall refer only to the 10 district asylums which are the subject of the Report of the Inspector General of Prisons for the year 1834. The following statement, furnished to us by the Board of Control, shows the date of opening, the cost of building, and the number of beds provided in ten district asylums up to the year 1835.

Name of Asylums	When opened.	Cost, including Cost of Site. £ s. d.	No of Beds.
Richmond (Dublin) -	—	74,000 0 0	361
Armagh - -	1824	19,900 4 5	104
Limerick - -	1827	26,630 18 1	150
Belfast - - -	1829	45,794 12 7	264
Londonderry - -	1829	26,090 15 4	120
Carlow - - -	1832	22,333 10 4	104
Maryborough - -	1833	24,176 3 0	104
Ballinasloe - -	1833	42,644 3 2	250
Waterford - -	1835	16,868 1 9	100
Clonmel - - -	1834	22,326 14 5	60
Total - -		332,207 5 1	1,637

App. C 4, p. 223.

From this statement it appears that down to 1835 the expenditure in providing 1,837 beds was 332,207*l*., or upwards of 181*l*. per bed. To justify this large outlay it should be shown that these institutions were not only nominally provided, but were strictly maintained, for curative purposes. Yet nothing is more remarkable in the history of district asylums in Ireland than is the way in which from the beginning they have been turned from the main purpose of their construction, and allowed to become places of detention for hopelessly incurable imbeciles, rather than hospitals for the curative treatment of lunacy. Hardly less remarkable is the fact that, although such a change in the character of asylums was long ago apprehended, has been from time to time brought prominently into notice, and been complained of as a serious evil, no effective attempt has yet been made to apply a remedy.

So far back as 1817, Dr. Cleghorn, an eminent physician attached to Swift's Hospital, stated to the Committee that sat in that year, "Places of this kind, unless under strict " rule for a limited term of residence, beyond which no patient should be allowed to " remain, will shortly become asylums for mad people, and not hospitals or places for the " cure of insanity."

It will be seen that even at the early period to which we are now referring these apprehensions were most unhappily realised. It will be also shown, by an unbroken chain of perfectly conclusive evidence extending from that time to the present year,—

That nearly all the district lunatic asylums have been constantly overcrowded with chronic incurable cases, who have occupied the beds that were originally provided for curative cases:

That asylums have been from time to time enlarged, at great expense, very far beyond the necessities for asylum accommodation for curative purposes:

That although the provision of auxiliary buildings, in which harmless incurable cases might be maintained at much less cost than in asylums, has been frequently suggested, no attempt has been heretofore made to make such provision:

That although several years ago the Legislature made provision for the classification of asylums, and the Inspectors of Lunacy concur with other witnesses of the highest authority in thinking that such classification would be attended with the utmost advantage—would in fact meet the difficulties of asylum administration—yet not only has no attempt ever been made to give effect to the provisions of that law, but the Lunacy Inspectors appear to have been unaware of its existence.

In 1834, upon the date of inspection, there were in the Richmond Asylum 272 cases, of whom 103 were classed as "incurable." The Belfast Asylum was at the same date reported to be "much crowded from the accumulation of incurable cases." In the Londonderry Asylum, "the accommodation of which is not sufficient for the wants of " the Province," there were 115 incurables out of 147 on the books. In the Carlow Asylum there were thirty-four (34) considered to be "curable;" fifty-seven (57) "incurable." Dr. Phelan, who was at much pains to collect information upon the subject, sums up the general result thus:—

"Of 2,448 lunatics confined in district and other asylums and in gaols at the end of 1834, only 624 were curable cases and 1,824 incurable."

The effect of this overcrowding with incurable cases was precisely what Dr. Cleghorn had apprehended. So far back as 1838 the Inspector General of Prisons reports:—

"The number of incurable cases remaining in the Londonderry Asylum is an evil it would be very desirable to get rid of, as they occupy the rooms and prevent the admission of recent cases when most hope exists of recovery; and this, should the malady be on the increase, would finally close those asylums, and some remedy must soon be applied. The intelligent Medical Officer of this institution suggests that a provincial asylum should be erected for incurables only, and states the vast numbers still unprovided for as an unanswerable reason. This or some other addition to the present buildings must be resorted to."

In the Report of the Limerick Asylum for 1838 it is stated:—

"Though we have been enabled to afford accommodation to nearly fifty more than the number for which the house was originally intended, yet we find it inadequate to the wants of the district, *chiefly because of the progressively increasing number of incurables,—an evil by which our sphere of usefulness is much circumscribed, and which often obliges us, however reluctantly, to refuse admission to applicants who, could they be received, would most probably be cured, but are now, under these painful circumstances of exclusion, compelled to remain at home under the care of persons who, for the most part, are ignorant of the mode of treating them, and generally inflict such usage as strengthens the disorder, and diminishes the chance of recovery when vacancies for their reception occur in the Asylum.*"

Mr. Jackson, the manager of the Armagh Asylum, writing in 1834, observes:—

"We felt the serious inconvenience of being obliged to admit chronic (incurable) cases, and, I may say, have never been able finally to overcome the difficulty that the receiving of a large number from the gaols caused on the first opening of the asylum. It strikes me that these institutions are not adequate at present to relieve all the lunatic poor; that they are equal to meet all curable and violent cases, I have no doubt, provided they were relieved of their present incurables, which would be of great advantage and public convenience."

The Manager of the Londonderry Asylum writes:—

"There is no asylum in the district to which incurable patients could be transferred, but the Governors are of opinion that such an establishment is indispensable, as the present asylum is totally inadequate to accommodate the number of lunatics in this district, for whom provision should be made at the public expense."

Equally strong was the opinion of the physician of the Carlow Asylum, who, writing in the same year, says:—

"Our house is now filled by old established confirmed cases, in which neither moral nor medical management can effect a restoration to reason. I think great and important alterations ought to be made in these institutions, and that a class of patients should alone be admitted that are capable of cure."

Such is an outline of the growth and condition of Irish Asylums down to the date of the Report of the Committee of the House of Lords, 1843.

The experience of Lunacy administration during the interval from that year to 1857 was apparently not regarded by the Government as satisfactory, and a Royal Commission was issued in the latter year to inquire into the state of the law, the management of asylums, and the condition and treatment of lunatic poor. The Commission comprised Sir Thomas Redington, Mr. Andrews, Queen's Counsel of the Irish bar, Mr. Lutwidge and Mr. Wilkes, two of the English Lunacy Commissioners, and Sir Dominick Corrigan. The inquiry was full and searching, and the Report is a most valuable record of information, and of the matured opinions of men distinguished by ability, and qualified by special knowledge and experience for the duty entrusted to them. To the proceedings of that Commission we shall refer only so far as they bear upon the state of asylum and workhouse accommodation, and the suggestions that we shall take leave to submit to your Grace for its improvement.

During the period from 1843 to 1857 the number of lunatic asylums was increased from 10 to 16, affording additional accommodation to 1,760 patients. The cost of these six additional asylums was 261,995*l*. as appears by this statement furnished to us by the Board of Control.

Name of Asylum.	When first opened				
	Date.	Cost, including Cost of Site			Number of Beds
		£	s.	d.	
Cork - -	1852	79,827	1	5	500
Kilkenny - -	1852	24,920	12	1	150
Killarney - -	1852	38,354	8	3	250
Mullingar - -	1855	37,716	15	9	300
Omagh - -	1853	41,407	12	2	310
Sligo - - -	1855	39,769	0	7	250
Total - -	- -	261,995	10	3	1,760

App. C 4, p. 228.

The evidence given before the Commission of 1857 by the Inspectors of Lunacy, Mr. White and Dr. Nugent, as well as that given by the Medical Superintendents of the several asylums, all lead to the same conclusion, that at that date, when the asylums had been thus increased from 10 to 16, and some of them only recently opened, they were crowded with those classed as "probably incurable." Of the 3,824 lunatics who were in the asylums at the date of the Commission, no fewer than 2,656 were of the class "probably incurable." This state of things led the Commissioners to report:— App. C 17, p. 254.

"At present the district asylums are to a great degree deprived of their utility as curative hospitals for the insane, by the large proportion of probably incurable cases which they contain."

There was not an asylum in Ireland at that time with one exception, Waterford, in which the number of "probably incurable" did not far outnumber the "probably curable." In some of them the "probably curable" did not exceed 25 per cent. of the whole. Without going minutely through this evidence, we may say that the difficulty of asylum management, attributable to the overcrowding of the establishments, is correctly stated by one of the Inspectors of Lunacy, Mr. White, who, being asked—

"What is the practice of the Boards generally, with reference to the discharge or otherwise of incurable cases?" replies, "They often make an effort to get rid of incurable cases; and we may direct the manager to write to the families of the parties or their friends, and to try and have them taken away by them, with the view of making room for recent cases. We have done that repeatedly, and have freed the asylums partially of such cases; but, generally, they are left upon the asylum, and there are many incurable cases, old chronic cases, that cannot be sent away. There is no one belonging to them, and it would be cruel, in fact, to send them out, though they are perfectly harmless. In some instances we do it in order to throw them upon the poorhouses; and there is so much unwillingness on the part of the poorhouse people to receive them, that they are sent back."

The additional accommodation thus provided within that brief period, at so great a cost, was virtually provided for incurables. Dr. Nugent, who was examined before the Commission of 1857, being asked,—

"What is your opinion upon the question of the removal of a number of the present chronic and harmless imbeciles in asylums, in order to make room for recent incurable cases?" replies—

"I think there are a great many lunatics in asylums who might be removed from them,—harmless, quiet persons; but I would not remove every harmless, quiet person, because he happened to be harmless in the asylum."

"What provision would you make for those removed?"

"I would erect additional asylums,—plain substantial buildings,—where you could insure the safe custody of such persons, and at the same time have for them a moderate amount of appliances. I think it would be well to have one in each district. There is expense in sending them to a distance, which would be the result of having only provincial institutions."

Instead of adopting that very reasonable course when it might have been adopted with ease and advantage, the Government, at the suggestion of the Inspectors, erected those six additional asylums, virtually, as we have said, for the accommodation of 1760 incurable patients at a cost of 261,995*l*.

It is true that Dr. Nugent, having been asked—

"Have you ever recommended to the Government the erection of such an institution?" replies

"Yes, we have constantly suggested it."

"I believe a power exists under the present law for the establishment of such institutions?"

"Yes."

"Has that power ever been exercised?"

"No. We have enlarged the Belfast and other asylums."

This single case of the enlargement of the Belfast Asylum here referred to will serve to illustrate the futility of those "suggestions" that were "constantly made" to the Irish Government.

Dr. Robert Stuart, the Medical Superintendent of the Belfast District Asylum, a witness before the Commission of 1857, states that "a very large proportion of the "inmates were incurable;" that "out of 330 inmates, only 74 are considered curable;" that, "the number of vacancies, therefore, which the institution can offer to the "district depends upon the number of cures that may take place out of 74 inmates "or the deaths amongst the incurables;" that, in his opinion, it would be most desirable "to erect a separate building in a distinct locality for the care of the incurable,—those "having a kind of vegetative existence." In the same year, 1857, there appeared in the annual Report of the Inspectors a "suggestion," which is referred to in the last Report, that—

"The question was deserving the consideration of the Executive of how far the separation of the "insane from the sane would ensure to the former more care and comfort than they can possibly enjoy "in ordinary workhouses. By the erection of distinct auxiliary buildings a desirable object would be "obtained, as, on the removal of many chronic and incurable inmates occupying a great deal of valuable "room in several District Asylums, the latter could be more beneficially devoted to recent or acute "cases of lunacy, and then *efficiently serve as hospitals for the cure of insanity, instead of being mere receptacles for the safe-keeping and maintenance of hopeless patients*."

To no asylum in Ireland did these observations apply with more force than to Belfast. Built for 284 inmates at a cost of 45,798*l*., this asylum was subsequently (in 1857) enlarged by the addition of 96 beds at a cost of 22,109*l*., this large and expensive accommodation being mainly as "a receptacle for the safe-keeping and maintenance of "hopeless patients." The inevitable increase of that class led again to the erection, not of "a plain substantial building" as an auxiliary to the existing asylum, but of a new asylum for the county of Down for 300 inmates at a cost of 60,377*l*. Nor, unless a complete change be made in the system, does the expenditure seem likely to end there; for we find the same results in both asylums, accompanied in one by the usual recommendation—a new Asylum,—the number of inmates being:—

Belfast - - - -	108	curable.
	281	incurable.
	50	idiots and epileptics.
Total - -	439	

being 19 in excess of the proper accommodation as stated in the last annual report of the Lunacy Inspectors.

Down - - -	71	curable.
	212	incurable.
	20	idiots and epileptics.
Total - -	303	

being three in excess of accommodation provided. Already in the case of Belfast the Inspectors "are of opinion that the wisest course for adoption would be "found in erecting an asylum to hold 260 beds for the county of Antrim itself." If the Irish Executive should listen to this proposal, the Governors of that asylum may repeat what was said by one of their body, Sir Robert Ferguson, so far back as 1857:—

"The Government seem to me not to have paid sufficient attention to the fact that a large proportion "of those admitted as curable or dangerous sink down into chronic, incurable or harmless patients, "and no houses or wards have ever been built to relieve the district asylums of these cases, so that "they might be open for the reception of curable and dangerous patients and recent cases. From the "want of attention to some such system the result is that all the incurable patients have been and are "supported at large expense."

Such is the conclusion to be drawn from the whole of the evidence on that branch of the inquiry that was given before the Commissioners of 1857, and which led to the recommendation in their Report that portions of workhouses, provided with all proper internal fittings, should be appropriated for a certain class of the "probably "incurable."

That recommendation was not attended to, but within the brief period of three years—from 1866 to 1869—six additional asylums were erected, at a total cost of 292,155*l*., to provide accommodation for 1,769 patients. This is the statement furnished to us by the Board of Control:—

Name of Asylum.	When first opened				
	Date.	Cost, including Cost of Site.			Number of Beds
		£	s.	d.	
Ennis - - -	1868	51,316	8	6	260
Letterkenny - - -	1866	37,887	5	3	300
Downpatrick - - -	1869	60,377	6	5	300
Castlebar - - -	1866	34,903	14	11	250
					31
Monaghan - - -	1869	57,662	5	5	340
Enniscorthy - - -	1868	50,006	0	6	288
Total - - -	- -	292,155	1	0	1,769

Nor is this all. A still further expenditure of 348,976*l*. has, according to the return furnished to us, been authorised or incurred in addition to existing asylums.

The progress of yearly expenditure on district asylums during the last ten years is thus exhibited:—

Year	Daily Average of Patients maintained	Expenditure			Average Cost of Maintenance per Head.			Valuation of Ireland	Poundage Cess
		£	s.	d.	£	s.	d.		
1868	5,670	153,53[illegible]	9	7	24	10	11	13,109,311	2 42
1869	6,256	140,034	10	11½	22	7	4½	13,162,246	2 55
1870	6,557	166,927	15	4	25	6	2	13,205,416	3 03
1871	6,850	177,895	1	11	25	9	2	13,351,807	3·21
1872	7,107	174,345	4	2½	23	16	7	13,381,676	3·13
1873	7,251	187,536	5	11	25	10	3	13,417,922	3 35
1874	7,497	190,311	15	2	25	2	1	13,430,675	3·39
1875	7,756	190,139	17	9	24	15	0	13,490,789	3·25
1876	7,[illegible]	[illegible]	1[illegible]	5	24	15	[illegible]	13,[illegible]	3·41
1877	8,103	200,046	3	11	24	13	9	13,552,250	3 54

Referring to the total expenditure, the Inspectors of Lunacy in their last Annual Report observe:—

"Suffice it to say, that the sum expended on the establishment of proper district asylums, and the purchase of land attached to them, may be set down in round numbers, up to the close of last year, at a million two hundred and fifty thousand (1,250,000*l*.)"

the "proper district asylums" above referred to being occupied at the date of the report by 1,911 "probably curable" cases, and 6,272 "probably incurable." We have already called your Grace's attention to the fact that from the date of the Commission down to the present day the objectionable practice of crowding asylums with incurable cases, unsuitable for admission, has continued to prevail even to a greater extent than before. Indeed, some of these asylums have, according to the Reports of the Inspectors of Lunacy, almost assumed the character exclusively of places of detention for hopelessly demented. Thus, the Killarney Asylum contained, on the 31st December 1877, 16 "probably curable" cases, and 238 "probably incurable." That asylum, originally built for 250 inmates, at a cost of 38,354*l*., is now being further enlarged at an additional cost of 10,000*l*. The class of inmates for whom this lavish outlay has been incurred may be inferred from the fact that on the 31st December 1877, of the "probably incurable" to whom we have referred, 47 had been in for two years and under five, 56 over five years and under 10, 23 over 10 years and under 15, and 66 upwards of 15 years. Similarly it may be observed that Omagh Asylum, built in 1853 at a cost of 41,407*l*., and subsequently enlarged in 1871 at a cost of 21,200*l*., contained, on the 31st of December 1877, 327 "probably incurable" lunatics, of whom no fewer than 109 were in the asylum upwards of 15 years, each pauper costing a larger sum per week than a labouring man can manage to earn as wages for the maintenance of himself and a numerous family.

The Annual Reports of the Inspectors contain abundant and striking evidence of the recent overcrowding of asylums with unsuitable cases, leading of course to fresh proposals for erecting new buildings or enlarging the old ones.

From these reports year after year, and from the successive records of each asylum, there is the same complaint, the monotonous repetition of "overcrowding with incurable and unsuitable cases," and the consequent necessity of increased asylum accommodation. We cite a few examples, more for the purpose of illustrating the character than the extent of the evil complained of.

18th Report, The Inspectors in the 18*th Annual Report* complain that—

p. 5. "Under the recent Act 30 & 31 Vict. no less than 979 persons have been committed by magistrates
p. 6. to asylums as 'dangerous lunatics,' fully one half of whom were found harmless, idiotic, or imbecile, and therefore unsuitable cases to be classified or treated under the denomination of 'dangerous lunatics,' and who are thus fixed upon the public rates for support and maintenance."

p. 8. "Of the 979 persons admitted into asylums as dangerous lunatics by warrant of justices in the year 1868, as against 351 admitted by warrant of the Lord Lieutenant in the previous year, a large proportion exhibited no symptoms whatever to justify their committal, some of them being described as 'blind,' 'crippled,' 'helplessly paralysed,' 'deaf and blind with great debility,' their committal as 'dangerously insane' being under such circumstances opposed to reason and common sense."

"Many of the above unfit subjects were sent from workhouses, and after a short residence in asylums were discharged and sent back to their unions as not being proper cases for asylum relief.

In their 19th Report the Inspectors write, speaking of Belfast,—

p. 10. "Here, as in Armagh, much inconvenience has been experienced from overcrowding."

p. 14. "There is a want of room here [Clonmel], and beds have to be made upon the floors for dangerous lunatics when they arrive; * * * and here, as elsewhere, are to be found amongst the alleged 'dangerous lunatics' several who were reported to be tranquil and unsuitable, one a harmless idiot, and one not insane."

"The admissions [to Ennis Asylum] during the year amounted to 63, 33 being committed as alleged dangerous lunatics under the Act, and of these latter 16 are reported to be 'tranquil and unsuitable.'"

p. 18. "This Asylum (Killarney) having over 30 patients beyond the number for which it was originally designed, is manifestly unable to meet the demand upon its resources."

p. 24. "Of the 39 persons committed as dangerous lunatics during the year, a considerable number are returned as tranquil and unsuitable." [Omagh.]

"Of the 17 persons committed as dangerous lunatics, 10 are reported to have been unsuitable cases." [Waterford.]

The Inspectors write,—

20th Report, p. 18. "25 were committed under the Act as dangerous lunatics; and of these no less than 16 are returned as 'tranquil and unsuitable,' and one 'apparently not insane.'"

22nd Report, p. 6. "Undoubtedly the Medical charities of Ireland, as an institution at large, are unsurpassed, probably not equalled in any other country; but its adaptation in detail to the exigencies of the population admits of improvement, certainly as regards the insane poor, who, instead of being placed with reference to two distinct classes, are at present alike located in the same institution, the incurables hopelessly demented, idiots, and epileptics constituting a large percentage of inmates in establishments more properly intended for curable and acute cases. A double disadvantage arises therefrom: with an overcrowding of asylums a heavier expenditure is incurred without proportional benefits; an expenditure, too, progressively advancing."

23rd Report, p. 11. "We might adduce an instance where it was recently in contemplation by a board of governors to send about twenty paupers to a district asylum from their then abode, on an examination of whom scarcely one seemed a proper subject for removal."

"In the course of the year many harmless and incurable lunatics were committed as dangerous, thus threatening to occupy the entire accommodation to the exclusion of suitable cases." [Clonmel Asylum.] p. 31.

"We consequently took occasion to observe that were the admissions suitable cases, though it was to be regretted there was not space sufficient for them, no reasonable objections could be raised, but upon finding that the crowded state of the asylum arose from the indiscriminate committal of dangerous lunatics, so called, be they blind, dumb, or debilitated by old age, without proper inquiry, we felt it incumbent upon us to complain against this monopoly as it were of accommodation, tending as it did to exclude legitimate cases." [Cork.] p. 34.

The Superintendent of Limerick Asylum attributes the small percentage of cures "to the long duration of disease before admission, and to the overcrowded state of the "wards." p. 64.

"We regret, however, to observe that of the 24 males and 6 females committed as dangerous lunatics by justices of peace during the year, no less than 20 were considered as unsuitable cases by the Resident Medical Superintendent." p. 73.

"With respect to the accommodation in Irish district asylums, not simply meaning the numbers they are made to contain, it is much below requirements, as we have at present almost a thousand in them beyond their legitimate complement." 24th Report, p. 7.

"No doubt, extensive as have been the advantages derived from district asylums in Ireland, they would be still more perceptible but for their being in many instances congested with hopeless cases." p. 12.

"It cannot then be a matter of surprise, from the irregular and constant influx of chronic cases of insanity, and also of imbeciles and epileptics, to asylums, together with the difficulty of procuring their removal, that those institutions get crowded with hopeless inmates, to the exclusion unhappily, and not unfrequently, of regular applicants in the early or acute stages of mental disease, as evidenced by the fact that of the 7,741 inmates on the 31st of December last, the incurables numbered 5,243." 25th Report, p. 8.

These extracts contain but a very small portion of the evidence that might be cited from these Reports in support of the opinion we have expressed, but quite enough to justify our statement that the evil of overcrowding with incurable cases, which was complained of by the Committee of 1843 and the Commission of 1857, has continued to the present day not merely unchecked but in a more aggravated form than ever.

This table exhibits the progress since the date of the Commission, a period of twenty years, of this overcrowding with "probably incurable" cases.

Year ending 31st December	Lunatics in Asylums					
	Probably curable.			Probably incurable		
	Males.	Females	Total.	Males.	Females	Total.
1856	556	612	1,168	1,393	1,263	2,656
1857	588	599	1,187	1,381	1,288	2,669
1858, 1859	653	622	1,275	1,434	1,381	2,815
1860, 1861, 1862	557	566	1,123	1,659	1,606	3,265
1863	641	573	1,214	1,798	1,660	3,458
1864	660	617	1,277	1,805	1,647	3,452
1865	631	581	1,212	1,898	1,725	3,623
1866	633	621	1,254	2,028	1,788	3,816
1867	612	584	1,196	2,136	1,880	4,016
1868	802	718	1,520	2,329	1,967	4,296
1869	860	764	1,624	2,522	2,170	4,692
1870	984	830	1,814	2,590	2,251	4,841
1871	1,028	889	1,917	2,732	2,343	5,075
1872	1,044	854	1,898	2,861	2,381	5,242
1873	1,020	855	1,875	2,947	2,525	5,472
1874	879	824	1,703	3,193	2,609	5,802
1875	923	846	1,769	3,219	2,753	5,972
1876	1,000	828	1,828	3,340	2,905	6,245
1877	989	922	1,911	3,404	2,868	6,272

A constantly recurring complaint in the Reports of the Inspectors is that the Act 30 & 31 Vict. has led to this great increase of committals of unsuitable cases to asylums. That, no doubt, has been one effect of the Act. But it is to be observed, that in this respect it has simply increased an existing evil, and not produced a new one. But, admitting, as we must do, that this complaint is well founded, it is reasonable to ask, how otherwise are these unhappy people to be dealt with? It may be that they are, as alleged, "unsuitable cases" for treatment in establishments that ought to be reserved for curative purposes; but has any other accommodation been provided for them? Though not suitable cases for curative hospitals, they are at all events suitable cases for care and humane treatment; and not until provision for such treatment is made, ought the door of the Asylum to be shut against them. When the Inspectors complain, as they do in their Eighteenth Annual Report, that, under the 30 & 31 Vict., of 979 cases committed by magistrates fully one-half were unsuitable, exhibiting "no symptoms whatever to justify their committal as "dangerous," they urge the strongest argument in favour of the establishment of intermediate and auxiliary asylums. For, whether these and hundreds of similar cases are fit subjects or not for treatment in curative establishments to which their committal is pronounced by the Inspectors to be "opposed to reason and common sense," it cannot be supposed that the necessary certificates would have been signed, or that the magistrates would have committed them, if they had not been suitable cases for treatment in asylums of one sort or other. It appears from a table printed in the Appendix that within the last few years the number of committals by magistrates under the provisions of 30 & 31 Vict. has swelled the total number of admissions within ten years from 1,527 to 2,314. More than one half the admissions in 1877 were by magistrates under the provisions of the Act in question. However unsatisfactory this may be from the point of view of the Lunacy Department, it is useless to complain of it. It should be met, not by remonstrances and circulars to magistrates and repeated complaints by the Inspectors, but by making suitable provision for all such cases, taking care that those who are in a condition to pay for the maintenance of relatives should be compelled to pay according to their ability. The evil thus referred to cannot be more forcibly illustrated than it is by the following minutes of Dr. Nugent and resolution of the Governors of the Ballinasloe Asylum.

"The grand jury of the county Roscommon, I think, has most properly passed a resolution in regard to the tax, indeed I venture to say the illegal procedure through which lunatics are now sent to this asylum by magisterial warrants;—physicians too, I fear, certifying to the existence of dangerous lunatics when in truth none exist. Since the 1st of January fifteen reputed dangerous lunatics have been transmitted to this institution, of whom two only have evidenced the slightest indications of violence.

"There are in the asylum at present, from what I observe on going through the divisions with the resident and visiting physicians, fully twenty patients who could with common care be very well treated for in workhouses. I think it would be advisable that a list of the parties should be submitted to the next Board.

"(Signed) J. Nugent,
14th March 1868.

"* * * * * I must say I observed many who, it appears to me, were placed here unnecessarily,—harmless idiots and utterly demented and aged persons, who, with little or no trouble, could be well looked after in workhouses. Of 97 admissions in the course of the twelve months just expired, I find no less than 79 were effected by magistrates' warrants, the parties being represented, or rather deposed to, as dangerous, when the reverse would seem to be the case,—they being quiet and inoffensive on reception here. I cannot but think the justices of the peace too frequently exercise the powers vested in them without due consideration, the result of which is over-crowding asylums, and the subsequent necessity of costly enlargements, while the expense of maintenance is double. A female without feet was transferred a day or two ago from a poorhouse, under police armed escort, and thinly clad, no less than 46 miles. The master of the union would have acted correctly had he applied to the Board in the first instance. The rate-in-aid was intended for lunatics in the proper meaning of the term."

"(Signed) J. Nugent,
11th March 1876.

"District Lunatic Asylum, Ballinasloe.

"At a meeting of the governors of the above asylum, held on Monday, the 14th February 1876, the following minute was adopted.

"Moved by Captain O'Hara, D.L., seconded by Andrew N. Comyn, Esq., J.P.:—

"The resident physician having reported that many cases sent into the asylum under committal warrants, appearing to him to be by no means dangerous, and likely to yield to treatment, th governors call the attention of the magistrates of the county to the number of these cases sent in as dangerous lunatics. They impress upon the magistrates what has, perhaps, escaped their notice,—that many of these cases could have been sent in under the ordinary form of admission, which would enable the governors to make the relations of such patients contribute to their support, which they cannot do in cases sent in under warrants as dangerous lunatics, and would enable them also to discharge such cases as have yielded to treatment without the difficulty that is very properly imposed in dangerous committals. Unless the magistrates assist the governors in this, the governors cannot keep down this ever increasing burden on the ratepayers. That a copy of this be sent to each magistrate in the district. That a copy of this resolution be also sent to the Inspectors.

"R. V. Fletcher,
"Resident Medical Superintendent."

The suggestion that is sometimes made, to remit this class of cases to the workhouse, to turn them over to the guardians, so to speak, is one of questionable legality, and in the present condition of many workhouses of unquestionable inhumanity. Guardians cannot receive lunatics as lunatics except from the asylum and under very special conditions. The sending of this class of cases direct to the workhouse, even if it were legal, would be, from every point of view, most unjustifiable. An ordinary pauper sent to a workhouse, if suffering from any bodily disease—from fever or smallpox—is at once sent to the ward specially appropriated for such cases, and is suitably treated for his illness, whatever it may be. But for the pauper afflicted with the heaviest of human calamities there is, as a general rule, no special provision whatever beyond shutting him up under conditions that are as likely as not to increase and ultimately perpetuate his disease. It is a matter that should cause the most serious reflection in dealing with this question of pauper lunacy that not a few of those who are consigned to the "idiot ward" of the workhouse might, under an improved system, be cured and restored to society. Even in some workhouses, though the cases may be exceptional, that is found to be possible. If the case of Cork, referred to by Dr. MacCabe, shows efficient management in a particular instance, it also indicates the class of cases—"curable"—that are sometimes sent to workhouses. Dr. McCabe, Ev. 2101.

Unsuitable as is the accommodation for lunatics in Irish workhouses, it appears that on the 31st December 1877 there were in these establishments no fewer than 3,365 patients, who were thus distributed through the 163 workhouses of the whole country. There were—

2	workhouses	without any lunatics.
59	"	having 10 and under.
49	"	upwards of 10 and not more than 20.
21	"	upwards of 20 and not more than 30.
19	"	upwards of 30 and not more than 40.
6	"	upwards of 40 and not more than 50.
0	"	upwards of 50 and not more than 60.
7	"	upwards of 60.

As early as the passing of the Irish Poor Law the pressure of incurable cases upon the accommodation of asylums was sensibly felt, and as soon as the workhouses were opened efforts were made to convert them, partially at least, into receptacles for that class.

In 1842 a conference took place between the grand juries of the county and city of Dublin, at which the following resolution was adopted, and having been signed on behalf of the grand juries by Geo. A. Hamilton and Lord Brabazon, was forwarded to the governors of the Richmond District Asylum:—

"It being a matter of general notoriety that there are at this time numerous lunatics throughout the county, some in prison, some in workhouses, and some at large, who by proper treatment in the District Asylum might be restored to society, and on whose behalf frequent application for admission has been made, but who have not been admitted in consequence of the crowded state of the asylum, we proceeded to make inquiries as to the reasons of its being so occupied, and we have to report that Mr. Wrigley, the manager, states that of 292 inmates, 150 are declared incurable.

"We cannot but remark that the design of the asylum being to receive only curable cases of lunacy, it appears to be a departure from that design, and to entail a great additional expense on the counties of the district, that the asylum should be occupied by incurable lunatics to the exclusion of persons who by timely treatment might be restored."

Then follows a list of some 80 cases which are certified by the medical officer of the institution as "affected with chronic insanity, and, being tranquil and harmless, *might with perfect safety be placed in a workhouse or any similar establishments.*"

Writing so far back as 1843, the manager of the Clonmel Asylum says,—

"There are about 30 persons in this asylum who are perfectly harmless and hopelessly incurable; these harmless and incurable cases supported at 6*l* per head per annum (the highest rate per Cashel Poorhouse Return) in their respective poorhouses or elsewhere, would cost the county but 180*l.* per annum; whereas supported in the lunatic asylum they come to above 540*l.* per annum. Moreover they occupy beds that could be at the disposal of the governors for those whose attacks of insanity are recent, and therefore probably curable, but which by being kept out for want of room, as is at present the case with more than 25 applicants, are rendered difficult, if not hopeless, of cure by being deprived of that system of discipline and treatment, from which alone there is a prospect of relief. This matter, whether as regard economy or the interests of society, requires serious and immediate attention. If, however, these cases are not only to remain in the asylum, but such of a similar character as present themselves are to be received, the present buildings, new and old, will soon be found totally inadequate to meet even one-fifth of the applicants for admission, and your institution become a depôt of hopeless incurable patients instead of an hospital for the treatment and cure of insanity."

One of the earliest suggestions for transferring harmless lunatics to workhouses was made in a letter of Lord Eliot to the Poor Law Commissioners in September 1842. His

Lordship communicated to the Commissioners the following extract from a communication received from the Connaught Lunatic Asylum respecting the transfer to the different workhouses of several idiotic and harmless lunatics at present in that institution.

"There are several idiotic and harmless lunatics in this asylum who would be as suitably provided for in the workhouses of the different unions to which they respectively belong, as such a transfer would relieve the gaols of the lunatics confined therein. Lord Clancarty is anxious to know if Government could make an arrangement for so desirable an object."

The reply of the Commissioners is sufficiently important to be quoted at length.

My Lord, Dublin, 29th September 1842.

"I beg to acknowledge the receipt of your Lordship's letter of the 27th instant, enclosing an extract of a communication from the Connaught Lunatic Asylum respecting the transfer of certain idiots and harmless lunatics to the several union workhouses of the district.

"Our attention has been frequently drawn to this question, the means provided for the accommodation of lunatic persons being notoriously insufficient, and a strong desire in consequnce existing for transferring to the workhouses such cases of confirmed lunacy as are beyond the reach of medical treatment.

"To applications of this kind the Commissioners have invariably answered that the Irish Poor Relief Act made no provision for the relief of insane and lunatic persons, as such, but required that relief should be administered solely on the ground of destitution, and that if a really destitute person were an idiot or harmless lunatic he would be as fit a subject for admission to the workhouse, if the guardians so decided, as any other destitute individual.

"To provide for cases of this description, which it was presumed would be occasionally admitted, the Commissioners have caused idiot wards to be prepared in the several workhouses for the accommodation of persons of this class. There are, or rather there will be, 130 workhouses in all, and the number of idiotic and lunatic persons for whom accommodation will thus be provided in the several workhouses is 2,300.

"To this extent, therefore, will the lunatic asylums be relieved eventually, as the several workhouses come into full operation, without resorting to any forced or immediate transfer from one to the other, or from the gaols to which unfortunate individuals of this class are now sometimes committed for want of room in the lunatic asylums. Whether this will be sufficient to meet the wants of the country may perhaps be doubted, and my own impression is that it will not be found sufficient.

"I hope that your Lordship will not consider that I am going beyond the scope of the reference which has been made to me if I venture to state my views in reference to the lunatic asylums. These are generally large and admirable institutions, supported at a great expense, for the reception and medical treatment of lunatic and insane persons, very many of whom are therein cured, and thus restored to society; but they are not all cured or susceptible of cure, and, notwithstanding the use of every means which skill and science can devise, many remain hopelessly and incurably insane.

"It is obvious that cases of this latter description must accumulate in every lunatic asylum, and in fact all the asylums are crowded; and their capacity for the cure of insanity in its various forms is crippled by this accumulation of chronic cases. Hence the too frequent committal of lunatics to gaol as a place of security, and hence, too, the desire now manifested of relieving the asylums by transferring such cases to the workhouses.

"But do not these circumstances rather point to a defect in the original constitution of these asylums? Ought they not to have been so formed as to provide for the chronic cases which would necessarily remain, as well as for the cases susceptible of cure by skilful treatment? Ought there not, in short, to have been a chronic ward to every institution for the reception of such incurable cases as the friends and natural relations of the parties were unable to relieve it from?

"The addition of such a chronic ward or wards to a lunatic asylum would leave it open for the reception and treatment of curable cases. This would be the most important as well as the most expensive portion of its functions; for this the medical staff would be adapted, and the various officers and attendants would be appointed, whilst for the incurable inmates far less expensive arrangements would be necessary; in fact the usual staff of the institution, with a small addition of keepers, would be sufficient.

"I am fortified in this view by the experience we have had of the lunatic institution at Island Bridge, which your Lordship is aware was prepared under our superintendence, for the reception of the lunatics previously supported in the old House of Industry, and who were removed from thence on its being declared the workhouse of the North Dublin Union. There were then 350 of these lunatics in the house, and for these were prepared and fitted up, at no great expense, the old Artillery Barracks at Island Bridge, where these poor people have since been kept in a state of as much comfort as their unhappy condition is susceptible of; and they would be in no respect better off if placed in an asylum, being all incurables, similar to the chronic cases with which our lunatic asylums are now encumbered.

"To add a chronic ward to the present asylums would seem therefore to be the proper remedy for the evil complained of, instead of transferring the harmless patients to the workhouses, which were not intended for this purpose, and which, except to a limited extent, are not capable of affording the requisite accommodation.

"In some instances harmless lunatics discharged from the asylums have been received into the workhouses, but the guardians have always admitted such persons on the ground of their destitution, and not, because they were idiotic, epileptic, insane, or lunatic. The direct transfer of such individuals from one institution to the other would, however, be very different from this, and would be at variance with the provisions of the Poor Relief Act, inasmuch as the inmate of a lunatic asylum can hardly be said to be in a state of destitution.

"I have, &c.,

"Lord Eliot, M.P., &c. &c." (Signed) GEORGE NICHOLLS.

This letter conveys with clearness the views that have been always entertained by the Poor Law Commissioners upon the subject of retaining lunatics in workhouses. Amongst the applicants for relief on account of destitution there would always be found a proportion afflicted with mental disease. For these, when not dangerous, provision at the time considered to be suitable, was made in workhouses, where they were admitted simply on account of being destitute. Lunacy was regarded as an accident of their condition, just as any form of bodily ailment might be; but, unlike any person admitted on account of some bodily ailment, the lunatic, as we have already observed, does not receive treatment for his special disease. Except in the very few cases that have been transferred from asylums no legal declaration of lunacy is ever had in cases of admission to the workhouse. No matter what may be the character of the mental disease, whether incipient, of recent occurrence, "probably curable" or confirmed, "probably incurable," of foul personal habits, no account is taken, or for practical purposes can be taken, of the mental condition of the pauper. He is simply consigned to the lunatic or idiot ward, as is the able-bodied pauper to his special department.

In that ward or cell the lunatic is virtually a prisoner, without warrant for detention more than of committal.

According to the return furnished to the Select Committee of the House of Lords on the state of the lunatic poor in Ireland in 1843 accommodation was provided in the several workhouses for 2,347 idiots. In the larger workhouses this accommodation consisted of "cells" together with an associated dormitory; in the smaller workhouses of "cells" only. Thus in the Cork Workhouse, originally built for 2,000 inmates, the provision consisted of 14 single cells and an associated dormitory with 46 beds; total accommodation, 60. Generally in the smaller workhouses the accommodation consisted of three, four, or six cells, each cell for one or two inmates. The dimensions of these cells varied from 6′ 6″ × 7′ 6″ to 9′ 0″ × 8′ 6″.

In some of the larger workhouses the accommodation is much better; in others, the partition walls have been removed and the cells with the narrow corridor thrown into one room. Of these "cells" as places of permanent occupation by any class of poor we cannot speak in terms of too strong condemnation. When the late Lord Monteagle told the Parliamentary Committee on Medical Charities in Ireland that these cells were more suited for the imprisonment of malefactors than for the accommodation of idiot paupers he did not exaggerate their objectionable character.

Yet in many workhouses they exist as originally constructed, with their stone flooring, heavily bolted doors, and small apertures near the ceiling for light and ventilation.

Although in the preceding letter Mr. Nicholls states that the Commissioners had caused idiot wards to be provided in the several workhouses, such provision was not at first contemplated, nor was it included in the original plans. Mr. Wilkinson, the architect upon whose designs all the workhouses of Ireland were constructed, being asked "what was the extent of provision made in the workhouses for lunatic paupers?" replied, "There was no provision whatever in the original plans; it was an after provision." Asked again, "Was that accommodation so provided intended merely "as a place of safe custody for those who might become lunatic in the workhouses, "or was it with the view of becoming the permanent residence of lunatics?" Mr. Wilkinson replies, "No; it was intended to relieve the other inmates from a "disagreeable class of persons, a few being found in each establishment. It was "never thought they were proper places for them. They were, however, the only "places. There was no room in any other institution." [Evidence before Commission 1857, 11287.] Sir Alfred Power, examined before the same Commission, speaking of the lunatic wards, observes, "I certainly never thought them at all proper places for "the treatment of that class of patients, on account of the want of means for exercise "and employment, and the want of sufficient airing grounds."

The Select Committee of the House of Lords report, (1843):—

"At the present moment the number of lunatics confined in 69 workhouses is 471 suffering under various types of the malady, both curable and incurable, violent maniacs, idiots, epileptic patients. The evidence of Dr. Phelan, of Mr. Clark, and of the Inspectors General of Prisons, together with the Committee, 1843, p. xiv.

general plans subjoined to this report, exhibit but too strongly the inadequate and ill-considered nature of the establishments thus provided, unsuited in every respect for the reception of the insane.

The same Committee observe :—

p. xv "A witness perfectly competent to speak on the subject, from his experience as an Assistant Poor Law Commissioner, states that the workhouses are generally built on one design; that the lunatic wards consist mainly of one row of cells below, having in some cases larger rooms above, communicating with confined yards, admitting of no possibility of employment, and having but a limited space for exercise. No adequate classification can under such a system be enforced, neither is there any moral superintendence, or any distinct medical treatment; nor are there any attendants retained for the service of the insane, competent and instructed in such duties. p. xv. Without a total reconstruction of the workhouses, without the purchase of additional land, and the appointment of a new staff of officers, it would therefore be wholly impracticable to confine 2,300 insane persons in the present workhouses."

Same Committee (1843) :—

p. xvi. "He [Dr. Phelan] states that the arrangements made for the insane in the workhouses neither admit of their due classification, employment, nor amusement; that this impedes the introduction of a mild system of government; that the intermixture even of the harmless lunatics with paupers is objectionable, as they become the objects of derision and attack on the part of the young and idle, producing dangerous irritation and excitement."

The Committee say that if any doubt remained it would be removed by the following letter, which they quote :—

p. xvi. "Dublin, Sept. 23, 1842. Sir, the Poor Law Commissioners have had before them minutes of the proceedings of the Board of Guardians of the Clogheen Union on the 22nd ultimo, with reference to the resolution directing the master to inform the Governor of the Lunatic Asylum, Clonmel, that there is accommodation for two quiet lunatics in the workhouse. The Commissioners desire to state, that it would be very inexpedient to act upon it, or to admit any lunatics into the workhouse. The unfortunate persons here contemplated ought to be the inmates of an institution which admits of such arrangements as their peculiar case required, which arrangements cannot be made in a workhouse without much expense and difficulty; and incurable lunatics received from time to time into the workhouse would soon constitute a large and permanent class, to the detriment of the primary object of the establishment, which is the relief and prevention of pauperism under ordinary circumstances. By order of Board. Arthur Moore, Chief Clerk."

The Lunatic Asylums, Ireland, Commission (appointed 1856), page 18 of Report, say :—

"It appears to us that there can be no more unsuitable place for the detention of insane persons than the ordinary lunatic wards of the union workhouse. The unfortunate creatures have commonly no one to attend them but some of the other pauper inmates, who are but little capable, or little inclined, to concern themselves with looking to their wants or necessities. The result is, that the condition of these wards, and the lunatics detained therein, is usually most unsatisfactory. In many cases the bedding is ill-attended to, the persons of the lunatics were often most filthy, their clothing bad, and no effort at cleanliness was observable in this apparently condemned division of the workhouse. In some workhouses, however, the bodily condition of these afflicted beings was as carefully attended to as in an asylum, though we cannot say that in any their moral treatment was much studied."

Surgeon White, one of the Inspectors of Lunatic Asylums (Ireland), does not consider workhouses suitable places of detention for lunatics, although they may not be curable. "They have neither apartments nor appliances for such class of persons "in the poorhouses. The apartments are very indifferent; in fact, there is no comfort "for them at all." Dr. Nugent, the other Inspector of Lunatic Asylums, "is in the "habit of inspecting in each year the workhouses in which lunatics may be retained," and is of "opinion that the accommodation is very insufficient. The rooms "are exceedingly small; they are ill ventilated. The yards attached to what are "called the 'insane cells' in those workhouses are very restricted and gloomy, without "a current of air." Asked, "Have you found that the lunatics have frequently been "placed under restraint in the workhouses?" Dr. Nugent replies,—

"The very places themselves constitute places of restraint, the cells in which they are lodged being very narrow and miserable. * * * I have seen the lunatics under mechanical restraint. Would not say they have habitual recourse to it in poor-houses. Does not think they are sufficiently clad or fed, or sufficiently looked after. Cannot say that they are cruelly treated, but I can say that they are not sufficiently well treated. * * * Finds many violent patients detained in workhouses who ought to go into asylums." (Evidence, 739 et seq.)

19th Report, p. 28. "The means for out-door exercise and employment are very limited in most cases" (in workhouses).

20th Report. "The most marked deficiency in the treatment of the insane in poorhouses is generally referrible to a want of suitable airing courts or places for exercise and occupation."

23rd Report, p. 102. "From a paucity of those afflicted inmates, paid attendants are not employed to take charge of them; well conducted and intelligent paupers are substituted."

The Inspectors, speaking of the arrangements for lunatics in workhouses, say :—

25th Report, p. 8. "Still there are drawbacks in them, essentially so as regards want of space for exercise, day room accommodation, and suitable sleeping provision for the parties themselves, and those in charge of them."

"All in them [the workhouses] is cheerless, naked, and monotonous, though clean, orderly, and healthy; in fact, in strict accordance with what workhouses should be." 26th Report, p. 12.

"The arrangement for the accommodation of lunatics in workhouses is very insufficient. First and foremost, the rooms are exceedingly small: they are ill ventilated There is no conveniency whatever, either for the comfort or the custody of the lunatics. The yards attached to what are called the 'insane cells' are very restricted and gloomy. * * * The cells are very narrow and miserable." Evidence of Commission, 1843.

This evidence of the general unsuitability of workhouses under existing arrangements for the detention of insane poor we can most strongly confirm from our personal observation. We met with several cases of great neglect, and very few cases in which the arrangements of the idiot wards were not in some essential respect defective. The worst condition of workhouse lunacy is to be found in those unions,—often in remote parts of the country,—in which the number of lunatics is too few to induce the guardians to make proper provision for them, and yet too many to be allowed to remain without special provision for their care and supervision. These are precisely the cases of which, as they are left unvisited, the Inspectors of Lunacy can have no personal knowledge. The expediency, indeed we might say the absolute necessity, of bringing them together in reasonable numbers, appropriating and fitting up portions of workhouses for their accommodation, appears to us to be far more urgent and far more easy of adoption than it was in 1857, when the Royal Commissioners reported:— Dr. Hatchell's evidence, 1743-44, and Return in App. C 9, p. 244.

"The lunatic wards originally constructed in the modern workhouses for the reception of lunatics are not suitable for that purpose; and the temporary accommodation provided we generally found inadequate and objectionable. * * It has appeared to us, however, that a portion of the accommodation at present existing in some of the workhouses of Ireland might, under proper arrangements, be made available for quiet cases of imbecility or idiocy. We should propose, therefore, that one or more workhouses in each district (where the largest amount of space accommodation is likely to be permanently available) should be selected, and a portion thereof, or the whole, fitted up for the reception of the class of lunatics above referred to, with all proper internal fittings required in asylums, baths, &c., and should be provided with airing courts for such as may be enabled to take exercise."

We but repeat to-day the same proposal. The objections to it, heretofore urged, appear to have been made exclusively by the Local Government Board. The opinion of that department upon such a subject must carry great weight, and we desire to consider it with the respect to which the high character and the official services of Sir Alfred Power, its Vice-President, are so eminently entitled. So far as these objections have been yet stated, they are, we believe, expressed in two official communications. The first is addressed by the Poor Law Commissioners to Colonel Larcom, with reference to a communication from the Governors of the Londonderry Lunatic Asylum; the second is addressed by the Local Government Board to the Guardians of the Ballymena Union, with reference to a proposal to appropriate a wing of the Ballymena workhouse for the accommodation of a certain number of harmless lunatics to be transferred from the district asylum. To this Ballymena case we shall refer in a subsequent part of this Report.

In the letter to Colonel Larcom, dated the first of April 1856, the Commissioners observe:—

"When an application was made to them, at the close of 1854, by the Board of Guardians of the Monaghan Union, for permission to allow a portion of the union workhouse to be converted into barracks for the accommodation of the militia force, the Commissioners informed the Board of Guardians that they did not consider it within the scope of their authority to permit a workhouse, or any portion of it, to be appropriated for the purpose proposed, the buildings having been designed by the legislature for a totally different purpose. The Commissioners conceive that the objection entertained by them to the conversion of workhouse premises to barrack accommodation applies with equal force to the conversion of a workhouse into a lunatic asylum, inasmuch as it is not warranted by the existing state of the law."

Nevertheless, "the existing state of the law" remaining unaltered, the rule, though inflexibly maintained against pauper lunatics, was relaxed in favour of the military, portions of workhouses having been allowed in several instances to be appropriated for barrack accommodation.

Thus far it is clear that from the passing of the 1 & 2 Geo. 4. c. 33. down to the present day the asylum accommodation in Ireland, provided at a very great expense and avowedly for curative purposes, has come to be mainly appropriated for a class of inmates, "probably incurable," who could be as satisfactorily cared for in establishments far more cheaply constructed, and at a far less annual cost of maintenance. This is conclusively shown to have been the case down to 1843 by the Reports of the Prison Inspectors and of the Lords Committee that sat in that year; and from that date down to 1857 by the Report and evidence of the Commissioners appointed in that year. That it has been perpetuated, and exists to-day not only unamended but even in a more aggravated form than it did close upon half a century ago, is established, as we have just shown, from the Annual Reports of the Inspectors of Lunacy and of the Medical Superintendents of the various district asylums.

It further appears that although workhouses as at present constituted are admitted to be most unsuitable places for the detention of lunatics of any class, they contain more than one-fourth of the pauper lunacy of Ireland.

It would be of comparatively little importance to ascertain how this has been allowed to come about if the result of such inquiry might not tend to put a check upon the continuance of such a system.

Your Grace will have observed that the Inspectors of Lunacy have repeatedly expressed opinions favourable to the establishment of intermediate asylums. Although general suggestions to that effect have been occasionally made to the Government, we do not find in the correspondence relating to the formation of asylum districts and the building of asylums a single case in which a distinct proposal has been made and followed up to relieve an existing asylum from the pressure of incurables by providing intermediate accommodation for that class; nor have we any reason to suppose that such a suggestion will be made, or, if made, will be adopted, unless through the direct interposition of the Executive Government.

If the enormous expenditure involved was the only evil attendant upon the construction and enlargement of these asylums there might possibly be no sufficient ground to interfere with it so long as cesspayers submit patiently to such taxation. But it is clearly shown that the system operates most injuriously in two directions. The character of an asylum as a curative establishment is impaired by it, and admission has been unavoidably refused to cases that might derive benefit from curative treatment. The citations that we have made of the opinions of different authorities are very far indeed from exhausting the evidence that might be adduced in support of these views; but they are quite sufficient to establish, in the interest of the insane poor and of the tax-paying public, the necessity of such a change in the existing system as shall make more suitable provision for the one at less cost to the other. The means by which this may be done is indicated with sufficient distinctness in the evidence already referred to in this Report. We shall recapitulate them briefly, and state the grounds upon which we think they should be adopted.

Our proposals are :—

1st. That, in accordance with the provisions of section 15 of 8 & 9 Vict. c. 107, the existing 22 asylums should be so classified as that a certain number should be set apart as hospitals for the curative treatment of insanity.

2nd. The others should be appropriated as asylums for a certain class of chronic cases.

3rd. While for a third class, the quiet and harmless, provision should be made in portions of workhouses set apart and suitably fitted up for the purpose as auxiliaries.

The expediency of providing two classes of lunatic asylums has been advocated from a very early period of asylum administration. As far back as the year 1835 Dr. Phelan, to whose evidence we have already referred, called attention not merely to the evils of the then existing system, but to the necessity of correcting them by such a classification of lunatics as we now suggest. "It appears to me," Dr. Phelan wrote in 1835,—

"that many serious objections lie to the proposal of enlarging the district asylums merely for the accommodation of incurable lunatics, and that when these objections are examined they will be found so valid as perhaps to induce the proper authorities to hesitate in enlarging those institutions for that purpose only. It is now universally admitted that the treatment of curable insane persons will be most efficient when moral and medical management are judiciously combined, and that it frequently fails where the one happens to be defective, though the other be ever so carefully applied. This being the case, it is evidently desirable that the moral governor of a lunatic asylum should not have under his care a greater number of patients than he is capable of keeping constantly under close observation; otherwise, in proportion as that number increases, his means of observing their habits and dispositions diminish in an equal ratio. It must, therefore, be an objection to the enlargement of asylums which contain 100 or 150 lunatics, to have them made still larger, in order that chronic incurable cases may be admitted. If such be received, the moral governor's attention must be more or less occupied with them when he might be much more usefully engaged with *relievable* patients; but if he should not think it necessary to devote any attention to the incurable class, a very probable circumstance, but leave them to the care of an inferior person, merely considering that order, cleanliness, and some employment be observed, *then they are in no way benefited by removal to such asylums*, for this system could be as well adopted in the different counties to which they respectively belong, and at much less expense.

"Incurable lunatics, it is true, especially epileptics, frequently become very violent, requiring prompt coercion and restraint; and it is said that on this account it is desirable that such persons be in a superior asylum where this system of restraint is better understood and more readily enforced. But, from several years' close observation of this class of lunatics, I am quite convinced that the means necessary to restrain such violent incurables are so simple and so readily enforced that this argument, if such it may be called, carries no weight.

"Seeing that no advantages of any importance are likely to arise from crowding all the curable and incurable pauper lunatics of one or more counties into a district asylum, but, on the contrary, that certain disadvantages are sure to attend it, would it not be better that the latter class were provided for in local county institutions, if it be admitted, and I know not how any one practically acquainted with the subject can deny it, that all the purposes for which such patients are confined can be there as well accomplished?

"I would therefore suggest that no further addition be made to the district asylums, unless it be found necessary to enlarge them for the admission of a greater number of curable or relievable cases, and that, after due inquiry as to the probable number of pauper incurable lunatics, each county should be *compelled* to establish an institution large enough for their accommodation. This being done, the district asylums would be rendered much more useful, as, none but patients likely to be improved by moral or medical treatment being admitted, the entire and undivided attention of the manager and physician could be bestowed on them, and a better system of classification more easily adopted. Were this done, it should be an understanding that, according as the inmates of the superior institution become incurable, they should be admitted, with the consent of their friends, into the county asylum; and, on the other hand, if, as will sometimes occur, a patient in the latter show signs of improvement, he should be transferred to the former, that a fair trial may be given him."

Dr. Phelan then points out with clearness the large pecuniary saving that would be effected by such an arrangement, and urges with great force the benefit that would be conferred upon a large class who are too poor to pay for accommodation in private asylums, though able to contribute a portion of the cost of maintenance for relatives in district asylums.

In 1843 the Select Committee on Medical Charities recommended by resolution that—

"Either a ward for chronic and incurable cases be provided in every asylum, or that hospitals for incurable patients of every class should be established for districts of suitable size."

Referring to such a proposal, Lord Monteagle, who was examined before that Committee, observed—

"If you were to add to the existing lunatic asylums a ward sufficient to provide accommodation for the chronic cases, you must increase the size of those establishments very largely indeed * * * My opinion, therefore, is undoubtedly that it would be more advantageous if within the several districts you had separate establishments for the incurable cases, to which they could be sent from the various asylums, and where they could be managed under such physical and moral treatment as was best suited to those particular classes of malady."

Mr. White, who in 1843 was Inspector-General of Prisons, having the duty of inspecting asylums as well as prisons, gave evidence before the Committee of the House of Lords on the State of the Lunacy Poor in Ireland. He was asked—

"Do you not consider if an establishment was entirely appropriated to chronic and incurable cases they could be supported in that separate establishment at a lower rate than they are now supported in the district asylum?"

"I do."

"And by their transfer would there not be a space left in the district asylum for the application of the curative process to more recent cases?"

"Considerable."

"Therefore, the system would be more efficacious in its results, and more economy would be produced?"

"That is my opinion."

The Right Honorable Anthony R. Blake, examined before the same Committee, is asked—

"Do you consider the number of district lunatic asylums, which are ten, are adequate for the purpose?"

"From the inquiries which I have made I should be inclined to think that the number would be sufficient if you confine them strictly to the curable lunatics; but I do not think the number at all sufficient for curable and incurable lunatics, nor do I think it desirable that curables and incurables should remain permanently in the same institution."

"Do you mean by 'not the same institution' 'not the same wards?'"

"No; I think it would be desirable to have separate institutions for curable lunatics, because those curable lunatics require a degree of medical attention which the incurables do not."

Dr. Conolly, the distinguished Superintendent of the Hanwell Asylum, asked before the same Committee—

"Supposing the county of Middlesex were desirous of relieving Hanwell from the accumulation of incurable patients by way of extending its curative powers, do you think that would be most advantageously done by adding to the present building wards for the chronic and incurable cases, or by the transfer of those cases to some other place?"

"Undoubtedly by the transfer of them to another building."

The Reverend E. M. Clarke, who was chaplain of the gaol of the county of Donegal and local inspector of the prison, is asked—

"Are the Committee to collect from your evidence that the accommodation provided for the lunatic poor in Ireland at the present moment in that district is inadequate to the necessity of the case, as well as imperfect in three cases out of four?"

"Certainly."

"How would you propose to remedy this inconvenience?"

"By a separate distinct establishment for incurable cases, by which the district asylums would be relieved from such cases."

"You have stated that in your judgment a separate establishment ought to be provided for the incurable; how would you propose such an establishment to be provided?"

"I would propose that a depôt (as it were) should be formed in some convenient situation, to which a certain number of district asylums could send their incurable cases."

Our object in referring to this evidence, which, were it necessary, we could greatly strengthen from other sources, is not simply to enforce the expediency of removing incurable cases from curative establishments, but to show that this view was entertained so far back as 1835, and was subsequently urged by witnesses of the highest authority. Nor was it thrown out merely as a suggestion. A definite scheme for giving effect to it was laid before the Lords' Committee of 1848. That scheme, suggested by Mr. Clarke, to whose evidence we have just referred, is worth reproducing as an illustration of the more reasonable views of asylum organisation that prevailed upwards of 30 years ago.

PROPOSED DISTRICTS for ASYLUMS for INCURABLE LUNATICS and IDIOTS.

COUNTIES.	Number from each at present in District Asylums.		Number of Incurable Cases in each, calculated at Two-thirds.	Number allowed to each Asylum for Incurables.
NUMBER 1.				
Antrim	125			
Armagh	50			
Donegal	85			
Londonderry	69			
Fermanagh	21			
Monaghan	31			
Down	124			
Tyrone	62			
		567	378	500
NUMBER 2.				
Galway	88			
Mayo	73			
Sligo	46			
		207	185	300
NUMBER 3.				
Roscommon	40			
Leitrim	34			
Cavan	23			
Meath	31			
Westmeath	48			
Longford	22			
King's County	48			
Louth	21			
		267	178	400
NUMBER 4.				
Queen's County	30			
Wicklow	27			
Kilkenny	31			
Wexford	44			
Kildare	52			
Carlow	42			
Dublin	203			
		449	298	500
NUMBER 5.				
Tipperary	101			
Waterford	115			
Clare	118			
Limerick	132			
		466	310	500
NUMBER 6.				
Cork	433			
Kerry	99			
		532	356	
		2,486	1,655	2,700
Total incurable in confinement 1st January 1848				2,474
Excess				226

Speaking of this scheme, Mr. Clarke observes—

"Though six districts have at present 2,448 in the district asylums and in the Cork Asylum, the proportion of incurable cases calculated at two thirds is 1,635. The number I propose those establishments to accommodate amounts to 2,700. According to the return made by the Inspectors General of Prisons (1842) the total of incurable cases confined not only in district asylums but in private asylums, in gaols, and everywhere else, amounted to 2,474, and the six establishments which I propose would accommodate 226 above that number."

If the principle of that proposal had been adopted when it was made, and been applied from time to time to meet the increasing want of lunacy accommodation, not only would a very large expenditure have been saved, but more suitable provision would have been made for the different classes of insane poor. Unless that principle be adopted now, late though it be, the history of the next 30 years will simply be a repetition of the last. The Committee of the House of Commons which in 1868 inquired into the Grand Jury Presentments in Ireland, reporting with reference to "the great and increasing expense of lunatic asylums," observes—

"There are at present 23 lunatic asylums in Ireland, and *unless some alteration be made as to the class of persons sent to them a considerable number of new asylums will have to be erected.*"

Although, several years before this Report was made, a Royal Commission had suggested what we suggest now, that a considerable number of "the class of persons sent to them" should be sent to workhouse auxiliaries, and though legislative provision was subsequently made for giving effect to the suggestion, yet the recommendation of the Commission and the provision of the law have to the present day been equally disregarded. Nor can we see much reason to suppose that any change in the direction indicated will be effected, except, as we have already said, through the interference of the Executive. For although the lunacy which is cared for in asylums is essentially a part of the general pauperism of Ireland, the Local Government Board is not responsible for the control of it, nor has that department any direct interest in the improvement of asylum administration. The Inspectors of Lunacy, on the other hand, have no personal or official knowledge of the unhappy condition of a large class of the lunatics in workhouses, and may not, therefore, be sufficiently alive to the urgent need of improving it. So long as there is no interference with the existing arrangements of workhouses, the Local Government Board appear to be satisfied; and so long as the Lunacy Inspectors can succeed in securing assent to the erection or enlargement of costly asylums, no serious effort will apparently be made to give effect in any other direction to proposals of which they have themselves constantly approved. It will, indeed, we cannot refrain from observing, be a grievous calamity to the most afflicted and helpless class of the poor, and a well-founded cause of complaint to the already "awfully mulcted cesspayers," to adopt Dr. Nugent's expression, if any want of departmental support or co-operation should be allowed to retard improvements provided for by legislation, recommended by every competent authority as yet consulted upon the subject, and that we venture to hope we shall be able to satisfy your Grace are at once both economical and practicable.

According to the last Report (the 27th) of the Inspectors of Lunacy, the total number of lunatics of which that department has cognizance was,—under care 12,380, thus distributed :—

	Males.	Females.	Total.
In public or district asylums - - -	4,393	3,790	8,183
In the Dundrum or central asylum for criminals	133	34	167
In Lucan Government asylum - - -	4	18	22
In private asylums - - - -	249	387	636
In poorhouses - - - -	1,268	2,097	3,365
Amounting to an aggregate of	6,047	6,326	12,373

In addition to these, there was, according to a corrected return furnished to us through the kindness of Colonel Hillier, Inspector General of Constabulary, and of Captain Talbot, the Commissioner of Metropolitan Police, 6,709 lunatics at large, making a total of 19,082. We do not propose to refer to the lunatics in the Dundrum Asylum for Criminals, in Lucan Government Asylum, or in private asylums. Our observations will apply exclusively to lunatics in district asylums, in workhouses, and "at large." App. C 14, p. 252.

The 8,183 lunatics in asylums are thus distributed :—

Asylums.	Counties comprised in present Districts.	Present Accommodation.			Remaining in Asylums on 31st December 1877.		
		M.	F.	Total	M.	F.	Total.
Armagh	Armagh	88	74	162	109	78	187
Ballinasloe	Galway, Roscommon, town of Galway	276	160	436	237	187	424
Belfast	Antrim, Carrickfergus (town)	240	180	420	237	202	439
Carlow	Carlow, Kildare	125	125	250	115	107	222
Castlebar	Mayo	175	125	300	167	110	277
Clonmel	Tipperary (N. and S. R.)	210	175	385	203	172	375
Cork	Cork (including city Cork)	250	250	500	382	364	746
Down	Down	150	150	300	179	124	303
Ennis	Clare	130	130	260	137	121	258
Enniscorthy	Wexford	144	144	288	149	120	269
Kilkenny	Kilkenny and city	108	108	216	124	104	228
Killarney	Kerry	110	110	220	169	108	277
Letterkenny	Donegal	175	175	350	185	123	308
Limerick	Limerick and city	250	250	500	211	226	437
Londonderry	Derry	156	106	262	154	108	262
Maryborough	King's and Queen's	130	130	260	132	114	246
Monaghan	Monaghan and Cavan	216	198	414	198	158	356
Mullingar	Westmeath, Meath, Longford	200	200	400	233	199	432
Omagh	Tyrone, Fermanagh	256	254	510	279	210	489
Richmond	Dublin, Wicklow, Louth, Drogheda (town)	505	595	1,100	493	568	1,061
Sligo	Sligo and Leitrim	187	143	330	179	142	321
Waterford	Waterford and city	150	150	300	121	145	266
	Total	4,231	3,932	8,163	4,393	3,790	8,183

It will be seen from this statement that the gross numbers in the 22 asylums exceeded the nominal accommodation by 20. It will also be seen that of the 22 district asylums, as many as 12 contained upwards of 300 inmates each, seven of them containing upwards of 400 inmates.

"We entertain strong objections," say the Commission of 1857, "to the erection of asylums upon too large a scale; and although we are aware that the patients who are considered incurable may call for comparatively little of the resident medical officer's time, yet there are few, if any, asylums in Ireland where the number of beds in the existing buildings, supposing them all to be occupied by cases not considered incurable, is not more than equal to the extent of attendance which can be afforded by any one individual." Dr. Nugent says, "I consider a building that would accommodate 250 or 300 inmates to be a reasonably sized asylum for the efficient treatment of insanity."

Yet the latest improvement appears to have been to enlarge the Cork asylum so a to accommodate 750 inmates. Of 746 inmates in that asylum at the date of the last Report of the Inspectors 489 are classed as "probably incurable."

From the unequal distribution of cases, the numbers in some of these asylums are much more in excess of the accommodation than in others. In no single asylum in Ireland, however, does the number of "probably curable" approach the amount of available accommodation. It is safe to say that not more than 30 per cent. of the insane in Irish asylums are suitable subjects for "curative" treatment. If, then, certain asylums could be set apart exclusively for the curative treatment of 2,500 cases, the remainder, amounting to less than 6,000, might be distributed in the other asylums, and in a certain number of auxiliaries in connection with workhouses.

Of the 5,683, the "probably incurable," a large proportion may be suitably accommodated in the workhouse auxiliaries, to which we shall refer presently. Thus, as we believe, ample accommodation may be provided for the whole of the indoor lunacy of Ireland at almost a fractional outlay in proportion to what must be incurred in order to meet the usual requirements of the department of lunacy administration.

Our first suggestion is that the 22 existing asylums should be classified; a certain number being appropriated as hospitals for the curative treatment of the insane, the others as asylums for the care and maintenance of chronic lunatics.

The classification of asylums, recommended in Ireland more than 40 years ago, was provided for by subsequent legislation. By the 15th section of the 8 & 9 Vict. c. 107. the Lord Lieutenant, with the advice and consent of the Privy Council, is empowered to

"order that any existing asylum may be exclusively appropriated for the sole and exclusive reception, custody, and treatment of a particular class of pauper lunatics distinguishable by the nature and character of the disease, and whether recent in its origin, or chronic, or whether considered curable or incurable."

That this provision of the Act has never been applied, can only be accounted for by the fact of its existence having been overlooked by the Inspectors of Lunacy. Dr. Hatchell, apparently unaware of the provision in question, being asked whether the advantage that would result from the classification of asylums would be sufficient to justify an application for powers to effect it, replies that he "thinks it would." It "never suggested itself to him to make such a classification, nor did he ever hear his "colleague say so." The opinion of Dr. Nugent as to the advantage of such classification is still more distinct. He is asked— Dr. Hatchell, Ev. 1692–3. Ev. 1694.

"Do you think it would be desirable to give, to whatever authority might exist for the supervision of lunacy, legislative power to classify lunatic asylums?" Dr. Nugent, Ev. 2221.

"I think it would be very judicious to do so."

"And if such power existed, do you think the lunacy inspectors would avail themselves to a considerable extent of such a power?" Ev. 2222.

"Certainly."

"And possibly some asylums may have an excess of incurable cases from the want of such a power?" Ev. 2223.

"Not only may have an excess, but positively have an excess, from want of such a power."

"But giving this power, and leaving it to the discretion of the Board, would it be useful?" Ev. 2224.

"Certainly. By doing that, you arrive at the great point."

"Do you think that the power of classifying lunatic asylums, if it were given by legislation, and the making of provisions of a nature that I shall call your attention to just now, would prevent the building of lunatic asylums upon the same scale as they have been built upon during the last thirty years?" Ev. 2227.

"I think it would to a very considerable extent."

Other witnesses, not less entitled by their position and experience to speak with authority upon such a subject, give evidence still more emphatic in favour of classifying asylums in the way we propose. Dr. Robertson, the medical superintendent of the Monaghan District Asylum, Dr. Lalor, of the Richmond Asylum, Dr. Patrick Cullinan, visiting physician of the Ennis Asylum, Dr. Daxon, of the Ennis Asylum, and Dr. Berkeley, of the Mullingar Asylum, all men of great experience, approve of the proposal; as does also Dr. MacCabe, one of the inspectors of the Local Government Board, who, as medical superintendent of the Dundrum Criminal Asylum and the Waterford District Asylum, has had ample opportunities of forming an opinion upon the subject. Dr. Robertson is of opinion that the classification of asylums in accordance with the provision of the 8th and 9th Vict. c. 107. would "fully meet" the difficulty of providing for the great increase of lunacy. Dr. Lalor is of opinion that the removal of the presumably incurable cases would facilitate the working of the establishment as a curative hospital; that the interchange of patients, sending the presumably curable to one establishment, and the incurable to another, "would be a great improvement," "a wonderful improvement on the present system." Dr. Daxon thinks that if accommodation could be provided elsewhere for a large per-centage of the incurable cases of his asylum, the advantages of the asylum as a curative establishment would be very much increased. Dr. Berkeley thinks that the classification of asylums to which we are referring "would be most desirable on the grounds of public policy and economy." This view Dr. Berkeley has long consistently entertained, and has frequently urged in his communications with the governors of his asylum. Dr. MacCabe, asked whether, in his opinion, the classification of asylums, appropriating a certain number as curative establishments, and others for the detention and care of presumably incurable cases, replies, without hesitation,— Dr. Robertson, Ev. 1541–3. Dr. Lalor, Ev. 1864. Ev. 1860. Ev. 1865–6. Dr. Daxon, Ev. 2376. Dr. Berkeley, Ev. 2318. Ev. 2317. Dr. MacCabe, Ev. 2057.

"I have not the slightest doubt on the subject It would enable the existing staff of the asylum to devote themselves to the care of individual curative cases, instead of having their attention distributed over a large number, the vast preponderance of which are incurable. You could give all the care to the curable if you got rid of the incurable."

Dr. Patrick Cullinan has for many years considered the expediency of making other provision for the class of lunatics in workhouses, and long since proposed that there should be a separate asylum for them. The Ennis Asylum is not crowded, as the harmless and incurable are drafted to the workhouses by the Resident Medical Superintendent. There are in the asylum 258 patients, of whom 204 are chronic and incurable cases, besides 16 epileptics;—cases, in fact, that require only such care and attention and discipline as may be necessary for their comfort and bodily health, and on whom a curative treatment would be thrown away. There are 158 quiet and orderly, but insane. Dr. Cullinan would not be disposed to transfer more than 67 of these to a workhouse auxiliary. This number he has fixed as the result of a census he has made. This would leave a balance of 187 incurables, many of whom are only moderately tranquil. Dr. Cullinan certainly thinks that if accommodation could be found elsewhere for this balance of incurables, less those that might be kept for the service of the house, it would be advantageous for this asylum to be made a curative hospital. He thinks that the establishment of three classes of asylums,—1st, for the curable,—2nd, for the reception of chronic insane, requiring special care, and whom it might be desirable to place where the accessions for restraint might be brought to bear in cases of relapse or emergency,—and, 3rd, the workhouse auxiliaries for harmless and incurable, would be based on sound theoretical and technical principles.

The last witness to whom we shall refer as favourable to the proposal to classify asylums is one who gives to it the sanction of the highest authority. Sir Dominick Corrigan was a member of the Commission which inquired into the condition and management of Irish lunatic asylums, and took an active part in its proceedings. His opinion, therefore, is not simply that of a witness of the highest professional position and attainments, but of one who has had special opportunities of ascertaining the defects of Irish lunacy administration, and of appreciating any suggestion for remedying them. As the evidence of the other witnesses to whom we have referred is supported by the authority of Sir Dominick Corrigan, a leading member of the former Commission, the proposal to classify asylums is submitted to your Grace with the greater confidence as to its expediency. Looking to the evidence before us, it is impossible to doubt that the efficiency of asylums as curative establishments is impaired by the pressure upon them of incurable chronic cases, or that the retention in them of cases that could be satisfactorily treated in establishments much less expensively managed, is the main cause of the great expenditure in the erection of new asylums. In reply to the question—

Dr. Nugent, Ev. 2296.

"To classify the asylums, and reserve to the proper authorities the mode of doing that, you think, would be the best organisation of lunacy administration that could be obtained?"

Dr. Nugent replies,—

"Yes; the impression on my mind for many years has been so. I consider that the public at large were awfully mulcted from sending individuals to asylums, and maintaining them there at 24*l*., when they would be as well taken care of for 14*l*. or 12*l*."

Sir D. Corrigan, Ev. 2292.

Assuming then that the classification of asylums is, as Sir Dominick Corrigan expresses it, "most desirable," there remains only to consider whether it is practicable, and how it can be best effected.

There are in Ireland, as we have already stated, 22 district lunatic asylums which afford accommodation for 8,168 patients. The total number in them on the 31st December 1877 was 8,183, thus classified:—

Probably curable, 1,911. Probably incurable, 6,272.

The following tabular statement is a fair estimate of the whole of the lunacy of all classes to be provided for. For cols. 1 and 2 we would appropriate, as we have just observed, certain asylums, selected as the most suitable. In addition to the patients under treatment in these curative establishments there would be retained in each of them a certain proportion, probably 50 males and 50 females, from cols. 3 and 4. From the remainder of cols. 3 and 4 we would appropriate the other asylums,—providing for cols. 11 and 12 (which represent the sums of cols. 5, 6, 7, 8, 9, and 10), in workhouse auxiliaries.

Asylum District.	Counties.	Class I. For Care or Treatment in District Asylums. Lunatics in District Asylums. Probably Curable. M. 1	F. 2	Class II. Chronic Incurable requiring special Care. M. 3	F. 4	Class III. For Care in the New Workhouse Auxiliary Asylums. Chronic Insane for transfer to Auxiliary Asylums. M. 5	F. 6	Already in Workhouses 31st Dec. 1877. M. 7	F. 8	Say One tenth of the Lunatics at large. M. 9	F. 10	Total of Class III. M. 11	F. 12
Province of Ulster.													
Armagh	Armagh	34	23	65	51	10	4	16	43	13·5	6·8	39	54
Belfast	Antrim	67	41	139	137	31	24	134	314	27·0	15·4	192	353
Downpatrick	Down	43	28	116	79	20	17	52	96	22·4	17·9	94	131
Letterkenny	Donegal	20	16	116	77	49	30	35	49	21·2	17·3	105	96
Londonderry	Londonderry	20	19	131	97	3	2	32	53	14·1	7·4	49	62
Monaghan	Cavan	4	4	89	64	14	11	24	26	13·4	6·7	51	46
	Monaghan	9	6	75	69	7	4	15	35	10·4	5·7	32	45
Omagh	Fermanagh	27	20	47	28	9	13	6	17	9·2	8·9	24	36
	Tyrone	66	49	104	75	27	24	54	30	15·3	13·3	96	67
		290	206	882	667	170	129	348	663	149·1	95·5	686	790

Asylum District	Counties.	Class I. For Care or Treatment in District Asylums. Lunatics in District Asylums. Probably Curable M. 1.	Class I. Probably Curable F. 2.	Class II. Chronic Incurable requiring special Care M. 3.	Class II. Chronic Incurable requiring special Care F. 4.	Class III. For Care in the New Workhouse Auxiliary Asylums. Chronic Insane for transfer to Auxiliary Asylums M. 5.	Class III. Chronic Insane for transfer to Auxiliary Asylums F. 6.	Class III. Already in Workhouses 31st Dec. 1877. M. 7.	Class III. Already in Workhouses 31st Dec. 1877. F. 8.	Class III. Say One-tenth of the Lunatics at large. M. 9.	Class III. Say One-tenth of the Lunatics at large. F. 10.	Total of Class III. M. 11.	Total of Class III. F. 12.
PROVINCE OF MUNSTER.													
Clonmel - -	Tipperary -	17	20	147	116	59	38	51	96	16·8	14·6	107	148
Cork - -	Cork - -	84	109	257	229	40	33	106	246	30·7	21·3	177	300
Ennis - -	Clare - -	16	19	102	86	17	16	72	127	15·1	7·7	104	151
Killarney - -	Kerry - -	10	6	149	93	10	9	13	22	10·8	6·6	34	40
Limerick - -	Limerick -	16	22	173	167	20	17	65	111	13·3	7·8	98	136
Waterford - -	Waterford -	58	64	53	73	10	6	39	92	6·8	5·1	56	103
		206	240	881	777	156	121	346	694	93·3	64·5	575	880
PROVINCE OF LEINSTER.													
Carlow - -	Carlow -	24	6	20	31	5	2	13	19	4·8	3·5	22	24
	Kildare -	17	22	46	37	4	7	20	39	8·0	5·6	32	39
Enniscorthy -	Wexford -	10	8	138	107	6	0	56	60	14·2	7·8	75	73
Kilkenny - -	Kilkenny -	54	44	27	37	43	25	23	46	9·8	11·6	86	81
Maryborough -	King's Co. -	20	16	29	26	22	8	24	38	8·4	6·4	54	52
	Queen's Co. -	18	15	29	44	16	5	21	29	6·3	4·5	43	39
Mullingar - -	Longford -	16	12	33	24	2	6	10	18	3·7	2·8	16	26
	Meath -	25	14	62	57	3	5	36	53	10·7	8·6	49	67
	Westmeath -	24	14	61	36	7	9	28	30	6·5	8·1	39	47
Richmond - -	Dublin -	103	166	112	90	142	218	133	228	9·9	4·2	285	445
	Louth -	13	15	23	6	25	21	36	60	7·3	5·1	67	86
	Wicklow -	22	16	9	8	21	16	12	41	5·2	4·2	23	63
		344	350	586	525	296	324	435	649	96·1	70·4	826	1,044
PROVINCE OF CONNAUGHT.													
Ballinasloe - -	Galway -	30	30	111	44	17	29	37	54	15·5	13·4	70	96
	Roscommon -	50	60	19	22	10	12	31	49	10·4	7·6	51	69
Castlebar - -	Mayo -	17	10	135	92	15	8	35	44	11·4	10·3	61	62
Sligo - -	Leitrim -	25	16	58	41	19	22	15	12	7·6	6·7	42	41
	Sligo -	25	17	35	14	22	30	21	32	7·5	6·8	51	68
		147	116	353	223	63	101	139	191	52·4	44·3	275	336
TOTAL—ULSTER - - -		290	205	883	667	170	129	348	563	149·1	95·5	666	790
MUNSTER - - -		206	240	861	777	136	121	346	694	93·3	64·5	575	880
LEINSTER - - - -		344	350	586	525	296	324	435	649	96·1	70·4	826	1,044
CONNAUGHT -		147	115	353	223	63	101	139	191	52·4	44·5	275	336
		987	911	2,704	2,192	665	675	1,268	2,097	392·9	275·0	2,344	3,050

Having then, in the first instance, to make provision for the "probably curable," we would appropriate for their accommodation such asylums as, from locality and structural arrangements, may be considered the best adapted for the purpose. These asylums should be the curative hospitals of separate districts, which should comprise, in addition, certain asylums for such incurable cases as might require special care, and of workhouse auxiliary asylums for harmless demented cases. By that distribution provision would be made for the treatment of the whole of the curable cases, leaving a reasonable number of vacant beds in each of the hospital asylums. Of the "probably incurable," upon a very moderate calculation, 1,860 may be removed to the auxiliary asylums that we propose in connection with workhouses. The remainder of the "probably incurable" would be distributed among the existing district asylums, being considered suitable cases for those establishments. The relief that would be afforded to the district asylums by the accommodation provided in workhouses would, not only without impairing, but as we believe by increasing, the efficiency of lunacy administration, leave a margin of spare room in asylums of both classes, so large as to obviate for many years to come the necessity of continuing the expenditure in the erection and enlargement of asylums which has been going on for so long a time upon so lavish a scale.

The detailed arrangements of such a classification of asylums as we propose would, of course, be left to whatever department may be ultimately charged with the lunacy administration of the country. Although we have satisfied ourselves that it can be carried into effect in every district in Ireland, we do not propose to enter into the details of how it can be done, further than may be necessary for the purpose of illustration. We take for that purpose the portion of Ireland in which there appears to be at present the most urgent need of additional asylum accommodation. For a considerable time the Inspectors of Lunacy have been insisting upon the necessity of building a new asylum for Londonderry, a new asylum for the county of Antrim, and of greatly enlarging the asylum of Armagh. We think it can be shown that the existing asylums, together with portions of workhouses, which can very well be appropriated to the purpose, could amply provide for the whole of the lunacy of the province of Ulster. If this be practicable in a district in which the want of accommodation appears to be most urgent, there can be no reason to doubt that as the necessity arises it may be also done in other districts.

The province of Ulster contains 44 unions distributed through the nine counties. It contains seven district lunatic asylums, affording accommodation for 2,418 inmates.

As there are in the seven district asylums of the province of Ulster only 496 lunatics of the class "probably curable," the obviously expedient course would appear to be to set apart say two of the existing asylums as hospitals for the curative treatment of that class. There would remain 1,848 of the "probably incurable," &c, class. Of these 200 would be retained for domestic and farm work in the curative hospitals. For a certain proportion of these who might require special care and treatment, the other asylums would afford ample accommodation.

There are, as we have said, 44 workhouses in the province. Distributed through these workhouses, in the very unsatisfactory way to which we have already called attention, there are 911 cases. Having carefully examined the capabilities of these workhouses, we have no hesitation in saying that if the Local Government Board and Inspectors of Lunacy would concur in the arrangement, and co-operate in giving effect to it, such portions of these could be set apart as would fulfil the conditions that can be reasonably insisted upon in auxiliary asylums for harmless and incurable lunatics, and would be sufficient to receive the whole of the workhouse lunatics of the province, together with those who might be declared suitable for transfer from asylums. In this way, as we have observed, provision might be made for curative treatment in hospitals, and for the care and treatment of lunatics of one class in asylums, and of another class in workhouse auxiliaries. The cost of adapting the portion of workhouses that might be selected would not exceed 15*l*. per bed. The cost of carrying out the suggestions of the Inspectors of Lunacy in this province would probably not be less than 160*l*. per bed, which means a perfectly unnecessary expenditure of at least 80,000*l*., without making any better provision for lunatics in workhouses.

By way of illustration we submit the following statement of the requirements of the province of Ulster, and the provision that might be made for it. Two asylums, say Belfast and Monaghan, might be appropriated as curative hospitals; the other five asylums, for such patients as might require special care; and in twenty workhouses accommodation could be provided for 1,680 chronic "probably incurable" cases. The preceding tabular statement shows that there are to be provided for in asylums of—

	Curable. Class 1.		Incurable. Class 2.		Harmless and Incurable. Class 3.		Total	
	Males	Females	Males	Females	Males	Females	Males	Females
	290	206	882	667	666	790	1,838	1,663
Total -	496		1,549		1,456		3,501	

Accommodation available.

Hospitals.

Name.	Present Accommodation.		Numbers to be provided for. Under Treatment.		Numbers to be provided for. For Service		Spare Room		
	Males	Females	Males.	Females	Males.	Females.	Males.	Females.	
Belfast -	240	180	145	103	50	50	45	27	
Monaghan	216	198	145	103	50	50	21	45	
Total -	456	378					66	72	{ Total spare room in hospitals.
			Class 1.		Of Class 2.				

Asylums.

Total of Class 2 - - - 882 males 667 females.
Taken for service in hospitals 100 „ 100 „

782 „ 567 „ { Balance to be accommodated in asylums.

Names.	Present accommodation. Males.	Present accommodation. Females.
Armagh - - -	88	74
Letterkenny - -	175	175
Downpatrick - - -	150	150
Londonderry - -	156	106
Armagh - - -	256	254
Total - -	825	759
Spare Room - - -	43	192

Auxiliaries.

The number of harmless lunatics to be provided for in the new workhouse auxiliaries is 1,456.

Ample separate accommodation can be found for them in the under-mentioned unions; and at comparatively trifling cost, more accommodation, if required, could be provided.

Name of Union.	Approximate Accommodation	Remarks.
Belfast - - -	240	School buildings.
Ballymena - - -	120	
Ballymoney - -	50	
Larne - - - -	100	
Banbridge - -	50	
Lisburn - - -	75	
Lurgan - - -	100	
Magherafelt - -	60	
Londonderry - -	50	
Limavaddy - - -	50	
Letterkenny - -	100	
Dunfanaghy - -	120	
Ballyshannon - -	50	
Lisnaskea - -	120	
Irvinestown - - -	60	
Cookstown - -	50	
Clones - - -	50	
Monaghan - -	100	
Armagh - - -	60	
Castleblayney - -	75	
Total - -	1,680	

The exact appropriation of this accommodation by sexes must be determined by the authority under which the scheme would be carried out.

In like manner we should propose, in addition to the hospitals and asylums, to appropriate portions of the following workhouses:—

MUNSTER.—Kilrush, Bandon, Cork, Midleton, Youghal, Dingle, Kenmare, Listowell, Croom, Limerick, Newcastle, Clonmel, Roscrea, Dungarvan.

LEINSTER.—Dublin (South), Edenderry, Tullamore, Ballymahon, Dunshaughlin, Navan, Trim, Abbeyleix, Delvin, Enniscorthy, Gorey, Shillelagh.

CONNAUGHT.—Glennamaddy, Oughterard, Portumna, Manorhamilton, Castlebar, Claremorris, Westport, Dromore West, Sligo, Tobercurry.

Should the necessity for further accommodation of this character arise, it can be provided to a considerable extent in other workhouses.

The map opposite affords an illustration of the probable distribution of the three classes of institutions in each province under the scheme submitted.

That the proposal to classify asylums will not be very heartily supported may perhaps be anticipated. To give effect to it will, no doubt, be attended with difficulty, and will involve trouble; and the ground is, so to speak, pre-occupied; and this is just one of those cases in which it would be much easier to organise a new system than to adapt an established system to altered circumstances. In their 23rd Report the Inspectors of Lunacy observe:—

"No doubt, did auxiliary institutions exist, as originally suggested by us many years ago, to which patients might be transferred, and taken back in cases of dangerous relapse, a costly asylum accommodation need not be extensive."

But instead of the "auxiliary institutions," which, if they existed, might be so easily utilised, we have to deal with costly asylums furnished with all modern appliances and improvements. To appropriate such buildings simply as places of detention for chronic lunatics may seem to be a very extravagant application of means to an end. But, though it may not be avowed, that is in fact what is done at present; and the change we propose will, at all events, have the recommendation that it removes any ground for proceeding further in the same mistaken direction.

The proposed classification would of course be an innovation upon the established policy of lunacy administration in Ireland, which appears to be simply to provide more accommodation instead of making the best of the accommodation already provided. There is also the objection which has been sometimes urged of seeming to treat mental disease, no matter what may be its character or duration, as hopelessly incurable. When it is considered, however, that on the 31st December 1877 there were amongst the "probably incurable" lunatics in Ireland 5,036 who were thus classified,—

Residence in asylums,—

Over 2 and under 5 years - - -	1,386
Over 5 and under 10 years - - -	1,817
Over 10 and under 15 years - - -	846
Over 15 years - - - -	987

it cannot, we think, be reasonably alleged that there would be practically any injustice in removing the great majority of these poor people to asylums for chronic incurable cases. The objection to which we have referred was put most strongly by a very eminent authority, Dr. Connolly, the medical superintendent of the Hanwell Asylum, upon the ground, to use his own expression, that it is important keep up a feeling of hope even in the incurable. He, however, admits that the objection is more in a change of name, and might be met by avoiding the expression "incurable." Another objection, suggested by an authority whose opinion is entitled to every respect, is, that the asylums which would be appropriated to chronic cases would come to be regarded as of an inferior class, and would involve the lowering of the status of the medical superintendent and other officers. A mode of compensating for any apparent distinction of the sort might be easily suggested; but as Dr. Hatchell, who referred to the probability of such an objection being made, very justly observed, if the thing was right to do, no prejudice of that sort should be allowed to stand in the way of doing it.

Dr. Hatchell, Ev. 1658.

Our next proposal is the establishment of workhouse auxiliaries.

Although, as we have shown in another part of this Report, the workhouse accommodation has been greatly overstated in the sealed orders of the Local Government Board, there is yet a very large amount of available room which is wholly unappropriated. Under the sudden pressure of pauperism workhouses were enlarged; detached

MAP
of
IRELAND,
SHEWING
THE PROPOSED LUNACY DISTRICTS
WITH THEIR RESPECTIVE
PITALS, ASYLUMS, & AUXILIARY ASYLUMS,
FOR THE INSANE.
NORTH CHANNEL
SLIGO
LEITRIM
MAYO
ROSCOMMON
GALWAY
IRISH SEA
ST GEORGES
CHANNEL
Districts Tinted
Hospitals
Asylums

the University of

hospitals built in some unions; while in others commodious and substantial sheds were erected; so that there is hardly a county in Ireland in which there may not be found a considerable amount of building which, owing to the changed circumstances of the country, is not only absolutely useless but a source of annual expenditure to keep in repair. While this is so, there is a constant demand for a most extravagant expenditure upon lunatic asylums to accommodate a class of people who, it is admitted by every competent authority, could be suitably maintained in these unappropriated buildings. In the very workhouses too, in which such accommodation might be provided, the lunatic poor are incarcerated without consideration either to their legal rights or the claims of humanity; for, as we have already observed, the law does not authorise the forcible detention of lunatics in a workhouse, nor can any one approve of their detention in such places as the cells to which many of them are now unavoidably consigned.

If, in accordance with the recommendation of the Royal Commission of 1857 which we repeat, portions of certain workhouses selected in different districts can, without impairing the efficiency of poor law administration, be appropriated for the accommodation of those harmless, demented chronic cases which are now scattered through what are called the "lunatic wards," and for the large number of the same class who might be transferred from asylums, it is needless to say that an enormous improvement would be thus effected in lunacy administration. The ratepayers of the country could no longer complain of having to maintain large buildings for which they know there is no present use, and for which they believe there can be no reasonable prospect of any future use in connection with the relief of the poor; suitable provision would be made for the associated accommodation of the lunatics who are now scattered through the various workhouses; and the necessity would be obviated of continuing that lavish expenditure in the erection of new asylums or the enlargement of old ones that is the subject of such general complaint.

We have visited every workhouse in Ireland, and satisfied ourselves by inspection and inquiry that there is, as we have just observed, a considerable amount of accommodation which, without interfering with the requirements of poor law administration, might be appropriated for the reception of harmless chronic lunatics. That opinion would, as we believe, be supported by the Guardians as well as by the local representatives of the Central Department.

With a view to ascertain the structural capabilities of a certain number of these workhouses, we availed ourselves of the assistance of Mr. Wilkinson, the architect of the Board of Control, who was also the architect of the Poor Law Commissioners under whose direction nearly the whole of the workhouses were built. A more competent authority we could not consult. We are able from our own observations to fully confirm the statement in the report of that gentleman, printed in the Appendix, as to C 10, p. 248. the general condition of the workhouses which were erected under his supervision. Mr. Wilkinson has furnished us with reports on buildings connected with eight workhouses, each of different type or class of building. The structures inspected and reported on by him are chiefly what were erected in the famine years as additions to the original workhouses and which can of course be now more easily dispensed with. The way in which they may be adapted is explained in Mr. Wilkinson's reports, and clearly indicated in the plans that accompany them.

It has been suggested that such an appropriation of portions of workhouses as we propose would not be legal, and it has been distinctly stated that, even if technically legal, it would not be in accordance with the intention of the legislature.

The question of the legality of this proposal has been determined by the opinion of the law adviser of the Government. Such an appropriation of portions of workhouses would be authorised by the words of the statute.

But it would not be, it has been contended, in accordance with "the intention of the legislature;" it was never contemplated that lunatics should be congregated in workhouses in such numbers, the intention of the legislature being simply that they should be "dispersed" amongst the neighbouring unions. Such was the construction put upon the Act by the Local Government Board, and, being forced upon governors and guardians by the decision in the Belfast and Ballymena case, has been a main cause of the measure being up to the present time practically inoperative. There is, it is true, nothing either in the preamble of the Act, or in the proceedings of Parliament upon its introduction or during its progress, to indicate the precise intention of its framers. As, however, a very serious evil existed, and had frequently been pressed upon the notice of the executive, it is only reasonable to assume that the intention of the framers of the Act was to supply a remedy for it.

Nor as to this are we left in doubt, for we can state that the object of the Act was to enable boards of guardians to make arrangements for the care and maintenance of lunatics who might be remitted to them from district asylums. It certainly could not have been intended that this should be done by "dispersing" them amongst neighbouring unions. Such "dispersion" is in fact one of the chief causes of the very unsatisfactory condition of that class of poor in the majority of workhouses. Even if they had been recognised as a class requiring and entitled to special treatment, their numbers distributed through scattered workhouses were too few to induce guardians to make suitable arrangements for their accommodation. An Act to provide for the "dispersion of individual cases among the workhouses surrounding the district asylum," would have been a piece of purposeless if not mischievous legislation. It is only by associating them in such numbers as will justify the outlay necessary to adapt wards, provide airing courts, and appoint paid attendants that satisfactory arrangements can be made in parts of workhouses for the care and proper treatment of any number of that class of the poor. The governors of the Belfast asylum having renewed their application we were called upon to submit our observations upon it for the consideration of your Grace. We did so in a communication, dated September 14, 1878, which is printed in the Appendix. We have the satisfaction to find that the opinion of the law adviser is in accordance with our views, and that the Local Government Board have accordingly sanctioned the proposal to transfer a certain number of harmless lunatics from the Belfast asylum to the Ballymena workhouse.

App. C 14, p. 252. In addition to the lunatics who are under care in asylums and workhouses, there are 6,709 lunatics "at large."

As to the actual condition of that very numerous class but little authentic information is available. An annual return is made by the constabulary, in which is set forth certain particulars,—the name of the lunatic, the character of the mental disease, the religion, and the class of life.

A more intelligent or better organised body of men than the Irish constabulary there is not in the public service. The duties imposed upon them they discharge with zeal and ability. But the duty of collecting the statistics of lunacy, of making a return that for practical purposes can be of any value, is one for which they are not qualified, nor for the discharge of which, even if qualified, have they adequate means or authority. They have personal knowledge indeed, as we had ample proof in the course of our inquiries, that a so-called "lunatic" is resident in such or such a house, is a member of a family of the "lower," or "middle," or "upper" class, and is of such a "religion." They have some hearsay knowledge that the alleged lunatic is "harmless," or what is termed a "softie," or is sometimes "troublesome." As to the treatment of the lunatic, they have the same sort of hearsay knowledge,—they know what "the neighbours say." But even if they had authority to enter private houses and inquire into the condition of an afflicted member of a family, they are wholly incompetent, whatever may be their intelligence, to furnish the sort of information that can be of any real value. Yet the returns of the constabulary appear to be the sole authority for a very remarkable table which is printed in the Annual Report of the Lunacy Inspectors, from which it would appear that of the total 987 are "lunatics," 4,479 "idiots," and 1,243 "epileptic imbeciles." Such a return made by professional men would, no doubt, be valuable, and might, during the mere process of classification, be turned to incalculable benefit. As it is, the return can hardly be other than misleading.

But if the constabulary cannot be expected to furnish accurate returns of the mental condition of so-called lunatics classified as "lunatics," "idiots," "epileptic imbeciles," still less, we venture to suggest, ought they to be required to furnish information as to the treatment of lunatic poor by their families or friends. There would be obvious impropriety, as well as public inconvenience, in making such an inquiry a matter of police. Yet it ought to be undertaken. Without assuming the existence of cruelty or gross neglect in the treatment of this class of poor, or without doing any injustice to the kind and charitable feeling that is ordinarily extended to them by all classes,—by the humbler classes especially,—it is yet certain that, owing to thoughtlessness, ignorance, inability to control them, narrow resources of large and struggling families, great misery is often inflicted upon these helpless beings. The Royal Commission of 1857 obtained a return of "Lunatics at large" at that time, which professed to exhibit the condition as to treatment of that class. From that return it appeared that of the total number 3,352, no fewer than 1,583 are returned as "neglected." While within the last 20 years the number of that class has increased by more than 100 per cent.—from 3,352 to 6,709,—we doubt whether there would be found to be any diminution in the proportion of those who may be still classed as "neglected." It is but a little while since the following letter was addressed to the Inspectors of Lunacy :—

"Gentlemen, I beg to acquaint you of a most distressing case I witnessed in Ireland a few days ago, and to request—if within your province—to give such directions as will remove such an outrage on common decency. Dr. Robertson.

"On approaching a small farmhouse at a place called * * * * near * * * * in the county * * * * I heard a most peculiar howling noise, and to my horror, when I came near the house I saw a lunatic *stark naked*, confined to a room and looking through the wooden bars that closed the windows, for there was no glass whatever. He is about 19 years of age, and I heard from his mother that up to 10 or 11 years he was a most intelligent boy, but at that age he suddenly lost the power of speech and became moody and abstracted, wandering about the fields alone, and constantly uttering a low muttering noise, and with incessant tendency to mischief. By careful watching the family prevented him injuring himself or others, until of late he has got so strong and unmanageable, and his inclination for destruction is so great, that they have been obliged to confine him in the room I have described. He breaks the window directly it is glazed, tears his bed clothes into shreds, and wont allow a stitch of clothing to remain on his body; besides his habits are most disgusting. It is really a sad case, and the more so as there are two grown-up sisters in the house. I was unable to direct the parents what steps to take in order to have him removed so as to receive some treatment, but promised I would write to request that you would advise them how to act. The name of the family is . . .

"I have the honour to be, Gentlemen, your obedient servant . . . ."

The Incumbent of the parish having been communicated with by the Inspectors, replied :—

"The case is indeed only suited for a lunatic asylum. The form which his lunacy has assumed is most shocking and is detrimental to morality. He is, as you have been informed, confined in a room in a small farmhouse. His family have been compelled to do so because of the manner in which he tears all his clothes, even the strongest homespun linen is little better than a piece of paper in his hands. As this is his constant employment. He is in a constant state of nudity, the only intermission of it being the short period during which he is asleep. The consequence of the confinement is manifesting itself in failing appetite. I am of opinion that he should be removed to a place where he might have proper care and be under medical treatment."

And, happily, owing to this accidental interference of an English tourist, he was so removed, and placed under the admirably efficient care of the medical superintendent of the Monaghan Asylum. We took occasion ourselves to visit several of these cases in different parts of the country. Some of them we found in a deplorably neglected condition; others disturbing the arrangements of a whole family, the head of which would willingly contribute a small sum towards maintenance in some suitable place of refuge. It admits of no doubt that many a case, if taken in hand at an early stage, might have been restored to society instead of lapsing into hopeless incurable insanity. Serious evil often results from the freedom with which idiots of both sexes are permitted to wander abroad, often teased and goaded to frenzy by thoughtless children, often the victims of ill-treatment or the perpetrators of offences far worse. The interests of the public no less than of the insane require that means should be adopted to ascertain that all of that class are properly cared for. This can only be done by substituting the visit of a medical man for that of the constable, and a professional report for the incomplete return that is now made. If it were the duty of the dispensary medical officer to visit and report upon the condition and treatment of every "lunatic" within his district, as it is the duty of district medical officers, in consideration of a moderate fixed remuneration, to visit and report upon the condition of pauper lunatics in England, incalculable benefit would be conferred both upon the patients and the general public. The visit of the medical man, instead of being received with suspicion or hesitation, would be welcome as that of a friend, in most cases known to the family, to whom all necessary information would be freely communicated. By such means too the statistics of lunacy at large might be made as complete as are those of the asylums.

It appears from the return made by the constabulary that of the total number of lunatics "at large," 1,886 are of the middle class. It may fairly be assumed, we think, that of the 4,662 who are returned as the "lower class" at least 25 per cent. would be in a position to contribute something towards the maintenance of members of their family in an asylum. Indeed, we believe that no greater boon could be conferred upon that class than by rendering asylums available to them upon reasonable terms. Their case cannot be stated more fairly or more forcibly than it was stated by Dr. Phelan nearly 50 years ago, when the circumstances of it were far less urgent than they are at present. App. C 14, p. 252.

"We know," Dr. Phelan wrote in 1835, "that insanity is a disease that affects others who are not paupers in as great a proportion as it does the latter, and it would appear but just and expedient to provide for the cure or improvement of the former, if it can be done without interfering with the latter, who have the first claims on our sympathy and protection. If we divide the population of a county into three classes, the insane of the first, or most wealthy, we shall suppose to be able to pay the sum demanded at private asylums, the minimum of which is, I believe, about 30*l.* a year; those of the second class will be able to pay from 10*l.* to 20*l.*; the third are paupers. In the second class, we shall find a considerable number of curable and incurable insane, a fact which the experience of several years fully warrants me in asserting. Now, by the present laws, this class is inadmissible to district institutions unless as paupers; and the operation of the law is this, and always must be so:—one of the family of a small farmer, shopkeeper, or comfortable tradesman, becomes insane, and requires the discipline of a well regulated asylum; his friends are willing to pay according to their circumstances, which enable them to give from 10*l.* to 25*l.* a year, but no private institution will admit him for that sum, and they cannot, without injury to their families, pay 30*l.* They, therefore, apply to have the lunatic admitted into the district asylum as a pauper. Observe, then, what happens; if he be admitted, the public are charged with 20*l.* a year for the support of a person both able and willing to pay that or a somewhat smaller sum; but if refused, being unable to pay the higher premium for a private asylum, the friends are obliged to keep the unfortunate lunatic in his own family, or to consign him to the treatment of unfit persons, whose want of judgment, and perhaps of feeling, soon convert a curable into an incurable case. Now, ought either alternative be allowed? Is it desirable to *facilitate* the pauperizing of such as are not paupers in any sense of the word, or who do not desire to be so considered? And should we not rather afford them the opportunity of avoiding such an alternative? But, on the other hand, the class I allude to peculiarly deserves our best attention. Amongst them are to be found industry, morality, integrity, and other good qualities, in a far greater proportion, perhaps, than amongst any other. When afflicted by so frightful a malady as insanity, therefore, a single case of which we know to be quite sufficient to break up the comforts and to impede the industry of a family, should not every assistance be afforded them consistently with the convenience of the public? Now, if this can be done without in the least interfering with the claims of the third class, by the admission of the curable patients of the second, at such rates as their respective friends can afford to pay, is it not evident that two advantages must result; first, lunatics who may, and often will, be otherwise excluded, receive the benefit of a good asylum, and next, the public are paid for the benefit so conferred. Independent of these considerations, it should be recollected, that the second class contributes largely to the support of the district asylums, and for this, and many other reasons, have strong claims on the public.

"Now, if incurable lunatics and idiots be kept in distinct establishments, such curable cases as occur amongst this second class might be conveniently accommodated in the present district asylums, which could then be made available for all who are unable to pay the sum usually charged in private institutions. And if it should at any time happen, that the curable lunatics of the third or pauper class were so numerous as to entirely or nearly fill them, there could be less objection to increase the buildings, when the whole of these two classes would be benefitted by such increase, and a considerable part of the annual expense borne, not by the public, but by individuals, as in the English lunatic asylums."

We shall only add that the opinions of all the authorities whom we consulted as witnesses upon the subject are in perfect accordance with these views. Not the least advantage of the scheme that we submit to your Grace would be to throw open hospitals and asylums to a most deserving class of people who are now virtually without any such resource, though in sore need of it.

According to the report of the constabulary, to which we have already referred, the number classed as "idiots" who are at large amounted to 4,479. The condition of that class of the lunatic poor has within the last few years attracted a good deal of attention—not more certainly than it deserves. Lord O'Hagan made a most forcible appeal, chiefly on their behalf, to the Legislature in the last session. Subsequently an Act, "The poor afflicted persons relief (Ireland) Act, 1878," was passed, which affords some facilities for making provision for that class. If the arrangement of asylum districts, and the classification of lunatics be adopted in accordance with our recommendation, the occasion would appear to be most opportune for making some distinct provision for the care and maintenance of idiots. Already the Superintendent of the Richmond Asylum has organised a department for the treatment of idiots in that establishment. A similar arrangement might be very well made in Cork for the province of Munster; in Belfast or Monaghan for Ulster; and probably in Ballinasloe for Connaught. But in whatever localities, or whether or not in connection with existing asylums, such institutions appear to be greatly needed.

There are no institutions connected with lunacy administration in England that deserve higher commendation than those that are specially devoted to the care and treatment of idiots. In no respect is the lunacy administration of Ireland so defective.

Your Grace having been pleased to call for the observations of the Local Government Board upon the proposal to appropriate portions of certain workhouses as auxiliary asylums, and of the Inspectors of Lunacy upon the proposal to classify asylums, the replies have been communicated to us, and are printed in the Appendix to this Report.

App. C 1, p. 220.

App. C 2, p. 221.

If a proposal which we submit for the consideration of your Grace be adopted, and the Lunacy Department be transferred to the Local Government Board, the views of Sir Alfred Power as to the constitution of auxiliary asylums would, we presume, be submitted as a matter of course to that authority as the most competent to advise upon them. It is probable that suggestions which are offered in contemplation of action being taken upon them by another department might be modified if the Vice-President of the Local Government Board were himself responsible for giving effect to his own views. For a system of administration that might be advantageously adopted if the whole were brought under the control of the Local Government Board, would be complicated and embarrassing if auxiliary asylums were placed, as district asylums are now, under a distinct and separate jurisdiction. We may, therefore, leave the minute of Sir Alfred Power without observation at present, beyond expressing our satisfaction that it seems to convey general approval of the appropriation of vacant workhouse buildings as auxiliary asylums.

It is most satisfactory to us to find that our proposals are so accurately appreciated and so fully assented to as they are by Dr. Hatchell. App. C 2, p. 319.

If it should be determined to give effect to our recommendations, the suggestion of Dr. Hatchell as to the designation of the different classes of asylums would, no doubt, be adopted by whatever authority might be ultimately charged with the reorganization of Lunacy administration.

The opinions of Dr. Nugent are entitled to the consideration that may be claimed for great experience, and to the respect that is due to zealous efforts during a long official life on behalf of the lunatic poor of Ireland. As the weight of his authority might tend to prejudice the proposals which we have the honour to submit to your Grace, we may be allowed, in examining his objections, to refer to the policy of Lunacy administration, with which his influence appears to have been more especially identified.

By no one has the expediency of classifying asylums been more forcibly stated than it has been by Dr. Nugent. The principle of such classification is laid down in a reply given in the course of his evidence before the Select Committee on Grand Jury Presentments (Ireland) so far back as 1868:—

"It is much better," he observed, "to have a class of people in one house, all receiving nearly the same treatment, than to have different gradations of treatment in the same asylum."

We have already directed the attention of your Grace to the evidence given by Dr. Nugent before this Commission, in which he expressed his approval of the suggestion to classify asylums, which he considered would be an improvement of sufficient importance to justify an application for legislative power to give effect to it. Still stronger is Dr. Nugent's opinion in favour of organising auxiliaries, and so relieving asylums from the pressure of unsuitable cases that could be as satisfactorily treated in the wards of workhouses. Yet he can hardly be expected, if we may judge from the communication which he has addressed to your Grace, to co-operate in any practical attempt to classify district asylums, or to organise workhouse auxiliaries. App. C 2, p. 349.

It is true that the classification of asylums has not been adopted in England. But Dr. Nugent, in calling attention to that fact, seems to have overlooked that the law has not provided for such classification in England as it has in Ireland. Nor, indeed, may we be permitted to say, does the legalised practice of England furnish examples either in Lunacy administration or in Poor Law administration, that in Ireland can be adopted with advantage. There are anomalies in the Lunacy administration of both countries, and it is a mistake to infer that because asylums are not classified in England, English ratepayers are not dissatisfied, or that the existence of a defective system there can be fairly appealed to to reconcile common sense to the continuance of it in Ireland. What Dr. Nugent said 10 years ago is felt to be hardly less applicable to England now than it was to Ireland then:—

"If you take the treatment of a lunatic in a lunatic asylum in Ireland, and contrast his position with what it was before he entered the asylum, you will find that you have brought him as it were from a hovel into a palace."

So long as residence in the "palace" is essential to cure, no considerate or humane person would grudge the expenditure; but when it is felt that the present state of Lunacy administration in England is open to the same objections to which Dr. Nugent called attention 10 years ago in Ireland, it is not surprising that serious efforts should be now made to apply a remedy to an evil of such magnitude. A very large class of the permanent occupants of the "palace" who have been brought to it from the "hovel" are, as Dr. Nugent describes them, "utterly demented, and merged into idiotcy or imbecility,"—"who afford no hope of recovery." It is only within the last few weeks that the detention of such cases in English asylums has elicited an energetic protest from an influential quarter; and already Parliamentary notice has been given of the introduction of a Bill in the course of the present Session, with a view to checking an abuse, the existence of which in England is referred to by Dr. Nugent apparently to justify its continuance in Ireland. Sir Edward Kerrison writes on November 1st:—

"Patients suffering from acute or curable mania should naturally occupy the principal attention of the medical officers, but now the numerous chronic cases thrust upon them completely deluge our asylums. It is true that efforts have been made to separate these two classes, but in a very expensive way. There are buildings for chronic cases now in course of erection, which, with the land, will cost nearly 150*l* a bed."

To one of these buildings Dr. Nugent thus refers:—

"In Norfolk, owing to a similar deficiency of accommodation (it being confined to 720 beds), the county magistrates assembled in 1876 to meet requirements. Various propositions were discussed. Three workhouses being available,—one with 25 acres of land attached to it, a second with 12, the third with four,—after a careful examination of each with the Government surveyor, a committee of justices decided on purchasing for 4,300*l.* 24 acres of land contiguous to the asylum, as a site for new buildings, at an estimated cost of 28,000*l*, for 250 inmates, 'of the harmless, aged, and imbecile classes;' —an arrangement, it may be parenthetically observed, which would seem not to be unfavourably regarded by some Irish boards."

"What," asks Sir Edward Kerrison, "is the reason for this unnecessary expenditure on poor idiots, imbeciles, epileptics, and others of this sad class?" * * * "It is the irresponsible authority of the Lunacy Commissioners which really stands in the way of a sensible solution of this question, affecting, as it does, every county and borough in England. Visiting justices and their surveyors well know that unless plans of buildings can pass the Lunacy Commissioners their work will be in vain. The central authority speak of less expensive buildings, but sanction expensive ones."

The Irish Inspectors, we may observe, have constantly recommended "plain, substantial buildings" for chronic cases; but the Lunacy Department has invariably insisted upon the erection of costly asylums instead.

The complaint of Sir Edward Kerrison is still more forcibly repeated by Mr. Rodwell, member for Cambridgeshire, who has just given notice of his intention to introduce a Bill to remedy the evil complained of.

With reference to an observation in Dr. Nugent's minute, we desire to observe that there is no ground whatever for attributing to us, as would appear to be done by inference, a desire to restrict in any way the accommodation for lunatics in Ireland. The whole scope of the suggestions which we have the honour to submit to your Grace is to increase accommodation,—but accommodation of a suitable character. As Sir Edward Kerrison, Mr. Rodwell, and hundreds of others have observed in England, we observe in Ireland, that the cesspayers—

"are continually called upon to provide space, accommodation, and even luxuries, which are utterly wasted upon many of the inmates of the asylum; and it savours of mockery to put poor helpless creatures, who need but food and lodging, into the palatial residences it is now the fashion to build. It is ludicrous to insist upon acres of recreation ground for the crazy, helpless, and infirm, who seek but quiet and repose."

It is to remedy such just cause of complaint that our suggestions are directed. We cannot think then that Dr. Nugent's objection to our proposal is at all strengthened by his reference to the absence of classification of asylums in England. It is not, however, so much to the principle of classifying asylums that Dr. Nugent directly objects, for, as we have already observed, he, in common with his colleague and every other witness who gave evidence upon the subject, approves of it. It is only when the principle comes to be applied that objections are raised. As these objections, though addressed more particularly to the proposal of classification that was suggested simply to illustrate our proposal, would, if sustained, apply to any scheme of classification whatever, it will, we doubt not, be satisfactory to your Grace to be assured and to have it shown that they are founded upon misapprehension.

p. 222. "It is proposed by the Commissioners," Dr. Nugent observes, "to convert seven of the existing district asylums into hospitals for curatives alone; the aggregate accommodation in them extending to 3,577 beds. Thus *in limine*, as one of the main objects intended through the medium of this arrangement is to secure an increased or more available provision for the insane generally, that object is frustrated by the loss of 1,666 beds, or the difference between 1,911 'curable' and the total accommodation, 3,577 beds," in these seven asylums.

The selection of particular asylums as "curative hospitals" was simply a suggestion made, as we have said, for the purpose of illustrating our proposal, and without presuming to anticipate the detailed arrangements that may be ultimately made by the Executive. But, assuming that the distribution of asylums will be that to which Dr. Nugent's objection is addressed, it is not the fact that there would be the loss of 1,666 beds, or, as we believe, of any beds at all.

In the first place, in addition to the patients under treatment, there would be retained in each asylum, in accordance with the suggestion of Dr. Robertson, 100—

50 males and 50 females—of the class who now perform the household and farm work of these establishments. That number could, of course, be increased, if desirable. Thus the number is at once brought up from 1,911 to 2,611, reducing the vacancies to 966. But as one great advantage of the proposal submitted to your Grace is that it would afford to hundreds of families of the middle and lower middle class the priceless advantage of asylum treatment for afflicted relatives, and as there are too surely many of the lowest class amongst the lunatics "at large" who would also be fit subjects for curative treatment, there need be little fear that the accommodation would exceed the demand for it. There certainly need be no such apprehension if the curative asylums are selected with reference to the probable requirements of the several districts. As the selection would, no doubt, be made by the Executive after full and careful inquiry, asylums the most suitable for the purpose, both from size and locality, would be appropriated as curative hospitals, due weight being given to objections of the character that Dr. Nugent urges to such a selection as that of Belfast. The great benefit that would be conferred by the classification of asylums upon "paying" patients is not overlooked by Dr. Hatchell, who refers to it as one of his reasons for approving of the proposal. It must be borne in mind that in Ireland the class of people to whom we refer are without any resource except the district asylums—a great deal of the accommodation of which is necessarily occupied by patients for whom it was not originally provided. As Dr. Nugent draws some conclusions from the amount and character of lunacy accommodation in England, it is important to observe that he leaves out of account altogether the amount of accommodation that is afforded by private establishments, which has no equivalent in Ireland, and the extent to which it is made available by boards of guardians. On the 29th of September 1877 there were in England no fewer than 6,410 pauper lunatics, towards whose maintenance relatives contribute in sums varying from 1*s*. per week up to the total cost of maintenance. The amount received by guardians as repayment in the course of the year was no less than 65,479*l*. 5*s*. 7*d*. About 800 were maintained in establishments other than district asylums. If a comparison can be made between English and Irish lunacy the preceding facts would seem to establish that in Ireland not only is there a great want of accommodation for a class of patients whose friends could contribute something towards their maintenance, but that many of that class are now kept wholly at the public expense; for it appears that the total number of paying patients in the 22 asylums is only 223, and the total amount received from them is 3,511*l*. 12*s*. 7*d*.

The other objection that is made by Dr. Nugent to the classification of asylums in the way proposed is apparently, but only apparently, of much greater weight. The difficulties that might arise are thus described:—

"A female, after her first confinement, is stricken by puerperal mania, resident in the town of Sligo, or on a farm adjoining the asylum, to the erection and maintenance of which her family and that of her husband had been contributing since its occupation, and as an hospital inferior to none in the three kingdoms. Instead of being placed there, not a mile from her dwelling, and close to her friends, she is to be transferred to Ballinasloe, a distance of 80 miles by car, an utter stranger, three days on the road, and perhaps escorted by police, who, though kindly and considerate, are not suitable companions for a delicate woman on so long a journey. If sent by railroad, before reaching her destination she will have traversed about 120 miles, passing through six different counties, Sligo, Leitrim, Longford, Westmeath, Roscommon, and Galway; recovered, be it at the termination of three months, or eight months, or of any other period, or if pronounced incurable at the close of a couple of years, a return journey under all the circumstances attendant on going and coming with result, at an expense of probably 10*l*." p. 225.

Any proposal, however reasonable, might be easily discredited if tested by an extreme case, still more by an imaginary case. The simple answer here is that every lunatic should be conveyed in the first instance to the nearest asylum (not being a workhouse auxiliary), the medical superintendent of which should determine within a reasonable time whether the case should be retained or sent to another asylum. The worst that could happen in such a case would be a transfer from one asylum to another. If that proposal be examined, not from the point of view of "making difficulties," as the common phrase is, but in the spirit of another common phrase, "where there's a will there's a way," the arrangement could really present no practical difficulty. All those distressing circumstances to which Dr. Nugent so feelingly refers would be avoided. The poor woman "stricken by puerperal mania" would be sent at once to Sligo, to be transferred at the discretion of the medical superintendent, or retained there upon his responsibility.

It may be objected that by this arrangement every asylum would in fact continue to be a curative hospital. In every asylum, no doubt, it would be desirable to have a certain number of single rooms for cases of emergency. But the occasions would be few in which suitable cases could not be sent to the curative asylum; and their detention, when thought desirable, need not affect the general character of the institution. Opposed to this view, however, Dr. Nugent refers to the case of the Waterford district in these terms :—

"The Waterford district affords, perhaps, the strongest objections to the proposed arrangement. The institution there is an object of satisfaction to the governors and ratepayers. Over 20,000*l.* have been recently laid out on additions and improvements, much though the influence of an English Lunacy Commissioner, the Hon. D. Fortescue, resident in the neighbourhood. The city, at its furthest point in a direct line, is scarcely a mile from the buildings, which, erected on a salubrious and open site, are replete with modern appliances. This asylum, the fresh admissions into which last year amounted to 56, would become of little value when most required, viz., in the early stages of insanity ;—the affected, at great inconvenience and no small expense, having to be transported as it were from home, fully ninety miles, to another city, and, being thus deprived of the personal sympathy and visits of their relatives, become exposed to the depraving influences of their neglect, although unavoidable."

It is easy to understand how the influence of such opinions should lead to the multiplication of asylums built at an enormous cost, practically for the accommodation of incurable idiots. It is not easy, however, to reconcile them with the evidence given before this Commission by Dr. Nugent, as by all other medical witnesses, in support of the proposal to classify asylums. For the objection in the Waterford case would apply equally to any other arrangement that might involve the necessity of sending recent cases "from home" to any locality where they "would be deprived of the "personal sympathy and visits of their relatives, and be exposed to the depraving "influence of their neglect."

The Waterford district does, no doubt, as Dr. Nugent states, "afford the strongest objections," or, as we may put it, present the greatest difficulties that our proposal is likely to encounter. It is on that account the more incumbent on those who examine the proposal to state the facts carefully, and not in such a way as to suggest, however unintentionally, unfounded conclusions. When the facts are fairly stated and fully considered, we do not think that the difficulties of even the Waterford district, great as they may be, will be found at all so formidable as Dr. Nugent would make them appear.

The Waterford Asylum, your Grace is informed, is only a mile from the city; the fresh admissions to it the last year amounted to 56; the asylum would become of little value when most required, viz., in the early stages of insanity, the affected at great inconvenience and no small expense having to be transported, as it were, from home fully ninety miles to another city. Such is the statement that Dr. Nugent makes with reference to the Waterford district.

It is remarkable how much inaccuracy is compressed into these few sentences. The whole force of the objection lies in the assumptions that the 56 cases are suitable cases for curative treatment; that they all come from the city or the immediate neighbourhood: and that, if sent to the curative hospital, they would have to be "transported" to a distance of ninety miles. What, however, are the facts?

Of the admissions (57, not 56) there are only 26 classed as "curable," 31 being "incurable." Of the 26 "curable" cases, 10 only are from Waterford. That is certainly a very different state of facts from what is suggested by Dr. Nugent's statement.

Again, instead of the whole 57 cases being admissions from Waterford, as many as 34 came from distances varying from 10 to 50 miles. Five "curable" cases came from a distance of 30 miles. If "transported" to Cork the distance would have been 43 miles. Two came from a distance of 37 miles, the distance to Cork being actually less, only 33; two came from a distance of 40 miles, while if "transported" to Cork the distance would only have been 26 miles. The greatest distance that any one of the "curable" cases (excluding those from Waterford) was conveyed was 50 miles. Had he been "transported" to Cork the distance would only have been 33½ miles.

We by no means underrate the importance of having the means of curative treatment easily accessible to an important populous city like Waterford. But for that purpose a few suitable wards might be set apart, as we have already suggested in noticing the case imagined by Dr. Nugent in Sligo.

If we should appear to have unduly trespassed upon the indulgence of your Grace by referring at so much length to the objections of Dr. Nugent to our proposal to classify asylums, we trust that a sufficient justification for doing so will be found in our desire to examine impartially the grounds upon which it is sought to prejudice a proposal which is not made without much consideration, and after the most careful inquiry.

It is not to the classification of asylums only that opposition from the Lunacy Department, as at present constituted, may be anticipated. If the organisation of workhouse auxiliaries is likely to check the building or enlargement of asylums, the work, if done at all, would probably be best done independently of that Department. While fully appreciating the zeal and success, as set forth in their annual Reports, of that Department, in providing asylum accommodation for all classes of lunatics in Ireland, there would appear to be but slight ground for counting upon co-operation in establishing workhouse auxiliaries. Not that Dr. Nugent does not appear to be sensible of the advantage of them, and of the necessity of organising them. The expression of his views in that sense is always clear and forcible. It is only when a distinct proposal is made that difficulties present themselves, and it is found to be "impracticable"—less desirable than building a new asylum or enlarging an old one.

Upon several occasions Dr. Nugent has urged the expediency of disembarrassing asylums of chronic incurable cases by transferring them to workhouses, and he has occasionally succeeded in relieving pressure upon asylums by inducing Boards of Governors to arrange with guardians to receive lunatics of that class, even where no special provision had been made for their accommodation in the workhouses to which they were sent. In his evidence before the Select Committee on Grand Jury Presentments (Ireland) Dr. Nugent says:—

"There are many poorhouses unoccupied. Where they are in a wholesome healthy situation, and where there is a quantity of ground attached to them, I see no difficulty whatever in adding to them a certain number of rooms, and putting one or two attendants to every 40 or 50 patients, and to the patients having a better dietary than is afforded to the ordinary paupers of the institution. They could be maintained, perhaps, in that way at 10*l.* or 11*l.* per head, whereas in the ordinary lunatic asylums they would cost double that amount, totally irrespective of the cost of building accommodation for them."

From this general statement he proceeds to give a particular case in illustration:—

"The County of Cork Asylum was built for 500 patients, and within the last six months the number of patients has increased by 60. It is quite clear that the asylum is too small, and you must do one of two things: you must either make increased accommodation for another class of lunatics, or you must build another asylum in the western part of the county. Adjoining the asylum at Youghal there was an immense establishment for an agricultural school, with fine buildings utterly unoccupied, and with 30 acres of ground. Why should not that be taken and made a receptacle for hopeless chronic cases?"

Why? indeed. The only intelligible reason would seem to be that to have so appropriated it would have rendered unnecessary the subsequent enlargements of the Cork Asylum at an expense of 28,768*l.*

The reason assigned for not taking it is so obviously unreal that we feel constrained to notice it; the more so as the proposal is one which after full inquiry we are prepared to submit for your Grace's approval. In the 23rd Report (for 1874) of the Inspectors of Lunacy it is stated:—

"Some years ago, in order to meet demands on the asylum, as an alternative arrangement being in favour of converting the Youghal Model School into a receptacle for chronic and old cases, in which also idiots and certain of the epileptic classes could be located, we brought the question under the consideration of the Board, but perhaps upon a thorough inquiry into the advisability of this plan the situation might interpose difficulties, the principal one consisting in the fact that it is at the extreme eastern side of the county, and distant over 100 miles from portions of the district where such provision would be most useful."

If the object was to relieve the asylum of chronic incurable cases, no building better suited for the purpose could have been selected; it is commodious, well laid out, with sufficient land, upon an open healthy site, and within about an hour's railway journey of Cork. But the Inspectors had been for some time advocating the erection of another district asylum for the West Riding, as well as the enlargement of the existing asylum. The appropriation of the Youghal School would have obviated the necessity of either, and so, although it was expressly proposed by Dr. Nugent after specially visiting the school, that it should be appropriated as "a receptacle for chronic and old cases, as well as for idiots and certain of the epileptic classes," it is found that there is "a very fair objection to such an arrangement, inasmuch as Youghal is situated at the extreme end of the East Riding." Had the district asylum which it was proposed to relieve been situated at the extreme end of the West Riding there might be something, though (as the removals would be once for all) not much in the objection. But as the school was, so to speak, at the very door of the asylum, which it was intended to relieve and which was then overcrowded with "incurables," we are not surprised to find that the true objection to the arrangement was that its adoption would interfere with the further extension of the asylum. In a minute of December 17th, 1878, communicated to us, Dr. Nugent says, "The Board did not wish to incur the "expense of a separate staff, considering it better to enlarge the asylum." They have enlarged the asylum, however, at a cost of probably 10 times what would have been sufficient to adapt the school, and have necessarily increased the salaries of their staff in proportion to the increased accommodation. In this, as in other cases, the Lunacy Department were profuse in admissions of the expediency of providing auxiliary asylums that might be economically managed; but so soon as there appears to be a fair prospect of a proposal being practically adopted "a very fair objection" to it is sure to be presented, and it is summarily thrown aside in favour of a more expensive, though not more efficient arrangement.

Of this mode of disposing of such proposals another illustration is furnished by the case of Armagh, to which we desire to refer, chiefly because the arrangement which was proposed there and subsequently rejected is one of those that we submit for your Grace's favourable consideration.

For some years before the opening of the asylum at Monaghan, the Armagh Asylum (the joint establishment of the two counties) was much overcrowded. Not long after the separation the Inspectors became satisfied that the asylum, which had heretofore served two counties, was wholly insufficient for the requirements of one. Additional land was purchased, and a proposal made for considerable additions to the Armagh Asylum. Against this a good deal of opposition was manifested by the local representative bodies, magistrates cesspayers, and board of guardians. They represented to the Government that, without incurring the great expense of enlarging the asylum, sufficient accommodation could be afforded by transferring a certain number of suitable cases to the workhouses of Armagh and Lurgan under the provision of the 38 & 39 Vict. c. 67. This suggestion was rejected upon the advice of the Inspectors that "it was neither practicable nor desirable," an opinion, they go on to say, in which "they are supported by the resolution of the Board of Governors of January 8th, 1877."

On the 31st of December 1877, there were in the Armagh Asylum 187 patients, of whom 121 were "probably incurable.". Of these, 50 were in the asylum over five years and under 10, 21 over ten years and under 15, and 16 upwards of 15 years.

The workhouses of the Armagh and Lurgan unions have been visited and carefully examined by us, with a view to ascertain the practicability of adapting them as auxiliary asylums. As the result of our own inspection and of Mr. Wilkinson's report upon the Armagh Workhouse we have no hesitation in stating that suitable accommodation could be provided in them for considerably more than the total number of incurable cases in the asylum in 1877. Upon what grounds the Inspectors came to the conclusion that it was "neither practicable nor desirable" to give effect to the provision of the 38 & 39 Vict. we have no means of knowing. From their own reports, however, we do know that when no legal authority existed for transferring lunatics from asylums to workhouses, Boards of Guardians were asked with their approval to receive them. But as soon as it became lawful to remove them, it was no longer either "practicable or desirable" to do so. And this is said of an asylum with reference to which the Inspectors, but a few years before, excuse the fewness of cures by stating "the small number of cures is not to be wondered at, for out of the 167 "inmates at the commencement of the year no less than 152 were stated to be in-"curable;" and magistrates are remonstrated with by the governors about sending in unsuitable cases.

Col. McKertie, Ev. 2007–2009.

Notwithstanding the opinion of the Inspectors, we feel bound to record our opinion that it would be difficult to find a case in which it would be at once so "practicable and so desirable" to give effect to the Act that has been referred to as in this asylum, overcrowded with incurable cases, and in the neighbourhood of such workhouses as Armagh and Lurgan.

The deliberate opinion of the Board of Governors is, no doubt, entitled to great respect. But the resolution which is referred to in this case as "supporting the opinion of the Inspectors" can only be regarded as the echo of Dr. Nugent's representation. Indeed the resolution states as much in so many words :—

"Resolved that, having heard from Dr. Nugent an explanation of the provisions of the Act 38 & 39 Victoria, cap. 67. of the percentage of lunatics that could be removed to workhouses, we are of opinion that any utilising of the workhouse at Lurgan or Armagh would not justify the governors in allowing the asylum to continue in its present state, and that the contemplated enlargement and improvements be proceeded with immediately."

We may observe that in determining the percentage of cases that can be removed from asylums to workhouses the nature of the accommodation which will be provided in the "auxiliaries" must be taken into account. The Inspectors have probably left that out of consideration, as no doubt the medical superintendents of some asylums have done in the returns which they have made to us.

To the case of Belfast and Ballymena it is not necessary for us to refer, as the circumstances are fully stated in the correspondence which is printed in the Appendix. Dr Nugent was under a misapprehension when he stated that the governors had changed their opinion upon the expediency of transferring a certain number of the inmates of the asylum to the workhouse of the Ballymena workhouse. As the Local Government Board have assented to the arrangement, it is to be hoped that no further difficulty may be experienced in giving effect to it.

App. C 8 p. 241.

Dr. Nugent Ev. 2200.

Before we close our observations upon the subject of Auxiliary Workhouse Asylums, we desire to refer to an objection that may possibly be urged to our proposal. Our suggestion, as we have explained, aims not merely at providing accommodation for a certain class of "incurables" from asylums, but at providing better accommodation for the lunatics who are now in workhouses. In the face of the evidence that we have cited of the unsuitability of workhouses for the detention of lunatics of any class, it may seem unreasonable to anticipate that it might still be held that the accommodation is sufficiently good to obviate the necessity of any change. In support of that view, statements may, no doubt, be quoted from the Reports of the Inspectors of Lunacy, which, if left unexplained, might lead to very erroneous conclusions.

The Inspectors of Lunacy can have but very imperfect knowledge of the condition of lunatics in many workhouses. Of 163 workhouses in Ireland, it would appear from a statement published in the Appendix which has been furnished to us by the Lunacy Department, 73 have been left unvisited for three years, 11 for two years, and 23 for more than a year. This, as the Inspectors have often explained, is unavoidable, owing to the number of the workhouses, and the great distance of many of them. Still it is important that the fact should be borne in mind in estimating the weight to be attached to the opinions to which we shall now refer, and which can apply to only a limited number of workhouses.

App. C 9, p. 244.

In their Report for 1871, the Inspectors, speaking of workhouses generally, say,—

> "We are happy to state that gradual but active amelioration is taking place in favour of the insane in workhouses, and that, as a rule, they are exceptionally well nourished, well clad, and their comfort fairly regarded. Day-rooms are being prepared in many where none previously existed, and special attendants are placed over them."

Reporting in 1873 they observe,—

> "For many years there has been a gradual improvement, which has now assumed a marked character, in the condition of the lunatic inmates in poorhouses, where they are treated with much consideration."

Writing of the insane in workhouses in 1875, the Inspectors state,—

> "It may be safely said that from year to year a progressive amelioration has been noticeable in the condition of the mentally affected in the poorhouses of Ireland, who, as a rule, have come to be recognised in a proper light, and made objects of kindly consideration by boards of guardians They are afforded an exceptional dietary, with animal food from three to six days in the week. Their clothing and bedding are improved, and personal cleanliness more carefully looked after. When the number of insane is large, separate apartments, with a paid attendant for each sex, are usually provided; or well-disposed paupers, encouraged by some additional domestic allowance, are employed, and, when grounds or open airing yards are available, full opportunity for exercise is afforded. In a few workhouses we have found many of the imbecile and idiotic industriously employed in day rooms set apart for them, and we not unfrequently learn from both masters and matrons that some of them are of the most useful and willing of the inmates."

In his Report on a visit to Galway workhouse in July 1876, Dr. Nugent writes that the insane "are comfortably located in a new ward, and kindly looked after."

Writing in December 1867 of the insane in the Roscrea workhouse, Dr. Hatchell states that he found the wards "particularly clean, orderly, and well ventilated. The "patients appear to be most carefully and kindly treated. On looking over the "hospital and house in general, the entire keeping and management of it reflects "great credit on the master and the other officers." Dr. Nugent, upon a visit in May 1869, found "the insane inmates of this workhouse kindly looked after." Dr. Hatchell visited this workhouse again in May 1877, and wrote of the insane, "They appear "to be very carefully attended to; their dormitory is kept particularly clean, orderly, "and well ventilated."

Upon a visit to the Fermoy workhouse in July 1865, Dr. Nugent wrote: "It [the "workhouse] appears to me equally well constructed and well conducted, and, from "what I observed, I am sure the imbecile * * * are carefully looked after." Of the same workhouse Dr. Nugent reported in July 1867 that the inmates were "kindly "attended to;" "the establishment for order, cleanliness, and ventilation deserve full "commendation."

In March 1868 Dr. Nugent again visited Fermoy workhouse, the management of "which was particularly good, and the classification much to be approved of. * * * "The various departments were very clean and orderly. * * * I consider the insane "to be kindly treated and carefully attended to. Their food is good and liberal."

Dr. Hatchell visited the Mountmellick workhouse in August 1872, and stated that the insane were "evidently taken very great care of, and their wards are particularly "clean and orderly." In August 1873 Dr. Hatchell paid another visit to this workhouse, and reported that the idiots, &c., "are kept in very creditable order, and the "inmates are evidently carefully attended to, being well clad and clean in their persons." Dr. Hatchell again, in September 1874, "inspected the idiot wards, and found "them clean, orderly, and well attended. The inmates appear to be carefully attended "to in every respect. The general condition of their wards is creditable to the master "and matron."

Dr. Nugent in April 1874 visited the insane inmates in the Cork workhouse, and reported that "personally they appear to be carefully and considerately treated, "their dietary, as a rule, ample and nutritious." Speaking of the same class upon a visit to this workhouse in July 1877, Dr Nugent states "they appear to be carefully "and kindly attended to, their personal cleanliness duly looked after; the dietary is "good and ample, the great majority getting animal food four times in the week."

Dr Nugent visited the insane inmates in the Belfast workhouse in November 1872, and wrote:—

"They, as hitherto observed by me, are kindly and considerately treated; the scale of dietary being ample in quantity, with a liberal allowance of animal food. Their personal cleanliness is, I am informed, duly attended to. They get baths once a week."

Upon a visit to this workhouse in November 1877, Dr. Nugent found—

"The room which they [the insane] occupy by day is clean, warm, and comfortable; their dormitories are duly and well ventilated. * * * The dietary I consider to be ample."

Dr. Hatchell visited the Cashel workhouse in May 1867, and found the idiotic inmates "carefully attended to"; and Dr. Nugent inspected it in June 1869, when he found "the insane inmates in this workhouse very carefully attended to; they appear "to be comfortably located and well clad."

At Tipperary workhouse, which Dr. Nugent visited in July 1873, he considered the insane "to be, as hitherto, carefully looked after, well clad, and on an ample dietary." In March 1875 Dr. Nugent found "the inmates of the lunatic wards kindly looked after, "and on a very good dietary." Dr. Hatchell visited this workhouse in June 1876, and reported that he had—

"Inspected the idiots and epileptics. They appear to be very well cared for and looked after; and their wards are kept in most creditable order, being particularly clean and well ventilated. The articles of food, such as bread, milk, and meat, were of most excellent quality. The general condition of the house, and hospital in particular, reflects much credit on all concerned in the management thereof."

Dr. Nugent inspected the insane inmates of the Waterford workhouse in July 1876, and found them "carefully and kindly attended to, and on a liberal scale of diet. I "do not consider any of them need transference to the district asylum." Dr. Nugent visited this workhouse again in March 1878, when he reported that the insane "appear "to be very humanely attended to, and are reported to me as not giving trouble."

Dr. Nugent, on his visit to the Carrick-on-Suir workhouse in March 1877, wrote:— "They [the insane] appear to be carefully looked after, as hitherto, and on a nutritious "dietary;" and on his visit in August 1877 he found "the insane kindly attended to. "The rooms which they occupy are clean and well ventilated, and their bedding and "wearing apparel in good order."

Dr. Hatchell paid a visit to the Kilmallock workhouse in June 1867, and "inspected the lunatic and idiot wards, and found them in a very creditable state, "being clean, orderly and well ventilated. This class appears, as stated by some of "them, to be most kindly and carefully treated, both by the master and matron." Dr Nugent visited this workhouse in March 1875, and reported that the insane "appear "to be kindly looked after, and, from what I learn, their personal cleanliness is duly "attended to."

Upon his visit to the Youghal workhouse in August 1867, Dr. Nugent reports:— "I visited the lunatic inmates here, and found they are kindly treated, and on the best "diet, with extras;" and upon his visit in July 1873, the lunatic inmates "appear to "be carefully and kindly attended to." Dr. Hatchell also visited this workhouse in September 1874, and found the insane inmates carefully attended to, the wards very clean and well ventilated, and the food of good quality.

Dr. Hatchell, upon his visit to the Newcastle workhouse in December 1869, wrote:—"The idiots appear to be most carefully and kindly treated; the wards are kept warm, "clean, and well ventilated." Dr. Hatchell visited this workhouse again in June 1875, and was of opinion that the idiots were fairly and kindly treated; "their wards are in "creditable order."

Upon a visit to the Clonmell workhouse in September 1873, Dr. Nugent reported on the insane inmates that they "personally appear to be kindly attended to; they "are on a better diet than the ordinary paupers, and are well clad."

Dr. Hatchell visited Coleraine workhouse in September 1871, and reported that he had "inspected the lunatic and idiot wards, and found them in very creditable order, "being clean, orderly, and well ventilated * * * I examined the soup; it is of "excellent quality, and the allowance liberal." Dr. Nugent also visited this workhouse in November 1875. He saw and examined all the insane inmates; they "appear "to be very kindly looked after, well fed, and their personal cleanliness duly attended "to."

Dr. Nugent inspected the insane in the Balrothery workhouse in October 1876, "who appear to be kindly and carefully looked after; and I am informed their "personal cleanliness is daily attended to."

Upon a visit to the North Dublin workhouse in October 1874, Dr. Nugent wrote:—

"The various apartments occupied by the insane classes are remarkably clean, and the bedding in them good and ample;—they themselves appearing to be treated with great consideration, and afforded a very liberal dietary,—three meals daily, with meat six times in the week for dinner. They are also well clad."

Upon his visit to this workhouse in May 1876, Dr. Nugent, speaking of the insane, reports that "all appear to be very carefully looked after, well clad, cleanly in their "person, and supplied with a good dietary, getting animal food six days in the "week."

Dr. Nugent visited the Rathdown workhouse in April 1875, and reported:—

"I find all [the insane] to be carefully attended to, and their wearing apparel and bedding good, while their personal cleanliness is duly regarded. The ordinary dietary—three meals daily—on which they are placed, is ample and nutritious."

Dr. Hatchell also visited this workhouse in October 1877, and reported "very "favourably on the general condition" of the lunatic department. "The several day "rooms and dormitories are kept very clean and well ventilated." The general "appearance of the insane is satisfactory as to cleanliness, clothing, and health."

Upon a visit to the South Dublin workhouse in April 1873, Dr. Nugent wrote of the lunatic wards:—

"I cannot but consider their present state as being highly satisfactory. A scrupulous cleanliness, with good ventilation, is maintained in them. The bedding is ample in quantity, and of good quality, while the patients themselves appear to be carefully and kindly looked after. * * * Night watches are regularly kept up in each ward. * * * A liberal dietary continues to be supplied."

Dr. Nugent, visiting this workhouse again in October 1874, states that since his previous visit—

"Various minor alterations and improvements have been effected in the lunatic wards, which are kept in a very orderly and cleanly state, and with a due regard to ventilation. The patients themselves are well clad, and appear to have their personal comforts fully attended to."

When Dr. Nugent visited this workhouse in July 1875, he reported that all the insane "appear to be very carefully looked after, well nursed, and maintained with a "due regard to cleanliness in dress and person."

Dr. Nugent visited Thomastown workhouse in July 1875, and found "the lunatic "inmates very kindly looked after and kept, with a due regard to their personal "cleanliness, both in dress and bedding." Dr. Nugent visited this workhouse again in February 1877, and found "the insane inmates very kindly looked after, and on a "good scale of dietary"; and in a visit in September 1877 he reported that the insane were "very carefully looked after, and cleanly in their personal appearance. "Their bedding too is ample and suitably kept."

Dr. Nugent visited the Callan workhouse in July 1865, and "found the imbecile "epileptic classes carefully looked after, and their dietary good." He reported again in September 1872, that "they appear to be carefully looked after, and, I understand, "give no trouble, being very tranquil." Also in April 1875 Dr. Nugent writes, "they "appear to be kindly and carefully treated in this union, and on good dietary."

Upon a visit to the Navan workhouse in April 1872, Dr. Nugent found the lunatic inmates "most kindly attended to, well clad, clean, and supplied with a generous dietary." Dr. Nugent visited this workhouse again in February 1874, and reported:—

"I find, on my present visit to the wards allocated to the insane, that the inmates are treated with every consideration; they are well clad, looked after, and allowed a liberal dietary."

Upon another visit to the workhouse in November 1876, Dr. Nugent found that the insane were—

"carefully and most humanely attended to. The rooms occupied by them are orderly and well ventilated, and their personal cleanliness looked after. The dietary is good and ample, with a fair allowance of animal food."

Dr. Nugent visited the Kells workhouse in December 1868, and found "the inmates "of the insane wards carefully looked after, with a fair and full dietary." When Dr. Nugent visited this workhouse in November 1876, the insane appeared "to be "kindly attended to, and are on a fair diet; their personal cleanliness is duly looked "after."

Dr. Nugent paid a visit to the insane of the Parsonstown workhouse in June 1872, and was "quite satisfied they are carefully and kindly attended to;" and on a visit in June 1874 they were "very carefully attended to; their dietary is good, and their "personal cleanliness and bedding duly looked after."

Dr. Nugent inspected the insane in the Mullingar workhouse in June 1873, when they appeared "to be kindly looked after, and are on a good scale of diet." In November 1876 he found them "kindly looked after, and on a fair dietary;" and in October 1877 they were "on a fair scale of dietary, and kindly looked after in other "respects."

Dr. Hatchell visited the Rathkeale workhouse in June 1876, and reported that the insane appeared "to be carefully and kindly treated."

Dr. Nugent visited Dundalk workhouse in December 1876, and found the insane "duly looked after." In May 1877 he found the rooms well ventilated, the patients' clothing fair, and their personal cleanliness not neglected; and in November 1877, when he reported that "the dietary is good and ample. Under all circumstances I "consider these inmates to be carefully and kindly looked after."

Dr. Nugent found the insane in Drogheda workhouse in April 1876 "well clad, "and on a good dietary, getting animal food three times a week, and their meals "ample in quantity daily. The bedding is good and clean." Upon another visit in October 1876, he saw and examined all the insane. "They are kindly treated, and "their creature comforts attended to;" and they were "carefully looked after," when Dr. Nugent visited the workhouse in May 1877.

Dr. Hatchell, upon a visit to Abbeyleix workhouse in February 1868, found the insane wards "clean and orderly and also comfortable, having good fires in each; "the allowance of food, I find, on inquiry, to be liberal;" and on a visit in August 1875, the insane "appear to be carefully treated and attended to; their wards are kept "and orderly."

In July 1873 Dr. Hatchell visited the Wexford workhouse, and made the following report:—

"I have this day inspected the idiot wards of this union, and have every reason to be satisfied with the care and attention the inmates receive, and the extreme cleanliness and order that prevails throughout the several dormitories and day rooms. The dietary is very liberal. I saw some of the articles of food, which was good."

In November 1873. Dr. Hatchell again visited this workhouse, when the insane appeared "to be carefully and kindly attended to, placed on good nutritious dietary, "and personally clean." Dr. Hatchell paid another visit to this workhouse in March 1874, and reported that the insane—

"Appear to be taken very good care of, being well clad, and the allowance of food is very liberal. I examined some of the articles of food, such as bread, milk, &c., and found them of most excellent quality. The dormitories are in most creditable order, being particularly clean, orderly, and well ventilated, reflecting great credit on the parties in charge."

Dr. Nugent visited Gorey workhouse in April 1875, when the insane appeared "to be very kindly attended to, and are kept with becoming cleanliness;" and in February 1876, and reported that the insane were "very humanely attended to in "the infirmary, have liberal dietary with animal food, and are personally kept clean "and orderly." Dr. Hatchell also visited this workhouse in December 1876, and wrote:—

"I am happy to report that they [the insane] appear to be carefully attended to, and their ward are kept in very creditable order, being clean, orderly, and well ventilated."

In August 1875 Dr. Nugent visited the Enniscorthy workhouse, and found the insane "carefully and kindly attended to, and on good dietary;" and in September 1876 he again visited the workhouse, when the insane appeared "to be very kindly "attended to, and on a good scale of dietary." Dr. Hatchell also visited this workhouse in November 1876, and reported that the insane were "carefully "attended to."

Dr. Nugent visited the Downpatrick workhouse in November 1873, and considered that the insane "are comfortably located, on a good dietary, cleanly in person, and "altogether most humanely treated."

The insane in the Lisburn workhouse appeared, upon Dr. Nugent's visit, "to be "kindly looked after, their cleanliness duly attended to, and on a fair dietary."

Dr. Nugent visited Monaghan workhouse in August 1874, when the insane were "evidently carefully looked after and kindly treated;" in June 1875 they were "humanely attended to, and kept with cleanliness;" and in May 1877 they were "duly attended to, and on a good dietary."

Dr. Nugent inspected the insane wards of the Enniskillen workhouse in October 1873, and found the inmates "humanely treated and on a good dietary; their personal "cleanliness being duly attended to." Dr. Hatchell also visited this workhouse in May 1874, when he found the idiot wards "in most creditable order, being very clean, "orderly, and comfortably furnished. The inmates appear to carefully and kindly "treated. Their allowance of food is liberal." Dr. Hatchell visited this workhouse again in September 1877, when he reported the insane to be carefully attended to; "and their wards are kept very clean, orderly, and well ventilated, having a homely "and comfortable appearance. The diet is liberal."

Dr. Nugent visited the Armagh workhouse in July 1866, and found the insane classes "carefully looked after. Their sleeping rooms and bedding I consider to be "very clean." Dr. Hatchell visited this workhouse in 1875. He reports that the idiot wards were "in most creditable order, being remarkably clean and well ventilated. "I have no doubt as to their [the insane] being most carefully attended to in all "respects."

Dr. Nugent visited this workhouse again in May 1876, and reported that the insane were "evidently well cared for; cleanly, both in person and dress, and on a nutritious "scale of dietary. I am happy to learn they give no trouble,—the best proof of kindly "treatment."

Dr. Nugent visited Castleblayney workhouse in June 1872, when he considered the insane to be "very carefully looked after, well fed, and with due regard to their "personal cleanliness;" and when he visited the workhouse again in May 1876, they "were carefully treated and on good diet."

In June 1871 Dr. Hatchell visited the Dunfanaghy workhouse, and felt "quite "satisfied that they receive every attention and kindness they require. Their wards "are kept clean and well ventilated."

The Carrickmacross workhouse was inspected by Dr. Hatchell in July 1871, when he found the idiots "having all the appearance of being most carefully and kindly "treated. The clean and orderly state their wards are kept in reflects credit on both "the master and matron." Dr. Hatchell, upon another visit in July 1872, writes: "The idiot wards are kept very clean, and the inmates carefully attended to."

Dr. Hatchell visited Sligo workhouse in September 1877, and reported that all the insane "appear carefully attended to. Their wards, particularly on the female side, "are kept clean and orderly."

Dr. Nugent inspected the insane patients of the Boyle workhouse in August 1873, and found them "carefully attended to, and, as before, not requiring any special "treatment." In March 1875 he also reported the insane as "being kindly attended "to." Dr. Hatchell also paid a visit to this workhouse in March 1877, when the insane appeared to be "very carefully attended to in every respect, which, together with the "general state of the several dormitories, dayrooms, &c., which are orderly and well "ventilated, reflect credit on the master and the other officers of the institution."

Dr. Hatchell inspected the idiots of the Newport workhouse in May 1868, and found them "carefully treated."

Dr. Nugent found the insane in Castlebar workhouse in December 1875 "to be "carefully and kindly attended to, and on a very good scale of diet."

Dr. Nugent found the insane "comfortably attended to" in Ballina workhouse in August 1871.

Dr. Hatchell visited Mount Bellew union in August 1862, when all the idiots, &c. appeared to be "well cared and attended to. The workhouse in general is particularly "clean, orderly, and well ventilated." Again, in September 1868, he "found this class "very carefully attended to. Every part of the house that I visited was very clean, "orderly, and well ventilated."

Dr. Nugent paid a visit to the Mallow workhouse in September 1875, and found "the inmates of the idiot wards kindly attended to." Upon a visit in November 1875, Dr. Hatchell found them "carefully attended to, and their wards in very creditable "order." In June 1877 Dr. Hatchell paid another visit to this workhouse, when the insane appeared "to be very carefully attended; and their wards, particularly that on "the female side, are kept clean, orderly, and well ventilated."

These are certainly most satisfactory statements, highly creditable to guardians, workhouse officials, and to the supervision of the Local Government Board. The value of them, however, consists, not in showing that the better accommodation of workhouse "auxiliaries" may be dispensed with, but in the evidence which they afford of the administrative capacity of those who would be responsible for the management of these institutions.

The real obstacle, however, to giving effect to the changes we suggest, if they should meet with your Grace's approval, will be found to consist in the present constitution of the Lunacy Department in Ireland. So far back as 1857 Dr. Nugent urged strongly the expediency of reconstituting the lunacy administrative body, and a distinct proposal for a complete change was one of the recommendations made by the Commission of 1857. If auxiliary asylums are to be established in connection with workhouses, the Local Government Board must necessarily exercise authority over the management of them. For reasons that are forcibly put in the evidence given before us, great difficulties would probably arise if the lunacy administration were controlled from two separate departments. We therefore think that the administration of the whole pauper lunacy in Ireland should be placed under a department of the Local Government Board. It is true that in England the administration is placed under a distinct Board, the Lunacy Commissioners. But, as Sir Robert Ferguson observed before the Commission of 1857,-

"There are very great differences between the two countries, which must be attended to, or the whole question may be thrown into confusion, and the working of the Lunacy Asylum Act might be impeded."

And certainly nothing could be more calculated to impede it than by dividing the responsibility of administration between two separate departments. Such a change as we now suggest was, we believe, contemplated under the administration of a predecessor of your Grace in the Viceroyalty. It would certainly not involve any ultimate addition of expenditure, whilst it would provide for the efficient inspection of the three classes of lunatic asylums by officials directly responsible, as are the inspectors of the Local Government Board, to that department.

CONCLUSION.

In conclusion, we beg most respectfully to submit to your Grace, with reference to each of the several matters referred to us for inquiry:—

I. That, for the reasons which are fully set forth in a preceding part of this Report, it would not be expedient that any Poor Law Union in Ireland should be dissolved and amalgamated with those adjoining.

II. That it would not be proper or advisable to dispense wholly with any existing workhouse in Ireland:

That portions of certain workhouses may be dispensed with and appropriated for the accommodation of a certain class of lunatics:

That it would not be proper or advisable to appropriate portions of workhouses so dispensed with for the accommodation of any other class of destitute poor from other unions.

III. That additional workhouse buildings are not required, as the existing accommodation, where not adequate to the wants of particular unions, can easily be rendered so. The overcrowding of infirmaries which is at present the chief defect may be remedied, and at the same time better means of classification be provided, by the removal of chronic cases to suitable apartments in the main building, and of lunatics to auxiliary asylums:

The appropriation of children's or school buildings belonging to the workhouses at Dublin, Belfast, Cork, and Limerick for auxiliary asylums is suggested, both because the buildings are suitable for such purpose, and also with a view of providing funds for the establishment of separate schools in those urban unions:

That in certain places which are remote or difficult of access, of which Achill Island and the Island of Innishboffin may be referred to as illustrations, it is expedient that hospitals should be established:

That the establishment of cottage hospitals, as recommended by some of the Inspectors of the Local Government Board, may be left to the discretion of Boards of Guardians, guided by such suggestions as they may receive from the central department.

IV. That portions of certain workhouses and detached buildings which can be dispensed with may be advantageously appropriated for the accommodation of a certain class of lunatics in the manner fully set forth in a preceding part of this Report.

V. That, subject to the suggestion immediately preceding, it does not appear to be expedient to make any change in the distribution of any other class of the destitute poor.

VI. That for the better care, relief, and treatment of the poor who are lunatic, idiotic, or imbecile in mind, or otherwise afflicted with mental disease, it is expedient that a complete reorganisation of the whole lunacy administration be effected. For which purpose, as is fully set forth in the last part of this Report, we recommend—

1st. That under the provisions of sec. 15. of 8 & 9 Vict. cap. 107, the existing district asylums should be classified, reserving one or more, as may be required, in each province, as "lunatic hospitals," especially for the curative treatment of the insane;

2nd. That the remaining district asylums should be appropriated as "lunatic asylums" for the accommodation of the chronic insane requiring special care. A certain number of this class would be accommodated in the "lunatic hospitals," as about fifty of each sex would be required for the service of those establishments; Dr. Robertson. Ev. 1526, 1529.

3rd. That the inspection of the "lunatics at large" should be made one of the duties of the dispensary medical officers, who should be remunerated for this duty, and whose certificate that any one of this class is neglected or improperly cared for, should be made the ground for action by the lunacy authorities;

4th. That the accommodation for the third or harmless class, who are at present in "lunatic asylums," in "workhouses," or "at large" in a neglected state, be provided by the appropriation of spare workhouse buildings, a sufficiency of which is to be found in each province, thus also meeting the very general complaint of guardians being compelled to maintain superfluous workhouse accommodation; and

5th. That for the present all expenditure upon the building or enlargement of district asylums be suspended.

Thus each province would be provided with three classes of lunatic establishments, *i.e.*, with one or more lunatic Hospitals, in which undivided attention could be given to the curative treatment of lunacy in its earliest stages,—with first-class lunatic Asylums in which the chronic cases requiring special care would be treated, and with second-class or "workhouse auxiliary asylums" for harmless cases not requiring special care. The first-class asylums, with their Superintendents and staffs, would still be available for the reception on first committal of urgent cases, and, worked in concert with the hospital establishments, would receive their cases when they are classed as probably incurable, and, would, in their turn, pass on cases, when they became harmless, to the workhouse auxiliary. All classes of the lunatic poor would thus be provided for.

These latter institutions it is proposed should be fitted in every way that is requisite for the class of cases for which they are destined, *i.e.*, with good dormitories (with a proper proportion of single rooms or cells), cheerful day rooms, bath-rooms, lavatories, and good airing courts; gardens or land for exercise and spade-labour should be available in all cases. They should also, as recommended by Dr. Robertson, Dr. M'Cabe, Dr. Berkeley, Dr. Cullinan, and Dr. Daxon, be provided with a sufficient staff (2 to every 50 or 60) of paid trained attendants.

The cost of effecting the proposed classification of lunatics, though small when it is considered that suitable asylum accommodation will be provided for nearly 5,000 additional lunatics, would nevertheless, if our suggestion be adopted, be considerable. In unions such as Dublin, Cork, Belfast, and others, if school buildings are appropriated as auxiliary asylums, it will be necessary to compensate the guardians to such an amount as would enable them to provide adequate school accommodation elsewhere. The cost of adapting portions of workhouses as auxiliaries should not be estimated at less than 15*l*. per bed.

Having regard to the pressure of local taxation and to the difficulty of adjusting the charge, in the first instance, for adapting these buildings for use as auxiliary asylums, this expenditure, we submit, should if possible be provided from another source.

In connection with such changes as we have recommended in the course of this Report, we beg leave to submit to your Grace some conclusions to which we have been led in the course of our inquiry, and some considerations to which it appears to us to be important that the attention of your Grace should be directed.

Irrespective of the advantages to be gained, under the scheme submitted, in the *curative* treatment of lunacy, considerable economic advantages may also be anticipated.

In order to arrive at an approximate estimate of the cost under the system proposed, it will be making a liberal provision if we estimate the cost per head of inmates of the *curative* establishments at 26*l*. per annum. The average over the whole of Ireland for the past few years having been about 24*l*. 10*s*.

It is not easy accurately to estimate the cost of the second-class establishments. Under good management it certainly ought eventually to become considerably less than the minimum cost per head in asylums under the present system, which in the year 1877 was 19*l*. per head. To be on the safe side, we may estimate it at 20*l*. per annum.

Dr. McCabe, Ev. 2108.

The cost in the workhouse auxiliaries can be fairly estimated. In the Cork workhouse the cost of lunatics per head per week is, for maintenance and clothing, 3*s*. 6*d*., and under the head of establishment charges, 1*s*. 4*d*.; in the South Dublin Union, in which there were 206 lunatics during the year ending March 1878, and in which they are well kept and cared for, the weekly average cost of their maintenance was 3*s*. 8*d*.; and according to a return presented to Parliament last session (No. 250, Sess. 1878,), the average weekly cost of maintenance for the whole of Ireland was 2*s*. 11½*d*., so we may safely estimate the maintenance charge at 4*s*. per head per week

The cost under the head of "establishment charges" in the auxiliaries should not on an average exceed 1*s*. 6*d*. per head per week. In these they should, as any other class of inmate for which separate accommodation is provided, be charged with their share of the workhouse establishment charges, slightly increased as they will be by additions to certain salaries, and by those of the lunatic attendants. We may, therefore, estimate their cost at 5*s*. 6*d*. per head per week, or 14*l*. 6*s*. a year. Applying these figures to the numbers it is proposed to deal with, we have their annual cost:—

	£
In curative hospitals, 1,911 + 700 for service = 2,611 at 26*l*. a year -	67,886
In first-class asylums, 4,912, less 700 for service of hospitals = 4,212 at 20*l*. a year - - - - - - -	84,240
In workhouse auxiliaries, 5,400 at 14*l*. 6*s*. a year - - - -	77,220
Total - - - - -	229,346

The actual cost of maintenance, &c., in district asylums for the year 1877 for 8,102 patients ("the daily average number maintained from public funds,") was 200,046*l*.; and if we estimate the cost of maintaining the 3,367 lunatics in workhouses at the moderate figure of 11*l*. per head per annum, we then have the total cost of maintaining 11,469 lunatics for one year under the present system standing at 237,083*l*.

It would thus appear that, under the proposed system of classification, the condition of a large number of this unhappy class of beings may be ameliorated, and the *whole* of the lunatic poor of Ireland adequately provided for, at a much less cost than that now entailed in dealing inadequately with a portion of them only; while, at the same time, relief, under the head of "establishment charges," will be afforded to the smaller rural unions, in connection with which auxiliary asylums may be established.

The wants of the lunatic poor in Ireland having been provided for before the establishment of a Poor Law, the expenses incurred were made chargeable to the county cess, which charge falls altogether (except in the case of new holdings created since the passing of the Land Act) on the occupier of the land. When the Poor Law was introduced, it was enacted that the charge should be shared between the owner and occupier. Thus it results that all the lunatics in asylums are charged on "county cess," and those in workhouses on "poor rates."

The charge upon the cess, as has been already shown, has gone on increasing rapidly; and although relief has been given by Treasury grant, at the rate of 4*s.* per head per week, in support of lunatics in asylums, the net charge, after deducting that grant, amounted, in 1877, to the same high figure as that cited by the Select Committee on Grand Jury Presentments in their Report as a very heavy charge in 1867.

The first year in which this relief was given was in 1875; the grant was at the rate of 75,930*l.* per annum; in 1876, it was 77,907*l.* per annum; in 1877, it was 80,380*l.* per annum, and it is steadily on the increase, as may be judged by the exposition already given of the increase of lunacy.

We recommend that, under the scheme submitted, the manner of making the grant should be approximated to that prevailing in Scotland: where the grant is "half the cost of maintenance," such maintenance in no case to exceed 8*s.* Thus the grant to asylums generally amounts, as in Ireland, to 4*s.* per head; but in the workhouse auxiliary asylums it varies from 3*s.* to 2*s.* 6*d.* per head per week.

Under the scheme submitted, it is suggested that this might be met by making the grant, in cases necessarily detained for curative or other purposes in the hospitals, at the resent rate of 4*s.*; to those in the first-class asylums, 3*s.*; and to those in workhouse auxiliaries, 2*s.* Such an arrangement would, in a very slight degree, increase the grant in the first instance, and would cause its growth to be much slower than under the present system.

Supposing all the lunatics for whom it is proposed to provide had been under treatment in 1877, the grant, on scale suggested, would probably have been as under:—

	£
1,911 curables + 700 for service = 2,611 in "lunatic hospitals," at 4*s.* per head per week - - - - - -	27,155
4,212 incurables requiring special care in "first-class lunatic asylums," at 3*s.* per head per week - - - - -	32,854
5,400 harmless, in workhouse auxiliaries, at 2*s.* per head per week - -	28,080
Total - - - - - -	88,089

Thus, with an addition of less than 8,000*l.* to the capitation grant, all classes of pauper lunatics, including over 4,000 additional, would be admitted to its benefits.

Deducting this capitation allowance from 229,346*l.*, the estimated cost of maintenance of the whole pauper lunacy of Ireland, we find that 141,257*l.* remains, and if from it we deduct 48,000*l.*, the charge for adequately providing for the lunatics already in workhouses, and therefore already chargeable to the "poor rates," we have, in round numbers, a balance of 93,000*l.*, which must be met, as against 120,000*l.*, the actual amount chargeable to "county cess" for considerably smaller numbers in the year 1877.

In order to secure efficiency in the management of each class of asylum in connection with the others, it appears essential that these different systems of charge should be done away with, and that the source from which the charge, or the balance of the charge, should be drawn should be the poor rates. Indeed had asylums been established after the introduction of the Poor Law, it is to the "poor rates" that they would, no doubt, have been chargeable.

When the Irish Church Disestablishment Bill was introduced, Mr. Gladstone suggested "provision for lunatics" as one of the principal objects to which the surplus funds could be appropriated. As the period appointed for the execution of the duties entrusted to "The Commissioners of Church Temporalities in Ireland" will soon expire, a fund from that source will be then available, and the appropriation of a portion of it to the purpose named would greatly facilitate the changes that we suggest and recommend them to general approval. Hansard, vol. 194, p. 459 *et seq.*

For the efficient working of the scheme, it will be necessary to obtain the power to move resident medical superintendents from one asylum to another without their losing their services (as reckoning for superannuation), and their salaries also should be fixed on a proper scale, and not left dependent, as they now are in a great measure, upon the number of beds for which their asylums are built.

If, in accordance with our suggestions, auxiliary asylums are organised, the control and management of them will become a very important part of lunacy administration. It would, we think, be most inexpedient to take it out of the hands of boards of guardians. It would be not less undesirable that hospitals and asylums for lunatics of different classes should be under the control of one central department, and auxiliaries of another. We are, therefore, of opinion, that the whole lunacy administration of Ireland should be under the general control, as Poor Law and sanitary administration is, of the Local Government Board.

We deem it right to direct the attention of Your Grace to the fact that the large expenditure which had been sanctioned to provide additional asylum accommodation at Armagh has been, at our suggestion, suspended for the present, and that the question of providing additional accommodation at Armagh, Londonderry, and Belfast, where it is most urgently required, is held over pending the decision of the Government upon the recommendations which are submitted to Your Grace in this Report.

In submitting this Report to Your Grace, we desire to acknowledge the great assistance which was afforded to us by the Inspectors of the Local Government Board, acting in accordance with instructions from Sir Alfred Power; by the several officials of the Lunacy Department; as also by clerks and other officials of the several unions throughout the country.

To the Secretary of the Commission, Mr. H. A. Robinson, we are especially indebted for the very zealous and efficient manner in which he discharged the duties of his office, involving great labour in the preparation of the several statistical returns which form so important a portion of the Appendix to this Report.

We have the honour to be
Your Grace's obedient servants,

W. LE POER TRENCH. (L.S.)
ANDREW DOYLE. (L.S.)
CHARLES SHARMAN CRAWFORD. (L.S.)

February 7th, 1870.

POOR LAW UNION INQUIRY COMMISSION.

MINUTES OF EVIDENCE.

INQUIRY AT CAVAN.—TUESDAY, 11TH DECEMBER, 1877.

CAVAN. Dec. 11, 1877.

Before Major Hon. WILLIAM LE POER TRENCH, R.E. (Chairman); ANDREW DOYLE, Esq., and CHARLES SHARMAN CRAWFORD, Esq., Commissioners.

Mr. GRIER, Clerk of Cavan Union, examined.

Mr. Grier.

1. Will you produce the resolutions of the guardians with reference to the question of the amalgamation of Cavan Union with others in the county?—The first resolution on the subject was passed at a meeting of the Board of Guardians of the Cavan Union, held on Tuesday, the 25th April, 1876, when on the motion of Mr Henry Fair, seconded by Mr. Edward Kennedy, it was unanimously adopted —

"RESOLVED—That, owing to the great decrease of pauperism, a petition be presented to Parliament, praying that the existing Poor Law be changed so as to amalgamate the unions in this county, the Cavan Workhouse being sufficiently large to contain double the number of paupers in the county. Resolved—that a copy of this resolution be forwarded to every Board of Guardians in Ireland, requesting their co-operation and support."

This was the resolution of the Board of Guardians of the Cavan Union, which was communicated to the various Boards of Guardians in the country afterwards. That is the original resolution, upon which all this question of amalgamation commenced.

2. That is to say, within the last two years. There was a previous one, though?—Yes, in 1857, and on the 30th May, 1876, another resolution was passed, unanimously adopting a petition to Parliament on the subject of amalgamation, a copy of which was forwarded to every Board of Guardians in Ireland, and a copy of which I now hand in.

3. That is the petition of 1876?—Yes. The third resolution was adopted on the 16th January, 1877, and it adopted a copy of the same petition to Parliament, extended. This resolution, I presume, it is unnecessary to read.

4. It is the same petition, with some addition?—Yes; the addition of the sentence relating to fever hospitals.

5. Well, we will take that as read. Now, who represents the Cavan Union in support of the resolution that it is desirable to amalgamate Cavan with the parts of other unions in this county?

Mr. *Edward Kennedy*.—I do.

EDWARD KENNEDY, Esq., examined.

Edward Kennedy, Esq.

6. You are a guardian of the Cavan Union, I believe?—Yes. Deputy Vice-Chairman and Chairman of Finance.

7. How long have you been a guardian of the union, Mr. Kennedy?—I think seven or eight years vice-chairman, but I was a guardian a long time before that.

8. How long have you been a guardian?—I suppose about eleven years altogether.

9. You moved the resolution in favour of amalgamation?—I did.

10. Upon what ground, may I ask you?—On the following grounds: The house was built in 1841, capable of holding 1,234 in-door paupers. On the 29th September, 1848, there were 1,007 paupers, including the auxiliary houses. We were obliged during the famine years to have auxiliary houses about the country here. Well, the lowest number of inmates, which was the 1st November in the present year, was 237, and the number of paupers at present in the entire union is 594.

11. In-door and out-door?—Yes.

12. At what date?—The 1st November in the present year. Well, the number of indoor paupers, including those in the outlying houses, viz.—eight or nine of our paupers in the Enniskillen Workhouse, in Bailieborough, 148; in Oldcastle, 85; in Bawnboy, 69; in Cootehill, 69; and at present in Cavan, 283—makes a total of 664 in-door paupers in the entire union.

13. In-door paupers?—Yes; 664 entirely in-door paupers. Well, the Cavan Workhouse alone is capable of holding 1,234, so after receiving all the paupers in the above workhouses, it would still leave room in the Cavan Workhouse alone for 534 additional inmates.

14. That is a large margin?—Yes. Is there any other question you desire to put to me?

15. We are desirous of getting all the information we can, and knowing the grounds upon which the proposal for amalgamation has been made and submitted to the other Boards of Guardians. So far as you have stated, now, I take it that the sole ground was that the workhouse was capable of accommodating 1,234, when in point of fact, you would have only 664 if all the unions were united?—Yes; that is precisely the way the matter stands.

16. With reference simply to the question of accommodation?—Yes.

17. No other ground?—We have additional ground for 534, provided they were all in the house here.

18. That would appear so from your statement. Is there any other ground?—On the ground of economy—saving the rates and keeping down taxation. I would also suggest baronial divisions, if we carry amalgamation.

19. Well, it is time enough when the question of amalgamation is disposed of to refer to that. We are simply dealing with the question of amalgamation, and not of baronial divisions. Well, that is all I wish to say.

20. If it happened that the Cavan Workhouse had been built for, we will say 600, instead of 1,234, would you still desire amalgamation?—Certainly.

21. Upon what ground?—Provided the house was originally built for that number.

22. I say, suppose the workhouse had been built to accommodate 600 instead of 1,234, would you still be in favour of amalgamation?—I would. I would take it on this ground—that all the outlying houses would be proportionately smaller and contain a fewer number.

23. If the Cavan Workhouse could accommodate no more than 600, would you still propose amalgamation?—I am for the principle.

24. What principle?—The principle of economy.

CAVAN. Dec. 11, 1877.

Edward Kennedy, Esq.

25. I am at present speaking of the accommodation simply. If the Cavan Workhouse were capable of accommodating only 600, would you still, on the ground of having room, propose amalgamation?—I don't think there would be much necessity for it, for the cost of maintaining 600 would be smaller——

26. I repeat that I am speaking simply of the question of accommodation. You put your application for amalgamation upon the ground of having large spare accommodation?—Certainly.

27. I ask you, if you had not that large accommodation would you still propose amalgamation?—I would

28. Supposing the workhouse were only capable of accommodating 664, would you think it desirable to unite all the electoral divisions of this county without leaving any margin whatever for accidental purposes?—These are contingencies which are provided for in the memorial before you. We suggest that there still should be provision for fever cases, any contingencies like fever or epidemics, and that the nearest dispensary medical officer should get an increased salary for attending to that duty.

29. With reference to the Cavan Workhouse being capable of accommodating 1,234 inmates, what steps have you taken to ascertain whether that is an accurate calculation of the space?—The architect, I believe, has shown that. It was built to accommodate that number.

30. Have you any other evidence of the fact, or of the accuracy of the statement that the house is capable of accommodating 1,234 inmates, except the fact that it had been declared to be, at the period of the famine, capable of holding that number?—It is perfectly well known what every workhouse in Ireland is built to contain. I based my statement on that fact alone. That is a thing generally understood in every union.

31. Have you ever gone through the wards of this workhouse with a view of ascertaining?—No.

32. Are you a member of the visiting committee?—I am, but not for that purpose. I may inspect the house.

33. But surely the visiting committee is bound to examine and report upon the state of the house every week?—Yes, they do, but there is no necessity when they find things are going right.

34. How can they know things are going right if they don't examine them?—So they do very frequently.

35. I merely wish to know whether you had made this examination with a view of ascertaining whether that amount of accommodation is provided?—I have not. I did not think it was necessary.

36. This is the sheet (produced) which has been issued, and upon which the accommodation of this house is founded?—Yes.

37. Take, for example, room No 3 on that list. It is eighty feet by sixteen feet six inches?—Yes.

38. Would you look at the number of people stated to be accommodated in that. I think the number opposite it is ninety-five?—It is ninety-five.

39. Now, in a room eighty feet long and sixteen feet six inches wide, can you tell me how would you place ninety-five people?—I cannot tell you.

40. Do you think it would be possible to do it?—It has been done.

41. I see the figures "95," but what I ask you is—do you think it possible to place ninety-five human beings in a room eighty feet long to sleep?—I don't think it would be of adults, but the majority of the inmates in this house are juveniles.

42. But that room is one for adults?—Yes

43. I ask you would it be possible to place ninety-five adults in a room eighty feet long and sixteen feet in width to sleep in it?—I don't think it would.

44. It would appear, then, that the calculation of space upon which you rely is incorrect?—I did not calculate the space at all.

45. You took it for granted?—Yes

46. Suppose it was shown you, from careful examination of every room in the house, that you could not accommodate more than about 600, would you still be of opinion that this amalgamation should be carried out?—I would.

47. Without enlarging the workhouse?—We could not do it without enlarging the workhouse.

48. If the house was only built for 600, you must increase the size of the workhouse to carry out amalgamation?—I don't say that, for the great majority of the inmates are young

49. I referred to adults. I pointed out a room eighty feet long, which was said to be capable of accommodating ninety-five persons. I ask you, could you place in that room that number?—I could not say.

50. Could you place in that room more than thirty people?—I don't know. I respectfully submit that I don't think that at all affects the question embodied in that memorial. We go for amalgamation in a general manner. If it is carried it should be met, even if this house were bound to be cleared.

51. Just so. What I want to ascertain is whether or not the statement that this house is capable of accommodating 1,234 is borne out by the fact?—I fancy the Poor-Law Commissioners, at that time, would be the best authorities on the subject, for they were the parties who gave the order for the work to be done, and got the house built.

52. What I wish to ascertain from you, Mr. Kennedy, is this. If the workhouse were only capable of accommodating 600 inmates, would you still be in favour of amalgamation on the ground of accommodation?—I would; even if it went to the extent of enlarging the house.

53. Does any guardian present wish to put any question to Mr. Kennedy? If so, I will be very glad to put it for him?—(No answer).

54. Then we will leave the question of accommodation as it is. Have you, Mr Kennedy, made any calculation of the probable saving that would be effected by your proposed scheme?—I had not time

55. How long has this question of amalgamation been under consideration—since 1876?—Yes, and before that.

56. And yet you have not had time to make any calculation?—We wanted to sound the voice of the country on the principle, and I am happy to tell you we got affirmative answers from nearly every Board of Guardians in Ireland.

57. We may, for the moment, put aside the affirmative answers, and merely ask have you made any calculation of the financial effect of this amalgamation?—It would be a very difficult thing to do.

58. Either for Cavan Union or any of the other unions, have you any?—I have not.

59. Then you have represented that a considerable saving would be effected without having made any calculation to satisfy yourself that such would be the fact?—I think it is palpable to any person that it must be so. You must know it as well as myself, that amalgamation will lead to economy.

60. That is exactly one of the questions we must not assume?—I assume it.

61. You assume it, but are you prepared to give any reason for it?—The reason is that you have a staff of officers in every one of these houses who are comparatively idle—the houses being comparatively empty. I don't think it is fair to the ratepayers that these officials should be kept in these different workhouses doing nothing, if there is room for all the intern paupers to come into this house.

62. We must not assume that that is so—that there is room for them, until we have gone into the accommodation of the workhouse—not the accommodation as it is in these sheets, but the accommodation as is actually exists?—I know.

63. You say you are Chairman of the Finance Committee?—Yes.

64. Have you any idea of what the establishment charges are?—Mr. Grier, the clerk, will tell you.

65. I want to know have you any idea of the poundage for establishment charges?—I don't know.

66. Is it sixpence in the pound?—I don't know.

67. Mr. *Grier*.—It is not three halfpence

CAVAN
Dec 11, 1877.
Samuel Saunderson, Esq., J.P.

SAMUEL SAUNDERSON, Esq., J.P., examined.

68. You are a guardian of the Cavan Union?—Yes.

69. *Ex officio*?—Yes.

70. Did you sign the petition in favour of amalgamation?—No, I don't think I was here that day, but I was in favour of it.

71. Are you in favour of the proposed scheme of amalgamation of all the electoral divisions in the county Cavan?—Of all the electoral divisions of Cavan—no, but that is a matter of detail afterwards. I am in favour of amalgamation generally, but I have not considered the whole scheme in detail.

72. You have not considered that scheme?—No, it is only amalgamation generally. My idea is not amalgamation by which the other workhouses should be closed altogether. I say to unite the electoral divisions, but not to do away with the powers of other guardians in other divisions, not to exclude them from the trouble, but that everything should be conducted here. What I consider the great advantage of having amalgamation—of having a larger number or all the able-bodied paupers here is this—that first of all we are in a very central position; next, we have railways coming in on all sides from Belfast, Dublin, and other places, from which stores, coals, and other things are got, so that we ought to be able to provide them at a cheaper rate. At Cootehill there is another railway by which the workhouse there can be supplied, but Bawnboy Union is several miles away from any railway station, where, when they cannot get coals, they have to burn turf, which is a very expensive fuel. There would be a great saving that way. Of course, it would be necessary to have some provision for the sick paupers. I don't think the guardians ever meant that all the sick from all the unions should be brought here, only that the able-bodied should be brought in here and kept at a much lower rate than they are when they are scattered as they are now—that the staffs in the other unions may be reduced, I will say, to half—I will not say more than that.

73. You spoke of Bawnboy. Are you a representative of that union also?—No; I only spoke of it in illustration.

74. Then do I understand you to support the Cavan scheme of amalgamation?—Yes, to a certain degree.

75. All the four unions are embodied in the resolution of the guardians?—The guardians did not exactly enter into the particulars of how it should be done.

76. That is the question I should like to enter into with you?—Their whole object is to reduce the expenses.

77. Their whole object is to reduce the expense?—Certainly; but not at the expense of the poor of the county.

78. In fact the idea of your Board is this, that they can form a county union by amalgamating these various unions, and that that can be done without inflicting any hardship on the poor?—Exactly.

79. And that you will effect a considerable saving to the rates thereby?—Yes.

80. You are of opinion that that can be done without any hardship to the poor?—I think so.

81. As regards the saving to the rates, have you any idea of the amount that would be saved?—No, I was not aware until the other day that I would be examined, and I did not prepare any particulars, but those I will give you afterwards.

82. With regard to the practicability of the proposal, have you made any examination into details as to how it would work?—I can quite understand its practicability. I have not entered into details or figures as to the practicability of the matter. I don't see the least difficulty about it.

83. Would you allow me to ask would you dissolve Bailieborough Union, Cootehill Union, and Bawnboy Union?—If you tell me what you mean by dissolving them.

84. To do away with these unions completely, having one board for the county Cavan. Would you make that board absolutely a board of all the Cavan unions, or what is your meaning?—No, do you mean to dissolve the Boards of Guardians?

85. Yes, would you dissolve the other Boards of Guardians?—No.

86. Then you would still preserve the Boards of Guardians?—Certainly.

87. And do away with the workhouses?—There must be some provision for the sick and infirm.

88. I think it would be more satisfactory, as the petition which has been put in embodies the views of your board. I should then like to examine you upon it. Your resolution was:—

"That the petition adopted last June by the Cavan Board, with the addition of the sentence relating to fever hospitals, be sent to all the unions in Ireland, asking their co-operation, and that the petition on the subject, signed by all the guardians of this union, be forwarded to the county members."

That was the resolution of the 16th of last January; but the previous resolution appears to have been on the 25th April, 1876, and it runs as follows:—

"Resolved—That, owing to the great decrease of pauperism, a petition be presented to Parliament praying that the existing Poor Law be changed, so as to amalgamate the unions in this county, the Cavan Workhouse being sufficiently large to contain double the number of paupers in the county. Resolved—That a copy of this resolution be forwarded to every Board of Guardians in Ireland requesting their co-operation and support."

That, then, is the substance of your proposal as regards this county?—Yes.

89. I will now read the petition adopted by this board and presented to Parliament, and handed in by Mr. Grier:—

"To the Right Honourable and Honourable, the Knights, Burgesses, and Citizens of the United Kingdom of Great Britain and Ireland, in Parliament assembled.

"The Petition of the Guardians of the Poor of the Cavan Union, in the County of Cavan.

"Humbly Sheweth—That, immediately after the famine years—in the year 1850—the Poor Law Commissioners increased the number of poor-law unions in Ireland, and made additional provision for the reception of very large number of in-door paupers, to provide for circumstances which have never since arisen in this country, thus entailing a very large and unnecessary expenditure in the maintenance of union buildings and payment of workhouse officers, which, as it appears, might, to a great extent, have been avoided.

"That, at the present time, in consequence of the decrease of pauperism, through emigration and other causes, the accommodation for workhouse inmates is enormously in excess of the requirements of the country.

"That, in the opinion of your petitioners, one county workhouse would, in most instances, afford ample room for the paupers of such county.

"That, in order to provide against any epidemic, the present Union fever hospitals be kept open, and a moderate sum be paid the medical officers of the dispensary districts in which such fever hospitals are situate for attendance on the patients therein.

"That, in any cases in which a long journey to the workhouse might be injurious to persons of advanced age, the present system of out-door relief, judiciously administered, would meet such cases.

"That the workhouse of this Union is quite large enough to accommodate double the number of paupers receiving relief in the county of Cavan.

Your Petitioners therefore pray your Honourable House will cause a re-arrangement of the boundaries of poor-law unions in Ireland, so as very considerably to reduce the number of workhouses by making a central house for each county.

"And your Petitioners, as in duty bound, will ever pray.

"Signed on behalf of the Board of Guardians."

90. Mr. *Kennedy*.—That was passed unanimously by the board, there was no dissentient.

91. When we received your board's resolution in reply to our queries, the resolution not being as full in its expression as the petition, we referred to you on the subject, and we asked with reference to the views expressed, whether your board proposed that all the electoral divisions within the county Cavan should be united into one union, having one central house for such union, or whether the board simply proposed, without reference to the parts of the county situated in other unions, that the four unions named—viz., those of Bawnboy, Bailieborough, Cootehill, and Cavan—should be amalgamated. The answer we

CAVAN.
Dec. 11, 1877.
Samuel Saunderson, Esq., J.P.

received from your board was signed by Mr. Grier, clerk of the union. It was as follows:—

"In reply to your letter of the 10th instant, I am directed by the Board of Guardians to inform the Commissioners that the guardians intended in their resolution that all the electoral divisions in the county Cavan should be attached to one central house in the county."

That is the proposition put before us by the board, and that is the proposition we desire now to inquire into. I have asked you in connexion with it, whether such a proposition could be carried into effect without inflicting hardship on the poor, and your answer was that it could?—Yes.

92. You also said you thought it would produce certain advantages in saving the rates?—Yes.

93. But at present you are not able to give figures to say what the saving could be?—Yes.

94. I will now take the statements in your petition *seriatim*. First, it states—"That immediately after the famine years—in the year 1850—the Poor-Law Commissioners increased the number of poor-law unions in Ireland, and made additional provision for the reception of a very large number of in-door paupers, to provide for circumstances which have never since arisen in this country, and thus entailing a very large and unnecessary expenditure in the maintenance of union buildings and payment of workhouse officers, which it appears might to a great extent have been avoided. That, at the present time, in consequence of the decrease of pauperism, through emigration and other causes, the accommodation for workhouse inmates is enormously in excess of the requirements of the country." Have you any facts or statistics that you can state in reference to this statement?—Yes, in this workhouse now there are not half the number.

95. Mr. *Kennedy*.—There are 298 in this house at present.

96. (To witness).—The figures you draw your conclusions from are those representing the numbers now in the house, and the number this house has accommodated?—Yes; precisely.

97. There is a decrease of pauperism throughout the whole county mentioned here?—Yes.

98. Have you any figures applying to the whole county under this head?—The number in the house has decreased, and therefore that is a decrease of pauperism.

99. My question refers to the pauperism of the whole county?—In every house in the county it is so.

100. What steps have you taken to ascertain what the requirements of the county are?—Simply by adding the numbers in each house; 800 all over.

101. Did the clerk make inquiries for you?—Yes.

102. What is the present state of your house?—Between 200 and 300.

Mr. *Grier*.—298 last Saturday.

103. *Witness*.—The present numbers in all the unions is something under 800.

104. Is that in the four unions?—Yes.

105. Give me them in detail, by unions. How many are there in your own house?—283; and this number was made up of some who were admitted on the 1st and 9th inst.

106. How many in Bawnboy?—Sixty nine.

107. In Bailieborough?—148.

108. In Cootehill?—100.

109. In Enniskillen?—Nine of ours belonging to this county.

110. That is nine belonging to the electoral divisions of Enniskillen, in the county Cavan. Has that information been furnished to you by authority? Yes, by the Clerk of the Enniskillen Union.

111. Does that number include any proportion of the union at large paupers?—No; these are the actual paupers that would be transferred to us.

112. How many in Kells?—They have not produced the number for Kells.

113. How many in Granard?—Thirty-two.

114. Do the figures which you have given us for Bawnboy and Cootehill, refer exclusively to the parts of these unions within this county?—Yes; they have been furnished by the clerks of these unions, that is the only guarantee that they are correct.

115. You have given us a total of how many?—796.

116. Have you got this total subdivided into the various classes that paupers are always divided into—able-bodied males and females; aged and infirm males, aged and infirm females, &c.?—No.

117. Have you any information on this head?—No.

118. Then you have not gone into the question of their classification?—No.

119. But are you not aware that under the Poor Law rules paupers have to be separately accommodated by classes?—(No answer.)

120. Would you propose that each electoral division should return its elected guardians to look after its interests?—Certainly.

121. Do you know how many electoral divisions there are in the county?—(No answer.)

122. Our secretary tells me there are ninety-one divisions. I apprehend there would be one guardian for each?—There would be two for Cavan.

123. I suppose if we doubled this number we should have the number of the new board, that is including *ex officios*?—Yes, but in any of our statements we have not proposed that one board should meet here.

124. I am examining you on the proposal before us?—I don't think you will find it is proposed by it that the Board should meet here.

125. Your resolution would appear to contemplate it. It affirms that the workhouse of this union is adequate to accommodate the poor of the county, and recommends that the workhouses of Bailieborough and Bawnboy should be closed, but the hospitals kept up?—Yes.

126. I presume the general transaction of business would be at the board-room of the new union?—I don't think so. Of course the guardians here will correct me if I am not right, but I don't think we ever contemplated the getting of all the guardians to come here every week.

127. What did you contemplate?—It is a very simple arrangement. What I think we wished for was, that all the able-bodied (of course we exclude the sick, as we mentioned) paupers should be sent in here; that in the places where the houses were closed the guardians were to have their meetings, and send their paupers in here.

128. Do I understand you to say that you propose that the guardians should hold their meetings at their present workhouses?—No; the workhouses we propose to do away with, but to have hospitals.

129. For accidents and infectious diseases?—And for the infirm. There are poor feeble people who come here sometimes in a dying state. It would be impossible that such people could be removed here from a distance. But the persons who could come here would be persons likely to live for a long time—yet still infirm. In certain cases they should come here, and the other unions should be only charged with the actual cost of providing for them here, and of course with a fair proportion of household expenses. That is what we propose. We should leave all the unions to their own guardians to deal with such matters as out-door relief, their own contracts, &c. If, at the time of taking contracts here, it was necessary that they should come here, let them come here; but we never proposed to take away the responsibility from the other guardians.

130. In fact, you don't propose to dissolve the other boards?—No.

131. But you propose to retain only one workhouse for the county?—One workhouse.

132. And you now say that the other unions should still retain their boards, keeping separate accounts. Your proposal would now appear to be, simply that these other boards should "board out" their able-bodied paupers, or those capable of being removed here?—Yes.

133. Would you then propose that guardians from

CAVAN Dec. 31, 1877. — Samuel Sanderson, Esq., J.P.

those unions should serve on your board to watch the interests of their poor?—Well, that is, of course, a matter of detail, that they could attend if they wished; but simply we don't intend to interfere with their outdoor relief, or their provisions for the sick. All we propose is that we should take charge of their able bodied paupers and all the others who could come here.

134. I apprehend you are giving us your own views, after your own notion of what was intended, rather than explaining the views of the board as communicated to us?—Well, I think I am.

135. This idea of "boarding out" paupers, and keeping the other boards in existence is not the same as the proposition sent us. Have you any further remarks to offer in explanation of your "boarding out" scheme?—Any question you wish to ask me I shall be happy to answer.

136. Under your system what do you think the saving would be—I will take Bailieborough Union, from which you would bring the able-bodied paupers here. In the first place, may I ask do you know the proportion of able-bodied paupers in the house, and of infirm and sick?—No, I am not aware.

137. Are you not aware that the number of able-bodied paupers in every one of the workhouses in the north of Ireland is very small in proportion to the sick and infirm?—I am aware in this house—I have been over it constantly—and have seen that the number of sick and infirm who would not be able to be removed to a central house is small, and I believe it is the same in the other unions.

138. Supposing your scheme is carried out I want to know what saving would take place—say in the Bailieborough Union. Would you be able to dispense with the services of the chaplain there—would you have no religious services in the workhouse?—What I propose would be an infirmary, and there would be a chaplain still.

139. Then you would not do away with the chaplain—you would not save that expense?—We would save a great deal of expense.

140. Would you do away with the clerk of the union?—I believe each of these places could have a clerk for half the salary these officers are getting now.

141. Would you reduce the salary?—Yes.

142. In what way would you reduce the salary of the clerk—in what way would his duties be diminished?—I think they would be very much diminished.

143. Show me on what ground they would be diminished, because the clerk's duties are very little affected by the number in the house?—I think the clerk's duties are keeping the books, writing up accounts, and keeping an account of everything, and he has to attend daily.

144. He may have to attend daily, but it makes very little difference to the clerk of the union whether there are many or few in the workhouse?—I think the clerk will tell you differently.

145. Well, the clerk of the Bailieborough Union gets £80 a year; how much would you save of that?—I think if you got a man at £40 a year, he would do it then for that.

146. Would you do away with the master?—Yes, I think you could.

147. Would you do away with the matron?—No; you would require the matron.

148. You think the master might be done away with?—I do.

149. Well, we need not say much about the school masters for they are paid by Government grant. The medical officer would be retained?—Yes.

150. Would you have the porter retained?—I suppose not; I suppose he might be done without.

151. The infirmary nurse, would you retain her?—Yes.

152. The fever hospital nurse?—Yes.

153. The two relieving officers?—Yes.

154. And the rate collectors—of course they must be retained?—Yes.

155. These are all the officers in the Bailieborough Union. You say there might be some saving in the chaplain—you say the master might be dispensed with—and you say the clerk might be something cheaper—the whole thing would be under £100 a year if you could save all these?—My reason for saying you could save all this is—we have in this town an infirmary which has at present an average of about 40 patients. Well, I think that would be quite as many—would be a great deal more than in some of these places—and we carry it on with a very much reduced staff. We have no master; the matron does it all. We have three nurses in the infirmary, and one porter. We have our meetings there, and I think the thing could be carried on in exactly the same way in all these towns.

156. I went over this list of officers in the Bailieborough Union with you *seriatim*?—Yes.

157. And you gave me an answer as to the whole of them?—Yes.

158. And I don't think you could make any further reduction?—Well, supposing I say £100 a year, and I suppose the reduced cost of paupers to be another £100 a year—that would be a great saving of the rates of Bailieborough Union.

159. Did I understand you to say there would be a saving to the guardians?—If we had all the guardians together we could get our contracts cheaper. I think we could get our provisions here—being in the centre of the country, with railways from Belfast and other places—at a cheaper rate than in the other unions.

160. It is desirable that the exact scheme of the guardians should be understood. Were you in the room when Mr Kennedy was examined?—Only during the latter part of his evidence.

161. He said distinctly his scheme was the amalgamation of the whole of the unions in the county Cavan into one union. Do you agree to that proposal?—Yes, so far as I have stated.

162. Is your proposal to retain the several unions as they now exist, and simply to make this house a boarding-house for a certain class of paupers—as I understand that is your proposal?—I suppose it would come very nearly to that.

163. Would it not come absolutely to that?—Well, I suppose so.

164. Don't you see the difference between constituting all the unions one union, and simply retaining the workhouse of this union for a certain class of paupers who could be carried here, while you would be leaving the other unions as auxiliary unions for a class of persons who could not be carried to this house—that is your proposal?—Yes. Of course, we were not prepared with a scheme, and the necessary evidence cut and dry, as to what we propose, but we thought that by all the unions consulting together a great reduction could be made.

165. This scheme has been before the Board of Guardians of the Cavan Union since 1837. It has been more recently fully before the board in 1876 and 1877?—Yes.

166. Yet, Mr Kennedy says he has not had time to enter into a calculation of the expenses. What I want to know is whether you have had time to come to any agreement as to what you mean? Mr Kennedy thinks that he meant one union for the whole county. You state that you mean four unions for the whole county, with one workhouse for one purpose, and three workhouses for other purposes. Is not that a fair statement of Mr Kennedy's proposal and yours?—I think Mr. Kennedy and myself agree. You call them workhouses—we call them infirmaries.

167. Mr. Kennedy does not agree with you, inasmuch as he would dissolve the whole of the other unions—Bawnboy, Bailieborough, and Cootehill?—I think if you explain to Mr Kennedy what you mean by dissolving the other unions, you will find that is not so. I don't think Mr. Kennedy ever meant that all the responsibility should be taken from the other unions.

Mr *Kennedy*.—No.

Cavan.
Dec. 12, 1877.
Samuel Saunderson, Esq., J.P.

168. Then you did not mean a scheme of amalgamation; it is not an amalgamation of unions, but simply what may be called an amalgamation of one class of paupers in this workhouse?—Well, yes; but we consider that that is an amalgamation of unions, if we get their paupers here.

169. Do you consider it an amalgamation of unions if you only bring one class of paupers to this workhouse, leaving the other paupers in the other workhouses, and not at all interfering with the electoral divisions of the other unions. Is that your idea of amalgamation?—Certainly, we don't confine ourselves so that we must not interfere with other unions at all, because when it becomes practically worked out, we would find that parts of other unions lie in here, and that they should all come out to form the county union. That is for after-consideration.

170. Are you prepared to state whether or not you mean to amalgamate—that is to reconstitute the union by taking in—by absorbing—into the Cavan Union the electoral divisions which now constitute the other three unions in the county?—So far as I have stated, most decidedly yes.

171. But what you have stated is, that you desire to leave the whole responsibility of their local administration to the other boards of guardians—that is, to leave them as they are now?—Certainly.

172. And simply to make this a boarding-house for their paupers?—Yes.

173. Of a particular class?—Of all the paupers of the county—able bodied——

174. Exactly that this should be constituted a workhouse for a certain class?—Yes.

175. And that there should be four boards of guardians still existing, and that the four unions should be represented by these four boards of guardians?—Yes.

176. That is your idea of amalgamation?—Yes.

177. Those numbers which you gave us—69 for Bawnboy, 148 for Bailieborough, and so on, represent the entire number of inmates in those houses, and not the able-bodied only?—Yes.

178. I thought you gave those as the actual numbers you proposed to transfer first?—No.

179. Excepting only those who remained suffering from accidents or infectious disease?—Precisely; and of course any one in a bad state, in a dying state, who could not be removed.

180. Then you would keep up the whole machinery of the other unions, except those few officials you mentioned in connexion with Bailieborough, for care of the sick and those suffering from infectious diseases and occupying the accident ward?—The infirmary I think I said—not the whole of the staff of the other unions.

181. With the exception of those you then specified, you would retain all the officers?—Yes, all those which were found absolutely necessary to conduct an infirmary where there would be a very small number of people.

182. It would still be within the discretion of the several boards of guardians whether they would retain certain officers or whether they would not retain them in the several unions?—Certainly.

183. If they found it necessary to retain the clerk of Bailieborough Union at £60 a year, it would be perfectly competent for the guardians to do so, and not to reduce it to £40 at your suggestion?—Yes. We don't want them to do so. The simple object of the Cavan guardians was to reduce the rates in every way we thought it could be done—in as simple a form as possible.

184. What benefit do you think would accrue to the Cavan Board of Guardians from this, in any point of view—for you get no increased valuation to support your establishment expenses?—I beg your pardon, we get all these paupers here, and of course all the other unions will have to bear their expenses.

185. They will pay you for nothing but their charge here, but you will get no increased establishment expenses?—Oh, certainly.

186. How can you. Your union remains the same, and you will only have the same area to bear the establishment expenses?—I beg your pardon, each of the paupers from the several unions will be charged for.

187. You don't understand, apparently, what I mean. I say the valuation remains exactly as it is at the present time?—Certainly.

188. And it is the same valuation that bears the establishment charges?—Certainly.

189. Will you get any increased valuation for that purpose?—I don't think you quite understand me. Suppose we have 300 paupers additional in here. Each of these paupers cost about 3s. 3d. a week per head. Along with that, we will charge a certain percentage in the way of household charges; and won't that reduce our charges.

190. That is another point, but I say, with regard to the valuation of your union, it would remain just as it is at present?—Yes.

191. Suppose you have a staff of six officers, and that you have to pay them—we will take in illustration—£400 a year. That is raised on the rateable value of the Cavan Union—that would continue to be raised on the rateable value of the Cavan Union?—No.

192. On what rateable value?—Upon those paupers.

193. It would be raised on the rateable value, and as counterbalancing that you calculate on a certain source of profit, 3d., 4d., or 6d., or whatever it would be, but the whole of your rateable value would continue to be exactly the same as that on which you would raise your £400 a year. But your whole profit—whatever the amount—would consist of a capitation profit?—Precisely. I suppose we would not require to raise £400 a year if we got a capitation profit.

194. You think the capitation profit would make a sensible help?—A sensible help to the ratepayers.

195. Have you made any calculation of the addition the actual cost of maintenance would make. Would it be more than sixpence per head?—I have not entered into these particulars. That must be a matter of arrangement hereafter.

196. Do you not know that at present there is no legal power to allow you to bring paupers from other unions?—Yes, and that was the reason we sent forward this petition.

197. You would have the law altered in order to give you power to give non-resident relief, for they would be removed to this union from the other unions?—Yes, but they would be all in this county.

198. Have you made inquiry from the other unions whether they would be consenting parties to your proposition?—No. I believe several of them are not consenting parties.

199. Have you studied the matter as regards its effects upon the poor—those requiring relief, and the distances they would have to travel to obtain it?—Yes.

200. We will take the electoral division of Kells, which is in this county?—Yes.

201. Do you know how far that electoral division is from its own workhouse?—The nearest point in the county Cavan is about four miles, and I suppose the farthest point is about eight.

202. Do you know how far that electoral division is from your workhouse?—Well, the farthest point is about twenty miles.

203. Taking the centre of it, it is twenty-seven. Do you think it would be for the benefit of the poor of that electoral division to have amalgamation?—I do. If they were able to come here I don't think there would be the least difficulty in bringing them here; if there was a proper vehicle I think the very farthest point of the Cavan Union is not so far as twenty-seven miles from here.

204. Take the Crossbane electoral division of the Bailieborough Union. I see by a return I have before me that it is seven miles from Bailieborough, and twenty-three from this; that Enniskeen is two and half miles from its own workhouse, and twenty-seven miles from this; do you think amalgamation in

CAVAN *Dec. 11, 1877.* Samuel Saunderson, Esq.

these cases would be advantageous?—That is the farthest; that may be very favourable to the Bailieborough house, and unfavourable to this.

205. Take the nearest one—Termon, it is thirteen miles from this, and nine miles from its own house? Well, we bring paupers longer distances than that at present. It would be no great hardship to paupers.

206. Enniskillen ought also be considered. How would you manage about the paupers from that union?—We have a railway direct from Enniskillen.

207. Would you propose to send your paupers by rail?—If it were found necessary—yes.

208. Would you propose that the Enniskillen Union should retain its workhouse?—Oh there are only nine of our paupers there, and the taking of them would not influence the workhouse there at all.

Mr. JAMES DUIGNAN examined. Mr. Duignan.

209. Are you an elected guardian of this union?—Yes.

210. For what electoral division?—Killeshandra.

211. How long have you been connected with the Poor-Law?—I think I must appeal to the clerk—three, four, or five years, I think.

212. You have a good knowledge of this question, and of the wants of the county?—I have what they call a natural knowledge; I don't know whether it is efficient or not. There is something natural about it, and I want to express myself about it.

213. You have heard these resolutions read, I think?—Yes.

214. I believe you are one of the parties who signed the petition to Parliament?—Yes.

215. You therefore are in favour of the proposal to form a "county" union?—Yes.

216. In fact for extending the area of taxation of what we may call the new Cavan Union over the whole county?—Yes.

217. Can you tell me the valuation, population, and area of the present Cavan Union?—I cannot indeed.

218. I may then tell you that the area of your present union is 160,662 acres; the population 53,556, and the valuation is £112,802. The new union proposed would have an area of 466,220 acres (the whole area of the county), the population 140,735, and the area of taxation you propose would be considerably more than double what it is at present—it would be £271,918. Were you on this board when it presented a petition to Parliament in 1857?—Yes.

219. That petition was, as you are aware, very much in the same terms as the last petition. As you have, I understand, taken an active part in this movement, you are aware, I presume, that repeated resolutions have been passed on this subject?—Yes.

220. Both before and during 1876?—Yes.

221. I think also that you have, with the view of calling public attention to the subject in Ireland, circulated the proposal embodied in your board's petition to Parliament among all the other unions in Ireland?—Yes, I think so.

222. Do you know how they received it?—I do not.

223. Do you know how many of them approved of it?—I do not.

224. By a paper I have before that seventeen of them did so. You are aware that considerable efforts were made to call the attention of the public to your scheme, and that the Cavan proposal is practically the one before the country?—Yes.

225. Are you of opinion that that proposal could be carried out really without inflicting any hardship on the poor of the county Cavan?—Yes.

226. Would good financial results be attained?—Yes.

227. Have you any figures to show the financial results you expect?—I don't say I can show figures, but I can show common sense.

228. At present your poundage on establishment charges is $2\frac{1}{4}d$ in the pound; your cost of maintenance need not be considered. It is the cost of establishment that is mainly affected by amalgamation?—Yes.

229. Do you believe that by the proposed extension of this union you would materially reduce this charge?—Yes.

230. What are the requirements of this county as regards the accommodation for paupers—will you take the answer given by Mr. Saunderson as correct, from what he stated the number at present accommodated would appear to be 796?—Yes.

231. Then you say 796 is the number you would accommodate here?—I am not with Mr. Saunderson there.

232. Did he not give the actual number?—He gave his own opinion.

233. He gave the figures which the clerk said were correct?—Well, I will give you figures.

234. Do so, and state the number in the county to be relieved, and for whom accommodation would be required.—I agree with Mr. Saunderson as to these figures of the number to be relieved. That was perfectly right.

235. Would you also propose that each electoral division should keep its representatives?—I would.

236. Then the number of elected representatives to manage the working of this great county union would be the number of elected guardians of electoral divisions in the county?—Yes.

237. With a corresponding number of *ex officios*?—Oh, I don't know.

238. The Board would consist of these elected guardians and the *ex officio* guardians. You who are so well acquainted with the working of the poor-law, do you not know that it is administered by elected and *ex officio* guardians in equal proportion?—Indeed I am aware that there are elected guardians and that there are *ex officio* guardians. The question is, you want to put them on a level, and I don't understand their being on a level. We see there is a certain number of elected and a certain number of elected by way of parallel or equal number.

239. You are aware that under the regulations of the poor-law the numbers are the same?—I never knew that before. I am very glad to hear it. That is information I never knew indeed.

240. You are aware, therefore, that the number of guardians for this great union would be over 180—twice ninety-one?—Yes.

241. Have you made any inquiry what effect this proposal of yours would have on the aged, infirm, and sick requiring relief?—I have contested the thing in my own mind, and I think it would be a benefit to the farmers and the ratepayers of the county to have amalgamation, and I think the poor would not suffer in the slightest degree, by establishing or keeping a room and a dispensary doctor to attend it, and a lady to attend it—we may say woman—you may give her what title you like; and the infirm and sick could be entertained there until they would be forwarded here, and if not, of course they would have the doctor to send them to heaven or elsewhere as well as in the workhouse. That is the effect of it now, if you had what you would call in the advertisement a good matron or woman.

242. In fact you would appoint a good woman or matron to assist the dispensary doctor to look after the sick and all hospital cases in the outlying unions?—I would make the dispensary doctor do it; I would have to pay the woman, of course, but that is all I would do.

243. Would you not increase the dispensary doctor's salary?—Yes, we might give him something.

244. How are your sick and infirm conveyed to this house at the present time?—Why, they walk some of them.

245. Supposing they cannot walk, how do you convey them?—We have a car or cart.

246. And horse?—Yes.

247. You have a car and horse here for the purpose of conveying the sick and infirm requiring relief?—Yes.

CAVAN
Dec 12, 1877
Mr. Duignan

248. How would you provide for the transmission of these sick and infirm, of the same class that now uses your horse and cart, from the more distant parts of the county?—Well, I live in Killeshandra, nine miles away, and I sent four children here last Saturday.

249. Is that your own division?—Yes. I wrote for the car here, and the car came out for them.

250. But there are many electoral divisions which are at a much greater distance from this workhouse. How would you provide for bringing the sick, aged, or infirm from these places—would you have cars for each district?—No; none but the one car.

251. Do you think one car would do the work of the entire county?—I admit there might be a letter this morning, perhaps two letters, and the car could not go to the two places the same day, but I think it could go the day following. I think the horse is often idle here, and that he has not to go more than once a week—fifty-two days a year—and we have to feed the horse.

252. Now with regard to the conducting of the business of your proposed union, do you think the attendance of guardians would be good?—Yes.

253. From distant electoral divisions?—I do. I think every division should have its own to look after.

254. And you think the gentlemen from the distant parts of the county would come here and attend regularly?—Oh, yes, what would ail them.

255. Would you have the relieving officers to attend here on board days?—I think so.

256. You would continue that rule. But do you think it would be possible for the relieving officers in charge of distant electoral divisions to attend here?—If the guardians would attend I don't think it would be necessary for them, and if they would not, I don't know how the poor would be minded then.

257. Then you would not propose a change in the law to render it unnecessary for the relieving officer to attend the Board?—No, I think it is necessary he should attend here.

258. Do you think that the applicants for relief from the distant parts of the county should attend also, and appear before the Board?—No, it is not necessary for them to attend. They don't attend here; they have not to apply here; the guardians represents that class of people in need of relief.

259. Of relief in the house?—No, of those outside.

260. I am speaking of those applying for relief and whose admission into the house may be ordered, would you cause them to attend here?—I don't understand you. I don't see how those who apply for admission to the house, could get into it before they come to it.

261. Then you would have all applicants for relief come before the Board as usual?—No, I am at a loss there.

262. Surely, every time you have a Board day here, you are aware that all the cases for admission are brought before the Board?—Yes.

263. And the people are there to appear if called upon?—Yes.

264. Then you would continue that system. You would have them from all parts of the country to attend?—Yes, I would bring them there, and just exhibit them.

265. You would bring them here?—Yes, I say I would have them attend there. I would be anxious to see them there, to see whether they really were destitute.

266. In your petition you say this house is adequate to accommodate double the number of paupers receiving relief within the county. What accommodation do you consider it affords—for 1,234 is not it?—Yes.

267. Your answer is 1,234?—Yes.

268. You have given us the gross number, can you subdivide that number under the different classes—able-bodied male and female; aged male and female, hospital, infirmary, &c.?—I cannot.

269. Have you ascertained the feeling of any of the other guardians or boards on the subject of amalgamation?—I have.

270. Had you communication with those at Bailieborough, Bawnboy, and Cootehill?—I will not say I had with all, but with some.

271. And did they express their willingness?—Yes.

272. The boards?—I did not say the boards, I say the guardians I spoke to, they joined in the opinion I had possessed, and do possess at the present time, upon amalgamation, but I did not meet the guardians of this division or that division outside of Cavan.

273. Your communications were private?—Yes.

274. With individual guardians. You were not acting on the part of this Board in communicating with the others?—No.

275. Your petition goes on to say, "That in any cases in which a long journey to the workhouse might be injurious to persons of advanced age the present system of out-door relief, *judiciously administered*, would meet such cases." Is that your opinion?—Yes.

276. Can you describe to us what you consider "a judiciously administered system of out-door relief?"—I do not understand you.

277. The words of your petition are, "The present system of out-door relief, *judiciously administered*, would meet such cases." Will you give me your idea of a judiciously administered system of out-door relief?—I will as far as I can, of course. I told you, I think, before that I sent for the car last week, and sent four children here.

278. That was for in-door relief, for admission into the house?—It was.

279. We are speaking of out-door relief, to which your petition especially alludes?—Very well.

280. These four children were for in-door relief?—They were.

281. Then that case does not illustrate the question. I want to know what you would recommend about out-door relief?—Well, I approve of it.

282. You approve of out-door relief generally?—Yes.

283. Do you know how many cases of out-door relief there are in Cavan Union?—I do not indeed.

284. Would you say there are fifty people in the whole union receiving relief out of the workhouse?—Above that.

285. Are there 100?—I think so.

286. Are there 200?—I think not. I think Cavan has eighty-two or eighty-six.

287. What are the class of persons to whom you give out-door relief?—The persons who need relief.

288. Of course you would not give it unless you considered that they wanted it. Take, for instance, a widow, without any belongings, having no friends to maintain her. What would you allow her?—All I would give would be one shilling.

289. Would she have no other means of subsistence?—I think not.

290. How could she live on that shilling?—She could get some little off her neighbours.

291. What would pay her rent?—I calculate that all these have free houses.

292. And that no part of that shilling goes to the payment of rent?—In very few cases.

293. And if it be stated here that that shilling has gone, in point of fact, for the payment of rent, do you believe that that would be an inaccurate statement? Is it a fact or not?—Well, I have no doubt there are some who may have to pay a shilling a week.

294. Have you any doubt there are a great number of poor people who are receiving 1s. a week from this union, and that that 1s. is for the rent of their cottages?—No, I would not say that. There are some cases where they have to pay 1s. a week, but not many.

295. They are not a very considerable number?—No.

296. How many do you relieve in the town of Cavan alone, or what is the weekly relief given by the relieving officer in the town of Cavan alone?

297. Mr. *Kennedy*.—It generally costs £18 to £20 a week.

298. It is upon an average 1s. a week per head?

299. Mr. *Kennedy*.—In some cases it is 2s.

300. Mr. *Saunderson*.—But Mr. Duignan says he would only give 1s. a week.

301. I will take the average at 1s. a week, we should say the average would be only 9½d a week. Well, we will now take the case of Mary Wear, a widow with four children, that is five in a family. (To witness).—What would you give that family to live upon?—I will tell you. That will depend greatly on the circumstances how I know that she can exist.

302. Suppose she had no ostensible means of living—what would you give her for herself and her four children?—I think I would give them 5s.—one shilling each.

303. And you think if the guardians only gave 3s. that it would be inadequate relief—would you consider that to be sufficient?—I would not.

304. Well, it happens to be 3s. a week that they give. I will take 200 cases out of this list of 250, where the parties are only getting on an average 1s. a week. Now, here is the case of James Gorman, who has a family of seven children. In the case of a man stricken down by illness, with a family of seven children, what would you call judicious relief to that family of eight?—That depends on the circumstances. Was the wife capable of doing anything?

305. There was no wife?—God help him.

306. What I want to know is this. Here is a man stricken down by sickness, with a family of seven children. We are inquiring into what is the system of judicious relief that you would like to give the benefit of to the other unions in this county. There is a family of eight—what would you consider judicious relief in that case?—I would think 12s. a week would be little enough.

307. Then you would add 9s. 6d. to the sum that family is actually getting. That family is actually getting only 2s. 6d. What is the system under which you think the poor of this union could be judiciously relieved at the rate of 1s. per head per week to persons having no other means of existence?—Having no other means of existence?

308. Yes, having no other means of existence?—Oh, I would give 1s. 6d.

309. If they had no other means of existence?—Oh, I think you are robbing me of my own knowledge there.

310. The relieving officer will tell by-and-by whether the fact be so or not—that the poor applying to this union for relief, when they have nothing else to live upon, they get 1s. a week—that the circumstances of the case are stated to this board that they want the relief, and that it is given in most cases for the payment of the rent. Is not that so?

Mr. Kennedy.—It is.

311. Is it not the fact that the 1s. a week is really given to the paupers for the payment of rent?

Witness.—No; not in my district.

312. But in your district it is, Mr. Kennedy.

Mr. Kennedy.—It is.

313. *Mr. Saunderson.*—I may say that I have attended this board very often, and I never heard that before—that the 1s. a week was given for the payment of rent.

314. They appear to be getting it every day. Now, Mr. Duignan, when I asked you how they could live on 1s. a week, you answered me, with the assistance of their neighbours. Is it not the fact that the 1s. a week is given to many poor people who are obliged to beg their subsistence in addition? Is that so within your knowledge?—No, it is not.

315. And if the relieving officer states that the 1s. a week is given in point of fact to people who beg through the country—is that, within your knowledge, the fact or not?—It would not be the fact. As a guardian, I would not give a shilling a week to a beggar.

316. But you would give the 1s. a week to persons who had no other means of making out a subsistence except by the kindness of their neighbours?—Yes.

317. You think they could live upon the kindness of their neighbours and your 1s. a week?—Yes; and by their own exertions.

318. Here is a woman on this list named Biddy Fitzpatrick, who gets 1s. a week. She is eighty years of age. What exertion could that woman make?—She and her husband get 2s.

319. There is no husband. She is disabled—tell me how does she live on that 1s. a week?—I know nothing about her.

320. *Mr. James Reilly.*—She is begging.

321. That is an illustration. Am I not quite right then in saying that the 1s. a week is given in relieving mendicants? A gentleman states that the woman is begging.

322. *Mr. Reilly.*—There are seven receiving relief in that division. She is the only one that is begging.

323. I happened to light upon the case in which a woman could not obviously make any exertion. That is the history of many cases in which I apprehend it will be found that the 1s. a week is given in aid of begging. Perhaps one has said enough at present to ascertain what is meant by a judicious system of out-door relief—given partly for the payment of rent, and partly to assist people in begging—altogether insufficient to maintain any poor person who has no other means of existence. Two-and-sixpence is given where you yourself admit 12s. would be adequate relief—2s. 6d. is the amount given for a family of eight people?—I mean for the eight people 12s.

324. Yes; but the guardians differ from you. They give only 2s. 6d.?—That may be quite clear, and I will explain it to you in a moment. In the town of Killeshandra, where I live, you will get a man and his wife and two or three children. The wife is a grand knitter, and can knit and earn money. The poor man may have no employment, and he makes application to the guardians upon the question of his distress. He will get a document signed by six or seven ratepayers of the electoral division, saying he wants out-door relief. He won't get the out-door relief until the ratepayers sign that, and then let the ratepayers pay.

325. Then the relief is given upon the certificate or requisition of the six or seven ratepayers?—Yes, with my own judgment. Then I give them 2s. a week—1s. for himself and 1s. for his wife. Of course if he has a family I give them an additional sum. I find that he and his wife can live very comfortably on that 2s. a week. The wife will come and buy thread from your humble servant to knit, and then she gets money for her work; and have we the right to saddle the guardians with the cost of keeping these people altogether, when the wife can earn money that way?

326. I want to know whether the relief is given after examination of the case by the relieving officer, or upon examination of the case by a number of ratepayers?—It is by the wisdom and prudence of the guardians.

327. Well, then, that is what you consider a judicious system of out-door Poor-Law relief—that a number of ratepayers sign a memorial in favour of some persons in their district or electoral division getting relief, and that the guardians are bound to attend to that?—I believe they are, because they (the ratepayers) have to pay the money.

328. Do you think that the scheme proposed would increase the amount of out-door relief to be given in the country on account of the distance from this house?—No, I don't think it would. We have four houses in the county Cavan, and we have officers and ladies and gentlemen in the four houses, and here we have a house which it is represented to me will accommodate 1,200. Isn't it a monstrous thing, and a hardship on us, to let us have one house at Cootehill, another at Bawnboy, and so on, when there is no necessity for them—when there is one house here capable of accommodating double the number of paupers. It is said that the officers in these places must be allowed compensation. Well, I know that that compensation would take away a great deal of the saving, but then, when these people would disappear out of this world, would not the next generation be free from the burthen of taxation, and what we are labouring under at present.

CAVAN
Jan 11, 1877.
Mr Duignan.

CAVAN.
Dec. 11, 1877.
Mr. Duignan.

329. Still you would consider it reasonable to give compensation?—I don't know. I don't think I have a right to go into that.

330. Would not you think it reasonable to give compensation in such a case as that?—I am with you in that.

331. Do you happen to know the case of an officer of a union, who served a union for as long as twenty-seven years, who broke down in the service of the Board of Guardians, who applied for a superannuation allowance and was refused, and who is now an inmate of the workhouse of that union. Do you know that case?—I do.

332. The matron of this workhouse. Is it a fact that the late matron of this workhouse is now an inmate as a pauper of this workhouse, after a period of twenty seven years' service?—Well, I understand she is.

333. But still you think it would be only reasonable to allow such compensation or superannuation allowance to officers who would lose their appointments by this amalgamation?—Aye; and how did she lose her appointment?

334. By having served you too long, and, perhaps, too assiduously?—Too long!

335. Twenty-seven years is a long period?—It certainly is so.

336. Well, we will leave it as it is?—I think it is better for you too.

337. Are you unable to say in any way, what the saving would be either to this union or to the other unions of the county by amalgamation, have you any calculation; can you show the amount of the poundage that would be saved in any one case—the Cavan Union or the others?—I am unable to show you that, but I will show you why amalgamation would be a saving. You have servants in four houses, and you would do away with them——

338. I want to know have you any figures to lay before us?—I have not.

339. Mr. *John Nixon*, J.P.—Would the Commissioners ask this gentleman how he proposes to bring paupers from Blacklion (Eskey) here?

340. You know the electoral division of Eskey (Blacklion). How would you propose to bring paupers from that division here. It is on the borders of the county Cavan?—(*Witness*) I would have a little covered cart.

341. Do you know the distance they would have to travel to come here?—I do not.

342. Thirty-eight miles?—Exactly.

343. How long would you expect them to be on the road?—I would convey them here in the twenty-four hours.

344. Mr. *Nixon*.—Why, I left home yesterday morning, and I only got here last night by train.

345. *Witness*.—You might not have one case there in six months—there might be one solitary case there in the six months—and you have a horse and cart that could bring them.

346. Mr. *Nixon*.—Will you kindly take the division of Dowra, in the Enniskillen Union.

347. The average of the centre of Dowra I find put down at about thirty-four miles.

348. Mr. *Nixon*.—And that is across the mountains.

349. Yes, that is by the mountain road, it would be more coming round by Swanlinbar and Florence Court.

350. Mr. *Nixon*.—It would be forty miles by Swanlinbar.

351. You would bring poor persons that distance to this house for relief?—(*Witness*) I would bring them fifty miles, and keep them comfortable too. Of course there would be an hospital, and it would be understood the dispensary doctor would attend the infirm—that is, those who would not be able to travel.

352. In their own houses?—In Bawnboy, Cootehill, and so forth.

John Nixon, Esq.

JOHN NIXON, Esq., examined.

353. You are an *ex officio* member of the Enniskillen Union?—Yes, and many years an elected guardian of the Enniskillen Union.

354. You have heard the proposal to amalgamate all the unions in this county into one for poor-law purposes?—Yes.

355. As a representative of Enniskillen Union, will you tell us your opinion of this proposal?—I can only talk as regards these eight divisions. It would be a very great hardship on the poor and sick, and on the ratepayers generally. The guardians could not attend here. It would not be possible. We require to leave home the day before to come here, and would get back late at night. Our rates are low, and we are satisfied. The elected guardians are quite unanimous in wishing to remain with Enniskillen, and I think if the ratepayers of the electoral divisions were polled, they would elect to remain with Enniskillen; and we come here to protest against any change being made.

356. Did you receive any communication from the Cavan Board regarding this proposition, and asking your adhesion to it?—Yes.

357. Did you return an answer?—I am not aware.

358. Was the subject discussed at your board?—Yes.

359. And was the resolution arrived at that you should attend here and protest against it?—Yes.

360. Have you anything further to add?—Yes.

361. Mr. *Saunderson*.—Does he represent the board, or are these his own individual opinions?

362. Do I understand you to say that you are deputed by the board?—Yes; I am deputed by the board, and I know the opinion of the eight elected guardians of these divisions, and I know the opinion of the ratepayers.

363. Your board is what you represent?—The board could not interfere.

364. You are here as the representative of your board, and of the eight divisions of your union situated in this county?—Yes.

365. There are two schemes—one for amalgamating all the unions, and the other for merely making this a boarding-house. Do their objections apply equally to both of those proposals?——

366. Mr. *Saunderson* (handing in document).—I will ask you to read that communication from the Enniskillen Board of Guardians to our Board of Guardians.

367. This appears to be an official document received from the clerk of the Enniskillen Poor-Law Union, and addressed to the clerk of this union:—

"Poor-Law Office, Enniskillen,
"10th May, 1877.

"William Henry Morrison, clerk of Union, executive sanitary officer and superintendent registrar,

"To Joseph D. Grier, Esq., clerk of the Union, Cavan.

"SIR,—The Board of Guardians of the Enniskillen Union had under consideration at their meeting yesterday, the resolution on the subject of amalgamation adopted by the Board of Guardians of the Cavan Union at their meeting on the 25th ult., when it was moved by Mr. Jeremiah Jordan, seconded by Mr. George Wills, and unanimously resolved—that this board approves of the principle of amalgamation, and directs their clerk to inform the Cavan Board of Guardians of their sympathy with them in the movement.

"By order,
"WILLIAM HENRY MORRISON."

368. *Witness*.—Quite so; that refers altogether to amalgamation with the Irvinestown Union and the Lisnaskea Union, and not at all with the Cavan Union.

369. That is a resolution in favour of the principle of amalgamation?—In favour of the principle.

370. Not in favour of this scheme?—Not in favour of this scheme.

371. Mr. *Saunderson*.—That is the communication from the Enniskillen to the Cavan Board.

372. *Witness*.—We approve of amalgamation, but not of these schemes. Of course, I speak of the amalgamation with Cavan.

CAVAN. *Dec. 11, 1877.*

James Bracken, Esq.

JAMES BRACKEN, Esq., *ex officio* guardian, examined.

373. You are an *ex officio* guardian of the Enniskillen Union?—Yes; and I have been an elected guardian.

374. You have heard the proposition that has been put before this Commission?—Yes, I have.

375. What is your opinion of the effect it would have on the portion of Enniskillen proposed to be put in this county union?—I was asked at the last board meeting (Lord Belmore in the chair), with Mr. Nixon, to attend here as a deputation, and protest against it. That was passed unanimously. I have spoken to several of the elected guardians of these eight divisions, and they think it would be most injurious. I spoke to them at Enniskillen on Tuesday last.

376. On Tuesday last the subject was brought before your board, and they unanimously passed a resolution asking Mr. Nixon and you to represent them here?—Yes.

377. And you say to protest against the proposal?—Against these eight divisions being put into this union.

378. What about is the distance of these divisions?—The distance from Enniskillen is about ten Irish miles.

379. And the distance from Cavan?—Would be about forty.

380. Would that be over the mountains or coming round by road?—By coming round by the road. The Enniskillen Guardians were always of opinion it would be wise to put part of Irvinestown and Lisnaskea into their own.

381. Then what I understand you to say the guardians approved of was not amalgamation with the Cavan Union, but an extension of their own?—Yes, by taking a slice off Lisnaskea and Irvinestown.

The Lord of Dartrey.

The Earl of DARTREY examined.

382. You are Chairman of the Cootehill Union?—I am.

383. The subject of amalgamation has been brought before your board?—Yes; and was fully discussed.

384. I see by the papers that returned to us by your board, that you expressed an opinion at that time. Shall I read it?

Witness.—If you please.

385. Lord Dartrey having been asked as Chairman of the Cootehill Board of Guardians, "whether, having regard to the extent, population, necessities of the sick and destitute poor, and Poor Law in the union of Cootehill, it would be expedient to dissolve such union and amalgamate it with any of the adjoining unions; and if so, what portions should be annexed to each of such adjoining unions,"—answered—

"I am of opinion that it would not be expedient to dissolve the union of Cootehill.

"First, because there are very few facilities for the inhabitants of the union to communicate with the poor-houses in the adjoining unions, Castleblayney being the only one with which there is direct railway communication, and even that is at a considerable distance, so that the attendance of guardians from the Cootehill district would be very uncertain, and we should practically have no control over the expenditure of our rates, and the management generally of our Poor-Law business would be left in the hands of the guardians of the other unions.

"Secondly, there would be little or no saving of expenditure, for though something might be economised in the salaries of officers, there must be considerable outlay in conveyance of paupers and travelling expenses of relieving and other officers that must be retained. Also it would be financially objectionable for us to be aggregated to other unions where the rates are higher than in our own, as is the case in all the surrounding unions.

"Lastly, it would be extremely grating to the feelings of the poor to be removed so far from the locality where all their friends reside, and in the case of patients who ought to resort to the fever hospital, the distance would be a positive bar to their making use of it, and consequently there would be great danger of the spread of infection through the patients remaining with their families in their own homes."

386. Are we to understand, my lord, that this is your opinion upon the subject of amalgamation generally?—I should wish to state that before I sent off that reply to the Commissioners I read it out to the Cootehill Guardians, and the board were unanimous in approving of the opinion therein contained. As to the statement respecting the average rates in our union—during the past seven years they vary from 6*d.* to 8½*d.* in the pound. The average rate at present over the whole union is 8½*d.* in the pound, and I think that that being the case it is clear that we are lower rated than any of the coterminous unions in either the counties Cavan or Monaghan, and therefore it would not be for the advantage of the ratepayers to be financially associated with any of them. There is another remark I beg leave to make—that is, that there appears to me to be a very great discrepancy between the idea of amalgamation, as originally put forth, and some of the schemes we have heard mentioned in this room, but whichever scheme might be adopted I am satisfied that the difficulty, expense, and inconvenience of managing so large a district from one centre would be enormous, and I very much doubt whether so complicated a machine could ever be managed by an elected board. I have no more to say unless the Commissioners wish to ask me for any other information about Cootehill Union, which I shall be happy to give them.

387. As a rule, I believe you set your faces at Cootehill against out-door relief?—Out-door relief is given on only a very limited scale. I believe it is only given where the doctor certifies the patient should not be removed.

388. There are 428 cases in Cavan, while there are only seventy in Cootehill?—Seventy this year. I cannot speak to the figures, but my impression is that our out-door relief does not come to more than one guinea in the week.

389. Have you any hesitation, my lord, in giving your opinion that the low rate in your union may be partly ascribed to your having a strict system of administering out-door relief?—I think that very much contributes to it.

390. Lord *Dartrey.*—We may register ourselves, gentlemen, as protesting against the proposed scheme of amalgamation.

391. Against the two proposals?—Yes, my own opinion would be that amalgamation in some cases would be good. In my opinion it would be well to reconstruct the areas of unions in some cases without dissolving the unions altogether.

392. That is merely increasing the area of the union by a readjustment of the electoral divisions?—Yes. I don't think such a scheme of amalgamation as has been ventilated here would be productive of the slightest good, either to the poor or to the ratepayers.

Philip Smith, Esq.

PHILIP SMITH, Esq., examined.

393. CHAIRMAN.—Are you an elected guardian?—No, I am an *ex officio* guardian of the Cootehill Union, but I was formerly an elected guardian. I quite agree with Lord Dartrey that our low rates is owing to the strict look-out the guardians keep in the matter of out-door relief by giving it only to persons who are temporarily ill, and who cannot be removed to the workhouse.

CAVAN. Dec. 11, 1877.

Philip Smith, Esq.

394. You think that such a strict system of granting out-door relief, if adopted in Cavan, would tend to reduce the rates?—I have not the slightest doubt but it would. I know it has in Cootehill.

395. Very much if applied to Cavan?—I have not the slightest doubt of it.

396. Do you think it would tend much to increase the number of inmates in the house?—I hardly think it would.

397. Do you think it would decrease the pauperism of the union?—Yes.

398. The general pauperism, without materially increasing the number of inmates?—Yes.

Mr. M'Manus.

Mr. Eugene M'Manus examined.

399. I am one of the Granard guardians. I don't mean to convey that I represent the union or the Board of Guardians. We would come in under this scheme as the Scrabby division. I have been an elected guardian for many years, and I am now an *ex officio* guardian of Scrabby.

400. Are you deputed by the guardians?—No, I came here to express my individual opinion. My opinion is in favour of amalgamation, so far as I can understand the term. I claim the annexation of Scrabby to Cavan, first of all, on the ground of the distance between Granard and Cavan. The distance is nearly equal from Scrabby to Cavan as from Scrabby to Granard; secondly, on the ground that, as a rule, the rates in Cavan have as a rule been lower, while ours in Granard have as a rule been high. I recollect in 1846 and 1847 our rates were 16*s* in the pound, and only for the rate in aid we could not have got along at all; and even to-day we have a rate of 2*s.* 4*d.* in the pound which I would call very high. I would earnestly impress on the Commissioners that Scrabby would be very much benefited by having it annexed to Cavan instead of to Granard. I believe it is the wish of the ratepayers that it should be so, and I believe it is the wish of the elected guardians also.

401. The distance of the centre of your electoral division from Granard is about seven and a half miles?—Quite so.

402. And what is the distance from this union?—Eight or nine miles.

403. I find it is fourteen and a half measured on the map?—Yes, but those are English miles—ten Irish miles. Well, I am sure there is a portion of Scrabby electoral division nearer Cavan than Granard.

404. And you desire to have it transferred to Cavan on the ground of distance and saving of expense?—Yes, the saving of expense to the ratepayers, and I think the poor also would be benefited by the change.

405. And your opinion simply refers to the annexation of your own electoral division with this Cavan Union?—Yes. I would be in favour of it.

406. Are you in favour of uniting the whole of the electoral divisions of the county Cavan into one union?—I am, on the score of economy. I am not prepared to go into that question now. I am only speaking of Scrabby. I have heard the opinions of gentlemen here more competent to form an opinion than I on the broader question.

Mr. O'Reilly.

Mr. Patrick S. O'Reilly examined.

407. What union do you represent?—I come here as a ratepayer of Granard Union, representing Scrabby and some of the neighbouring electoral divisions of the Granard Union in the county Cavan. I think I will be able to satisfy you that both the paupers and the representatives of these electoral divisions of the Granard Union in the county Cavan, can just as conveniently come to Cavan as to Granard. There are five of these electoral divisions, and they are split up by railways. One at the extreme end, Ballywillan, is fifteen miles by rail, and Lough Dawan is not more than eleven and a half miles from here. I know many of the guardians live not more than a mile and a half, and some of them not more than 200 yards from these railway stations. There is no portion of the county Cavan which could be more conveniently represented on this board than these outlying portions which are now attached to the Granard Union.

408. That is your opinion as a ratepayer?—That is my opinion as a ratepayer, and it is also the opinion of the ratepayers of Lough Dawan, some portion of which I think is only seven miles from Cavan.

409. The question is not so much whether particular electoral divisions might be united with Cavan, but whether the amalgamation of the whole of the electoral divisions into one union would be for the benefit of all?—That sweeping change of making the whole of the unions into one—I would not go so far as that. We were considering that amalgamation to some extent should be carried out, and we thought that if a scheme of amalgamation was to be applied to any county in Ireland, it should be to Longford and Granard, and that it should be such a scheme as would take from Granard Union the electoral divisions in the county Cavan and give them to Cavan Union. I am opposed to any sweeping change, but I believe that one workhouse in the county Longford is more than two in Cavan, because you have double the population and double the area. I may add that our rates are always excessive. The utmost extravagance is carried on by the Granard Board of Guardians.

410. Have you any idea of the amount of outdoor relief you give in the Granard Union?—It is unlimited.

411. I believe there is no judicious system of giving it?—No; and to that we must attribute our high rates.

Mr. Higgins.

Mr. William Higgins examined.

412. You are clerk of the Granard Board of Guardians?—Yes.

413. Have you been deputed by your board to come here?—Yes; by resolution passed upon the reading of your letter of the 19th November. In accordance with the resolution of the Board of Guardians I wish to hand in the following statement:—

"Granard Union, December 11th, 1877.

"Gentlemen,—I beg most respectfully to submit to you the following resolution, adopted by the Board of Guardians of the Granard Union on the 28th November last at a very full meeting (twenty-four guardians present), on the subject of detaching five of the electoral divisions of the Granard Union and joining them to the Cavan Union, as proposed by the Board of Guardians of the latter union. On your letter of the 19th of November last being read, the board resolved 'That the clerk attend on the 11th December, 1877, to state the views of the board to the Commissioners.—This board is of opinion that in place of giving to Cavan Union the electoral divisions in that county in the Granard Union the old boundary of the union should be restored.—Signed, Edward More O'Farrell, Chairman; William Higgins, clerk of the union.'

"In accordance with the above direction I earnestly and respectfully direct your attention to the proposal above quoted, namely, to form one union by combining all the electoral divisions in the county Cavan. This proposal to make the union of Cavan nearly three times its present extent—to give it an area of 477,360 statute acres, a net annual value of £271,130, and a population of

CAVAN
Dec. 12, 1877.

Mr Higgins.

140,876—is disapproved of by the Granard Board of Guardians. The greatest length of the new union would be fifty-one Irish miles, forming an inaccessible centre of relief to numerous cases to the poor and sick, and a consequent negation of relief to a great extent to the workhouse and the hospitals attached thereto. The guardians of the Granard Union would regard the severance of the electoral divisions in question as a breach of good faith with them, as it would reduce the net annual value of their union by nearly one seventh of the whole. Again, from the position of the Granard workhouse, situate almost at the extreme boundary of the county Longford, and within one five-eighth miles of the boundary of the county Cavan at Tullyquillan, it was evidently the intention of the original Boundary Commissioners under the poor-law, that a considerable portion of the county Cavan should be always included in the Granard Union, the workhouse being more convenient to the poor and sick than Cavan workhouse. If it were otherwise intended a position more central in the county Longford would have been selected for Granard workhouse and hospitals. The electoral divisions which the proposed arrangement of boundaries would detach from Granard Union are Drumhummin, Kilcogy, Kilgolagh, Loughdawne and Scrabby; their net annual value in the aggregate is £11,781, and their population is 6,038. These electoral divisions are so situate (as a reference to the map will show) as to render the Granard workhouse and hospitals easy of access to the poor, infirm, and sick of this district. The boundary of Kilcogy electoral division approaches, at Tullyquillan, to within one five-eighth miles of Granard workhouse. This townland is about thirteen and a half or fourteen miles from Cavan workhouse, Carronbeg, in the same division, extends to within two miles of Granard workhouse. This townland is about thirteen miles from Cavan workhouse. The boundary of Kilgolagh electoral division at Brackleagh, nigh the railway at Ballywillan, in the county Longford, is about three miles from Granard workhouse, the same townland, which is not the most distant from Cavan workhouse in this division, is about thirteen or fourteen miles distant from that centre. The boundary of Scrabby electoral division at Cranaghbegh, in the county Cavan, is about five and a quarter miles from Granard, and between twelve and thirteen miles from Cavan workhouse. Considering, therefore, the great expense of maintaining horses, vans, &c., for removing the infirm and the sick such long journeys, and also the great danger to the sick and to the public health by want of prompt removal in cases of contagious diseases, the guardians are persuaded that feelings of humanity and economy will suggest an abandonment of the scheme. The guardians deem this a good time to ask on behalf of the ratepayers of Scrabby electoral division the restoration to that division of the townlands of Dungim and Knockatchy valued in 1850 at £313 17s 6d, and also the restoration to Loughduff electoral division of the townland of Drumcor, valued in 1850 at £107 6s (when added to Cavan Union). The proposal to disturb the boundary of the union suggests inconvenience in the future arrangement and management of the medical charities districts, as well as in the registration, sanitary, and vaccination districts. I therefore beg to repeat the views of the Board of Guardians of this union—'That the proposal of the guardians of the Cavan Union, if carried into effect, would inflict great hardships on the poor and sick—would be an injustice to the ratepayers of Granard Union and a contravention of the original intention of the poor-law, by which it was never designed to construct unions of such enormous extent, as would prove a great hindrance to the poor, infirm, and sick obtaining relief with facility.' I have the honour to be, gentlemen, your very obedient servant,

"WILLIAM HIGGINS,

"Clerk of Granard Union, for the Board of Guardians.

"The Poor-Law Union Inquiry Commissioners,
"Cavan Workhouse."

Witness—These are the views I have been directed to put forward.

414. Is not Scrabby a very poor electoral division?—It is.

415. I find here in the report that for the two half years—September and March—there were 69 in one half year and 63 in the other, paupers relieved in that district, that is 132 in all for that division, while in the workhouse there were only 25 in the one half-year and 19 in the other, making a total of 44, on which establishment charges were made, so that the great charge on the Scrabby electoral division would come under the head of out-door relief?—Certainly.

416. So that it would affect them very little whether they were in the Cavan or Granard Union?—Quite so.

417. I see by this return that you give more in Ballymahon—you relieve 386 there, and in Longford 164, and in Granard 123. What class of paupers is it you give out-door relief to in the Granard Union?—In some cases the aged and infirm; in other cases because of their being disabled, or out of employment.

418. According to law, but is it a fact that you give small sums such as 1s to a very considerable number of people to pay their rents?—I am not aware of that.

419. What is the average amount given?—I think about 1s 6d, and I think that in distributing this relief the guardians do everything in their power to afford it to those who are real objects for relief, and entitled to it by law.

420. Do they not give relief in Granard Union to a very considerable number of poor upon the ground that it is cheaper to keep them out of the workhouse than to maintain them at the cost of maintenance, &c., in the workhouse?—I can hardly say I ever heard of out-door relief being given on that ground.

421. You have not heard the guardians decide to give 1s. or 1s 6d out-door relief to the paupers because it would cost more to bring the recipients into the workhouse and keep them there?—No, sir.

422. Mr. *O'Reilly*.—I invariably heard that given as a reason.

423. Mr. *Eugene M'Manus*.—And so did I.

424. Mr. *O'Reilly*.—I have often heard it put on that very ground, that it is cheaper to keep them out of the workhouse and give them out-door relief than to bring them into the workhouse and keep them there.

425. (To Witness).—How do you account for the discrepancy as to the matter of fact between the two guardians who have last spoken and yourself. Are they stating what is not the fact?—Well, I have heard such statements made, but the relief was never given on that ground, and the statements were never ratified by the board.

426. Is the relief given by the board of guardians upon the ground that it is cheaper to give it than to support the paupers in the workhouse?—Mr. *O'Reilly*.—The way it is done is this, sir. The out-door relief is recommended by a particular guardian, and the board do not object, and that guardian when he is speaking to the others about proposing this always says it is cheaper to give him so and so—it is not half what it would cost to keep him in the house, and the proposition is always carried.

Witness.—That may be. I believe it to be true, in fact, but it is not formally done.

427. You believe it to be true that the suggestion is made?—Yes, I have often heard it.

428. And following the suggestion the relief is given, but it is not—the granting of it is not put with the ground of granting it—on the minutes?—I have known it to be refused almost invariably when it is asked for on that ground.

Mr. *O'Reilly*.—I never knew it to be refused in one case.

Mr. THOMAS BATTERSBY examined.

Mr. Battersby.

429. You are an elected guardian of Oldcastle?—I am an elected guardian and vice-chairman of the Oldcastle Union Board, and I am also deputed by that board to come here.

430. To attend this meeting?—Yes.

431. You have heard the observations that have been made here?—I have.

432. And the proposition for the creation of one union for the county?—Yes.

433. And with regard to that what opinion are you deputed to express?—The opinion of our board is decidedly that it would not be a wise measure either for us or for Cavan.

434. You think it would not be to the advantage of your poor?—No; decidedly not.

435. And are you deputed in fact to protest against the formation of this proposed county union?—I cannot say I am deputed to protest against it, but we

CAVAN
Dec 11, 1877.
Mr. Battersby.

considered when such a thing was going on that we should know about it, and that it was the duty of our board to send some one down to express our opinion on it, if we were asked, and nothing more

436. And your opinion is unfavourable to it?—Yes, entirely. We get on very well. Our union I believe is as well managed as most unions, and the people are very well satisfied as far as the management of it goes.

437. And you have by far the lowest rate of out-door pauperism in the county?—Yes.

438 You only give out-door relief to sixty three, while the numbers for other unions in the county are 475, 807, 700?—Yes.

439. And your rates are low?—Yes.

440. And your pauperism low?—Yes.

441. And you ascribe that to the fact that you set your faces against the indiscriminate giving of out-door relief?—Certainly, I think there is nothing that strikes more at the root of the poor-law system than this indiscriminate giving of out-door relief. It is the blot on the system in my opinion We set our faces against it as far as possible on our board, but of course we give it when we think the cases for which it is applied are satisfactory and necessary cases.

442. And when you give out-door relief you don't give doles, but substantial relief, not merely relief in aid of mendicancy?—Yes.

443. Would you be apprehensive if the union was made very large, so that many of the paupers lived at long distances, that it would tend to increase the giving of out-door relief in that union?—Undoubtedly it must do so, I would say. The situation of the workhouse being more difficult to reach, it would be necessary to give out-door relief more largely, and, as I have said, there is nothing in my opinion more ruinous under the Poor-law system.

444 If those electoral divisions were annexed to Cavan would it be possible, in your opinion, for the guardians of such outlying districts to attend the meetings of the board at Cavan?—I think you would get very few to attend. Even as we are, and where the guardians have only to come four or five miles, their attendance is very irregular.

445. Take the electoral division of Virginia, which is twenty-eight miles from here, do you think the elected guardians would attend regularly from there?—No, I doubt it very much

P. Maguire, Esq.

PATRICK MAGUIRE, Esq., examined.

446 Are you an elected guardian?—I am; and deputy vice chairman of the Bawnboy Union.

447. I understand that you attend here in consequence of this proposal for amalgamation, and to express the opinion of your board?—I have been nominated as one of five to attend here for that purpose

448. You have been present during the inquiry that has taken place?—Yes.

449 And what is the opinion that you desire to express on the part of the Bawnboy Board?—When the application was made by this board for amalgamation, when the petition was sent forward to Bawnboy to get the concurrence of the guardians there, they would not entertain it at all It did not occupy them two minutes. They unanimously rejected it on its being read

450 That is the petition on the question of amalgamation?—Yes

451 Has what you have heard during the progress of this inquiry altered your opinion?—Certainly not

452. And that opinion was formed upon the first application made by this board?—Yes

453. Was there not a second application?—No; but other guardians moved themselves about it, but they never intended to amalgamate with Cavan, but to absorb with Mohill Union

454. They simply intended to extend the area of their own union?—Of the Mohill Union.

455 Were you here when the proposition made by Mr. Saunderson was explained by him?—I was here during his evidence.

456 We may say there have been two propositions put forward to-day, one has been the Cavan proposition of one entire union for the county—a central union for the county—to that you give, I believe, your disapproval?—Yes.

457. And there was then the other suggestion that Bawnboy and other unions within the county might board their paupers out here. Have you given your attention to that, and do you object to that also?—I don't see how it could be worked or lessen our expenses in any way.

458. Do you think it would be practicable to carry it out at all?—I cannot see how it would be.

459 Would you be satisfied to have paupers from your union boarded out or taken to adjoining unions and maintained there, you paying simply a capitation grant?—Not at all

460 Without being represented at the board would that be an objection?—Certainly, and a very serious objection

461. And can you point out any other objection?—I think the spirit of the Poor-law was that it contemplated the relief of the poor, and this would be very injurious to the poor For instance, I would mention that our Chairman was to have been here to-day, but the stormy character of the weather has detained him, although he has his carriage to come in, and if it detained him in his carriage, how could the poor be brought a similar distance in an open cart without injury to them

462 You are of opinion that it is against the spirit of the Poor-law?—Yes.

463. And would entail hardship on the poor?—Yes.

464. Are you aware that at one period, before certain workhouses were built, the boarding out of a certain number of paupers in other workhouses was sanctioned for a limited period—that is for a period of three years during the building of these workhouses?—No, I was not aware.

465 You are not aware that that was the fact?—No.

466 Nor that it gave rise to interminable disputes within the unions sending their paupers to those workhouses and the guardians of those unions where they were sent?—No; but I can easily see that it must lead to disputes

467. But you are not aware that that is the case—that during the time certain houses were being built, the transfer of paupers to other workhouses, which was sanctioned for a limited period led to interminable disputes in reference to cost of maintenance and other things—that the scheme was found to work badly altogether—that is not within your knowledge?—No.

468 But you could imagine a case such as this, suppose some of the paupers of your union taken into this workhouse under the arrangement proposed by Mr Saunderson, and that after their discharge, but before their return to your union, they applied for re-admission, in such a case, to what union would you consider these paupers chargeable?—I don't know.

469. Would not great difficulties, as to chargeability, be likely to arise in such cases?—Certainly; they must arise as to chargeability.

Mr M'Govern.

MR. JAMES M'GOVERN, examined.

470 You are Clerk of the Bawnboy Union?—Yes.

471. Are you deputed to attend here to-day?—Yes.

472 And what opinion have you to express on the part of your board?—The board on taking into consideration the Commissioners' letter about this inquiry, appointed five gentlemen to represent them here to protest against the amalgamation of that portion of the county Cavan which is portion of our union with Cavan, on

CAVAN
Dec 13, 1877
Mr M'Govern.

the ground of the very great inconvenience it would entail in the removal of paupers here, and also that it would favour the extension of out-door relief. They also stated that it would be an impossibility for the guardians to attend here to the interests of the electoral divisions which they represent, and that in fact they would lose all control over the expenditure of that portion of their union if it were so transferred.

473. Does out-door relief prevail in your union?—Yes.

474. Largely?—Well, to a pretty large extent

475. Is care taken that such cases that you may have heard quoted to-day, should be guarded against?—Yes. We have very rarely a disallowance of sums granted for out-door relief by the auditor, which shows that it is only in proper cases that out-door relief is granted.

476. That is legal cases?—Yes

477. There is a distinction between relief that is, strictly speaking, legal and relief that is expedient or judicious.

Mr. HENRY FARIS examined.

Mr Faris.

478. Are you an elected guardian of Cavan Union?—I am an elected guardian of several years standing.

479. Do you approve of what we may call "the Cavan proposal?"—It was I brought it before the board at first, that was in 1876. My idea of it at that time was simple, it was that it would tend to save expense to the ratepayers, and not act injuriously to the poor. It will not take long to explain.

480. How long did you say you have been a guardian?—About twenty-six years.

481. You say you first brought it before the board—were you on the board in 1857 when the question was mooted?—Yes; it was Mr Burroughs took it up at that time He was our member.

482. Mr Burroughs, you say, was your chairman?—Yes, he was.

483. And your member at that time also?—Yes; he was.

484. And he was a man whose opinion should carry great weight in a matter of this kind?—Yes Then in 1876 I brought it before the board again, and the proposition I made was simply this that we should make our county house the parent house and take home the paupers of the rural districts to it. I did not think of Cavan alone, but of Cork, Waterford, and all the other like towns in Ireland, to take home the paupers of the outlying districts to the parent house For instance, from Bawnboy, Bailieborough, and Cootehill here That was the proposition I brought before the board, and which was adopted by the board Mr. Saunderson proposes that there should be an hospital kept at each of these houses and that only the able-bodied paupers should be kept here But I don't see the use in having such an hospital at all It would simply be knocking down one house and building up another. To remedy the inconvenience I proposed—and it was sanctioned by the board—to get a nice spring car, covered overhead, with a bed inside to hold two or three people, one say at Bawnboy, another at Bailieborough, and another at Cootehill, under the care of the relieving officer at each of these places; and in case there was a pauper to be removed who was sick or infirm you could hire a donkey or a horse to bring the persons here, which would be a great improvement on the present mode of conveyance, and I don't see how any inconvenience could arise then. I hear of distance talked of. Now the division I represent, it is only fourteen Irish miles from where I sit now to the extreme end of it, and Bawnboy is not more, and Bailieborough and Cootehill are not a very great deal more, and from the other odd outlying districts of the county not thirty paupers would come from them to this house. Then as to the matter of the expense, saving to the ratepayers is all we have to consider, and I think there would be an immense saving to the ratepayers. Take, for instance, the amount that is expended in paying the officers in Bawnboy workhouse. Take the chaplain's salary, the doctor's fees, coals, candles, rations to officers, &c., add up that. Take Cootehill in the same way, take Bailieborough in the same way, and add these sums together, and you will find it will come to a good sum; and I cannot see why, with the changes we propose, there would not be a saving of 5*d.* or 6*d.* in the pound to the ratepayers. I demur altogether to saying that we must have a doctor to watch over the infirmary at these outlying places. We want no doctor and no infirmary, for if a man takes ill to-morrow or meets with an accident, say at the extreme end of my division or even in the county Leitrim, the first thing is to come here with a ticket They get the ticket in the distance, and they are brought in a car at present without a ha'porth over them. I have known a man to be brought in that way with a broken leg, a long way, to this workhouse They are brought at present long distances without inconvenience, and it is nonsense to talk of that being injurious to the poor through the closing of these hospitals

485. You would give them up altogether—you would give up these hospitals?—Yes

486. You would only have the one workhouse and no hospitals?—Yes

487. You would bring them all here, irrespective of distance, convenience, or condition?—Yes. Of course you will not find any of the guardians of the workhouses which are proposed to be closed in favour of this scheme; they will all oppose it, because there is not a guardian who is not influenced by contractors in some way, and it is not the interest of contractors to close them If they are not influenced by contractors they will be influenced by officials. I know a case recently where a guardian, who very seldom attends the meetings, came up at the request of an official for the official's own purpose Then as to giving compensation——

488. That you would not approve of?—It is all moonshine.

489. You would be opposed to it?—Decidedly, it is opposed to common sense.

490. To superannuate an old officer?—Yes. For instance if a farmer pays his rent for fifty years who compensates him when he is unable to work his lands any longer? A shopkeeper works for thirty years and breaks down, who compensates him?

491. Are we to assume that all these guardians—Lord Dartry and others—have all personal interests?—All these guardians examined to-day are influenced by third parties I have given you a case in point, they are influenced one way or another.

492. Listen to this expression of opinion—"The distance of many of the electoral divisions is such that neither guardians nor relieving officers could attend the Board without serious interruption to their duties. The applicants for relief coming from remote divisions suffer the greatest hardships, when from want of room they are unable to gain admission to the workhouse, and are obliged to return to their own locality."—I think the union in some directions might be curtailed with advantage

493. Would you call that "moonshine?"—That could not happen

494. Still a gentleman whose opinion you spoke of just now as being entitled to weight—Mr. Robert Burroughs—did express the opinion I have just read?—That could not happen I say.

495. Still it is the opinion of a gentleman you thought entitled to considerable weight?—He might not have considered the question.

496. You have, no doubt, some figures prepared to communicate to us in support of your proposition?—No.

CAVAN. Dec. 11, 1877. Mr. Parle

497. But as I understand, you would even shut up fever hospitals, and if a fever case was reported from Blakey or Blacklion you would bring that fever case here to the Cavan Union?—I would, because I would have that covered car to convey the patients in.

498. Or from Kingscourt on the other side?—I would, because I know that cases come here from Cloon, in the county Leitrim, on the usual tickets.

Mr. M'Cann

Mr. JAMES M'CANN, examined

499. You are an elected guardian of the Cavan Union?—I am

500. And you signed the memorial, I find, in favour of amalgamation?—Yes, I did, and I beg to state that on reconsideration of the matter and from the arguments I have heard here to day, I think that amalgamation would be injurious I signed the petition but have since considered the matter more seriously, and I think that an amalgamation of the whole county would be a great inconvenience and entail great sufferings on the poor in the lower part of the county on the removal here I wish therefore to express my distinct withdrawal from the petition. As to Mr. Saunderson's proposition—that of having several different boards of guardians in different parts of the county with one workhouse, I do not approve of it.

501 You do not think it is a desirable or practicable scheme?—I believe it would be altogether unworkable

Dr Moore.

Dr. MOORE, Medical Officer of the Cavan Union, examined.

502. You are medical officer, of the Cavan Union?—Yes.

503. How long have you held that position?—I have been twenty years here and eleven years in Bailieborough.

504. And you know, from your acquaintance with this house, pretty well what the accommodation of this workhouse is?—Yes

505. For the various classes of the poor?—I do.

506. Do you recollect when the accommodation was fixed at 1,234 (that has been referred to to-day) by Dr. Brodie?—Well I recollect Dr Brodie once coming with me and measuring the wards in the infirmary, taking the cubic space there, and I pointed out to Dr Brodie what I considered an error in his measurement. For instance, we will suppose this was a room we measured; it will contain so many cubic feet of air, but in order to arrive at a proper estimate of its accommodation you must take the superficial area as well, unless it is intended to sling hammocks in the room and let them sleep one over the other

507. You showed him that before this cubic space was arrived at?—Yes, but that was only in reference to the infirmary. I went over no other part of the house with him.

508. But you did with me on Saturday?—Yes.

509. And we looked at most of the rooms—at all of them in fact in this part of the house and in the infirmary also?—Yes.

510. Now, dealing first of all with the accommodation provided for persons in health, there is the No. 1 dormitory which is eighty feet long?—That is the female infirm ward.

511. It is eighty feet long Do you recollect the number of beds that you, as medical officer, said might be properly placed in that ward?—Well, there are thirty-two in it.

512. No, thirty, I think you said, allowing five feet for each bed, that is two feet six inches for a bed, and two feet six inches for the space between each, and then there would be sixteen on one side and only fourteen on the other as you had to deduct two, one for the fireplace and one for the door?—Yes

513. Then that would be only 16 and 14—30?—Yes; I think that is what we arrived at.

514. And that I find is set down in the cubic accommodation as at fifty-three?—Yes

515. And as medical officer, knowing the necessities of the class of people who are in that ward, would you consider it proper to place more than thirty people in it?—Certainly not. Thirty-two is the greatest number I would ever place in it. We have had thirty-two in it.

516. But when you have had thirty-two in it, was it not over-crowded by two beds at least?—Yes.

517. Has it come to your knowledge, from time to time, that the particular class of inmates, for whom that ward is provided, have been necessarily removed to other wards contrary to your wishes, that is to say, have been taken to other wards when you would have wished to place them there?—Well, they are constantly complaining of having to go up stairs.

518. To leave their own wards because there is not room, in point of fact, in their own wards for them, that is a constant complaint?—That is a constant complaint—that is, in the winter time. I have heard this complaint frequently in the winter time

519. It does not apply to time, but to the question of accommodation, because in the summer as well as in winter there may be an influx of pauper inmates Come now to No 3 ward, that is the ward above that infirm ward, that is also eighty feet in length?—That just contains about the same amount of cubic space—perhaps less?

520. It contains more cubic space, but it is the same superficial or floor space?—Pardon me, I don't think that is right.

521. You are quite correct, I find it contains the same cubic space. Well, thirty beds is the number that would be allotted for that room also?—Yes

522 Would you consider it capable of holding ninety-five people? Would it be possible to place ninety-five people in that ward?—If you ask me the question, I can explain that I have seen it so crowded with less that number, that the medical officer had to creep in between the people and separate the sick from the dying. That was in the famine years.

523. That is to say, when the medical officer had to creep in between the people?—I did it myself, going in on my hands and knees, separating the living from the dead

524 But we are speaking now of the state of things, when the question before the Commission is whether or not this workhouse contains accommodation for 1,234 people. There is a ward—the first ward estimated to contain fifty three, and you say it cannot contain more than thirty; the second is estimated to contain thirty, and you say it cannot contain more than sixteen, No 3 is estimated to contain ninety-five, and you put it down at thirty, No. 4 estimated to contain fifty-four, and you have put it down as sixteen, nine on one side and seven on the other—going through the whole——

Witness—Won't it be well to answer the question with reference to the ward for the infirm?—The ward you asked me would it contain ninety-five, I have given only portion of an answer, that the two wards contain the same cubic space, but that is not available space.

525. Your answer applies to all those on the female side?—Yes.

526. And, Dr. Moore, it is practically of the same character. The whole space available for healthy inmates, including the probationary wards, which is put down in the certificate of accommodation at 890, can according to your measurement accommodate only 480, that is to say, the workhouse, as far as the portion of it for healthy inmates is concerned, is capable of containing 400 short of the certified accommodation. That I believe is the conclusion you arrived at?—Yes; that is about correct.

527. Well then, passing to the infirmary. As a medical man, speaking from your general experience of the infirmary and not of exceptional periods, when the rate of sickness is low, are you satisfied with the accommodation that is afforded in that infirmary?—There is no doubt there is one thing I am dissatisfied about, and I objected to it at the time, and that is taking the two wards, one the children's ward and the other the women's ward, and appropriating them for lunatics.

528. On the female side you had two very good wards?—Yes. The children's ward and the women's ward.

529. And owing to the increase of the class of lunatics upon that side you were compelled to lessen the infirmary accommodation by taking these two wards for lunatics, and that has left you deficient in accommodation for female patients?—Yes; in some instances.

530. You are liable at any time to have more than you can accommodate?—Yes.

531. And is it not a fact that at times you are compelled to receive patients in the body of the house who ought properly to be in the infirmary, because of want of accommodation there?—Yes; for some days at times.

532. Because you have not suitable accommodation always in the infirmary?—Yes; that frequently happens.

533. With the male sick as well as the females?—Yes.

534. Then we may take it you are of opinion that the accommodation both at the male and female side is short of the wants of the union, as these wants are frequently brought under your notice?—Well, I would not go as far as that. We can generally send a man down to the body of the house sufficiently convalescent to make room for another coming in. We always make room for the sick coming in by removing the convalescent to the body of the house.

535. That is by a contrivance?—Yes; in the way I have mentioned.

536. But suppose you, as a medical man, had the distribution of the hospital space, would you not feel that it was imperatively necessary to have sufficient accommodation—to always keep the sick and convalescent from the healthy, and that you should have the skin diseases in a separate ward, and wards for dirty cases, ulcers, &c.?—Well, we at no time had any exceptional demand for accommodation of that kind. We have very few cases of that kind except ophthalmia.

537. But you are liable to it?—Yes.

538. And you have no special accommodation for such cases?—Well, we have an ophthalmic ward and a lying-in ward.

539. We have been speaking of a proposed amalgamation of other unions with Cavan—what would you say if it was proposed to increase the number of sick and infirm threefold here?—You would have to increase the infirmary accommodation.

540. You would have to build?—Either to build or to set apart some other portion of the house for them.

541. Is there any other part of the house that could be set apart for that purpose?—Not that I know of. I think such a union would be very unwise.

542. Would it not entail a vast deal of suffering upon the poor and additional expense on the ratepayers in providing accommodation and supervision?—If you could make use of the attic story it could be done, but you would have to get a lift to bring them up, and have additional attendants.

543. And if you did so, then you would cut off the margin, so to speak, that you have for dealing with able-bodied pauperism in case of any sudden influx?—Yes; certainly.

CAVAN.
Dec. 11, 1877.
Dr. Moore.

544. Now, with reference to your male lunatics, are you satisfied with the accommodation provided for them?—No, decidedly not. They have always been a blot on the infirmary. The epileptics and the lunatics are placed together in the male infirm ward.

545. Irrespective of that, looking merely to their own comfort and the reasonable accommodation that ought to be provided, do you think the accommodation in the male lunatic department is good?—I think first of all that there is no proper accommodation in the workhouse at all for pauper lunatics.

546. Would you go one step further, and say you think the accommodation for the lunatics in the workhouse is absolutely improper?—I would not go so far as that.

547. Not even as regards the accommodation for the male lunatics?—Well, that is improper in my estimation, because I don't consider that these cells are proper places for lunatics. It is well known and generally accepted among medical men that lunatics should be treated in large, airy rooms, and that they should have the ordinary comforts provided for them. There is no fire-place in these separate cells—there is the fire-place at one end for the entire of them.

548. Are these cells which exist here in point of fact worse than you would expect to see in a gaol or lock-up?—They are.

549. And absolutely improper places to confine people in—people of any class?—Certainly; if I had my choice I would not put them there.

550. But you are driven to it from the want of accommodation elsewhere?—Yes.

551. And if the union was so enlarged as to bring into this workhouse a considerably larger number of that class, could you devise any means of dealing with them?—Well, if there were fire-places broken out into those large rooms up stairs, and other comforts provided there, that class would be far better off than they are.

552. But still you would decrease the accommodation for other classes in the workhouse by such a move?—Certainly.

553. And you would take them to a department of the house where they would have no access to the yard or gardens?—Oh, they could have access to the yard or gardens.

554. When this space accommodation of 1,234 was arrived at was not the fever hospital taken into consideration as being capable of accommodating 146 people?—It was.

555. Fever patients?—Yes, scarlatina or any infectious disease.

556. But you cannot take that into account in making the general calculation of the house accommodation?—If there be one fever case in that hospital the hospital then would be obliged to be used for that purpose. It would be segregated from the calculation of workhouse accommodation.

557. And the same with the probationary wards—if you had two or three people coming in—no more than two or three, would you consider it proper to place them in the ward already occupied as an ordinary part of the workhouse?—I don't understand you.

558. Suppose the probationary wards were occupied as an ordinary part of the workhouse by the aged or the infirm or by children, would you think it right or proper to put paupers in there who have just come in, before being brought into the house?—No; for they might be suffering from disease which they might spread on going in there.

559. Quite so; therefore the probationary wards set down as capable of holding twenty-nine each cannot be considered as forming any portion of the available space of the workhouse for ordinary purposes?—No; the object of them is to prevent any infectious disease spreading in the house through—to prevent, in fact,

CAVAN
Dec. 11, 1877
Dr. Moore

the germ of disease or anything of that kind getting into the house by the medium of persons just come in.

560. And, therefore, that cannot be taken as in any way forming a part of the ordinary accommodation of the workhouse?—No

561. Then in point of fact the available accommodation of the workhouse, set down in the estimate at 890 for healthy inmates, is reducible to 480, according to the actual space, and the infirmary, instead of being for 109, would be taken down to eighty four?—Yes; according to this measurement

562 And the lunatic wards—you have told us what you think about them?—I would remark that I don't know about the healthy part of the house I never measured it, and I don't know so well about the accommodation there

563 Further than that you measured it on Saturday with me?—Certainly, certain rooms of it we did, and they could contain no more, I think, than the number set down yesterday, except in case of emergency, when they could be a little crowded, of course

564 Precisely, but when a board of guardians invite the whole county to come here, and when they are speaking of house accommodation for 1,234, and that their actual accommodation is very little over one half that—would you still, if such a union were made, have spare rooms for cases of emergency?—Oh, certainly not—I think not. I do not think you could put any more into the rooms than we saw yesterday—than the numbers we fixed upon to be comfortably and healthfully accommodated

565. That is, of course, that in the time of epidemic, or of any such emergency, all matters of convenience might have to give way, and there would be of necessity overcrowding, but that as a general rule, the numbers you have quoted are the greatest number that could properly be accommodated in this workhouse?—I think so

566 Those sheds that were built for a temporary purpose—do you think those ought to be continued as a permanent part of the accommodation of the workhouse?—No, they are not available in winter time

567. And that is at the time that you have the greatest necessity for them, when there is the greatest pressure on the workhouse accommodation?—Yes, but I think they might be made available by putting on substantial roofing and making the buildings more substantial.

568. That is in fact rebuilding the thing, substituting a substantial building for the shed that is there at present?—Well it would amount to that—they are not available at present.

569. The question of accommodation, Dr Moore, was that upon which your opinion we thought would be of value, and we were anxious to ascertain whether the guardians had not, naturally enough, been led into a great misconception of the actual accommodation of this workhouse, when they put forward the statement that they had room for 1,234, when in point of fact they had hardly half that available space?—Yes, they took the measurement of the Commissioners naturally enough, and I recollect very well going over with Dr. Brodie, as I have said, and pointing out that although the cubic space was so much, he should also take into account the superficial space before he arrived at any calculation of the accommodation.

570. Very well, there is another question. You have a great deal of experience going about among the people of the county?—Yes.

571 I think you may naturally anticipate, I should say, a very considerable increase of sickness and pauperism this time of the year?—I never saw the country looking worse since the famine time

572 And the period would therefore be particularly ill chosen for making any reduction in the accommodation of the workhouse. Do you think so?—I think it would.

573 The accommodation arrived at and now mentioned, 480—is arrived at on the supposition that every room is to be occupied as a sleeping room?—Yes.

574. And there is no deduction made for those rooms for day rooms?—I think there is an error there. At the men's side there is a day-room that they never sleep in

575 In this calculation of space upon which the opinion of the guardians is founded, every room in the house is treated as a dormitory, and there is no room left for day-room for the able-bodied, and if you looked to the return you will find that to be the fact?—I don't think that was ever the intention of the Board, or that there should be no day-rooms, and it is not the practice at present

576 Dr *Burke*, L.G.I.—May I ask through the Chairman if you signed, as Medical Officer of this workhouse, the accommodation certificate and approved of it, when the accommodation was taken by Dr. Brodie, the Inspector of the time?—I cannot recollect that

577. (Document handed to witness) Is that your handwriting?—As I have said, I protested against the accommodation put down for the infirmary.

578 Will you read that?—(Reads document) "I am of opinion that the numbers specified in column 6 of this return are reasonable"

579. In justice to Dr. Brodie, who is no longer Inspector of this district, I thought it necessary to show that Dr Moore signed and approved of that return which is now alleged to be fallacious.

580. Dr *Moore*—I may be allowed to remark that I never went over any part of the house except the infirmary with Dr Brodie.

581. Dr. *Burke*.—Did you ever since that make any report to the guardians of the accommodation?—No

582. In justice to Dr. Moore it should be noted that the opinion prevailed and was upheld for a considerable time, that the accommodation of workhouses was to be gauged solely by the rule of cubic space, and it was not until comparatively recently that it was found that the floor space should also be taken into consideration as well, and probably Dr Moore accepted that return and signed it as a matter of form, it being framed according to the then prevalent ideas.

James Benison,
Esq., J.P.

JAMES BENISON, Esq, J.P., examined.

583 You are Chairman of Bawnboy Board of Guardians?—Yes

584. Your union has already been represented by the deputy vice-chairman and your clerk, who, having heard what passed at this inquiry, have expressed an opinion which I take to be in direct opposition to amalgamation May I ask have you been present during the discussion?—No, I had a long way to come, and it has been a dreadfully wet day, and although I had intended to be here when the inquiry commenced, I have been detained until the present, but I went over the whole matter with the clerk and the other gentleman who represented the union here, who were opposed to amalgamation as they have represented to you on various grounds, principally I would say that it would be very disadvantageous to the poor—that amalgamation would not answer the purposes for which the Poor-Laws were made. For instance, how are we to bring our poor some twenty miles here? How are they to be looked after on the road? In fact, I regard it in addition to its being a great hardship on the poor people, bringing them such a distance, the expense would be enormous, greater than under the present system. I have brought down a carefully compiled statement here, which you hereafter might look into, and on all which you may rely as being perfectly accurate. It embraces the statistics of the union almost from its beginning until the present.

585. We shall be glad to look into it, and if you have any other observations to make we shall be glad

CAVAN. Dec. 11, 1872. James Benison, Esq., J.P.

to hear you?—I have only to state, and that most emphatically, we are opposed to amalgamation.

586. And particularly to the scheme of the Cavan Board?—Yes; the return which I have handed in will give you the electoral divisions which are situated in Leitrim and Cavan, and an epitome of our house down to the present, and a *resumé* of our receipts from the outside, and I think you will find on the whole our management has been most judicious.

587. Have you been long Chairman of your union?—No, I have been vice-Chairman for a long time, but I have been Chairman for only seven years.

588. Then you have a large experience in the administration of the Poor-Law—what, in your opinion, would be the result of a large extension of out-door relief?—Shall I speak as regards our own union.

589. If you please?—I have reason to think that the system of out-door relief has been carried too far in our union. Our expenditure has been between £500 and £600 a year.

590. For out-door relief?—Yes. It is too enormous. It has been carried too far in my opinion, but it is very hard to meet these cases when they are brought forward, but certainly I must say if that £500 a year was wiped out of the amounts, we might have at least fifty more inmates in the house than we have at present.

591. Then you agree with the members of the Cavan Board that the doling out of out-door relief prevents people coming into the house?—I think it does prevent them coming into the house, that is just what I have stated, but still I think the out-door relief system is carried too far in our union.

592. When out-door relief is given in your union is the amount large enough to support the recipient?—No; the sums given only vary from 1*s.* to 1*s.* 6*d.* and 2*s.* 6*d.*

593. And do you think if that was withdrawn all the recipients would go into the workhouse?—Well, some would go in.

594. The really destitute would come in?—Yes, the really destitute.

595. Suppose the Cavan part of Bawnboy was amalgamated with the Cavan Union, and that parties to get relief from the workhouse had to come in from Swanlinbar, don't you think that the out-door relief would be increased there—that is to say, that the people would obtain out-door relief rather than be sent such a distance to the workhouse?—Yes.

596. The tendency would be to increase the out-door relief rather than send them such a distance to the workhouse?—I think that would be the tendency.

597. Is it of recent growth—the out-door relief in your union?—Well, it has increased within the last year or two. It is the last year I have been speaking of.

598. Has not the pauperism of your union been very much increased by giving out-door relief?—Well, yes. My own opinion is that such relief should not be given except under medical certificate, or where there is real distress, and in very many cases I know that a very few shillings for a few weeks will enable the head of a family who is stricken down with illness to tide over the period of sickness and prevent him and his entire family going into the workhouse.

599. Mr. *Martin.*—Allow me to say with reference to the out-door relief for Belturbet, there is a diversity of opinion, and in my opinion if the system of out-door relief was judiciously administered it would be a saving to the ratepayers and less trouble to the union. By judicious management, I take it that a great deal would depend on the various guardians and the relieving officers, and that more would depend on the endeavours of all ratepayers as well as the guardians to prevent imposition. The names of those receiving out-door relief in our union are published quarterly. The ratepayers can at once see whether anyone is obtaining relief whom they consider not entitled to it. If they discover that they can communicate with the guardians and the matter is set right at once. That has been done in my experience over and over again. I may say I have never recommended anyone for out-door relief without making very full inquiry and obtaining an opinion from the neighbours who knew the circumstances of the applicant thoroughly. Of course a great number of those who received out-door relief would not come into the workhouse, but if a third of them came in it would in my opinion be more expensive to maintain them there than to give all out-door relief.

Mr. JOHN BYRNE examined.

Mr. Byrne.

600. You are relieving officer of Cavan union?—Yes.

601. And have been so for how long?—For many years.

602. What is your district?—It is the upper end and larger half of the union, covering about 144 square miles.

603. Including the town of Cavan?—Yes, and other towns.

604. And you have a large number of out-door poor upon your list for relief?—Yes; I give from £11 to £14 a week.

605. Do you pay much money in Cavan itself?—Yes; about three-fourths of it.

606. Do you pay that much in the town of Cavan?—Yes.

607. What is the average payment in the town of Cavan to paupers in receipt of out-door relief? A shilling a week is the general run.

608. May I ask you whether that shilling a week is to your knowledge most frequently given for the payment of rents?—I believe it is—in three out of every four cases.

609. That is in three out of every four cases in which this shilling a week is given for out-door relief it is used for the payment of rents?—It is given for rents—that is their own statement to me. They are waiting for me to go up with the money to enable them to pay their rents.

610. Does it happen to be within your knowledge that upon any occasion relief is given for the payment of rents through the influence of any person or persons interested in the payment of the rent?—It does happen, and the way it is done is this:—Persons get up a memorial and get it signed by others in the locality, in favour of giving out-door relief to a certain person, and that memorial is sent in here, and very often the signatures and the memorial itself are all in the one handwriting. Here is one (produced) I got to-day, and it is all in the one handwriting, and I get hundreds of them in the month; then the guardians consider them and make their ruling.

611. I need not ask you whether you consider that a judicious administration of out-door relief?—No, as far as I am concerned, my ideas are opposed to that, and I have had thirty years' experience of it, and what I would like to do with it is, where there would be deserving cases and all those entitled to it, I would give them 2*s.* 6*d.* or 3*s.* a week—something substantial, but I think 1*s.* a week is only a kind of penal servitude for these persons—simple starvation—for they cannot live on it.

612. When you speak of the payments of rents—of those persons waiting for this dole of 1*s.* a week until you arrive with it, until they pay their rents, you know something of their habitations that these moneys are required for—will you describe to me what class of residences are these which these rents have been required for?—I inspect a number of them as sub-sanitary officer, and the most of them the down rain is coming in. Some of them (the houses) are narrow—say about eight feet to twelve feet, for three or four of a family to live in. They would be, in my opinion, many of them unfit for to put animals in.

CAVAN
Dec 11, 1877.
Mr Byrne.

613. And it is within your knowledge that rents are being paid for such habitations out of the rates—for habitations, as you say, unfit for human beings?—Yes, to pay the rent or some of it, for sometimes the rent is over 1s. a week.

614. Is it within your knowledge, Mr Byrne, that many of these people receive relief in aid of begging?—I know they are obliged—many of them—to eke out their subsistence by begging through the country, for I have met them going out to beg after I have paid them their weekly shilling

615. You have met them going out to beg?—Yes, numbers of them. They beg to get a living, and they pay their rent with the out-door relief.

616. They are obliged to beg for their subsistence?—Yes; a good number of them.

617. And you, as a relieving officer, when you attend the Board of Guardians here don't you tell them of these things?—I am not allowed to express an opinion save and except upon some occasion when it is asked. I have no discretion in the matter. For instance, there have been sixteen cases put on the book to-day for next week, and my opinion has not been asked about one of them. My opinion is never consulted except by the chairman and vice-chairman. They are the only two gentlemen who consult me. The whole matter is carried by one member of the board proposing that such-and-such a person should get relief, and by another guardian seconding it, and the body carrying it.

618. It is proposed by guardians interested in the giving of the relief?—Yes, interested through individuals outside

619. One supporting the other to-day, and getting supported again?—Yes; and, in my opinion, it is a simple act of cruelty to give many of these poor people a shilling a week.

620. There are one or two cases here on one week which I am rather curious to know about. I observe here the name of a blind man upon the list—Patrick Mulvany—fifty years of age: he gets 1s a week. Is he living with any friend?—He is getting 1s 6d, and that 1s. 6d. is well applied. He lives with his sister.

621. The next case to that is the case of Catherine Hyland, sixty-five years of age. She gets only 1s a week?—I know her. That woman was put on entirely in despite of the advice I gave in the matter. I would not willingly give her out-door relief at all, because she had two daughters, and each of them has become a prostitute.

622. We need not go into that; but she has been getting out-door relief in despite of your advice?—Yes, and in despite of my efforts for four years. She is not in Cavan. I brought her before the board on one occasion and had her struck off the list, and then I went away to the seaside, and when I came back I found she was on again in despite of my opinion.

623. Have you any doubts that the effect of giving relief in such a case is that it is most corrupting and demoralising to the neighbourhood?—I believe it is giving a reward to vice, and makes the virtuous poor in the neighbourhood look upon the system of doing it as unjust and unfair. That was my idea.

624. And altogether you are of opinion that the pauperism of this union might be much diminished if there was a more judicious administration of relief, and that such would not entail the slightest hardship on the poor?—I am; not the slightest hardship to the poor. There are cases in which money should be given where it is not given, and there are cases in which it is given where it is only encouraging idleness by giving it.

625. That is that you have very frequently met, as relieving officer—the agent of giving relief—in cases where, according to your opinion, no relief ought to be given, and that it is withheld in cases where, according to your opinion, relief ought to be given?—There are ten or twelve cases I would have had under relief at present, and I believe there is about twenty per cent. of those on out-door relief that should not be on at all.

626. That is your idea from your knowledge of the district, and from your experience?—Yes; that though these people get on the books here without my knowledge, I make it my business to inquire who they are and why they got on, and then I make a representation about it to the board. Those who get on to-day, I will see about them before Saturday next.

627. But to-day, when the guardians placed them on through these memorials you knew nothing about them?—Nothing at all.

628. And you say three-fourths of the memorials that come forward are a counterpart of that one you have produced?—Yes; all in the one handwriting—memorials, signatures and all. All the names are signed by the one person.

629. These names are put on your book to-day. I want to know are they put on for out-door relief at once, or in order that you should make inquiries about them first?—They are put on my book to-day for out-door relief at once

630. Have you not reported them to the board previously?—No, when I get these memorials I enter them in the application book without knowing anything about them. The memorials are sent before the board, and the guardians give it to them on the memorials

631. That is, you get a memorial, and on receipt of it you enter the case in your application and report-book, and that application and report-book is brought before the board without your knowing anything more about the party?—Nothing more about the party.

632. Do you not investigate the cases before you bring them before the board?—No; I do not. All the names are entered into my book that is brought before the board with the memorials, and on the memorials being read the guardians give the relief; that is the way the thing is done generally.

633 (To Mr Grier)—These memorials which have been produced by Byrne here, are they a part of your records?—No.

634. We may take this with us as an illustration of the working of your system?

635 Mr. *Grier*—Yes; there are some genuine signatures there. I know them to be genuine signatures.

"To the Board of Guardians, Cavan Union.

"We, the undersigned inhabitants of the townland of Derrylahan, most humbly showeth that Bridget Brady, of said townland, is in a most destitute way, and very much needs relief. Hoping the guardians will be kind enough to consider her situation

"LUKE M'CAVEY,
"FARRELL SMITH,
"PATRICK BELL,
"JAMES BYRNE.

"Dated 10th December, 1877."

636. But in fact the system of out-door relief here appears to be a system of applications by a certain number of ratepayers and not by the pauper to the relieving officer, and the case investigated by him.

637. *Witness*.—I am not consulted at all.

638. Mr. *Grier*—Of course the relieving officer sometimes brings cases forward himself.

639. But as a rule is it not the fact that the relief is granted in the manner stated by Byrne—that is, the application is made not by the pauper to the relieving officer, but by a certain number of ratepayers through memorials?

Mr. *Grier*.—Well, latterly it is more the habit to send these memorials to the board.

640. How long is it since this system of giving relief upon applications by memorials came into existence?—Within the last two years.

641. Does it prevail now to a considerable extent?—Yes, to be the prevalent way.

642. The relieving officer is, so to speak, put aside, and relief is administered on memorials.

643. Mr. *Grier*—But if the relieving officer considered that the relief ought not to be given, the guardians would not give it.

644. His evidence appears to be that the guardians would not listen to his opinion at all, but that they simply make their rule on reading the memorials.

645. Mr. *Grier*.—Oh, sometimes they would listen to him.

CAVAN
Dec. 11, 1877.
Mr. Mulligan.

Mr RALPH MULLIGAN, Master of Cavan Workhouse, examined.

646. You know this workhouse, of course, very well?—I do, sir.

647. And you are acquainted, I think, with the mode that Dr. Moore and I took to ascertain the accommodation of the several wards?—Yes.

648. And from your knowledge of the dimensions of these wards do you think the calculation we came to with reference to the accommodation was well founded?—I do.

649. Can you mention any case in which you have been put to serious inconvenience, owing to particular parts of the house being overcrowded?—Well, the infirm wards, that is, male and female, are often so overcrowded that I have to put some of the people up-stairs, and some old people don't like going up-stairs.

650. That is, in order to find room for certain cases you are obliged to remove infirm people to the able-bodied wards?—Yes.

651. With reference to the actual space of these rooms, would it be possible, do you think, to put more than thirty people into a ward of 80 feet long—that is, sixteen on one side, and fourteen on the other?—I think not.

652. I think we took it that there was two feet six inches for the bed, and two feet six inches for the space between?—The beds are between two and three feet, the ticks come beyond the beds a little.

653. But didn't we take it that five feet was allowed for each bed, and the space between?—Yes.

654. And on that measurement you say it would not be possible to put more than sixteen on one side of the room, and fourteen on the other side of the room?—Yes.

655. And that would be thirty instead of ninety-five, as is given in the estimated space accommodation?—Yes.

656. And unless the people were packed you could not put more than thirty in that apartment?—No.

657. Has any inconvenience arisen, to your knowledge, from the want of accommodation in the infirmary?—Well, sometimes the patients have to wait a few days in the body of the house before room could be made in the infirmary.

658. Have you ever heard of an instance of the nurse being obliged to put two sick people into one bed?—Yes.

659. And to put them on the floor?—Yes; I heard her state so.

660. And have you any reason to doubt that such is the fact?—No.

661. With reference to the idiots, both in the male and female side, you have heard Dr. Moore state two of the best wards of the infirmary have been taken for their accommodation on the female side?—Yes.

662. You have another ward there, have'nt you?—Yes; that belonged to the lunatics in the first instance.

663. And the cells were removed, and it is now one large room for women of bad character?—Yes.

664. That is their day-room?—Yes.

665. And the adjoining shed is the room in which they sleep?—Yes.

666. Was that shed formerly occupied with children?—Not that I recollect; not since I came here.

667. But is it within your knowledge that it was occupied by children?—No; it must have been before 1847, but I saw it used for spinning purposes in the year of the famine.

668. But now it is used as a sleeping ward for that class of people?—Yes.

669. That is a shed built up against the wall merely?—Yes.

670. The male idiots' shed is altogether, according to Dr Moore's opinion, unfit for the occupation of the class of people who are in it?—Yes, I heard him state so.

671. And what is your own opinion?—I think that if there could be a better place it would answer better.

672. That is a very safe opinion; but still you think that there ought to be a better place supplied, as I gather from you?—Yes.

673. Then we come to the conclusion that instead of having accommodation for 890 in the healthy part of the house, the number is reduced to 480—isn't that the number that could be properly accommodated in this house?—Yes; according to that measurement.

674. According to the measurement of floor or superficial space?—Yes.

675. Giving five feet for each bed?—Yes.

676. And the number then is reduced on that measurement from 890 to 480?—Yes.

677. The fever ward is rarely altogether unoccupied?—Very seldom unoccupied, except for a day or two at a time. I never knew it to be unoccupied, in fact. There was always one or two patients in it.

678. You have now some people in the female side of the probationary ward—could you put them into that ward if it was occupied by any of the usual occupants of the workhouse?—No.

679. So that the probationary ward, like the fever ward, must be taken out of account in calculating the accommodation of the workhouse?—It must. It has not, and never could be, used as an ordinary portion of the workhouse.

680. And could not be so used?—No.

681. It then comes to this, that in the healthy department we have accommodation for 480, instead of the estimated number of 890, and in the hospital accommodation for eighty-four, instead of for 109?—Yes.

682. What day-room accommodation have you?—The only accommodation on the male side of the ground floor is one room next to the infirm ward, and the inside ward would be too crowded if I allowed them to divide the two wards.

683. Isn't that ward occasionally used as a sleeping room—the ward at this side of what is called the infirm ward—the ward which is forty-five feet long, adjoining the eighty-five feet ward?—No; it is considered as such, and comes into the accommodation, and, therefore, ought to be deducted from the accommodation.

684. Then, on the women's side the same ward was originally intended as a day-room for all classes of females?—It was.

685. But it is now occupied as a nursery?—It is.

686. The room that was prepared as a nursery was found too small?—Yes; it is now occupied by adult females.

687. And the room adjoining the infirm female room is, in point of fact, given up altogether to mothers of children, with their children at breast?—Yes.

688. Have you any separate day-room for able-bodied women?—No.

689. The aged and infirm, and the mothers and able-bodied are congregated together in one day-room?—Yes.

690. Is there separate nursery accommodation for illegitimate children?—No.

691. Are the mothers of legitimate and of illegitimate children, with their children at breast, associated together?—Yes.

692. On the men's side is it the case that the aged, infirm, and the able-bodied have the one room in common?—Yes; they mix at the fire together.

CAVAN
Dec. 11, 1877

Mary Eliza Kenny.

MARY ELIZA KENNY, Nurse, examined.

693 Have you ever found any inconvenience, and if so, state what it is, owing to the small size or insufficient accommodation in your part of the workhouse?—I often had to go in next other beds and to put two persons into one bed

694. Have you ever been obliged to put beds on the floor?—No.

695. But you have been obliged to put two persons sick, into one bed, owing to the want of room?—Yes.

696 You have two children in one bed, I think, at present, with itch?—No, not at present.

697. On Saturday you had?—Yes.

698 But you have no skin disease ward in the workhouse that you could put children suffering from skin disease apart from other children?—No; we have to mix them all up together, and they often take the infection one from the other.

699 And that is owing to the fact of your not having a separate ward for such cases?—Yes.

700 If the lunatics were removed from both sides do you think it would be then possible to provide such accommodation as would enable you to keep cases of this kind separate?—I think so, unless the number of cases increases more than since I came to the place.

701. But if there were any considerably larger number brought into the infirmary you then could not deal with them?—No, I think not

---

Jane Anderson.

JANE ANDERSON examined.

702. You are nurse of the female lunatics' shed?—Yes.

703. Am I right in stating that you have been obliged sometimes, owing to limited accommodation in that department, to put beds on the floor?—Yes, sir.

704 And can you state any other inconvenience that you have experienced owing to the want of accommodation in the lunatic wards?—Yes, the want of cells—more cells for the dangerous lunatics.

705 You have none except these two large cupboards, I might call them?—Yes, that is all.

706. And you find it difficult to keep dangerous lunatics separate from others, owing to the want of accommodation?—Yes.

707. That is one of the inconveniences you have experienced?—Yes.

708 And you have been obliged to place beds on the floor also, owing to the crowded state of the department?—Yes

709. Although you have taken the best part of the infirmary?—It was not I that did it, sir.

710 But still, even with that accommodation taken from the infirmary, you have not sufficient room at times for patients in your department?—It would be better if I had more room, sir

711. And regarding that separation ward——?—I have not the supervision of it, sir.

MONAGHAN
April 15, 1878

INQUIRY AT MONAGHAN.—MONDAY, 15TH APRIL, 1878.

Before ANDREW DOYLE, Esq., and CHARLES SHARMAN CRAWFORD, Esq., Commissioners.

712 This inquiry, as the Guardians are aware, arises out of certain resolutions that have been passed by the Guardians of the Monaghan Union. There are present some gentlemen who have come from other unions, and who are probably not aware of the nature of those resolutions, so that I had better read them now. First of all, on the 5th of September last, the Guardians of this Union passed the following resolution:—

"That this Board is unanimously of opinion that two unions would be sufficient for this county. Which of the two existing unions to be abolished the Local Government Board can decide on further inquiry, but we recommend that the unions of Monaghan and Castleblaney be continued."

That resolution was re-considered upon the 14th of November by the guardians, and this resolution was adopted on that date:—

"The subject of Union Amalgamation having been this day again discussed and the votes of the Board having been taken, 3 voted for amalgamation, 5 against it, and 7 did not vote. It was resolved 'that there be no amalgamation of unions.'"

Upon the 12th December following this resolution was adopted:—

"The amalgamation of Poor Law Unions having been this day again discussed, amalgamation was carried by a majority of one—5 voting for and 4 against it."

It is then out of those resolutions that this inquiry originates, and Mr. CRAWFORD and myself are here for the purpose of hearing any guardians who may wish to state their views on the subject of resolutions. The first thing we would desire to know is, what is the particular scheme of amalgamation referred to in these resolutions, and when that has been explained to us, we should like to learn the grounds upon which the particular scheme of amalgamation has been resolved upon.

Mr William Woods, P.L.G.

Mr. WILLIAM WOODS, P.L.G., examined.

713. How long have you been a guardian of the Monaghan Union?—Some twelve months or better

714 What electoral division do you represent?—Ankettell Grove.

715 What is the particular scheme of amalgamation that you think it would be desirable to adopt in this union?—The scheme of amalgamation I am not prepared to go into, but I know that the feeling of the public generally—the ratepayers—is in favour of amalgamation.

716. Well, will you be good enough to explain, what you mean by amalgamation?—We were all very much in favour of one workhouse for the county; but as a trial we would be much inclined to retain two of them at present. I believe, as far as I am concerned, that one would be sufficient for the whole county Monaghan.

717 As an experiment you would be disposed to retain two, to begin with, but you think that one would be sufficient?—Yes, exactly.

718 Forming the whole county into one union?—Yes

719 Do you mean, then, that all the electoral divisions of the county Monaghan should be constituted one union, to have as a commencement two workhouses, with the view of having one workhouse ultimately for the whole?—I would not say ultimately one—I would give the two a trial, and retain them if found to work well

720. Then do you mean that you would amalgamate the whole of the electoral divisions of the county Monaghan into one union, having two workhouses for that one union?—I have not studied the matter suffi-

MONAGHAN, *April 16, 1872*.

Mr William Woods, P.L.G.

ciently to give a proper answer to that; but my general opinion is that two workhouses are sufficient for the whole county.

721. Are we to understand that, the subject having been fully considered at three meetings of the Board, you have not formed any definite opinion as to details?—No, I have not; but Mr. Kelly, who is the mover of these resolutions, asked a friend of his, Mr. Roberts, who is a guardian in the Clogher Electoral divisions that are situated in this County to give an explanation.

722. We will hear him presently. As you see, we are desirous of knowing what it is that the majority of the guardians mean by amalgamation. I understand you to say that it is to combine the whole of the electoral divisions of the county Monaghan into one union for the whole county—having two workhouses?—I would be inclined to confine the amalgamation to Monaghan itself—not divided into the county Fermanagh or the county Tyrone, or any other county.

723. You mean to include all the electoral divisions of the county Monaghan only?—Yes.

724. Then how many electoral divisions are there in Monaghan county, can you tell me?—I don't know.

725. Have you made any calculations at all?—Not the least.

726. Have you made no calculation of the population which would be comprised in your proposed new union?—No.

727. Or of the rateable valuation?—No, I have not.

728. Nor of the pauperism?—No; I have not gone into the subject at all, so far as calculation is concerned.

729. But does not the whole scheme depend upon calculations?—No doubt; but I thought after we resolved on amalgamation that the Poor Law Board or the Commissioners would make the calculation.

730. For your information I may tell you that there are seventy-two electoral divisions in the four County Monaghan unions, and that of those seventy-two, fifty-five are in the county. There are fifty-five electoral divisions, and your proposal is to combine these into one union?—I would be inclined for that course.

731. That is your scheme?—Yes.

732. To have one union consisting of the fifty-five electoral divisions of the county Monaghan?—Yes.

733. Well now, will you state, for our information, upon what grounds do you think it would be desirable to effect an amalgamation of the whole of the electoral divisions of the county Monaghan into one union?—I say that ultimately, I believe, that one workhouse would be quite sufficient for the county, but I would not go so far as that at present. I only propose for two workhouses at present. However, Mr Kelly, the mover of the resolutions for amalgamation is now come. He has given it a great deal more consideration than I have, and you might hear him.

734. We will hear Mr Kelly presently, but as you are under examination now I should like to know what were your reasons for concurring with him, that forming the whole of the electoral divisions into one union for the county is desirable?—As I said in the early part of this conversation, I have not given it sufficient consideration to answer the question; but I believe the ratepayers are unanimous in wishing for amalgamation.

735. Upon what grounds?—On the ground of saving—that it would certainly be a saving to the ratepayers to have an amalgamation.

736. Are you in the habit of attending the meetings of this board?—I suppose I am an average attender.

737. Is it the custom of this board that persons applying for relief should attend before the board?—Yes, any that are asked.

738. But they have the right to attend?—Yes.

739. And as a rule, do you think it desirable that they should attend?—I think it is desirable if the poor have any complaints to make that they should come here and be heard.

740. And that the guardians should investigate the matter?—Certainly.

741. But do you think that the poor who are applicants for relief would be able to attend from the most distant parts of the county, either this board or the board at Castleblaney to make their applications?—That is not what I mean—I mean complaints from inmates of the house.

742. But take the case of the out-door paupers applying for relief?—Oh, the relieving officer is the proper person there to see whether the claims are just or not.

743. And do you think it is not desirable that the poor should attend here and make their applications or statements before the board?—I do not; I think that each guardian would be quite able to ascertain the wants of the poor in his own district, assisted by the relieving officer.

744. And that the decisions of the board upon the applications should be made, not in the presence of the poor persons applying for relief, but, so to speak, behind their backs?—I believe investigation into their cases by the guardians and the relieving officer is sufficient.

745. Do you think it would be desirable, at all events, for the poor to attend here or at Castleblaney, if the whole county was formed into one union?—They don't attend here at all even now. It is unnecessary for them to attend, I believe.

746. Mr. *Mitchell*, Clerk of the Union.—They come before the Board of Admission.

747. *Witness*.—I believe they don't come before this board—at least I have not, from my experience, observed that they came here until after they were admitted.

748. Then it may be taken for granted that the poor—if the county was formed into one union—would not have an opportunity of attending the meeting of the board at which their application was to be considered?—Oh, certainly not. The poor in the lower end of this county could not come into Monaghan or Castleblaney until they were admitted, and then there would be arrangements made for bringing them to the workhouse.

749. At all events, the distance would be too great to expect them to apply either at Castleblaney or here from remote distances?—Oh certainly.

750. So much for the interests of the poor. Now how do you think it would affect the interests of the ratepayers—this proposed amalgamation?—It would save expense, which would be an advantage to the ratepayers.

751. And have you made any sort of calculation as to what the saving would be?—I have not, but in spite of any arguments or any calculations that could be brought forward, I do say there must be a saving. Figures are all very well, but as the old adage goes, if we went into figures and calculations, we would never put a plough in the land.

752. Your opinion is that we ought to take it for granted, without any figures or calculations, that there would be a saving?—I do—on the broad basis of the subject. I have always been of opinion that there would be a considerable saving the first year and a greater saving for a very considerable number of years.

753. But is not it reasonable to ask you to state for our information, upon what grounds do you form that opinion?—Well, by lessening the number of officers to begin with—the clerks, the doctors, and the clergymen and so forth. As I said in the beginning, I am not prepared to go into figures at all, but speaking with the public in general, everyone seemed to believe that there must be a saving, and it can be put in figures here, I have no doubt.

754. You don't seem to have gone into any part of the scheme in detail?—No.

755. And that is all you have to say, I presume?—Yes, at present.

MONAGHAN.
April 18, 1878.

Mr. John Kelly.

Mr. JOHN KELLY examined.

756. Are you an elected Guardian of the Union?—I am, and there are gentlemen here of course more learned in these things than I am; but from my experience these thirty years on committees and as a member of the Board, I moved in the matter, having given great consideration to the subject for a long time. I had a talk about amalgamation here about twenty years ago, but I did not know as much about the question then as I do now, although public opinion was then as it is now—that amalgamation would create a saving.

757. Let us not have a speech, please, but answer a few questions. First of all, what do you mean by amalgamation—what is your scheme?—What I always thought of it was to amalgamate those union workhouses into one or two. I say two, but a great number of the ratepayers consider that one would do.

758. Don't mind the opinion of the ratepayers at present—what do you mean by amalgamation?—Well, I would consider that two union workhouses would do for the county of Monaghan.

759. And do you think that the whole county Monaghan—that all the electoral divisions ought to be amalgamated into one union?—I thought the scheme must affect adjoining unions and adjoining counties—that they would have to be amalgamated also.

760. But Mr. Woods is of opinion that all the electoral divisions of the county Monaghan should be united into one union—is that your opinion?—My meaning is that we have adjoining counties and adjoining unions and to amalgamate them (the electoral divisions) with the union most convenient—to the house that is nearest to them, as far as possible. And as you asked Mr. Woods about the outlay ——

761. Don't mind that for the present; we are first endeavouring to ascertain what you really mean by amalgamation, and I confess I am not able yet to arrive at what your opinion is—you speak of the amalgamation of workhouses and the amalgamation of adjoining counties, but do you mean that all the electoral divisions of the county of Monaghan should be amalgamated into one union to be called the Monaghan Union?—I would say into two unions, and some of the outlying divisions should be amalgamated into other counties or unions—any of them that would suit or fit.

762. Then you would take the Fermanagh portion of the Clones Union and send it, may be, to Enniskillen?—To the nearest workhouse that would be retained.

763. And keep the Monaghan electoral divisions for the Monaghan unions?—Yes, unless that we considered some of those divisions nearer other unions, or other workhouses in other counties.

764. But if they were nearer other unions in other counties, would you then send them into other counties?—Yes, I consider amalgamation to that effect—that is my opinion of it; but I did not go into the figures here.

765. We will ask you about the figures presently. What one is endeavouring to ascertain now is this—what do you mean by amalgamation, what is your scheme of amalgamation. You have considered the subject you say for some twenty years. Upon three different occasions the matter has been the subject of discussion at the board. It has, apparently, been very fully considered, and you must have arrived at some decision as to what you mean by amalgamation, and we want to know whether you advocate an amalgamation of all the electoral divisions of the county?—Yes, into two unions.

766. What are the two you would retain for the entire county?—Well, we looked over the map, and it was said—not that we confirmed it, only it was considered that Monaghan and Castleblaney, judging from the map, should be the two. I do not give it rashly that those should be the two workhouses, but it was considered by the board and we left it to the Commissioners to arrange that—we did not think it was for us to do.

767. Have you any idea about what the Castleblaney Board think of that scheme?—No.

768. Or the guardians of Clones Union?—Well, I I have not. But there is not a workhouse in the county the officials of which would not make a stand against it being closed. Then the officers influenced the guardians. It is natural that persons making something out of these places would wish to see them continued, and would wish to hold their situations. But the poor ratepayers are the sufferers.

769. You say Monaghan and Castleblaney would do for the county Monaghan?—I think so, according to the opinion of the board.

770. Well, there are four union workhouses situate in the county Monaghan at present—Monaghan, Castleblaney, Clones, and Carrickmacross?—Yes.

771. And of course after you only keep Monaghan and Castleblaney, you do away with Clones and Carrickmacross?—Of course.

772. Here you have nothing to say to Carrickmacross, because if it was amalgamated no part of it would come to this union, Castleblaney being between it and this—isn't that the case?—I believe it is. I did not just go into the details or the distances between those unions.

773. The Clones Union being dissolved, you would get the Monaghan electoral divisions of that union?—Of course, I suppose we would.

774. Do you know what the valuation of those divisions that you would thus get from the Clones Union is?—I cannot tell that, but I was going to introduce Mr. Roberts here, who can throw more light over it. He might be able to satisfy the Commissioners and the ratepayers both. I would propose that you examine him, as he can find you the figures and all better than I can. But in a bulk way I say amalgamation would be a saving. Mr. Roberts can give you figures for that.

775. Would you propose to make any change in the Cootehill Union?—That is what I say—adjoining unions. I would send the poor to the nearest workhouse, having only two in Monaghan. Then if it was necessary under that to do away with Cootehill and bring the paupers here it should be done.

776. Would you do anything with the Clogher union—there are three electoral divisions of it in this county—would you disturb it? They are giving outdoor relief there now and some in Clones. The three divisions there, I suppose, must come into Monaghan workhouse?—I think so, but I cannot give an opinion "all out." Taking it in the lump, and taking the opinion of the ratepayers generally, we want amalgamation. I myself in this workhouse did propose a county meeting to get the opinion of the ratepayers, but others did not move, and I did not think it proper to take upon my own shoulders the responsibility of calling such a meeting. I then considered it better to leave it over for some time longer, as I was not any great man for a meeting. I never stood at any meeting in ——

777. Very well; now as to the saving by amalgamation. Would it cause any saving on what you pay for in-door relief in this union—would it lessen the pauperism of the union?—I believe it would in a way, but let me explain ——

778. Would it lessen in-door relief—answer that, yes or no?—Explain the question again.

779. Would your own electoral divisions have less in-door relief to pay for if you were amalgamated?—I do consider they would.

780. How so. Would you have less poor to pay for in each of the Monaghan electoral divisions because others were added?—No, but we have a great deal of tramps and vagrants going about, and if we had not so many workhouses they would not have a house so convenient to come to, and would stay at home in their own countries. We are taking them now from England and Scotland. They come over here, vagrants apply at the workhouses and in they go, and we cannot put

MONAGHAN, April 18, 1878.

Mr. John Kelly.

them out We don't know who they are, but we cannot put them out, and on that very score if half the workhouses were done away with we would not have so many tramps

781. Is one of your reasons for wishing to have amalgamation that you think the poor would be less inclined to come into the workhouse from long distances—that they would have a less chance of getting in than at present?—I think when we got the destitute poor into it they would not leave us, but if those tramps had not so many houses we would not have so many of them about. When they have a house in Clones, another in Castleblaney, another at Carrick, and this one here they just go tramping about from one to another.

782. Then you think the poor would have less, or rather should have less facility for getting into the workhouse?—Well, when we never had a workhouse we had less poor and better times I remember those poorhouses building, and there has not been a bit of luck since They were built in Ireland to house the poor, but they have been nuisances and for bad luck and that occurs from one source or another.

783. Do you think it would be desirable to give more out-door relief in consequence of amalgamation—to relieve the poor at their own houses instead of at the workhouses?—I think we could feed the poor at less expense with out-door relief and without the workhouses at all. We are now paying a large sum of money here each year for officers and so forth that if we were feeding the poor with, we could feed them and support them better if we never had a workhouse at all. And another thing I look to is this, we have divisions I know divisions in my own district, that there has not been a pauper out of in this workhouse these two or three years back and yet there is 6d and 7d in the pound taxed on that division. Mr. Patton there can state that to you. And where is that money going to? It is quite plain to the ratepayers that they are blinded in these affairs

784. Do you think Mr. Kelly, or do you not, that it would be desirable to give more out-door relief in consequence of amalgamation than you give now?—I dont approve of out-door relief, and I was always opposed to it here from 1847. That was the year of the stirabout, and we gave a great deal of out door relief then in the expectation that the Government would assist us, but they did not give us a penny, and our rate was 3s. 6d in the pound.

785. I don't think we can learn much more from you Mr. Woods referred us to Mr Kelly, the mover of these resolutions in favour of amalgamation, and now Mr. Kelly refers us to Mr. Roberts—perhaps we may get more information from him.

Mr WILLIAM ROBERTS examined.

Mr William Roberts.

786. You appear on behalf of the Clogher Board of Guardians?—Yes, and this is a statement which I have prepared showing what we would save by amalgamating

787. Have you been authorised by them to attend here?—Yes, and their opinion is all summed up here in this letter (produced).

788. Perhaps you will let me have a copy of the letter, or leave me the letter itself? (Original handed in). That is the opinion of the Clogher people and of the whole county at large.

789. I want to know, and will you be good enough to tell me, whether you are authorised to come here on behalf of the Clogher Board of Guardians—have they passed any resolution to that effect?—No.

790. Then how do you come, as a ratepayer merely? —Yes, and as a guardian.

791. Not on behalf of the Clogher Board of Guardians?—Certainly.

792. Have they authorised you to come here?—Well, we had no resolution about it.

793. Have they passed any resolution in favour or against amalgamation?—They called a meeting upon the amalgamation question.

794. The board had a meeting?—Yes, and the guardians did not attend properly, and I put a motion on to rescind it ——

795. To rescind what?—They had a meeting you know, and they carried it by one of a majority against amalgamation.

796. Yes, that is what I thought, they sent us a resolution against amalgamation?—Yes, and we got up meetings—five meetings and ——

797 Meetings of the Board?—No, Sir, but of the different divisions.

798 We have nothing to do with the divisions—only with the board of guardians, did the board ever rescind their resolution against amalgamation?—No, sir, they passed the resolution.

799. Against amalgamation?—Yes, by one of a majority

800 At all events they passed the resolution—a majority of the guardians were opposed to amalgamation, and you are here now, not on behalf of the Board but to give your own individual opinion?—Yes, in a certain sense.

801. And what is the certain sense—let us know? I will tell you. After that resolution we then called five meetings, large meetings of the ratepayers of five or six divisions, and it was all carried unanimously in favour of amalgamation. And then what we did was this—we sent up to the Local Government Board and that answer came down in return, that the matter was to be considered here by you

802. Very well—the Clogher Board of Guardians are opposed to amalgamation, but you and certain meetings that were got up are in favour of amalgamation. Will you explain what it is that you and those meetings mean by amalgamation?—The amalgamation of one union with another and the closing of one workhouse and sending the paupers to another.

803. And do you mean that you would take all the electoral divisions that are in the county of Monaghan but in the union of Clogher—would you take them out of the Union of Clogher and unite them to Monaghan?—There are three of the divisions of Clogher belonging to this county

804 And would you take them out of Clogher and unite them to Monaghan?—Yes

805. And what would you do with the other divisions of Clogher?—Unite them with another union that would be convenient.

806. What union is convenient?—Both the workhouses are about ten miles from either of these divisions, and I would be guided by considerations of convenience

807. Which of the unions would it be convenient to amalgamate, the Fermanagh electoral divisions of Clogher Union with—is it Enniskillen?—I will tell you. When I brought forward my motion to rescind the resolution against amalgamation Mr. Macartney was there, and my motion was declared informal in consequence of me posting it, and I lost my position. But Mr Macartney, the member of Parliament for Tyrone, desired me to move the resolution, and I did so—that three divisions in our union within eight or nine miles of this town should be added to the Monaghan Union

808. And what was the result?—We lost that Then we got meetings called and memorials forwarded from the meetings to the Local Government Board

809. You want three electoral divisions of the Clogher Union to be added to the Monaghan Union? —What we want now is general amalgamation, and I am here to prove that it would lead to a saving.

810. Do you mean by amalgamation one union for the whole county?—Two unions for the whole county

MONAGHAN, April 15, 1878.

Mr William Roberts

and three unions in Tyrone where there are seven workhouses at present.

811. Confine yourself to the county Monaghan if you please. You would have two unions for it? — That is my view.

812. How would you form those two unions?—With Castleblaney and Clones, or Monaghan

813. You would form one at Monaghan and the other at Castleblaney?—Yes, or at Clones—it is very near the one district

814. That is you would carry Monaghan over to Clones?—No, I couldn't do that, but I would amalgamate them together.

815. Where would you have the workhouses?—One at Monaghan and another at Castleblaney, say.

816. And you would take the Monaghan divisions of Clones and add them to Monaghan?—Yes.

817. But the guardians of Clones are opposed to that, and yet you would take the divisions from that union and break it up?—No, I would not break it up ——

818. Do you mean that you would not meddle with the Clones Union at all?—I would make it larger if I could

819. Would you not move those divisions of Clones that are in the county Monaghan—would you leave them still in Clones Union?—I would not be very anxious whether they would be moved or not. I would leave Clones as it is, because it is too small an area as it is I would add to it from other unions.

820. I asked you what you meant by amalgamation, and you said two unions for the county Monaghan. Then I asked would you take the divisions of the county Monaghan that are in Clones and unite them in your proposed new county unions, and you say no, you would leave Clones as it is?—I would.

821. Then what do you mean by saying you would form two unions of Monaghan as a whole county?—I would amalgamate all Ireland as a general question.

822. Oh, you would amalgamate all Ireland?—Yes, there are 163 unions and I would make 81 of them

823. Well, carrying out that scheme as applied to this particular inquiry that we are conducting now, you would have the whole of the electoral divisions of the county Monaghan formed into two unions?—Certainly

824. Then if you would take the whole of the electoral divisions of Monaghan, how could you do that and leave Clones undisturbed?—Well, I would unite Clones and Lisnaskea or whatever is most convenient. It is a great general question.

825. But you cannot deal with the thing as a great general question We are dealing with the particular question arising here?—I have been a guardian for thirty six years, and have had frequent conversations with the ratepayers about this.

826. Then as you have had such a lengthened experience, perhaps you can tell us how you propose to deal with the Clones Union?—I would take Carrickmacross, Monaghan, Castleblaney and all into consideration, and I would fix those unions wherever it would be most convenient For instance, Castleblaney is within eleven miles of this town ——

827. But what would you do with the Clones Union—how many electoral divisions are there in that union?—Why, you could put three into one if you chose.

828 How many electoral divisions are there in Clogher Union?—I don't know.

829 How many in the Monaghan Union?—I am not sure. And you don't know how many there are in Clones?—No.

830. There are sixteen, and seven of these are in the county of Monaghan Would you take those seven electoral divisions out of their present union and put them into Castleblaney or Monaghan?—Yes, whichever was most convenient.

831. And what would you do with the other eleven?—They would go to Fermanagh or elsewhere.

832. Then if the Clones Guardians tell you that it is the general opinion of that Board and of the ratepayers that sent them there that such a break up would be against the interests of the ratepayers and the poor, and attended with no possible advantage, would you still be of opinion that it should be broken up? I would submit that to the Government that stuck up those houses.

833. But if you say that the five meetings are to be considered, the Board should also be considered?—We confined that altogether to Tyrone, and our opinion is that there should be three workhouses there instead of seven. I think the practical matter is the saving, and I can show you if there was there would be a saving here of 6d in the pound on the rates.

834. We will go into that question presently, but with reference to a matter that must interest you as a guardian of the poor, let me ask you how do you think the poor would be affected by amalgamation?—I don't think they would be injuriously affected They might have to come longer distances, but if you kept a couple of horses to bring in the feeble or the sick paupers it would do, for those who could walk there would be nothing to hinder their coming 9 or 10 miles, as in fact they do now in Clogher.

835. What is the distance of the most remote portion of the Clogher Union from the workhouse?—Ten miles.

836. And you think that the poor could walk that distance?—The able-bodied can, and do; but we keep a machine to convey the sick or feeble. I don't think, however, that there has been £5 spent in the last two years drawing in paupers.

837. And fever cases and infectious cases of every description, you would send them all over here—10 miles?—Yes, the same as is now done in Clogher. But, sir, if you would allow me I will state the effect of this. The principal thing to be understood here is this—supposing that this house was closed and added to another union what would you have to pay after the amalgamation had taken place?—I have it all here—you would have the doctors to pay, the rate collectors, and the cost of feeding the paupers. You will have to do that no matter where you go to.

838. I will ask you one or two questions about that.

Witness.—I never thought that any person could fix these unions except the Government—those who struck them out, and if they want a general scheme of amalgamation, my opinion is that they should blot out all these unions, and strike out new ones

839. Begin again?—Certainly, sir, it would be better.

840 You say, Mr Roberts, that you have formed some calculation as to what the saving would be by an amalgamation?—I have.

841. And what is the amount that you estimated would be saved?—I will show it in one moment.

842 You handed in a paper here, but it is quite unintelligible—what do you say the saving would be?—I will show you in one moment. First, what have you to pay for here.

843. Are you taking the expenses of the Monaghan Union?—Yes, I confine myself to that exclusively.

844. I have got here the expenses of the Monaghan Union for one year, ending March, 1877, is that what you are dealing with?—Yes, I will confine myself to that

845. Do you know what the union paid in in-door relief in that year?—I think I do, I find in that year—if I am accurate—from the abstracts belonging to this house that the total expenditure for the relief of the destitute poor was——

846. I am asking as to the cost of the in-door relief?—I will give you my figures—£4,282.

847. That is the total expenditure for the whole year?—Yes, that is what was spent here last year.

848. I have the total here, deducting the part that is paid by Parliamentary grant, and I find that it comes to £3,658, the balance is the Parliamentary grant, isn't that so?—I did not deduct that at all, I followed where it comes out, the total expenses for the relief of the destitute poor, and I take the medical

MONAGHAN.
April 15, 1878.

Mr William Roberts.

officers, &c., and I have a list of the medical officers, and every penny you would have to pay supposing amalgamation was carried out, that is what you would have to pay whether you amalgamated or not, and the saving, as I make it out, is about 6*d.* in the pound.

849. Can you tell me what the amount of the "establishment" expenditure for that year was?—I think £924, sir.

850. That, I should think, is quite correct. Do you know the part of that that was paid by Parliamentary grant, and therefore did not come upon the ratepayers of the union at all?—I did not get into that.

851. I can tell you that when the amount of the Parliamentary grant was deducted, the establishment charge was £817?—Well, we look upon the Parliamentary grant as a clear proof that the British Government think we are paying too much, and that they ought to help us.

852. Do you know how much £817 is upon the valuation of the Monaghan Union?—No, I can't say.

853. £817 comes to 2½*d.* on the valuation of the Monaghan Union. 2½*d.* is the poundage rate. If you amalgamated, is there any other item of the account, except on the establishment charges, where the present Monaghan Union would gain by the amalgamation?—(No answer).

854. Would it gain on anything else?—It would save three clergymen for instance.

855. Those come into the establishment expenses—all the salaries and rations of officers, and all the printing, &c., are included in establishment charges—would there be a saving on anything else?—You mean of the establishment charges.

856. Yes, that is all that would be saved by an amalgamation, isn't that the fact?—I suppose you see this clearly yourself, if amalgamation was carried out.

857. Will you answer me please, can there be a saving on anything except the establishment charges?—On all the officers, master, matron, and everyone.

858. They are all included in the establishment charge, can there be a saving on anything else—that is all included in the 2½*d.* in the pound?—Then what do you mean more?

859. I want to know can you point to any other charge in the union, except the establishment charge, which would be reduced by amalgamation—it is a plain question, would there be less out-door relief, for instance, charged on the Monaghan Union?—Won't you be done with Mr. Mitchell (the Clerk) for one, which I would be sorry for.

860. Mr. *Mitchell.*—I am included in the establishment charges.

861. I have put a very plain question—you say that the whole establishment charge is 2½*d.* in the pound, and I ask can you save anything at all outside of that, and you answer me that you would save the master and the clergy and the clerk their salaries, but they are all included in the 2½*d.*?—I never looked at it in that light.

862. All the salaries of officers, and the printing and stationery, and all the items that are general, are included in the establishment charges, and you say they come to what?—To £924.

863. And that after deducting the Parliamentary grant represent a poundage rate of 2½*d.* in the union?—Yes.

864. Can you show a saving then on any other item—would you save anything on the medical charities for instance?—Not a penny.

865. Or on the sanitary expenses?—Not a penny

866 Or on the in-door or out-door relief?—We cannot do that.

867. Then the whole saving would be on the establishment charge which comes at present to 2½*d.* in the pound—isn't that the utmost possible advantage the union could get by amalgamation—2½*d.* in the pound?—Apparently it is as you put it, but it is no such thing as I calculate it. I beg your pardon for one moment, and I will tell you the advantages that would be derived. Here you hand the medical officers £570.

868. That is included in the establishment charge, isn't that so?—These are charges you must keep up. The doctors we can't do without, but if there was amalgamation we would not require the same number But after allowing for medical officers, poor rate collectors, relieving officers, and all necessary charges, as I show on the paper I handed in, you would, if carried out in this union, have a saving in Monaghan of [illegible]*d* or 6*d.* in the pound

869. Oh! you are making a mistake. You are leaving the cost of maintaining the paupers out of view entirely. What we ask is, exclusive of the establishment charges, could anything be saved by amalgamation.

870. I can show you that 6*d.* in the pound would pay all the expenses in the Monaghan Union, and if you do away with the workhouse, you won't have so many pensions to pay shortly.

871. Are you aware what the expenditure has been here for the last ten years?—No, but I can show you there must be a saving.

872. Mr. *Mitchell.*—In the ten years a 7*d.* rate would have paid the whole thing.

873. *Witness.*—My calculation is that £1,966 would cover all—how much is that in the pound on the valuation?

874. Mr *Mitchell.*—It would be 5*d* in the £, but you have forgotten the Union paupers altogether.

875 You have been asked whether the total establishment charges being 2½*d.* in the £, you can calculate upon any saving except that 2½*d.* Outside that 2½*d.* in the £, can you show us any saving?—Sure, the very moment you closed the house doesn't the establishment cease here.

876. Well, the establishment expenses that ceases would be only 2½*d.* in the £?—Doesn't it cease the moment you close here.

877. And how much is that?—£900, odd.

878. And how much in the £—is it more than 2½*d.* in the £? There is not a man here but can tell that—divide the union valuation into it and you will have it at once. It is 2½*d.* But as I make it out, 6*d.* in the £ would cover everything—the whole expense of the union, and you paid 1*s.* last year. If you deduct 6*d* out of that, what will the saving be?

879. Mr. *Mitchell.*—We never paid 1*s.* in the £ since the bad times—not for the last 30 years

880 You, Mr. Roberts, are here on behalf of the Clogher Union; there are gentlemen here on behalf of the Monaghan Union, who can speak more accurately about the saving. Have you anything else to say?—Very well, ask them, but I am able to show that 6*d.* in the £ would pay all the expenses in the Monaghan Union.

881. Leave that to the Monaghan Guardians.

Mr. James Mitchell.

Mr. JAMES MITCHELL, Clerk of the Monaghan Union, examined.

882. We will take a year's expenditure of the union—the year ending March, 1877. Can you tell us what was the amount spent in in-door relief in that year?—£1,093 5*s.* 11*d.*

883. What did that come to at the poundage rate?—2¾*d.*

884. Was there any out-door relief?—No, none.

885. The establishment charge, independent of the Parliamentary grant, is how much?—£817 5*s.* 3*d.*

886. That is all that was charged to the union, and what was that on the poundage rate?—2½*d.*

887. We will come to the medical charities—what was that charge on the union?—£593 0*s.* 7*d.*

888. And what was that upon the rates?—1½*d.*

MONAGHAN. April 25, 1878. — Mr James Mitchell.

889. Take all the other expenses—what was the balance? £1,152 16s. 11d., and in that sum there was £550 for the National School teachers, and £97 18s 9d under the Cattle Plague Act.

890 How much did that come to upon the valuation?—$2\frac{1}{4}d$.

891. That made the total expenditure of the union for the year how much?—£3,656 8s. 8d.

892. And that comes to a poundage of how much, on the whole union?—$9\frac{7}{16}d$.

893. And that $9\frac{5}{16}d$. included the grant to school teachers and the expenses under the Cattle Plague Act, which were extraordinary and not ordinary expenses?—Certainly, I cannot say extraordinary now, because as long as we determine to remain contributing under the School Teachers' Act, we are liable to that charge, and the other is imposed by statute.

894 Very well; you can tell, Mr. Mitchell, from your knowledge of the accounts, what would be the effect of amalgamation in the expenditure—we will suppose now, that the Clones union was going to be amalgamated with this, at least, the electoral divisions of Clones that are in the County Monaghan, and I have included also one of the Fermanagh divisions, Rosslea, because it comes nearer Monaghan than what it does to Lisnaskea. The valuation of the new divisions would be £37,840; well, I want to know if those electoral divisions are added to the Monaghan Union, what would be the effect in reducing your expenditure—could it possibly reduce the amount of the indoor relief?—I believe not.

895. The same number of paupers from the same divisions would come in?—Yes, and there must be out-door relief given if there is amalgamation

896 You think there must be out-door relief?—I think there must be.

897. Very well, the establishment charges comes next, we will leave that for the present. Would it make any change in the medical charities part of the expenditure?—No.

898. That could not be altered?—No.

899. And in all the other expenses would there be any saving—excepting the establishment charges for the present—by amalgamation?—I believe not.

900. Very well, the total saving then would be on the establishment charge?—Yes.

901. Which are at present as you have said, £817, representing a poundage rate of $2\frac{1}{4}d$.?—Yes, but I believe all those officers could not be done away with.

902. Wait now, supposing you got an additional valuation of £37,840 put on the union, do you believe that would increase the establishment expenses here—would it not necessitate additional relieving officers, and would not the salaries have to be increased?—Certainly, I believe it would.

903 Don't you believe that it would increase your establishment charges then?—It would, to a certain extent.

904. If you got the additional valuation here, would I be wrong in supposing that your establishment expenses might be increased £100?—At least that, I think

905 You think it would be at least that?—Yes, at least.

906. So that it would be £917 in place of £817 at the present moment—well, do you know what the poundage of the establishment charge in the new union would be supposing you added £100 to it?—Well, it would be $\frac{1}{4}d$. on the present valuation, about.

907. I can tell you it would reduce your establishment charge here from $2\frac{1}{4}d$., which it is at present, to $1\frac{7}{8}d$., and it would give to the union a benefit of $\frac{7}{16}$ths of a penny, which is the least fraction over $\frac{1}{8}d$. in the pound do you see that the union would gain anything more than that $\frac{7}{16}$ths of a penny by amalgamation?—I don't think it would benefit at all.

908. But could it possibly save more than that—is that not a fair calculation?—I have not made the calculation, but I should say that must be correct.

909. And there could not be a saving in any other way except by the additional valuation that you get to the union to throw your establishment expenses on?—No, there could not

910. Well, I have made the calculation, and that would reduce the establishment expense by, as I say, from $2\frac{1}{4}d$. in the pound to $1\frac{7}{8}d$., which is exactly $\frac{7}{16}$ths of a penny, which would be the gain to the Monaghan Union

911. Assuming that the increase to your establishment charges would be only £100.

912. Yes, whereas the increase to the valuation comes to nearly £40,000

913. *Witness.*—But I believe that the out-door relief would more than compensate for that gain.

914. More than compensate for the small saving?—Certainly.

915. Mr. *Roberts*.—But it would be for the Guardians to say whether they would give out-door relief at all or not.

916 *Witness.*—Yes, but people could not be expected to come such distances for relief. Mr. Roberts talks about the rates in the Monaghan Union being 1s in the pound—until the school teachers came on the rates some years ago, our rates were never more than $7\frac{1}{2}d$. in the pound. If you deduct the sums paid to the teachers, and under the Cattle Plague Act, you will find that $7\frac{1}{2}d$ would do now even.

917. Mr *Kelly*.—But it would be better if we were only paying 4d., and it stands to reason that we must save by amalgamation.

918 *Witness*—Yes; but you must keep the poor before your minds too

919 Have you any doubt, Mr. Mitchell, that the extension of area that is proposed would be introducing into this union the administration of out-door relief?—I believe it would, and I think the out-door relief a bad system. It is a test that the people are in poverty if they come in here, whereas it is no test their receiving out-door relief.

920. Whether the principle of out-door relief be good or bad, it is a fact that you would have it introduced into this union if the area was enlarged?—We must have it then.

921. It is desirable to ascertain what are the opinions of the boards of guardians that would be affected by this, and as the chairman of the Cootehill Board is present, I will ask him what is his opinion?

The Earl of Dartrey.

The EARL OF DARTREY examined.

922. I believe the Commissioners are already well aware of the opinions of the Cootehill Board, because they were fully explained at the recent inquiry held in Cavan. I may say, however, that my board are of the same opinion now as then—they consider that it is not in the interests of the ratepayers to amalgamate, and that it would entail great hardships upon the poor

923. I suppose we may assume that the views given at the Cavan inquiry with reference to the effect in Cootehill, applies to the proposed amalgamation in this union also?—Certainly.

924. The Guardians of the Cootehill Union are decidedly opposed to amalgamation; they think it would not serve the interests of the poor or the interests of the ratepayers; and, therefore, they have expressed themselves against it at the Cavan inquiry and here, through their chairman, Lord Dartrey.

925. Yes. There was a board of 27 and we were unanimous. I may state the considerations which weighed with us. In the first place, we would rather keep the management of our affairs in our own hands. In the next place, the saving would be infinitesimal when you take into consideration the extension that would be given to out-door relief by dividing the country into large districts, and when regard is had

Monaghan. April 16, 1878.

The Earl of Dartrey.

to the amount that would have to be paid as compensation to officers who would be discontinued and the cost of conveying paupers, allowance to relieving officers for travelling expenses, and a large number of increased costs that would have to be put against any saving made. Also, we think, it would be a great hardship upon the poor, sending them out of their own districts to be relieved, and that it would be very detrimental to them to have to go long distances to apply for relief. As I said before, it would entail great hardships on the poor without yielding any corresponding advantage to ratepayers. These were our chief reasons for opposing amalgamation.

Mr. Woods re-examined.

Mr. Woods.

926. *Witness*.—So far as out-door relief is concerned, I think it will become general to refuse it altogether. It is only an encouragement for people to hang about and not look for a living.

927. But don't you think that the larger the district is the more necessity there would be for out-door relief?—I think not; in my opinion it would lead to our having the genuine poor in our workhouses—people who really need relief, and not tramps or shams.

928. Do I understand by that observation that you regard the distance of the workhouse as a proper additional test of destitution; that it should be imposed as an additional test of destitution?—I think if we had workhouses at a farther distance, we would have less paupers.

929. That is if you make it more difficult for the poor to get to the workhouse, you would have less paupers?—I think we would. There seems to be great stress laid upon bringing the paupers long distances. Might I ask, Mr. Mitchell, the distance this house is from the most remote part of Monaghan Union?

930. Mr. *Mitchell*.—It is about 10 miles.

931. *Witness*.—And did you ever hear of any pauper suffer by having to come that distance; was such a thing ever brought up at the board?

932. Mr *Mitchell*.—No, I think not, but though the most remote parts of the union are nine or ten miles away, very few people might come that distance.

933. What would you think of distances like 17 miles, and 16 miles, and 18 miles, and 16½ miles; and some of those electoral divisions that are included in the proposed amalgamation would be of that distance; how would you propose to bring paupers from Drumully—I believe it is 16 miles to Monaghan?

934. Mr. *Woods*.—It should be given to the nearest workhouse or union, and there would be a workhouse even after amalgamation nearer than that.

935. Mr *Richard D Smith*.—Some in the Clones divisions of Monaghan have to go seven miles to the workhouse for relief, and I don't see how poor people could travel seven miles—they would starve on the road.

Witness.—The general opinion of the ratepayers in this union is in favour of amalgamation. And it will be carried yet, in my opinion, if it is not at the present moment, for the ratepayers are for it. And it is evident that we are the only liberal union in the county, for we are satisfied to give up Monaghan if it is so arranged,—for the sake of the benefits to be derived from amalgamation, we will go to Carrick if you like.

936. Mr. *Edward Richardson*.—What about the infirmary, that must be kept open, I suppose?

Yes, if amalgamation were effected it would be necessary to keep in the several existing unions—in all that it is proposed to abolish—an infirmary for fever and exigency cases.

937. *Mr. Richardson*.—Than that would reduce the $\frac{1}{12}$th of a penny, saving to less than nothing, I suppose.

John Brady, Esq., J.P., Chairman of the Clones Board, examined.

John Brady, Esq., J.P.

938. Will you be so obliging as to state what the opinion of the Clones Board with reference to this proposed scheme is, and the grounds for that opinion?

939. I was not present at any discussion of the question until August, 1877, and upon that occasion there was a notice sent out that the subject of amalgamation would be considered in consequence of certain questions that were sent down from the Poor Law Union Inquiry Commissioners to ascertain the views of the Board. The circular was issued for the purpose of convening of all Boards of Guardians, and upon that occasion there were 16 members present. Well, some of the guardians at first sight, without entering into the details of the question or appearing to understand it, were of opinion *in globo* that it would be a good thing to amalgamate the union, and that general expression seemed to pervade a certain portion of the Board. I was in the chair, and I said—Gentlemen, this is a very serious question, and have you considered how it can be carried out practically and with benefit to the people—the poor—for whom the poor law was instituted? And, after some discussion, we unanimously came to the conclusion that it would be premature and very hazardous to recommend an amalgamation under the circumstances. If amalgamation is advocated I, for one, would like to hear the argument in its favour. I am open to conviction, if it can be proved to my mind that it can be safely done, but up to this I have never heard good reasons given why the present system should be broken up without our having a better system laid before us. As far as I have considered the matter, and I have given it some consideration, and I would be as anxious as anybody to see my way to reducing the expenditure, provided the purposes intended by the poor law are achieved; but, as far as I have considered the matter, I cannot see how amalgamation would better matters. I would, as I have said, be glad of any information that would throw light on the subject. In the first place, with regard to Clones Union—the Board of which are unanimous on the matter—what is to be done with that and other existing unions? Those who advocate the breaking up of Clones Union have not told me what they are going to do with Clones house. If we knew that we would be in a position to say something upon the subject. What is to be done with it? Is it to be kept up? Is a person to be paid for keeping it up? Until we know more we think it is neither safe nor wise to break up a system that is working cheaply and well, and giving general satisfaction. We even think—but we are not going to dictate to any other union—we think that in Clones we hold a position that entitles us to great consideration. We are in a central position geographically, and we have a better railway communication to Clones than any town in the county Monaghan or any of the adjoining counties, and we see no reason why we should be broken up and handed over to other Boards of Guardians. True, if houses were now to be built it might be different, it would be another question where they should be put; but I don't see why Clones should now be closed, when the building is not required for any other purpose. I am old enough to remember when Clones Workhouse was too small, and when we had an auxiliary house, and we

MONAGHAN.
April 15, 1878.

John Brady, Esq., J.P.

don't want to paint the future too black, but it is within the range of possibility, at all events, that bad times might come again. Our idea is, we are satisfied to leave well alone. Instead of complaining that we have only about 100 paupers, we are very thankful that we have not 200 or 300. It is a very fortunate thing, we think, that there are so few in our house; but even the small number we have would have to be sent somewhere, and, seeing that our management is good and our expenses moderate, we prefer keeping them ourselves, being of opinion that under no system could we expect much saving. I don't intend to draw a distinction between any union and ours with regard to expenditure, but for the last 5 years our general average poundage rate has been 7½d. I got a return from the Master for the last five years—1873, '74, '75, '76, and '77. Our whole expenses of the establishment don't exceed £560. Well, we say that we can scarcely expect to be in a better position than that. We are very willing to make the change if it can be shown that we would benefit. We want to save money, but we don't want to deprive the poor of the asylum which the law has directed that we should provide for them. I must say that I very often feel most grateful in my own mind when I see poor creatures coming into such a place in their latter days, and people sometimes who have been in better circumstances—coming to a place where they can get relief and support and a more comfortable living than they could have outside. Then if these workhouses were placed at larger distances from the poor requiring relief, how are they to be sent there? Frequently they are unable to walk, and the expenses of sending them by car would be a large item, while many would be deprived of what is a pleasant feeling—a house such as that to go to in their own district. Then if their house was broken up their officers must be superannuated—it is not likely that they will walk about their business without claiming it—that is not my experience, at all events—and, in addition, those unions which are retained and enlarged will have to be officered by persons having much larger salaries than are paid now. Of course the paupers must be provided for wherever they go, and query, would they be provided for at less expense in Monaghan than in Clones. I am not going with that question, but officers would have to be increased and better paid for attending to a larger number. Then the question of supervision is an important element. At present we have a very excellent supervision in the principle of divisional rating and divisional representation, for I have observed that from time to time guardians from the different divisions are very anxious to superintend their affairs and see that they are conducted as cheaply and as moderately as possible, though I have never known them to deny a person properly chargeable to the division relief in the union. Increase your area, and I do not think the supervision would be at all equal. It may be said that representatives would still be sent from districts to the new Board, but we find that with 30 or 40 of a Board it is very difficult to get a meeting. It is only on special occasions—I will not say more than that—that we have a very large attendance, and therefore I don't think that from a distance such as would be embraced in an amalgamation of Clones with Monaghan that there would be a good attendance of guardians. Then, if it would result in the appointment of paid guardians, that would be deplored by all, for we have had in this very county a little experience of paid guardians. Our rates were considerably increased when we had them, and the people who before that had talked of paid guardians were very glad to return to the unpaid. I have no objection, if gentlemen pleased, that they should send Monaghan to Clones, but I have a very great objection that Clones should come to Monaghan. It is all very well for people to recommend amalgamation, but everyone likes to keep his own. We don't want to interfere with any one. We only want to be left alone—we are satisfied as we are, and want no change, unless some better system is shown to us. We have as compact a little union as can be found. I got the Master of the Workhouse to make out a very rough sketch of it to-day [produced], and you will see that it comprises a much larger part of Fermanagh than of Monaghan. We are in two counties—in Fermanagh and in Monaghan—and we are very nearly equal in the valuation of each division. We have £29,072 in Monaghan and £28,233 in Fermanagh, making a total of £57,305, while the area in Monaghan is 27,709 acres and in Fermanagh 45,700—because there is a great deal more mountain land in that county. For that very reason a very large number of the inmates of our house are from Fermanagh—there is more pauperism and destitution in mountain districts than in more favoured localities. The question then will naturally arise, as we are in two counties, if we are to be divided in two, what is to be done with our Fermanagh half?

940. If I may interrupt you—It is the proposal of the amalgamationists that the Fermanagh portion should be sent to another union in the county Fermanagh, and the dislocated portions of the county Monaghan in that union are to be carried over to Monaghan.

941. *Witness.*—In valuation they are very nearly equal sir, and we don't know what union they are going to send the Fermanagh half to. We have £28,000 worth of property in Fermanagh in one Union.

942. I fancy their scheme is to let those electoral divisions take care of themselves—it is not part of their duty, they consider to think of that here.

943. I can only speak for myself—at the same time none of my brother guardians have differed from me in opinion; and according to the best light I have upon it and the information I have obtained, I cannot see under existing circumstances, where the saving would be. As I have said 7½d. in the pound covers all our expenses, and has done so, as an average, for five years past, and if people would just deal with the matter in a practical way, enter into detail and work the question out, there would not be so strong a feeling in favour of amalgamation at present.

944. Are you a contributory union under the Teachers' Act?—Yes, and we continue to be contributory.

945. And 7½d. covers everything?—Yes.

946. If you had been here earlier you would have been promised a saving of 6d. in the £ out of that 7½d.

947. Nonsense. We consider ourselves very well off at present, and don't grudge the money. Certainly our number of inmates is small—I would be glad if we had only 20, if it suited the poor people—but we have had more than we have at present, sometimes up to 150. In 1873 our expenditure was under 7½d. in the pound, but I took an average of 5 years for 3 of these we were contributory to the teachers, and for the other two we were not contributory, and the average total rating was 7½d. in the pound. We paid last year somewhere about £380 or £390 to be contributory to our schools. We wish to give the children of the rising generation a good education, and though we have been met in that with some opposition, it has been always carried and we have continued to be contributory. I don't look upon Sanitary work as part of the poor law business or as properly affecting the poor laws. The sanitary measure is not a poor law bill at all, and I don't talk about our workhouses in reference to that. If I take into account the sanitary business and the other duties put on us, it would influence me very much more against amalgamation, because then what is to be done with our sanitary business? but I think that is extraneous to the question under consideration, with regard to the poor.

948. Yet if Boards constituted as Boards of Guardians are having functions of sanitary administration given them, do you consider these functions could be as well carried out from Monaghan in the division

MONAGHAN, April 15, 1872.

John Brady, Esq., J.P.

of your union which it is proposed to bring here, as from Clones?

949. Oh no, but the view I take of it is that that is a matter that should be dealt with outside the poor law.

950. But simply as affecting local self-government so to speak you could have no centre for your sanitary business except from Monaghan.

951. Which would not be at all in my opinion desirable. Had I been here earlier I intended asking a question about that—what is to be done with this sanitary business. I think that is a very serious reason against change too—we in Clones ought to know more about our sanitary business than any board assembled 10 or 12 miles distant. If a question with regard to the sewage of Clones came up here for instance, and we happen to have no guardian or representative here, they would be quite at sea and would not know what to do with it. I am sorry that such things are thrown upon Board's of Guardians. I am not at all presuming to be a judge, but my idea is that the poor law was intended as a measure of relief, and that it is being extended to things with which we, as poor law guardians, ought to have nothing to do.

952. We may take it for granted that the views you have expressed with regard to amalgamation are the views of the whole of your board?—Quite so. There are two gentlemen with me here, Mr Wall a magistrate and a gentleman of experience in connexion with property, and Mr. Fitzgerald. They are present here and may be examined, but we have no second opinion upon the subject.

953. We are very much obliged to you for your very clear statement of the views of your board. I don't know whether any gentlemen here wishes to ask you any question by way of information—not discussion.

954. Mr. *Woods*.—It is quite clear that Mr. Brady wishes to stick to Clones—he is very selfish?—Oh no, we think the present system a good one, it has been tried and we don't want to abandon it for a new and untried system.

955. Now, the guardians of the Monaghan Board should understand that all the other unions that would be affected by it are opposed to the proposal of amalgamation, and that—as far as we have to do—the whole scheme of amalgamation, as it is before the Commission, is a proposal made by five guardians of this Union and opposed by four guardians of this union, and unanimously by the guardians of all the other unions. That is the position in which the question of amalgamation in Monaghan stands.

956. Mr. RICHARDSON.—It ought to be perfectly understood that it is only one class of the ratepayers of this union that wish to have amalgamation.

957. I rather gathered from Mr. Kelly that one effect of amalgamation would be an extension of outdoor relief, and that was an object to be aimed at—that it was rather desired by a certain class of ratepayers that there should be more outdoor relief—that the outdoor relief should assume more the character of charity than of poor law relief.

958. Mr. *Kelly*.—We talked over that, but we can't get amalgamation now that is clear, and I will call a county meeting, and if there is not 20 to 1 for amalgamation, in this union, or in the county either, I will never say another word for it.

959. Mr. *Woods*.—Mr. Richardson is quite wrong about the feeling of the ratepayers. There are 20 respectable ratepayers standing at the door now, to give an explanation here if they are summoned in. They are waiting there for the purpose—20 of them; and we could get hundreds from all parts of the county the same way of thinking.

960. If they can give any evidence or information we would be glad to hear them.

961. The Earl of *Dartrey*.—I apprehend that a great number of the ratepayers are in favour of it because they have never considered it, and have never been told the results that would flow from it. But if they went into it, or had it properly explained to them, they would find that there is very little ground for supposing that there would be a saving to the public.

962. *Witness*.—Might I say one word on that point? When coming down to the train to-day at 12 o'clock I met a gentleman, an educated gentleman and a man of property. He asked me where I was going, and I said "To Monaghan; there is to be an inquiry there about amalgamation." Well, said he, you are in favour of that, surely. I said, I am open to conviction, and would you give your reasons for thinking that there should be amalgamation. Well, said he, there's the jails amalgamated. But said I, the jails are not on the same footing at all, can you give me another reason? Won't it lessen expense; would not the officers be sent about their business that are doing nothing, he asked. Show me it will effect a saving, I said, and I will go with you; I am anxious for a saving, if possible. Then, he said, one or two things. I bowled him over on each, and he sung dumb. I asked, would you break up this Board and send it to Clones? No, said he, I would not do that. What would you do, have you ever calculated the saving that would arise? No, said he, I have not calculated that at all. So you see that what Lord Dartrey has said is correct, people talk about amalgamation and clamour for it without knowing what it rightly means, or calculating the cost and the saving and drawing a line between the one and the other.

Mr. WOODS re-examined.

Mr Woods.

963. The gentlemen who have been most active in advocating it here, have not, either from want of time or power—I know not which—to make the inquiry, gone into figures. As they stated, they have not originated any plan of amalgamation. They talked of an amalgamation of the whole county into one union or into two unions, but they have not, I think, considered it quite as fully as they might reasonably be expected to have done. Can you give us any information upon the subject?—We did not go into the details at all.

964. But this being brought before the ratepayers of the county as a question of figures it did seem desirable that the persons advocating amalgamation should have taken the trouble of stating how it might come out in figures?—I think if they had they might have brought it out in a very favourable light indeed.

965. I don't think you can suppose that Mr. Crawford is wrong in his figure—is that what you mean?—Oh, no; but this whole meeting is in favour of matters remaining as they were, and they have brought them out in figures, I won't say one-sided, but it is very like it.

966. If you can see any mistake in the figures we would be glad to have it pointed out.—Well, I think the distance paupers would have to come in the event of amalgamation has been overstated.

967. Do you know the distance of Clonkellan electoral division from Monaghan?—No.

968. Well, it is 16½ miles?—But it is only 21 miles from here to Carrick, and if you divided that district it would be only 10½ miles to one workhouse or another.

969. Is there any other gentleman who wishes to give any evidence? (No Answer).

970. *Witness*.—There has been a good deal said about pensioning off the officers and that sort of thing, but if matters stand as they are we will have two batches of officers to pension off ere long.

971. But if you abolish an office you must give

Monaghan. April 18, 1878.

Mr. Woods.

compensation, whilst the question of superannuation is within the discretion of the guardians.—Certainly, at present; but the existing officers will be pensioned off, and the new officers who would come in would be pensioned off too. It is hardly worth while, however, detaining the meeting.

972. Mr. *Kelly*.—I live 10 miles from here—on the verge of Tyrone, and I don't consider that the carriage of paupers from that district has cost us £3 these 25 or 38 years; and there is Mr. Mitchell there, and if he calculates he will find I am right.

973. Mr. *Mitchell*.—We have a donkey and cart here, and it costs nothing at all.—We send it for them.

974. Mr. *Kelly*.—If we once got the really destitute to the workhouse they won't leave it, and then if we had fewer workhouses we would not have so many tramps coming from England and Scotland here. If they had a distance to go from one union to another they would not be on the tramp so often, and surely we are not bound in Ireland to pay for these tramps from other nations and countries?

The inquiry then terminated.

Ennis. May 8, 1878.

Inquiry at Ennis.—Wednesday, 8th May, 1878.

Before Major the Hon. W. Le Poer Trench, R.E. (Chairman), Andrew Doyle, Esq., and Charles Sharman Crawford, Esq.

975. Gentlemen, you are doubtless aware of the object of our meeting. We issued circulars to the different Boards of Guardians on the 6th August last, and on the 22nd August we received your reply to the effect:—

"That in the opinion of the Guardians of Ennis Union portions of the unions of Killadysert, Corrofin, Ennistymon, and Tulla might be added to the Union of Ennis with great advantage and economy of management. As to the particular portions which should be added, the Guardians will be prepared at the proper time to submit their suggestions to the Commissioners."

One of the Commissioners, Mr. Crawford, visited the various unions in this county, and having formed his opinion as to what he thought most desirable to be done attended a meeting of this board last February, when I think he discussed the matter with you. On that occasion the board appears to have passed a resolution—"Proposed by Colonel M'Donnell, seconded by Colonel Butler, and resolved, That having heard the very clear and lucid statement of Mr. Crawford, one of the Commissioners, we are still of opinion nevertheless that it would be advantageous to absorb portions of the unions named." This being the case, the present inquiry has become necessary, as, if we are to arrive at other conclusion than that arrived at by Mr. Crawford, further data must be supplied. Having, therefore duly advertised our intention we have now come here for the purpose of receiving such evidence as any members of the board desire to tender in support of the opinion formed in favour of amalgamation. Of course alterations of this nature cannot be proposed without causing a good deal of difference of opinion, and we must also take into consideration the answers of the other unions to the queries sent to them. In the case of the Corrofin union the answer was distinctly "No." They are unanimously against being dissolved or amalgamated with any other union. In the case of Killadysert the answer was a direct negative as to the expediency of dissolving the union and amalgamating it with any other—"That we give a direct negative reply to the first query of the Poor Law Union Inquiry Commissioners relating to the expediency of dissolving this union and amalgamating it with the adjoining unions to which the townlands thereof belonged up to the year 1850." The resolutions were passed in August, and there has been a considerable interval since, and a new election of guardians has taken place. The ratepayers have had an opportunity of reconsidering the opinion expressed by their guardians. The subject was brought before the new Board on the 7th of May, 1878, when a resolution was carried by 5 to 3, in the affirmation of that I have just read.

Thos. Greene, Esq., J.P.

Thomas Greene, Esq., J.P., examined.

976. You are Deputy Vice-Chairman of this union?—Yes.

977. You have been so for some time?—Yes, for about twenty years.

978. You desire that amalgamation should take place?—Yes, I think it would be for the interest of the ratepayers of Ennis as well as those outside of it.

979. Are these the grounds on which you desire it?—Yes.

980. What advantage do you expect will accrue from it?—I first take the position of the union and its extent. On reference to the map you will see that at one side it extends to Bunratty, about 14 miles from Ennis, and that at the north west side it extends only five or six miles. Then if you go on towards the Gort side, due north, we extend 7 or 8 miles, and then we join Killadysert at the other side a very short distance. I don't think we could increase our area more than it is at the Limerick side. Here is Ennis (indicating boundary of union on a map) and we extend down to Bunratty bridge. Tulla comes very close to us, and there is an angle there nearly opposite the Shannon. Taking in a large portion of the Tulla union and going up to Corrofin close to the union, I think a good deal of both these districts could be added; they consist of large farms not populously inhabited and consequently with very few paupers in them, and by amalgamating these portions of the two unions no detriment could arise to parties seeking relief for they would not have to go near the same distance as paupers from the Bunratty side suffer from. I am interested as a land agent in all the surrounding unions, and it is not selfish on my part, although it may appear selfish on the part of the board to recommend amalgamation for the purpose of saving themselves, but I say where the interests of a community are concerned people must put their private feelings under foot, and give their opinion fearlessly and honestly to the best of their belief.

981. That is your desire, to extend the area of this union by taking in portions of the adjoining unions?—Yes. With regard to the Killadysert Union I agree with the Board there in favour of not amalgamating, and I will tell you why. There is a large extent of sea-board along there, if I may so call it, to Kilrush, it is a very wild, extensive district, and I think it would be very wrong to carry the poor through that district into Kilrush—a very long distance, and through such a country, and therefore I think Killadysert, even in the interests of the poor, ought not to be interfered with.

982. What would be the distance to Kilrush?—Seventeen or eighteen miles, if not more.

983. That you consider would be wrong?—That I consider would be wrong for those seeking to enter the workhouse, or seeking medical or hospital relief.

984. Then you think Killadysert should be left untouched?—Yes; though our rates might not be reduced so far as establishment charges are concerned, I think the gain would be four-fold more to the two unions that would be added to us. Our valuation is about £74,000, and of course the larger your valua-

Ennis May 8, 1878.

Thos. Greene, Esq., J.P.

tion the smaller the rate for establishment charges. The other unions have a smaller valuation as compared with ours, and even adding £4,800 or £5,000 from each of them, it would make, instead of £74,000, say £84,000 of a valuation, and I think that with that basis the establishment charges of the portions to be added would scarcely be one-third of what they are at present, while those of Ennis, if we took that selfish view of it, would be considerably increased; and that view was presented to us by the very able statement of Mr. Crawford on the last day we had the pleasure of meeting him.

985. Have you made any calculation as to the extra number of inmates your proposal would bring into your house?—I set out by stating that very few paupers would come in from these districts, as is shown by the numbers in the workhouses from these portions. I say a great part of the districts are grazing land, not inhabited by the class of paupers who become workhouse inmates. In fact, everyone you find there is a farm labourer, and when distress arises it could be met by out-door relief in place of indoor.

986. Your proposal appears not to be for the amalgamation of the two unions, but simply a proposal for the extension of Ennis Union at the expense, so to speak, of certain electoral divisions of other unions?—Yes, of Corrofin and Tulla.

987. It is not a distinct proposal to amalgamate the unions, but to attach to this union so much of those adjoining as would benefit you?—If I broached such an opinion as that Tulla and Corrofin should be added to Ennis Union I would be laughed at, but what I propose is to add portion to Ennis, and the remaining portions to go to Ballyvaughan and Scariff, so as to make it as convenient as possible to parties likely to seek indoor relief or otherwise.

988. These unions, as you are aware, being unwilling to give up those portions you are anxious to have amalgamated with yours?—I would be slow to take them against their will, but where there is a necessity it cannot be helped. I admit that probably if I were a Corrofin man I would say, "Do not amalgamate," because we must admit there is a large expenditure of money in these unions; and in a country like Ireland, circumstanced as we are, it is the desire, and the wish, and the duty I might say, of those resident in it to obtain the circulation of money in every district, and to prevent the centralisation as far as possible of expenditure. We must know that in a country village or town the expenditure of £2,000 or £3,000 a year must be, and it is, the life blood of the prosperity of the people.

989. One effect, as I understand one of your answers, of the extension of the area of the union would be to necessitate the giving of out-door relief in certain cases?—No, the necessity would exist whether the extension took place or not, but the circumstance of their being farm labourers would render out-door relief suitable to relieve sudden distress instead of indoor relief, for numbers of them would not take indoor relief. There was a question raised with regard to lunatics, but I think that that is outside this matter altogether, and I offer no opinion about it, because if a union is dissolved or amalgamated that is a question that must arise, and I believe it is beyond your control or ours to say what it may be converted into, but I think it doesn't come into our discussion here.

990. Do you know what the establishment expenses of the Ennis Union are at the present time, after the deduction of the part paid by Parliamentary grant?—£1,314.

991. Do you know the amount of the establishment charges, and the poundage they come to, in the union?—I think it was 5d. on the last rate in this union.

992. Are you aware of the poundage of the establishment charge in the Corrofin Union?—I think it is 2d. over Ennis.

993. You have not got the figures?—No.

994. Or in Tulla?—No. Why we have not got the figures is this:—The Chairman and I were deputed at last meeting as a committee to prepare an answer and to get up the statistics. Of course we could have got them from the unions, but we thought perhaps you would be kind enough to forward the figures and calculations as prepared by Mr. Crawford on the occasion of his last visit here; but our time was so short, the meeting deputing the Chairman and I having only been held on Wednesday, that the thing had to be worked by wires, and ended in our being unprepared.

995. You had nearly three weeks' notice of our intention to hold the inquiry, and I think you might have taken steps to prepare your case a little earlier. Mr. Crawford will be most happy to give you the information asked, but he was desirous of working out the expenses from your point of view, and to know what grounds you had for arriving at your conclusions.

996. I have the establishment charges of all the Unions, independent of the Parliamentary Grant. Ballyvaughan establishment charges come to 6d. in the £. Corrofin comes to 5½d. in the £. Ennis to 4½d. Ennistymon to 5¼d. Killadysert to 5¾d. Kilrush to 5¾d. Scariff to 5¾d., and Tulla to 4¾d. These are the poundages of the establishment charges of the Unions after the Parliamentary Grant for the year ending March, 1877.

997. (To *Witness*).—I think that one of the grounds on which you also base your application for amalgamation is that you consider the workhouse here has ample accommodation for increased numbers?—No.

998. Have you considered that question of accommodation?—I have. Of course, by a late measurement, our accommodation has been reduced very much, but still we would be prepared, if necessity arose, to enlarge our house. We have at the West side here, a farm of 6 or 8 acres. We could build on that, and we have land at the other side, which is available and could be easily got.

999. You would be willing to expend what might be necessary for additional buildings?—Yes, and I think it would be of advantage, for in any new buildings we could devote our present hospitals which are in the centre of the house to the use of healthy paupers, and build new hospitals outside with any other addition that would be required. I don't think any increase of officers would be required for the Union by reason of any increase we could expect in the number of paupers coming from the portions of other unions to be added to ours.

1000. But you are clearly of opinion that if the present measurements be accurate, and if this change was made, the house, looking to its present structural arrangements would be insufficient for the accommodation of the union?—No, not insufficient and I think if it proved to be insufficient we have the means of enlarging it and giving ample accommodation to any that would be likely to come. It should be remembered that at the time this house was built, this country contained a population of eight millions of people, and the population of this union was nearly double what it is at present. There was then in this town 10,000 or 11,000 inhabitants, the population is now 6,500. I have before me one of the minute books of January, 1849, and I find we then had 2,004 paupers in the house. Science makes progress every year and with it there is a progress in the amount of accommodation given to each inmate, and thus the accommodation of the house has been reduced by increasing the measurements allowed to each person, and even apart from that I think it would be of advantage to have the hospital outside the house and the entire space of the house devoted to the use of the healthy inmates, and when we can get the money so cheap and pay it back by instalments, the additional expense would be very little to the union; perhaps not more than a halfpenny in the £.

1001. Still, the Workhouse as it exists at present, is in the opinion of the medical officer and of Major Trench, altogether insufficient in certain departments?

I don't know of any report from the medical officer on the books to show it is insufficient, and I don't think there is a Board in Ireland that has been more willing at all times to accede to any report or suggestion of the medical officer than this Board, and every required accommodation has been given and every latitude allowed in every way. No officer whose duty it was to look to this matter has been restrained in any way in the effort to make the house as comfortable as possible I speak in presence of Major Butler, who has been chairman here for many years.

1002. You say you are aware that recently on our application the house has been remeasured?—Yes.

1003. And that the accommodation was fixed under a new schedule?—But a great portion of our sheds, on which a large amount of money has been expended, are perfectly useless now for the accommodation of the poor. There is for instance, a large portion devoted to the Ennis dispensary; the medical officer has got his waiting room and surgery there to save the expense of a house, and there are other portions not used for the accommodation of the poor, so that we are not confined to the measurements of the house, for it is very likely these were not measured at all, and we would probably be able to accommodate 100 in them

1004. You, or your chairman, stated since we came into this room that you could not understand on what principle the accommodation of your house had been reduced upon the recent measurement I will take one of your dormitories, No 3, on the male side of the house, second floor, and by means of it show you how misleading the old accommodation returns are. You are aware that that room is 95 feet long, 17 feet wide and 14ft 6in. high?—Yes.

1005. Are you aware that the room is certified to accommodate 93? Now I should like you to assist me in making a little calculation so as to see how much wall space each pauper would be allowed for his bed. Now multiply 95 feet by two and what is your result?—190 feet

1006. Now deduct from that 5 feet for doorway and 7 feet for the staircase and what have you left?—178 feet

1007. Divide that by 93, which is the number for which the room is certified?—Well, that will be 2 feet for each

1008 No, not even that, it will give less than 2 feet for each inmate?—That is not our argument We think that where the ward was built for 93, to take one third off would be quite sufficient, that would reduce it to 62.

1009 The new measurement under the schedule, (which is a digest of the minimum space accommodation required in England and Scotland), reduces the accommodation of that room not to 62 but to 31, and it is little enough. It is the maximum number, and the minimum space

1010 How is that ward occupied now?—There are only 24 or 25 in it.

1011. But, at the same time, there are in that room certain cases that have been removed from hospital, and which Dr Cullinan would say are very improper cases to be placed in that room, and it appears they have been put there simply from want of proper hospital accommodation?—That is the first time that has appeared, it was never reported to us as a board before

1012. You frequently inspect the house, and you are, doubtless, well acquainted with these details?—Yes, I inspected it formerly oftener than now

1013. Do you know the attic rooms?—Yes, I was through them about a month ago It was suggested by the doctor to make certain changes.

1014. Do you think these rooms in their present condition are proper rooms to be occupied as dormitories. You are aware they have no ceiling—there is nothing but the slates between the people and the open air, and that they are consequently, very hot in summer and very cold in winter. Do you then think these attics should be considered as accommodation to be counted upon for use in a normal state of affairs?—If the matter was brought before us I would be certainly in favour of having a ceiling made—not a flat ceiling, but a cone ceiling.

1015. Do you know the height of the rooms to the wall-plate is scarcely five feet?—I think it is children that are put into these attics now.

1016 Do you know how the attic on the women's side is now occupied—I think some of the paupers there are infirm?—No, it is occupied by the mothers with children

1017. In the present condition of your house are you able to provide separate accommodation for the unmarried mothers and for the married mothers?—No. We have not tried that The only classification we have tried is as to persons of immoral character, these we keep separate, and if they reform we allow them back into the body of the house again.

1018. But is there no difference made between mothers of legitimate and of illegitimate children?—No, but is it so in other unions?

1019. It ought to be so, and in many instances there is accommodation separately provided, but not everywhere They ought, however, to be separated?—Until recently when an alteration was made in the ward these classes were separated, but the ward occupied by the unmarried mothers had to be given up; but I would like to remark that there are a great number of sheds that have not been brought into the measurement that are house property; they are now converted into other uses by us in consequence of having more than sufficient room

1020. I find that a great extent of the shedding has been included in the measurements. Some of them are used as straw stores, and for other purposes?—They are not included in the 560 accommodation return.

1021. You are right, as the accommodation return under the new measurements inclusive of the sheds appears to be for 726

1022. But it must be borne in mind when any portion of the house is overcrowded the house is overcrowded You cannot shift the sick into the healthy department or the children into the adult wards. Therefore, if the hospital is crowded, the house is crowded So with all the classes, and if you take in the aggregate and say that 750 is not overcrowded, it is not sufficient. The house may be overcrowded in some parts, as it was this morning in the hospital, and it is not enough to say there are so many less than the aggregate for whom you have accommodation so long as any one class exceeds the accommodation provided?—The portion I refer to can be made a healthy portion We have more than sufficient room at that side The houses have been converted as I have told you, and as Mr. Doyle has suggested we could turn that again into use for the healthy without overcrowding any portion of the place, and have sufficient accommodation for increased numbers.

1023 Do you consider that the representatives of the ratepayers in giving their answers to our queries may be considered as giving the answers of the ratepayers they represent?—Yes, but still, as Mr. Fitzgerald our vice-chairman has often said, the ratepayers don't always agree

1024 *Witness* —I have spoken frequently to parties from different parts of the union, and they have always complained of the high rates, and the non necessity that existed of keeping up workhouses with so few in them, and that if these unions were amalgamated or absorbed into others their rates would be so much less.

1025. But it appears that you have found nobody who could work that out on paper, and who could show that this proposed amalgamation would produce this saving?—That could be easily done. Our valuation is about £74,000, and our establishment charge is fourpence one-fourth, and if you take £10,000 for the new divisions added to Ennis from

Ennis,
May 8, 1878.

Thos. Greene,
Esq., J.P.

these other unions I speak of, and add that £10,000 to the £74,000, see what relief we give the unions added to us by giving them a basis of £84,000 to raise the rate from.

1026. Do you think this union would benefit by it?—I do. The state of things is very much altered from what it was. Every expenditure now ratified by Parliament is put on the rates, and the rates instead of being called poor rates ought to be called something like a consolidated fund. Whereas formerly if we only contributed for the poor rate we were done, but where these mandatory charges are increasing every year it would be a great advantage to have such a large basis to start from.

1027. Then one of your grounds is that this extended area would reduce the amount of mandatory charges?—Yes.

1028. Well, what are these mandatory charges you speak of?—There are a great many lately put on by the Government, the expense of jurors lists, and other expenses.

1029. Will your proposed amalgamation reduce this expense?—No, but if you have to raise the sum the larger the valuation the less must be the rate per pound.

1030. But if you extend the area you extend the charges as the number of jurors lists must be increased to include the jurors in the extended area?—No.

1031. Do you mean to say that in extending the area you do not increase the number of jurors which the extended area would include?—There is a certain number the clerk has to return, and if you make the return in a certain area you do not increase the number of names.

1032. If, for instance, you extend your area to include part of Corrofin, and take up the rural district of Ruan, will not the clerk have to include in his returns the names of the jurors resident in Ruan?—Yes.

1033. And will not that increase his labours?—No; it is a mere bagatelle, for it is by the hundred he is paid and so many afterwards.

1034. Your valuation of the Ennis Union is £74,004, and your establishment charges $4\frac{1}{4}d.$ I calculated that if the part of Tulla Union was brought back to you, which was originally taken away, it would raise the valuation by £15,750, making a total valuation of £89,754. Now, how much do you suppose that would reduce your establishment charges in Ennis Union?—If you add portion of Corrofin, say the two divisions of Ruan and Muckenagh, which make £4,989 more, that makes a total valuation of £94,743 and one penny in the pound on that would realize something about £400 over the whole valuation.

1035. What would be the effect of this on the Ennis Union?—It might reduce ours perhaps one penny or three farthings in the pound.

1036. Do you think your establishment charges would be at all increased if you get portion of Corrofin and Tulla added to you?—No.

1037. Would you not have an additional relieving officer to pay?—Yes.

1038. Would that not increase the establishment expenses?—Yes, take two relieving officers at £50.

1039. Do you say there would be no additional establishment charges supposing the area of the union was increased by those parts of Tulla and Corrofin?—There would be a little, but it would be counterbalanced by the gain. For instance, a relieving officer is at present in the establishment charges for Corrofin.

1040. I am speaking of the Ennis Union?—It is a mere bagatelle, it might add a farthing. Corrofin comes to us with one penny in the pound in excess of ourselves, and in the fivepence one-fourth Corrofin includes one relieving officer, and that I am allowing for. Then, if you spread that over the whole the effect will not be much. It will be still greater gain for Corrofin, and equally so for Tulla.

1041. I am asking the effect it will have on the Ennis Union. Your establishment charges for March, 1877, were £1,315. Do you think I am wrong in my estimate that if you get that large addition of area to the union your establishment charges would be brought up to £1,400?—Yes, I say in round numbers it would be about that.

1042. Suppose your new establishment charges were £1,400, what would be the poundage then of the establishment charge on the new union?—It would be about fourpence.

1043. At present it is about fourpence farthing?—Yes.

1044. What would the profit be to the Ennis Union?—It is fourpence farthing at present; by the increased area we increase the valuation to £94,743.

1045. And increase the establishment expenses to £1,400?—One penny in the pound will realize £400; threepence in the pound realizes £1,200; and a halfpenny realizes £200. That is threepence halfpenny to realize £1,400, so that Ennis must save three farthings, and Corrofin a penny three farthings. If there is to be a gain I think in the present altered state of the country, where pauperism is on the increase, the property of the country requires that the burden should be made as light as possible, without infringing on the privileges of the poor who seek relief.

1046. I think when I was examining you a few minutes ago about the accommodation you gave me to understand that you were aware that it had been considerably, though not unduly reduced. Under the new schedule 95 is the amount of your hospital accommodation. To-day you have 100 in your hospital. I am, therefore, disposed to agree with you that if any portions of the other unions were amalgamated with yours you would be obliged to build. Now, if you build, would you propose that the charge of the new building should fall on Ennis or upon the whole of the newly constituted union?—The union as it would exist.

1047. Then you would make Corrofin, for instance, which protests against amalgamation, and which already has its own workhouse within easy reach of the poor, pay for providing the necessary extra accommodation here?—I don't think the necessity has arisen for building.

Colonel Butler.

Colonel BUTLER examined.

1048. The board's mind is made up on the subject. You could not persuade us that three establishments are cheaper than one, and until you prove that you will not convince us while we have one house perfectly capable of doing all that is necessary. I was chairman of this board for twenty years during the worst of the times, and I can answer for it we did our duty then. Now the case is altered. We have only 457 in the house. We had over 2,000 then; besides that, the system has been brought in of giving out-door relief, and thus a number of parties who would be getting relief in the house then are now on out-door relief, and with reference to some remarks that were made by Mr. Doyle a few minutes ago about overcrowding—I don't think it is a fair way of putting it to say that because one ward is overcrowded the whole house is overcrowded. I don't think it is exactly logical.

1049. But suppose, the fact to be that the hospital is full, and that the medical officer required room for a dozen other cases, how would you propose to deal with this dozen other cases?—The medical officer would point out some portion of the house that could be used. I believe it has been done sometimes. I would leave that to the medical officer, to report to the board, and they would take steps to remedy it.

1050. In fact you think he would recommend

ENNIS, Aug. 8, 1878.

Colonel Butler.

the temporary use of some other portion of the building for the purpose?—Yes, it was done before.

1051. You were just saying it would greatly reduce the expense if you had one instead of three houses in this county?—Yes, if you ——

1052. Have you given your attention to the subject and calculated in detail what the saving would be?—You will see that no man of common sense would require any calculation. The plain, broad question is, will it cost more to keep up three establishments than one.

1053. Have you considered the necessities and comfort of the poor? If you extend your area very much, and knock three unions into one, have you thought of the distances they will have to travel to get relief?—They would not have great distances.

1054. But suppose you extend your area by knocking three unions into one?—Suppose by extending our area we get additional portions added to the union we are willing, as we have ample accommodation, to build, if we want it.

1055. What would be the distance of the most distant electoral division you propose to add to the new workhouse in Ennis?—Bunratty is the furthest point, and that would be about thirteen Irish miles, and the Corrofin Union comes within two miles of Ennis. The only thing I have to add is to lay down the broad principle that three houses cost more than one. I have property in the other unions proposed to be amalgamated.

Dr. Cullinan.

Dr. CULLINAN examined.

1056. You have been medical officer of this union for a good many years?—Thirty-seven years.

1057. You have been here, in fact, since its formation?—Yes.

1058. I suppose when the union was first formed it was contemplated that those to be accommodated would be principally "able-bodied"?—Yes.

1059. And the dormitories were rather constructed for the purpose of affording shelter to large numbers than for the purpose of being used as a workhouse in the modern sense of the term?—Yes, there is a good deal of difference in the purpose for which they were contrived then and what they are used for now.

1060. During the time of the famine the house was overcrowded?—It was very overcrowded at that time.

1061. And the majority of the people accommodated were able-bodied, and driven in through distress?—Quite so.

1062. At that time was your aged and infirm class very numerous?—All classes were very numerous. Several beds contained two or three persons together. There was very severe distress, and the mortality was excessive, but the able-bodied were in the largest number. They were not generally able bodied, they were reduced to the last point.

1063. By starvation?—Yes, they would have been able-bodied under other circumstances.

1064. Now, that the condition of the country has changed, is it not a fact that the infirmaries are full?—Yes.

1065. And that the major portion of the inmates of the workhouse consist of "the sick," and the "aged and infirm?"—That is quite so.

1066. I suppose that to some extent the accommodation originally set apart for ordinary able bodied is comparatively unused by them?—Yes, but it is inadequate for the present class of inmates.

1067. Have you not been obliged, as time went on, to convert a good deal of what was originally intended for able-bodied paupers into accommodation for aged and infirm?—Certainly.

1068. And, notwithstanding that conversion, is it not a fact that very recently you have been obliged to move mothers with children into one of the attics to give further room for the aged and infirm?—That was not done by my direction. When I saw that the infirm females were exceedingly overcrowded I directed that the attic should be occupied by the mothers, but the children were put in afterwards without my direction.

1069. Was this change brought about by direction of a committee of this board who met to consider the question?—I made a report that the infirm womens' department was very much overcrowded, and a committee was deputed to inquire into the matter, and they directed that a certain portion of the attics should be occupied by certain classes of able-bodied women, as I intended by the mothers, but it was occupied afterwards by the children, with their mothers.

1070. Is not the infirmary intended for acute cases?—Yes; but there are general cases of infirmity there also.

1071. Is not the fever hospital kept exclusively for infectious cases?—Not exclusively. It is also used for acute cases.

1072. Is not your infirmary crowded?—The female side is very crowded.

1073. Have you got a labour-room separate?—Yes.

1074. Are the convalescents kept in the same room after confinement?—They remain for about a month afterwards in that room.

1075. In the infirm ward are there not cases that are more properly suited to the hospital than the infirm ward—cases of dysentery?—They are not allowed to remain in the infirm wards. After a day or two I have them transferred, and my colleague acts in the same way.

1076. But is it a fact that there are cases in the infirm ward which, if you had room you would remove into the female hospital?—Yes.

1077. Cases that properly belong to the female hospital?—Yes.

1078. And that you are compelled to keep in the infirm ward because there is not room in the hospital?—There are some females in the infirm ward who owing to the confined space, become unsuited to the place, and they should be removed to the hospital.

1079. Do you consider that attic a proper place for any class of people to sleep in during either winter or summer?—The word proper is a relative term. I think it is much better than a crowded room, and in that sense I consider it a proper place, and I prefer it to crowded accommodation for the use of any patients.

1080. Are we speaking of the same room—the attic—where the women and children are?—Yes, I prefer to see anybody in the attic rather than in the infirm wards, where they are crowded.

1081. But suppose you had infirm wards in proper condition would you consider the attic a proper place?—Certainly not. They have been for a long time overcrowded.

1082. You would dispense with the attics if you had sufficient room besides?—Yes.

1083. With regard to the fever hospital, has it at any time been overcrowded?—Not for many years. We have had very little fever for many years. In January, 1849, we had 93 cases of fever; in January, 1878, we had 12.

1084. In the fever hospital you have 12 cases, which appears to be the minimum number referred to, but is that fever hospital practically useless for any other purpose than fever patients. Would you put any other patients into the hospital if there was typhoid in it already?—The distinction you make is very proper; if there was typhoid I would be very slow to put it in contact with persons not suffering from contagious diseases and accidents.

1085. Are extern and non-pauper patients admitted to the fever hospital?—Yes.

1086. In the 12 at present are there any externs?—Yes, they came from outside chiefly.

Ennis May 9, 1918. Dr Callinan.

1087. They have not arisen within the walls of the house?—No, we have very little from the house.

1088. Did you say that you would prefer to use those attics as sleeping rooms rather than the rooms under them?—Yes, in their present state. The space below is entirely overcrowded. It is the infirm female wards and the female hospital are overcrowded.

1089. Did you ever report to the board that this part of the house were overcrowded?—Frequently.

1090. When?—My report book is there; I even laid out a scale of space.

Captain George O'Callaghan, examined.

Capt. George O'Callaghan

1091. I am Chairman of Tulla Union. I simply wish to state that I think the feeling of the ratepayers is against amalgamation, though at a meeting of the board I think the proposal for amalgamation was carried by a majority of one. I wish simply to state the views held by those who are against amalgamation. First of all, the present buildings would have to be given up or used as hospitals; secondly, there would not be the same surveillance over the expenses as at present, and there would be many expenses put upon us—to keep up a medical officer, to have paid nurses instead of the workhouse free nurses, there should besides be ambulances to bring in patients, and they should also do what they and we are very much opposed to, namely—pay a large rate in aid for Ennis. That I believe exists. (Mr. Vesey Fitzgerald interrupting said that no rate in aid had been levied.)

1092. (*To Witness.*) Yes, you are quite right. There has been a rate in aid under the late act? - We pay something less than a farthing, but then we should have to pay a very large rate in aid for Ennis. Then the officers could not be dispensed with, unless by compensating them for many years to come. There would also be a very large sum expended in increasing the accommodation of this house. Of course that would, no doubt, aid the town of Ennis very much, but it would afford no aid to Tulla or Corrofin, and, at the same time, contracts would be taken away from these small towns for they could not compete with Ennis, but that is no argument. At the same time everything being equal I think the ratepayers in small towns ought to get an opportunity of making money by small contracts. It has been stated here that there is a feeling, a sentiment among the people in these country parts, that their union should not be broken up. What I expected was a plain statement from the chairman how it would affect our pockets. If amalgamation will reduce our rates I am for it. If it is shown there will be no decrease I prefer leaving things as they are. I think that is the feeling of most people in Tulla Union. It is simply a question of pounds, shillings, and pence.

1093. I think Mr. Crawford attended at Tulla, and so far as statistics are concerned he explained the matter fully?—Yes. But I believe the statistics did not contemplate what would be doubtless necessary—to maintain hospitals at such places when the workhouses had been done away with.

1094. No, the calculations were independent of that, and independent also of any superannuation.

1095. Do you think extensions of the area would have any effect on the attendance of guardians at Ennis?—Decidedly.

1096. Do you think the guardians representing these additional divisions would be disposed to attend?—I think it would tend very much against their attendance.

1097. Do you think the poor who have to attend to make applications for relief would be facilitated by the change?—No. Of course there are greater facilities for attending at Tulla.

1098. If part of Tulla was brought here would the other part be taken to Scariff?—Yes.

1099. Is there part of it close to Scariff?—Yes.

1100. Would Tulla itself be close?—It is about 10 miles.

1101. Tulla was originally in the Scariff Union, I understand?—Yes.

1102. And it is about 10 miles from Tulla itself?—Yes.

Pierce O'Brien, Esq., Ex officio Guardian, Tulla Union, examined.

Pierce O'Brien, Esq.

1103. It was on my notice of motion that the resolution was carried in Tulla for the purpose of amalgamating a portion of it with Ennis. We succeeded by a majority of two out of twenty-two or twenty-three Guardians. I will state the reasons I wish to have the portion of Tulla I represent added to Ennis. For instance, in one of the divisions I hold in Tulla the rate is quite as large as in the division I hold in this Union, while the one is a twelve months rate and the other is only a six months rate, in fact, the one is only half the other.

1104. Which is your electoral division?—Quin is the particular one: Quin and Spancilhill.

1105. And you state that you have to pay twice as much in the one as in the other?—Yes. For a long time I did attend both Boards, but I have not attended Tulla much lately, and from my experience of the way both unions are managed, I decidedly prefer the management of Ennis to that of Tulla in many respects. There are many other reasons which I cannot exactly bring forward at present, which would make one prefer being added to Ennis. From my knowledge of the Guardians, I think they would be as well disposed to attend the weekly meetings in Ennis as in Tulla. I am speaking of the portion to be added to Ennis and not the portion to be added to Scariff.

1106. Do you think at the present time there are any people receiving relief from Quin who ought not to receive relief?—There are. I went one day to investigate that matter and I am afraid there are people receiving relief who ought not to be.

1107. Do you think out-door relief is too much given in Quin?—I think so, the elected Guardian says he has done everything in his power to prevent it but that he cannot.

1108. Do you think the outdoor cases and the relief given to persons who ought not to receive relief, are sufficient to cause the extra expense complained of?—No. I think it must be the management of the union.

1109. Do you think the amount of pauperism and the amount of relief to be given would be less if Quin was in this union instead of in Tulla?—No. We are most liberal in Ennis, but I think the contracts might be more favourable in Ennis and the management better.

1110. How is it that the cost is 3s. $8\frac{1}{4}d.$ here and in Tulla 3s. $8\frac{1}{4}d.$?—Here beef tea is given to the inmates at certain times, which adds a little to the cost.

Ennis. May 8, 1878.

ROBERT SPAIGHT, Esq., examined.

Robt. Spaight, Esq.

1111. Are you a Guardian?—I am an ex-officio Guardian of Tulla Union.

1112. Do you attend here by direction of the Tulla Board?—Yesterday a resolution was passed at the Board, when there was a very large meeting and the Chairman, Vice-chairman, and I, were asked to attend here to-day to protest against amalgamation. We do not think it would be for the interests of the ratepayers. We would be for amalgamation if it would decrease the rates. There are a great many gentlemen here who think that if these Workhouses were done away with, they would have no rates to pay, but for the very good reasons stated by Mr. Crawford, we do not think it would be so. I am a very large ratepayer, and if I thought amalgamation would effect the rates I would be in favour of it.

1113. That is if it effected something substantial?—Yes.

1114. Three farthings or a penny you would not consider substantial?—No. I would be a Guardian in both Scariff and Ennis, and I could not attend either boards; the distance is too far.

THOMAS LUCAS, Esq., Vice-chairman Ennistymon Board of Guardians, examined.

Thomas Lucas, Esq.

1115. I have been deputed to come here to ask some questions as to the removal of some parts of the townlands of this union—Ballyae, Fermoyle, and Clooneen. There was a notice from Ennis Union that it was intended to take part of our union, and there was a resolution passed at our Board:—"That we beg to direct the attention of the Poor Law Union Inquiry Commissioners to our reply on the 28th August last to their inquiries as to the subject of the amalgamation of the union, and to state that we are opposed to the proposal of the Ennis Union Board of Guardians, namely, that portion of this union be added to theirs." The Board of Guardians are quite opposed to have any portion of their union amalgamated with Ennis.

MAJOR C. W. STUDDERT, Chairman of Corrofin Union, examined.

Major C. W. Studdert.

1116. I appear with the Deputy-chairman and Deputy Vice-chairman to protest against amalgamation, and there was a resolution passed as follows:—"The Board of Guardians of this union unanimously object to any portion of their union being annexed to that of Ennis, as they are of opinion that an examination of the statistical information received by the Commissioners of Inquiry from clerks of unions will show that little or no saving (if any) could be effected by amalgamation, while very great hardship and injury to the sick and destitute poor would result therefrom. The Board feel that the interests of the poor, which they are bound to protect, should not be overlooked through a desire to effect what would appear a doubtful saving to the ratepayers. Amalgamation would entail the following expenses, which should be incurred, and which would more than counterbalance any supposed saving:—(1.) The erection of additional building accommodation. (2.) Increase of officers' salaries for increased duties. (3.) Conveyance of sick and infirm persons to the workhouse, by reason of the increased distance they would have to travel. (4.) Superannuation of officers of dissolved unions. Another objection to amalgamation would be that the guardians, owing to the long distances they would have to travel, would not attend regularly at the meetings of the Board, and could not, therefore as efficiently watch over the interests of the poor and the ratepayers. Another matter which the Board desire to bring under the notice of the Commissioners is that 1,286 applications for relief were made to them during the year ended 25th March, 1878, which were considered and decided on by them as follows:—

Provisional admissions to workhouse confirmed	183
Ordered to the workhouse	403
Provisional out-door relief confirmed	73
Ordered out-door relief	604
Refused relief	23

In submitting the above figures the guardians hope that some idea may be formed of the injury which would be inflicted on the poor if such large numbers should be obliged to travel long distances to another workhouse to seek relief. In conclusion, the Board would observe that they do not see that sufficient reason exists for dissolving the union; the guardians hold their weekly meetings regularly; the wants of the poor are duly attended to, the ratepayers are satisfied with the management of its affairs, which are efficiently and economically administered, and on these grounds the Board respectfully protest against amalgamation."

1117. Do you know the number of inmates there are in the Corrofin Workhouse?—155 on last Saturday.

1118. Do you know the proportion of sick and infirm?—Yes, 91, and 3 in the fever hospital.

1119. There are 108 altogether classed among the sick and infirm?—Yes, and during the year there were 129 persons admitted in sickness, 12 of whom were suffering from fevers or other dangerous contagious diseases, 150 suffering under other diseases, 12 suffering from accidental injury. There were 130 admitted who were not sick (exclusive of births). The total number admitted during the year was 259. The number of persons treated in the workhouse and fever hospital during the year ending 29th September, 1877, were—fever and other dangerous contagious diseases, 13; other diseases, 183; accidentally injured, 13. Total, 209.

MR. JOHN CHAMBERS, elected Guardian Kilradysart Union, examined.

Mr. Chambers.

1120. Are you deputed by your Board to attend here?—Yes; I am the Western guardian, and the Eastern guardian is here also. There was a rumour that there would be an adjournment of this inquiry to this day week, and therefore we did not come as well prepared as we would like to be.

1121. You represent the part that would go to Kilrush, and the other guardian represents the part that would go to Ennis. Are you deputed by the Board to come here?—No, they did not ask us.

1122. And you come here of your own notion?—Yes, as a representative of the ratepayers.

1123. You represent the Electoral Division of Kilmurrey, the one adjacent to Kilrush?—Yes.

1124. What is your feeling on the subject of amalgamation?—The ratepayers of the whole Kilradysart Union, unless those interested, are for amalgamation. Whether it will effect a saving or not I don't know, but in 1875 and 1876 our rates were 6d., 7d., and up to 11d.

1125. In your electoral division?—Yes; and for the last three years they were 12d., 14d., and 15d.

1126. Do you wish to be amalgamated?—Yes; I have abstracts to prove that for the last three rates made we have only four paupers from my division, and 7s. was given in out-door relief.

1127. Are you aware how these accounts are made up?—Yes; I have the abstracts here.

1128. Do you know what the whole expenditure was in Killadysart Union for the year 1877?—I do.

1129. In March, 1877, it was 2s. 2d. in the £ in Killadysart; the expenditure in Kilrush for the same period was 2s. 2½d., being a halfpenny more than you paid, while the whole expense in Ennis Union was 2s. 0½d. So that Kilrush was only a halfpenny more than Killadysart, and Kilrush was twopence over Ennis. There is, therefore, not so much difference between you. Do you think it would reduce the expenses if you were transferred to Kilrush?—I do.

1130. Can you show it by figures in any way?—No, I have no figures. I can only show the abstracts for the last four years.

1131. In Kilrush the Establishment charges were 5⅛, and in Killadysart 2⅛?—We have only four paupers, and we consider it a great hardship to have to pay so heavy a rate.

1132. But the other charges would remain the same?—The present levy is 15d., whereas in 1875 and 1876 it was only 6d. and 7d.

1133. Do you know that new charges have been put on the poor-rates since then?—I do.

May 8, 1878. Mr. Chapman.

Mr. THOMAS MOYLAN examined.

Mr Thos. Moylan.

1134. What electoral division do you represent?—I represent the Lissan electoral division.

1135. Are you deputed to attend here?—No.

1136. What have you got to say on the subject of amalgamation?—We consider the rate too high, and it is rising daily, and, as amalgamation was offered, I came to see what could be done.

1137. Can you show us how amalgamation would reduce your rates?—No.

1138. By statistics or otherwise?—I could not.

CHARLES GEORGE MAHON, Esq., ex-officio Guardian, Killadysart Union, examined.

Chas. Geo Mahon, Esq.

1139. I adopt in full every expression used by Captain O'Callaghan and Mr. Speight. I would be for amalgamation if I thought it would save expense, but I am satisfied it would not. I adopt their views also as to the distance patients would have to travel, and I think it would be a great inconvenience to the poor. Our chairman holds these views, and he wrote a statement in which his views were embodied.

The inquiry then closed.

INQUIRY AT MILLSTREET.—FRIDAY, MAY 10TH, 1878.

MILLSTREET. May 10, 1878.

Before Major the Hon. W. LE POER TRENCH, R.E. (Chairman), ANDREW DOYLE, Esq., and CHARLES SHARMAN CRAWFORD, Esq.

Gentlemen. We have attended here in consequence of a resolution of this board which was passed on the 28th February last. A series of questions was sent out when our commission was first appointed, and the answer given by this board to our question as to whether it would be expedient that the union should be dissolved was—"The board are of opinion this union should be dissolved and amalgamated with the unions of Kanturk, Macroom, and Killarney." Since then my two colleagues have each, on two different occasions, met this board and conferred with them and have, I think, given every information in their power with regard to the financial consequences of the proposed change. I find that the following resolution was adopted by you, after having seen my colleagues:

"Resolved that the Commissioners be requested to hold an inquiry into the question of amalgamation of this union with the three adjoining unions as formerly as we cannot continue to pay the exorbitant rates at present assessed, and likely to continue, the average being from 3s 4d to 3s. 6d for several years, being nearly twice larger than the average rates of Munster; the Board is decidedly of opinion, having given deep and earnest consideration to the question, that the accomplishment of that object would not bear harshly on the poor as the remotest parts of the proposed amalgamated districts would be as near to their respective workhouses as many districts of the adjoining unions."

There are three other unions involved in this question, and we are now prepared to hear whatever evidence is offered by the guardians of this union in support of their resolution, and on behalf of the other unions affected.

JOHN HOWARD, Esq., examined.

John Howard, Esq.

1140. You are, I understand, deputy vice-chairman of this union of Millstreet?—At present I am vice-chairman.

1141. Are you an ex-officio guardian?—No; always an elected guardian since the formation of the union, about twenty-eight or thirty years ago.

1142. Do you desire amalgamation?—I do, Sir.

1143. Will you be good enough to explain on what grounds?—I think the first grounds are these—The valuation of our union is very low, our rates are excessive, and consequently owing to our low valuation, they are likely to continue so, inasmuch as since the formation of the union they have been so. We see no reason to expect the rates to be lightened. I may say, perhaps, it was never intended to have a union in Millstreet.

1144. That is hardly the question. You have a union in Millstreet, and we are now dealing with the question of dissolving it.—The reason we got it was there was so much pauperism and distress and death existing through the country at the time. We had no union here, and so many required relief, and so many died, that the workhouses adjacent were not able to afford immediate relief to the number of applicants, and it was consequently considered perfectly necessary at that time to have many auxiliary houses formed in this town. At that time the part of the town as you come into it and drive up from the lower part to the bridge up here, that part was altogether formed into auxiliary houses exclusively, and a temporary shed had been built a little outside the town, at a place we call the tanyard, and besides that there was a large house belonging to Mr Morris, which was also made available for a temporary house. Seeing that the amount requiring relief was excessive at the time—as well as I remember there were in all these sheds nearly 3,000 persons at the time with a great number relieved outside—it was deemed advisable by some of the intelligent and leading persons in this locality who take a decided interest in the welfare of the people, to recommend to the Commissioners to build a workhouse, seeing it was quite

MILLSTREET.
May 16, 1872.
John Howard, Esq.

necessary to have it within reach of these people, not knowing how long that state of the country would exist. We find now, thank God, that the pauperism which existed then does not still exist, nevertheless the rates continue high, inasmuch as many of the people we had at that time in the sheds and auxiliary houses got disabled—maimed or blind, and some of them are here to this day, and are chargeable to my own division The population has gone down now, and though it has gone down pauperism has not gone down to that extent also; and we see very plainly from the enormous and excessive rates we have had to pay all along, and are likely to continue, that ultimately this union if not bankrupt, will, at all events verge on it or very near it, the rates are so excessive and high. If you look to the other unions, as I see from the last return of Thom, you will see that where the average rate in Mill-street Union amounted to 3s. 5d., all over Ireland there was not a union, with the exception of one, that went over 3s, and that went up to 3s 2d If you look you will find that few unions in Ireland average 2s, while many commenced at 5d, 6d., and 8d. I think it is only right to say that as pauperism exists and the rates are so high here, we could fairly and justly claim amalgamation with the unions from which we have been severed. If through any fault of ours or the management of this union by the guardians the rates have become excessive it may be a fair excuse for adjacent unions not to take pity on us again, but we being formerly part and parcel of them, and having been severed from them when the distress of the times required it, and when that distress is over now, and we see that our rates are not going down as the population does. I claim it as a right—in fact, a charitable right—for these persons to take charge of us, and be united with them again, as it was through no fault of ours these excessive rates were incurred. We got the fag end of the three unions, where, if failure of crops or potatoes existed throughout the country, we are likely to have a fair share of it, being in a remote district

1145. You say as to pauperism that while the population has gone down the pauperism has not gone down?—No, it has not gone down *pari passu*.

1146. Then so far as pauperism has not gone down you don't think the necessity for giving relief has decreased?—The necessity for giving relief exists still, inasmuch as the people who are in the house are relieved.

1147. Pauperism has not gone down, and there are as many to be relieved as before?—Not as fully as it ought, for there are many relieved who might not be.

1148. Do you mean to convey that this union workhouse is used by many who should not be relieved?—I think they could manage outside it. They come in for a time in winter, and then branch away again in summer, and we have to complain of many of them

1149 I think you mentioned that the valuation was very low?—Yes, it is only £27,000

1150 And you compared your rates with the rates in other parts of Ireland?—I did.

1151 You say that your valuation is low Are you not aware that the valuation in Ireland is uneven, and if it is low in one district and somewhat higher in another the district where the valuation is low has apparently higher rates, inasmuch as the poundage is higher?—What makes the great difference is that the staff expenses of this union take as much money as the staff of the Macroom Union. They have a large valuation. Here the expense has to be borne by £27,000 or £28,000, while in Kanturk it is spread over £80,000 That alters the case very much. We are £27,000, and when we pay 3d it never costs them more than a halfpenny When this union was formed it was considered at that time that fuel could be easily had, having so many bogs in the locality, but when that was tested it was found from various causes, the wetness of the season, and the price of the labour, that turf was more expensive than coals, and we had to give up burning turf altogether, and the house is now supplied with coals. That is one thing which those who were anxious to get this union were mistaken in. Then, again, it was considered that milk could be easily had, but we found that that also was a mistake, and we do not now get the milk from the locality, as there is not enough of it here The skim milk is supplied mostly by one contractor, who is obliged to bring it from Cork The man lives in the district, but in order to supply the full amount he must go to Cork for it in the winter and bring it up here He is the only contractor. There is no competition

1152. Then, is it on the ground of economy you advocate amalgamation?—Yes

1153. How do you propose to divide your unions amongst these other unions?—Now, so far as I am concerned, that is a thing to which I did not give much consideration

1154 Do you agree with the resolution the board passed?—I do partly agree with it, but it occurs to me that if the electoral divisions comprising the town of Millstreet went to Kanturk it would be more convenient for the inhabitants of Millstreet, and easier of access.

1155 You think it better that the whole union should go to Kanturk?—I would not say the whole of it I would let the portion that went with Macroom before go with Macroom now Perhaps Kanturk would not take all the unions, and there might not be room for all, but there was portion of this union went with Kanturk already, and I say let part still go to Macroom Kilcorny went formerly with Macroom.

1156. Didn't Drishane also go formerly with Macroom?—No, only Kilcorney

1157. The sub division proposed by the board was Coomlegane, Drishane, Crinnaloo, and Kilcorney to go to Macroom?—Kilcorney and Crinnaloo formed one division at the time they were united with Macroom, and when they were separated from Macroom Kilcorney was divided, and portion of it formed Crinnaloo division So far my opinion goes with regard to Millstreet and Crinnaloo, but I don't think I am an authority at all on that subject.

1158. But from your local knowledge you do not disapprove of the sub-division proposed in the regulation?—No, I don't disapprove of it I think the remaining portion of the union went to Kanturk before.

1159. You have recommended Caherbarnagh and Knocknagree to go to Killarney?—Yes, if advisable It is said it would be inconvenient to Millstreet people to go to Kanturk I think there are portions of each of the adjoining unions further away from the workhouses than any part of the new union, and as far as any part of the present union.

1160 Are there any other such centres of population as Millstreet now in Kanturk Union, and at a distance from the workhouse?—No, I am not aware of any Newmarket is far away, but not so large as Millstreet.

1161. Have you any statistics to show the class of paupers that would have to be provided for by Kanturk supposing it took the districts you propose to transfer to it?—What I think is that at present it would be advisable to leave sick persons in hospital here, for it would be most difficult to remove them instanter I would for some time leave a hospital here—as long as reason and utility would recommend.

1162. What class would you propose to transfer to Kanturk?—I would leave the fever patients who would not be convenient to the other town or sudden cases, such as a man with a broken leg

1163 In fact you would leave the hospital here for fever and accident cases?—Yes, if necessary.

1164. Then of the inmates at present here which would you transfer?—The whole of them with the exception of any that it would be dangerous to remove. Those whose health would guarantee their safety I would remove.

1165. Have you made any inquiry at Kanturk as to their willingness to receive your paupers?—From the few guardians I spoke to I think there is no objection, but I can't speak for all of them.

1166. Have you made any inquiry as to the capability of the Kanturk Workhouse to receive the paupers

MILLSTREET.
May 13, 1878.
John Howard, Esq.

transferred from you?—From what I know myself of the Kanturk Workhouse I think it did at one time contain a very large number, and I think it would have to contain a less number now than it did in former times Therefore I think the room ought to be there. I understand there is accommodation there for 1,100, and we will be far short of that number.

1167. Of the numbers you would have to transfer from here, how many are there in the house at the present time?—269.

1168 Can you tell me the numbers in each class of which this 269 is composed?—On the 8th May there were 51 healthy inmates, 113 infirm, and 107 sick, total 271

1169 107 in the hospital?—Yes This is a return of the state of the house for the last six years, viz 1873: —1st January, healthy 90, infirm 92, sick 158, total 340, 1873, 1st July, healthy 85, infirm 55, sick 137, total 387, 1874—1st January, healthy 121, infirm 81, sick 137, total 339, 1st July, healthy 50, infirm 59, sick 131, total 240, 1875—1st January, healthy 107, infirm 122, sick 124, total 353, 1st July, healthy 55, infirm 83, sick 100, total 238, 1876—1st January, healthy 114, infirm 112, sick 85, total 311; 1st July, healthy 52, infirm 98, sick 89, total 239, 1877—1st January, healthy 90, infirm 110, sick 68, total 268; 1st July, healthy 34, infirm 96, sick 96, total 226, 1878.—1st January healthy 65, infirm 139, sick 92, total 296, 8th May, healthy 51, infirm 113, sick 107, total 271.

1170 Do you know what accommodation Kanturk Workhouse has for the sick and infirm class?—I do not, but as they had accommodation for 1,000 or 1,100, they must have more accommodation than would answer what would be sent by us, especially if we sent some to Macroom and some to Killarney The Kanturk Guardians can answer better however, for I could hardly answer for other than my own union.

1171 With regard to the portion you propose to transfer to Macroom Do you not think the natural features of the country (the mountain which intervenes) would rather impede the means of transporting paupers?—There is as good a road there as any where else.

1172. Over the mountains?—Yes There is a good road Part of Kilcorney is only 8 miles from Macroom.

1173 Have you made any calculation of the estimated saving that would accrue to the part of the union that would go to Kanturk?—No, I have not exactly made any calculation, but I know and believe that ultimately there would and ought to be a large saving

1174 Do you know what the establishment expenses of your own union are?—They are something about 7*d*

1175. After deducting the parliamentary grant what does the union pay for establishment expenses?—About 7*d*, but I could not exactly tell

1176 Would it surprise you to find that after deducting the Parliamentary Grant for the year ending March, 1877, the charge was 5½*d*?—It would not, for if you made the calculation it is correct, and I made no calculation.

1177 Do you know what the establishment charge in Kanturk is?—No, I don't, but I would not be surprised if it would be a good deal higher than ours

1178. Do you know that the excess of expenditure in this union over Kanturk union is derived nearly altogether from your excess of poverty; that it is on the indoor maintenance charge that your union exceeds Kanturk?—Yes, I know it must go far on the way to do it.

1179. Take the year ending March, 1877, the charge for indoor maintenance in the Kanturk union was 11¾*d*, in your union it was 1*s* 7*d*, showing a difference of 7¼*d*. on the in-maintenance. Do you think you would get a reduction of that amount paid for in-maintenance by going to Kanturk?—Oh, I know we would get a reduction of a portion of it.

1180. How would you get it—by reducing the number of parties relieved?—The valuation of Kanturk.

1181 That has nothing to say to it. Do you think you would have less indoor maintenance charged on the union?—Certainly I do

1182. Do you think the amount of relief given in this house, chargeable to this union, would be diminished?—I think it would be, for I see there are many applicants here who could do without relief if relief were not so accessible. Of course, any one who requires it, should get it, but there are many relieved who would not look for it in Kanturk. Persons come in here with a sore hand, or anything of that kind, and they would not look for relief if they had to go to Kanturk or Macroom When they get the habit of coming in to us, some of them come and spend the winter, and do the best they can in the summer I may candidly tell that, perhaps as you distinctly say, it is not the difference of union maintenance our gains at present would be derived from, but what makes me so anxious for the amalgamation of this union is that, I say, we were severed without any fault of ours from these unions formerly when it was quite necessary and charitable to do so I say the tendency of the Government now is different from what it was then with regard to the chargeability of paupers I say the tendency of the Government lately is for union rating That was not in contemplation at that time, and I say it is not fair for the adjacent union or Government to do any act that would injure us materially on account of their intentions of having union rating I say if we were united to those unions to which we formerly belonged, and would still belong, were it not for the exigency of the times—we were divided in order to bring relief to those who were dying, and but for that, we would still remain part and parcel of them If we have the union that existed originally, we will derive something from that, something that we won't derive if left to ourselves in Millstreet It is not treating us fairly if we are left here. That is the principal reason.

1183 Do you know the difference between the average rating in the union and the three other unions of Killarney, Macroom, and Kanturk?—I do.

1184 Tell me what the average poundage is?—I know very well the last argument I used won't avail unless the gentlemen attending from Kanturk Union (and it is an important fact, and I confide in the justice of these gentlemen attending from other unions), unless they do what is just, and I say they are incapable of doing anything unjust or unfair

1185 Answer my question, please. That is another matter altogether?—Millstreet rates for the last four years.

1186 What do you mean by the Millstreet rates?—I am giving you the Millstreet, Kanturk, and Macroom average rate for the last four years. I find the last average rate in Millstreet, in 1877, was 2*s*. 11½*d* That is 3*s* I may say Kanturk average was 1*s* 5½*d*, and the average of Macroom, 1*s* 4*d*. I have not got Killarney return. I may also tell you that for 1876, Millstreet was 2*s* 6*d*, Kanturk, 2*s* 8*d*.; Macroom, 1*s*. 2*d*., for 1875, Millstreet was 2*s*. 8*d*, Kanturk, 2*s*. 1½*d*, Macroom, 1*s* 3½*d*, and for 1874, Millstreet was more than doubled, 4*s*. 6*d*, Kanturk, 1*s* 11½*d*.; and Macroom 1*s* 3*d* Therefore, I think, you will not be surprised, seeing the excessive rates, at our reasonable request to have something done to save us from them.

1187. Your valuation, I think you said, was as low as £27,576?—Yes

1188 And your expenditure for relief on the valuation of the poundage is 2*s* 7*d*.?—Yes

1189. Well taking such a union as Bantry, for instance, which has only a valuation of £21,000, or £6,000 less than yours, where the poundage is only 1*s* 3*d*. or less than half of yours Have you ever considered any reason why Bantry should be so much less than Millstreet?—I have not Of course it must be caused by the number relieved in the house.

1190. Do you think the number relieved out of the

MILLSTREET.
May 16, 187[illegible]
John Howard, Esq.

house is any test of the expenditure in any union, or that it illustrates in any way the cost to the ratepayers—the greater or less amount of outdoor relief?—The greater amount of outdoor and indoor relief you give, of course it adds to it.

1191. If you find in Millstreet you give ten times as much outdoor relief as in Bantry, would that tend to clear up in your mind why Millstreet is so much in excess of Bantry?—I think a union is not so essential in Bantry.

1192. There are two unions nearly equal in valuation, one £27,000, and the other £31,000. Bantry being at the disadvantage Bantry gives 1s. 3d., and you give 2s. 7d. Looking for a reason for that, I find that you give ten times as much outdoor relief in Millstreet as in Bantry, and I naturally conclude that that is one reason why the expenditure in Millstreet is so much greater? Is the population as great in Bantry as it is in Millstreet?—If the population be not as great, the amount of relieve should not be as great.

1193. The amount of indoor relief?—The outdoor relief too; for if they have not the population they don't want the relief. Bantry is a remote district.

1194. What is the amount of your outdoor relief as compared with the indoor relief—the comparative amount for the year in Millstreet?—I have not calculated that.

1195. You have 280 odd in the house, and the number receiving outdoor relief is 325, so that, in fact, you are in excess of your indoor relief?—Yes.

1196. Don't you think that would, to some extent, account for the larger expenditure in this union?—I don't think it would, for I think if we were to stop the outdoor relief, and have the number brought into the house, the expenditure would be far higher, and I think many families getting relief is a saving. If you stopped relief fathers of families would die, and a greater number of widows and orphans should inevitably be relieved in the house, and they are the class to whom this board is anxious to give relief, and I may add that the guardians are very slow (and have formed a resolution on the subject) to give outdoor relief to single persons.

1197. At all events you, with a population of 14,592, give ten times as much outdoor relief as Bantry, whose population is 16,330. So that you see the population of Bantry is higher, and yet their outdoor relief is all these times less than yours, and your poundage on your relief is rather more than twice as much as on Bantry. Take another union—the Union of Skull. The valuation is only £15,000—(you give seven times nearly as much outdoor relief as they give)—and yet their poundage is only 1s. 9d., and they don't complain?—They don't because they have not the applicants.

1198. You complain very much in this union of the weighty expenditure, and in other unions the expenditure appears to be considerably less, and all other things being equal except the outdoor relief, one naturally thinks that the greater extent of outdoor relief in this union is the cause of your greater expenditure?—No, we would be worse off if we did not relieve them, in fact the family we relieve with 5s. or 6s. outside would cost £1 in the house.

1199. That is a very old story?—Well, it is worth something.

1200. And is the system you think it would be desirable to apply to the other unions, with which your union to be amalgamated—outdoor relief in the same proportion?—If I were a guardian in the other unions I would use my own discretion, but I could form no opinion now what other unions should do. We give outdoor relief with another motive: if these children were reared in the workhouse they would be almost perfectly useless for work outside afterwards. They do not grow up as healthy and as strong, nor are their habits, so far as manual labour goes, improved in the house at all. Each of these children would form portion of the family if reared outside, and being taught something as they grow up; they are taken by the farmers and fed, and positively without any effort whatever they cease to become burdens on the union.

1201. Then you think amalgamation would extend that beneficial system of outdoor relief, and for that, among other reasons, you desire to see amalgamation?—Not for that reason, but anywhere I was guardian I would continue that system as it is for the good of the applicants.

1202. I think I understood you to say that the shutting up of this house would reduce pauperism considerably, inasmuch as the convenience would not be so great for the poor to receive relief?—I do not give that as a reason.

1203. In certain cases then?—It would not be worth shutting up the house if it made relief inaccessible.

Horace Townsend, Esq.

HORACE TOWNSEND, Esq., Examined.

1204. I appear here as the representative of my partner, Mr. Hussey. We are agents for a large area in this division and up to the present we have been strongly in favour of amalgamation on the ground that the area taxed is so small that it must always be heavily rated. Of consequence our judgment is formed on that general basis. We have not gone into the statistics. The area is a very small one, and it has practically been always a highly rated union, and the probability is it will always be so. We are in favour of anything that would make a change, thinking that possibly any change would be an improvement, as it could not make us worse.

Mr. Hegarty.

MR. JEREMIAH HEGARTY, examined.

1205. Are you an elected guardian?—Yes.

1206. Have you been long a guardian?—No, I am rather a new guardian. This is my second year.

1207. You have heard the proposal made as regards amalgamation?—Last August when the matter was before this board they were unanimous, at that time I was one of the parties who was anxious for amalgamation, and for this reason—it was stated plainly that the saving would be from 8d. to 1s. in the £. I also asked our respected Chairman at the time whether an hospital would be maintained here, and he was not then in a position to give that information, so when we had Mr. Doyle here last February I repeated my question, and he left that impression on my mind and on the mind of the whole board that there should be an hospital maintained here. The matter has caused me a good deal of consideration and anxiety since last August, first, because I represent a division which is about one-sixth of the rateable property of the union.

1208. Which Electoral Division is that?—Drishane, and of course the interests of the ratepayers there ought to be the foremost part of my consideration, and in addition to that, I may say that anything that would tend to lessen taxation in this union, provided it did not press unduly on the poor, would be a great relief to myself. I believe I may say I am the largest rated guardian in this union, and I pay a large amount of taxes in the union, so it would be a great relief to me if I saw that taxation could be reduced without pressing unduly on the poor. With this information before me I came to the conclusion that the very same staff of officers should be maintained in this house if we had to keep an hospital here, either for fever patients or for the fever and infirm inmates of the union. The only officers we could dispense with would be either the master or clerk, the schoolmaster and schoolmistress. I put down the saving to be effected by these reductions at £150, that would reduce the establishment charges a very small item, and as regards that we would have to pay our proportion of the establishment charges of Killarney, Kanturk, and Macroom. Of course they should pay their share of the establishment charges here, so I saw that in the place of saving there would be a decided loss in that respect. I began to ask myself what would be saved by this amalgamation, and I proposed to my brother guardians here, "give me some tangible reason for breaking up the union." If they could show me a large amount of saving without pressing on the poor I would go with them, but in the absence of that information, which I thought they would be able to make out, I went tee-totally against amalgamation. I may say, and I say it advisedly in the presence of two of my principals, that a very large proportion of the constituency I represent have strongly urged me to oppose amalgamation. I heard a great deal about the ratepayers being in favour of this move, and I was prepared to see the country *en masse* here to support it. I have taken statistics from the Annual Report of the Local Government Board for 1876, and, I have not alone confined my inquiries to that report, I have looked into two previous and two after reports of the same board as to the positions of the unions whose interests are involved. By the report ending Sept. 1876, I find that Kanturk had in the workhouse 1,303 paupers, with 904 persons on out-door relief, total 2,207; the collective number of days was 151,793, the average daily number of inmates in the house 415, total cost of provisions and clothing £4,214; the weekly average cost was 3s. $10\frac{1}{4}d.$, the valuation of that union is £76,462. In Macroom the number of inmates in the house was 791, and on out-door relief 142, total 933, the collective number of days 82,355, average daily number of paupers in the house 225; total cost of provisions and clothing £1,928, weekly average cost 3s. $3\frac{1}{4}d.$, valuation £63,000. In Killarney the number of inmates in the house was 1,052, the number on out-door relief 908, total 1,960, the collective number of days 118,885, average daily number of paupers in the house 325; total cost of provisions and clothing £3,231; weekly average cost 3s. $9\frac{3}{4}d.$; valuation £76,000. In Millstreet the number of inmates in the house was 1,012, the number on out-door relief 366, total, 1,378, collective number of days, 95,002, average daily number of paupers in the house, 260, or 40 daily more than Macroom, while the collective number of days was 13,000 more than Macroom. The cost of clothing and provisions was £2,311, and the average cost 3s. $4\frac{1}{4}d.$ The cost of our inmates is more than in Macroom. Their average is the lowest of the four unions, 3s. $3\frac{1}{4}d.$, but if you take the average weekly cost of the three other unions you will find the average cost is about 5d. under the average cost of the others. The valuation of Kanturk is £76,462, Macroom, £63,000, Millstreet, £27,847; and Killarney, £76,000. I come now to a very serious question, the parties interested who are desirous of amalgamation say always, "It is the staff of the house that is doing the whole thing." Now, as to the poundage rate required for the establishment charges of the different workhouses, I find the poundage rate in Kanturk is $3\frac{3}{4}d.$, Macroom 3d.; Millstreet, $5\frac{1}{2}d.$, Killarney, $5\frac{1}{4}d.$ That varies from your calculation, and is accounted for in this way:—The establishment charges are put down at £773 17s. 2d., but that is reduced this year under the heading of salaries by £80, and still further reduced by half the salaries out of the Parliamentary Grant, and half the medicines, and that would leave £624 17s. for the establishment charges this year and the year before. $5\frac{1}{2}d.$ in the £1 will produce £630, or a fraction over what is required for the establishment charges.

1209. Do you say there has been a reduction of salaries?—Yes, by about £80. We reduced the clerk's salary about £60, and the master's by £10, and the matron's by £10. That is why there is a slight change. The poundage rate required for establishment charges in Killarney is $5\frac{1}{4}d.$, and that is very little over what the establishment charges are in Macroom. If you transfer these portions of this union to the three adjoining unions there will naturally be some increase in the establishment charges there, and without guaranteeing the accuracy of the calculation I say about three farthings in the £1. Some people say it would not be so much. That would make Kanturk $4\frac{1}{2}d.$ leaving the portion that would go to Kanturk to gain one penny in the £1 on the establishment charges. If I add three farthings to the Macroom charge that would make $3\frac{3}{4}d.$, so that the portion to go to Macroom would gain a penny-three-farthings. If I add three farthings to the Killarney charge that would be 6d., so that the portion to go to Killarney would actually lose a half-penny by the transaction. I happen to belong to one of these unions, and I say the amount to be saved in this way would not warrant the guardians to recommend the breaking up of the union, and sending it to the neighbouring unions. I heard our vice-chairman say a while ago that at the time of these sheds, and the introduction of the union here, that we had about 3,000 people here, and he stated soon afterwards that while the population had gone down pauperism did not go down to the same extent. He must have made some mistake for the two statements are perfectly inconsistent, for I find there are only 269 paupers in the house, and that is very different from 3,000 which he said before. Having that large number in the house, and seeing the class of people who would be affected by the change, I don't think the chance of economising the rate by 1d. and 3s. 4d. in the two unions would justify this union in breaking up the establishment.

1210. I see on the 25th February, 1878, there were 350 in the house?—I will come to that in a minute. I say that the miserable amount of saving to be effected on that head would not justify this board of guardians or the owners of property who are the parties actually more interested than the ratepayers themselves, for they pay half the rates. If I find in addition that guardians state as I know they did, that if you remove relief out of the reach of the poor you will certainly not have much pauperism in the union, that is not a very philanthropic way of looking at the question; that is no way of looking to the economy of the rates. I am a guardian, and am largely interested in the reduction of the rates, but I am bound first to be a guardian of the poor and afterwards a guardian of the ratepayers, and I believe I have given as much time to the affairs of this union as any man in the place. There is nothing that economy could recommend so far as I am concerned I have not done. I have a return here and it is certainly a very powerful argument I think on my side against amalgamation. It is for five years, from the 1st January, 1873, to the 1st February, 1878. On the 1st January, 1873, we had 90 healthy inmates in the house, including young children who were healthy, 98 infirm, and 158 sick, making 256 sick and infirm, and showing that the house is altogether used by the sick and infirm—the very class they could not conveniently move about. In 1874 there were 21 healthy inmates, 81 infirm, and 137 sick, making 218 sick and infirm; in 1875 there were 107 healthy, 122 infirm, and 124 sick, making 246 sick and infirm; in 1876 there were 114 healthy, 112 infirm, and 85 sick, making 197 sick and infirm; in 1877 there were 98 healthy, 110 infirm, and 68 sick, making 178 sick and infirm; and in 1878 there were 65 healthy, 139 infirm, and 92 sick, making 231 sick and infirm. This shows that the healthy inmates are decreasing, while the infirm and sick are increasing. This may be used by my friends on the other side as an argument that that was the period of the year when

MILLSTREET, Aug. 19, 1878.

Mr. Hegarty.

MILLSTREET
May 10, 1878
Mr Hegarty

the house would be full because that was the time when want was most prevalent But I take the 1st July in each year, and I find that whilst the healthy inmates have decreased, there is scarcely any diminution in the sick and infirm—the very class that would require relief in this house. There was a very ingenious statement—of course I owe that to the cleverness and ingenuity of my friend, Mr Murphy—in the resolution passed on the 28th February, asking for an inquiry. He said any portion of this union to be transferred would not be a bit further off than portions of the adjacent unions were at present from headquarters If he looks to the facts before him he will find that that was not an argument likely to have weight with the Commissioners To compare a mountainous place like Williamstown, in the Kanturk Union, to a populous place like Millstreet, that has not more than 1 to 50 in Millstreet, which is increasing every year in population and prosperity. A great deal of that is owing to Mr Townsend here and the resident owners of property, who have done so much to improve the town, and therefore increase the population. I think it would be rather unfair to compare a place like this to a mountainous place, or a district union far away from accommodation

1211 Did you put your objection to that resolution on record?—I did object to it in the same way as I do now, with statistics and that kind of thing

1212. Then you do not think it would be for the interests of the ratepayers that the union should be dissolved?—I am totally against dissolution of the union, not only for the sake of the ratepayers, whose interests we are bound to look after, but in the interests of the poor But let me put it to you in this way if we had a bad epidemic, such as unfortunately we had this year, and if hospital accommodation was not within easy distance, what would be the result?

1213 Had you an epidemic this year?—We had a very bad one The house was full of fever for a long time, and in addition to that a great many of the ratepaying community availed themselves of the skilful treatment they received at the house, and in that way a great deal of the disease was checked, and it left without any fatal case.

1214. Mr Haward contemplates having an hospital here

1215 What I understand that you wish to convey by your reference to the epidemic is that you consider an hospital here would be necessary?—It could not be done without. It is absolutely indispensable that an hospital should be maintained, and if you had an hospital there should be the same staff and there would be no saving, while the change would entail fearful hardship on the poor who should be removed to the Killarney Union, and be taken a distance of 17 miles from the extreme end of the district. It would not be of advantage in the way of economy either. It would be morally impossible to get guardians to come here every week to look after the place, and what would be the consequences? There might be a poor woman or a family go to the board for relief. The local guardians would not be there, and the board would have to go on the statement of the relieving officer, who, perhaps, would not know much about the case, and the district from which these parties came would be injured

1216 You mentioned, as one strong point of your case, that the distances from portions of the union proposed to be attached to Macroom are such that you think it would be a great hardship on the poor to have to attend at Macroom for admission or relief?—Yes

1217. You also say the attendance of guardians would be bad?—Yes; there is certainly nobody has more experience than I have

1218. The distance from Millstreet to Macroom would be too great, and the same objection applies if it was joined to Kanturk?—The very same; the fever patients might die on the road

1219. The distance from the extreme point being seventeen miles?—Yes

1220 Over a mountain road?—It is a good public road In winter is it bad? Sometimes it is rugged enough in winter, and very inclement It is one of the worst roads to travel over in winter.

John Howard,
Esq

JOHN HOWARD, Esq., re-examined.

1221. Supposing your proposal to annex a large portion, if not the whole, of Millstreet to Kanturk, necessitated the enlargement of Kanturk Union Workhouse, and the erection of additional buildings and extensive alterations, would you think it right that the Millstreet Union should bear the expense of such additional buildings or alterations?—Certainly it should

1222. While they have their buildings here and available?—Of course, I don't see any necessity for that

1223 But should it arise?—They ought to bear part of it, as they share the profits they should share the loss, but such a contingency would never arise.

1224 When you said that the population had gone down, but that pauperism had not, I suppose what you meant was that when the great distress was over, and the famine had passed away, and the district had returned to its normal condition, the population decreased, but that pauperism did not decrease in proportion?—Not to the benefit of the union at all events.

Richard Ashe,
Esq.

RICHARD ASHE, Esq., examined

1225. Are you a guardian of the Macroom Union?—Yes

1226. You are deputed by the board of that union to attend here?—Yes, but I am not able to give you any material evidence in addition to what has been given already I believe the statistics of Mr Hegarty are very nearly correct The Macroom Board object very strongly to the amalgamation, principally on the ground of the very great expense it would entail on Macroom, in addition to its present rate for the support of the paupers that would be thrown upon it by the divisions added from Millstreet, if the proposal was carried out. I believe the proposal is to amalgamate with Macroom the divisions of Kilcorney, Coomlagane, and Crinaloo. Well Crinaloo and Kilcorney were originally part of the Macroom Union, and we would not object to them, and we might agree to take them if it was found necessary. The distance of Macroom from them is not so great as it is from them to Millstreet, for there is a short cut across the mountains by a capital road. If it was found necessary to carry out the proposal that might very well be done; but if we get these two Millstreet divisions we would be saddled with an enormous amount of pauperism that has already swamped the Millstreet Union, and would add some 3d or 4d to our average rate I don't think that would be fair to the Macroom Union I don't think it would be fair to entail on the sick and infirm the necessity of going the additional distance from Millstreet to Macroom. In addition to that the Macroom Workhouse is, I understand, quite incapable of affording the necessary accommodation Our medical officer, Dr Crook, is here, and will be able to give full information on that point, and give his reasons for stating it The house was originally built, I believe, to afford accommodation to a much greater number than are in it at present; but from the alteration of times, and the necessity of affording relief to a different class of persons

KILLARNEY. May 18, 1876.

Richard Ashe, Esq.

now to what it was originally intended to accommodate, it has become quite insufficient to afford any additional relief at present. These are the principal reasons why the Macroom Guardians object to the amalgamation. Our officers are here and they can give reasons for saying that the house is insufficient.

1227. Did you say you would be swamped by the paupers from Kilcorney and Crinnaloo?—No; Drishane and Coomlagrane. Before the building of this house we had portion of Kilcorney and Crinnaloo, the other portions belonged to Killarney and Kanturk, and I think the fairest way would be to resort back to the original status.

Dr. WARREN CROOKE, examined.

Dr. Warren Crooke.

1228. You are medical officer of Macroom Union I believe?—Yes.

1229. The statement made by the Deputy from your Union was to the effect that the Workhouse there, though constructed for a comparatively large number of inmates, would be incapable of taking into it the paupers that would be transferred from this union in the event of amalgamation taking place?—Certainly.

1230. Can you state why it would be insufficient?—It was constructed to accommodate able-bodied and sick and infirm in about equal proportions. That proportion has been altogether changed. We have very few able-bodied people now, and the accommodation suitable for them in high and lofty rooms, up stone stairs, is partly occupied, and these rooms would not be suitable for the sick and infirm. We have scarcely convenient accommodation for our own sick and infirm. We have some vacant rooms at the top of the house, but they are totally unfit for the sick and infirm.

1231. Have you appropriated any portion of the able-bodied accommodation for the sick and infirm?—We have.

1232. And having done that you could not now accommodate any more of those classes?—No.

1233. In fact, the wants of your own union take all the room you have?—We want more room to accommodate the sick and infirm.

1234. Do you think that the distance of the districts it is proposed to annex to your union, would be found objectionable?—The distances the paupers have to come are most objectionable, they are very great for fever and weak infirm cases, and even at present the distance from which they are brought to our Workhouse is very objectable.

1235. Mr CRAWFORD.—Even in your own union you think the sick suffer from the distance?—Yes, they come from a long distance.

1236. And you find it has an injurious effect on them?—Certainly.

Mr. DANIEL MURPHY, P.L.G., Kanturk Union, examined.

Mr. Daniel Murphy.

1237. I am deputed with two other Guardians to give the views of my union.

1238. You have heard the proposal with regard to amalgamation, tell me what the views of your board are on the subject?—Yes, and our board think if they get thirteen electoral divisions they would not object, but if the division of Drishane and Coomlagrane are added we would object to them strongly. There are some other divisions which, if we got, we would not object to.

1239. Those immediately adjoining which have no paupers?—Yes.

1240. Are you acquainted with the state of your house?—I am.

1241. Do you know the state of the hospital wards and infirm wards?—I am not thoroughly acquainted with them for the reason that recently one of your Commissioners was there and took statistics.

1242. I wanted to know whether you could give evidence as to the state of your wards and the amount of accommodation available?—No, I could not.

1243. Could either of the gentlemen who came with you do so?—No.

1244. Then in short, Kanturk objects to amalgamation unless it gets a certain number of electoral divisions that are exactly adjoining it?—Yes.

1245. Could you name them?—I can. They are Cullen, Derragh, Doonasleen, Keale, Rathcool, and Skagh.

1246. Is there anybody from Kanturk who could speak of the accommodation there?—No.

Reverend ARTHUR GRIFFIN, examined.

Rev. Arthur Griffin.

1247. Do you attend with a deputation of ratepayers?—I attend, knowing the opinion of a great number of ratepayers with regard to the question.

1248. You are a ratepayer yourself?—I am, and I have formed a very strong opinion on the subject besides. If I could be convinced that taxation would be considerably lessened in this union without serious detriment to the poor I would be inclined, as a ratepayer, to vote for the amalgamation of this union with the Killarney, Kanturk, and Macroom Unions, but until these points are clearly proved I feel myself bound as ratepayer, parish priest, and chaplain to this workhouse to oppose any such step. That the rates would be considerably decreased I do not believe. That the hardships on the poor of the union would be immensely increased I am convinced. If this union is broken up I take for granted every officer connected with the union, with the exception of the dispensary doctors and relieving officers, would be entitled to compensation for disturbance. This would amount to a large sum, and should be levied on the union I suppose. Are we to pay it all at once, or is it to be spread over a certain number of years? In either case it would entail very heavy taxation. The transport of the sick poor from their homes to this workhouse, though miserably defective, is a small expense to the union, whereas the conveyance of these poor people to Killarney, Kanturk, and Macroom from distant townlands in this union would cost a considerable sum in the year. I shall leave to others more conversant than I am with statistics to point out items that would increase taxation. But I may add that the guardians themselves would be very heavily taxed throughout the year by this change both as to time and money. At present it costs them little time and no money to attend here on board days as they are all near home, but if they have to go to Killarney, Kanturk, and Macroom they lose the entire day, and cannot make the journey without considerable expense; and I doubt they would be willing to sacrifice both. I am sure the consequence would be that after a short time we would have no representation on these boards, and this would lead to serious inconvenience for the ratepayers and the poor. For the ratepayers, because guardians having no interest in the place could do as they liked with the taxation of this place; for the poor, because they would have no one to represent their various cases, and therefore may get no relief, either indoor or outdoor. A great

MILLSTREET
May 30, 1878.

Rev. Arthur Griffin.

improvement has been, during the past few years, effected in the sanitary state of Millstreet, but if we were at the mercy of another board of guardians I fear little more would be done. As to the grave and serious injury inflicted on the poor by the change, anyone of a thinking mind must come to the conclusion that it would be simply outrageous; but perhaps some guardians do not mind that if they could strike off a shilling in the pound on their valuation. I remarked to a guardian some time since, when there was question of this amalgamation, that it would be a dreadful hardship for poor people to go to either of these three towns for relief from some townland in this union, and what was his humane answer? "Oh," said he, "that is just the very thing we want, the journey would be too long, and they would not go at all, and there would be a saving to the rates." I was really astounded at this answer, and said in reply, "Clearly in your eyes the poor are to starve if it saves a trifle from the rates, but the Poor-laws take a more humane view, and entitle the pauper to better treatment than you are inclined to extend to him." This is a sample of what may occur if this amalgamation takes place. I said before that the transport of the sick poor to the workhouse is miserably bad; they are brought in open carts, even in inclement weather, though Mr. Horsely, the inspector, stated here about a year ago that an ambulance should be provided for the purpose. Now, if this is a hardship on the poor, how much greater will it be if they have to travel in the same way to Killarney, Kanturk, and Macroom? We had an outbreak of typhus fever here during the spring and the hospital here was largely availed of, where I believe everyone recovered, under the able treatment of Dr Leader, our late medical attendant. Would all these people consent to be removed from their homes and taken to Killarney, Kanturk, and Macroom? I say ten of them would not go, and the consequence would be a dreadful plague in the town and country, and loss of life. I may be again told that their not going would be a saving to the rates. I deny it, for though hospital expenses may be saved, many families would be left without a father, and would eventually be thrown on the rates as a heavy burden. The doctor who so successfully brought all these poor people over the fever which attacked them will tell you that he could not expect the same success if he had to attend them in their own badly-ventilated or badly-kept houses or cabins. I heard someone say that an hospital should be kept open here even if this splitting up of the union takes place. If so, where is the saving? Are not two thirds of the poor people in this house in the hospital or infirmary, and must not a staff be paid to attend this hospital? The doctor, chaplain, matron, and nurses must be paid their salaries, and where then is to be the great saving? There is another matter which concerns us all in this business—the splitting up of the union would seriously damage our little town. Though we are paying heavy rates, nearly every shilling of the money is spent back in the town. Divide the union, and every shilling of our money will go to Killarney, Kanturk, and Macroom. I doubt very much if so much money is taken away from the town that landed proprietors would get the same smart rents they are getting at present from shopkeepers for the lands they hold adjacent to the town. Looking at it from every point of view, it appears to me the idea of amalgamating this union with Killarney, Kanturk, and Macroom is mischievous, and would, if carried out, inflict most grievous injuries on the poor of the district. With regard to the expenditure of this house I may say I have been chaplain here for the last five or six years, and I think, from my observation, a great deal of the large expenditure is entirely due to the mismanagement of the house, and I have seen, as I have reported to the board on more than one occasion, as much waste in the shape of eggs and bread as would support the entire house for a day. I have seen heaps of bread over the heads of the people in the wards hardened with age, and not fit for use, and I have seen eggs in heaps together over the heads of the patients, not used by them, and I believe afterwards taken down to the town and sold. I believe also there has been, in most instances, a most reckless expenditure in outdoor relief. I saw, about three or four years ago, one woman come into my church. She was from Mr. Howard's district (he was not a guardian then), and she was decked out with ribbons, yet she was receiving outdoor relief.

Mr. Howard.—I was a guardian since the formation of the union.

Rev. Mr. Griffin.—You were not a guardian then, for there were paid guardians at the time.

1249. In saying that do you represent not merely your own opinion, but the opinion of a considerable body of ratepayers?—I have been speaking to a great many ratepayers, and they all think that in the interests of the poor, even if they were to save a little themselves, it would not be fair.

Mr. James Cooper.

Mr. JAMES COOPER examined.

1250. Are you an ex-guardian of this union?—Yes.

1251. Have you any fact bearing on the proposal before us that you desire to communicate to us?—I have this one fact, which is a very tangible one, we are now saddled with a large population, and we should look to the interests of the poor first. I take Mr. Hegarty's view. I was twenty-two years a guardian. I represented Drishane for twenty one years, and I say without premeditation that many a death would have occurred during that time had I not been a guardian.

The inquiry then closed.

GLENNAMADDY
June 11, 1878.

INQUIRY AT GLENNAMADDY, COUNTY OF GALWAY.—TUESDAY, JUNE 11, 1878.

Before Major the Hon. WM. LE POER TRENCH, R.E. (Chairman), ANDREW DOYLE, and CHARLES SHARMAN CRAWFORD, Esquires.

1252. This Commission as I presume you are all aware, gentlemen, in consequence of the cry for amalgamation throughout the country, has been appointed to inquire into the question generally, to ascertain what grounds there are for the various applications made for amalgamation. In August last, this union had queries sent to it, the same as were sent to all the unions. After considering them, the following resolutions appear to have been arrived at by your board. On the 4th September last it was proposed by Mr Wm Neary, seconded by Mr Stephen J. M'Donagh and resolved—"That the Glennamaddy "Union Workhouse be amalgamated with the adjoining "unions." That was adopted, not unanimously, but by majority of 9 to 7. The answer to the query sent to us with that resolution states:—"The Guardians of Glennamaddy Union consider it would be expedient to "dissolve this Union and amalgamate it with Tuam, "Castlerea, Roscommon, and Mount Bellew Unions, "the portions to be annexed to each of the adjoining "unions to be determined after consulting with the "Commissioners." There appears to have been a second meeting held here in reference to this question on the 27th November, 1877, when the following resolution was proposed by Mr Roe, seconded by Mr. M'Donagh and adopted unanimously:—"That in the

GLENNAMADDY June 11, 1878.

"event of this union being amalgamated with the "adjoining unions, it will be necessary to discontinue "the Hospital attached to the Workhouse, and have "the sick paupers therein removed to the respective "unions to which they may be chargeable, and to dis- "pose of the workhouse and grounds for the benefit of "the union, and in the event of superannuation being "granted to any of our officers that same be borne "jointly with unions with which we may amalgamate." On the 22nd of January in this year the question was again before the Board, when it was proposed to rescind the resolution in favour of amalgamation. There was a very close division upon an amendment proposed by Mr Martin M'Donnell and seconded by Mr. William Newry, to the effect "that the resolution be not "rescinded," for on a poll being taken it appears that the amendment was only carried by 7 to 6. The expressed opinion of this Board is still therefore in favour of amalgamation—7 to 6 being the numbers last voting for it.

ROBERT GLANCY, Esq., J.P., examined.

Robert Glancy, Esq., J.P.

1253. Are you an Ex-officio or an Elected Guardian of this union?—I am an Ex-officio Guardian of the Glennamaddy Union, and also a Guardian of the Castlerea Union.

1254. Do you desire that this Union should be broken up and amalgamated with the adjoining unions?—Yes.

1255. Will you be good enough to say on what grounds?—It would be a saving. I am a ratepayer in both Unions—I pay rates in three divisions of Castlerea Union, and in three divisions of this Union, and I find that the rates here are double what they are in Castlerea.

1256. It is therefore with the view of effecting a saving of poor-rates that you desire amalgamation?—Yes, saving expenditure. I can give you an account of the rates in my divisions in both Unions for the last four years.

1257. Please do so?—Well, taking Castlerea first—in Ballynagar division in 1874 the rate was 6*d.* in the pound, in '75, 11*d.*

1258. In the same division?—Yes. In '76 it was 11*d*, and in '77, 8*d*. In Castlekean, in the same Union, it was in '74, 6*d* in the pound, in '75, 7*d*; in '76, 7*d*; and in '77, 8*d*. In Ballyduff, in the same Union, it was in '74, 6*d.*, in '75, 7*d*; in '76, 7*d.*; and in '77, 11*d*. Now in this Union, Glennamaddy, the rates were—in Ballynakill, in '74, 2*s.* in the pound; in '75, 1*s* 4*d*, in '76, 1*s.* 5*d.*, and in '77, 1*s.* 4*d*. In Creggs they were, in '74, 1*s.* 8*d*, in '75, 1*s.* 9*d.*; in '76, 1*s.* 9*d*, and in '77, 1*s* 8*d*. And in Toberroe, they were, in '74, 2*s.* 6*d.*; in '75, 2*s*; in '76, 1*s* 5*d.*, and in '77, 1*s.* 7*d.*

1259. Are you a ratepayer in all those divisions?—Yes.

1260. Have you a statement of the rates in the other divisions of these Unions?—I don't exactly understand you.

1261. Have you any return of the relative expenditure of the various divisions of the two Unions?—No. I only took what their respective cess was, not the expenditure.

1262. Only the rating?—The rating is all I took. I have not the valuation of either, and I merely took those figures as being concerned with the divisions I am interested in.

1263. Is there a larger pauper population in these three electoral divisions you have named in Castlerea than in the three corresponding divisions of Glennamaddy?—I would say in one of them, Ballynagar. There are a good many paupers getting both out-door relief and in the house, but not so many from the others.

1264. To what cause do you attribute the difference in charge?—One is a much larger Union, and we all know that when the establishment charges are spread over a larger area the cess will be less.

1265. Do you know what the establishment charges in Castlerea are?—I am not prepared exactly to say.

1266. Can you say what they are in Glennamaddy?—No, I did not look at that either.

1267. Do you know, Mr Glancy, that supposing this Union was amalgamated, two of the divisions you mention, Ballynakill and Creggs, would not go to Castlerea at all—that they would probably go to the Union of Roscommon? Do you know how Roscommon stands?—Not at present. At one time I was a cesspayer there too, but I don't think we would be better off there than in Castlerea.

1268. But are not those divisions much nearer Roscommon than Castlerea?—No; on the contrary, the whole of Ballynakill is nearer to Castlerea, and half of Creggs is nearer to Castlerea also.

1269. Is Castlerea their market town?—It is the market town for all Ballynakill.

1270. I think when I was here last some representative of the property with which you are connected desired that Creggs, in the event of this Union being dissolved, should be attached to Roscommon?—The greater part of Creggs, you will find, is nearer to Castlerea than to Roscommon, or at all events as near, while Ballynakill is much nearer.

1271. Do you know what the establishment charges are in any of these Unions?—No.

1272. Do you attribute the difference in cost between your Glennamaddy electoral divisions and the Castlerea electoral divisions to the establishment charges?—Yes; and to the higher price paid for different articles that are got here.

1273. The higher prices paid here at Glennamaddy?—Yes. Higher prices must be charged here, because there is more cartage on the goods. In Castlerea there is a railway station quite close to the Workhouse, and the result is, supplies may be got much cheaper there than here.

1274. In fact, the contracts are obtained on better terms in Castlerea than here?—Yes, that must be.

1275. Is it not the case that the difficulty in getting contracts taken here has been such that you have been obliged to get a guardian to supply milk?—Yes; I have been asked as a guardian to supply milk. There (document handed to Chairman) is a resolution I got some time ago on the subject.

1276. Do you know the difference between the cost of maintenance here and in Castlerea?—No, I really did not look at it.

1277. I have a return taken from the annual Report of the Local Government Board before me—are you aware what the average weekly cost per head of inmates in the Glennamaddy Workhouse is?—No.

1278. I see here that it is 3*s* 8*d* for the year 1877, and in the same year for Castlerea I find it was 3*s.* 9½*d.* and for Roscommon 4*s* 3½*d* and for Tuam, which is also interested in this question of amalgamation—4*s* 2¾*d*—so that altogether your cost of maintenance is lower here than in the unions with which you propose to amalgamate.

1279. Assuming that proportion, or disproportion between expenditure to be correct, and it is taken from the official returns, would you still be of opinion that in the cost of "in" maintenance your divisions would save anything by a transfer to another union?—On those statistics one would say not.

1280. You take, we will say, three electoral divisions of one union and three electoral divisions of another and finding that the cost—the rating in the three electoral divisions in Castlerea is much lower than in the three from this union, you calculate that the higher would be brought down to the level of the lower divisions by a transfer of those divisions?—No, not to the lowest level exactly, but they would be brought lower.

1281. Taking for instance one of the divisions—where you have a rating of 11*d* in the pound, how much of that 11*d*, think you, would be saved by a transfer of that electoral division from this union to Castlerea

GLENNAMADDY
June 11, 1878.
—
Robert Glancy, Esq., J.P.

union ?—I really did not look into it that way—I should say fully 3*d* at all events

1282. Now, out of that 11*d*, 8*d* was expended in relief to the poor and the establishment charges come to 3*d*—do you mean to say that the 8*d* which is given in relief to the poor would be less—is that your view of it, that there would be a saving in that portion of the expenditure which was relief to the poor ?—I should say there must be some saving

1283. But would there be any saving in the relief to the poor ?—Yes, if you get the contracts cheaper in one union than another there must be a saving

1284. Then the saving would be the difference between the cost of maintenance here and in Castlerea—that is if you had ten paupers here and ten in the Castlerea union, the saving would be the difference in the cost of maintenance in the two establishments ?—No, because the establishment charges are spread over a larger area.

1285. Leaving the establishment charges out of the question and taking so much of the expenditure as is paid for relief to the poor ?—There would be a saving—not a large saving—but there would be a saving if you get the supplies cheaper

1286. Have you any idea as to how much of that 11*d*—taking that as the expenditure of a particular electoral division—is for outdoor relief and how much for "indoor" maintenance ?—I cannot say.

1287. Or have you made any calculation or any inquiry as to the proportion which is establishment charges or the proportion that is relief to the poor ?—I made no calculations whatever.

1288. But came generally to the conclusion that because the rating in a particular division is so much less, the transfer of other divisions to that union would effect a saving ?—I have no doubt it would

1289. Is it not perfectly plain that the only saving that could be effected would be a saving in the establishment charges ?—That is not the case if you get supplies cheaper in one union than in the other.

1290. There would be also you think a saving in the cost of "in" maintenance ?—Yes

1291. Do you know the difference between the cost of "in" maintenance here and in Roscommon or in Castlerea ?—I don't know, but I think they get everything cheaper there

1292. (*To the Master of the Workhouse*)—What is the cost of maintenance in this Workhouse—food and clothing, without establishment charges ?—The average cost is 2*s* 3*d* (it was 3*s* 4*d*. for the last week), and about 6*d*. a week for clothing.

1293. Included in that ?—No, not included, that is simply the average cost of provisions, the hospital and all. The cost in all is only 2*s* 0½*d*

1294. *Witness*—And you don't suppose that the outdoor relief, which is almost a fixed quantity in these unions, could be diminished ?—Not much, although I don't think they give as much outdoor relief in Castlerea as in this union

1295. Have you ever calculated how much of the union pauperism—of the paupers not chargeable to a division, but to the whole union, would be thrown upon those electoral divisions that you would propose to transfer from this to Castlerea or Roscommon ?—I have never made such a calculation.

1296. Are there any details or figures, Mr. Glancy, that satisfies you in your own mind that there would be a saving by amalgamation, more than the general impression that the rate for a particular division in one union being so much less than in a particular division of another union, that therefore by a transfer of the division from this union to the other you would save—you have made no calculation of how that would be effected at all ?—No, except that I suppose the larger the union is the lower the rates must be.

1297. You say that outdoor relief is less in Castlerea ?—Much, I think.

1298. I find here, from the abstracts for the year ending the 25th March, 1877, that in the Glennamaddy union it was 2*d* and in the other it was 1⅕*d*—that is the difference between the two on the average over the union

1299. Four-fifths of a penny is the difference—that is not very much ?—I know the outdoor relief is very much increased for the last two or three years in Castlerea.

1300. I have taken the year 1877 ?—There was a large increase in that year.

1301. Have you considered the question of amalgamation from any other point of view than the ratepayer's point of view—saving money ?—No.

1302. How would it affect the poor, think you ?—I cannot see how it would affect them very much, except in the few divisions adjoining the workhouse here

1303. But the paupers of this immediate union would be much worse off for accommodation, would they not ?—Those few divisions about here would be of course, the paupers there would have more trouble and inconvenience going over to Castlerea or Mount Bellew, but some of the other divisions are as near to these other unions as to this. I mean the outside divisions of Glennamaddy.

1304. Would you think it desirable or necessary to keep up an hospital here ?—I don't think it would be at all necessary. I think there should be conveyances for fever patients and for the infirm to Castlerea or the other unions

1305. The sick and the infirm and the people of this immediate neighbourhood requiring to be taken into hospital or the infirmary for infectious diseases, you think it would be just as well to carry them to Castlerea as here ?—For people in hospital it would be better to have them here of course. It is unpleasant to remove people out of hospital

1306. Would you not think it more than unpleasant—something approaching inhumanity to compel that removal ?—I should say so.

1307. Then don't you think it would be necessary to keep up an hospital here of some sort ?—It would be the humane way of looking at it.

1308. From the pauper's point of view it would be desirable to keep it up; though from the ratepayer's point of view it might be dispensed with. In the resolution that was sent to us it was suggested that if there was an amalgamation this house should be disposed of for the benefit of the union ?—I was not present when that was passed

1309. The house, I suppose you are aware, is vested in the Local Government Board as trustees for the union, and is not the property of the guardians to dispose of ?—I am.

1310. So that they would not have the fund received from the sale of the house, if amalgamation was effected ?—I am well aware of that fact

1311. In the event of this house being vacated, do you know of any use to which it could be turned ?—No

---

Mr. Martin M'Donnell.

Mr. Martin M'Donnell examined.

1312. You are an elected guardian, are you not, of this union ?—Yes.

1313. And you are well acquainted with the working of the poor law ?—Yes.

1314. You are aware that your board has passed a resolution (by 7 to 6 on the last division,) in favour of amalgamation ?—Yes.

1315. You are, I understand, in favour of amalgamation ?—I have been.

1316. You say "you have been," pray have you changed your mind on the subject ?—I don't know that I have changed my mind

1317. Then you are in favour of it ?—Yes; it would be for the interest of some people, of course, that we should continue this union; and for myself, personally, I don't see that it would be a saving for me to go to Castlerea to discharge the duties I have discharged here, but the results would be beneficial to the ratepayers, because there would be a very large saving. I have gone over the books, and my statistics are these. I went on the principle that the saving I will mention would arise subject to the deductions that would be liable to turn up on amalgamation. The figure I laid down as the saving to this union was £985.

1318. Per annum?—Yes; they were based on this principle—The medical officer gets £50 a year for his attendance in this house; the clerk gets £80 (these are charges to be dispensed with in the event of amalgamation); the returning officer gets £10, the master's salary and rations we put at the figure of £80, the matron's £55, that includes payment and rations, the nurse £45, the porter £30, the chaplain £60; fuel and light, say £100; miscellaneous (as taken from the books, and that must in every such instance exist), half-yearly, £200.

1319. Then for the whole year that is £400?—Yes.

1320. Do you know what that is made up of?—The books here can tell; I will read the items separately, if you like. (Reads)—A donkey and man (yearly) for carrying milk here, £40; painting, (yearly) say, £25, that is only done once in three years, but it costs £25 for each year as an average, and that gives you the figure of £985. In round numbers you may say 7¾d. in the pound; and if my calculations are right, they apply in the same ratio to every union in Ireland.

1321. What is the valuation of this union?—£31,870, but you must take this question of amalgamation as a whole——

1322. We are now dealing with this union, and you had better stick to it. You state that your estimated saving is £985?—Yes, that is my estimated saving here annually; in fact the whole of the establishment charges——

1323. And more, in fact. Will you give us the details of the £400 exclusively miscellaneous charges, the items you read out did not amount to £985?—I have them down correctly from the books, but it would take a long time to give you all the items. (Reading from books.) Here you have Cullen for wine, 2s.; Keogh, for pigs, £9; Carroll, for carriage on coal, £1 16s.; Carroll, for railway freight, 4s.; Glancy, milk for pigs, £1 17s. 6d.; Coghlan, on account of painting, £10; Coleman, wages and driver, £3——

1324. Are these charges to maintenance or establishment?

1325. *The Clerk of Union (Mr. Edmond Smith)*—A great number of them, nearly all, are establishment charges.

1326. *Witness*—Coleman again for driving, £3 15s.; Coleman, wages and driver, £1 5s.——

1327. Do you mean to say that the whole of the items you are reading now come under the head of miscellaneous charges, and can be dispensed with?—Yes, you don't want them.

1328. And do they amount to £400 a year?—Yes, I took them out before, every one of them, and they come to £200 half-yearly. I only went into one half-year. Then there are law expenses, and some little things of that kind; Keogh, farm expenses, £4, and then comes the salaries again.

1329. But you are not to include the salaries again in these miscellaneous charges?—The salaries will, I contend, be saved by amalgamation.

1330. But surely you cannot save them twice over—you have already put them down separately?—I only mention the items as I meet them in the books.

1331. But they go, don't they, to make up the £400?—No, that is exclusive of salaries. I gave you the salaries first, as I have them in the list before me. Then turbary and light and one thing and another we take at £100. But the salaries are entirely exclusive of these items, or these items are exclusive of the salaries.

1332. And the first salary you mentioned was the medical officer's £50 a year?—Yes. GLENNAMADDY. June 11, 1878. — Mr Martin M'Donnell.

1333. You would save the whole of that?—I would say so.

1334. And you would not have to contribute any portion of the salary of the medical officer of the union to which you would be transferred?—That is a matter for future arrangement.

1335. Does not your calculation assume that you would have to pay nothing for the medical officer of the new union into which you would be transferred?—It assumes this, that in the whole, for this house, there would be a saving of £985, and that amounts to 7¾d. in the pound. Then, of course, we have to take our proportion of the augmented salaries of the other union.

1336. Therefore if you add your proportion of the augmented salaries you must deduct it from that £985?—Precisely.

1337. Then you would not have a saving of £985?—Just so. I gave you the gross saving.

1338. You could not have a saving of £985 if you must set on the other side of the account a certain proportion of the salaries of all the officers of the other union to which you would be transferred—a portion of the salaries of the medical officer, of the clerk, of the master, of the matron, and so forth?—Decidedly not.

1339. And would not that reduce your £985?—It would, of course. I gave you the gross, not the net saving.

1340. To how much would it reduce your £985?—I never calculated that.

1341. You never considered that at all?—No, that is for the board to consider.

1342. You said deliberately that it would save £985 a year, and you admit that you must pay a proportion of the salaries of all those officers in the other union, but don't deduct that from the £985?—Certainly not, I made out merely what answered my own purposes, and I left you and the board to make out the remainder.

1343. That is evident enough—have you any further details to give us?—Three of our Electoral Divisions would go into the Castlerea Union according to the arrangement discussed when the Hon. Major Trench was here before.

1344. What three Electoral Divisions—would you mention the three please?—Perhaps I am wrong in that. Of course we would have to take our proportion of the additional salaries paid to the officers in that other union.

1345. But are you aware that you in putting down the saving at 7¾d. in the pound cover the entire establishment charges of this union?—That would be the saving.

1346. And, in fact, that is the entire establishment charge?—No, it is not—it is merely things we would not require in the future if we had amalgamation.

1347. What have you here that you would not require in another house?—We have nothing, but I take it for granted that the other houses to which we would be amalgamated have already their standing staff.

1348. But about your miscellaneous charges, which of them would you not require there?—You have them all existing there too.

1349. Does not your miscellaneous charges include fuel?—Yes, they do.

1350. Well, will you not require more fuel in another place if you have more cooking and more day and night rooms?—I don't suppose you will require a great deal more. All the people we have in this house would be scattered over three or four others.

1351. And how many have we here?—*The Clerk of Union.*—We had 137 last night.

1352. What else in the miscellaneous charges would you save—give me another item?—The Clerk.

1353. He is included in the salaries to be saved?—Well, I cannot mention the miscellaneous charges, but you have them here in the books.

GLENNAMADDY June 11, 1878.

Mr Martin M'Donnell.

1354. You know what exists here and what could be dispensed with—£400 is a very large sum to save in miscellaneous items?—But it is not the less true, and it is quite plain. If you get the Clerk to go over them he will make it all right. I went over them myself item by item. We would not want a donkey and cart for drawing milk at all events.

[Clerk requested to go over the miscellaneous items in book.]

1355. Is the donkey and cart used for any other purpose than drawing milk—is it used to bring in sick paupers?—I dare say it would be.

1356. And would you not require a donkey and cart, or even a better conveyance to take your sick poor from this to Castlerea?—They have a conveyance at Castlerea, and at all the other unions, which would be plenty for us.

1357. Do you think the drivers would be able to do the extra work without being paid for it?—No, but the proportion would be small on us all.

1358. The £40 that you have put down for the donkey and man who carries in milk and sick paupers is put down independent of your miscellaneous charges?—Yes.

1359. Your estimate of saving appears to be very strange. I will now refer you to your printed audited accounts. Are you aware what the amount of the establishment charge was here for the half-year ending September, '76?—I think that is the one I took.

1360. From these certified returns it appears to have been £389 11s 6d. Do you know what it was for the following half-year?—I took the miscellaneous charges at £200 a half year and the rest becomes a fixed figure.

1361. I have given you the establishment charges up to September, '76; for the next half-year it was £347 7s 11d., or a total of £736 19s. 5d for the year, according to the audited accounts?—Yes, that is about my figure too.

1362. Now, do you know how much of that is repaid by Parliamentary Grant and not chargeable to the rates?—I don't know—the Clerk had better answer that—I have not gone into the question.

1363. Then, in fact, you don't know what the establishment charges are?—Yes, I think I took them out accurately.

1364. Do you know, for instance, who pays the salary of the Schoolmistress?—The Consolidated Fund.

1365. And half the Medical Officer's salary?—The same fund.

1366. Very well, deduct those items, which amount to £50 and you will find that the establishment charge is £686 19s 5d., and that on the valuation of £31,870 gives what poundage do you suppose—it gives a poundage of 5¼d.; that was your entire establishment charge for the year. Now, with those figures before you—taken from the audited accounts—will you show us how you make out that 7¼d. would be saved on establishment charges?—£985 I made it out on everything, and here (document produced) is my calculation, showing the salaries, fuel, light, miscellaneous, and all that, taken from the books, and which I contend would all be saved.

1367. Before you go further, do you mean to say that no part of the salaries is included in the miscellaneous?—I do.

1368. The clerk is taking it out now, but I see that the half-year's salary of every officer is included in that account?—That may be so, but I have not touched them. You may see them marked with a cross there, and I passed them over. I took long enough to see it before, and I now leave it to you.

1369. Are we to understand distinctly from you that you did not calculate what portion of the salaries of officers you would have to bear in another union, suppose you were amalgamated?—I did not.

1370. Don't you believe it would be quite fair to deduct from your £985 the proportion you would have to bear of the salaries of the officers of the new union?—I did not do so.

1371. Don't you think it would be fair to do that, when you say that £985 would be saved, isn't it contrary to the fact inasmuch as you must have to pay your proportion of the salaries of the officers of the other union?—I never considered the question otherwise than that there would be a saving here of £985.

1372. But take the details of that. You say you save £50, the medical officer's salary—that is his whole salary?—Yes.

1373. And if you have to pay a portion of the medical officer's salary of the other union you will not save £50?—No.

1374. Supposing even you saved £900, establishment and other expenses in this union, how much would this particular union save exclusive of the other unions?—1d. in the pound on the valuation gives £133.

1375. I want to know how much in the rating of this union do you suppose would be saved by the saving of that £900?—I will give you it as near as I can do it.

1376. Will you just state the amount if you please?—I cannot do it unless I explain.

1377. Give the amount first, and then explain afterwards?—I should say 6d. in the pound would be saved.

1378. Don't you know that that £900, if saved, would not be only saved to this union, but the saving would be spread over all the other unions with which it would be amalgamated. All would be gainers?—They would.

1379. Very well, do you know what the valuation of this union, and all the other unions with which it is proposed to be amalgamated is?—I never gave attention to that question.

1380. I can tell you. The valuation of the five unions, Glennamaddy, Mount Bellew, Roscommon, Tuam, and Castlerea, comes to £285,555, and 1d. in the pound on that valuation produces £1,190, so that your saving of £900 would be much under 1d. in the pound over the whole area?—Very well, give us that 1d.

1381. The saving, spread over the whole area, you see, would be considerably under 1d. in the pound, even supposing that whole £985 to be saved?—That is as far as the whole goes, but surely the saving won't be in this isolated union only, and the other unions are to benefit by our saving we must also benefit by theirs. We want to save ourselves and not to go into the details of what 1d. in the pound is in all the other unions round us.

1382. As a matter of fact, with reference to the £400 per annum for "miscellaneous" you were asked whether you had included in that the salaries which you had previously given separately, and you said not?—As a matter of fact I included no salaries.

The CLERK having examined the books states that the following salaries included in witness's miscellaneous item:—

Officers' Salaries—Yearly.

Rev Mr. O'Brien,	£80 0 0
Dr Hodkins,	80 0 0
The Clerk,	50 0 0
The Master,	50 0 0
The Matron,	25 0 0
The School Mistress,	25 0 0
The Nurse	14 0 0
The Porter,	14 0 0
Relieving Officer	10 0 0
	£328 0 0

1383. And it would appear that the total amount of the miscellaneous in the ledger is £371, not £400?—That is for the half-year.

1384. And it includes salaries for the half-year amounting to £161?—That may be.

1385. And £164 out of £371 does not give a total of exactly £400?—I took my items out of the books, and there are various things in the books besides—law, expenses, &c., that I took out.

1386. It was on your motion that the Board arrived at the resolution in favour of amalgamation, was it on

GLENNAMADDY
June 11, 1878.

Mr. Martin M'Donnell.

your figures that they proceeded?—Well, we had two or three discussions on the subject, and the last day it was proposed to reject amalgamation, which was voted for before.

1387. And I see you were the mover of the amendment in favour of amalgamation. Was it on your representations that the Board by a majority adopted it?—No, I think they arrived at it on their own opinion.

1388. But it was moved by you yourself, Mr M'Donnell, and seconded by Mr. Neary, when you stated, I suppose, the figures you are now giving us?—Yes, but I did not go into the miscellaneous that day. I don't think we had so full a detail of the saving that was likely to arise.

1389. But still it was on the representations you made that the proposition in favour of amalgamation was carried?—Just so.

1390. Would you consider it necessary to keep an hospital here if the house was closed?—No, if you did that we would have no saving at all of any consequence.

1391. If you kept an hospital here you would make no saving at all?—No, if you proposed keeping an hospital here I would vote for holding the union on as it stands.

1392. And you think that in the interests of the poor the hospital could be dispensed with here?—I do. I think the places about are near enough to the other unions.

1393. Are you a member of the visiting committee of this union?—I have been from time to time, and I have not attended to my duties well, I am sorry to say.

1394. Do you know what the condition of affairs in the infirmary is?—I always thought the condition of every part of the house admirable.

1395. Have you recently been among the sick, or the aged and infirm people there?—I have not.

1396. Do you think if you went in and found some score of people there, whom it would be almost a cruelty to remove out of the place, you would not come to the conclusion that it was desirable to keep a place of refuge for them here or an hospital of some sort?—I tell you fearlessly and truly if I thought it a cruelty to remove anyone from here I would not do it.

1397. Well, considering that, have you ever made any inquiry amongst the people themselves, or asked the medical officer what he thought of removing these poor people from this house to Castlerea and Roscommon?—I have not.

1398. I think if you had done so your opinion might have been different?—Well, people become wedded to a place and never like to leave it, so the inmates are biased witnesses.

1399. But in spite of that you would like to remove them. Do you think one consequence of extending the union in that way would be that you would be obliged to give more outdoor relief here?—I do not; we are very liberal in outdoor relief here already indeed.

1400. Yes, but don't you think you would have occasion to become still more liberal if the proposed amalgamation was carried out?—If I was to express my own opinion I would willingly give more outdoor relief than we generally give.

1401. More in quantity?—More in numbers, and in quantity too. We often fish for a salmon and take up a pinkeen, and I think if we gave more outdoor relief it would be reversing that order, and would save the rates in the end.

1402. What is the average outdoor relief you give here?—I could not tell you that.

1403. Does it exceed 1s. 2d. per head per week?—The clerk will tell you that.

1404. On looking over the books I find that in the greater number of cases 1s. is given, and in some cases 1s. 6d., but probably the average might be taken at 1s. 2d.; do you think 1s. 2d. a week to a poor person to provide rent, clothing, food, and fuel is adequate relief?—I do not, and I was never an advocate for it, and never will be; it is a poor thing to live on.

1405. But still that is the average—1s. 2d. You are aware that there are a vast number of cases in which 1s. a week outdoor relief is given?—I am aware of it, and I think it is too little.

1406. You think that too little?—I do.

1407. Do you think, in point of fact, that the poor people who get that relief are compelled to beg to eke out their existence?—It is only a subsidy in favour of begging—that is all.

1408. Then, in fact, the outdoor relief of this union is subsidising mendicancy, as you put it?—The drift of my language would mean that, but I may tell you that a poor person getting that 1s. a week tries to eke out a miserable existence by it, and would rather eke out that existence with 1s. than come in here no matter how well you care them. I would leave them where they are and give them more.

1409. But outdoor relief is of such a character that an extension of the area of the union would be an extension of the system?—I don't think it would tend that way at all, but if it did I don't think we would be worse off.

1410. It would be no detriment?—No; I think it would be far better to extend the system a little than to have 137 people in this house, built to accommodate over 600 with officers, and incidental expenses in the same ratio.

1411. Have you considered whether this house could be turned to any other purpose?—I never considered it, but I heard it mooted that it was intended to use it as an auxiliary asylum for insane people, and that I think would be a boon to people; at present a good many people have to come long distances to reach the county asylum, at Ballinasloe. This county is the largest in Ireland but one, and it is a long distance from Clifden to Ballinasloe, and if you had one in the centre of the province here—there is not one at all in Mayo—it would be of great use.

1412. Has this Board of Guardians much sanitary work to do?—It does all that is laid down for them.

1413. And would you be satisfied to transfer the sanitary work of this union to Roscommon and Castlerea?—As to the convenience of getting at these places, you could easily do it.

1414. But what do you think the effect of that would be; do you think the board at Castlerea or Roscommon could discharge the sanitary duties of this immediate district?—I think they might do it as well as we do.

1415. That is an equivocal kind of answer?—I was only answering according to my feelings.

Mr. William Neary.

Mr. William Neary examined.

1416. You are an elected guardian?—Yes, for Ballynakill Electoral Division.

1417. And you were the seconder of the resolution of Mr. M'Donnell, which was carried, and, therefore, I presume you are in favour of amalgamation?—I am.

1418. Be kind enough to state on what grounds?—Principally on the ground that there would be a saving to the union, which Mr. M'Donnell estimates at 7d., but which you, Mr. Chairman, said, when down here, would be about 1½d. in the pound.

1419. Have you gone into the figures yourself?—No.

1420. I think you told me that Mr M'Donnell made the calculations on which you based your resolution?—Yes.

1421. And it was in fact on the figures that he put forward at that time that you voted?—Yes, having in my own mind the usefulness of it. I gave it serious attention too. I thought could any hardship possible

GLENNAMADDY. June 11, 1878.

Mr. William Keary.

arise to the poor, and I really did not see how they could

1422. You went on the grounds of economy?—Yes, without any hardship to the paupers

1423. The idea that there would be a large saving was one ground, and your belief that it would inflict no hardship on the poor was the other?—Yes, that it would inflict no hardship on the poor, and that it would work a large benefit to the ratepayers I think the area of this union is entirely too small for the establishment expenses incidental to it

1424. You belong to the Ballymagar Electoral Division?—Yes.

1425. Then supposing that division was sent to the Roscommon Union, would you still be in favour of amalgamation?—In principal I would, because there would be a saving in the other, and the greater number of the division, but personally I would not, for I went in for sending it to Castlerea Union to which, I believe, it formerly belonged.

1426 Do you know what the rate of expenditure is in the Roscommon Union?—No; I never went into the statistics of the surrounding unions at all. I took that from Mr M'Donnell.

1427 I may tell you that the average poundage expenditure in the Roscommon Union is 1s. 10d, and here it is 1s. 6½d. a year, the year ending March, 1877, so that this union is 3½d cheaper than Roscommon for that year?—I am not at all anxious or ambitious to get into the Roscommon Union I may say, but I am for getting into Castlerea; at the same time I would not be against amalgamation in principle, if I had to go into the Roscommon Board—in principle, though personally, I would gain nothing

1428. When I was here on the last occasion, you remember that so far from admitting the possible saving as being 7½d. in the pound, as made out from Mr M'Donnell, I showed you that there might be a saving—a possible saving—in the establishment charges of about 2d?—2½d is my recollection of it Independent of that, do you know what the average cost per head per week is of the pauper inmates at Glennamaddy?—Yes, 3s. 8d.

1429. And in Roscommon it is 4s. 5½d.?—I never contemplated an amalgamation with Roscommon at all

1430 Then, assuming that the proposal introduced a transfer of your division to Roscommon, you would not be in favour of it?—I would, on principle, though I had to pay as much. One division should not stand in the way of benefitting the other seventeen or eighteen electoral divisions of the Union.

1431 Have you considered whether the attendance of guardians, from say your division, would be as good if you were transferred to Roscommon, to look after the interests of the ratepayers, as it is here at present?—I have, and from my knowledge I think it would, and in the case of other divisions, much better than at present For instance, the divisions that go into Roscommon or Castlerea, the gaurdians would go there rather than come here, because these are the market towns.

1432 Are you aware that the possible saving of about 3d. in the pound, estimated when I was here before, was exclusive of any provision for a hospital here?—I am, because I was against having an hospital

1433. Do you not think that it would be a hardship on the poor, accustomed all their lives to come here for hospital treatment, to have to travel these considerable distances in search of relief?—No; it would not be hard on the poor outside, and I think I had it from the doctor that no great hardship would arise to the sick. In fact, at present people have to come as far to this Workhouse as they would have to go to the other Unions, except in the case of the division in which the house stands For instance, part of Ballymagar and Cregg are nearer Roscommon and Castlerea than here.

John Lloyd Bagot, Esq., J.P.

JOHN LLOYD BAGOT, Esq., J.P., examined.

1434. Are you an ex-officio guardian of this Union?—Yes.

1435. Have you heard the proposal to amalgamate this Union with those surrounding it?—Yes.

1436. Are you in favour of amalgamation?—Certainly.

1437 On what grounds?—The great saving that would be effected in the management of the Union, by having it amalgamated with others.

1438 Are you in favour of amalgamation on the ground of economy *only*?—That is one ground; and the next is the impossibility, almost, of getting contracts here We have to get meat from Dunmore, eight or nine miles from here, and very often it is nothing better than carrion. Another reason is that the guardians have no business here, except to attend the Board meetings. There is no market here.

1439. Is not Glennamaddy a market town?—There is a small market here, but it is not the market town. In fact, there is no market in it except for eggs.

1440. What is the market-day here?—Wednesday.

1441. And the Board day is Tuesday?—Yes.

1442. If the Board day was changed to Wednesday, would that not be an advantage?—No, every day but Monday, I think, was tried.

1443. Then it appears you are in favour of amalgamation on three grounds—the saving, the difficulty of getting contracts here, and the difficulty of getting guardians to attend?—Yes, often there is not a Board here at all

1444. Now, on the head of saving, what saving do you anticipate?—I anticipate about the same as Mr. M'Donnell.

1445. Do you adopt his figures?—Yes; I do Further, I say that though the house is vested in the Local Government Board at present, it is for the benefit of the ratepayers It is not their absolute property—they are only trustees for the ratepayers.

1446. Did this Union pay for this house?—I think we did. We had to pay in Roscommon, Castlerea, and Tuam, a large sum for their houses; and I think you will find we have paid for this house.

1447. Do you mean to say that the electorial divisions of those unions were called upon to pay their proportions when they left?—Yes

1448 At the time this union was formed are you sure that you did not get credit from those unions on account of that?—We got some, but not the full proportion of our outlay.

1449. Would you not have to pay the same amount back to them now that you got from them at that period in the event of amalgamation?—No, the wear and tear of the house would have to be taken into account. Then whatever this house and grounds brought the money would come to us.

1450 You mentioned just now the difficulty of getting contracts here. Do you think that the consequence would be that the cost of maintenance would be cheaper elsewhere?—Yes. I know that only for the kindness of Mr Clancy, and of the guardians we could get no milk here. We used to get milk here more than one-third water.

1451. Notwithstanding your statement as to your difficulty in obtaining contracts do you know what the cost of maintenance in the adjoining unions is compared with the cost here?—I' heard it mentioned here before to-day, but I know that the Roscommon people treat the poor a great deal better than we do here

1452. You reside at Ballymoe, on the border of Castlerea Union—do you not?—No, at Aughrane at present. My theory is that the small unions cannot afford to pay the necessary staff—it is too heavy a burden on the ratepayers

GLENNAMADDY, June 11, 1878.

John Lloyd Bagot, Esq., J.P.

1453. Your third objection was the difficulty of getting guardians to attend here?—Yes.

1454. And in support of that objection you mentioned that frequently there are no boards here?—Yes—frequently no board.

1455. Is there any return showing the number of board days in the year on which there was no board?—*The Clerk of the Union.*—There were 36 meetings held during the year ending March, 1878, out of 52 summoned, and in the previous year 39 out of 52.

Witness.—And sometimes you will find there was only a quorum, the consequence is that the business is badly done.

1456. Would you keep up an hospital here, Mr. Bagot?—No, I think not. If fever or any epidemic broke out it would be easy to put up a temporary hospital, but a permanent one is not required.

1457. Would you have no hospital to meet an accidental case of fever?—I don't see the necessity for one.

1458. I don't mean an epidemic, but say three or four cases breaking out?—No, I think not. I may say that the Ballymoe division, the extreme end, is within two miles of Castlerea, and it is eight miles from here, and in place of coming here I would even go to Roscommon, though it is ten miles there.

Mr. M'Donnell

Mr. M'DONNELL re-examined.

1459. I beg leave, Mr Chairman, to correct Mr Bagot in one or two things. First of all I have seen as good meat here as in any workhouse in the Province, and certainly our maintenance here is lower than in other of the adjoining unions, as shown by the statistics you have quoted. That proves what I beg to state that our contracts here have been cheaper than in these other unions, and not as Mr. Bagot says higher.

Dillon Hughes, Esq.

DILLON HUGHES, Esq., examined.

1460. Your are Vice-Chairman of this union?—Yes.

1461. And you have been a long time connected with the union, have you not?—Yes, since its formation.

1462. You have heard this proposal to dissolve the union, and amalgamate it with those adjoining—are you in favour of that?—No, I am not, I am against it.

1463. Why are you against it?—Because I think there would be no saving effected, and because I think it is only right that the men who have property in the county should come here and do their business, and not be leaving it to other guardians elsewhere to do.

1464. When you say that do you mean that representatives of property and the representatives of the ratepayers here would not be likely to attend at the other boards?—I do, because I would be unlikely myself to go nearly as often if I had to go to Mountbellew. May be I would not go there once in three months. I object to the proposal also on the grounds of its being inconvenient for the removal of the poor; it would be very much against the interests of the poor having them handed about to Castlerea, Mountbellew, Tuam, and Roscommon, and I think they would not get the same attention in those places at all that they get here, or that they ought to get. I have seen how they were treated before in Castlerea.

1465. Before the formation of this union?—Yes.

1466. Was there great inconvenience found there then?—Yes; and numbers died from fever and pestilence from the crowding of such a number of the poor people together.

1467. I presume when you say that they died from pestilence that you allude to the famine period when the houses were very crowded?—Yes.

1468. But now is there not plenty of vacant space?—I dare say there is now, though I don't know what the numbers are in Roscommon.

1469. I doubt if your objection on the plea of over-crowding in the present instance would hold; but as to the distances do you think they would be found inconvenient?—Yes, and I don't at all agree with Mr M'Donnell's statistics. He gives you the debtor account, but not the credit side at all. He does not take into account either the proportion of salaries elsewhere which we would have to pay, or the retiring allowances which we would have to provide for in the case of amalgamation.

1470. When you say "retiring allowances" do you mean superannuation?—Yes, they should be superannuated, and the cost of keeping this house, which should be kept up in some way, even if there was no workhouse, would amount to something.

1471. When you say "kept up," do you mean kept up for the benefit of the poor as an hospital?—Yes, and if it was kept up as an hospital there could be no possibility of any saving. All the witnesses agree to that, even Mr. M'Donnell, when pushed to it.

F. F. Cullen, Esq.

F. F. CULLEN, Esq., examined.

1472. Are you a guardian of this union?—Yes, I am the deputy vice-chairman, and I entirely concur in Mr. Hughes' observations. I may add that I would consider it very inhuman to dispense with the hospital here. I don't think it could be done away with without very great injustice and hardship to the poor.

1473. Do you think that by maintaining the hospital the union could otherwise be done away with?—Of course it could, but that would be no saving to us.

1474. Do you think it would be a benefit?—No.

James Browne, Esq., J.P.

JAMES BROWNE, Esq., J.P., examined.

1475. You are a guardian of this union, are you not?—I am for the last twenty years or so.

1476. You have heard or read of the proposal for amalgamation?—Yes, I heard the proposal made.

1477. Are you in favour of it?—No, I am in favour of the union remaining as it is.

1478. Will you say on what grounds you have arrived at that conclusion?—Well, I don't think that the estimate of those who go in for amalgamation would be realised.

1479. Then you don't think that economy would be the result of amalgamation?—No, I don't think it would at all, and in the interests of the poor I very much would prefer seeing the union remain as it is.

GLENNAMADDY, June 11, 1878.

Mr Patrick Kennedy.

Mr. Patrick Kennedy examined.

1480. Are you an elected guardian of this union?—Yes

1481 Are you in favour of amalgamation?—Yes.

1482. On what grounds?—Well, you lead the people here to infer that we were influenced in voting for amalgamation from the figures Mr. M'Donnell brought up, but that is not so. We had our own minds perfectly made up, and when you were here before that was mentioned—before ever Mr. M'Donnell made out those details, for which we are very thankful to him. They are very creditable to him. Now, my simple opinion is this—the valuation of this union is too low to support a staff sufficient for the house——

1483. Be good enough to state concisely on what grounds you desire amalgamation.—Well, I tell you that it would bring about a great saving without any hardship to the poor. But the evidence taken to day has tended to show that we are very inconsiderate with respect to the poor, and it is not right. There are no more humane or deserving guardians than those here—none who pay more attention to the wants of the poor——

1484. Have you any statement or evidence to submit bearing on the question before us?—Well, as I said, the valuation is too small, and the rates too low to take proper care of 130 paupers The house was never made for that; and then, if it is said that we want to disregard the wants of the poor, I must reply that that is not our intention at all.

1485. Are you on the visiting committee of this house?—I have been—several times.

1486. Then, I may inform you on my own part, and I think I may say on that of my colleague, Mr. Doyle, who inspected the house with me, that it appeared to us that the management of your hospital and of the house generally was very good, and the inmates appear to be in every way exceedingly well manity or consideration for the poor, it appears to us that the whole interior of the house is extremely well managed

1487. We ask you as we have asked other witnesses what is your opinion as to the hardship, or the reverse, of removing the poor from this house and the immediate neighbourhood to other and more remote workhouses?—Anything that would be a hardship to them we would be the last to do; but there are other things beyond that—the paupers in the house will not last for ever, and we must look into futurity. The famine brought bad enough times to us, but we are to look forward.

1488. Do you mean that the paupers who are in the house now have been here since the time of the famine?—No.

1489. But that the house was created in consequence of the famine?—No, but that the paupers are created in consequence of the house and the famine. If the house was not here the paupers would not be so numerous. The house was built in a time of necessity, and now when there is no necessity the house should be done away with. It is all very well to say that if there was amalgamation it would inconvenience the poor hereabouts—that they would have too far to go to a workhouse, but they are inconvenienced just the same now in coming from the outskirts of our union here.

1490. Do you think, as a matter of fact, that is would be as convenient for a sick person to go to Castlerea or Roscommon from this union as to come here?—This district is not the whole union of Glennamaddy. I say it would be nearer for the people of Ballymagar to go to Castlerea In a general way the whole will be benefited by it, though those just about this house won't

1491 Then, would you be in favour of keeping up an hospital here?—No, certainly not. There is nothing to justify it, and people would rather go to the union hospital—they would be better cared.

1492 You don't think that a detached hospital could be kept up here with efficiency?—No; it is the last thing we should think of It is to be understood that there would be proper hospital accommodation, and comforts, and care in the other places. Here we are out of the world for comforts. Only that we got Mr. Glancy to oblige us we wouldn't even have milk. Nature never intended this place for a workhouse, it is so out of the world. Besides, you have it now as plain as that two and two make four that the voice of this board is for amalgamation

1493 Seven to six voted for it on the last occasion?—Was not that a majority, and is not that enough But don't lead the other gentlemen who have the honour of coming with you, and who were not here before, to think that it was Mr. M'Donnell that inclined us by his figures and took our heads away; we are all sure it would lead to a saving, and you admitted that yourself, as clear as light, the last time you were here

---

Mr Patrick M Morgan.

Mr. Patrick M. Morgan examined.

1494. Are you an elected guardian of this Union?—Yes, from the electoral division of Kilcroan.

1495 And you have heard the proposition to dissolve this union and amalgamate it?—Yes.

1496. Are you in favour of that not.

1497. State your reasons for opposing it?—I think it would be a great hardship on the poor, and a most inhuman thing to bring them to far distant unions while they could be well cared for here, as they are, and I think the saving would be very inconsiderable—2d in the pound at most, and even that very doubtful

1498. And as representing the ratepayers in your district, and the interests of the poor there, do you think they would desire to see amalgamation carried?—I think the poor ratepayers would have things remain as they are, but I think the large ratepayers—the land owners—would, perhaps, be for amalgamation

1499. In your electoral division?—Yes, because the majority of the poor are the friends of the poorer ratepayers.

FOUR COURTS, DUBLIN, JULY 25, 1878.

DUBLIN, July 25, 1878.

Before Major the Hon W. LE POER TRENCH, R.E., Chairman; ANDREW DOYLE, Esq., and CHARLES SHARMAN CRAWFORD, Esq., Commissioners.

JOHN CHARLES ROBERTSON, Esq., M.D., examined.

Dr. John C. Robertson.

1500. You are the Medical Superintendent of the Monaghan District Lunatic Asylum?—I am.

1501. How long have you been?—Ten years.

1502. In what position connected with lunacy, if any, had you been before you came to Monaghan?—I was first Assistant Medical Officer of the Essex County Lunatic Asylum, after that of the Devon County Lunatic Asylum, and after that of the Hanwell Asylum.

1503. And thence you came to Monaghan?—Yes.

1504. So that you have had a great deal of experience in connexion with lunacy administration?—About twenty-three years' experience.

1505. Has the Monaghan Lunatic Asylum been over crowded since you have had charge of it?—Not yet, from the quantity of spare room we had originally.

1506. The Monaghan Asylum was built for the purpose, I think, of relieving the Armagh Asylum?—It was.

1507. It was supposed, was it not, when the Monaghan Asylum was built that the Armagh Asylum would be for many years at least, sufficient for that district?—I suppose so; but that is not within my knowledge.

1508. The Monaghan Asylum is built in blocks, I think?—Yes, in blocks.

1509. What number is Monaghan Asylum capable of accommodating?—At present it can accommodate 414 bed patients.

1510. Equally divided between males and females?—Very nearly, I think; there may be fifteen beds more for the men.

1511. Then we may put it at 214 for men and 200 for women?—Yes.

1512. With sufficient accommodation for attendants in addition?—Scarcely sufficient for attendants, but we could do with it.

1513. There is a large proportion of the cases, is there not, in the Monaghan Asylum that are classed as incurable?—Yes.

1514. Can you state about what proportion the incurable cases bear to the curable?—No, I could not state that accurately unless I had the returns before me.

1515. However, you will be good enough, some time before our inquiry closes, to give us a statement of the numbers of the curable and incurable cases?—Yes, as far as my memory goes there are at present about twenty-five curable patients in the asylum.

1516. Out of what total number?—Out of 365.

1517. You have 340 incurables and twenty-five curables?—Yes.

1518. Do you find that the presence of so large a class of incurables in the asylum impairs in any way the efficiency of the asylum as a curative establishment?—Certainly.

1519. Irrespective of the room taken up by the incurable cases, are you of opinion that the presence of so many incurables in the asylum operates injuriously in preventing the efficient administration of the institution as a curative establishment?—I do.

1520. Suppose there was accommodation provided elsewhere, of a character that would be satisfactory to you as a medical superintendent, for incurable chronic cases, would you see any objection to the removal of that large number of incurable cases from your asylum?—None, provided a certain number of the chronic patients were left to assist in the working fo the asylum.

1521. That is provided a certain number of useful patients were left to carry on the work of the asylum?—Yes.

1522. How many do you think of the inmates of the asylum are at present usefully employed—begin with the men?—Seventy.

1523. And these seventy are incurable cases, or a large proportion of them?—The greater proportion—more than four-fifths.

1524. Are these seventy so employed from the necessities of your farm, or is their employment part of your curative system?—It is part of my curative system, and furthermore the necessities of the asylum, the cleaning of the house, and so forth, requires it.

1525. And if they were removed you would probably be unable to find amongst the other inmates of the house the means of carrying on your farm operations, and your domestic work in the house?—That is so.

1526. What proportion, can you form any idea, of these seventy would you be compelled to keep, as a working staff, let us call it?—Fifty.

1527. You would consider that in an asylum of that size it would be necessary to retain fifty harmless incurable cases, that, except for their being retained for useful purposes in the asylum, might otherwise be removed to auxiliary asylums?—Yes.

1528. And of women, for laundry and household work, and so forth, have you any idea of what proportion you would require to retain?—Well there is about the same number of women employed.

1529. And the same remark with reference to their removal applies to women as to men?—Yes.

1530. Your asylum at Monaghan is built on a different system, is it not, from the ordinary run of District Lunatic Asylums?—It is, being in blocks.

1531. Do you think that the same proportions of incurable patients for the services of the establishment would be necessary in the other asylums as in yours with its detached blocks?—Yes.

1532. Suppose the Monaghan Asylum was appropriated exclusively as a curative establishment in addition to the curable patients, you would require to retain in the house 100 incurables for the purposes of the place?—Yes.

1533. And that would leave accommodation for how many curable cases?—About 314.

1534. Then putting it in round numbers you would have accommodation, leaving you a sufficient number to carry on the work of the establishment for 300 curable lunatics in the house?—Yes.

1535. The asylum could afford accommodation for 300 lunatics, retaining in the house a sufficient number out of the incurable class to carry on all the necessary works?—Yes.

1536. Now in dealing with the incurable cases that might be removed from the asylum, would you be satisfied from what you know—taking the Monaghan Union as an illustration—to remove a certain proportion of these to an auxiliary asylum composed of the fever ward of the Monaghan Workhouse and the building which is known as the nursery, now which I think you have seen?—Yes.

1537. If these buildings were put into order by the architect of the department—Mr. Wilkinson—upon his plans, would you be satisfied that a certain number of those that would be removed from the Monaghan Asylum might be sent there?—Yes.

1538. That would be for one class, which I think in the returns you were good enough to furnish us with, would be class A?—Yes.

1539. The chronic, harmless and quiet cases?—Yes.

1540. In addition to them there is another class of cases that I think are regarded by the Medical Superintendents of asylums as requiring special care?—Yes.

DUBLIN. July 26, 1878. — Dr John C. Robertson

1541. You know of course, Dr Robertson, that there is power given to set apart certain asylums if necessary, for the Classification of lunatics?—I was not aware.

1542. That is provided by the 8th and 9th Vic cap. 107. I will read Section 13:—

> "Be it enacted that in order to provide for the more effectual treatment of pauper lunatics by a better classification of the same, it shall and may be lawful for the Lord Lieutenant or other Chief Governor or Governors of Ireland by and with the advice and consent of Her Majesty's Privy Council in Ireland, from time to time, and at all times whenever and so often as shall seem expedient to him or them so to do, to direct and order that any existing asylums, or additional buildings which may be made to existing asylums under the provisions of this Act shall and may be exclusively appropriated for the sole and exclusive reception, custody, and treatment of a particular class of the said pauper lunatics, distinguishable by the nature and character of the disease, and whether recent in its origin or chronic, or whether considered curable or incurable."

Referring to so much of the provisions it appears to have been contemplated that certain asylums might be set apart in Ireland for the detention of chronic cases and certain other asylums set apart for the treatment of curable cases?—Yes

1543. Do you think it would be desirable to give effect to that provision of the Act by setting apart certain asylums in Ireland for chronic cases?—I do

1544. Then suppose it was practicable to provide for the whole of the lunacy of Ireland in three classes of asylums—a certain number of district asylums as curative establishments, certain other asylums as places of detention for chronic incurable cases, and a third class auxiliary asylums composed of wings or portions of workhouses adapted for the purpose, do you think that that arrangement would meet the difficulty of providing from time to time for the great increase of lunacy which appears from the reports of the Inspectors of Lunacy?—I think it would meet it fully.

1545. You are of opinion that it would meet it fully?—Yes.

1546. Have you any reason to think, that by making additional room in the district asylums means might be afforded for the treatment of paying patients of a class between the wealthy who are able to send to private asylums and the poor who are removed into district asylums?—I have.

1547. And that that would in fact be a great boon to a large class of people who are at present without any means of providing for the treatment of members of their families who are lunatics?—It would be a great boon, much the same as in Scotland where that is carried out in the Royal asylums

1548 You think the practice that exists in Scotland might be advantageously extended to Ireland for the treatment of such a class?—With certain modifications

1549. What modifications would you suggest?—I would limit such accommodation to the poorer middle classes.

1550 The classes who might pay probably the bare cost of maintenance, or a little above it?—About £1 a week or so—not more than cover every expense.

1551. Have you many of the class of paying patients in your asylum?—Five.

1552 Does any difficulty attend the admission of patients of that class?—Considerable difficulty and delay is experienced in admitting pay patients—especially acute cases In the first instance the forms when perfected are submitted to the Board of Governors, who meet but once a month, and the admission approved by them, then the form has to be forwarded to the Inspector's office for their approval, and when returned to the Resident Medical Superintendent, approved, he can then notify the patient's friends, that the lunatic can be admitted.

1553 If the case is acute and urgent, can he be admitted provisionally or must he wait the approval of the Board and Inspectors?—He can be admitted provisionally, but then there is some trouble in making the friends fill up the forms agreeing to pay the sum stipulated

1554 Have you any experience of the extent to which idiotcy, as distinguished from lunacy, exists in the asylums in Ireland?—Merely judging from Monaghan asylum—I have no other experience.

1555 Do you think if an asylum like Monaghan was set apart as a curative establishment, that it would be possible to retain a portion of it for the education and treatment of idiots?—Yes, being built in blocks, it would.

1556 And suppose that architectural and structural arrangements could be made for the purpose in other asylums do you think that it would be possible to extend that arrangement to other asylums as well?—Yes—but not to all asylums.

1557. To curative asylums?—Not to all curative asylums I think, for idiots are so few.

1558 But you think if a census of the idiot population, who are amenable to educational influences, could be got that it would be desirable to make provision—be the extent of the provision more or less according to the number—that it would be desirable to make provision in the curative establishments for their treatment and education?—Yes.

1559. Your asylum is managed as are all the asylums in Ireland, by a Board of Governors?—It is.

1560. How many are there in the Board?—Thirty-three

1561. Are they very regular in their attendance at your monthly meetings?—Latterly they have been—I may say, yes.

1562. Is the asylum regularly visited?—It is not.

1563. Isn't there a provision made in the regulations of the Privy Council for the regular visiting of the asylums by the visitors?—There is.

1564 Is that in your asylum, as I believe it is in most others, a form which is really not observed?—About six times in the year the place is visited—I don't know how to answer the question.

1565. Are the visitors from among the Governors?—Yes.

1566. The rule of the Privy Council is, I believe, that the asylum shall be visited a certain number of times by the Governors, and that visiting you say is not regular?—No

1567. May we take it that in your asylum the visiting is, without being what would be called a thorough examination of the establishment, yet useful, as it gives persons an opportunity of making complaints if they have any to make and enable the visitors to see whether the house is in proper order or not?—Yes

1568. How frequently is your asylum visited by the Inspectors of Lunacy?—Quarterly.

1569. Is it an associated visit?—No, a single visit.

1570. Is notice given of the intention to visit or is the visit made unexpectedly?—Sometimes notice is given, but it is oftener unexpectedly.

1571. Are you satisfied with the mode of appointing officers—subordinate officers or officials in Lunatic Asylums?—I am not.

1572. The subordinate officers are appointed by the Governors?—They are.

1573. And what do you think is the objection to the appointment of such officials by the Governors?—The officials consider themselves independent of the control of the responsible officers—the medical superintendents—to a great extent

1574 And you are of opinion that they ought to be absolutely responsible to him as he is responsible for the management of the house?—I am.

1575. Do you think that the selection and appointment of the warders and servants ought to be left with the Medical Superintendent, subject to the approval of the Board of Governors?—I am.

1576. Practically is that the case in your asylum?—It is

1577 The Governors of your asylum, we take it, recognise the expediency of leaving these appointments in your hands, and practically do leave them in your hands?—Yes

1578 But if they took the appointment into their

own hands, you probably would apprehend that some inconvenience would arise from the selection of persons less efficient than you would appoint yourself?—Yes

1579. Have you ever known any inconvenience to arise, on account of the present system of appointing subordinate officers?—No, but I think it might.

1580. In the auxiliary that are proposed in connexion with workhouses, looking to the classes of inmates that would be removed from the asylums and from the different workhouses, what proportion of attendants would you say it would be desirable to have in those auxiliary asylums?—Very much would depend upon the structural arrangement of the buildings, but I should say one in thirty would be sufficient

1581. You think that where there were sixty inmates that two attendants would be sufficient?—If it was one ward—yes.

1582. Do you mean one associated ward?—Yes

1583. For 60 beds?—Yes—one ward for 60.

1584. But suppose there were four associated wards so arranged that there might be an attendants room between each two, and say two day-rooms or even one day-room, do you then think that one in thirty would be sufficient for that class?—It would, but less attendants than one in 30 could not superintend the sanitary arrangements, &c.

1585. Assisted by a certain number of the best conducted paupers from the workhouse?—If they were to get the help of well conditioned paupers from the workhouses, then one nurse could take charge of more patients. I really think that one man could take charge of the number I mentioned but certainly no more.

1586. Say that one warder for thirty and that the warder should get the assistance of a couple of paupers, men of good character, capable of doing a moderate amount of work—that would be sufficient?—That could be done.

1587. In the suggestion that is implied in the questions that have been put to you, it is contemplated that a certain number of lunatics should be removed from the curative district asylums to the intermediate asylums and also to workhouse asylums—do you think that it would be beneficial, or that it would be otherwise if the control of the whole lunacy department was divided between two authorities?—I think it would be highly inconvenient.

1588. You think it would be highly inconvenient?—Highly inconvenient

1589. You think without noticing what the authority might be, that the whole lunacy administration ought to be under one department?—Most certainly.

1590. You are strongly of that opinion?—Strongly.

1591. Do you agree with an opinion that was expressed by Dr Nugent in a communication made by him, that great inconvenience and conflict of authority would arise if there were two authorities having the control of lunacy?—I do.

1592. What are the arrangements now with reference to retiring allowances of all classes connected with lunatic asylums?—They are under the Civil Service Act—I forget which Act it is, and they must serve 10 years before service can count; after that the pension is at the rate of one-sixtieth per annum of their whole service, with allowances considered.

1593. That is to say, an officer who has served nine years and from any cause other than misconduct, retires from the service; is obliged to leave the service, we will say from illness, accident or incapacity, would not be entitled to a pension?—That is so

1594. Do you think that that is, as far as it goes, a hardship?—Not so much that, because I think there ought to be a limit to service before a man is entitled to a pension, but a gratuity might be given in such a case.

1595. You think that it ought to be within the discretion of the Governors, to give a gratuity in such a case?—Yes, furthermore the Medical Superintendent being appointed when he is of full age; sometimes not till he is thirty or thirty-five, his pension begins to count at that age, whereas the Civil Service men begin at eighteen or twenty: when they enter, and there is no clause by which a certain number of years could be added to our service.

1596. Do I understand you to say that the pension of a Medical Superintendent commences, not from the period of his service but from a certain year of his age?—No, from the period of his service but he is rarely appointed until he is elderly.

1597. But if it happened that a man was appointed at 23, the fact of his being so young would make no difference in the calculation of his pension subsequently?—No.

1598. Then I gather from what you say that you think the medical superintendents of asylums being professional men, that when they have served a period that would entitle them to retire, they should have added on to their term of service a certain number of years, as in the case of certain other servants in the public service?—Yes.

1599. For instance, a barrister being in the public service in England, if he retires from certain employments, is entitled to have seven years added on to the period of his service—that is what you mean?—Yes

1600. You think that a similar arrangement should be made with reference to the medical superintendents of asylums in Ireland?—Yes; and that they should be put upon the same footing as the second class civil servants

1601. And that their whole period of service should count, no matter how changed about?—It should.

1602. At present if a medical superintendent is in one asylum and appointed to another, he loses the advantage, does he not, of his service in the previous appointment?—He does

1603. And if a man has served twenty years in one asylum, and is promoted to another, that twenty years is left out of the period of his service in calculations for a pension?—It is.

1604. And you think that that is an obvious injustice that ought to be removed?—It ought to be removed, certainly.

1605. And the service be regarded as a continuing service in the public service, and not in a particular asylum?—Exactly so

1606. And the reason of all this is that you are county officers and not servants of the crown, or rather members of the civil service?—Yes, we receive our appointment from the Lord Lieutenant, and are paid by the county or counties.

1607. What is the general mode of admission to a lunatic asylum?—There are two modes. One mode is upon a house form, application being made to the superintendent to forward one to the friends of the patient: the other is where the relatives, or some person, makes an information, or declaration before two magistrates that the lunatic is dangerous. Then he is committed upon warrant as a dangerous lunatic

1608. Is that power of admitting upon a magistrate's warrant one, that within your knowledge, is very much abused, when I say abused, I mean is it one under which cases that are really not dangerous are admitted as dangerous?—A few have been, not many.

1609. It is alleged in the reports of the lunacy inspectors—the annual reports—that several asylums that are named have become over crowded in consequence of the number of harmless lunatics that have been sent as dangerous, when in point of fact they are not dangerous, and not fit subjects at all for asylum treatment?—That has not been my experience. I look upon that act as a very valuable one, because through it I have been enabled to get patients in a more recent stage of insanity—patients that otherwise, I think, friends would have detained longer at home

1610. Patients in an earlier stage?—Yes.

1611. Upon the other hand does it not give a facility to friends to send in as dangerous lunatics to occupy

DUBLIN
July 22, 1878.

Dr John C. Robertson.

the place of curable cases, persons who are really not dangerous, and not susceptible of curative treatment?—It does. I have had two or three such cases sent to my asylum.

1612. Is it not a fact that the friends of lunatics, committed by the magistrates as dangerous lunatics, enter into no engagement for their removal when cured and cannot be called upon to contribute to their support?—Yes, it is so, and cannot be called upon to contribute to their support if capable; but should the patient become quiet and be considered not dangerous, the Board of Governors can order the patient to be discharged, though still insane, reference was made on this subject to the inspectors, and the opinion of the law officers obtained regarding it.

1613. Let me refer you to a passage or two in the report of the Inspectors of Lunacy to illustrate what I mean. This is one of many observations to the same effect. Speaking of a particular asylum the Inspectors say —

> "The resident physician justly complains of the undue advantage taken by parties in forcing a class of patients into the asylum under committal warrants, well knowing that in such cases admission cannot be refused and that many of them are more suited for workhouses, thus not only adding to the overcrowded state of the house, but occupying the room of urgent and suitable cases."

That passage conveys a complaint in that particular case that is repeated over and over again of other asylums—but that is not within your experience?—No.

1614 In that same asylum in the report for 1870, the Inspectors say, that of the thirty-nine persons committed as dangerous lunatics during the year, a considerable number are returned as tranquil and unsuitable?—That has not been my experience.

1615. Here is a passage referring to another asylum:—

> "The house is estimated to contain 596 patients, whereas upon the 31st of December there were actually in it 687, or 91 over the proper number, the daily average for the year being 661 or 65 beyond the prescribed limit. We consequently took occasion to observe that were the admissions suitable cases, though it was to be regretted there was not space sufficient for them, no reasonable objection could be raised, but upon finding that the crowded state of the asylum arose from the indiscriminate committal of dangerous lunatics so called, be they blind, dumb or debilitated by old age, without proper inquiry, we felt it incumbent upon us to complain against this monopoly as it were of accommodation, tending as it did to exclude legitimate cases."

There are many other passages to the same effect in the reports of the Inspectors, but that is not your experience?—No, the number of cases that are unsuitable, being sent to Monaghan asylum under that Act are very few indeed.

1616. And probably to that care upon the part of the magistrates may be ascribed the fact that your asylum is not over-crowded at present?—Very possibly.

1617 Having regard to the number of lunatics returned by the constabulary in the return which was published in the annual reports of the Inspectors of Lunacy, do you believe that there are a considerable number of lunatics at large who might be advantageously removed into asylums?—Oh! yes.

1618. As an illustration of that you were good enough to send to us some time ago the particulars of one case that came within your own knowledge?—I did.

1619. And we may refer to that correspondence which you have furnished us with, and annex it as part of your evidence?—Yes.

Dr. George Wm. Hatchell.

GEORGE WILLIAM HATCHELL, ESQ., M.D., examined.

1620 How long have you been in your present position as inspector of lunatic asylums?—I was appointed on the 24th June, 1857.

1621. And during the period of your service you have had the best means of knowing the condition of lunatic asylums?—Certainly.

1622. Has there been a constant and continuous overcrowding of the asylums within your experience?—In some—most of them, certainly. They are always crying out for more room and additional accommodation, and there have been additional asylums built consequently within that time.

1623. In consequence of the overcrowding?—Yes

1624. Has this overcrowding been of chronic, and probably incurable cases?—I think they have accumulated. That is a question often put to me by professional men and outsiders, as to the increase of lunacy. Lunacy appears to increase more than it really does, inasmuch as it accumulates, it doesn't kill in the same way as other diseases. I should say to a certain extent exempts them from other diseases, and, although there be many cures, still it accumulates, and eventually an asylum becomes overcrowded.

1625. With incurables?—Yes.

1626 Would you say that as much as 70 or 75 per cent of the inmates of an asylum at any one time are classed as probably incurable?—Well, I would; it comes very nearly to that.

1627. I think that is the result of the statement in your annual reports?—Yes. I think something about two-thirds.

1628. I think it has been frequently stated in the reports at about two-thirds?—I think that comes within the number.

1629. The approximate number?—That I should say would be about the number.

1630. The crowding by such cases is alleged to interfere very much with the efficiency of the asylums as curative establishments Have you any doubt about that?—None in the world.

1631. That a consequence of the asylums being crowded with chronic and probably incurable cases is to impair their efficiency in curable cases?—I think it does, because it causes crowding in the curable cases, which is very injurious. For instance, put a number of refractory and curable cases into a ward at the same time, that is injurious. Limerick was a particular instance of that. There there are the worst refractory patients I ever saw anywhere, because they are overcrowded with acute curable cases. Of course then they become refractory.

1632 And has it the effect of distracting the attention of the medical superintendent?—It prevents him concentrating his curative powers on curable cases

1633. And in that respect it impairs the efficiency?—Of the entire establishment.

1634. From your experience, what suggestion would you make with the view to relieve the asylums from the burden of the incurable or probably incurable cases?—Well, you know that is a question one has been thinking over many years, and it is in a nutshell. Make an establishment apart from the curable cases for the treatment of the incurable cases. Whether you make that in immediate proximity, and in addition to the lunatic asylums, or convert other establishments, it should be done.

1635. The suggestion has been frequently made as we gather from one of your reports to provide separate establishments for the incurable cases?—Yes.

1636. Have you formed any decided opinion yourself as to whether it would be better to increase the asylums, or take advantage of vacant space in other

Dublin.
July 25, 1878.
Dr. George
Wm Hatchell.

institutions?—That becomes a question of pounds, shillings, and pence. One would be expensive and the other not. It is a nice question to say the case that is curable and the case that is not curable, because people have been cured long after they were given up as incurable, but I don't think an establishment set apart for apparently incurable cases prevents a man being cured if proper management is used. Then, if you were to ask me which was the more perfect of the two arrangements to make, I would be disposed to say an establishment built for the purpose of these incurable cases in the proximity of the lunatic asylum, and placed under the same supervision.

1637. Or under similar supervision?—Yes, under similar: the same would be too much perhaps.

1638. One gathers from you that there is a difference in the character of the lunatics who are probably incurable, that there are some hopelessly demented, and others that might be supposed to offer some reasonable grounds for hope?—Some never have a mind and others have a diseased mind.

1639. Congenital idiots?—Yes, and those who were born without a mind.

1640. You know the character generally speaking of the lunatic inmates of workhouses?—I do.

1641. Would it be in your opinion desirable to collect from the several workhouses of certain districts all that class, and deal with them there in considerable numbers instead of having them scattered in two's and three's through asylums, and dealing with the matter as to workhouses only for many reasons. From your knowledge of the workhouses you have no difficulty in assenting to the opinion expressed by the Commissioners in 1856 that the condition of lunatics in workhouses is most unsatisfactory?—I think so. In the first place you see them placed at the end of a long passage with a fire-place, and then you have the dark ill-ventilated cells, where generally two of them are in a space that ought not to have more than one certainly, and they are on the diet of the house which is very objectionable in cases; then they are in charge of paupers; there is no paid person in charge except the master and matron; there is no other paid person in the house.

1642. Are you not under some misapprehension about that?—In some cases I know they are paid—in Derry and Belfast I believe they are paid.

1643. There is no objection to have them paid where there is a sufficient number to justify their being paid?—I know they are paid in this way: "Have you charge of these lunatics?"—"Yes, sir," and if a woman is there, I say: "You should give her better diet," and I find she does get better diet, and if there is a man he gets tobacco, but I don't call that paying.

1644. But in wages many of them?—Oh yes, I know some are paid.

1645. Bearing in mind the condition of these people as you represent them, do you not think it would be desirable to take them out of the workhouse into some other building?—I think it would be most desirable.

1646. You think that would be a great improvement?—Most certainly.

1647. Have the inspectors of lunacy ever recommended that, or taken any steps to see whether such an arrangement could be carried out?—Well, I think, yes, at one time I think it was recommended by the inspectors to take the poor-house at Corrofin so far back as Mr. Cardwell's time as chief secretary, and I remember Sir Alfred Power coming up with myself and colleague, and discussing with the chief secretary on the subject, and it ended in Sir A. Power convincing the chief secretary that the Corrofin workhouse could not be given up for the purpose.

1648. Has the fact ever been brought to the notice of the inspectors that there is a good deal of unoccupied space in many of the workhouses?—I am aware of the fact that workhouses capable of accommodating 800 or 1,000 people, have not 200 in them, and it is a great waste of space that would be better occupied.

1649. Have the inspectors ever made any attempt to induce the Government to appropriate that space?—I don't think so.

1650. Do you think that space could in certain cases be appropriated?—Most assuredly I do.

1651. Look, for example, at this drawing (map produced), here is a sketch of what might be done in Oughterard. The pink coloured lines would be the place appropriated with the adjoining yards for lunatics?—I understand that perfectly.

1652. Well, suppose that that building could be set apart for a certain number of lunatics in the Oughterard Workhouse, and suppose that there was a sufficient staff of attendants; that the day-room was sufficient, that the airing ground was sufficient, that the supervision was sufficient, would you have any hesitation in recommending a certain number of harmless and probably incurable lunatics in asylums to be removed there and associated with the same class of the inmates from Workhouses?—No, because if they were taken the same care of as if they were left in the asylum, I don't see any reason why they should not be removed.

1653. We should not speak of having the same care, but of the care they would require?—Suitable arrangements made for their care.

1654. As Dr. Nugent expresses it—their "creature comforts" attended to?—Yes, with a wash-house and other requisites.

1655. Have you any hesitation in saying that a large per-centage of the probably incurable cases from asylums could be associated with the workhouse lunatics or imbeciles in an establishment of that sort?—I think not, because they are pretty much of the same class.

1656. There is another class described as a little above them, not absolutely of the "probably incurable" class, and yet not proper subjects for a curative establishment; would you think it desirable to have some intermediate asylum between that and the curative establishment?—Now, there are a great many incurables that I don't look upon as completely demented; they are very quiet and orderly, and useful in the asylums. These are people, I think, it would be as well to leave in the asylums.

1657. For useful purposes?—Yes.

1658. A sufficient number of them?—Such as the Institution would require, otherwise you would have to go in for paid labour.

1659. That is not exactly the class I refer to?—I think I know what you mean. We have got a low class of lunatics thoroughly demented—the incurable lunatic. Now, you want an incurable lunatic of a higher class—of a higher order of intellect, and you ask me then would an intermediate establishment be desirable, and I answer you I don't think it would be required.

1660. You think that the workhouse asylum, that is the unappropriated portion of the workhouse—the wings of the house; detached hospitals and sheds, that could all very well be appropriated for the purpose would be quite adequate in point of accommodation for the reception of that class?—I would not be disposed to mix that class with the other class we have been talking of.

1661. Then it was that class we have been talking of that I want to know whether you would suggest any class of building for them?—I think it would be desirable.

1662. Would you think it practicable from what you know of the asylums and the arrangements, and the proportions of different classes in certain asylums to give up, say one asylum or two in a district for that class, and convert another into a curative hospital for the district?—At first sight that looks right, but when you come to look at the working of it I am afraid it would not work satisfactorily. In the first place it would remove the curative hospital too great a distance from parts of its own district.

1663. Would it necessarily be so—as an illustration take Maryborough. Suppose you were to convert it into an asylum for curables, and to draft all the incurables from that asylum to, let us say, the nearest adjacent asylum?—Kilkenny would be the nearest

DUBLIN, July 25, 1878.

Dr. George Wm. Hatchell.

1664. Well, take Kilkenny as an example—as an asylum for incurable cases. Send the whole of the incurable cases from Maryborough to Kilkenny, and the whole of the curable cases from Kilkenny to Maryborough, would there be any difficulty about that arrangement?—The only thing is that violent curable cases would have a longer distance to travel than in the present district. Whereas mad people in Kilkenny, instead of being sent direct to the asylum, have to come all the way into Maryborough, and I think in that way I would be afraid to try to take away the curative idea out of any of these asylums—that is to convert them into incurable hospitals.

1665. Would there be any difficulty about removing the chronic cases, dismissing the idea of their being any curable cases there, from Kilkenny to Maryborough and the incurable cases from Maryborough to Kilkenny?—There would be no difficulty. The only difficulty, I think, is that an asylum of its character—incurable—would be objectionable. It would be a slur on the medical officer to get all the incurable cases—and to trust one man, to all appearances, and not another, would annoy them. I think all the medical officers of the place would object to it, but I don't know that they would.

1666. Apart from the feelings of the officers, if you had to begin *de novo*, and had all those asylums to deal with, what then?—There would be less difficulty then.

1667. Would there be any difficulty then?—Well, you could appoint men, then, and they would know what they were taking.

1668. Is it simply out of deference to the opinion of the medical man you speak?—When you come to adopt an improved system, I would not allow anything to stand in the way of it.

1669. Apart from the feelings of the medical man, do you think that would be an improved system; it is a classification of lunatics?—I clearly see it.

1670. Already you have 75 per cent. of that class in the asylums. Every asylum is virtually, according to the reports of the inspectors, a place of detention rather than a hospital, and, according to the evidence that we have already received, its efficiency as a curative asylum is impaired. The question then is, whether, by bringing all the cases of one class or character together, you could not have a better establishment and more economical?—I don't see how you could diminish the staff of the existing asylums.

1671. That is another consideration; if it could be proved there is no pecuniary advantage in doing it, of course it would fall to the ground?—I don't see any objection in principle to it.

1672. Except the objection that it would be establishing an inferior class of asylums?—It would, and it would be establishing a fact which does not exist—that that class of person we speak of is incurable, and if a medical man gets that into his mind he will make no attempt to cure, he would say, "I am left in charge of incurable people, and I take no trouble about them."

1673. Would it not put a medical man on his mettle to try whether he could not cure where it was supposed they were incurable?—That kind of rivalry might do if they were to gain anything by it.

1674. Let us hope they would be influenced by higher motives than that. Apart from that you have indicated already that you have three classes to deal with. First, the workhouse lunatics, two other classes still in asylums, and in order to preserve the asylums as curative establishments and to avoid the necessity of constant increase in buildings for incurable cases, virtually you would remove that class to an intermediate asylum; they would not necessarily be incurable, but they are a type of case that don't require the same care as in the curative establishments?—Well, they require the same care, but perhaps not the same vigilance or the same anxiety that acute curable cases would, but then I think they require the same attention and the same watching as to the moment they became getting better so as to follow it up.

1675. Well, you would have the means of doing that in these asylums if they were appropriated for the purpose?—I would. I don't see any decided objection. I am only raising these little apparent difficulties in order that we may thrash the subject thoroughly. I would rather do that than ride off by saying, "Oh, do it, there's no difficulty will arise," and then have these difficulties arising afterwards.

1676. And we are, I'm sure, much obliged to you; the first difficulty you suggested was rather one of sentiment—the feeling of the medical superintendents, that they would feel their status was lowered, that the medical superintendent of one of these asylums would be in fact an inferior officer to the one in charge of the curative establishment?—I think he would consider he was selected in consequence of being thought so.

1677. If it so happened that the particular asylum selected was obviously selected on other grounds—was selected for its suitability and arrangement?—I certainly would not select them on account of their medical officers, let that be clearly understood.

1678. Are the other difficulties local?—Yes.

1679. For instance, take Armagh. You were very anxious to make some improvement there. I don't know whether you have made them?—There was a step towards it.

1680. Take then such an asylum as Monaghan. Suppose you made that a curative establishment, sending the "probably incurable" from Armagh to Monaghan, Armagh Asylum being an old building, inferior in its structural arrangements, I dare say you would consent to the enlargement of Armagh with reluctance?—I originally thought it would be better to take it down altogether, and to build an asylum in a better site, it is surrounded by buildings, and is close to the town and railway.

1681. But, having it there, don't you think that, as an illustration of what is meant, it would be desirable to make that asylum receive the overflow of Monaghan?—That is my opinion.

1682. That is one illustration. Would you see any difficulty about that arrangement?—No.

1683. And if you had Armagh Workhouse, which is capable of accommodating a considerable number of the class we first spoke of, and the Armagh Asylum, which is capable of accommodating a large number of the other cases, because there are very few of the "curable" cases in Armagh, and if they were sent to Monaghan would it not be beneficial to the district?—It would.

1684. And ultimately effect probably a considerable saving in other large asylums?—It would probably save the enlargement of Armagh Asylum, which otherwise will be enlarged, provided the building there be carried out.

1685. But, applying that to the whole country, don't you think that if that scheme was carried out it would for a very considerable time obviate the necessity of increasing the asylum buildings throughout the country?—Certainly, if we confine ourselves to the poor-houses alone I think it would, and it would make the supervision much easier so far as the inspectors are concerned.

1686. But suppose, on a careful calculation of the number of the various classes to be accommodated, it was found that sufficient accommodation could hardly be found in poor-houses, probably for four-fifths or less than that, still there would be a number, it would be almost necessary and certainly desirable to provide for in the asylums—don't you think a certain number of the asylums could be given up for that purpose?—I think so, because the curable cases in asylums are small in number, and one large asylum like Monaghan would hold a large number.

1687. It would hold the cases of the district?—It would, and so with Omagh and Derry, that would be the upper, middle, and lower classes. The middle class which calls for the inferior asylums as to buildings and sites, the upper class being the curable cases, which are to be kept where there is plenty of land and plenty of room. The locality would necessarily be as a matter of course of importance, that would be the first thing.

1688. Take Richmond asylum, that is a very large building, capable of accommodating a very large number?—There are over 1,000 in Richmond Asylum now.

1689. Of that 1,000 there are 60 per cent. of incurable, and you could appropriate an asylum within easy distance in point of time, or such a distance as Carlow (although Carlow might, perhaps, be considered too good an asylum to appropriate for the purpose), and suppose you could send a number of the incurable cases to the workhouse, the middle class to Carlow, and preserve Dublin for curative cases alone, don't you think that would be a great improvement on the existing system?—I do.

1690. Do you see any practical difficulty in carrying that out—suppose a certain number could be provided for in the workhouse, do you see any difficulty in providing for what you designate the middle class by appropriating one or more asylums for the purpose?—No. Mullingar is almost too good a place for our middle class, at the same time it would be the nearest relief to that class. Then Carlow would be the next in the neighbourhood, although it is not in the district.

1691. Still the Lord Lieutenant has power to make a district?—Yes.

1692. Do you think the advantage, suppose you looked at it from the point of view that suggested this question, would be sufficient to justify the legislation with the view to such classification of asylums?—Well, if it is right to do it, it is right to get power to do it.

1693. Well, that is putting the question in another way. Do you think it a sufficient improvement to ask for power to do it?—I think it is.

1694. That is simply an illustration. It has never suggested itself to the inspectors to make such a district themselves?—No, it never suggested itself to me, and I don't think I ever heard Dr. Nugent say so.

1695. The suggestion has always taken the form of enlarging the asylum?—Yes.

1696. Wherever you have an asylum crowded with chronic cases, instead of suggesting any other mode of relief the suggestion of the inspectors has been always to increase the asylums?—We make the same division of patients—first, second, and third; upper, middle, and lower—in the asylums, which you want to make by the separate buildings.

1697. In point of fact, are you able to make that classification?—We are able to do so, because we keep violent acute cases very nearly together, and quiet cases pretty well together, and then we keep these low idiots (epileptic) together.

1698. That is the classification of accommodation. Is there any classification that affects the expenditure—any classification of diet?—No; they all cost the same. The only classification is the classification of rooms.

1699. But the classification that affects the ratepayers is not considered at all?—No; it can't be considered.

1700. Curable cases are of necessity mixed with the others?—Yes; because they are fewer in number, and it is not easy to discover the curable at once.

1701. Several of the districts were broken up within your time?—Yes, for instance, Carlow was separated from Wexford, and Letterkenny from Derry.

1702. Practically, was there much inconvenience otherwise than the inconvenience of overcrowding before the district was broken up?—That was all.

1703. Your duty as inspector involves the visiting of all asylums four times a year?—Yes—that is, within the last three years.

1704. And it also involves the duty of visiting all the workhouses?—Yes.

1705. But on going into the number, we see that these are not in point of fact visited?—No; except some of the principal ones. Sometimes I find it is a waste of time and money, going to look at two or three patients and taking three or four days to do it.

1706. Still, would it not be important in the case of two or three in a remote workhouse to visit them and see their condition?—No doubt, and that is the way I have satisfied myself. I have done a turn of duty with the view of laying the ground for such an alteration of their condition, as is indicated in the questions put—whether it would not be necessary to visit them, to see whether those in some of the remote workhouses were in a condition that no humane persons would allow them to remain in longer than they could help—don't you think visiting necessary?—Yes; and I have often said to the master—"What a pity these people could not be put together and looked after, instead of being huddled up here, and stowed away somewhere else, and no care at all, except that they are fed, and generally not too well fed, and clothes put on them."

DUBLIN,
July 23, 1878.

Dr. George
Wm. Hatchell.

1707. Suppose the asylums—taking Richmond Asylum as an illustration—were relieved from the great mass of incurable cases, do you think any advantage might be derived from the lower and middle class being taken in as paying patients—the people who would be able to pay?—Most decidedly. It would make room in the curative hospital or asylum.

1708. Don't you think that that would be an object to bear in mind in any alteration suggested—that accommodation might be afforded for a class of patients for whom there is no asylum now?—I think that would be a great boon.

1709. You think the advantage that would be conferred on the class of poor people who might pay a small sum, but who yet are unable to pay the sum they are required to pay in private asylums, would go to relieve the burden of the incurable cases?—Yes; and most of these cases are acute curable cases. There are very few incurable cases among them, and we learn that from private asylums, and from that of Lucan Spa Asylum, which is a sort of intermediate pay asylum, and if there was a branch asylum thrown open for that class a number of cases might be sent in the earlier stages. I think it would be most desirable. I think an asylum set apart for such cases, and made Governmental, would be the right thing to do.

1710. Would not a portion of an asylum, say portion of Richmond asylum, or a block of the asylum we were speaking of (Monaghan) do?—There is a kind of objection among that class of poor respectable people who could not pay as much as a private asylum wants, to send them to a pauper asylum, and these people have told me so themselves. I don't say it is a well-founded objection, for if a man or woman becomes mad they don't know where they are until they become well or convalescent.

1711. The idea of pauperism has very much disappeared in connection with asylums in Ireland?—Very much so. A very large number put in as paupers are not paupers, but there are some people who are very sensitive about that subject. The majority are not.

1712. It is a prejudice that would wear out, and more rapidly if there was a classification of the asylums?—More rapidly. I am quite sure a great many would send their friends to a curative asylum who would not send them to an asylum with a number of idiots.

1713. If there was a curative hospital instead of an asylum, that prejudice would be broken down?—No doubt the best way would be to have a curative hospital.

1714. Would you say a ward in each province for the reception of that class?—A building separate from the other with more comfortable furniture and more like a private asylum.

1715. To use a common phrase they should get the worth of their money?—And more than that, they should have a dining-room as well furnished as their own, and not like a gaol. Some place more like home.

1716. You trust altogether to the constabulary returns for the lunatics at large?—We have no

DUBLIN
July 26, 1878.

Dr George
Wm. Hatchell.

means at all of knowing how many they are except from them.

1717. And your knowledge even of the number is only approximate?—We take it from the constabulary returns.

1718. But you don't know how they get them?—I believe the constabulary returns are exact.

1719. They have no legal authority to go into houses and make inquiries?—They know the reputed lunatics. Ask any old constabulary man in Ireland how many people are in that house living, and he will tell you every one of them.

1720. As to the condition of these people the constabulary returns simply class them as middle class, upper class, and lower class?—Yes.—For instance, if a country gentleman has a member of his family insane, and if he wishes to keep him at home, the constabulary man knows he is there, and he is looked upon as the upper class.

1721. Do you ever make any visit round to the lunatics at large?—No, for it would take one to go to a town and stay there for a week before you would find them out. It would take a long time. I had the curiosity to try it.

1722. Some of these lunatics in Dublin are in a deplorable state?—Oh yes; I visited one or two myself that I heard of—possibly a dozen altogether, and I found them so, but I could not interfere, they were with their own people.

1723. You found them in a bad condition?—I found them in bed, not exactly badly treated, but not in the way they ought to be.

1724. No attention paid them?—No.

1725. And grossly neglected in the cases you came across?—Yes.

1726. Could you suggest any means of dealing with that which is a very great evil?—My idea is this; that the moment a man becomes a lunatic he ought to become a child of the State; his people ought to have nothing to do with him.

1727. Except to pay for him I hope?—Except to pay for him if they are able to pay, but he should be at once taken out of the hands of his own people.

1728. In England the state of the law is as you know that every pauper lunatic is visited twice a year by the medical officer of the district in which he resides, and if upon his report he is returned as a proper subject to be sent to an asylum, or to be removed to the workhouse, he is at once removed, and if his people are capable of paying, they pay. Do you think such an alteration of the law in Ireland, extending it not to paupers, but to lunatics at large would be practicable?—I think it could be abused.

1729. In what way would the abuse arise?—In the first place twice a year is very seldom to see men confined in a private house.

1730. The visits would be too few?—Yes, too few, and secondly if the party wished to keep them at home I think the doctor would not be pressing very much the other way.

1731. But supposing it was the duty of the dispensary medical officer to visit all the lunatics within his district, and make a report to your department?—First—that it would be his duty to visit four times a year or more, and then to report once in three months to our officer, giving the name and address, and symptoms and everything connected with the lunatic, and his opinion as to his treatment. Then it would be in the power of the inspector to go down unexpectedly, take a list, and visit them to see that that report is right or not.

1732. That is what in some cases was done by the Lunacy Commissioners in England. When the medical officers' reports were sent in, if they saw indications that certain cases required to be visited they went down at once and saw whether such cases were unfit to be at large, and they decided to have them removed into asylums at once?—The advantage of that would be that supposing an inspector went down and made it a point to go through these lunatics, having seen that they were reported as being well taken care of, and that he found them otherwise, I would then recommend their being sent to an asylum, for I would not put much trust in people's promises to take care of a patient.

1733. Then that is the only suggestion you could probably make as to obtaining more information and dealing in a more satisfactory way with the class of lunatics at large?—Yes.

1734. With reference to your own department, do you think if the inspectors were relieved, or if your department were relieved from all the duties of inspection, that the administrative duty connected with the lunacy department would be sufficient to occupy the time of your department?—Well, you see inspection gives us great power in the office because we know from observation what is going on in the country, and we would then only know that by letter.

1735. If you had a staff of inspectors under you liberating you from the duty of inspecting, and if you devoted your time exclusively to administrative work you might be able to initiate, perhaps, and ultimately carry out improvements such as you have indicated, and have really never been done?—I don't think that so much has had anything to do with preventing our ideas being carried out as what was done by some of the boards.

1736. Which boards?—the Board of Governors.

1737. But supposing the inspector to make a report to you—supposing these alterations have been effected, and your inspector reports that certain things are not satisfactory you satisfy yourselves from personal inquiry, or put confidence in your inspector. Surely you would have power to act there?—No, that is the very thing we have not, and that should be remedied. We should be armed with a greater power than we have, and be able to say, "A inspected the asylum, and reported to us, and recommended so and so." We should have the power of carrying out that more than at present.

1738. Have you any difficulty in getting governors to carry out reasonable improvements?—The greatest possible difficulty. I have been obliged to go round them individually and collectively, but probably you will not have the same men on the board twice in succession. The board says it is quite ready, and the thing is put off until next meeting, and at the next meeting there is only one man present who was at the first meeting, and then perhaps they pooh pooh it, and the whole thing is thrown overboard.

1739. Suppose an inspector had charge of a single district for a considerable time, was permanently attached to that district, as it were, so as to gain the personal influence which constant intercourse gives, don't you think, looking to the constitution of boards of governors, that it would be possible to induce any body like that to adopt any reasonable suggestion?—So far as the inspectors are concerned I think they would, but these members are so frequently opposed to each other that sometimes they will oppose a thing because it is supported by others.

1740. That applies to all boards where you have different feelings and you have antagonism engendered, but still Inspectors of the Local Government Board find that by their personal influence with boards they were able to bring them round to any reasonable suggestion?—That is the only way we could do it.

1741. Do you think the obstructiveness of the governors, if I may use such a word, is so much as to justify handing over the authority to the department?—I would suggest that if a county was divided into districts and worked as it is, or by sub-inspectors—call these commissioners and the others inspectors—and if the inspector writes up recommending certain alterations or additions to be made, and if that is opposed by the board and they adhere to their opposition, which ten to one they do, because it is a matter of pounds, shillings, and pence to these men, then I think if another inspector went down and corroborated the first, that improvement or alteration ought to be enforced because these gentlemen frequently don't know anything; they are very often men who have not been round their own asylum once in the year and never were in another asylum, yet still they throw in their opposition to the men who are continually going from one asylum to the other and recommending improvements. Often I have suggested the improvements existing in England and Scotland and they say, "Oh, these people are too well off. Look at them at home. They are better off here than at home." That is the answer they give.

1742. That is the very ordinary form for the objection to take?—Some people think them too well treated, yet look at the class of people at Spike Island, and what care is taken of them.

1743. At present you cannot visit the workhouses they are so numerous?—I cannot do them all nor anything like them.

1744. Nor one-third of them?—Nor one-third of them.

1745. But they ought to be visited. Suppose the paupers of the different workhouse asylums were brought together in different numbers, say 40 or 50, and the asylums remained to be visited also, do you think two inspectors—yourself and Dr. Nugent—could possibly visit them a sufficient number of times?—I think so, if they were reduced to that.

1746. If they were reduced to 80 altogether say?—Exactly, and I think it is about 100 times I visited in the year.

1747. Would not that imply that your duty ought to be inspectorial exclusively, and have no administrative duty in addition?—The difficulty is that our office requires an inspector to be there to give instructions and sign documents, &c., &c.

1748. You want an administrative officer as in the Local Government Board?—Yes, some one ought to be there. That arrangement would make the matter more fixed and certain and each man would know what he had to do; for instance, if a country was divided between two, each would have 12 or 13 asylums. The inspector would have 40 asylums under his care, and he would be in constant attendance. He would know where he was going. I lost a week nearly in going to Belmullet, and I find, perhaps, when I get there three idiots, and that takes a good deal of time.

1749. For such workhouse asylums as are now suggested here how many inspectors would you think necessary?—I think two would be enough. I think one would not be enough. The present system is very systematic. The inspections should, however, be made at irregular intervals.

1750. They are quarterly visits now?—Yes, formerly we inspected this way. I went to Enniscorthy this day, say, and three days hence I would be in Belfast. I am saying this without meaning anything against the institutions. I might say to Dr. Nugent I found so and so there, and he would go to that asylum in two or three days hence, and we kept them on the *qui vive*.

1751. Have you ever visited the institution attached to the Limerick Workhouse, in which there are fifty or sixty incurables, and were you satisfied with it?—No, I think it is improved latterly. When I was there seven or eight years ago it was unsatisfactory.

1752. Don't you think that in such an establishment attached to a workhouse it would be absolutely necessary to keep them "up to the mark"?—I do.

1753. And more than two visits would be necessary to keep them up?—Yes; but one workhouse would require only one visit, where others would require three or four, particularly these overgrown workhouses like Limerick, Derry and Belfast.

1754. Then holding your inspector responsible for the efficiency of these workhouse auxiliaries you would give him discretion to visit as often as he liked?—I would.

1755. But would you not think it desirable to lay down a minimum number of visits?—Certainly.

1756. Do you think two would be sufficient?—I think two would do for the minimum, and as often afterwards as he thought necessary.

DUBLIN. July 24, 1878. Dr George Wm. Hatchell.

1757. If he was responsible for forty institutions he would take care to visit them a sufficient number of times?—If there were sub inspectors, or local inspectors, or provincial inspectors the way would be to take his report of the lunatics at large, in the workhouse, or in the asylums, and let the head of the department go to a particular workhouse, having the sub inspector's report there, and see whether he has reported faithfully, and if he suggested anything to see whether they are carrying it out, and then there ought to be full power given to some authority to see his suggestion carried out, otherwise things are forgotten and laid there. Sometimes suggestions made by inspectors lie over for five or six years.

1758. You say report the lunatics at large. Do you contemplate the inspectors should inspect the lunatics at large?—Not the inspectors, but the local officers—the dispensary medical officer for instance.

1759. With reference to the admission of patients to asylums, there has been a good deal of complaint made in the reports of the Inspectors that this is too great—admitting as dangerous cases, persons who are not dangerous?—No doubt, the magistrates are very thoughtless, instead of waiting for the regular house form they sometimes commit where the man is not dangerous at all. They come up and swear before a magistrate that a man is a dangerous lunatic and he is committed at once.

1760. Don't you think that the house form if magistrates were bound to wait for it would be sufficient safeguard?—That might not meet every case. There might be really cases of dangerous lunatics that ought to be brought at once. More depends on the good sense and proper feeling of the magistrates, but magistrates, like a great many other people in the world, they don't take the trouble of reasoning on the matter.

1761. Don't you think the trouble of imposing any particular form on the medical officer, and holding him responsible for the insufficiency of it, would give security?—I do; and I would make it part of his responsibility, for the magistrate has very little opportunity of judging of the facts of the case.

1762. Here is the certificate of the medical officer on the form of committal, would you read it?—(*Reads*)—"I certify that —— whom I visited on —— day of —— and into whose case I specially personally inquired, is now a dangerous lunatic, and I am of opinion from the nature of his malady that he is a fit subject for speedy admission into —— Lunatic Asylum, under the provisions of the Act 30 and 31st Vic., cap. 118, section 10." Well, you know here is a man signing he is a dangerous lunatic, he is the medical officer, and he is the most responsible man.

1763. That is the doctor?—Yes.

1764. He is bound to state some facts within his own knowledge. He is bound to fill in the other form below?—I think he ought to be held responsible that it is correct.

1765. And would you fix the responsibility on him?—It is very hard to do that, besides a man might be extremely dangerous for 24 hours, and cease to be so afterwards, and if a man is labouring under the effects of drink, such as *delirium tremens*, he might become dangerous in the street or in his own house and smash people's heads, and the doctor hearing that as he continually does, signs that certificate, and the moment the man is in the asylum he is perfectly sound after a couple of days—after he gets some sleep.

1766. You think that a proper case to send to a lunatic asylum?—I think for the safety of the public it is.

1767. Don't you think the police would be able to treat such cases?—They are not always certain whether it is delirium tremens. It might aggravate matters very much if not.

1768. Medical superintendents have, as a rule, the reputation of not at all objecting to cases of delirium tremens?—I will tell you why—it fills up a list of

DUBLIN
July 25, 1878
Dr George Wm. Hatchell.

cures uncommonly well, they very soon cease to be troublesome, they are put into a padded room, and they are very little trouble

1769. And the per-centage of cures is made large?—Yes, and you cannot blame them for that.

1770. Are they returned as affected with delirium tremens?—It is under the head of acute mania. The moment a man is admitted suffering from delirium tremens I would shave his head, and thus punish him when he is discharged.

1771. In your annual report and classification of cases delirium tremens cases are included under the head of acute mania?—They are.

1772. Do you think it would be desirable to have them determined, and to institute a sub-class entirely devoted to cases of delirium tremens?—Well, if it would have a deterrent effect I think it would.

1773. With a view of ascertaining the number of cures?—Yes; inasmuch as he would know then whether a man was merely a case of recovery from delirium tremens, or a case of recovery from mania.

1774. It would give a better idea of the action of curative asylums?—Yes, for we all know that these cases get better by themselves—at least the majority of them.

1775. Is it within your knowledge that many cases are sent to asylums under these committals of dangerous lunatics that ought not to be sent?—Yes. A great many cases are reported to us, and when we come our rounds they say, "He is sent in as dangerous, but we have not seen any signs of it yet."

1776. Do you think the friends of these people are interested in sending them in on this form, inasmuch as once they are certified as dangerous lunatics they are relieved of all expense?—Well, I think they do it more with the idea of getting rid of the man, being troublesome.

1777. That is the case where they are dangerous?—Women are never sent in with delirium tremens.

1778. I speak of this large number of cases returned to these asylums. I should not be at all surprised. I think it is very probable, because on the ordinary form they undertake to take out the patient when cured, and under this form there is no undertaking whatever?—No doubt that is one of the reasons for taking that short cut. They thus have the man taken up by the police, and put into an asylum as a dangerous lunatic.

1779. Do you think it would be advantageous to adopt in connexion with the lunatic asylum a department for the cure and education of idiots?—Certainly.

1780. There is no recognised classification now for educational purposes, unless it is done by some of the medical superintendents themselves, but you don't recognise it as part of your administrative machinery?—No. It has been done in the Richmond by Dr Lalor, and in Sligo, but they seldom do it in the asylums generally.

1781. Do you think it were more desirable to establish it in one of these curative establishments, if they are set up, as a branch for the educational purposes, or have a branch set apart altogether?—A branch set apart altogether, because the men calculated to carry on such a branch would not be found amongst the general class.

1782. Then you would probably lay hands on some asylum, and devote it exclusively to the education of idiots?—Yes; and the same thing is done near London, and they have one near Lucan. You would be astounded to hear how they answer in that one near Lucan. I have watched the progress of cases of children who came there with no mind at all, and who now answer in arithmetic and geography, and have become human beings; but I would never press them with their education.

1783. Would you be indisposed to leave the management of that third class of which you spoke in the hands of the Guardians?—I would.

1784. Would you have the governing body composed of members of the Board of Guardians and of the Board of Governors?—Many of the guardians are governors of the district lunatic asylum.

1785. Do you think they would form a good governing body?—Why have guardians at all. Why not compose that body alternately of members of the Board of Governors.

1786. Would it not be difficult to take part of the poorhouse without giving the guardians some authority?—The dietary and clothing should, for instance, be taken out of their hands. Some of the Board of Guardians are governors.

1787. But they would be selected from those who are not; would they not constitute a sufficiently independent body?—Well, they would have their board.

1788. And it would be probably the day the guardians meet?—It would not be the same day as the board of governors of the asylum meet. I would not let these people be in the hands of the guardians only.

1789. The analogy would be the dispensary committee: for the management of the dispensaries you create committees?—Yes.

1790. There would be apparently no reason why a lunacy committee should not be constituted in the same way?—Yes, but then who would be their medical officer?

1791. The medical officer of the workhouse?—Would the master of the workhouse have charge of these people?

1792. It would depend on the size; if it was only a branch of the house there appears to be no reason why it should be taken out of the hands of the master?—They are generally respectable men.

1793. Where you have a workhouse, as in Dublin, where it is large you don't think of taking it out of the charge of the master, and if it is to your satisfaction?—Yes. Then you would have these divided into sections?

1794. In Monaghan there is a fever hospital completely detached, capable of accommodating fifty: devote that to men exclusively with two caretakers?—Yes, but where would you put the women.

1795. If there was no other way we would send the women to Clones which is close by, but it happens there is a wing of the house at Monaghan?—It is not desirable to have the men and women completely separated, because the women do all the washing and the men the labour.

1796. The land of the workhouse might be made available in all cases?—Yes, but would the cooking be done in the same way?

1797. That would depend on the locality, in Youghal for instance, they have two hundred inmates?—I once pointed that out as an auxiliary asylum to Cork.

1798. And was it taken up?—No, it fell to the ground for some reason.

1799. Are you acquainted with the Belfast poorhouse?—Yes.

1800. And you know where the lunatics are located?—Yes.

1801. In the Infirmary building?—Yes.

1802. You know the small room recently told off for the lunatics?—Yes.

1803. Close, dark and damp?—Yes.

1804. Don't you think they would be better out of that if suitable accommodation could be provided elsewhere?—I do.

1805. Do you happen to know the school built at Belfast, it is situated just beyond the infirmary?—No, I don't remember it.

1806. But the accommodation in Belfast you certainly do not think suitable?—No, it is overcrowded.

1807. Do you know the North Dublin Union?—Yes, well.

1808. You know where the lunatics are located there?—Yes, very badly located.

1809. And you are aware there is no classification or separate rooms?—Yes.

1810. Do you know the place called the madman's lock?—I do.

1811. Do you think that desirable?—I do not.

DUBLIN
July 25, 1878.

Dr George Wm Hatchell

1812. Do you know the South Dublin Union?—I do.

1813. Are the lunatics better located there?—Yes.

1814. Have they separate rooms?—Yes

1815 Are you well acquainted with the buildings of the South Dublin Union?—Only the lunatic department.

1816. Do you know the boys' building beyond the lunatic department?—No.

1817. In the South Dublin Union female lunatic departments, do you know the yards that connect the departments?—Yes.

1818 Don't you think these yards are rather confined?—Yes, and I think they should have a view from them. They should not be like ball-courts or prison yards. I would put them outside where they could see the world. It is a great matter even to an idiot when he has got a space to look at, instead of having merely four walls. I think it is half the means of treatment

1819. You know Cork workhouse?—I do

1820. Do you recollect how the lunatics are located there?—I do.

1821. Do you know how the males are located?—Yes.

1822. With a small confined yard?—Yes, passing through a building to another yard and down under ground.

1823. Don't you think it would be a desirable thing to have them removed to a more suitable site?—I do. In Cork they are away in a back building under ground.

1824. Do you know the girls' school at Cork?—I do. I remember the place very well.

1825. Here is a plan of the Cork workhouse (plan produced); are you acquainted with the girls' school?—Yes.

1826. Do you think that they with the piece of ground in front would make a good place if it could be detailed for one class of lunatics?—I do, I know that place very well. It was Dr. King suggested that place for the girls.

1827. And you think if the girls could be provided for elsewhere that would be a desirable place for the male lunatics?—I do.

JOSEPH LALOR, Esq., M.D., examined.

Dr. Joseph Lalor.

1828. You are medical superintendent of the Richmond Lunatic Asylum?—Yes

1829. How long have you held that office?—Since 28th September, 1857

1830. Were you not in the lunacy service before that time?—I was first appointed in Kilkenny to the county prison, and in connexion with that there was an old asylum under an old Act—a house of industry in which there were about fifty lunatics. I was visiting physician to that in 1846 in Kilkenny. Then in 1852 I was appointed to the district lunatic asylum, on its being opened in February, as resident medical superintendent.

1831. Is the Richmond Lunatic Asylum full now?—No. There are about fifty or sixty vacancies.

1832. Its total accommodation being?—1,100.

1833. Of the patients in the asylum you have, comparatively speaking, but a small proportion of probably curable cases?—Yes

1834. Do you happen to know the numbers?—I made a careful analysis of the curable and incurable cases in the house in March and April last, and forwarded a classified return thereof to you afterwards in July last, and this return gave 139 males and 212 females, or a total of 351 curable cases these The numbers at present differ, I should think, but little.

1835. Your asylum is very extensive?—Yes it covers a large space of ground

1836. Do you find the large number of incurable cases interferes with the efficiency of the asylum as a curative establishment?—I don't think it interferes with the efficiency of the asylum as a curative establishment, but I think there is a great deal of room occupied by incurable *and unimprovable cases*, and those requiring special care—cases that might be appropriated to curable cases and improvable cases.

1837. Then you think it might be advantageous to your establishment as a curative hospital if a considerable proportion of the incurable cases could be removed to suitable accommodation elsewhere?—Not to my establishment; but it would be a *public* advantage.

1838. It would extend the advantages of your asylum as a curative establishment to substitute for the incurable and unimprovable cases now in it others capable of cure or improvement or requiring special care?—Places left vacant were filled by curable cases

1839. I suppose you would not like to denude your asylum altogether of incurable cases, do you not find that a large number of them are useful for the service of the establishment?—Yes. It would increase the expense of management and working very considerably if we had no cases under treatment but curable cases.

1840. Then you prefer to keep a certain number of incurable cases; a proportion of useful hands for the ordinary work of the establishment?—It would make my establishment more useful, and in that sense more advantageous, if the places left vacant by the removal of incurable and unimprovable cases and those not requiring special care were occupied by others of a different nature In reference to that I wish to make a general explanation: One general division of lunatics is "curable," and another "incurable" I think that is the idea, but there is an intermediate class—the "improvable."

1841. Is that the class you would keep for the services of the establishment?—I think if our establishment were to retain all the improvable and curable cases, we need keep very few incurable cases, for I think in the improvable and curable cases there would be a sufficient number to assist in the management of the asylum. I think we would require to keep very few of the totally incurable and unimprovable

1842. Have you any idea of the number in your house, of the "improvable" class?—In the return I was called upon to make the divisions were curable and incurable, and I did not go beyond that.

1843 I suppose the improvable are included under the head of probably incurable?—To some extent

1844. You have had so much experience in different parts of the country, that I dare say you have had at times under your observation the lunacy wards of workhouses?—Yes, I was medical officer of Kilkenny Workhouse, from its opening in 1842 until 1852, when I was appointed to the district lunatic asylum, and as one of the officials of the workhouse I had an opportunity there of inspecting the lunacy wards and I have visited several other workhouses.

1845. Then you are doubtless aware that throughout the country there are a very considerable number of imbeciles and idiots accommodated in workhouses?—I am aware of that from the blue books.

1846. But from your own knowledge?—From my own knowledge, I should say the famine fever of 1846 cleared every one of them out of Kilkenny Workhouse, and I am under the impression it carried them off out of every other workhouse asylum.

1847 But the class has been renewed since?—Yes, and I see from the blue books that there is a considerable number of lunatics in workhouses now.

1848 Don't you think it would be desirable for the comfort and proper caring of these people to have them brought together in such numbers, as to enable them to be suitably treated, and properly cared for, instead of being kept in ones and twos, as at present?—Circumstanced as workhouses are, and as they are likely

K

DUBLIN
July 24, 1872.
Dr. Joseph Lalor

to be for some time, I think it would be very undesirable to have lunatics mixed up with sane paupers in workhouses

1849. Then you think it desirable to remove them?—Yes, to special establishments.

1850. If this class of lunatics were brought together, in numbers varying, say from fifty to sixty, into buildings provided with suitable day rooms, dormitories, lavatories, and all the other requisites for an auxiliary lunatic asylum, do you not think they could be well and suitably cared and treated in them?—I think they might, but in reference to the number fifty or sixty, I have an opinion—I know I don't agree with the majority of persons acquainted with the subject—but I have an opinion that it is better to have them in large numbers in an institution than in small. I think fifty or sixty treated as a class, could not be so well treated as a larger number in a larger asylum.

1851. You prefer large numbers, as at Leavesden and Caterham?—Yes.

1852. But suppose a number of this class, be it large or small, were brought together into auxiliary workhouse asylums; is there not a considerable number of a somewhat similar class in the lunatic asylums that might be treated together with them, that is of the "hopelessly insane," who are harmless to themselves and to others?—I should suppose a large number. In reference though to ascertaining the incurable and the unimprovable in workhouses or at large, I think there should be some sufficient test. I think they should be kept a time under treatment before saddling them with the title of incurable.

1853. You mean that before drafting any lunatics into such establishments as those to which our questions are pointing, you would ascertain in a curative establishment or an establishment under properly qualified officers whether they were fit and proper persons to transfer into the auxiliary?—Yes. Take lunatic asylums under a proper system a sufficient trial would then be made, and I would not ask a further test, and if the medical officer declared the case to be incurable, I would consider that sufficient, but lunatics in workhouses and out of workhouses have not had any chance of treatment, and I think it desirable to give them treatment before putting a name upon them, and stamping them as incurables.

1854. You think in fact that all the lunatics now in workhouses should be passed through some test before being stamped as suitable cases for these auxiliaries?—There should be inspection certainly and time to see whether the cases were curable or incurable.

1855. Then it appears that there is a class of lunatics in the workhouses which could be considerably increased from the present inmates of lunatic asylums—from those you were kind enough to enter under Class A in the returns you furnished us with?—Yes. Now, between that class and the curable and improvable class there is, I apprehend, another class, who are most probably incurable, but who would require some special care on account of their being either noisy or dangerous to themselves or others, and who might have to be kept under some more strict guardianship than could be given in the workhouse auxiliaries we have been speaking of?—There is such a class. Looking at the case in one point of view as regards the individual, and giving the individual whatever chance he can have of being cured or improved, there is one class that I think ought to be detained in curative establishments, that is a class of cases for whom there is a chance of being improved or cured. There is another class for whom there is not the least chance of improvement or cure, but in whose case it is necessary for the well-being of the public and of other institutions that they should be kept in curative establishments. Those curative and improvable establishments should be for the curable cases, and for incurable cases who require special care and supervision.

1856. A certain proportion of them?—Yes. In other words, I don't think any patient ought to be sent to an intermediate asylum—non-curative asylum or workhouse asylum—who requires special care or attention. Although they may be perfectly incurable, they ought to be kept in curative establishments—that is, I think they ought to be kept in special establishments suited to them; they ought not to be mixed up with the quiet, harmless, and incurable. I would send the quiet, harmless, and incurable to asylums.

1857. And the other class ought not to be mixed with the workhouse class?—No, and the question is, whether you would give them an intermediate asylum, using the word in its general sense, and then comes the question, whether the class that are incurable, but requiring special care should be kept in curative establishments or establishments for themselves. I am inclined to think they should be kept in curative establishments. They include cases that are occasionally quiet and harmless. They are incurable, but require special care—not always, but only occasionally; but when they do require special care, medical or moral, it is the same sort of care as the acute and curable, and there would be an advantage in putting them into an establishment with the acute and curable cases.

1858. But I don't see what special advantage you point out under such an arrangement?—I consider it a special advantage not to multiply special institutions more than is unavoidable.

1859. Then you would not create new institutions for the purpose?—No, particularly new buildings; and then the same classes of officers would be best adapted to treat curable cases and those requiring special care.

1860. Suppose that the Richmond Asylum, for instance, had this class of harmless workhouse lunatics (Class A) removed from it, and also this intermediate class of which I have been speaking (Class B), and suppose that in some other districts the asylums were made available for the reception of the intermediate class, leaving Richmond to be used as a curative establishment—do you not think that these district lunatic asylums, furnished, as they are, with a fair staff and means of internal organisation and control, would meet the case, and be found suitable for improving and treating these people (Class B) without creating fresh buildings?—I think that class would have insufficient care in such an asylum; and if room could be made for them in the curative establishments it would be attended with greater advantage on the whole. There is another matter. I take it you accept as the meaning of curative establishments, those where cases are treated which are absolutely curative, and also cases capable of being improved.

1861. This other establishment would still retain improving patients, although not themselves specially curative establishments?—I think it would be well to treat curable and improvable cases in the same establishments with those requiring special care.

1862. Are you aware that in some of the workhouses, the lunatic wards are looked upon by their medical officers as curative establishments?—With regard to the cases that are considered incurable, sometimes recoveries will take place under the most adverse circumstances.

1863. You never give up a lunatic as entirely hopeless—you always consider an improvement may possibly be made?—Yes, even in incurable establishments.

1864. Do you not think that such a classification as I suggest would improve the character of the "curative" which would be the main establishment?—As a curative establishment, it would.

1865. Would you not effect a larger per-centage of cures?—Oh, certainly.

1866. Would not that be a great object to gain?—That would be a great object so far as the character of the establishment, for a large proportion of cases, is concerned, but so far as the whole amount of cures is concerned, it would not be any gain.

1867. But when I say improve the per-centage of cures, I don't mean simply to compare your asylum as it is, and as it might be as a partly curative establishment, but taking lunacy in Ireland as a whole;

DUBLIN
July 25, 1878.
Dr Joseph Lalor.

would not the institution of curative establishments, where undivided attention could be given to the curing of patients, result in the effecting of a greater number of cures than would be likely to result if things were left as at present?—I think it open to great question.

1868. In that way there would be indirectly economy for the greater the number of cures, the less the number that would drift into chronic insanity?—The question of economy must include the consideration of the system which will effect the greatest number of cures of the total number of insane, and not merely the number of cures in any asylum, be it called curative or by any other name.

1869. You are aware that in the asylums throughout the country generally, a considerable portion of the accommodation consists of single cells—do you think for this intermediate class B, associated dormitories, with a small proportion of single cells would suffice?—I think for curative establishments as well as those you speak of a far less proportion of single cells would be exceedingly desirable.

1870. You think that in one of the second class or intermediate asylums (which at present are limited in their accommodation by their interior being cut up, and laid off in cells), if a large quantity of the cell accommodation were abolished, and replaced by associated dormitories a great deal more suitable accommodation could be provided in these establishments?—I think the accommodation in asylums, call them by what name you will, would be improved by reducing the quantity of cell accommodation. I took up, lately, the twenty-second Report of the Inspectors for the year 1872. It is the last report, in which they gave the number of single rooms in asylums, and totting table No. 34, I found the number of single apartments in all the asylums in Ireland was 1,029 for males, and 984 for females, and the accommodation of all the asylums at that time was 7,989, call it 8,000, that is twenty-five per-cent. of single rooms; now I think that is not only useless but a positive disadvantage. I have a very strong opinion that putting lunatics into single cells is of much disadvantage as a general rule, just upon the same principle, that if you have a dog that is fierce, you make him twice as fierce by keeping him chained up. Man is a social animal; to keep a man in a single room is calculated to make him morose; therefore I think it is most desirable not taking the economy view of the question alone but for the good of the patient, that the proportion of single cells in the curative establishments, and in establishments for lunatics should be very limited.

1871. And in that way the accommodation might be greatly increased?—Yes, and in Paris after a very careful consideration by a commission issued by the late Emperor, that course was adopted. There were six asylums established for the city of Paris, and I visited one of them in 1869, and from my own personal observations I ascertained that it was built for 600, and for the 600 there were only twenty single rooms and on the day I visited it there were only five in the single rooms, so that twenty was more than sufficient, and that was at the rate of about three single rooms for every 100 patients in a curative establishment.

1872. Do you know whether it was then used wholly as a curative establishment?—Many of our asylums were built as curative asylums, but have degenerated into being places chiefly for the custody of incurables. Take Killarney for instance. There are 16 curable patients out of a total of 238, although it was originally intended to be a curative establishment. Possibly this asylum in Paris may have been built as a curative establishment, and yet have become a receptacle for incurables?—Well, the incurables taken by themselves would require less than twenty cells, than the argument is still the same, and the fact remains that in an asylum for 600 patients only five were in single cells at the time of my visit.

1873. In your asylum have you many paying patients?—Very few—10.

1874. To what class of life do they belong?—It is as follows—(reads from book). *No class* in seven cases; the other three consist of one barrister, one gentleman, and one clerk.

1875. I suppose we may term the whole as middle class?—Yes, the total sum received from them is £212 18s. 8d., being an average of £21 per head. The highest payment is £28, and the lowest £12 10s. Under the Privy Council rules, paying patients are not to be taken for more than half the cost.

1876. Have you ever been obliged to refuse admission to paying patients in consequence of want of accommodation?—Our last increase of accommodation was seven or eight years ago, and on the 1st of this year the exact number was remaining in the asylum 1,061, accommodation 1,100. That is, we had thirty-nine vacancies. We have something more now—about 50 or 60.

1877. Is it not the case that under the Privy Council rules, two applicants for admission may appear, the friends of one of them being able and willing to pay, while the friends of the other may be able but *unwilling* to pay, and that in such a case you are bound to receive the patient whose friends are *unwilling* to pay in preference to the patient whose friends are willing to pay?—I have no experience of that for some years.

1878. You are obliged to give priority in all cases to the poor or pauper class?—Yes.

1879. I see the wording of the Privy Council Rule is that "no paying patient shall be admitted into any district lunatic asylum as long as there shall be unsatisfied the application of any pauper lunatic," so that the unwillingness constitutes a qualification for admission?—The 38th and 39th Victoria, chap. 37, passed in the year 1875, very properly gave power to boards of Governors to recover from the lunatics whose friends had the means of paying. Now that that is the law I would do away altogether with the Privy Council Rule of admitting paying patients. I would throw no obstacle in the way of admitting the insane. I would take in all, and if they were able to pay I would make the friends pay under this Act, if not able to pay they should be free.

1880. Letting them understand on admission that they will be called on to pay?—Yes, I regret to say that power is not acted on. That 16th clause is not carried out, or very little carried out. In my asylum I brought it under the attention of my board some years ago, and made a list of the patients whose friends I thought were able to pay although these patients were sent in as paupers, and the Board had two or three cases put into the hands of their solicitor, but there was some difficulty in the way and it was not acted on. There were thirty or forty patients in the asylum at the time, whose friends came under the operation of the 16th clause.

1881. From whom you could get £300 or £400 a year probably?—Yes.

1882. Is it within your knowledge that there is a considerable class of lunatics who belong to middle class families that don't like to have their friends treated in a pauper asylum, and would be glad to avail themselves of accommodation by paying a fair and reasonable amount if such accommodation was provided in a public establishment, people who cannot afford the expense of private lunatic asylums?—I am sorry to say I think there is very little of such proper spirit amongst the people. My experience is that people say, "If I pay will my friends get better treatment?" and under the Privy Council rules they are not allowed to get better treatment, and when they find this they let the thing go, as they say there is no advantage from paying. There is a great objection amongst people to let it be known that their friends are in an asylum.

1883. Do you think there are many lunatics kept at home in consequence of this delicacy of feeling?—Yes; why a great many are kept at home during the curable period is owing to their friends not wishing to run the chance of having it known that a relative is in an asylum.

DUBLIN.
July 25, 1878.
Dr. Joseph Lalor.

1884. They don't wish the stigma of lunacy to be introduced into the family?—Exactly.

1885. Then it is not the sentimental feeling only, as to sending their friends to a pauper asylum, but the having it known there is a demented member of the family?—Yes. There are some cases in which there is the proper pride not to have a person supported as a pauper who is not so.

1886. Do you think that if within your asylum separate wards were set apart for such a class of people they would avail themselves of the arrangement?—I dare say they would; but it would be a great disadvantage in a certain sense.

1887. Why?—I think from experience that this mixture of paying at small stipend and non-paying patients is a question of great trouble and difficulty.

1888. But I speak of setting them apart from the non-paying patients, their being charges at a proper and reasonable rate?—That would be taking the Scotch system. I have turned that matter over in my mind at different times, and I think the Scotch system of having paying and non-paying patients in the same institution appears to have a great many advantages, and I am inclined to think well of it.

1889. Have you not given a great deal of attention to the cure and improvement of idiots?—I have.

1890. Have you been able to get good results?—I think so.

1891. What is the nature of the results you have obtained—are the people you treat and cure fitted to return to society?—There are cases, in the common acceptation of the term, which are looked upon as idiots, that is what we technically call cases of dementia, in which after recovery from the acute stage of mania they fall into a state of weakmindedness, and I think in classifying lunatics, are often set down as idiots. I think education amongst that class is often reckoned a very great advantage; and some of them are able by education and training to resume the duties of life, and support themselves.

1892. And others are very difficult to improve?—Some. Take the congenital idiot or imbecile, I think you may put down the number improved so as to be made self-supporting as nothing. Even in the splendid establishments you have in England it is so.

1893. But their condition can be greatly improved?—They can be made cheerful, happy, contented, properly conducted, and orderly, in place of being a more degraded and miserable class. Large classes of the lower animals are very happy and contented, and intelligent and useful.

1894. Do you think if classification of asylums was carried out it would be a desirable thing in connexion with it to have in each province a portion of an asylum set apart for the improvement of the class of idiots you refer to?—A re-arrangement of asylum districts would, I think, be desirable; but obsolete territorial distinctions would not, in my mind, form a good basis for such arrangement. Other factors must be taken into account in making such a re-arrangement. Other Government buildings and lands as well as district asylums and workhouses are likely to be available for the use of lunatics and idiots and imbeciles—for instance, gaols and model farms. Some of the latter in particular would, from what I know, be very suitable for institutions for the training and education of idiots and imbeciles. I should hope that the central authority for organizing the treatment of the insane may have the option of appropriating them to such purposes, and that they will not be alienated to purposes other than Governmental, or not to the best advantage for the tax-paying community, that they may be applied as beneficially as possible and as profitably for the curtailment of fresh outlay and the avoidance of additional taxation. In this point of view amongst others, I ventured some years back to recommend, in a paper I read before the Medico Psychological Association, an interchange of action and views between different Government departments more than appears to exist at present. In reference to legislation as to a better arrangement in reference to the insane, and of districts and institutions, and of further provision for their care, I think that legislation might with great advantage be confined to the organization of a central authority, and of local managing bodies, as I believe is done by the English Metropolitan Asylums Act, leaving the organization and carrying out of the system in all its details as much as possible at the discretion of those bodies. By so doing, contingencies impossible to foresee at present can be met as they arise in a way far more satisfactory than they could be by fast statutable provisions. As an illustration, I would take the principles laid down by myself for legislation, that the insane, as insane, should all be treated in two classes of institutions, viz: one, First Class, for curable and improvable cases of lunacy, and those requiring special care, and for the training and education of imbeciles and idiots, chiefly of the juvenile classes; and, secondly, asylums for the incurable and unimprovable. Now, whilst I think these are good general principles, I can foresee that when they come to be worked out into practice it may be found that juvenile idiots and imbeciles in place of being treated in the first-class asylums of their districts, with curable and improvable insane and those requiring special care, might from a variety of circumstances be placed with more economy and general advantage in institutions with larger areas and accommodation, and with a proportion of quiet and harmless lunatics incurable and unimprovable, but who would form a cheap and good auxiliary, not only for many domestic and other like purposes, but as assistants in teaching and training. No statute can provide by express enactments for such contingencies as well as a central body empowered and competent to deal with such questions as they arise.

1895. Now, with regard to the admission of cases to your asylum. Before the passing of the Act, 31st Victoria, under which they at present commit dangerous lunatics direct to the asylum, they used to have to pass through prisons?—Yes.

1896. Do you find that since the passing of that Act the number of dangerous lunatics committed has much increased?—Considerably more are sent in since the passing of that Act than before.

1897. Do you think all that are sent in under that warrant as "dangerous lunatics" ought be sent in as such?—Legally, I think they ought. There may be a few cases not sent in properly according to the Act, but they are rare exceptions.

1898. Then the magistrates in your district look carefully after this?—I think they do, and I think they exercise the discretion they ought to exercise under the Act of Parliament. I know that persons—official persons—hold opposite views, and I think the reason is, they confound the ordinary meaning of the word dangerous with the legal meaning. Under the 30th and 31st Victoria, dangerous lunatic is a person dangerous in a special and legal sense. He is a person, according to the words of the Act, "taken under circumstances denoting derangement of "mind, and the purpose of committing some offence "for which, if he was sane, he would be indictable;" and under that Act of Parliament the magistrates have no discretion but to comply with the letter of the Act if there is an affidavit made before them that the person is taken under circumstances denoting derangement of the mind and a purpose of committing an indictable offence, and I have never found a case in which the Act was not complied with in that respect. Then, as regards the symptoms of insanity that is ascertained in the way prescribed by the Act by the nearest dispensary doctor, and the Act having been complied with the magistrate has no discretion but to commit the person to the lunatic asylum. Some persons in viewing the question assume the meaning of dangerous to be dangerous in the ordinary sense of the term, as likely to injure themselves or others. The Act is not interpreted in our district in that sense of the word, nor should it be. With regard to the increased number of admissions under the 30th and 31st Victoria,

DUBLIN.
July 25, 1878.
Dr. Joseph Lalor.

I think it is an immense advantage, because before that Act there was a great number of persons kept out who ought to be sent into lunatic asylums, but there was not sufficient machinery for doing so. I think the 30th and 31st Victoria gave machinery for sending persons to lunatic asylums that was very much wanted before. We never had nor have we now the power given in England of relieving officers looking after the lunatics in their district, and being bound, if they suppose there is a pauper lunatic in the district, to visit him. We in Ireland have never had such means as that. It is only in cases in which the lunatic or idiot is chargeable to the poor rates that the relieving officer is bound to report?—There is a provision, I believe, in England, that if it comes to the knowledge of the relieving officer that there is any wandering lunatic not properly taken care of, he is to take steps.

1899. He is not to initiate steps of inquiry. In case of pauper lunatics in England they are visited twice a year, and the relieving officer reports on them, whether they are properly treated or not; and if he reports that they are not properly treated, they are removed to the asylum?—There is no such provision in Ireland.

1900. But you have no such class in Ireland?—We have wandering lunatics in Ireland.

1901. Well, is there no machinery to deal with the wandering lunatic?—No, not under the 30th and 31st Victoria, and there should be such a power given. That Act could only be set in motion by the voluntary act of some person, there is no officer to do it, and there should be. Either the police or some official party should be obliged to take cognizance of these things, and not leave the Act to be set in motion by voluntary act. There are two disadvantages. The Act is sometimes set in motion very improperly through spite or spleen, and very often the Act is not set in motion where it ought to be, because it is left to voluntary action. I don't think that ought to be so. The police, the poor law officers, or some officials should have the power.

1902. You think there should be some means of committing the wandering lunatic, and that the same machinery under which the dangerous idiot is committed should apply to the wandering lunatic?—Yes. I think some party connected with the state ought to have the duty.

1903. Has not this form under the 30th and 31st Victoria to a great extent, in the rural districts at all events, superseded the usual house form?—Yes.

1904. Don't you think a great number are admitted under this form who might be admitted under the ordinary house form?—I think so; but whether it would be more advantageous to have them admitted in one way than the other is a question. Those committed under the form for dangerous lunatics are on the whole a more curable class, and it is a better form of committal than the house form.

1905. Why?—Because in one sense under the house form, there is sometimes a delay of a month for the Board, that is one disadvantage.

1906. But in cases of urgency you are obliged to receive—the admission is of necessity immediate?—Yes, but the police are more accessible than the Governors or the Resident Medical Superintendent, and there is greater facility afforded under the 30 and 31 Victoria; I think there is also a greater safeguard; I think the form of committing dangerous lunatics is a greater safeguard than the house form; this may be the case in Dublin, for here we have divisional paid magistrates; and without saying anything against unpaid magistrates, paid magistrates have the advantage of being professional men and lawyers.

1907. Still you must know from the Reports of Inspectors that fully eighty per cent. of the persons sent to asylums under that form are unfit?—I don't know on what ground that is stated. The Inspectors give a number of unsuitable cases for the asylum—they give that return in one asylum but it cannot refer to all; for instance for years I have not given a return of any as unfit. Of course, as I said, the city of Dublin is almost altogether administered by divisional magistrates; the interpretation acted on, I believe, by my *confrères*, the Resident Medical Superintendent, is this—that nobody ought to be sent to a district lunatic asylum unless they are dangerous in the ordinary sense of the term, I disagree with that altogether. If you take the number of cures you find the number is considerably greater of those sent in under the 30 & 31 Victoria than under the other forms of admission.

1908. That would argue in favour of the other contention, the less suitable the more likely the cure. Under the ordinary form, is it in your discretion to take in the patient provisionally?—It would be incorrect to return as cured those who were never insane.

1909. On the ordinary form, I think the friends of the lunatic are bound to present the lunatic at your asylum door—they have to pay the expenses to the door?—The wording of it is exceedingly obscure, practically that is never done, the patient is never brought until an order has been made for admission.

1910. Who pays the expenses of the lunatic?—His expenses are paid by the friends. I thought you meant there was an opportunity of inspection to see whether the person applied for is absolutely insane.

1911. On the ordinary form there is an undertaking to remove, by the friends when the lunatic is taken in, that I suppose is desirable?—It is not operative, we have tried to enforce it, and failed.

1912. Is there no Act of Parliament to support that engagement?—No.

1913. I do not see that on the form for the committal as a dangerous lunatic, there is any undertaking whatever?—No, but what is still more forcible—as soon as the resident physician thinks the party is cured, out the patient goes; the door is opened and out he must go.

1914. Would not the same law apply, to the case of persons admitted under the ordinary form?—No, because the engagement between the board, and the parties implies an understanding acted on by the Board, and not, I am sorry to say, always acted on by the friends. The Governors consider that they should perform their part of the contract, and not send out the person until the friends come for him.

1915. Then you have at present some cured persons who were admitted under the ordinary form and you cannot get rid of them, and you have no cases recovered remaining who were admitted under the dangerous lunatic warrant?—Precisely.

1916. With regard to the lunatics at large, have you ever thought over any way of bringing them under inspection?—I think it ought to be the duty of the relieving officer, and of the constabulary to report any case they think is insane, either wandering or not wandering, to report to some officer.

1917. They do as a matter of fact report the existence of cases, that is so far as to make a return?—Oh, yes, that is, of reputed lunatics occasionally, I believe, yearly only.

1918. How would you deal with that class, 3,000, or 4,000 reputed lunatics at large; would you have them visited, and if so, by whom?—I think the police, the relieving officer, and the dispensary officer ought to look after these cases, and should have power, as they have in some cases in England under the advice of the medical officer, either to treat a person outside, or send the person to the workhouse or a lunatic asylum, and if a person is treated outside, then the medical officer has to visit them twice a year, and he is paid for his visits.

1919. Your machinery would be that the constabulary should make a return of the name and address of every reputed lunatic, that the medical officer should visit all the cases within his district, and in any case where there appears to be any neglect, he should give notice to the relieving officer to act as officer of the guardians.

1920. And have them removed to the asylum?—Yes; or workhouse, or otherwise dealt with, as he thought best.

DUBLIN.
July 25, 1878.
Dr Joseph Lalor.

1921. That would entail considerable machinery and expense I think, if that was done, very few of the dangerous lunatics under the 30th and 31st Victoria would be done away with, and the medical officers of the dispensaries would have to be fee'd?—As in England.

1922. In England it is only as to pauper lunatics, but here you would include the whole lunacy at large?—All poor lunatics should be looked after by the authorities, and all necessary expenses paid out of the public funds.

1923. With regard to lunatic attendants, do you find any difficulty in obtaining officers under the present regulations?—There is no difficulty in obtaining attendants.

1924. Or in retaining them?—None. I don't find any.

1925. Since 1869, there has been a change in the system of employing lunatic officers, before that the appointment was in the hands of the resident medical superintendent, subject to the approval of the Governors?—Yes, I think so, in the case of attendants.

1926. That system has been changed now?—I am not positive about the fact, but at present the Board of Governors appoint, but practically they leave it in my hands in general.

1927. But not the dismissal?—No not the dismissal. The practice in my asylum is generally this: When there is a vacancy for an attendant I select and put a person on trial for a month, and if I think the party efficient I report so to the board. If the month is not sufficient, I keep the probationer for a longer time, or whatever time I consider necessary, and if I don't consider him fit I don't ask the leave of the board for his disposal, as never having been appointed regularly my power to dismiss has never been disputed where the engagement has been on trial only.

1928. And your exercise of that power has worked well?—Yes.

1929. Do I understand you to say you find no difficulty in obtaining officers, including teachers? What is your plan as to teachers?—Teachers so called rank as officers, and are appointed by the board. As to school attendants, there are nine who teach. One of them was in a long time. I did not engage her with the view to teaching, she had been brought up in the workhouse, and she used to assist the paid workhouse teacher in the teaching. I got her from the workhouse, and I think there could be young girls of that class got who had been trained, and had experience in teaching in workhouses.

1930. As monitresses?—Yes. There was another girl who had been assisting her uncle, who had a school in London, and there she learned training. There is a third who became an attendant through reverse of circumstances. She is a lady with very high feeling, which I consider very commendable, she struggled to maintain herself, she had been well educated and had been a governess, and she applied for the situation of ordinary attendant. These are three out of the nine, the other six I got from schools in connection with the National Board, or under care of the sisters of Mercy and sisters of Charity. Several years ago I got some school attendants directly from Marlborough street model schools, under the National Board, and they were not satisfied with the place, they were not satisfied to act as attendants and they left after some time. I applied since then—I always had a very high respect for the National Board of Education, and had a good many friends among the authorities there, and I know they would do anything they could to get persons for me. I have applied several times to them latterly and they say their monitresses would not go to the asylum, that there is a limited number of them, and that they have better situations for them, so that that source of supply is stopped. That is as regards the females. As regards the males, I have four. I got three out of the Industrial school at Artane.

1931. These are persons who are attendants, and combine with their other duties that of teaching?—Yes; the fourth is a pensioner who had charge of the school in his regiment, before he left the army.

1932. What workhouse was it you got the female teacher, of whom you speak so highly from?—The North Dublin.

1933. And she has turned out in every way satisfactory?—Yes, she is a first class attendant now.

1934. Now supposing that the three classes of asylums of which we spoke in the early part of your examination were established, do you think it would be desirable that that third class, or workhouse auxiliary, into which our class A, is to be drafted, should be under the same superintendence and management as the others?—With the view to efficiency in each, I think it would be very desirable if all the lunatic asylums should be under one management.

1935. I do not mean under one Board of Governors, but under one central authority?—Yes, two authorities would be undesirable, I think it is one of the reasons why lunatic asylums in Ireland are not more advanced than they are; (they are advanced very much), but I think if they were under one central authority they might be more advanced.

1936. If the whole lunacy administration of the country was under one head, it would be in a more satisfactory condition?—Yes, that is my opinion; two or three years ago, I read a paper before the Medical Psychological Association, in which I expressed that opinion.

1937. You are an advocate for large asylums?—Yes.

1938. Would you consider that in the Richmond Asylum 1,000 cases under treatment as patients in a curative hospital, would be too many?—Curable and improveable, I don't think it would be.

1939. No, apart from improveable, do you think if you had simply for curative purposes 1,000 persons in your asylums would that be too many?—I don't think it would.

1940. Would you as a Medical Superintendent consider 1,000 curable cases too many?—If for individual supervision as Medical Superintendent, I think 1,000 curable cases too many.

1941. I don't mean for your supervision as head of the establishment, but for your personal supervision?—I do think it would be too much.

1942. How many assistants have you in Richmond Asylum?—One assistant, and one resident apothecary.

1943. Suppose the whole of the improvable cases, and of the incurable cases were removed and their places supplied by purely curable cases—cases under treatment as in hospital for mental disease—what assistance do you think you would require?—It depends entirely on what you mean by curative and hospital. If you mean by curable cases cases for medical treatment, the administration of drugs——

1944. No, the person to whom you would be applying the ordinary means of cure. How many do you think it would be desirable to have in any one asylum?—I don't think I could fix the limit of the number. I would certainly say from my own experience that 1,000 would not be too many, and I think 2,000 would not be too many.

1945. The Commissioners of lunacy who inquired into the subject expressed a strong opinion that lunatic asylums ought not to contain more than 200 cases, and your opinion is that 1,000 cases would not be too much, if it was converted from an asylum having a certain number of incurable into an hospital, for the treatment of mental disease?—I think it would not be too many.

1946. You, as head of the establishment, with an adequate staff of assistants, could deal with 1,000 curable cases? I could, and I could exemplify that for you.

1947. Let me ask you first. Suppose from crowded surrounding asylums the cases that are classed in this asylum as probably curable were drafted into your asylum, and the probably incurable cases drafted from your asylum to the other asylums, and your asylum was thus converted into an hospital for the treatment of mental disease, do you think you could manage 1,000 cases of that class?—I do.

Dublin.
July 26, 1878.

Dr. Joseph Lalor.

1948. And it would not be too much for you?—No. I would expect I could manage them more advantageously.

1949. In point of fact, having an asylum devoted exclusively to curable cases?—Curable and improvable—remember I make that distinction.

1950. As I understand your answers to some questions, lunacy is divisable into three classes. There is the class of incurable imbeciles, that we would suppose would be removed to workhouse auxiliaries with all the appliances for the proper treatment of that class. Then there is the class you call improvable; and I understood you to agree to the suggestion that that class might be removed to one of the existing asylums, and that asylum converted into an asylum for the treatment of the improvable class. Remove that improvable class, and leave your asylum to be simply an asylum for curative purposes?—I never meant to express such an opinion. I think improvable and curable ought to be treated in the same asylum. I am distinctly strongly of that opinion.

1951. What is your classification of improvable cases. Is it Class B that was returned by you to us?—You cannot give a definition of the improvable class.

1952. But instead of giving a definition can you give the number of probably curable and improvable?—I think the curable would be about one-third to one-fourth, and the incurable would be two-thirds or three-fourths.

1953. Two-thirds or three-fourths of the whole?—About that.

1954. Take the probably curable cases as 25 per cent. of the whole, and the probably incurable as about 75 per cent., of that 75 per cent. what per-centage, according to your view, would be of the class improvable?—Something about one-third or one-fourth.

1955. That is to say, that in your own asylum, taking 25 per cent. curable cases, then there would be 25 per cent. improvable, and that would leave 50 per. cent. to be taken away?—Yes.

1956. Then, of these improvable cases may we assume the larger number would be retained for household purposes—that is, for farm purposes, the women for servants and that class of work for which they are useful?—It was something like that I meant to express some time ago, that if the improvable class were left with us, you might not leave any incurables.

1957. It was with the view of clearing up any difficulty that might arise afterwards that I asked the question. Suppose you have 1,000 in your asylum, you would say in round numbers as an approximate calculation that 500 would be sent out and 500 retained, and of that 500 you retained, 250 would be probably curable, and the other 250 would be improvable?—I think there would be about 200 curable and 300 improvable.

1958. Do you think if there was an interchange of patients, if from asylums with facilities of communication you transferred a number of curable cases, and sent in return incurable cases—do you think that would be an improvement on the existing arrangement?—A very great improvement.

1959. And suppose upon a calculation of all the numbers throughout the country, it would be practicable to divide the country into districts, retaining certain numbers for curative establishments on the basis you have just indicated, and a certain other number, for incurable asylums, cases that require better treatment than the workhouse, and yet not such expensive treatment as that in the curative establishment, do you think would that enable an advantageous distribution or classification of lunatics to be made throughout the country?—I think it would be advantageous—a wonderful improvement on the present system.

1960. Being an advocate for large asylums, you rather objected to these smaller asylums where fifty or sixty patients were, but if it so happens there is much spare accommodation broken up in the building capable of accommodating only fifty or sixty, what would be your objection to placing fifty or sixty males in a suitable building, perfectly well arranged with baths, and so forth, with, say two male attendants and suitable supervision—would you think that would be an objectionable arrangement on account of the smallness of the number?—I did not say objectionable; I say a larger number would be better.

1961. But simply regarding their care and comfort, you do not see any objection?—No, not absolutely, but relatively.

1962. The smallest number could be almost apart from pauper administration, and it would be better to have the smallest number, which would prevent you having any connection with the workhouse?—I have often expressed my opinion that lunatics might be treated in workhouses from some points of view, better than in lunatic asylums; for there is this advantage you would be bringing the influence of the sane on the insane, which I think is very advantageous, but I don't think in the present state of matters, such a thing is practicable. I hope, however, the day will yet come when the insane will be treated in the same institution with the sane, and that there will be mutual benefits to the parties—that the insane will derive the good influences that are to be derived from intercourse with their sane fellow-beings, and that the sane will derive the good charitable lessons that are to be derived from being associated with their insane fellow-creatures, and be taught to treat them humanely instead of as at present treating them with scoff, and ridicule.

1963. You have not had much experience of workhouses?—I was from 1842 until 1853 one of the officers of the Kilkenny Workhouse.

1964. The idea of mixing insane with sane is in opposition to the suggestion made by us, and therefore it may as well be referred to, do you think the mixing of three or four or five insane, of troublesome habits, dirty habits it may be, with the sane amongst whom there would be many disposed to annoy them or tease them or in the winter season not let them near the fire, in fact taking advantage of their weakness, do you think these are disadvantages, to which they might be liable.—I meant to say that taking the existing circumstances of workhouses, the circumstances of lunatics, and the circumstances of sane paupers in a public institution, and the circumstances of insane paupers in a public institution, such an idea is impracticable, but in the growth of time I think such a thing as treating classes of sane and insane paupers in the same institution or institutions may be found not only practicable but useful.

1965. If you can find a number of benevolent persons combining to allow lunatics to associate with them of course it would be different, but in workhouses you have a different class of people to deal with?—Yes. As to the comparison between large and small asylums in reference to the moral treatment of insanity, and the influence of education and training, I have had a very long experience, and bestowed much thought to the subject. Earlswood Asylum holds about 800, and I believe it is an admirable institution. I believe the training of idiots and imbeciles is not one bit more difficult than the training of the insane of other classes, and then supervision by one head is not a bit more difficult. All the authorities at Earlswood, I believe, if they were asked, would tell you that they would consider that asylum far more suitable for idiots and imbeciles, with a total of 800, than if there was four asylums with 200 each. I have no doubt that is what they would say.

1966. Earlswood is for children?—Yes, altogether.

1967. And they are put there for a few years, and put out again, whether cured or not?—Yes, and the same idea ought to be carried out in lunatic asylums. With regard to the removal to curative hospitals for curable cases you must remember that a person is sent in labouring under acute insanity, which may be only temporary or of a nature with a tendency to natural cure, or very easily cured by medical means, and to send that case up at once to one of the large asylums would meet a strong practical and sentimental objection. There ought to be time given to the local asylums conveniently situated, as at present, for treatment of cases from their neighbourhood. They should keep

DUBLIN
July 25, 1874.
Dr Joseph Lalor.

the case for a reasonable time, and if it is not cured or improved, then it should be sent to an asylum with full appliances to treat such cases by all medical and moral means, including education and industrial employment, by skilled and competent hands, in continuous care of the patients. With regard, then, to the curative establishment, I give a period of three years to them, inasmuch as I treat curable and improvable together, and if at the end of two years they were not able to show some improvement in the patient, and if the patient was quiet and harmless, I would transfer him to the workhouse.

1968. Do you have many cases known as ordinary *delirium tremens* under treatment in the Richmond Asylum?—Not many. There are cases from time to time.

1969. But you don't have many of them?—Not many.

1970. I suppose they are cured and discharged very rapidly?—They might be discharged very rapidly, but our rule is to keep a patient for two months, unless there is some special reason to the contrary to test the permanency of the cure. In the case of *delirium tremens* it is also advantageous to give them a lesson.

1971. Do you shave their heads?—No.

1972. Do you treat them as a special class?—No. In reference to the classification (I wish to mention) into different forms of mania dementia, and all that, it is not a classification of my own. It is the classification contained in their admission papers, and it is a very imperfect classification.

1973. Is the classification in the report simply the classification in which they are entered?—In my own case it is simply the classification under which they enter, and I believe it is so in the other asylums.

1974. Then it is called by that name which it received from the doctor who certifies that the person is insane?—Precisely, and it is so registered, and the return is taken from the register.

1975. Don't you think it would give a more accurate idea if the resident doctors reconsidered it?—I do. The name of the disease might be perfectly right when the patient was admitted, but then the disease changes. Almost always cases of mania, if not recovered, end in dementia. In reference to the increased accommodation, I referred to single rooms I thought objectionable. There is another question, and a very large question, in reference to providing accommodation. I think there might be very large increased accommodation provided in addition to the other advantages to be obtained by converting these single rooms into associated day-rooms and dormitories. In connection with that return, I alluded to before on the 22nd report of the inspectors, I wish to give you what increased accommodation there might be had in lunatic asylums, and what expense it could be done for. I give the number of single cells in this return, and I think they are something about the same proportion at present, at about 2,000; that would be at the rate of 25 per cent., that would be one out of every four. I consider that one out of twenty would be a quite sufficient proportion, and then if you take 2,013 as the entire number of single rooms, and if you reduce that by taking 16 out of every 20, that would be four-fifths, and that would give 1,600 as the number. That would be 400 cells, leaving 1,600 to be removed, and you would double the accommodation by removing them. The removal of 1,600 cells would give extra 1,600 beds at an expense of £20 per head.

1976. It would not cost so much?—I have not made the calculation exactly, but large accommodation would be gained at a cost of about £20 per head or less. You could not erect a new building for less than £80 per head. I have here a map (produces map) of the old district asylum; it was all cells, and here it is (produces another map) as it has been altered by me. I removed three-fourths of the cells. In some divisions, many more might be advantageously removed.

Col. M'Kerlie.

Colonel JOHN GRAHAM M'KERLIE examined.

1977. You are Chairman of the Board of Control and Correspondence?—I am senior member of the Board for General Control and Correspondence, and for superintending and procuring the erection and establishment of asylums for the lunatic poor in Ireland.

1978. Can you give us a general account of the duties that are performed by the Board?—The present Board was formed pursuant to the Act the 18th and 19th Victoria, 1855; and its formation was the result of an inquiry held by the late Sir Thomas Reddington into the mode of conducting business by the former Board, which was composed of a considerable number of gentlemen. I don't remember the original number, but ultimately it dwindled down practically to only two, Sir Richard Griffith and the late Mr. John Radcliffe, who, being also members of the Board of Works, carried on the works of these days. They erected six entirely new asylums, and what is now called the new Richmond Asylum may be called a seventh; it is a separate and distinct asylum. Their operations, I may say, were a good deal cavilled at, and they were considered to have incurred unnecessary expenditure in some matters. A Commission of Inquiry was appointed—I don't know exactly in what year, but it must have been about 1854—consisting of the late Mr. Donaldson, Architect, of London, and Mr Wilks, who was one of the Lunacy Commissioners in England. They held an inquiry into various matters which had been complained of, resulting in a remission on the part of the Treasury, under the authority given by this Act, to which I have referred, to the amount of about £17,000 in respect of these asylums I have mentioned. As I have stated, there were only two members practically remaining of the old Board of Control, which had consisted of a considerable number. Though I myself was here during the latter part of the period referred to, as a member of the Board of Works, I was not a member of the Board of Control; I became so on its being reconstituted by the Lord Lieutenant in Council. Upon its re-formation, Sir Richard Griffith was Chairman of the Board of Works, and consequently became senior Commissioner of the new Board.

1979. It has been stated before the Commissioners of Lunatic Asylums that that Board ceased to exist upon the termination of its work—that is, that it was not replaced, and that having discharged the duty for which it was appointed, it then ceased to exist?—That is scarcely quite correct. In fact, the passing of the Act to which I have referred was the result of the inquiry held by the commission presided over by the late Sir Thomas Reddington. On the formation of the new Board, I was appointed one of the members. Of course, I was junior member.

1980. Under Sir Richard Griffith?—Yes, with two inspectors of lunatic asylums. I took some interest in the matter, of course, upon being appointed one of the members, and I gave some attention to the subject. I drew up these rules or instructions for planning and designing asylums. (Rules produced, and handed in.)

1981. What were the duties that devolved on the Board when you were appointed?—The duties of the Board were to take into consideration all applications for extended accommodation for the lunatic poor, either in the formation of entirely new districts and building, or in the extension of existing buildings.

1982. By whom is application for extended accommodation generally made?—Jointly, I may say, by the Boards of Governors and the inspectors of lunatic asylums. When any such propositions are brought forward, either for the formation of new asylums or adding to existing asylums, the matter is referred to the Board of Control.

1983. But before the reference to the Board of Control was the formation of the new district agreed upon by the Lord Lieutenant in Council?—No; the reference is that of the recommendation from the inspectors that a new district should be formed, and the Government or the Lord Lieutenant call on the Board of Control for a report.

1984. Then something more than a building reference was made to the Board of Control. They were referred to for advice upon the formation of the new district?—Yes; whether it was a desirable thing to form a new district or not. The Board then obtain all the necessary information by calling for statistics to enable them to form an opinion, and then enter very closely into the subject before expressing any opinion on it. Then, in accordance with the result of their consideration, they recommend the Government to adopt such a course as appeared to be expedient. Having got the statistics, they form an opinion, and advise the Government accordingly.

1985. What statistics did you get?—We got from the inspectors a statement of the number of known insane in the district. Supposing it is a district which it is proposed to divide, comprising perhaps three counties, we obtain from them a statement of the present accommodation for the insane poor, the number who are known to be at large or otherwise provided for in the district, and looking also to the geographical features of the district, we take into consideration whether it would be advisable to form an entirely new district, and provide a separate establishment for it. Having submitted that report to the Government, we await their instructions as to further proceedings. The step then taken by the Government would be to give public notice, I apprehend, of their intention, and then having heard objections (I am now speaking from what I believe to be the course of procedure; I have no actual knowledge of the fact for I don't remember), and having considered the subject fully, notice is given in the Gazette of the formation of the new district having been determined on.

1986. Is that notice given in anticipation of the building of the establishment?—Yes, in anticipation of the building consequent on the formation of the new district. The next step then is to select a site on which the institution should be established, we endeavour to ascertain from local sources where a proper site could be obtained, sometimes from the county surveyor or medical gentlemen resident in the district, or other source. We then proceed to visit it ourselves with our architect, and having visited the sites, if more than one, we determine on that which is most desirable to acquire, and take the necessary steps for doing so. The next measure taken is as to the erection of the building. We have an architect attached to the Board of Control, Mr. Wilkinson, who was formerly architect to the Poor Law Commissioners, and is a pensioned officer of that Board, and who now receives a salary as architect to the Board of Control. We think it right to give the Board of Governors in existing districts, or in those about to be formed, the option of employing an architect themselves, of course informing them at the same time that if they elect to choose their own architect they will be subject to the usual fees of architects, while on the other hand, if they leave the erection of the building to our architect, the charge will be only half of the usual cost. In four out of the entirely new asylums which we have built, the Board of Governors have availed themselves of the permission to select their own architect.

1987. That is of the establishments that have been built since you became a member of the Board?—Yes, four out of six. In the other two they expressed a wish that our own architect should be employed. The result of that has been that the cost to the districts has been considerably greater where they selected their own architect. I cannot tell the exact per-centage, but it is something like 30 per cent.

1988. What was the cost per bed?—The average of the two we erected ourselves was £123, and in the four which the local gentlemen carried out themselves, under their own architect, it amounted to £182. These sums include all the costs of purchase of land, law costs, building, furniture fittings, incidental expenses, and everything else. The same practice is followed where we add to old asylums. The proposition for the addition originates with the Board of Governors, generally, at the suggestion of the inspectors, who were *ex-officio* members.

1989. Who were *ex-officio* members. Are they not now?—No; they attend as inspectors.

1990. Well, they attend their meetings as inspectors and advise the Governors, and it is upon these occasions they point out the necessity of additions to the asylums. Then a memorial is forwarded by the Board of Governors, sometimes to the Board of Control, sometimes to the Government. In the event of its being addressed to the Government it is forwarded to us, and in either case we make the necessary inquiries as to the necessity for the addition.

1991. Does it come direct to you or through the inspectors?—Direct to us. We have obtained statistics, as I have before mentioned, of the number in the asylum and the number outside.

1992. Do you include in this latter the number in the workhouses?—Yes, the number in the workhouses. We have then a careful inspection made of the existing buildings, to ascertain what they are fairly calculated to accommodate. On this basis we lay down in our instructions, and having satisfied ourselves as to the necessity for the additional accommodation, we report to the Government, giving approximately an estimate of the cost.

1993. You speak of the Government afterwards communicating with the Board of Governors and the Boards of the new districts. Is it not the grand juries of the counties or counties of cities embraced in the new districts with which the Government communicates. Boards of Governors will not, at this period of the proceeding, have been formed in the new districts?—Yes, the notice of the intention to add to the asylum is gazetted, and we then proceed, as before stated, to carry out the works either through our own architect or an architect chosen by the Board of Governors. Formerly, until the present year, indeed, money was advanced out of the consolidated fund and made repayable nominally in 14 years, but practically in 16 years by instalments.

1994. With interest?—Without interest. The Public Works Loans Act of last session alters that by making the advances subject to interest at 3½ per cent, and while naming 14 years as the time for repayment, the Treasury reserve to themselves the power of extending it to a longer period not exceeding 20 years, if circumstances renders it desirable to do so.

1995. What is the exact nature of the inquiries you make as regards the accommodation available in, and the probable requirements of a district?—Take for instance the case of Limerick. It was enlarged within the last two or three years. We got plans of the existing buildings and we had a careful inspection of them by our architect, and a calculation made by him on the basis of the accommodation which we consider necessary, and the amount of space required for each individual. He also looks into the nature of the accommodation the building affords as regards its general suitability, and he then reports to the Board what in its present state it could accommodate, and how the existing accommodation might be increased by converting single rooms into associated rooms, and by other means. Upon this data we are enabled to say what number of patients the building will accommodate, and then taking that number from the whole number, the inspectors point out to us that it is necessary to provide accommodation, for we are in a position to have plans prepared for the additional extension required.

1996. Is the number for which you propose accommodation furnished by the inspectors?—Entirely by the inspectors.

1997. You said in a previous part of your evidence that you received information as to the number of the lunatics in the district *including the lunatics at large*?—Yes, That information we receive from the

L

DUBLIN July 25, 1878.
Col. M'Kerlie.

inspectors and they name to us a number which they think it necessary to provide for. We have questioned the necessity for the amount of accommodation they proposed, and I rather think in one or two cases (I speak from memory) we questioned the necessity for the number they proposed.

1998. Do you happen to recollect whether in calculating the probable requirements of a district they take into consideration any per-centage of the lunatics at large?—That is the principal ground on which they base the calculations. I apprehend it is almost entirely so. There are statistics provided I believe by the constabulary, and I remember in the case of the Co. Clare I felt dissatisfied with the statistics, and an effort was made to obtain special statistics on the separation of the counties, that is to say we proposed to employ the constabulary or probably the medical officers of poor law unions to report what number of lunatics were in the several unions and their condition. I remember perfectly well proposing that, but there was a difficulty in carrying it out.

1999. Did they observe upon the condition of the lunatics at large as well as upon the class in the workhouses?—The report referred to was only proposed to be prepared by the constabulary and other persons competent to inquire.

2000. Is there any means of ascertaining how far the inspectors are making the calculation of the necessity for the additional accommodation take into consideration the wants of the lunatics at large. Say 1,000 at large, and 400 in a particular assigned district, do the inspectors include any per-centage, of these or make any sort of inquiry to ascertain how far provision should be made for the lunatics at large?—I am unable to answer that. My belief is that they have gone on the general average throughout the country without venturing to subdivide it into special districts. We know there are special districts in which lunacy exists more than in others, and they have expressed their belief on that subject. The practice is, however, to go on the general average throughout the whole country, at the same time taking into consideration the number in the workhouses.

2001. Have they not also been guided by the gradual increase in the number of lunatics in asylums from year to year, and in that way been enabled to form some idea of the probable requirements?—I could not say, they give the numbers, but they don't give the means by which they arrive at the numbers.

2002. Do you know whether they include the lunatics in workhouses in their returns of the numbers for whom accommodation should be provided in the new lunatic asylums?—I think the best answer I can give you will be to show you one of the returns thus furnished to us.

A RETURN of the NUMBER of INSANE PERSONS of all DENOMINATIONS in the COUNTY of ARMAGH on the 31st December, 1871, showing how they were then located.

How Located.	Denomination	Male	Female.	Total	TOTAL. Male	TOTAL. Female.	TOTAL. Total
In district. Lunatic asylums,	Idiots,	16	0	16			
	Lunatics,	83	68	151	96	71	167
In poor-houses,	Idiots,	9	14	23			
"	Lunatics,	12	23	35	21	37	58
At large,	Idiots,	27	20	47			
"	Epileptic lunatics,	10	14	24			
"	Lunatics,	6	5	11	43	39	82
	Gross total,				160	147	318

Office of Lunatic Asylums, Dublin Castle,
31st February, 1872.

(Signed), W. J. CORBET, Chief Clerk.

2003. You are aware there was an Act passed, the 38 and 39 Victoria—giving power to Boards of Governors with the consent of the Local Government Board and the Inspectors, to transfer harmless lunatics to workhouses?—Yes, I am aware of that.

2004. Have there been applications for the enlargement of asylums or the construction of new asylums, since the passing of that Act?—Yes, several; the case of Armagh will afford an answer to your question.

2005. When considering the question of accommodation, has this new means of providing for harmless and incurable been brought under your notice by the inspectors?—Yes especially in the case of Armagh, a memorial was addressed to the Lord Lieutenant on the subject.

2006. Of the increased accommodation required at Armagh?—Yes, objecting to the additional building proposed there on the ground that accommodation could be provided in the workhouse under the Act referred to.

2007. Was the addition first proposed before the passing of that Act or after?—The addition was proposed before the passing of the Act, but delays having occurred in making these additions, the Act was passed before much progress had been made. There was first of all a memorial from the Board of Guardians of Armagh Union, signed by Sir James Stronge, Chairman. This is the petition. (Reads)—

"The petition, &c., humbly sheweth that the Governors of the Armagh District Lunatic Asylum, have taken measures to increase the quantity of land and the building of that establishment, and they have gone so far as to obtain an inquisition to ascertain the value of certain lands required for the proposed addition at the inquisition held at Armagh, on Tuesday, the 28th day of November, last, the jury awarded the large sum of £3,500 for about twelve statute acres of medium quality of land (being about £300 per acre), which outlay does not include the large prospective sum to be expended upon the building which will be required, that your memorialists further beg leave to submit to your excellencies, that the Board of Guardians proposed to the Governors of the said asylum to relieve that institution of a large number of the harmless lunatics confined therein, and to appropriate a portion of the workhouse for their accommodation, which could be done without any inconvenience at a very small expense and which offer fully meets the approval of the district poor law inspector; this proposition is not without precedent as other unions have adopted a similar course, your memorialists humbly pray that your excellencies will be so good as to interfere, to prevent further proceedings being taken by the Board of Works, until a full investigation be instituted as to the reasonableness and economy of the above proposals, and your memorialists as in duty bound will ever pray."

That was referred to us from the Castle on the 19th December, 1876, then came another memorial referred to us from the Castle on the following 17th of January, it is a memorial from the Board of Governors of the Armagh District Asylum, passed at a meeting held on Monday, 8th January, 1877, His Grace the Lord Primate in the chair. It is as follows.

(Reads)—

"Resolved, that having heard from Dr Nugent, an explanation of the provisions of the Act 38 & 39 Victoria, cap. 67, of the per-centage of lunatics that could be removed to workhouses we are of opinion that any utilising of the workhouse at Lurgan or Armagh would not justify the Governors in allowing the asylum to continue in its present state, and that the contemplated enlargements and improvements be proceeded with immediately."

That was sent to us and the following letter was sent in reply. (Reads)—

"Armagh District Lunatic Asylum,

25th January, 1877.

SIR,—In reply to your letter of the 23rd inst. having reference to your previous letters of the 19th ult., and 17th instant, the one enclosing a copy of a memorial from the Armagh Board of Guardians, praying that for reasons therein stated the contemplated acquisition of additional ground, and the extension of the building of above asylum might be stayed; and the other a copy of a resolution of the Board of Governors of the asylum in favour of their being proceeded with, and in reply also to your reference of the 2nd inst. to memorials from the magistrates and cess-payers assembled at the late presentment sessions of Co. Armagh relative to the subject (file No. 1964 herewith returned) the Board beg to submit the following observations for the information of His Grace the Lord Lieutenant. The Lunatic Asylum at Armagh up to the year 1869 received the insane poor from a district composed of the three counties of Armagh, Cavan, and Monaghan. In that year the new asylum was erected at Monaghan for the separate use of the two latter counties, and the old asylum at Armagh was then appropriated to the exclusive use of the county of Armagh for the service of which it was then supposed it would be found amply sufficient. As time went on, however, it was found to provide inadequate accommodation for the insane, even of the reduced area, and to be deficient in many of those appliances, and the means of employment and recreation which had been introduced into new asylums, and were deemed necessary in the modern and improved treatment of the insane. Accordingly in the year 1863 on the application of the Board of Governors and the recommendation of the inspectors, the Board of Control, after full inquiry, submitted for the future consideration of the Government whether new day rooms, a recreation hall, an improved laundry, as well as additional accommodation in sleeping rooms for 60 patients should be provided, and also additional land—10 acres in extent—should be acquired; the whole cost of which was £10,968 17s 9d. The recommendations have been approved, and the necessary loans authorised. Again in 1873 on its being found by the Board of Governors that a still further addition to the asylum was needed to meet the requirements of the continually increasing number of patients we applied to the Board for authority to have plans prepared to provide for the increased accommodation which appeared to be necessary, the matter was in progress when the attention of the Commissioners was called by the Government (by reference from the Under-Secretary, dated 10th February, 1873, file No. 2735) to the Inspector's report for the year 1873, which refers to the inadequacy of the accommodation at the asylum afforded. In consequence of that communication the Board have in the meantime satisfied themselves from the return received from the inspectors (copy of which is enclosed) of the necessity for the proposed extension, and obtained the sanction of the Government thereto, the plans and specifications for the work were pushed forward as much as circumstances admitted, and now they are so far matured as to admit of tenders for their execution being immediately called for. At the same time steps have been taken for the acquisition of an additional extent of land (12 acres) for the institution, such having been recommended by the inspectors as desirable on the application of the Board of Governors, and in which the Board have concurred. It is the latter point—the purchase of the land—which has given rise to the question now raised as to the necessity for the contemplated additions to the building or land. Different public bodies memorialised the Government all pointing to the Act of 38th & 39th Victoria cap. 67, as providing a means of avoiding the expenditure which the proposed additions will involve by removing certain portions of the patients to workhouses, while at the same time they protest against the exorbitant price to be given for the additional land under the award of the jury called together to determine the question under an order to do so by inquisition. In regard to the first of these grounds of objection the Board are advised by the inspectors that it is neither practicable nor desirable to provide in the workhouse for the extra number of patients now in or likely to require admission into the asylum beyond what it is fairly calculated to hold, and in this they are supported by the resolution of the Board of Governors dated the 8th inst. While it may be proper for the Government to give further inquiry with reference to the particular acts now in question in regard to the bringing into operation the act quoted, it yet appears to the Board that the additions contemplated cannot be dispensed with and that it is advisable they should be authorised to proceed with the step of calling for the tenders for the work. With regard to the question of the value of the land, it, as before stated, has been submitted to the determination of a jury. The Board beg to enclose copies of the valuation made by the duly qualified valuator appointed by them to ascertain the value and of the amounts awarded by the jury in each corresponding item."

I have the honour to be, sir,

Your obedient servant,

FREDK. L. WEBER, Secretary.

"To T. H. Burke, Esq.,
Under-Secretary, Dublin Castle."

The latter part of the letter only refers to the land.

2008. It appears then that the Board of Guardians and the magistrates and cess-payers assembled at presentment sessions were anxious that this building should not take place?—Yes.

2009. Was there any letter addressed by the inspectors to your Board advising you that it was neither desirable nor practicable to transfer harmless lunatics to the workhouse?*—It must be amongst the papers on the file. I will endeavour to find it.

In connexion with the general question, I may add that we are now purchasing fifty additional acres for the Downpatrick Asylum. That was applied for by the Board of Governors. They had, we considered, an adequate quantity of land for the number of patients. Our calculation of the extent of land required—based on the information derived from English sources—was in the proportion of one acre to six patients, male and female, and in establishing the asylum at Downpatrick that was the proportion of land allowed; but within the last two years they desired to acquire an additional fifty acres, and we are in treaty about it—in fact, have agreed to purchase.

Dublin, July 23, 1878.

Col. M'Kerlie.

2010. With the view of enlarging the asylum?—No; merely for the purpose of employing the patients—a sort of dairy establishment. It was a proposal pressed very much by the Board of Governors, and very strongly urged by the inspectors, to which we demurred a good deal at first.

2011. But you are bound now?—I think so.

2012. What was the acreage they had before?—About fifty acres, as near as possible.

2013. I suppose they cannot get that less than £100 an acre?—It will cost about £7,000. It belongs to Mr. Mulholland, and he has agreed to take £5,000, but then there are the tenant's interests besides to be met.

2014. On the original plans, on which most of these asylums were built, was not nearly all the accommodation composed of single cells?—There was a very large proportion of them. There were very few rooms which provided accommodation for more than three or four.

2015. The fresh instructions drawn up by you very much reduced the proportion of single cells?—Yes; and since that we have endeavoured, wherever it is practicable, to introduce large associated rooms for perhaps sixteen or twenty patients, or more.

2016. That is in new buildings?—Yes.

2017. Has not the accommodation in many of the old buildings been increased by getting rid of these cells, and replacing them by associated rooms?—Yes; especially so in Richmond.

2018. In that way a good deal of extra accommodation has been obtained?—Yes.

2019. And you think a good deal more could be thus obtained?—No; I think nearly all has been converted that could be. Wherever we have been making additions to asylums it has been in the way of large dormitories and day rooms. There is scarcely an instance of additional cells being provided. It has also been in the way of recreation halls and chapels, and places for religious worship, improved laundries, and generally improved accommodation for the patient.

2020. Have you had any other instance besides that at Armagh, in which difficulties have been raised as to the proposal to utilise workhouse accommodation for harmless lunatics?—The only other case in which such have arisen, I think, is Derry. A proposition was made there, and I think it was on the same grounds it was objected to.

2021. Except as to the arrangement of the building, have you any control over asylums at all?—None whatever, over either discipline or management. None whatever as regards the curative treatment, or the discipline, or internal economy; but we consider it our duty to see that no structural alterations are made without our consent.

* This it is found was a verbal communication, no letter appearing to have been received by the Board.

DUBLIN
Aug. 5, 1878.
Dr Frederick MacCabe

FREDERICK MACCABE, Esq., Physician and Surgeon, examined.

2022. You are at present one of the Inspectors of the Local Government Board?—Yes.

2023. How long have you been Inspector?—Since April, 1876.

2024. Before then you were connected with the lunacy department?—Yes.

2025. In what capacity?—From 1865 to 1872, I was Medical Superintendent of the Waterford District Asylum. From 1872 to 1876, I was Resident Physician and Governor of the Criminal Lunatic Asylum in Dundrum.

2026. Then you have had eleven years experience of lunacy administration, first as medical Superintendent at Waterford, and then as physician at Dundrum?—I have.

2027. And you have had the subsequent experience as Local Government Board Inspector?—I have.

2028. Your district is the Cork District and that comprises all the Cork and some of the Waterford Unions?—Some of the Cork.

2029. It is called the Cork District?—It is, to be precise it includes eleven unions in Cork, one in Limerick and two in Waterford.

2030. Are you acquainted with the structural arrangements, and the arrangements for classification of the inmates of all these workhouses?—As far as two years experience enables me to be.

2031. You have been communicated with I think by this Commission with the view of revising the accommodation, and Schedule A, containing a table of the space requirements for healthy and sick in the different workhouses has been sent to you?—Yes.

2032. Have you examined any of the workhouses in your district, with the view of ascertaining how far that schedule would be applicable in fixing the accommodation of inmates in the workhouses?—Yes, one I particularly examined, Mallow Workhouse, and went over the measurements of each department in it according to the existing limitation order and then contrasted it with the measurement under Schedule A.

2033. The result of the examination in the Mallow case was a certain reduction?—Oh, yes, a very considerable reduction.

2034. You have been good enough to send to the Commissioners a statement of the measurement according to the sealed order, and the corrected measurement under Schedule A?—Yes, I sent in a return in each, after working out all the calculations for Mallow. I applied the same rules to the other workhouses without going into individual calculations for each department; I was satisfied it would produce a tolerably accurate result.

2035. That is you found the reduction amount to a certain per centage in Mallow, and applying the same rules of measurement, you worked out the measurements in other cases?—Yes.

2036. May we assume there would be very little variation between the actual accommodation under this schedule, and the assumption according to the Mallow case, that there would be so much per cent?—I think so.

2037. We may assume that the accommodation in the whole of your unions would be reduced according to the scale you found it necessary to reduce to in the case of Mallow?—Quite so.

2038. Speaking generally of the accommodation for lunatics in workhouses in your district, are you satisfied with it in amount, and character. Do you consider it insufficient in quantity and defective in structural arrangements?—I am very strongly of that opinion.

2039. May we assume that there is no workhouse in your district in which, speaking from your experience in connexion with lunatic asylums, you would not feel you had reason to be dissatisfied with the accommodation provided for lunatics?—With one exception. Within the last few months a new block of buildings has been opened in Cork, the accommodation for the male lunatics in that building is very fair, with that exception, the accommodation is defective in quantity and quality.

2040. Then with the exception of the provision for the male lunatics in Cork which is quite recent, the arrangements are in your opinion defective if not objectionable?—Altogether.

2041. Have you considered the expediency of removing the lunatics from a certain number of these workhouses to some separate portion of any one workhouse, or two or three workhouses that might be fit for the purpose?—I have given the subject a good deal of consideration.

2042. And what conclusions have you arrived at?—I arrived at the conclusion that by removing all the lunatics distributed over my different unions and placing them either in vacant buildings or vacant blocks of workhouses, or some two or three workhouses, an immense advantage would be conferred on the workhouses from which they were removed, and unspeakable advantage would be conferred on the lunatics themselves. The advantage conferred on the workhouses from which they were removed would be by affording additional space to the sick and aged and infirm, and the advantage that would be conferred on the lunatics would be that in an intermediate institution devoted exclusively to their treatment they would have a better chance of fair treatment, fair dies, and above all proper attendance.

2043. Would you see any objection to appropriating a certain proportion of these blocks of buildings you have spoken of, for males, and a certain other proportion for females; do you think such a classification would be attended by any inconvenience?—I think not.

2044. That is your opinion as one having experience in the treatment of lunacy?—Yes. I not only think it would not be attended with disadvantage, but I think, as the Commission probably intend that the intermediate asylums should be conducted on a scale of greater economy than district asylums, that economy would be promoted by a separation as to sex.

2045. With reference to the economical management of them have you any doubt that the lunatics removed into blocks of buildings so arranged and with the necessary appliances could be maintained with much less cost than in lunatic asylums?—I am perfectly satisfied of that.

2046. If you had one of these asylums with 60 patients would you consider that two female paid attendants, with such assistance as could be derived from the better class inmates in the workhouse, would be sufficient for the supervision of these asylums?—I think that whenever the number exceeded 90 the proportion of one attendant to 30 would be fair, but as you would have to provide against the contingency of one being ill or one going out on leave, I think it would always require a staff of two.

2047. So that no matter how small the number of patients in one of these asylums or auxiliary asylums you think two properly qualified attendants should be always provided?—Yes.

2048. And where the asylum was arranged for the reception of 60, two paid attendants with such assist-

Dublin, Aug. 8, 1878.

Dr. Frederick MacCabe.

ance as they could get from the workhouse inmates would be sufficient?—I think they would, but I should like the Commission to understand that if there were only 30 patients I would still have two paid attendants provided.

2049. To revert to an answer you gave this moment you referred to the advantage that would be conferred on the workhouses by the removal of the lunatics as affording additional infirmary accommodation, is it your experience within your own district that the infirmary accommodation, as a rule, is deficient?—Clearly so.

2050. Is it not a fact that originally the infirmaries were designed simply as hospitals for the sick of the workhouse itself, and that the great bulk of the accommodation was intended for able bodied, and that in the course of time the whole of the arrangements of workhouses have been disarranged by there being few able bodied and an excess of aged and sick in the infirmary?—That is so.

2051. And the result is that within your experience the infirmary accommodation is most unsatisfactory. In point of accommodation you are compelled in almost every workhouse to have recourse to expedients in order to supply the defect of infirmary accommodation?—That is so.

2052. There are very few workhouses in which the removal of the lunatics or those who are classed as lunatics and idiots would not afford additional infirmary accommodation probably, sufficient to meet the requirements for some time?—In many it would.

2053. Do you think in those it would not afford that assistance immediately it would not be possible by redistributing the inmates through the departments of the house you might re arrange the house so as to afford additional accommodation for the aged and infirm sick?—I think a good deal could be done in that direction.

2054. By some slight structural alterations you might probably appropriate some of the rooms in the wings on each side for aged and infirm, and transfer a certain number of that class from the infirmary, thus retaining the infirmary exclusively for hospital purposes?—That might be done.

2055. Does your own experience of Waterford justify us in assuming that that asylum has been constantly overcrowded?—Constantly while I had charge of it. I had to bring that subject several times under the notice of the Governors of the asylum, and eventually during my time, a large structural addition was built.

2056. Did not all the overcrowding consist of overcrowding by chronic and what are termed in the reports "probably incurable" cases?—Entirely so.

2057. If there was suitable accommodation provided elsewhere; not referring at this moment to what it might be, but if there was suitable accommodation provided for a large percentage of that class elsewhere, have you any doubt that it would be for the advantage of lunacy administration to have that class removed from the asylums, leaving the asylums simply as hospitals for curative treatment?—I have not the slightest doubt on the subject, it would enable the existing staff of the asylums to devote themselves to the care of individual curable cases instead of having their attention distributed over a large number, the vast proportion of which are incurable. You could give all the care to the curable if you got rid of the incurable.

2058. And as a matter of administration are you of opinion that it would be attended with advantage that the medical superintendent of an asylum should be able to devote his attention exclusively to curative treatment?—That is my opinion.

2059. The returns we have received from the various lunatic asylums, exhibited, as probably you are aware, something like a per-centage of 70 per cent. on the whole, as being probably incurable. Suppose it were practicable, or suppose it were legal to appropriate certain asylums for the reception of incurable cases; reserving certain other asylums as curative hospitals; would you consider that that arrangement would be attended with advantage. If you had three classes we will say; the district asylum for curative purposes and we will keep the intermediate asylums for cases that would not be properly cases for curative treatment, and yet not cases you would like to transfer to the workhouse intermediate asylums, but cases between the two. Do you think such a classification of asylums as is indicated in that question would be attended with advantage?—I think that would be the best arrangement that could possibly be made, because amongst the probably incurable cases in asylums, there are no doubt many—a good many—who would not be suitable for workhouses, and if you provide a class of institution intermediate between the two you would exactly meet all the requirements of the country.

2060. I might say that opinion has been strongly expressed by Dr. Hatchell and Dr. Nugent, and by the medical superintendent of the Mullingar asylum, in a passage of his report to which your attention I think has been called, and we assume that you having experience of lunacy in workhouses and asylums are strongly of that opinion?—I am very strongly of that opinion.

2061. Besides the cases that are classed as curable do you consider there is another class that might be put down as improvable?—Clearly so.

2062. You would class those that were improvable along with the curable cases?—I would. Perhaps the best way to answer that question is to say that in the returns which are now made officially, those that are put down in asylum returns as curable, are cases in which there is a reasonable hope of complete recovery and restoration to society, and probably of becoming working members of society again, but amongst those who are probably incurable take them in the workhouse, there is a very large proportion of that class who with proper care would be improvable, they would be improvable in habits, and morally and mentally sufficiently improvable to make them very useful in the intermediate asylum without there being any reasonable hope of their being restored to society.

2063. If these asylums that constituted portions of workhouses were under the management of Boards of Guardians, and the asylums proper were left under the management of Boards of Governors, do you think there would be any difficulty likely to arise from the separate jurisdiction exercised by Guardians and otherwise?—I think there would not be much difficulty in that way, because the members of Boards of Governors of district asylums are nearly all ex-officio members of the Board of Guardians, and indirectly they have the same interest at heart—keeping down the rates; and I think they would be very willing to help the Guardians by an interchange of patients.

2064. Would you think it a good arrangement that a committee analogous to the Dispensary Committee should be constituted partly of members of the Boards of Guardians and partly of members of the Boards of Governors—the nearest residents to the workhouse asylum should have the management of the workhouse asylum, instead of leaving it to the whole Board of Guardians?—If I were to answer from my experience of dispensary committees, I should be disposed to say no; for I know that when gentlemen are associated together to perform duties of that kind it is exceedingly hard to make them meet. I would be more disposed to consider that a working plan would be to make Boards of Guardians—where the asylums are attached to their institutions—the controlling body, letting the Board of Governors nominate any number of their own body to attend the meetings of the Guardians for the supervision of the asylum.

2065. Would it not be better to have a distinct committee for the management of the workhouse asylum; that committee to be composed of Guardians and Governors representing the interests of both, and were likely to bring both into co-operation, rather than have two distinct authorities, who might not be

DUBLIN,
Aug. 5, 1878.

Dr. Frederick MacCabe.

inclined to agree sometimes?—I think it would be the best plan, if you could induce them to meet.

2066. Well, the analogy of the Dispensary Committee. I simply refer to that as an illustration of the character of the committee, apart from the Board of Guardians, and not at all as implying that you would have the same difficulty to encounter in their meeting. If the Guardians met, and had to appoint three members of their Board on the Committee, they would probably appoint three who would attend to the business?—That is likely.

2067. The ordinary attendance of the members of such a committee to the business of the unions would necessitate their frequent attendance close to the auxiliary asylum. This is different from the case of the Dispensary Committees, their place of meeting being often remote from the workhouse. Do you not think that these more favourable conditions would have the required effect upon their meeting?—It would probably. Attendance at the asylum to perform the duties would be different from the case of the Dispensary Committee meetings.

2068. As to the constitution of the governing body or the controlling authority at head-quarters, do you think it would be practicable to carry on the administration of two sets of totally distinct asylums by distinct authorities—one under the Local Government Board, and the other under the Lunacy Department?—I think not. It appears to me success would depend on co-operation between the two classes of institution. You will have patients that ought to be transferred from the county asylum to the intermediate asylum, because they have ceased to be any longer probably curable; and other patients who, through the manifestation of dangerous tendencies, ought at once to be transferred to the county asylum, and if you have two different controlling authorities you can't well expect that prompt interchange to take place.

2069. And for the purpose of carrying out a scheme of that sort if it should be recommended, and for administering it, your opinion is, I gather, that there ought to be one central authority for the control of the whole, that is that the lunacy administration should be brought under one authority, be that authority what it may, either the existing authority, or the creation of a new authority?—I am very strongly of that opinion.

2070. You furnished us with a return, exhibiting the accommodation that could probably be afforded in your district of the class of lunatics in the workhouses at Mallow, Middleton, Youghal, and Cork, could be removed. Do you think, from your experience of these unions, that the taking of the portion, to which you called attention, and which we had an opportunity of inspecting, would in any way either actually or prospectively interfere with the administration of the poor-law. Begin at Mallow. Do you think if the fever hospital at Mallow, and a wing on the left hand side—the female wing—if either or both of those were taken, it would interfere with or impair the poor-law administration in any way?—Mallow is the one I am most doubtful about. The pressure there is often very great, even under the old limitation order, of the division of space, we are very much overcrowded in portions of that house.

2071. Suppose the interference at Mallow was confined to taking the fever hospital, would that cause any inconvenience, provided the small infectious hospital that lies between the town and the workhouse, was enlarged and fitted up as a fever hospital for the workhouse?—I don't think it would. I have gone carefully into the returns of fever for the last fifteen or twenty years, and I have never found the amount of fever prevalent exceed the amount of accommodation that fever hospital by suitable addition might be made to afford.

2072. And there are sheds near that which could be adapted for small-pox patients in emergency?—Quite so.

2073. So that for infectious cases between that hospital and these sheds, there would be provided sufficient accommodation, taking the present fever hospital for lunacy purposes?—I think so.

2074. But the taking of the female wing you think possibly would be attended with inconvenience?—I do, in this way, that after going over the accommodation as I did in Mallow, side by side with Schedule A, I find we are greatly overcrowded in Mallow, and I think the principles laid down in Schedule A ought to be applied to all, but it would be impossible to apply them if you took away that wing from Mallow.

2075. It would be impracticable to apply to Mallow strictly the arrangement contemplated by this schedule if you took away that wing?—Yes.

2076. But in Middleton?—That can be taken, I think, without any inconvenience.

2077. Bandon?—That can clearly be taken, for there is a very large hospital to fall back upon.

2078. Youghal?—The auxiliary building would make an excellent lunatic asylum.

2079. That is the industrial school?—Yes.

2080. In Cork you have made provision for the males, which you consider satisfactory, but for female lunatics it is not so?—Thoroughly unsatisfactory.

2081. Would you consider the male accommodation satisfactory as a permanent arrangement in Cork. Do they not occupy space in a wing that is really intended for another class?—Quite so; they are placed side by side with the blind. The Blind Epileptics and Lunatics occupy one portion of the block. In the answer I am making I am making it subject to the very strong opinion that lunatics ought not to be in workhouses at all, but suppose the lunatics remain in Cork Workhouse, I say the arrangement in Cork for male lunatics is the best that could be made. It is equal to the accommodation in many asylums, except as to attendance.

2082. But for females it is not so?—No.

2083. You are well acquainted with the school building in Cork?—Yes.

2084. With reference to the education of children in workhouses are you disposed to draw any distinction between the character of the workhouse training, and the bringing up of children in small purely rural unions, and large towns such as Cork. That is to say would you consider the arrangements for the education of children in such a workhouse as Middleton or Mallow upon the whole satisfactory?—It is difficult to answer that question, because at times the educational condition of the children depends so much on the individual teacher. If you take Middleton for example I say yes, it is satisfactory, for not only is the literary education, but the industrial training of the children is very well attended to.

2085. There is great diversity in the character, not of the literary education but the instruction of the children—their industrial training?—That is what is stated to be generally deficient.

2086. And do you consider that in large workhouses of large towns like Cork, Waterford, and Limerick that the very character of the building is adverse, that there are adverse influences at work which it would be desirable to remove?—If you permit me I should like to answer that by saying my experience is so limited that my opinion would not be of much value. I have made a good deal of inquiry on the subject from those who ought to know, and some of the most experienced I have spoken to are strongly averse to having children trained in large workhouses like that at Cork. My own experience has not been sufficient for I have not seen the results of the training, and they complain constantly that in large workhouses like the Cork workhouse, those they have done their best to train, industrially and otherwise, have always a tendency to come back to the workhouse. They stay out for a time, but they look upon the workhouse as their home, and they return to it; but those statements are not borne out by my own limited experience.

2087. That objection has been strongly urged before a committee of the House of Commons by at least

DUBLIN. Aug 5, 1873.

Dr. Frederick MacCabe.

three witnesses from Cork with respect to the Cork workhouse. Mr Mahony was one, and Mrs. Woodlock another I think, and they gave as the result of their experience what you state

2088. But suppose the children (the girls) could be removed from Cork workhouse, do you think that that building could be well adapted for the reception of a certain number of female lunatics?—It could undoubtedly be adapted.

2089 Could it be well adapted?—I think with some slight internal alterations it might, it has nice bathing arrangements and good sanitary arrangements. It could be adapted.

2090. With a protecting wall built along the railway?—Yes, that would be absolutely necessary.

2091. Do you think that that could be advantageously appropriated for that purpose if arrangements could be made for the removal of the children to a distinct building apart from the workhouse?—I think so

2092. Your hospital accommodation at Cork I think, is habitually overcrowded?—We have a very full hospital indeed; it is frequently overcrowded

2093. The accommodation given to female lunatics adjoins the female hospital?—It does

2094. It would be very advantageous to the house if that accommodation could be added to the female hospital?—Yes.

2095. The male hospital is likewise very much overcrowded?—Yes.

2096. The situation of the boy's school is such that if it could be vacated it would be a very desirable addition to the male hospital?—Yes, it would make an excellent male hospital.

2097. You think it would be an admirable hospital for males? -We require it at this moment.

2098. So it would be very advantageous for the internal arrangements of the Cork workhouse, if accommodation could be provided for the boys elsewhere?—We could occupy their space. I know the anxiety of the Cork Guardians would be to get rid of their lunatics, if possible, and we could make use of both spaces if we had them.

2099. Both the boys and girl's space, and if the girl's space was available it would be useful for female lunatics?—It would be better than at present for our female lunatics They are at present in the middle of the buildings, where we want space for the infirmary patients.

2100 Whether they be removed to the girl's department or not it is desirable to have the female lunatics removed out of the workhouse?—I think it is essential, for if the Commissioners consider for a moment, when I took charge of the Waterford asylum in 1865 there were only 160 patients in it We have got nearly that number of lunatics within the walls of Cork workhouse, so we have a lunatic asylum within the workhouse, and it is also to be borne in mind that under the existing state of the law, lunacy constitutes no claim to poor law relief. They come in as destitute persons, not as lunatics. The Guardians admit them on the plea of destitution, and really and truly they look upon it as beyond their function to provide accommodation at all for them.

2101. Speaking of the efficiency or inefficiency of these asylums that are contemplated in workhouses, is it within your experience that the curative treatment or the improving treatment of some of the workhouses is satisfactory, Cork for instance?—Very satisfactory in Cork, for instance, I have taken a great deal of trouble in regard to the lunatic department in Cork Workhouse I have got a very good nurse at the head of it, and the patients were set to work to occupy them, sewing, and in a variety of ways. I took the trouble of getting returns last year and I found that of the female lunatics thirty-two per cent. were sent home recovered

2102. You have got a good nurse at the head of that department in Cork?—Excellent.

2103. How many lunatics have you; and can you say what is their average weekly cost under the heads of maintenance and establishment charges?—I think the day before yesterday we had 150- -100 females, 50 males, and the cost was, under the head of maintenance, 3s 6d. per week, and under the head of establishment charges, 1s. 4d. per week.

2104. What supervision have you besides that head nurse?—She has now one paid assistant only, the rest of the work is done by people from the house.

2105. And very satisfactorily done?- -Very satisfactorily done.

2106. And suppose you had that head nurse and two assistants, would you consider that in an ordinary workhouse asylum sufficient?—It would be amply sufficient, and the proof is, we have in Cork Workhouse, cases of acute mania that are not suitable for the place and still with that staff we are able to manage very well, and have a fair proportion of recoveries, and a great deal of needlework turned out for the rest of the institution.

2107. A certain amount of inconvenience might be anticipated if asylums were classified in the way suggested in one or two questions put to you from the distance of the asylum for patients who were to be admitted. Would you anticipate any such difficulty if asylums were classified in the way suggested?—I think there would be no practical inconvenience under any classification you made with the proviso that where recent cases were admitted, particularly under magistrates' warrants, they should be directed to be taken as at present to the nearest district asylum

2108. Recent cases of any class?—Of any class

2109. That is to say that your opinion is that all recent cases should be taken as a rule to the nearest of the two district asylums, not to the workhouse, but to the nearest asylum?—Quite so.

2110. And if necessary transferred from the asylum that would be retained for chronic cases to the curative establishment?—Precisely.

2111. You don't think there would be any practical difficulty if that arrangement existed owing to the distance?—No more than at present, but I think it would be necessary to make that arrangement, for it is within my personal knowledge that magistrates sometimes commit late in the evening under the 30 & 31 Victoria, cap. 118, the constabulary are communicated with, and they take charge of the alleged dangerous lunatic, and they may deliver the lunatic in the middle of the night. If it was absolutely necessary only to deliver that patient at the curative or first class asylum, I don't know how they would dispose of him for the night, and you might have to return to the defective arrangement which induced Lord Mayo to pass that Act, before that Act they were to be committed to the nearest goal to await the transfer.

2112. That would imply that Ireland should be divided into large districts, each district to comprise a curative establishment; one other establishment for chronic cases, and others for workhouse cases?—Yes.

2113. And your view is that all recent cases should be transferred to the nearest of the first one or two (we will call them A and B), and not to the workhouse asylums?—Not to the workhouse asylums.

2114. These transferred to the asylum B, should, if the medical superintendent was of that opinion, be transferred to the curative establishment?—And as a rule it would be safest that lunatics committed under magistrates' warrants should go to class A, for I assume in class A you would have a much more expensive staff so far as attendants perhaps is concerned.

2115. Still that would involve inconvenience as to distance, if all cases committed under magistrates' warrants were sent to Class A, it might happen that the patient should pass the door of Asylum B in going to Asylum A?—There is that objection.

2116. Would there be any objection to turn into Asylum B, and leave the patient there to await the result of the examination?—I am speaking of a permanent arrangement The only reason I make the remark is that patients committed under magistrates' warrants are, to a certain extent, prisoners. They are not in the position of the ordinary lunatic, and the medical superintendent is bound to take care of them, and see that they don't make their escape. That is the reason

DUBLIN
Aug 5, 1878
Dr Frederick MacCabe.

why I say it would be well to place them eventually in Asylum A, where there is a large class of attendants.

2117. If these were removed from Class A, do you think you could confer any advantage on private patients who desire to avail themselves of the lunatic asylums?—I think so. I think if the suggestion I gather from the questions means the dividing of the county between three classes of asylums—Class A. The curative establishment, Class B. The intermediate asylum, and Class C. The workhouse asylum. I think you would have sufficient vacancies in Class A to take in the whole of the private cases.

2118. And you think that would be a great gain to the middle class, who are not rich enough to pay for a private asylum, and yet, although willing to pay, have no asylum to receive them?—Yes; not merely a matter of opinion, but it is within my knowledge for years, that one of the greatest wants in Ireland is a class of intermediate asylum, suited to private patients of moderate means.

2119. Do you mean a curative asylum for the intermediate or middle class?—Yes.

2120. Do you think that accommodation could be satisfactorily afforded by the removal of the large class, we speak of from district asylums?—I think so. If you take the number of patients now accommodated as private patients in Ireland, and if you take the amount of space which the re-arrangement of district asylums and the establishment of workhouse asylums would give, you cannot fail to see there would be ample accommodation.

2121. But do you think the character of the accommodation would be such as would be satisfactory to the families of that class?—I think it would. That is the result of my experience. I have had private patients in district asylums under my care, and I never heard or knew of their friends complaining of the treatment or the condition they were in.

2122. Your experience has not led you to suppose that the character of it, as an asylum to which poor people were admitted, would operate to prevent middle class people coming in?—No, I have had frequent applications from persons who were quite beyond the range of the county asylum. I think if that feeling existed in some, it would be counteracted by the feeling of others when they knew that the asylum was a place where they would have proper treatment.

2123. You think the number sent would break down the prejudice?—I think it would. I don't think any prejudice would be found. If you stated to-morrow that private patients would be received at such a rate per inmate, you would, I think, have applications coming in at once.

2124. Have you any experience of the extent and character of the lunatics at large, or the nature of their mental disease?—Not the slightest. I have never visited any of them. I think from what I have been able to gather from others, they appear to be weak-minded, quiet people.

2125. But you have no knowledge of them?—I have no personal knowledge of them.

2126. In the early part of your examination, you said you thought the removal of the lunatic class, and the re-classification or the re-appropriation of accommodation of workhouses, would provide sufficient infirmary accommodation for the ordinary wants of the Union?—Yes, in some workhouses.

2127. There is in nearly every Union good fever hospital accommodation?—Yes.

2128. And the appropriation of buildings, we have alluded to, would still leave a sufficiency of fever hospital accommodation. May I ask you, is there within your district, as a rule, separate provision made for the reception of small-pox cases?—As a rule, there is not. I should like to say, I think you must have misunderstood part of my answer before. I did not intend to say that the removal of lunatics from workhouses would always make sufficient hospital accommodation.

2129. Combined with the re-appropriation of accommodation within the house?—Even combined with that.

2130. Combined with the accommodation in another part of the house, into which some who are now in the infirmary might be transferred?—Yes. I think that might provide sufficient accommodation in some workhouses.

2131. Is there no regular and separate accommodation for small-pox patients in each Union?—Not in each, but in several of my workhouses there are sheds reserved for that purpose—for instance, at Cork and Middleton. We have sheds at other places that could be appropriated to that purpose.

2132. Do you consider it desirable that suitable sheds should be provided?—I think they should be in every workhouse.

2133. Looking at the schedule, and applying it with your experience of public buildings, do you think it a fair calculation of space to allow for these various classes?—I do.

2134. Both as a Poor Law Inspector, and as a professional man, that is a standard of accommodation you think might be reasonably insisted on, except in extraordinary emergencies, in all workhouses?—I think so.

2135. Is there any suggestion which you, from your experience, would desire to lay before the Commissioners in reference to any of the subjects about which we have been speaking?—The only suggestion I should like to make to the Commissioners would be this, that in carrying out their views, if they are carried out, it would be of great importance to see that in the first instance suitable cases are sent to the workhouse intermediate asylums.

Aug 5, 1878.
Dr Nugent.

JOHN NUGENT, Esq., M.D. examined.

2136. You are one of the Inspectors of asylums?—Yes.

2137. How long a time?—Over thirty years.

2138. You have a very intimate knowledge of the condition of the asylums in Ireland?—Well yes, I have had the opportunity at least.

2139. Is it not a fact that there has been constant, and continuous overcrowding of the lunatic asylums in Ireland?—Yes, it is in this way, and requires considerable explanation. If you take the original construction of asylums, and the number of patients for whom they were intended, there is not an asylum almost in Ireland that is not overcrowded with the exception of two or three, one of which I notice is Carlow, and the other Wexford; with the exception of these two, I believe they are all overcrowded beyond their normal capabilities; the result of which has been the conversion of rooms and apartments from purposes for which they were originally intended; and it would seem that Boards of Governors look upon the number they can accommodate so far as bedding is concerned, and if they can crowd into a house a large number of people, not giving them a sufficient quantity of atmospheric area, they put it down as accommodation, whereas with the increased number of these bedrooms and dormitories, as a necessary consequence, all the accessories of the establishment become overcrowded, for example, day-rooms, corridors, facilities for washing, water-closets, such not increasing *pari passu*, with the number of inmates.

2140. My question referred rather to the past?—That I presumed, and it was even stronger in the past, but it continues in the present.

2141. That is what I wished to ascertain, whether the building of asylums—the multiplication of them, if I might use the expression—was the result of the overcrowding which you have explained?—Originally, when the population of Ireland was over seven millions of inhabitants (about the year 1828), from that to 1833 or 1834, there were nine asylums built, and these were competent and capable of containing something under 1,000 patients. For five or six years those asylums were not filled; but as soon as people at large became aware of the benefits accruing from the proper treatment of lunatics, there was a greater pressure on lunatic asylums, and the result was that in many of the old asylums, as I said before, they converted rooms that were intended for workshops, and day-rooms, and recreation rooms into bedrooms, and they filled those bedrooms with patients, utterly indifferent as to their accommodation.

2142. The overcrowding, we gathered from the evidence of your colleague and from your own reports from time to time, has been in consequence of the number of incurable lunatics retained in the asylums?—Yes.

2143. Of the probably incurable?—The inference is very clear, if every case was a case of bodily disease the patient either succumbs or recovers, but it is totally different with mental disease, for out of the number attacked, forty will on the average remain uncured.

2144. Do you mean forty per cent?—Forty out of every 100, the result is that the asylums become filled with that class of patients, at the same time, I wish it to be understood as the result of my experience that these forty patients remaining incurable require the same treatment, the same care, the same anxious consideration as a general rule as those who have benefited by the treatment and were removed cured.

2145. In the various reports made from time to time by the Lunacy Inspectors it may be taken as generally represented that about seventy-five per cent. of the inmates of an asylum in any given month are of the class of probably incurable?—I should say about that fully.

2146. That is if we go into an asylum and there are 500 say in that asylum, what I understand you to say is that 380 will be incurable and 120 curable?—Oh, fully the former.

2147. Seventy-five per cent. is what I think was alleged, more than were in the reports published?—Yes. We always put it under in the reports, for I think in reporting it is better to understate than to exaggerate.

2148. It is frequently alleged in the reports that these cases are not suitable cases for asylum treatment?—Yes, for numbers, in consequence of the mode of committal of lunatics to asylums. In the first instance they are very often people who were insane for a considerable time, and they are sent in as dangerous lunatics. They are admitted as curable cases, consequently, the curability of the case may be associated with transmission to the asylum, because the physician who certifies always puts it down that "so and so is a fit subject for admission to an asylum, and is likely to derive benefit therefrom," though the party may be incurable; and it is in that way that asylums have lost, to a certain extent, their utility, inasmuch as persons are sent into asylums who have no hopes of recovery—persons who are utterly demented, quiet and tranquil. Very often, I regret to say, I find that so. I will produce a case in point. I was in Monaghan six or eight weeks ago. I was going round the asylum and two patients were brought in—brother and sister—as being insane, and on the certificate as likely to recover, and I said to the physician—Dr Robertson, a Scotch gentleman—"why that woman is not insane, it is the last stage of fever she is in—the delirium of fever is on her." I left that night, and I asked him to oblige me by telegraphing to me what way the woman was, and I had a telegram next day that she was dead. The brother was also labouring in the delirium of fever, but not to the same extent. He remained in the asylum and was then sent out. I adduce this to show that people are sent into asylums who are not insane or proper persons to be sent, and they, to a certain extent, fill the asylums. I have known old women of 70 sent in.

2149. As dangerous?—Yes; and I have known men turned 80 being sent in as dangerous, because they might have broken a pane of glass. It is the false system of transmitting lunatics, as *per se*, into lunatic asylums that has led to the overcrowding.

2150. That false system, as you call it, is of recent origin, I think?—With the increase of asylums, gentlemen in the country, when they see persons insane, say, "Here is a large building, and a fine building, we will send them to it," without examining particularly into the cases, and I think you, Major Trench, will recollect my bringing up instances, when the asylum at Ballinasloe was enlarged, some time ago. Application was made from a union—Glennamaddy—to our office, to remove eight or ten lunatics who were very bad, and ought to be sent to the asylum.

2151. Were they in the workhouse?—Yes, and I went down to Glennamaddy, and saw six or eight old people lying in their beds, one drinking a cup of tea, when I observed, "These are not subjects to be transferred, they are all decrepit, it would not do to fill an asylum with such people." They remained there, and, I suppose, died there.

2152. Have you many of that class in the asylums throughout Ireland?—I think there are. I think governors are beginning to glean now, they are more particular about the admissions. I believe it was at my suggestion the boards of governors entered into an arrangement with the boards of guardians that they will not take patients from the poorhouse into an asylum unless on the express condition that when called upon they would take them back when they cease to be troublesome.

2153. Have they any legal power to make that condition?—I think they have.

2154. Under what Act?—It is recognised by the Privy Council rules, as to the admission of patients into asylums. Of course they are bound to take a patient back when called on. If you look at the admission paper you will find the first portion of it is a statement of the name of the person, then the nature of the disease, then the signature of the clergyman or magistrate identifying the person, and then an engagement by their friends or relatives to remove them from the asylum when called upon.

2155. But we are not speaking of relatives or friends?—But we put the guardians who seek for admission naturally in the position of the friends or relatives, in fact they become stronger, for they are the responsible persons.

2156. They sign an undertaking to remove, on the ordinary form?—Yes.

2157. I understood you to say that asylums were beginning to get greatly crowded with inmates committed upon the dangerous lunatic form of warrant?—Over that we have no control, it being under an Act of Parliament.

2158. The asylums, since the commencement, have been overcrowded through that class of cases?—Through the instrumentality of that mode of committal.

2159. But as to the reason for forming new districts and building new asylums, was it not that the existing asylums were overcrowded and the necessity arose for additional accommodation?—Not only that they were overcrowded, but that the accommodation in them was not equal to the *bona fide* normal wants of them. We have reason to assume now—as the statistics of insanity are so clear, and beyond all doubt all through Europe, I think, and in no place are they better collected than in this country,—that in the population at large you will find so many persons fit to be placed under control.

2160. If in the asylums there is so large a proportion of probably incurable cases, would you think it desirable to remove them from asylums to any species of intermediate building?—There are certain classes I would remove, but remember this fact: an individual being in an asylum tranquil, well conducted, quiet—provided that man has a delusion, and provided the delusion is of such a character that it will condone any crime or offence he perpetrates—that man, if he is properly looked after, if he has a feeling there is a control on him, that he is watched, well fed, has

Dublin, May 8, 1878.

Dr Nugent.

proper and suitable employment; these will continue as a rule tranquil and in good bodily health I say it is essential that that man should be kept in an asylum, in nine cases out of ten, because you run a risk if you send him from the asylum of producing insanity a second time in an acute form; you destroy the tranquility of mind afterwards, and render the man, beyond yea or nay, a dangerous member of society.

2161 Dealing with such a case as that, would you have any objection to substitute *an* asylum for *the* asylum—a proper place?—If you make an intermediate asylum, and make that in every respect equivalent to the primitive asylum; if you establish an intermediate asylum for persons of the kind, giving them an acre of ground to every six or eight, and if you afford them all the facilities for employment, and all the attendance necessary to protect them, I think you will have a primitive asylum. The principle I go upon is this—I am only giving my honest opinion, the result of my experience, and what I conscientiously think good for society, and for the protection of the individual—I consider if you deprive a lunatic of his liberty and social enjoyment, and all the other *et ceteras* that belong to free man, you deteriorate his condition, and the party who deprives him of them is undoubtedly bound to look after his well being to the fullest extent. You cannot deteriorate the condition of a person who has been in an asylum for twelve or fourteen years. It is not morally right or christian-like subsequently to place him in a worse position than he occupied before.

2162 I remember being struck by a phrase of your own, used either at an inquiry or in one of your reports, that "provided the creature comforts of a large class of those who were in asylums were attended to properly, they might with advantage be removed to some establishment where they could be maintained at a cost of one-third less"?—Certainly, I thoroughly agree with you, and I adhere to that opinion still, that there is a class of people in lunatic asylums, who are utterly inert, whose mental condition is such that if they were served up with water, cabbage, or the best soup, would be incapable of appreciating the difference. If you meet the comforts of these people to such an extent that they are not deprived of anything reasonable, the question arises what should the Government do on a subject affecting the expenses of the country

2163. The hopelessly demented class?—Yes. You will see persons sitting quite inert. They will remain so until an attendant comes and takes them away I think it is wrong that a regular institution should be filled with that class of lunatics

2164. One may gather from you that you say there are three classes of patients?—Certainly.

2165 There is a class who are essentially of the curable description?—On whom you are operating to effect a cure.

2166. And therefore fit for an hospital for the treatment of mental diseases?—Precisely.

2167. There is then the second class who require vigilance and attention and care as to their personal cleanliness; and the third class—the demented class? —Yes

2168 For the first class of cases there could be no doubt an asylum should be retained as a curative establishment?—Yes.

2169 For the second class, do you think some intermediate building might be provided in which the care that you have so forcibly indicated as being necessary might be bestowed, the intermediate building to be apart from the curative asylum?—If you put them in a similar or the same position to what they were in before

2170 Not in the same position, but relatively in a similar position?—Then you do it on the principle of economy and very naturally.

2171. Not altogether on the principle of economy; I did not mean to suggest that to you?—But the principle of economy has always been strong in my mind in the treatment of lunacy I never disintegrate from my mind that the taxation of the country should be as limited as is consistent with propriety in the maintenance of these cases

2172. Suppose you have three asylums, and a certain number, say, of the first class in one of them, and in the other two a certain number of the same class, and suppose you have in each of these asylums a certain number of the middle class for whom special care is necessary, and you have a certain number of the third class—the hopelessly demented class—would it be practicable to draft all the curable cases to one asylum, reserving the second or the second and third for the middle class, giving to them that care and attention which is necessary, but more economically administered than in the curative establishment, and transferring the third class or hopelessly demented to an intermediate asylum?—Well, if you ask me my opinion, I honestly tell you I would only have two asylums altogether—one for utterly demented, and for epileptic idiots I think it would be essential that in the regularly constituted asylum you should have persons who are tranquil and quiet for the reasons I have given Then there is on the principle of economy a very important consideration, and that is that the class of people who are not the curable class are really the working class in the asylum, and it is they who lower the expenses. We will take women—women of that class are employed in the laundries, in the corridors, and in knitting, and sewing Similarly with regard to the men if you have fifty or sixty acres of ground. If we are to endeavour to make these asylums self-supporting you may do it through the tranquil lunatics, and if you have not that class, you must employ persons to cultivate the ground, and to perform those menial duties which the quiet perform I have been for upwards of 30 years on terms of intimacy with the lunatics, and I have been in the habit of addressing them by their christian names. I have often said to one of them, "Where is poor so and so," and I have been told, "Oh he has broken out in the most terrific fashion He has nearly killed a man. Here he is in the wildest state of delirium." So that if you removed that man and others of the same sort, you should have a sort of railway communication to bring them backward and forward. I think that proper treatment consists in quietness and reasonable enjoyments.

2173 But above that class necessary to discharge the household duties of a large establishment are there not a considerable number besides who might properly be removed to this separate class of asylums?—Yes, I have always corrected myself by saying there is such a class—the utterly demented

2174 That is the third class, but you would not think is advisable to have any asylum between the auxiliary asylum for the demented class, and the curative establishment?—No.

2175. What is the objection to that?—First, I am sure you would deteriorate the condition of the persons by removing them, and secondly on the ground of economy, I believe it is more economic to have them all in one asylum.

2176 With reference to the first, we will take, as an illustration, an asylum that has given some trouble to arrange, or trying to arrange—the Londonderry Asylum Suppose that instead of building a new asylum at Derry, you were to take that asylum and to remove the class of probably incurable cases, (the second class cases) into that asylum and remove the curable cases from Londonderry to Monaghan or Omagh. or any other curative establishment, retaining Derry as the asylum for that second class, what would be the objection?—I see a very strong objection, first and foremost as to removing the patients. Take Derry as the Asylum, you have there an asylum built for 109 patients, you have 270 patients in it; you have, in Derry, a stone rolling up the hill, for you have to roll it against public opinion; you have five or six acres of ground about the place, you have the worst constructed house for a curative establishment, you have

DUBLIN Aug. 1, 1878.

Mr. Nugent.

a kitchen for 270 people not more than two-thirds of the size of this room, you have not the materials at Derry for making anything of it, consequently you must go elsewhere, and then the question arises what is the best to be done? Isn't it better to build an asylum for the whole county, instead of sending patients elsewhere?

2177. Now take any other asylum. There the asylum is obviously unfit for curative purposes?—Or for any purpose at all.

2178. You would not accept Derry for a limited number of that second class of patients?—No.

2179. You would not allow this 109 to be placed in it?—No.

2180. On what ground?—I think if you want to keep 109 in it, there is no facility, according to modern improvements, for the maintenance of that number there.

2181. Not for the maintenance of 100 patients of that class where their creature comforts could be attended to, you would not accept Derry as an asylum suitable for that purpose?—Not to the denial of the building of a public institution for the county.

2182. The question was not with the view of avoiding building but was simply as an illustration. Have you any objection to putting 109 idiots of the demented epileptics or of that class into it?—I would have no objection.

2183. But you object to have it as an asylum for any class?—Except the third class.

2184. Take Richmond Asylum and convert that into a curative establishment, transferring the incurable cases from Richmond to the nearest asylum, say Carlow or Mullingar?—You can't do that, if you transfer them to Carlow or Mullingar, you will have to build.

2185. Would that be the only objection?—That would be one. I see great difficulties in the way; you are removing them out of their own county.

2186. Without reference to the amount of accommodation, would there be any objection in principle to making that redistribution of asylums?—I have gone over Richmond Asylum very minutely with the physicians. There are in that asylum 1,070 patients; I have asked Dr. Lalor and Dr. Banks, how many men in this asylum do you think could be removed from it, and they said five or six per cent. to an ordinary workhouse.

2187. Removed to where?—They say with the exception of five or six per cent. the rest of the patients would require the same careful treatment and looking after, the same amount of employment no matter where they went.

2188. Is that the opinion of Dr. Lalor?—I believe so.

2189. That only five or six per cent. could be removed to any intermediate asylum?—If the intermediate asylum has all the comforts, all the advantages, and all the facilities of employment, that are in the primary asylum; of course if the ratepayers or the Government insist to do it, I could not raise an objection to any number being so removed.

2190. But suppose Carlow was absolutely empty, and that you had an opportunity of transferring to Carlow the probably incurable lunatics of the second class, would you think that a desirable arrangement to make?—To a certain extent, I might.

2191. To what extent?—Provided it was not to the detriment of the employment.

2192. Would it be to the detriment?—I think it would.

2193. In what respect?—I think the men employed there, with the exception of sixty or eighty patients, are all employed beneficially in some way or other, or if they are not, the nature of their malady is such as to require constant care and watching.

2194. Then seventy-five per cent. of the lunatics in asylums in Ireland, being of the class that is probably incurable, can you make any suggestion besides building new asylums or enlarging existing asylums at an enormous cost, for relieving asylums from that condition?—Yes, I have been always thoroughly impressed with the conviction that there are persons in asylums who could be maintained one-third cheaper elsewhere, consequently what I would do with cases like that—I think it highly inexpedient, that of all the poorhouses in Ireland, one poorhouse in a district should not be allocated to this class of persons and then you have an asylum provided, there is ground enough attached to it for the idiots and thoroughly demented.

2195. But suppose you had that accommodation provided in connexion with poorhouses or in suitable buildings. Do you think sufficient relief could be afforded to the asylums by finding accommodation elsewhere so as to leave asylums to be as nearly as possible curative establishments?—I think so.

2196. In well organized districts?—In Mullingar I think there is ample. In Sligo too there is ample. Belfast asylum I don't think is suitable for the requirements of the borough and district. After fifteen years battling and contesting with the Derry Board I think it is an injury to the city of Derry, and a greater one to the lunatics of the county, to have such an establishment there, because a curative asylum could be built a couple of miles off, which would be better for the district at large.

2197. Suppose proper accommodation was provided elsewhere for the demented class, you don't think that would be sufficient to accommodate the others?—No.

2198. There is a very intelligent physician connected with the Belfast asylum, and in discussing the question with him, as we are here, he said he had reason to know that many of the gentry were thoroughly of opinion that for such a town as Belfast the asylum was too small?—There are very few in that asylum you could remove out of it. I don't think there are twenty patients in Belfast asylum that could be removed.

2199. Would that be the opinion of the Board of Governors?—I think the Board of Governors of the Borough of Belfast would be very glad to be relieved by having a few of them removed.

2200. Is it not a fact that a few years ago it was by the consent of the Lunacy Inspectors, the Governors at Belfast, and the Board of Guardians of the Ballymena Union that about 120 lunatics might be transferred from Belfast to that Workhouse?—There was only accommodation provided for thirty. I am now speaking as to a matter of fact, there were not more than thirty or forty. A very extraordinary fact connected with the district is that the Board of Governors of Belfast object to send them away, and many of the Guardians object to have them in the house.

2201. Speaking of Ballymena and Belfast is it not a fact that the Governors themselves considered that they were not fairly treated in having the scheme provided, and then allowed to fall to the ground?—They allowed it to fall to the ground themselves. An Act of Parliament which was passed when you, Major Trench, were Secretary to Sir Michael Hicks Beach, was to the effect that when lunatics were transferred from workhouses to asylums with the sanction of the Inspectors and the Local Government Board, and by arrangement come to between the Governors of the asylum and the Guardians of the poorhouse, they would be paid for, but there were not a dozen cases in Ireland, although we have given our full approval of the matter.

2202. Is it not a fact that provision could have been made in Ballymena workhouse with the consent of the Governors, with the consent of the Lunacy Inspectors, and with the approval of the Inspector of the Local Government Board for that district for the transfer of 120 lunatics from Belfast to Ballymena, and that a difficulty raised by the Local Government Board prevented that being carried out, but in principle it was carried out. An architect, Mr. Lanyon from Belfast, made plans which were approved by you and sanctioned by the Governors, and owing to the difficulty with the Local Government Board it was not carried out?—Yes, but I think the whole expenses of the thing is represented as £120.

2203. No, the accommodation was for 120 inmates?

Dublin. Aug. 5, 1878. — Dr. Nugent.

—They prepared originally a plan and sent in a bill to us for £240 for putting up baths and other requisites. It was sent to the Board of Control, and we said let the Local Government Board arrange with the Guardians; we have nothing to say to it.

2204. At all events you approved of the transfer of 120 lunatics?—No, excuse me, I was always against it. We approved on principle of this, that if the medical man was not against it, and if the Board of Governors on one hand, and the Guardians on the other consented, we should make no objection.

2205. But did not the Lunacy Inspectors give their consent to sending 120 lunatics from Belfast to Ballymena?—Oh never.

2206. You would not object to this classification of asylums, to appropriate one asylum for curative cases, and the other or two others for the reception of the middle class (we will call it) of lunatics from that asylum?—The view I would wish to press on that point is that I go on the principle that there are persons in lunatic asylums who could be as well treated without injury to them, and that at one third less, elsewhere. As far as my experience goes it would be quite a mistake to assume that although there are only forty curable cases, with forty cases of tranquil patients, that these forty tranquil cases could be sent out. That must be left to the judgment and discretion of the physicians of the asylums. Then there is another class of patients—the demented and utterly hopeless cases—who can be looked after very well in the secondary asylums.

2207. Take the judgment and discretion of the medical superintendent, and suppose Dr. Lalor told you there are fifty persons who might very well be transferred to Kilkenny or Mullingar, leaving Richmond Asylum for purely curative purposes?—But surely Kilkenny and Mullingar are much better as curative asylums, being of recent construction.

2208. That is beside the question; what we wish is to ascertain your opinion as to whether supposing the Richmond Asylum was devoted purely as a curative hospital for the insane, retaining there only such a staff of incurables as would be necessary for the service of the institution, its benefits as a curative asylum would not be much increased?—No.

2209. You think that the curative capabilities of that asylum are not deteriorated by its being overcrowded by incurable cases?—No, certainly not.

2210. You think the presence of a large proportion of incurable cases taking up a large amount of valuable space deteriorates in no way the chances of recovery of curable cases?—No, for the more curable cases you have to diffuse amongst quiet incurable cases the better for the former.

2211. Suppose a certain number of quiet incurable cases were kept in that Richmond Asylum, who would be able to do the work of the establishment in the manner you speak of, and that it was proposed to transfer the violent cases, who are incurable, to Mullingar or some other asylum, would you see any objection to such transfer?—If you send them to Mullingar, and they are as well looked after, I would have no objection. They would be almost better looked after at Mullingar, because it is more spacious.

2212. You said just now that you thought the transfer of this class of incurables—this second class that requires more special care and attention—to an intermediate asylum would deteriorate their condition; why do you come to that conclusion?—Because if they had not all the comforts they had before——

2213. But we are assuming they should still have all necessary comforts. The proposal is to re-classify your patients simply? Suppose you sent them from asylum A which is crowded, and suppose there are in that asylum A 190 patients—60 curable, 60 in *statu pupillari*, that you cannot pronounce idiotic or demented, then there are 70 who are doubtful—they form class D we will say. In that class we will put the epileptic incurables—persons who had previously intellects, but had become demented from old age, &c.——

2214. Suppose we group all those into one class and call them the B class of incurables?—That class of incurables—idiotic incurables—who require far more caution, and who are more dangerous to themselves, I would not remove.

2215. That class B of incurables you would not remove to workhouse auxiliaries?—No.

2216. You would prefer to transfer them to such an asylum as Mullingar?—What is the use of transferring them. I would keep them where they are. I see a parcel of idiots who would murder you or anybody else if they had a chance. Take the epileptic sitting quietly at table, walking about for two months perfectly tranquil, perfectly amenable, in his senses an educated man; he gets a sudden attack of insane epilepsy, and he murders the man next him, or perhaps himself. Therefore, the appearance of that individual in an asylum is morally and physically speaking no criterion by which to judge him or to say I will remove that man merely because he is tranquil, and so I say that the utmost care and caution are required for tranquil well conducted epileptics who are subject to sudden attacks. Well, there is a man who, although imbecile and epileptic, I would keep in the very best constructed asylum. Then there are idiots who are very violent and very dangerous; I would keep them in the primitive asylum. Then there are demented people who have delusions of that fixed nature, who are utterly demented; these are persons who require, though they are idiots, that constant supervision for their own safety, and if you go into an asylum and ask A, B, or C, he will say "Look at that poor creature; he is the most dangerous patient here. Don't go near him."

2217. Is not the treatment of these cases subject to the discretion of the medical superintendent?—Precisely, and you go to him and ask him how many of these would he conscientiously allow to leave the asylum, or to leave the care and attention that they are now subject to and the kindly treatment. How many of them could he safely remove from the asylum? I will put the issue on that as regards the medical men of Ireland, and as regards this institution it will depend, I should say, upon what they report.

2218. But suppose the medical superintendent of a District Asylum thinks his asylum could be rendered purely a curative establishment, such as you seem to have been aiming at all your life?—I don't think there are many curative cases. I think these asylums would be enough if slightly eased——

2219. The point we want to come to is the practicability of classifying asylums, and to ascertain whether great benefits cannot be gained by such classification. First, to the curable cases, by bringing them together in the early stages in purely curative establishments, associating them therein only with such other classes of lunatics as may be deemed desirable for a curative treatment, and next, by the drafting into intermediate asylums those cases requiring special care of which you have just been speaking—asylums in which they would have every care, and in which the existing machinery would still be available for their constant employment, but in which they might be maintained more economically than in the curative hospitals. The question is whether the classification could or could not be carried out, and if not we want to see what your objection to it would be?—I have no objection. If you make intermediate asylums, and make them on a par with the primitive asylums, I have no objection.

2220. Giving to the inmates such comforts as they could appreciate, and putting them under such care as would meet any sudden outburst?—I see no objection.

2221. Do you think it would be desirable to give to whatever authority might exist for the supervision of lunacy, the legislative power to classify lunatic asylums?—I think it would be very judicious to do so.

2222. And if such a power existed, do you think the lunacy inspectors would avail themselves, to a considerable extent, of it?—Certainly.

Dublin, Aug. 8, 1878.

Dr. Nugent.

2223. And possibly some asylums may have an excess of incurable cases from want of such a power?—Not only may have an excess, but, positively, have an excess from want of such a power. No doubt all the kindly feelings creditable to human nature were enlisted on the part of the executive and legislature; but Acts of Parliament prepared by lawyers, however *legally* well-worded and definite, could not be up to the mark.

2224. But giving this power and leaving it to the discretion of the board, would it be useful?—Certainly. By doing that you arrive at the great point.

2225. We have arrived at the conclusion that it would be desirable to give the power?—I think it is most unsatisfactory. Nothing could be more ridiculous or improper than having one person coming up and forcing another into a lunatic asylum. Two magistrates are sitting together, a complainant comes up: "This woman is a desperate woman, she swore she would kill her children," and may be she has had the misfortune to break a pane of glass. A doctor called in certifies "That she would be benefited by being sent to an asylum."

2226. Before the power was given it was a subject of constant complaint in your reports?—That was as to cases sent in from gaols as dangerous. To classify the asylums and reserve to the proper authorities the mode of doing that, you think would be the best organization of lunacy administration that could be obtained?—Yes; the impression on my mind, for many years, has been so. I consider that the public at large were awfully mulcted, from sending individuals to asylums and maintaining them there at £24, when they could be as well taken care of for £14 or £16. That is the real point—combining economy with the utmost idea of benevolence, and it is the worst thing you could do to make these costs excessive.

2227. Do you think that the power of classifying lunatic asylums, if it was given by legislation, and the making of provision of a nature that I shall call your attention to just now, would, in point of fact, prevent the building of lunatic asylums upon the same scale as they have been built upon for the last thirty years?—I think it would, to a very considerable extent, but there is another point which is a necessity, so far as I am able to form an opinion. Every district, whether it contains one county or two counties, should have, *in limine*, a well organized asylum.

2228. A curative asylum?—A regularly well-constructed curative asylum, such as you see in England, Wales, and Scotland, and that that asylum should be, as far as possible, made from the necessities of the case, to receive curable cases and cases which, if they were not under proper surveillance might prove dangerous to society at large and to themselves. Then you will see there is a large class of the community who are insane, and who might be located elsewhere at a less rate, and the only issue between us is on the question of two intermediate asylums. I would have a primitive asylum, and I would have a drafting asylum, into which cases could be removed from the primitive asylum when they became *effete* and unable to move about or be useful.

2229. You pass them through your primary asylum into a second asylum?—Yes, and get rid of one class as the wave of the other comes in.

2230. The condition of lunatics in workhouses you know a good deal about, and you have condemned it very strongly in some of your reports?—Yes.

2231. Do you think it would be practicable, and if practicable, that it would be advantageous, to collect the lunatics from the several workhouses in a county and remove them to some portion of one workhouse selected for the purpose?—I rather think it would be beneficial. I think they would be under more central control.

2232. Here is a ground plan of Monaghan workhouse. A portion of it it is proposed to convert into an asylum for 50 men, and it is proposed to take this wing of the house, giving a large airing court, and to convert that into a similar establishment for 50 women, completely shut off from the workhouse itself?—Would they give up that portion of the workhouse, for there are not more than five or six in Monaghan, and only one in Clones, I think.

2233. The question is whether you would give your approval to such an arrangement?—Without reference to any particular asylum, I have always been of opinion that in every district in Ireland, as an alleviation to the original asylum, that the poor should be under the same roof. As far as I can judge of the Monaghan asylum, it is very well circumstanced—Monaghan and Cavan.

2234. And suppose Monaghan was arranged for 50 males and 50 females, I dare say there are a few in the Monaghan asylum that could be transferred?—Very few, I think. Dr Robertson told me he did not think there were eight or ten he could recommend to be removed. In principle, I thoroughly agree with that. In Kilkenny there is a workhouse at a place called Callan. Well, twenty years ago I asked the board to utilize the building there. It is an almost uninhabited workhouse, that could accommodate over 100 patients, with plenty of ground.

2235. Where would you find 200 patients—from Kilkenny?—No. I daresay there are about forty or fifty in the Poorhouse of Kilkenny, and I think there are five or six in Callan, seven or eight at Thomastown, and there were six at Castlecomer.

2236. For those establishments, more or less not precisely workhouses but auxiliary lunatic asylums, would you think it desirable that some different supervision should be exercised than over the workhouses?—Certainly.

2237. What sort of supervision would you substitute in lieu of the Board of Governors, would you think a committee analogous to the dispensary committee desirable?—I think in such a place as Monaghan you might very well leave it to the local governors.

2238. Would not you associate with them some of the Board of Governors?—There are generally a couple of local guardians on the Board of Governors.

2239. Suppose this power of classifying lunatic asylums was in existence, and these auxiliary asylums in workhouses were created, and a certain class of asylums were retained for curative purposes only, do you think some organization of the central department as existing at present, would be efficient in dealing with that new organisation of lunatic asylums throughout Ireland?—Certainly, it should be more definite than at present.

2240. You think that no new organization of the department would be necessary?—Certainly not; under the Act of Parliament the inspectors are to visit every union in Ireland in which there are lunatics, and it would naturally alleviate their trouble if they had them in one poorhouse in the district.

2241. But, suppose the inspectors were relieved altogether from the duty of inspecting, and had simply the administrative duties to perform, would that be advantageous?—I think if the inspectors did not saw the asylums would go to the bad in six months. When I came to be connected with the lunatic institutions of the country there were 2,500 lunatics under treatment. I have lived to see accommodation for 8,600, and I undertake to say that the 8,600 are principally owing to personal exertions with the Boards of Governors, and I could not undertake that without being personally cognizant of the requirements. I think two inspectors are quite enough to visit the asylums in Ireland.

2242. And would be quite enough to visit all the intermediate asylums as well?—Yes, quite able.

2243. Don't you think such an institution would require a greater amount of visiting than the present institutions?—The Lunacy Commissioners in England only go once, and we go four times.

2244. Don't you think these subsidiary institutions would require a good deal of inspection to keep them up to the mark?—I have reason to believe the insane are treated with great kindness in workhouses. I

DUBLIN.
Aug. 4, 1875.
Dr. Nugent.

think as far as the limited capabilities of the workhouse admit they are so treated.

2245. They are left altogether to the physicians who have authority to order them what they think fit, and if there is any deficiency it is a fault on the part of the medical man?—I don't think there is any.

2246. And you think the system of treatment is satisfactory?—I do. I think the Local Government Board have endeavoured all through to administer to their comforts as far as the law gives them power. Take for example Loughlinstown poorhouse. It is a gratification to look at it. There they are admirably fed and well taken care of. I have often met patients in that house, and knowing them very well, I have said "would you rather be here than at the asylum," and they would say they would rather be there, because they wish to associate with people who have reason.

2247. Still people who have reason don't like to associate with them?—Yet that is a reason. The man knows he is insane, and he likes to associate with those who are sane. Sometimes on visiting these poorhouses I write reports when I see any necessity, but I think, as a general rule, they are very well looked after.

2248. You are not able yearly to visit every workhouse?—No; neither are they in England.

2249. Do you know what are called cells in poorhouses?—They are very bad. They are doing away with them in a great measure.

2250. But you don't approve of them?—No; and it is upon that broad principle that I would like to see that class congregated together in a large district, because they would be better looked after and have paid attendants.

2251. What knowledge have you of the lunatics at large?—I think that is a myth to a very great extent. I think the number is exaggerated.

2252. Do you not think some means ought to be taken to obtain more accurate information concerning their condition?—In my own county (the county Kilkenny) I am setting on foot, through the clergymen and through the doctors, a movement to let me know the different parties in their localities who are really insane. The way we have obtained the information hitherto was through the Constabulary. The extraordinary thing that shook my confidence was that every year they came to nearly the same point, and I tested it. I sent you a return of the persons supposed to be insane on the Clancarty property for you to make inquiries about it. I sent the same to Cavan, and I was informed that some of them are ideal—some of them got 10s. a week for working. They are weak minded, but many are at work every day.

2253. Could you suggest any means of obtaining better information as to that class, to enable them to be dealt with in a manner beneficial to themselves and to the community?—I think you wrote to me about that and I think I suggested that the wisest plan would be to get the doctors immediately under the Poor Law Board to send in from their different districts their own returns.

2254. The dispensary doctors?—Yes.

2255. Then you think it desirable that better information should be obtained?—As an interesting and practical fact it would.

2256. In England you are aware every district medical officer is bound to visit periodically every lunatic pauper, and to make a return in a prescribed form that he is properly treated if he is so. But that only applies to lunatic paupers. Do you think it should be rendered obligatory on dispensary doctors to visit every person of unsound mind and to make periodical reports?—I think it would be a very desirable step if the Local Government Board wrote to every medical man all through Ireland in the different dispensary districts to state *bona fide* who in his district was a lunatic, the name and age, and to ascertain what was the character of the insanity.

2257. And whether he was well treated or neglected?—Well I don't think they are ill treated in this country.

2258. Not ill-treated, but a great many of them are neglected. I could take you to some in the city of Dublin who are grossly neglected?—Perhaps you could get twenty or thirty there, but it would be better to get the returns fixed all over Ireland, and to get the medical officer to find the name of each individual.

2259. The question applies rather to dealing permanently with that class who are at large, not merely for the purpose of ascertaining the number?—In England they have the power, here they have not.

2260. That is only as to pauper lunatics, I speak of the lunatics at large who are not paupers?—I don't know how you could deal with them.

2261. You have no suggestion to offer about that?—No, if they are non paupers I don't see what you can do with them against the wish of their family.

2262. You have spoken in approval of the way in which lunatics are treated in the workhouses?—As a general rule.

2263. In the North Dublin Union they are very kindly treated?—Oh, very.

2264. Do you think the accommodation there suitable?—No.

2265. Do you know the "madman's lock?"—I know it well. They are well fed.

2266. Do you know the cells in the madman's lock?—Yes.

2267. Are they not very objectionable?—Yes. I am anxious in any way to extend as far as possible the accommodation for the demented idiots and epileptics, and I think that would be best affected by allocating a whole poor-house for that class, and the larger you have the house the more you can draft in of outsiders.

2268. But you cannot suggest any means of coming at the outside class?—No.

2269. They have no separate yards for these classes?—No, but they have a sort of airing ground.

2270. Not for each sex?—The women use it at one time and the men at another. There are very nice walks in a grassy field.

2271. Suppose the asylums could be relieved in the way proposed—by classification of the utterly demented class and the class immediately above them—do you think any facility would be afforded by that means for giving the advantage of asylum treatment to private paying patients of the middle class?—There is an asylum now nearly built near Dublin. That is the idiots' asylum. That asylum is raised very little in price above the ordinary lunatic asylum expenses, which will be say £26. You would not take persons into an asylum under £26 or £28, and my opinion is you ought to charge them £30. At this asylum they take them in at £40, but there are very few of that middle class in Ireland. You have not in Ireland what is in England and Wales, the same well-to-do intermediate middle class.

2272. Still there is a concurrence of testimony that it would be desirable to afford this accommodation?—They are gradually increasing. The best proof of it is that last year we got from paying patients in district asylums £3,400, and the year before only £1,800, so that they are gradually coming into it, and I am sure in the year we admit twenty or thirty paying patients to the asylums.

2273. But do you think paying patients have been prevented from coming in through the overcrowding of the establishments?—The rule is this—that no paying patient is admitted unless there is a margin of vacancies, and he is admitted on the condition that as soon as his bed becomes requisite he must be removed. The way in which they are admitted is by application to the Board of Governors, and they are not admitted without the sanction of the inspectors.

2274. Do you think if these asylums were re-classified in the manner already indicated and that some of the hospital wards in the first class, or curative establishments, could be set apart for the reception of patients whose friends are willing to pay, that you would thereby be enabled to meet a want largely felt?—I think it would in England, but it is not congenial to the feelings of the Irish.

DUBLIN, Aug. [illegible]

Dr Nugent.

2275. Do you mean that they are unwilling to pay?—Yes They say that "If we go into a public asylum, why go in with the disgrace, while we are paying," so they go in and don't pay.

2276. But if they are able to pay, should they not be made to pay?—Well, but that is a very hard case. I was asked that question in the House of Commons. There was one gentleman whom I knew, and he asked me, "Don't you think it is right they should pay?" Well, I said, I know several of your tenants who have a beneficial interest under you of £100 Well, suppose that man has a wife and three or four children, he has been for 20 or 30 years paying for the maintainance of the asylum, and would it not be an unfair thing that that man and his family, who have been paying for the support of the asylum, should (if his child becomes insane) be called upon to pay for one child £20 a-year.

Sir DOMINIC CORRIGAN, Bart, M.D., examined.

Sir Dominic Corrigan.

2277 You were upon the Commission appointed to inquire into the Lunacy Question in Ireland in 1857?—Yes

2278. The report they presented met with your full assent?—Yes, the only part I differed from was that about the physicians

2279. We have now to deal with the provision made for the care and treatment of lunatics, and more especially with the accommodation provided. In your report you very strongly condemned the accommodation as at that time provided in the workhouses?—Yes.

2280. You are aware that some of your recommendations were not acted upon, and that the accommodation in workhouses is much the same now as then?—O'Connell used to say · "If it took twenty-one years to do nothing, how long would it take to do anything."

2281. Among your recommendations was one that workhouse asylums or wards should be established, and that it should be competent to any Board of Governors of asylums after the establishment of such wards to direct any person of the hopelessly insane class to be transferred thereto?—Yes.

2282. We have carefully examined all the workhouses in Ireland, and we are prepared to make recommendations not merely in the abstract as to the desirability of establishing such wards, but we propose submitting a scheme pointing out the actual buildings that can be appropriated for the purpose. We have had some of these examined by an architect and plans made of the alterations necessary to suit them for the accommodation of lunatics of the class referred to This is the plan of one of these buildings—of a detached building at Lisburn workhouse (map produced) which we propose to appropriate. Will you kindly look into the arrangements proposed and say if you think them suitable?—There could be no objection to that.

2283. It, in fact, carries out in detail a recommendation you made in 1857?—We are both going in the same groove.

2284 There is in every district in Ireland a certain number of workhouses that have wings. Without accumulating lunatics in any one of these, might they not be distributed in fifties and sixties instead of being scattered in threes and fours, and being in some cases grossly neglected?—I concur in your view entirely.

2285. We allude to lunatics very many of whom are at present badly housed in various workhouses throughout the country, numbering over 3,000. At the time your commission sat they numbered about 1,700, so that there is now nearly double the number with the same accommodation. So far as the workhouses are concerned, you approve of the scheme?—Certainly.

2286 The inmates of the lunatic asylums proper, then, may be divided into two classes: those under "curative treatment," those who are designated as the "probable incurable;" the latter class forming the large majority, seventy-five per cent. This latter class may be subdivided into two classes, viz, those who are subject to paroxysms of violence and who require special care and treatment?—They are generally epileptic

2287. Yes, and those who are very much of the same class, as we find in the workhouse, i e, cases that are harmless to themselves and to others, and past all hope of cure?—Yes.

2288. When you had the subject before you in 1857, you found the asylums much crowded with these latter classes, and I think you went so far as to recommend that special accommodation should be provided for them?—Yes

2289. At that time there appears to have been a proposal afloat, that accommodation should be provided out of the District Asylums for the whole of the class of incurables, and that proposal did not meet with your approval, I see here you are of opinion that as far as possible all cases except those who are imbecile, and hopeless and completely harmless, should be treated in *District Asylums* We have a proposal before us to classify these District Asylums. Would you see any objection to, as it were, re-classify the asylums, say in one district where there are three asylums—make A an asylum, or rather an hospital, for the treatment of curable cases where the undivided attention of the medical staff and others could be given to the curable cases in their early stages, and make the other two district asylums, B and C, available for the "probable incurable," or chronic cases, of the class that you stated you would wish to keep in the district asylums, and for whom you might not consider the expensive paraphernalia of a curative hospital necessary; this classification of the district asylums, with the addition of the workhouse auxiliary, would give us three classes of asylums in every district, one is for recent cases that are presumed to be curable, the workhouse auxiliary for imbeciles and the other for epileptics or dangerous?—Yes, these require special care and treatment.

2290. These asylums connected with workhouses should be for the hopelessly demented, quite harmless imbeciles?—That I quite approve.

2291. That the district asylums should be so classified as to appropriate one for curable cases, and retain the other for a section of the seventy-five per cent which is about the proportion we find in the several asylums of incurable cases?—Yes, but not imbeciles.

2292. We may assume that you have three classes to deal with; the curable class you would leave in the curative hospitals; another class which requires nearly the same vigilance and personal attention in the other district asylums; and you have a third class who might be removed into these workhouse auxiliary asylums. The suggestions we are making is to so classify the asylums as to make a sufficient number of curative asylums throughout Ireland, and to distribute the other two classes?—I think that would be most desirable.

2293. The two inspectors assented to that as a very desirable arrangement to make they were apparently not aware they had power to classify asylums in that way?—Well, I think we agree that the classification is most desirable No. 1 we call recent or curable cases, No. 2 are violent cases, or those requiring special care, but not fit subjects for a curative treatment. Then all the third class are imbeciles.

2294 The third being fed, so to speak, from the workhouse and the overflow of the asylums?—Oh, yes.

2295. Then there is another class that was brought under your notice in 1857, and that is the class of lunatics "at large" You made a recommendation in connection with them?—That the Irish Law should be assimilated to the 16th and 17th Victoria, cap 97 With respect to those cases, which would give the constabulary and the police power to arrest and bring before the magistrates every person wandering at large and deemed to be a lunatic, and that every justice of

DUBLIN.
Aug. 8, 1878.
Sir Dominic Corrigan.

the peace should have power on sworn information on having such person brought before him to have such person placed in asylum for treatment

2296. Nothing was done on that recommendation at all?—Nothing. I think in giving any power to the police it would be well to take measures that the power should be exercised carefully indeed. For instance, in the suburb to which I frequently go at present there are two or three lunatics in the town who are not an annoyance to anybody. They stand there with their backs to the wall until they get something to eat.

2297. Would you think it desirable to give the police any jurisdiction at all, or would you think it more desirable to bring these lunatics, as a class, under surveillance so far as visiting and reporting to the medical gentlemen of the different dispensaries?—I would be very chary about giving the police any power.

2298. You would probably think it better to give the power to the dispensary medical officer?—I would not give him the initiative power either.

2299. But make it his duty to report whether they are properly cared for, and have some power to deal with them if they were neglected or ill treated?—I would give him power to report cases to the sessions or magistrates. I think it might make the police unpopular. Some might be too meddling, and some might do nothing at all. On the whole, I would keep the police out of it.

2300. Would you approve of applying the principle of the English law to the case of the lunatics at large in Ireland? Under the English law, as you are aware, every pauper lunatic is visited periodically by the medical officer of the district who makes a report on the prescribed form, stating whether the lunatic is properly cared for or is neglected or ill treated. Upon that report being received by the Local Government Board if it is that the lunatic is not neglected he is not interfered with; but if the report be unfavourable, the lunatic is, if necessary, removed to an asylum, or steps are taken to see that he is properly taken care of. In Ireland there is no means of knowing whether the lunatics at large, amounting to 3,000, are neglected or ill treated. We have visited several cases where there was no doubt they were grossly neglected. The poor creatures were in the most abject state of dirt and filth, and in such a condition that there could be no question about the propriety of interfering with them. If that be the case with a considerable number, the question arises what machinery you would put in motion for their protection. Not the police, you say, but then there appears to be no means between the police and the dispensary officer. The relieving officer would not be a competent or proper person to give an opinion on the subject. If a list was furnished to the dispensary officer and it was obligatory on him to visit twice a year and report, he should receive a fee for it. You would then have security that every lunatic was visited by a competent person, and from his acquaintance with the people in the district, you would have security that these people were visited, and, if necessary, cared for?—Who would be the authority to take the initiative?

2301. The list of reputed lunatics would be furnished as at present by the constabulary; the constabulary are a sufficient machinery to obtain the names and addresses of all reputed lunatics, and that list would simply be returned to the dispensary officer; a list of the persons it would be his duty to visit. At present the constabulary make out a list for the Lunacy Inspectors, they give the name and address, the age, and the class to which they belong, of every lunatic in Ireland. If they were to make that return to a responsible officer who would make a report and visit them twice a year, you would have ample proof that the person was looked after?—And the duty of the police would not go further than that?

2302. The duty of the police would be to start them, and once the thing was started it would be all in the hands of the dispensary medical officer?—I see no objection whatever to giving the police that power.

2303. To give the names?—To give them and not to go further.

2304. But seeing there is so large a number of lunatics at large, and that they are of various classes in different degrees of insanity and some of them in a very abject state of neglect, and some of them possibly ill treated, don't you think some means of ascertaining whether these people are properly cared for, should be devised?—I think you have suggested that already.

2305. It is suggested rather with a view to ascertain how far it meets your approval?—I think it does.

2306. I don't know whether you could suggest any better means of protecting these people?—Your suggestion as you have explained it, seems to be very good and as much as you could do.

2307. From that class probably the inmates of the asylums would be recruited on the certificate of the medical officer. Now, with regard to the management and administration of these asylums, if once started, do you not think it would be desirable that these workhouse auxiliary asylums should be under the same head and management as the district lunatic asylums of the country, would you recommend that they should be placed under two different heads?—No, you should take care that the heads under which they were put should not come into collision with the Board of Guardians, &c.

2308. It would be very desirable that the head under which these auxiliaries might be placed, should work in harmony with the Local Government Board?—Oh, yes, it would never do if the Inspectors came down and suggested one system, and the Board suggested another, and got into a squabble.

2309. Do you think that the danger of difficulty arising would be such as to render it advisable to place all these asylums under the Local Government Board, or under a Department working directly in connection with the Local Government Board?—I rather lean to that view.

2310. That is to create within the Local Government Board a sub-department having the control of the lunacy administration of the whole of Ireland, district asylums, subsidiary asylums, and the inspection of the lunatics at large, that they should be all under one department, and that department in direct communication with the Local Government Board?—I think so. I would be greatly afraid to make a department totally separate from the Poor Law.

2311. You think it would be better that the lunacy department should be a department of the Local Government Board?—Yes, that would be better, and I see no objection to the medical officer of the workhouse being the attendant of the auxiliary.

MULLINGAR.
Aug. 9, 1878.
Dr. Henry Berkeley.

HENRY BERKELEY, Esq., M.D., examined.

2312. You have been Resident Medical Superintendent of Mullingar Asylum for some time I believe?—The house was built in 1852; I was appointed then and have continued ever since.

2313. Previous to your appointment had you any other experience?—I have had considerable experience in private life.

2314. You have thus had a very lengthened experience in the care and treatment of lunatics?—Yes.

2315. What is the amount of accommodation afforded by your asylum?—The accommodation is intended for 400, but the numbers have increased from time to time there are at present 464 in the house.

2316. Is it not a fact that a large percentage of those in the house are considered to be incurable?—No doubt, we have furnished returns to your Commission giving full particulars. I believe in the whole of Ireland 75 per cent may be said to be incurable.

MULLINGAR Aug. 9, 1872.

Dr. Henry Berkeley.

2317. Do you consider that the efficiency of your asylum, as a curative establishment is impaired by its being crowded with incurables?—There is not a doubt of it, I have held that opinion for many years, in fact I have suggested a separation of the classes, as far back as 1866

2318. If for the purpose of such a separation of classes it was found practicable to make a classification of asylums, appropriating, some for the treatment of curable cases and others for the reception of incurables, would you consider such an arrangement advantageous?—I think it would be most desirable both on the grounds of public policy and economy.

2319. We have asked you from time to time for returns of the curables and incurables in your asylum, and have asked you to classify the latter under two heads, one the "harmless," and the other the "chronic incurables" requiring special care?—Yes, I have furnished them to your Commission.

2320. Will you be good enough to throw your eye over this plan of a class of building, which we propose to appropriate as an auxiliary asylum? Do you think that buildings arranged on this model would be suitable for the reception of harmless incurables?—Yes, admirably.

2321. Here is another plan (Oughterard), for harmless incurables of the class at present in workhouses. This auxiliary would consist of ranges of shed buildings, admirable shells capable of being well fitted up, arranged as indicated on the plan for the reception of those classes. They would in this, and in all cases, be provided with separate dormitories, day-rooms, lavatories, and yards, and a certain proportion of single rooms or cells, rooms for attendants, and in fact with all the accessories for the proper supervision of lunatics?—A most judicious arrangement, I remark on this plan (Monaghan), that on the ground floor, there are separate dining and day-rooms; this is an excellent arrangement I would always have a dining room otherwise it is most dirty. I recollect before we had one it was next to impossible to keep any sort of order

2322. But there would be no objection in our auxiliaries to the dining-room being also used as a day room?—It would make a capital day-room.

2323. Are you acquainted with the class of accommodation generally provided for the insane throughout the country in workhouses?—Well I have been in some of them, one of them at least, Mullingar here It was a miserable place to keep them in—want of room, want of attendance, want of proper arrangements, and I think it most desirable that the class should be moved elsewhere to better accommodation

2324. Could not a considerable number of the class of harmless, of which we asked you to make a return, be associated with the workhouse class?—No doubt they could.

2325. Between that class and the curable, have you not a certain other class which though incurable are liable to fits of violence and excitement, and therefore require special care and attention?—Yes, I know exactly the class you mean

2326. Supposing the district asylums were divided into two classes, one class being appropriated as purely curative establishments, and the other for the reception of the class just described, would you be satisfied with such an arrangement?—Yes, I would prefer to keep that class in district asylums

2327. Now, with regard to attendance, what proportion of attendants do you think should be placed in charge of the inmates of these new auxiliary asylums?—One to fifteen we have, but they would not require so many.

2328. Would you think two to sixty would be sufficient for the harmless class?—I don't think it would if they were in charge of those of dirty habits, they always require additional attendance.

2329. Supposing such assistance was given by employing for the purpose some of the inmates of the workhouse?—With that assistance the number you mention would, no doubt, be sufficient, and the arrangement would also be a saving of expense

2330. With regard to the reception of patients I believe your practice is to accommodate them when first received in single cells until you ascertain their disposition; for that reason you would consider a considerable proportion of cells necessary in a curative establishment?—Yes.

2331 Afterwards, when you know the patient, do you think association is desirable?—Oh, yes.

2332 Of the class of chronic incurables that you like to detain in the district asylums, do you think they would be better, as a rule, accommodated in single cells or in associated dormitories?—I think there ought always to be cells commensurate with the number you have in the house

2333 But when their proclivities are ascertained, and they become classed as incurables, do you think as large a proportion of cells would be necessary in district asylums, into which they would be drafted as in the curative establishments?—Well, perhaps not

2334 Have you many paying patients in your house?—More than in any asylum in Ireland. We return more money than they do at Richmond.

2335. Do you think there is a want of proper asylum accommodation in Ireland for the middle classes—I mean a class that cannot afford sending their relatives to the expensive private asylums, and do not like sending them to pauper lunatic asylums?—As far as I know here the accommodation is sufficient, they are taken much better care of here than they would be at a private asylum I don't think any one will deny that.

2336. Do you think, under the present circumstances, the accommodation is such as to enable the middle classes to send their relatives in for treatment early on the first symptoms of the disease, when there is a greater probability of recovery?—I think the accommodation is good enough.

2337. Have you ever had to refuse admission to a pay patient for want of room?—Never from want of room, though I have been obliged to refuse admission through the Privy Council rule We have to get first the liberty of the Board of Governors, and then we must send for the sanction of the Inspectors of Lunatic Asylums I don't think anything should be required beyond the liberty of the Board of Governors.

2338. Do you think that, supposing this was made a curative establishment, and a wing was set apart for the special care of these classes, it would be a beneficial arrangement?—Indeed it would be, and it would make a great deal of money. They would rather come here than to any asylum in Ireland; if such an arrangement as that was made, it would be a source of large revenue.

2339. Do you think that giving such facility it would result in cases being sent in in the earlier stages of insanity?—I do.

2340. And that there would be as a consequence a larger per-centage of cures?—No doubt of it.

PATRICK CULLINAN, Esq., M.D., examined.

ENNIS Aug. 7, 1872.

Dr. Patrick Cullinan.

2341. What official appointments do you hold?—I am Medical Officer of Ennis Union, Visiting Physician of the District Asylum, Surgeon to the Gaol, and District Medical Visitor of Lunatics in Chancery.

2342 How long have you held these offices?—I have been 37 years Medical Officer of the Workhouse, 32 years at the gaol, and 10 or 11 at the asylum—since that institution opened, in fact; and Lord Chancellor's Visitor of Lunatics for 15 years.

2343. Now, to deal with the question of accommodation. You are acquainted with the sealed order under which the accommodation of workhouses is limited by the Local Government Board?—I am.

2344. Do you know the principle upon which they

Ennis
Aug. 9, 1878.
Dr. Patrick Cullinan.

were based?—It was chiefly or exclusively with regard to cubic space. Floor space and wall space were not taken into account.

2345. Have you had your attention called to the fact that the numbers given in the returns are considerably in excess of the actual numbers that could be accommodated?—Yes; and at the time the accommodation was being fixed I repeatedly remonstrated with the Inspector of the Local Government Board against the scanty amount of accommodation which he proposed to assign, I said that in my opinion it was quite insufficient. I was informed that my opinion would be placed on record, and that if I ever found the workhouse to be overcrowded, the Local Government Board would, at once, on my reporting the fact, prevent such overcrowding, and on that understanding I signed the returns. Now, for instance, on looking at this copy of the sealed orders, I see that the male dormitory No. 3, second pair, which is 95 feet in length, and which, deducting for entrance door and fire-place, would afford available wall space of 178 feet nett, is entered as affording accommodation for ninety-three inmates, which would afford less than 2 feet wall space per head; this illustrates my statement that wall space was not considered.

2346. Consequently these returns may be said to be misleading?—Undoubtedly so.

2347. Have you had under your consideration Schedule A of minimum space requirements for various classes drawn up by this Commission?—Yes.

2348. Looking at that Schedule would you, from your experience as a medical man and a workhouse official, consider that it lays down a fair and reasonable space for the various classes therein named?—Yes, I consider it fair enough and reasonable generally, but decidedly insufficient for the class of "Mothers with infants."

2349. What allowance do you think should be made for that class?—I am of opinion that dormitory space of 800 cubic feet with its appropriate allowance of wall and floor space, and of 450 feet for day rooms should be given. Children, from the activity of their functions and their greater tendency to disease, require ample space.

2350. What space do you think should be allowed between the beds of able-bodied?—I should like to see between 2 and 3 feet. On looking at the Schedule again, I would say that 3 feet 9 inches is very fair allowance of wall space for children.

2351. With these exceptions do you think the schedule satisfactory?—Yes, I think its requirements very reasonable.

2352. From your experience as medical officer of the workhouse and as visiting physician of the lunatic asylum, do you consider that the accommodation provided in workhouses for the insane is suitable or satisfactory?—It is quite unsuitable in every respect; it is very defective.

2353. Have you ever considered the expediency of making other provision for the class of lunatics in workhouses?—I have considered it for many years.

2354. Would you have any objection to the creation of auxiliary asylums by the appropriation of vacant wings, or detached buildings of workhouses, for the purpose?—I have long since proposed that there should be separate asylums for the workhouse class of lunatics. I think it would be a good thing to appropriate portions of existing lunatic asylums for that purpose, if it could be done, as I greatly fear that in workhouses sufficient attention would not be paid to them.

2355. But if these workhouse buildings were so altered and fitted up as to provide suitable day-rooms, dormitories, lavatories, yards, and a proper proportion of single cells, with accommodation for a suitable number of skilled attendants, do you think they would be found suitable?—I think they would; if there were such radical changes as you mention.

2356. Suppose that an auxiliary such as I have described was fitted up for the reception of say 60 inmates, would you consider that two paid attendants, properly qualified, with the assistance of workhouse inmates, would be sufficient for the care of such a number?—I think that would be a fair proportion of paid attendants.

2357. Do you consider the Ennis Asylum crowded?—No; there has been no material increase in the numbers since it was opened.

2358. Is not this the result of the resident medical superintendent drafting out the harmless and incurable to the workhouses?—Yes. We get rid of that class as fast as we can.

2359. Does not the majority of inmates in the asylum consist of chronic and incurable cases?—Yes. There are, out of 258, 204 of that class, besides 16 epileptics.

2360. Cases in fact that require only such care and attention and discipline as may be necessary for their comfort and bodily health, and on whom a curative treatment would be thrown away?—Exactly so.

2361. Would you think it advantageous for the medical officer of a lunatic asylum to be placed in a position to give his undivided attention to curable cases?—It would be very important and desirable. His attention is now distracted by the various calls upon his time and care.

2362. The incurable class, of which I see there are 204 in the house, may, I presume, be divided into two heads, viz., those suitable to the workhouse lunatic class, and those requiring special care and supervision?—There are 138 quiet and orderly, but insane. I would not be disposed to transfer more than 67 of these to a workhouse auxiliary. This number I have fixed as the result of a census I have made. This would leave a balance of 137 incurables, many of whom are only moderately tranquil.

2363. Then if accommodation could be found elsewhere, say in another district asylum, for this balance of incurables, less those you would wish to keep for the service of the house, do you think it would be advantageous for this asylum to be made a curative hospital for the insane?—Yes, certainly; and the presence of the small proportion of the harmless incurables would be useful for the convalescents, by their association with them.

2364. You may perceive that our questions have been tending towards the establishment of three classes of asylums—1st, for the curable, 2nd, for the reception of chronic insane, requiring special care, and who it might be desirable to place where the accessories for restraint might be brought to bear in cases of relapse of emergency, and 3rd, the workhouse auxiliaries for harmless and incurable. Do you think that the establishment of such institutions and of such a classification would be advantageous?—I think the classification of the institution you have named, and which I would call "curative," "protective," and "sustentative," would be based on sound theoretical and technical principles.

2365. Now, with regard to the administration of such institutions, do you think that the administration of the existing asylums under the new classification, and of the new or workhouse auxiliary class, could be efficiently carried on under two district authorities?—I think they would work better and be managed more harmoniously under one authority. The transfer of cases from one class of asylum to another would be managed better, the whole being under one administration than under two.

WILLIAM DAXON, Esq., M.D., examined.

Ennis. Aug. 8, 1878. Dr. Wm Daxon.

2366. You are the resident Medical Superintendent of Ennis District Lunatic Asylum, I believe?—I am.

2367. What accommodation does it afford?—For 260 inmates, 130 of each sex.

2368. What is the number at present in the house?—132 males and 123 females; there might be one more or less of either sex.

2369. Then your house is very nearly full?—Full at the male side. Two over the legitimate number.

2370. I have been given to understand that to avoid crowding and asking for additions you have been obliged, from time to time, to transfer a number of harmless incurable lunatics to the different workhouses in your county?—When I require room I send them to the workhouse.

2371. Have you drafted many to the workhouses?—A good number; forty-three since the opening of the Asylum about ten years ago.

2372. Of the number at present in your house how many do you class as probably curable?—Forty-five are classed at present as probably curable; but I cannot give you that as strictly accurate, as we only class them at the end of the year, and that was last year's computation.

2373. You have, therefore, a large proportion of incurables?—Yes, very large.

2374. I see, by the return you furnished us with, that you have fifty one of that class, who have been for over fifteen years under asylum treatment?—Yes.

2375. I suppose that if they pass five years without recovering, you class them as probably incurable?—Two years we generally say.

2376. Now, suppose that accommodation could be provided elsewhere for a large percentage of your incurable class, and that they were replaced by curable patients, would not the advantages of your asylum as a curative establishment be very much increased?—I think so.

2377. Supposing it were found practicable to classify the district asylums, and to have some of them as purely curative establishments, with the requisite proportion, only for the service of the house, of harmless incurables or improvable patients, the other district asylums being appropriated for that class of incurables requiring special care and supervision, cases that are ordinarily quiet, but not suitable for transfer to workhouses, as being liable, if not rather carefully watched, to break out. Would you think such a classification advantageous to the lunatic poor?—I dare say there would be a larger proportion of cures; but you must bear in mind with reference to curables, who are very violent, that the fact of their being violent does not militate against their being cured.

2378. Of your incurable class, you have a considerable number in the house that are very similar to the class that are at present located in workhouses?—Yes a very large number.

2379. Now, if auxiliaries could be established in connexion with the workhouses, provided with all the requisites for such establishments—day rooms, dormitories, and proper proportion of single cells, lavatories, yards, &c.,—do you consider that a large proportion of incurables could be removed to them from the asylums throughout the county?—Yes, a very large number. I myself could send you sixty.

2380. And supposing that we had established auxiliary asylums, such as I have already described, would you consider that two properly trained paid attendants, with such assistance as could be given by respectable paupers from the workhouse, would be sufficient for the care of say sixty of the class of which we have been speaking?—Yes, if you had one large day room, I have a room here, one division in which there are forty, and I have only two ordinary attendants, assisted by the tailor to take charge of them.

2381. Now, supposing the public lunatic establishments of this country were constituted under the following heads—e. g. the district asylums (divided into curative hospitals and asylums for a special class of the chronic insane) and workhouse auxiliaries, do you think that these different classes of institutions could be successfully administered under two distinct governing bodies?—I think they would be apt to clash as to the class of patient that should be kept back or transferred from the one to the other. I sent a man twelve months ago to the Ennistymon Workhouse, and he was sent back to me yesterday, committed as a dangerous lunatic. He came in on a warrant on the ground of his having assaulted the porter. The want of suitable accommodation made them send him back. Had a proper establishment been formed there would have been no need to have sent him back here.

2382. Irrespective of this case, in illustration of the defective accommodation provided in workhouses, do I understand you to say that you think it desirable that the administration should be under one head?—Yes, and that there should be frequent inspection of these auxiliary establishments.

2383. In what manner and on what forms are lunatics admitted to the asylum?—If on the house form, they are obliged to come before the Board, but I have a discretionary power to take them in; they are also admitted as dangerous lunatics, and some are sent in on a warrant of the Lord Lieutenant.

2384. Is not the majority sent in as dangerous lunatics?—Yes, a large majority, and several of them are not dangerous at all.

2385. You are aware that the Lunacy Inspectors have frequently reported to that effect?—Yes.

2386. Could you suggest any amendment to the form of warrant to guard against this abuse?—No, I think the warrant is well enough.

2387. Do you think the medical certificate could be amended?—No, the doctor who certifies, says it is a case for immediate admission. He cannot see from a cursory view of the patient, whither he is dangerous or not.

2388. If the doctor who signs it simply signs it on the statement of the person who brings in the lunatic, would it be an advantage to devise some mode of making the declaration more stringent, or to compel him to make a declaration under the statute of the grounds on which he arrives at his conclusions?—I can't say; there was a man came in here one Saturday as a dangerous lunatic and I discharged him the following Saturday as an unfit case, and he was certified as a dangerous lunatic.

RICHARD BOURKE, Esq., Local Government Inspector, examined.

Limerick. Aug. 8, [illegible] [illegible] Bourke.

2389. You are Local Government Inspector of this district I believe?—Yes.

2390. What are the counties comprised in your district?—The whole of County Clare, North Riding of Tipperary, and the greater portion of County Limerick.

2391. Speaking generally of the accommodation provided for lunatics in the workhouses, in your district are you satisfied with it?—I think there is great room for improvement. In some houses it is better than in others, but in none of the houses in my district is there the structural accommodation requisite for the proper care of lunatics; idiots and epileptics are perhaps sufficiently well cared for.

2392. Are they generally associated with other classes?—No mostly in by themselves.

2393. Take Rathkeale as an instance, what is your opinion of the accommodation there?—I think Rath-

LIMERICK. Aug. 5, 1878.

Mr Richard Bourke

keale looks worse than it really is, because you have to go down five or six steps, if you recollect; but supposing you were not obliged to do that, but entered on a level, it would be a sufficiently lofty apartment The cells have been converted into one large dormitory.

2394 Have you ever considered the expediency of appropriating detached buildings or other parts of the workhouses for the better accommodation of these workhouse lunatics?—Yes, I have had occasion more than once to consider the accommodation of these classes of inmates in several workhouses with a view to its improvement, for example, it was at my suggestion that the female lunatics of the Limerick Workhouse were removed and put into the separate building they now occupy, their removal afforded us some additional room for the male occupants, but their condition is not entirely what I would like to see.

2395 I believe at Kilrush, Ballyvaughan, Scariff, and other places in your district there are ranges of buildings not at present occupied?—Yes.

2396. What is your opinion as to their suitability for this class of lunatics?—With regard to Kilrush I have long been of opinion that the sheds there with the ground attached would be admirably adapted for the treatment of lunatics and epileptics, and in my half-yearly reports to the Local Government Board I have frequently during the last two years brought the subject forward, and the Local Government Board have entirely agreed in the views I laid before them, and strongly urged on the board of guardians the propriety of fitting up portions of these sheds, and removing to them the lunatics, who are very indifferently accommodated where they are This recommendation has been renewed to the Kilrush Board within the last three weeks

2397 Are there any other buildings within your district that might be spared?—I need hardly refer to Roscrea, as I believe that has already been fixed upon as very suitable, both wings could well be spared without interfering with the classification of the workhouse, that is my opinion, but it must be remembered that these buildings were built at the time of very great pressure, they were very well suited for the number of children then in the schools, but they are now unnecessarily large.

2398. At Ballyvaughan, I think, you said there was some shedding?—There is a considerable amount of shedding at Ballyvaughan situated at the other end of the town that would do very well, but I don't think the Scariff building would be very suitable

2399. With regard to the Limerick Workhouse you said that one building there was given up at your instance to the female lunatics?—Yes, that building affords ample accommodation

2400. Is there not another building similar to it at its back?—Yes.

2401 How is that occupied?—It was occupied as a nursery for many years, but within the last few months there has been a change, and that was merely for a temporary emergency, consequent on the prevalence of small-pox

2402 Since that pressure—which was caused, I understand, by the occupation of the fever hospital for small-pox cases—I believe that sheds have been put up for the reception of small-pox patients. Do you not think that, in the event of another outbreak, a sufficiency of these sheds should be provided to meet it, so that the fever hospital could be left to its proper use?—I think it extremely desirable that hospital accommodation should be provided to meet other epidemics as well as fever

2403. Supposing that arrangements could be made for the proper accommodation of the children of Limerick Union outside the walls of the house, do you think that the nursery building, before referred to, which is at the back of your female auxiliary asylum could be advantageously appropriated for another auxiliary asylum?—Certainly These buildings have good yards, &c, and all appliances, and if the children were removed from the workhouse the re-arrangement could be made so as to make this building available

2404 Would the removal of the children from the workhouse be found beneficial, as tending to afford additional accommodation for other classes?—The removal of a large number, such as is represented by the children, must of necessity be advantageous

2405 Your infirmaries, I believe, are crowded?—They are

2406. Then the removal would be advantageous as affording additional accommodation for the sick?—Yes.

2407 With regard to the training of workhouse children, will you please tell me what is the system pursued and to what inspection are they subject, with a view of ascertaining their literary and industrial progress? -The inspection, as far as we are concerned, is exclusively carried on by the Inspector himself. Of course, the Guardians direct it, but the superintendence is entirely confined to the Inspector of the District

2408 I understand that the National Education Board, through their Inspector, only take cognizance of the literary training of the children?—Yes; but they also pass examinations in the girls' schools as to needlework

2409 That is the girls' training, but is not the industrial training of the boys entirely under the supervision of the District Inspector?—Yes, almost entirely.

2410 Is there any system laid down under which their industrial training is worked?—Each Union works according to the requirements of its particular principles, but the general direction of the arrangements is the same everywhere The training in agriculture is given in the working of the land around the workhouse, and is carried on with more or less efficiency Now—Roscrea is an example—the largest part of the work (some five or six acres) is done by the boys, and I will not hesitate to say a better farm could not be found in the United Kingdom Boys in large numbers are taken out periodically from the workhouses; and in my district I have had returns prepared, showing the number of boys and girls who have been discharged since my last visit, and those who have been returned from service, and I can confidently state that the percentage of returns is extremely small, and I argue from that that they get on well

2411 So far, it seems that the education of the children in rural Unions works well?—I think so

2412 But in urban districts, such as Limerick and other populous towns, would you not consider it advantageous to remove the children to schools to some little distance from the walls of the workhouse, and, where possible, into the country?—Yes; I don't think there can be the slightest doubt about that The associations are very disadvantageous; and the further you remove children, the better you can bring them up.

2413 There is one other question I wish to ask you, and that is, with regard to the accommodation returns as at present fixed under the sealed orders of the Local Government Board; were not the numbers in those returns arrived at by a rough computation of cubic space?—Not a rough computation, an accurate computation of cubic space.

2414 That is, of cubic space only, but without any regard to floor or wall space?—That is so.

W. H. NEWELL, Esq., LL.D. Secretary to the Board of National Education, examined.

2415. Is not the inspection of the workhouse schools throughout Ireland conducted under the Board of National Education?—Yes; with the exception of a few of these schools which are not National.

2416. Can you name the unions not having schools in connection with your board?—Five; Dublin South, Dungarvan, Gortin, Kilkeel, and Stranorlar Unions.

2417. Is not the education in these workhouse schools in connexion with your board, conducted under the same rules and regulations as in ordinary national schools, that is united secular, and separate religious instruction?—Exactly the same.

2418. Your department has furnished us with a return giving details of the "results examinations" in workhouse schools for year 1877-78. In it I see set forth the numbers of passes in the following classes:—"1st class," "2nd class," "3rd class," "4th class," "5th class (first stage)," "5th class (second stage)," and "6th class"—Will you give in detail the course of instruction in each of these classes?—I can best do this by handing you a copy of the programme of examination in each subject for each class (appendix B 3, p. 177.) The amount of knowledge required in each case is the minimum.

2419. I see that "agriculture," "book-keeping," and "needlework" are subjects in which children in the more advanced classes are examined. Does your department take any cognizance of the industrial training of the children further than what may be said to be included under the foregoing heads?—No.

2420. How is the children's knowledge of agriculture ascertained?—Merely by questions on the lessons. It is only *rote* knowledge.

2421. What is included under the head of "needlework"? Does it include a knowledge of "cutting out"?—Yes, when pupils reach fifth and sixth classes. I believe the number examined in these classes in needlework last year was under 100 girls.

2422. Is any credit given for "washing" and "making up linen"?—None.

2423. In fact your department confines its inspection almost altogether to the literary instruction of the children, and does not take any cognizance of the industrial training beyond the theory of farming, book-keeping, and the needlework and knitting taught the children?—It is just as you say.

2424. Has your department anything to do with the appointment of teachers in workhouse schools?—Nothing, but the inspectors are required to state whether the teachers they find in charge are qualified or not.

2425. Are the teachers appointed obliged to have certificates?—Unless the teacher is classed according to the regulations of the Commissioners of National Education he, or she, is not recognised by them; but frequently the guardians retain the services of teachers, even for years, who possess no certificate. I knew one case in which a teacher was retained for over fourteen years although there was no evidence of her fitness as tested by examination. At present there are forty two unclassed teachers employed in workhouse national schools. The Commissioners of National Education are powerless to remove them, but always report the facts to the Local Government Board. Teachers who submit to examination and fail are removed, but many who decline to be examined are retained by the guardians. The Local Government Board do not insist upon the candidates, in every case, passing the necessary examination.

2426. What number of teachers, principals and assistants, are there attached to workhouse schools?—There are in all 286 at present employed, but how many of these are assistants I am not sure. I think 108 are males and 178 are females. Of the males two are first class; twenty three second class; sixty-eight third class; and fifteen not classed. Of the females four are first; thirty-seven second, 110 third class; and twenty-seven are unclassed.

2427. Then there are forty-two unclassed teachers. Does your department ever have occasion to call attention to the inefficiency of teachers—and if so, what is the course followed?—Yes, if pronounced incompetent, the Local Government Board insists on the teachers being dismissed, but other shortcomings are not, I believe, visited with penal action. A copy of the report is sent to the guardians who, as a rule, do nothing.

2428. What is the average number of pupils to each teacher?—On the average twenty-three to each teacher, about half the number to each teacher of an ordinary National school.

2429. Your department has furnished us with returns in which the results earned in "workhouse" and "ordinary" schools are reduced to money value and contrasted. From these it appears that the average amount earned by each pupil, according to the established scale, was in each of the following subjects, as follows:—

Subject.	Workhouse Schools s.	Workhouse Schools d.	Ordinary Schools s.	Ordinary Schools d.
Reading,	1	11½	1	11¾
Spelling,	0	9½	0	9¼
Writing,	1	1½	1	1¼
Arithmetic,	1	5	1	4¾
Grammar,	0	8½	0	6¾
Geography,	0	8½	0	7¼
Agriculture,	1	3	1	1¼
Book-keeping,	1	5	1	4¼
Needlework,	1	0¾	1	3¼

Could you supplement this by supplying a column showing the possible earnings in each of these subjects?—The average sum earned is set out for all the pupils of all the classes collectively, while the fee varies for each class, therefore the possible earnings in each subject could only be given correctly by making the return refer to each class. This is a return showing the actual average earnings, and the possible average earnings in each subject in ordinary and workhouse schools, taking into account the varying rates in each class:—

—	Workhouse Schools: Average per Pupil. s.	d.	Workhouse Schools: Possible Average per Pupil. s.	d.	Ordinary Schools: Average per Pupil. s.	d.	Ordinary Schools: Possible Average per Pupil. s.	d.
Reading,	1	11½	2	2½	1	11¾	2	3
Spelling,	0	9½	1	0	0	9¼	1	0
Writing,	1	1½	1	2¼	1	1¼	1	8½
Arithmetic,	1	5	1	10¾	1	4¾	2	0
Grammar,	0	3½	0	10	0	6¾	0	11¾
Geography,	0	8½	1	1	0	7¼	1	1¾
Agriculture,	1	3	2	2½	1	1¼	2	4
Bookkeeping,	1	5	2	7	1	4¼	2	7¾
Needlework,	1	0¾	1	3½	1	3¼	1	4½

2430. The workhouse schools appear to have kept up a good comparative average, notwithstanding the fact that their possible earnings were, under all heads, except that of spelling, less than in ordinary schools?—Yes, but it must be borne in mind that of the 4,105 children examined, only 275, or 6·7, were above fourth class, while in the ordinary National schools the number was 16·8, or, if we include the fourth classes, the proportions will be as 20 to 31; or, in other words, of the workhouse pupils 80 per cent were in the junior classes, but in the ordinary National schools only 69 per cent. Extra subjects, too, are rarely taught in workhouse schools.

2431. You say that these results are the average of the earnings in all the classes collectively; could you furnish us with the details of the "numbers *examined*" and the "numbers passed" in *each class*, with the "rate" and "money value gained" in each, both for the workhouse and ordinary schools?—Yes, I beg to hand in such a return (Appendix C. 5, p. 184.)

2432. Are infants included in the numbers examined for results?—Generally they are included, but not in these returns.

DUBLIN. Nov. 27, 1878.

Dr. Newell.

2433. Can you tell me the per-centage of infants to the total number of pupils that were examined in "ordinary" and in "workhouse" National schools?—In ordinary National schools, 17·6. In workhouse National schools, 23·6.

2434. Your department has also furnished us with a very interesting return of the per-centage of pupils *passed* to numbers examined in ordinary and in workhouse schools; could you also give us these per-centages *by classes*?—Yes, I beg to hand in the return. (Appendix C. 6, p. 184.)

2435. How often are the workhouse schools inspected?—Once yearly for results.

2436. Are inspectors especially detailed for this duty in your department?—No. Each inspector deals with the workhouse National schools that may happen to be in his district. There are sixty-two school districts, and only two are without a workhouse school; but in one district there are six workhouse schools; in one, five; in nine, four; in twenty-three, three; in fifteen, two; and in eleven, one workhouse school.

2437. Do you think that it would be advantageous to the children were their industrial and literary training conducted under one head, as in the English Poor Law Department?—Most advantageous and most desirable. The Inspectors of National Schools feel that their inspection is often of little value, because the teachers are not the servants of the Commissioners of National Education, nor, indeed, in any sense amenable to their control, which is indirect, feeble, and frequently nil. Inspection is, I fear, in some cases discharged in a perfunctory manner. It should be performed by officers directly connected with the Department of State to which the schools belong—by officers who could devote their whole time and energies to the schools—taking cognizance not only of the literary proficiency of the classes, but of the educational, technical, and moral training—examining the institutions patiently, and not in a hurried manner, once a year—studying and comparing the methods pursued in schools of this class, and of schools akin to them in other countries; and bringing directly under the notice of the responsible authorities suggestions for their improvement. The Inspectors of National Schools are at present nominally serving two masters. Formerly the Poor Law Inspectors were required to examine these schools.

2438. Supposing that the inspection of these schools in all departments, both industrial and literary, was conducted by either your department or under the Local Government Board, how many inspectors, do you think, would suffice for the efficient performance of this duty in the 163 Unions in Ireland?—Two.

2439. Are you aware that there are a good many children of inmates of workhouses "hired out" to service?—I am aware; but I have no definite knowledge of the facts.

2440. But has your department no official knowledge of this class of child, and is any attention paid to their education?—None. We know nothing officially of them.

2441. You are aware that in various Unions there is a large number of "orphans and deserted children" placed out to nurse?—Yes.

2442. An undertaking is entered into by the nurse that such children shall attend at the nearest National school, and fees are paid for them by the guardians—is any especial notice taken of those children, and is any report furnished concerning their progress by your inspectors?—No report is necessarily forwarded. An inspector might examine a National school in which some of these boarded-out pupils were present, and remain ignorant of the fact. This is the circular addressed to inspectors on this subject:—

"SIR,—We have to inform you that the Commissioners of National Education have received a communication from the Local Government Board relative to the examination of orphan and deserted pauper children who are lodged and boarded out of the Workhouses, and who are required to attend school, and to be annually examined by an Inspector of the Commissioners.

"The Regulation adopted by the Local Government Board, with the approval of His Grace the Lord Lieutenant, is as follows:—

"'The child shall, when of sufficient age to attend school, be made to attend the nearest National School, or other public school, and to remain there during the ordinary school hours; and a certificate of such attendance, signed by the Teacher, and showing the days of absence, shall be given to the Relieving Officer each month, provided that if the school be not a National School the child shall be examined annually by an Inspector of the Commissioners of National Education at a convenient time and place, and the results of the examination reported to the Board of Guardians.'

"The Commissioners have intimated to the Local Government Board that with regard to "boarded-out" pauper pupils attending schools that are not National, their District Inspectors will be prepared to examine them at the Workhouse nearest or most convenient to them.

"Also, that the Inspector will give at least one month's notice of his intended examination, when it will be for the Poor Law authorities to secure the attendance of the "boarded-out" children, and the Inspector will, in each case, leave an abstract of the answering of each of the children with the Master of the Workhouse in which the examination is held.

"You will accordingly be good enough to comply with these regulations, and note in your Weekly Journals whenever you hold an examination of boarded-out pauper children who attend public schools that are not National.

"As nearly all the Workhouses have National Schools attached to them, we presume that in many cases you will have the opportunity of examining the children referred to along with the Workhouse pupils at the Annual Results Inspection."

And this is an extract from a report of one of our head inspectors on the Kilnaminsha National School, which shows that in one instance, at least, the boarded-out children attended school very irregularly:—

"Two orphan children, Michael and Anne J. Connor, are placed to board with Mrs. Callan, of Canniberg, near Kilnaminsha School, Co. Monaghan. They have been pupils of this school since 2nd October, 1876, during which period the boy has attended school only on 151 days, and the girl on only 150 days. Of these attendances 67 and 64, respectively, were made during the six months ended 31st March, 1877, but during the following year, ended 31st March, 1878, the boy made only 56 attendances, and the girl 60, and, as a consequence, neither was examined at the Results Examination of the school in April last.

"During the quarter ended 30th June, 1878, the boy attended on only 17 days, and the girl on 23; and the day of my visit (23th July) was the first day on which they had been at school during this month. They are evidently well cared for by Mrs. Callan, who is paid 2s. a week for each, and they present a clean and healthy appearance, but they are not regularly sent to school, which is the more to be regretted as they are intelligent children, especially the girl. The Relieving Officer, Mr. Nugent, made enquiries of the Teacher in June respecting their attendance at school, and wrote to her last week on the subject. I think it right, however, to bring the facts under the notice of the Commissioners. The excellent and humane practice of placing children from Workhouses to board in the country would lose much of its value if sufficient precautions were not taken to ensure their attendance at school."

I think that in every case the teacher should send monthly to the clerk of the union in which the school is situated a manuscript from the rolls of the pupils' attendance. This could be checked by the inspector.

2443. Would you see any objection to these "boarded-out" children—although on the school rolls of ordinary schools—attending the examinations at the workhouse schools?—No objection, except that the arrangement would be somewhat inconvenient in dealing with the official returns to the Education Office. Double payments should be guarded against.

APPENDIX.

TABLE OF CONTENTS.

APPENDIX A.—POOR RELIEF

APPENDIX B.—INDUSTRIAL TRAINING FOR CHILDREN.

Appendix C.—Lunacy.

APPENDIX.

APPENDIX A.

POOR RELIEF.

No. 1.—List of Queries addressed to Boards of Guardians by the Commissioners relative to Amalgamation, with analysis of Replies thereto.

No. 1. Whether, having regard to the extent, population, necessities of the sick and destitute poor, and proper administration of the Poor Law in the Union of ———— it would be expedient to dissolve such Union and amalgamate it with any of the adjoining Unions; and if so, what portions should be annexed to each of such adjoining Unions?

No. 2. In the event of Query No. 1 being answered in the negative, would it be desirable to dispense wholly or in part with the use of the existing Workhouse of the Union, and have the destitute poor accommodated in the Workhouse of any adjoining Union; and if so, what Union or Unions?

No. 3. Is any additional Workhouse or Hospital accommodation required in the Union for the adequate relief of the destitute poor, and especially the sick poor, arising from any portion of the Union being too remote from the Workhouse, thereby entailing undue hardship upon the poor?

Replies.

(a) Unions suggesting their own Dissolution and Amalgamation with Adjacent Unions.—

Ardee, Baltinglass, Belmullet, Cookstown, Glenamaddy, Gortan, Millstreet, Newport, Oughterard, Portumna, Skull. (11.)

Of the eleven unions above-mentioned, five passed resolutions rescinding previous ones, which, with the original resolution, are subjoined.

Ardee.

1st—"That it is desirable the Ardee union should be dissolved and amalgamated with the adjoining unions, viz.—

Drogheda, (To embrace Elec Divisions of)	Dundalk, (To embrace Elec Divisions of)
Dromin,	Tallonstown,
Dunleer,	Mansfieldstown,
Callan,	Strabannon,
Grangefelth,	Castlebellingham,
Drumcar,	Clonkeen.
Ardee.	
Navan, (To embrace Elec Divisions of)	Carrickmacross, (To embrace Elec Divisions of.)
Killary.	Drumcondra."

Carried unanimously.—11th Sept., 1877.

2nd—"That the resolution of the Board passed on 11th Sept last, recommending the dissolution of the Ardee union and amalgamation with neighbouring unions, be rescinded."

Carried unanimously.—1st January, 1878.

Baltinglass.

1st—"As this union is so small, and its boundaries run to such short distances from the neighbouring union workhouses, viz., from Shillelagh 5¼ miles, from Carlow 3½ miles, from Athy 5 miles, and from Naas about 6 miles, distances measured on map from point to point, it is better adapted to be dissolved, divided, and amalgamated with those Unions. To Naas the electoral divisions of Togher, Hollywood, Tober, Dunlavin, Donard, Lugglass, and Rathsallagh, to Athy the divisions of Ballitore, The Grange, Stratford, Donaghmore, Hartstown, Tuckmill, Badstown, Baltinglass, Talbotstown, and Carrigeen, to Carlow, Rahill, Rathvilly, Tucknall, Kinneagh, Williamstown, and Graney, to Shillelagh the divisions of Humewood, Ballinguile, Imaal North, Imaal South, and Rathdangan (the union bounding all except Humewood), and if such allotment were made the distances from the several workhouses to the outbounds of the divisions so allotted would be less than at present exists between Baltinglass union workhouse and the northernmost points of both Hollywood and Togher"—16th September, 1877.

2nd—"That having discussed the propriety of the amalgamation of this union, and having heard the lucid statement of Mr Commissioner Crawford, we are of opinion that it would be highly impolitic, under existing circumstances, to advocate any such amalgamation."—15th January, 1878.

Belmullet.

"The Board of Guardians are unanimously of opinion that the entire of this union ought to be amalgamated with Ballina, as was originally the case."

John Casey, Chairman.

30th August, 1877.

Letter from the Commissioners to the Guardians of the Belmullet Union.

Four Courts, Dublin,
30th June, 1878.

Sir,—The Poor Law Union Inquiry Commissioners have had under consideration the resolution passed by the Belmullet Board of Guardians on the 30th August, in reply to the queries sent to them, in which the guardians state as their opinion that the entire of the union should be amalgamated with Ballina, as was originally the case.

The Commissioners have referred to the representations which were made to the Boundary Commissioners at the time at which the separation of Belmullet from Ballina, and its formation into a separate union was recommended, and find that the following statements were made at that period

Ballina.

William Atkinson, D.L. and J.P., states, "That during the last six months prior to the dismissal of the guardians, of the six guardians chosen for the two electoral divisions of Binghamstown and Belmullet only one attended on one board-day, and that was for the purpose of getting a friend of his appointed master to the auxiliary workhouse just then about being established in Erris.

I would say that forty-six miles from Ballina to Belmullet, or even from Ballina to Dromore West, would be too far to require applicants for relief to attend the board, and return to their homes on the same day"

Richard Hamilton, Temporary Poor-law Inspector;—"I am informed that while the affairs of this union were managed by elected guardians—the guardians for Belmullet and Binghamstown electoral divisions, scarcely ever attended the board—their doing so would occupy them three days in each week—one day going to Ballina, one day returning, and at least one day to attend the board. It would be impossible for the re-

APPENDIX A.
Poor Relief.

lieving officers in this district to perform their duties and attend at board at Ballina. The distance decidedly prevents the applicants for relief who desire to attend the board from doing so without serious inconvenience. The union workhouse is sixty miles distant from parts of the district. I am decidedly of opinion that Belmullet and Binghamstown electoral divisions should be formed into a separate union, because I find even an auxiliary workhouse here on a small scale cannot be properly managed by a board who hold their meetings at Ballina."

Colonel Knox-Gore, Belleek.—"The greatest misery and inconvenience used to result to the applicants for relief coming from the two remote electoral divisions of Binghamstown and Belmullet, and would likely no doubt have been attended with much loss of life but for the auxiliary workhouse established in Erris."

William J Hamilton, Temporary Poor Law Inspector —"The size of the union is most decidedly such as to prevent guardians and relieving officers from attending the board without serious interruption to their other duties There is, perhaps, no union in Ireland which can be compared to the Union of Ballina in this respect—before the present auxiliary workhouse was taken at Binghamstown persons had to travel 120 miles—i e, sixty to the house and sixty back—before their applications could be personally inquired into by the guardians."

William Gardner —"The extent of the union is sufficient from its great size to prevent the inhabitants to feel a community of interest, and to co-operate for their general welfare

It appears from the above statements that the distance of the western portion of the union, from Ballina, formed what might be considered an insuperable barrier to the attendance of guardians at the meetings of the board—an absence from home of three days and two nights being necessary on the part of each guardian who attended—the same remark being applicable to relieving officers, rate collectors, and other parties required to attend the board"

If the distance were thus so great as to prevent the attendance of guardians, it is self evident that the removal of the poor to the Ballina Workhouse, even under the best arrangements which could be made, would be attended with the greatest hardship, particularly in the case of the aged and infirm, it being manifest that such a removal could not even be thought of in the case of the sick.

The pauperism of the union exists for the greatest degree in the part of the union the most remote from Ballina, as is shown by the fact that for the year ended 25th March, 1877, 29,004 collective days relief were charged against the three divisions of Belmullet, Binghamstown North, and Binghamstown South, whilst only 11,730 days were charged against all the other twelve divisions of the union

The average number in Workhouse for the last few years has not been inconsiderable, having amounted to 124 in the year 1873, 136 in 1874, 146 in 1875, 130 in 1876, and 134 in 1877

Mr. Crawford found when he visited the workhouse in January last, that out of 121 inmates, 35 were classed as infirm, and 36 as hospital patients.

The number of admissions to the workhouse for the year ended 25th March, 1877 was 197.

Under these circumstances the Commissioners are decidedly of opinion that it is necessary that hospital accommodation must be retained at Belmullet for all cases of sickness occurring in the district, and such being the case, it would appear impossible to reduce in any very great degree the establishment expenses, in the event of amalgamation with Ballina, as it would be probably still found necessary to retain nearly all the existing officers, viz , a clerk, chaplain, master, matron, medical officer, porter, nurse, &c , so that a very small amount of saving would result from the change.

The establishment charges of the Belmullet Union, deducting the portion defrayed by Parliamentary grant, amounted, for the year ended March, 1877, to £599, from which, however, may be further deducted the sum of £50, being an excess over the average amount of workhouse repairs charged in the half-year ended 25th March, 1877, thus leaving the average establishment charge on the union at £550, to raise which amount a rate of 1s. in the pound is necessary.

The establishment charge in the Ballina Union at the present time is at the rate of 3½*d.* in the pound on the valuation, which would be raised to 5*d.* in the event of amalgamation, and thus being compelled to bear its proportion of the Belmullet establishment expenses, whilst the Belmullet Union would undoubtedly profit to something approaching to 7*d.* in the pound, by having its establishment charges reduced from 12*d.* to 5*d.*, the Belmullet Union thus gaining 7*d.* in the pound, at the expense of Ballina, which would lose 1½*d.*

Although the Belmullet establishment expenses appear to be very high in proportion to the valuation of the union, the Commissioners have reason to believe that the present valuation is very low and greatly under the present letting value, and that if a revaluation of the union was made, the poundage rate required to defray the establishment charge would be greatly reduced.

The Commissioners are of opinion that the alteration proposed by the Guardians, by removing the union to so great a distance from its workhouse, would probably be productive of a large increase in the amount of outdoor relief

It appearing under these circumstances that the amalgamation proposed by the Guardians (being productive of very small saving on the whole) would only effect a transfer of the burden of establishment expenses from the union at the expense of Ballina, the Commissioners are not, as at present advised, of opinion that the case is one in which they can recommend the scheme proposed by the Guardians being carried out.

I am, Sir, your obedient servant,

H A Robinson, Secretary.

The Clerk of the Union, Belmullet.

Cookstown.

1st—"That the first query should be answered in the affirmative.—12th August, 1877.

2nd—"That the Guardians of the Cookstown Union are of opinion that amalgamation with any other union would not be conducive primarily to the interests of the poor of this union, and secondly that it would not be to the ratepayers' interest that such amalgamation should take place"—15th December, 1877.

Glenamaddy.

1st—"The Guardians of Glenamaddy Union consider it would be expedient to dissolve this Union and amalgamate it with Tuam, Castlerea, Roscommon, and Mount Bellew Unions, the portions to be annexed to each of the adjoining unions to be determined after consulting with the Commissioners."—4th September, 1877.

2nd—"That in the event of this union being amalgamated with the adjoining unions, it will be necessary to discontinue the Hospital attached to the Workhouse, and have the sick paupers therein removed to the respective unions to which they may be chargeable, and to dispose of the workhouse and grounds for the benefit of the union, and in the event of superannuation being granted to any of our officers that same be borne jointly with unions with which we may amalgamate"—27th November, 1877.

Gortin.

1st—"Resolved by the majority of this Board that the Union be dissolved and amalgamated with the adjoining Unions of Omagh and Strabane. The Electoral Divisions of Crockanboy, Fallagh, Glenchiel, Glenlark, Gortin, Mounthamilton, Moyle, Plumbridge, and Tremoge(?)dan, to be annexed to Omagh Union, and the Divisions of Glenroan, Lisles, Longhash, and Strangawilly to be annexed to the Union to Omagh Union.—11th September, 1877.

2nd—Resolved unanimously:—"That having heard Mr. Crawford's explanation, we are of opinion that the whole question be left in the hands of the Poor Law Inquiry Commissioners to say and decide whether it would be for the advantage of this Union to amalgamate with the adjoining Unions."—19th December, 1877.

Millstreet.

1st—"The Board are of opinion that this Union should be dissolved and amalgamated with the adjoining Unions of Macroom, Kanturk, and Killarney."

Observations.

This Union was formed at the time of and after the famine, the Union of Kanturk, from which the principal portion was taken, had at the period vast numbers on out-door relief and its workhouse overcrowded. The population has diminished from 23,151 to 14,592 in the years from 1841 to 1871.

With the aid of railway and other improved communications the distances for removal of the sick would not be greater than it is at present.

It would afford great relief to the charge for establishment if the amalgamation was adopted by the Local Government Board.

M'Carthy O'Leary (Chairman)

25th September, 1877.

2nd—Resolved:—"That the Commissioners be requested to hold an inquiry into the question of amalgamation of this Union with the three adjoining unions as formerly, as we cannot continue to pay the exorbitant rates at present assessed and likely to continue, the average being from 3s. 4d. to 3s. 6d for several years, being nearly twice larger than the average rates of Munster. The Board is decidedly of opinion, having given deep and earnest consideration to the question, that the accomplishment of that object would not bear harshly on the poor, as the remotest parts of the proposed amalgamated districts would be as near to their respective workhouses as many districts of the adjoining unions."—28th February, 1878.

Newport.

1st—"The whole of this Union to be amalgamated with the Unions of Castlebar, Westport, and Belmullet.

"The Electoral Divisions of Achill, Corraun Achill, Doolga and Slievemore to the Union of Westport. The Electoral Divisions of Ballycroy North and Ballycroy South to the Union of Belmullet. The Electoral Divisions of Derrylohin, Glenhest, Newport East, Newport West, and Trahmore to the Union of Castlebar."—12th September, 1877.

Observations.

As regards No. 1 Query this Board remarks that a new line of steamers has commenced to run weekly from Westport to Achill Sound, affording every facility for the transmission of paupers from that District to Westport Union.

With regard to No. 3 Query this Board beg very particularly to point out the great facility afforded by the healthy situation and large capacity of the building and good order of this workhouse for the reception of the harmless idiots of the county, and beg that this matter should be considered, and would be ready to furnish further details if called for.

2nd—Resolved unanimously:—"That this Board is of opinion that the amalgamation of this Union with any other union would be no appreciable saving, while it would be detrimental to the interests of the destitute poor requiring relief."—9th January, 1878.

Oughterard.

1st—"We are unanimously of opinion that this union should be dissolved and amalgamated with Galway, Ballinrobe, Clifden, and Westport Unions, and we would suggest that the Electoral Divisions of Oughterard, Wormhole, Lettermore, Letterford, Gorumna, Crumheen, and Camus, should be added to the Galway Union, that Clunbur, Cong, Curr, and Ross should be added to the Ballinrobe Union, and that Letterbreckan should be added to Westport and Turlough to Clifden Union."—27th November, 1877.

2nd—Resolved:—"That, understanding that it is proposed to appropriate parts of Workhouses for the reception of harmless lunatics, we beg to call the attention of the Poor Law and Lunacy Commission to the fact that this union has long ranges of buildings and sheds which would be eminently suited for this purpose. That by utilising available buildings and employing, as could be done, some of the staff, a reduction might then be made in the rates, as far as the Rate-payers of the Union is concerned, and that we adopt this arrangement if it is found impossible to dissolve the union and amalgamate it with others."

J. Gillmore, Clerk of Union.

25th July, 1878.

Portumna.

1st—Having applied for the amalgamation of this union, we think it would be expedient to dissolve it now, and to add portions of it to Ballinasloe and Loughrea, this small union being formed of divisions taken from the above mentioned unions, with the exception of Coose and Drumin, which were taken from Scarriff. As to the administration of Poor Law in this union, information can be more effectually procured by a visit of the Commissioners to the Workhouse on a day appointed, of which timely notice may be given.

Observations.

We would not like to have an hospital established in Portumna, it would soon be almost as costly as the present workhouse, and would be a receptacle for women of bad characters, as the workhouse is now to a great extent, and the Commissioners are particularly requested to take notice of this matter. Coose and Drumin, the southern extremity of Portumna Union were formerly part of Scarriff Union, but we would not like that these divisions be again added to Scarriff—because they adjoin the division of Woodford in the Loughrea Union, and form a portion of the Dispensary District. Loughrea is also, we think, a better managed union than Scarriff.

Portumna Union is very small and the staff expenses unusually high, and it is impossible to manage it properly, the contractors instead of opposing each other as elsewhere, combine, and no one in the neighbouring towns will bid against them, for instance the butchers are now getting 8d. per pound for meat here, while good sound half fed beef and mutton only cost 6d. in other unions which is as good or better than the meat used by soldiers at mess.—September, 1877.

Signed on behalf of the Board,

Westmeath, Chairman.

2nd—Resolved:—"That having statistically inquired into the subject of this union's amalgamation, this committee believes it would not be for the benefit of the union that such would take place, for the following reasons, viz.:—1st, We consider that it would entail great hardship on the poor of the union by removal to distant workhouses; 2nd, That after having carefully considered the statistics bearing on the matter, they find that the saving on a portion of the union which would be transferred to Ballinasloe would be virtually nil, and the portion which would be transferred to Loughrea very small, and that even this small saving would most likely disappear, when they consider the additional cost of the removal of the paupers such long distances, and the keeping up of an auxiliary hospital here."—12th January, 1878.

APPENDIX A.

Poor Relief

SCHULL.

"The Board are unanimously of opinion that it would be desirable to amalgamate with the Skibbereen and Bantry Unions in the following proportions. The electoral divisions of Kilcoe and Ballybawn, to be annexed to Skibbereen, the remainder of the union to that of Bantry."—25th September, 1877.

LETTER from the COMMISSIONERS to the BOARD of GUARDIANS of the SCHULL UNION.

Four Courts,
Dublin, 4th July, 1878.

SIR,—The Poor Law Union Inquiry Commissioners have had under consideration the resolution passed by the Skull Board of Guardians on the 25th September last, in reply to the queries sent to them, in which the Guardians state that "they are unanimously of opinion that it would be desirable to amalgamate with the Skibbereen and Bantry Unions in the following proportions:—The electoral divisions of Kilcoe and Ballybawn to be annexed to Skibbereen—the remainder of the Union to that of Bantry.

The Commissioners have referred to the representations which were made to the Boundary Commissioners at the time at which the separation of Skull from Skibbereen and its formation into a separate Union was recommended, and find that statements to the following effect were made by the chairman and vice-chairman of the Skibbereen Union:—

ARTHUR PERCY AYLMER, Rosscarbery.—"The size and circumstances of the union are such as to prevent the guardians and relieving officers from attending the Board of Guardians without the interruption of their duties and employments, and the applicants for relief in most of the eastern electoral divisions are prevented by the extreme distance from attending the Board without the most serious inconvenience to themselves, and cost to the electoral divisions. The great extent and all the circumstances render it quite impossible for the inhabitants of the distant electoral divisions to have any community of interest or to cooperate successfully for the general welfare."

DANIEL MCCARTHY, Vice-Chairman of the Board of Guardians—"The general opinion is, that the size of the Union is inconveniently large, and the distance that guardians and relieving officers have to travel to the workhouse is so great as to be attended with much inconvenience and interruption to their other duties. When it is considered that the western applicants for relief have to come a distance of thirty miles, the inference to be drawn is that the inconvenience to applicants for relief must also be very serious; indeed, in some instances, the long journey has been attended with fatal consequences to the applicants coming from the extreme western electoral divisions."

THOMAS SOMERVILLE, Chairman of Board of Guardians—"The Union is very large—its extreme length about forty-five miles, its greatest breadth about ten—the guardians from either extremity are unable to attend the Board of Guardians with regularity, and as a journey of twenty or twenty-five miles to the workhouse in wet and cold weather on one of the carts of the country with a wretched horse, occupies seven or eight hours, I must think such exposure injurious to the health of the applicant for relief, and that the law should endeavour to bring indoor relief nearer to the poor man. The alteration I should propose would be the cutting off from either end of the Union—the eastern divisions to be formed into a small union with part of the Bandon Union annexed, and on the other extreme the western divisions to be formed into another union with the workhouse in the village of Skull—if which alterations were carried out few applicants for relief would have to go a greater distance to their workhouse than seven or eight miles. I beg to refer you to a map of the Union. The last year's experience induces me to recommend these divisions. We ought to be prepared for future failure in our crops. We incurred much expense in fitting up hired houses for the applicants for indoor relief. There was much difficulty in founding the supplies of food and clothing, additional labour imposed on the officers to keep up their books. When a family would go out the man was in one place, the wife in another, the daughter in another, and the son in another, and confusion in the Register. Paupers walked off with Union clothing—no means of restraining them from committing plunder on the inhabitants in the neighbourhood of the hired houses, as there were no surrounding walls. No means of putting them to work; in fact the houses were merely used by the paupers as lodgings whose inmates were under no control, and the county gaol, built for 300 had 1,400 crowded into it, which prevented the offenders from being punished as they ought, and held out no terrors for them, and the dining-hall at the workhouse, too small to accommodate those quartered in its vicinity, enabled the paupers to walk in and get food as it suited their convenience."

It appears from these statements that the distance of the western portion of the old Skibbereen Union from its workhouse was, as might naturally be expected, productive of the greatest inconvenience both to the guardians and to the poor who had occasion to apply for relief, the extreme end of the Union being about thirty six miles away.

The inconvenience to guardians and poor which was experienced in the old Skibbereen Union would be found to apply equally to the proposal now made to amalgamate all the western portion of the Union to Bantry—its distance from Bantry and Skibbereen being nearly identical.

During the year ended the 25th March 1877, there appear to have been 114 admissions to the Skull workhouse, which had an average number of inmates amounting to 92.

The establishment charges of the Skull Union for the year ended March, 1877, deducting the sum defrayed by Parliamentary grant, amounted to £442—being a charge of 7d. in the pound on the valuation.

In the event of amalgamation the Commissioners are of opinion that it would not be possible to effect a saving of more than one-half of this amount—as they consider it would be absolutely essential to keep up an hospital at Skull for *all* cases of sickness arising in the western portion of the union—as their removal to Bantry would be attended with great hardship and suffering to the patients; the cost of this hospital, together with the increased cost of the establishment expenses of the Bantry Union, occasioned by so large an addition, precluding the possibility of any greater saving.

The average establishment charge in the Skibbereen Union, after the deduction of Parliamentary grant, amounts to about £1,050, being a charge on the union of 5¾*d*. in the pound on the valuation.

On a similar calculation the average charge of establishment in the Bantry Union amounts to £430, being a charge on the union of 4¾*d* in the pound.

If the proposal of the Skull Board of Guardians were carried out, the Skibbereen Union, by the addition of the two Electoral Divisions of Ballybawn and Kilcoe, would have their valuation increased by £3,331, which would reduce their establishment charge from 5¾*d*. to 5½*d*. in the pound—being a saving of ¼ of a penny in the pound only.

In the case of the Bantry Union the valuation would be raised to £33,040, but, as has been previously mentioned, the Commissioners are of opinion that the Bantry establishment charge would be increased by at least one-half of the charge of the present Skull Union, that is, by £220—the effect of which would be to leave the establishment charge of the new Bantry Union the same as at present, that is, at 4¾*d*. in the pound.

It would thus appear that with respect to the establishment charges the effect would probably be to benefit the Skibbereen Union, by reducing the charge from 5¾*d*. to 5½*d*., being a saving of ¼ of a penny in the pound, whilst Bantry would receive no advantage whatever.

The portion of Skull Union going to Skibbereen might be benefitted to the extent of a small fraction under 2d in the pound, whilst that portion going to Bantry might receive benefit to the extent of a small fraction over the same amount

Looking to the small pecuniary advantage which might be derived from amalgamation in the reduction of establishment expenses, the Commissioners, as at present advised, are decidedly of opinion that such a saving would but badly compensate for the great inconvenience which would be produced to Guardians and Officers in attending to their duties, for the probable necessity of the extension of a system of out-door relief, and for the hardship inflicted on applicants for relief who would be obliged to go to such a distance from their homes for that purpose.

I am, sir, your obedient servant,

H A. ROBINSON, Secretary.

The Clerk of the Schull Union.

---

(5)—UNIONS suggesting the DISSOLUTION of ADJACENT UNION and adding portion of DISSOLVED UNION to their own.

Abbeyleix, Athlone, Ballinasloe, Ballymoney Bandon, Carrick-on-Shannon, Carrick-on-Suir, Castlebar, Cavan, Dundalk, Dunfanaghy, Dungannon, Ennis, Ennistimon, Listowel, Magherafelt, Monaghan, Mountmellick, Nenagh, Oldcastle, Omagh, Roscrea, Sligo. (23)

ABBEYLEIX.

1st—4th September, 1877—That our clerk be authorized to communicate to the Clerk of the Castlecomer Union that the board of guardians of this union believe it would be of advantage to the ratepayers of both unions if an amalgamation could be arranged, and that he, the Clerk of the Castlecomer Union, be informed that we will be prepared to receive any portion of the Castlecomer Union which is contiguous to this union, and we would be glad to learn the views of the Castlecomer Board on the subject.

That a committee, consisting of Messrs. John Lyster, J P., Richard Caldwell, J P, and Robert Owen, be appointed to arrange with the Donaghmore Board in regard to the addition of that union, or any part of it, with this union

2nd—18th September, 1877—That, considering fully our position as guardians of the poor, we are willing to receive into this union so much of the adjoining unions as may be given up to us, believing that the interest of the destitute poor, and the welfare of this union with the proposed additions would be equally improved by such a change.

ATHLONE.

The Board are of opinion that at least on the West Meath side of the union the area might be considerably enlarged.

Portions of the Ballinasloe, Roscommon, and Ballymahon Unions formerly belonged to this union, and with advantage to the ratepayers, and without injury to the poor the union might be extended so as to reach on the N.E. side of Ballymahon, and on the S.E. Ferbane. The latter is in the Parsonstown Union, and the former in the Ballymahon Union; about equal distances from Athlone and Longford Workhouses; and the board are of opinion that the necessity for the latter union has long since passed.

CASTLEMAINE, Chairman.

BALLINASLOE.

That this board is of opinion that some arrangement might be made by which amalgamation might be carried out between the Union of Ballinasloe and neighbouring unions, as there is accommodation in Ballinasloe Workhouse for 1,300 inmates, whereas the average number of paupers for many years has been under 300.

JOHN D'ARCY, Clerk of Union.

BALLYMONEY.

That the said queries be answered in the negative and that under the head of "observations" the following remarks be sent up.

That, as regards the question of the amalgamation of unions this Board is of opinion that the time has come when it might, with great advantage, be carried out in several cases

That since the introduction of the Irish Poor-law in 1838 the circumstances of the country have greatly changed, not only has there been a great decrease in the population, but there has been a marked improvement in the condition of the people, arising from abundant employment at remunerative wages for all conditions of agricultural and skilled labour, one of the consequences of which is to be seen in the reduced number of inmates, no less than in the character of the inmates themselves, our workhouses being occupied almost exclusively either by the very young or very old and infirm, and taking this house as a fair specimen of others, with accommodation as regards space for above 700 inmates (with officers and establishment in proportion) and having for the last five years only an average number of inmates of about 125, we think that a judicious amalgamation of unions similarly circumstanced might be advantageously carried out.

Taking the county of Antrim as an example, we find that it has seven workhouses, namely—Belfast, Lisburn, Antrim, Larne, Ballymena, Ballycastle, and Ballymoney. We are aware, of course, that some of these unions embrace portions of the neighbouring counties, whilst those of other counties include portions of county Antrim. Nevertheless, we are of opinion that two, or at most three, workhouses, besides that at Belfast, would be found amply sufficient for the relief of the poverty of the county, thus effecting large savings in establishment and other incidental charges.

In case of such amalgamation being carried out, we would suggest that one of the smaller workhouses might, with advantage, be devoted to the reception and care of the increasing number of lunatics and imbeciles whose unhappy condition might be improved and ameliorated by being kept in a proper place, and with suitable attendance and care.

BANDON.

"Although negativing the first query as regards the dissolution of this particular union, we beg to observe that we consider the amalgamation of neighbouring unions with this union advisable."

S. R. TRESILIAN, Clerk of the Union.

CARRICK-ON-SHANNON.

"We deem the amalgamation of unions advisable, and consider that this union should at least be restored to its original area, as we fail to understand why it was that at the alteration of unions in 1851 the boundary of this union was limited on one side to less than three miles from the workhouse, whereas on the other side it extends over twenty miles from it.

And, at the same time, we would respectfully invite the attention of the Commissioners to the suitability of this union for a central one The workhouse was originally built to accommodate more than three times as many inmates as have been relieved in it at any one time for twenty years past, and from its size, healthful position, and being easy of access, can readily accommodate the inmates of some neighbouring unions, and thus save the expense of these establishments. We would suggest that the existing fever hospitals be continued under the care of the dispensary medical officers."

A. O'CONNOR, Clerk of Union.

CARRICK-ON-SUIR.

The Board consider it inexpedient to dissolve this union, and are of opinion that a good portion of the Kilmacthomas, Thomastown, Callan, and Clonmel unions might be annexed thereto.

APPENDIX A.
Poor Relief.

This Board is of opinion that the workhouses of Ireland would be quite sufficient for its present requirements, having regard to the number of poor and its population, by having them situated so that the area of each union should extend according to a radius of ten miles from each workhouse. This scale would give about 102 workhouses to Ireland, and having regard to the workhouses on the coast, and making provision for any special circumstances that may arise in particular localities, the Board is further of opinion that 120 workhouses would be amply sufficient for the requirements of the country. It seems absurd, to the Board, to be maintaining a staff of officers for workhouses where there are less than an average of 120 paupers relieved, and they desire to draw the attention of the Commissioners to the last annual report of the Local Government Board, in which it will be seen that there are as many as 38 union workhouses in which the average numbers of any do not exceed 120, and which, if taken together, do not exceed 96, and that in the same unions the average numbers on out-door relief was only 113, whilst the salaries and rations of the officers of the same unions amounted to an annual average of £454 each, which is equivalent to £2 3s. 5d., for each person relieved, both indoor and outdoor

Referring further to the same report, it will be observed that the average numbers relieved in each workhouse in Ireland was 268, and the average numbers on out-door relief 406, making an average total of 674 in each union, and an average cost on that number for salaries and rations of officers of £1 3s 5d for each person relieved, against £2 3s. 5d as above quoted, if, therefore, 120 union workhouses are found to suffice and the remaining unions amalgamated, an annual saving of £20,000 may be effected in salaries alone, and the necessities of the destitute poor in all probability just as carefully and as efficiently attended to. In making these observations the guardians have fully in view the difficulties that may arise in certain localities from excessive population, destitution, or other causes, and they are further of opinion that if the area quoted may be considered excessive, that intermediate hospitals may be provided for the treatment of contagious diseases, such hospitals to be supported by joint contributions from adjoining unions.

FRANCIS HOGAN, Chairman.

18th August, 1877.

CASTLEBAR.

We believe that at least one of the unions of the county might be dissolved, and added to the adjoining unions with advantage to this union and the others concerned.

CHARLES O'MALLEY, Chairman.

25th August, 1877.

CAVAN.

This Board is of opinion that the workhouse of this union is quite adequate to accommodate the poor of this county, and they recommend that the workhouses at Bailieborough, Bawnboy, and Cootehill be closed, but that the hospitals of those unions be kept open for the reception of persons suffering from accidents and infections.

THEOPHILUS THOMPSON, Vice-Chairman.

28th August, 1877.

LETTER from the COMMISSIONERS to the CLERK of CAVAN UNION.

FOUR COURTS,
10th November, 1877.

SIR,—Referring of the reply of the Guardians of the Cavan Union to the queries addressed to them by the Poor-law Union Inquiry Commissioners, and also to the printed copy of the petition of the guardians to Parliament, dated 25th January, 1877, the Commissioners observe in the queries that under the head of "observations" the guardians state that the workhouse of the Cavan Union is quite adequate to accommodate the poor of this county, and in their petition the guardians express their opinion that "one county workhouse would in most cases afford ample room for the purposes of such county"; and they conclude their petition by praying that Parliament will cause a re-arrangement of the boundaries of poor-law unions in Ireland, so as very considerably to reduce the number of workhouses by making a central house for each county.

I am directed to inquire with reference to the views thus expressed, whether the Guardians of Cavan Union propose that all the electoral divisions, that are within the County of Cavan, should be united with one union, having one central house for such county union, or whether they simply propose that without reference to the county boundaries, the four unions should be amalgamated?

I am, Sir, your obedient servant,

H. A. ROBINSON, Secretary.

The Clerk of the Union, Cavan.

LETTER from the CLERK of the CAVAN UNION, to the COMMISSIONERS.

Poor Law Office, Cavan,
15th November, 1877.

SIR,—In reply to your letter of the 10th inst., I am desired by the Board of Guardians, to inform the Commissioners that the Guardians intended that all the electoral divisions in County Cavan, should be attached to one central workhouse for the County.

I have the honour to be,

Your obedient Servant,

JOSEPH GRIER, Clerk of the Union.

The Secretary, Poor Law
Inquiry Commissioners, Four Courts.

DUNDALK.

In the opinion of this Board the County should contain only two workhouses, viz., this house and Drogheda. Dundalk Workhouse was built to accommodate 848, the number at present is reduced to 778. Our present average number of inmates seldom exceeds much over 200, consequently we have ample accommodation for all the paupers that would be likely to apply for admission under the proposed altered circumstances.

We may add that both Dundalk and Drogheda are favourably situated for the attendance of the great majority of the Guardians for the proposed amalgamated unions.

SAMUEL BRADFORD, Chairman.

10th September, 1877.

DUNFANAGHY.

We are in favour of amalgamation provided it can be shown to us that it would amount to a considerable reduction in the rates, and would dispense wholly with the workhouse, and send the paupers to Letterkenny Workhouse.

Observations.

Owing to the healthy position of the Dunfanaghy Workhouse, being situated so near to the sea shore, and having other advantages as regards its sanitary and drainage arrangements, we are of opinion that the Letterkenny and Milford Unions could advantageously be amalgamated with this one, as the workhouse here holds 450 inmates, and would accommodate all the destitute poor in each of the unions, and both the workhouses at Letterkenny and Milford, could be set with advantage for such purposes as barracks for the militia, or as a county infirmary, which would be more central, and we do not at present see in what way the workhouse here (in the event of it being left vacant), could be utilised or let with advantage in a locality so remote as this is.

DUNGANNON.

The Guardians of the Dungannon Union are of opinion that owin to its central position it would be found most undesirable that this union should be dissolved or amalgamated with any adjoining union

Observations.

The Guardians of the Dungannon Union are unanimously of opinion that amalgamation of unions is most desirable But looking to the geographical position of this union, and taking into account that since the formation of this union, railway communication now exists to Pomeroy District and a new line of railway is at present being constructed to Cookstown, and taking also into account that the indoor paupers of the seven unions of the county Tyrone, namely, Omagh, Strabane, Castlederg, Gortin, Clogher, Dungannon, and Cookstown, average only about 950, the Guardians are of opinion that three workhouses, say Dungannon, Omagh, and Strabane, since these have accommodation for 3,000 inmates, would more than afford ample accommodation for the entire county.

JOHN BOYD, Clerk of Union.

13th September, 1877.

ENNIS.

1st. "That in the opinion of the Guardians of Ennis Union, portions of the unions of Killadysert, Corrofin, Ennistymon and Tulla might be added to the Union of Ennis with great advantage and economy of management. As to the particular portions which should be added, the Guardians will be prepared at the proper time to submit their suggestions to the Commissioners.

2nd "That having heard the very clear and lucid statement of Mr. Crawford, one of the Commissioners, we are still of opinion nevertheless, that it would be advantageous to absorb portions of the unions named."

ENNISTYMON.

It would not be desirable or expedient in the opinion of the Board of Guardians to dissolve the union and amalgamate it with any of the adjoining unions.

Observations

The Board of Guardians consider it would be advisable to amalgamate with Ennistymon the portions of the Unions of Ballyvaughan and Corrofin which originally belonged to Ennistymon Union

AUGUSTUS HOGREVE, Chairman.

28th August, 1877.

LISTOWEL.

This Union gets on well as it is, but if desirable would not object to having the northern portion of this Barony now forming part of the Glin Union added to Listowel as was the case previous to 1850.

GEORGE SANDES, Chairman.

23rd August, 1877.

MAGHERAFELT.

We do not consider it would be adviasable to dissolve the Union of Magherafelt, but see no objection to a portion of Cookstown Union being amalgamated with it.

Observations.

We beg to remark that we consider it adviasable that the Sanitary matters connected with contributory areas such as Cookstown, Pomeroy, Stewartstown, and Coagh, should be managed locally by Town Commissioners or otherwise, and not dealt with by the Board of Guardians.

J. H. McCAUSLAND, Chairman,
JOHN STEELE, Clerk.

August, 30th, 1877.

MONAGHAN.

"That this Board is unanimously of opinion that two unions would be sufficient for this county. Which of the two existing unions to be abolished the Local Government Board can decide on further inquiry, but we recommend that the Unions of Monaghan and Castleblayney be continued."

5th September, 1877.

"The subject of Union Amalgamation having been this day again discussed, and the votes of the Board having been taken, 3 voted for amalgamation, 5 against it, and 2 did not vote It was resolved 'that there be no amalgamation of unions.'"

14th November, 1877.

"The amalgamation of Poor Law Unions having been this day again discussed, amalgamation was carried by a majority of one—5 voting for and 4 against it."

JAMES MITCHELL, Clerk of Union.

12th December, 1877.

MOUNTMELLICK

That the Board are of opinion that the time has arrived when the amalgamation of unions in Ireland can be advantageously carried out with benefit to the heavily taxed ratepayers, and without inconvenience to the sick and destitute poor, by keeping the hospitals in the several unions open for the sick

As regards this union we believe that there is more room in the Workhouse than would be required for the accommodation of all the paupers in the county.

ROBERT GOODBODY, Clerk of the Union.

20th September, 1878.

NENAGH

The Guardians would not object to the amalgamation of that part of the Borrisokane Union which formerly belonged to the Nenagh Union.

J. HINSTON SHEEHAN, Clerk of Union.

24th August, 1877.

OLDCASTLE.

That in the opinion of this Board it would not be expedient to dissolve this union, but as regards the Union of Delvin of which a part was taken from this union, and in which Union of Delvin at the time of the last printed return on the 30th September, 1876, there were only 88 destitute poor getting relief, we are of opinion the said union ought to be dissolved, and the portion thereof taken from this union restored hereto in which there is accommodation for 600 paupers.

THOMAS F JENKINS, Clerk of Union

27th August, 1877.

APPENDIX A.
Poor Relief.

OMAGH.

We do not think that Omagh Union should be dissolved, but are strongly of opinion that the smaller Unions of Gortin, Castlederg, and Clogher, might be advantageously dissolved and portions of them should be added to, and amalgamated with the Unions of Strabane, Omagh, Dungannon, and Monaghan.

That in Omagh Workhouse for the past three years the average daily number of inmates did not exceed 206, whereas there is building accommodation therein for 820.

That there is hospital accommodation for 168, whilst the average number of patients for the like period did not exceed 60.

We think that the hospital accommodation now attached to those workhouses whose dissolution we have recommended might be kept open for the accommodation of the sick poor of their respective districts, and be placed under the charge of the medical officer of the dispensary district in which they are respectively situate.

THOMAS ELLIS, Chairman of the Board.

8th September, 1877.

ROSCREA.

It would be utterly impossible, having regard to the adequate relief of the destitute poor, to dissolve the Roscrea Union, or to divide it amongst the adjoining unions.

Observations.

In the year 1849 the Roscrea Union, comprising a valuation of £109,996, relieved in its workhouses 6,087 paupers; and the necessity of making provision for such large numbers more conveniently to their dwellings, led to the formation of the Donaghmore Union, which was chiefly an offshoot from Roscrea. The numbers relieved indoor by the divided unions in 1850 were respectively—

Roscrea Union, . .	5,623
Donaghmore Union, .	739
	6,362

The numbers belonging to both unions, and accommodated in the workhouses of Roscrea Union, at the time of alteration, June 1850, being—

Roscrea Paupers, . . .	1,704
Donaghmore Paupers, .	492
	2,196

This condition of the country has been so materially changed, that while the expense of maintaining and supervising the several workhouses cannot be proportionately reduced, the small number of paupers relieved indoor by each union renders it quite obvious that the necessity for separate establishments has ceased, and that Donaghmore might be again merged in Roscrea Union, with manifest advantage to both. The paupers relieved in 1876, as stated in the Report of the Local Government Board for 1877 are—

Roscrea Union, . . .	130
Donaghmore Union, . . .	100
	230

While Roscrea Union Workhouse has accommodation for 985 paupers, and a permanent fever hospital for 36 patients, making in all room for 2,021 persons

That the smaller union should be annexed to the larger might be admitted at first sight, but the disproportionate expenditure in the smaller union is so clearly evidenced by the excessive cost entailed for its separate maintenance, that no doubt can be entertained as to the propriety of such an arrangement as the Roscrea guardians would now propose.

In the tables of the Local Government Reports for the last three years, the average excess in Donaghmore, on Roscrea Workhouse, in the item of food and clothing alone, is *two shillings and one penny per head per week*. This excess, upon the average collective days, of paupers actually relieved, amounts to £500 per annum, representing a poundage rate of three pence on Donaghmore Union. If united to Roscrea the saving would be still more, for it is well known that the larger the number maintained, the lower is the cost per head.

Again, in the columns headed "officer's" salaries and all other Poor Relief," the average expenditure is set down as—

	£
Roscrea Union, . . .	1,204
Donaghmore Union, . . .	1,005

Of this latter, certainly half—more likely three fourths—would be saved by having the unions amalgamated; but in these items also it may be assumed that another three pence in the £ would be added to the saving in food and clothing of Donaghmore.

That this saving of sixpence in the pound is correct is further shown by the tables in the three yearly reports already referred to for the average total expenditure is—

	s.	d.	
In Roscrea Union, . .	1	1	per £ on the valuation.
Donaghmore, . .	1	7	
Difference, . .	0	6	

And the average expenditure for poor relief only is—

	s.	d.	
In Roscrea Union, . .	0	10	per £ on the valuation.
Donaghmore, . .	1	4	
Difference, . .	0	6	

A question which will weigh considerably with the Commissioners of Inquiry will doubtless be, whether the proposed amalgamation is likely to entail hardship on the poor in seeking relief at a workhouse more distant than that to which they had been accustomed to resort.

The Roscrea Union Workhouse would still be the centre of a radius of ten or at the most eleven statute miles from the furthest part of the proposed amalgamated union. Such a radius would include the towns of Borris-in-Ossory and Rathdowney, which formerly belonged to the Roscrea Union, and would even include the village of Coolrain in Mountmellick Union—the bounds of which extend to within six miles of Roscrea Workhouse. This portion of Mountmellick Union—or the electoral division of Marymount, which is at least sixteen miles from the workhouse of that union—could be advantageously added to Roscrea—the workhouse of which lies so near, while the whole, or the greater part of Donaghmore Union, which was formerly comprised in Roscrea, could be re-united to it without any inconvenience.

The local circumstances of medical and sanitary expenditure have not been taken into account in the foregoing calculation, as these must necessarily remain the same; only such items as can be clearly reckoned on for saving have been included. The transmission of paupers to the workhouse presents no difficulty, as the numbers are so small, and the persons now relieved generally remain more continuously without taking their discharge. To the ratepayers the amalgamation would be by no means objectionable, as from the districts referred to the general tendency is to Roscrea for marketing and mercantile purposes.

To Roscrea Union the addition would, of course, be some advantage—extending the area of taxation for establishment and other general chargeabilities.

It is, therefore, resolved unanimously,—that the Poor Law Union Inquiry Commissioners be requested to recommend that the Electoral Division of Marymount in Mountmellick Union, and the entire of

Donaghmore Union, or such portion of it as formerly belonged to Roscrea, be added thereto, thus forming a compact and conveniently circumstanced union—the valuation of which would then be about £114,566, the population about 28,593, and the area about 173,548 acres or 16½ miles square, in the centre of which the workhouse is situate.

Passed unanimously.

JOSEPH GRIFFITH, Chairman.

6th September, 1877.

Note.

The Donaghmore Union was, until 8th June, 1850, comprised in the Roscrea Union, with the exception of the townlands of Clonouseen, Keeloge South, and Springhill, which were severed from Mountmellick Union, and the townlands of Beckfield South, Coolfin, Kilbeedy, Beckfield North, Coolfin, Electoral Division of Grantstown, except Garryduff, Electoral Division of Kildellig, except Braska, Kildellig and Kilcotton, which are detached from Abbeyleix Union.

SLIGO.

The Sligo Union extends eighteen miles north and south, and poor relief is administered without any hardship on the poor within that area. It may, therefore, be a matter for the consideration of the Government whether the boundaries can be extended to a radius of eighteen miles—this would include all the divisions of Dromore West to within eighteen miles of Ballina—to which union the western portion of Dromore West may be amalgamated, and would bring us to within a short distance of the town of Tobercurry. The south-western portions of the latter union may be divided between the Swineford and Ballina Unions.

To the east by extending the boundaries, the Manorhamilton Union might possibly be divided between this union and that of Enniskillen.

The Board offer these suggestions for the consideration of the Commissioners.

EDWARD H. COOPER, Chairman.

4th September, 1877.

(c.)—UNIONS not suggesting AMALGAMATION but ALTERATION of BOUNDARIES of existing UNIONS by having some Electoral Divisions or Townlands from ADJACENT UNIONS added to their area.

Bailieborough, Ballinrobe, Carlow, Carrickmacross, Claremorris, Corrofin, Donegal, Donaghmore, Dunmanway, Gorey, Gort, Irvinestown, Kilmacthomas, Kilrush, Lismore, Macroom, Naas, Tullamore (18).

BAILIEBOROUGH.

A portion of the Kells Union comes as close as two and a-half miles from this workhouse and ten miles from Kells.

Of the Cavan Union within five miles of this workhouse and eleven miles from Cavan.

Of the Cootehill Union within three miles of this workhouse and seven miles from Cootehill.

Of the Oldcastle Union within four miles of this workhouse and eight from Oldcastle.

In the year 1850 there were four electoral divisions taken off this union, namely—Ardagh, Newcastle, Maybolgue, Tullyarran—and also portions of other divisions; and we are of opinion if these electoral divisions and portions which are situated closer to our workhouse than are to the present union to which they are attached, were restored to our union it would be very much more to the advantage of the union and accommodation of the paupers.

R. G. ADAMS, Chairman.

10th September, 1877.

BALLINROBE.

The Board begs to observe that there are several electoral divisions of the Oughterard Union situate in the barony of Ross, and lying on the side of Lough Corrib, adjoining the Ballinrobe Union, which in the event of the dissolution of the Oughterard Union ought to be restored to the Ballinrobe Union, which has ample workhouse and hospital accommodation. These several electoral divisions, namely—Cloonbur, Cong, Cur, Letterbrickaun, and Ross—are separated from the Oughterard Workhouse by the large Lake Corrib, rendering it impossible to give the sick poor relief in the workhouse hospital of that union, while the populous electoral divisions of that part of the union above referred to are relatively near the Ballinrobe workhouse.

THOMAS MAY, Clerk of Union.

8th September, 1877.

CARLOW.

The guardians beg to state that from the character and importance of this commodious building, which is scarcely second to any other workhouse in Ireland, and as such has been frequently reported on favourably by the Local Government Board Inspectors, in our opinion the only change required is to have it augmented from the adjoining unions, and it is the unanimous opinion of the guardians that this would be most desirable, which would prove a great advantage and economy to the general administration of the house.

The average number of paupers annually in the house is about 350, and it is competent to accommodate 859.

The hospital accommodation is in keeping with the house, being large and extensive, and more than sufficient for present requirements.

R. CLAYTON BROWNE, Chairman.

30th August, 1877.

CARRICKMACROSS.

It would not be expedient to dissolve this union, but we believe large portions of all the adjoining unions could be advantageously added to it.

BERNARD M'CAUL, Clerk of Union.

4th September, 1877.

CLAREMORRIS.

The Board, taking into consideration the central position of the workhouse of this union, and the accommodation it affords, are of opinion that a few of the electoral divisions of the neighbouring Unions of Ballinrobe and Swineford might advantageously be added to this union, more particularly as this house has been built on the newest plan, and on an excellent sanitary site.

CORROFIN UNION.

The Board of Guardians of this Union unanimously object to any portion of their union being annexed to that of Ennis, as they are of opinion that an examination of the statistical information received by the

APPENDIX A.
—
Poor Relief.

Commissioners of Inquiry from clerks of unions will show that little or no saving (if any) could be effected by amalgamation—while very great hardship and injury to the sick and destitute poor would result therefrom. The Board feel that the interests of the poor, which they are bound to protect, should not be overlooked through a desire to effect what would appear a doubtful saving to the ratepayers.

Amalgamation would entail the following expenses, which should be incurred, and which would more than counterbalance any supposed saving :—

1. The erection of additional building accommodation.

2. Increase of officers salaries for increased duties

3 Conveyance of sick and infirm persons to workhouse, by reason of the increased distance they would have to travel

4 Superannuation of officers of dissolved union.

Another objection to amalgamation would be that the guardians, owing to the long distances they would have to travel, would not attend regularly at the meetings of the Board, and could not therefore as efficiently watch over the interests of the poor and the ratepayers.

Another matter which the board desire to bring under the notice of the Commissioners is, that 1,286 applications for relief were made to them during the year ended 25th March, 1878, which were considered and decided on by them as follows :—

Provisional admissions to workhouse confirmed,	183
Ordered to the workhouse,	403
Provisional out-door relief continued,	73
Ordered out-door relief,	604
Refused relief,	23

In submitting the above figures the guardians hope that some idea may be formed of the injury which would be inflicted on the poor if such large numbers should be obliged to travel long distances to another workhouse to seek relief

In conclusion, the Board would observe that they do not see that sufficient reason exists for dissolving the union. The guardians hold their weekly meetings regularly—the wants of the poor are duly attended to—the ratepayers are satisfied with the management of its affairs, which are efficiently and economically administered—and on these grounds the Board respectfully protest against amalgamation

JONAS STUDDERT, Chairman,
JOHN THOS LINGARD, V.C.,
E CAHILL, D.V.C.,
JOHN M'GAW.

Board Room, Corrofin Workhouse,
May 2nd, 1878.

Observations.

The Board of Guardians of Corrofin Union infer that one of the objects which the Government have in view is the placing of hospital accommodation within convenient distance from the residences of the sick poor, and with the view of securing this very desirable end, and supplying a want long felt, they would beg to recommend a revision of the areas of the neighbouring Unions of Ballyvaughan, Ennis, and Ennistymon, in the hope that the portions of those unions (as the following return will show) which are nearer to Corrofin workhouse than to the hospitals of the unions to which they at present belong be annexed to the Corrofin Union. The adoption of this course would, the guardians are of opinion, afford easy facility for the relief of the sick poor, and probably obviate the necessity of providing additional hospital accommodation in the remote portions of the unions referred to.

JONAS STUDDERT, Chairman

13th September, 1877.

LIST of TOWNLANDS in the neighbouring Unions of Ballyvaughan, Ennis, and Ennistymon, proposed to be annexed to Corrofin Union.

BALLYVAUGHAN UNION, Carron Electoral Division.

Townlands.	Distance from Corrofin Workhouse.	Distance from Ballyvaughan Workhouse.
	Miles.	Miles.
Cappaghkennedy,	6½	11½
Ballymoney,	7	9
Croaghwell,	7	10
Teeskagh North,	7	11
" South,	7	11
Glencolumbkille North,	7	12
" South,	7	12
Knockaunes Lower,	6	12
" Upper,	6	12

CASTLETOWN, Electoral Division.

Townlands.	Distance from Corrofin Workhouse.	Distance from Ballyvaughan Workhouse.
Carron,	6	10
Castletown,	5½	11
Clooncoose,	4	11½
Commons,	6	10
Crossagh,	4	10
Termacalvin,	5	10
Meggaboy,	5	9
Noughaval,	5	9
Sheeg-o-donnell East,	5	9
" West,	5	9

ENNIS UNION, Dysart Electoral Division.

Townlands.	Distance from Corrofin Workhouse.	Distance from Ennis Workhouse.
	Miles.	Miles.
Ahasla,	4	6
Ballycullinan,	2	5
Ballinagunnaghtagh,	3½	5
Cashna,	3	6
Clooney,	2	5
Cloontohil,	2½	4½
Dromoland,	3	5
Dromsallagh,	2½	5
Dysert,	2	6
Gortnacurka,	3½	6½
Knockanure,	3	6½
Knockmore,	3½	6
Knockvragh,	2	5
Mollaneen,	2½	6
Mevanties,	3½	7
Scalleen,	3½	6

ENNISTYMON UNION, Clooney Electoral Division.

Townlands.	Distance from Corrofin Workhouse.	Distance from Ennistymon Workhouse.
	Miles.	Miles.
Carhumeere,	4	6
Loughnagowan,	3½	5½
Warren,	4	6

Unanimously adopted.

JONAS STUDDERT, Chairman.

13th September, 1877.

Countersigned,
D. SULLIVAN,
Clerk of Corrofin Union.

DONEGAL.

That the Donegal workhouse is quite sufficient to accommodate the paupers of that portion of Ballyshannon Union which is in the county of Donegal (which would make the union on that side conterminous with the county of Donegal), and also a considerable portion of the Glenties Union, without enlarging the district to any undue distance from the centre at Donegal.

D. C. PEARSON,
Clerk of the Union.

25th August, 1877.

DONAGHMORE.

The Guardians are of opinion that it would be inexpedient to dissolve the Donaghmore Union, but that it is desirable that the area should be extended by the addition of portions of Kilnaseer, Cahir, and Castletown electoral divisions of Abbeyleix Union, and part of the Mountmellick Union, which are much more convenient to the Donaghmore Workhouse than to those at Abbeyleix and Mountmellick. A portion of Roscrea and Urlingford Unions might also be added to this Union, unless there be an objection on the grounds of being situate in different counties.

A portion of Kilnaseer electoral division is within three statute miles of this workhouse, while it is over ten from Abbeyleix; and Cahir electoral division is eleven Irish miles from Abbeyleix, and only six from Donaghmore.

We believe that the Poor Law Boundary Commissioners would have recommended that several of the townlands in these divisions should have been included in this Union originally, were it not that it was proposed to form a Union of Mountrath, which idea was abandoned at the last moment, and the townlands which otherwise would have been placed in Donaghmore Union were left unaltered.

CASTLETOWN OF UPPER OSSORY,
Chairman.

21st September, 1878.

DUNMANWAY.

We, the Committee appointed by the Board of Guardians of the Dunmanway Union to consider the queries submitted by the Poor Law Union Inquiry Commissioners respecting the proposed amalgamation of Unions, unanimously agree that the three queries should be answered in the negative. This Union was one of the original unions formed under the Poor Law Act, when first introduced into Ireland, and was chosen for this purpose on account of its very central position. Even in the event of a diminution in the rates by an amalgamation with other unions (which we doubt) we still could not recommend it, as we consider that in consequence of the great distance to be traversed and the large and poor population of this district, the absence of a workhouse here would be a practical denial of relief to the destitute poor. In the event of the suppression of any of the other unions, which were formed during the famine years—to wit, Clonakilty—to form which a considerable portion of our union, as originally formed, was taken from us, we would suggest that the following electoral divisions of that union be added to Dunmanway Union—viz., Ardfield, Arrigadeen, Cahirmore, Castleventry Coolcraheen, Kilkerranmore, Knox, Rathbarry, Rosscarbery, and Rossmore, as all the above electoral divisions are nearer to Dunmanway than to either Skibbereen or Bandon.

In the event of the reconstruction of any of the neighbouring unions, we would recommend that the following electoral divisions of the Skibbereen Union be detached from it, and attached to the Dunmanway Union—viz., Bredagh, Drinagh, Drimoleague North and Drimoleague South. These electoral divisions lie much nearer to the Workhouse of Dunmanway than to that of Skibbereen.

With respect to the Bandon Union, we recommend that the following electoral divisions be taken from it and added to the Dunmanway Union—viz., Bengour and Teadies.

With regard to the Macroom Union, we recommend that the electoral divisions of Ballingeary and Inchegeela be taken from it and added to the Dunmanway Union.

As regards Bantry Union, we recommend that the townland of Glounacarney, in the electoral division of Kealkil, be added to this union.

Should all or any of these additions be made to the Dunmanway Union, there would be more than sufficient workhouse and hospital accommodation in the union, the workhouse having been originally built to accommodate four hundred (400) and additional accommodation for four hundred (400) having been added during the famine year.

Signed on behalf of the Committee,
E. A. SHULDHAM, Chairman.

28th September, 1878.

GOREY.

The Guardians of this Union are unanimously of opinion that this Union should *not* be dissolved, but *that several townlands might be added* to this from other Unions with advantage.

W. M. KIRK, Chairman.

GORT.

We consider it undesirable to make any change in this house, but it might be desirable to add portions of other Unions to this.

A. BELLEW NOLAN, Chairman.

25th August, 1877.

IRVINESTOWN.

The Guardians consider it would be greatly to the advantage of the sick and poor of the Killadeas Division of the Enniskillen Union, were that division added to this Union.

FRED. D'ARCY, Vice-Chairman.

5th September, 1877.

KILMACTHOMAS.

The Guardians are of opinion that the townlands which, on reference to the map, are shown to be nearer to Kilmacthomas than the Unions in which they are at present situated, might with advantage to the public be added to the former Union.

KILRUSH.

Generally, we are of opinion that the Poor Law Unions which were in existence in this county prior to the potato famine are quite sufficient for the requirements of the destitute poor.

R. W. C. REEVES, Chairman.

1st September, 1877.

LISMORE.

In the opinion of the Lismore Board of Guardians it would be desirable to re-annex to Lismore Union that portion of the County Waterford which was some years since detached from it to form part of the Youghal Union.

By Order,
MAURICE HEALY, Clerk of Union.

28th September, 1877.

MACROOM.

The Guardians desire to call attention to the fact that portion of Dunmanway Union is within two miles of Macroom, and that the poor of that district are greatly inconvenienced by being attached to Dunmanway.

T. T. HEALY, Clerk of Union.

1st September, 1878.

NAAS.

That in the opinion of this Board there are certain townlands comprised at present in the Baltinglass Union in the Togher, Lugglass, and Hollywood Electoral divisions that would be more conveniently included in the area of the Naas Union.

G. MOLLOY, Clerk of Union.

5th September, 1877.

TULLAMORE.

That, having considered the subject of the foregoing queries, we are of opinion that it would not be expedient to dissolve this union, or amalgamate any portion of it with an adjoining union. If any change should be made, we consider that the district about Ballycumber, Castlearmstrong, and Bellair should be placed in this union, and we believe it would be more advantageous to the poor of these districts for the purpose of relief in the workhouse, being much nearer this than Parsonstown Union, in which they are now situate.

GEO. RIDLEY, Chairman.

11th September, 1877.

(d.)—UNIONS expressing an OPINION in favour of AMALGAMATION generally

Kilmallock, Longford, Rathdrum (3).

KILMALLOCK.

We approve of the amalgamation scheme, as we consider there are too many workhouses in Ireland, and the amalgamation or re-arrangement will effect a large saving to the ratepayers. Whenever the amalgamation shall take place we hope that the Commissioners will recommend that one of the closed workhouses in each province be set apart for the accommodation of idiots and harmless lunatics, with a special set of officials to attend to them, as they cannot be properly attended to in ordinary workhouses.

R. QUIGLEY, Clerk of the Union.

20th September, 1877.

LONGFORD.

We are not opposed to the principle of amalgamation; we believe that the boundaries of unions should be revised, and that the boundaries should be conterminous with those of counties.

GRANARD, Chairman.

5th Sept., 1877.

RATHDRUM.

The guardians are in favour of amalgamation of unions where it can be carried out without inconvenience to the sick and destitute poor, but they do not think this union could be amalgamated without such inconvenience.

But they consider they could accommodate a portion of the paupers of some of the adjoining unions, if such should be thought advisable by the Commissioners.

(e.)—UNION expressing OPINION against AMALGAMATION, but in favour of having its poor accommodated in another workhouse (1).

KILLALA.

We are of opinion that the poor of this union should be accommodated in the neighbouring union of Ballina, so as to do away with a great portion of establishment charges.

ERNEST KNOX, Chairman.

(f.)—UNIONS ANSWERING QUERIES in the NEGATIVE and SUGGESTING no ALTERATION of BOUNDARIES (104).

Antrim,	Dingle,	Milford,
Armagh,	Downpatrick,	Mitchelstown,
Athy,	Drogheda,	Mohill,
Ballina,	Dromore West,	Mountbellew,
Ballycastle,	Dublin, North,	Mullingar,
Ballymahon,	Dublin, South,	Naas,
Ballymoney,	Dungannon,	Newcastle,
Ballyshannon,	Dunshaughlin,	New Ross,
Ballyvaughan,	Edenderry,	Newry,
Balrothery,	Enniscorthy,	Newtownards,
Banbridge,	Enniskillen,	Parsonstown,
Bantry,	Fermoy,	Rathdrum,
Bawnboy,	Galway,	Rathkeale,
Belfast,	Glenties,	Roscommon,
Borrisokane,	Glin,	Scarriff,
Boyle,	Granard,	Shillelagh,
Cahersiveen,	Kanturk,	Skibbereen,
Callan,	Kells,	Strabane,
Cashel,	Kenmare,	Stranorlar,
Castleblayney,	Killadysert,	Strokestown,
Castlecomer,	Kilkeel,	Swineford,
Castlederg,	Kilkenny,	Thomastown,
Castlerea,	Killarney,	Thurles,
Castletown,	Kinsale,	Tipperary,
Celbridge,	Larne,	Tobercurry,
Clifden,	Letterkenny,	Tralee,
Clogheen,	Limerick,	Trim,
Clogher,	Limavady,	Tuam,
Clones,	Lisburn,	Tulla,
Clonmel,	Londonderry,	Urlingford,
Coleraine,	Loughrea,	Waterford,
Cootehill,	Lurgan,	Westport,
Cork,	Mallow,	Wexford,
Croom,	Manorhamilton,	Youghal.
Delvin,	Midleton,	

(g.)—UNIONS in which the GUARDIANS were equally divided in opinion (1).

INISHOWEN.

(h.)—UNIONS which were undecided (2).

CLONAKILTY, LISNASKEA.

No. 2.—LIST OF QUERIES addressed to the INSPECTORS of the LOCAL GOVERNMENT BOARD by the COMMISSIONERS with reference to the circumstances of the UNIONS in their respective Districts, and the REPLIES of the INSPECTORS thereto.

1.—Is the workhouse adequate to the general wants of the union? If not, in what respects is it deficient?

2.—(a.) Is the general accommodation for the sick poor in the workhouse sufficient? (b) Are there infectious wards attached to the workhouse?

3.—Is there a school attached to the workhouse? (b). Are the educational arrangements satisfactory?

4.—What is the distance (by road or rail) of the workhouse from the centre of the most remote electoral division of the union?

5.—Would it be practicable to provide for the reception of the indoor poor of the union in the workhouse of any of the adjacent, and if so, what union?

6.—Can you suggest any alteration in the existing boundaries of the union that can be advantageously made, having due regard to the proper administration of the Poor Laws, as well as to the necessities of the sick poor?

REPORT FROM MR. R. BOURKE TO THE COMMISSIONERS.

ENNIS.

1.—I consider the workhouse adequate to the general wants of the union.

2.—The general accommodation for the sick poor is sufficient, taking into account the single-storied buildings used in connexion with the infirmary. There is a fever hospital consisting of two fine wards, separate from the infirmary, and a convalescent ward.

3.—There is a male and female school, of which the arrangements are, in my opinion, satisfactory.

4.—The distance by road from the centre of Dromline Electoral Division to the workhouse is about twelve statute miles, and longer if any part of the journey is performed by rail.

5.—It would, in my opinion, be so inconvenient as to be almost impracticable to accommodate the poor of Ennis Union in any other workhouses.

6.—No alteration of boundaries occurs to me likely to be attended with advantage.

TULLA.

1.—The workhouse is adequate to the general wants of the union.

2.—I consider the general accommodation for the sick poor in the workhouse sufficient. There are infectious wards which have supplied all necessities up to the present time.

3.—There is a boys' and girls' school, each having its own teacher, and they are fairly conducted.

4.—About 11 or 12 miles.

5.—It might be practicable to provide for the reception of the indoor poor of the union in Scariff, but it would demand extension of infirmary space.

6.—I am not aware of any alteration of boundaries of the union that are called for by the proper administration of the Poor Law.

SCARIFF.

1.—I am not aware of any serious deficiency in the workhouse.

2.—The accommodation in the infirmary is, upon the whole, sufficient. But the infectious wards used by the guardians are deficient in many respects, and objections are entertained on grounds of expense to fitting up an excellent fever hospital standing on the grounds, but not used since the famine.

3.—The distance by road (there are no rails) from the centre of Cahermurphy Electoral Division to the house may be about twelve statute miles.

5.—I think not.

6.—I can suggest no alteration of boundaries that would act favourably on the administration of the poor law, or be advantageous to the poor.

KILLADYSERT.

1.—The workhouse is quite adequate to the wants of the union.

2.—The accommodation for the sick is sufficient, and there is a wooden shed used for the treatment of fever and other contagious diseases. Though the accommodation in this shed is rough, and the space limited, it has hitherto proved sufficient.

3.—There is a combined school, conducted by a female teacher, and considering the limited numbers and the youth of the children, I think this arrangement sufficient.

4.—Between nine and ten miles.

5.—It might be practicable to divide the union, and annex one-half to Ennis and one to Kilrush, but the extreme distances would probably be fifteen or sixteen miles.

6.—As long as this workhouse remains, I think it conveniently placed for the union as now existing, and I know of no change in boundaries that would improve it in this respect.

CORROFIN.

1.—The workhouse is abundantly adequate to the wants of the union.

2.—The accommodation for the sick is sufficient, and there is a good detached hospital for infectious cases.

3.—There is a combined school under a female teacher, which is sufficient under the circumstances.

4.—The distance from the middle of Barton Electoral Division (which is the furthest from the workhouse) is probably about ten miles.

5.—It might be practicable to add four electoral divisions to the Ennis Union, and the remaining five to Ennistymon, though the increase in the sick would press somewhat on the infirmary space of both of these workhouses, and the distance from the furthest electoral division to its workhouse would be increased from six to sixteen miles.

6.—If the workhouse of Corrofin be preserved, I know of no desirable change of boundary in the interests of the poor.

BALLYVAUGHAN.

1.—The workhouse is adequate to the general wants of the union.

2.—The accommodation for the sick poor has, by various changes in the building, been rendered sufficient, but it differs from other workhouse in having no good infirmary. What was originally intended for one is now an hospital for fever and contagious diseases, and it is not altogether commodious.

3.—The educational arrangements, consisting of a combined school under one female teacher, are sufficient for the class of children attending.

4.—Between ten and twelve miles I should say, but in such a wild mountainous place there may be roads unknown to me.

5.—I think it would be quite impracticable with any regard to the comfort and due of the poor to provide for the reception of indoor paupers in any adjacent union. Ennistymon or Gort would both be distant from twenty to twenty-five statute miles from various parts of the Union of Ballyvaughan, and Corrofin could scarcely hold the combined poor of both places.

6.—I can suggest no alteration of boundaries.

KILRUSH.

1.—The workhouse is adequate to the wants of the union.

2.—All the hospital arrangements are good, and ample separate accommodation is available for cases of fever or other contagious diseases.

3.—There is a school for boys and another for girls, both well conducted.

4.—The distance from the centre of Kilballyowen Electoral Division is about sixteen or seventeen miles by crossing a ferry, and nineteen or twenty miles all by road.

5.—I see no practicable mode of disposing of the indoor poor otherwise than in the present workhouse.

6.—The distances are so great that the only change I could suggest would be to separate the six western-mosts electoral divisions, and construct hospital accommodation for their sick poor at Carrigaholt.

ENNISTYMON.

1.—The workhouse is adequate.

2.—The accommodation for the sick is not limited, and there are contagious wards separated from the main hospital.

3.—The school for boys and girls, under one woman, is fairly efficient; and a single teacher is enough for the work.

4.—The farthest distance may be eight or nine miles.

5.—I see no means by which the poor of this union could be removed from their own workhouse to any adjacent one without great hardship and inconvenience.

6.—The union boundaries seem to me about as well arranged in reference to their connexion with Ennistymon itself as they can be.

LIMERICK.

1.—The workhouse is, in my opinion, adequate to the general wants of the union.

2.—The accommodation for the sick poor is amply sufficient, and an excellent fever hospital is connected with the workhouse.

3.—The schools are commodious and well conducted.

4.—The distance (by road) from Doon, west, may be about fourteen statute miles.

5.—It would be altogether impracticable to provide for the reception of the indoor poor in any adjacent workhouse.

6.—No alteration in existing boundaries occurs to me as in any essential respect desirable.

RATHKEALE.

1.—The workhouse is adequate to the general wants of the union.

2.—The accommodation for the sick poor is sufficient, and a good infectious hospital is attached to the workhouse.

3.—There are schools for boys and girls, tolerably well conducted.

4.—Pallaskenry, which is probably the most distant Electoral Division, is about twelve statute miles.

5.—I see no means of adequately providing for the indoor poor in any adjacent workhouse.

APPENDIX A.
Poor Relief.

6.—The union seems well arranged; and I am not aware of any change of boundaries required for the due administration of the law, or the better accommodation of the sick poor.

CROOM.

1.—The workhouse is adequate to the general wants of the union.

2.—The sick poor are sufficiently accommodated, and there are infectious wards.

3.—There is a mixed school, under charge of a female teacher; it is tolerably conducted.

4.—Castletown is the furthest Electoral Division, and its centre may be between nine and ten statute miles from the workhouse.

5.—It would, no doubt, be practicable to distribute the indoor poor of the union in the adjacent unions of Rathkeale, Kilmallock, Newcastle, and Limerick.

6.—Assuming Croom Workhouse to be maintained, I see no changes specially called for in the present boundaries.

GLIN.

1.—The workhouse is adequate.

2.—The accommodation for the sick poor is good and sufficient, and there is an excellent detached hospital for the treatment of infectious diseases.

3.—There is a boys' and a girls' school, and the educational advantages are as good as in most unions.

4.—Dunmoylan, east, which is the most distant Electoral Division, is about eight or nine miles from the workhouse.

5.—It might be practicable to put the indoor poor into either of the adjacent workhouses of Newcastle or Rathkeale, but it would be highly inconvenient.

6.—The union boundaries are convenient enough.

NENAGH.

1.—The workhouse is adequate in every respect.

2.—The hospital accommodation is excellent, and a fine hospital exists for infectious diseases.

3.—The schools are good and in all respects sufficient.

4.—The workhouse is tolerably central, Abington Electoral Division being the furthest off, its centre being about twelve or fourteen miles.

5.—I do not think the indoor poor could be adequately provided for in the workhouses of any adjacent unions.

6.—The existing boundaries are generally convenient.

BORRISOKANE.

1.—The workhouse is adequate to the general wants of the union.

2.—There is sufficient infirmary accommodation, and a good fever hospital about quarter of a mile distant.

3.—The school is a mixed school for boys and girls, and is tolerably well conducted.

4.—The furthest electoral division is about eight miles off.

5.—There would be nothing impracticable in providing for the indoor poor in the adjacent Unions of Nenagh and Parsonstown.

6.—The workhouse occupies a central position in the union, and no change of boundaries seems desirable.

ROSCREA.

1.—The workhouse is in every respect adequate.

2.—The infirmary and fever hospital are both sufficient in extent and accommodation.

3.—The schools are good, and the educational arrangements satisfactory.

4.—The most remote electoral division is Bourneyfarney, and the distance from Roscrea may be between ten and twelve miles.

5.—I do not think it would be practicable to provide for the indoor poor in any adjacent workhouse.

6.—I am not aware of any change in boundaries called for by the proper administration of the poor laws.

PARSONSTOWN.

1.—The workhouse is adequate in all respects to the wants of the union.

2.—There is sufficient infirmary accommodation, and an excellent hospital for contagious diseases.

3. The schools are good.

4.—The distance from the most remote electoral division cannot be less than from fifteen to sixteen statute miles.

5.—I consider it would not be practicable to provide adequately for the indoor poor in any of the adjacent workhouses.

6.—Parsonstown does not occupy a central position, and it is possible that some change of boundaries might be of advantage, but I do not feel competent at present to suggest any.

REPORT FROM MR. W. P. O'BRIEN TO THE COMMISSIONERS.

9 Goldsmith terrace, Bray,
6th August, 1877.

SIR,—The Local Government Board having forwarded to me certain queries, answers to which, from their inspectors, are desired by the Commissioners appointed to make inquiry into Poor Law Unions and Workhouses in Ireland, I have the honour to send you herewith my replies—prepared for greater convenience in a tabular shape—in regard to the fourteen unions which comprise my present district.

In returning, as I have in every instance done, a negative answer to query No. 5, I desire to explain that I do not intend to convey that it would not be perfectly practicable to provide for the present number of inmates in the workhouses of some of the unions in others adjacent to them, having regard merely to the extent of accommodation available, but only that it would not be possible, in my view of the question, to do so, conveniently, with a due regard to general convenience and the interest of those concerned.

In replying to query No 6, it will be seen I have not felt myself in a position to suggest any alteration of the existing boundary of any of the unions to which this return relates; but if, as the inquiry proceeds, such changes should be proposed, as may possibly happen, in other quarters, I will be happy, should the Commissioners so desire, to furnish them with the best information in my power upon any representation which may be submitted to them with this object.—

I have the honour to be, Sir,

Your obedient servant,

W. P. O'BRIEN,
Local Government Inspector

H. A. ROBINSON, Esq.

[TABLE

Mr. O'Brien's District.

Union		Query 1	Query 2. a.	Query 2. b.*	Query 3	Query 4.	Query 5.	Query 6.	Observations.
1. Athy,		Yes	Yes	Yes.	Yes.	11	No.	No.	
2. Balrothery,	(a)	Yes.	Yes.	Yes	Yes.	10	No.	No	(a) One school now found sufficient for both sexes in this workhouse.
3. Baltinglass,		Yes.	Yes.	Yes.	Yes.	20	No	No.	
4. Carlow,		Yes.	Yes.	Yes	Yes	18	No.	No.	
5. Celbridge,	(b)	Yes	Yes	Yes.	Yes.	18	No.	No.	(b) Same observation applies here.
6. Dublin, North,	(c)	Yes.	Yes	No	Yes	6	No.	No.	(c) In Dublin all infectious cases are treated in city hospitals.
7. Dublin, South,	(c)	Yes	Yes.	No.	Yes.	10	No.	No	
8. Enniscorthy,		Yes	Yes.	Yes.	Yes.	10	No.	No.	
9. Gorey,		Yes	Yes.	Yes.	Yes.	14½	No	No	
10. Naas,		Yes.	Yes.	Yes.	Yes.	15	No.	No	
11. Rathdown,		Yes.	Yes.	Yes.	Yes	8	No.	No.	
12. Rathdrum,		Yes	Yes.	Yes.	Yes.	18	No.	No	
13. Shillelagh,		Yes.	Yes.	Yes	Yes.	14	No.	No.	
14. Wexford,	(d)	Yes.	Yes (see note).	Yes.	Yes	19	No.	No.	(d) During the past year the infirmary accommodation proved somewhat inadequate, and the expediency of increasing it permanently has been under consideration.

* There is a separate fever hospital attached to each workhouse in my district except in Dublin (N. and S.)

Report from Mr. W. J. Hamilton to the Commissioners.

Piltown, Piltown,
3rd August, 1877.

Gentlemen,—I beg to send herewith replies to the questions received by me yesterday, and at the same time to submit to you a memorandum in detail, having reference to the subject generally—it is one in which I naturally take great interest—the opinions I have formed are not hasty ones, indeed there is nothing new in them.

I would only add that I shall be most glad to give you any assistance in my power.

I have hesitated to specify particular unions for particular purposes until I have more light as to what area of unions should be included in the reception of any particular classes of inmates, if my own district were to be an area I should exactly know which Workhouses to appropriate to the purposes I have specified, and I do not doubt that the several Boards of Guardians would in time give the suggestions favourable consideration.

I think there would be general objection to any alteration in existing boundaries, but even if there were not, I am not prepared to recommend any, for the reasons I have stated in my memorandum on the subject.

I have the honour to be, gentlemen,
Your obedient servant,
W. J. Hamilton

To the Commissioners to inquire
into Poor Law Unions.

Names of Unions, Area, Population in 1871, in Mr. W. J. Hamilton's District.

	Area, Acres	Population, 1871
Tipperary,	179,966	42,891
New Ross,	177,791	39,946
Cashel,	156,623	22,309
Thurles,	142,251	31,475
Waterford,	125,719	57,310
Clogheen,	118,427	22,247
Carrick-on-Suir,	112,630	26,173
Kilkenny,	110,248	31,193
Abbeyleix,	107,167	19,949
Thomastown,	107,577	18,817
Callan,	104,011	20,764
Clonmel,	84,610	24,069
Urlingford,	76,149	12,620
Kilmacthomas,	64,478	18,399
Castlecomer,	57,820	14,802
Donaghmore,	51,060	8,859

Average area, 111,861 acres; average population, 25,933.
There are 76 dispensary districts, including 108 dispensaries.
The average area of unions in England and Wales is 57,509 acres, average population, 34,295.
Average of unions in Ireland, 127,729; average population (1871), 32,204

Union.		No. 1.	No. 2.	No. 3. a.	No. 3. b.	No. 4.	No. 5.	No. 6.
						Miles by road		
Tipperary,		Yes.	Yes	Yes	See mem.	About 13½	Not the entire in any one adjacent union. See mem.	I do not desire any of the existing unions absorbed. Every arrangement that I would suggest is perfectly feasible with existing areas of administration. See mem.
New Ross,		Yes.	Yes.	Yes	"	" 15½		
Cashel,		Yes	Yes	Yes	"	" 13		
Thurles,		Yes.	Yes	Yes	"	" 12		
Waterford,		No. See note *.	No. See note †.	Yes.	"	" 10½		
Clogheen,		Yes.	Yes	Yes	"	" 10		
Carrick-on-Suir,		Yes.	Yes.	Yes	"	" 8		
Kilkenny,		Yes	Yes	Yes.	"	" 10½		
Abbeyleix,		Yes.	Yes	Yes.	"	" 12		
Thomastown,		Yes	Yes.	Yes	"	" 9		
Callan,		Yes.	Yes.	Yes	"	" 9		
Clonmel,		Yes	Yes.	Yes	"	" 8½		
Urlingford,		Yes.	Yes.	Yes	"	" 10		
Kilmacthomas,		Yes.	Yes. See note ‡.	Yes.	"	" 7		
Castlecomer,		Yes.	Yes.	Yes.	"	" 6		
Donaghmore,		Yes.	Yes.	Yes.	"	" 6½		

* Every winter since I have known this union (3½ years) there has been a want of suitable accommodation for one or more classes—sick, idiots, children, &c., and temporary and sometimes objectionable expedients have had to be resorted to.

† There is a deficiency of accommodation for the sick poor at times. There are some temporary buildings that ought to be replaced. In winter there has always been pressure.

‡ Last winter there was pressure on this hospital, but there is plenty of spare accommodation in the union building.

The area of this district is 1,780,183 acres The population in 1871 was 414,915. It contains 16 unions The workhouse buildings will accommodate, according to the scale of cubic feet allowed for each class, 14,519 inmates, exclusive of fever hospitals.

There are 19 fever hospitals, affording accommodation for 971 patients, according to the existing limitation orders

The total indoor accommodation is therefore (14,519 plus 971) for 15,490.

The number in receipt of indoor relief on the 24th March, 1877, was 5,397, including 1,706 sick in the infirmaries, and 136 in the fever hospitals

The number in receipt of indoor relief on the 25th March, 1876, was 5,343, including 1,638 in infirmaries, and 150 in fever hospitals, and the number in receipt of indoor relief on the 27th March, 1875, was 5,671, including 1,736 in infirmaries, and 103 in fever hospitals.

		Including Sick.	Fever Cases
March 24, 1877,	5,397	1,706	136
" 25, 1876,	5,343	1,638	150
" 27, 1875,	5,671	1,736	103

The total maximum numbers relieved indoor, in the winter of 1876-77 were 5,710

The allowance of cubic space for each class is, in every instance, somewhat less than the scale recommended by the cubic space committee for metropolitan workhouses, which is as follows—850 cubic feet for each sick person, 1,200 for lying-in women; 1,200 for cases of an unusually offensive character; 700 for infirm persons occupying the same room day and night; 500 for infirm persons able to leave their dormitories during the day; and day-room accommodation at the rate of 200 for each person; 300 for the able-bodied, and day-room besides In practice, of late years especially, nearly all classes of inmates have had far more, or at least quite as much space as the above There have been exceptions at times of pressure; for instance, in Waterford union in particular, some of the wards for sick, for lunatics, and idiots, and for children, have been occupied to the full extent of the limitation orders, and at times there has been no margin for anything In nearly all of the other workhouses in my district there has been no pressure which has not been easily met by temporary arrangements.

I have always endeavoured to have fewer beds in the wards than the sealed orders authorise, regarding those orders more as a limit for times of emergency than for ordinary times when ample space can be had by a little management The allowance for the sick is only 500 cubic feet, which is low enough, and ought never to be diminished In estimating the amount of space, the supply of light, ventilation, and pure air without draughts and at an equable temperature, are the really important considerations

Where the arrangements in these respects are perfect, or nearly so, I do not attach undue importance to the mere question of cubic space; where they are not so, I do not believe that any amount of space will compensate: where there is a good lofty room with windows on both sides, good aspect, ventilators, neither drains nor walls to interfere with the free current of country air, I should not care much about a few cubic feet one way or the other, provided the superficial area in each ward were regulated according to the surrounding circumstances. These conditions vary in different workhouses, according to sites, &c., and it will not do to depend altogether on fixed scales. It may be well, therefore, in estimating the amount of available accommodation, and for the removal of any temporary buildings which may be desirable to take the large allowance as a guide, and, allowing the increased space for each class, there will remain, in almost every portion of the district, more than ample accommodation for any amount of destitution and sickness which is ever likely to need it.

Such a superabundance of accommodation has led to a general belief that there would be no practical inconvenience in closing some of the workhouses, especially the smaller houses such as Castlecomer, Donoughmore, Kilmacthomas, and Urlingford, and, reverting to the areas which were originally deemed to be sufficient for the purposes of relief; and it is generally thought that this would be followed by such a saving in establishment and some other charges as would be a substantial relief to the ratepayers.

Any proposal which, without interfering with the due relief of the poor, would at the same time decrease the burdens of the ratepayers, is entitled to favourable consideration, and in this spirit I approach the subject.

In each of the above unions there is a fever hospital and an infirmary. There are no other hospitals for the sick poor.* In cases where there is ability to pay, reasonable payment is enforced, and thus, too, a large amount of hospital relief is given to classes above the destitute poor Any one who has been brought in contact with the practical relief of the sick must know that persons going to hospital "in serious illness, especially in fever or with fractured limbs, suffer more or less in removal, and that their sufferings are frequently in proportion to the distance of removal," that the removal of fever patients after a certain stage is, where the distance is long, almost certain death. It is, therefore, necessary to offer every facility for the admission of contagious cases The health of others is moreover endangered by keeping such cases in dwellings unsuited either for the cure of disease, or prevention of the spread of infection. Fresh air, cleanliness, and separation are essentials. Separation at least cannot be had in the cabins of the poor, or even in the majority of houses—hence disease spreads, and often runs free course.

So convinced am I of the benefit of even auxiliary hospitals, that I have taken every opportunity to urge their establishment, or their continuance, on the grounds that they give timely and acceptable relief, especially when remote from a centre with which there is not much intercourse, and because they are readily availed of when a distant hospital would either not be at all, or too tardily so, in which case the isolation which is so important in the treatment of contagious fevers would be utterly impracticable.

In the following extracts from an article in the *Times*, the importance of making provision for the treatment of contagious diseases is very ably stated. Any person who has had practical experience must know what a faithful picture it is.—

"Every one who has any practical knowledge of the poor must have been struck by their peculiarly unhappy condition on the occasion of sickness. Frequently with only one bed-room, and rarely with more than two, the whole family sleep and breathe in an atmosphere of contagion Owing to the additional expenses which sickness entails, they are often even worse fed than usual, and those who are not at first attacked are thus predisposed to contract the disease Moreover, if it be the father who falls ill, the wages of the family are gone, if it be the mother, she has no one to nurse her, the children are neglected, and the food is ill prepared Even when the mother is not the person attacked, the labour of nursing, in addition to her other work, is alone sufficient to prostrate her, proper nursing, in fact, in any case, is an impossibility. There are neither the appliances, nor the time, nor the strength, nor the quiet, nor the food for it. The poor sufferers get their medicine, and that is about all the medicinal help they receive If the neighbours help, as in their generosity they often do, they incur the peril of spreading the illness among their own families, and indeed the mere proximity of one family to another is alone sufficient to propagate it

"The London poor, in spite of their crowdings, suffer less, perhaps, from this peculiar aggravation of their lot than the poor in some parts of the country, for the sick may be always removed either to the fever or small pox hospital, or to a separate ward of the workhouse infirmary. In the country they have rarely any such opportunity, and they must live through the disease in their unhealthy cottages, with such scanty attendance as the parish doctor, with a large district under his charge, can afford to give them An admirable illustration, however, of the manner in which the evil might be obviated, was described in our columns some time ago A sort of hospital was established in a village in the simple shape of a clean, well ventilated cottage. To this cottage the sick

* There are County Infirmaries at Kilkenny and Cashel. The Leper Hospital at Waterford, and the Houghton Fever Hospital at New Ross.

were removed from their crowded homes, there they were brought under a regular and efficient system of nursing, and could be attended by the parish surgeon more conveniently, and therefore more effectually, than when scattered over the parish."

A case is then particularised where "four persons, husband, wife, and two children, were found all lying sick of typhus, in one low room, attended only by a poor old woman who entreated to be released from her deadly task. The mother and one of the children died very shortly afterwards. The history of the case is as follows:—The mother sickened first; her sister came from the country to nurse her, but fell ill herself and returned home, where she gave the disease to her brother. The family were then visited by the mother of the husband; she did not fall ill herself, but she conveyed the fever to her home, where her son died, and the two sisters and the father also fell ill; a girl employed at a neighbouring house gave some assistance and she carried the disease to two of her mistress's children. Falling ill herself, she was sent home, and there formed another focus of infection. Two neighbours then visited the house: the one has since lost her son; of the other the husband and son have been dangerously ill. It will be observed that, exclusive of the house in which the fever broke out, two persons have died, and ten others have fallen ill; and all because for want of a nurse the sick had to be visited by persons from healthy families."

In another case an outbreak of fever in a village appears to have run with frightful rapidity through at least five families, and for the most part the progress of the disease is traced to direct personal contagion. "One family of five persons, consisting of the father and four children, were found sleeping in one room 12 feet by 9, in a most squalid house, surrounded by filth, and the four children were all sick. A poor woman had been paid by the Guardians two shillings a week to act as nurse to this sick family; the result was, that her own boy fell ill of the disease. The family in which the outbreak originally occurred was visited by two neighbours: one of these is now left a widow, with two suffering children; the other is dead. As to the family itself, when the Inspector called, the mother lay helpless in one room, and the son in another, while the daughter had gone to take the father his dinner." In the last case "a poor woman, who has since died of typhus, lay for some time, not merely without nursing, but even without any medical attendance."

Without waiting to reflect on such revelations, it may be sufficient to point out "the hopelessness of these poor people obtaining proper nursing, and how grievously the danger of each case must have been aggravated for the want of it; and in the next place, that in all probability the greater part of this suffering and death might have been avoided if some provision had existed for at once isolating, under proper care, the persons who were first attacked. The contagion is traced from family to family as one neighbour goes to the assistance of another. The first case is like a lighted stick in the midst of a bundle—it must be separated at once from the others. Even when this is done, a spark may linger, and another and another stick may have to be removed—leave them together, and the fire is not only sure to spread, but it is far more violent in each particular case." In short, "to remove the sick person and to disinfect the house offers the only effectual means by which the disease can be prevented from spreading, while the same plan affords the best chance for the sufferer's recovery." "In some place specially adapted for his reception he may be well nursed and carefully watched."

Such a place, conspicuous for the successful treatment of contagious diseases, exists in every union in my district, and from time to time has played its part in preventing the spread of disease and many other ways. *I do not believe it would be possible to close any one of these hospitals without the certainty of lamentable consequences.* It would, indeed, in my opinion, be more true economy to increase the facilities for the treatment of contagious diseases by increasing the number of cottage hospitals, and seeking in every possible way to overcome prejudices which still interfere, more or less, with the free use of such hospitals by any class unable to secure segregation in their own dwellings.

And not only do I hold that fever wards should be increased, but I contend that the existing facilities for ordinary hospital treatment cannot safely be interfered with. If anything, they ought to be increased in large unions, and generally in the direction of *pay cases* especially. "Ordinary houses do not allow separation, quiet and attendance that shall not interfere with rest—the hospital of the house, even under favourable circumstances, must be all comprised in one room, everything has to be remembered, to be understood, if possible, to be sent for, to be discussed, and to be performed before the eyes of the sufferer: ordinary attendants soon weary, flag, and sleep, and sometimes shrink with terror or disgust when anything serious is to be done—the cry for a nurse when none is to be found—the case not understood—drugs in which nobody puts the least faith—the delay in obtaining the commonest appliances, when found necessary—all this is the daily business of a hospital."

Surely where hospitals already exist, and are equally conspicuous as fever hospitals for the good they do, it would be an incalculable injury to close them on the mere ground of economy. "Economy of money, possibly, but at the cost of health and life. Economy ought not to be permitted to override the dictates of humanity in the case of actual disease—the truest economy is to cure the sick pauper as rapidly as possible. It is short-sighted parsimony which converts a curable into an incurable case, or spreads contagious disorders by refusing to isolate those affected with them." Most of the workhouses are now hospitals rather than workhouses properly so called. They receive of course "a fluctuating body of vagrants, and now and then an able-bodied labourer, but their permanent inmates are orphan and deserted children, destitute and deserted women, old and decrepid people of both sexes, idiots, and imbeciles, and patients afflicted with every variety of disease, acute and chronic, curable and incurable."

Experience has helped to "sift the classes which have to be dealt with, and to discriminate between the innocent and helpless, and the confirmed vagrant and hopeless idler, and there are few who do not think that the appliances and comforts bestowed upon these sick, aged, and infirm, and children, are strictly in accordance with what is right, cries for more humanity, and more expenditure at one time, and cries for a more stringent and deterrent system at another, are not now so common as they used to be." There is a general disposition to do everything that is essential for curing the sick poor and restoring them to health: at the same time it is right to remember that a large proportion of the ratepayers are nearly as poor themselves, and therefore any unnecessary expenditure or waste is unpardonable.

If I could regard the maintenance of these hospitals as unnecessary expenditure, nothing would induce me to say a word in favour of their being retained as such, but I have no sort of doubt that it would be as fatal policy to close them as it would be to close the fever hospitals. I feel bound, therefore, to record my deliberate opinion that *neither fever hospitals nor ordinary workhouse hospitals can be safely closed in any portion of my district.*

There will still remain an amount of available accommodation, taken as a whole, which ought to render further building operations on a large scale wholly unnecessary, and at the same time facilitate improvements in the relief of certain classes of indoor poor.

In the suggestions which I am about to make I should be glad to elicit the opinions of those affected, to the utmost possible extent, so that I might collect and consider their views. It has been well said that "the most benumbing thing to the intellect is routine," and I know that generally, and I think properly, there is a deeply rooted objection to change. I have no authority to consult anyone, and therefore my suggestions have not been subjected to the criticism which is so useful; however, as I am unwilling to interfere with the independent action of Boards of Guardians, as they exist, and my proposals are for permissive rather than compulsory powers, I hope there is nothing fairly objectionable in any of them.

I propose —

1. That there shall be a combined attempt to train a suitable staff of assistant nurses for the sick.

2. That there shall be separate and improved accommodation for harmless lunatics, and for idiots and imbeciles.

3. That orphan and deserted children, between the ages of 5 and 15 shall be trained in union industrial training schools.

4. That tramps and vagrants, and one or two other classes, shall in some respects be subjected to different rules and regulations from other classes.

5. That section 7 of 25 and 26 Vic., c. 83, be extended, so as to include workhouse infirmaries, and enable Boards of Guardians to send cases requiring sea air and sea bathing to workhouses on the sea coast, and likewise that sec. 14 of the 6 & 7 Vic., c. 92, be amended so far as to leave to the Boards of Guardians' discretion as to the age of deaf and dumb and blind, who may be sent to institutions duly approved of.

6. That power be given to amalgamate workhouses, with a view of thus preventing the over-crowding of any particular class, and the more perfect relief of particular classes of inmates.

All of these changes are consistent with existing areas and arrangements, which admit of more effective local surveillance as well as of more real and ready assistance of relief to those who need it than larger areas would. The area of the smallest known in my district (Donoughmore) is 51,060 acres. The average area of the unions in England and Wales is 57,502 acres. Every other Union in my district is above this average. The average area of Unions in my district is 111,261 acres, nearly double the size of the average of Unions in England and Wales.

That the suggested changes will much effect expenditure, one way or the other, I do not anticipate, beyond the economy which is allied to efficiency, and going to the roots of evils rather than making provision for their maintenance and growth.

1st. As to a trained staff of assistant nurses. Of late years especially there has been difficulty in many Unions in providing suitable attendants for the sick; I have frequently adverted to it, any person who has the supervision of sick wards has experienced more or less the difficulty I have referred to, it is one which I apprehend can only be met by a regular system of training, and the sooner the mere fact that a woman is able-bodied ceases to be regarded and recognised as the qualification for the office of attendant on the sick, the better. I have often seen poor women thus placed, doing their best to do justice to the sick, and to their young infants, sometimes not a month old.

I think that all attendants on the sick should be trained, and at least be of good character, free from any incumbrance, able to read, and that they should invariably be paid servants.

In September, 1868, I said "the evil of the present system of assistant nurses is increasing year by year, and sooner or later a less objectionable class of nurses will have to be appointed." I referred a few days ago to a Union where some of the assistant nurses had infants in arms, "who cry when their mothers leave them, and disturb the patients." Again, in 1870, I said, "in this as in many other workhouses there is not much to choose from now. No able-bodied woman of good character, at all handy, and without young children, need enter or remain in a workhouse." Hence the selection is often limited to unmarried women with young children.

In point of fact the reason why the present class of attendants are inmates of the workhouses at all under the existing circumstances of the country, is because too many of them have failed in some of the qualifications essential to the position of a fit and proper attendant on the sick. Miss Nightingale has so ably laid down these qualifications that the more publicity and consideration they receive, and the more Boards of Guardians are educated to them, the better for all parties. She says, "no person should be employed as a wardswoman who is not sober, honest, truthful, trustworthy, punctual, quiet, and orderly, cleanly and neat, patient, cheerful, and kindly."

Such persons should then be trained:—

1. In the dressing of blisters, burns, sores, wounds, and in applying fomentations, poultices, and minor dressing.

2. In the application of leeches externally and internally.

3. In the administration of enemas for men and women.

4. In the management of trusses and appliances in uterine complaints.

5. In the best methods of friction to the body and extremities.

6. In the management of helpless patients, that is to say, moving, changing, personal cleanliness of, feeding, keeping warm, or cool, preventing and dressing bed sores, managing position of.

7. In bandaging, making bandages and rollers, lining of splints, &c.

8. In making the beds of patients, and removal of the sheets whilst the patient is in bed.

9. In attending at operations.

10. To cook gruel, arrowroot, egg flip, puddings, and drinks for the sick.

11. To understand ventilation, or keeping the ward fresh by night as well as by day. That cleanliness is observed in all the utensils, those used for secretions as well as those used for cooking.

12. To make strict observations of the sick in the following particulars:—The state of secretions, expectorations, pulse, skin, appetite, intelligence, as delirium or stupor, breathing, sleep, state of wounds, eruptions, formation of matter, effect of diet, or of stimulants and of medicines.

13. And to learn the management of "convalescents."

Miss Nightingale further points out the source from which such a class of attendants may be obtained.

This source is readily available, and if it were in time turned to use, there would be no want of fit and proper attendants for the sick, not only in the workhouses but in the country generally, a want which at one time or another almost everybody has experienced.

The appointment of nuns as nurses is an important step in the direction of improving the class of wardswoman, and hence I look favourably on the movement.

As to harmless lunatics, idiots, and imbeciles, there were, in April last, in my district, 187 in separate departments, and 100 with other inmates. Most of these are harmless imbeciles, many of them very helpless and requiring special care.

In 1859, I said, "I would once more say that I trust these arrangements are not to be regarded as a permanent provision for this class of persons, and that it is only pending further legislation on the subject that the responsibility of taking charge of them is to be borne by the Poor Law authorities; for it must be remembered that few workhouses are regularly visited by the Guardians, and this class, of all others, should be most carefully and regularly visited and looked after, inasmuch as they are generally unable to complain of ill-treatment." In 1867, I said, "I did not intend to limit some observations I had made to any particular case. That they were merely a repetition of views I had repeatedly submitted for consideration. There was then no alternative in the case of a destitute dangerous lunatic but to admit him to the workhouse, however unsuitable the accommodation, &c., &c. The law does not enable Boards of Guardians to detain any person of weak intellect in the workhouse, and when such persons apply for their discharge, as they frequently do, it is not easy in practice to deal with them. As a rule, all persons of weak intellect are more or less incapable of taking care of themselves; and in practice it is found generally necessary to refuse to accede to such requests, and if it is right, as I believe it is, that such requests should be refused where there may be reasonable grounds to suppose that harm to the person of the pauper is apprehended, it would be more satisfactory to those who have to deal with such cases if it were clearly made legal to detain them under competent authority; though I say this I do not desire to be understood as regarding such an arrangement, as anything more than an improvement on the existing, for which there is no authority that I know of. If there were proper means of supervision and recreation, for poor persons of these classes, and that Boards of Guardians were regularly to visit them I should not so much care. At lunatic asylums they have paid and intelligent attendants, newspapers, musical instruments, games, cheerful day rooms, good exercising grounds, and they are much more frequently visited by the Board of Governors than they are by Guardians in workhouses.

Again in 1868 I observed, "it is probable from the tendency of the observations of Dr Nugent, in this and in other workhouses, that the new asylums will not relieve the workhouses in any degree. I trust, therefore, that Boards of Guardians may by degrees be induced to provide better supervision, better accommodation, and better means of recreation and amusement than at present exists, so far as I have had experience.

Again in 1874 I said, "I strongly object to any cells in Workhouses. *I think that lunatics and idiots who require separate confinement are not fit cases for workhouses.* Where they can properly mix with others I think they are far happier. Where they cannot, they should be at least fit cases for the wards, same as are provided for others. There is neither the staff nor the appliances in most workhouses for the proper treatment of idiots and lunatics requiring restraint."

For these reasons I should be glad to see a classification as follows:—

Harmless male lunatics—harmless female lunatics.
Harmless male idiots and imbeciles—harmless female idiots and imbeciles.

I think that all the cases of each of these classes could be better treated in selected workhouses, portions being fitted up specially for them, having a due regard to their respective requirements, and to the recommendations contained in a report of a special committee of the Charity Organisation Society, presented to the Council on the 15th of January last. Such fittings need not be expensive. The amount of suitable accommodation which would thus become available would enable Boards of Guardians to send from workhouses without any delay or difficulty cases which require either treatment or restraint, and greatly relieve both the lunatic asylums and the workhouses.

3. That orphan and deserted children between the ages of 5 and 15 years shall be trained in Union Industrial Schools.

I am aware that under the School Districts Order, an experiment in this district was not successful in consequence of parents objecting to their children being sent to a workhouse any miles distant, however, in the cases of ordinary industrial schools, I have frequently seen children altogether unconnected with the localities, and I have no doubt that orphans and deserted children, and possibly others, would not object to being sent to schools where there would be increased facilities for training them in habits of intelligence, industry, and goodness, without some of the drawbacks which now exist.

I think one such school for boys and another for girls could be most beneficially established in selected localities for each district.

There has been general testimony to the advantages of industrial training schools, and those I have visited, in Ireland especially, have so favourably impressed me that I should be glad to see a movement in this respect amongst the Irish Unions, similar to that in England.

Such schools need not interfere with boarding out, where practicable, the great object being to strike at the root of pauperism, and to raise the "religious, moral, and social character of the children." Next to the influence of a good home, and domestic life, I would place a good industrial school, and I think one such school for boys and another for girls might easily be established in selected unions where good influences prevail, and where the surroundings might almost be similar to those in an ordinary industrial school.

The number of children available for such schools is not open to the objection that the "assembling of a large number of children facilitates the spread of infectious diseases, when once it has broken out or been introduced within the walls."

I should very much like to see a few village schools for workhouse children on such a system as I have advocated in pamphlets written by me on the subject of military industrial training schools.

4. That tramps and vagrants, and one or two other classes, shall in one or two respects be subjected to different rules and regulations from other classes.

There have not been in workhouses, of late years, so many tramps and vagrants, or single able-bodied men, and other objectionable classes as formerly. Nevertheless, in some localities the evil still exists, more or less, vagrancy and idleness are regular professions. Parties travel systematically about the country from union to union, sometimes spreading disease, both of body and mind. They are not always destitute discharged soldiers, ticket-of-leave men, men who will not work, and men who cannot work, blind, maimed, &c., persons who frequent races, fairs, markets, &c. They seldom remain more than one night in each workhouse, and they sometimes visit a workhouse twice a year. I believe that if each casual had to wait over the following Board day, to appear before the Board of Guardians, if so desired by them, an effectual stop would be put to all the objectionable part of the present system. I should be glad to see legal provision to this effect. In England there is power of detention to some extent: "The method employed for some time past has been to detain habitual vagrants, and set them to work. Two metropolitan unions having discontinued this wholesome practice, soon proved its necessity by the result of its discontinuance. In one case vagrancy increased 38 per cent. One benefit of the practice is the regular identification of census and vagrancy." As to interference with the liberty of the subject, the casuals have the best of it now. No destitute poor person could fairly object to have to wait for a few days. Some Boards of Guardians would probably view the matter differently, and think it cheaper to let them go, as at present, but most sturdy tramps would avoid those workhouses where delay was imposed.

In England the instructions as to food are "the food supplied to the inmates of the vagrant wards should be sufficient for their actual necessities, but not such as either in quantity or quality would tend to increase the number of applicants or encourage imposture.

In Ireland no such distinction is made. I think that while a workhouse should be made as far as possible cheerful and kindly "for the sick, the suffering, the old, and the young, it should be made as fairly deterrent as ever, for destitution caused by idleness and vagrancy. Professional vagrants, like the pauperism of certain classes, are "weeds of noxious growth," and require stringent and stern measures to root them out, whereas, "poverty and sickness are visitations

APPENDIX A. — Poor Relief.

of the Almighty, and require different treatments." I think it is bad enough not having them always under supervision. The master's hands are too full to give them much of his time.

The fact that any young able-bodied men should seek relief under present circumstances, is I think *prima facie* evidence of how much the most of them require to be looked after closely. If they were kept from any attractive work— confined to their own yard, breaking stones mashed, a regular task, and under supervision of a steady paid servant day and night, the number would be reduced to a minimum.

5. That the Guardians powers under the 7th Sect., 25 and 26 Vic. 83, be extended so as to include workhouse infirmaries, and thus enable Boards of Guardians to send cases requiring either sea air or sea bathing to workhouses on the sea coast, and that sec 14 of 6 & 7 Vic., c. 92, be amended.

The Medical Officer of New Ross Workhouse reported the remarkable improvement of some children since their removal to the sea coast, at Waterford too, the step was attended with such satisfactory results that the Guardians have frequently repeated it.

In August, 1867, I said I sincerely wished there were facilities for such treatment in the inland unions, for there are few workhouses in which there are not cases where sea air and sea bathing alone can restore health and strength.

Such a mode of treatment is commonly prescribed for certain classes of diseases. I would submit that until cases of this description can be so treated from workhouse infirmaries it cannot be said that everything has been done to save life, and if the existing law is defective, as I apprehend it is, in this respect, it might be possible upon a representation of facts to have the Guardians powers under the 7th Sect., 25 and 26 Vic., c. 83, extended so as to enable them to send to any hospital or infirmary, whether an union infirmary or otherwise, any inmate of a workhouse whose case might require sea air or sea bathing.

I said that judging by many years experience I should not apprehend either abuse or any unwillingness on the part of a large majority of Boards of Guardians to do what was right.

Cases of hardship have come under my notice in consequence of the limit of age as fixed by the 6 & 7 Vic., c. 92, as regards deaf and dumb and blind, and I think the foregoing observation applies equally to those classes.

I think too, that by having pay-wards in those union hospitals, which are remote from county infirmaries, many sick persons who will not avail themselves of the existing arrangements would do so with incalculable benefit to themselves and to others, and without any additional expense to the ratepayers. A want which is generally felt might thus be supplied, without destroying or lessening the feeling of independence which ought to prevail.

6. That power should be given to Boards of Guardians to amalgamate workhouses with a view of preventing the over-crowding of any particular class, and the more perfect relief of particular classes of inmates, keeping in view the check of pauperism, "how best to relieve want, and how to promote thrift; stringent and stern measures are required on one side, kindness, gentleness, and mercy on the other." The greater the discretion left to Boards of Guardians the better, so far as indoor relief, but not so as regards outdoor; there is but little danger of fictitious pauperism in the one, every possible danger in the other; out-door relief is far more injurious in its consequences than indoor, it often tends to want of forethought, thriftless habits, self indulgence, idleness, and drink. Every county will have as many paupers in it as it is willing to support. If "out-door relief be sown over a union a crop of pauperism must be expected," whereas the most comfortable hospital arrangements will rarely *induce people to qualify for admission to them*.

"No one will get his leg broken or bring a fever upon himself for the sake of being kindly nursed or skilfully doctored." The real difficulty is to get them in, not to keep them out.

In one of the best unions in my district out-door relief is unknown and unexpected, hence the workhouse is more promptly and more timely availed of. There is no union in which the poor are better cared, or in which I feel less apprehensive of any case of unshoved suffering. The unions in which out-door relief is waited for are the dangerous unions in this respect. If anything, there should be a premium on thrift rather than on improvidence. In many cases, now, a thrifty person gets no assistance where an improvident person does, and rates go "partly in aid of destitution, or to supplement poor wages," except in cases of sickness or accident, aged and infirm, or widows with two or more children, all relief should be given as far as possible in workhouses. With certain classes the more closely the principles of a Poor Law are adhered to the less mischief will be done in the way of undermining independence, and even in the cases of those to whom the Irish Poor Law authorises out-door relief, the Guardians might reasonably require before granting it that they should be of "good character, able to satisfy them that their destitution was not caused by improvidence or intemperance, and that while independent they had done all in their power to make provision against times of sickness or want of employment, and there should be visible means of a suitable dwelling and of available understanding, and I should be glad to see such relief given by way of loan, as in the case of indoor relief, they would probably check the present tendency to seek relief for aged parents by classes who in former times took a pride in supporting them.

Husbands and wives in workhouses, when either is infirm, sick, or disabled by any injury, or above the age of 60 years, might be permitted to live together as in England.

Guardians should be permitted to pay at their discretion for the outfit and expenses of children going to any suitable employment, such as the army, navy, domestic service, &c.

As to disputes or misunderstandings between Boards of Guardians respecting the details of expenditure for any of the purposes suggested they may be provided for by legislation or by regulations. A union clearing house would not probably encounter any greater difficulties than a railway clearing house, and the administration of a common fund for the relief of certain classes of indoor poor would, I believe, result in efficiency and consequently in economy.

W. J. HAMILTON.

3rd August, 1877.

REPORT FROM MR. R. HAMILTON TO THE COMMISSIONERS.

UNIONS in Co. DONEGAL, viz :—

Ballyshannon, Donegal, Dunfanaghy, Glenties, Inishowen, Letterkenny, Milford, Stranorlar.

1, 2. Yes.

3. A school is attached to each of the above workhouses.

4 In Glenties and Dunfanaghy the distance is about twenty miles. In the other unions of the County of Donegal about twelve miles.

5. I don't think so.

6. No.

STRABANE.

1. There is not suitable accommodation for idiots, but in other respects the accommodation is sufficient.

2, 3. Yes.

4. About ten miles.

5, 6. No.

The accommodation for the sick poor is only sufficient for the Strabane Union. There is no spare room for the sick poor of an adjoining union.

ENNISKILLEN.

1. There is a want of suitable accommodation for the idiot class, but the guardians are about to fit up a place for them.

2, 3. Yes.

4. I think it must be twenty miles.

5. No.

6. I think that some of the district divisions in the County Cavan might be taken off Enniskillen, and added to Bawnboy Union.

OMAGH.

1, 2, 3. Yes.

4. About fourteen miles.

5, 6. No.

MONAGHAN.

1, 2, 3. Yes.

4. About ten miles.

5, 6. No.

IRVINESTOWN.

1, 2, 3. Yes.

4. About ten miles.

5, 6. No

LISNASKEA.

1, 2, 3. Yes.

4. About eleven miles.

5. I don't think so.

6. No.

CLONES.

1, 2, 3. Yes.

4. I am not quite sure as I have no map of the union, but I suppose about ten miles.

5. I don't think so, but I believe the guardians think it could be arranged. Monaghan and Lisnaskea are the adjoining unions.

6. No.

CASTLEDERG.

1, 2, 3. Yes.

4. About nine miles.

5. I don't think so.

6. No.

CLOGHER.

1, 2, 3. Yes.

4. About ten miles.

5. I don't think so, but the guardians are of a different opinion. Monaghan is the only adjacent union where spare accommodation could be provided for the sick poor of Clogher Union.

6. No.

GORTIN.

1, 2. Yes.

3. No; the children are sent to Omagh Workhouse under School District Order.

4 About twelve miles.

5. If there was room in the adjoining workhouses of Strabane and Omagh for the sick poor, the inmates might be sent to these workhouses, but there is not any spare room in the above-mentioned workhouses for sick inmates.

6. No.

COLERAINE.

1, 2, 3. Yes.

4 About twelve miles.

5. No

6. I cannot.

The accommodation for the sick in Coleraine Workhouse is only sufficient for the union. The subject of amalgamation of unions has been discussed by the Board, and I am under the impression the guardians are in favour of it, but I don't consider it can be carried out, except by making additions or alterations in the buildings of the receiving unions.

LONDONDERRY and LIMAVADY.

1, 2, 3. Yes.

4. About twelve miles

5, 6. No.

I am not aware of the views of guardians on the subject of amalgamation, but I don't consider it practicable in the county Derry Unions.

August 11, 1877. R. HAMILTON.

REPORT FROM DR. BRODIE TO THE COMMISSIONERS.

Galway, September, 1877.

GENTLEMEN,—In submitting the accompanying replies to the queries addressed to me by the Local Government Board on the subject of union amalgamation, I may be permitted to observe that so many and conflicting opinions will be offered, that it will be rather difficult to fix upon a course that would answer the peculiar circumstances of every union; some seeking for amalgamation, while others may be opposed to any alteration in existing boundaries, or system of external or internal arrangements being satisfied to "let well enough" alone.

The principal objects to be obtained are, if practicable, a retrenchment of the expenses at present necessary for keeping up certain establishments, while the numbers relieved therein have dwindled down to a mere fraction compared with former years, and the anomaly of the same staff of officials, or nearly so, being required to superintend the workhouses now-a-days as in the years 1847, 1848, and 1849.

One of the oft-suggested changes is, that the several unions throughout Ireland should revert back to the original boundaries as fixed upon in the first introduction of the Poor Laws in 1839, and convert the new workhouses into some other more beneficial and advantageous concerns than at present. This subject agitated the several boards of guardians in no small degree in the year 1857; and the answer then received by the deputation of the boards from the Lord Lieutenant, namely, "that the interests of the poor would be the first matter to be attended to," applies as well at the present day.

Any change or alteration that would impose additional hardship or inconvenience upon the sick poor, the infirm, or the helpless poor ought, and I am convinced will meet with the strongest opposition upon the part of those who administer the law.

The substitution of a more extended system of outdoor relief for the existing indoor relief would not be an improvement in the Poor Laws, but would, in my opinion, prove in the end a regular abuse of the original intention and spirit of the law of relief.

In conclusion I may be permitted to add that in making any alteration of the present boundaries of unions, it would be well to keep in mind the desirability of making the divisions conterminous with the counties, and to avoid, as far as practicable, having any electoral division situate in more than one barony. This would be found advantageous in relation to the future arrangement of the fiscal business of counties.

I remain, gentlemen, your obedient servant,

T. BRODIE, L. G. Inspector.

To the Commissioners of Poor Law Inquiry.

GALWAY.

1. The workhouse is quite adequate for the general wants of the union. The total available accommodation is 860, present number of inmates 394; in receipt of outdoor relief 51.

2. There is a fever hospital attached to the workhouse, located on an efflux of Lough Corrib, a short distance from the workhouse; it consists of two stories with two chief wards in each. The building is capable of accommodating forty-four patients.

3. There are schools attached, one for male and the

Appendix A.
Poor Relief.

other for female children, in which the children are instructed by a male and female teacher, the course of instruction is satisfactory.

4. The distance by road of the workhouse from the centre of the most remote electoral division of the union is eighteen statute miles

5. To transfer the paupers to any of the adjacent union workhouses would almost amount to a practical denial of relief.

6. I cannot suggest any alteration in the existing boundaries of the union that could be advantageously made, having due regard to the proper administration of the Poor Law, as well as to the necessities of the sick poor

Ballinasloe.

1. The Ballinasloe workhouse is quite adequate for the general wants of the union. The total accommodation is 1,359; present number of inmates, 243; number of persons receiving outdoor relief, 3.

2. There is sufficient accommodation for the sick poor. A fever hospital is attached, and on the workhouse grounds, capable of accommodating ninety-eight persons.

3. There are schools attached, one for male and the other for female children, in which the children between the ages of two and fifteen are instructed by a male and female teacher, the course of instruction is on the whole satisfactory.

4. The distance by road of the workhouse from the centre of the most remote electoral division is sixteen statute miles.

5. It would not be practicable, much less expedient, to provide for the reception of the indoor poor of the union in the workhouse of any adjacent union.

6. I cannot suggest any alteration in the existing boundaries of the union that can be advantageously made, having regard to the proper administration of the Poor Law, as well as to the necessities of the sick poor.

Loughrea

1. The workhouse is quite adequate for the general wants of the union The total accommodation is 818; present number of inmates, 104, number of persons in receipt of outdoor relief, 33.

2. Sufficient accommodation is provided for the sick poor Wards are attached in which infectious diseases are treated. No cases of fever under treatment at present.

3. A school has been at all times connected with the workhouse, in which the children between the ages of two and fifteen are instructed, at present by a schoolmistress; the course of instruction is satisfactory, but the children are of too tender years to derive that benefit which might otherwise result.

4 The workhouse is distant from the centre of the most remote electoral division (Colmanstown), fourteen Irish miles

5. It would be practicable to provide for the reception of the inmates in another union workhouse, but not desirable,—not many benefits could result from such a course, and the project would, I am convinced, meet strenuous opposition from the guardians, ratepayers, and the poor people

6 I could not suggest any alteration in the existing boundaries of the union that can be advantageously made, having due regard to the proper administration of the Poor Law, as well as to the necessities of the sick poor.

Gort.

1 The workhouse is quite adequate to the general wants of the union. The total accommodation is 780, present number of inmates, 176; in receipt of outdoor relief, 27

2 The accommodation for the sick is amply sufficient. There is a fever hospital on the premises, detached from the main building, with accommodation for fifty-one patients

3. There are two school-rooms attached to the workhouse, but at present the education of all the children (male and female) is conducted by one female teacher, and this arrangement has been found satisfactory

4. The workhouse is distant from the centre of the most remote electoral division about fourteen statute miles.

5. I do not think it would be at all practicable to provide for the reception of the inmates in any of the adjacent unions without great hardship to the sick poor The nearest is twelve miles distant from the Gort workhouse.

6. I could not suggest any alteration in the existing boundaries of the union that can be advantageously made, having due regard to the proper administration of the Poor Law, as well as to the necessities of the sick poor

Portumna.

1. The workhouse is quite adequate for the general wants of the union The total accommodation is 576; present number of inmates, 124; in receipt of outdoor relief, 27

2. Sufficient accommodation is provided for the sick poor; wards are attached in which infectious diseases are treated.

3. There is a school attached in which the children, male and female, are instructed by a female teacher, the arrangements are satisfactory.

4. The distance (by road) of the workhouse from the centre of the most remote electoral division of the union is ten miles.

5 and 6. It would, no doubt, be practicable to provide for the indoor poor of this union in the workhouses of the adjacent unions of Ballinasloe and Loughrea, but then arises the question of expediency Ballinasloe is distant fifteen Irish miles from Portumna, and Loughrea nearly an equal distance. The Portumna Guardians, with their Chairman, the Earl of Westmeath, are anxious to have their union dissolved and amalgamated with Ballinasloe and Loughrea, the proposal will not be favourably entertained by the Loughrea Board. I must leave to the Commissioners to judge of the expediency, or otherwise, of the proposed amalgamation

Tuam

1. The workhouse is quite adequate for the wants of the union. The total accommodation is 742, present number of inmates, 222, in receipt of outdoor relief, 351.

2. The general accommodation for the sick poor is sufficient, a fever hospital is attached to the workhouse grounds, capable of accommodating forty-eight persons.

3. There is a school attached; the educational arrangements are satisfactory.

4. The distance (by road) to the centre of the most remote electoral division of the union is about fourteen Irish miles.

5. It would not be practicable, much less expedient, to provide for the reception of the indoor poor of the union in the workhouse of any adjacent union. Galway is distant sixteen Irish miles from Tuam

6. I could not suggest any alteration in the existing boundary of the union that can be advantageously made, having due regard to the proper administration of the Poor Law, as well as to the necessities of the sick poor.

Mount Bellew.

1. The workhouse is adequate to the wants of the union; its total accommodation is 586. Average daily number of inmates relieved during the past year was 100; in receipt of outdoor relief, sixteen.

2. The general accommodation for the sick is sufficient; the present number on medical officers' books is thirty-eight, of whom thirty-two are aged and infirm persons. There are infectious wards capable of accommodating twenty two persons, these wards are at present unoccupied.

3 There is a school attached; present number (boys', girls', and infants') attending is seventeen.

4. The distance (by road) of the workhouse from the centre of the most remote electoral division of the union is about seven Irish miles.

5. No doubt it would be practicable to provide for the reception of the indoor poor of this union in the workhouses of the adjacent unions. Glennamaddy is the nearest, being about nine Irish miles (by road) from Mount Bellew Workhouse. Ballinasloe is distant about twelve Irish miles from Mount Bellew Workhouse. The Chairman of the Mount Bellew Union, Lord Clonbrock, who takes a deep interest in its well working, is strongly opposed to amalgamation with Ballinasloe or Glennamaddy.

6. Same answer as to query 5.

GLENNAMADDY.

1 The workhouse is quite adequate for the general wants of the union. The total accommodation is 592; present number of inmates, 117, in receipt of outdoor relief, 82.

2 There is sufficient accommodation provided for the sick poor, wards are attached in which infectious diseases are treated.

3. There is a school attached in which the children (male and female) are instructed by a female teacher; the arrangements are satisfactory.

4. The distance (by road) of the workhouse from the centre of the most remote electoral division of the union is ten miles.

5. It would, no doubt, be practicable to provide for the reception of the indoor poor of this union in the workhouses of some of the adjacent unions, but then arises the question of expediency The guardians at their meeting, on Tuesday last, declared in favour of amalgamation with the Unions of Tuam, Mount Bellow, Castlerea, and Roscommon. The first named is distant twelve Irish miles from Glennamaddy; the second, twelve, the third, twelve; and the fourth an equal distance I must leave to the Commissioners to judge of the expediency of the proposed amalgamation.

6 The townland of Cloonadarragh, forming portion of this union, but situate in the county of Roscommon, has been transferred to Castlerea Union.

OUGHTERARD.

1. The workhouse accommodation is quite adequate for the requirements of the union The total accommodation is 848, present number of inmates, 84, in receipt of outdoor relief, 0.

2 There are infectious wards capable of accommodating twenty-two persons, but the medical officer does not consider them suitable for the purpose, and treats fever cases in wards of the infirmary building

3. There is a school attached—the education of the children (male and female) is conducted by a female teacher; this arrangement has been found satisfactory.

4 The distance (by road) of the workhouse from the centre of the most remote electoral division of the union is, at least, twenty miles.

5 and 6. It would, no doubt, be an advantage to the sick poor residing in that portion of the barony of Ross situate in the Oughterard Union, if the electoral divisions comprising that barony were transferred to the Ballinrobe Union The Cong and Clonbur electoral divisions of the Oughterard Union are situate within six or seven miles of the Ballinrobe workhouse, whilst the workhouse of Oughterard is sixteen miles distant from the centre of these divisions. But it must be borne in mind that the total valuation of the Oughterard Union is only £15,044; under any circumstance, the townland of Ballykine Lower, the only townland in the county of Mayo and barony of Kilmain belonging to the Oughterard Union, should be added to the barony of Ross, it being already in the electoral division of Clonbur, in said barony of Ross, in Ballinrobe Union. The valuation of Ballykine Lower is £121 5s.

CLIFDEN.

1. The workhouse is quite adequate for the general wants of the union. The total accommodation is 822, present number of inmates, 120; in receipt of outdoor relief, 47.

2. There is a detached fever hospital on the workhouse grounds, capable of accommodating thirty-two.

3. There is a school attached—the education of the children (male and female) is conducted by a female teacher; this arrangement has been found satisfactory.

4. The distance (by road) of the workhouse from the centre of the most remote electoral division of the union is eighteen or twenty miles

5. I do not think it would be at all practicable to provide for the reception of the indoor poor of this union in any of the adjacent workhouses, without great hardship to the sick poor, the nearest (Oughterard) is distant twenty-five Irish miles from Clifden.

6. I cannot suggest any alteration in the existing boundaries It would be an advantage to the poor people residing in the Island of Innisboffin, if a small hospital could be procured for the treatment of fever cases occurring on the island, which is a considerable distance from the mainland, and inaccessible in bad weather.

ROSCOMMON.

1. The workhouse is quite adequate for the general wants of the union The total accommodation is 849; present number of inmates, 271, in receipt of outdoor relief, 237.

2. There is a detached fever hospital on the workhouse ground, capable of accommodating fifty-eight

3 There are schools attached, one for male and the other for female children, the course of instruction is satisfactory.

4 The workhouse is distant eight miles from the centre of the most remote electoral division of union.

5. It would not be expedient to transfer the paupers to any of the adjacent union workhouses.

6 I cannot suggest any alteration in the existing boundaries of the union that could be advantageously made, having due regard to the proper administration of the Poor Laws, as well as to the necessities of the sick poor. The union is sufficiently extensive for the purposes for which it is intended.

STROKESTOWN.

1 The workhouse is adequate to the general wants of the union. The total accommodation is 636; present number of workhouse inmates, 157, number in receipt of outdoor relief, 342

2 The accommodation for the sick is sufficient; there is a detached fever hospital on the workhouse grounds, capable of accommodating forty-four patients.

3. A school has been at all times connected with the workhouse in which the children between the ages of five and fifteen are instructed; the arrangements are inexpensive and satisfactory.

4. There is no line of railway passing through the union. The distance (by road) to the centre of the most remote electoral division is about nine statute miles.

5. It would not be practicable, much less expedient, to provide for the reception of the indoor poor of the union in the workhouse of any adjacent union, Roscommon, which is the nearest workhouse, is thirteen statute miles, Castlerea and Boyle eighteen each, Carrick-on-Shannon fourteen, and Longford seventeen from Strokestown

6 I am unable to suggest any alteration in the existing boundaries of the union that can be advantageously made, having due regard to the proper administration of the Poor Laws, as well as to the necessities of the sick poor.

CASTLEREA.

1. The workhouse is quite adequate for the general wants of the union. The total accommodation is 868, present number of inmates, 179, in receipt of outdoor relief, 0.

2. Sufficient accommodation is provided for the sick poor. There is a detached fever hospital on the workhouse grounds, capable of accommodating forty.

3. There are schools attached, one for male and the other for female children, in which the children are instructed by a male and female teacher; the course of instruction is satisfactory.

4. The workhouse is distant fourteen miles from the centre of the most remote electoral division of the union.

5. It would not be expedient to transfer the indoor paupers to any of the adjacent union workhouses.

6. I cannot suggest any alteration in the existing boundaries of the union that could be advantageously made, having due regard to the proper administration of the Poor Laws, as well as to the necessities of the sick poor.

BALLINROBE.

1. The workhouse is quite adequate for the wants of the union; the total accommodation is 647; present number of inmates, 202, in receipt of outdoor relief, 60.

2. The general accommodation for the sick is sufficient, there is a fever hospital attached to the workhouse containing accommodation for forty-four persons.

3. There is a school attached. Educational arrangements are satisfactory.

4. The distance by road of the workhouse from the centre of the most remote electoral division, Owenbrin, is twenty six miles.

5. It would not be practicable, much less expedient having regard to the requirements of the sick poor.

6. The Ballinrobe Union is sufficiently extensive for the purposes for which it is intended. It would no doubt be an advantage to the sick poor resident in that portion of the barony of Ross situate in the Oughterard Union, if the electoral divisions comprising that barony were transferred to Ballinrobe Union; the Cong and Cloonbur electoral divisions of Oughterard Union are situate within six miles of the Ballinrobe Workhouse, whilst the workhouse of Oughterard is over sixteen miles distant from the centre of these divisions, but it must be borne in mind that the total valuation of the Oughterard Union is only £15,044.

ATHLONE.

1. The workhouse is quite adequate for the general wants of the union; the total accommodation is 876; present number of inmates, 230; in receipt of outdoor relief, 123.

2. Sufficient accommodation is provided for the sick poor. There is a detached fever hospital on the workhouse grounds; accommodation, sixty-six.

3. Male and female schools, arrangements satisfactory.

4. The workhouse is distant from the centre of the most remote electoral division of the union fourteen miles at the Roscommon side, and seven miles at the Westmeath side.

5. It would not be practicable, much less expedient, to provide for the reception of the indoor poor of this union in the workhouse of any adjacent union.

6. The Athlone Union is sufficiently extensive for the purposes for which it is intended, and I could not suggest any alteration of the existing boundaries that can be advantageously made, having due regard to the proper administration of the Poor Laws, as well as to the necessities of the sick poor.

T. BRODIE.

REPORT FROM DR. ROUGHAN TO THE COMMISSIONERS.

LARNE, CO. ANTRIM.

1. Yes.
2. (1) Yes. (2) Yes.
3. Educational arrangements satisfactory. School attached.
4. Nineteen miles.
5. It might; but I question much whether it would be expedient to do so. I think the inconvenience that would result from so doing would not be compensated by the small saving that might take place.
6. If concentration of any of the unions in Antrim must take place this is the only union whose boundaries could at all be altered, by attaching the electoral divisions of Ardclinis, Glencloy, Glenarm, Carncastle, Kilwaughter, Larne, to Ballymena Union, and the remaining southern division to Antrim.

BALLYCASTLE.

1. Yes.
2. (1) Yes. (2) Yes.
3. Educational arrangements satisfactory. Schools attached.
4. Eighteen miles.
5. I think not.
6. I am not in a position to suggest any alterations in the existing boundaries of the union.

BALLYMONEY.

1. Yes.
2. (1) Yes. (2) Yes.
3. Educational arrangements satisfactory. Schools are attached.
4. Twelve miles.
5. I think not.
6. I am unable to suggest any alteration in the existing boundaries of the union that would be advantageous as far as the administration of the Poor Laws is concerned.

BELFAST.

1. Yes, quite adequate.
2. (1) Yes. (2) Yes.
3. Educational arrangements satisfactory. Schools attached.
4. Seven miles.
5. No.
6. I cannot suggest any alteration in the existing boundaries of Belfast Union.

BALLYMENA.

1. Yes.
2. (1) Yes. (2) Yes.
3. Educational arrangements satisfactory. Schools attached.
4. Ten miles.
5. I think not.
6. I am not in a position to suggest any alteration in the boundary of the present union.

ANTRIM.

1. Yes, quite adequate.
2. Yes, quite sufficient, and infectious wards are attached.
3. Yes, the educational arrangements are quite satisfactory. Schools attached.
4. Ten miles.
5. I think not.
6. I am not in a position to suggest any alteration in the existing boundaries of the union.

DROGHEDA.

1. Yes.
2. (1) Yes. (2) Yes.
3. Arrangements satisfactory.
4. Eight miles.
5. I think not.
6. I am unable to suggest any alteration in the existing boundaries of the union.

ARDEE.

1. Yes.
2. Yes (1.) Yes (2.)
3. Yes. Educational arrangements satisfactory.
4. Eleven miles.
5. I think not.
6. I am unable to suggest any alterations in the existing boundaries of this union.

DUNDALK.

1. Yes.
2. Yes (1.) Yes (2.)
3. Yes. Educational arrangements satisfactory
4. Sixteen miles.
5. I think not.
6. I cannot suggest any alterations in the existing boundaries of this union.

MAGHERAFELT.

1. Yes.
2. Yes (1.) Yes (2.)
3. Yes. Educational arrangements satisfactory
4. Fourteen miles.
5. I think not.
6. I am unable to offer any suggestion as to alterations being practicable in the existing boundaries of this union.

DUNGANNON.

1. Yes.
2. Yes (1.) Yes (2.)
3. Yes. Educational arrangements satisfactory
4. Ten miles.
5. I think not.
6. If concentration of unions in some instances is determined on, this union might be amalgamated with Cookstown, keeping Dungannon as central workhouse, and attaching a few outlying divisions to Clogher Union.

COOKSTOWN.

1. Yes
2. Yes (1.) Yes (2.)
3. Yes. Educational arrangements are satisfactory.
4. Eleven miles.
5. If amalgamation of unions is decided on, I think this union might be amalgamated with Dungannon, adding a few electoral divisions to the Gortin Union
6. Answer to Query 5 includes this.

ARMAGH.

1. Yes.
2. Yes (1.) Yes (2.)
3. Yes. Educational arrangements satisfactory.
4. Twelve miles.
5. Certainly not.
6. I am unable to suggest any alterations in the existing boundary of this large union.

LURGAN.

1. Yes.
2. Yes (1.) Yes (2).
3. Yes. Educational arrangements satisfactory.
4. Fourteen miles.
5. I think not.
6. I am unable to suggest any alteration in the existing boundaries of this union.

NEWTOWNARDS.

1. Yes.
2. Yes (1.) Yes (2.)
3. Yes. Educational arrangements satisfactory.
4. Thirteen miles.
5. I think not.
6. I am unable to suggest any alterations in the existing boundary of this union.

LISBURN.

1. Yes.
2. Yes (1.) Yes (2.)
3. Yes. Educational arrangements satisfactory.
4. Ten miles.
5. I think not.
6. I am unable to suggest any alterations in the existing boundaries of this union.

DOWNPATRICK.

1. Yes.
2. Yes (1.) Yes (2.)
3. Yes. Educational arrangements satisfactory.
4. Fourteen miles.
5. I think not.
6. I am unable to suggest any alterations in the existing boundary of this union.

KILKEEL.

1. Yes
2. Yes (1.) Yes (2.)
3. Yes. Educational arrangements satisfactory
4. Sixteen miles.
5. I think not.
6. I am unable to suggest any alterations in the existing boundaries of this union.

BANBRIDGE.

1. Yes.
2. Yes (1.) Yes (2.)
3. Yes. Educational arrangements satisfactory.
4. Seventeen miles.
5. I think not
6. I am not able to suggest any alterations in the existing boundaries of this union

NEWRY.

1. Yes.
2. Yes (1.) Yes (2.)
3. Yes. Educational arrangements satisfactory.
4. Eighteen miles.
5. I think not.
6. I am not able to suggest any alteration in the existing boundaries of this union.

GEORGE F. ROUGHAN.

August 14, 1877.

REPORT *from* Dr. BURKE, to the Commissioners

BAILIEBORO'.

1. It is adequate
2. It is sufficient There are infectious wards attached
3. There is a school attached. The educational arrangements are satisfactory.
4. About six miles.
5. It would not, so far as I can judge.
6. I have none to suggest.

BALLYMAHON

1. It is adequate.
2. It is sufficient. There are infectious wards attached.
3. There is a school attached. The educational arrangements are satisfactory.
4. About eight miles.
5. It would not, so far as I can judge.
6. I have none to suggest.

CARRICKMACROSS.

1. It is adequate
2. It is sufficient. There are infectious wards attached.
3. There is a school attached. The educational arrangements are satisfactory.

Appendix A.
Poor Relief.

4. About nine miles.
5. It would not, so far as I can judge.
6. I have none to suggest.

CASTLEBLAYNEY.

1. It is adequate.
2. It is sufficient. There are infectious wards attached.
3. There is a school attached. The educational arrangements are satisfactory.
4. About eight miles.
5. It would not, so far as I can judge.
6. I have none to suggest.

CAVAN.

1. It is adequate.
2. It is sufficient. There are infectious wards attached.
3. There is a school attached. The educational arrangements are satisfactory.
4. About twelve miles.
5. It would not, so far as I can judge.
6. I have none to suggest.

COOTEHILL.

1. It is adequate.
2. It is sufficient. There are infectious wards attached.
3. There is a school attached. The educational arrangements are satisfactory.
4. About nine miles.
5. It would not, so far as I can judge.
6. I have none to suggest.

DELVIN.

1. It is adequate.
2. It is sufficient. There are infectious wards attached.
3. There is a school attached. The educational arrangements are satisfactory.
4. About ten miles.
5. I think it would be practicable to do so in the workhouses of the adjoining Unions of Granard, Oldcastle, Kells, and Trim by the amalgamation of certain electoral divisions taken from each of which Unions I have learned the Union of Delvin was formed.
6. I have none to suggest.

DUNSHAUGHLIN.

1. It is adequate.
2. It is sufficient. There are infectious wards attached.
3. There is a school attached. The educational arrangements are satisfactory.
4. About eight miles.
5. It would not, so far as I can judge.
6. I have none to suggest.

EDENDERRY.

1. It is adequate.
2. It is sufficient. There are infectious wards attached.
3. There is a school attached. The Educational arrangements are satisfactory.
4. About ten miles.
5. It would not, so far as I can judge.
6. I have none to suggest.

GRANARD.

1. It is adequate.
2. It is sufficient. There are infectious wards attached.
3. There is a school attached. The Educational arrangements are satisfactory.
4. About twelve miles.
5. It would not, so far as I can judge.
6. I have none to suggest.

KELLS.

1. It is adequate.
2. It is sufficient. There are infectious wards attached.
3. There is a school attached. The Educational arrangements are satisfactory.
4. About twelve miles.
5. It would not, so far as I can judge.
6. I have none to suggest.

LONGFORD.

1. It is adequate.
2. It is sufficient. There are infectious wards attached.
3. There is a school attached. The Educational arrangements are satisfactory.
4. About twelve miles.
5. It would not, so far as I can judge.
6. I have none to suggest.

MOUNTMELLICK.

1. It is adequate.
2. It is sufficient. There are infectious wards attached.
3. There is a school attached. The Educational arrangements are satisfactory.
4. About fifteen miles.
5. It would not, so far as I can judge.
6. I have none to suggest.

MULLINGAR.

1. It is adequate.
2. It is sufficient. There are infectious wards attached.
3. There is a school attached. The Educational arrangements are satisfactory.
4. About twelve miles.
5. It would not, so far as I can judge.
6. I have none to suggest.

NAVAN.

1. It is adequate.
2. It is sufficient. There are infectious wards attached.
3. There is a school attached. The Educational arrangements are satisfactory.
4. About nine miles.
5. It would not, so far as I can judge.
6. I have none to suggest.

OLDCASTLE.

1. It is adequate.
2. It is sufficient. There are infectious wards attached.
3. There is a school attached. The Educational arrangements are satisfactory.
4. About seven miles.
5. It would not, so far as I can judge.
6. I have none to suggest.

TRIM.

1. It is adequate.
2. It is sufficient. There are infectious wards attached.
3. There is a school attached. The Educational arrangements are satisfactory.
4. About nine miles.
5. It would not, so far as I can judge.
6. I have none to suggest.

TULLAMORE.

1. It is adequate.
2. It is sufficient. There are infectious wards attached.

3. There is a school attached. The Educational arrangements are satisfactory.

4. About eleven miles.

5. It would not, so far as I can judge.

6. I have none to suggest.

T. H. BURKE, L.G.I.

13th August, 1877.

REPORT from Mr. W. ARMSTRONG, to the Commissioners.

Chaffpool, Ballymote,
8th August, 1877.

GENTLEMEN,

The Local Government Board having forwarded to me certain queries with regard to the several Unions in my district, and directed me to forward to you the answers thereto, I have the honour to transmit for your information a list of the several queries, together with my replies thereto.

I have the honor to be, gentlemen,
Your obedient servant,
W. ARMSTRONG, *Inspector.*

The Commissioners of Enquiry into
Poor Law Unions, &c.,
Four Courts.

BALLYSHANNON.

1. The workhouse is quite sufficient.

2. The Hospital accommodation is good. There is a separate Fever Hospital.

3. The school appears well conducted.

4. The centre of the most remote electoral division is about twenty statute miles distant from the workhouse by road.

5 I do not think any of the adjoining workhouses would be available for the reception of the in-door poor; but I think Mr. R. Hamilton should be consulted on this point.

6. I can offer no suggestions as to altering the boundaries of the Union.

BAWNBOY.

1. The workhouse is quite sufficient.

2. The Hospital accommodation is sufficient. There are separate male and female fever wards.

3. The school appears well conducted.

4. The workhouse is about twenty miles distant by road from the centre of the most remote electoral division.

5. I do not think any adjoining workhouses would be available.

6. I can suggest no alterations in the boundaries of the Union.

BOYLE.

1. The workhouse is quite sufficient.

2. The Hospital accommodation is very good. A separate Fever Hospital.

3. The schools, male and female, are well conducted.

4. The centre of the most remote electoral division is about eighteen or nineteen statute miles distant from the workhouse by road.

5. I do not consider any adjoining workhouse available.

6. I can suggest no alteration of the boundaries of the Union.

CARRICK-ON-SHANNON.

1. The workhouse is quite sufficient.

2. The Hospital accommodation is very good. There is a separate Fever Hospital.

3. The schools (male and female) are, I believe, well conducted.

4. The centre of the most remote electoral division of the Union is about twenty statute miles distant from the workhouse by road.

5 Boyle and Mohill workhouses are about nine and eleven statute miles distant, respectively; but I do not think any change desirable.

6. I cannot suggest any alteration in the Union boundaries.

MANORHAMILTON.

1. The workhouse is quite sufficient.

2. The Hospital accommodation is good. There is a separate Fever Hospital

3. The school is well conducted.

4. The centre of the most remote electoral division is about seventeen statute miles distant from the workhouse by road.

5. I do not consider any adjoining workhouse available.

6. I can suggest no alteration of the boundaries of the Union.

MOHILL.

1. The workhouse is quite sufficient.

2. The Hospital accommodation is good. There is a separate Fever Hospital.

3. The schools (male and female) are, I believe, well conducted.

4. The centre of the most remote electoral division is about sixteen statute miles from the workhouse by road.

5. I do not consider any of the adjoining workhouses available.

6. I can suggest no alteration in the boundaries of the Union.

KILLALA.

1. There is sufficient accommodation for the inmates, but the house is very old, being formerly the Bishop's palace.

2. There is fair Hospital accommodation, but no separate Fever wards.

3. School fairly conducted.

4. The most remote electoral division is about twenty statute miles distant from the workhouse.

5. I think all the in-door poor of the Union might be accommodated in Ballina workhouse, about seven statute miles distant.

6. The only suggestion I can offer is, to amalgamate the Union with Ballina.

BELMULLET.

1. The workhouse is sufficient.

2. The Hospital is sufficient, but there are no separate Fever wards.

3. The school appears fairly conducted.

4. The centre of the most remote electoral division of the Union is, I am informed, about twenty-three statute miles distant from the workhouse.

5. I do not consider any adjoining workhouses available.

6. I can offer no suggestion as to the boundaries of the Union.

SWINEFORD.

1. The workhouse is quite sufficient.

2. The Hospital accommodation good. A separate Fever Hospital.

3. The school appears well conducted.

4. The centre of the most remote electoral division, "Doocastle," is about fourteen or fifteen miles distant from the workhouse.

5. It might be practicable to provide for the in-door poor in Tobercurry, Claremorris, Castlebar and Ballina Unions, but I do not think it would be desirable.

6. I can suggest no alteration of the boundaries of the Union.

Appendix A
Poor Relief.

NEWPORT.

1. The workhouse accommodation is quite sufficient, but very inconveniently situated, being at the extremity of the Union, being about eight miles from Westport, and eleven or twelve from Castlebar.

2. The Hospital accommodation is good. There are two separate fever wards.

3. The school appears well conducted.

4. The centre of the most remote electoral division of the Union is about thirty-two statute miles distant from the workhouse.

5. The inmates might possibly be accommodated in Westport, Castlebar and Belmullet workhouses, but there are great difficulties in the way, owing to distances, inlets of the sea, and mountains.

6. I cannot suggest any alteration of the boundaries of the Union.

BALLINA.

1. The workhouse is quite sufficient. Part at present is occupied by military.

2. The Hospital accommodation is sufficient, and there is a separate Fever Hospital

3. There are male and female schools, which I believe are well conducted.

4. The centre of the most remote electoral division is, I should say, about twenty miles distant from the workhouse by road.

5. I do not consider the houses of any adjoining Unions available.

6. I cannot suggest any alteration in the boundaries of the Union.

CLAREMORRIS.

1. Workhouse quite sufficient.

2. Hospital accommodation good. Separate Fever Hospital.

3. School well conducted.

4. The centre of the most remote electoral division is about twelve miles by road from the workhouse. There is, however, rail to Ballyhaunis, which is quite close.

5. It might be practicable to provide for the in-door poor in Castlebar and Swinford workhouses; also, possibly, in Ballinrobe and adjoining Unions in the counties of Galway and Roscommon, which are not in my district, but I do not think any change desirable.

6. I cannot suggest any alteration in the boundaries of the Union.

CASTLEBAR

1 The workhouse is quite sufficient. A large number of sheds have been unoccupied for years.

2. The Hospital accommodation is very good. There is a separate Fever Hospital.

3. The school appears well conducted.

4. The centre of the most remote electoral division is, I should say, about twelve miles distant from the workhouse by road.

5. I do not think it would be advisable to provide for the in-door poor in other workhouses.

6. I cannot suggest any alteration in the boundaries of the Union.

DROMORE WEST.

1. The workhouse is quite sufficient.

2 The Hospital accommodation is good. Part is vacant, and set apart for Fever patients.

3. The school is fairly conducted.

4. The centre of the most remote electoral division is about thirteen miles distant from the workhouse.

5. It might be possible to provide for the reception of the inmates in Sligo and Ballina workhouses. The mountains would be an objection to any being accommodated in Tobercurry; but I do not consider any change desirable.

6. I cannot suggest any alteration in the boundaries of the Union.

SLIGO.

1. The workhouse is quite sufficient.

2. The Hospital accommodation good. No separate wards for infectious diseases, but some wards could be used if required. Fever patients are sent to the County Fever Hospital, which is quite close.

3. There are male and female schools, which I believe are well conducted.

4. The centre of the most remote electoral division is about sixteen or seventeen miles distant from the workhouse by road.

5. I do not consider the houses of any adjoining Unions available.

6. I cannot suggest any alteration in the boundaries of the Union.

TOBERCURRY.

1. The workhouse is quite sufficient.

2. Hospital accommodation good. Separate Fever wards, but rather small.

3. There is one school, which is well managed.

4. The centre of the most remote electoral division is, I should think, about fifteen miles from the workhouse

5. I hardly think so.

6. I cannot suggest any alterations.

WESTPORT.

1. The workhouse is quite sufficient for the Union.

2. The Hospital accommodation is good, and there is a separate Fever Hospital.

3. There are male and female schools, which I believe are well conducted.

4. The centre of the most remote electoral division from the workhouse is about twenty miles by road.

5. I do not think the workhouses of any adjoining Unions available.

6. I cannot suggest any alteration of boundaries.

W. ARMSTRONG.

6th August, 1877.

REPORT from Dr. MACCABE, to the Commissioners.

Blackrock, Cork,
2nd August. 1877

GENTLEMEN,—I have the honour to acknowledge the receipt, through the Local Government for Ireland, of a list of Queries referring to Union Workhouses, and I beg leave to forward herewith the answers referring to the fourteen Union Workhouses in my District.

I have the honour to be Gentlemen,
Your obedient servant,
FREDERICK MACCABE, L.K., Q.C.P.
Local Government Inspector, Cork District.

To the Commissioners for inquiring into Poor Law.

BANDON.

1. Adequate.

2. Sufficent. There is a detached Hospital for infectious diseases.

3. Yes.

4. North, eight miles, road. South, five miles, road. East, four miles, road. West, eight miles, road.

5. In my opinion it would not.

6. No.

CLONAKILTY.

1. Adequate.

2. Yes.

3. Yes.

4 North, four and half miles, road. South, four and half miles, road. East, seven and half miles, road. West, seven miles, road.

5. In my opinion it would not.

6. No.

CORK.

1. Adequate.
2. Yes. And in addition excellent detached Hospitals for fever, small-pox, &c.
3. Excellent schools for Boys and Girls. Yes.
4. North, eleven miles, road. South, seven miles, road. East, nine miles, rail or steamer. West, nine miles, road.
5, 6. No.

DUNMANWAY.

1. Adequate.
2. Yes
3. Yes. Fairly satisfactory.
4. North, nine miles, road. South, three and half miles, road. East, nine miles, two miles, road, seven miles rail. West, nine miles, road.
5. In my opinion it would not.
6. No.

FERMOY.

1. Adequate.
2. Yes.
3. Yes Quite satisfactory.
4. North, seven and half miles, road. South, seven and half miles, road. East, nine miles, road. West, nine miles, rail.
5. In my opinion it would not
6. I think that two Townlands situated respectively in Castlerichard and Tallow Electoral Divisions of Lismore Union (County of Waterford), ought to be added to Curraglass Electoral Division in this Union (County of Cork), so as to render the Union and County boundaries conterminous

KINSALE.

1. Adequate.
2, 3. Yes.
4. North, seven miles, road. South, six miles, road. East, ten miles, road. West, six miles, road.
5. In my opinion it would not
6. No.

MACROOM.

1. Adequate.
2. Yes. There is a detached Hospital for the reception of infectious cases.
3. Yes.
4. North, ten miles, road. South, six miles, two by road, four by rail. East seven and half miles, road. West, fourteen miles, road.
5. In my opinion it would not.
6. I cannot—but I consider the Western extreme of this Union, very distant from the workhouse.

MALLOW.

1. Adequate
2. Yes. There is a detached Hospital for the reception of infectious cases.
3. Yes.
4. North, about fourteen miles, eight by road, and six by rail. South, about six miles, road. North-east, about nine miles, three by road, and six by rail. North-west, about nine miles, three by road, and six by rail.
5. In my opinion it would not.
6 No.

MIDDLETON.

1. Adequate.
2. Yes. There is a detached Hospital for the reception of infectious cases.
3. Yes.
4. North, seven and half miles, road. South, seven and half miles road. East about six miles, two by road, and four by rail. West, about six miles, three by road, and three by rail.
5. In my opinion it would not.
6. No.

MITCHELSTOWN.

1. Adequate.
2. Yes. There is a detached Hospital for the reception of infectious cases
3. Yes.
4. North, about eleven miles, road. South, about three and half miles, road. East, about four and half miles, road. West, about ten miles, road.
5. In my opinion it would not.
6. No.

YOUGHAL.

1. Adequate.
2. Yes. There is a detached Hospital for the reception of infectious cases.
3. Yes
4. North, eight miles, road (Bridge across). North-east, twelve miles, road. North-west, fifteen miles, road. South, eight miles, road East, fourteen miles, road (by Bridge, sick van, &c.), and ten miles, road (by ferry, on foot). West, nine miles, rail.
5. In my opinion it would not.
6. No.

KILMALLOCK.

1. Adequate.
2. Yes, with one exception; an additional room is required in the lying-in ward. There is a detached Hospital for the reception of infectious cases.
3. Yes.
4. North-east, about seventeen miles, road (or via Knocklong eight by road, and nine by rail). South-east, about thirteen miles, road. South-west, about thirteen miles, five by road, and eight by rail. East, about eleven miles, two by road, and nine by rail. West, about ten miles, road.
5. No.
6. No.

DUNGARVAN.

1. Adequate.
2. Yes There is a detached Hospital for the reception of infectious cases.
3. Yes. Fairly satisfactory.
4. North, about sixteen miles, road. South, about twelve miles, road. East, about seven miles, road. West, about thirteen and half miles, road.
5. In my opinion it would not.
6. No.

LISMORE.

1. Adequate.
2. Yes. There is a detached Hospital for the reception of infectious cases.
3. Yes.
4. North, about seven miles, road (rail in construction). South, about nine miles, road. East, about ten miles, road. North-west, about twelve miles, three by road, and nine by rail.
5. In my opinion it would not.
6. The whole of this Union lies in the County of Waterford, except one small Townland in the south corner of Castlerichard Electoral Division and another in the North-west corner of Tallow Electoral Division. I think those two Townlands ought to be added to Curraglass Electoral Division, in Fermoy Union and County of Cork, to which they naturally belong; the arrangement would have the advantage of rendering the Union and County boundaries conterminate.

F. MACCABE,
Local Government Inspector.

2nd August, 1877.

Appendix A.

Poor Relief.

KILLARNEY, *September 12th*, 1877.

GENTLEMEN,—Adverting to the queries submitted to me with reference to the subject of your inquiry into Poor Law Unions and Workhouses in Ireland, I have now the honor to transmit herewith answers to those queries for each of the Poor Law Unions comprised in my district.

I have the honor to be, gentlemen, your very obedient servant,

SAMUEL HORSLEY, L.G.I.

To the Poor Law Union Inquiry Commissioners, Ireland.

UNIONS IN DISTRICT.

BANTRY.	KENMARE.	NEWCASTLE.
CAHIRCIVEEN.	KILLARNEY.	SKULL.
CASTLETOWN.	LISTOWEL.	SKIBBEREEN.
DINGLE.	MILLSTREET.	TRALEE.
KANTURK.		

BANTRY.

1. The Workhouse is adequate to the general wants of the Union.

2. It is. Yes, a fever hospital for the accommodation of forty patients.

3. Yes, a mixed school under a competent schoolmistress. The educational arrangements are fairly satisfactory.

4. Twenty statute miles (by road) from the centre of Sheep's Head Electoral Division.

5. I think not; the bulk of Bantry Union is too remote from either of the Workhouses of the two adjacent unions of Skull and Skibbereen.

6. No, as it is, the sick poor are in many cases a long distance from hospital relief.

CAHIRCIVEEN.

1. Yes.

2. Yes There are no infectious wards attached to the Workhouse; but there is a fever hospital with accommodation for forty-nine patients, at a distance of about two and a-half statute miles from it, and this hospital is in the possession and under the control of the Board of Guardians

3. Yes, a mixed school under a female teacher. The educational arrangements are sufficient, the children being generally of very tender years

4. About eighteen statute miles (by road) from the centre of Maum Electoral Division in one direction, and about the same distance from the centre of the Electoral Division of Ballinskelligs in an opposite one.

5. I think not, for the same reason as that given in the case of Bantry Union.

No; the geographical formation of the country is against the disturbance of the existing boundaries of the union; it is mountainous and in many parts difficult of access.

CASTLETOWN.

1. Yes.

2. Yes. But there are no infectious wards separate from the Workhouse Infirmary or general hospital, though two wards therein are, when necessary, devoted to infectious cases. There were some timber sheds on the workhouse site for the treatment of infectious and contagious disease, but the Board of Guardians suffered them to fall into perfect decay, and they are no longer available for the purpose.

3. There is a mixed school taught by a careful and competent female teacher The educational arrangements are upon the whole sufficient.

4. About twelve statute miles from the centre of Kilnamanagh Electoral Division.

5 No; the workhouses of the two adjoining unions of Bantry and Kenmare are much too distant from this union to be made available, and the Boards of Guardians of all three unions are averse to a change in the existing boundaries.

6. No.

DINGLE.

1. Yes, quite adequate.

2. Yes. There are two wards in the general hospital or infirmary for the treatment of infectious disease, and when necessary there are some vacant shed buildings which could be made available without much expense, for the reception of infectious and contagious cases.

3. There is a mixed school conducted by a remarkably well qualified schoolmistress; and the educational arrangements are satisfactory.

4. About seventeen statute miles (by road) to the centre of the Electoral Division of Lack, and about the same distance to the centre of the Electoral Division of Castle Gregory.

5. I think not, without the greatest possible hardship to the applicants for, and the recipients of relief.

6. I cannot; in this case as in that of the Cahirciveen Union, the geographical formation of the country would not, I think, admit of any material alterations in the existing boundaries.

KANTURK.

1. It is adequate.

2. It is sufficient in extent, but the wards though numerous are small and confined in the male hospital, and do not present perfect facility for constant supervision of the pauper attendance on the part of the paid nurses. There are infectious wards, but not separate from the general hospital accommodation, that is, in a detached building.

3 There is a male school, and also a female school, under a competent schoolmaster and two competent schoolmistresses. The educational arrangements are satisfactory upon the whole

4. About thirteen statute miles by road from the centre of the Electoral Division of Newtown.

5. I think not.

6. No, the union is already very extensive, embracing an area of about 293 square miles.

KENMARE.

1. Yes, it is adequate.

2. The general accommodation for the sick poor is sufficient; and there is a detached building (or fever hospital) affording accommodation for forty-nine patients labouring under infectious or contagious disease.

3. There is a mixed school conducted by a competent schoolmistress. The educational arrangements are sufficient.

4. Twenty-one statute miles by road from the centre of the Electoral Division of Castlecove.

5. It would not.

6. No; all the workhouses of the coterminous unions are too far removed from the workhouse of this union to render any change in its existing boundaries expedient.

KILLARNEY.

1. Yes, there is no deficiency in this respect.

2. The general accommodation for the sick poor in the workhouse is sufficient; but there are no infectious wards—properly so called—except for cases of skin disease, &c., which are treated in isolated wards Cases of fever and contagious disease are transferred to the "Killarney Fever Hospital," (distant about a quarter of a mile from the workhouse), the Board of Guardians paying for their maintenance and treatment therein, by agreement with the trustees of said hospital.

3. There is a male, and also a female school in the workhouse, conducted by a head and an assistant schoolmaster, and by a head and an assistant schoolmistress. The educational arrangements are satis-

factory, and a few boys are instructed out of school hours in shoemaking and tailoring by a master shoemaker and a master tailor.

4. Eighteen statute miles by road from the centre of the Electoral Division of Carragh.

5. I think not, looking to the distance of those workhouses from the Killarney one.

6. Not unless Mill-street Union were to be dissolved and its area re-distributed between the unions of Kanturk and Macroom, in which case it might be practicable to annex a small portion of the existing area of Mill-street to that of Killarney.

LISTOWEL.

1. Yes.

2. The general accommodation for the sick poor in the workhouse is sufficient. There is a detached fever hospital on the workhouse premises for the accommodation of forty-three patients.

3. There is a mixed school for male and female children conducted by a competent schoolmistress. The educational arrangements are fairly satisfactory.

4. Eleven statute miles by road from the centre of the Electoral Division of Killury.

5. No, especially if the same Poor Law Union is not to be partly in one county and partly in another.

6. No, I think the existing area of the union is sufficiently extensive and compact for all practical purposes.

MILLSTREET.

1. It is adequate to the general wants of the union.

2. The general accommodation for the sick poor in the workhouse is sufficient, and there is a fever hospital detached from the other workhouse buildings, providing accommodation for fifty-eight patients.

3. There is a male and also a female school attached to the workhouse, conducted by a competent schoolmaster and a competent schoolmistress. The educational arrangements are satisfactory.

4. About six statute miles by road from the centre of the Electoral Division of Crinaloo.

5. I think the indoor poor might, as far as accommodation for the healthy is concerned, be received into the workhouses of Kanturk, Killarney, and Macroom, and that no special hardship would result to them therefrom; but there has always been a very large number of sick in the Millstreet Hospital as compared with the number of healthy inmates of the workhouse, and I think it more than doubtful whether accommodation for them could well be provided in the union workhouses I have mentioned, except at a considerable outlay and some hardship to the sick themselves, and I further think that the saving financially to the Mill-street union rate-payers, would not counterbalance the evils that would probably result from an impaired local supervision in regard to the administration of relief.

6. The reply to this question would depend greatly upon whether the Mill-street union is to be dissolved or re-constructed.

NEWCASTLE.

1. Yes quite adequate.

2. The general accommodation for the sick poor is ample; and there are infectious wards attached to the workhouse with accommodation for fifty patients, and it could be largely increased with scarcely any additional expense.

3. Yes, there is a mixed school for male and female children, under a competent schoolmistress and an assistant schoolmistress.

4. About seventeen statute miles by road from the centre of Mountcollins Electoral Division.

5. I think not advantageously.

6. No.

SKIBBEREEN.

1. The workhouse is adequate to the wants of the union.

2. It is sufficient, and there are separate male and female wards attached to the workhouse.

3. Yes; a mixed school for boys and girls, under a competent schoolmistress and an assistant schoolmistress. The educational arrangements are pretty satisfactory.

4. Nearly ten statute miles by road from the centre of the Electoral Division of Gorthnasoreeny, and a like distance from the centre of the Electoral Division of Clonnkeen.

5. I think not, with any advantage to the adjoining unions.

6. I cannot.

SKULL.

1. Yes, quite adequate.

2. The general accommodation for the sick poor is sufficient; there are good slated detached sheds on the workhouse land, close to the principal entrance to the workhouse; they are at present unoccupied, but could be made available in a few hours, if necessary, for infectious diseases.

3. There is a mixed school under a competent female teacher. The educational arrangements are not unsatisfactory.

4. Fourteen statute miles by road from the centre of the Electoral Division of Crookhaven.

5. I think not; the workhouses of Bantry and Skibbereen Unions are too remote from the Skull one.

6. No, the boundaries of the union as at present constructed are, I think, well arranged.

TRALEE.

1. The workhouse is adequate to the general wants of the union.

2. The general accommodation for the sick poor in the workhouse is sufficient. There are no infectious wards attached to the workhouse, the fever hospital being occupied now by male infirmary patients. The fever and contagious disease cases are transferred from the workhouse to the Tralee Fever Hospital, and treated and maintained there in a set of good slated shed buildings in the possession of the Board of Guardians.

3. There is a school for male and also one for female children, conducted by a schoolmaster and a paid monitor, and by a schoolmistress and an assistant schoolmistress, respectively; all the teachers are well qualified.

4. Twenty-four statute miles by road from the centre of the Electoral Division of Gneeves.

5. I think not; the workhouses of the adjoining unions are too remote to admit of this being done advantageously for the poor.

6. I am unable to offer any suggestions for altering the existing boundaries of the union, I believe they were very well considered by the Boundary Commissioners previous to returns made to an order of the House of Lords, dated 7th day of March, 1854.

SAMUEL HORSLEY,
Local Government Inspector.

September 12th, 1877.

No. 3.—MEMORIAL praying for the AMALGAMATION of CASTLECOMER UNION with that of ABBEYLEIX.

To the Commissioners of the Poor Law Union Inquiry.

The humble petition of the Ratepayers of the Electoral Divisions of Ballyraggett, Attanagh, Clobarinka, Kilmaleck, Mothel, and Muckalee, in the Castlecomer Union, showeth that your Petitioners believe that by effecting an amalgamation of the said union with that of Abbeyleix, a considerable reduction could be made in the cost of administering the law

APPENDIX A.

Poor Relief.

for the Relief of the Poor, without in any degree impairing its efficiency; your Petitioners are convinced that the staff of Officers which is at present kept up in either one of the aforesaid unions would be amply sufficient to attend to the number of paupers now relieved in both, and that by the amalgamation which they respectfully suggest the expense of nearly the whole of one staff could be saved. In support of their suggestion your Petitioners submit that from the diminution of the population since the union areas were last defined, the subsequent increased demand for labour, and the higher rate of wages, the numbers in the poorhouses have considerably diminished, so that many of them now are comparatively empty, and that consequently the cost of the staff, on the establishment charges as they are termed, have become absurdly disproportionate to the amount required for the actual support of the destitute poor. Your Petitioners submit for your information the poundage of the expenditure on the valuation in their union for both these purposes for the years ending September 29th, 1875 and 1876:—

1875, Poundage expenditure for In-door, Out-door Relief, and Clothing . . .	1s 6d in the pound.	
" " Establishment Charges	0s 3½d.	"
1876, For Indoor, Outdoor Relief & Clothing	1s 3¾d.	"
" " Establishment Charges	0s. 9½d.	"

("Establishment charges" are exclusive of Medical Charities, Vaccination, Registration, and Sanitary Charges.)

and they would ask your kind notice of the fact that the Establishment Charges as shown by these figures average more than one-third of the expenditure on the relief of the destitute poor. With reference to the general question, your Petitioners would submit that, as regards area, population, and valuation, Castlecomer Union is less than half the average size of the Unions in Ireland, the figures being as follows:—

	Castlecomer Union	Average of Unions in Ireland
Area,	57,793 statute acres.	124,742 statute acres.
Population,	15,937 (Census of 1861)	35,552 (Census of 1861).
Valuation,	£38,150	£80,697

and that with the exception of the two Unions of Skull and Donaghmore, Castlecomer is the smallest rural union in Ireland.

Your Petitioners further respectfully submit that no geographical objections exist to the amalgamation of the two unions which they suggest and that from their local knowledge of the districts they are convinced that it would be in no way detrimental to the interest of the Poor. Under these circumstances your Petitioners hope that your honourable Board, will, after due inquiry, see fit to recommend the amalgamation of the Castlecomer Union with that of Abbeyleix, and by so doing lighten the heavy burden of taxation imposed upon them by the support of the present system, and as in duty bound your Petitioners will ever pray.

Arthur Kavanagh, M.P., Carlow Co., Ballyragget.
Gerald J. Brennan, Ballyragget.
Thomas Walsh, Ballyragget.

And about 200 others.

REPLY of the COMMISSIONERS.

Four Courts, Dublin,
23rd July, 1878.

SIR,—The Poor Law Union Inquiry Commissioners have given their best consideration to the Memorial of the ratepayers of several divisions of the Castlecomer Union, urging the abolition and amalgamation with the adjoining Union of Abbeyleix, but are unable to find any advantages arising from such a course as would compensate for the inconvenience and hardship which must necessarily arise from the breaking up of an established Union, and the dissolution of a Board of Guardians whose proceedings the Commissioners believe to have been judicious and satisfactory.

The Commissioners note that the ground upon which the demand for amalgamation is based, and the chief point upon which stress is laid, is, that the result would be—"Reduction in the cost of administering the Poor Law, without in any degree impairing its efficiency." In this view the Commissioners are unable to concur.

Having regard to one point urged by the Memorialists in favour of amalgamation, viz., the small size of the Union, the Commissioners desire to observe that the area of Castlecomer is 57,830 acres, which, though under the average of Irish Unions, is larger by over 300 acres than the average area of Unions in England and Wales.

The Commissioners find—taking as their basis the year ended the 25th March, 1877—that the pauperism of the Union is in a great measure concentrated in the Castlecomer Electoral Division.

In the above year, out of 48,337 collective days relief given in the Workhouse, no less than 34,323 were charged to that division, whilst only 5,443 were charged to all the other divisions of the Union, and as fully a proportionate part of the collective days charged to the Union at large arose from parties coming in from Castlecomer Electoral Division, it would therefore appear that more than five-sixths of the Workhouse relief was given to parties belonging to that Division.

The numbers admitted to the Workhouse for hospital treatment, and the numbers treated in the Fever Hospital for the last five years, are shown on the subjoined table:—

Year ended.		Workhouse Infirmary.	Fever Hospital.
September, 1873,	.	124	89
" 1874,	.	121	61
" 1875,	.	131	192
" 1876,	.	171	168
" 1877,	.	160	99
		707	609

Looking to the amount of disease and suffering indicated by the above return, and taking into consideration the quarter of the union in which they arise, the Commissioners are not able to concur in the statement contained in the memorial that amalgamation with Abbeyleix "would be in no way detrimental to the interest of the poor," as on the contrary they believe that such a proceeding would entail undue hardship upon large numbers of sick and infirm, by necessitating a removal to such a distance, and they would therefore not feel justified in recommending any measure which would not leave provision for the continued treatment of Fever Hospital and Workhouse Infirmary cases at Castlecomer.

Supposing that it were deemed expedient to amalgamate the two unions, while still maintaining this provision for the sick at Castlecomer, the saving in rates would fall far short of that hoped for by the petitioners, as a considerable staff would still have to be kept up in connexion with the Fever Hospital and Infirmary, and the saving in the salaries and rations of the few officers whose services might be dispensed with, though it might amount to from £200 to £300 a year, would have to have set against it the cost of the superannuation which they would naturally expect, and with the enlarged area increased outdoor relief, with its train of evils, would certainly follow.

Irrespective of the foregoing considerations, there is yet another ground upon which it would appear to the Commissioners to be highly inexpedient to dissolve the Union of Castlecomer and unite it with that of Abbeyleix, and that is the insufficiency of accommodation in the workhouse of the latter union for the destitute poor of the two unions.

The numbers in receipt of relief in the two unions on the 15th February of the last three years, irrespective of those in Fever Hospitals and Probationary Wards, were as follows:— Appendix A. Poor Relief.

	Sick in Infirmary		Healthy							Total.
			Aged and Infirm		Able-bodied.			Children.		
	Male	Female	Male	Female	Male.	Female	Mothers with Infants	Male	Female	
1875 { Castlecomer,	24	23	27	16	5	6	3	26	13	146
1875 { Abbeyleix,	22	21	31	25	–	3	4	30	15	128
Total,	46	44	58	41	5	9	7	56	31	277
1876 { Castlecomer,	18	17	25	20	4	8	6	28	21	148
1876 { Abbeyleix,	19	18	35	30	1	–	10	16	24	150
Total,	37	35	45	50	5	8	16	44	45	305
1877 { Castlecomer,	20	15	10	29	2	10	4	27	19	136
1877 { Abbeyleix,	21	20	30	34	–	–	4	25	21	157
Total,	41	35	40	64	2	10	8	52	40	293

The above table shows the numbers for whom accommodation would have been required supposing the Castlecomer house to have been abolished

It may be supposed by the Petitioners that the house at Abbeyleix can afford ample accommodation for the foregoing numbers, inasmuch as its accommodation under the existing sealed orders is (exclusive of fever hospital accommodation) certified at 619, and the gross totals of the foregoing only amount to 277, 305, and 293 (or less than half the certified accommodation).

Even were the accommodation returns referred to reliable, it would not necessarily follow that spare accommodation would be found available for the classes for which it might be required.

In the construction of these workhouses the class for which the greatest amount of dormitory accommodation was provided was the able-bodied, comparatively little provision being made for the aged and infirm, the class which is now the most numerous.

This will be seen from the following table, showing the accommodation certified under the sealed orders:—

Abbeyleix Accommodation under Sealed Order of 1861.

	Male	Female
Infirmary,	66	67
Aged and Infirm,	15	15
Healthy Able-bodied,	180	156
Children,	60	60
Total,	321	298
	619	

Accepting the foregoing figures as correct, it will be seen that but little margin would be left in the infirmary and children's department, and a large portion of the able-bodied accommodation would have to be appropriated for the aged and infirm: but it has been found that these figures cannot be accepted as reliable.

In the house at Abbeyleix, for instance, there are two wards, Nos 3 and 4, 27 feet 10 inches in length by 15 feet 4 inches in width, each of them certified to accommodate 28 inmates, which would allow less than 2 feet of wall space per bed. The Commissioners have been obliged to take into consideration the whole question of accommodation, and the regulations under which it should be calculated The result, they have no doubt, will go to show that Abbeyleix workhouse would be totally incapable of receiving the destitute poor of the two unions, and maintaining a proper classification, much less of receiving them, and keeping in reserve in each class such a margin of spare accommodation as should, in all cases, be kept to meet such emergencies as would be the consequence of a potato or fuel famine, or any other unforeseen calamity

Under all the circumstances the Commissioners feel that they would not be justified in complying with the prayer of the Petitioners, by recommending the amalgamation of Castlecomer Union with that of Abbeyleix.

I have the honour to be, Sir,

Your obedient servant,

H. A. Robinson, Secretary.

Arthur Kavanagh, Esq., M.P.

Oughterard Union.

Oughterard Union.

No. 4.—Letter from Mr. William Burke to the Commissioners.

Lisloughry, Cong, 22nd January, 1878.

Sir,—That portion of the Oughterard Union lying on the north and north-west of Lough Corrib, comprising the Electoral Divisions of Cong, Ross, Curr, and Letterbrickane originally belonged to the Ballinrobe Union, and were taken from this Union to form the Union of Oughterard, with other Electoral Divisions on the Oughterard side of the lake, which then belonged to the Galway Union.

The greater portion of the Electoral Divisions lying on the north side of Lough Corrib are much nearer to Ballinrobe Workhouse than to Oughterard. The lake separating those Electoral Divisions from Oughterard causes great inconvenience and loss to the poor of the district, the sick poor are deprived of the advantage of the Workhouse Hospital, and cases have occurred of persons dying in the attempt to carry them in open boats across the lake The lake is eight miles across to Oughterard; it is often very dangerous for boats to cross in rough weather The distance by road from part of Cong Electoral Division is thirty-four statute miles to Oughterard, while it is only seven miles to Ballinrobe.

The lake makes such a separation of these Electoral Divisions from the Oughterard Workhouse that it is admitted by all who have heard the case stated to be a great hardship to continue the arrangement as it now stands, while the inhabitants have, by a memorial presented to the Local Government Board, strongly expressed their opinion that the junction of these Electoral Divisions to the Oughterard Union is a great hardship to the poor, especially to the sick poor, and they have strongly recommended the restoration of them to Ballinrobe Union.

I know the district well, and I was at one time a Guardian of the Oughterard Union for several years, and I am now a Guardian of the Ballinrobe Union, and I strongly recommend the dissolution of the Oughterard Union and the restoration of the several Electoral Divisions I have named to the Ballinrobe Union.

I have the honour to be, Sir, your obedient servant,

WILLIAM BURKE.

The Honorable William Le Poer Trench,
Chairman of the Poor Law Union Inquiry Commission.

COTTAGE HOSPITALS.

No. 5.—COPY of LETTER addressed by the COMMISSIONERS to the LOCAL GOVERNMENT INSPECTORS, and their REPLIES.

Dublin, 9th March, 1878.

SIR,—The attention of the Poor Inquiry Commissioners has been directed to the alleged insufficiency of hospital accommodation in some parts of Ireland, and it has been suggested that it might be advisable to provide, in certain districts to be hereafter determined, one or two rooms in connexion with or adjacent to existing dispensaries, in which cases of infection might be more conveniently treated than by removal to the hospital of the Union Workhouse.

I am to request that you will be good enough to advise the Commissioners whether, in the district under your supervision, there are any places in which, in your opinion, such provision would contribute to the better administration of medical relief.

I am, Sir, your obedient servant,

H. A. ROBINSON.

REPORT from R. HAMILTON, Esq.

Culmore, Londonderry, March 4, 1878.

SIR,—In reply to your letter of the 26th ult. requesting me to advise the Poor Law Inquiry Commissioners whether there are any places in the district under my supervision in which it would be advisable to provide one or two rooms in connexion with the existing dispensaries, where cases of infectious diseases might be treated, I beg leave to say that accommodation of the contemplated description would, I think, be useful at Moville, on Lough Foyle, in Inishowen Union, and at Rathmullan, on Lough Swilly, in Milford Union.

There are anchorages off both these places, where vessels constantly lie; and, I may say, there is no accommodation within reasonable reach of either of them to which sailors suffering from disease could be removed. Moville is 13 or 14 miles from the union hospital, and Rathmullan 8 miles from it.

Dungloe, in Glenties Union, is also a place where, in my opinion, a provision of the kind would contribute to the better administration of medical relief; it is about 21 miles from the nearest hospital—Glenties. There has been some severe outbreaks of disease in this village, and the want of an hospital on the spot has been much felt, and has been the subject of correspondence with the Local Government Board; but the union is already so heavily taxed, the Guardians strenuously opposed any additional burden on the rates, and I have no doubt they would do the same again.

It would, I think, be desirable to have a few beds in every village for the treatment of urgent cases of illness; and, if the recommendation of the Commissioners is likely to be one of a general character, I will furnish them with a list of the places I would name; but I apprehend there will be considerable difficulty in carrying out such a scheme. 1st. In procuring suitable rooms; and, next, in providing for the proper care and nursing of the sick. I have, therefore, merely suggested in this letter the places which struck me as being most in need of such a provision.

It has been found almost impossible to rent or hire houses in remote places for hospital purposes, as the inhabitants are generally strongly opposed to having infectious diseases treated in their neighbourhood; and I apprehend that, wherever the plan is carried out, suitable buildings will have to be erected.

I have the honour to be, Sir, your obedient servant,

R. HAMILTON.

H. A. Robinson, esq., Secretary,
Poor Law Inquiry Commissioners,
Dublin.

REPORT from W. ARMSTRONG, Esq.

Carrick, 4th March, 1878.

SIR,—Referring to your letter of the 26th ultimo relative to providing accommodation for infectious diseases at, or near some of the existing dispensary buildings, I have the honour to state for the information of the Poor Law Union Inquiry Commissioners that most of the dispensaries in my district are held in small houses. Some are attached to the Union Workhouse buildings, and I am not aware of any I could recommend to be used for the purpose.

I am, Sir, your obedient servant,

W. ARMSTRONG, Inspector.

The Secretary,
Poor Law Union Inquiry Commission.

REPORT from R. BOURKE, Esq.

Mornfields, Lisnagry, Limerick,
16th March, 1878.

SIR,—In reply to your letter of the 12th inst. requesting me to state for the information of the Poor Law Inquiry Commissioners, whether there are within the district under my inspection, any localities where small hospitals for the treatment of infectious diseases might advantageously be established in connexion with dispensaries, I have to state that there are portions of the Unions of Limerick and Kilrush where the distance from the Workhouse Infirmary is so great that some such provision would be of the utmost importance to the sick poor.

In the Union of Limerick, the Electoral Divisions of Doon West and Cappamore are between 15 and 18 statute miles from the Workhouse, and in Kilrush the Divisions of Kilballyowen, Rahona, and Tullig, are at a still greater distance from the Union Infirmary. It is obvious that moving persons such distances while labouring under severe forms of sickness, or severe accidents, in vehicles of the kind which can alone be provided in those localities, must lessen the patient's chance of recovery, whilst adding considerably to their suffering, and I am aware that medical officers have in some instances declined the responsibility of ordering such removals.

I therefore consider that provision of the kind indicated in your letter would be of the utmost value as the villages of Cappamore (Union of Limerick), and Carrigaholt (Union of Kilrush), in both of which there is already a dispensary and resident physician.

I may perhaps be allowed to point out that if these sick wards were placed under the charge of a qualified midwife, whose services were available throughout the district, a double object would be attained, and the management need not be attended with much expense. A trifling addition to the rent now paid for the dispensary would secure the requisite accommodation, and no further permanent staff than the midwife would be required.

I would venture to add that these wards, though primarily available for the reception of contagious cases, might occasionally be used for the treatment of poor persons suffering under dangerous forms of sickness or severe accidents.

I am, Sir, your obedient servant,

R. BOURKE.

H. A. Robinson, esq.

REPORT from W. HAMILTON, Esq.

Fiddown, Piltown,
14th March, 1878.

SIR,—I have the honour to acknowledge the receipt of your letter of the 12th inst. relative to the provision in certain districts of one or two rooms in connexion with or adjacent to existing dispensaries, &c.

The subject is one to which I referred in my letter to you of the 3rd of August last. All of the unions in my district are referred to in the memorandum which accompanied that letter, and I will now refer to them in the order in which they are there given.

Tipperary Union.—I think that in Tipperary Union a cottage hospital at Cappagh and another at Emly would be found of advantage. I would say Thomastown were it not that the medical officer resides at Tipperary.

New Ross Union.—There is already a building available at Campill; I would prefer Arthurstown. I would likewise suggest Fethard (Wexford), Carrickbyrne, and Glyn, or Tinnahinch, unless the sick can be relieved at Graiguenamanagh, in the adjacent union of Thomastown, or probably St. Mullins, but the medical officer resides at Borris.

Cashel Union.—I would suggest Dundrum, Fethard (Tip.), and Killynaull.

Thurles Union.—I would suggest Templemore and Borrisoleigh.

Waterford Union. — Dunmore, Tramore, and Mullinavath.

Clogheen Union.—There is already a building available at Cahir very suitable in every respect.

Carrick-on-Suir Union.—There is already a fever hospital at Portlaw to which the Guardians can send patients. I should like to see a cottage hospital at Piltown, but there is no urgent necessity for it.

Kilkenny Union.—There are already fever hospitals at Gowran and Freshford.

Abbeyleix Union.—I should like to see cottage hospitals at Durrow, Castletown, and Timahoe.

Thomastown Union.—I should like to see a cottage hospital at Graiguenamanagh.

Callan Union.—I should like to see cottage hospitals at Kilmagarry, Ballingarry, and Mullinahone.

Clonmel Union.—I am not aware that there is any urgent need of a cottage hospital in this union. Ballymacarbery is the only locality I have any doubt about.

Urlingford Union.—I should like to see a cottage hospital at Ballyragget (in Castlecomer Union) made available for the Balleen dispensary district. A cottage hospital towards New Birmingham, in the Kilcorkey dispensary district, would, I think, be of benefit. Very little fever in this union.

Kilmacthomas Union.—I should like to see cottage hospitals at Stradbally and Bonmahon.

Castlecomer Union.—I should like to see a cottage hospital at Ballyragget, open to a portion of Urlingford Union.

Donaghmore Union.—I should like to see a cottage hospital at Borris-in-Ossory, but this is not urgent.

I have the honour to be, sir,

Your most obedient servant,

W. J. HAMILTON.

The Secretary, Poor Law Union
Inquiry Commission, Ireland.

APPENDIX A.

Cottage Hospitals.

REPORT from W. P. O'BRIEN, Esq.

42, Waterloo-road, 14th March, 1878.

SIR,—I have the honour to acknowledge the receipt of your letter of the 12th instant, and in reply desire to state that while I am fully sensible that the more accessible hospital accommodation is rendered for the sick poor the better it will in every way be, and the more readily will it be availed of by them, there is no part of my present district in which it appears to me a necessity exists for making such an arrangement as that referred to by you.

In each of the rural unions included in my present district there is a commodious hospital set apart for the exclusive treatment of infectious diseases, and in two of them—viz., Carlow and Enniscorthy—there are, in addition to this, four fever hospitals, maintained in places situated at a distance from the centre of this union. Few, if any, of the dispensaries known to me would afford accommodation adapted to hospital purposes, and I do not think it would be practicable to provide it anywhere without incurring a considerable expense, both in providing a building, however limited, and maintaining it in such a condition of efficiency as would, in my opinion, be indispensable in the case of any recognised institution, for the management of which the public authorities had rendered themselves responsible.

The workhouse hospitals in my district are, upon the whole, placed in central, convenient, and easily accessible positions; and having regard to the fact that covered spring vans are now very generally available at all times for the removal of the sick, whenever they are called into requisition for that purpose, I am not, as at present advised, prepared to suggest that any of the Boards of Guardians with which I am officially connected should be invited to make such arrangement as that described.

I have the honour to be, Sir,

Your obedient servant,

W. P. O'BRIEN.

H. A. Robinson, Esq., Secretary, Poor Law
Union Inquiry Commissioners, Dublin.

REPORT from Dr. BURKE.

57, Mountjoy-square, Dublin,
16th March, 1878.

SIR,—I have the honour to acknowledge the receipt of your letter of the 12th inst. relating to the alleged insufficiency of hospital accommodation in some parts of Ireland, as being brought under the notice of the Poor Law Union Inquiry Commissioners to whom it has been suggested that it might be advisable to provide in certain districts one or two rooms in connexion with, or adjacent to, existing dispensaries in which cases of infection might be more conveniently treated than by removal to the Workhouse Hospital, with reference to which I beg to state for the information of the Commissioners that in the eighteen Unions comprising the district under my supervision, and containing eighty-two dis-

APPENDIX A.

Cottage Hospitals.

pensaries, there is not an instance in which I would recommend the establishment of an hospital in connexion therewith, as being necessary or advisable for the treatment of cases of infectious disease, for which purpose the several fever hospitals attached to the workhouses afford not alone ample accommodation but proper means of isolation where necessary, which I must doubt could be efficiently carried into effect by the establishment of an hospital attached to a dispensary where the sick poor of the district must necessarily assemble for medical advice and treatment, as well as children to undergo the ordeal of vaccination.

I am, Sir,

Your most obedient servant,

T. H. BURKE,

Local Government Inspector.

H. A. Robinson, esq., sec.,
Poor Law Union Inquiry Commissioners,
Custom House, Dublin.

REPORT from DR. MACCABE.

Blackrock, Cork, 25th March, 1878.

SIR,—I beg to acknowledge the receipt of your letter of the 9th instant on the subject of the alleged insufficiency of hospital accommodation in some parts of Ireland, and requesting me to state, for the information of the Poor Law Union Inquiry Commissioners, whether, in my opinion, the provision of one or two rooms in connexion with, or adjacent to, existing dispensaries, for the local treatment of cases of infectious diseases, in preference to the removal of such cases to the hospital of the union workhouse, would contribute to the better administration of medical relief.

Before submitting to the Commissioners the considerations which have suggested themselves to me in connection with this subject, I think it right to state that I have been for not quite two years in charge of this district, and that my knowledge of the more remote portions of several of my unions is very imperfect. The short period over which my personal experience extends, and my defective knowledge of those portions of my unions most distant from the workhouses ought therefore to be borne in mind in weighing the value of the observations which I have the honour to offer.

I beg leave to state that in my opinion the establishment in certain portions of unions remote from workhouses of village hospitals, as suggested by the Commissioners, for the treatment of fever and other infectious diseases, would confer a great advantage upon the sick poor, and it may perhaps be well for me to indicate the situations in which cottage hospitals would appear calculated to confer benefit in the district with which I am connected:—

Cork Union.—The Glenville Depôt of Carrignavar North Dispensary District, in Cork Union, is very far from the Cork Workhouse, and I submit that a cottage hospital would be desirable at that point, it being understood that such cottage hospital should receive patients from the southern part of the adjoining union of Fermoy.

The Vicarstown Depôt of Dripsey Dispensary District, in Cork Union, is another point at which a cottage hospital might with advantage be established.

Fermoy Union.—The Watergrasshill Depôt of Rathcormac Dispensary District might have a cottage hospital near it, if one is not established at Glenville, as suggested under the head of Cork Union.

A cottage hospital at Ballynoe Dispensary would be a great advantage to the south-western portion of Fermoy Union, and to the north-west extremity of Youghal Union adjoining it (Valeraml and Ardagh Electoral Divisions of Youghal Union).

Kinsale Union.—The Carrigaline Dispensary of Kinsale Union is very far from the Union Workhouse, and I think that a cottage hospital established there would confer benefit upon the sick poor. It ought, however, upon terms to be arranged between the Unions, to be also made available for the population of the Carrigaline Electoral Division of Cork Union.

Macroom Union.—A Dispensary Depot ought, I think, to be established at Beolanageary, in Inchegeelah Dispensary District, and with it a cottage hospital to receive cases from the western extremity of Macroom Union (from Sheveragh on the northwest to Bealanageary on the south-west), and also to take patients from Bealanageary, Coolmountain, and Teerelton Electoral Divisions of Dunmanway Union, which adjoins Macroom.

At the north-eastern extremity of Macroom Union I think a depot and a cottage hospital would be desirable at the village of Donaghmore in Kilcullen, Electoral Division of Macroom Union.

Mallow Union.—The question of establishing a cottage hospital in connection with Churchtown, Depot of Buttevant Dispensary District, appears to me to deserve consideration.

Mitchelstown Union.—I think a cottage hospital might, with advantage, be established at Ballylanders, Depot of Galbally Dispensary District.

Dungarvan Union.—I think the Seskinan Dispensary might, with advantage, have a cottage hospital attached to it.

I have the honour to remain, Sir,

Your obedient servant,

F. MACCABE, Local Government Inspector.

H. A. Robinson, esq., Secretary,
Poor Law Union Inquiry Commission.

REPORT from S. HORSLEY, Esq.

Killarney, April 23rd, 1878.

SIR,—Adverting to your letter of the 12th ultimo, addressed to me by direction of the Poor Law Union Inquiry Commissioners, I beg to report that the scheme therein indicated for providing auxiliary accommodation for the treatment of cases of infectious disease could not, in my opinion, for the following reasons, be advantageously put in practice—except, perhaps, in one or two cases—in the dispensary districts within the unions under my supervision:—

1. The difficulty, amounting almost to an impossibility, of obtaining—without building—in the dispensary districts farthest removed from the workhouse hospitals, suitable miniature hospital accommodation near the medical officer's residence.

2. The difficulty of procuring careful, trustworthy, and efficient nurses for such establishments.

3. The difficulty of establishing such a system of discipline and supervision as would preclude the relatives and friends of patients from resorting, at all times and hours, to these auxiliary hospitals, ostensibly for the purpose of ascertaining their condition, but oftentimes from less worthy motives; and also the abuse which, I think, would, in remote places, arise by the admission of patients labouring under other than really infectious cases.

4. The large additional taxation—though this should not be considered when proper medical treatment of the sick absolutely requires it—which would, I fear, infallibly result from carrying into practical effect a system which, in this country, would afford too much scope for the exercise of the jobbing propensities to which the humbler classes are, I am sorry to think, already too prone.

5. Upon the whole—although small hospital accommodation might possibly be obtained at the following places. Crookhaven, in the Skull Union; Abbeyfeale, in the Newcastle Union; and Sneem, in the Kenmare Union—I think that, if really good invalid carriages or ambulances were provided for the conveyance of the sick from all parts of the union to the work

house hospital, there would be no real necessity for smaller or intercepting establishments.

I have the honour to be, Sir,

Your very obedient servant,

SAMUEL HORSLEY, L.G.I.

The Secretary,
Poor Law Union Inquiry Commission,
Four Courts, Dublin.

REPORT from DR. BRODIE.

1, Palmyra Terrace, Galway,
8th December, 1878.

SIR,—In reply to your inquiry, "whether there was any necessity in my district for additional fever hospital accommodation in places remote from the workhouse," I beg to state that the place in my district most requiring fever hospital accommodation is the Island of Inishboffin, situate in the Clifden Union, county of Galway; the nearest point of the mainland, Cleggan, is distant, say 8 miles from the Island, and an equal distance from the union workhouse hospital. Often, in bad weather, all communication between the Island and the mainland is interrupted for several consecutive days. For some years past fever of a bad type has appeared amongst the islanders, and the patients suffering from the disease have to be treated in their miserable cabins. There is a dispensary medical officer residing on the Island, and if a dispensary building, capable of containing, say 6 beds for the reception of patients suffering from fever or other contagious disease, could be procured on the Island it would, I have no doubt, be hailed as a boon both by the medical officer and the poor islanders.

Very truly yours,

T. BRODIE.

To H. Robinson, esq., Secretary.

REPORT from DR. ROUGHAN.

Belfast, December 14th, 1878.

GENTLEMEN,—In reply to your communication on the subject of the establishment of cottage hospitals in districts remote from the union workhouses in my charge, I beg leave to say that hospitals of this kind are very much needed—1st, Cushendall, in Ballycastle Union; 2nd, Portaferry, in Newtownards Union; 3rd, Newcastle, in Kilkeel Union; and 4th, Carlingford, in Dundalk Union. There are many other localities which would derive much convenience from having small hospitals established in them, but I have only mentioned those, which from distance and geographical position, place them altogether beyond the reach of hospital accommodation.

I have the honour to be, gentlemen,

Your obedient servant,

G. F. ROUGHAN.

[STATISTICAL TABLE

APPENDIX A.

Poor Relief.

No. 6.—STATISTICAL TABLE showing the progress of the PAUPERISM and

Years.	Valuation.	Population.	Average Daily Number on Receipt of Relief. In-door	Out-door, under 10 Vic. c. 31	Total	Ratio of In-door to Out-door.	Expenditure for In-Maintenance and Clothing	Out Relief under 10 Vic. c. 31.	Total	Expenditure under Medical Charities Act, exclusive of Vaccination.	Total of Cols. 10 and 11.	Poundage On Amount in Col. 10.	On Amount in Col. 12.	Percentage of Paupers to Population. In-door.	Out-door	Total
1.	2.	3.	4.*	5.	6.	7.	8.†	9.	10.	11.	12.	13.	14.	15.	16.	17.
Province of Ulster.																
ANTRIM UNION. Area, 117,109 acres.							£	£	£	£	£	d.	d.			
1851	101,289	41,778	288	.	288	.	1,255	.	1,255	.	1,255	3	3	·7	.	·7
1853	101,289	41,329	288	.	288	.	1,249	.	1,249	694	1,943	3	4½	·5	.	·5
1855	101,289	40,887	263	.	263	.	1,412	.	1,412	602	2,014	3¼	4¾	·6	.	·6
1857	101,187	40,492	216	.	216	.	1,237	.	1,237	615	1,852	3	4¼	·5	.	·5
1859	101,140	40,077	293	.	293	.	1,403	.	1,403	640	2,043	3¼	4¾	·7	.	·7
1861	101,308	39,683	297	.	297	.	1,791	.	1,791	630	2,421	4¼	5¾	·7	.	·7
1863	121,708	38,904	409	.	409	.	2,787	.	2,287	772	3,059	4½	6	1·0	.	1·0
1865	121,790	38,160	338	.	338	.	2,011	6	2,017	763	2,780	4	5½	·9	.	·9
1867	121,444	37,416	291	1	292	.	2,122	3	2,125	793	2,918	4¼	5¾	·7	.	·7
1869	121,518	36,673	334	3	337	.	2,448	5	2,453	804	3,257	4¾	6½	·9	.	·9
1871	122,216	35,929	295	26	321	11 to 1	2,118	94	2,212	814	3,026	4¼	5¾	·8	·1	·9
1873	122,014	35,929	290	61	351	4·8 to 1	2,449	221	2,670	821	3,491	5¼	7	·7	·2	·9
1875	123,086	35,929	250	96	346	2·6 to 1	2,174	539	2,713	807	3,520	5¼	6¾	·7	·2	·9
1877	123,054	35,928	241	98	341	2·4 to 1	2,082	471	2,553	810	3,363	5¼	6½	·6	·3	·9
BALLYCASTLE UNION. Area, 102,214 acres.																
1851	38,640	20,963	202	.	202	.	826	.	826	.	826	5	5	·9	.	·9
1853	38,640	20,701	137	.	137	.	582	.	582	297	889	3½	5½	·6	.	·6
1855	38,640	20,439	124	.	124	.	612	.	612	314	926	4¼	5¾	·5	.	·5
1857	39,642	20,177	118	.	118	.	650	.	650	378	1,024	4	6¼	·5	.	·5
1859	38,638	19,915	117	.	117	.	671	.	674	529	1,203	4¼	7¼	·6	.	·6
1861	39,567	19,653	175	.	175	.	1,114	.	1,114	382	1,496	6¾	9¼	·8	.	·8
1863	44,776	19,420	200	.	200	.	1,236	.	1,236	407	1,633	6¾	9	1·0	.	1·0
1865	41,423	19,194	186	.	186	.	813	.	813	362	1,304	4¾	6¼	·7	.	·7
1867	43,565	18,966	119	.	119	.	936	.	936	345	1,312	5¼	7¼	·6	.	·6
1869	43,566	18,736	124	.	124	.	948	.	948	477	1,425	5¼	7¾	·6	.	·6
1871	43,605	18,507	114	.	114	.	823	.	823	533	1,356	4¾	7¼	·6	.	·6
1873	44,804	18,507	127	.	127	.	1,323	.	1,323	687	1,910	6¾	10¼	·6	.	·6
1875	44,126	18,507	108	.	108	.	924	.	924	471	1,395	5	7¼	·5	.	·5
1877	44,656	18,507	94	1	95	.	785	11	785	463	1,248	4	6¾	·5	.	·5
BALLYMENA UNION. Area, 161,244 acres.																
1851	100,360	71,623	239*	.	239	.	817	.	847	.	847	2¼	2¼	·3	.	·3
1853	100,360	72,557	177	.	171	.	720	.	720	719	1,440	1¾	3¼	·2	.	·2
1855	100,360	73,552	245	.	245	.	1,296	.	1,296	838	2,134	3¼	5¼	·3	.	·3
1857	101,145	74,367	204	.	202	.	1,066	.	1,066	751	1,817	2½	4¼	·2	.	·2
1859	102,093	75,582	235	.	235	.	987	.	987	878	1,865	2¼	4¼	·3	.	·3
1861	102,210	76,307	336	.	336	.	1,651	.	1,651	825	2,471	3¾	5¾	·4	.	·4
1863	116,594	75,570	347	2	349	.	2,709	11	2,720	810	3,530	5¼	7¼	·7	.	·7
1865	118,720	74,844	445	10	455	42·5 to 1	2,580	20	2,610	897	3,507	5¼	7¼	·6	.	·6
1867	119,070	74,318	362	112	474	3 to 1	2,694	334	3,028	1,038	4,066	6¼	8¼	·5	·1	·6
1869	121,407	72,482	377	281	658	1·4 to 1	2,540	403	2,928	1,114	4,043	5¼	8	·5	·4	·9
1871	122,100	71,466	288	647	935	1 to 2·1	2,091	898	2,989	1,148	4,137	5¼	8½	·4	·8	1·2
1873	124,097	71,446	298	659	958	1 to 2·2	2,284	1,100	3,414	1,075	4,489	6¾	8¾	·4	·9	1·3
1875	123,618	71,446	307	571	828	1 to 1·8	2,415	1,026	3,341	1,074	4,415	6¼	8¾	·4	·7	1·1
1877	126,270	71,466	333	608	910	1 to 1·8	2,671	1,085	3,756	1,176	4,932	7¼	9¼	·4	·9	1·3
BALLYMONEY UNION. Area, 137,316 acres.																
1851	71,918	42,414	293	1	294	.	1,066	.	1,066	.	1,066	3½	3½	·7	.	·7
1853	71,913	42,251	169	1	169	.	536	3	539	408	1,047	1¾	3¼	·3	.	·3
1855	71,916	42,084	155	1	156	.	855	3	858	560	1,418	2¾	4¾	·3	.	·3
1857	72,240	41,917	125	3	128	41 to 1	604	14	618	672	1,290	2¼	4	·3	.	·3
1859	72,310	41,750	129	5	134	26 to 1	599	24	623	594	1,217	2	4	·3	.	·3
1861	72,313	41,583	166	13	181	13 to 1	865	86	951	631	1,582	3¼	5	·4	.	·4
1863	80,510	40,882	241	41	282	6 to 1	1,740	115	1,855	675	1,530	4	5¼	·6	·1	·7
1865	80,729	40,181	218	29	247	7 to 1	892	149	1,041	638	1,689	3½	5	·5	.	·5
1867	81,101	39,782	193	62	250	3 to 1	1,070	203	1,273	636	1,889	3¾	5¼	·5	·1	·6
1869	81,407	39,182	169	116	285	1·5 to 1	987	342	1,329	617	1,946	4	5¾	·4	·3	·7
1871	81,510	39,582	145	176	321	1 to 1·2	821	490	1,311	650	1,962	3¾	5¾	·4	·4	·8
1873	81,944	39,582	134	219	353	1 to 1·6	1,489	378	1,867	741	2,608	4¾	6¾	·3	·6	·9
1875	82,286	38,580	120	210	330	1 to 1·6	861	379	1,540	779	2,219	4¾	6¾	·3	·5	·8
1877	82,537	38,582	135	256	391	1 to 1·9	843	642	1,485	780	2,315	4¼	6¾	·3	·7	1·0
BELFAST UNION. Area, 49,173 acres.																
1851	316,897	125,862	1,601	.	1,601	.	7,294	.	7,294	.	7,294	5½	5½	1·2	.	1·2
1853	316,897	129,416	1,485	.	1,485	.	9,334	.	9,334	1,869	11,203	7	8½	1·1	.	1·1
1855	316,897	133,170	1,873	.	1,873	.	14,082	.	14,082	2,039	16,121	10¾	12¼	1·4	.	1·4
1857	301,845	136,921	1,479	.	1,479	.	9,832	.	9,832	1,940	11,772	7¼	9¼	1·1	.	1·1
1859	414,681	140,679	1,150	.	1,150	.	7,101	.	7,101	2,040	9,141	4¼	7	·8	.	·8
1861	487,845	144,427	1,186	.	1,194	.	7,843	.	7,843	2,063	9,906	4¼	7	·8	.	·8
1863	576,107	156,061	1,541	.	1,541	.	10,041	.	10,041	2,151	12,192	6¼	7¾	·9	.	·9
1865	404,857	167,885	1,414	.	1,414	.	9,340	.	9,350	2,282	11,632	6	7¼	·8	.	·8
1867	451,893	179,829	1,780	.	1,780	.	14,061	.	14,061	2,815	16,876	7¼	8¾	1·0	.	1·0
1869	529,551	190,065	1,455	8	1,363	181·2 to 1	16,230	24	16,583	2,435	18,968	7¼	8¾	·7	.	·7
1871	567,580	202,171	2,378	12	2,390	198 to 1	17,485	71	17,506	3,109	20,615	7¼	8¾	1·1	.	1·1
1873	563,271	202,171	2,444	16	2,460	187 to 1	20,310	104	20,434	3,378	23,792	8¼	10	1·2	.	1·2
1875	601,474	208,171	2,854	18	2,872	142 to 1	21,446	71	21,517	3,702	24,935	8½	10¼	1·3	.	1·3
1877	621,276	208,151	2,013	21	2,034	96 to 1	17,088	83	17,071	4,104	21,075	7	8¼	1·0	.	1·0

* This includes the children at nurse.

† This includes the estimated cost of children at nurse.

EXPENDITURE of each POOR LAW UNION in IRELAND since the year 1851.

Years	Valuation.	Population.	Average Daily Number in Receipt of Relief: In-door.	Out-door, under 10 Vic. c. 31	Total	Ratio of In-door to Out-door.	Expenditure for: In Maintenance and Clothing	Out Relief under 10 Vic. c. 31	Total.	Expenditure under Medical Charities Acts, exclusive of Vaccination.	Total of Cols. 10 and 11.	Poundage: On Amount in Col. 10.	On Amount in Col. 12.	Per centage of Paupers to Population: In-door.	Out-door	Total
1	2	3	4	5	6	7	8	9	10	11	12	13	14	15	16	17
PROVINCE OF ULSTER—continued.																
LARNE UNION. Area, 117,609 acres.							£	£	£	£	£	d.	d.			
1851	73,738	34,677	282	.	282	.	1,063	.	1,063	.	1,063	3½	3½	·8	.	·8
1853	73,834	34,240	226	.	226	.	1,031	.	1,031	426	1,457	3¾	4½	·6	.	·6
1855	73,838	34,041	214	.	214	.	1,099	.	1,099	470	1,569	3½	5	·6	.	·6
1857	77,943	34,283	196	.	196	.	951	.	951	526	1,477	3	4½	·5	.	·5
1859	84,177	34,883	177	.	177	.	977	.	977	487	1,464	3½	4½	·5	.	·5
1861	74,348	35,087	216	.	216	.	1,313	.	1,313	573	1,886	4½	6¼	·6	.	·6
1863	87,432	34,840	291	.	291	.	1,740	.	1,740	610	2,350	4½	6½	·8	.	·8
1865	89,364	34,812	256	1	257	.	1,301	3	1,304	809	2,113	4	5½	·7	.	·7
1867	91,548	34,475	242	1	243	.	1,694	3	1,697	697	2,408	4½	6½	·7	.	·7
1869	82,918	34,528	278	2	280	139 to 1	1,293	6	1,299	848	2,147	5	6½	·8	.	·8
1871	92,499	34,401	243	13	256	20 to 1	1,898	42	1,940	842	2,782	5	7	·7	.	·7
1873	93,689	34,401	236	17	253	14 to 1	1,992	68	2,060	705	2,765	5½	7	·7	.	·7
1875	94,769	34,401	210	51	269	4·2 to 1	1,868	207	2,075	905	2,880	5½	7½	·6	·1	·7
1877	93,277	34,401	204	31	235	6·6 to 1	1,619	221	1,840	700	2,600	4½	6¾	·6	·1	·7
LISBURN UNION. Area, 119,868 acres.																
1851	133,674	68,785	393	.	393	.	1,195	.	1,195	.	1,195	2½	2¾	·4	.	·4
1853	133,674	68,409	261	.	261	.	1,106	.	1,106	748	1,854	2	3½	·3	.	·3
1855	133,674	68,022	378	.	378	.	1,745	.	1,745	842	2,587	3½	4½	·6	.	·6
1857	133,541	67,649	279	.	279	.	1,181	.	1,181	777	1,958	2½	3½	·4	.	·4
1859	133,790	67,281	286	1	287	.	1,120	5	1,125	824	1,949	2	3½	·4	.	·4
1861	134,220	66,852	348	1	349	.	1,362	4	1,366	894	2,260	2½	4	·5	.	·5
1863	134,444	66,446	413	.	413	.	1,894	.	1,894	829	2,723	3½	4½	·6	.	·6
1865	134,884	64,915	365	5	370	73 to 1	1,863	28	1,891	808	2,699	2½	4	·5	.	·5
1867	135,133	62,580	284	1	285	.	1,816	4	1,820	896	2,716	2½	4	·4	.	·4
1869	166,528	61,147	306	2	308	153 to 1	1,776	42	1,818	937	2,755	4	5½	·5	.	·5
1871	167,767	59,714	264	13	277	20 to 1	1,791	78	1,869	992	2,861	3½	4	·4	.	·4
1873	168,889	59,714	246	43	289	5·6 to 1	1,911	259	2,170	1,043	3,213	3	4½	·4	.	·4
1875	169,432	59,714	241	91	332	2·6 to 1	1,824	482	2,306	1,108	3,414	3½	4½	·4	·2	·6
1877	171,100	59,714	234	117	351	2 to 1	1,670	542	2,212	1,070	3,282	3¼	4½	·4	·2	·6
ARMAGH UNION. Area, 164,216 acres.																
1851	166,082	86,418	375	.	375	.	1,836	.	1,836	.	1,836	2	3	·4	.	·4
1853	166,092	85,294	284	.	284	.	865	.	865	1,091	1,956	1½	3	·3	.	·3
1855	166,092	84,173	325	.	325	.	1,689	.	1,689	807	2,496	2½	3½	·4	.	·4
1857	166,308	84,089	251	.	251	.	1,335	.	1,335	1,056	2,391	2	3½	·3	.	·3
1859	166,888	81,931	306	.	306	.	1,515	.	1,515	1,108	2,623	2½	4½	·4	.	·4
1861	166,843	80,810	341	.	341	.	2,070	.	2,070	1,109	3,179	3	4½	·4	.	·4
1863	166,611	79,147	497	.	497	.	2,945	.	2,945	1,058	4,003	4½	5½	·6	.	·6
1865	203,209	77,484	360	2	362	.	2,194	17	2,211	1,231	3,442	3½	4½	·4	.	·4
1867	202,855	75,821	326	.	326	.	2,138	.	2,138	1,070	3,208	3½	5½	·4	.	·4
1869	203,174	74,156	319	.	319	.	2,190	.	2,190	1,163	3,353	3½	4	·4	.	·4
1871	201,467	72,496	340	1	341	.	2,330	6	2,336	1,293	3,629	3½	4½	·4	.	·4
1873	203,925	72,495	321	1	322	.	2,406	10	2,416	1,725	4,141	3½	4½	·4	.	·4
1875	204,694	72,495	291	1	292	.	3,408	10	3,418	1,521	4,939	4	5½	·4	.	·4
1877	201,307	73,495	284	2	286	142 to 1	2,326	19	2,345	1,297	3,642	2¾	4	·4	.	·4
LURGAN UNION. Area, 79,813 acres.																
1851	94,416	69,860	350	.	350		1,401	.	1,401	.	1,401	3½	3½	·5	.	·5
1853	94,416	67,807	251	.	251		1,262	.	1,262	652	1,914	3½	5	·3	.	·3
1855	94,416	69,405	415	.	415		2,691	.	2,691	607	3,298	6½	8½	·6	.	·6
1857	95,775	70,918	301	.	301		1,694	.	1,694	698	2,392	4½	5½	·4	.	·4
1859	97,763	72,421	348	.	348		2,216	.	2,216	848	3,064	5½	7	·4	.	·4
1861	99,178	73,030	428	.	428		2,633	.	2,633	681	3,314	6½	8	·5	.	·6
1863	103,076	73,124	695	.	695		4,521	.	4,521	849	5,370	10½	1s. 0½d.	·9	.	·9
1865	132,205	72,222	535	.	545		3,832	.	3,832	887	4,719	7	8½	·7	.	·7
1867	135,010	71,539	418	.	418		3,259	.	3,259	848	4,107	5½	7½	·5	.	·5
1869	137,064	70,718	440	.	440		3,533	.	3,533	1,004	4,537	6½	8	·6	.	·6
1871	138,892	69,916	354	.	354		2,728	.	2,728	881	3,609	4½	6½	·5	.	·5
1873	140,288	69,916	395	.	395		3,575	.	3,575	1,125	4,700	6	8	·5	.	·5
1875	140,873	69,916	412	.	412		3,621	.	3,621	1,252	4,873	6½	8½	·6	.	·6
1877	141,085	69,916	390	1	391		3,349	8	3,357	1,160	4,560	5½	7½	·5	.	·5
BAILIEBOROUGH UNION. Area, 63,809 acres.																
1851	39,357	26,497	701	.	701	.	2,568	.	2,568	.	2,568	1s. 4d.	1s. 4d.	2·7	.	2·7
1853	39,367	23,811	351	.	351	.	1,671	.	1,671	482	2,153	10½	1s. 1½d.	1·5	.	1·5
1855	39,457	25,178	182	.	182	.	784	.	784	393	1,177	4½	7½	·8	.	·8
1857	38,384	24,445	90	.	90	.	577	.	577	404	981	3½	6½	·4	.	·4
1859	39,398	23,783	97	.	97	.	667	.	667	427	1,094	4	6½	·4	.	·4
1861	40,437	23,879	145	.	145	.	877	.	877	450	1,327	5½	8	·6	.	·6
1863	39,856	24,877	173	2	175	86 to 1	1,153	5	1,158	452	1,610	7	9½	·7	.	·7
1865	39,169	24,273	143	2	145	71·5 to 1	984	7	991	468	1,459	6	8½	·6	.	·6
1867	39,570	24,273	173	10	183	14·2 to 1	1,132	46	1,178	407	1,585	7½	10½	·6	.	·6
1869	40,364	23,471	138	19	157	7 to 1	1,244	60	1,304	478	1,782	7½	10½	·5	·1	·6
1871	39,563	26,072	121	24	145	5 to 1	1,026	129	1,155	504	1,659	7	10	·4	·1	·5
1873	40,570	26,072	140	32	172	5 to 1	1,357	100	1,457	472	1,929	9	1s. 0d.	·5	·1	·6
1875	39,372	26,072	134	30	164	4·5 to 1	1,281	175	1,456	544	2,000	8½	1s. 0d.	·5	·1	·6
1877	40,089	26,072	133	50	183	2·6 to 1	1,260	284	1,544	531	2,075	8½	1s. 0½d.	·5	·2	·7

APPENDIX A.

Poor Relief.

No. 6.—STATISTICAL TABLE showing the progress of the Pauperism and

Years	Valuation	Population	Average Daily Number in Receipt of Relief: In-door	Out-door under 10 Vic. c. 31	Total	Ratio of In-door to Out-door	Expenditure for: In Maintenance and Clothing	Out Relief under 10 Vic. c. 31	Total	Expenditure under Medical Charities Acts, exclusive of Vaccine fees	Total of Cols. 10 and 11	Poundage: On Amount in Col. 10	On Amount in Col. 12	Percentage of Paupers to Population: In-door	Out-door	Total
1	2	3	4	5	6	7	8	9	10	11	12	13	14	15	16	17
Province of Ulster— *continued*																
BAWNBOY UNION.							£	£	£	£	£	d.	d.			
Area, 105,612 acres.																
1851	37,518	29,404	276	.	276	.	834	.	834	.	834	6½	6½	·9	.	·9
1853	37,518	28,414	158	.	158	.	601	.	601	456	1,057	4⅞	8½	·6	.	·6
1855	37,518	26,863	143	.	143	.	962	.	962	347	1,309	6½	8½	·5	.	·5
1857	37,674	27,346	116	.	116	.	794	.	794	358	1,152	5	7½	·4	.	·4
1859	37,518	27,097	109	.	109	.	640	.	649	401	1,041	4½	6½	·3	.	·3
1861	38,570	26,008	138	10	148	13·8 to 1	978	64	1,042	460	1,502	6½	8½	·5	.	·5
1863	38,683	26,246	208	82	290	2·5 to 1	1,370	308	1,678	444	2,122	10½	1s. 1½d.	·8	·3	1·1
1865	39,678	25,686	164	67	231	2·5 to 1	1,007	178	1,185	460	1,645	7½	10	·6	·3	·9
1867	39,165	25,136	153	95	248	1·6 to 1	1,018	309	1,327	395	1,722	8	10½	·6	·3	·9
1869	39,544	24,566	128	92	217	1·4 to 1	858	200	1,059	488	1,547	6½	9½	·4	·3	·8
1871	39,020	24,008	96	184	280	1 to 2	884	341	1,225	491	1,726	7½	10½	·4	·8	1·1
1873	39,684	24,006	105	183	288	1 to 1·6	1,093	487	1,580	519	2,099	9½	1s. 1½d.	·4	·6	1·1
1875	39,684	24,006	118	208	326	1 to 1·7	1,073	506	1,579	487	2,066	9½	1s. 1½d.	·5	·8	1·3
1877	39,816	24,006	85	209	294	2·4 to 1	790	506	1,384	479	1,782	8	10½	·3	·9	1·2
CAVAN UNION.																
Area, 16,074 acres.																
1851	94,966	66,991	1,170	.	1,170	.	3,461	.	3,461	.	3,461	8¾	8¾	1·7	.	1·7
1853	94,985	65,329	624	12	646	53 to 1	2,390	29	2,419	851	3,270	6¼	8¼	·9	.	·9
1855	94,985	63,657	382	.	382	.	2,060	.	2,060	569	2,649	5⅛	6⅝	·6	.	·6
1857	94,905	61,892	238	1	239	.	1,484	8	1,492	615	2,107	5½	6	·3	.	·3
1859	110,961	60,327	207	1	208	.	1,329	9	1,338	709	2,047	3	4½	·3	.	·3
1861	111,125	58,665	249	14	263	17 to 1	1,779	21	1,800	825	2,625	3½	5½	·4	.	·4
1863	111,311	57,962	236	6	242	39 to 1	1,962	35	1,997	800	2,797	4½	6	·4	.	·4
1865	111,370	56,662	298	.	298	.	1,875	2	1,877	772	2,649	4	5½	·5	.	·5
1867	111,288	55,662	293	1	294	.	1,925	27	1,952	920	2,872	4¼	6¼	·5	.	·5
1869	111,126	54,662	406	1	407	.	2,251	27	2,278	813	3,091	4½	6½	·6	.	·6
1871	111,946	55,662	263	30	293	8·6 to 1	2,060	76	2,134	948	3,082	4⅛	6½	·5	.	·5
1873	111,410	53,662	276	168	444	1·6 to 1	2,478	467	2,945	985	3,929	6½	8½	·5	·3	·8
1875	112,674	54,662	308	131	439	2·3 to 1	2,673	587	3,260	1,064	4,294	6½	9½	·6	·2	·8
1877	112,880	53,662	278	257	535	1 to 1	2,257	723	2,980	1,175	4,155	6¼	8½	·5	·5	1·0
COOTEHILL UNION.																
Area, 105,846 acres.																
1851	57,098	44,444	762	.	762	.	2,577	.	2,577	.	2,577	10¾	10¾	1·7	.	1·7
1853	57,946	43,173	368	.	368	.	1,289	.	1,289	489	1,778	5½	7½	·8	.	·8
1855	57,098	42,304	211	.	211	.	1,213	.	1,213	511	1,724	5½	7½	·5	.	·5
1857	57,165	41,233	151	.	151	.	932	.	932	482	1,414	4	6	·3	.	·3
1859	70,620	40,163	129	.	129	.	670	.	670	495	1,165	2¼	4½	·3	.	·3
1861	71,283	39,098	156	.	156	.	775	.	775	475	1,250	2½	4½	·3	.	·3
1863	71,480	38,206	178	.	178	.	904	.	904	480	1,388	3½	4½	·4	.	·4
1865	71,985	37,317	154	.	154	.	744	.	744	488	1,232	2½	4	·4	.	·4
1867	72,164	36,429	162	.	162	.	863	.	863	329	1,192	3	5	·4	.	·4
1869	72,166	35,541	155	.	155	.	903	.	903	538	1,421	3¼	5	·4	.	·4
1871	77,146	34,653	123	6	129	20·5 to 1	719	21	740	706	1,446	2½	4½	·3	.	·3
1873	72,347	34,653	131	19	150	7 to 1	1,026	68	1,094	497	1,591	3½	5¼	·3	·1	·4
1875	72,987	34,653	116	19	135	6 to 1	996	65	1,061	574	1,635	3½	5½	·3	·1	·4
1877	72,564	34,653	95	20	115	4·7 to 1	752	90	842	604	1,446	2½	4½	·3	·1	·3
BALLYSHANNON UNION.																
Area, 128,814 acres.																
1851	35,606	35,544	292	.	292	.	958	.	958	.	958	6½	6½	·8	.	·8
1853	35,606	34,889	242	.	242	.	867	.	867	525	1,392	6	9½	·7	.	·7
1855	36,603	34,287	181	.	181	.	1,291	.	1,291	345	1,646	8½	11	·5	.	·5
1857	33,602	33,588	71	.	71	.	441	.	441	347	788	3	5½	·2	.	·2
1859	35,602	32,838	89	.	89	.	546	.	546	362	908	3½	6¼	·3	.	·3
1861	35,802	32,161	131	.	131	.	758	.	758	385	1,149	5	7½	·4	.	·4
1863	35,696	31,404	183	.	183	.	1,062	.	1,062	385	1,447	7¼	9¾	·5	.	·5
1865	39,482	30,680	164	.	164	.	899	.	899	411	1,310	4½	6½	·5	.	·5
1867	60,091	29,836	194	.	194	.	1,109	.	1,109	412	1,521	4½	6	·6	.	·6
1869	50,281	29,082	206	.	206	.	1,189	.	1,189	438	1,627	5½	7½	·7	.	·7
1871	50,246	28,308	181	.	181	.	1,037	.	1,037	480	1,517	5	7½	·6	.	·6
1873	50,380	28,308	160	.	160	.	1,277	.	1,277	600	1,877	6	9	·5	.	·5
1875	50,380	28,308	179	.	179	.	1,070	.	1,070	644	1,714	6	8½	·6	.	·6
1877	50,894	28,308	143	.	143	.	1,016	.	1,016	587	1,603	5	8	·5	.	·5
DONEGAL UNION.																
Area, 168,408 acres.																
1851	27,742	34,190	296	.	296	.	1,096	.	1,096	.	1,096	9½	9½	·8	.	·8
1853	27,742	24,546	153	.	153	.	361	.	361	536	897	5	9½	·6	.	·6
1855	27,762	28,974	94	2	96	.	392	11	403	335	738	3½	6	·3	.	·3
1857	27,758	28,403	73	3	76	.	288	16	304	418	722	2½	6½	·2	.	·2
1859	23,988	31,690	57	3	60	.	349	20	369	448	817	3½	6½	·1	.	·1
1861	33,926	31,756	86	6	92	14·3 to 1	513	20	533	407	940	3¾	6½	·3	.	·3
1863	33,918	30,518	128	20	148	6·4 to 1	704	70	774	392	1,166	5½	8¼	·4	·1	·5
1865	33,994	29,540	130	18	148	7·2 to 1	774	56	830	517	1,345	5½	9½	·4	·1	·5
1867	34,021	29,382	114	79	193	1·4 to 1	658	180	838	503	1,441	6	10¼	·4	·2	·6
1869	34,021	24,874	119	15	134	8 to 1	877	44	921	601	1,522	6½	10½	·5	.	·5
1871	34,130	27,716	77	33	110	2·3 to 1	641	90	731	774	1,505	5¼	10½	·3	·1	·4
1873	34,213	27,716	82	11	93	7·4 to 1	849	35	884	649	1,533	6¼	9	·3	.	·3
1875	34,380	27,716	92	22	114	4·2 to 1	608	84	692	678	1,370	4½	9½	·3	·1	·4
1877	34,386	27,716	86	80	166	1·1 to 1	584	176	760	750	1,510	5½	10½	·3	·2	·6

Expenditure of each Poor Law Union in Ireland since the year 1851—*continued.*

Years	Valuation	Population	Average Daily Number in Receipt of Relief. In-door	Out-door, under 10 Vic. c. 31	Total	Ratio of In-door to Out-door	Expenditure for In Maintenance and Clothing	Out Relief under 10 Vic. c. 31	Total	Expenditure under Medical Charities Acts, exclusive of Vaccination	Total of Cols. 10 and 11	Poundage. On Amount in Col. 10	On Amount in Col. 12	Per centage of Paupers to Population. In-door	Out-door	Total
1	2	3	4	5	6	7	8	9	10	11	12	13	14	15	16	17
Province of Ulster—continued.																
Dunfanaghy Union.							£	£	£	£	£	d.	d.			
Area, 125,175 acres																
1851	10,716	17,320	85	.	85	.	368	.	368	.	368	8¼	8¼	·5	.	·5
1853	10,716	17,201	41	.	41	.	177	.	177	199	376	4	8½	·2	.	·2
1855	10,716	17,332	42	.	42	.	252	.	252	251	503	5½	11¼	·2	.	·2
1857	10,716	17,383	22	.	22	.	153	.	153	231	384	3½	8½	·1	.	·1
1859	11,155	17,324	22	.	22	.	147	.	147	202	349	3¼	7½	·1	.	·1
1861	11,190	17,426	38	.	38	.	250	.	250	256	506	5½	11	·2	.	·2
1863	11,236	17,153	47	.	47	.	333	.	333	206	539	7	11½	·2	.	·2
1865	11,285	16,984	51	.	51	.	267	.	267	224	491	4½	10½	·3	.	·3
1867	11,278	16,815	55	.	55	.	315	.	315	271	586	6½	1s. 0½d.	·3	.	·3
1869	11,398	16,646	45	.	45	.	336	.	336	295	631	7¼	1s. 1½d.	·3	.	·3
1871	11,423	16,477	33	.	33	.	246	.	246	303	549	5¼	11½	·2	.	·2
1873	11,437	16,477	41	.	41	.	317	.	317	399	716	6½	1s. 2½d.	·2	.	·2
1875	11,506	16,477	31	.	31	.	314	.	314	319	633	6½	1s. 1d.	·2	.	·2
1877	11,583	16,477	31	.	31	.	284	.	284	473	757	6	1s. 3½d.	·2	.	·2
Glenties Union.																
Area, 259,719 acres																
1851	16,100	40,108	199	.	199	.	649	.	649	.	649	9½	9½	·5	.	·5
1853	16,100	40,114	159	.	159	.	474	.	474	448	922	7	1s. 1¾d.	·4	.	·4
1855	16,109	40,125	160	.	160	.	540	.	540	328	868	8	1s. 0¾d.	·3	.	·3
1857	16,074	40,136	76	4	80	19 to 1	433	14	447	357	804	6½	1s. 0d.	·2	.	·2
1859	19,540	40,147	104	6	110	17 to 1	567	22	589	434	1,023	8½	11½	·3	.	·3
1861	19,572	40,159	117	9	126	13 to 1	640	37	727	466	1,193	9	1s. 2½d.	·3	.	·3
1863	18,632	39,710	170	12	182	14 to 1	900	73	973	492	1,465	1s. 0d.	1s. 6½d.	·4	.	·4
1865	18,862	39,264	124	11	135	11 to 1	771	32	803	475	1,278	9½	1s. 3¼d.	·3	.	·3
1867	18,700	38,820	135	9	144	15 to 1	825	43	868	567	1,435	10¾	1s. 5¾d.	·3	.	·3
1869	19,727	38,375	121	11	132	11 to 1	652	58	700	716	1,416	8½	1s. 5¼d.	·3	.	·3
1871	19,825	37,930	102	14	116	7·3 to 1	620	38	658	640	1,298	7½	1s. 3¾d.	·3	.	·3
1873	18,802	37,930	106	22	128	4·8 to 1	751	81	832	930	1,762	10½	1s. 9½d.	·3	·1	·3
1875	20,010	37,930	111	47	158	2·3 to 1	756	108	864	900	1,766	10½	1s. 10½d.	·3	·1	·4
1877	20,126	37,930	115	34	149	3·2 to 1	721	124	845	860	1,705	10¾	1s. 9¾d.	·3	·1	·4
Inishowen Union.																
Area, 158,450 acres.																
1851	38,987	28,962	478	.	478	.	1,230	.	1,230	.	1,230	8	8	1·2	.	1·2
1853	36,987	25,712	188	.	188	.	567	.	567	737	1,304	3½	8½	·5	.	·5
1855	36,987	22,466	127	.	127	.	526	.	526	490	1,016	3½	6½	·4	.	·4
1857	36,987	24,210	87	.	87	.	423	.	423	612	1,035	2¾	6¾	·3	.	·3
1859	37,082	23,974	88	.	88	.	406	.	406	639	1,045	2½	7	·3	.	·3
1861	37,382	22,729	113	2	115	56·5 to 1	599	2	601	690	1,291	4	8	·5	.	·5
1863	37,853	22,125	198	6	204	33 to 1	986	32	1,018	630	1,648	6½	10½	·9	.	·9
1865	37,927	21,532	186	17	203	11 to 1	979	65	1,044	712	1,756	6½	11¼	·8	·1	·9
1867	38,120	20,919	168	39	207	4·3 to 1	1,098	109	1,207	708	1,815	7½	11½	·8	·1	·9
1869	38,614	20,316	155	51	206	3 to 1	981	157	1,138	713	1,851	7¼	11½	·7	·2	1·0
1871	38,675	19,714	143	64	207	2·2 to 1	853	233	1,086	671	1,757	6¾	11	·7	·3	1·0
1873	38,800	19,713	179	64	243	2·8 to 1	1,218	248	1,473	768	2,241	9	1s. 1¾d.	·9	·3	1·2
1875	39,064	19,713	142	88	230	1·6 to 1	1,042	320	1,378	808	2,186	8¼	1s. 2d.	·7	·5	1·2
1877	39,125	19,713	154	144	298	1·1 to 1	1,066	404	1,470	993	2,463	9	1s. 3¼d.	·8	·7	1·5
Letterkenny Union.																
Area, 101,247 acres.																
1851	31,050	20,685	171	.	171	.	601	.	601	.	601	4½	4½	·8	.	·8
1853	31,050	20,216	87	.	87	.	423	.	423	502	925	3¼	7¼	·4	.	·4
1855	31,050	19,870	73	.	73	.	428	.	440	348	776	3¼	6	·3	.	·3
1857	31,343	19,524	47	.	47	.	317	.	317	326	643	2¼	5	·2	.	·2
1859	30,827	19,278	51	.	51	.	379	.	379	368	747	3	6	·3	.	·3
1861	30,371	18,982	85	.	85	.	708	.	708	374	1,082	5½	8½	·4	.	·4
1863	30,634	18,585	131	.	131	.	912	.	912	434	1,436	7¼	10½	·7	.	·7
1865	30,180	18,209	147	.	147	.	909	.	909	352	1,261	7¼	10¼	·8	.	·8
1867	30,314	17,889	125	.	125	.	1,030	.	1,030	481	1,471	8	11½	·7	.	·7
1869	30,943	17,476	109	.	109	.	947	.	947	421	1,368	7¼	10½	·6	.	·6
1871	30,944	17,113	102	.	102	.	944	.	944	417	1,361	7¼	10½	·6	.	·6
1873	30,963	17,113	117	.	117	.	1,051	.	1,051	500	1,551	8¼	1s. 0d.	·6	.	·6
1875	31,000	17,113	103	.	103	.	870	.	870	548	1,418	7¼	11½	·6	.	·6
1877	31,080	17,113	98	.	98	.	933	.	933	354	1,287	7¼	10	·5	.	·5
Milford Union.																
Area, 111,385 acres.																
1851	30,999	31,482	271	.	271	.	1,003	.	1,003	.	1,003	8¼	8¼	·8	.	·8
1853	30,469	30,589	159	.	159	.	447	.	447	582	1,029	3½	7½	·5	.	·5
1855	30,888	30,224	130	.	130	.	607	.	607	536	1,143	4¾	9	·4	.	·4
1857	31,087	29,558	140	.	140	.	722	.	722	484	1,206	5½	9¼	·4	.	·4
1859	28,830	29,891	77	.	77	.	446	.	446	375	821	3¾	6¾	·3	.	·3
1861	28,846	28,226	87	.	87	.	613	.	613	382	995	5	8¼	·3	.	·3
1863	28,473	27,743	136	.	136	.	785	.	785	591	1,376	6½	11½	·5	.	·5
1865	29,678	27,263	118	.	118	.	718	.	718	689	1,407	5¾	11½	·4	.	·4
1867	29,528	26,781	116	2	118	58 to 1	801	13	814	715	1,529	6½	1s. 0¼d.	·4	.	·4
1869	29,682	26,400	116	25	141	4·6 to 1	778	46	824	713	1,537	6¾	1s. 0½d.	·4	·1	·5
1871	29,042	25,819	97	41	138	2·4 to 1	670	36	706	484	1,190	5¾	11½	·4	·1	·5
1873	29,646	25,819	94	28	122	3·3 to 1	791	54	845	704	1,549	6¾	1s. 0½d.	·4	·1	·5
1875	29,364	25,819	89	24	113	3·7 to 1	677	42	719	761	1,480	6	1s. 0d.	·3	·1	·4
1877	29,837	25,819	68	20	88	3·4 to 1	541	58	600	743	1,343	4¾	10¾	·3	·1	·3

Appendix A.
Poor Relief.

No. 6.—STATISTICAL TABLE showing the progress of the Pauperism and

Years.	Valuation.	Population.	Average Daily Number in Receipt of Relief. In-door	Out-door, under 10 Vic. c. 31.	Total.	Ratio of Indoor to Outdoor.	Expenditure for In-Maintenance and Clothing	Out-Relief under 10 Vic. c. 31.	Total.	Expenditure under Medical Charities Acts, exclusive of Vaccination.	Total of Cols. 10 and 11.	Poundage. On Amount in Col. 10.	On Amount in Col. 12.	Per-centage of Paupers to Population. In-door	Out-door	Total.
1.	2.	3.	4.	5.	6.	7.	8.	9.	10.	11.	12.	13.	14.	15.	16.	17.
Province of Ulster—continued.																
STRANORLAR UNION.							£	£	£	£	£	d.	d.			
Area, 121,150 acres.																
1851	29,182	21,970	212	.	212	.	567	.	567	.	567	4½	4½	·9	.	·9
1853	29,182	21,570	115	.	115	.	287	.	287	287	574	2½	4½	·5	.	·5
1855	29,182	21,172	69	.	69	.	229	.	229	277	506	1¾	4¼	·3	.	·3
1857	29,0?9	20,774	56	.	56	.	180	.	180	271	451	1½	3¾	·2	.	·2
1859	29,513	20,375	58	.	58	.	172	.	172	289	511	1⅓	4	·2	.	·2
1861	29,593	19,978	60	.	60	.	249	.	249	330	579	2	4¾	·3	.	·3
1863	29,846	19,701	93	.	93	.	513	.	513	372	885	4	7¼	·4	.	·4
1865	29,781	19,430	90	.	90	.	424	.	424	363	787	3½	6½	·5	.	·5
1867	29,816	19,157	74	.	74	.	435	.	435	387	822	3½	6¾	·4	.	·4
1869	29,865	18,884	87	.	87	.	473	.	474	469	942	3¾	7½	·4	.	·4
1871	29,941	18,611	72	.	72	.	365	.	365	461	826	3	6½	·4	.	·4
1873	31,110	18,611	68	.	68	.	344	.	344	494	837	2½	6½	·3	.	·3
1875	31,681	18,611	49	.	49	.	364	.	364	444	808	3	6¼	·2	.	·2
1877	30,140	18,611	63	2	65	31·5 to 1	334	6	300	493	8??	3	6¾	·3	.	·3
BANBRIDGE UNION.																
Area, 120,130 acres.																
1851	122,018	75,297	263	.	263	.	1,462	.	1,462	.	1,462	2¾	2¾	·4	.	·4
1853	122,049	74,418	223	1	224	.	1,006	5	1,011	617	1,628	2	4¼	·3	.	·3
1855	122,018	73,541	317	26	343	12·2 to 1	1,611	61	1,672	635	2,106	2¾	4½	·4	.	·4
1857	120,198	73,368	189	14	203	13·5 to 1	1,036	67	1,103	637	1,740	2¼	3½	·3	.	·3
1859	120,145	72,599	180	39	219	4·6 to 1	964	174	1,138	660	1,798	1¾	3½	·2	.	·3
1861	120,496	71,818	234	31	265	7·5 to 1	1,414	175	1,589	677	2,266	2½	4½	·3	.	·3
1863	121,018	70,688	301	43	344	6·9 to 1	1,826	190	2,016	724	2,740	4	5¼	·4	.	·4
1865	130,760	69,446	215	99	314	2·2 to 1	1,368	387	1,755	675	2,430	2½	3½	·3	·1	·4
1867	137,003	68,228	174	136	310	1·3 to 1	1,417	394	1,811	864	2,675	2½	4½	·2	·2	·4
1869	141,254	66,995	210	154	364	1·4 to 1	1,576	527	2,101	899	3,001	3¾	4¾	·3	·2	·5
1871	138,982	65,764	194	147	341	1·3 to 1	1,335	359	1,694	834	2,528	3	4½	·3	·2	·5
1873	138,318	65,768	202	184	386	1 to 1	2,026	700	2,726	802	3,528	4¾	5½	·3	·3	·6
1875	150,080	65,768	200	275	475	1 to 1·4	1,962	727	2,689	979	3,668	4	5½	·3	·4	·7
1877	140,349	65,768	251	212	463	1·2 to 1	2,076	668	2,744	892	3,636	4¾	5¼	·4	·3	·7
DOWNPATRICK UNION.																
Area, 147,488 acres.																
1851	165,892	62,776	431	.	431	.	1,697	.	1,697	.	1,697	2½	2½	·6	.	·6
1853	165,392	62,613	362	6	368	55 to 1	1,541	44	1,585	788	2,373	2¼	3¼	·5	.	·5
1855	165,391	61,498	309	14	323	22 to 1	1,516	68	1,584	790	2,484	2¼	3¼	·5	.	·5
1857	165,385	60,291	250	24	274	10 to 1	1,425	89	1,514	847	2,361	2¼	3½	·4	.	·4
1859	165,483	58,150	266	9	275	29 to 1	1,455	61	1,516	944	2,450	2¼	3½	·4	.	·4
1861	165,591	57,803	296	14	310	21 to 1	1,988	94	1,082	859	2,941	2¾	4¼	·5	.	·5
1863	166,498	57,304	346	17	363	20 to 1	2,217	109	2,326	941	3,267	3¼	4¾	·6	.	·6
1865	170,949	56,630	273	14	287	19 to 1	1,822	86	1,908	897	2,805	2½	4	·5	.	·5
1867	171,969	55,974	295	24	319	8·3 to 1	2,185	129	2,314	916	3,230	3¼	4½	·5	.	·6
1869	174,135	55,300	311	22	333	10 to 1	2,331	128	2,459	973	3,432	3¼	4¾	·6	.	·6
1871	174,592	54,614	263	22	285	12 to 1	2,107	99	2,206	994	3,200	3½	4½	·5	.	·5
1873	175,166	54,644	280	29	309	9·6 to 1	2,462	110	2,572	1,028	3,701	3½	5	·5	.	·6
1875	176,170	54,644	229	19	248	12 to 1	1,913	94	2,007	1,131	3,1??	2¾	4½	·4	.	·4
1877	176,273	54,644	212	22	234	9·7 to 1	1,734	102	1,836	1,029	2,865	2½	3¾	·4	.	·4
KILKEEL UNION.																
Area, 81,843 acres.																
1851	37,141	24,726	130	.	130	.	490	.	490	.	490	3¼	3¼	·5	.	·5
1853	37,141	24,302	98	.	98	.	307	.	307	349	656	2	4¼	·4	.	·4
1855	37,141	23,859	76	.	76	.	395	.	395	370	765	2½	5	·3	.	·3
1857	37,493	23,458	64	.	64	.	276	.	276	366	642	1¾	4¼	·3	.	·3
1859	37,184	24,035	63	3	66	.	267	13	280	401	681	1¾	4¼	·3	.	·3
1861	37,381	21,614	84	.	84	.	418	.	465	406	871	3	5½	·4	.	·4
1863	47,447	22,448	94	2	96	47 to 1	494	16	510	436	946	2½	6	·4	.	·4
1865	39,981	22,095	110	4	114	26 to 1	570	30	540	494	1,044	4	6½	·5	.	·5
1867	40,494	21,793	116	1	117	.	760	9	769	460	1,229	4¼	7½	·5	.	·5
1869	40,880	21,519	87	2	89	43 to 1	847	23	870	542	1,162	3¾	7	·4	.	·4
1871	41,049	21,346	87	2	89	43 to 1	836	13	849	540	1,089	3¾	6¼	·4	.	·4
1873	41,779	21,346	101	1	102	.	678	19	697	489	1,186	4	7	·4	.	·4
1875	41,641	21,346	94	3	97	31 to 1	610	16	626	535	1,161	4¼	6¾	·4	.	·4
1877	42,103	21,346	78	6	84	13 to 1	555	20	575	499	1,074	3¼	6	·4	.	·4
NEWRY UNION.																
Area, 127,827 acres.																
1851	128,184	84,576	621	.	621	.	2,008	.	2,008	.	2,008	3¾	3¾	·7	.	·7
1853	124,884	82,515	478	7	485	68 to 1	1,776	13	1,484	1,040	2,524	2¾	4¾	·6	.	·6
1855	124,594	81,470	527	10	537	52·7 to 1	2,642	37	2,680	1,048	3,745	5¼	7¼	·6	.	·6
1857	124,905	78,417	335	6	341	56 to 1	1,443	74	1,517	1,104	2,6??	3	5	·4	.	·4
1859	124,606	76,334	331	9	340	149 to 1	1,491	38	1,529	1,177	2,657	3	6¼	·4	.	·4
1861	124,846	74,411	361	14	375	25·8 to 1	2,011	99	2,110	1,108	3,218	4	6¼	·5	.	·5
1863	125,479	75,899	463	149	612	3·1 to 1	2,159	407	2,566	1,151	4,017	5¼	7¾	·6	·2	·8
1865	126,752	73,417	446	127	573	3·5 to 1	2,719	481	3,200	1,090	4,290	6¼	8¼	·6	·1	·7
1867	130,136	74,871	408	104	512	4·1 to 1	3,056	394	3,450	1,209	4,651	5½	7	·5	·1	·7
1869	132,651	72,875	513	168	681	3·0 to 1	3,798	324	4,121	1,247	5,368	6¾	8¾	·7	·2	·9
1871	164,642	72,079	425	217	642	2 to 1	4,127	583	4,745	1,451	6,186	6¾	7¾	·6	·3	·9
1873	161,604	72,079	431	214	645	2 to 1	3,495	643	4,178	1,488	5,663	6¼	8¼	·6	·3	·9
1875	164,440	72,079	389	219	608	1·8 to 1	3,018	786	3,801	1,604	5,410	5½	8	·5	·3	·8
1877	165,181	72,079	354	180	534	2·0 to 1	3,074	579	3,658	1,668	5,321	5¼	7¼	·5	·2	·7

Expenditure of each Poor Law Union in Ireland since the year 1851—*continued.*

Year	Valuation	Population	Average Daily Numbers in Receipt of Relief: In-door	Out-door, under 10 Vic. c. 31	Total	Ratio of Indoor to Outdoor	Expenditure for: In Maintenance and Clothing	Out Relief under 10 Vic. c. 31	Total	Expenditure under Medical Charities Acts, exclusive of Vaccination	Total of Cols. 10 and 11	Poundage: On Amount in Col. 10	On Amount in Col. 12	Percentage of Paupers to Population: In-doors	Out-doors	Total
1	2	3	4	5	6	7	8	9	10	11	12	13	14	15	16	17
Province of Ulster— *continued.* **Newtownards Union.** Area, 93,947 acres							£	£	£	£	£	d.	d.			
1851	129,092	56,784	419	.	419	.	1,630	.	1,630	.	1,630	3½	3½	·7	.	·7
1853	129,542	56,112	340	.	340	.	1,314	.	1,314	599	1,913	2½	3½	·6	.	·6
1855	129,542	55,411	390	.	390	.	2,077	.	2,077	631	2,708	4	5	·7	.	·7
1857	119,573	54,770	302	.	302	.	1,642	.	1,642	671	2,313	3¼	4¾	·5	.	·5
1859	118,674	54,000	296	.	296	.	1,435	.	1,435	718	2,153	2¾	4½	·5	.	·5
1861	118,485	53,428	495	.	495	.	2,900	.	2,900	870	3,770	5¾	7¾	·9	.	·9
1863	119,791	52,387	614	4	618	153 to 1	3,714	17	3,731	902	4,613	7½	9¼	1·1	.	1·1
1865	126,650	51,848	441	12	453	37 to 1	2,761	40	2,801	994	3,795	5¼	7¼	·8	.	·8
1867	124,3[illegible]	50,309	454	56	510	8 to 1	3,065	183	3,248	1,002	4,250	6	8	·9	·1	1·0
1869	140,923	49,279	481	203	685	2·3 to 1	3,707	697	4,404	1,002	5,406	8	10	·9	·4	1·3
1871	11[illegible],694	48,281	358	326	684	1·1 to 1	2,476	903	3,379	972	4,364	6	7¾	·7	·7	1·4
1873	135,286	48,231	363	398	761	1 to 1·1	3,007	1,397	4,404	998	3,362	7¾	9¼	·7	·8	1·5
1875	140,620	48,211	443	361	788	1 to 1·1	2,996	1,323	4,319	1,100	5,419	7½	9¼	·7	·6	1·5
1877	137,943	48,281	354	391	745	1 to 1·1	3,090	1,358	4,448	1,060	5,508	7¾	9½	·7	·8	1·5
Enniskillen Union. Area, 203,643 acres																
1851	87,265	51,414	692	.	692	.	1,973	.	1,973	.	1,973	5½	5½	1·3	.	1·3
1853	87,265	51,067	416	.	416	.	1,595	.	1,595	665	2,260	4¼	6¼	·8	.	·8
1855	87,265	50,729	276	.	276	.	1,536	.	1,536	740	2,276	4¼	6¼	·5	.	·5
1857	89,948	50,201	197	.	197	.	1,017	.	1,017	692	1,709	2¾	4 7/12	·3	.	·3
1859	89,294	49,942	190	.	190	.	1,480	.	1,480	763	2,243	4	6	·3	.	·3
1861	90,880	47,718	248	.	248	.	1,493	.	1,493	594	2,087	4½	5½	·5	.	·5
1863	90,671	48,471	306	.	306	.	1,716	.	1,716	707	2,423	4½	6½	·6	.	·6
1865	104,750	47,368	271	.	271	.	1,670	.	1,670	728	2,398	3¾	5½	·5	.	·5
1867	104,653	46,045	279	.	279	.	1,859	.	1,859	768	2,627	4¼	6	·6	.	·6
1869	105,046	44,882	305	.	305	.	2,142	.	2,142	834	2,976	5	6¾	·6	.	·6
1871	106,114	41,709	236	.	236	.	1,687	.	1,687	817	2,504	3¾	5¾	·5	.	·5
1873	106,337	44,109	229	.	229	.	2,051	.	2,051	876	2,927	4½	6½	·5	.	·5
1875	104,406	44,[illegible]09	255	.	255	.	2,061	.	2,061	931	2,992	4½	6¾	·5	.	·5
1877	105,791	43,859	270	3	273	90 to 1	1,827	18	1,845	876	2,721	4¼	6¼	·6	.	·6
Irvinestown Union. Area, 75,919 acres																
1851	43,875	25,673	183	.	183	.	540	.	540	.	540	3	3	·7	.	·7
1853	43,875	25,004	103	.	103	.	376	.	376	340	716	2	4	·4	.	·4
1855	43,875	24,488	67	.	67	.	351	.	351	350	701	1¾	3¾	·2	.	·2
1857	43,875	23,906	73	.	73	.	384	.	384	365	749	2	4	·3	.	·3
1859	43,875	23,317	57	.	57	.	307	.	307	399	706	1¾	3¾	·2	.	·2
1861	43,875	22,798	119	.	119	.	563	.	563	401	964	3	5¼	·5	.	·5
1863	43,875	22,105	155	.	155	.	813	.	813	411	1,224	4½	6¾	·7	.	·7
1865	48,393	21,484	163	.	163	.	880	.	880	438	1,308	4½	6½	·7	.	·7
1867	48,446	20,863	123	.	123	.	832	.	832	352	1,184	4¼	6	·6	.	·6
1869	48,583	20,213	128	.	128	.	789	.	789	376	1,165	3 11/12	5¾	·6	.	·6
1871	48,540	19,921	93	.	93	.	631	.	631	482	1,113	3¼	5½	·4	.	·4
1873	48,643	19,791	106	.	106	.	964	.	964	496	1,460	4¾	7¼	·5	.	·5
1875	48,717	19,521	105	.	105	.	848	.	848	597	1,445	4¼	7¼	·5	.	·5
1877	48,781	19,881	110	.	110	.	821	.	821	489	1,310	4	6¼	·5	.	·5
Lisnaskea Union. Area, 96,751 acres.																
1851	46,906	29,165	348	.	348	.	1,192	.	1,192	.	1,193	6¼	6¼	1·1	.	1·1
1853	46,906	28,448	178	.	178	.	664	.	664	437	1,101	3½	5½	·6	.	·6
1855	46,906	27,724	123	.	123	.	641	.	641	498	1,039	3½	5½	·4	.	·4
1857	46,906	27,160	82	.	82	.	509	.	509	405	1,004	2¾	5	·3	.	·3
1859	46,906	26,486	87	.	87	.	517	.	517	498	1,015	2¾	5½	·3	.	·3
1861	46,906	25,829	163	.	163	.	673	.	673	495	1,168	3½	6	·6	.	·6
1863	46,906	25,429	159	.	159	.	925	.	925	489	1,414	4¾	7¼	·6	.	·6
1865	57,879	25,082	124	.	124	.	763	.	763	491	1,254	3¼	5¼	·5	.	·5
1867	57,814	24,692	110	12	122	13 to 1	864	17	881	530	1,411	3¾	5¾	·4	.	·4
1869	57,763	24,232	133	18	151	7 to 1	1,019	30	1,049	594	1,643	4¼	6¾	·5	.	·5
1871	57,796	23,842	79	56	140	1·6 to 1	810	115	925	551	1,476	3¾	6	·3	·2	·5
1873	57,865	23,442	95	86	181	1·1 to 1	862	129	991	626	1,617	4¼	6¾	·4	·3	·7
1875	57,925	23,062	92	79	171	1·1 to 1	947	135	1,073	627	1,700	4½	7	·4	·3	·7
1877	57,961	22,842	152	111	263	1·3 to 1	797	167	964	584	1,548	4	6 7/12	·6	·4	1·0
Coleraine Union. Area, 112,396 acres.																
1851	76,867	43,071	298	.	298	.	1,116	.	1,116	.	1,116	3½	3½	·6	.	·6
1853	76,867	42,526	212	.	212	.	864	.	864	559	1,423	2 11/12	4½	·5	.	·5
1855	76,867	42,055	232	3	235	77·3 to 1	1,219	.	1,219	614	1,833	3¾	5¾	·5	.	·5
1857	76,547	41,544	143	1	144	.	934	.	934	607	1,541	3	4¾	·3	.	·3
1859	77,431	41,083	169	3	172	56 to 1	801	15	816	658	1,474	2½	4½	·4	.	·4
1861	90,[illegible]	40,462	275	11	286	25 to 1	1,664	46	1,700	647	2,347	4½	6¼	·6	.	·7
1863	91,421	40,281	316	26	342	12 to 1	1,936	131	2,067	689	2,776	5¼	7¼	·7	.	·8
1865	92,619	39,844	289	40	329	7·2 to 1	1,906	141	2,047	608	2,655	5¼	6¾	·7	·1	·8
1867	93,653	39,427	305	61	366	4·9 to 1	2,161	154	2,315	734	3,049	6	7¾	·8	·1	·9
1869	94,638	34,130	323	87	400	3·7 to 1	2,169	334	2,483	758	3,241	6¼	8¼	·8	·2	1·0
1871	97,409	38,773	265	100	365	2·6 to 1	1,684	435	2,119	825	2,944	5¼	7¼	·6	·3	·9
1873	97,778	38,775	236	147	384	1·6 to 1	1,946	599	2,545	886	3,431	6¼	8½	·6	·4	1·0
1875	99,018	38,775	229	217	446	1·1 to 1	1,914	851	2,765	965	3,731	6¾	9¼	·6	·5	1·1
1877	99,853	38,773	232	211	444	1·1 to 1	1,668	986	2,654	840	3,494	6½	8½	·6	·5	1·1

No. 6.—STATISTICAL TABLE showing the progress of the Pauperism and

Years.	Valuation.	Population.	Average Daily Number in Receipt of Relief. In-door.	Out-door, under 10 Vic. c. 31.	Total.	Ratio of Indoor to Outdoor.	Expenditure for In-Maintenance and Clothing.	Out Relief under 10 Vic. c. 31.	Total.	Expenditure under Medical Charities Acts, exclusive of Vaccination.	Total of Cols. 10 and 11.	Poundage On Amount in Col. 10.	On Amount in Col. 12.	Percentage of Paupers to Population. In-door.	Out-door.	Total.
1.	2.	3.	4.	5.	6.	7.	8.	9.	10.	11.	12.	13.	14.	15.	16.	17.
Province of Ulster—continued.																
LIMAVADY UNION.							£	£	£	£	£	d.	d.			
Area, 152,712 acres.																
1851	67,064	33,920	321	.	321	.	1,136	.	1,136	.	1,136	4	4	·9	.	·9
1853	67,064	32,791	197	.	197	.	824	.	824	440	1,264	3	4½	·6	.	·6
1855	67,064	32,885	163	.	163	.	718	.	718	493	1,211	2½	4¼	·5	.	·5
1857	67,180	32,099	103	.	103	.	399	.	399	447	846	1½	3	·3	.	·3
1859	66,460	31,568	60	.	60	.	377	.	377	266	643	1¼	2¼	·2	.	·2
1861	66,891	30,907	110	.	110	.	499	.	499	549	1,048	1¾	3¾	·3	.	·3
1863	68,087	30,275	154	.	154	.	739	.	740	545	1,284	2¾	4½	·5	.	·5
1865	67,457	29,848	150	.	150	.	822	.	822	574	1,395	3	5	·5	.	·5
1867	67,343	29,030	173	.	173	.	860	.	860	487	1,347	3	4¾	·6	.	·6
1869	68,117	28,393	179	.	179	.	854	.	854	527	1,381	3¼	5¼	·6	.	·6
1871	68,267	27,764	141	.	141	.	672	.	672	676	1,348	2½	4¾	·5	.	·5
1873	64,698	27,764	134	.	134	.	869	.	869	698	1,567	3	5¾	·5	.	·5
1875	68,710	27,764	136	.	136	.	849	.	849	711	1,560	3	5½	·5	.	·5
1877	68,829	27,764	133	.	133	.	864	.	874	788	1,662	3	5¾	·5	.	·5
LONDONDERRY UNION.																
Area, 112,866 acres.																
1851	115,620	62,418	573	.	573	.	1,961	.	1,961	.	1,961	4	4	·9	.	·9
1853	115,622	61,805	476	.	476	.	1,842	.	1,842	1,169	3,071	3¾	6¼	·8	.	·8
1855	115,622	61,201	493	.	494	.	2,852	.	2,852	1,051	3,903	6	8¼	·8	.	·8
1857	116,288	60,597	369	.	369	.	2,190	.	2,190	996	3,186	4½	6½	·6	.	·6
1859	127,198	59,994	410	.	410	.	1,979	.	1,979	1,101	3,080	3¾	5¾	·6	.	·6
1861	131,255	59,389	475	.	475	.	2,175	.	2,175	1,160	3,335	4	6	·8	.	·8
1863	135,611	59,263	406	.	406	.	2,445	.	2,445	1,199	3,644	4½	6½	·7	.	·7
1865	142,406	59,136	442	3	445	147·3 to 1	2,239	14	2,253	1,351	3,604	3¾	6	·7	.	·7
1867	150,941	59,010	416	1	417	.	2,515	4	2,519	1,195	3,714	4	6	·7	.	·7
1869	145,706	58,884	449	1	450	.	2,481	4	2,485	1,143	3,628	4	6	·7	.	·7
1871	147,714	58,758	376	1	377	.	2,540	4	2,434	1,466	4,000	4½	6½	·6	.	·6
1873	149,309	58,758	414	1	415	.	2,78[illegible]	5	2,784	1,695	4,391	4¾	7	·7	.	·7
1875	152,486	58,758	374	1	375	.	2,4[illegible]	4	2,469	1,645	4,108	3¾	6¼	·6	.	·6
1877	153,612	58,758	349	.	349	.	2,237	.	2,237	1,536	3,743	3½	5¾	·6	.	·6
MAGHERAFELT UNION.																
Area, 155,804 acres.																
1851	74,024	64,292	315	.	315	.	1,049	.	1,049	.	1,049	3¼	3¼	·4	.	·4
1853	74,024	64,228	174	.	174	.	612	.	612	627	1,239	2	4	·3	.	·3
1855	74,081	64,134	153	.	153	.	698	.	698	577	1,275	2¼	4¼	·2	.	·2
1857	74,076	64,040	128	.	128	.	618	.	618	578	1,196	2	3⅞	·2	.	·2
1859	89,784	63,946	148	.	148	.	700	.	700	616	1,316	1¾	3¾	·2	.	·2
1861	89,679	63,852	150	.	150	.	800	.	800	695	1,495	2¼	4	·2	.	·2
1863	90,019	62,188	216	.	216	.	1,247	.	1,247	639	1,886	3¼	5	·3	.	·3
1865	90,147	61,778	206	1	207	.	1,081	5	1,086	673	1,759	3	4¾	·3	.	·3
1867	90,488	60,745	176	2	178	88 to 1	1,194	11	1,205	701	1,906	3¼	5	·3	.	·3
1869	90,607	59,708	198	2	200	74 to 1	1,282	10	1,292	746	2,038	3¼	5¼	·3	.	·3
1871	91,218	58,674	170	4	174	42 to 1	1,088	17	1,105	717	1,822	3	4¾	·3	.	·3
1873	91,347	58,673	219	1	220	.	1,703	7	1,710	703	2,413	4½	6¼	·3	.	·3
1875	91,046	58,673	197	3	200	48 to 1	1,548	14	1,614	800	2,418	4¼	6¼	·3	.	·3
1877	91,833	58,673	298	4	302	74·5 to 1	1,405	20	1,425	942	2,367	3⅞	6¾	·5	.	·5
CARRICKMACROSS UNION.																
Area, 60,660 acres.																
1851	46,780	28,169	1,235	.	1,235	.	4,637	.	4,637	.	4,637	1s. 11¾d.	1s. 11¾d.	4·3	.	4·3
1853	46,789	27,066	458	.	458	.	1,477	.	1,477	464	1,941	7½	10	1·6	.	1·6
1855	46,789	25,849	224	.	224	.	1,132	.	1,132	345	1,477	5¾	7½	·8	.	·8
1857	46,791	24,680	136	.	136	.	609	.	609	360	969	3¼	5	·5	.	·5
1859	46,940	23,417	131	.	131	.	607	.	607	385	992	3¼	4⅞	·5	.	·5
1861	46,810	22,354	136	.	136	.	893	.	893	383	1,276	4¼	6¼	·6	.	·6
1863	44,263	22,010	146	.	146	.	951	.	951	364	1,315	4¼	6½	·6	.	·6
1865	46,645	21,670	128	.	128	.	791	.	791	369	1,160	3¾	5½	·6	.	·6
1867	47,842	21,330	120	.	120	.	917	.	917	400	1,317	4½	6½	·5	.	·5
1869	48,983	20,990	108	.	108	.	777	.	777	418	1,195	3¾	5¾	·5	.	·5
1871	49,471	20,650	99	.	99	.	772	.	772	405	1,177	3¾	5¾	·4	.	·4
1873	50,031	20,650	124	.	124	.	1,149	.	1,149	480	1,629	5½	7½	·6	.	·6
1875	50,106	20,650	108	.	108	.	1,030	.	1,030	471	1,501	5	7¼	·5	.	·5
1877	50,244	20,650	114	3	117	38 to 1	1,146	11	1,157	489	1,646	4½	8	·5	.	·5
CASTLEBLAYNEY UNION.																
Area, 94,215 acres.																
1851	62,840	46,639	536	.	536	.	2,326	.	2,326	.	2,326	9	9	1·1	.	1·1
1853	62,340	45,684	342	.	342	.	1,552	.	1,552	449	2,001	6	7¾	·7	.	·7
1855	62,840	44,716	227	.	227	.	1,373	.	1,373	483	1,856	5¼	7¼	·5	.	·5
1857	62,862	43,748	158	.	158	.	1,113	.	1,113	471	1,584	4¼	6	·3	.	·3
1859	60,913	42,780	146	.	146	.	894	.	894	490	1,384	3½	5½	·3	.	·3
1861	64,329	41,812	162	.	162	.	1,110	.	1,110	448	1,558	4¼	5¾	·4	.	·4
1863	64,761	41,614	232	.	232	.	1,446	.	1,446	504	1,950	5¼	7¼	·6	.	·6
1865	74,204	41,420	197	8	205	24 to 1	1,025	21	1,046	505	1,551	3¼	5	·4	.	·4
1867	74,383	41,226	188	4	192	47 to 1	1,370	37	1,407	497	1,904	4½	6¼	·4	.	·4
1869	74,481	41,032	177	8	185	22 to 1	1,178	53	1,231	633	1,864	4	6	·4	.	·4
1871	74,838	40,838	172	29	201	6 to 1	1,162	134	1,296	678	1,934	4	6¼	·4	.	·4
1873	74,731	40,838	175	74	249	2·3 to 1	1,403	255	1,658	749	2,409	5¼	7¼	·4	·1	·6
1875	75,410	40,838	162	54	216	3 to 1	1,103	198	1,300	709	2,009	4¼	6¾	·4	·1	·5
1877	75,426	40,838	163	81	244	2 to 1	1,127	281	1,408	747	2,155	4¼	7	·4	·2	·6

Expenditure of each Poor Law Union in Ireland since the year 1851—*continued*.

Years.	Valuation.	Population.	Average Daily Number in Receipt of Relief: In-door	Out-door, under 10 Vic. c. 31	Total	Ratio of Indoor to Outdoor	Expenditure for: In Maintenance and Clothing	Out Relief under 10 Vic. c. 31	Total	Expenditure under Medical Charities Acts, exclusive of Vaccination	Total of Cols. 10 and 11	Poundage: On Amount in Col. 10	On Amount in Col. 12	Per centage of Paupers to Population: In-door	Out-door	Total.
1.	2.	3.	4.	5.	6.	7.	8.	9.	10.	11.	12.	13.	14.	15.	16.	17.
Province of Ulster—continued.																
CLONES UNION.							£	£	£	£	£	d.	d.			
Area, 73,302 acres.																
1851	47,458	28,365	405	.	405	.	1,426	.	1,426	.	1,426	7½	7½	1·4	.	1·4
1853	47,638	28,247	203	.	203	.	868	.	868	449	1,317	4 7/10	6½	·7	.	·7
1855	47,598	28,231	169	.	169	.	614	.	614	352	966	3 3/10	4 7/10	·5	.	·5
1857	47,635	28,215	97	.	97	.	667	.	667	848	1,515	3 3/10	5½	·3	.	·3
1859	47,069	28,189	108	.	108	.	782	.	782	351	1,133	3½	6½	·3	.	·3
1861	47,769	28,184	112	.	112	.	731	.	731	332	1,063	3 3/10	5½	·3	.	·3
1863	58,082	27,187	136	.	136	.	886	.	886	368	1,254	3½	5½	·5	.	·5
1865	57,146	26,192	115	.	115	.	745	.	745	350	1,095	3½	4½	·4	.	·4
1867	56,820	25,197	122	.	122	.	852	.	852	284	1,136	3¾	4½	·4	.	·4
1869	56,844	24,303	130	.	130	.	925	.	925	444	1,369	4	5½	·5	.	·5
1871	56,874	23,207	106	.	106	.	762	.	762	463	1,225	3½	5¼	·4	.	·4
1873	56,985	23,207	94	.	94	.	750	.	750	468	1,218	3½	5½	·4	.	·4
1875	57,087	23,207	94	.	94	.	661	.	661	481	1,142	2¾	4 7/10	·4	.	·4
1877	57,306	23,207	76	.	76	.	637	.	637	447	1,084	2¾	4½	·3	.	·3
MONAGHAN UNION.																
Area, 112,728 acres.																
1851	98,002	49,028	479	.	479	.	3,487	.	3,487	.	3,487	3s. 0½d.	3s. 0½d.	·9	.	·9
1853	98,002	48,350	252	.	252	.	3,150	.	3,150	594	3,744	1s. 5d.	2s. 1d.	·5	.	·5
1855	96,093	47,687	197	.	197	.	1,381	.	1,381	610	1,991	9¼	1s. 1½d.	·4	.	·4
1857	94,085	47,016	162	.	162	.	1,046	.	1,046	566	1,612	6	9	·3	.	·3
1859	93,066	46,245	150	.	150	.	874	.	784	618	1,402	4½	7¼	·3	.	·3
1861	93,469	46,874	165	.	165	.	980	.	980	549	1,529	2½	4	·3	.	·3
1863	94,516	44,785	198	.	198	.	1,073	.	1,073	687	1,760	2¾	4½	·4	.	·4
1865	93,529	43,738	177	.	177	.	935	.	935	618	1,553	2¾	4	·4	.	·4
1867	93,782	42,767	180	.	180	.	1,082	.	1,082	618	1,700	3	4½	·4	.	·4
1869	98,847	41,788	163	.	163	.	1,053	.	1,053	665	1,718	2 7/10	4½	·3	.	·3
1871	98,408	40,829	158	.	158	.	981	.	981	759	1,740	2½	4¼	·3	.	·3
1873	93,077	40,829	158	.	158	.	1,178	.	1,178	826	2,004	3	5½	·3	.	·3
1875	94,029	40,828	169	.	169	.	1,176	.	1,176	882	2,058	3	5½	·4	.	·4
1877	94,474	40,829	154	.	154	.	1,155	.	1,155	945	2,100	2 7/10	4 7/10	·4	.	·4
CASTLEBLAYNEY UNION.																
Area, 61,705 acres.																
1851	21,627	18,739	141	.	141	.	335	.	335	.	335	4	4	·7	.	·7
1853	21,627	18,478	73	.	73	.	211	.	211	198	409	2½	4½	·3	.	·3
1855	21,627	18,298	54	.	54	.	163	.	163	192	355	1¾	4	·2	.	·2
1857	21,613	17,978	43	.	43	.	148	.	148	183	331	1¾	3½	·2	.	·2
1859	21,613	17,728	47	.	47	.	165	.	165	200	365	1¾	4	·2	.	·2
1861	25,673	17,478	48	.	48	.	168	.	168	208	376	1½	3½	·2	.	·2
1863	26,081	17,245	78	.	78	.	313	.	313	244	557	2½	5¼	·4	.	·4
1865	26,019	17,010	83	.	83	.	339	.	339	244	583	3¼	5¼	·4	.	·4
1867	25,157	16,777	63	.	63	.	293	.	293	249	542	2¾	5	·3	.	·3
1869	25,813	16,546	80	.	80	.	321	.	321	282	603	3	3½	·4	.	·4
1871	25,625	16,311	70	.	70	.	337	.	337	212	549	3¼	5	·4	.	·4
1873	25,168	16,311	71	.	71	.	388	.	388	312	700	3½	6½	·4	.	·4
1875	24,780	16,311	72	.	72	.	351	.	351	311	662	3¼	6	·4	.	·4
1877	26,246	16,311	66	.	66	.	397	.	397	333	730	3 7/10	6¾	·4	.	·4
CLOGHER UNION.																
Area, 101,679 acres.																
1851	49,422	31,630	327	.	327	.	1,893	.	1,893	.	1,893	8	8	1·0	.	1·0
1853	49,422	30,834	186	.	186	.	899	.	899	484	1,383	5	7½	·6	.	·6
1855	49,438	30,018	164	.	164	.	1,043	.	1,043	436	1,479	5½	8½	·5	.	·5
1857	42,112	29,302	130	.	130	.	1,047	.	1,047	419	1,466	5½	8½	·4	.	·4
1859	43,442	28,488	185	.	185	.	561	.	561	407	968	3¼	5¼	·7	.	·7
1861	43,739	27,572	117	.	117	.	737	.	737	428	1,165	3¼	5	·4	.	·4
1863	55,770	27,095	165	.	165	.	1,124	.	1,124	431	1,555	4¾	6½	·6	.	·6
1865	55,707	26,621	126	3	129	42 to 1	850	9	859	441	1,300	3¾	5¾	·4	.	·4
1867	55,879	26,147	117	7	124	16·7 to 1	920	27	947	497	1,444	4¼	6¼	·4	.	·4
1869	56,082	25,674	123	12	135	10·3 to 1	1,026	47	1,073	544	1,617	4½	7	·5	.	·5
1871	56,146	25,190	117	17	134	6·9 to 1	900	43	943	575	1,518	4	6¼	·4	·1	·5
1873	56,266	25,190	120	33	153	3·7 to 1	1,089	108	1,197	582	1,779	4½	7½	·5	·1	·6
1875	56,724	25,190	110	41	151	2·7 to 1	909	163	1,072	582	1,654	4½	6½	·4	·2	·6
1877	56,723	25,190	129	61	190	2·1 to 1	1,192	260	1,452	643	2,095	6½	8½	·5	·2	·7
COOKSTOWN UNION.																
Area, 96,720 acres.																
1851	46,636	38,883	230	.	230	.	808	.	808	.	808	3¼	3¼	·5	.	·5
1853	46,616	38,657	170	.	170	.	676	.	676	485	1,161	3½	5	·4	.	·4
1855	54,836	38,441	161	.	161	.	849	.	849	471	1,320	3 7/10	5½	·4	.	·4
1857	57,317	38,205	128	.	128	.	729	.	729	489	1,218	3	5	·3	.	·3
1859	57,516	[illegible]	130	.	130	.	787	.	787	477	1,264	3	5	·3	.	·3
1861	61,420	37,488	137	.	137	.	873	.	873	451	1,324	3½	5¼	·4	.	·4
1863	61,761	37,226	245	.	245	.	1,270	.	1,270	467	1,737	5	6¾	·6	.	·6
1865	61,880	36,635	145	.	145	.	784	.	784	452	1,236	3	4½	·4	.	·4
1867	62,229	35,977	145	.	145	.	854	.	854	612	1,466	3¼	5½	·4	.	·4
1869	62,711	35,319	176	1	177	.	893	5	898	439	1,337	3½	5	·5	.	·5
1871	63,069	34,661	136	2	138	68 to 1	809	9	818	533	1,351	3¼	5¼	·4	.	·4
1873	64,136	34,661	124	5	129	20 to 1	822	27	849	604	1,453	3½	5½	·3	.	·3
1875	63,468	34,661	125	10	135	12 to 1	791	76	867	545	1,412	3½	5½	·3	.	·3
1877	63,648	34,661	101	16	117	6·3 to 1	653	115	768	611	1,379	3¼	5½	·3	.	·3

APPENDIX A. — Poor Relief.

No. 6.—STATISTICAL TABLE showing the progress of the Pauperism and

Years	Valuation	Population	Average Daily Numbers in Receipt of Relief: In-doors	Out-doors, under 10 Vic. c. 31	Total	Ratio of Indoor to Outdoor	Expenditure for: In Maintenance and Clothing	Out Relief under 10 Vic. c. 31	Total	Expenditure under Medical Charities Acts exclusive of Vaccination	Total of Cols. 10 and 11	Poundage: On Amount in Col. 10	On Amount in Col. 12	Per centage of Paupers to Population: In-door	Out-door	Total
1	2	3	4	5	6	7	8	9	10	11	12	13	14	15	16	17
Province of Ulster—continued.																
DUNGANNON UNION.																
Area, 102,847 acres.							£	£	£	£	£	d.	d.			
1851	89,231	54,282	266	.	266	.	800	.	800	.	800	2½	2½	·4	.	·4
1853	89,231	51,891	169	.	169	.	575	.	575	529	1,104	1½	3	·3	.	·3
1855	89,831	51,230	214	.	214	.	1,002	.	1,002	686	1,778	3	4½	·4	.	·4
1857	89,929	52,918	163	1	166	.	871	2	873	678	1,551	2½	4½	·3	.	·3
1859	89,928	52,772	164	1	166	.	809	5	814	720	1,534	2½	4½	·3	.	·3
1861	91,361	51,893	211	4	218	53 to 1	1,270	10	1,280	603	1,883	3½	5	·4	.	·4
1863	92,316	50,710	258	7	265	36 to 1	1,606	45	1,651	726	2,377	4½	6½	·5	.	·5
1865	92,260	49,530	235	6	241	39 to 1	1,484	30	1,514	699	2,213	4	5½	·4	.	·4
1867	92,513	48,310	235	20	245	11 to 1	1,591	113	1,709	813	2,522	4½	6½	·4	.	·5
1869	92,874	47,170	258	26	286	8·5 to 1	1,673	162	1,835	829	2,664	4½	5½	·5	.	·6
1871	92,913	45,990	218	77	295	3 to 1	1,342	228	1,570	844	2,414	4	5½	·4	·1	·6
1873	93,347	45,990	210	107	435	2·6 to 1	1,916	403	2,321	840	3,161	6	8½	·4	·2	·7
1875	93,433	45,990	210	139	357	1·5 to 1	1,694	748	2,145	627	3,392	6½	8½	·4	·3	·7
1877	93,784	45,990	204	146	350	1·4 to 1	1,775	443	2,388	680	3,068	5½	7½	·4	·3	·7
GORTIN UNION.																
Area, 111,963 acres.																
1851	16,890	17,301	163	.	164	.	479	.	479	.	579	9	9	·9	.	·9
1853	15,898	17,166	61	.	61	.	284	.	284	246	530	4½	4½	·3	.	·3
1855	15,890	17,031	47	.	47	.	290	.	290	151	441	4½	6½	·2	.	·2
1857	15,710	16,898	50	.	50	.	288	.	288	153	441	4½	6½	·3	.	·3
1859	15,710	16,761	55	.	58	.	254	.	254	174	428	4	6½	·3	.	·3
1861	15,873	16,626	54	.	54	.	337	.	337	260	597	6	7	·3	.	·3
1863	19,445	16,410	59	.	59	.	598	.	598	236	834	7	10½	·3	.	·3
1865	19,264	16,191	69	.	69	.	334	.	334	245	579	4½	7½	·4	.	·4
1867	19,415	15,978	50	.	50	.	373	.	373	230	593	4½	7½	·3	.	·3
1869	19,421	15,762	48	.	48	.	346	.	346	240	586	4½	7½	·3	.	·3
1871	19,427	15,546	45	.	48	.	360	.	360	272	640	4½	8	·3	.	·3
1873	19,531	15,546	49	.	49	.	410	.	410	281	691	5	8½	·3	.	·3
1875	19,580	15,546	47	4	51	12 to 1	387	35	422	316	738	5	9	·3	.	·3
1877	19,610	15,546	50	4	54	12·5 to 1	376	5	381	320	703	4½	5½	·3	.	·3
OMAGH UNION.																
Area, 174,217 acres.																
1851	75,157	58,497	490	.	490	.	1,925	.	1,925	.	1,925	6½	6½	·8	.	·8
1853	75,157	55,764	316	4	320	79 to 1	1,318	10	1,328	497	1,825	4½	5½	·5	.	·5
1855	75,167	55,032	244	3	247	81 to 1	1,409	8	1,417	599	2,016	4½	6½	·4	.	·4
1857	75,421	54,800	227	3	230	75 to 1	1,316	13	1,329	686	1,962	4½	6½	·4	.	·4
1859	75,547	53,588	190	5	195	38 to 1	877	24	901	686	1,587	2½	5	·3	.	·3
1861	80,821	52,846	227	.	227	.	1,446	23	1,369	649	2,018	3½	5½	·4	.	·4
1863	90,462	51,898	341	3	344	113 to 1	2,077	21	2,098	649	2,747	5½	7½	·6	.	·6
1865	90,948	50,856	318	6	324	53 to 1	1,638	56	1,694	613	2,307	4½	6½	·6	.	·6
1867	90,977	49,417	255	16	271	16 to 1	1,501	59	1,560	619	2,179	4½	6	·5	.	·5
1869	91,446	48,276	251	18	269	14 to 1	1,467	56	1,523	754	2,277	4	6	·5	.	·5
1871	92,401	47,139	189	19	208	10 to 1	1,166	44	1,210	853	2,063	3½	5½	·4	.	·4
1873	92,916	47,139	204	26	230	8 to 1	1,247	107	1,354	673	2,024	3½	5½	·4	.	·4
1875	93,820	47,139	203	25	228	8 to 1	1,267	123	1,390	925	2,315	3½	5¾	·4	.	·4
1877	94,138	47,149	202	34	236	6 to 1	1,317	149	1,466	883	2,349	3½	5½	·4	.	·4
STRABANE UNION.																
Area, 155,718 acres.																
1851	82,890	49,167	479	.	479	.	1,681	.	1,681	.	1,681	4½	4½	·9	.	·9
1853	82,890	48,948	279	12	291	23 to 1	1,207	28	1,215	620	1,835	3½	5½	·5	.	·6
1855	83,970	46,987	245	.	245	.	1,244	.	1,244	582	1,816	3½	5½	·5	.	·5
1857	83,428	45,686	167	.	167	.	900	.	900	599	1,502	2½	4½	·3	.	·3
1859	83,930	44,715	123	8	125	44 to 1	621	15	635	580	1,215	1½	4½	·3	.	·3
1861	94,780	42,694	189	.	189	.	1,043	.	1,043	681	1,724	2½	4½	·4	.	·4
1863	94,646	42,792	257	12	269	21 to 1	1,613	46	1,655	708	2,463	4½	6	·6	.	·7
1865	95,402	41,994	297	12	309	25 to 1	1,835	27	1,862	764	2,625	4½	6½	·7	.	·7
1867	95,825	41,146	279	54	333	5 to 1	1,754	101	1,855	724	2,579	4½	6½	·7	·1	·8
1869	96,057	40,720	269	145	414	1·8 to 1	1,965	239	2,204	832	3,036	5½	7½	·6	·3	1·0
1871	96,589	39,510	247	221	468	1·1 to 1	1,682	363	2,045	828	2,873	5½	7½	·6	·5	1·1
1873	96,578	39,510	237	225	462	1 to 1	1,908	446	2,354	835	3,189	5½	8	·6	·5	1·1
1875	96,697	39,510	244	244	488	1 to 1	1,991	478	2,471	896	3,367	6	8½	·6	·6	1·2
1877	96,279	39,510	244	230	474	1 to 1	2,210	547	2,757	992	3,749	6	9	·6	·6	1·2
Province of Munster.																
BALLYVAUGHAN UNION.																
Area, 71,030 acres.																
1851	12,140	8,145	846	.	846	.	2,635	.	2,635	.	2,635	4s. 4½d.	4s. 4½d.	10·4	.	10·4
1853	12,141	7,079	847	.	847	.	1,917	.	1,917	261	2,178	2s. 3½d.	2s. 7½d.	8·0	.	6·9
1855	13,141	7,614	237	.	237	.	1,168	.	1,168	130	1,298	1s. 11½d.	2s. 2d.	3·0	.	3·0
1857	17,293	7,349	129	.	129	.	867	.	867	80	947	10½	11½	1·8	.	1·8
1859	19,347	7,084	100	.	100	.	609	.	609	86	695	7½	8½	1·4	.	1·4
1861	19,348	6,919	133	.	133	.	911	.	911	75	986	11½	1s. 0½d.	1·9	.	1·9
1863	19,316	6,596	162	.	162	.	967	.	967	119	1,086	1s. 0½d.	1s. 2½d.	2·5	.	2·5
1865	19,535	6,375	159	.	159	.	1,245	.	1,245	111	1,356	1s. 3½d.	1s. 5d.	2·5	.	2·5
1867	19,320	6,164	151	.	151	.	1,189	.	1,189	114	1,303	1s. 2½d.	1s. 4½d.	2·4	.	2·4
1869	19,336	5,884	175	.	175	.	1,318	.	1,340	130	1,480	1s. 4½d.	1s. 6½d.	2·9	.	2·9
1871	19,463	4,712	145	.	145	.	1,189	.	1,189	138	1,327	1s. 2½d.	1s. 4½d.	2·5	.	2·5
1873	19,416	4,712	161	25	186	6·4 to 1	1,570	48	1,618	141	1,759	1s. 7d.	1s. 9½d.	3·6	·4	3·2
1875	19,460	4,712	163	6	169	27·1 to 1	1,451	54	1,505	147	1,732	1s. 5d.	1s. 9½d.	2·5	·1	2·6
1877	19,496	4,712	258	6	264	43 to 1	1,412	42	1,454	134	1,588	1s. 6d.	1s. 7½d.	4·5	·1	4·6

Expenditure of each Poor Law Union in Ireland since the year 1851—*continued.*

Years	Valuation.	Population.	Average Daily Number in Receipt of Relief: In-door.	Out-door, under 10 Vic. c. 31.	Total.	Ratio of In-door to Out-door.	Expenditure for: In Maintenance and Clothing.	Out Relief under 10 Vic. c. 31.	Total.	Expenditure under Medical Charities Acts exclusive of Vaccination.	Total of Cols. 10 and 11.	Poundage: On Amount in Col. 10.	On Amount in Col. 12.	Per centage of Paupers to Population: In-door.	Out-door.	Total.
1.	2.	3.	4.	5.	6.	7.	8.	9.	10.	11.	12.	13.	14.	15.	16.	17.
Province of Munster—*continued.*																
Corofin Union. Area, 61,886 acres.							£	£	£	£	£	d.	d.			
1851	11,450	9,272	862	.	862	.	2,538	.	2,538	.	2,538	4s. 6d.	4s. 6d.	9·2	.	9·2
1853	11,460	9,941	485	.	485	.	1,479	.	1,479	130	1,609	2s. 7½d.	2s. 11¼d.	4·8	.	4·8
1855	11,460	8,757	160	.	160	.	745	.	745	125	870	1s. 4d.	1s. 6d.	1·8	.	1·8
1857	20,440	8,460	79	.	79	.	467	.	467	95	562	5¼	7	·9	.	·9
1859	20,350	8,163	66	.	66	.	421	.	421	90	511	5	6¼	·8	.	·8
1861	20,370	7,866	91	.	91	.	586	.	586	117	703	7	8¼	1·1	.	1·1
1863	20,385	7,711	131	.	131	.	879	.	879	168	847	10½	11¾	1·7	.	1·7
1865	20,385	7,807	144	.	144	.	804	.	804	123	927	9½	11	1·8	.	1·8
1867	20,385	7,403	127	.	127	.	926	.	926	125	1,051	11	1s. 0½d.	1·7	.	1·7
1869	20,405	7,269	124	.	124	.	909	.	909	138	1,047	10¾	1s. 0¼d.	1·7	.	1·7
1871	20,410	7,095	114	9	123	12·6 to 1	869	20	889	143	1,032	10¼	1s. 0¼d.	1·6	·1	1·7
1873	20,419	7,095	110	39	149	2·8 to 1	1,053	202	1,255	148	1,403	1s. 2d.	1s. 4½d.	1·5	·5	2·0
1875	20,428	7,095	119	75	194	1·6 to 1	1,120	224	1,344	151	1,495	1s. 3¼d.	1s. 5½d.	1·7	1·0	2·7
1877	20,434	7,095	130	85	215	1·6 to 1	1,230	245	1,475	139	1,614	1s. 3½d.	1s. 7d.	1·9	1·1	3·0
Ennis Union. Area, 132,504 acres.																
1851	48,783	48,230	2,940	.	2,940	.	10,042	.	10,042	.	10,042	4s. 1½d.	4s. 1½d.	6·0	.	6·0
1853	48,683	48,417	1,704	.	1,704	.	5,862	.	5,862	438	6,300	2s. 4½d.	2s. 6d.	3·7	.	3·7
1855	48,684	41,167	824	.	824	.	4,553	.	4,553	475	5,028	1s. 10½d.	2s. 1d.	1·9	.	1·9
1857	72,397	37,737	442	.	442	.	2,406	.	2,406	485	2,891	8	9½	1·2	.	1·2
1859	73,601	34,927	370	.	370	.	1,892	.	1,892	348	2,240	6¼	7¼	1·1	.	1·1
1861	72,404	30,397	394	.	394	.	2,509	.	2,509	726	3,235	8¼	10¾	1·3	.	1·3
1863	72,553	29,423	484	.	484	.	2,649	.	2,649	686	3,335	8¾	11	1·6	.	1·6
1865	72,649	28,669	423	.	423	.	2,443	.	2,443	678	3,121	8	10¼	1·5	.	1·5
1867	72,801	27,956	445	.	445	.	2,150	.	2,150	664	2,814	10¼	1s. 0¼d.	1·6	.	1·6
1869	72,746	27,846	448	1	449	448 to 1	3,467	9	3,476	641	4,117	11½	1s. 1½d.	1·6	.	1·6
1871	72,680	26,530	417	63	480	6·6 to 1	3,471	149	3,620	770	4,390	1s. 0d.	1s. 2½d.	1·5	·2	1·8
1873	72,721	25,530	407	167	574	2·4 to 1	3,752	422	4,174	640	4,814	1s. 1½d.	1s. 3d.	1·6	·6	2·2
1875	73,697	25,530	413	188	601	2·2 to 1	3,724	557	4,281	686	4,967	1s. 2d.	1s. 4½d.	1·6	·7	2·3
1877	74,696	26,530	434	220	654	1·9 to 1	3,814	685	4,499	677	5,176	1s. 2½d.	1s. 4¼d.	1·6	·8	2·4
Ennistymon Union. Area, 99,281 acres.																
1851	20,872	31,812	2,745	.	2,745	.	9,881	.	9,881	.	9,881	9s. 5¾d.	9s. 5¾d.	8·7	.	8·7
1853	20,882	30,297	1,471	.	1,471	.	4,514	.	4,514	524	5,038	4s. 4¼d.	4s. 10¼d.	4·8	.	4·8
1855	20,882	26,955	536	.	536	.	2,954	.	2,954	342	3,296	2s. 10d.	3s. 2d.	1·8	.	1·8
1857	34,452	27,870	327	.	327	.	2,073	.	2,073	375	2,448	1s. 2½d.	1s. 4¾d.	1·1	.	1·1
1859	34,984	26,514	251	.	251	.	1,480	.	1,480	434	1,914	10¼	1s. 1¼d.	·9	.	·9
1861	35,709	26,078	281	.	281	.	2,014	.	2,014	406	2,420	1s. 1½d.	1s. 3¾d.	1·0	.	1·0
1863	35,877	24,691	382	.	382	.	2,332	.	2,332	421	2,753	1s. 3¾d.	1s. 6½d.	1·5	.	1·5
1865	35,923	24,347	350	.	350	.	2,143	.	2,143	452	2,595	1s. 2d.	1s. 4¾d.	1·4	.	1·4
1867	35,900	24,623	318	.	318	.	2,513	.	2,513	466	2,979	1s. 4¾d.	1s. 7¾d.	1·3	.	1·3
1869	35,991	24,629	314	.	314	.	2,555	.	2,555	497	3,052	1s. 4½d.	1s. 8d.	1·3	.	1·3
1871	35,985	22,855	263	63	326	4·2 to 1	2,345	104	2,449	531	2,980	1s. 3¾d.	1s. 7¾d.	1·1	·3	1·4
1873	30,859	22,356	195	29	224	6·7 to 1	2,485	111	2,596	499	3,095	1s. 4¼d.	1s. 8d.	1·1	·1	1·2
1875	36,843	23,355	265	76	341	3·5 to 1	2,609	261	2,870	522	3,392	1s. 6¼d.	1s. 10¼d.	1·1	·3	1·4
1877	35,896	22,358	252	119	371	2·1 to 1	2,378	461	2,839	505	3,344	1s. 6¾d.	1s. 9¾d.	1·1	·5	1·6
Killadysert Union. Area, 82,819 acres.																
1851	14,908	16,807	1,090	.	1,090	.	6,827	.	6,827	.	6,827	7s. 9¾d.	7s. 9¾d.	6·5	.	6·5
1853	14,966	16,067	823	.	823	.	2,640	.	2,640	378	3,018	3s. 6½d.	4s. 0½d.	5·1	.	5·1
1855	15,308	15,329	421	.	421	.	2,109	.	2,109	214	2,323	2s. 9d.	3s. 0½d.	2·7	.	2·7
1857	25,182	14,481	185	1	186	.	971	1	972	194	1,166	9¼	11	1·3	.	1·3
1859	25,166	13,673	141	2	143	.	757	2	759	229	988	7¼	9½	·9	.	·9
1861	24,209	13,268	132	.	132	.	937	.	937	246	1,183	9	11¼	1·0	.	1·0
1863	25,231	13,051	159	2	161	79·5 to 1	1,026	1	1,027	249	1,276	9¾	1s. 0¼d.	1·2	.	1·2
1865	25,111	12,841	132	14	146	9·4 to 1	866	20	886	297	1,183	8½	11	1·0	·1	1·1
1867	25,087	12,661	143	20	163	7·1 to 1	1,173	46	1,219	297	1,516	11¾	1s. 2½d.	1·1	·1	1·2
1869	25,114	12,421	112	58	170	1·9 to 1	977	138	1,115	298	1,413	10¾	1s. 1½d.	·9	·4	1·3
1871	25,241	12,211	123	83	206	1·5 to 1	1,165	217	1,382	240	1,622	1s. 1d.	1s. 3½d.	1·0	·7	1·7
1873	25,373	12,211	120	124	244	·9 to 1	1,104	377	1,481	281	1,763	1s. 2½d.	1s. 4½d.	1·0	1·0	2·0
1875	25,309	12,211	143	139	282	1·0 to 1	1,421	309	1,730	267	1,997	1s. 4¼d.	1s. 6¾d.	1·2	1·1	2·3
1877	24,625	12,211	147	169	316	·8 to 1	1,418	479	1,897	316	2,213	1s. 6d.	1s. 9d.	1·2	1·4	2·6
Kilrush Union. Area, 13,047 acres.																
1851	53,994	51,287	3,354	.	3,354	.	9,879	.	9,879	.	9,879	5s. 11¾d.	5s. 11¾d.	6·5	.	6·5
1853	53,224	40,930	1,986	.	1,986	.	6,301	.	6,301	409	6,710	3s. 9½d.	4s. 0½d.	4·9	.	4·9
1855	54,225	47,199	888	.	888	.	4,071	.	4,071	474	4,545	2s. 4½d.	2s. 8d.	1·8	.	1·8
1857	51,638	45,170	434	.	434	.	2,406	.	2,406	429	2,835	11¼	1s. 1¼d.	·9	.	·9
1859	51,980	42,103	265	.	265	.	1,619	.	1,619	404	2,023	7½	9¼	·6	.	·6
1861	52,062	41,130	315	1	316	.	2,048	21	2,069	672	2,741	9½	1s. 0½d.	·7	.	·7
1863	52,168	40,091	447	29	476	15 to 1	2,874	132	3,006	389	3,395	1s. 1¾d.	1s. 4d.	1·1	.	1·1
1865	52,097	39,648	463	36	499	12·8 to 1	3,051	162	3,213	679	3,892	1s. 2¾d.	1s. 6d.	1·1	.	1·2
1867	52,074	38,093	312	44	356	7·1 to 1	2,890	204	3,094	671	3,765	1s. 2¼d.	1s. 5¼d.	·9	·1	1·0
1869	52,074	37,008	316	101	417	3·1 to 1	2,456	341	2,797	676	3,473	1s. 1d.	1s. 4d.	·8	·3	1·1
1871	52,008	35,078	257	111	368	2·3 to 1	2,419	358	2,777	725	3,502	1s. 0¾d.	1s. 4d.	·8	·3	1·1
1873	52,346	35,978	205	227	432	·9 to 1	2,853	778	3,631	756	4,387	1s. 4¾d.	1s. 8¼d.	·5	·6	1·2
1875	52,510	35,978	308	165	473	1·9 to 1	2,802	682	3,484	672	4,161	1s. 4d.	1s. 7¼d.	·8	·4	1·3
1877	52,447	35,978	326	290	616	1·1 to 1	2,923	659	3,582	895	4,477	1s. 5d.	1s. 8½d.	·9	·8	1·7

APPENDIX A. —— Poor Relief.

No. 6.—STATISTICAL TABLE showing the progress of the Pauperism and

Year	Valuation	Population	Average Daily Number in Receipt of Relief: In-door	Out-door, under 10 Vic. c. 31	Total	Ratio of In-door to Out-door	Expenditure for: In Maintenance and Clothing	Out Relief under 10 Vic. c. 31	Total	Expenditure under Medical Charities Acts, exclusive of Vaccination fees	Total of Cols. 10 and 11	Poundage: On Amount in Col. 10	On Amount in Col. 12	Percentage of Paupers to Population: In-door	Out-door	Total
1.	2	3	4	5	6	7	8	9.	10	11.	12	13	14	15	16.	17
Province of Munster—continued.																
SCARIFF UNION. Area, 86,290 acres.							£	£	£	£	£	d.	d.			
1851	18,190	22,597	2,301	.	2,301	.	5,831	.	5,831	.	5,831	5s 10½d	5s 10½d	10·2	.	10·2
1853	18,190	21,189	1,457	.	1,457	.	4,034	.	4,034	411	3,485	3s 4½d	3s 9½d	6·8	.	6·8
1855	18,190	19,603	516	.	516	.	2,422	.	2,498	244	2,866	2s 7½d	2s 11½d	2·6	.	2·6
1857	20,167	18,484	239	.	239	.	1,140	.	1,149	207	1,397	10½	1s 1½d	1·3	.	1·3
1859	25,708	17,018	179	.	179	.	1,014	.	1,044	295	1,339	9½	1s 0½d	1·0	.	1·0
1861	25,730	15,971	128	.	128	.	1,447	.	1,447	304	1,741	1s 1½d	1s 4½d	·8		·8
1863	25,767	15,977	235		235	.	1,483		1,462	302	1,764	1s 3½d	1s 4½d	1·5	.	1·5
1865	25,696	14,946	209	.	209	.	1,317	.	1,347	319	1,666	1s 0½d	1s 3½d	1·4		1·4
1867	25,685	14,615	197	.	197	.	1,407	.	1,407	372	1,779	1s 1½d	1s 4½d	1·3	.	1·3
1869	25,712	14,284	181	.	181	.	1,400		1,400	377	1,777	1s 1d	1s 4d	1·2	.	1·2
1871	25,784	13,985	167	.	167	.	1,724		1,424	418	1,743	1s 0½d	1s 4½d	1·2	.	1·2
1873	25,773	13,858	185	.	185	.	1,694	.	1,694	516	2,210	1s 3½d	1s 8½d	1·3		1·3
1875	25,738	14,053	175	.	175	.	1,863		1,635	414	1,919	1s 2½d	1s 6½d	1·2		1·2
1877	25,769	13,813	160	.	160	.	1,656	.	1,356	411	1,967	1s 2½d	1s 6½d	1·2		1·2
TULLA UNION. Area, 84,679 acres.																
1851	21,628	19,282	1,890	.	1,890	.	6,496		6,496	.	6,496	6s 0½d	6s 0½d	9·8	.	9·8
1853	21,694	18,575	844	.	844		2,907	.	2,947	233	3,179	3s 3½d	3s 0½d	4·5	.	4·5
1855	21,848	17,171	468	.	463	.	2,198		2,198	287	2,485	2s 0½d	2s 3½d	2·6	.	2·6
1857	22,470	17,167	238	.	238		1,444	.	1,454	400	1,784	10½	1s 1d	1·3	.	1·3
1859	22,481	16,463	202	.	202	.	1,166		1,166	438	1,614	8½	11	1·2		1·2
1861	22,418	15,739	235		235		1,074	.	1,074	344	2,018	1s 8½d	1s 2½d	1·4		1·4
1863	22,658	15,351	304		304		2,013	.	2,013	398	2,411	2s 2½d	1s 5½d	2·0	.	2·0
1865	22,634	14,864	329	6	335	54·8 to 1	1,741	3	1,744	395	2,139	1s 6½d	1s 8½d	2·2		2·2
1867	22,659	14,587	298	49	347	6·1 to 1	2,467	124	2,591	409	2,900	1s 6½d	1s 11½d	2·0	·4	2·4
1869	22,679	14,160	300	66	366	4·5 to 1	2,374	135	2,510	412	2,762	1s 8½d	1s 8½d	2·0	·4	2·4
1871	22,030	13,763	240	68	308	2·9 to 1	2,084	200	2,284	446	2,730	1s 4½d	1s 1d	1·7	·4	2·1
1873	22,704	13,765	238	74	312	3·3 to 1	2,251	245	2,496	489	2,985	1s 6½d	1s 9½d	1·7	·5	2·2
1875	22,742	13,763	225	84	309	2·7 to 1	2,143	243	2,386	478	2,871	1s 5½d	1s 9d	1·6	·6	2·1
1877	22,760	13,763	216	101	317	2·1 to 1	2,080	320	2,400	482	2,888	1s 5½d	1s 9½d	1·6	·7	2·3
BANDON UNION. Area, 101,694 acres.																
1851	69,876	38,102	930	.	930		2,894	.	2,894	.	2,895	10	10	2·5	.	2·5
1853	69,076	31,984	590		590	.	2,075	.	2,076	470	2,545	7½	9	1·9		1·9
1855	67,016	30,789	389	.	389	.	1,975		1,975	508	2,484	6¾	8¾	1·2	.	1·2
1857	69,394	29,493	201	.	201	.	1,390	.	1,390	618	1,983	4½	6¾	·7	.	·7
1859	69,647	28,896	161	.	161	.	861	.	861	682	1,543	4½	6½	·5	.	·5
1861	70,279	27,900	159	.	159		1,311	.	1,314	615	1,924	4½	6½	·6	.	·6
1863	70,371	26,907	184		184	.	1,154	.	1,154	564	1,718	4	6	·7		·7
1865	70,603	26,615	191	.	191	.	1,490	.	1,490	652	2,143	5	7½	·7	.	·7
1867	70,608	26,234	203	.	203	.	1,601	.	1,601	650	2,261	6	7½	·8	.	·8
1869	70,956	26,031	215	.	215	.	1,699	.	1,699	717	2,416	6½	8½	·8	.	·8
1871	72,598	25,749	184	.	183	.	1,512	.	1,512	671	2,183	5	7½	·7	.	·7
1873	72,968	25,739	217	.	217	.	2,091	.	2,091	784	2,875	6½	9½	·8	.	·8
1875	73,680	25,739	207	.	207	.	1,785		1,785	711	2,496	6	8½	·8	.	·8
1877	74,596	25,739	186	.	186	.	1,513		1,515	738	2,253	5	7½	·7	.	·7
BANTRY UNION. Area, 106,853 acres.																
1851	20,828	19,406	1,273	.	1,273	.	3,673	.	3,673	.	3,673	3s 6½d	3s 6½d	6·5	.	6·5
1853	20,079	18,795	685		685	.	2,350	.	2,369	371	2,740	2s 3d	2s 7½d	3·5	.	3·5
1855	20,870	18,088	355		353	.	2,010	.	2,010	234	2,244	1s 11½d	2s 1½d	1·9		1·9
1857	20,168	17,880	177		177	.	1,002	.	1,002	262	1,264	11½	1s 2½d	1·0		1·0
1859	20,809	16,477	122	.	122	.	618	.	616	461	944	7	10½	·7	.	·7
1861	20,795	16,964	108	.	108	.	848	.	848	236	888	7½	10½	·7	.	·7
1863	20,056	16,627	135	.	135	.	718	.	718	330	1,048	8½	1s 0½d	·8	.	·8
1865	20,919	17,119	116	.	116	.	606		606	351	957	7	11	·7	.	·7
1867	21,016	16,186	110	2	112	55 to 1	721	7	728	374	1,102	8½	1s 0½d	·7	.	·7
1869	20,211	16,256	114	3	117	38 to 1	710	11	721	418	1,139	7	1s 1½d	·7		·7
1871	21,271	16,570	91	9	100	10·1 to 1	555	34	589	435	895	6½	9½	·6	·1	·7
1873	21,565	16,560	104	21	125	4·9 to 1	776	72	848	406	1,254	9½	1s 2½d	·6	·1	·7
1875	21,493	16,530	142	19	161	7·5 to 1	915	60	975	401	1,376	11	1s 3½d	·8	·1	·9
1877	21,697	16,530	104	11	115	9·4 to 1	696	27	723	484	1,107	8½	1s 0½d	·6	·1	·7
CASTLETOWN UNION. Area, 74,445 acres.																
1851	11,891	18,299	691	.	691	.	2,019	.	2,019	.	2,019	3s 10½d	3s 10½d	3·1	.	3·1
1853	11,784	17,836	444	.	444		1,550	.	1,550	367	1,917	2s 7½d	2s 8d	2·5	.	2·5
1855	14,804	16,886	296	.	296	.	1,441		1,441	227	1,668	2s 0½d	2s 4½d	1·8	.	1·8
1857	14,150	15,484	204	.	204	.	1,079	.	1,079	303	1,387	1s 6½d	1s 9½d	1·3	.	1·3
1859	17,474	15,118	149	.	149	.	925	.	925	254	1,179	1s 0½d	1s 4½d	·9	.	·9
1861	15,525	15,076	245		245	.	1,020	.	1,020	253	1,273	1s 4d	1s 7½d	1·6	.	1·6
1863	15,578	14,808	173	.	173	.	1,029	.	1,029	301	1,330	1s 4d	1s 8½d	1·2	.	1·2
1865	15,109	14,276	140		140	.	806	.	806	314	1,123	1s 0½d	1s 5½d	1·0	.	1·0
1867	15,660	14,606	146		146	.	935	.	984	285	1,230	1s 1½d	1s 6½d	1·0	.	1·0
1869	15,800	14,476	155	1	156		962	18	978	274	1,248	1s 2½d	1s 7d	1·0	.	1·0
1871	15,899	14,323	96	2	98	46·5 to 1	888	15	903	289	1,192	1s 1½d	1s 6d	·7	.	·7
1873	16,001	14,353	140	14	154	10 to 1	1,009	50	1,059	302	1,361	1s 4d	1s 8½d	1·0	.	1·0
1875	14,850	14,326	133	21	154	6·3 to 1	952	67	1,019	429	1,448	1s 4½d	1s 9d	·9	·1	1·0
1877	14,860	14,326	155	17	172	9·1 to 1	1,055	53	1,058	444	1,437	1s 6½d	2s 0½d	1·0	·1	1·1

Expenditure of each Poor Law Union in Ireland since the year 1851—*continued*.

Years	Valuation.	Population.	Average Daily Number in Receipt of Relief: In-doors	Out-doors, under 10 Vic. c. 31	Total.	Ratio of Indoor to Outdoor	Expenditure for: In-Maintenance and Clothing	Out Relief under 10 Vic. c. 31	Total	Expenditure under Medical Charities Acts, exclusive of Vaccination	Total of Cols. 10 and 11.	Poundage: On Amount in Col. 10	On Amount in Col. 12	Per centage of Paupers to Population: In-door	Out-door	Total.
1.	2.	3.	4.	5.	6.	7.	8.	9.	10.	11.	12.	13.	14.	15.	16.	17.
Province of Munster—continued.																
CLONAKILTY UNION.							£	£	£	£	£	d.	d.			
Area, 80,811 acres.																
1851	49,659	31,480	972	.	972	.	1,645	.	1,645	.	1,645	5	5	1·7	.	1·7
1853	49,159	30,844	314	.	315	.	976	.	976	246	1,222	4½	6	1·0	.	1·0
1855	49,460	30,200	220	.	220	.	1,074	.	1,074	240	1,314	5¼	6½	·7	.	·7
1857	49,920	29,866	146	.	146	.	811	.	811	272	1,083	4	5	·5	.	·5
1859	48,700	28,912	146	.	156	.	732	.	732	265	997	3½	4½	·5	.	·5
1861	49,704	28,308	187	.	187	.	1,073	.	1,073	276	1,349	5¼	6½	·6	.	·6
1863	49,875	27,985	239	.	239	.	1,270	.	1,270	266	1,536	6¼	7½	·8	.	·8
1865	49,915	27,701	179	.	179	.	1,181	.	1,181	267	1,448	5¾	7	·6	.	·6
1867	50,088	27,417	205	.	205	.	1,455	.	1,455	348	1,803	7	8½	·7	.	·7
1869	50,283	27,133	222	.	222	.	1,604	.	1,604	368	1,972	7½	9¼	·8	.	·8
1871	50,418	26,849	214	.	214	.	1,562	.	1,562	388	1,950	7½	9¼	·8	.	·8
1873	50,794	26,849	248	.	245	.	2,069	.	2,069	393	2,462	9¾	11½	·9	.	·9
1875	50,903	26,849	212	.	262	.	1,816	.	1,816	477	2,293	8½	10¾	·9	.	·9
1877	50,900	26,849	141	3	144	47 to 1	1,860	70	1,880	454	2,334	8¾	11	·5	.	·5
CORK UNION.																
Area, 174,685 acres.																
1851	260,684	167,460	4,626	.	4,626	.	13,809	.	13,809	.	13,809	11½	11½	2·7	.	2·7
1853	280,634	164,302	3,825	.	3,825	.	14,618	.	14,618	2,514	17,132	1s. 0½d.	1s. 2½d.	2·3	.	2·3
1855	246,481	159,157	3,082	.	3,082	.	19,472	.	19,472	2,331	21,806	1s. 4½d.	1s. 8½d.	1·9	.	1·9
1857	287,001	155,012	2,220	.	2,220	.	14,529	.	14,529	2,487	17,066	1s. 1d.	1s. 2½d.	1·4	.	1·4
1859	280,194	150,867	1,808	.	1,808	.	11,682	.	11,682	2,782	14,464	9¾	1s. 0d.	1·2	.	1·2
1861	299,187	146,729	2,485	.	2,485	.	20,188	.	20,188	2,871	23,064	1s. 4½d.	1s. 6½d.	1·7	.	1·7
1863	297,951	146,058	2,518	33	2,551	76·3 to 1	17,617	.	17,617	3,077	20,694	1s. 2d.	1s. 4½d.	1·7	.	1·7
1865	306,804	140,384	2,483	294	2,777	8·4 to 1	18,731	776	19,407	3,245	22,712	1s. 3d.	1s. 6½d.	1·7	·2	1·9
1867	313,930	144,715	2,653	248	2,901	10·7 to 1	24,574	549	25,123	4,336	29,459	1s. 7¼d.	1s. 9½d.	1·9	·1	2·0
1869	321,116	144,040	2,578	267	2,845	9·6 to 1	22,423	448	22,871	3,606	26,257	1s. 5½d.	1s. 7½d.	1·78	·18	1·9
1871	327,480	144,477	2,041	318	2,359	7 to 1	20,407	295	20,702	4,792	24,494	1s. 3¼d.	1s. 6d.	1·5	·2	1·7
1873	328,752	143,377	2,290	424	2,714	5·4 to 1	24,549	912	25,461	3,681	29,133	1s. 6½d.	1s. 9½d.	1·6	·3	1·9
1875	330,720	143,277	2,228	544	2,831	3·1 to 1	21,637	1,412	23,049	4,317	27,366	1s. 4½d.	1s. 7½d.	1·5	·4	1·9
1877	339,975	143,377	2,318	1,062	3,470	2·2 to 1	22,814	2,590	25,304	3,796	29,190	1s. 5½d.	1s. 8½d.	1·6	·7	2·3
DUNMANWAY UNION.																
Area, 163,917 acres.																
1851	32,595	20,439	557	.	557	.	1,296	.	1,296	.	1,296	9½	9½	2·7	.	2·7
1853	31,595	19,690	307	.	307	.	998	.	998	341	1,339	7½	9½	1·6	.	1·6
1855	32,595	18,935	164	.	164	.	924	.	924	269	1,193	6¾	8¾	·9	.	·9
1857	32,558	18,270	108	.	108	.	585	.	585	248	833	4¼	6¼	·6	.	·6
1859	32,806	17,495	70	.	70	.	403	.	403	345	748	3	5½	·4	.	·4
1861	32,601	16,160	99	.	99	.	558	.	558	349	907	4¼	6¾	·6	.	·6
1863	32,679	16,941	145	4	149	34 to 1	901	10	911	370	1,281	6¾	9½	·8	.	·8
1865	32,719	17,132	108	3	111	36 to 1	671	39	710	375	1,085	5¼	8	·6	.	·6
1867	32,820	17,306	134	2	136	67 to 1	922	16	938	384	1,322	6¾	9¾	·8	.	·8
1869	32,871	17,483	150	3	153	50 to 1	970	19	989	464	1,450	7½	[illegible]	·9	.	·9
1871	32,989	17,646	130	5	135	26 to 1	1,207	44	1,251	416	1,667	9¼	1s. 0½d.	·7	.	·7
1873	33,040	17,666	122	66	188	2 to 1	1,216	153	1,369	444	1,813	10	1s. 1¼d.	·7	·4	1·1
1875	33,124	17,666	133	28	161	4·8 to 1	1,340	57	1,397	468	1,865	10¼	1s. 1½d.	·8	·1	·9
1877	33,199	17,666	163	67	230	2·4 to 1	1,181	195	1,376	449	1,825	10	1s. 0½d.	·9	·4	1·3
FERMOY UNION.																
Area, 165,365 acres.																
1851	98,768	44,930	1,745	.	1,745	.	4,071	.	4,071	.	4,071	11¼	11¼	3·9	.	3·9
1853	98,763	43,632	853	.	853	.	2,701	.	2,701	713	3,414	6½	8¼	1·9	.	1·9
1855	98,768	42,134	477	.	477	.	3,129	.	3,129	645	3,774	7½	9¼	1·1	.	1·1
1857	98,706	40,756	306	.	306	.	1,839	.	1,839	671	2,510	4½	6½	·7	.	·7
1859	98,087	39,358	215	.	215	.	1,402	.	1,402	694	2,096	3½	5	·5	.	·5
1861	99,788	37,960	282	.	282	.	2,132	.	2,132	683	2,815	5¼	6¾	·7	.	·7
1863	101,792	36,924	364	.	364	.	3,367	.	3,367	704	4,071	8¼	9½	1·0	.	1·0
1865	102,048	35,890	331	.	331	.	2,976	.	2,976	748	3,684	5¾	7¼	·9	.	·9
1867	102,251	34,854	303	.	303	.	2,189	.	2,189	820	3,009	5¼	7	·8	.	·8
1869	102,387	33,819	273	.	273	.	1,996	.	1,996	723	2,719	4¾	6¼	·8	.	·8
1871	103,089	32,784	296	.	296	.	1,825	.	1,825	878	2,708	4¼	6¼	·9	.	·9
1873	103,184	32,784	299	.	299	.	2,636	.	2,636	907	3,553	6¼	8¼	·9	.	·9
1875	105,390	32,784	267	.	267	.	2,292	.	2,292	809	3,101	5¼	7¼	·8	.	·8
1877	104,893	32,784	295	6	301	49·1 to 1	2,406	58	2,464	565	3,029	5¾	8	·9	.	·9
KANTURK UNION.																
Area, 186,563 acres.																
1851	74,108	41,801	2,980	.	2,980	.	9,279	.	9,279	.	9,279	2s. 6d.	2s. 6d.	7·1	.	7·1
1853	74,108	40,360	1,084	.	1,084	.	4,837	.	4,837	647	5,484	1s. 3¾d.	1s. 5¾d.	2·7	.	2·7
1855	74,108	38,920	863	.	863	.	4,680	.	4,680	516	5,196	1s. 3d.	1s. 4¾d.	2·2	.	2·2
1857	74,448	37,480	523	.	523	.	3,295	.	3,295	556	3,851	10¾	1s. 0½d.	1·4	.	1·4
1859	74,815	36,040	356	.	356	.	2,122	.	2,122	649	2,771	6¾	8¾	·9	.	·9
1861	75,007	34,600	447	.	447	.	2,611	.	2,611	650	3,261	8¼	10½	1·3	.	1·3
1863	75,112	34,300	524	351	875	2·5 to 1	3,324	554	3,878	679	4,557	1s. 0½d.	1s. 2½d.	1·7	·7	2·4
1865	75,308	33,879	505	280	785	1·8 to 1	3,283	541	3,824	641	4,465	10½	1s. 1½d.	1·5	·9	2·4
1867	75,311	33,518	515	253	768	2·0 to 1	4,021	519	4,540	653	5,193	1s. 2¼d.	1s. 4½d.	1·5	·7	2·2
1869	75,464	33,187	480	234	751	2·1 to 1	3,535	572	4,107	647	4,754	1s. 1d.	1s. 3¼d.	1·5	·7	2·2
1871	76,263	32,796	404	414	818	·9 to 1	3,352	679	4,031	764	4,794	1s. 0½d.	1s. 3d.	1·2	1·2	2·4
1873	76,544	32,796	474	644	1,118	·7 to 1	4,649	1,061	5,710	811	6,521	1s. 2½d.	1s. 8d.	1·4	1·9	3·3
1875	77,040	32,796	441	524	965	·8 to 1	4,301	1,093	5,344	842	6,186	1s. 4½d.	1s. 7d.	1·2	1·6	2·8
1877	77,289	32,796	405	386	791	1·0 to 1	4,606	776	5,384	819	6,203	1s. 2½d.	1s. 5d.	1·2	1·1	2·3

Appendix A.
Poor Relief.

No. 6.—Statistical Table showing the progress of the Pauperism and

Years	Valuation	Population	Average Daily Number in Receipt of Relief: In-door	Out-door, under 10 Vic. c. 31	Total	Ratio of In-door to Out-door	Expenditure for: In Maintenance and Clothing	On Relief under 10 Vic. c. 31	Total	Expenditure under Medical Charities Acts, exclusive of Vaccination	Total of Cols. 10 and 11	Poundage: On Amount in Col. 10	On Amount in Col. 12	Per-centage of Paupers to Population: In-door	Out-door	Total
1.	2	3.	4	5	6	7	8	9	10.	11	12.	13.	14	15	16	17
Province of Munster—continued.																
Kinsale Union.							£	£	£	£	£	d.	d.			
Area, 79,367 acres.																
1851	57,944	30,051	709	.	709	.	1,824	.	1,824	.	1,824	8	8	2·3	.	2·3
1853	57,944	26,609	519	.	519	.	1,935	.	1,935	410	2,345	8	9¾	1·9	.	1·9
1855	57,944	27,506	330	.	330	.	1,539	.	1,539	382	1,921	6¼	8	1·2	.	1·2
1857	57,705	26,[illegible]	154	.	154	.	895	.	895	454	1,349	3¾	5½	·6	.	·6
1859	57,902	25,090	227	.	227	.	690	.	690	460	1,150	2¾	4¾	·8	.	·8
1861	57,704	23,897	198	.	198	.	913	.	913	487	1,400	3¾	5¾	·8	.	·8
1863	57,869	24,[illegible]	180	.	180	.	1,056	.	1,056	443	1,500	4¼	6¼	·7	.	·7
1865	58,014	24,128	204	.	204	.	1,123	.	1,123	470	1,593	4¾	6¾	·8	.	·8
1867	58,168	24,290	179	.	179	.	1,389	.	1,389	441	1,830	5¾	7½	·7	.	·7
1869	58,729	24,441	158	.	158	.	1,700	.	1,700	504	2,204	7	9	·6	.	·6
1871	58,148	24,394	133	.	133	.	1,148	.	1,148	555	1,703	4¾	7	·5	.	·5
1873	58,121	24,394	111	.	111	.	1,171	.	1,171	570	1,741	4¾	7¼	·4	.	·4
1875	58,215	24,394	128	1	129	.	1,116	10	1,126	628	1,754	4¾	7¼	·5	.	·5
1877	59,238	24,394	136	.	136	.	1,137	.	1,137	610	1,747	4¾	7	·5	.	·5
Macroom Union.																
Area, 179,168 acres.																
1851	61,482	37,394	1,479	.	1,479	.	4,834	.	4,834	.	4,834	1s 6¾d	1s 6¾d	3·9	.	3·9
1853	61,482	35,184	965	.	965	.	4,487	.	4,487	421	4,908	1s 5½d.	1s. 7¼d	2·7	.	2·7
1855	61,482	34,874	606	.	606	.	2,883	.	2,883	515	3,398	11¼	1s 1¼d	1·7	.	1·7
1857	61,683	33,613	309	.	309	.	1,883	.	1,883	610	2,493	7¼	9¾	·9	.	·9
1859	62,041	32,451	210	.	210	.	1,380	.	1,380	566	1,916	5¼	7½	·7	.	·7
1861	62,165	31,040	189	.	189	.	1,581	.	1,581	663	2,243	6¼	8¾	·6	.	·6
1863	62,250	30,989	236	.	236	.	1,540	.	1,540	649	2,189	6	8½	·7	.	·7
1865	62,434	30,571	225	.	225	.	1,456	.	1,456	694	2,150	5½	8¼	·7	.	·7
1867	62,470	30,793	250	.	250	.	1,749	.	1,749	695	2,444	6¾	9¼	·8	.	·8
1869	62,484	30,653	257	.	257	.	1,821	.	1,821	693	2,514	7	9¾	·8	.	·8
1871	62,920	30,544	240	.	240	.	1,779	.	1,779	699	2,478	6¾	9½	·8	.	·8
1873	63,091	30,544	281	.	281	.	2,429	.	2,429	689	3,118	9¼	11¾	·9	.	·9
1875	63,470	30,544	249	33	282	7·6 to 1	2,351	43	2,394	693	3,087	9	11½	·8	·1	·9
1877	63,516	30,544	287	70	357	4·1 to 1	2,452	125	2,577	741	3,318	9¾	1s. 0½d.	·9	·2	1·1
Mallow Union.																
Area, 149,364 acres																
1851	98,858	42,862	1,470	.	1,470	.	4,938	.	4,938	.	4,938	11¾	11¾	3·4	.	3·4
1853	99,800	41,475	773	.	773	.	2,696	.	2,696	727	3,423	6½	8¼	1·8	.	1·8
1855	99,858	39,959	441	.	441	.	2,051	.	2,051	695	[illegible]	6¾	8	1·1	.	1·1
1857	102,029	38,563	277	.	277	.	1,687	.	1,687	750	2,437	4	5¾	·7	.	·7
1859	104,697	37,167	268	.	268	.	1,297	.	1,297	764	2,061	3	4¾	·6	.	·6
1861	107,663	35,[illegible]	279	.	279	.	1,993	.	1,993	846	2,839	4½	6¼	·7	.	·7
1863	107,645	34,824	382	.	382	.	2,308	.	2,308	1,061	[illegible]	4¾	7¼	1·1	.	1·1
1865	107,893	33,[illegible]	434	1	435	.	2,739	9	2,748	1,063	3,811	6¼	8½	1·3	.	1·3
1867	108,141	32,965	422	23	445	18·4 to 1	3,472	23	3,495	1,192	4,687	7¾	10¾	1·3	.	1·3
1869	108,188	32,040	419	111	530	3·8 to 1	3,220	73	3,293	1,078	4,373	7¼	9¾	1·3	·3	1·6
1871	108,405	31,112	378	260	638	1·1 to 1	4,297	397	3,694	1,098	4,792	8¾	11¾	1·2	1·0	2·2
1873	105,184	31,112	466	434	892	1·0 to 1	4,450	603	5,053	1,048	6,101	11½	1s. 1¾d.	1·4	1·4	2·8
1875	105,976	31,112	399	429	828	·9 to 1	3,193	851	4,044	1,163	5,207	9¼	11¾	1·3	1·3	2·6
1877	106,581	31,112	412	451	863	·9 to 1	3,381	826	4,207	1,141	5,348	9½	1s. 0d.	1·3	1·4	2·7
Midleton Union.																
Area, 111,009 acres.																
1851	91,502	44,039	1,805	.	1,805	.	5,290	.	5,290	.	5,290	1s 1¾d	1s 1¾d	4·1	.	4·1
1853	91,502	42,470	1,356	.	1,356	.	4,670	.	4,670	908	5,578	1s 0¼d.	1s 2½d	3·2	.	3·2
1855	91,502	40,892	879	.	829	.	4,449	.	4,449	641	5,090	11¾	1s 1¼d	2·0	.	2·0
1857	91,632	38,408	597	.	597	.	2,386	.	2,386	812	3,198	6¼	8½	1·5	.	1·5
1859	91,633	37,724	496	.	496	.	2,076	.	2,076	777	2,853	5¼	7½	1·3	.	1·3
1861	91,830	36,140	406	.	405	.	2,540	.	2,540	874	3,414	6¾	9	1·1	.	1·1
1863	92,516	34,902	427	18	445	23·7 to 1	2,484	35	2,519	860	3,379	6½	8¾	1·2	.	1·2
1865	92,668	34,845	359	52	411	6·9 to 1	2,000	138	2,137	897	3,044	5¼	8	1·05	·15	1·2
1867	92,739	33,698	348	95	443	3·7 to 1	2,475	239	2,614	1,000	3,694	6½	9½	1·05	·29	1·3
1869	92,726	31,661	344	163	507	2·1 to 1	3,297	431	3,728	926	4,654	8½	1s. 0d.	1·1	·5	1·6
1871	93,249	30,404	296	227	523	1·3 to 1	2,143	603	2,746	920	3,666	7	9¼	·98	·75	1·7
1873	94,083	30,404	337	391	728	·8 to 1	2,789	1,042	3,831	1,060	4,891	9¾	1s. 0½d	1·1	1·3	2·4
1875	94,215	30,404	329	383	712	·8 to 1	2,431	907	3,338	971	4,309	8¼	11	1·08	1·25	2·3
1877	94,330	30,404	308	440	748	·7 to 1	3,342	1,201	4,553	1,083	5,636	11¼	1s. 2d.	1·0	1·4	2·4
Millstreet Union.																
Area, 74,906 acres.																
1851	24,362	17,281	1,702	.	1,702	.	5,480	.	5,480	.	5,480	4s 6¼d	4s 6¼d	9·8	.	9·8
1853	24,362	16,768	840	.	840	.	2,873	.	2,873	196	3,069	2s. 4¼d	2s 6¼d	5·0	.	5·0
1855	24,[illegible]	16,273	561	.	561	.	2,897	.	2,897	210	3,107	[illegible]	[illegible]	3·4	.	3·4
1857	25,344	15,761	263	.	263	.	1,872	.	1,872	205	2,077	1s 5½d	1s 7¾d	1·6	.	1·6
1859	25,364	15,299	199	.	199	.	1,380	.	1,380	255	1,635	1s 0¾d	1s 3¼d	1·3	.	1·3
1861	26,651	14,797	255	.	255	.	1,955	.	1,955	235	2,190	1s 6¾d	1s 8¾d	1·7	.	1·7
1863	26,097	14,756	382	.	382	.	2,715	.	2,715	279	2,994	2s 1¼d	2s 3¾d	2·6	.	2·6
1865	26,128	14,715	325	56	381	6 to 1	2,160	82	2,348	278	2,626	[illegible]	[illegible]	2·2	·4	2·6
1867	26,152	14,674	309	80	389	3·9 to 1	2,345	244	2,589	265	2,854	1s 11¼d	2s 2¼d	2·1	·5	2·6
1869	26,154	14,[illegible]	285	158	443	1·8 to 1	2,727	304	3,031	316	[illegible]	1s 11¼d	2s 2¼d	1·9	1·0	2·9
1871	27,252	14,[illegible]	285	217	430	1·2 to 1	2,281	407	2,688	265	2,950	1s 11¼d	2s 2¼d	1·8	1·4	3·2
1873	27,349	14,[illegible]	342	186	528	1·8 to 1	3,265	453	3,918	319	4,237	2s 10¼d	3s 1¼d	2·3	1·3	3·6
1875	27,477	14,582	282	115	397	2·3 to 1	2,621	157	2,778	300	3,078	2s. 0¾d	2s 2d	1·7	·7	2·5
1877	27,655	14,392	288	156	438	1·3 to 1	2,478	353	2,831	319	3,045	1s. 11d	2s. 1½d.	1·7	1·3	3·0

Expenditure of each Poor Law Union in Ireland since the year 1851—*continued*.

Years	Valuation.	Population.	Average Daily Number in Receipt of Relief: In-door.	Out-door, under 10 Vic. c. 31.	Total.	Ratio of In-door to Out-door.	Expenditure for: In-Maintenance and Clothing.	Out-Relief under 10 Vic. c. 31.	Total.	Expenditure under Medical Charities Acts, exclusive of Vaccination.	Total of Cols. 10 and 11.	Poundage: On Amount in Col. 10.	On Amount in Col. 12.	Per-centage of Paupers to Population: In-door.	Out-door.	Total.
1.	2.	3.	4.	5.	6.	7.	8.	9.	10.	11.	12.	13.	14.	15.	16.	17.
Province of Munster—continued.																
Mitchelstown Union. Area, 86,957 acres.							£	£	£	£	£	d.	d.			
1851	48,404	27,369	1,584	.	1,584	.	2,278	.	2,273	.	2,273	11½	11½	5·6	.	5·6
1853	48,484	26,363	780	.	780	.	2,371	.	2,371	537	2,908	11¾	1s. 2¼d.	3·0	.	3·0
1855	48,484	25,450	615	.	615	.	3,085	.	3,085	387	3,472	1s. 3¼d.	1s. 5¼d.	2·9	.	2·9
1857	48,452	24,846	230	.	230	.	1,429	.	1,429	384	1,813	7½	9½	·9	.	·9
1859	48,498	23,631	183	.	183	.	1,144	.	1,144	480	1,624	5¾	7¾	·8	.	·8
1861	48,818	22,747	226	1	227	.	1,438	4	1,442	441	1,883	7¼	9¼	1·0	.	1·0
1863	48,876	22,348	261	1	262	.	1,578	6	1,584	442	2,026	7¾	10	1·2	.	1·2
1865	48,810	21,946	237	.	237	.	1,293	3	1,296	444	1,740	6¼	8½	1·1	.	1·1
1867	48,938	21,545	244	1	245	.	1,456	6	1,462	427	1,889	7¼	9½	1·1	.	1·1
1869	49,007	21,148	248	1	249	.	1,549	11	1,560	478	2,038	7¾	10	1·1	.	1·1
1871	49,095	20,748	228	3	231	76 to 1	1,503	32	1,535	484	2,019	7¾	9¾	1·1	.	1·1
1873	48,980	20,748	205	5	210	37 to 1	2,117	50	2,167	482	2,649	10½	1s. 1d.	1·0	.	1·0
1875	49,110	20,745	233	4	237	58·2 to 1	1,771	30	1,801	488	2,289	8¾	11¼	1·1	.	1·1
1877	48,128	20,745	216	4	220	54 to 1	1,635	38	1,673	464	2,137	7¾	10¼	1·0	.	1·0
Skibbereen Union. Area, 114,963 acres.																
1851	44,587	38,069	2,186	.	2,186	.	6,076	.	6,076	.	6,076	2s. 8¼d.	2s. 8¼d.	5·6	.	5·6
1853	44,587	35,828	1,134	.	1,134	.	3,572	.	3,572	606	4,178	1s. 7¼d.	1s. 10¼d.	3·1	.	3·1
1855	44,560	35,790	546	.	546	.	2,730	.	2,730	458	3,188	1s. 2¾d.	1s. 5¼d.	1·5	.	1·5
1857	44,712	34,670	309	.	309	.	1,739	.	1,739	431	2,170	9¼	11¾	·9	.	·9
1859	44,712	33,841	237	.	237	.	1,448	.	1,448	641	2,089	7¾	11¼	·7	.	·7
1861	44,787	33,412	214	.	214	.	1,802	.	1,802	561	2,363	9¾	1s. 0¾d.	·7	.	·7
1863	44,900	32,306	357	.	357	.	2,412	.	2,412	579	2,991	1s. 0¾d.	1s. 4d.	1·1	.	1·1
1865	45,123	32,000	257	.	257	.	1,727	.	1,727	568	2,295	9¼	1s. 0¼d.	·8	.	·8
1867	45,218	31,795	316	.	316	.	2,419	.	2,419	588	3,007	1s. 0¾d.	1s. 3¾d.	1·0	.	1·0
1869	45,345	31,589	281	.	281	.	2,075	.	2,075	579	2,654	11	1s. 2¼d.	·9	.	·9
1871	45,010	31,485	261	.	261	.	2,200	.	2,200	689	2,889	11¾	1s. 3¼d.	·8	.	·8
1873	45,834	31,385	305	.	305	.	2,810	.	2,810	599	3,409	1s. 2¾d.	1s. 5¾d.	·9	.	·9
1875	45,049	31,385	260	72	332	3·7 to 1	2,476	145	2,621	723	3,344	1s. 1¼d.	1s. 5¾d.	·8	·2	1·0
1877	46,018	31,385	323	87	410	3·7 to 1	2,769	184	2,953	733	3,686	1s. 2¾d.	1s. 7d.	1·0	·2	1·3
Skull Union. Area, 67,169 acres.																
1851	14,213	16,418	849	.	849	.	2,458	.	2,458	.	2,458	3s. 5¼d.	3s. 5¼d.	5·1	.	5·1
1853	14,213	15,914	262	.	262	.	2,039	.	2,039	363	2,372	2s. 11d.	3s. 1½d.	1·6	.	1·6
1855	14,218	15,411	156	.	156	.	706	.	706	169	875	1s. 0d.	1s. 2¼d.	1·0	.	1·0
1857	14,275	14,908	90	.	90	.	438	.	438	175	613	7¼	10¼	·6	.	·6
1859	14,801	14,406	74	.	74	.	464	.	464	300	764	7½	1s. 1d.	·5	.	·5
1861	14,309	13,902	65	.	65	.	506	.	506	287	793	8¼	1s. 1d.	·5	.	·5
1863	14,483	13,747	115	.	115	.	620	.	620	281	901	10¼	1s. 2¾d.	·8	.	·8
1865	14,557	13,506	137	.	137	.	574	.	574	246	820	9¼	1s. 1¼d.	1·0	.	1·0
1867	14,651	13,443	93	.	93	.	698	.	698	277	975	11¾	1s. 4d.	·7	.	·7
1869	14,657	13,291	102	.	102	.	700	.	700	245	945	11¾	1s. 3¼d.	·7	.	·7
1871	14,729	13,189	98	6	104	16·3 to 1	693	43	736	248	984	1s. 0d.	1s. 4d.	·7	.	·7
1873	14,980	13,139	102	7	109	14·6 to 1	744	47	791	290	1,081	1s. 0¼d.	1s. 5¼d.	·7	.	·8
1875	15,011	13,139	125	5	130	25 to 1	810	43	853	302	1,155	1s. 1¼d.	1s. 6¼d.	·9	.	·9
1877	15,219	13,139	91	66	157	1·4 to 1	679	150	829	272	1,101	1s. 1¼d.	1s. 5¼d.	·7	·5	1·2
Youghal Union. Area, 70,924 acres.																
1851	57,212	33,826	333	.	333	.	4,109	.	4,109	.	4,109	1s. 5¼d.	1s. 5¼d.	1·0	.	1·0
1853	57,272	31,581	993	.	993	.	3,373	.	3,373	558	3,931	1s. 2¼d.	1s. 4¼d.	3·1	.	3·1
1855	57,218	29,640	745	.	745	.	4,125	.	4,125	504	4,629	1s. 5¼d.	1s. 7¼d.	2·5	.	2·5
1857	57,194	27,201	389	.	389	.	2,380	.	2,380	555	2,935	10	1s. 0¼d.	1·4	.	1·4
1859	57,187	26,360	288	.	288	.	1,714	.	1,714	572	2,286	7¼	9½	1·1	.	1·1
1861	57,444	24,701	344	12	356	28·6 to 1	2,380	19	2,399	751	3,150	10	1s. 1¼d.	1·3	.	1·4
1863	58,301	24,151	401	56	457	7·1 to 1	2,577	176	2,753	706	3,459	11¼	1s. 2d.	1·6	·2	1·8
1865	58,449	23,626	326	179	505	1·8 to 1	2,415	276	2,691	678	3,369	10¼	1s. 1¼d.	1·3	·7	2·1
1867	58,948	23,045	357	203	560	1·7 to 1	2,867	406	3,273	760	4,033	1s. 1¼d.	1s. 4¼d.	1·5	·8	2·4
1869	59,782	22,807	348	294	642	1·1 to 1	2,668	588	3,256	703	3,959	1s. 1¼d.	1s. 4d.	1·5	1·3	2·8
1871	60,641	21,960	284	296	580	1·1 to 1	2,432	508	2,940	746	3,686	11¾	1s. 2¾d.	1·3	1·1	2·4
1873	60,787	21,960	323	231	554	1·4 to 1	2,975	508	3,483	789	4,272	1s. 1¼d.	1s. 4¾d.	1·5	1·0	2·5
1875	60,700	21,960	237	166	403	1·3 to 1	2,159	311	2,470	761	3,231	9¾	1s. 0¼d.	1·0	·7	1·8
1877	60,545	21,960	250	199	449	1·4 to 1	2,138	376	2,514	771	3,285	10	1s. 1d.	1·2	·9	2·1
Cahirciveen Union. Area, 200,710 acres.																
1851	21,747	29,264	1,833	.	1,834	.	6,901	.	6,901	.	6,901	5s. 4¼d.	5s. 4¼d.	6·1	.	6·1
1853	21,747	28,682	1,008	.	1,008	.	3,470	.	3,470	847	4,317	3s. 2¼d.	4s. 0d.	3·5	.	3·5
1855	21,747	28,000	423	.	423	.	1,975	.	1,975	412	2,387	1s. 10d.	2s. 2¼d.	1·5	.	1·5
1857	21,716	27,068	163	.	163	.	1,055	.	1,055	458	1,513	11¾	1s. 4¾d.	·6	.	·6
1859	21,847	26,136	119	.	119	.	617	.	617	462	1,079	6¾	1s. 1¼d.	·4	.	·4
1861	21,865	25,904	245	.	245	.	1,029	.	1,029	455	1,484	11¼	1s. 4¼d.	·9	.	·9
1863	21,637	25,129	181	.	181	.	1,137	.	1,137	541	1,678	1s. 0¼d.	1s. 6¼d.	·7	.	·7
1865	21,656	25,181	140	.	140	.	871	.	871	580	1,451	9½	1s. 4¼d.	·5	.	·5
1867	21,783	25,170	121	.	121	.	1,139	.	1,139	472	1,611	1s. 0¼d.	1s. 6d.	·5	.	·5
1869	21,808	25,750	123	25	148	4·9 to 1	1,076	160	1,236	637	1,873	1s. 1¼d.	1s. 8¼d.	·5	·1	·6
1871	22,327	26,148	127	34	161	3·7 to 1	929	191	1,120	733	1,853	1s. 0¼d.	1s. 8d.	·5	·1	·6
1873	23,278	26,148	120	55	175	2·1 to 1	1,180	327	1,507	744	2,251	1s. 4¼d.	2s. 0¼d.	·5	·2	·7
1875	22,588	25,148	112	63	175	1·8 to 1	1,147	445	1,592	748	2,340	1s. 4¼d.	2s. 0¼d.	·4	·3	·7
1877	22,757	26,148	105	73	178	1·4 to 1	944	375	1,319	602	1,921	1s. 2d.	1s. 8¼d.	·4	·3	·7

Appendix A.
—
Poor Relief.

No. 6.—Statistical Table showing the progress of the Pauperism and

Years.	Valuation.	Population.	Average Daily Number in Receipt of Relief: In-door	Out-door, under 10 Vic. c. 31	Total	Ratio of Indoor to Outdoor.	Expenditure for: In Maintenance and Clothing	Out Relief under 10 Vic. c. 31	Total	Expenditure under Medical Charities Acts, exclusive of Vaccination	Total of Cols. 10 and 11.	Poundage: On Amount in Col. 10.	On Amount in Col. 12.	Per centage of Paupers to Population: In-door	Out-door.	Total
1.	2.	3.	4.	5.	6.	7.	8.	9.	10.	11.	12.	13.	14.	15.	16.	17.
Province of Munster—continued.																
Dingle Union. Area, 125,653 acres.							£	£	£	£	£	d.	d.			
1851	32,791	38,725	2,884	.	2,884	.	9,181	.	9,841	.	9,531	5s. 4½d.	5s. 4½d.	10·8	.	10·8
1853	32,791	30,549	1,460	.	1,460	.	4,694	.	4,694	469	5,163	2s. 1½d.	2s. 6¼d.	5·4	.	5·4
1855	32,791	28,930	709	.	709	.	2,369	.	2,309	342	2,541	1s. 9¼d.	1s. 11¼d.	2·6	.	2·6
1857	33,574	27,076	313	.	313	.	1,723	.	1,723	364	2,085	1s. 0¼d.	1s. 10¼d.	1·2	.	1·2
1859	33,640	27,106	220	.	220	.	1,119	.	1,119	370	1,488	11½	1s. 2¼d.	·8	.	·8
1861	32,808	27,312	276	.	276	.	1,491	.	1,491	396	1,887	1s. 3½d.	1s. 8d.	1·0	.	1·0
1863	33,676	25,905	321	.	321	.	1,821	.	1,821	432	2,343	1s. 7¼d.	1s. 11½d.	1·2	.	1·2
1865	32,808	24,490	210	.	210	.	1,069	.	1,069	484	1,543	11½	1s. 4¼d.	·8	.	·8
1867	33,801	24,075	196	.	196	.	1,400	.	1,400	488	1,888	1s. 2¼d.	1s. 8d.	·8	.	·8
1869	33,607	21,880	166	.	166	.	1,031	.	1,031	485	1,516	11	1s. 4¼d.	·7	.	·7
1871	32,683	20,245	153	.	158	.	1,188	.	1,188	714	1,900	1s. 0¼d.	1s. 8d.	·7	.	·7
1873	32,725	20,245	182	.	182	.	1,607	.	1,607	604	2,211	1s. 3d.	1s. 11¼d.	·9	.	·9
1875	32,706	20,245	164	.	164	.	1,304	.	1,304	728	2,080	1s. 1¼d.	1s. 9¼d.	·8	.	·8
1877	32,887	20,245	158	.	158	.	1,197	.	1,197	734	1,931	1s. 0¼d.	1s. 1¼d.	·7	.	·7
Kenmare Union. Area, 190,182 acres.																
1851	18,646	21,382	2,319	.	2,319	.	9,279	.	9,279	.	9,279	10s. 0¼d.	10s. 0¼d.	10·9	.	10·9
1853	18,626	20,751	1,089	.	1,089	.	4,091	.	4,091	365	4,456	4s. 5¼d.	5s. 0¼d.	5·0	.	5·0
1855	18,646	20,252	612	.	612	.	2,701	.	2,701	376	3,077	2s. 11d.	3s. 4d.	3·0	.	3·0
1857	18,621	19,184	321	.	321	.	1,619	.	1,619	387	2,006	1s. 9d.	2s. 2d.	1·6	.	1·6
1859	18,272	18,244	202	.	[illegible]	.	1,153	.	1,153	334	1,646	1s. 2¼d.	1s. 9¼d.	1·1	.	1·1
1861	18,606	16,785	228	.	228	.	1,419	.	1,413	413	1,826	1s. 6¼d.	1s. 11¼d.	1·1	.	1·1
1863	18,563	14,762	166	.	166	.	1,379	.	1,379	430	1,809	1s. 6d.	1s. 11¼d.	·9	.	·9
1865	18,609	16,861	174	1	175	.	1,846	9	1,055	427	1,482	1s. 1¼d.	1s. 7¼d.	·9	.	·9
1867	18,726	14,910	161	1	162	.	1,226	9	1,234	482	1,716	1s. 3¼d.	1s. 10¼d.	·9	.	·9
1869	18,740	13,429	161	.	161	.	1,097	.	1,097	586	1,683	1s. 2d.	1s. 9¼d.	·9	.	·9
1871	18,707	18,348	150	35	185	1·2 to 1	940	61	1,001	547	1,548	1s. 0¼d.	1s. 8d.	·7	·1	·8
1873	19,078	18,348	140	59	199	2·4 to 1	1,076	141	1,217	561	1,778	1s. 3¼d.	1s. 10¼d.	·7	·3	1·0
1875	19,210	18,448	132	76	208	1·3 to 1	873	166	1,015	590	1,643	1s. 1d.	1s. 8¼d.	·7	·4	1·1
1877	19,270	18,348	108	90	198	1·3 to 1	760	230	990	564	1,561	1s. 0¼d.	1s. 7¼d.	·5	·6	1·0
Killarney Union. Area, 251,257 acres.																
1851	67,858	49,770	2,902	.	2,902	.	10,064	.	10,064	.	10,064	2s. 11¼d.	2s. 11¼d.	5·8	.	5·8
1853	67,858	48,571	2,481	.	2,481	.	5,410	.	5,410	663	6,073	1s. 7¼d.	1s. 9¼d.	5·0	.	5·0
1855	67,858	47,426	728	.	728	.	4,115	.	4,115	596	4,711	1s. 2¼d.	1s. 4¼d.	1·7	.	1·7
1857	69,474	46,279	384	2	386	192 to 1	2,759	9	2,268	664	2,942	7¾	10¼	·8	.	·8
1859	69,476	45,133	288	2	290	144 to 1	1,834	23	1,857	776	2,633	6¼	9¼	·6	.	·6
1861	71,120	44,987	281	2	283	140·5 to 1	2,475	18	2,493	787	3,275	8¼	11¼	·7	.	·7
1863	72,240	44,078	402	33	435	31·7 to 1	3,234	78	3,413	829	4,192	11¼	1s. 2d.	·9	.	·9
1865	71,288	44,169	405	46	451	8·8 to 1	2,791	185	2,976	626	3,602	9¼	1s. 0¼d.	·9	·1	1·0
1867	72,282	44,369	367	54	421	6·8 to 1	3,171	205	3,376	827	4,403	11¼	1s. 2¼d.	·8	·1	·9
1869	72,289	44,331	388	99	467	3·4 to 1	2,787	382	3,169	831	4,000	10¼	1s. 1¼d.	·7	·2	·9
1871	78,530	44,443	326	179	505	1·8 to 1	3,015	605	3,620	1,010	4,630	11¼	1s. 2¼d.	·7	·4	1·1
1873	75,834	44,443	354	330	684	1·7 to 1	3,914	1,100	5,014	996	6,010	1s. 4d.	1s. 7d.	·8	·7	1·5
1875	75,728	44,444	298	385	681	·9 to 1	3,461	1,218	4,689	862	5,551	1s. 2d.	1s. 5¼d.	·7	·8	1·5
1877	76,885	44,443	315	431	746	·8 to 1	3,139	1,466	4,805	938	5,743	1s. 0¼d.	1s. 6d.	·7	·9	1·6
Listowel Union. Area, 181,208 acres.																
1851	80,678	45,261	2,799	.	2,799	.	12,391	.	12,391	.	12,391	4s. 10¼d.	4s. 10¼d.	6·2	.	6·2
1853	80,681	41,807	1,495	.	1,494	.	4,764	.	4,764	321	5,084	1s. 10¼d.	2s. 0d.	3·6	.	3·6
1855	80,676	40,863	684	.	684	.	2,883	.	2,884	403	3,208	1s. 11¼d.	1s. 8¼d.	1·7	.	1·7
1857	80,567	38,219	211	.	211	.	1,007	.	1,007	504	1,511	4¼	7¼	·5	.	·5
1859	80,659	37,875	134	.	134	.	653	.	653	447	1,100	3	5¼	·3	.	·3
1861	80,901	36,381	119	.	178	.	831	.	881	467	1,418	4	6¼	·3	.	·3
1863	81,1[illegible]	36,079	206	.	206	.	1,536	.	1,538	504	2,092	7¼	9¼	·5	.	·5
1865	81,491	35,640	248	.	248	.	1,709	.	1,709	641	1,951	5¼	8¼	·7	.	·7
1867	81,490	35,101	243	.	243	.	1,809	.	1,809	755	2,549	5¼	1s. 6d.	·7	.	·7
1869	81,044	34,780	171	.	171	.	1,165	.	1,165	703	1,869	3¼	5¼	·5	.	·5
1871	82,046	34,263	158	.	158	.	1,206	.	1,206	674	1,880	3½	5½	·4	.	·4
1873	81,683	34,786	140	.	140	.	1,311	.	1,311	780	1,891	3¾	5¼	·4	.	·4
1875	82,083	34,789	134	.	134	.	1,115	.	1,115	694	1,809	3¼	5¼	·4	.	·4
1877	82,336	34,288	109	.	109	.	877	.	877	683	1,560	4	7¼	·3	.	·3
Tralee Union. Area, 271,834 acres.																
1851	82,891	58,548	4,438	.	4,438	.	14,107	.	14,107	.	14,107	3s. 4¼d.	3s. 4¼d.	8·2	.	8·2
1853	82,891	51,248	2,467	.	2,467	.	8,886	.	8,886	1,055	9,941	2s. 1¼d.	2s. 4¼d.	4·8	.	4·8
1855	82,891	55,808	1,196	.	1,196	.	6,273	.	6,273	701	6,974	1s. 6¼d.	1s. 8¼d.	2·1	.	2·1
1857	81,508	54,656	611	.	611	.	2,955	.	2,955	789	3,744	8¼	10¼	1·1	.	1·1
1859	82,553	53,384	435	.	435	.	2,273	.	2,273	870	3,143	6¼	9¼	·8	.	·8
1861	82,891	52,068	534	.	534	.	3,218	.	3,218	866	4,083	9¼	11¼	1·0	.	1·0
1863	84,135	51,619	689	.	689	.	4,027	.	4,027	865	4,892	11¼	1s. 2d.	1·3	.	1·3
1865	84,687	51,172	632	.	632	.	3,943	.	3,948	1,126	5,068	11¼	1s. 2¼d.	1·2	.	1·2
1867	84,819	50,726	643	.	633	.	4,577	.	4,577	1,065	5,642	1s. 1d.	1s. 4d.	1·3	.	1·2
1869	84,846	50,276	564	.	564	.	4,211	.	4,211	1,044	5,255	11¼	1s. 3d.	1·1	.	1·1
1871	84,877	49,831	418	.	418	.	3,403	.	4,403	1,038	4,441	9¼	1s. 0¼d.	·8	.	·8
1873	85,470	49,831	435	.	435	.	4,090	.	4,090	1,073	5,163	11¼	1s. 2¼d.	·9	.	·9
1875	85,772	49,831	529	.	529	.	4,148	.	4,148	935	5,183	11¼	1s. 2¼d.	1·0	.	1·0
1877	85,680	49,531	518	7	525	73·7 to 1	4,377	60	4,437	1,223	5,660	1s. 0¼d.	1s. 3¼d.	1·0	.	1·0

Expenditure of each Poor Law Union in Ireland since the year 1851—*continued*.

Years.	Valuation.	Population.	Average Daily Number in Receipt of Relief: In-door.	Out-door, under 10 Vic. c. 31.	Total.	Ratio of In-door to Out-door.	Expenditure for: In Maintenance and Clothing.	Out Relief under 10 Vic. c. 31.	Total.	Expenditure under Medical Charities Acts, exclusive of Vaccination.	Total of Cols. 10 and 11.	Poundage: On Amount in Col. 10.	On Amount in Col. 12.	Per-centage of Paupers to Population: In-door.	Out-door.	Total.
1	2	3	4	5	6	7	8	9	10	11	12	13	14	15	16	17
Province of Munster—continued.																
Croom Union.							£	£	£	£	£	d.	d.			
Area, 81,386 acres.																
1851	62,170	27,258	1,501	.	1,501	.	3,326	.	3,326	.	3,326	2s. 9½d.	1s. 9½d.	5·5	.	5·5
1853	62,271	26,060	676	.	676	.	2,393	.	2,393	715	3,071	11½	1s. 2d.	2·5	.	2·5
1855	62,471	24,881	394	.	394	.	2,121	.	2,121	486	2,018	8½	10	1·6	.	1·6
1857	62,634	23,600	172	.	172	.	1,172	.	1,172	491	1,663	4½	6½	·7	.	·7
1859	62,798	22,488	149	.	149	.	1,003	.	1,003	497	1,500	3¾	5½	·6	.	·6
1861	63,018	21,172	188	.	188	.	1,375	.	1,375	487	1,862	5	7½	·9	.	·9
1863	63,844	20,348	244	.	244	.	1,881	.	1,881	541	2,422	7½	9½	1·2	.	1·2
1865	64,157	19,886	241	.	241	.	1,861	.	1,861	485	2,346	7	9	1·2	.	1·2
1867	64,158	18,704	235	.	235	.	2,003	.	2,003	488	2,548	7½	9½	1·2	.	1·2
1869	63,747	17,892	271	16	287	16·9 to 1	1,944	30	1,982	540	2,532	7¾	9½	1·5	.	1·6
1871	63,301	17,060	223	64	287	3·5 to 1	1,940	105	2,045	567	2,612	7¾	10	1·3	·3	1·6
1873	63,540	17,060	233	85	318	2·7 to 1	2,208	238	2,446	555	2,991	9¼	11½	1·5	·5	1·8
1875	64,108	17,060	229	146	375	1·5 to 1	2,134	421	2,555	608	3,163	9½	11¾	1·3	·8	2·1
1877	64,068	17,060	233	207	440	1·0 to 1	2,001	581	2,582	531	3,113	9½	1s. 0d.	1·3	1·2	2·5
Glin Union.																
Area, 70,176 acres.																
1851	27,916	17,631	1,697	.	1,697	.	3,970	.	3,970	.	3,970	2s. 10½d.	2s. 10½d.	9·6	.	9·6
1853	27,917	17,257	733	.	733	.	1,991	.	1,991	317	2,308	1s. 5¼d.	1s. 7¾d.	4·1	.	4·1
1855	27,917	16,680	367	.	367	.	1,336	.	1,336	225	1,561	1s. 1½d.	1s. 3¼d.	2·7	.	2·7
1857	27,800	16,501	164	.	164	.	664	.	664	250	914	5¾	8	1·0	.	1·0
1859	27,884	16,126	103	.	103	.	478	.	478	314	792	4	6¾	·6	.	·6
1861	27,473	15,740	105	.	105	.	724	.	724	369	1,093	6¼	9½	·6	.	·6
1863	27,918	15,480	167	.	167	.	917	.	917	314	1,231	8	10¾	1·0	.	1·0
1865	27,891	15,310	156	23	179	6·7 to 1	937	29	966	310	1,276	8½	11	1·0	·1	1·1
1867	27,918	15,240	149	76	225	1·9 to 1	1,334	214	1,548	307	1,855	1s. 1¼d.	1s. 4d.	·9	·5	1·4
1869	27,806	14,870	156	7	163	20·7 to 1	1,118	10	1,128	286	1,414	9¾	1s. 1d.	1·0	.	1·0
1871	28,242	14,859	123	27	150	4·6 to 1	1,051	79	1,130	286	1,416	9¼	1s. 1d.	·8	·2	1·0
1873	28,409	14,859	132	49	181	2·7 to 1	1,360	139	1,499	306	1,805	1s. 0½d.	1s. 3½d.	·8	·4	1·2
1875	28,830	14,859	145	71	216	2·0 to 1	1,497	197	1,694	351	1,945	1s. 1d.	1s. 4¼d.	1·0	·4	1·4
1877	28,130	14,089	164	16	178	8·0 to 1	1,493	16	1,509	336	2,000	10¾	1s. 3¼d.	1·0	·1	1·2
Kilmallock Union.																
Area, 140,805 acres.																
1851	177,708	48,779	3,748	.	3,748	.	13,133	.	13,133	.	13,133	[illegible]	[illegible]	7·6	.	7·6
1853	177,708	46,951	2,087	.	2,087	.	6,974	.	6,974	789	7,763	1s. 1¼d.	1s. 2¾d.	4·4	.	4·4
1855	177,786	45,085	970	.	970	.	4,786	.	4,786	814	5,600	9	10½	2·1	.	2·1
1857	180,275	43,255	552	.	552	.	3,270	.	3,270	780	4,050	6	7¼	1·3	.	1·3
1859	179,640	41,587	417	.	417	.	2,805	.	2,818	895	3,708	5½	6¾	1·0	.	1·0
1861	179,931	39,539	565	.	565	.	4,200	.	4,396	841	5,139	7½	8¼	1·4	.	1·4
1863	182,182	38,422	670	2	678	335 to 1	5,103	21	5,134	952	6,086	9½	11	1·7	.	1·7
1865	181,920	37,705	625	33	658	18·9 to 1	4,603	64	4,667	929	5,596	8½	10¼	1·6	·1	1·7
1867	180,493	36,758	641	164	805	3·9 to 1	5,300	417	5,717	932	6,649	10¾	1s. 0½d.	1·7	·4	2·1
1869	182,747	35,871	619	440	1,059	1·4 to 1	5,123	1,232	6,355	1,063	7,418	11¼	1s. 1d.	1·7	1·2	2·9
1871	182,991	34,954	473	634	1,107	·9 to 1	4,880	1,304	6,184	1,018	7,202	11½	1s. 1d.	1·3	1·8	3·1
1873	185,711	34,954	629	648	1,277	·9 to 1	6,406	1,506	7,912	1,117	9,029	1s. 0½d.	1s. 2¼d.	1·8	1·8	3·6
1875	185,768	34,954	666	656	1,322	1·0 to 1	6,205	1,465	7,670	1,276	9,014	1s. 1½d.	1s. 2¾d.	1·8	1·8	3·7
1877	186,876	34,954	672	641	1,313	1·0 to 1	6,096	1,451	7,574	1,238	8,702	1s. 1¼d.	1s. 2¾d.	1·9	1·8	3·7
Limerick Union.																
Area, 101,455 acres.																
1851	183,780	110,628	5,519	.	5,519	.	21,249		21,249	.	21,249	2s. 3¾d.	2s. 3¾d.	5·	.	5·
1853	184,709	106,648	4,192	.	4,192	.	16,173		16,173	1,165	17,338	1s. 9d.	1s. 10½d.	3·9	.	3·9
1855	184,709	102,866	2,273	.	2,273	.	10,379	.	10,379	1,325	11,704	1s. 1½d.	1s. 3¼d.	2·2	.	2·2
1857	185,168	96,688	1,416	.	1,416	.	6,696	.	6,696	1,415	8,111	8¾	10½	1·5	.	1·5
1859	184,884	94,708	1,040	.	1,040	.	5,845	.	4,845	1,646	7,492	7½	9½	1·1	.	1·1
1861	185,371	90,729	1,679	.	1,679	.	11,532	.	11,532	1,711	13,243	1s. 3d.	1s. 5¼d.	1·7	.	1·7
1863	188,276	88,463	1,893	1	1,894	.	12,807	3	12,600	1,706	14,309	1s. 4d.	1s. 7¼d.	2·1	.	2·1
1865	189,549	86,146	1,784	62	1,846	28·7 to 1	11,183	173	11,356	1,578	12,901	1s. 2½d.	1s. 4¼d.	2·	·1	2·1
1867	190,603	83,840	1,548	654	2,202	2·3 to 1	10,779	1,195	11,974	1,835	13,809	1s. 2¾d.	1s. 5¼d.	1·8	·8	2·6
1869	191,510	81,344	1,707	232	1,939	7·3 to 1	12,822	1,145	13,967	1,650	15,017	1s. 5½d.	1s. 7½d.	2·1	·3	2·4
1871	191,863	79,248	1,496	396	1,892	3·7 to 1	12,829	973	13,790	1,833	15,623	1s. 4½d.	1s. 6¾d.	1·8	·5	2·3
1873	192,761	79,248	1,646	651	2,297	2·5 to 1	15,042	1,702	16,819	1,794	18,613	1s. 10½d.	1s. 11¼d.	2·	·8	2·8
1875	194,765	79,248	1,479	748	2,227	1·9 to 1	12,339	2,001	14,340	1,680	16,020	1s. 5¾d.	1s. 7¾d.	1·8	1·	2·8
1877	194,876	79,248	1,396	906	2,302	1·5 to 1	13,275	2,647	15,922	1,753	17,675	1s. 7¾d.	1s. 9¾d.	1·8	1·1	2·9
Newcastle Union.																
Area, 143,023 acres.																
1851	60,480	36,196	3,304	.	3,304	.	12,686	.	12,686	.	12,686	4s. 2½d.	4s. 2½d.	9·3	.	9·3
1853	60,459	33,309	1,630	.	1,630	.	5,977	.	5,977	862	5,849	1s. 8d.	1s. 11¼d.	4·5	.	4·5
1855	60,480	34,209	964	.	964	.	5,516	.	5,516	512	6,028	1s. 10d.	2s. 0d.	2·2	.	2·2
1857	60,401	33,453	479	.	479	.	2,923	.	2,923	511	3,434	11½	1s. 1¾d.	1·3	.	1·3
1859	60,188	31,…	278	.	278	.	1,444	.	1,444	607	2,051	5¾	8¼	·8	.	·8
1861	60,631	31,094	340	5	345	68 to 1	2,254	17	2,271	690	2,961	9	1s. 0¾d.	1·1	.	1·1
1863	60,175	31,330	273	18	291	15·7 to 1	2,551	87	2,638	640	3,278	10½	1s. 1d.	1·3	.	1·3
1865	60,289	31,834	303	65	368	4·6 to 1	2,293	167	2,460	709	3,050	9¾	1s. 0¼d.	·9	·2	1·1
1867	61,806	30,769	276	116	392	2·3 to 1	2,196	369	2,555	708	3,263	10¼	1s. 1¼d.	·9	·3	1·2
1869	61,007	30,494	248	185	433	1·3 to 1	2,130	610	2,740	769	3,499	10¾	1s. 1¾d.	·8	·6	1·4
1871	61,245	30,196	244	172	416	1·4 to 1	2,719	660	3,379	733	4,112	1s. 1¼d.	1s. 4¼d.	·8	·5	1·3
1873	61,367	30,196	285	230	515	1·2 to 1	2,907	686	4,098	804	4,397	1s. 2d.	1s. 4¾d.	·9	·8	1·7
1875	61,464	30,196	300	228	528	1·3 to 1	2,951	768	3,694	829	4,463	1s. 2d.	1s. 5½d.	1·	·7	1·7
1877	61,475	30,196	270	287	557	·9 to 1	2,603	856	3,459	737	4,196	1s. 1¼d.	1s. 4d.	·9	·9	1·8

No. 6.—Statistical Table showing the progress of the Pauperism and

Years.	Valuation.	Population.	Average Daily Number in Receipt of Relief: In-door.	Out-door, under 10 Vic. c. 31.	Total.	Ratio of In-door to Out-door.	Expenditure for: In-Maintenance and Clothing.	Out-Relief under 10 Vic. c. 31.	Total.	Expenditure under Medical Charities Acts, exclusive of Vaccination.	Total of Cols. 10 and 11.	Poundage: On Amount in Col. 10.	On Amount in Col. 12.	Per centage of Paupers to Population: In-door.	Out-door.	Total.
1.	2.	3.	4.	5.	6.	7.	8.	9.	10.	11.	12.	13.	14.	15.	16.	17.
Province of Munster—continued.																
Rathkeale Union. Area, 79,092 acres.							£	£	£	£	£	d.	d.			
1851	55,274	28,725	1,691	.	1,691	.	6,339	.	6,339	.	6,339	2s. 3½d.	2s. 3½d.	5·3	.	5·3
1853	55,274	27,391	880	.	880	.	3,026	.	3,026	668	3,694	1s. 1¼d.	1s. 4d.	3·	.	3·
1855	55,275	26,042	415	.	415	.	2,010	.	2,010	638	2,648	8¾	11	1·6	.	1·6
1857	55,770	24,725	191	1	192	.	1,161	8	1,169	589	1,758	5	7½	·8	.	·8
1859	55,091	23,269	185	9	194	66·5 to 1	776	14	790	672	1,462	3¼	6¼	·8	.	·8
1861	55,547	22,095	258	29	287	9·1 to 1	1,735	146	1,881	649	2,530	8¼	11	1·1	·1	1·2
1863	55,198	21,231	408	26	434	15·6 to 1	2,206	115	2,321	642	2,963	10	1s. 0¾d.	1·8	·1	1·9
1865	55,461	20,487	261	138	399	1·8 to 1	1,820	470	2,290	600	2,890	8½	1s. 0½d.	1·3	·6	1·9
1867	55,461	19,528	280	172	452	1·6 to 1	2,448	592	3,040	606	3,646	1s. 1¼d.	1s. 3¾d.	1·4	·9	2·3
1869	55,655	18,719	254	265	519	0·9 to 1	2,889	950	3,249	625	3,884	1s. 2d.	1s. 4¼d.	1·3	1·4	2·7
1871	55,760	17,884	221	277	498	0·8 to 1	2,300	1,300	3,600	633	4,242	1s. 3½d.	1s. 6¼d.	1·2	1·5	2·7
1873	55,897	17,884	225	413	638	0·5 to 1	2,372	1,540	3,912	646	4,558	1s. 4¾d.	1s. 7¾d.	1·3	2·4	3·7
1875	56,115	17,884	181	459	640	0·4 to 1	1,749	1,794	3,543	654	4,197	1s. 3¼d.	1s. 6¼d.	1·	2·5	3·5
1877	56,235	17,884	204	471	675	0·4 to 1	1,875	1,906	3,781	664	4,445	1s. 4d.	1s. 6¾d.	1·2	2·6	3·8
Borrisokane Union. Area, 41,800 acres																
1851	41,564	19,307	961	.	961	.	3,368	.	3,368	.	3,368	1s. 7½d.	1s. 7½d.	4·9	.	4·9
1853	41,564	18,242	477	.	477	.	1,725	.	1,725	361	2,086	9	1s. 0d.	2·6	.	2·6
1855	41,564	17,117	208	.	208	.	1,060	.	1,060	282	1,342	6¼	7¾	1·2	.	1·2
1857	41,560	15,902	116	.	116	.	718	.	718	328	1,046	4¼	6	·7	.	·7
1859	41,461	14,887	109	.	109	.	668	.	668	374	1,042	3¾	6	·7	.	·7
1861	41,361	13,740	119	.	119	.	841	.	841	355	1,196	4¾	6¾	·8	.	·8
1863	41,437	13,284	162	.	162	.	892	.	892	375	1,267	5¼	7¼	1·2	.	1·2
1865	41,420	12,848	185	.	185	.	906	.	906	277	1,183	5¼	7¼	1·3	.	1·3
1867	41,244	12,492	145	.	145	.	1,032	.	1,032	385	1,417	6	8¼	1·1	.	1·1
1869	41,243	11,956	126	.	126	.	1,037	.	1,037	425	1,462	6	8½	1·0	.	1·0
1871	41,341	11,510	117	.	117	.	988	.	988	409	1,397	5¾	8	1·0	.	1·0
1873	41,397	11,510	118	.	118	.	1,097	.	1,097	483	1,580	6¼	9¼	1·0	.	1·0
1875	41,400	11,510	109	.	109	.	961	.	961	454	1,415	5¼	8¼	·9	.	·9
1877	41,397	11,510	120	.	120	.	1,058	.	1,058	494	1,552	6¼	8¾	1·0	.	1·0
Carrick-on-Suir Union. Area, 112,630 acres																
1851	76,269	37,752	909	.	909	.	3,958	.	3,958	.	3,958	1s. 0½d.	1s. 0½d.	2·4	.	2·4
1853	76,260	35,398	692	.	692	.	2,758	.	2,758	887	3,645	8¾	11½	1·9	.	1·9
1855	76,269	34,755	516	.	516	.	2,705	.	2,705	602	3,307	8½	10½	1·5	.	1·5
1857	76,268	33,358	315	.	315	.	1,803	.	1,803	591	2,394	5¾	7½	·9	.	·9
1859	76,468	31,781	310	3	313	.	1,816	16	1,832	644	2,476	5¾	7¾	·9	.	·9
1861	76,887	30,294	423	3	426	.	2,949	60	3,009	581	3,590	9½	11½	1·4	.	1·4
1863	77,475	29,657	484	30	514	.	3,272	157	3,429	692	4,121	10¾	1s. 0¾d.	1·6	·1	1·7
1865	77,911	29,421	465	34	499	.	3,343	137	3,480	692	4,172	10½	1s. 0¾d.	1·6	·1	1·7
1867	78,392	28,985	476	37	513	.	3,939	242	4,181	674	4,855	1s. 0¾d.	1s. 2¾d.	1·7	·1	1·8
1869	78,851	28,540	437	84	521	.	3,532	450	3,982	659	4,601	1s. 0d.	1s. 2d.	1·5	·3	1·8
1871	78,986	28,113	328	178	506	1·8 to 1	2,937	474	3,410	706	4,116	10½	1s. 0¾d.	1·1	·7	1·8
1873	79,281	28,113	276	167	443	1·6 to 1	2,858	312	3,170	731	4,001	10¼	1s. 0¾d.	·9	·6	1·5
1875	79,436	28,113	236	192	448	1·3 to 1	2,782	398	2,788	670	3,458	8½	10½	·9	·6	1·5
1877	79,416	28,113	278	259	537	1·1 to 1	2,141	639	2,780	760	3,540	8¾	10½	·9	·9	1·8
Cashel Union. Area, 156,723 acres.																
1851	165,116	45,869	3,413	.	3,413	.	12,991	.	12,991	.	12,991	2s. 3¼d.	2s. 3¼d.	7·5	.	7·5
1853	165,116	44,001	2,115	.	2,115	.	7,284	.	7,284	845	8,129	1s. 4¾d.	1s. 6¾d.	4·8	.	4·8
1855	165,116	40,835	1,172	.	1,172	.	6,276	.	6,276	545	6,821	1s. 2¼d.	1s. 3¾d.	2·8	.	2·8
1857	106,102	38,948	619	.	619	.	4,025	.	4,025	557	4,582	9¼	10¼	1·6	.	1·6
1859	106,[illegible]	35,897	448	.	448	.	2,813	.	2,813	640	3,453	6¼	7¾	1·2	.	1·2
1861	106,[illegible]	34,527	483	.	483	.	3,313	.	3,313	828	4,141	7½	9¼	1·4	.	1·4
1863	107,608	32,700	544	19	563	48·3 to 1	3,515	68	3,583	691	4,274	7¾	9½	1·7	.	1·7
1865	107,643	31,873	528	33	561	16· to 1	3,545	104	3,649	718	4,218	7¾	9½	1·6	·1	1·7
1867	107,671	31,616	511	88	599	5·8 to 1	4,394	410	4,805	727	5,150	10¼	1s. 0¾d.	1·7	·2	1·9
1869	107,712	30,919	504	182	686	2·8 to 1	4,313	636	4,949	794	5,743	11	1s. 0¾d.	1·7	·6	2·3
1871	107,878	29,392	489	401	790	1·2 to 1	4,324	1,473	5,797	841	6,638	1s. 1d.	1s. 2¾d.	1·6	1·3	2·9
1873	107,719	29,392	484	402	886	1·1 to 1	4,769	1,547	6,316	948	7,258	1s. 2d.	1s. 4¼d.	1·6	1·5	3·0
1875	107,407	29,883	412	412	824	1· to 1	3,839	1,338	5,177	938	6,115	11¾	1s. 1½d.	1·4	1·4	2·8
1877	107,[illegible]	29,392	413	376	789	1·1 to 1	3,876	1,279	5,155	913	6,068	11½	1s. 1¼d.	1·4	1·3	2·7
Clogheen Union. Area, 115,218 acres.																
1851	62,575	33,274	1,466	.	1,466	.	4,234	.	4,234	.	4,234	1s. 4¼d.	1s. 4¼d.	4·4	.	4·4
1853	62,873	31,869	982	.	982	.	3,562	.	3,562	442	4,004	1s. 1¼d.	1s. 3¼d.	3·1	.	3·1
1855	64,873	30,064	367	.	367	.	2,696	.	2,696	448	3,144	10	1s. 0d.	1·2	.	1·2
1857	62,777	28,159	297	.	297	.	2,044	.	2,044	473	2,517	7¾	9¾	1·	.	1·
1859	62,089	26,864	201	.	201	.	1,186	.	1,186	430	1,616	4½	6¼	·7	.	·7
1861	62,917	25,349	189	.	189	.	1,417	.	1,417	426	1,843	5¼	7	·7	.	·7
1863	62,948	24,649	220	.	220	.	1,434	.	1,434	446	1,880	5¼	7	·9	.	·9
1865	62,936	24,049	215	.	215	.	1,491	.	1,491	484	1,975	5¾	7½	·9	.	·9
1867	64,267	23,440	236	.	236	.	1,866	.	1,866	427	2,293	7	8½	1·	.	1·
1869	64,285	22,848	258	.	258	.	2,007	.	2,007	422	2,427	7½	9¼	1·1	.	1·1
1871	64,571	22,247	243	.	243	.	2,067	.	2,067	423	2,490	7¾	9¼	1·	.	1·
1873	64,769	22,247	267	.	267	.	2,766	.	2,766	453	3,219	10¼	1s. 0d.	1·2	.	1·2
1875	64,632	22,247	238	.	238	.	2,283	.	2,283	460	2,743	8½	10¼	1·	.	1·
1877	64,031	22,247	272	.	272	.	2,261	.	2,261	485	2,746	8½	10¼	1·0	.	1·0

Expenditure of each Poor Law Union in Ireland since the year 1851—*continued.*

Year.	Valuation.	Population.	Average Daily Number in Receipt of Relief: In-door.	Out-door, under 10 Vic. c. 31.	Total.	Ratio of In-door to Out-door.	Expenditure for: In-Maintenance and Clothing.	Out-Relief under 10 Vic. c. 31.	Total.	Expenditure under Medical Charities Acts, exclusive of Vaccination.	Total of Cols. 10 and 11.	Poundage: On Amount in Col. 10.	On Amount in Col. 12.	Per-centage of Paupers to Population: In-door.	Out-door.	Total.
1.	2.	3.	4.	5.	6.	7.	8.	9.	10.	11.	12.	13.	14.	15.	16.	17.
Province of Munster—continued.																
Clonmel Union. Area, 86,446 acres.							£	£	£	£	£	d.	d.			
1851	72,321	36,984	2,462	.	2,462	.	9,533	.	9,533	.	9,533	2s. 7½d.	2s. 7½d.	6·6	.	6·6
1853	72,221	35,985	1,778	.	1,778	.	7,911	.	7,911	793	8,704	2s. 2½d.	2s. 4½d.	5·	.	5·
1855	72,221	35,406	1,258	.	1,258	.	6,872	.	6,812	839	7,451	1s. 10½d.	2s. 0½d.	3·7	.	3·7
1857	71,632	31,617	921	.	921	.	4,846	.	4,856	641	5,497	1s. 4½d.	1s. 6½d.	2·9	.	2·9
1859	71,738	29,838	540	.	540	.	3,146	.	3,146	763	3,909	10½	1s. 1d.	1·8	.	1·8
1861	72,070	28,039	676	.	676	.	4,154	.	4,154	684	4,838	1s. 1½d.	1s. 4½d.	2·4	.	2·4
1863	70,898	27,740	781	18	798	52 to 1	4,641	30	4,681	773	5,444	1s. 3½d.	1s. 6½d.	2·8	.	2·9
1865	70,869	26,459	677	12	688	56·4 to 1	4,437	35	4,472	739	5,111	1s. 2½d.	1s. 5d.	2·6	.	2·6
1867	71,262	25,869	638	33	671	19·3 to 1	4,916	84	5,102	836	5,938	1s. 5½d.	1s. 8d.	2·0	.	2·6
1869	68,663	24,679	587	41	628	14·3 to 1	4,619	105	4,724	881	5,573	1s. 4½d.	1s. 7½d.	2·3	·2	2·5
1871	68,708	24,099	439	84	523	7·2 to 1	3,929	218	4,147	902	5,049	1s. 2½d.	1s. 5½d.	1·9	·2	2·1
1873	70,107	24,099	496	159	655	3·1 to 1	4,502	422	4,924	854	5,778	1s. 5d.	1s. 7½d.	2·	·7	2·7
1875	70,362	24,069	494	179	673	2·7 to 1	4,293	478	4,771	867	5,638	1s. 4½d.	1s. 7½d.	2·	·7	2·7
1877	70,600	24,069	428	279	707	1·5 to 1	3,690	494	4,184	900	5,084	1s. 2½d.	1s. 5d.	1·8	1·1	2·9
Nenagh Union. Area, 183,050 acres.																
1851	91,456	50,465	2,949	.	2,949	.	8,492	.	8,562	.	8,562	1s. 10½d.	1s. 10½d.	5·8	.	5·8
1853	91,456	48,077	1,561	.	1,561	.	6,243	.	6,243	750	6,993	1s. 4½d.	1s. 6½d.	3·2	.	3·2
1855	91,487	45,589	919	.	919	.	4,983	.	4,983	648	5,621	1s. 1d.	1s. 2½d.	2·	.	2·
1857	91,289	42,148	537	.	537	.	3,403	.	3,403	607	4,010	9	10½	1·2	.	1·2
1859	90,894	40,701	438	.	438	.	2,300	.	2,300	796	3,096	6	8¼	1·	.	1·
1861	89,972	38,277	418	.	418	.	4,164	.	4,154	812	4,966	11	1s. 1½d.	1·	.	1
1863	90,708	37,768	569	3	572	189·6 to 1	4,054	18	4,072	769	4,841	10½	1s. 0½d.	1·5	.	1·5
1865	90,744	36,349	548	1	549	.	4,083	17	4,100	825	4,925	10½	1s. 1d.	1·5	.	1·5
1867	90,756	36,325	466	22	488	21·1 to 1	3,748	103	3,851	852	4,703	10½	1s. 0½d.	1·3	.	1·4
1869	90,769	34,721	393	268	648	1·4 to 1	3,103	487	3,590	788	4,378	9½	11	1·1	·7	1·8
1871	93,391	33,206	391	424	815	0·9 to 1	3,113	812	3,925	788	4,714	10	1s. 0½d.	1·2	1·2	2·4
1873	93,469	33,306	363	502	865	0·7 to 1	3,534	1,086	4,620	840	5,460	11	1s. 2d.	1·1	1·5	2·6
1875	93,688	33,306	340	274	614	1·7 to 1	3,003	1,166	4,169	848	5,014	10½	1s. 0½d.	1·	·8	1·8
1877	93,941	33,306	294	581	875	0·5 to 1	2,829	1,306	4,135	894	5,029	10½	1s. 1d.	0·8	1·7	2·6
Roscrea Union. Area, 118,488 acres.																
1851	68,859	33,442	1,193	.	1,193	.	4,379	.	4,379	.	4,379	1s. 3½d.	1s. 3½d.	3·5	.	3·5
1853	68,949	31,496	568	.	563	.	2,148	.	2,148	480	2,628	7½	9½	1·7	.	1·7
1855	68,939	29,331	355	.	355	.	2,081	.	2,081	379	2,430	7½	8½	1·2	.	1·2
1857	69,218	26,176	226	.	226	.	1,426	.	1,426	418	1,844	5	6½	·8	.	·8
1859	69,479	26,421	164	.	164	.	990	.	990	442	1,432	3½	5	·6	.	·6
1861	70,155	24,888	227	1	228	.	1,594	9	1,604	479	2,083	5½	7½	·9	.	·9
1863	70,100	23,728	265	8	273	33·1 to 1	1,772	41	1,813	508	2,321	6½	8½	1·1	.	1·1
1865	70,068	24,012	258	10	268	25·8 to 1	1,737	50	1,787	579	2,366	6½	8½	1·1	.	1·1
1867	70,041	21,886	224	30	254	7 to 1	2,041	119	2,160	551	2,711	7½	9½	1·0	·1	1·1
1869	69,865	20,960	192	44	236	4·4 to 1	1,963	201	2,164	482	2,646	7½	9½	·9	·2	1·1
1871	71,654	20,034	162	88	243	2 to 1	1,611	354	1,965	601	2,567	6½	8½	·8	·4	1·2
1873	71,700	20,034	146	99	245	1·5 to 1	1,597	448	2,045	590	2,635	6⅞	8½	·7	·5	1·2
1875	71,648	20,034	181	90	271	1·4 to 1	1,338	409	1,747	582	2,329	5½	7½	·6	·5	1·1
1877	71,680	20,034	128	103	231	1·2 to 1	1,280	442	1,722	643	2,355	5½	7½	·6	·5	1·1
Thurles Union. Area, 143,351 acres.																
1851	84,860	48,338	2,103	.	2,103	.	8,189	.	8,189	.	8,189	1s. 11½d.	1s. 11½d.	4·3	.	4·3
1853	116,860	46,089	1,117	.	1,117	.	3,655	.	3,655	741	4,396	10½	1s. 0½d.	2·4	.	2·4
1855	94,869	43,483	628	.	628	.	3,202	.	3,202	842	4,744	9	10½	1·4	.	1·4
1857	87,067	41,106	398	.	398	.	2,408	.	2,408	873	[illegible]	6½	9½	·9	.	·9
1859	87,768	38,838	475	.	475	.	1,897	.	1,897	762	2,659	5½	7½	·9	.	·9
1861	90,474	36,182	377	.	407	.	2,244	.	2,344	726	3,068	6½	8½	1·0	.	1·0
1863	69,824	35,216	438	.	438	.	2,515	.	2,515	723	3,238	6½	8½	1·2	.	1·2
1865	69,901	34,280	322	1	323	.	1,941	12	1,953	771	2,724	4½	7½	·9	.	·9
1867	69,956	33,315	276	16	292	17·2 to 1	2,023	69	2,092	764	2,856	5⅞	7½	·8	.	·8
1869	69,926	32,410	255	10	265	25·5 to 1	2,110	62	2,172	852	3,024	5½	8	·7	.	·7
1871	69,967	31,475	235	3	248	78·3 to 1	1,984	20	2,004	432	2,436	5½	7½	·7	.	·7
1873	69,967	31,475	233	22	255	10·6 to 1	2,170	59	2,230	873	3,132	6	8½	·7	.	·8
1875	90,036	31,475	205	48	253	4·3 to 1	1,844	184	2,018	856	2,973	5½	8	·6	·1	·8
1877	90,016	31,475	200	70	270	2·9 to 1	1,813	328	2,141	959	3,100	5½	8½	·6	·2	·8
Tipperary Union. Area, 179,988 acres.																
1851	181,129	60,268	3,484	.	3,484	.	12,363	.	12,363	.	12,363	1s. 10½d.	1s. 10½d.	5·7	.	5·7
1853	194,130	57,754	1,676	.	1,676	.	5,061	.	5,061	1,003	6,084	9 1/16	10½	2·9	.	2·9
1855	184,120	55,140	773	.	773	.	4,457	.	4,457	770	5,227	8	9½	1·4	.	1·4
1857	186,308	52,876	441	.	441	.	2,610	.	2,610	917	3,527	4½	6½	·8	.	·8
1859	133,722	48,812	355	.	355	.	2,231	.	2,231	935	3,166	4	5½	·7	.	·7
1861	135,722	47,286	425	.	425	.	3,397	.	3,397	913	4,310	6	7½	·9	.	·9
1863	137,763	46,425	475	19	494	18·7 to 1	4,176	67	3,243	950	4,193	5½	7½	1·0	.	1·0
1865	137,702	45,530	412	60	476	6·5 to 1	3,119	326	3,445	929	4,371	6	7½	·9	·1	1·0
1867	138,430	44,677	444	144	588	3·2 to 1	3,407	468	3,875	958	4,837	6½	8½	1·0	·3	1·3
1869	139,701	44,008	433	155	588	3 to 1	3,723	461	4,185	1,896	6,075	7 1/16	10½	·9	·3	1·3
1871	140,806	42,841	428	204	632	2·1 to 1	3,609	567	4,176	1,067	5,244	10½	9	·9	·3	1·3
1873	141,247	42,961	476	285	761	1·7 to 1	4,718	882	5,600	1,166	6,766	9½	11½	1·1	·6	1·7
1875	141,920	42,961	505	360	870	1·4 to 1	5,034	969	6,004	1,138	7,141	10½	1s. 0d.	1·1	·8	2·0
1877	142,082	42,961	487	461	948	1·0 to 1	4,752	1,365	6,117	1,045	7,162	10½	1s. 0d.	1·1	1·1	2·2

Appendix A.
Poor Relief.

No. 6.—Statistical Table showing the progress of the Pauperism and

Years	Valuation	Population	Average Daily Numbers in Receipt of Relief: In-door	Out-door, under 10 Vic. c. 31	Total	Ratio of Indoor to Outdoor	Expenditure for: In-Maintenance and Clothing	Out Relief under 10 Vic. c. 31	Total	Expenditure under Medical Charities Acts, inclusive of Vaccination	Total of Cols. 10 and 11	Poundage: On Amount in Col. 10	On Amount in Col. 12	Percentage of Paupers to Population: In-door	Out-door	Total
1	2	3	4	5	6	7	8	9	10	11	12	13	14	15	16	17
Province of Munster—continued.																
Dungarvan Union. Area, 94,044 acres.							£	£	£	£	£	d.	d.			
1851	53,403	31,[illegible]	1,244	.	1,244	.	3,317	.	3,317	.	3,317	1s. 9¼d.	1s. 9¼d.	3·9	.	3·9
1853	54,404	29,838	938	.	938	.	4,416	.	3,416	589	4,005	[illegible]	1s. [illegible]	3·1	.	3·1
1855	54,404	28,160	[illegible]	.	682	.	2,933	.	2,933	434	3,[illegible]	1s. 1¼d.	1s. 3½d.	2·0	.	2·0
1857	63,294	27,103	397	.	397	.	2,008	.	2,008	464	2,472	9	11¼	1·0	.	1·0
1859	53,301	25,721	249	.	249	.	1,414	.	1,414	498	1,911	6¼	8¾	1·0	.	1·0
1861	53,504	24,448	308	.	308	.	2,094	.	2,094	581	2,677	9¼	11¾	1·2	.	1·2
1863	53,948	24,840	402	52	454	7·7 to 1	2,795	187	2,982	557	3,489	1s. 1½d.	1s. 3¼d.	1·6	·2	1·8
1865	58,935	23,951	285	19	304	15 to 1	1,958	54	2,012	564	2,576	9	11½	1·2	.	1·3
1867	54,877	22,[illegible]	420	96	516	4·4 to 1	3,074	322	3,436	580	3,916	1s. 3d.	1s. 5¼d.	1·8	·4	2·2
1869	53,984	22,184	463	151	614	3 to 1	3,[illegible]	411	4,337	618	4,955	1s. 7¾d.	1s. 10½d.	2·0	·6	2·7
1871	53,871	21,860	339	187	526	1·8 to 1	2,9[illegible]	[illegible]	3,484	578	4,012	1s. 3d.	1s. 6d.	1·5	·8	2·4
1873	54,911	21,889	363	229	592	1·7 to 1	3,662	815	4,477	648	5,125	1s. 5d.	1s. 11d.	1·6	1·0	2·6
1875	53,830	21,869	371	218	589	1·7 to 1	3,800	677	4,477	749	5,346	1s. 6d.	1s. 11¾d.	1·6	·9	2·6
1877	52,990	21,969	361	184	545	2·0 to 1	3,568	555	4,123	673	4,796	1s. 6¾d.	1s. 8¾d.	1·5	·9	2·5
Kilmacthomas Union. Area, 64,478 acres.																
1851	35,312	18,729	353	.	353	.	1,916	.	1,916	.	1,916	8¼	8¼	1·9	.	1·9
1853	35,317	18,074	316	.	316	.	1,203	.	1,203	389	1,595	8¾	10¾	1·7	.	1·7
1855	35,319	17,479	229	.	229	.	1,341	.	1,387	286	1,673	9¼	11¼	1·3	.	1·3
1857	35,271	18,184	100	.	109	.	850	.	850	255	1,105	5¾	7¼	·6	.	·6
1859	35,309	16,189	90	.	90	.	637	.	637	282	919	4¼	6¼	·5	.	·5
1861	35,335	15,194	141	.	141	.	1,323	.	1,243	285	1,608	8½	10¾	·9	.	·9
1863	38,416	15,075	203	.	203	.	1,475	.	1,475	316	1,791	9¼	11¼	1·3	.	1·3
1865	41,425	14,846	203	18	221	11·3 to 1	1,327	52	1,379	310	1,689	9¼	11	1·4	·1	1·5
1867	40,439	14,287	207	85	292	2·3 to 1	1,381	211	1,592	306	2,198	11¼	1s. 1½d.	1·4	·6	2·0
1869	44,418	13,818	190	151	349	1·3 to 1	1,621	441	2,062	300	2,362	1s. 2d.	1s. 4d.	1·4	1·1	2·5
1871	34,743	13,360	156	203	359	·7 to 1	1,474	463	1,937	343	2,280	1s. 1¼d.	1s. 4d.	1·1	1·5	2·6
1873	34,725	13,390	117	247	364	·7 to 1	1,816	577	2,393	363	2,756	1s. 4½d.	1s. 7½d.	1·3	1·8	3·1
1875	34,473	14,500	164	168	332	·9 to 1	1,500	451	1,951	322	2,273	1s. 1½d.	1s. 4d.	1·1	1·2	2·4
1877	34,440	14,599	179	144	423	1·2 to 1	1,651	318	1,970	493	2,463	1s. 1¼d.	1s. 3¼d.	1·3	1·1	2·4
Lismore Union. Area, 97,140 acres.																
1851	49,976	27,077	1,226	.	1,226	.	3,505	.	3,505	.	3,505	1s. 5½d.	1s. 5½d.	4·4	.	4·4
1853	49,978	25,[illegible]	906	.	906	.	2,939	.	2,939	486	3,425	1s. 2⅛d.	1s. 5d.	3·4	.	3·4
1855	49,976	24,[illegible]	616	.	616	.	3,671	.	3,671	447	4,118	1s. 5[illegible]	1s. 7¼d.	2·5	.	2·5
1857	49,[illegible]	24,847	394	.	394	.	1,915	.	1,914	469	2,[illegible]	9¼	11¼	1·6	.	1·6
1859	49,786	23,091	232	.	232	.	1,427	.	1,427	482	1,909	7	9¼	1·0	.	1·0
1861	49,757	20,845	235	.	235	.	1,673	.	1,673	480	2,153	8	10¼	1·0	.	1·0
1863	49,974	20,449	288	12	300	24 to 1	2,010	22	2,032	518	2,550	9¾	1s. 0¼d.	1·4	.	1·4
1865	49,782	20,037	237	20	257	11·8 to 1	1,810	31	1,841	506	2,347	9	11¼	1·1	.	1·2
1867	49,785	19,614	245	38	283	6·5 to 1	1,774	80	1,854	560	2,414	9	11¼	1·2	·2	1·4
1869	49,702	19,248	213	62	275	3·4 to 1	1,686	198	1,884	518	2,402	9	11¼	1·1	·3	1·4
1871	49,729	18,[illegible]	181	90	271	2 to 1	1,647	193	1,840	525	2,365	9	1s. 0d.	1·0	·4	1·4
1873	49,865	18,834	198	101	299	1·9 to 1	1,908	268	2,173	606	2,779	10¼	1s. 1d.	1·0	·5	1·5
1875	49,854	15,814	141	74	215	2·6 to 1	1,619	151	1,771	643	2,414	8¾	11¼	1·4	·3	1·8
1877	49,885	10,[illegible]	195	63	258	3·1 to 1	1,751	105	1,856	664	2,520	9	1s. 0d.	1·3	·3	1·9
Waterford Union. Area, 125,719 acres.																
1851	140,139	68,299	2,146	.	2,146	.	8,189	.	8,189	.	8,189	1s. 2d.	1s. 2d.	3·1	.	3·1
1853	139,820	65,724	1,183	11	1,703	102 to 1	8,244	22	8,260	921	9,181	1s. 2½d.	1s. 4½d.	2·6	.	2·6
1855	140,939	64,025	1,513	11	1,524	137·4 to 1	8,788	49	8,837	803	9,640	1s. 3½d.	1s. 4½d.	2·4	.	2·4
1857	140,497	6[illegible]	1,078	51	1,129	21·1 to 1	6,290	107	6,397	866	7,263	11	1s. 0¼d.	1·7	.	1·8
1859	141,015	60,[illegible]	835	146	981	5·7 to 1	4,370	205	4,575	947	5,[illegible]	8½	9¾	1·3	·2	1·6
1861	143,486	58,[illegible]	946	295	1,241	3·2 to 1	7,448	556	8,004	1,088	9,092	1s. 1¼d.	1s. 3¼d.	1·6	·5	2·1
1863	145,312	58,116	1,033	411	1,444	2·5 to 1	6,709	1,035	7,744	1,099	8,843	1s. 0¼d.	1s. 2¼d.	1·7	·7	2·5
1865	145,686	57,916	940	510	1,450	1·7 to 1	6,071	1,802	7,873	1,454	9,327	1s. 1d.	1s. 3¼d.	1·6	·8	2·5
1867	145,949	57,716	883	731	1,614	1·2 to 1	6,871	1,691	8,562	1,491	9,853	1s. 2¾d.	1s. 4¼d.	1·5	1·2	2·7
1869	147,296	57,316	916	780	1,696	1·2 to 1	5,664	1,775	7,444	1,271	8,665	1s. 0¾d.	1s. 1¼d.	1·5	1·3	1·7
1871	148,236	57,316	647	878	1,770	·7 to 1	6,9[illegible]	2,061	8,[illegible]	1,597	10,382	1s. 3¼d.	1s. 5¼d.	1·4	1·6	3·0
1873	150,065	57,316	943	1,105	2,048	·8 to 1	8,648	2,146	10,782	1,442	12,224	1s. 6¼d.	1s. 7¾d.	1·6	1·9	3·5
1875	151,068	57,316	936	1,054	1,990	·9 to 1	8,356	2,721	10,577	1,650	11,[illegible]	1s. 4¼d.	1s. 6¾d.	1·5	1·8	3·4
1877	150,915	57,316	960	1,083	2,041	·9 to 1	8,430	2,216	10,646	1,610	12,256	1s. 5d.	1s. 7¾d.	1·6	1·9	3·5
Province of Leinster.																
Carlow Union. Area, 105,867 acres.																
1851	147,871	63,853	2,054	.	2,044	.	8,377	.	8,377	.	8,377	1s. 1¼d.	1s. 1¼d.	4·1	.	3·1
1853	147,071	61,303	1,362	4	1,366	315·3 to 1	5,467	19	5,486	1,309	6,777	8¾	11	2·[illegible]	.	2·[illegible]
1855	147,071	[illegible]	816	7	823	116·5 to 1	6,210	170	6,380	1,011	7,441	10¼	1s. 0d.	1·3	.	1·4
1857	149,025	[illegible]	497	8	405	49·6 to 1	2,6[illegible]	41	2,647	971	3,618	4¾	5¾	·7	.	·7
1859	148,189	34,189	349	8	357	43·6 to 1	1,951	48	2,000	1,048	3,057	3¼	4¾	·6	.	·6
1861	149,796	31,[illegible]	459	23	5[illegible]	19·6 to 1	2,590	184	2,735	1,040	3,775	4¼	6	·7	.	·7
1863	146,759	[illegible]	433	131	564	3·3 to 1	3,250	313	3,563	1,111	4,714	6¼	7¾	·8	·2	1·1
1865	148,066	49,418	431	277	648	3·3 to 1	3,291	559	3,850	1,343	5,[illegible]	6¾	8¼	·9	·4	1·3
1867	148,171	48,[illegible]	465	225	650	1·2 to 1	4,249	436	5,185	1,060	6,244	8¾	10	·9	·5	1·4
1869	148,344	47,[illegible]	404	451	855	·9 to 1	2,792	1,679	4,071	1,036	6,107	7¾	9¾	·9	·9	1·8
1871	150,836	45,[illegible]	331	691	852	·5 to 1	3,055	1,774	5,451	1,361	6,692	8¾	10¾	·7	1·3	2·[illegible]
1873	150,278	45,335	372	689	1,061	·5 to 1	4,504	2,078	6,582	1,333	7,915	10¼	1s. 0¾d.	·8	1·5	2·3
1875	150,[illegible]	45,[illegible]	347	701	1,048	·5 to 1	3,741	2,0[illegible]	5,759	1,414	7,194	9½	11¾	·8	1·5	2·3
1877	150,500	45,345	419	499	1,918	·7 to 1	4,260	2,092	6,352	1,366	8,018	10¼	1s. 0¼d.	·9	1·3	2·2

Expenditure of each Poor Law Union in Ireland since the year 1851—*continued.*

Years	Valuation	Population	Average Daily Number in Receipt of Relief: Indoor	Outdoor under 10 Vic. c. 31	Total	Ratio of Indoor to Outdoor	Expenditure for: In-Maintenance and Clothing	Out Relief under 10 Vic. c. 31	Total	Expenditure under Medical Charities Acts exclusive of Vaccination	Total of Cols. 10 and 11	Poundage: On Amount in Col. 10	On Amount in Col. 12	Percentages of Paupers to Population: Indoor	Outdoor	Total
1	2	3	4	5	6	7	8	9	10	11	12	13	14	15	16	17
Province of Leinster—*continued.*																
Balrothery Union.							£	£	£	£	£	d.	d.			
Area, 75,139 acres.																
1851	87,589	23,748	441	.	441	.	2,181	.	2,181	.	2,181	6	6	1·7	.	1·7
1853	87,588	23,094	431	.	431	.	2,112	.	2,112	845	2,957	5½	8	1·7	.	1·7
1855	87,448	24,797	309	.	309	.	2,065	.	2,065	847	2,912	5¼	8	1·6	.	1·6
1857	87,106	23,510	185	.	185	.	1,169	.	1,169	784	1,953	3¼	5½	·8	.	·8
1859	88,042	22,764	148	.	148	.	943	.	943	841	1,784	2½	4¾	·6	.	·6
1861	86,191	22,016	174	.	174	.	1,529	.	1,529	819	2,348	4¼	6	·7	.	·7
1863	86,180	21,636	204	.	204	.	1,922	.	1,922	916	2,838	5	7½	·9	.	·9
1865	84,461	21,536	170	.	170	.	1,292	.	1,292	920	2,212	3½	6¼	·8	.	·8
1867	94,843	20,046	183	4	186	45 to 1	1,719	.	1,719	961	2,680	4½	6¾	·9	.	·9
1869	94,720	20,436	227	8	235	28·3 to 1	2,054	14	2,068	823	2,891	5½	7¾	1·1	.	1·1
1871	94,819	20,066	223	60	283	3·7 to 1	1,821	146	1,967	957	2,924	5	7¾	1·1	·3	1·4
1873	94,536	20,070	195	152	347	1·2 to 1	2,114	490	2,604	1,144	3,748	6½	9½	1·	·7	1·7
1875	95,087	20,066	123	174	297	0·7 to 1	1,385	470	1,855	1,117	2,972	5	7½	·6	·8	1·4
1877	95,204	20,060	130	229	359	·6 to 1	1,238	778	2,016	1,163	3,179	5	8	·6	1·1	1·7
North Dublin Union.																
Area, 69,759 acres.																
1851	317,531	135,146	2,417	.	2,417		10,721	.	10,721		10,721	8½	8½	1·7	.	1·7
1853	312,531	145,[illegible]	2,657	.	2,657		11,616	.	11,616	1,675	13,291	10½	11½	1·9	.	1·9
1855	312,531	144,981	2,785	.	2,785		19,057	.	19,057	1,961	21,018	1s 2¾d	1s 4¼d	2·	.	2·
1857	313,784	134,897	2,389	.	2,389		14,246	.	14,246	1,905	16,151	11	1s 0¼d	1·7	.	1·7
1859	315,108	134,113	1,830	.	1,830	.	10,977	.	10,977	2,090	13,067	8¼	10	1·3	.	1·3
1861	319,744	134,729	1,769	.	1,769	.	14,089	.	14,089	2,142	16,231	10½	1s 0¼d	1·3	.	1·3
1863	320,944	134,608	1,958	.	1,958	.	16,428	.	16,428	2,452	18,880	1s 0¼d	1s 2¼d	1·4	.	1·4
1865	327,731	134,476	2,015	.	2,015	.	17,564	.	17,564	2,473	20,037	1s 1d	1s 2¾d	1·5	.	1·5
1867	328,610	134,447	2,150	.	2,150	.	18,477	.	18,477	2,496	20,973	1s 1¼d	1s 3¼d	1·6	.	1·6
1869	331,431	134,219	2,077	.	2,077		17,911	.	17,911	2,728	20,639	11¾	1s 1d	1·5	.	1·5
1871	331,265	134,091	2,146	.	2,146		19,053	.	19,053	3,347	22,400	1s 2d	1s 4¼d	1·6	.	1·6
1873	351,640	134,091	2,094	.	2,094		20,310	.	20,310	3,485	23,795	1s 1½d	1s 3¾d	1·5	.	1·5
1875	360,253	134,091	2,084	.	2,084		18,926	.	18,926	3,870	27,196	1s 1¼d	1s 2¾d	1·5	.	1·5
1877	358,017	134,091	2,189	.	2,189		20,773	.	20,773	3,645	24,410	1s 2¼d	1s 4¼d	1·6	.	1·6
South Dublin Union.																
Area, 43,060 acres.																
1851	470,959	197,125	2,985		2,985		14,911		14,911		14,911	7¼	7¼	1·5	.	1·5
1853	479,070	190,056	3,109	189	3,298	16·4 to 1	14,409	330	14,739	2,923	17,662	8¼	9¾	1·5	·1	1·6
1855	479,049	198,853	3,374	461	3,835	7·4 to 1	20,918	1,991	22,909	3,233	26,142	1s 2¾d	1s 4¼d	1·7	·2	1·9
1857	492,174	189,867	2,950	258	3,208	11·4 to 1	18,872	611	19,483	2,674	22,157	9½	11	1·6	·1	1·6
1859	497,774	200,[illegible]81	2,237	241	2,478	8·6 to 1	12,505	341	12,846	2,665	15,511	6¼	7½	1·1	·1	1·2
1861	509,344	201,694	2,467	445	2,912	5·5 to 1	20,542	845	21,387	2,647	24,034	10	11¾	1·2	·2	1·4
1863	517,439	201,780	2,732	605	3,337	4·5 to 1	23,350	822	24,172	2,987	26,159	11¼	1s 1¼d	1·3	·3	1·6
1865	524,132	200,828	3,355	556	3,911	6·0 to 1	29,681	927	30,608	3,106	33,714	1s 1¾d	1s 3¼d	1·7	·2	1·9
1867	518,443	199,372	3,434	705	4,139	4·9 to 1	34,495	1,900	36,395	3,111	39,506	1s 4d	1s 5¼d	1·7	·3	2·
1869	535,075	199,056	3,571	429	4,000	8·3 to 1	31,030	263	31,293	3,130	34,423	1s 2¼d	1s 3¼d	1·7	·2	1·9
1871	567,925	199,812	3,266	535	3,801	6·2 to 1	31,218	354	31,588	3,060	34,[illegible]	1s 2¼d	1s 4¼d	1·6	·3	1·9
1873	606,796	199,812	3,033	519	3,552	5·8 to 1	34,274	911	35,185	3,952	39,137	1s 1¼d	1s 3¼d	1·5	·2	1·7
1875	616,256	199,512	3,203	421	3,674	7·6 to 1	32,278	713	32,990	4,063	37,653	1s 1¼d	1s 2¾d	1·6	·2	1·8
1877	621,580	199,512	2,921	425	3,346	7·0 to 1	29,750	704	30,454	4,441	34,895	11¾	1s 1¼d	1·5	·2	1·7
Rathdown Union.																
Area, 61,516 acres.																
1851	162,460	45,146	494	.	494		2,309	.	2,309		2,309	3½	3½	1·	.	1·
1853	162,460	49,172	573	.	573		3,015	.	3,015	1,474	4,489	4½	7¼	1·1	.	1·1
1855	162,460	50,304	530	.	530		3,960	.	3,960	1,217	5,177	5¾	7½	1·	.	1·
1857	164,491	51,226	425	.	425		2,832	.	2,832	1,431	4,263	4¼	6¼	·8	.	·8
1859	171,916	52,284	317	.	317		2,292	.	2,292	1,352	3,644	3¼	5	·6	.	·6
1861	191,744	53,296	348	.	348		3,052	.	3,052	1,294	4,346	4	5½	·6	.	·6
1863	201,834	53,578	469	.	469		3,915	.	3,915	1,451	5,366	4¾	6½	·8	.	·8
1865	214,087	53,656	491	.	491		4,345	.	4,345	1,509	5,854	4¾	6½	·9	.	·9
1867	220,204	54,136	544	.	544	.	5,143	.	5,143	1,712	6,855	5½	7½	1·	.	1·
1869	228,376	54,410	491	.	491	.	4,367	.	4,367	1,722	6,089	4½	6½	·9	.	·9
1871	238,676	54,637	508	.	508	.	5,566	.	5,566	2,171	7,736	5½	8½	·9	.	·9
1873	246,209	54,097	533	.	533	.	6,417	.	6,417	2,028	8,445	6¼	8¼	·9	.	·9
1875	248,204	54,097	559	.	559	.	6,649	.	6,649	2,019	8,668	6½	8½	1·	.	1·
1877	251,394	54,097	551	.	551	.	6,731	.	6,731	1,995	8,726	6¼	8¼	1·0	.	1·0
Athy Union.																
Area, 160,254 acres.																
1851	89,837	37,671	875	.	875	.	3,046	.	3,046	.	3,046	7½	7½	2·3	.	2·3
1853	88,487	34,719	583	13	596	45·0 to 1	2,460	38	2,498	627	3,125	6	8	1·6	.	1·6
1855	99,597	33,887	492	4	496	118·6 to 1	2,664	30	2,694	844	3,538	6½	8½	1·3	.	1·3
1857	104,371	31,895	329	19	348	17·3 to 1	1,901	115	2,016	852	2,868	4½	6½	·9	.	·9
1859	104,437	34,403	235	46	281	4 to 1	1,327	160	1,487	621	2,108	3½	4¾	·7	·1	·8
1861	108,614	33,910	279	101	380	2·7 to 1	1,690	452	2,142	909	3,051	4¾	7¼	·8	·3	1·1
1863	108,744	32,594	334	182	516	1·8 to 1	2,207	479	2,686	895	3,581	6	7	1·	·6	1·6
1865	109,908	31,949	360	188	548	1·9 to 1	2,314	467	2,779	934	3,713	6½	8½	1·1	·6	1·7
1867	108,824	31,289	360	160	520	2·2 to 1	2,857	565	3,422	1,039	4,461	7½	9½	1·1	·5	1·6
1869	108,881	30,142	316	284	600	1 to 1	2,645	730	3,375	1,170	4,545	7	10	1·	·9	1·9
1871	108,156	27,825	297	254	551	1·1 to 1	2,820	1,018	3,838	1,193	5,031	8½	11	1·	·9	1·8
1873	108,893	29,015	301	431	732	0·7 to 1	4,062	1,235	4,987	1,104	6,131	9¼	1s 0d	1·	1·4	2·4
1875	107,897	30,026	308	377	685	0·8 to 1	3,063	1,119	4,182	1,107	5,289	9¼	1s 0¼d	1·	1·2	2·2
1877	109,846	30,025	311	400	711	·8 to 1	4,134	1,257	5,386	1,230	6,616	11½	1s 1¼d	1·0	1·3	2·3

Appendix A. — Poor Relief.

No. 6.—Statistical Table showing the progress of the Pauperism and

Years.	Valuation.	Population.	Average Daily Number in Receipt of Relief: In-door	Out-door, under 10 Vic. c. 31.	Total	Ratio of Indoor to Outdoor	Expenditure for: In Maintenance and Clothing.	Out Relief under 10 Vic. c. 31.	Total	Expenditure under Medical Charities Acts, exclusive of Vaccination	Total of Cols. 10 and 11.	Poundage: On Account in Col. 10	On Amount in Col. 12	Per centage of Paupers to Population: In-door.	Out-door.	Total.
1	2	3	4.	5.	6	7	8	9	10	11	12	13	14.	15.	16.	17.
Province of Leinster—continued.																
Celbridge Union							£	£	£	£	£	d.	d.			
Area, 86,856 acres.																
1851	107,478	22,547	337	.	337	.	1,984	.	1,984	.	1,984	4½	4½	1·4	.	1·
1853	107,478	21,964	243	.	245	.	1,278	.	1,278	1,068	2,346	2½	5½	1·1	.	1·1
1855	107,470	21,369	213	.	214	.	1,738	.	1,738	639	2,377	5½	5½	1·0	.	1·0
1857	109,593	20,769	159	7	167	22·7 to 1	1,340	47	1,447	686	2,033	3	4½	·9	.	·9
1859	109,890	20,173	174	4	177	43 to 1	1,184	24	1,209	631	1,836	3½	4½	·8	.	·8
1861	114,275	19,889	212	66	277	3·2 to 1	1,870	277	2,147	678	2,825	4½	6	1·0	·4	1·4
1863	114,674	19,278	187	146	333	1·3 to 1	1,501	406	1,987	772	2,679	4½	5½	·9	·7	1·6
1865	114,708	18,974	221	158	379	1·4 to 1	1,806	627	2,433	789	3,222	5⅛	6½	1·2	·8	2·0
1867	114,789	18,670	233	171	404	1·3 to 1	2,479	591	3,070	756	3,826	6½	8	1·2	·9	2·1
1869	114,668	18,366	170	164	334	1· to 1	1,888	590	2,478	849	3,327	5½	7	·9	·9	1·8
1871	114,609	18,062	168	204	372	0·8 to 1	2,014	784	2,797	911	3,708	6	7½	·9	1·1	2·0
1873	114,607	18,062	160	247	407	0·6 to 1	2,056	802	2,858	890	3,698	6¼	8½	·9	1·3	2·2
1875	114,674	18,062	157	253	406	0·6 to 1	1,979	968	2,950	844	3,688	6½	8	·8	1·4	2·2
1877	114,890	18,062	158	251	409	0·6 to 1	1,998	965	2,956	826	3,786	6½	8	·8	1·4	2·3
Naas Union																
Area, 216,629 acres.																
1851	140,450	44,862	1,835	.	1,835	.	4,382	.	4,382	.	4,382	7½	7½	3·8	.	3·8
1853	140,450	43,830	672	8	680	109 to 1	3,378	23	3,401	1,107	4,508	5½	7½	1·5	.	1·5
1855	140,450	42,630	439	36	475	15 to 1	3,150	160	3,310	803	4,113	5½	7	1·2	·1	1·3
1857	142,344	41,026	418	53	436	7·9 to 1	2,210	125	2,335	769	3,104	4	5½	1·0	·1	1·1
1859	142,642	40,818	338	52	391	6·5 to 1	1,773	120	1,893	887	2,779	3½	4½	·7	·1	·8
1861	148,410	39,900	372	89	461	3·7 to 1	2,257	251	2,508	766	3,274	4	5½	·8	·2	1·0
1863	150,890	40,680	452	144	496	2·4 to 1	2,391	401	2,992	786	3,778	4½	6	·9	·3	1·2
1865	151,230	41,300	332	275	607	1·2 to 1	2,478	672	3,150	888	4,038	5	6½	·8	·6	1·4
1867	151,609	42,440	354	350	704	1 to 1	3,100	827	4,046	1,133	5,179	6½	8½	·8	·8	1·6
1869	151,780	43,820	317	387	704	0·8 to 1	2,662	1,000	3,662	1,080	4,942	5½	7½	·7	·9	1·6
1871	151,891	44,187	293	598	891	0·5 to 1	2,661	1,353	4,014	1,137	5,151	6½	8½	·7	1·1	1·8
1873	152,417	44,187	336	514	850	0·6 to 1	3,283	1,565	4,848	1,183	6,031	7½	9½	·7	1·2	1·9
1875	152,573	44,187	317	593	910	0·5 to 1	3,480	1,768	5,248	1,381	6,630	8½	10½	·7	1·3	2·0
1877	152,637	44,187	345	584	929	0·6 to 1	3,988	1,936	5,924	1,397	7,321	9½	11½	·8	1·3	2·1
Callan Union																
Area, 104,011 acres.																
1851	73,046	32,748	1,446	.	1,446	.	5,655	.	5,655	.	5,655	1s. 6½d.	1s. 6½d.	4·7	.	4·7
1853	73,046	31,395	853	159	1,012	5·3 to 1	3,224	226	3,450	544	3,994	11½	1s. 1½d.	2·7	·5	3·2
1855	73,046	28,787	618	61	679	8·5 to 1	3,046	190	3,236	454	3,690	10½	1s. 0½d.	1·9	·2	2·1
1857	72,983	28,181	367	44	411	9 to 1	2,460	108	2,568	486	3,049	8½	10	1·4	·1	1·5
1859	72,952	26,323	263	32	295	8·2 to 1	1,584	68	1,652	452	2,104	5½	7	1·	·1	1·1
1861	73,204	24,969	315	39	354	8 to 1	2,304	115	2,419	529	3,048	8½	10	1·3	·1	1·4
1863	73,230	24,138	373	164	537	1·9 to 1	2,238	346	2,614	544	3,158	8½	10½	1·5	·7	2·
1865	73,758	23,297	300	189	489	1·6 to 1	2,172	484	2,656	660	3,296	8½	10½	1·3	·8	2·
1867	73,750	22,446	293	264	587	1·1 to 1	2,558	560	3,117	533	3,650	10½	1s. 1d.	1·3	1·2	2·5
1869	73,225	21,605	256	292	548	1 to 1	2,549	730	3,279	486	3,795	10½	1s. 0½d.	1·1	1·3	2·7
1871	73,405	20,764	239	341	580	0·7 to 1	2,364	780	3,144	585	3,729	10½	1s. 0½d.	1·2	1·6	2·8
1873	73,405	20,764	294	345	639	0·8 to 1	2,925	877	3,802	579	4,381	1s. 0½d.	1s. 2½d.	1·4	1·4	2·8
1875	73,485	20,764	284	342	630	0·8 to 1	2,688	868	3,556	539	4,095	11½	1s. 1½d.	1·4	1·6	3·
1877	72,973	20,764	273	407	680	0·6 to 1	2,558	1,178	3,736	548	4,274	1s. 0½d.	1s. 2d.	1·3	1·9	3·3
Castlecomer Union																
Area, 57,839 acres.																
1851	32,677	18,479	237	.	237	.	1,152	.	1,152	.	1,152	8½	8½	1·3	.	1·3
1853	32,677	17,903	136	609	745	2 to 1	731	1,007	1,741	338	2,079	1s. 1½d.	1s. 3d.	·7	3·4	4·1
1855	32,577	17,485	210	30	240	7 to 1	1,810	107	1,917	345	2,259	1s. 2½d.	1s. 4½d.	1·2	·2	1·4
1857	32,094	16,951	130	55	185	2·4 to 1	1,121	216	1,334	345	1,680	10	1s. 0½d.	·8	·3	1·1
1859	32,851	16,444	104	93	197	1·1 to 1	808	496	1,314	385	1,699	10	1s. 1d.	·6	·5	1·1
1861	32,101	14,937	134	196	330	1·5 to 1	1,257	636	1,893	367	2,259	1s. 2½d.	1s. 3d.	·8	1·2	2·
1863	33,110	14,810	159	229	388	1·5 to 1	1,425	760	2,185	400	2,585	1s. 4½d.	1s. 7½d.	1·0	1·5	2·5
1865	32,112	15,983	148	188	342	1·3 to 1	1,227	508	1,735	318	2,053	1s. 1d.	1s. 3d.	·9	1·2	2·1
1867	33,101	14,956	152	244	396	1·6 to 1	1,473	673	2,095	378	2,473	1s. 8d.	1s. 6½d.	1·0	1·6	2·7
1869	32,130	14,679	186	238	394	1·9 to 1	1,270	723	2,023	438	2,427	1s. 3d.	1s. 6½d.	·9	1·7	2·7
1871	32,228	14,383	145	248	393	1·7 to 1	1,535	734	2,269	451	2,740	1s. 8d.	1s. 8½d.	1·0	1·7	2·7
1873	32,406	14,803	151	235	383	1·7 to 1	1,584	742	2,326	464	2,790	1s. 8½d.	1s. 6½d.	·9	1·6	2·5
1875	32,429	14,396	142	214	356	1·5 to 1	1,606	780	2,386	498	2,884	1s. 8½d.	1s. 8½d.	1·0	1·5	2·5
1877	32,417	14,803	135	218	348	0·6 to 1	1,563	704	2,267	493	2,760	1s. 8d.	1s. 8½d.	·9	1·5	2·4
Kilkenny Union.																
Area, 110,948 acres																
1851	97,297	46,718	1,702	.	1,702	.	7,836	.	7,836	.	7,836	1s. 7½d.	1s. 7½d.	3·8	.	3·8
1853	97,297	44,457	1,356	.	1,360	.	6,353	.	6,335	982	7,765	1s. 3½d.	1s. 6d.	3·0	.	3·0
1855	97,297	42,295	982	.	982	.	6,756	.	6,756	738	7,494	1s. 4½d.	1s. 6½d.	2·3	.	2·3
1857	100,883	39,068	686	.	686	.	4,584	.	4,584	826	5,389	10½	1s. 0½d.	1·7	.	1·7
1859	100,883	37,741	652	3	654	326 to 1	4,262	16	4,273	891	5,166	10½	1s. 0½d.	1·7	.	1·7
1861	100,985	35,489	621	344	965	1·8 to 1	4,260	701	4,960	894	5,854	11½	1s. 2d.	1·7	·9	2·7
1863	99,783	34,667	638	326	964	1·7 to 1	4,507	711	5,218	963	6,181	1s. 2½d.	1s. 2½d.	1·8	·9	2·8
1865	99,983	33,778	606	484	1,090	1·3 to 1	4,667	910	5,577	852	6,429	1s. 1½d.	1s. 3½d.	1·8	1·3	3·1
1867	100,904	32,815	714	583	1,297	1·2 to 1	5,168	1,160	7,028	863	7,891	1s. 4½d.	1s. 7d.	2·1	1·8	3·9
1869	100,948	32,064	502	777	1,279	·6 to 1	4,875	1,486	6,361	1,008	6,669	1s. 1½d.	1s. 2½d.	1·5	2·4	3·9
1871	100,245	31,198	621	777	1,788	·7 to 1	5,068	1,574	6,642	966	7,608	1s. 4d.	1s. 6½d.	1·6	2·5	4·1
1873	100,550	31,195	599	801	1,400	·7 to 1	5,900	1,971	7,379	987	8,766	1s. 7d.	1s. 8½d.	1·9	2·5	4·4
1875	100,397	31,188	515	644	1,159	·8 to 1	5,100	1,795	6,895	1,087	7,986	1s. 4½d.	1s. 7d.	1·6	2·0	3·7
1877	100,323	31,193	495	552	1,047	·8 to 1	5,276	1,683	6,958	1,053	8,061	1s. 4½d.	1s. 7½d.	1·6	1·8	3·5

Expenditure of each Poor Law Union in Ireland since the year 1851—*continued.*

Years	Valuation	Population	Average Daily Number on Receipt of Relief: In-door	Out-door, under 10 Vic. c. 31	Total	Ratio of In-door to Out-door	Expenditure for: In-Maintenance and Clothing	Out-Relief under 10 Vic. c. 31	Total	Expenditure under Medical Charities Acts, exclusive of Vaccination	Total of Cols. 10 and 11	Poundage: On Amount in Col. 10	On Amount in Col. 12	Per-centage of Paupers on Population: In-door	Out-door	Total
1	2	3	4	5	6	7	8	9	10	11	12	13	14	15	16	17
Province of Leinster—*continued.*																
Thomastown Union.							£	£	£	£	£	d.	d.			
Area, 107,477 acres.																
1851	65,245	27,298	580	.	580	.	3,840	.	3,840	.	3,840	1s. 2¼d.	1s. 2¼d.	3·2	.	3·2
1853	65,245	26,117	361	31	392	18·2 to 1	2,675	57	2,682	414	3,106	9¼	11¼	2·1	·1	2·2
1855	65,245	24,830	339	18	357	18·8 to 1	2,214	48	2,262	413	2,675	8½	9¾	1·3	·1	1·4
1857	65,006	23,761	240	22	262	10·9 to 1	1,680	50	1,730	451	2,180	6¼	8	1·	·1	1·1
1859	64,964	22,583	215	34	249	6·4 to 1	1,428	68	1,496	476	1,972	5½	7¼	1·	·1	1·1
1861	64,683	21,405	227	53	280	4 to 1	1,817	100	1,925	493	2,419	7¼	9¼	1·2	·2	1·3
1863	64,955	20,085	244	78	322	3·1 to 1	1,851	170	2,021	457	2,478	7½	9¼	1·1	·4	1·5
1865	64,967	20,360	217	147	434	1·9 to 1	2,160	273	2,433	484	2,867	9	10¼	1·3	·7	2·0
1867	65,790	19,861	269	166	435	1·6 to 1	2,177	287	2,494	485	2,900	9	10¼	1·3	·8	2·1
1869	65,790	19,481	242	181	423	1·3 to 1	1,917	438	2,355	476	2,781	8½	10	1·2	·9	2·1
1871	65,946	18,817	271	212	483	1·2 to 1	1,771	459	2,230	473	2,703	8	9¾	1·4	1·1	2·5
1873	66,284	18,817	231	321	552	1·4 to 1	2,101	665	2,766	514	3,280	10	11¾	1·1	1·7	2·9
1875	66,362	18,817	220	298	518	1·3 to 1	2,018	663	2,681	504	3,185	9¾	11½	1·1	1·6	2·7
1877	66,241	18,817	231	234	465	0·8 to 1	1,884	577	2,461	497	2,958	9	10¾	1·1	1·3	2·4
Urlingford Union.																
Area, 75,149 acres.																
1851	45,208	19,631	840	.	840	.	3,632	.	3,632	.	3,632	1s. 7¼d.	1s. 7¼d.	4·3	.	4·3
1853	45,208	18,849	507	5	512	101·4 to 1	2,233	17	2,250	395	2,650	1s. 0d.	1s. 2d.	2·7	.	2·7
1855	45,208	18,013	295	6	301	49 to 1	1,854	16	1,871	405	2,276	9¾	1s. 0d.	1·6	.	1·6
1857	45,225	17,187	157	6	163	26·1 to 1	1,116	16	1,132	418	1,550	6	8¼	·9	.	·9
1859	45,270	16,536	125	19	144	6·6 to 1	870	40	910	423	1,333	4¾	7	·8	·1	·9
1861	45,314	15,325	164	10	174	16·4 to 1	1,365	66	1,431	427	1,858	7½	9¾	1·	·1	1·1
1863	45,762	14,943	184	62	246	3· to 1	1,490	206	1,646	457	2,073	8¾	11	1·2	·4	1·6
1865	45,798	14,364	164	51	215	3·2 to 1	1,184	204	1,390	450	1,840	7½	9¾	1·1	·3	1·4
1867	45,484	13,782	174	61	235	2·9 to 1	1,375	182	1,557	439	1,996	8	10¼	1·3	·5	1·8
1869	45,488	13,783	171	52	223	3·3 to 1	1,513	185	1,698	546	2,244	8	10½	1·3	·4	1·7
1871	45,469	12,623	161	74	235	2·2 to 1	1,616	249	1,865	517	2,372	9¼	1s. 0¼d.	1·3	·6	1·9
1873	45,475	12,623	157	112	269	1·4 to 1	1,717	355	2,072	516	2,588	11	1s. 1¾d.	1·3	·9	2·1
1875	45,490	12,623	138	112	250	1·2 to 1	1,425	365	1,790	530	2,310	9½	1s. 0¼d.	1·1	·8	1·9
1877	45,491	12,623	144	117	261	1·2 to 1	1,534	391	1,925	471	2,396	10	1s. 0¾d.	1·1	·9	2·0
Edenderry Union.																
Area, 172,407 acres.																
1851	94,309	29,791	813	.	813	.	3,162	.	3,162	.	3,162	9	9½	2·8	.	2·8
1853	93,589	28,500	712	16	728	44·5 to 1	2,861	29	2,890	784	3,674	7½	9½	2·5	.	2·5
1855	93,589	27,227	492	9	501	54·6 to 1	2,921	30	2,951	689	3,640	7½	9¼	1·8	.	1·8
1857	93,976	25,916	415	1	416	415 to 1	2,447	10	2,457	678	3,135	6¼	8	1·6	.	1·6
1859	94,849	24,645	287	4	291	71·7 to 1	1,855	36	1,891	711	2,602	4¾	6½	1·3	.	1·3
1861	95,187	23,354	316	24	340	13·2 to 1	2,319	66	2,385	662	3,047	6	7½	1·4	·1	1·5
1863	94,345	22,755	321	26	347	12·3 to 1	2,211	75	2,286	692	2,978	5¾	7½	1·4	·1	1·5
1865	95,261	22,025	273	27	300	10 to 1	1,642	49	1,691	681	2,370	4¼	6	1·2	·1	1·3
1867	95,271	21,482	207	48	255	4·1 to 1	1,487	141	1,628	763	2,371	4	6	·9	·2	1·1
1869	96,324	20,909	276	57	333	5 to 1	1,637	105	1,742	745	2,487	4½	6¼	1·4	·1	1·5
1871	96,420	20,166	183	63	245	3 to 1	1,603	280	1,783	634	2,627	4½	6¼	·9	·3	1·2
1873	95,494	20,166	180	119	299	1·5 to 1	1,747	303	2,050	964	3,014	5¼	7½	·9	·5	1·4
1875	95,540	20,166	227	127	354	1·7 to 1	1,867	192	2,059	939	2,998	5¼	7½	1·1	·6	1·7
1877	95,580	20,166	176	216	392	1·5 to 1	1,636	252	2,188	984	3,172	5¼	8	·8	·6	1·4
Parsonstown Union.																
Area, 230,457 acres.																
1851	87,177	49,681	1,227	.	1,227	.	4,184	.	4,184	.	4,184	11½	11½	2·7	.	2·7
1853	87,177	47,590	770	.	770	.	3,159	.	3,159	919	4,078	8¾	11¼	1·6	.	1·6
1855	87,177	45,520	394	.	394	.	1,547	.	1,547	621	2,168	4¼	6	·7	.	·7
1857	101,228	43,470	234	.	234	.	1,529	.	1,529	640	2,169	3¾	5¼	·5	.	·5
1859	101,977	41,430	230	.	230	.	1,416	.	1,416	755	2,171	3¼	5¼	·5	.	·5
1861	101,995	39,350	276	.	276	.	2,159	.	2,159	645	2,804	5	7	·7	.	·7
1863	102,325	37,912	341	.	341	.	2,084	.	2,084	827	2,911	4¾	6¼	·9	.	·9
1865	102,206	36,514	310	.	310	.	2,183	.	2,183	641	2,824	5¼	7	·8	.	·8
1867	102,143	35,040	314	.	314	.	2,437	.	2,437	916	3,353	5¾	7½	·9	.	·9
1869	102,036	33,618	288	.	288	.	2,477	.	2,477	912	3,389	5¾	8	·8	.	·8
1871	102,516	31,261	266	.	266	.	2,180	.	2,180	902	3,082	5	7	·8	.	·8
1873	102,495	31,262	239	.	239	.	2,411	.	2,411	863	3,274	5½	7¾	·7	.	·7
1875	102,560	32,251	244	.	244	.	2,308	.	2,308	1,073	3,375	5¼	7¾	·7	.	·7
1877	102,587	32,251	238	19	257	.	2,238	73	2,261	1,043	3,374	5¼	7¾	·7	.	·7
Tullamore Union.																
Area, 155,396 acres.																
1851	80,846	41,180	1,351	.	1,351	.	5,979	.	5,979	.	5,979	1s. 5¾d.	1s. 5¾d.	3·7	.	3·7
1853	80,855	39,535	991	256	1,247	3·5 to 1	4,145	391	4,536	857	5,393	1s. 1½d.	1s. 4d.	2·5	·6	3·1
1855	80,855	37,923	597	112	709	5·3 to 1	4,891	271	5,162	687	5,849	1s. 3d.	1s. 5¼d.	1·6	·3	1·8
1857	80,916	36,311	414	6	420	69 to 1	2,800	6	2,806	623	3,429	7	9	1·2	.	1·1
1859	81,018	34,699	368	2	370	184 to 1	2,031	4	2,035	667	2,702	6	8	1·0	.	1·0
1861	81,314	33,087	394	6	400	64 to 1	2,878	16	2,894	590	3,488	8	10	1·1	.	1·2
1863	82,460	32,132	440	33	473	13·3 to 1	3,052	180	3,232	787	3,949	9½	11½	1·3	·1	1·4
1865	82,881	31,219	429	112	541	3·8 to 1	3,695	291	3,986	653	4,739	9	11	1·4	·3	1·7
1867	84,435	30,306	429	214	643	2 to 1	3,905	530	4,435	650	5,085	1s. 0¾d.	1s. 2¼d.	1·4	·7	2·1
1869	82,487	29,363	350	235	585	1·5 to 1	2,994	555	3,549	712	4,262	10¼	1s. 0¾d.	1·2	·7	2·0
1871	81,995	28,420	354	273	627	1·3 to 1	2,934	946	3,880	778	4,612	11¼	1s. 1½d.	1·2	1·0	2·2
1873	81,988	28,420	343	349	692	1· to 1	3,036	1,226	4,262	755	5,008	1s. 0d.	1s. 2¾d.	1·2	1·2	2·4
1875	83,095	28,420	313	348	661	1· to 1	2,874	1,293	4,167	814	4,983	1s. 0d.	1s. 2¼d.	1·1	1·2	2·3
1877	83,174	28,420	354	355	709	1· to 1	2,852	1,611	4,463	749	5,212	1s. 1d.	1s. 3¼d.	1·2	1·2	2·4

APPENDIX A.

Poor Relief

No. 6.—STATISTICAL TABLE showing the progress of the Pauperism and

Years	Valuation	Population	Average Daily Number in Receipt of Relief: In-door	Out-door, under 10 Vic. c. 31	Total	Ratio of In-door to Out-door	Expenditure for: In-Maintenance and Clothing	Out Relief under 10 Vic. c. 31	Total	Expenditure under Medical Charities Acts, exclusive of Vaccination	Total of Cols. 10 and 11	Poundage: On Amount in Col. 10	On Amount in Col. 12	Percentage of Paupers to Population: In-door	Out-door	Total
1	2	3	4	5	6	7	8	9	10	11	12	13	14	15	16	17
Province of Leinster—continued.																
BALLYMAHON UNION.							£	£	£	£	£	d.	d.			
Area, 100,196 acres.																
1851	62,309	26,268	604	.	604	.	2,885	.	2,885	.	2,885	1s. 1½d.	1s. 1½d.	2·3	.	2·3
1853	62,180	25,405	497	.	497	.	1,626	.	1,626	259	1,885	7½	8½	1·9	.	1·9
1855	62,509	24,676	172	.	172	.	1,210	.	1,210	278	1,488	5¼	6½	·7	.	·7
1857	62,488	24,747	108	.	108	.	687	.	687	293	980	3½	3¾	·4	.	·4
1859	62,487	23,918	105	.	105	.	706	.	706	321	1,027	3½	4	·4	.	·4
1861	67,460	23,029	152	6	158	27 to 1	1,084	58	1,138	288	1,440	4½	5½	·6	.	·6
1863	62,840	21,426	172	12	184	14·3 to 1	1,227	63	1,290	361	1,651	5	6½	·8	.	·8
1865	62,107	20,766	174	28	202	6·2 to 1	1,317	96	1,413	355	1,768	5½	7	·8	·1	·9
1867	62,169	20,164	152	20	172	7·6 to 1	1,376	85	1,460	362	1,721	5½	6½	·7	·1	·8
1869	62,134	19,446	145	19	164	7·1 to 1	1,187	84	1,271	364	1,635	5	6½	·7	·1	·8
1871	61,978	18,786	125	30	155	4·1 to 1	1,134	173	1,308	403	1,749	4½	6½	·7	·1	·8
1873	61,843	18,786	131	41	172	3·1 to 1	1,419	244	1,663	486	2,149	6¼	8½	·7	·2	·9
1875	61,910	18,786	118	87	205	1·4 to 1	1,175	274	1,449	430	1,878	5½	7½	·6	·5	1·1
1877	61,916	18,786	109	122	231	·9 to 1	1,180	258	1,438	440	1,878	6	7½	·5	·7	1·2
GRANARD UNION.																
Area, 134,003 acres.																
1851	68,910	41,473	1,534	.	1,544	.	3,043	.	3,046	.	3,046	1s. 6d.	1s. 6d.	3·7	.	3·7
1853	66,919	40,127	784	.	784	.	2,463	.	2,463	753	3,216	9½	11½	1·9	.	1·9
1855	66,919	39,861	356	.	356	.	2,081	.	2,088	508	2,596	7½	9½	·9	.	·9
1857	64,348	38,215	248	.	248	.	1,484	.	1,484	613	2,097	4½	6	·6	.	·6
1859	64,747	37,129	216	.	216	.	1,295	.	1,295	658	2,073	4	6½	·5	.	·5
1861	64,854	36,043	210	1	211	210 to 1	1,749	3	1,761	719	2,478	5	7	·6	.	·6
1863	64,578	35,561	274	228	502	1·2 to 1	1,981	599	2,580	786	3,296	7½	9½	·8	·6	1·4
1865	64,623	34,089	291	288	579	1 to 1	1,816	641	2,457	718	3,175	7	9	·8	·8	1·6
1867	64,680	34,597	278	684	962	·4 to 1	2,166	1,174	3,240	751	3,991	8½	11½	·8	1·9	2·7
1869	64,925	34,175	249	491	740	·4 to 1	1,878	1,209	3,182	799	3,981	9	11½	·7	1·6	2·3
1871	64,955	34,645	212	621	833	·3 to 1	1,934	1,573	3,507	857	4,364	10	1s. 0½d.	·6	1·9	2·5
1873	65,213	34,663	233	643	874	·3 to 1	2,413	1,751	4,164	880	5,046	11½	1s. 2½d.	·7	1·8	2·6
1875	65,416	31,099	210	646	856	·3 to 1	1,974	1,086	3,060	892	4,449	10½	1s. 1½d.	·6	1·9	2·5
1877	65,481	33,833	236	618	849	·3 to 1	1,943	1,890	3,833	978	4,811	10½	1s. 1½d.	·6	1·9	2·5
LONGFORD UNION.																
Area, 109,981 acres.																
1851	54,917	37,655	1,289	.	1,289	.	3,165	.	3,165	.	3,165	1s. 10½d.	1s. 10½d.	3·5	.	3·5
1853	55,857	35,193	616	.	616	.	2,051	.	2,051	496	2,547	8½	10½	1·7	.	1·7
1855	55,917	35,354	287	.	287	.	1,443	.	1,443	341	1,784	6½	7½	·7	.	·7
1857	50,126	34,478	229	.	229	.	1,521	.	1,521	351	1,874	6½	7½	·6	.	·6
1859	50,108	33,616	208	.	208	.	1,276	.	1,476	311	1,587	5½	6½	·6	.	·6
1861	52,948	32,757	251	1	252	251 to 1	1,909	15	1,924	307	2,231	7½	9	·7	.	·7
1863	58,460	32,110	397	13	410	30·5 to 1	2,572	67	2,639	312	2,951	10½	1s. 0d.	1·2	.	1·2
1865	59,620	31,465	402	42	444	9·6 to 1	2,789	148	2,937	388	3,315	1s. 0½d.	1s. 1½d.	1·3	·1	1·3
1867	59,374	30,830	340	94	444	3·7 to 1	2,590	254	2,774	373	3,147	11½	1s. 0½d.	1·1	·3	1·4
1869	59,440	30,175	318	182	500	2· to 1	2,391	349	2,730	457	3,037	11	1s. 0½d.	1·2	·4	1·6
1871	60,778	29,830	280	220	509	1·3 to 1	2,820	662	3,482	389	3,231	11½	1s. 1½d.	1·0	·7	1·7
1873	59,691	29,830	280	417	697	·6 to 1	3,521	847	3,463	451	3,814	1s. 1½d.	1s. 4½d.	1·0	1·0	2·0
1875	60,105	29,530	275	343	617	·8 to 1	2,569	537	3,106	496	3,602	1s. 0½d.	1s. 2½d.	·9	1·1	2·0
1877	60,080	29,830	220	288	508	·8 to 1	2,684	750	2,716	509	3,225	11½	1s. 1d.	·7	1·0	1·7
ARDEE UNION.																
Area, 96,211 acres.																
1851	93,081	32,768	609	.	609	.	2,389	.	2,383	.	2,383	8½	8½	1·8	.	1·8
1853	94,081	31,273	449	.	449	.	1,940	.	1,890	617	2,507	5	6½	1·4	.	1·4
1855	93,081	29,775	317	.	317	.	1,797	.	1,797	688	2,485	6½	9½	1·7	.	1·7
1857	92,804	28,278	213	.	213	.	1,542	.	1,542	692	2,234	4	5½	·8	.	·8
1859	92,890	27,751	228	.	228	.	1,484	.	1,484	672	2,156	4½	5½	·9	.	·9
1861	93,778	25,384	266	251	567	1 to 1	2,189	243	2,552	652	3,204	6½	8½	1·2	1·1	2·3
1863	93,786	24,642	350	.	350	.	2,319	.	2,319	710	3,019	5½	7½	1·5	.	1·5
1865	94,796	24,682	300	123	423	2·5 to 1	2,498	738	3,336	711	4,047	8½	10½	1·2	·5	1·7
1867	93,960	23,483	292	113	405	1·8 to 1	3,070	864	3,674	735	4,437	9½	11½	1·1	·5	1·7
1869	93,761	22,882	290	290	580	1· to 1	3,157	1,149	4,306	761	5,070	11	1s. 1d.	1·3	1·1	2·4
1871	91,096	23,362	250	541	801	·5 to 1	2,841	1,605	4,346	797	5,143	11	1s. 1½d.	1·1	2·4	3·5
1873	94,084	22,363	262	643	905	·4 to 1	2,955	1,908	4,863	869	5,732	1s. 0½d.	1s. 2½d.	1·1	3·0	4·0
1875	94,145	22,262	221	593	814	·4 to 1	2,800	1,607	4,407	872	5,279	11½	1s. 1½d.	1·0	2·6	3·6
1877	94,134	22,383	215	415	630	·5 to 1	2,542	1,396	3,938	897	4,835	10	1s. 0½d.	·9	1·9	2·8
DROGHEDA UNION.																
Area, 90,045 acres.																
1851	118,228	47,240	605	.	606	.	2,955	.	2,388	.	2,884	4½	4½	1·2	.	1·2
1853	116,221	45,761	590	80	670	7·4 to 1	2,826	97	2,923	884	3,807	6	7½	1·3	·1	1·4
1855	116,222	44,376	460	14	474	40 to 1	3,424	70	3,494	890	4,324	7½	9½	1·2	.	1·2
1857	119,790	42,701	392	32	424	12 to 1	2,796	96	2,892	775	3,667	5½	7½	·9	.	·9
1859	119,657	41,808	440	99	539	4 to 1	2,913	245	3,158	880	4,038	6½	8½	1·	·2	1·3
1861	124,940	39,881	494	548	1,042	1 to 1	4,080	800	4,880	823	5,683	9½	11	1·3	·6	2·
1863	121,468	35,799	467	498	965	1 to 1	3,901	948	4,849	818	5,758	9½	11	1·1	1·1	2·2
1865	126,783	37,781	396	719	1,115	·5 to 1	2,727	1,163	3,890	852	4,742	7½	9½	1·	1·9	2·9
1867	124,497	36,763	404	883	1,287	·5 to 1	2,974	1,142	4,116	835	4,961	8	9½	1·1	2·4	3·5
1869	124,377	44,745	429	940	1,369	·4 to 1	3,719	2,044	5,764	899	6,663	11	1s. 0½d.	1·2	2·6	3·8
1871	124,708	34,727	396	917	1,333	·4 to 1	3,292	2,434	5,726	1,050	6,776	11	1s. 1d.	1·1	2·7	3·8
1873	124,879	34,787	363	1,029	1,392	·3 to 1	3,479	2,584	6,063	1,014	7,077	11½	1s. 1½d.	1·	3·0	4·0
1875	124,810	34,787	358	775	1,134	·4 to 1	3,318	2,122	5,840	1,089	6,929	11½	1s. 1½d.	1·	2·2	3·2
1877	124,801	34,787	360	825	1,185	·4 to 1	3,626	2,060	5,686	1,128	6,818	11	1s. 1d.	1·0	2·5	3·5

Expenditure of each Poor Law Union in Ireland since the year 1851—*continued.*

Years	Valuation	Population	Average Daily Number in Receipt of Relief: In-doors	Out-doors, under 10 Vic. c. 31	Total	Ratio of In-door to Out-door	Expenditure for: In Maintenance and Clothing	Out Relief under 10 Vic. c. 31	Total	Expenditure under Medical Charities Acts and Acts for Vaccination	Total of Cols. 10 and 11	Poundage: On Amount in Col. 10	On Amount in Col. 12	Percentage of Paupers to Population: In-door	Out-door	Total
1	2	3	4	5	6	7	8	9	10	11	12	13	14	15	16	17
Province of Leinster—continued.																
DUNDALK UNION. Area, 104,484 acres.							£	£	£	£	£	d.	d.			
1851	98,046	34,716	676	.	676	.	2,775	.	2,775	.	2,775	6¾	6¾	1·9	.	1·9
1853	99,096	39,549	487	.	487	.	1,871	.	1,871	846	2,817	4½	7	·9	.	·9
1855	99,916	39,869	368	6	374	61 3 to 1	2,296	21	2,317	843	3,160	5¾	7½	·7	.	·7
1857	99,956	40,594	257	6	263	42 8 to 1	1,857	21	1,878	882	2,480	5¾	6	·6	.	·6
1859	98,856	40,222	272	19	291	14 3 to 1	1,874	89	1,963	887	2,850	4¾	7	·6	.	·6
1861	101,916	48,820	278	37	315	7 5 to 1	1,940	330	2,368	876	3,244	5¾	7½	·6	.	·7
1863	101,906	46,337	343	58	401	6 0 to 1	2,451	148	2,599	903	3,502	6¾	8¾	·7	·1	·8
1865	103,001	46,362	280	68	348	5 0 to 1	1,786	231	2,017	994	3,011	4¾	7	·6	·1	·7
1867	103,440	44,979	268	185	453	1 4 to 1	2,406	302	2,807	1,067	3,874	6¾	9	·6	·4	1·0
1869	104,271	45,690	420	241	554	1·4 to 1	2,515	678	3,141	1,018	4,159	7¾	9½	·7	·5	1·2
1871	105,069	45,401	296	319	665	·8 to 1	2,367	1,074	3,441	1,109	4,550	8	10½	·6	·6	1·4
1873	105,036	45,401	294	448	741	·6 to 1	2,712	1,411	4,123	1,109	5,232	9½	1s. 0d.	·6	1·0	1·6
1875	105,736	45,401	275	476	751	·6 to 1	3,237	1,471	4,708	1,130	4,819	6¾	11	·6	1·0	1·6
1877	105,736	45,401	246	510	756	·4 to 1	2,209	1,656	4,865	1,385	6,096	8¾	11½	·5	1·1	1·6
DUNSHAUGHLIN UNION. Area, 106,259 acres.																
1851	104,693	17,168	478	.	478	.	2,138	.	2,138	.	2,138	4¾	4¾	2·8	.	2·8
1853	104,693	16,591	433	115	548	3 8 to 1	2,027	340	2,367	569	2,936	5¾	7	2·6	·7	3·4
1855	104,694	15,242	299	56	363	5 4 to 1	2,016	290	2,306	554	2,860	5¼	6¾	1·9	·4	2·3
1857	104,708	15,311	202	42	244	4 8 to 1	1,296	141	1,437	544	1,981	3¼	4½	1·4	·2	1·6
1859	104,694	14,729	177	42	219	4 2 to 1	1,060	103	1,163	522	1,685	2¾	3¾	1·2	·2	1·4
1861	104,740	14,969	147	53	200	2 8 to 1	1,179	171	1,350	515	1,815	3	4	1·0	·4	1·4
1863	104,864	13,615	171	66	237	2 6 to 1	1,306	225	1,531	513	1,838	3	4½	1·2	·5	1·7
1865	105,487	13,120	172	54	227	3 0 to 1	1,306	208	1,504	497	2,001	3½	4½	1·3	·4	1·7
1867	105,000	12,631	170	78	248	2 2 to 1	1,146	651	1,797	484	2,281	4¼	5	1·3	·6	1·9
1869	104,973	12,130	160	91	251	1 7 to 1	1,413	667	2,080	446	2,526	4½	5½	1·3	·7	2·0
1871	105,615	11,647	153	117	270	1 3 to 1	1,544	464	1,997	651	2,638	4½	6	1·3	1·0	2·3
1873	106,623	11,647	168	171	339	·9 to 1	1,843	794	2,637	607	3,244	6	7½	1·4	1·5	2·9
1875	106,614	11,647	155	184	338	·8 to 1	1,808	831	2,639	648	4,027	6	7½	1·3	1·6	2·9
1877	106,081	11,647	199	139	338	·7 to 1	1,828	824	2,662	645	3,217	6	7½	1·7	1·2	2·9
KELLS UNION. Area, 106,292 acres.																
1851	88,046	41,335	917	.	917	.	3,895	.	3,895	.	3,895	10½	10½	2·2	.	2·2
1853	88,658	29,944	684	.	684	.	3,624	.	3,624	739	4,363	7½	9¾	2·3	.	2·3
1855	88,658	26,853	429	.	429	.	3,585	.	3,585	426	4,011	9¾	11	1·6	.	1·6
1857	84,761	27,312	227	4	231	56 7 to 1	1,408	7	1,415	497	2,052	4	5½	·8	.	·8
1859	84,910	25,871	186	.	186	.	1,281	.	1,281	497	1,778	3½	4½	·7	.	·7
1861	84,916	24,640	170	.	170	.	1,401	.	1,401	566	1,967	3¾	5¼	·7	.	·7
1863	88,182	24,615	259	1	260	.	2,310	5	2,295	474	2,769	5¾	6	1·0	.	1·0
1865	89,276	24,416	261	2	263	130 to 1	2,204	19	2,223	515	2,840	5¾	8	1·1	.	1·1
1867	89,277	22,939	225	15	238	15 to 1	2,040	86	2,180	535	2,646	6¾	7½	1·	.	1·
1869	91,391	22,442	219	37	256	6 to 1	1,497	276	1,773	637	2,410	4½	6	·9	·2	1·1
1871	94,425	21,895	203	102	305	2· to 1	2,123	430	2,553	896	3,451	6¾	8½	·9	·5	1·4
1873	94,410	21,895	246	206	452	1 1 to 1	2,519	876	3,395	892	4,287	8½	11	1·1	·9	2·0
1875	95,485	21,895	240	185	425	1 2 to 1	2,141	879	3,020	869	3,919	7½	10	1·0	·9	1·9
1877	96,583	21,895	197	240	437	·8 to 1	3,158	1,046	4,204	899	4,103	8	10½	·9	1·1	2·0
NAVAN UNION. Area, 84,466 acres.																
1851	96,147	27,660	729	.	729	.	3,398	.	3,398	.	3,398	9	9	2·6	.	2·6
1853	96,187	26,524	686	5	690	119 0 to 1	3,219	27	3,246	484	3,730	8¼	9¾	2·2	.	2·2
1855	96,187	26,290	449	27	476	16 6 to 1	3,446	89	3,535	359	3,894	8½	9¾	1·8	·1	1·9
1857	96,414	24,936	283	18	301	14 5 to 1	1,950	79	2,029	388	2,417	5	6	1·1	.	1·1
1859	96,478	23,152	246	51	297	[illegible] to 1	1,749	144	1,803	648	2,339	4½	5¾	1·0	·2	1·2
1861	97,716	21,981	278	195	473	1·4 to 1	1,811	409	2,220	526	2,746	5¼	6¾	1·2	·9	2·1
1863	97,791	21,461	241	213	454	1· to 1	1,950	480	2,430	434	2,863	6	7	1·1	1·0	2·1
1865	97,704	20,910	229	273	502	·8 to 1	2,090	655	2,745	430	3,175	6¾	7¾	1·1	1·3	2·4
1867	97,703	20,381	271	288	559	·9 to 1	2,654	661	3,315	422	3,737	8¼	9	1·3	1·4	2·7
1869	97,722	19,845	242	346	588	·7 to 1	2,428	860	3,288	469	3,757	8	9¼	1·3	1·7	3·0
1871	97,822	19,311	219	481	700	·4 to 1	2,443	1,346	3,678	487	4,165	9	10¼	1·1	2·5	3·6
1873	94,680	19,311	233	523	756	·4 to 1	2,414	1,741	4,155	549	4,704	10½	11½	1·2	2·7	3·9
1875	97,490	19,311	231	453	684	·5 to 1	2,510	1,765	4,275	641	4,916	10½	1s. 0d.	1·2	2·3	3·5
1877	91,285	19,311	187	464	651	·4 to 1	2,325	1,696	4,020	584	4,604	9¾	11½	·9	2·3	3·4
OLDCASTLE UNION. Area, 83,912 acres.																
1851	52,386	30,289	1,083	.	1,083	.	3,507	.	3,507	.	3,507	1s. 4d.	1s. 4d.	3·7	.	3·7
1853	51,436	28,145	687	.	687	.	2,560	.	2,560	346	2,906	11½	1s. 1¼d.	2·4	.	2·4
1855	51,386	27,034	423	2	425	211 to 1	3,162	4	3,166	393	3,549	10	11½	1·6	.	1·6
1857	52,860	25,901	244	.	244	.	2,725	.	2,725	433	3,158	1s. 0¼d.	1s. 2½d.	·9	.	·9
1859	52,021	24,772	194	.	194	.	1,258	.	1,258	509	1,747	4¾	6¾	·8	.	·8
1861	52,012	23,857	208	.	208	.	1,656	.	1,656	417	2,073	5¾	6	·9	.	·9
1863	52,012	23,219	243	.	243	.	1,676	.	1,676	452	2,129	6¼	8¼	1·0	.	1·0
1865	53,164	21,782	211	.	211	.	1,450	.	1,450	460	1,910	6¾	7½	·9	.	·9
1867	53,184	21,245	210	4	214	52 to 1	1,725	16	1,741	489	2,230	6¾	8¾	·9	.	·9
1869	53,184	21,906	211	.	211	.	1,720	.	1,720	484	2,204	6¾	8¾	1·0	.	1·0
1871	53,201	21,471	181	5	186	36 to 1	1,569	47	1,616	546	2,162	6¾	8¾	·9	.	·9
1873	52,132	21,471	180	15	195	13 6 to 1	2,039	40	2,079	558	2,647	8	10¼	·8	.	·9
1875	52,729	21,471	187	8	195	24 to 1	1,942	61	2,004	477	2,480	7¾	10	·9	.	·9
1877	52,463	21,471	193	14	207	13 8 to 1	1,914	29	1,943	585	2,528	7¾	10	·9	.	·9

No. 6.—STATISTICAL TABLE showing the progress of the Pauperism and

Years	Valuation	Population	Average Daily Number in Receipt of Relief: In-door	Out-door, under 10 Vic. c. 31	Total	Ratio of In-door to Out-door	Expenditure for: In-Maintenance and Clothing	Out-Relief under 10 Vic. c. 31	Total	Expenditure under Medical Charities Acts, exclusive of Vaccination	Total of Cols. 10 and 11	Poundage: On Amount in Col. 10	On Amount in Col. 12	Percentage of Paupers to Population: In-door	Out-door	Total
1	2	3	4	5	6	7	8	9	10	11	12	13	14	15	16	17
Province of Leinster—continued																
TRIM UNION.							£	£	£	£	£	d.	d.			
Area, 119,518 acres.																
1851	87,985	29,904	547	.	547	.	2,374	.	2,374	.	2,374	6½	6½	1·8	.	1·8
1853	87,255	28,268	418	62	480	9·8 to 1	1,917	86	2,003	612	2,615	5½	7½	1·5	·1	1·6
1855	87,259	26,979	265	16	281	16·5 to 1	1,601	145	1,746	496	2,242	4¾	6¼	1·0	.	1·0
1857	107,090	25,682	223	33	256	7·0 to 1	1,545	72	1,607	566	2,173	3½	4¾	·9	·1	1·0
1859	107,801	24,538	195	46	241	4·3 to 1	1,270	76	1,352	561	1,913	3	4¼	·8	·1	·9
1861	106,908	22,819	294	146	440	1·5 to 1	1,712	273	1,985	612	2,597	4¼	5¾	·9	·6	1·5
1863	106,840	22,341	244	265	509	·9 to 1	2,007	484	2,491	602	3,093	5½	6¾	1·1	1·1	2·2
1865	108,873	21,586	271	307	578	·9 to 1	2,396	487	2,883	580	3,463	6¼	7½	1·3	1·4	2·6
1867	108,068	20,401	259	397	656	·6 to 1	2,575	840	3,415	708	4,123	7½	9	1·2	1·9	3·1
1869	108,929	20,216	235	342	507	·7 to 1	2,603	879	3,482	662	4,144	7¼	9	1·1	1·7	2·8
1871	108,843	19,511	236	391	597	·6 to 1	2,632	882	3,514	595	4,009	7¼	8¾	1·2	1·8	3·0
1873	108,900	19,341	206	375	581	·5 to 1	2,969	694	3,663	715	4,378	8½	10½	1·0	2·0	3·0
1875	108,840	19,341	196	391	587	·5 to 1	2,576	867	3,443	774	4,217	7½	9½	1·0	2·0	3·0
1877	109,046	19,341	185	399	584	·5 to 1	2,494	911	3,405	805	4,210	7½	9½	1·0	2·0	3·0
ABBEYLEIX UNION.																
Area, 107,166 acres.																
1851	64,327	27,729	807	20	827	43 to 1	3,661	84	3,745	.	3,745	1s. 2d.	1s. 2d.	3·1	.	3·2
1853	64,427	26,084	516	15	531	39 to 1	2,681	76	2,757	712	3,469	10½	1s. 1d.	2·1	.	2·2
1855	64,317	25,508	299	.	299	.	1,918	3	1,921	577	2,498	7¼	9½	1·1	.	1·1
1857	65,724	24,532	185	3	188	62 to 1	1,191	14	1,205	562	1,767	4½	6½	·7	.	·7
1859	65,571	23,466	151	3	154	50 to 1	877	14	891	.	.	4¼	.	·6	.	·6
1861	66,079	22,400	177	5	182	35 to 1	1,307	20	1,327	630	2,044	4¾	7¼	·7	.	·8
1863	66,011	21,901	203	43	246	5 to 1	1,486	115	1,601	496	2,097	5½	7½	·9	.	1·1
1865	64,911	21,419	213	82	295	2½ to 1	1,590	245	1,835	747	2,582	6¾	9½	1·0	.	1·4
1867	64,911	20,494	193	143	336	4 to 3	1,680	401	2,081	608	2,686	7¼	9¼	·9	.	1·7
1869	68,964	20,480	169	169	338	1 to 1	1,374	496	1,870	641	2,511	6½	9	·8	.	1·7
1871	65,947	19,949	137	184	321	3 to 4	1,337	454	1,791	770	2,561	6¼	8½	·6	.	1·6
1873	66,434	19,949	178	189	367	3 to 4	1,512	787	2,299	838	3,137	8½	9¾	·8	.	1·8
1875	67,947	19,949	142	232	374	2 to 3	1,561	810	2,371	778	3,149	8¼	11½	·7	.	1·8
1877	67,493	19,949	155	206	361	·7 to 1	1,746	755	2,501	751	3,252	8½	11½	·8	.	1·8
DONAGHMORE UNION.																
Area, 51,060 acres.																
1851	36,071	12,395	382	.	382	.	1,331	.	1,331	.	1,331	8½	8½	3·0	.	3·0
1853	36,071	11,736	236	.	236	.	830	.	830	211	1,041	5½	7	2·0	.	2·0
1855	36,071	11,178	139	.	139	.	1,035	.	1,035	195	1,230	6¾	8	1·2	.	1·2
1857	37,384	10,680	66	.	66	.	589	.	589	198	787	3¾	5	·6	.	·6
1859	35,535	10,087	58	.	58	.	482	.	482	227	709	3¼	4¾	·6	.	·7
1861	40,098	9,304	68	.	68	.	615	.	615	281	896	3¾	5¼	·7	.	·9
1863	40,129	9,275	89	.	89	.	778	.	778	235	1,013	4¾	6	·9	.	1·0
1865	40,160	9,046	94	4	98	23 to 1	791	40	831	303	1,134	4	6¾	1·0	.	1·1
1867	40,164	8,817	83	14	97	6 to 1	911	75	986	277	1,263	6	7½	1·0	·1	1·2
1869	40,173	8,728	96	11	107	8·9 to 1	1,106	57	1,163	274	1,437	7	8¾	1·1	·1	1·2
1871	40,200	8,330	85	29	114	3 to 1	1,110	107	1,217	328	1,543	7¾	9	1·0	·3	1·3
1873	40,846	8,330	84	42	126	2 to 1	1,433	171	1,604	333	1,937	9½	11½	1·0	·5	1·5
1875	40,864	8,359	81	66	147	1·2 to 1	1,345	197	1,542	273	1,815	9	10¾	·9	·8	1·7
1877	40,968	8,330	107	58	165	1·9 to 1	1,436	183	1,619	317	1,936	9½	11½	1·2	·7	1·9
MOUNTMELLICK UNION.																
Area, 200,684 acres.																
1851	94,098	50,168	1,283	.	1,283	.	4,396	.	4,396	.	4,396	11	11	2·5	.	2·5
1853	95,089	48,340	813	.	813	.	3,374	.	3,374	921	4,295	8½	11	1·7	.	1·7
1855	95,089	46,460	511	.	511	.	3,295	.	3,295	633	3,928	8¼	10	1·1	.	1·1
1857	98,740	44,920	314	.	314	.	2,141	.	2,141	788	2,929	5¼	7	·7	.	·7
1859	94,426	42,600	332	1	333	332 to 1	2,191	4	2,195	709	2,904	5½	7¼	·8	.	·8
1861	101,795	40,400	440	1	441	440 to 1	2,984	16	3,000	757	3,757	7	8¾	1·1	.	1·1
1863	101,600	40,073	481	7	488	68·3 to 1	3,579	33	3,612	894	4,506	8¼	10¾	1·2	.	1·2
1865	101,792	39,346	526	27	553	19·4 to 1	4,164	441	4,605	807	5,341	10¾	1s. 1d.	1·3	·08	1·4
1867	101,950	38,019	468	116	584	4 to 1	3,887	222	4,109	962	5,071	9½	1s. 0d.	1·2	·3	1·5
1869	101,918	37,382	414	269	683	1·7 to 1	3,929	685	4,614	940	5,554	10¼	1s. 0d.	1·1	·6	1·7
1871	101,091	37,165	335	328	663	1 to 1	2,846	1,187	4,033	914	4,947	11½	1s. 0¼d.	·9	·9	1·8
1873	102,287	37,165	340	448	788	·8 to 1	3,774	1,421	5,184	967	6,101	12½	1s. 2¼d.	·9	1·2	2·1
1875	102,348	37,165	367	511	878	·7 to 1	3,646	1,814	5,460	948	6,408	12½	1s. 2d.	·9	1·4	2·3
1877	102,255	37,165	348	496	844	·7 to 1	3,879	1,844	5,723	1,075	6,798	1s. 1¼d.	1s. 4d.	·9	1·4	2·3
ATHLONE UNION.																
Area, 130,768 acres.																
1851	86,930	46,817	1,378	.	1,378	.	4,064	.	4,064	.	4,064	1s. 5¼d.	1s. 5¼d.	2·9	.	2·9
1853	86,382	45,487	1,043	.	1,043	.	4,189	.	4,189	779	4,968	1s. 2¼d.	1s. 5¼d.	2·3	.	2·3
1855	86,492	43,811	514	.	514	.	2,388	.	2,388	637	3,025	7½	10½	1·1	.	1·1
1857	86,204	45,797	336	.	336	.	1,958	.	1,958	548	2,501	5¼	7	·7	.	·7
1859	86,882	46,803	279	.	279	.	1,391	.	1,391	756	2,142	3¾	6	·5	.	·6
1861	86,011	39,823	317	.	317	.	2,032	.	2,032	713	2,745	5¼	7½	·8	.	·8
1863	78,160	38,160	356	1	357	356 to 1	2,300	13	2,313	661	2,974	6	8	·9	.	·9
1865	86,484	37,036	382	6	388	63·6 to 1	1,940	16	1,964	689	2,645	5¼	7½	·9	.	·9
1867	86,145	35,809	341	5	346	68·2 to 1	2,458	22	2,480	637	3,117	6¾	8½	·9	.	·9
1869	86,621	34,764	344	3	347	114·6 to 1	2,307	31	2,338	800	3,088	6	8	1·0	.	1·0
1871	86,357	33,013	298	37	335	8 to 1	2,424	126	2,551	960	3,511	7	9¾	·9	·1	1·0
1873	[illegible]	33,612	272	75	347	3·6 to 1	2,643	313	2,976	1,006	3,982	8	10½	·8	·2	1·0
1875	86,386	32,612	225	88	313	2·8 to 1	2,047	321	2,368	1,067	3,435	6½	9½	·7	·2	·9
1877	86,488	30,019	246	102	348	2·4 to 1	2,164	492	2,656	967	3,623	7½	10	·7	·3	1·0

Expenditure of each Poor Law Union in Ireland since the year 1851—*continued.*

Years	Valuation	Population	Average Daily Number in Receipt of Relief. In-door	Out-door, under 10 Vic. c. 31	Total	Ratio of Indoor to Outdoor	Expenditure for In Maintenance and Clothing	Out Relief under 10 Vic. c. 31	Total	Expenditure under Medical Charities Acts, exclusive of Vaccination	Total of Cols. 10 and 11	Poundage. On Amount in Col. 10	On Amount in Col. 12	Percentage of Paupers to Population. In-door	Out-door	Total
1	2	3	4	5	6	7	8	9	10	11	12	13	14	15	16	17
Province of Leinster—*continued.*																
DELVIN UNION.							£	£	£	£	£	d.	d.			
Area, 74,775 acres.																
1851	52,851	13,636	200	.	200	.	755	.	755	.	755	3½	3½	1·2	.	1·3
1853	52,851	13,136	161	.	161	.	676	.	676	341	1,017	3	4½	1·0	.	1·0
1855	52,851	11,736	157	.	157	.	1,038	.	1,038	204	1,242	4¾	6	1·0	.	1·0
1857	52,573	14,386	118	.	118	.	767	.	769	299	1,068	3½	4½	·8	.	·8
1859	52,881	13,936	101	.	101	.	599	.	599	352	951	2¾	4¼	·7	.	·7
1861	52,883	13,536	157	.	157	.	1,175	.	1,175	291	1,466	5½	6¾	·9	.	·9
1863	52,850	13,195	159	4	163	65·7 to 1	1,443	36	1,479	368	1,846	6½	8	1·2	.	1·2
1865	52,420	12,858	133	4	137	33·2 to 1	1,135	19	1,154	394	1,548	5¼	7	1·0	.	1·0
1867	52,970	12,521	146	8	154	18·2 to 1	1,317	36	1,353	477	1,730	6¼	7½	1·2	.	1·2
1869	53,028	12,184	116	12	128	9·6 to 1	1,169	31	1,200	426	1,626	5¼	7½	·9	·1	1·0
1871	53,011	11,847	131	31	162	3·8 to 1	1,176	49	1,225	453	1,678	5½	7½	1·0	·2	1·2
1873	53,128	11,847	131	57	188	2·3 to 1	1,210	196	1,405	437	1,842	6¼	8¼	1·1	·5	1·6
1875	53,114	11,847	89	71	160	1·2 to 1	994	207	1,201	408	1,609	5¼	7¾	·7	·6	1·3
1877	53,163	11,847	110	60	170	1·8 to 1	1,106	200	1,306	486	1,792	6	8	1·0	·5	1·5
MULLINGAR UNION.																
Area, 208,401 acres.																
1851	133,032	51,221	1,323	.	1,323	.	4,789	.	4,789	.	4,789	6¾	6¾	2·6	.	2·6
1853	142,893	48,515	1,016	.	1,016	.	4,180	.	4,180	835	5,015	7½	9	2·0	.	2·0
1855	152,022	47,812	693	.	694	.	4,445	.	4,445	600	5,045	7½	9	1·4	.	1·4
1857	154,763	46,109	476	.	476	.	3,434	.	3,434	685	4,119	5¼	6¼	1·0	.	1·0
1859	154,030	44,406	341	.	341	.	2,191	.	2,191	840	3,031	3½	4½	·8	.	·8
1861	154,283	42,703	309	.	309	.	3,044	.	3,044	819	3,863	4¾	6	·8	.	·8
1863	157,716	41,429	467	.	467	.	3,570	.	3,572	844	4,416	5¼	6¾	1·1	.	1·1
1865	157,280	40,356	431	.	431	.	3,221	.	3,221	764	4,085	5	6	1·0	.	1·0
1867	157,530	39,183	405	8	413	50·6 to 1	3,461	138	3,599	898	4,497	5¼	6¾	1·0	.	1·0
1869	157,417	38,010	367	73	440	5·0 to 1	3,220	214	3,465	1,030	4,495	5¼	6¾	·9	·2	1·1
1871	157,220	36,837	474	316	640	1·0 to 1	2,894	873	3,767	1,111	4,878	5¾	7½	·9	·9	1·8
1873	157,373	36,837	454	581	1,035	·8 to 1	3,721	1,754	5,475	1,123	6,598	8¼	10¼	·9	1·6	2·8
1875	157,550	36,817	345	604	945	·5 to 1	4,433	1,846	5,279	1,090	6,369	8	9¾	·9	1·7	2·6
1877	157,769	36,837	365	890	1,255	·4 to 1	3,644	2,353	5,997	1,240	7,237	8½	11	1·0	2·4	3·4
ENNISCORTHY UNION.																
Area, 194,690 acres.																
1851	109,400	53,863	1,367	.	1,367	.	6,338	.	6,333	.	6,333	11¾	11¾	2·5	.	2·5
1853	109,400	51,666	1,032	.	1,032	.	4,185	.	4,185	885	5,070	9½	11	2	.	2
1855	109,400	48,471	701	.	701	.	4,216	.	3,716	658	4,374	9¾	8½	1·4	.	1·4
1857	109,400	47,276	438	.	438	.	2,382	.	2,382	473	2,783	5¾	7	·9	.	·9
1859	108,898	46,081	334	1	335	.	1,350	11	1,361	711	2,072	4¼	6¾	·7	.	·7
1861	109,505	42,866	350	43	393	8 to 1	2,632	157	2,789	775	3,564	6¾	7½	·8	·1	·9
1863	109,398	42,217	326	150	476	2 to 1	2,693	472	3,165	754	3,919	6¾	8¼	·8	·3	1·1
1865	109,617	41,550	411	169	580	2 to 1	2,694	446	3,140	797	3,937	6¾	8¼	·9	·4	1·3
1867	109,124	40,857	345	297	642	1 to 1	2,572	798	3,370	728	4,098	7¾	9	·8	·7	1·5
1869	109,574	40,322	304	281	585	1 to 1	2,400	885	3,285	930	4,214	7¾	8½	·7	·6	1·3
1871	109,716	39,557	206	389	618	·6 to 1	2,778	1,306	4,080	1,104	4,684	7¾	10¼	·7	·9	1·6
1873	110,450	39,557	328	609	937	·5 to 1	2,814	1,910	4,724	1,095	5,819	10¾	1s. 0¼d.	·8	1·5	2·3
1875	110,400	39,557	391	591	982	·7 to 1	2,757	1,812	4,569	1,129	5,698	10	1s. 0½d.	·7	1·4	2·1
1877	110,360	39,557	274	569	843	·5 to 1	2,884	1,830	4,714	1,216	5,927	10¼	1s. 1¼d.	·6	1·4	2·0
GOREY UNION.																
Area, 129,706 acres.																
1851	78,451	31,261	1,060	.	1,060	.	4,499	.	4,499	.	4,499	1s. 2d.	1s. 2d.	3·4	.	3·4
1853	78,452	29,984	784	4	788	196 to 1	3,044	17	3,061	450	3,511	9¼	10¾	2·6	.	2·6
1855	78,453	28,700	518	1	519	518 to 1	2,847	5	2,852	475	3,327	8¾	10¼	1·8	.	1·8
1857	78,825	27,425	346	1	347	346 to 1	1,812	9	1,821	368	2,189	5½	7¼	1·2	.	1·2
1859	78,519	26,141	268	2	270	134 to 1	1,398	16	1,414	535	1,949	4¼	6	1·	.	1·
1861	78,674	24,857	230	8	238	28·7 to 1	1,604	17	1,621	543	2,164	5	6½	·9	.	·9
1863	78,791	24,527	268	91	359	2·9 to 1	1,835	234	2,069	598	2,667	6¾	8¼	1·1	·3	1·4
1865	78,807	24,197	285	134	419	1·8 to 1	1,860	356	2,196	491	2,747	6¾	8¼	1·1	·6	1·7
1867	78,954	23,867	298	277	575	1	2,684	782	3,466	702	4,168	10½	1s. 0½d.	1·2	1·2	2·4
1869	79,080	23,537	311	45	356	7	2,807	98	2,905	614	3,519	8½	10¾	1·3	·2	1·5
1871	79,216	24,707	250	45	295	5·5 to 1	2,515	93	2,608	684	3,292	8	10	1·	.	1·2
1873	79,823	23,707	240	58	298	4·1 to 1	2,707	179	2,836	678	3,514	8¼	11¼	1·	·2	1·3
1875	80,120	23,907	237	59	296	3·8 to 1	2,046	137	2,186	708	2,879	6¼	8¾	·9	·3	1·2
1877	80,142	24,907	221	77	298	2·8 to 1	2,106	235	2,341	664	3,005	7	9	·9	·3	1·2
NEW ROSS UNION.																
Area, 177,781 acres.																
1851	108,613	56,454	1,634	.	1,634	.	7,516	.	7,516	.	7,516	1s. 5d.	1s. 5d.	2·9	.	2·9
1853	106,614	53,430	1,365	430	1,790	3·1 to 1	6,340	724	7,064	1,625	8,689	1s. 4d.	1s. 7¾d.	2·5	·8	3·3
1855	106,614	50,409	849	12	861	70·7 to 1	2,159	87	2,246	1,079	3,325	5¼	7½	1·6	.	1·6
1857	105,440	47,388	604	23	627	26·3 to 1	3,580	63	3,643	900	4,543	8¼	10¼	1·3	·1	1·4
1859	105,440	44,437	481	57	538	8·4 to 1	2,708	217	2,925	854	3,739	6¾	8½	1·1	·1	1·2
1861	105,808	41,876	496	301	797	1·6 to 1	3,862	1,044	4,906	900	5,806	11¼	1s. 1½d.	1·2	·7	1·9
1863	105,050	41,166	572	515	1,087	1·1 to 1	4,243	1,710	5,953	1,094	6,957	1s. 1½d.	1s. 4d.	1·4	1·2	2·6
1865	104,516	40,002	573	298	869	1·9 to 1	4,360	1,201	5,561	1,169	6,759	1s. 1d.	1s. 3½d.	1·4	·7	2·1
1867	104,738	40,616	577	406	983	1·4 to 1	4,907	1,398	6,305	1,049	7,431	1s. 2¼d.	1s. 5d.	1·4	1·	2·4
1869	104,496	40,230	503	298	801	1·8 to 1	4,184	1,213	5,396	1,069	6,466	1s. 0¼d.	1s. 0¾d.	1·2	1·	2·2
1871	104,325	39,944	419	425	844	·9 to 1	4,814	1,464	6,278	1,124	6,402	1s. 0½d.	1s. 2½d.	1·0	1·	2·0
1873	105,410	39,944	368	310	678	·9 to 1	4,462	1,667	6,099	1,037	7,092	1s. 1¾d.	1s. 4½d.	1·1	1·3	2·4
1875	104,635	39,944	414	733	1,147	·5 to 1	4,864	1,870	5,738	1,184	6,942	1s. 1¼d.	1s. 3¼d.	1·0	1·9	2·9
1877	104,426	39,944	420	928	1,348	·5 to 1	4,125	1,845	5,970	1,248	7,206	1s. 1¼d.	1s. 6¼d.	1·0	2·1	3·1

Appendix A.
Poor Relief.

No. 6.—Statistical Table showing the progress of the Pauperism and

Years	Valuation	Population	Average Daily Number in Receipt of Relief: In door	Out door, under 10 Vic. c. 31	Total	Ratio of Indoor to Outdoor	Expenditure for: In Maintenance and Clothing	Out Relief under 10 Vic. c. 31	Total	Expenditure under Medical Charities Acts, inclusive of Vaccination	Total of Cols. 10 and 11	Poundage: On Amount in Col. 10	On Amount in Col. 12	Per-centage of Paupers to Population: In-door	Out door	Total
1	2	3	4	5	6	7	8	9	10	11	12	13	14	15	16	17
Province of Leinster—continued.																
Wexford Union.							£	£	£	£	£	d.	d.			
Area, 126,801 acres.																
1851	105,486	52,308	1,153	.	1,153	.	4,712	.	4,712	.	4,712	10¾	10¾	2·2	.	2·2
1853	105,486	50,747	1,062	1	1,063	.	4,703	4	4,707	857	5,564	10¾	1s. 0¾d.	2·	.	2·
1855	106,418	48,992	743	1	744	.	4,594	4	4,598	874	5,472	10½	1s. 0½d.	1·4	.	1·4
1857	106,812	47,237	551	2	553	265 to 1	3,456	12	3,465	848	4,313	8	9¾	1·1	.	1·1
1859	106,207	45,483	406	5	411	[illegible] to 1	2,3[illegible]	25	2,3[illegible]	861	3,2[illegible]	5¾	7½	·9	.	·9
1861	106,374	43,727	437	20	457	21·8 to 1	2,916	125	3,041	801	3,842	6¾	8½	1·	.	1·
1863	106,518	44,110	476	20	496	23·8 to 1	3,451	124	3,575	814	4,189	8	11	1·1	.	1·1
1865	106,380	42,494	466	68	534	7·1 to 1	3,408	272	3,670	880	4,550	8¾	10¼	1·1	·2	1·3
1867	106,920	41,870	532	218	750	2·2 to 1	4,144	562	4,806	933	5,639	10¾	1s. 0¾d.	1·2	·5	1·7
1869	107,103	41,252	491	315	806	1·5 to 1	3,978	682	4,785	914	5,699	10¾	1s. 0¾d.	1·2	·7	1·9
1871	107,108	40,845	447	560	1,007	·8 to 1	4,035	1,514	5,349	998	6,347	1 0	1s. 2½d.	1·1	1·3	2·4
1873	107,115	40,846	504	620	1,124	·8 to 1	4,653	1,804	6,459	1,085	7,584	1s. 2¾d.	1s. 5d.	1·2	1·5	2·7
1875	107,[illegible]	40,846	503	538	1,041	·9 to 1	4,869	1,647	6,516	1,050	7,526	1s. 2½d.	1s. 5½d.	1·2	1·3	2·5
1877	107,[illegible]	40,848	489	566	1,016	·8 to 1	4,624	1,468	6,092	1,062	7,154	1s. 1½d.	1s. 4d.	1·1	1·3	2·4
Baltinglass Union.																
Area, 139,107 acres.																
1851	73,446	27,324	751	.	751	.	3,065	.	3,065	.	3,065	10	10	2·7	.	2·7
1853	73,446	25,364	495	1	496	495 to 1	2,077	4	2,081	586	2,667	6½	8¼	1·8	.	1·8
1855	73,446	25,206	345	1	346	345 to 1	2,259	5	2,264	577	2,841	7¼	9¼	1·4	.	1·4
1857	73,585	24,148	238	3	241	79·3 to 1	1,865	7	1,872	519	2,391	6¼	7½	·9	.	·9
1859	73,258	22,940	190	2	193	95 to 1	1,880	14	1,894	616	2,510	6¼	6½	·8	.	·8
1861	73,288	22,037	213	13	226	15·6 to 1	1,820	69	1,889	684	2,483	6¼	8¼	1·	.	1·
1863	73,285	21,734	259	40	299	6·4 to 1	2,186	127	2,4[illegible]	565	2,308	7¼	9¼	1·2	·1	1·3
1865	73,409	21,418	275	104	379	2·6 to 1	2,278	291	2,569	667	3,216	8¼	10¼	1·2	·5	1·7
1867	73,304	21,186	284	176	460	1·6 to 1	2,715	477	3,192	623	3,815	10¼	1s. 0¼d.	1·3	·8	2·1
1869	73,582	20,709	244	194	447	1·4 to 1	2,437	483	2,920	600	3,520	9¼	11¼	1·2	·9	2·1
1871	73,734	20,433	208	450	658	·5 to 1	2,251	851	3,102	601	4,708	10½	1s. 0½d.	·9	1·7	2·6
1873	73,731	20,403	213	418	631	·5 to 1	2,390	1,024	3,414	728	4,142	11	1s. 1½d.	1·	1·3	2·3
1875	74,054	20,401	183	480	663	·3 to 1	2,137	1,454	3,591	745	4,336	11¼	1s. 1¼d.	·9	2·4	3·3
1877	73,887	20,406	169	379	548	·4 to 1	1,886	1,168	4,029	832	3,880	9¾	10¾	·8	1·8	2·6
Rathdrum Union.																
Area, 227,841 acres.																
1851	128,216	47,861	874	.	874	.	3,259	.	3,259	.	3,259	6½	6½	1·8	.	1·8
1853	128,216	46,965	679	32	711	21·2 to 1	2,621	55	2,676	882	3,558	5¼	6¾	1·4	·1	1·5
1855	128,216	46,069	593	44	637	13·4 to 1	3,218	84	3,297	928	4,225	6¼	8	1·2	·1	1·3
1857	128,868	44,173	371	50	421	7·4 to 1	2,029	73	2,102	864	2,966	4	5½	·8	·1	·9
1859	127,576	44,277	264	36	300	7·3 to 1	1,754	57	1,811	985	2,796	3¼	5¼	·6	.	·6
1861	127,990	43,381	311	96	407	3·2 to 1	2,346	200	2,546	930	3,476	4¾	6½	·7	·2	·9
1863	127,918	42,365	333	193	526	1·7 to 1	2,668	478	3,136	1,008	4,144	5¾	7¾	·7	·4	1·1
1865	126,540	41,149	349	302	651	1·1 to 1	2,645	761	3,406	1,087	4,486	6¾	9½	·8	·7	1·6
1867	130,477	40,855	393	497	890	·7 to 1	3,870	1,077	4,947	1,011	5,958	9¼	11	·9	1·2	2·1
1869	129,296	39,621	396	546	893	·6 to 1	3,415	1,300	4,715	1,284	6,000	8¾	11¼	1·0	1·5	2·5
1871	127,884	37,487	313	558	871	·5 to 1	3,401	1,378	4,818	1,243	5,956	8½	11	·8	1·5	2·3
1873	131,348	37,807	263	677	940	·4 to 1	2,927	1,467	4,394	1,366	5,760	7¾	10¼	·7	1·7	2·4
1875	133,790	37,807	290	592	882	·4 to 1	3,103	1,512	4,615	1,297	5,912	8¾	10¾	·8	1·5	2·3
1877	130,827	37,807	268	670	948	·4 to 1	2,916	1,650	4,563	1,370	5,933	8½	10¾	·7	1·7	2·5
Shillelagh Union.																
Area, 110,1[illegible] acres.																
1851	50,108	24,179	659	.	659	.	2,533	.	2,7[illegible]	.	2,9[illegible]	10¾	10¾	2·8	.	2·8
1853	50,105	23,174	480	.	480	.	1,726	.	1,795	311	2,106	8¾	10	2·0	.	2·0
1855	50,105	22,170	472	.	472	.	1,608	.	1,608	434	2,042	7¾	9¾	1·5	.	1·5
1857	50,049	21,178	210	.	210	.	1,191	.	1,191	416	1,607	5½	7¼	1·0	.	1·0
1859	50,100	20,181	171	.	171	.	838	.	838	458	1,296	4¾	6¼	·8	.	·8
1861	50,110	19,183	165	.	164	.	895	.	895	437	1,327	4¾	6¾	·8	.	·8
1863	50,030	18,917	180	.	180	.	888	.	888	411	1,299	4¾	6	·9	.	·9
1865	50,092	18,652	185	.	185	.	1,034	.	1,034	432	1,466	4¾	6¼	1·0	.	1·0
1867	50,105	18,387	204	.	204	.	1,421	.	1,421	419	1,840	6¾	8¾	1·1	.	1·1
1869	50,071	18,122	210	.	210	.	1,330	.	1,330	419	1,749	6¼	8¼	1·1	.	1·1
1871	50,082	17,857	215	.	215	.	1,728	.	1,748	404	2,152	8¼	10¼	1·2	.	1·2
1873	50,323	17,857	209	.	209	.	2,167	.	2,167	413	2,580	10¾	1s. 0¾d.	1·2	.	1·2
1875	50,314	17,857	194	.	193	.	1,904	.	1,904	402	2,306	9¼	11	1·1	.	1·1
1877	50,[illegible]	17,857	210	.	210	.	2,087	.	2,087	400	2,487	9¾	11¼	1·1	.	1·1
Province of Connaught.																
Ballinasloe Union.																
Area, 160,507 acres.																
1851	68,982	35,069	965	.	965	.	3,101	.	3,101	.	3,101	11¼	11¼	2·6	.	2·6
1853	68,[illegible]	34,491	619	.	619	.	2,513	.	2,513	560	3,073	9	11	1·7	.	1·7
1855	68,[illegible]	32,917	345	.	345	.	1,797	.	1,797	555	2,352	6¼	8¼	1·0	.	1·0
1857	68,[illegible]	31,643	237	.	237	.	1,304	.	1,304	568	1,872	4¾	6¾	·7	.	·7
1859	70,439	30,767	265	.	265	.	1,411	.	1,411	702	2,113	4¾	6¾	·8	.	·8
1861	72,366	28,193	236	.	236	.	1,634	.	1,634	709	2,343	5	7	·8	.	·8
1863	78,645	27,411	246	.	246	.	1,680	.	1,680	728	2,408	5¼	7¼	·9	.	·9
1865	78,727	26,631	240	.	240	.	1,663	.	1,663	776	2,439	5	7½	·9	.	·9
1867	78,743	25,851	263	.	263	.	2,009	.	2,010	712	2,722	6¼	8½	1·0	.	1·0
1869	78,770	24,871	288	1	289	.	2,182	.	2,182	814	3,006	7	9¼	1·1	.	1·1
1871	78,712	24,391	250	2	252	125 to 1	2,016	.	2,016	853	2,869	6¼	8¾	1·0	.	1·0
1873	78,648	24,291	248	2	250	124 to 1	2,316	12	2,328	805	3,133	7¾	10¼	1·0	.	1·0
1875	78,676	24,291	289	1	290	.	2,634	21	2,655	800	3,455	8¾	10¾	1·1	.	1·1
1877	78,807	24,291	258	8	263	30·4 to 1	2,321	54	2,375	868	3,243	7½	10	1·0	.	1·0

Expenditure of each Poor Law Union in Ireland since the year 1851—*continued.*

Years	Valuation	Population	Average Daily Number in Receipt of Relief: In-door	Out-door, under 10 Vic. c. 31	Total	Ratio of Indoor to Outdoor	Expenditure for: In-Maintenance and Clothing	Out Relief under 10 Vic. c. 31	Total	Expenditure under Medical Charities Acts, exclusive of Vaccination	Total of Cols. 10 and 11	Poundage: On Amount in Col. 10	On Amount in Col. 12	Percentage of Paupers to Population: In-door	Out-door	Total
1	2	3	4	5	6	7	8	9	10	11	12	13	14	15	16	17
Province of Connaught—continued. CLIFDEN UNION. Area, 192,884 acres							£	£	£	£	£	d.	d.			
1851	10,773	26,389	1,928	.	1,928	.	6,847	.	6,847	.	6,847	12s 8½d	12s 8½d	7·6	.	7·6
1853	10,773	26,408	481	.	481	.	1,404	.	1,404	660	2,064	2s 1½d	3s 11d	1·7	.	1·7
1855	10,773	26,281	189	.	189	.	1,018	.	1,018	452	1,470	1s 10½d	2s 6½d	·7	.	·7
1857	16,080	26,154	113	.	116	.	733	.	733	368	1,101	11	1s 4½d	·5	.	·5
1859	16,144	25,677	89	.	92	.	592	.	592	508	1,100	8¾	1s 4¼d	·4	.	·4
1861	16,249	25,000	113	.	113	.	826	.	826	377	1,203	1s 0½d	1s 5½d	·5	.	·5
1863	14,725	25,444	103	61	164	1·7 to 1	965	61	1,026	471	1,497	1s 2½d	1s 9½d	·6	·1	·7
1865	16,886	25,048	126	15	141	8·6 to 1	787	57	844	563	1,407	11½	1s 5½d	·5	.	·5
1867	17,193	25,182	121	20	141	6 to 1	916	100	1,016	569	1,585	1s 2½d	1s 10½d	·5	·1	·6
1869	17,181	25,176	144	56	200	2·6 to 1	984	96	1,080	388	1,468	1s 2½d	1s 10½d	·6	·2	·8
1871	17,397	25,210	136	56	192	2·2 to 1	939	90	1,029	670	1,699	1s 2¼d	1s 10½d	·5	·2	·7
1873	17,471	25,720	126	147	273	·8 to 1	1,093	177	1,270	676	1,946	1s 5½d	2s 2d	·5	·6	1·1
1875	17,180	25,720	112	52	164	2·2 to 1	988	131	1,119	720	1,839	1s 3d	2s 0½d	·5	·1	·6
1877	17,696	25,370	117	64	181	1·8 to 1	852	149	1,001	775	1,776	1s 4½d	2s 0d	·5	·2	·7
GALWAY UNION. Area, 197,467 acres.																
1851	61,228	61,578	2,817	.	2,817	.	8,465	.	8,465	.	8,465	2s 9½d	2s 9½d	4·6	.	4·6
1853	61,228	59,528	1,653	.	1,653	.	5,379	.	5,379	1,108	6,487	1s 9d	2s 1½d	2·8	.	2·8
1855	63,276	57,274	720	.	720	.	3,557	.	3,557	689	4,276	1s 2d	1s 4½d	1·2	.	1·2
1857	62,571	55,124	378	.	313	.	2,000	.	2,000	652	2,652	7½	10½	·7	.	·7
1859	62,676	53,478	290	.	290	.	1,665	.	1,665	876	2,541	6½	9½	·6	.	·6
1861	63,818	50,621	297	.	296	.	2,567	.	2,567	871	3,438	9½	1s 1d	·6	.	·6
1863	63,491	49,438	493	11	504	41·2 to 1	3,194	25	3,219	921	4,140	1s 0d	1s 3½d	1·0	.	1·0
1865	64,344	48,098	486	3	489	162 to 1	3,271	33	3,304	851	4,155	1s 0½d	1s 3½d	1·0	.	1·0
1867	65,461	46,740	510	21	531	24·3 to 1	3,770	76	3,846	940	4,786	1s 2d	1s 5½d	1·1	.	1·1
1869	65,134	45,281	438	28	466	15·5 to 1	4,103	126	4,229	936	5,165	1s 3½d	1s 6½d	1·0	.	1·0
1871	65,428	44,022	372	45	417	8·3 to 1	2,781	163	2,944	871	3,815	10½	1s 2½d	·8	·1	·9
1873	65,578	44,022	372	57	429	6·5 to 1	3,305	203	3,508	879	4,387	1s 1½d	1s 4d	·8	·1	·9
1875	66,350	44,012	363	63	426	5·8 to 1	3,194	244	3,438	1,172	4,610	1s 0½d	1s 4½d	·8	·1	·9
1877	66,170	44,012	391	64	455	6·1 to 1	4,098	287	3,385	1,153	4,538	1s 2d	1s 6d	·9	·1	1·0
GLENAMADDY UNION. Area, 100,987 acres																
1851	21,635	23,063	602	.	602	.	2,471	.	2,471	.	2,471	2s 3½d	2s 3½d	2·0	.	2·0
1853	21,636	22,185	201	2	203	100·5 to 1	1,171	6	1,177	333	1,510	1s 1d	1s 4½d	·9	.	·9
1855	21,646	21,305	139	1	140	139 to 1	852	10	862	251	1,113	9½	1s 0½d	·6	.	·6
1857	21,916	23,077	103	4	107	25·7 to 1	640	20	660	264	924	5	7	·4	.	·4
1859	21,823	22,748	85	2	87	42·5 to 1	556	20	576	286	862	4½	6½	·4	.	·4
1861	21,826	22,459	124	6	130	20·6 to 1	797	26	823	301	1,124	6½	8½	·6	.	·6
1863	21,882	21,829	185	17	202	10·9 to 1	1,738	64	1,802	204	1,906	10	1s 0½d	·8	·1	·9
1865	21,884	21,660	162	15	177	10·8 to 1	1,033	63	1,096	310	1,406	8½	10½	·8	.	·8
1867	21,876	21,241	188	31	219	6 to 1	1,348	100	1,448	317	1,765	11	1s 1½d	·9	·1	1·0
1869	21,881	20,988	173	43	216	4 to 1	1,466	104	1,570	328	1,898	11½	1s 1½d	·8	·2	1·0
1871	21,886	20,473	164	52	216	3·1 to 1	1,198	188	1,386	330	1,716	10	1s 1d	·8	·2	1·0
1873	21,890	20,823	133	85	218	1·6 to 1	1,495	240	1,735	364	2,099	1s 1d	1s 4½d	·6	·4	1·0
1875	21,808	20,438	118	33	151	3·6 to 1	1,317	206	1,523	457	1,910	11½	1s 2½d	·6	·1	·7
1877	21,871	20,420	96	106	202	·9 to 1	1,098	269	1,297	381	1,678	9½	1s 0½d	·5	·5	1·0
GORT UNION. Area, 167,919 acres.																
1851	36,068	28,787	1,962	.	1,962	.	6,487	.	6,487	.	6,487	3s 0½d	3s 0½d	7·5	.	7·5
1853	36,085	25,139	948	.	948	.	3,150	.	3,150	353	3,503	1s 9d	1s 11½d	3·7	.	3·7
1855	36,085	23,973	328	.	328	.	1,381	.	1,381	276	1,657	9½	11	1·3	.	1·3
1857	[illegible]	22,815	147	.	147	.	1,046	.	1,046	291	1,337	5½	7½	·6	.	·6
1859	44,014	21,558	140	.	140	.	874	.	874	417	1,291	4½	6½	·7	.	·7
1861	45,144	20,401	129	.	129	.	911	.	911	361	1,272	5	7½	·7	.	·7
1863	43,120	19,946	184	.	184	.	1,167	.	1,167	357	1,524	6½	8½	·9	.	·9
1865	44,198	19,498	169	.	169	.	1,147	.	1,147	375	1,522	6½	8½	·8	.	·8
1867	44,179	18,862	151	.	158	.	1,283	.	1,283	358	1,636	7½	9	·8	.	·8
1869	44,718	18,478	191	2	193	90·5 to 1	1,388	10	1,398	348	1,911	8½	10½	1·0	.	1·0
1871	45,249	17,974	165	5	160	32 to 1	1,150	17	1,167	349	1,516	6½	8½	·8	.	·8
1873	48,294	17,978	149	4	153	37·2 to 1	1,386	18	1,404	300	1,904	7½	10½	·8	.	·8
1875	44,978	17,978	148	2	150	74 to 1	1,270	6	1,276	516	1,746	6½	8½	·8	.	·8
1877	44,230	17,913	186	8	194	24·2 to 1	1,327	60	1,387	545	2,132	8½	11½	1·0	.	1·1
LOUGHREA UNION. Area, 193,764 acres																
1851	80,161	60,493	1,491	.	1,491	.	4,446	.	4,446	.	4,446	1s 6d	1s 6d	3·8	.	3·8
1853	80,461	56,365	802	.	802	.	2,132	.	2,132	549	2,681	6½	10½	1·8	.	1·4
1855	69,362	31,312	283	.	308	.	1,397	.	1,397	449	1,846	4½	7½	·9	.	·9
1857	80,442	32,771	148	.	148	.	779	.	779	401	1,180	2½	4½	·4	.	·4
1859	74,000	31,000	95	.	95	.	589	.	589	375	964	1¾	2¼	·3	.	·3
1861	74,772	29,780	115	.	115	.	611	.	611	436	1,046	2	3½	·4	.	·4
1863	75,879	28,800	148	.	148	.	847	.	847	465	1,312	2½	4½	·5	.	·5
1865	75,489	28,045	156	.	156	.	895	.	895	438	1,333	2½	4½	·5	.	·5
1867	75,414	27,496	153	1	154	153 to 1	1,103	1	1,104	459	1,563	3½	5	·6	.	·6
1869	75,443	26,949	125	3	128	41·6 to 1	1,015	12	1,027	494	1,521	3½	4½	·5	.	·5
1871	74,498	26,492	115	7	122	16·3 to 1	967	24	991	545	1,536	3	4½	·4	.	·4
1873	75,480	26,482	101	20	141	5 to 1	1,189	80	1,271	699	1,969	3½	6	·4	·1	·5
1875	76,216	25,602	126	31	157	4 to 1	1,087	250	1,337	548	1,885	4	6	·5	·1	·6
1877	75,314	24,608	106	32	138	3·3 to 1	1,077	107	1,184	585	1,769	3½	5½	·4	·1	·5

APPENDIX A.

Poor Relief.

No. 6.—STATISTICAL TABLE showing the progress of the Pauperism and

Years.	Valuation.	Population.	Average Daily Number in Receipt of Relief: In-door.	Out-door, under 10 Vic. c. 31.	Total.	Ratio of In-door to Out-door.	Expenditure for In Maintenance and Clothing.	Out Relief under 10 Vic. c. 31.	Total.	Expenditure under Medical Charities Acts, exclusive of Vaccination.	Total of Cols. 10 and 11.	Poundage: On Amount in Col. 10.	On Amount in Col. 12.	Percentage of Paupers to Population: In-door.	Out-door.	Total.
1.	2.	3.	4.	5.	6.	7.	8.	9.	10.	11.	12.	13.	14.	15.	16.	17.
Province of Connaught—*continued.* MOUNTBELLEW UNION. Area, 102,454 acres.							£	£	£	£	£	d.	d.			
1851	31,794	32,790	683	.	683	.	2,227	.	2,227		2,227	1s 4½d	1s 4½d	·3		·2
1853	31,794	22,216	379	.	379	.	1,247	.	1,247	434	1,681	9½	1s 0½d	1·4	.	1·4
1855	31,794	21,646	185	.	185	.	992		992	351	1,343	7½	10½	·8	.	·8
1857	40,404	21,076	118	.	118	.	641	.	641	372	1,013	3¾	6	·5	.	·5
1859	40,459	20,806	101	.	101	.	504	.	504	333	837	3	5	·5	.	·5
1861	40,453	19,956	120	.	120	.	738	.	738	446	1,184	4½	7	·6	.	·6
1863	40,494	19,801	173	.	173	.	900	.	900	480	1,380	5½	8	·9	.	·9
1865	40,477	19,389	181	2	183	90·5 to 1	1,096	20	1,116	412	1,528	6½	9 1/10	·9		·9
1867	40,450	19,027	144	3	147	48 to 1	1,010	23	1,033	417	1,450	6	8½	·7	.	·7
1869	40,421	18,726	147	6	153	73 to 1	1,040	45	1,093	501	1,594	6½	9½	·8	.	·8
1871	40,600	18,425	151	7	158	21·6 to 1	1,067	40	1,107	533	1,640	6½	9½	·8	.	·8
1873	40,456	18,473	111	7	118	16 to 1	1,072	41	1,113	479	1,592	6½	9½	·6	.	·6
1875	40,460	18,429	88	14	102	6·3 to 1	972	40	1,012	537	1,549	6	9½	·5	·1	·6
1877	40,455	18,423	97	14	111	7 to 1	841	93	934	546	1,470	5½	8½	·5	·1	·6
OUGHTERARD UNION. Area, 172,686 acres.																
1851	11,630	18,089	1,183	.	1,183	.	4,513		4,513		4,513	7s 10d	7s 10d	6·2	.	6·2
1853	11,620	19,016	490	.	490	.	1,550	.	1,550	493	1,943	2s 9d	3s 4½d	2·5	.	2·5
1855	11,620	19,016	154	.	154	.	591		591	251	842	1s 0½d	1s 5½d	·8	.	·8
1857	14,429	18,018	85	.	85	.	463	.	463	323	786	7¾	1s 1d	·4	.	·4
1859	14,429	19,013	64	.	64	.	328	.	328	316	644	5½	10½	·3	.	·3
1861	14,429	19,013	71	.	71	.	499		473	373	845	7¾	1s 2d	·4		·4
1863	14,470	19,131	112	3	115	37·3 to 1	685	5	690	467	1,157	11¼	1s 7½d	·6	.	·6
1865	14,577	19,249	116	3	119	38·6 to 1	585	17	602	416	1,018	10	1s 5d	·6		·6
1867	14,610	18,467	127	12	139	10·6 to 1	903	60	963	421	1,103	1s 4d	1s 11½d	·6		·7
1869	14,935	19,486	139	11	150	12·6 to 1	919	67	986	425	1,411	1s 3½d	1s 10½d	·7		·7
1871	14,933	19,907	131	28	159	4·7 to 1	940	130	1,070	608	1,688	1s 5½d	2s 3½d	·7	·1	·8
1873	14,989	19,807	117	4	121	29·3 to 1	1,080	53	1,133	536	1,669	1s 0½d	2s 3d	·6	.	·6
1875	15,054	19,807	119	4	123	29·7 to 1	972	40	1,012	396	1,408	1s 4½d	2s 1½d	·6	.	·6
1877	15,045	19,807	77	7	84	11 to 1	786	59	784	618	1,402	1s 0½d	1s 10½d	·4		·4
PORTUMNA UNION. Area, 77,008 acres.																
1851	28,802	19,747	720	.	720	.	2,100	.	2,100	.	2,100	1s 7½d	1s 7½d	3·6	.	3·6
1853	28,803	18,786	448	.	448	.	1,301	.	1,361	437	1,798	1s 2d	1s 6d	2·4	.	2·4
1855	28,809	17,823	214	.	214	.	1,033	.	1,033	279	1,312	9 1/10	1s 0½d	1·2	.	1·2
1857	34,794	16,861	99	.	99	.	616	.	616	249	865	4¼	6	·6	.	·6
1859	35,558	15,900	90	.	90	.	460	.	460	324	783	3¼	5½	·5	.	·5
1861	35,407	14,939	99	1	100	99 to 1	696	4	700	351	1,051	4¾	7½	·6		·6
1863	35,427	14,980	139	2	140	69·5 to 1	956	20	976	367	1,343	6½	9	·9	.	·9
1865	35,465	14,114	201	31	232	6·5 to 1	1,353	113	1,467	343	1,810	10	1s 0½d	1·4	·2	1·6
1867	35,510	13,708	161	13	175	14·8 to 1	1,376	56	1,476	259	1,735	8½	11½	1·2	·1	1·3
1869	35,516	13,308	146	13	159	11·2 to 1	1,234	40	1,274	308	1,582	8½	10½	1·1	·1	1·2
1871	35,726	12,906	136	11	147	12·3 to 1	1,069	49	1,118	297	1,415	7½	9½	1·0	·1	1·1
1873	35,557	12,906	128	20	148	6·4 to 1	1,390	75	1,465	319	1,684	9½	11½	1·0	·1	1·1
1875	35,520	12,906	139	16	155	8·7 to 1	1,325	64	1,409	347	1,766	9½	11½	1·0	·1	1·1
1877	35,824	12,906	134	29	163	4·9 to 1	1,377	107	1,319	345	1,664	9	11½	1·0	·3	1·2
TUAM UNION. Area 190,506 acres.																
1851	58,076	51,194	1,870	.	1,870	.	6,764	.	6,764		6,764	2s 4d	2s 4d	3·6	.	3·6
1853	58,076	48,840	845	.	845	.	3,150	.	3,150	714	3,864	1s 1d	1s 1d	1·7	.	1·7
1855	58,076	48,400	366	.	366	.	2,135	.	2,135	477	2,612	8½	10½	·7	.	·7
1857	58,689	47,140	224	.	224	.	1,180	.	1,180	304	1,774	4½	7½	·5	.	·5
1859	74,433	45,790	204	.	204	.	974	.	974	738	1,712	3	5½	·4	.	·4
1861	74,435	44,440	214	1	215	214 to 1	1,281	11	1,292	706	2,048	4	6½	·5	.	·5
1863	75,866	46,818	342	102	444	3·1 to 1	2,048	492	2,440	868	3,308	7¾	10½	·8	·2	1·0
1865	75,725	44,190	235	60	298	3·4 to 1	2,036	271	2,307	941	3,248	7½	10½	·8	·1	·9
1867	76,049	42,567	428	78	505	4·5 to 1	2,963	497	4,290	825	4,115	10½	1s 1d	·8	·1	·9
1869	74,658	41,244	324	75	399	4·3 to 1	2,512	348	2,860	863	3,723	9	11½	·8	·1	·9
1871	75,716	41,321	288	133	421	1·7 to 1	2,391	458	2,849	861	4,710	9	11½	·6	·4	1·0
1873	74,816	41,321	271	238	507	·9 to 1	3,432	1,001	4,433	891	4,694	10 1/10	1s 1½d	·6	·7	1·3
1875	76,714	41,321	201	224	424	·9 to 1	2,390	787	3,167	965	4,039	10	1s 0½d	·5	·6	1·0
1877	76,825	41,321	213	290	506	·7 to 1	2,330	1,007	3,387	917	4,304	10½	1s 1½d	·5	·7	1·2
CARRICK-ON-SHANNON UNION. Area, 100,730 acres.																
1851	33,837	35,318	390	.	390	.	2,342	.	2,342	.	2,342	1s 4½d	1s 4½d	1·7	.	1·7
1853	33,847	34,589	289	.	289	.	1,218	.	1,218	601	1,819	8½	1s 0½d	·8		·8
1855	33,837	34,851	191	.	191	.	957	.	957	335	1,292	6¾	8½	·6	.	·6
1857	33,837	33,158	139	.	139	.	639	.	639	377	1,016	4½	7½	·4	.	·4
1859	47,384	32,106	136	.	136	.	513	.	513	519	1,032	3½	6½	·4	.	·4
1861	47,303	31,677	178	.	178	.	800	.	800	489	1,289	4	6½	·5	.	·5
1863	47,481	30,933	179	.	179	.	1,049	.	1,049	517	1,566	5½	7½	·6	.	·6
1865	47,373	30,331	181	4	184	45·2 to 1	1,007	12	1,019	451	1,470	5½	8	·6		·6
1867	47,416	29,530	183	5	188	36·5 to 1	1,079	13	1,092	526	1,618	6½	8½	·6		·6
1869	47,448	29,827	218	4	222	54·5 to 1	1,362	29	1,441	625	2,166	7½	10½	·7	.	·7
1871	48,100	29,115	187	26	213	7·2 to 1	1,356	73	1,428	650	2,076	7½	10½	·6	·1	·7
1873	48,149	29,115	220	75	295	3 to 1	2,070	181	2,297	608	2,865	11½	1s 2½d	·8	·2	1·0
1875	48,170	29,115	128	83	211	1·4 to 1	1,697	261	1,958	614	2,572	9½	1s 0½d	·7	·3	1·0
1877	48,919	29,118	170	119	289	1·4 to 1	1,439	337	1,776	633	2,409	8 7/10	1s 0d	·6	·4	1·0

Expenditure of each Poor Law Union in Ireland since the year 1851—*continued.*

Years.	Valuation.	Population.	Average Daily Numbers in Receipt of Relief. In-door.	Out-door, under 10 Vic. c. 31.	Total.	Ratio of Indoor to Outdoor.	Expenditure for In-Maintenance and Clothing.	Out Relief under 10 Vic. c. 31.	Total.	Expenditure under Medical Charities Acts, exclusive of Vaccination.	Total of Cols. 10 and 11.	Poundage. On Amount in Col. 10.	On Amount in Col. 12.	Per-centage of Paupers to Population. In-door.	Out-door.	Total.
1.	2.	3.	4.	5.	6.	7.	8.	9.	10.	11.	12.	13.	14.	15.	16.	17.
Province of Connaught—continued. MANORHAMILTON UNION.							£	£	£	£	£	d.	d.			
Area, 144,847 acres.																
1851	45,043	34,604	427	.	427	.	1,206	.	1,206	.	1,206	6½	6½	1·2	.	1·2
1853	45,043	34,381	239	.	239	.	975	.	975	686	1,661	5¼	8¾	·6	.	·6
1855	43,943	33,250	154	.	154	.	734	.	734	435	1,169	3¾	6¼	·4	.	·4
1857	45,065	33,487	121	.	121	.	786	.	786	493	1,279	4¼	6¾	·4	.	·4
1859	45,060	33,115	101	.	101	.	749	.	749	548	1,297	4	7	·3	.	·3
1861	45,147	32,894	134	.	134	.	797	.	797	552	1,349	4¼	7¼	·4	.	·4
1863	43,289	32,257	177	.	177	.	1,019	.	1,019	533	1,552	5¾	8½	·5	.	·5
1865	43,310	31,882	154	.	154	.	911	.	911	542	1,453	5	8	·5	.	·5
1867	43,304	31,477	145	.	145	.	900	.	900	611	1,511	5	8¼	·4	.	·4
1869	43,307	31,073	143	.	143	.	950	.	950	613	1,563	5¼	8¾	·4	.	·4
1871	43,319	30,687	111	.	111	.	816	.	816	825	1,641	4½	7¼	·3	.	·3
1873	43,083	30,687	118	.	118	.	1,135	.	1,135	641	1,776	6¼	9¾	·3	.	·3
1875	44,418	30,667	125	.	125	.	1,076	.	1,076	607	1,683	6	9¼	·4	.	·4
1877	43,468	30,667	114	.	114	.	1,019	.	1,019	347	1,366	5¼	6¾	·4	.	·4
MOVILLE UNION.																
Area, 92,936 acres.																
1851	39,786	34,724	746	.	746	.	2,796	.	2,796	.	2,796	1s. 5d.	1s. 5d.	2·2	.	2·2
1853	39,736	31,415	262	.	262	.	1,007	.	1,002	665	1,667	6	10¼	·8	.	·8
1855	39,736	31,109	129	.	129	.	764	.	764	460	1,224	4¾	7¼	·4	.	·4
1857	39,731	30,883	119	.	119	.	742	.	742	504	1,246	4½	7½	·3	.	·3
1859	39,918	30,437	130	.	130	.	755	.	755	469	1,224	4½	7¼	·4	.	·4
1861	39,118	30,191	161	.	161	.	1,093	.	1,093	484	1,577	6¾	9¾	·5	.	·5
1863	39,143	29,694	256	1	259	256 to 1	1,682	14	1,696	467	2,163	10¼	1s. 1¼d.	·9	.	·9
1865	39,168	29,129	225	8	233	281 to 1	1,309	33	1,342	474	1,816	8	11	·8	.	·8
1867	39,176	28,704	206	10	216	20·6 to 1	1,468	28	1,496	498	1,990	9¼	1s. 1½d.	·7	.	·7
1869	39,164	28,709	190	51	241	3·8 to 1	1,367	133	1,500	494	1,994	9¼	1s. 1d.	·7	·2	·9
1871	39,514	27,714	174	183	357	·9 to 1	1,323	471	1,794	871	2,665	11	1s. 2¼d.	·6	·7	1·3
1873	39,540	27,714	178	227	405	·8 to 1	1,720	398	2,118	429	2,547	1s. 1¼d.	1s. 3½d.	·6	·8	1·4
1875	39,457	27,714	163	256	419	·6 to 1	1,398	553	2,151	597	2,748	1s. 1d.	1s. 4¾d.	·7	·9	1·6
1877	39,612	27,714	173	216	389	·8 to 1	1,415	539	1,934	632	2,566	11¾	.	·6	·8	1·4
BALLINA UNION.																
Area, 159,415 acres.																
1851	33,871	38,276	1,194	.	1,194	.	3,902	.	3,902	.	3,902	2s. 4¼d.	2s. 4¼d.	3·2	.	3·2
1853	33,881	34,717	512	.	512	.	2,177	.	2,177	427	2,604	1s. 3¾d.	1s. 6¾d.	1·5	.	1·5
1855	33,871	34,211	307	.	307	.	1,803	.	1,803	347	2,150	1s. 0¾d.	1s. 3¼d.	·9	.	·9
1857	33,839	33,705	277	1	278	.	1,976	8	1,984	482	2,466	1s. 2d.	1s. 4¾d.	·7	.	·7
1859	46,355	33,199	221	2	223	.	1,277	10	1,287	364	1,651	6¾	8½	·7	.	·7
1861	46,508	32,693	226	1	227	226 to 1	1,294	1	1,295	331	1,729	7¼	9	·7	.	·7
1863	46,545	32,445	308	.	308	.	1,844	.	1,844	431	2,278	9¾	11¾	·9	.	·9
1865	46,478	31,979	268	15	283	17·8 to 1	1,356	27	1,383	446	1,829	7¼	9½	·8	.	·8
1867	46,440	31,623	215	8	223	27 to 1	1,480	24	1,504	392	1,896	7¾	9¾	·7	.	·7
1869	46,440	31,267	195	29	224	6·7 to 1	1,276	68	1,344	438	1,782	7	9¼	·6	·1	·7
1871	46,434	30,911	157	28	185	5·6 to 1	1,005	60	1,065	411	1,476	5¾	7¾	·5	1	·6
1873	46,258	30,911	145	14	159	10·4 to 1	1,102	37	1,139	298	1,646	6½	8¾	·5	.	·5
1875	48,484	30,911	154	31	185	5 to 1	1,219	87	1,303	459	1,762	6¾	9¾	·5	·1	·6
1877	49,026	30,911	141	77	218	1·9 to 1	1,180	171	1,351	437	1,788	6½	8¾	·5	·2	·7
BALLINROBE UNION.																
Area, 144,895 acres.																
1851	58,765	37,703	1,739	.	1,739	.	5,552	.	5,552	.	5,552	2s. 10¾d.	2s. 10¾d.	4·6	.	4·6
1853	58,765	36,474	722	.	722	.	2,409	.	2,409	483	2,892	1s. 2¾d.	1s. 6d.	2·0	.	2·0
1855	58,766	35,245	302	.	302	.	1,549	.	1,549	326	1,875	6¼	7¾	·9	.	·9
1857	58,161	34,016	177	.	177	.	838	.	838	331	1,169	3½	4¾	·5	.	·5
1859	59,368	32,787	167	.	167	.	943	.	943	393	1,336	3¾	5½	·5	.	·5
1861	59,910	31,558	188	1	189	188 to 1	1,255	17	1,272	347	1,619	5¼	6½	·6	.	·6
1863	59,920	31,100	265	2	267	132·5 to 1	1,794	13	1,807	383	2,190	7¼	8¾	·8	.	·8
1865	59,982	30,644	315	1	316	315 to 1	1,790	25	1,815	587	2,402	7¼	9½	1·0	.	1·0
1867	60,228	30,188	269	9	278	27·3 to 1	1,939	44	1,983	620	2,603	7¾	10¼	·9	.	·9
1869	59,931	29,784	253	7	260	36·1 to 1	1,867	70	1,937	632	2,569	7¾	10¼	·9	.	·9
1871	59,896	29,776	234	7	241	33·4 to 1	1,910	65	1,975	584	2,559	8	10¼	·8	.	·8
1873	59,913	29,276	233	44	277	4·1 to 1	1,998	200	2,198	590	2,788	8¼	11¼	·7	·2	·9
1875	59,945	29,216	197	65	262	3 to 1	1,810	372	2,182	715	2,898	8¼	11½	·7	·2	·9
1877	60,116	29,216	194	56	250	3·4 to 1	1,821	306	2,127	655	2,782	8¼	11	·7	·2	·9
BELMULLET UNION.																
Area, 177,933 acres.																
1851	7,274	17,836	1,133	.	1,133	.	3,722	.	3,722	.	3,722	8s. 11¾d.	8s. 11¾d.	6·5	.	6·5
1853	7,274	17,288	282	.	282	.	944	.	944	251	1,195	2s. 7¼d.	3s. 3¼d.	1·6	.	1·6
1855	7,274	17,240	87	.	87	.	480	.	480	187	667	1s. 4d.	1s. 10¼d.	·5	.	·5
1857	10,035	17,192	44	.	44	.	317	.	317	187	504	7½	11¼	·2	.	·2
1859	10,717	17,144	52	38	90	1·4 to 1	371	35	406	306	712	9¼	1s. 4d.	·3	·2	·5
1861	10,751	17,096	99	1	100	99 to 1	778	2	780	257	1,037	1s. 5¼d.	1s. 11¼d.	·6	.	·6
1863	10,758	16,826	162	6	168	27 to 1	1,276	33	1,309	305	1,614	2s. 5¼d.	3s. 0¼d.	1·0	.	1·0
1865	10,753	16,559	121	4	125	30·2 to 1	620	16	636	411	1,047	1s. 2d.	1s. 9¼d.	·7	.	·7
1867	10,877	16,292	91	5	96	18·2 to 1	543	30	573	326	899	1s. 0¼d.	1s. 8d.	·6	.	·6
1869	10,677	16,025	116	5	121	23·2 to 1	716	38	754	330	1,084	1s. 4¼d.	2s. 0d.	·7	.	·7
1871	10,866	15,758	78	17	95	4·6 to 1	615	40	655	305	960	1s. 2¼d.	1s. 9¼d.	·5	·1	·6
1873	11,082	15,758	124	31	155	4 to 1	913	49	962	318	1,280	1s. 9d.	2s. 3¾d.	·8	·2	1·0
1875	10,440	15,758	137	21	158	6·5 to 1	1,055	79	1,134	277	1,411	2s. 1¾d.	2s. 7¼d.	·9	·1	1·0
1877	10,930	15,758	116	58	174	3·6 to 1	886	88	1,074	308	1,382	1s. 11¾d.	2s. 6¾d.	·8	·3	1·1

No. 6.—Statistical Table showing the progress of the Pauperism and

Years	Valuation	Population	Average Daily Number in Receipt of Relief: In-door	Out-door, under 10 Vic. c. 31	Total	Ratio of Indoor to Outdoor	Expenditure for: In-Maintenance and Clothing	Out Relief under 10 Vic. c. 31	Total	Expenditure under Medical Charities Act, exclusive of Vaccination	Total of Cols. 10 and 11	Poundage: On Amount in Col. 10	On Amount in Col. 12	Percentage of Paupers to Population: In-door	Out-door	Total
1	2	3	4	5	6	7	8	9	10	11	12	13	14	15	16	17
Province of Connaught—continued. Castlebar Union. Area, 140,298 acres.							£	£	£	£	£	d.	d.			
1851	33,839	36,898	1,383	.	1,388	.	5,122	.	5,122	.	5,122	3s 1½d	3s 1½d	3·8	.	3·8
1853	33,440	35,868	443	.	444	.	1,636	.	1,636	350	1,985	1s 0½d	1s 2½d	1·2	.	1·2
1855	33,290	34,946	271	.	271	.	2,105	.	2,105	214	2,319	1s 4½d	1s 4½d	·8	.	·8
1857	33,404	33,894	134	.	134	.	842	.	842	281	1,123	6	8	·4	.	·4
1859	45,490	32,927	127	.	127	.	639	.	639	302	941	3½	5	·4	.	·4
1861	45,519	31,790	155	.	155	.	838	.	838	284	1,122	4½	6½	·5	.	·5
1863	45,408	31,848	177	4	181	44·3 to 1	963	4	967	429	1,396	5¼	7½	·6	.	·6
1865	45,786	31,938	175	2	177	87·5 to 1	910	38	948	358	1,306	4½	6¾	·6	.	·6
1867	40,785	32,914	181	13	194	14 to 1	1,106	100	1,206	330	1,536	6¾	8¾	·6	.	·6
1869	45,880	32,892	152	29	181	5·2 to 1	1,010	131	1,148	484	1,632	6	8½	·5	·1	·6
1871	45,878	32,111	127	66	193	1·9 to 1	937	313	1,250	502	1,752	6½	9¼	·4	·2	·6
1873	45,986	32,171	110	129	239	·9 to 1	961	411	1,372	549	1,921	6¾	9½	·3	·4	·7
1875	46,270	32,171	114	117	231	1 to 1	848	830	1,678	480	2,158	8¾	11¼	·3	·4	·7
1877	46,350	32,171	111	110	221	1·0 to 1	864	309	1,173	504	1,677	6	8¾	·3	·3	·7
Claremorris Union. Area, 110,783 acres																
1851	27,783	33,006	668	.	668	.	2,984	.	2,984	.	2,984	2s. 2d	2s. 2d	2·0	.	2·0
1853	27,723	32,018	455	5	460	91 to 1	1,713	27	1,740	613	2,353	1s 3¼d	1s 7¾d	1·4	.	1·4
1855	27,788	32,821	256	1	257	256 to 1	1,327	11	1,348	361	1,709	1s 1½d	1s 4¾d	·8	.	·8
1857	27,659	32,444	176	.	176	.	919	.	919	385	1,304	8	10¾	·5	.	·5
1859	41,065	32,257	145	1	146	145 to 1	731	2	733	300	1,033	4¾	6	·4	.	·4
1861	41,189	32,070	145	2	147	72·5 to 1	928	15	943	298	1,241	5½	7¼	·4	.	·4
1863	41,827	31,916	155	.	155	.	926	.	926	356	1,282	5¼	7¼	·5	.	·5
1865	41,851	31,762	167	1	168	167 to 1	803	9	812	404	1,266	5¼	7¼	·5	.	·5
1867	41,878	31,608	135	.	135	.	985	1	987	319	1,276	5½	7¼	·4	.	·4
1869	41,910	31,454	141	2	143	70·5 to 1	1,025	14	1,039	361	1,400	6	8¼	·4	.	·4
1871	41,986	31,400	143	19	152	7 to 1	964	86	1,049	382	1,431	6	8¼	·4	·1	·4
1873	41,970	31,300	118	57	175	2 to 1	1,086	252	1,338	501	1,839	7¾	10½	·4	·2	·6
1875	42,106	31,300	131	51	182	2·4 to 1	1,150	254	1,404	529	1,933	8	11	·4	·2	·6
1877	43,104	31,300	148	55	207	2·8 to 1	1,283	206	1,489	500	1,989	8¼	11¼	·5	·2	·7
Killala Union. Area, 104,559 acres.																
1851	15,868	14,306	946	.	946	.	3,755	.	3,755	.	3,755	4s 9¾d	4s. 9¾d.	6·6	.	6·6
1853	15,868	14,257	382	.	382	.	1,622	.	1,622	280	1,902	2s. 1d.	2s 5¼d	2·7	.	2·7
1855	15,868	13,850	151	.	151	.	855	.	855	147	1,002	1s. 1¼d	1s. 3¼d	1·1	.	1·1
1857	20,416	12,845	67	.	67	.	495	.	495	295	790	5¾	9¼	·5	.	·5
1859	20,927	12,398	61	.	61	.	394	.	394	289	683	4½	8	·5	.	·5
1861	20,881	11,839	91	.	91	.	627	.	627	289	916	7¼	10¾	·8	.	·8
1863	20,871	11,510	158	18	176	9·9 to 1	984	63	1,047	297	1,344	1s. 0¼d	1s. 3¾d.	1·4	·1	1·5
1865	20,663	11,193	114	9	123	12·6 to 1	715	39	754	291	1,045	8¾	1s. 0¼d	1·0	·1	1·1
1867	20,371	10,876	99	18	117	5·5 to 1	820	61	881	285	1,106	10¼	1s. 1¼d	·9	·1	1·0
1869	20,808	10,559	69	27	96	2·5 to 1	585	96	681	332	1,013	8	11¾	·6	·3	·9
1871	20,504	10,242	84	49	143	1·7 to 1	641	156	799	382	1,188	9½	1s. 2d.	·8	·5	1·3
1873	20,698	10,242	59	69	148	1·8 to 1	697	115	812	305	1,117	9½	1s 1d	·9	·6	1·5
1875	20,684	10,242	77	60	137	1·3 to 1	679	131	810	458	1,268	9½	1s 2¾d.	·7	·6	1·3
1877	20,685	10,242	77	75	150	1·1 to 1	634	186	840	.	.	9¾	.	·7	·7	1·4
Newport Union. Area, 170,413 acres.																
1851	6,185	15,279	1,117	.	1,117	.	3,613	.	3,613	.	3,613	9s 10½d	9s 10½d.	7·2	.	7·2
1853	5,185	15,635	290	6	296	48·3 to 1	1,107	9	1,116	94	1,210	3s 8¼d.	3s 11¼d	1·8	.	1·8
1855	5,165	15,891	115	1	116	.	734	2	736	198	934	2s 9¼d	2s. 4¼d	·7	.	·7
1857	11,877	16,147	77	.	77	.	461	.	461	252	713	9¼	1s 2¼d	·5	.	·5
1859	12,729	16,403	76	.	76	.	417	.	417	246	663	7¾	1s 0½d	·5	.	·5
1861	12,749	16,660	81	.	81	.	430	.	430	304	734	8¼	1s 2¼d	·5	.	·5
1863	12,763	16,527	100	1	101	100 to 1	528	24	552	271	823	10¼	1s. 3¼d	·6	.	·6
1865	12,714	16,418	103	2	105	51·5 to 1	586	15	601	302	903	11¼	1s. 5d.	·6	.	·6
1867	12,740	16,289	103	4	107	25·7 to 1	594	10	610	430	1,040	11¼	1s. 7½d	·6	.	·6
1869	12,746	16,180	96	9	105	10·7 to 1	590	27	617	447	1,064	11½	1s 8d.	·6	.	·6
1871	12,949	16,081	68	22	90	3·1 to 1	527	51	578	478	1,044	10¾	1s 7¼d	·4	·1	·5
1873	14,107	16,081	69	11	80	6·2 to 1	565	25	590	463	1,053	11	1s 7¼d	·4	·1	·5
1875	14,100	16,081	82	2	84	41 to 1	700	35	735	445	1,170	1s 0½d	1s 9¾d	·5	.	·5
1877	14,100	16,081	80	16	86	5 to 1	692	26	718	440	1,158	1s. 1½d.	1s. 8¾d	·5	·1	·6
Swineford Union. Area 152,594 acres.																
1851	29,048	48,822	701	.	701	.	2,386	.	2,386	.	2,386	1s 7¾d.	1s. 7¾d	1·5	.	1·5
1853	29,048	47,838	302	.	302	.	982	.	982	662	1,644	8	1s 1¼d.	·6	.	·6
1855	29,548	48,854	174	.	173	.	921	.	921	403	1,324	7½	10¾	·3	.	·3
1857	29,708	49,970	126	.	126	.	624	.	624	379	1,003	5	8¼	·2	.	·2
1859	39,478	50,986	124	.	124	.	684	.	684	410	1,094	4	6¾	·2	.	·2
1861	40,394	52,004	161	.	161	.	1,005	.	1,005	516	1,521	6	9	·3	.	·3
1863	40,485	52,316	216	.	216	.	1,255	.	1,255	559	1,814	7½	10¾	·4	.	·4
1865	40,408	52,618	159	.	159	.	1,048	.	1,048	552	1,600	6¼	9½	·3	.	·3
1867	40,474	52,925	187	1	138	187 to 1	1,110	6	1,116	544	1,660	6¾	9¾	·3	.	·3
1869	40,489	53,232	148	4	152	37 to 1	1,147	42	1,189	747	1,936	7	11½	·3	.	·3
1871	40,459	53,540	141	46	187	3·1 to 1	1,123	121	1,244	845	2,089	7½	1s 0¼d	·3	·1	·4
1873	40,488	53,540	156	63	219	2·5 to 1	1,347	294	1,641	740	2,381	11	1s 2¼d.	·3	·1	·4
1875	40,766	53,540	177	51	228	3·5 to 1	1,451	196	1,647	714	2,361	9½	1s 2d	·3	·1	·4
1877	40,700	53,540	170	77	247	2·2 to 1	1,452	292	1,744	741	2,485	10½	1s. 2¾d	·3	·1	·4

Expenditure of each Poor Law Union in Ireland since the year 1851—*continued.*

Years.	Valuation	Population	Average Daily Number in Receipt of Relief: In-doors.	Out-doors, under 10 Vic. c. 31.	Total	Ratio of Indoor to Outdoor	Expenditure for: In Maintenance and Clothing	Out Relief under 10 Vic. c. 31.	Total.	Expenditure under Medical Charities Acts, and Vaccination.	Total of Cols. 10 and 11.	Poundage: On Amount in Col. 10	On Amount in Col. 12	Per-centage of Paupers to Population: In-doors.	Out-doors.	Total.
1	2	3	4	5	6	7	8	9	10	11	12	13	14	15	16	17
Province of Connaught—continued. Westport Union. Area, 175,808 acres.							£	£	£	£	£	d.	d.			
1851	22,346	36,282	1,061	.	1,061	.	6,186	.	6,186	.	6,186	5s. 6½d.	5s. 6½d.	3·4	.	3·4
1853	22,358	34,132	412	.	412	.	1,498	.	1,498	487	1,985	1s. 4½d.	1s. 9½d.	1·2	.	1·2
1855	22,364	32,468	231	.	231	.	1,422	.	1,422	411	1,833	1s. 3½d.	1s. 7½d.	·7	.	·7
1857	30,569	30,800	176	.	176	.	1,060	.	1,060	383	1,443	8½	11½	·6	.	·6
1859	30,659	28,744	147	.	147	.	827	.	827	496	1,323	6½	9½	·5	.	·5
1861	30,705	26,863	136	.	136	.	863	.	863	390	1,253	6½	9½	·5	.	·5
1863	30,672	26,445	213	4	217	53·2 to 1	1,311	.	1,311	417	1,728	10½	1s. 1½d.	·8	.	·8
1865	30,787	26,185	177	6	183	29·5 to 1	1,079	10	1,089	445	1,534	8½	1s. 0d.	·7	.	·7
1867	30,881	25,605	173	8	181	21·6 to 1	1,274	24	1,298	387	1,685	10	1s. 1d.	·7	.	·7
1869	30,171	25,185	192	6	198	32 to 1	1,352	17	1,369	450	1,823	10½	1s. 2½d.	·8	.	·8
1871	30,816	24,765	162	3	165	54 to 1	1,176	9	1,185	463	1,648	9½	1s. 1d.	·7	.	·7
1873	30,831	24,765	172	6	178	28·6 to 1	1,366	11	1,377	486	1,863	10½	1s. 2½d.	·7	.	·7
1875	31,112	24,765	164	8	168	17·1 to 1	1,244	33	1,277	438	1,715	10	1s. 1½d.	·6	.	·7
1877	31,134	24,765	138	2	140	69 to 1	1,047	16	1,063	527	1,590	8	10½	·5	.	·6
Boyle Union. Area, 139,696 acres.																
1851	63,601	49,473	699	.	699	.	2,484	.	2,484	.	2,484	9½	9½	1·2	.	1·2
1853	64,091	46,390	339	.	339	.	1,667	.	1,667	803	2,470	6½	9½	·7	.	·7
1855	63,691	46,187	266	4	270	66·6 to 1	1,284	7	1,291	591	1,882	4¾	7	·6	.	·6
1857	64,761	48,044	169	9	178	18·7 to 1	1,168	22	1,190	442	1,632	4¼	6	·4	.	·4
1859	72,437	47,901	190	12	202	15·8 to 1	1,791	32	1,823	755	2,578	6	7	·4	.	·4
1861	72,476	47,708	244	25	269	9·4 to 1	1,682	85	1,767	709	2,476	5	8½	·5	.	·5
1863	72,391	47,092	328	147	475	2·2 to 1	1,962	444	2,406	811	3,217	8	10½	·7	·3	1·0
1865	72,649	46,449	259	176	435	1·8 to 1	2,021	499	2,520	888	3,408	8½	11¼	·6	·4	1·0
1867	72,444	45,646	284	203	487	1·4 to 1	2,536	412	2,948	826	3,774	9½	1s. 0½d.	·6	·4	1·1
1869	72,624	44,943	285	187	472	1·6 to 1	2,042	452	2,494	927	3,421	8½	11½	·6	·4	1·1
1871	72,641	44,240	264	200	464	1·0 to 1	1,984	698	2,682	969	3,651	8⅞	1s. 0½d.	·6	·5	1·2
1873	73,508	44,240	258	248	506	1·0 to 1	3,439	667	4,106	942	4,048	10½	1s. 1½d.	·6	·5	1·1
1875	74,072	44,240	219	184	403	1·2 to 1	2,005	543	2,548	1,034	3,582	8½	11½	·5	·4	·9
1877	73,686	44,240	211	219	430	1 to 1	1,915	894	2,809	1,070	3,879	8½	11¼	·5	·5	1·0
Castlerea Union. Area, 162,368 acres.																
1851	61,199	46,988	834	.	834	.	3,446	.	3,446	.	3,446	1s. 1½d.	1s. 1½d.	1·8	.	1·8
1853	61,896	46,948	339	.	339	.	1,226	.	1,226	889	2,115	6½	9½	·7	.	·7
1855	61,899	46,882	262	.	262	.	1,474	.	1,474	413	1,887	5½	7½	·6	.	·6
1857	61,389	46,863	170	.	170	.	1,251	.	1,251	431	1,782	5	7	·4	.	·4
1859	70,696	46,828	134	1	135	134 to 1	919	2	921	547	1,468	3½	5	·3	.	·3
1861	71,075	46,788	177	.	177	.	1,306	.	1,306	510	1,816	4½	6½	·4	.	·4
1863	71,651	46,274	341	.	341	.	2,044	.	2,044	534	2,578	6⅞	8⅞	·7	.	·7
1865	71,716	45,768	308	.	308	.	2,149	.	2,149	571	2,720	7½	9½	·7	.	·7
1867	71,734	45,266	286	3	289	95·3 to 1	2,173	13	2,186	530	2,716	7½	9½	·6	.	·6
1869	71,708	44,747	243	5	248	48·6 to 1	1,866	18	1,884	536	2,420	6½	8½	·5	.	·5
1871	71,784	44,738	206	14	220	14·6 to 1	1,716	65	1,781	648	2,419	6	8½	·5	.	·5
1873	71,787	44,238	193	29	222	6·6 to 1	1,927	116	2,043	588	2,631	7	8½	·4	.	·5
1875	71,870	44,238	211	34	245	6·2 to 1	1,998	103	2,116	609	2,725	7⅛	9½	·5	·1	·6
1877	71,873	44,236	186	105	291	1·8 to 1	1,668	363	2,031	541	2,572	6½	8½	·4	·2	·6
Roscommon Union. Area, 114,067 acres.																
1851	41,785	34,846	1,485	.	1,485	.	6,223	.	6,223	.	6,223	2s. 11¼d.	2s. 11½d.	4·4	.	4·4
1853	41,786	32,589	706	.	706	.	2,589	.	2,589	496	3,085	1s. 2¾d.	1s. 5½d.	2·1	.	2·1
1855	41,795	31,028	406	5	411	81·2 to 1	2,589	7	2,596	315	2,911	1s. 3d.	1s. 4½d.	1·3	.	1·3
1857	41,805	28,540	291	4	295	72·7 to 1	1,761	9	1,770	367	2,137	10½	1s. 0½d.	1·0	.	1·0
1859	63,570	28,012	282	11	293	25·5 to 1	2,052	45	2,097	460	2,557	8	10	1·0	.	1·0
1861	63,648	26,504	317	39	356	8·1 to 1	2,460	165	2,625	463	2,915	9½	11	1·2	·1	1·3
1863	64,619	25,636	372	49	421	7·6 to 1	3,124	196	3,310	348	3,657	1s. 0½d.	1s. 2d.	1·4	·2	1·6
1865	64,364	24,089	391	46	437	8·5 to 1	3,300	111	3,411	352	3,763	1s. 0½d.	1s. 2d.	1·6	·2	1·8
1867	64,311	24,083	357	87	444	4·4 to 1	3,261	201	3,462	391	3,853	1s. 0½d.	1s. 2½d.	1·5	·3	1·8
1869	64,317	23,275	316	155	471	2·5 to 1	2,872	366	3,238	405	3,643	1s. 0d.	1s. 1½d.	1·4	·6	2·0
1871	64,393	22,468	324	184	508	1·7 to 1	2,924	477	3,401	450	3,851	1s. 0½d.	1s. 2½d.	1·4	·8	2·2
1873	64,447	22,468	280	207	487	1·3 to 1	3,152	781	3,933	451	4,384	1s. 2½d.	1s. 4½d.	1·2	·9	2·1
1875	64,482	22,468	257	213	470	1·2 to 1	2,981	710	3,698	488	4,186	1s. 1½d.	1s. 3½d.	1·1	1·0	2·1
1877	64,528	22,468	291	237	528	1·2 to 1	3,044	792	3,836	507	4,343	1s. 2½d.	1s. 4d.	1·3	1·0	2·3
Strokestown Union. Area, 90,036 acres.																
1851	36,524	30,288	935	.	935	.	3,883	.	3,883	.	3,883	2s. 1½d.	2s. 1½d.	3·0	.	3·0
1853	36,574	29,507	486	.	486	.	2,049	.	2,049	504	2,553	1s. 1½d.	1s. 5d.	1·7	.	1·7
1855	36,524	28,729	337	1	338	337 to 1	2,076	2	2,078	335	2,413	1s. 1½d.	1s. 4d.	1·1	.	1·1
1857	36,512	27,951	188	8	196	23·5 to 1	1,291	23	1,314	331	1,645	8½	10½	·7	.	·7
1859	50,712	27,173	192	10	202	19·2 to 1	1,226	59	1,285	340	1,625	6	7½	·7	.	·7
1861	50,817	26,396	317	34	351	9·4 to 1	1,679	164	1,843	378	2,221	8½	10½	·8	·2	1·0
1863	50,818	25,789	297	163	460	1·8 to 1	2,078	406	2,484	332	2,816	11½	1s. 1½d.	1·1	·7	1·8
1865	50,718	25,175	291	176	467	1·6 to 1	2,122	315	2,437	338	2,775	11½	1s. 1½d.	1·1	·7	1·8
1867	50,760	24,885	295	186	481	1·6 to 1	2,489	500	2,989	402	3,371	1s. 1½d.	1s. 3½d.	1·2	·8	2·0
1869	50,782	25,966	209	291	500	1·4 to 1	2,268	477	2,745	404	3,149	1s. 1d.	1s. 2d.	1·1	·9	2·0
1871	50,788	24,845	210	319	529	·9 to 1	1,670	511	2,181	469	2,650	10½	1s. 0½d.	·9	·9	1·8
1873	50,765	24,345	216	272	488	·8 to 1	2,140	699	2,839	439	3,278	1s. 1½d.	1s. 3½d.	·9	1·2	2·1
1875	50,778	23,345	166	276	442	·6 to 1	1,724	779	2,503	442	3,083	11½	1s. 2½d.	·7	1·2	1·9
1877	50,838	24,445	174	216	390	·8 to 1	1,825	814	2,639	519	3,178	1s. 0½d.	1s. 3d.	·7	·9	1·6

APPENDIX A. — Poor Relief.

No. 6.—STATISTICAL TABLE showing the progress of the Pauperism and Expenditure of each Poor Law Union in Ireland since the year 1851—*continued.*

Years	Valuation.	Population.	Average Daily Number in Receipt of Relief: In-door.	Out-door, under 10 Vic. c. 31.	Total.	Ratio of In-door to Out-door.	Expenditure for: In-Maintenance and Clothing.	Out-Relief under 10 Vic. c. 31.	Total.	Expenditure under Medical Charities Acts, exclusive of Vaccination.	Total of Cols. 10 and 11.	Poundage: On Amount in Col. 10.	On Amount in Col. 12.	Percentage of Paupers to Population: In-door.	Out-door.	Total.
1	2	3	4	5	6	7	8	9	10	11	12	13	14	15	16	17
Province of Connaught—*continued.* DROMORE WEST UNION. Area, 96,988 acres.							£	£	£	£	£	d.	d.			
1851	26,644	19,863	230	.	230	.	895	.	895	.	896	8	8	1·1	.	1·1
1853	26,644	19,272	151	.	151	.	673	.	673	437	1,110	6	10½	·8	.	·8
1855	26,641	19,181	110	.	110	.	771	.	771	281	1,052	7	9	·6	.	·6
1857	26,618	18,999	71	.	71	.	415	.	415	252	667	3½	6	·4	.	·4
1859	26,198	18,799	63	.	63	.	434	.	434	277	691	3½	4½	·3	.	·3
1861	26,293	18,698	86	.	86	.	560	.	562	240	808	3½	5½	·5	.	·5
1863	26,360	18,434	102	.	102	.	569	.	569	247	816	3½	5½	·6	.	·6
1865	26,687	18,261	97	.	97	.	514	.	514	287	801	3½	4½	·5	.	·5
1867	26,603	18,068	65	.	65	.	465	.	465	278	743	3	5	·4	.	·4
1869	26,601	17,915	77	1	78	77 to 1	533	10	543	292	835	3½	4½	·4	.	·4
1871	26,717	17,768	67	12	79	5·6 to 1	487	23	510	327	837	3½	5½	·4	.	·4
1873	26,771	17,742	73	7	80	10·4 to 1	509	21	530	418	948	4	6½	·4	.	·4
1875	26,856	17,742	88	8	96	11 to 1	689	18	707	397	1,104	4½	7½	·5	.	·5
1877	26,868	17,742	77	24	101	3·2 to 1	635	74	709	358	1,067	4½	7	·5	·1	·6
SLIGO UNION. Area, 143,828 acres.																
1851	85,306	88,384	1,259	.	1,259	.	3,543	.	3,543	.	3,543	1s. 2½d.	1s. 2½d.	2·1	.	2·1
1853	85,505	67,629	671	.	671	.	2,317	.	2,317	1,360	3,677	6½	10½	1·0	.	1·0
1855	85,905	58,697	424	.	424	.	2,774	.	2,774	1,221	3,995	7½	10½	·7	.	·7
1857	85,437	55,760	365	.	365	.	2,239	.	2,240	1,016	3,254	6	8½	·6	.	·6
1859	91,686	54,833	328	.	328	.	2,044	.	2,044	1,142	3,186	5½	8	·6	.	·6
1861	95,117	54,901	429	.	429	.	3,124	.	3,124	1,073	4,197	7½	10½	·8	.	·8
1863	95,880	52,670	502	5	507	100·4 to 1	3,173	11	3,184	1,594	4,778	8	10½	1·0	.	1·0
1865	95,893	51,440	446	41	487	10·9 to 1	2,763	119	2,882	1,161	4,043	7½	10½	·9	.	·9
1867	95,894	50,310	479	100	579	4·7 to 1	3,816	428	4,244	1,103	5,347	10½	1s. 1½d.	·9	·2	1·1
1869	95,991	48,980	411	119	530	3·4 to 1	3,058	347	4,405	1,079	4,484	8½	11½	·8	·2	1·0
1871	97,475	47,780	354	184	538	1·9 to 1	2,779	573	3,352	1,109	4,461	8½	11	·7	·4	1·1
1873	97,602	47,730	344	280	624	1·2 to 1	3,211	808	4,019	1,254	5,273	9½	1s. 1d.	·7	·6	1·3
1875	97,304	47,730	352	286	638	1·2 to 1	4,037	810	4,847	1,490	6,337	9½	1s. 1½d.	·7	·6	1·3
1877	97,844	47,730	338	330	668	1·0 to 1	2,863	891	3,754	1,190	4,944	9	1s. 0½d.	·7	·7	1·4
TOBERCURRY UNION. Area, 123,774 acres.																
1851	39,339	38,081	234	.	234	.	1,021	.	1,021	.	1,021	8½	8½	·9	.	·9
1853	30,249	36,806	83	2	85	41·5 to 1	340	4	353	357	710	2½	5½	·4	.	·4
1855	30,239	26,711	64	1	65	64 to 1	325	3	328	204	532	4½	6½	·2	.	·2
1857	30,249	27,076	60	1	61	60 to 1	455	2	460	291	731	3½	6	·2	.	·2
1859	40,388	27,341	67	1	68	67 to 1	403	4	407	393	800	3	4½	·2	.	·2
1861	40,417	27,657	88	5	93	17·6 to 1	651	21	672	330	1,002	4	6	·3	.	·3
1863	40,490	27,468	143	34	177	4·2 to 1	926	106	1,032	355	1,387	6½	8½	·5	·1	·6
1865	40,411	27,292	117	21	138	5·6 to 1	713	80	793	322	1,115	4½	6½	·4	·1	·5
1867	40,473	27,096	138	43	181	2·6 to 1	2,163	405	2,568	391	3,259	1s. 5d.	1s. 7½d.	·4	·1	·5
1869	40,465	26,910	99	47	146	2·1 to 1	573	178	751	454	1,205	4½	7½	·4	·1	·5
1871	40,524	26,724	94	70	164	1·3 to 1	565	260	825	429	1,254	4½	7½	·4	·2	·6
1873	40,517	26,724	113	131	244	·8 to 1	847	383	1,230	445	1,675	7½	10	·4	·5	·9
1875	40,635	26,724	121	169	290	·7 to 1	895	521	1,416	441	1,857	8½	11	·5	·6	1·1
1877	40,945	26,724	100	130	230	·7 to 1	807	496	1,303	433	1,736	8	10½	·4	·6	1·0

Establishment Poundage.

No. 7.—Return showing the POUNDAGE of the ESTABLISHMENT CHARGE, less Parliamentary Grant, for the year ending 25th March, 1877.

Unions.	Valuation.	Establishment Poundage	Unions.	Valuation.	Establishment Poundage	Unions.	Valuation.	Establishment Poundage
	£	d.		£	d.		£	d.
Armagh,	204,507	1½	Celbridge,	114,378	3½	Clogher,	86,878	2½
Antrim,	128,464	2½	Clogheen,	84,083	4	Castletown,	14,660	1½
Athlone,	88,480	3	Coleraine,	99,369	2½	Delvin,	53,185	3
Athy,	100,749	4½	Cashel,	107,728	3½	Dunshaughlin,	105,681	1½
Abbeyleix,	67,453	3½	Cork,	336,606	8½	Dunmanway,	43,159	4½
Ardee,	84,144	2½	Cootehill,	74,305	2½	Dublin South,	621,438	5½
Baltinglass,	73,277	4½	Callan,	72,873	3½	Dublin North,	391,854	4½
Ballymahon,	61,916	2½	Cookstown,	68,576	3½	Downpatrick,	177,512	1½
Bantry,	21,850	4½	Castleblayney,	73,438	2½	Dungarvan,	53,899	7
Boyle,	73,678	3½	Clones,	67,395	2½	Donaghmore,	40,936	4½
Banbridge,	160,340	2	Castlecomer,	82,421	6½	Dunfanaghy,	11,362	6½
Bawnboy,	39,518	3	Clonakilty,	30,944	2½	Dromore West,	36,808	2½
Ballyshannon,	50,593	2½	Carrick-on-Suir,	70,438	3½	Dungannon,	114,784	2½
Balrothery,	95,010	2½	Cavan,	138,853	2½	[illegible]	103,735	2½
Ballina,	49,125	3½	Clifden,	17,878	6½	Drogheda,	124,749	2½
Ballinrobe,	68,114	3½	Carlow,	130,300	2½	Dingle,	22,836	6½
Bailieborough,	40,137	4½	Corofin,	20,430	5½	Donegal,	34,488	3
Ballyvaughan,	18,465	6	Croom,	64,084	3	Edenderry,	63,380	2
Bandon,	73,809	2½	Carrick-on-Shannon,	48,219	4½	Ennis,	75,084	4½
Ballinasloe,	74,821	3½	Castlederg,	26,248	4	Enniscorthy,	110,360	5½
Ballymena,	126,370	3	Carrickmacross,	56,244	3½	Enniskillen,	105,790	7½
Belfast,	606,436	4	Castlebar,	46,340	4½	Ennistymon,	38,498	6
Ballymoney,	82,378	3	Cahersiveen,	22,797	7	Fermoy,	103,448	2½
Ballycastle,	44,298	3	Claremorris,	42,125	4½	Galway,	60,169	5½
Belmullet,	10,949	13	Castletown,	71,873	2	Glenamaddy,	31,610	5
Borrisokane,	41,644	4	Clonmel,	70,481	4½	Glenties,	20,125	6½

No 7.—Return showing the POUNDAGE of the ESTABLISHMENT CHARGE, less Parliamentary Grant, for the year ending 25th March, 1877—*continued.*

Appendix A.

Establishment Poundage.

Unions.	Valuation	Establishment Poundage	Unions.	Valuation	Establishment Poundage	Unions.	Valuation	Establishment Poundage
	£	d.		£	d.		£	d.
Glin,	28,421	5½	Lurgan,	141,969	2½	Rathdown,	349,912	2
Gorey,	80,397	2¾	Limavady,	68,796	2¾	Rathdrum,	130,826	2½
Gort,	44,219	4½	Macroom,	64,516	3	Rathkeale,	56,285	4¼
Gortin,	19,099	4½	Magherafelt,	91,833	2½	Roscommon,	84,838	4
Granard,	86,690	2¾	Mallow,	106,023	3	Roscrea,	71,096	3⅛
Inishowen,	38,113	4	Manorhamilton,	44,801	4½	Scarriff,	25,768	3½
Irvinestown,	48,791	3	Midleton,	86,410	2½	Shillelagh,	50,851	3½
Kanturk,	77,204	3¾	Milford,	29,036	3¾	Skibbereen,	43,894	7½
Kells,	94,400	2¼	Millstreet,	27,575	4½	Skull,	13,211	7
Kenmare,	19,369	7½	Mitchelstown,	49,153	3½	Sligo,	97,864	3
Kilkeel,	42,864	2½	Mohill,	39,488	5½	Strabane,	99,279	2¾
Kilkenny,	108,249	4⅝	Monaghan,	94,214	2¾	Stranorlar,	30,139	4
Killadysert,	25,694	5½	Mountbellew,	40,460	3½	Strokestown,	50,847	3½
Killala,	29,089	4⅞	Mountmellick,	102,283	3	Swineford,	40,700	4½
Killarney,	74,204	5½	Mullingar,	157,665	2½	Thomastown	65,940	3½
Kilmacthomas,	34,438	4½	Naas,	152,849	2½	Thurles,	80,016	3½
Kilmallock,	126,700	2¾	Navan,	97,865	2¾	Tipperary,	142,022	2½
Kilrush,	88,416	5¾	Nenagh,	94,004	2¾	Tobercurry	40,865	4½
Kinsale,	59,387	3¾	Newcastle,	61,681	5½	Tralee,	86,032	4⅛
Larne,	95,277	2¾	Newport,	13,168	10	Trim,	109,046	2½
Letterkenny,	81,959	4½	New Ross,	104,338	3½	Tuam,	76,934	3
Limerick,	[illegible]	5	Newry,	165,160	2	Tulla,	38,769	4½
Lisburn,	171,200	1½	Newtownards,	137,178	2	Tullamore,	80,178	3
Lismore,	49,885	4¾	Oldcastle,	62,463	2⅛	Urlingford,	45,491	3
Lisnaskea,	57,972	2½	Omagh,	94,240	2½	Waterford,	199,914	4½
Listowel,	52,258	3	Oughterard,	17,043	7½	Westport,	31,144	3½
Londonderry,	158,612	2	Parsonstown,	102,557	1½	Wexford,	107,768	3½
Longford,	66,079	4½	Portumna,	35,532	3	Youghal,	60,542	3½
Loughrea,	76,214	2½						

No. 8.—RETURN showing the AVERAGE WEEKLY COST per head for year ended 25th March, 1877

Average weekly cost.

ULSTER.	s.	d.	MUNSTER.	s.	d.		s.	d.		s.	d.
Bailieborough,	3	3	Killarney,	3	2½	Skull,	2	4½	Celbridge,	2	11½
Letterkenny,	3	1¼	Cork,	3	2¼	Clonakilty,	2	4	Parsonstown,	2	11¼
Bawnboy,	3	0½	Kilmacthomas,	3	2¼	Mitchelstown,	2	3½	Wexford,	2	11
Carrickmacross,	3	0½	Newcastle,	3	2	Midleton,	2	3¼	Longford,	2	10
Dunfanaghy,	3	0¼	Tulla,	3	1¾	Dunmanway,	2	2	Gorey,	2	10
Lisnaskea,	2	11¾	Dungarvan,	3	1½	Castletown,	2	1½	Athlone,	2	9½
Strabane,	2	10¾	Rathkeale,	3	1½	Kenmare,	2	1	Dundalk,	2	9
Clogher,	2	9½	Tipperary,	3	1¼				Thomastown,	2	8
Clones,	2	9	Ennis,	3	1						
Banbridge,	2	9	Killadysert,	3	1	LEINSTER					
Cavan,	2	8½	Glin,	3	1						
Antrim,	2	8½	Corrofin,	3	0¾	Donaghmore,	4	7			
Irvinestown,	2	8¼	Ennistymon,	3	0½	Athy,	4	1	CONNAUGHT.		
Belfast,	2	7½	Kanturk,	3	0½	Dunshaughlin,	4	0			
Ballycastle,	2	7	Millstreet,	3	0¼	Trim,	3	11	Roscommon,	3	7½
Milford,	2	6¾	Cahirciveen,	3	0¼	Naas,	3	10	Tuam,	3	6¾
Monaghan,	2	6½	Limerick,	3	0¼	Ardee,	3	9	Strokestown,	3	5¼
Downpatrick,	2	6¼	Clogheen,	3	0¼	Rathdown,	3	8¼	Ballinasloe,	3	3½
Newry,	2	6¼	Roscrea,	3	0¼	Abbeyleix,	3	7½	Castlerea,	3	3¼
Newtownards,	2	6	Thurles,	3	0¼	Balrothery,	3	6¾	Galway,	3	2¼
Dungannon,	2	6	Kilmallock,	3	0	Castlecomer,	3	6½	Glennamaddy,	3	1¾
Inishowen,	2	5¾	Cashel,	3	0	Delvin,	3	6½	Loughrea,	3	1½
Armagh,	2	5	Croom,	2	11½	Drogheda,	3	6¼	Claremorris,	3	1½
Larne,	2	4¾	Borrisokane,	2	11¼	Mountmellick,	3	6¼	Boyle,	3	1½
Enniskillen,	2	3½	Kilrush,	2	11	Carlow,	3	6	Ballinrobe,	3	0
Castleblayney,	2	3¼	Waterford,	2	11	Rathdrum,	3	6	Oughterard,	3	0
Cootehill,	2	2¾	Nenagh,	2	10½	Mullingar,	3	5¾	Killala,	3	0
Kilkeel,	2	2½	Macroom,	2	10	Urlingford,	3	5½	Mountbellew,	2	11
Gortin,	2	2½	Mallow,	2	9¼	Baltinglass,	3	5½	Portumna,	2	10¾
Coleraine,	2	2¼	Scariff,	2	9	South Dublin,	3	5	Carrick-on-Shan.,	2	9¾
Ballymena,	2	2¼	Kinsale,	2	8¾	Navan,	3	4½	Ballina,	2	9¾
Lurgan,	2	2¼	Bandon,	2	8½	Edenderry,	3	3¼	Dromore West,	2	9½
Ballyshannon,	2	2	Tralee,	2	8½	Ballymahon,	3	3	Manorhamilton,	2	9
Magherafelt,	2	2	Skibbereen,	2	8¼	Granard,	3	1¾	Sligo,	2	8¾
Donegal,	2	1¾	Clonmel,	2	8	North Dublin,	3	1¾	Tobercurry,	2	8½
Glenties,	2	1½	Ballyvaghan,	2	7¾	Kilkenny,	3	1½	Gort,	2	8¼
Cookstown,	2	1¼	Lismore,	2	7½	Kells,	3	1½	Swineford,	2	8
Lisburn,	2	0¾	Fermoy,	2	6¾	Tullamore,	3	1½	Mohill,	2	7½
Omagh,	2	0¼	Dingle,	2	6½	Enniscorthy,	3	1¼	Newport,	2	7
Limavady,	1	11½	Listowel,	2	6¼	Shillelagh,	3	1¼	Westport,	2	5½
Castlederg,	1	10¾	Carrick-on-Suir,	2	6	New Ross,	3	0½	Clifden,	2	5
Ballymoney,	1	10¼	Bantry,	2	5½	Oldcastle,	3	0½	Castlebar,	2	4½
Londonderry,	1	8	Youghal,	2	5¼	Callan,	2	11½	Belmullet,	2	3¼
Stranorlar,	1	6½									

No. 9.—Minimum Space Requirements in Workhouses.

Schedule recommended by the Commissioners.

Dormitories				Day Room.
Class.	Space.			Day Room.
	Wall	Floor	Cubic	
1	2	3	4	5
Sick.				
Ordinary,	6 feet.	80 feet.	800	
Lying in,	6 feet	80 feet	800	
Offensive, &c., cases,	6 feet.	80 feet.	800	
Healthy.				
"Aged and infirm," occupying one room by day and night.	6 feet	60 feet.	600	
"Do.," in rooms partially occupied by day and night.	5′ 6″	50′	500	Equal to one-fifth of total dormitory floor space.
Mothers with children,	5′ 0″	45′	450	Nurseries.
Able-bodied adults, both sexes,	4′ 6″	About 40′	400	Equal to one-third of total dormitory floor space.
Children,	3′ 9″	—	300	Equal to one-fourth of total dormitory floor space.

In measuring the cubic space of rooms immediately under the roof, half the height of the triangle formed by the roof, and a line drawn from point to point where it rests upon the walls, is to be deducted from the height of the ward.

The height of the wards is to be measured from floor to floor where there is no plastered ceiling, and from floor to ceiling where the latter is plastered.

Any height over 10 feet is not to be taken into account in calculating the cubic space in column 4.

Should the height of a ward be less than 10 feet, the space to be allotted in columns 2 and 3 must be increased, so as to ensure to each bed the minimum requirement of cubic space as laid down in column 4.

In calculating the wall space available for each bed the space occupied by fire-places and doors should not be included.

Copy of Memoranda submitting the above to Professional Opinion.

The Poor Law Inquiry Commissioners were instructed to inquire whether it would be expedient to dissolve any Poor Law Unions in Ireland, and to amalgamate them with other Unions.

The chief ground upon which such amalgamation was applied for by different Unions was that there was a superabundance of workhouse accommodation, and that the poor of three or four Unions might be conveniently accommodated in one workhouse.

With reference to this averment, the Commissioners had to inquire and ascertain whether such superabundance of accommodation does in fact exist. They found—1st, That the workhouses of Ireland were originally constructed with a view to test the destitution of the able-bodied poor, and that the main provision in them consisted of large dormitories—without corresponding provision of dayrooms.

2nd. That the provision for the sick had reference solely to an assumed per-centage of cases upon the ordinary indoor pauperism, and not to the admission of cases on account of sickness only.

3rd. That during periods of great distress the workhouses were made to hold, though they never could properly accommodate, numbers enormously in excess of their original allotment.

4th. That this original allotment was an appropriation in gross and not by classes. A workhouse was built to hold 800 or 1,000 people, but for a considerable time no attempt was made, or, perhaps, under the circumstances of the country, would have been made, to classify them with any degree of strictness, or to appropriate the rooms according to any fixed scale of accommodation.

5th. By degrees the whole character of the indoor pauperism of Ireland has changed. There are virtually no ablebodied poor in the workhouse. Aged and infirm, sick, and children now constitute the indoor pauperism of Ireland. Sickness as well as pauperism is now a ground of admission, and the infirmary has become more than ever an important department of an Irish workhouse.

This change in the character of indoor pauperism was followed by—if it did not lead to—an appropriation of workhouse room according to a fixed scale of so many cubic feet of space for each inmate.

No account was taken of anything else—neither of wall space or floor space, or the interference of fire-places, doors, gangways, or windows, or of the means of ventilation. The result of this mode of computing accommodation was, that by the sealed orders of the Local Government Board, guardians were authorised to place a thousand inmates in a workhouse that would be fully occupied by six hundred—fully occupied, that is to say, according to this schedule of accommodation.

The preceding statement is now submitted to you in order that you may advise the Poor Law Inquiry Commissioners,

1st. Whether, having regard to the health and the reasonable accommodation of the inmates of workhouses of the several classes specified, the scale is one of which you approve, and the adoption of which ought to be enforced by order of the Local Government Board.

2nd. Whether you consider that any modification, and if so, to what extent should be made in this schedule. With a view to assist you in advising the Poor Law Inquiry Commissioners on the preceding points, the following extract from their Draft Report is (confidentially) submitted to you.

Report of Sir Dominic Corrigan, Bt., M.D., M.R.C.S.E., F.K.Q.C.P.I.; J. T. Banks, Esq., M.D., H.F.K.Q.C.P.I.; and J. L. Holloway, Esq., M.D., M.R.C.S.E., D. Surgeon-General, A.M.D.

Gentlemen,—We beg to state that having given the subject submitted to us by the Poor Law Inquiry Commissioners for our advice and opinion the most full and careful consideration, we have arrived at the conclusion that, considering the circumstances and construction of the Irish workhouses, the schedule proposed by them is one which we approve, and which, in our opinion, ought to be adopted.

We have no doubt it is framed with a view of giving as liberal an allowance of space to the sick and healthy inmates of the workhouses as is attainable.

In calculating the cubic space alloted, no height over

ten feet is taken into account, and of this we highly approve.

Finding that owing to the limited accommodation in the infirmaries of the workhouses, it is impossible to provide dayrooms for the patients.

We consider that attention to proper ventilation is of paramount importance.

We desire to observe that unless there be a provision in dayrooms and hospital wards for a system of ventilation which shall insure constant interchange of air from without and within, and which shall be free from being interfered with by the inmates, it matters not how high the wards and dayrooms may be—the impure air from lungs and bodies of those within will ascend to the roof and will be detained in upper stratum, and return when cooled down, to be again breathed in a vitiated state. This evil is obviated by punched tin or zinc ventilators, through which a constant alternation of air is maintained by changes of temperature constantly in action between inner and outer air.

In the Report of the Commissioners of Health (Ireland), 1846, 1850, there is a simple but efficient plan of ventilation recommended, and to this plan, which is annexed, we call the attention of the Commission of Inquiry, observing at the same time that in the House of Industry (Government) hospitals with which two of us have for many years been connected, it has been tested by the experience of twenty-five years, and has been found to answer perfectly.

We subjoin an extract from the Commissioners' Report of 1852.

"A sheet of zinc or tin plate is punched (not drilled) with holes one-twelfth-inch diameter, and half an inch apart. Thus prepared, it is inserted in place of one pane of glass in every window, or every alternate window, as required, care being taken that the side on which the burra project is turned to the weather, so as to throw off the rain. Neither wire gauze nor perforated zinc of the ordinary kind will be found suitable, as both permit blasts of cold air and rain to pass through them; and the former is liable, after some time, to become choked with dust. Those who have had practical experience of the importance of ventilation to the sick, and of the difficulty of maintaining it, will appreciate the value of a simple plan that combines utility with cheapness, and which cannot be interfered with by the inmates of the hospital or dayroom."

We send for your inspection a zinc plate such as is described in the Report.

We have the honour to remain, gentlemen, your obedient servants,

D. J. Corrigan.

J. T. Banks.

James J. Holloway,
Deputy Surgeon-General, A.M.D.

Appendix A

Maximum Space Requirements.

No. 10.—Workhouse Accommodation in Cork District.

Letter from Dr. MacCabe to the Commissioners.

Workhouse Accommodation Cork District.

Blackrock, Cork,
25th March, 1878.

Sir,—On the 22nd of February last I had the honour of meeting two of your Commissioners in Mallow, and on that occasion I was requested to furnish them with a return of one or more of the union workhouses under my charge, showing the accommodation afforded under the measurements of cubic space as given in the existing Limitation Orders, and under the measurements as prescribed in Schedule A.

In carrying out the instructions of the Commissioners, I selected the Mallow Union Workhouse as a fair type of all the workhouses in my district (with one exception to which I shall presently refer). Mallow Workhouse is one of average size; a rough ground plan of that workhouse is in the hands of the Commissioners, and it has been visited and examined on, I think, three occasions by Mr. Andrew Doyle, one of the commissioners. The measurements under the Limitation Order referring to Mallow, may be stated to be generally applicable to all the workhouses in my district except Cork.

Cork Workhouse I have not included in my returns—it forms the exception to which I have alluded. Recent additions to the Cork Workhouse rendered it desirable to re-examine the accommodation, and, with the sanction of the Local Government Board, the cubic space was lately calculated and re-distributed upon a scale not inferior to that given in Schedule A.

Taking Mallow, therefore, as a fair example of the calculations under the old system as contrasted with the allowance of cubic space prescribed under Schedule A, and applying the result obtained in Mallow to the other workhouses in my district, the following approximate results are obtained:—

Name of Workhouse	Accommodation under Limitation Order	Accommodation under Schedule A.
Bandon,	1,008	594
Clonakilty,	807	473
Dunmanway,	631	370
Fermoy,	736	431
Kinsale,	636	385
Macroom,	703	412
Midleton,	753	441
Mitchelstown,	565	343
Youghal,	867	508
Kilmallock,	1,003	588
Dungarvan,	885	518
Lismore,	870	510

I venture to hope that these results will be considered sufficiently near the truth to answer the purposes of the Poor Law Union Inquiry Commissioners.

I have the honour to remain, sir,

Your obedient servant,

Frederick MacCabe,
Local Government Inspector.

H. A. Robinson, esq., Secretary,
Poor Law Union Inquiry Commission.

ENCLOSURE in foregoing—MALLOW UNION WORKHOUSE (CORK DISTRICT).

	Under Existing Sealed Orders							Under Schedule A.					
Dormitory or Day Room to be described as such, and distinguished by Numbers.	Dimensions of Room: Length	Width	Height	Contents, Cubic Feet	Portion of Workhouse in which situated, and whether Permanent or Temporary Building	Number the Ward is entitled to accommodate	Cubic Space allowed for each Occupant	Space available: Wall	Floor	Cubes	Number the Ward will accommodate	Proposed Appropriation.	Remarks
1	2	3	4	5	6	7	8	9	10	11	12	13	14
	Ft. In.	Ft. In.	Ft. In.				Feet.						
Healthy Inmates													
3 Dormitory,	26 6	14 11	14 11	4,840	Entrance building, permanent,	20	300	63	397	3,870	10	Healthy females,	Not quite 10.
3 "	42 11	16 7	10 7	6,977	Main building; permanent,	21	300	106	674	6,740	22	" adults.	
3 "	29 6	16 7	10 4	5,026	" "	17	300	58	486	4,860	13	" males	
4 "	53 6	16 9	15 8	13,316	" "	44	300	106	860	8,660	22	" adults.	
5 "	29 6	17 6	15 0	7,644	" "	25	300	59	501	5,010	13	" "	Over 12.
7 "	51 3	26 0	15 0	19,997	" "	66	330	107 6	1,326	13,260	44	" boys	
2 "	42 11	16 7	10 7	8,237	" "	81	300	106	674	6,740	22	" females,	Not quite 22.
3 "	29 6	16 7	10 5	5,026	" "	17	300	90	487	4,870	12	" women	
4 "	53 6	15 9	15 0	13,316	" "	44	300	106	901	9,010	22	" adults	
5 "	29 8	17 6	15 0	7,644	" "	25	300	58	401	4,010	12	" infants,	Over 12.
6 "	51 4	26 0	15 9	19,957	" "	66	300	102	1,320	13,200	33	" adults.	
3 "	79 8	16 4	15 7	20,160	" "	83	250	140	1,161	13,410	46	" children,	Not quite 46
4 "	60 0	16 4	16 7	17,356	" "	69	250	121	1,116	11,129	37	" girls.	
						553					305		
Aged and Infirm Inmates													
1 Ward,	43 6	16 4	11 11	10,316	Main building, permanent,	21	600	100	674	6,740	14	Aged and infirm males	
1 "	26 6	13 0	12 0	3,302	" "	7	400	69	304	2,840	5	" females,	Not quite 5.
2 "	26 5	18 5	12 9	4,844	" "	12	400	69	450	4,500	8	" "	
3 "	46 0	10 8	12 0	10,464	" "	21	500	206	674	6,740	14	" "	Over 14
1 "	72 9	17 11	10 6	13,576	"New building"; permanent,	27	500	244	1,296	12,960	21	" "	
2 "	20 6	17 11	8 7	4,487	" "	8	500	70	531	4,437	7	" "	
3 "	36 6	17 11	8 7	5,618	" "	11	500	78	687	5,893	9	" "	
						108					75		
Ordinary Sick,													
1 Ward,	21 10	16 10	11 9	4,318	Infirmary building, permanent,	9	500	63	374	3,740	6	Sick males	
2 "	20 7	16 10	10 11	4,379	" " "	11	400	55	433	4,330	5	"	
3 "	26 11	18 10	10 11	4,768	" " "	5	500	51	429	4,290	7	Sick patients,	Sex not stated
4 "	27 0	27 0	13 1	4,790	" " "	10	400	44	374	3,740	6	"	"
5 "	67 0	27 0	13 8	15,291	" " "	30	500	134	1,200	11,230	16	Sick males	
6 "	21 11	17 0	13 1	2,650	" " "	5	500	22	204	2,040	3	Sick patients,	Sex not stated (over 3)
7 "	12 2	17 2	13 1	2,729	" " "	4	500	24	204	2,040	3	Nurses,	Reckoned as healthy.
8 "	22 0	17 6	13 1	4,893	" " "	10	300	44	374	3,740	6	Sick females.	
9 "	67 0	27 0	13 8	15,243	" " "	30	300	134	1,180	11,880	19	"	
10 "	21 10	16 10	11 9	4,318	" " "	9	400	43	374	3,740	6	"	
11 "	22 0	16 11	11 0	4,094	" " "	8	500	44	374	3,740	5	Sick inmates,	Reckoned as healthy.
12 "	26 0	16 11	11 0	4,838	" " "	10	500	52	449	4,490	7	Prostitutes.	Reckoned as sick
						146					88		
Contagious Diseases, Fever Hospital													
1 Ward,	19 4	19 10	11 5	3,307	Fever hospital building, permanent.	7	500	44	281	2,810	3	Fever cases,	Over 3.
2 "	16 10	17 4	11 5	3,426	" " "	7	500	53	280	2,800	5	"	"
3 "	40 2	17 7	11 6	8,129	" " "	16	500	80	720	7,200	8	"	"
4 "	27 8	19 10	11 9	3,800	" " "	7	500	41	273	2,730	3	"	"
5 "	16 11	17 4	11 9	3,445	" " "	7	500	38	297	2,970	3	"	"
6 "	40 2	17 7	11 9	8,288	" " "	17	500	80	720	7,200	9	"	"
7 "	12 7	7 10	11 8	1,270	" " "	3	500	26	119	1,190	1	"	Over 1.
						64					31		
Auxiliary (County Fever Hospital) reserved for Small-pox.													
1 Ward,	16 0	16 4	10 4	2,700	Auxiliary building, permanent,	7	500	32	260	2,600	3	Reserved for dangerous contagious diseases	
2 "	13 1	20 9	10 4	2,487	" " "	5	500	24	240	2,400	3	" "	
3 "	16 6	20 3	10 3	3,321	" " "	7	500	32	320	3,200	4	" "	
4 "	16 3	20 4	10 3	3,390	" " "	7	500	32	338	3,380	4	" "	
5 "	10 2	20 0	12 4	2,500	" " "	5	500	20	200	2,000 say	3	" "	(3+)
6 "	20 2	12 0	8 10	2,380	" " "	5	500	40	240	2,400	3	" "	
						35					19		

MALLOW UNION WORKHOUSE—SUMMARY and OBSERVATIONS.

—		Number the Ward is entitled to accommodate	Number the Ward will accommodate
Sheet 1. Healthy inmates,		553	305
" Aged and infirm inmates,		108	75
Sheet 2. Ordinary sick,		146	88
" Contagious diseases ("offensive, &c.," cases),		64	31
" Auxiliary reserved for small-pox, &c. ("offensive, &c.," cases),		35	19
		905	551
Accommodation according to scale fixed in sealed order,	905		
" " Schedule A,	551		
Difference,	374		

Observations.—In calculating floor space and cubic space, it is right to remark that my calculations are not absolutely correct. Thus, when a room has measured 25·11 × 16·10 I have given the floor space as 26 × 17. I thought this reasonable as the cubic space (following the direction given in the table with which Major Trench favoured me) has in every instance been reduced by only allowing 10 feet for height, although in some rooms the height exceeded 15 feet.

A few temporary sheds have not been included, and a few day rooms have not been included, because both were excluded from the calculations in the sealed order returns, and to have included them would have destroyed the comparison between accommodation as given in the sealed order and as prescribed under Schedule A.

25th March, 1878.

F. M.

Appendix A

Letter from the Irish Medical Association

No. 11.—Letter from the Irish Medical Association to the Chairman of the Poor Law Inquiry Commissioners.

Royal College of Surgeons, Dublin,
13th day of April, 1878.

Sir—The Council of the Irish Medical Association beg to submit the following observations relative to abuse of Dispensary Medical Relief in Ireland, being aware that the Commissioners are anxious to obtain information concerning the present state of medical relief for the sick poor in Ireland, which may tend to make that system more efficient and less liable to be abused than it has hitherto been in many instances:—

When the Medical Charities' Act passed in 1851, the working classes in Ireland were in a very impoverished condition so far as medical relief was concerned, and were dependent upon institutions supported by voluntary contributions. The poor were in the habit of obtaining relief in these institutions by the mere recommendation of subscribers, irrespective of the degree of their poverty. Under these circumstances, on the passing of the Act, it was considered that dispensary medical relief should be easily obtainable, and that the Committee of Management of the dispensaries should have the power of ordering medical relief equivalent to that possessed by the managers and subscribers under the old voluntary dispensary system.

The state of things which existed at the time of the passing of the Medical Charities' Act has now passed away, and almost all the subscribers and managers of the old voluntary dispensaries have passed away, too. The working classes of Ireland are in a much better position than they were at that time, and the position of the Irish artisan, labourer, or cottier farmer, may now be considered as good, relatively, as the position of similar persons in England. Taking the present condition of the working classes in Ireland into consideration, the Council are of opinion that medical relief under the Poor Laws should be administered in Ireland upon similar principles to those acted upon in England, namely—that while every one too poor to pay for medical attendance should be able to obtain efficient attendance easily at the public expense, yet persons able to contribute towards the expense of medical attendance, either through provident dispensaries or sick clubs, or by direct fees to medical practitioners, should not be permitted to obtain gratuitous advice, except in cases of great emergency.

The Council have taken considerable pains to obtain the opinion of the Dispensary Medical Officers upon this question, and have ascertained that the abuse of dispensary medical relief, chiefly by visiting ("red") tickets, is almost universal, and especially great in the south and west of Ireland. They have also ascertained that tickets are so easily obtained that practically there is little difficulty, in the majority of districts, in any one procuring a ticket. They also find that there is great difficulty in getting improperly issued tickets cancelled by the Committee, partly on account of the *long intervals* between the meetings of the Committee, and partly through the unwillingness of the members of the Committee to censure their fellow-members by cancelling tickets issued by them. This is to a certain extent demonstrated by the small number of cancelled tickets reported to the Local Government Board. The report of the Board shows that the number of tickets cancelled is only about 500, out of a total of nearly three-quarters of a million per annum issued in the whole of Ireland, while the abuse of dispensary relief is notorious in almost every district.

The cancelling of tickets is almost useless, as the patient has had the attendance of the Dispensary Medical Officer, who is responsible for the case, which has generally terminated long before the Dispensary Committee holds a meeting, and tickets are frequently re-issued for the same individual immediately after the previous one had been cancelled. Therefore the Council consider that the following portion of section 9, cap. 68, 14 and 15 Vict.—"Provided always that if any person who shall obtain a ticket . . . . shall be declared by a majority of the members then present not to be a fit object for dispensary relief, the ticket shall be cancelled, and the *holder thereof disentitled to further relief*"—should be read and acted upon in its literal sense.

The Council regret to find, on inquiry, that little or but feeble attempts have been made by working people in Ireland to found sick clubs or provident dispensaries, as in England; and the Council attribute this want of independence on their part to the fact that so long as free medical attendance is obtainable by almost every one, as at present, there is no inducement to the people to provide for their own wants out of their own pockets. The inquiries of the Council with regard to gratuitous medical relief in England have proved that wherever free relief is too easily obtainable, either no attempt has been made to establish provident dispensaries, or where such an attempt has been made it has failed.

The Council also have ascertained that a large number of the Dispensary Medical Officers in Ireland are willing to attend comparatively poor persons at a reduced rate.

The Council are therefore of opinion that, in order to reduce as far as possible the present great abuse of dispensary medical relief, the following rules should be enforced:—

1. That gratuitous medical relief should not be afforded to any person entitled to vote at elections for Members of Parliament.

2. That gratuitous relief should be afforded only to those who are barely able to support themselves and their families during health.

Note.—Careful inquiries conducted in England have shown that—

- (*a*) Persons in receipt of over £2 a week are able to pay fees for medical advice, and may be left to arrange terms with their medical attendants.
- (*b*) Persons receiving at the rate of from £1 to £2 a week are sufficiently well off to provide for their medical attendance by means of provident dispensaries or sick clubs; as are also single persons in receipt of even less than £1 a week.

3. That persons able to provide for their medical attendance by provident dispensaries or sick clubs should be debarred from receiving gratuitous dispensary medical relief.

Note.—The Council consider it the duty of Poor Law Guardians and other local representatives of the people to take the lead in founding provident dispensaries, and even if necessary to subscribe funds for initiating such institutions. From the success which has been attained by these institutions in England, and the well known desire of medical men to help those who are willing to help themselves, there is little, if any, doubt that the services of medical officers (in most cases Dispensary Medical Officers) could easily be obtained for provident dispensaries, if established in Ireland.

4. That in cases of emergency medical relief "on loan" from the Poor Law Guardians might be granted to certain persons.

Note.—Medical relief on loan is intended by the Council to mean the granting of a ticket for medical attendance in case of emergency to a person who asserts his inability to pay, on condition that he shall, unless he produce proof of his inability to do so, pay to the Guardians such fee as the medical attendant would have been entitled to, had the person been attended as a private patient, which fee shall be collected by the Guardians for the medical attendant.

APPENDIX A.

Letter from the Irish Medical Association.

5. The issuer of a ticket should be held liable for the fee for medical attendance, in case he shall have wilfully or negligently issued a ticket to a person not entitled to gratuitous relief, it being found that the privilege of issuing medical relief tickets is not unusually exercised for the personal benefit of the issuer.

6. A person not entitled to gratuitous relief, who obtains a ticket by misrepresentation, should be punished for so doing.

7. That power should be given to the issuer of the ticket, or to any Justice of the Peace, to cancel a ticket shown to have been improperly issued or obtained.

8. Wardens, if such officers be necessary, should be ratepayers rated at, at least, £15, whose appointment shall be subject to the sanction of the Local Government Board.

Note.—The Council have ascertained that a great deal of the abuse of medical relief is owing to the careless manner in which the Wardens frequently exercise their functions, and the Council are of opinion that in all large towns and many rural districts Wardens are unnecessary.

9. The existing regulations of the Local Government Board relative to the issuing of tickets should be strictly enforced, viz., that all the particulars upon the ticket, and the signature thereto, should be written by the person entitled to issue the ticket, and not by deputy.

The Council believe that if the foregoing suggestions were carried out, the present abuse of dispensary medical relief would be reduced to a minimum, if not altogether abolished; and they direct the special attention of the Commissioners to clauses 6, 7, 8, and 9, as affording a prospect of immediately checking to a great extent the existing abuse.

The Council think that, with the disposition of medical men to accept reduced fees from persons of limited means, together with the establishment of provident societies, and the introduction of the system of relief on loan as a security against emergencies, that no danger need be apprehended that any sick poor person will be unprovided with proper medical attendance, if the foregoing suggestions were adopted.

I have the honour to be, Sir,

Your obedient servant,

JOHN H. CHAPMAN, *Hon. Secretary.*

MAJOR THE HON. W. LE POER TRENCH, R.E.,
Chairman, Poor Law Inquiry Commission.

APPENDIX B.

APPENDIX B.

Pupils examined for Results.

NATIONAL EDUCATION, IRELAND.

No. 1.*—TABLE showing the Number of Pupils examined for Results in Ordinary Schools and in Poor Law Union Schools during the year 1877–78, with the per-centage of Passes gained by the Pupils examined in each Branch, and the Average Money Value per Pass in each Subject for each Class of Schools respectively.

—	Reading		Spelling		Writing.		Arithmetic.		Grammar.	
	Ordinary Schools.	Workhouse Schools.	Ordinary Schools.	Workhouse Schools.	Ordinary Schools.	Workhouse Schools.	Ordinary Schools.	Workhouse Schools.	Ordinary Schools.	Workhouse Schools.
Number examined,	336,340	4,105	336,340	4,105	336,340	4,105	336,340	4,105	170,597	1,642
Per-centage of passes to number examined.	88·3	88·1	77·6	75·0	69·9	81·4	60·4	68·2	54·5	56·4
Average money value of passes,	1s. 11¾d.	1s. 11¼d.	9½d.	9½d.	1s. 1¾d.	1s. 1¼d.	1s. 4½d.	1s. 3d.	11¼d.	5½d.

—	Geography.		Agriculture.		Book-keeping.		Needlework.	
	Ordinary Schools.	Workhouse Schools.	Ordinary Schools.	Workhouse Schools.	Ordinary Schools.	Workhouse Schools.	Ordinary Schools.	Workhouse Schools.
Number examined,	170,207	1,649	26,657	368	11,816	88	113,126	1,123
Per-centage of passes to number examined.	52·5	65·3	46·0	55·5	53·3	68·6	88·0	95·5
Average money value of passes,	7½d.	8½d.	1s. 1¼d.	1s. 3d.	1s. 4½d.	1s. 8d.	1s. 5½d.	1s. 0¾d.

PER-CENTAGE of PUPILS examined for Results in each Class to the Total Number examined in all the Classes for Ordinary and Workhouse Schools respectively.

	Ordinary Schools.	Workhouse Schools.
Per-centage in Infants' grade,	17·6	23·7
" Class I.,	21·9	25·6
" " II.,	19·8	20·3
" " III.,	16·0	15·1
" " IV.,	12·0	10·3
" " V.,	11·3	4·3
" " VI.,	2·6	0·6

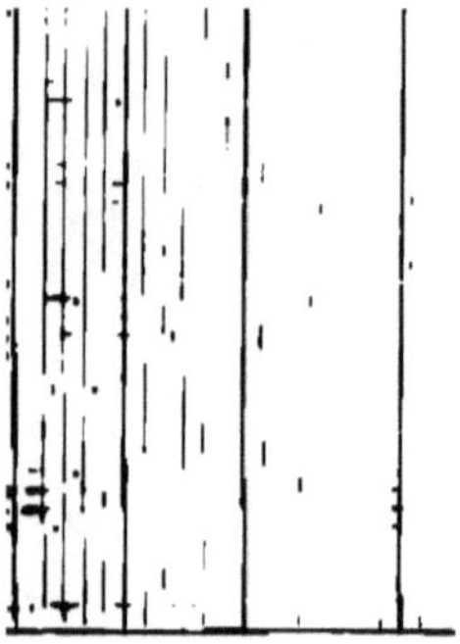

No. 3.—Programme of Instruction and Examination for National Schools.

Infants.

1. *Over 4 and under 6 years of age*:—To know the letters of the Alphabet, and to spell and read words of two letters.

2. *Six years and under 7 years of age*:—To read and spell to the end of Second Section of First Book.

First Class.

1. Reading.—To read correctly lessons in the latter half of the First Book.

2. Spelling.—(*a.*) To spell correctly the words arranged in columns at the head of the lessons in the First Book. (*b.*) To spell phrases or short sentences *selected from the lessons in the First Book.*

3. Writing.—To transcribe on slate any short sentence from the latter half of the First Book.

4. Arithmetic.—(*a.*) To read and set down numbers up to *and including* three places of figures. (*b*) To know the Addition Table. (*c.*) To add on slate or black board three numbers, each not exceeding two places of figures.

Second Class.

1. Reading.—(*a.*) To read correctly, and with due attention to pauses, the lessons in Second Book. (*b.*) To answer simple questions on the meanings of words, the subject-matter of the lessons, and to point out on the map places therein referred to. (*c*) To repeat at least four of the pieces of poetry correctly.

2. Spelling.—(*a.*) To spell orally the words arranged in columns at the head of the lessons in Second Book. (*b.*) To spell phrases or short sentences *selected from the lessons in Second Book.*

3. Writing.—(*a.*) To transcribe on paper, with correct spelling, any short sentence in Second Book to page 76. (*b.*) To exhibit in copy-books at least sixty pages of the *elementary numbers* of any approved series of copy-books, *written on sixty different days* since the preceding annual inspection—each page to be dated.

4. Arithmetic.—(*a.*) To read and set down any number up to and including four places of figures. (*b*) To know the Addition and *Subtraction* Tables. (*c.*) To work on slate questions in Simple Addition of not more than five addends of three places each, and easy questions in Simple Subtraction.

5. Needlework.—To know how to hem, *or* to do plain knitting.

Third Class.

1. Reading.—(*a.*) To read with ease and correctness the lessons of the Third Book. (*b*) To be fairly acquainted with the meanings of words, and the subject-matter of these lessons. (*c*) To repeat correctly five of the pieces of poetry contained in Third Book.

2. Spelling.—(*a*) To write from dictation on slate an easy sentence from the Third Book. (*b.*) To spell correctly the words arranged in columns at the head of the lessons.

3. Writing.—(*a.*) To transcribe on paper, with correct spelling, any four lines from the first half of Third Book. (*b.*) To exhibit in copy-books at least *one hundred* pages in round hand or elementary small hand, written *on one hundred different days* since the preceding annual inspection—*each page to be signed and dated by the pupil.*

4. Arithmetic.—(*a*). To read and set down any number up to *and including* six places of figures. (*b*) To know the Multiplication and Pence Tables. (*c.*) To work on slate or paper sums in all the Simple Rules, and also sums in Addition of Money not exceeding five addends.

5. Grammar.—To be well acquainted with the definitions of the Parts of Speech, and to distinguish the Parts of Speech in an ordinary sentence.

6. Geography.—To know the outlines and leading features of the Map of the World.

7. Needlework (Girls).—To know how to hem and to do plain knitting.

Fourth Class.

1. Reading.—(*a.*) To read with ease and correctness the lessons of the Fourth Book. (*b*) To be acquainted with the meanings of words, and the subject-matter of the lessons. (*c*) To repeat six of the pieces of poetry in Fourth Book correctly.

2. Spelling.—(*a.*) To write from dictation on paper a passage of six or seven lines selected from the Fourth Book. (*b*) To spell correctly the words arranged in columns at the head of the lessons.

3. Writing.—(*a*) To transcribe on paper, with correct spelling and punctuation, any six lines selected from the Third Book. (*b*) To exhibit in copy-books at least one hundred pages in fair small hand, *written on one hundred different days* since the preceding annual inspection—each page to be signed and dated by the pupil, and *to be kept neat and free from blots.*

4. Arithmetic.—(*a*) To know Numeration and Notation *well*, and all the *more useful* arithmetical tables. (*b.*) To perform *mentally* easy exercises in Addition and Subtraction, and to work on slate or paper, *accurately and speedily*, a sum of seven lines in Addition of Money. (*c.*) To work on paper questions in all the Compound Rules and Reduction.

5. Grammar.—(*a.*) To be well acquainted with the definitions of the Parts of Speech, and to distinguish the Parts of Speech readily and intelligently in any ordinary sentence. (*b*) To be well acquainted with the gender, number, and cases of nouns and pronouns, the comparison of adjectives, and the simple moods, tenses, &c., of verbs.

6. Geography.—(*a.*) To know the ordinary geographical definitions. (*b*) To be acquainted with the Maps of the World, Europe, and Ireland.

7. Agriculture* (Boys).—(*a.*) To answer intelligently on the subject-matter of the lessons in Part III. (Crops) of the Agricultural Class Book; or (*b*) Part I. of Introduction to Practical Farming (exclusive of Cottage Gardening).

8. Needlework (Girls).—To exhibit fair proficiency in hemming, stitching, and top-sewing, and in plain knitting.

* Optional for pupils of this class in *all* Schools—Town and Rural.

Fifth Class—First Stage.

1. Reading.—(*a.*) To read with fluency, correctness, and intelligence the first 200 pages of the Fifth Book of Lessons. (*b*) To answer intelligently on the subject-matter of the lessons read. (*c.*) To repeat correctly six of the poetical pieces in the prescribed portion of the Fifth Book.

2. Spelling.—(*a.*) To write from dictation, on paper, with correct spelling, an ordinary passage of *six or seven* lines from the Fifth Book. (*b*) To spell ordinary words and phrases selected from the prescribed portion of the Fifth Book.

3. Writing.—(*a.*) To write a neat legible hand with ease and freedom. (*b.*) To exhibit in suitable books one hundred pages of well-written school exercises, executed *on one hundred different days* since the preceding annual inspection—each page to be signed and dated by the pupil.

4. Arithmetic.—(*a.*) To know the numeration and notation of Decimals, and *all the arithmetical tables* in the Board's First Book of Arithmetic, and to be able to write out on paper any of the latter in correct form. (*b.*) To perform simple arithmetical questions *mentally*, and to work on slate or paper, *accurately and speedily*, a sum of ten lines of Addition of money. (*c.*) To work neatly, on paper, questions in Simple Proportion and Practice.

5. Grammar.—(*a.*) To be well acquainted with Orthography and Etymology. (*b.*) To parse simple sentences.

6. Geography.—(*a*) To understand longitude, lati-

tude, zones, &c. (b.) To know the *maps* of the Continents.

7. AGRICULTURE* (BOYS).—(a.) To answer intelligently on the subject-matter of the lessons in Parts III. and IV. of the Agricultural Class Book; or (b.) Parts I. and II. of Introduction to Practical Farming (exclusive of Cottage Gardening).

8. BOOK-KEEPING.—First Three Sets (Board's Treatise).

9. NEEDLEWORK (GIRLS).—To be proficient in sewing and knitting.

* Optional for pupils of this class in Town Schools.

FIFTH CLASS—SECOND STAGE.

1. READING.—(a.) To read with fluency, correctness, and intelligence the Fifth Book of Lessons (b.) To answer intelligently on the subject-matter of the lessons (c.) To repeat correctly six of the poetical pieces in the Fifth Book

2. SPELLING.—(a.) To write from dictation, on paper, with correct spelling, an ordinary passage of *six or seven* lines from the Fifth Book (b.) To spell ordinary words and phrases selected from the Fifth Book or the Girls' Reading Book.

3. WRITING.—(a.) To write a neat legible hand with ease and freedom (b.) To exhibit in suitable books *one hundred* pages of well-written school exercises, executed *on one hundred different days* since the preceding annual inspection—each page to be signed and dated by the pupil—*and at least thirty of these exercises to be letters on simple subjects*

4. ARITHMETIC.—(a.) To know the numeration and notation of Decimals, and *all the arithmetical tables*, and to be able to write out on paper any of the latter in correct form (b.) To perform simple arithmetical questions *mentally*, and to work on slate or paper, *accurately and speedily*, a sum of ten lines of Addition of Money. (c.) To work neatly, on paper, questions in Simple and Compound Proportion, Practice, and easy questions in Vulgar Fractions and Decimals

5. GRAMMAR.—(a.) To be well acquainted with Orthography and Etymology. (b.) To know the *principal* Latin roots, prefixes, &c. (c.) To parse simple sentences

6. GEOGRAPHY.—(a.) To understand longitude, latitude, zones, &c. (b.) To know the *Maps* of the Continents (c.) To be acquainted with the geography of the British Empire

7. AGRICULTURE (BOYS).*—To answer intelligently on the subject-matter of the lessons in Parts III. and IV. of the Agricultural Class Book, or (b.) Parts I. and II. of Introduction to Practical Farming.

8. BOOK-KEEPING.—First Five Sets (Board's Treatise)

9. NEEDLEWORK (GIRLS).—To be proficient in sewing and knitting, and in cutting out any simple article of dress.

* Optional for pupils of this class in Town Schools

SIXTH CLASS.

N.B.—Pupils presented for the *first time* will not be examined in Reading, Spelling, or the repetition of Poetry beyond the first 200 pages of the Sixth Book.

1. READING.—(a.) To read the Sixth Book with fluency, correctness, and intelligence, and to answer intelligently on the subject-matter of the lessons (b.) To repeat correctly six of the pieces of poetry in the Sixth Book.

2. SPELLING.—To write on paper in a free legible hand, and with correct spelling and punctuation, a *paragraph of six or seven lines* dictated from Sixth Book.

3. WRITING.—(a.) To exhibit in suitable books one hundred pages of *school exercises*, written in a good hand *on one hundred different days* since the preceding annual inspection. *Each exercise, as in the preceding classes, to be signed and dated by the pupil.* (b.) Specimens of ornamental Penmanship may be included amongst the exercises

4. ARITHMETIC, &c.—(a.) To be expert in mental calculation. (b.) To perform *accurately and speedily*, on slate or paper, a sum of twelve lines in Addition of Money. (c.) To work neatly, on paper, questions in any rule of arithmetic (including, *for boys only*, Involution and Evolution).

5. GRAMMAR.—(a.) To parse prose and poetry correctly (b.) To be acquainted with the principal roots, prefixes, and affixes employed in the formation of English derivatives (c.) To write, with correct grammar and composition, a simple letter on any subject suggested by Inspector.

6. GEOGRAPHY.—(a.) To be acquainted with the elements of Mathematical and Physical Geography (b.) To draw, *from memory*, an outline map of Ireland. (c.) To know the geography of the Continents and of the British Empire.

7. BOOK-KEEPING.—1st year—First Six Sets (Board's Treatise). 2nd year—The entire of Board's Treatise.

8. AGRICULTURE (BOYS).*—To answer intelligently on the subject-matter of the lessons in Parts I., III., and IV. of the Agricultural Class Book, or (b.) Introduction to Practical Farming.

9. NEEDLEWORK (GIRLS).—(a.) To be able to cut out any article of females' apparel (b.) To exhibit satisfactory proficiency in the different branches of plain sewing and knitting

* Optional for pupils of this class in Town Schools.

NOTES.

(a.) No results fee can be paid in respect of any pupil whose attendance at the school during the year ended on the last day of the month preceding the annual examination shall be less than ONE HUNDRED days Under no circumstances are Saturdays' attendance to be included.

(b.) No pupil may be presented for examination in a higher class than that in which he is enrolled

(c.) In evening schools attendance on FIFTY evenings will be accepted as qualifying a pupil for admission to examination for results *Under no circumstances should a day school pupil be presented for examination in an evening school.* (N.B.—In evening schools results fees will be paid for reading, spelling, writing, and arithmetic *alone* of the ordinary branches, and for those only when the proficiency in them is traceable to the instruction given in the evening school *Results fees will be paid in these schools for not more than two extra branches, and when such payment is made no fees will be paid for the ordinary branches in respect of the same pupil*)

(d.) A written exercise, signed and dated by the pupil, must be presented for every attendance for which credit is claimed in an evening school.

(e.) Pupils *above* four and *under* seven years of age, who make the necessary minimum number of attendances in the year, may be presented for inspection as infants. *Individual* examination of such pupils may be dispensed with in those schools ONLY in which there is *bonâ fide* provision made for the systematic training of infants. A pupil who has been presented once as an infant and who attains to seven years of age before the second examination for infants, may be again presented as an infant A pupil over seven years of age attending school for the first time (*i.e.*, not before examined for results) may be presented for examination in the second portion of the Infants' Programme, but only once.

(f.) In a thoroughly organised infants' school, with a separate staff, and in a separate room, a fee of 4*s* per pupil may be paid.

(g.) No fee shall be paid in an infants' school for any pupil in music or drawing; nor for any pupil presented in a class higher than second, unless the pupil has been in attendance in the infants' school two years or more, in which case the pupil may be presented while in this school in the third class, provided that at the close of the results year for which the examination is held, such pupil shall not have completed his ninth year.

(h.) Only *one fee for each subject* can be paid for a pupil in any class, no matter how long the pupil may remain in the class, except in the case of *infants*, and

APPENDIX B. Programme of Instruction and Examination.

of the fifth class (in which a pupil may be paid for twice, viz., once in each stage) and of *sixth* class pupils. Any pupil in first, second, third, or fourth class who earns for the teacher fees for reading, writing, *and* arithmetic, cannot again earn a fee for any subject in the same class. But if the pupil fails in any of these three subjects, he may be presented a second time in the same class, and earn fees in the subjects in which he failed previously, subject to conditions specified in notes (*i*) and (*m*). (N.B.—No fee can be paid for a pupil in the first or higher classes who passes in only *one* of the subjects specified in the above Programme.)

(*i*.) *Under no circumstances* can a pupil be presented for examination *for results fees* more than twice in the same class, except in the case of the *fifth* and *sixth* classes, and in that of *infants*.

(*j*.) A pupil who failed to pass in either stage of fifth class, may be presented again in the *same stage* for fees of subjects in which he previously failed; and a pupil who failed to pass in sixth class, 1st stage, may be again presented in the *same stage* for fees of those subjects in which he failed previously.

(*k*.) A pupil presented a second time in sixth class may earn results fees in any subject in which he obtains a "No. 1 *pass*," without being required to pass in an extra subject; if he succeed in an extra subject, fees for "No. 2 *passes*" may also be gained. A pupil presented oftener than twice in sixth class cannot earn results fees in Reading, Spelling, or Writing, but may earn fees on "No. 1 *passes*" in the other subjects, provided he also pass in *two* extra subjects.

(*l*.) In cases where it is found necessary by the Inspector to hold a results examination at a date less than eleven months after the date of the termination of the last results year, teachers will be allowed to present pupils again in the same class in which they passed at the previous examination, subject to conditions specified in notes (*i*) and (*m*). (N.B.—This privilege will not, however, extend to the presentation of pupils again in the *same stage* of fifth or sixth class in which they previously passed.)

(*m*.) No pupil of seven years of age or above who has been enrolled for a *year* in any class can be presented in a lower class than that in which he is enrolled; and under no circumstances can a pupil be presented in a lower class than that next below the class in which he is enrolled.

(*n*.) Result fees cannot be paid for needlework, cutting out, or sewing machine, in a *female* school in which there is a workmistress paid by the Board.

(*o*.) A pupil may select a number of lines of prose instead of half of the pieces of poetry required under the head "Reading," section (*b*), in the different classes, to repeat as an exercise of memory, *i.e.*, so many lines of prose, *and* so many lines of poetry, the total of both not to be less than 300 lines.

Paid Monitors.

(*p*.) Second class monitors and third class monitors are to be examined in their schools with their respective school classes for results fees. Teachers to be entitled to whatever they may earn in addition to the usual gratuities granted for their training and extra instruction. Second class monitors are not to be presented for examination in any class in which they had passed previously as pupils or as third class monitors; and those of third year of service are not to be presented in any class lower than sixth.

(*q*.) The attendance of paid monitors shall be marked on a separate roll, and included in the average daily attendance in all schools; monitors are not to be reckoned as pupils for capitation payments; first class monitors are not to be presented for examination as pupils at the results examination, except in the *extra subjects* allowed.

(*r*.) First class monitors may be presented in Classics or French, or in a *science* branch not included in any part of their prescribed course of instruction. Only two science subjects will be allowed to be taken in any one year.

(*s*.) Second and third class monitors presented for results examinations, are subject to the same rules as ordinary pupils, as far as those rules apply to them.

Extra Subjects:—

(*t*.) No fee will be paid for any pupil *presented* for examination in the same subject, within the previous twelve months, under the Department of Science and Art.

(*u*.) A fee of five shillings will be paid for every pupil in the fifth or sixth class, who, *having passed in reading, spelling, writing*, AND *arithmetic*, shall exhibit satisfactory proficiency in the course prescribed in geometry and mensuration. A similar fee will be paid for every pupil of the fifth or sixth class passing in the course prescribed in algebra, or in any other of the *approved* extra branches, subject to the conditions and limitations laid down in the Programme of Extra Subjects. The ordinary results fees accruing in schools where assistants are recognized will be apportioned on the principle of allocating to the head teacher twice as much as to any assistant. Results fees for extra subjects, if these subjects are taught during ordinary school hours, shall go into the common fund divisible among the teachers in schools where one or more assistants are employed. But when extra subjects are taught before or after the ordinary school hours, the results fees accruing will be payable to the teacher who gives the extra instruction.

(*v*.) The subject matter of any of the Board's Reading Lesson Books, or a subject included in any part of the ordinary Results Programme, cannot be recognised as an EXTRA subject for any class. Girls of the fifth and sixth classes, however, may be examined on the subject matter of the Girls' Reading Book *as an extra subject* in lieu of Book-keeping—the first half of the book for fifth class, and the second half for sixth class. Management of poultry, &c., will not be paid for as an extra subject where there is not a poultry yard attached to the school, available for, and made use of in the practical instruction of the pupils. Payment can be made only once for the same pupil in the use of the sewing machine, or *in the same subdivision of any extra branch*.

Notice must be given by the teachers to the District Inspector at the commencement of the results year, or as soon after as classes in the subjects shall have been formed, of the extra branches in which they purpose to present pupils for examination.

The Regulations of the Commissioners enable teachers possessing certificates of competency satisfactory to the Commissioners to earn results fees under each of the following heads:—

I. Vocal Music and Drawing; II., Classics and French; III., Geometry, &c., Algebra, or other approved branch of Science—Provided—(*a*.) That no fees shall be paid for more than two Extra Subjects (besides Vocal Music and Drawing) in the same class to the same teacher; this limitation does not, however, extend to Classics or to French. (*b*.) That Classics, French, Trigonometry, Navigation, Mechanics, or any of the Physical Sciences, be not taught to children *under ten years of age*.—(*c*.) That an extra fee of Two Shillings per Quarter shall be paid by each pupil and monitor for instruction in each extra branch referred to under (*b*).

By order,
Wm. H. Newell,
John E. Sheridan, } *Secretaries.*

Education Office,
Marlborough-street, Dublin,
August, 1878.

APPENDIX B

Programme of Extra Subjects

No. 4.—Programme of Extra Subjects for which Results Payments may be claimed in National Schools.

The regulations of the Commissioners enable teachers possessing certificates of competency satisfactory to the Commissioners to earn results fees under each of the following heads:—

I. Vocal Music and Drawing.
II. Classics and French.
III. Geometry, Algebra, or other approved branch of science.

Provided that:—(a) No fees shall be paid for more than two extra subject (besides Vocal Music and Drawing) in the same class to the same teacher. This limitation does not, however, extend to Classics, or to French. (b) That Classics, French, Trigonometry, Navigation, Mechanics, or any of the Physical Sciences be not taught to children *under ten years of age*. (c) That an *extra fee* of two shillings per quarter shall be paid by each pupil for instruction in each extra branch referred to under (b)

Vocal Music and Drawing.

I. Results fees will be paid according to the following scale:—(a) Vocal Music—For pupils presented in second class, a fee of one shilling and sixpence for each pass. (b.) Vocal Music and Drawing—For pupils presented in third or higher classes, fees equal to that paid for arithmetic in the class.

II. No fee will be paid for any pupil who is not a member of a regularly constituted class for instruction in the theory and practice of vocal music, or of a regularly constituted drawing class, in operation in the school.

III. No fee for vocal music or drawing will be paid in infants' schools, nor for any pupil in other schools who does not pass in reading, and at least two of the other ordinary subjects of instruction (viz., spelling, writing, arithmetic).

IV. The following is the minimum proficiency upon which pupils will be allowed to pass in the different classes:—

Vocal Music—Programme.

Second and Third Classes.

(a) To name the notes on the clef, and to sing the natural scale. (b) To sing with precision, in unison, any six approved school songs

Fourth and Fifth Classes.

(a) To define satisfactorily the various intervals in the diatonic scale (b) To read accurately any ordinary piece in common time (c) To join in at least three harmonized pieces.

Sixth Class.

(a) To exhibit a fair knowledge of the theory of the subject. (b) To transpose an easy passage from one key to another. (c) To take first and second parts in at least three harmonized pieces

Note 1.—No fees will be paid for pupils in second or third classes unless the pupils of the higher classes show a satisfactory proficiency.

2.—As pupils advance from class to class, they must exhibit a knowledge of at least two new songs in each class.

3.—If the Tonic Sol Fa system be pursued in any school, a programme of proficiency for each class must be submitted for the approval of the Board before the class can be presented for examination for results fees.

Drawing—Programme.

Third and Fourth Classes.

(a.) Free-hand drawing from the flat on paper, such as simple arrangements of straight lines, forming either simple familiar objects, or geometrical designs, or easy curved line ornament.

Fifth Class.

(a) Free-hand drawing, of a more advanced character, such as simple ornament, curved lines, or, (b) Easy practical geometry.

Sixth Class.

(a) Free hand drawing, of a still more advanced character, from the flat on paper, such as advanced ornament, higher practical geometry, or elementary drawing from objects in outline (b) Free-hand drawing from the model and from shaded examples.

Note.—If a pupil be presented a second year in sixth class, he may exhibit drawings from examples of landscape, figures, or animals, or *shading* from the model, perspective, and water colours. The proficiency must in all cases be satisfactory to entitle the pupil to a pass. Specimens of drawings to be forwarded by the Inspector to the Education Office with his report.

Classics and French.

The Commissioners of National Education have sanctioned the payment of results fees for Latin, Greek, and French, upon the following conditions:—

I. If these subjects be taught by a recognised National teacher, he must devote at least four hours per day, on five days in the week, to instruction in the ordinary English subjects.

II. Pupils learning Classics or French must also receive instructions for at least twenty hours weekly in the ordinary branches taught in the school.

III. Instruction in Classics and French, when given by the recognised National teachers must be given out of the ordinary school hours; but pupils, who have passed *once* in the *sixth* class, may be allowed to devote a portion of these hours to the *study* of their Classical or French lessons, provided that the routine business of the school be not interfered with.

IV. No pupil may be presented for examination in these branches who has not reached at least the *fifth* class.

V. No payment can be made for any pupil who has not made the necessary number of attendances, or for any pupil who fails to pass in *reading*, *spelling*, *writing*, and *arithmetic*.

VI. The course will extend over a period of three years, and a pupil can be presented only once for examination on the course for each year.

VII. For every pupil fulfilling the foregoing conditions who passes a satisfactory examination on the course prescribed for his year on the following programme, results fees will be awarded to the teacher:—In Latin, 10s., in Greek, 10s.; in French, 5s.

VIII. Payment of results fees for Classics or French will not debar a teacher from payment for two other approved extra branches, exclusive of vocal music and drawing.

Classics and French.—Programme.

Latin.—*First Year.*—Grammar, including syntax, Latin Delectus, or any similar elementary book. *Second Year.*—Two books of Cæsar, *or* two books of Virgil, *or* the Jugurtha of Sallust, or any approved course of equal difficulty. *Third Year.*—Not less than 500 lines of Ovid, Horace, or Juvenal, or of the Georgics of Virgil, *and* any book of Livy. An easy passage of at least 20 lines from the Third Book of Lessons to be translated into Latin prose.

Greek.—*First Year.*—Grammar, to the end of the regular verbs. *Second Year.*—Grammar, including syntax, Greek Delectus, and one book of Xenophon, either the Anabasis or the Cyropædia. *Third Year.*—Two books of the Iliad and a book of Herodotus.

French.—*First Year.*—Grammar, not including syntax, with 20 pages of a French vocabulary, or of an easy phrase book. *Second Year.*—Grammar, including syntax, with 20 additional pages of a phrase-book, and translation of two books of Telemachus, or Charles XII., or Chambaud's "Fables Choisies," edited by Du Gué. *Third Year*.—The Athalie of Racine, or any approved book of French poetry. Translation of an easy passage of English into French. Fair correctness of pronunciation.

NOTES (1).—The elementary books used during the first year must be approved by the Inspector.

(2).—Other books may be substituted for those prescribed for second and third years, but the sanction of the Commissioners for the change must be previously obtained.

SCIENTIFIC BRANCHES.

A fee of five shillings will be paid for every pupil in fifth or sixth class who, having passed in Reading, Spelling, Writing, AND Arithmetic, shall exhibit satisfactory proficiency in Geometry, &c., Algebra, or other *approved* extra branch, subject to the conditions and limitations laid down in the Programme for Extra Subjects.

The several branches of science for which results payments may be claimed are thus classified:—

I. Mathematical Science, comprising—1. Geometry and Mensuration. 2. Algebra. 3. Plane Trigonometry. *4. Navigation.

II. Mechanical Science, comprising—1. Mechanics. 2. Hydrostatics and Pneumatics. *3. Heat and the Steam Engine.

III. Physical Science, comprising—1. Physical Geography (*advanced course*). 2. Magnetism and Electricity. 3. Light and Sound. 4. Botany and Vegetable Physiology. *5. Zoology and Animal Physiology. *6. Inorganic Chemistry. *7. Geology.

The whole course of Physical Geography is required in one examination to constitute an extra branch, inasmuch as an elementary knowledge of the subject forms part of the regular programme for sixth class.

As regards Geometry and Algebra the course will extend to three examinations; for the other branches there will be two examinations, one elementary, the other more advanced.

It is strongly recommended that the pupils should have passed at least one examination in Geometry, and one in Algebra, before engaging in any of the other branches.

NOTE.—Physical Geography is not regarded as a subject for which an extra fee should be charged.

* The subjects marked with an asterisk are to be taken by pupils in the sixth class only.

GEOMETRY AND MENSURATION.

The entire course will be comprised in three examinations, as follows:—the first year's examination may take place while the pupil is in fifth class:—

FIRST EXAMINATION.—Euclid, Book I. Mensuration, area of rectilineal figures.

SECOND EXAMINATION.—(*In addition to above.*)—Euclid, Book II. Mensuration; circle—ellipse—zone—surfaces of the principal solids.

THIRD EXAMINATION.—(*In addition to above.*) Euclid, Books III. and IV., with the first eight propositions of Book VI. Mensuration; solidity of prism, cylinder, cone, and sphere—artificers' work—a general knowledge of the principles of land surveying.

ALGEBRA.

The entire course will be comprised in three examinations—the first may take place while the pupil is in fifth class:—

FIRST EXAMINATION.—Definitions—simple rules—computation of algebraic expressions—easy simple equations.

SECOND EXAMINATION.—(*In addition to above.*)—Simple equations, and problems producing them—simultaneous equations—algebraic fractions—involution and evolution—theory of integer indices—ratio and proportion.

THIRD EXAMINATION.—(*In addition to above.*)—Quadratic equations, and problems producing them—theory of fractional and negative indices—surds—arithmetical and geometrical progression—binomial theorem with integer indices.

APPENDIX B. — Programme of Extra Subjects.

PLANE TRIGONOMETRY.

Two examinations will embrace the course in this branch.

FIRST EXAMINATION.—Definitions—measurement of angles—trigonometrical functions—logarithms—use of logarithmic tables—formulæ for the solution of right-angled triangles—heights.

SECOND EXAMINATION.—(*In addition to above.*)—Four fundamental formulæ, with the more useful formulæ deduced from them—oblique-angled triangles—application to distances—description and use of theodolite and vernier.

NAVIGATION.

The course will comprise two examinations:—

FIRST EXAMINATION.—General knowledge of "Mathematical Geography"—rhumb line—difference of latitude—departure—course—correction of courses—plane sailing—middle latitude sailing—mariner's compass—variation—deviation—leeway.

SECOND EXAMINATION.—(*In addition to above.*)—Mercator's sailing—Mercator's projection and chart—the great principle of the chart, and in what its value consists—to determine a ship's place on the chart from her latitude and longitude, and *vice versâ*—to find the course and distance between two places on the chart—to compute a day's run—great circle sailing—oblique sailing.

(This subject should be preceded by a course of plane trigonometry, and it should be taught only after a pupil has reached the sixth class.)

MECHANICS.

FIRST EXAMINATION.—Matter—different states—laws of matter—natural forces—properties of bodies—momentum—equilibrium—action and re-action—composition and resolution of forces—lever, different kinds of—human arm as a lever—pulley—relation of P to W in lever and pulley—centre of gravity—toy figure explained—conditions to be satisfied by a balance—delicacy of balance—how obtained—double weighing.

SECOND EXAMINATION.—(*In addition to above.*)—Absolute unit of force—unit of work and horse power—systems of pulleys—wheel and axle—inclined plane—wedge—screw—relation of P to W in each—laws of motion—accelerated motion—laws of falling bodies—water hammer—feather and penny experiment—Atwood's machine—pendulum—terrestrial gravitation and the causes which modify it.

HYDROSTATICS AND PNEUMATICS.

FIRST EXAMINATION.—Pressure of non-elastic fluids—laws of pressure—bursting of rocks by pressure of small quantity of liquid. Hydrostatic paradox—Bramah's press—pressure of air—Magdeburg hemispheres—tumbler and card experiment—elasticity—air gun—barometer—construction of—specific gravity of solids—liquids—gases, how determined—pumps—suction pump—force pump—air pump—conveyance of water across valleys—syphon.

SECOND EXAMINATION.—(*In addition to above.*)—Expansion of gases—Boyle and Marriotte's law—pressure supported by a body immersed in a liquid—hydrostatic balance—specific gravity bottle—Nicholson's hydrometer—conditions of equilibrium of floating bodies—Cartesian diver—swimming—capillary phenomena—endosmose and exosmose—Torricellian vacuum—determination of heights by the barometer—aneroid barometer—balloons—parachute.

LIGHT AND SOUND.

FIRST EXAMINATION.—(1.) LIGHT—Undulating and emission theory—how objects are seen—intensity of light—law of inverse squares—velocity of light, how determined—shadows and penumbræ—laws of reflection—mirrors—formation of images by plane mirrors—use of concave mirrors in lighthouses—analysis of light—photometers.

(2) Sound—Sound waves, nature of them—density and elasticity of air, how affected by heat—velocity of sound through air, how determined—calculation of distance by light and sound—velocity of sound through water—law of inverse squares as applied to sound—reflection of sound—echo—whispering galleries.

Second Examination.—(*In addition to above.*)—(1.) Light—Kaleidoscope—concave spherical mirrors—meaning of term axis—principal focus—centre of mirror—refraction of light, illustrations of—different kinds of lenses—course of a ray of light through a converging and a diverging lens—optical structure of the eye and the condition of distinct vision—use of spectacles—solar spectrum—rainbow—stereoscope—magic lantern.

(2) Sound—Structure of the ear—difference between music and noise—musical notes—pitch and intensity—various methods of producing musical sounds—laws of vibration of strings and use of sound boards—laws of vibration of columns of air in pipes—ear trumpet—speaking trumpet.

Heat and the Steam Engine.

First Examination.—1. Heat—Theories as to the nature of heat—effects of heat—radiation—convection—conduction—good and bad conductors—metallic surfaces—when to be bright and when rough—absorption and transmission of heat—thermometers, how constructed—determination of the fixed points—expansion of solids—compensation pendulums—maximum density of water—freezing of deep and shallow water—salt and fresh water—vapour—dew—clouds.

2. Steam Engine.—Properties of steam—how produced—unit of heat—history of steam engine—Savary's engine—Newcomen's engine—difference between high and low pressure engines—horse power.

Second Examination.—(*In addition to above.*)—1. Heat—Differential thermometers—maximum and minimum thermometers—expansion of solids—of liquids—of gases—ventilation of mines and buildings—specific heat—how illustrated by experiment—latent heat and sensible heat—trace the successive effects of heat applied to ice below the freezing point till converted into steam—cooling effects of evaporation—how exemplified in different regions on the earth's surface—effects of specific heat of water on climate—freezing mixtures.

2. Steam Engine.—Watts' single acting engine—oscillating engine—fly wheel—parallel motion—eccentric—governor—propulsion of vessels by means of (1) paddlewheel—(2) screw—computation of the horse power of an engine.

Physical Geography.

Full Course—One Examination.—Form of the earth—motions—magnitude and measurement—distribution of land and water—zones—climates—temperatures—mountains—table lands—plains—deserts—rivers—lakes—tides and currents—atmosphere, its properties and uses—reflection—refraction—evaporation—clouds—rain—dew—hail—winds, three kinds of—hurricanes—cyclones—typhoons—hot winds—distribution of plants and animals—relation of horizontal and vertical distribution—different races of men and how distributed.

Magnetism and Electricity.

First Examination.—1. *Magnetism.*—Natural and artificial magnets—magnetic poles—theories of magnetism—magnetic induction—coercive force—explain experiments with iron filings, and with broken magnet.

2. *Frictional Electricity.*—History and general nature of—development by friction—electrical machines—conductors and non-conductors—two kinds of electricity, and how related to each other—Franklin's discovery.

3. *Dynamical Electricity.*—History of—different names for—Voltaic couple—explanation of action—origin of currents—simple experiments to show the existence of electric currents—Volta's pile.

Second Examination.—(*In addition to above.*)—1. *Magnetism.*—Mariner's compass—terrestrial magnetism; inclination—declination—magnetic intensity—magnetic equator and poles—magnetization—magnetic battery.

2. *Frictional Electricity.*—Best insulators—distribution of electricity—tendency to accumulate on corners and points, and to escape from them—induction—condensers—description of the Leyden jar as a condenser—electroscopes—thunder and lightning—lightning conductors.

3. *Dynamical Electricity.*—Different methods of originating the Voltaic current—Smee's battery—galvanometer—electric telegraph—chemical effects of the current—decomposition of water by the current.

Vegetable Physiology and Botany.

First Examination.—General structure of a flowering plant—distinction between flowering and flowerless plants—ascending and descending axis—functions of the several parts—root—stem—leaf—stipules—inflorescence—germination of bean—grain of wheat—three great classes of plants, with the characters of each—description of daisy, pea, primrose, and lily.

Second Examination.—(*In addition to above.*)—Vascular and cellular plants—various tissues of plants—various forms of root, stem, leaf, inflorescence, flower, fruit—cohesion, adhesion, and suppression of various parts of the flower—characters of ranunculaceæ—cruciferæ—leguminosæ—rosaceæ—umbelliferæ—labiatæ. Description and classification of the following plants:—Wheat; clover; rice; Indian corn; turnip; rhubarb; cucumber. Description of the following vegetable products, with the names and classification of the plants which yield them:—Opium—cotton—mustard—sugar—chocolate—tea—coffee—starch—jute—flax—cinnamon—pepper—galls—quinine.

Animal Physiology and Zoology.

First Examination.—*Animal Physiology.*—(*a.*) General build of the human body—human skeleton—names and position of the principal bones—composition of bone. (*b.*) Circulation of the blood—the heart and blood vessels—course of the circulation—valves of the heart—aorta—composition of the blood. (*c.*) Respiration—changes in the blood—venous blood—arterial blood—the lungs and their appendages—changes in respired air—mechanical movements of respiration—animal heat.

Zoology.—Characteristic differences between plants and animals—divisions of the animal kingdom—classes of the vertebrates.

Second Examination.—(*In addition to above.*)—*Animal Physiology.*—Digestion—mastication—teeth—the pharynx—stomach—intestines—secretion and excretion—liver—pancreas—the skin and its functions—the senses—organs of the senses—structure and movements of the eye ball—structure of the ear—animal mechanics.

Zoology.—A complete knowledge of the characteristic features of the sub-kingdoms, and classes of the animal kingdom—modification of the vertebrate skeleton in birds, reptiles, amphibia, and fishes—general nature of the skeleton or hard parts in the several groups of invertebrate animals—general form and nature of the organs of digestion, circulation, and respiration in the various classes of animals.

Inorganic Chemistry.

First Examination.—Matter—simple and compound—divisions of elementary bodies—symbols and atomic weights of the ordinary elementary bodies—to know the properties and mode of obtaining oxygen, hydrogen, and nitrogen—to know the chief properties and composition of water, air, ammonia, carbonic acid, muriatic acid, nitric acid, potash, and soda; and to give the chemical symbols for each—to understand the laws of chemical combination—allotropic modifications of elementary bodies—chemical affinity or force.

SECOND EXAMINATION.—(*In addition to above.*)—To understand the terms of chemical nomenclature and the use of the several prefixes and affixes employed—atomic weights and combining proportions—acids—alkalies—oxides—salts. To know the symbols and combining proportions of oxygen, hydrogen, nitrogen, chlorine, carbon, phosphorus, sulphur, silicon, iron, lead, mercury, sodium, potassium, calcium. To know the principal oxides, acids, and salts formed by the combination of these elements—to explain the ordinary experiments with oxygen, hydrogen, and chlorine.

GEOLOGY.

FIRST EXAMINATION.—(*a.*) Classes of rocks, aqueous, igneous, and metamorphic rocks—mode of formation of each—origin and composition of siliceous, argillaceous, calcareous, and carboniferous rocks—to be able to refer a specimen to its proper class. (*b.*) Agencies at work in *wasting* the land, and how they act—air—frost—ice—rain—rivers—the sea. (*c.*) Movement of the earth's crust—central heat—volcanoes and earthquakes—mountain chains—anticlinal and synclinal curves—faults—dip and strike of strata. (*d.*) Definitions of common geological terms.

SECOND EXAMINATION.—(*In addition to the above.*)—(*a.*) Palaeozoic rocks—names and order of the chief subdivisions of this group—their distribution in the British Islands—leading fossils in the various groups. (*b.*) Coal—its nature, origin, and distribution—its position in the stratified series—ores of metals found in palaeozoic rocks, and their mode of occurrence—probable origin of lodes. (*c.*) Mesozoic rocks—names and order of the chief members of this group—their distribution in the British Islands—principal fossils in the various groups—origin of chalk, rock salt, and gypsum. (*d.*) Cainozoic rocks—subdivisions—distribution in British Islands—principal fossils—nature, origin, and distribution of the boulder clay or glacial drift—bone caves, and their contents—fossils of the drift.

NOTES.

1. Result fees for extra subjects, if these subjects are taught during ordinary school hours, shall go into the common fund divisible among the teachers in schools where one or more assistants are employed. But when extra subjects are taught before or after the ordinary school hours, the results fees accruing therefrom will be payable to the teacher who gives the extra instruction.

2. The subject matter of any of the Board's Reading Lesson Books, or a subject included in any part of the ordinary Results Programme, cannot be recognised as an EXTRA subject for any class, except in the case of fifth and sixth classes. Girls may be examined on the subject-matter of the Girls Reading Book *as an extra subject* in lieu of Book-keeping—the first half of the book for fifth class, and the second half for sixth class. Management of poultry, &c., will not be paid for as an extra subject where there is not a poultry yard attached to the school, available for, and made use of in the practical instruction of the pupils.

3. Notice must be given by the teachers to the District Inspector at the commencement of the results year, or as soon after as classes in the subjects shall have been formed, of the extra branches in which they purpose to present pupils for examination.

4. Payment can be made only once for the same pupil in the use of the sewing machine; or in the same subdivision of any *extra branch*. In a female school in which there is a workmistress paid by the Board, results fees cannot be paid for needlework, cutting-out, or sewing machine.

5. A pupil presented a second time in sixth class may earn results fees in any subject in which he obtains a "*No. 1 pass*," without being required to pass in an extra subject; but if he succeed in an extra subject, fees for "*No. 2 passes*" may be gained. A pupil presented oftener than twice in sixth class cannot earn result fees in Reading, Spelling, or Writing, but may earn fees on "*No 1 passes*" in the other subjects, provided he also pass in two extra subjects.

6. First class monitors may be presented for results examinations in Classics or French, or in a *Science* branch not included in any part of their prescribed course of instruction. Only two science subjects will be allowed to be taken in any one year. Second and third class monitors may be presented as pupils for results fees in ordinary and extra branches.

7. In evening schools results fees will be paid for not more than two approved extra branches; and when such payment is made, no fees will be paid for the ordinary branches in respect of the same pupil.

8. No fee will be paid for any pupil *presented* for examination in the same subject within the previous twelve months under the department of Science and Art.

WM. H. NEWELL,
JOHN E. SHERIDAN, } *Secretaries.*

EDUCATION OFFICE,
MARLBOROUGH-STREET, DUBLIN,
August, 1878.

1877–8.

No. 5.*—A TABULATED STATEMENT exhibiting a comparison between the proficiency of the Pupils of Poor as indicated by the money value of the Passes gained

Statistics regarding infants

WORKHOUSE

	Reading				Spelling				Writing				Arithmetic				
	No. Examined.	No. Passed.	Rate.	Money value per Scale 1874-5	No. Examined	No. Passed	Rate	Money value per Scale 1874-5	No. Examined	No. Passed.	Rate	Money value per Scale 1874-5	No. Examined	No. Passed.	Rate.	Money value per Scale 1874-5	No. Examined
			s. d.	s.			s. d.	s.			s. d.	s.			s. d.	s.	
Class 1	1,377	1,153	2 0	2,310	1,374	1,047	1 0	1,037	1,373	1,149	1 0	1,149	1,376	943	1 0	943	.
" 2.	1,276	856	2 0	1,018	1,078	726	1 0	685	1,029	1,016	1 0	1,015	1,029	654	2 0	1,310	.
" 3.	919	710	[illegible]	[illegible]	912	844	1 0	844	919	794	1 6	1,191	918	80	[illegible]	1,400	919
" 4.	646	511	2 6	1,277½	555	434	1 0	434	555	534	1 [illegible]	801	586	284	2 6	710	535
" 5¹	196	182	2 6	455	180	164	1 0	164	195	189	1 6	283½	199	85	2 6	212½	189
" 5²	61	56	2 6	140	61	53	1 0	53	61	57	1 6	85½	61	21	2 6	57½	61
" 6.	15	15	2 6	37½	15	15	1 0	15	15	15	2 0	30	15	11	3 0	33	15
Total,	4,105	3,513	.	7,369	4,105	3,303		3,303	4,105	3,753	.	4,735	4,105	2,703	.	5,181	2,[illegible]
Average amount earned by each pupil in each branch, . .	s. d. 1 11¼	.	.	.	s. d. 0 9¾	.	.	.	s. d. 1 1¾	.	.	.	s. d. 1 3	.

ORDINARY

	Reading				Spelling				Writing				Arithmetic				
	No. Examined	No. Passed	Rate	Money value per Scale 1874-5	No. Examined	No. Passed.	Rate	Money value per Scale 1874-5	No. Examined	No. Passed.	Rate	Money value per Scale 1874-5	No. Examined	No. Passed.	Rate	Money value per Scale 1874-5	No. Examined
			s. d.	s.			s. d.	s.			s. d.	s.			s. d.	s.	
Class 1.	87,077	73,423	2 0	146,846	87,017	70,484	1 0	70,484	87,017	72,350	1 0	72,350	87,017	64,139	1 0	64,139	.
" 2.	74,737	67,362	2 0	134,404	79,178	59,007	1 0	59,007	74,776	70,353	1 0	70,353	79,720	63,951	2 0	127,902	.
" 3.	64,311	57,308	2 6	143,270	64,011	48,026	1 0	48,026	64,931	61,076	1 6	91,614	64,311	47,344	2 6	118,360	64,911
" 4.	49,006	43,909	2 6	109,772½	49,009	33,180	1 0	33,180	49,004	47,538	1 6	71,307	49,006	26,461	2 6	66,177½	49,006
" 5¹	29,437	27,706	2 6	69,265	29,877	24,049	1 0	24,049	29,432	27,940	1 6	41,929	29,437	15,722	2 6	39,305	29,397
" 5²	16,108	15,415	2 6	38,537½	16,108	14,183	1 0	14,183	16,108	15,398	1 6	23,097	16,108	9,622	2 6	24,055	16,104
" 6.	10,733	9,436	2 6	23,590	10,773	9,376	1 0	9,376	10,733	9,145	2 0	18,290	10,731	6,187	3 0	18,561	10,733
Total.	332,340	296,735	.	678,385	336,340	261,082		261,063	336,340	303,442	.	384,470	336,340	233,475	.	458,095½	170,397
Average amount earned by each pupil in each branch, . .	s. d. 2 11¼	.	.	.	s. d. 0 9¼	.	.	.	s. d. 1 1¾	.	.	.	s. d. 1 4¼	.

1877–8.

No. 6.*—TABLE showing the percentage of the numbers of pupils Passed to the numbers Examined in

Statistics regarding infants

	Reading		Spelling		Writing		Arithmetic	
	Percentage of Passes to number of Pupils examined in Class.		Percentage of Passes to number of Pupils examined in Class		Percentage of Passes to number of Pupils examined in Class.		Percentage of Passes to number of Pupils examined in Class	
	Ordinary Schools	Workhouse Schools	Ordinary Schools	Workhouse Schools	Ordinary Schools	Workhouse Schools	Ordinary Schools	Workhouse Schools
Class I, . . .	86 7	84 0	81·0	76 9	83·6	83 5	73·7	68 5
" II, . . .	95 4	86 1	75·0	76 7	90 7	90·0	61 2	76 9
" III, . . .	88 6	92 1	75 2	79 8	94 0	97 8	72 9	73 4
" IV, . . .	89 6	92 0	71·6	78 2	92 9	96 2	54 0	51 2
" V¹, . . .	93 1	91 3	80 6	82 4	93 5	95 0	52·8	42 7
" V², . . .	95 7	91 8	88·1	86 9	95 0	98 4	59 7	37 7
" VI, . . .	88·5	100·0	87·4	100·0	85 2	100·0	57 7	73·3
Total, . .	88 9	89·1	77 6	78 0	89 9	91 4	80 4	68 2

* Furnished by the Board

Law Union National Schools and the proficiency of Pupils in National Schools generally, for the years 1877-8, at the Results Examinations, according to Scale of 1874-5.

omitted in each case.

SCHOOLS.

Grammar.			Geography.				Agriculture.				Bookkeeping.				Needlework.			
No. Passed	Rate.	Money value per Scale 1874-5	No. Examined	No. Passed.	Rate.	Money value per Scale 1874-5	No. Examined.	No. Passed.	Rate.	Money value per Scale 1874-5.	No. Examined	No. Passed.	Rate	Money value per Scale 1874-5	No. Examined.	No. Passed	Rate.	Money value per Scale 1874-5
	s. d.	s.			s. d.	s.			s. d.	s.			s. d.	s.			s. d.	s.
.	.	.	.	.	.	.	.	.	.	.	.	.	.	.	.	.	.	.
.	.	.	.	.	.	.	.	.	.	.	.	.	.	.	491	433	0 6	216
471	0 6	245½	812	594	1 0	224	.	.	.	.	.	.	.	.	846	494	1 0	8[illegible]
235	1 0	245	555	375	1 0	375	155	74	2 0	158	.	.	.	.	375	311	2 0	479
307	1 6	166½	339	194	1 6	144	71	44	2 6	110	23	11	2 0	27½	70	47	2 6	117½
40	1 6	60	51	34	1 [illegible]	57	25	17	2 6	49½	5	4	2 6	10	21	21	2 6	52½
14	1 6	13½	18	11	1 6	16½	8	7	3 0	21	7	6	3 0	18	1	1	3 0	3
937	.	770½	1,443	1,077	.	1,154½	253	140	.	329½	35	21	.	55½	1,198	1,079	.	1,1[illegible]
		s. d.				s. d.				s. d.				s. d.				s. d.
.	.	0 9½	.	.	.	0 10½	.	.	.	2 3	.		.	2 6	.	.	.	1 0½

SCHOOLS.

Grammar.			Geography.				Agriculture.				Bookkeeping.				Needlework.			
No. Passed	Rate	Money value per Scale 1874-5	No. Examined.	No. Passed.	Rate	Money value per Scale 1874-5	No. Examined	No. Passed	Rate	Money value per Scale 1874-5	No. Examined	No. Passed	Rate.	Money value per Scale 1874-5	No. Examined	No. Passed.	Rate.	Money value per Scale 1874-5.
	s. d.	s.			s. d.	s.			s. d.	s.			s. d.	s.			s. d.	s.
.	.	.	.	.	.	.	.	.	.	.	.	.	.	.	.	.	.	.
.	.	.	.	.	.	.	.	.	.	.	.	.	.	.	34,[illegible]	32,250	0 6	16,140
35,276	0 6	17,694	64,[illegible]	36,7[illegible]	1 0	36,750	.	.	.	.	.	.	.	.	29,909	27,980	1 0	27,9[illegible]
23,640	1 0	23,600	47,[illegible]	26,741	1 0	26,741	10,041	4,8[illegible]	2 0	[illegible],843	.	.	.	.	22,[illegible]	20,918	1 6	31,[illegible]
16,275	1 6	24,342½	29,837	14,443	1 6	21,664½	7,951	3,541	2 6	[illegible],377½	3,179	2,473	2 0	4,355	15,480	13,120	2 0	31,[illegible]
10,[illegible]	1 4	15,31[illegible]	16,196	6,603	1 6	12,904½	4,078	2,304	2 6	[illegible],470	3,375	1,32[illegible]	2 6	4,[illegible]	7,169	4,[illegible]	2 6	17,110
7,079	1 6	10,642½	10,753	8,191	1 6	2,[illegible]	[illegible]	1,403	3 0	6,144	[illegible]	1,621	3 0	4,[illegible]75	4,353	4,154	3 0	12,4[illegible]
92,834	.	92,170	170,597	89,[illegible]		104,243½	26,057	12,[illegible]94	.	27,[illegible]0½	11,016	6,013	.	11,[illegible]15	113,1[illegible]6	104,237	.	146,928
		s. d.				s. d.				s. d.				s. d.				s. d.
.	.	0 4½	.	.	.	0 7½	.	.	.	2 1½	.	.	.	1 4½	.	.	.	1 8½

in each Branch in each Class for Poor Law Union National Schools and National Schools generally, 1877-8.

omitted in each case.

Grammar.		Geography.		Agriculture.		Bookkeeping.		Needlework.	
Percentage of Passes to number of Pupils examined in Class		Percentage of Passes to number of Pupils examined in Class		Percentage of Passes to number of Pupils examined in Class		Percentage of Passes to number of Pupils examined in Class		Percentage of Passes to number of Pupils examined in Class	
Ordinary Schools	Workhouse Schools	Ordinary Schools	Workhouse Schools	Ordinary Schools	Workhouse Schools	Ordinary Schools	Workhouse Schools	Ordinary Schools	Workhouse Schools
.	.	.	.	.	.	.	.	.	.
.	.	.	.	.	.	.	.	93·5	94·8
34·5	58·0	55·1	64·5	.	.	.	.	91·5	96·5
48·8	53·9	49·7	67·6	39·1	60·8	.	.	93·1	94·6
54·4	83·8	49·1	69·3	45·2	58·8	47·5	50·0	94·8	95·7
65·9	65·6	53·4	62·3	56·8	68·0	55·5	80·0	96·0	100·0
65·5	86·7	57·7	73·3	57·6	87·5	56·7	100·0	95·4	100·0
54·5	58·4	52·5	65·3	46·0	55·5	53·3	63·6	93·0	95·6

of National Education.

No. 7.—Return of Pauper Children Relieved in each County in Ireland, showing the Classes to which they severally belong.

COUNTIES.	In the House December 31st, 1876.				Admitted during the Year 1877.				Discharged during the Year 1877.				In the House December 31st, 1877.				Remaining of those in the House on December 31st, 1876, still remaining on December 31st, 1877.			
	Orphans and Deserted		With Parents		Orphans and Deserted		With Parents		Orphans and Deserted		With Parents		Orphans and Deserted		With Parents		Orphans and Deserted		With Parents	
	Under 4	Over 4	Under 4	Over 4	Under 4	Over 4	Under 4	Over 4	Under 4	Over 4	Under 4	Over 4	Under 4	Over 4	Under 4	Over 4	Under 4	Over 4	Under 4	Over 4
Antrim,	104	437	278	433	86	347	584	1,254	[illegible]	212	680	1,130	101	442	274	411	67	319	85	110
Armagh,	58	14	31	76	3	31	252	265	1	8	177	275	90	72	106	85	47	87	60	41
Cavan,	73	73	17	73	46	177	270	265	65	170	201	290	60	81	76	99	16	44	30	40
Donegal,	26	57	17	72	12	79	204	307	12	74	179	769	79	80	72	310	15	62	16	78
Down,	36	132	197	265	42	144	579	616	50	160	564	698	59	127	152	261	31	80	63	103
Fermanagh,	7	61	44	77	1	21	180	190	1	73	161	197	1	180	43	76	4	55	10	33
Londonderry,	27	183	65	77	11	89	310	266	10	61	177	227	25	185	90	92	15	100	35	35
Monaghan,	27	83	34	86	16	42	154	272	15	45	117	220	27	90	35	49	15	67	10	16
Tyrone,	24	160	101	108	14	95	462	610	10	90	465	601	77	133	149	208	10	41	41	56
Clare,	61	200	86	175	161	265	244	437	80	244	279	471	72	215	109	205	45	114	63	101
Cork,	173	823	446	865	161	781	1,485	2,000	120	654	1,295	1,060	212	896	608	783	121	473	168	204
Kerry,	87	191	107	134	101	189	208	281	71	171	202	280	67	109	100	163	92	93	41	60
Limerick,	51	345	145	307	81	209	276	575	51	175	281	863	51	246	120	329	38	136	47	104
Tipperary,	65	283	203	296	36	234	702	913	31	970	771	974	12	903	286	342	65	214	110	96
Waterford,	47	183	114	200	65	287	463	573	47	261	452	560	86	179	147	161	35	140	40	107
Carlow,	13	40	77	66	19	37	56	85	6	37	64	77	18	50	32	51	5	81	11	25
Dublin,	130	601	217	257	106	778	1,401	1,116	80	262	1,672	1,195	155	612	403	290	74	464	77	104
Kildare,	40	114	61	93	41	74	137	204	36	51	144	266	55	18	45	301	34	47	14	35
Kilkenny,	97	218	141	177	104	163	316	455	116	155	398	409	40	127	134	185	76	131	81	100
King's,	21	97	43	71	16	43	312	483	14	48	387	488	21	97	81	03	18	78	77	41
Longford,	5	88	43	69	13	60	175	116	5	83	167	199	27	66	65	94	7	65	23	74
Louth,	24	36	24	75	40	123	176	305	36	176	177	209	26	99	53	71	13	56	13	26
Meath,	20	96	79	56	11	20	258	433	11	47	251	287	25	70	75	94	18	63	31	21
Queen's,	15	50	46	67	22	51	117	276	20	64	144	265	13	65	36	77	10	28	14	27
Westmeath,	14	80	44	40	30	46	278	181	29	56	201	171	20	53	61	70	8	70	49	41
Wexford,	46	148	48	191	174	164	223	311	174	140	233	116	76	103	79	136	45	104	29	47
Wicklow,	16	84	57	113	13	81	301	348	30	80	810	358	17	46	54	131	11	45	40	64
Galway,	87	187	129	377	29	124	302	443	16	119	298	400	81	191	144	262	80	120	71	160
Leitrim,	13	97	29	84	14	37	70	55	14	47	43	39	11	77	80	50	11	74	8	76
Mayo,	26	112	83	187	34	120	344	475	30	238	633	334	63	109	120	176	32	63	37	66
Roscommon,	65	108	49	80	22	127	137	128	24	119	189	124	37	116	60	64	29	86	32	40
Sligo,	11	79	22	74	23	70	64	125	19	71	89	161	29	77	37	17	15	38	8	25
Total,	1,416	5,227	3,300	4,621	1,617	4,263	11,267	14,296	1,806	4,316	10,950	13,708	1,563	5,224	3,617	3,206	971	3,690	1,272	2,013

Appendix B.
Industrial Training.

No. 9.—Industrial Training for Children.

Copy of Letters addressed to the Clerk of each Poor Law Union, with a Summary of Replies.

Four Courts, Dublin,
Sir, 3rd July, 1878.

The Poor Law Inquiry Commissioners are desirous of obtaining information with reference to the system of Industrial Training for Children in the Workhouse of your Union. I am, accordingly, to request that you will be good enough to inform them—

1. What is the system of Industrial Training in the Workhouse of your Union?

2. Under whose supervision is it conducted?

3. Do the Guardians experience any difficulty in getting the children into service?

4. Upon what conditions as to wages, period of service, &c., are children sent out?

5. Are children apprenticed in your Union, and, if so, upon what conditions?

6. At what age are children generally sent into service, and do they, as a rule, retain their first places?

7. Does the practice prevail in your Union of sending children out for short periods of service—for such temporary employments, for example, as "herding?"

8. Are there any adult inmates in your Workhouse now who were brought up in it as children? If so, to what cause is their destitution attributable?

The Commissioners will feel obliged for any additional information that you can give, or for any observations that you may desire to offer upon the subject of the Education of Children in Workhouses, and I am to request that you will be so good as to let me have the enclosed form duly filled in and the information above required by the 9th inst.

I am, Sir, your obedient servant,

H. A. Robinson, Secretary.

To the Clerk of each Poor Law Union.

Antrim.

1. That, as regards this Workhouse, boys (who are regarded as eligible) are taught the trades of carpenter, shoemaker, and tailor. Girls are likewise taught sewing and knitting, also washing, and (as far as practicable) a knowledge of general "house work."

2. That the boys, as above, are taught under paid masters in the several departments named. The girls under the instruction of the schoolmistress, who is a very competent officer.

3. That the Guardians do not experience any difficulty in getting the children into service.

4. That when children (under 15) are hired, the conditions as to wages, nature of work, &c., are arranged before the Board, and, if practicable, with the concurrence also of the parent.

5. In some instances boys have, with the sanction of the Board, apprenticed themselves to trades. Conditions vary according to circumstances, but the Guardians satisfy themselves that same are proper and equitable in the several cases.

6. Children are seldom sent to service under the age of thirteen and a-half years, and the Guardians are particular to see that their education is considerably advanced before allowing them to go out as servants. In most cases they become re-engaged after first term has expired.

7. The Guardians object to allow children to go out as servants for a shorter period than six months, and in no instance do they allow a child to engage in temporary employment such as "herding."

8. There are only a few inmates in the Workhouse now who were brought up in it as children. Present destitution, in case of males, arises from delicacy of health, &c., and as regards females, it proceeds in one case from her having an illegitimate child, and in three other cases from mental infirmity.

M. A. Scott, Clerk of Union.

Ballycastle.

1, 2, and 3. None.

4. Hired for six months; to remain longer if all are satisfied.

5. No.

6. From ten to twelve years; generally retain their first places.

7. No.

8. Only one—ill health.

Charles M. Caughan, Clerk of Union.

Ballymena.

1. A class of boys, 12 in number, is specially trained in farming and gardening operations, all the boys being employed out of school and play hours in general work on the farm. The girls are taught to knit, sew, and wash.

2. The boys are under the immediate supervision of the schoolmaster, the girls under that of the schoolmistress, the master superintending the former, and the matron the latter.

3. No difficulty is experienced in getting the children of both sexes into service, in fact numerous applications for boys and girls have to be refused.

4. Boys are hired out as farm servants for no less a period than 12 months, at an average wage of 12s. 6d. a quarter, to be spent on them under the direction of the relieving officers, the employers undertaking to bring them back to the house if they do not suit.

5. No children are ever apprenticed in this union.

6. No children are sent into service under 12 or 14 years of age. A little more than one half of those sent out retain their first places.

7. No such practice prevails in this union as sending children out for short periods of service, such as "herding."

8. There are about half a dozen adult inmates at present in the house who have been in and out since they were children, they looking on the workhouse as their homes when they experience any difficulty in procuring employment.

My experience, extending over a period of 30 years, tends to convince me that a workhouse is not a good place to bring up children in. With very few exceptions I have never known those so reared ever turn out well. We have one sample of a young man, at present conducting clerk in a solicitor's office in town, and instructor of instrumental music to the workhouse band, who, if not born in the house, was certainly in it from infancy till he was 16 or 17 years of age; but I must say this is an exception, not a rule.

I believe the giving out children to nurse in the houses of small farmers, and keeping them there till they would be quite fit to do for themselves, a much better way of rearing them than keeping them in a workhouse; but this could, of course, only apply to deserted or orphan children of whom the guardians would have sole control, and for whose education and moral training due provision would be made.

G. A. Mathews, Clerk of Union.

P.S.—I omitted to state that, in my opinion, the band organised amongst the boys some years ago has been very beneficial in its results, a good number of them now occupying respectable positions as members of military and militia bands.

Ballymoney.

1. That girls are taught sewing and knitting under the supervision of the schoolmistress, they also help to wash out their own apartments, but it is not thought advisable that they should be brought much into contact with the female inmates.

The boys are taught agriculture, and do all the light work required on the farm, which contains 18 acres. The schoolmaster takes charge of them.

2. Answered in No. 1.

APPENDIX B. Industrial Training.

3. They do not.

4. The children are hired out for 12 months, at wages varying from 30s. to 40s., with food, lodging, and washing. Boys as agricultural servants, girls as house servants. The former give satisfaction in nearly every instance, the latter are frequently complained of as being useless.

5. Children have not been apprenticed in this union for the past 10 years.

6. From 12 to 14 years. Boys, as a rule, retain their first places, and are liked by their masters. Girls do not give so much satisfaction, in fact as servants they are a failure.

7. Children are never hired for a shorter period than 12 months.

8. Yes, one man of weak intellect, and three women. One of these is of weak intellect, the other two came back to the house after having been out for some time, and are now nursing their own infants, they are illegitimate children.

In conclusion I may state, that for the class of boys in the workhouse a better system of bringing up could not be found. They are much sought after by farmers, and look healthy and strong. There is something faulty in the management of the girls. If it were possible to give them some instruction in other departments, cooking for instance, besides knitting and sewing, it would be for their benefit, but under existing arrangements, whereby everything is cooked by steam, it would be difficult to manage this.

T. Bowes Hamilton, Clerk of Union.

LARNE.

1. The boys assist in weeding and any light work on the farm and grounds; the girls are taught to sew and knit; they mend their own clothing, and assist in scouring the floor of the school-room, and keeping it clean.

2. The boys under the supervision of the master and schoolmaster; the girls under that of the schoolmistress.

3. The Guardians have no difficulty whatever in getting the children into service, applications for them are much in excess of the supply.

4. Children usually go out to service when about 14 years of age, and are generally engaged for a year, the amount of wages being from £1 10s. to £3 for the year.

5. No children have been apprenticed for some years past. A few boys were apprenticed a good many years ago, generally for four years, the master providing the boy with clothing, board and lodging.

6. Children usually go to service at about 14 years of age, and generally retain their first places.

7. Children are never sent out for short periods for temporary employment such as "herding."

8. There is one woman in the house who was brought up in it. She has two illegitimate children, and she spends more than half of her time in the house. There is also a young man who comes in occasionally for a short time, and who was brought up in the workhouse. None of the other inmates were brought up in it as children.

A number of boys brought up in Larne Union Workhouse are now filling respectable situations. Several are teachers of National schools, one of them a first class teacher. One recently deceased, was for several years assistant clerk of a Poor Law Union. One at present occupies a situation in a mercantile house in Dublin, and is in receipt of a good income. As a rule, the boys who have been brought up in the Union have turned out well.

William Hay, Clerk of Union.

LISBURN.

1. The male children are occupied in the workhouse farm after school hours when not taken out to walk, and the female children are instructed in sewing, knitting, &c.

2. Both male and female children are under the supervision of their respective teachers.

3. The guardians have no difficulty in procuring service for the children.

4. They are hired by the quarter, and get from 10s. to 14s., according to age.

5. No children have been apprenticed for a number of years past.

6. Children are sent to service from 11 years of age up, and generally retain their first places.

7. There are no children sent out for short periods of service.

8. There are only two adult inmates in the house who were brought up in it as children—both are idiotic lunatics.

W. Sinclair, Clerk of Union.

ARMAGH.

1. The children are employed in the cultivation of about 2 acres of land.

2. The schoolmaster's.

3. No.

4. 12s. per quarter.

5. No.

6. At 12 years and upwards, and they retain their first places generally.

7. No.

8. Yes, a few, being the mothers of illegitimate children.

Wm. M'Master, Clerk of Union.

LURGAN.

1. Boys who are capable of learning are taught the tailoring and shoemaking trades, and all physically able are employed in farming operations on a limited scale.

The girls are taught to knit, sew, make up and repair articles of clothing, and to wash, &c.

2. Under the supervision of the schoolmaster and schoolmistress of the workhouse.

3. No difficulty whatever. The demand more than equals the supply.

4. Boys 10s., and girls 7s. 6d. per quarter.

5. We are not aware of any law empowering the guardians to apprentice children, except to sea service, under 14 & 15 Vic., cap. 35, and 17 & 18 Vic., cap. 104, which has not been acted on.

6. At ages varying from 10 to 14 years. They do not generally retain their first places.

7. No. Children are not sent out for the purpose of herding alone, although this may sometimes constitute a portion of their employment.

8. There are at present only three adults in the house who were brought up in it as children, one a woman with two illegitimate children, and the other two are male paupers who have always been on the sick list.

Referring to Query 6, I may mention that owing to the operation of the recent Act of Parliament extending the time to which orphans and deserted children may be boarded out, viz., up to thirteen years, I apprehend there will be few children to go out to service. From considerable experience as a poor law official, I believe that the parents of children in the workhouse, are generally reluctant to send their children out to service, preferring rather to keep them in the house.

I may also remark that I always considered it a defect in the Irish Poor Law that no provision has been made for apprenticing boys and girls to some suitable trade, by which they would be enabled to gain an honest livelihood, for under the present law they become emancipated from the control of the guardians at fifteen years of age; and on entering into the battle of life they are placed at a great disadvantage when compared with children of their own class and age, but who have not been brought up in the workhouse.

James Donaldson, Clerk of Union.

BAILIEBOROUGH.

1. Girls taught plain sewing and knitting
2. The school mistress.
3. No
4. From 8s. to 10s. per quarter, and from three to six months.
5. No.
6. From twelve to fourteen years, as a rule they do retain first places.
7. The practice does not prevail, but it happens sometimes
8. One in pregnancy, and two mental debility; total three girls.

THOMAS CLARKE, Clerk of Union.

BAWNBOY.

1. Female children are taught sewing and knitting, and also to clean out their dormitories.
2. The school teachers
3. None whatever.
4. No conditions are imposed, save that the amount agreed upon, will be paid, except in a recent case the hirer of a boy aged ten years consented to allow him to attend school three days in each week.
5. No.
6. From ten to fourteen years, as a rule they do retain their first places.
7. No.
8. Six females are at present inmates, one from idiotcy, one from bodily infirmity, viz.—loss of eyesight, two cases to widowhood, and two cases of having illegitimate children.

In conclusion, I beg to state that I am of opinion that Boards of Guardians should not hire children out of the workhouse at an earlier age than twelve years, and more particularly in the case of orphan and deserted children.

JAMES M'GOVERN, Clerk of Union

CAVAN.

1. About twelve boys are daily taught the tailoring business, the school girls are taught sewing, knitting, &c.; those over ten years of age are taught washing.
2. Under the supervision of the workhouse tailor the school teachers, and the matron.
3. The guardians do not experience any difficulty in getting the children into service
4. The workhouse master usually makes the agreement as to amount of wages. The period of service is, generally speaking, six months.
5. Boys who have learnt something of tailoring are the only inmates apprenticed (with the consent of parent or parents), the term is usually five years; the employer to provide food and clothing, no apprentice fee is given.
6. At twelve years. In most instances they retain their first places, almost the only exceptions are those children whose parent or parents continue to be inmates of the workhouse.
7. There very seldom occurs a case of the kind.
8. About fifteen of the present inmates were brought up in it as children. Their remaining is attributable to various causes, such as cutaneous diseases and hereditary complaints.

I may add that the children taught in the schools of this union are thoroughly instructed in the course prescribed by the Board of National Education.

JOSEPH D. GRIER, Clerk of Union.

COOTEHILL.

1. None Occasional weeding of ground, &c.
3. No.
4. About for half year, at trifling wages, about 10s.
5. No.
6. About an average of ten years old, and seldom return

7. No; always hired out.
8. Yes, three—one an idiot, one for her confinement, and one with sore leg.

ROBERT GRAHAM, Clerk of Union.

BALLYSHANNON.

In reply to your circular dated 3rd instant, I beg to state that there is no industrial training carried on in this workhouse. There are few applications for children for service, and there are not many in the house fit to send out. They are generally hired by the quarter—wages small, barely sufficient to keep them clothed. The children frequently stop but a short time in their places, and do not even put in one quarter in many cases. They are sent out when applied for, at from twelve to fifteen years of age. There are no children apprenticed to trades. Boys are sometimes sent out during spring and summer months to "herd." I don't think there is an adult inmate in the workhouse who was brought up in it as a child. I think there should be some steps taken to provide industrial training for children in workhouses, either by giving them trades or training them to farm work. They have nothing to do, and grow up lazy, and when they go out are not inclined to work, and do not care to keep their places, having the workhouse to fall back on when out of employment. I believe that Mr. Moore's bill, proposing to give Guardians power to send children to industrial schools, would be a most useful measure

J. B. CHISM, Clerk of Union.

DONEGAL.

1. Sewing; no boys fit for industrial training.
2. Matron.
3. No.
4. According to age, generally six months.
5. No.
6. About ten years of age.
7. Yes.
8. No.

DUNFANAGHY.

No school attached to Workhouse.

GLENTIES.

1. No industrial training.
3. The parents in all cases hire out their children as soon as they are fit for service.
4. The period of service is generally six months, the amount of wages is fixed by the parents and employer.
5. None of the children have been apprenticed
6. About twelve years, and with few exceptions retain their first place.
7. Herding is generally the employment for which boys are hired, and with few exceptions do not again return to the workhouse
8. There are two who have returned with illegitimate children.

WILLIAM BUCHANAN,
Acting Clerk of Union.

INISHOWEN

1. None, except household work and plain sewing.
2. The matron and schoolmistress.
3. No
4. Usually from twenty to thirty shillings for half a year.
5. No.
6. From ten years, as applied for, and they generally retain their places for the term agreed upon, and often return temporarily for a few terms.
7. Yes.
8 No.

ROBERT MOORE, Clerk of Union.

APPENDIX B.
Industrial Training.

LETTERKENNY.

1. Industrial training:—Boys, farm labour; Girls, knitting, sewing, washing, &c.

2. Boys under supervision of master; girls under schoolmistress.

3. No difficulty.

4. Half yearly, at current wages.

5. Children rarely apprenticed.

6. At first generally too young, being about twelve years, but, as a rule, they retain their first places. They return after first and second half-years to the workhouse, after which they generally remain at service permanently.

7. Yes.

8. Only three, and these are helpless imbeciles.

Education well attended to; but from the fluctuating attendance, owing to discharges and re-admissions, in such cases little progress can be made. In my opinion, there is a tendency to hire out children for "herding" at too young an age, and these, after being out for the half year, return to the workhouse, having forgotten much that they had previously learned.

JOHN STOREY, Clerk of Union.

MILFORD.

1. Sewing, knitting, washing linens, &c.; also farm work on land attached to the workhouse.

2. Matron, schoolmistress, and porter.

3. No.

4. Those children whose parents are in the workhouse, hire them out—the girls generally for domestic service, and the boys for farm work or herding.

Girls, according to their age and capabilities, receive from twenty-five to forty shillings for the half year, and boys from thirty to fifty shillings for the same period. The Guardians do not approve of hiring girls for herding, and it is not done in this Union.

5. No.

6. From thirteen years up to fourteen years. The Guardians, as a rule, do not approve of sending them out sooner than thirteen years.

7. No. Half a year is the shortest period.

8. One male—weak intellect.

W. REID, Clerk of Union.

STRANORLAR.

1. Boys trained in agricultural work on a farm of 12 acres. Farmers in consequence glad to hire them.—Girls, when old enough, trained in dairy work, and taught sewing in the school as children.

2. Training on farm under Master. Of girls by Matron and Schoolmistress.

3. No.

4. Conditions according to size and strength; not hired for shorter period than three or six months.

5. One only.

6. From 11 to 13 years old; they have retained their places with only one exception.

7. No.

8. One only since the Workhouse opened—the cause bad health.

The form as to number of children at different periods in Workhouse is enclosed.

ANDREW MILLAR, Clerk of Union.

BANBRIDGE.

1. Shoemaking and tailoring for the boys, and knitting and sewing for the girls.

2. A paid working shoemaker and tailor, and the schoolmistress.

3. No.

4. In the case of children whose parents are in the Workhouse, the parents alone arrange the terms. Orphan and deserted children are not hired out till they are 14 years of age, and then they make the best bargain they can for themselves.

5. No.

6. From eight years upwards.

7. No.

8. Four. Two are simple in mind, the other two have each a number of illegitimate children.

EDWARD WYLY, Clerk of Union.

DOWNPATRICK.

The system of Industrial Training is simply whatever knowledge of sewing, &c., and household duties the schoolmistress can impart to the girls, and the boys are taught farming, &c., in the grounds by the schoolmaster. The Guardians experience no difficulty in getting service for the children. They do not hire them out for a less period than one half-year, and will not hire them out at all until the children attain the age of thirteen years. The children, as a rule, retain their first places, and get on well. Some are apprenticed to trades, but not many latterly. There are but a few adult inmates in the Workhouse who were reared in it, and these are young women who were led astray after they had gone to service. We find the rule of not hiring for less than half a year to work well; also the one not to hire the children out early, that is before the age of thirteen years.

J. W. MONTGOMERY, Clerk of Union.

KILKEEL.

1. The female children are taught needlework, washing, &c., the boys are employed occasionally at suitable work on the Workhouse Farm.

2. The Master, Matron, and Schoolmistress.

3. No.

4. Various, according to circumstances.

5. None apprenticed, they invariably obtain situations as servants.

6. They do; some of them who were hired out six years ago are in the same places.

7. No.

8. There are none.

NEWRY.

1. That the boys are engaged after and before school hours at agricultural labour; and the girls at sewing, knitting, washing and household work.

2. The teachers.

3. None whatever.

4. At so much per quarter as arranged by the Master.

5. Not usually.

6. As a rule none leave before the age of twelve; they generally retain their first places.

7. No, seldom hired out for less than three months.

8. There are a few females, but no males, misconduct was the principal cause of their return.

Several hundred children, including both sexes, have been successfully trained in this Workhouse; and as a whole they have turned out well.

The demand for children for some time past has been greater than the supply.

Children under twelve would frequently be taken out, if permitted; but the Guardians refuse to hire out orphans or deserted children before they have an opportunity of acquiring a fair education for their position in life.

The children generally are very smart and intelligent, and learn rapidly at school.

JOSEPH BELL, Clerk of Union.

NEWTOWNARDS.

1. The boys are taught shoemaking, tailoring, and to assist in the tillage of the farm, which contains ten acres. The girls to wash, knit, sew, and keep their apartments clean.

2. Under the supervision of a master shoemaker and tailor, and the schoolmaster and schoolmistress.

3. The Guardians have no difficulty in getting the

children into service, the demand being greater than the supply.

4. The children are engaged for six months; the Guardians give a good outfit; wages nominal.

5. Boys are apprenticed, time dependent on age of boys, and length of time at trade in Workhouse. In no case length of apprenticeship exceeds five years.

6. The children are hired out at from thirteen to fifteen years of age. Very few of them return again to the house.

7. No; they are not sent out for short periods.

8. There are three adult males and two females in the Workhouse who were brought up in it as children. One of the males Deaf and Dumb, one an idiot, a third almost blind. One female has two illegitimate children, the other "very defective sight."

The Local Government Board issue all returns in *duplicate* with questions, numbered and printed with blanks to be filled up by Union Clerks, which very much facilitates them in furnishing the information required, and besides enables them to keep a copy of each return.

ROBERT BROWN, Clerk of Union.

ENNISKILLEN.

1. None.
3. No.
4. Monthly, at from 3s. 6d. to 4s. per month.
5. Occasionally, to printers for seven years.
6. Twelve to fourteen years, and they remove from place to place like other servants.
7. No.
8. Two; one a boy accidentally hurt, and the other a girl suffering from scrofula.

WM. HENRY MORRISON, Clerk of Union.

IRVINESTOWN.

1. The girls are taught sewing, &c., and the boys (who are able) assist in keeping the Workhouse grounds in order.

2. Under the supervision of the Master and Schoolmistress.

3. The Guardians have no difficulty in getting the children into service.

4. They are generally engaged for six months at from £1 to £1 10s.

5. No children have been apprenticed from this Union Workhouse.

6. Children are generally sent to service at from 10 to 12 years of age, according to capability. The majority retaining first place.

7. The usual period of service is from May to November, and seldom any engagement for a shorter period.

8. There are two adult inmates at present in this Workhouse, a male and female, the former being lame and unable to work, and the latter being now the mother of three illegitimate children.

I consider the system of periodical inspection under the National Board well suited to Workhouse Schools.

J. GRAHAM, Clerk of Union.

LISNASKEA.

In reply to your circular of 3rd inst., with reference to the industrial training of children in the Workhouse, I beg to say that there is no recognised system of industrial training carried out in this Workhouse, the ordinary education under a female teacher, and in a school in connexion with the National Board being all the children received.

There are no children apprenticed in the Union, children are sometimes hired out with farmers for a period of six months, the employer usually expending the wages in clothing for the child; who either returns to the Workhouse, or is re-hired at the expiration of the term.

There are a few adult inmates in the Workhouse who were brought up in it as children; their destitution is owing to some permanent infirmity which prevents them from being able to earn a livelihood.

J. O. R. HOEY, Clerk of Union.

COLERAINE.

1. Boys, farmwork; girls, sewing, housework, &c.
2. Workhouse School Teachers.
3. No.
4. Wages from 30s. to 40s. a year with board and washing.
5. Very seldom; but if so it depends on the trade. Say six years.
6. From 12 to 15 years; generally some return, however.
7. No.
8. A few cases—to having illegitimate children.

Nil.—Question very large, and admits of great argument.

WM. HENRY, Clerk of Union.

LIMAVADY.

1. The boys are taught agriculture on the farm, and the girls knitting, sewing, and household work.
2. The boys under the supervision of Schoolmaster, and the girls under the Matron.
3. They do not.
4. Market wages for children of their class, one year. Guardians require a written engagement that the person taking out the boy or girl shall keep same for a year.
5. No.
6. 14 years. They do.
7. No.
8. One, destitute through illness.

W. P. HUNTER, Clerk of Union.

LONDONDERRY.

1. The boys are trained to farm work, and the girls knitting and sewing.
2. The School Teachers.
3. No.
4. Sent to service from twelve years of age, boys engaged for six months, and girls by the month. Wages at the rate of £3 per year.
5. No.
6. Twelve years, yes.
7. Yes.
8. There are a few, but they are for the most part either lame or in infirm health.

I have only to add that the education of the children in this Workhouse appears to me to be properly attended to, all of whom are fairly educated when leaving the Workhouse.

I desire to mention that while the education of the children is carefully attended to, there are great difficulties in the way of their moral and industrial training, principally owing to the bad examples and associations of their parents or other relatives, most of whom, through their own misconduct, are inmates of the Workhouse.

It appears to me the only way to remedy this evil would be to have the children, say of a number of Unions, brought up together and educated in the same building, the cost of such to be paid by the several Unions in proportion to the number of children from each maintained therein.

J. T. RUSSELL.

MAGHERAFELT.

1. The boys are generally employed after school hours on the workhouse farm, and the girls also employed sewing, knitting, &c.
2. The schoolmaster and schoolmistress.
3. None whatever.
4. The guardians hire them out as servants for 12 months at wages averaging from £2 10s. to £3.

APPENDIX D.

Industrial Training.

5. Yes, boys are apprenticed for five years, receiving food and clothing for the time, and £1 at expiration of apprenticeship.

6. Children are generally hired out from 12 to 14 years old and as a rule retain their first places.

7. No.

8. None.

I beg to state that the schools are placed under the National Education Board.

JOHN STEELE, Clerk of Union.

CARRICKMACROSS.

1. Casual employment on the ground attached to the workhouse.

2. Under the master of the workhouse.

3. No.

4. From 10s. to 20s. for 6 months.

5. No.

6. About 12 years old. As a rule they return to the workhouse.

7. Yes.

8. No.

BERNARD M'CAUL, Clerk of Union.

CASTLEBLAYNEY.

1. The few able-bodied men and boys in the house are employed in cultivating the farm, and keeping the premises in order. The females are employed in making and mending clothing, and keeping the house clean. The females at school knit and sew.

2. The master, matron and schoolmistress.

3. No.

4. They are hired for the usual period of six months, on same terms as children outside.

5. No.

6. From ten to twelve years. Yes.

7. No.

8. Yes, a few who are subject to epilepsy, and unable to work.

S. M'BIRNEY, Clerk of Union.

CLONES.

1. No system of industrial training.

2. Nil.

3. No.

4. Persons taking them out promise to clothe them.

5. Not apprenticed.

6. From ten to fourteen years. No.

7. No.

8. None.

I have nothing to add to the above.

ALEXANDER BAILEY, Clerk of Union.

MONAGHAN.

In compliance with the circular of the Poor Law Inquiry Commissioners, dated 3rd inst., I beg leave to state that the only industrial training in the workhouse is that the girls are taught knitting and sewing, the boys in agriculture, the former under the supervision of the matron, and the latter under the schoolmaster. There are very few children to get into service, and consequently the supply is not near so great as the demand, the guardians have no difficulty in getting children of fourteen years (they object letting them go out sooner) into respectable farm-houses, and as a rule they never return to the workhouse. They receive at first only small wages not more than it takes to clothe them, the period for which they are engaged being generally six months, and then they make new engagements for themselves. None have been apprenticed. The guardians have at all times objected to let them out to herd, and when applied to for this purpose they will not let them go. It was found some years ago that children taken out for this purpose generally returned in bad health, and the loss greater to the union than keeping them in the workhouse. There are no adults in the workhouse who were brought up in it as children.

Enclosed herewith you have return asked for.

JAMES MITCHELL, Clerk of Union.

CASTLEDERG.

1. The boys are trained on the workhouse farm, and the girls are taught sewing and knitting, and other household work.

2. The training of the children are conducted under the supervision of the officers of the house, specially the master of the workhouse, and schoolmistress.

3. The guardians experience no difficulty in getting the children into service.

4. The children are generally hired out for the period of six months, at the average wages of about £2.

5. Children are not apprenticed in this Union.

6. Children are generally sent out to service about the age of fourteen years, and as a rule they do retain their first places.

7. The practice of sending out children for short periods of service such as herding does not prevail in this union.

8. There are no adult inmates in this workhouse at present who were brought up in it as children.

W. HAMILTON, Clerk of Union.

CLOGHER.

1. The girls are taught sewing, knitting, &c., and the boys are instructed on the farm, and in house work generally.

2. Under the supervision of the master and schoolmistress.

3. The Guardians do not experience much difficulty in getting the children into service.

4. The children are hired out at sums varying from ten shillings to two pounds for periods of service extending from three to six months.

5. There are no children apprenticed in this Union.

6. The children are generally sent into service from the age of nine to fifteen years, and, as a rule, retain their first places.

7. Children are sometimes sent out for short periods on temporary employment, but the practice does not prevail.

8. There are no adult inmates in this Workhouse who were brought up in it as children.

JOHN C. SCRAGGS, Clerk of Union.

COOKSTOWN.

I beg leave to acknowledge receipt of circular from the Poor Law Inquiry Commissioners, dated 3rd July, 1878.

With regard to query—

1. As to the system of Industrial Training for Children in this Workhouse, I have to remark that there is no agriculturist here, but the boys are generally employed on the farm at weeding, picking stones, &c.

2. It is under the master's supervision it is conducted.

3. I have to state that the Guardians do not experience any difficulty in getting the children into service.

4. As to the conditions upon which children are sent out, I am to state that the Guardians hire them out as ordinary servants, generally for half a year. They receive the usual wages. The Guardians have declined in some cases to hire them out below the current rate of wages, and also if the child is not of sufficient age.

5. I have to remark that we have no children apprenticed in this Union.

6. I may mention that the children are generally sent into service at the age of fourteen; they retain their first places as a rule.

7. As to the practice of sending children out for short periods of service, I beg to state in reply that the

children are sometimes hired out as herds, but not for a shorter period of service than six months.

Lastly. With regard to adult inmates in the Workhouse now who were brought up in it as children, I have ascertained that there are none of this class in the Workhouse of the Cookstown Union.

JOHN HUNTER, Clerk of Union.

DUNGANNON.

1. The Industrial Training in the Workhouse of the Dungannon Union consists chiefly in the girls being taught to sew and knit, and the boys at proper times being required to assist at weeding in the garden, and at the distribution of manure

2. The girls are under the constant supervision of the schoolmistress, and the boys under that of the master of the Workhouse There is no schoolmaster, and the average number of boys is about nine or ten.

3 The Guardians experience no difficulty in getting the children into service

4 The period of service is usually by the quarter or half year, and the wages are usually from a pound to twenty-five shillings per quarter This sum is generally expended in procuring a renewal of clothing for the children.

5 During the last nine years at least only one child has been apprenticed. This was a boy of fourteen, who was apprenticed for a period of five years to a tailor But the Guardians incurred no responsibility in the matter They only furnished him with an outfit of clothing, and they privately contributed towards his apprentice fee.

6. Children have occasionally been sent to service at the age of twelve, but from thirteen to fifteen is the usual age As a general rule they do not retain their first places.

7. The children are not sent out temporarily for such employments as "herding."

8. Of the adult inmates at present in the Workhouse there are three who have spent a considerable portion of their lives in the Workhouse Two of them are females with children, and one a male, whose general health and sight are bad. None of these persons, however, were brought up in the house.

JOHN BOYD, Clerk of Union.

GORTIN.

The Board of Guardians here send all children over five years of age to Omagh Workhouse to be educated and trained, and on account of this arrangement no system of Industrial Training has been adopted at this Workhouse.

With regard to queries (one to seven), contained in Poor Law Inquiry Commissioners' letter of the 3rd instant, I am unable therefore to give any really satisfactory reply, beyond stating the fact of the children being trained in every respect same as the children of the Omagh Workhouse In reference to query No. 8, no adult inmates are now in this Workhouse who were brought up in it as children.

DAN. M'FARLAND, Clerk of Union.

OMAGH.

1 and 2 The boys in the Workhouse of this Union are trained to agriculture under the supervision of the schoolmaster, and the girls to needlework, under that of the schoolmistress.

3. The Guardians experience no difficulty in getting the children into service.

4. The children are usually hired out for a period of six months, say from May to November, or November to May, the rate of wages being that given by farmers to other children engaged by them.

5. There is no apprenticing of children in this Union.

6. The children are sent out to service between the ages of ten and twelve years, and they generally retain their first places.

7. The children are not sent out for a shorter period than six months.

8. There are no adult inmates in the Workhouse now who were brought up in it as children.

W. J M'KNIGHT, Clerk of Union.

STRABANE.

1. The boys are taught agriculture, the girls sewing knitting, &c.

2. The agriculturist and schoolmistress.

3. No.

4 Various conditions—the usual period is six months.

5. No.

6. From ten to fourteen years of age. As a rule they do not retain their first places.

7. Yes, it prevails very much.

8. Two males; one idiotic and the other scrofulous.

DAVID M'ILHENNY, Clerk of Union.

BALLYVAUGHAN.

1. Cultivation of land the property of the Guardians.

2 The master of the Workhouse.

3 They do.

4. They are generally sent to service at 10s. each per quarter.

5. No.

6. At the age of fourteen years Occasionally retain their first places.

7. No.

8 There are several, chiefly females, whose destitution is attributable to their want of virtue, and their disinclination to work.

CORROFIN.

1. The industrial training in the Workhouse of this Union is, for girls, sewing, knitting, and occasionally laundry work, for boys there is no particular industrial training, but they are employed occasionally after school hours, in household work, such as serving coal, cleaning and repairing walks, &c. The industrial training of the girls is under the supervision of the schoolmistress.

3. The Guardians do not experience any difficulty in getting the children into service

4. The children are sent out to service at wages varying from 8s. to 15s. per quarter, with board and lodging.

5. No children are apprenticed to trades in this Union.

6. The children are generally sent to service from the ages of 13 to 15 years, and only leave their first places on obtaining higher wages elsewhere.

7 The children are not sent out for such temporary employment as herding.

8 There is only one boy in the Workhouse who had been brought up in it since his childhood, and who returned thereto after two or three short terms of service, his destitution is owing to his inability to work outside.

D. SULLIVAN, Clerk of Union.

ENNIS.

1. The system of industrial training in this Workhouse is tailoring and agriculture.

2. Under the supervision of M. Daly (master tailor) and P. Nash, agriculturist.

3. The Guardians experience no difficulty in getting children into service.

4. The conditions as to wages are regulated according to the service in which they are engaged. No period of service being named

5. No children are apprenticed in this Union.

6. The ages of children sent into service usually

APPENDIX B.

Industrial Training

vary from 12 to 15 years, and as a rule retain their places.

7. The practice does not prevail in this Union of sending children out for short periods of service.

8. There are two adult inmates in the Workhouse now who were brought up in it as children. The cause of their destitution being want of employment at the present time, having recently been disengaged.

ENNISTIMON.

1. The boys assist in cultivating the grounds, stone breaking, lime washing, and the other general work of the house. The girls assist to knit, sew, wash, cook, and in the general household work.

2. The boys under the supervision of the master—the girls under that of the matron and schoolmistress.

3. No.

4. Wages from 10s. to 15s. a quarter; period of service generally three months, which is the usual practice in this locality.

5. No.

6. At the age of twelve years and upwards, and as a rule if they do not continue in their first places at increased wages, they are employed by others.

7. No.

8. Yes, owing to delicacy of health, or weakness of intellect, and in a few instances to females having returned to the house, the mothers of illegitimate children.

JOHN O'LOUGHLIN, Clerk of Union.

KILLADYSERT.

1. That the system of industrial training in this Workhouse is confined to sewing and knitting.

2. That it is conducted under the supervision of the Matron and Schoolmistress as regards the women and girls, and under the supervision of the tailor as regards the boys.

3. The Guardians experience little difficulty in getting the children into service, according as they become sufficiently old and strong. The only difficulty exists in feeling themselves reluctant in allowing the children into the service of some of those who apply, lest they may not be comfortable or well treated in such places.

4. The hiring is generally quarterly, and the wages, being for beginners, necessarily small, varying from 7s. 6d. to 12s. 6d. per quarter with promises to increase the wages according as the children may be deserving and suitable.

5. The Guardians have no power of apprenticing children except sending them to sea, and have done so on one occasion; on another occasion, however, a child was apprenticed to a printer, but the boy's mother it was who executed the indenture, his father having been dead.

6. Children from about 11 to 14 years old are sent to service, as stated in answer to query 3.

7. Children are not sent out "herding" for short periods, nor otherwise than as stated in reply to query 3.

8. There are a few persons now in the Workhouse who were brought up in it as children, but their destitution is caused by delicacy and bodily ailments of various kinds.

ALEX. MACMAHON, Clerk of Union.

KILRUSH.

In reply to the queries in your circular of the 3rd instant, I have the honour to state that the industrial training in this Union is limited to teaching the school girls plain needlework and knitting, two of the schoolboys are taught tailoring, and the other boys work occasionally in the Workhouse grounds about two acres of grass and tillage. The Guardians experience no difficulty in getting the children to service when old enough. The wages vary from 10s. to 20s. per quarter, and they generally, with a very few exceptions, do not return to the Workhouse. The Guardians have no power to apprentice the children, the ages they generally go out to service is from 12 to 14 years. There are no adult inmates who were brought up in it just now.

AUGUSTUS WARREN, Clerk of Union.

SCARRIFF.

1. Boys work on farm when weather permits, and when there is work to be done, between 8 and 10 o'clock A.M., and 2 and 6 o'clock P.M. They also assist in the necessary household work such as drawing turf, sweeping yards, &c. Girls sew and knit during same hours, and any that are able, assist in washing, cleaning up establishment, &c.

2. Boys under master, schoolmaster, and porter; girls under matron and schoolmistress.

3. They do not.

4. Generally from 5s. to 10s. a quarter, for girls as well as boys. They are generally hired for three or six months certain, leaving it to the employer and employed to deal again if they wish or can agree.

5. No.

6. Between 11 and 15, but they are almost always applied to by employers before being sent out with them. They often do, but not always.

7. Never less than 3 or 6 months. (See query 4).

8. Yes, about 10. Blindness, idiotcy, and being crippled principally.

JOSEPH PARKER, Clerk of Union.

TULLA.

1. The school boys work on the farm attached to the Workhouse. The school girls assist in making the articles of clothing required for the female inmates.

2. Schoolmaster and Matron.

3. No.

4. 12s. to 15s. per quarter.

5. No.

6. From 12 to 15 years. The majority do not retain their first place.

7. No.

8. Yes, six males and seven females; all of whom are either blind, idiots, or cripples, except one male who has returned from serving in militia, and will leave when employment offers.

T. MURPHY, Clerk of Union.

BANDON.

1. The boys are taught digging, weeding, cleansing yards, &c., and five of them are learning trades, two shoemaking, and three tailoring; and the girls are taught knitting, sewing, washing, scrubbing, and general house-work.

2. The master, matron, and schoolmistress.

3. They do not.

4. From 10s. to £1 per quarter.

5. They are not.

6. From eleven years.

7. It does not.

8. Two cases caused by illness.

BANTRY.

1. The girls are taught sewing, knitting, &c. The grown girls are trained to the usual work of domestic servants. There is no system of industrial training for the boys.

2. Under the supervision of the Schoolmistress and Matron.

3. No. Farmers come to the Workhouse from time to time, and are glad to get children strong enough to go into their service.

4. There is no condition as to period of service, &c. The Guardians agree with the person taking a child from the Workhouse to have such child paid wages

according to what they consider the child's service may be worth.

5. No. A tradesman will not take a child without a fee, and the Guardians have not the power of appropriating the poor rates in such manner.

6 About 14 years of age As far as my knowledge goes they retain their first places.

7. No

8. There is only one Bodily infirmity.

RICHARD CROLY, Clerk of Union.

CASTLETOWN.

1. The school girls are trained to plain sewing and knitting, the grown girls to house-work.

2. The officers of the House.

3. They are taken out without the interference of of the Guardians

4 They are not sent out. They go out, and their friends bargain for them.

5. No.

6. They go out about the age of fourteen years, and remain out

7. No

8. No.

T. R. HARRINGTON, Clerk of Union.

CLONAKILTY.

1 and 2. That the male children are employed on the Workhouse farm under superintendence of the Workhouse master, the female children at sewing and knitting, under the schoolmistress.

3. Guardians experience no difficulty in sending out the children, on the contrary are frequently obliged to refuse applications for children who are either too young or delicate

4. No special period of service, wages are low, but quite equal to their value, the children are always cautioned to return to the Workhouse if not properly treated, and then inquiry is made.

5. No children apprenticed.

6. About twelve years is the usual time, but much depends upon size and strength of the child, some children stay, others soon leave their first place.

7. Children are never sent out for temporary employment

8. Six women are now in the Workhouse who were reared in it as children, each, with one or more illegitimate children, all were servants. No men

JOHN C. SPILLER, Clerk of Union.

CORK.

1. Industrial training cannot at present be said to be carried on as a system. Special female industrial superintendents were employed some time ago to train girls for domestic service, and proper appliances were provided for the purpose, but the number of school girls of a suitable age failing, the services of the last superintendent were dispensed with. Since then the girls are trained under the directions of the schoolmistresses in such occupations as may be fit for them, as sewing, knitting, washing, scouring, cooking, &c, such as the requirements of the school department demand

A limited number of boys are employed at tailoring and shoemaking, the remainder are engaged at regular hours daily assisting in the cultivation of the large vegetable garden of the Workhouse.

2. Under the schoolmistresses, master tailor, master shoemaker, and gardener.

3 No; but from the general imperfection of their training and habits as servants, they do not in most cases retain the situations they first obtain They get re-engaged, however, from time to time, the intervals being principally spent in the Workhouse.

4. The Guardians, when hiring out, exact part payment of the first quarter's wages from the employer to secure an interest on his part in the boy or girl. The children are generally employed from about the age of twelve years upwards The rate of wages averages about 10s. per quarter to commence with.

5 No.

6. See replies to queries 3 and 4.

7. No.

8 There are. not many, however. In the case of the males, who are few, their return is almost altogether attributable to bad health. In the case of the females ill health, a failure in their career as servants from incapacity or want of temper, or the misfortune of having become mothers of illegitimate children, cause their return to the Workhouse

GENERAL OBSERVATIONS.

From time to time the Guardians, feeling the want of industrial training for the juvenile inmates, established training institutions both inside and outside the Workhouse. These institutions failed, however, from causes not easy to specify, and the expenses were found not to be commensurate with the result. Some system, under which boys and girls— the latter especially— could be suitably trained to handicraft occupations, or for domestic service, is most desirable, and the Guardians believe that any institution for the purpose would be most likely to succeed, if separated or detached from the Workhouse, with power to the Guardians to retain the children therein for a definite period sufficient to complete their education in this regard. The power of the parent at present to quit the Workhouse at pleasure, and the obligation he is under of taking his children with him, destroy the hope of useful results from any system where the instruction of the child cannot be continuous till the object in view be attained.

J. M'GRATH, Clerk of Union.

DUNMANWAY.

1. The boys work on the farm after school hours, and the girls knit and sew during same time.

2. The boys are under the supervision of the master and porter, and the girls under that of the matron and schoolmistress

3. None whatever.

4. They generally get from 10s. to 15s. per quarter, and agree for quarter or half year.

5. They are not by the guardians, but in a few cases have been by their mothers after leaving the workhouse.

6. From 10 to 15 years of age, and they in general keep their places.

7 It does not

8 Two female inmates, one after being out five years, returned in bad health, and the other, having got married and buried her husband, returned with three children, being nearly blind, and could not support them.

PETER O'SULLIVAN, Clerk of Union.

FERMOY.

1. Shoemaking, tailoring, baking, sewing, knitting, and agriculture.

2. Under the supervision of the foreman shoemaker tailor, and baker, and that of the male and female school teachers

3. No, the demand is generally in excess of the supply.

4 Children, intended as farm or house servants, get from 15s. to 20s. per quarter, and are hired generally for a year.

5. There have been no apprenticeships.

6. From the ages of 12 to 15. Yes.

7. No

8 Not one.

J. W. HEALY, Clerk of Union.

APPENDIX B.

Industrial Training.

KANTURK.

1. No industrial training in male school. Needlework and knitting taught in female school.

2. Conducted under the supervision of the schoolmistress.

3. No difficulty experienced when children come to maturity.

4. A yearly engagement of service at current rate of wages.

5. No children apprenticed from this union.

6. From 12 years upwards. With few exceptions retain their places.

7. No child sent to service less than an annual engagement.

8. There are a few, owing to bodily infirmity, such as blindness, scrofula, &c.

JOHN SULLIVAN, Clerk of Union.

KINSALE.

1. For boys.—Daily work on farm so as to fit them for farm service. For girls.—Household work to train them as domestic servants.

2. Under the supervision of the master, matron, and schoolmistress.

3. No.

4. Children are generally sent out to farmers at 12s. per quarter, with board and lodging.

5. No.

6. From 10 years upwards. Generally.

7. No.

8. One male inmate, being physically unable to do hard work.

M. HEGARTY, Clerk of Union.

MACROOM.

1. The boys are occasionally employed in the gardens weeding and cleaning up the walks. The older girls are engaged sewing and mending the clothing and bedding.

2. The schoolmistress and assistant schoolmaster superintend the children.

3. As a rule there is difficulty in putting them out to service, as very few of them give satisfaction.

4. They are generally sent, the boys to herd cattle, and the girls to mind children, by the month or quarter, at very low wages.

5. No children have been apprenticed out in this union, the guardians power in this respect being very limited.

6. The age at which they go out to service depends a great deal on circumstances, their growth and disposition, 14 to 16 years may be put down as an average. They generally return from time to time to the workhouse.

7. This question is answered in No. 4.

8. There are adult inmates in the workhouse who have been brought up there as children. Several (females) have come to misfortune, and as a rule they are unsuited to enter into the struggle of life, and none of them retain that self-respect which even the humblest who have been reared in their own homes possess immeasurably above them.

I would suggest that a vast improvement would accrue from an extension of the Guardians' powers to apprentice out children to farmers, housekeepers, or tradesmen, as circumstances may from time to time offer inducements.

T. T. HEALEY, Clerk of Union.

MALLOW.

1. For girls, general household work, including sewing and knitting; for boys, tailoring and shoemaking, and occasionally at farm operations.

2. The schoolmistress, tailor, shoemaker, schoolmaster, and other officers.

3. Owing to the rule made by the guardians, by which it appears that an employer must have a valuation of £30 and upwards, there have been fewer applications for children as servants recently.

4. The conditions, &c., &c., appended hereto; wages from 12s. to 15s. per quarter.

5. No.

6. Over 12 years of age; no.

7. Yes; the guardians endeavour to make a year's term, and generally for "herding."

8. There are—fondness of the establishment which they consider a home, and owing to which a desire for ambition lies dormant in those inmates who, if that attachment to workhouse life had not been of long duration, should now be in respectable employments outside.

9. In regard to the subject of the education of children in workhouses, I beg to observe that, in my opinion, district schools for "orphan and deserted children" should be established in each county, and, perhaps, should be termed "industrial."

J. HANLEY, Clerk of Union.

MIDLETON.

1. Female children are instructed in washing, sewing, knitting, cleaning dormitories, &c. Male children, no available means of industrial training.

2. Industrial training of female children under supervision of schoolmistress.

3. They do not.

4. They are sent out to service to farmer's when applied for at 15s. for first quarter, subject to the approval of the board of guardians.

5. No.

6. About 14 years. As a rule they retain their first service.

7. No.

8. There are. Delicacy of constitution or mental weakness.

WILLIAM ROCHE, Clerk of Union.

MILLSTREET.

1. No special system of industrial training has been adopted in this Union for either boys or girls, but the boys are employed sometimes in cleaning their yards, schoolroom, and dormitories, and in autumn in weeding potatoes, turnips, and other crops grown in the plot of ground within the workhouse; while the industrial training of the girls is confined to occasional needlework, and knitting, assisting the adults in cleaning their yards, dormitories, and dining hall. They are also employed about two hours a week at laundry-work.

2. They are under the supervision of master and schoolmaster; the girls under that of schoolmistress and matron.

3. No, few are sent.

4. The usual conditions are that the person who hires gives the wages generally given to children of same age through the country; the periods of service seldom exceed half a year.

5. They are not apprenticed.

6. About twelve years. They generally retain their first places.

7. Yes. This seems to be the prevalent practice here.

8. There are twelve, of whom six are suffering from different phases of infirmity—lameness, epilepsy, &c.; four are blind, and two are nursing illegitimate children.

To the entire absence of a proper industrial training, and the consequent habit of idleness contracted by most of the above, may be attributed their destitution and infirmity.

T. M. O'CONNOR, Clerk of Union.

MITCHELSTOWN.

1. Knitting, sewing, household work, and boys occasionally employed on farm of workhouse.

2. The master and matron, schoolmaster and schoolmistress.

APPENDIX B. Industrial Training.

3. None whatever during the summer season, but in winter they do

4. The wages are from 7s. 6d. to 10s. for the three months which they are usually hired for in summer.

5. They are not.

6. From 10 to 12 years. Generally speaking they retain their places, and give satisfaction. Some are obliged to return during the winter months, and readily leave when offered employment.

7. The shortest period is three months. The boys are, as a rule, employed "herding," and the girls caring children. If they give satisfaction the hiring is continued.

8. There are four females who returned with illegitimate children. There are a few others who are obliged to remain in the house during ill health, such as scrofula and being idiotic.

R. FITZGIBBON, Clerk of Union.

SKIBBEREEN.

1. The boys are trained on the farm under the schoolmaster, the girls in the general work of the house, also sewing, making frocks, &c., &c., under the schoolmistress and assistant.

2. See No. 1.

3. Not until this year, when very few persons applied for either boys or girls.

4. Generally hired by the quarter, first at low wages.

5. No.

6. From 12 to 15 years of age; they generally retain their first place.

7. No.

8. None, except those who are afflicted either by mental or bodily infirmity.

The schools are at present conducted by a schoolmaster, schoolmistress, and assistant, and appear to be now in a very good state.

SCHULL.

1. The industrial training in the workhouse is confined to the employment of the females making and repairing the clothing of the inmates. The men and boys do a little at agriculture. The ordinary household work occupies nearly the entire time of the paupers.

2. Under the supervision of the master, matron, and schoolmistress.

3. The guardians do not experience any difficulty in getting the children into service. The demand for girls as servants is greater than the supply.

4. Wages paid quarterly.

5. Children are not apprenticed.

6. Children are taken out to service at from 10 to 15 years of age. As a rule they retain the first place until they can better their condition.

7. Children are not sent out for short periods of service.

8. There are no adults now in the workhouse who were brought up in it as children.

OBSERVATIONS.

It appears to me that workhouse children do not value the books and the education which they receive gratis as much as the children outside whose parents have to pay for them. The children should be instructed to set a higher value on what they receive.

JOHN EVANS, Clerk of Union.

YOUGHAL.

1. The boys are taught to mend their own clothes and boots, under the master tailor and master shoemaker, and the amount of work done by each is inspected by the master at six o'clock every evening, or in his absence by the schoolmaster. But when there is work to be done on the farm, suitable to their capacity, they do it, under the supervision of the schoolmaster. They also distribute coals every morning to the whole house, and sometimes clean windows. The girls are engaged at sewing, knitting, darning, washing in the laundry, cleaning dormitories, schoolroom, and chapel; also, in cleaning brasses, fire irons, and windows, and polishing boots. A few of the eldest assist in cutting out the clothing of the children, and work the sewing machine.

2. The boys, under the supervision of the master tailor, the master shoemaker, the schoolmaster, and the master, and the girls under the supervision of the schoolmistress.

3. They do not.

4. By the quarter, and with wages, from eight shillings upwards.

5. They are not apprenticed.

6. From ten years upwards, and generally retain their first places.

7. It does not.

8. There are three, on account of bodily infirmity.

I would most humbly suggest, for the future improvement of the education of workhouse children, that when the schools are found and reported as progressing satisfactorily, the teachers be awarded results or gratuities, as at present there is nothing to encourage the energetic teacher. The gratuities that were formerly given to deserving teachers were withdrawn when the result system was introduced, though, as a rule, the workhouse teachers have derived no benefit from that system, therefore, instead of their position being improved, it has been made the contrary, and as a natural consequence, the effect cannot be otherwise than injurious to the education of workhouse children.

M. ROMAYNE, Clerk of Union.

CAHIRCIVEEN.

1. Girls taught needlework and knitting. The boys are not trained to any industry.

2. The schoolmistress.

3. The Guardians do not, as a rule, take any steps to have the children sent into service.

4. See answer No. 3.

5. No instance of the kind has occurred in this Union during my term of office as clerk—a period of twenty years.

6. See answer No. 3.

7. No.

8. None now in the workhouse who were brought up in it as children.

D. A. O'CONNELL, Clerk of Union.

DINGLE.

1. Sewing and knitting for children.

2. The schoolmistress.

3. They are rarely taken out whilst children; when arrived at the age of fifteen, farmers and others take them out for three, six, nine, or twelve months, as the case may be, at wages rating from 15s. a quarter to £1.

4. See query 3.

5. Apprenticeship in the naval and mercantile services is only allowed—some cases of which occurred several years ago.

6. See query 3.

7. No; farmers and others apply to take them out. See query 3.

8. Only one boy (illegitimate) who was deserted by mother, and who received an injury on the arm when an infant.

PATRICK GREY, Clerk of Union.

KENMARE.

1. The female children are taught knitting, sewing, and housekeeping. The boys—no industrial training.

2. The schoolmistress.

3. No.

4. Children under fifteen years of age are not sent out from workhouse, but should they go out, they receive 15s. a quarter at an average.

5. No.

6. From thirteen to seventeen.

7. No.

8. Only two women.

Appendix D

Industrial Training

KILLARNEY.

1. One boy is employed at tailoring; one boy is employed at shoemaking, and about a dozen are occasionally employed in the workhouse garden. The female children are sometimes employed washing in the laundry, and making and mending their own clothes, and knitting and repairing stockings. Some of the female children are also employed as domestic servants to the workhouse officers and their families.

2. Under the supervision of the tailor, shoemaker, gardener, schoolmaster, and schoolmistress respectively.

3. No, the demand is greater than the number of children fit for service.

4. The conditions of the engagement are mutually agreed upon in each case, and then submitted to the Guardians for their approval.

5. The Guardians of this union do not apprentice any children.

6. The ages at which children first go to service from this workhouse vary from 12 to 16 years, and they seldom remain out of the workhouse permanently on their first engagement.

7. Yes, the children are allowed to go to service for short periods or otherwise, as they may happen to get employment, but they are not compelled to accept any engagement unless the Guardians approve of all the conditions, and consider them free from objection as to length of time or otherwise.

8. There are a few adult inmates in the workhouse who were brought up in it as children, and their destitution appears to be caused for the most part by delicate health, but in some instances their destitution may be traced to their inability or unwillingness to retain their employments.

EDMOND M'SWEENY, Clerk of Union.

LISTOWEL.

1. Girls are taught to sew, to wash rooms and clothes. Boys to work occasionally in a vegetable garden.

2. Under that of master and matron respectively.

3. No difficulty in getting employers for children amongst farmers.

4. About £3 a year. Sometimes for six months, usually for twelve months.

5. None of the children are apprenticed by the board; a few of them are taken by tradesmen.

6. Children are sent to service usually at fourteen years of age. They, in some cases, retain first place for a number of years.

7. This practice is discountenanced by guardians far as they can, though service for short periods, viz., six months, has been in some cases allowed.

8. One man, partially disabled and unfitted for work, one young woman, rather disinclined to go to service, and another having an illegitimate child.

J. M'CARTHY, Clerk of Union.

TRALEE.

1. Boys tailoring and shoemaking after school hours.

2. Under master tailor and shoemaker.

3. No.

4. From three to six months, at fifteen or twenty shillings per quarter.

5. Yes, upon agreement with the guardians.

6. Age from twelve to fifteen years. Yes.

7. Yes.

8. No.

JOHN G. STOKES, Clerk of Union.

CROOM.

1. Sewing and knitting for girls; farming work for boys.

2. Girls under schoolmistress and matron; boys under master.

3. No.

4. About 7s. 6d. per quarter.

5. Not apprenticed.

6. Eleven to thirteen years. They do.

7. No.

8. There are a few. All are more or less disabled.

GLIN.

1. No special system of industrial training has been adopted in this union for either boys or girls, but the boys are sometimes employed in cleaning their yards, schoolroom, and dormitories, and in autumn in weeding potatoes, turnips, and other crops grown in the plot of ground within the workhouse walls, while the industrial training of the girls is confined to occasional needlework, and knitting, assisting the adults in cleaning their yards, dormitories, and dining hall. They are also employed for about two hours a week at laundry work.

2. They are under the supervision of the master, or schoolmaster, the girls under that of the matron and schoolmistress.

3. No; few are sent.

4. The usual conditions are that the person who hires gives the wages generally given to children of the same age through the country; the periods of service seldom exceed half a year.

5. They are not apprenticed.

6. About twelve years, they usually retain the first places.

7. Yes, this seems to be the prevalent practice here.

8. There are twelve, of whom six are suffering from different phases of infirmity—lameness, epilepsy, &c., four are blind, and two are nursing illegitimate children. To an entire absence of a proper industrial training, and the consequent habit of idleness contracted by most of the above may be attributed their destitution.

KILMALLOCK.

1. The system of industrial training in this workhouse comprises that for the boys, baking, tailoring, shoemaking, carpentry, and farming, conducted under paid artisans, the master, and schoolmaster of the workhouse.

2. That of the girls, sewing, knitting, washing, and general house business, under the matron and school-teachers of the workhouse.

3. No, scarcely any difficulty in getting the children into service.

4. Period of service mostly by the quarter, but sometimes may be half-yearly or yearly; and rates of wages per quarter range from 12s. to 16s. for children under 15 years.

5. None for a long time apprenticed by the Guardians, but some are occasionally by the parents, parent, or other friend of the child, to a tradesman well known for good character.

6. Children are generally allowed to service from 11 to 16 years of age, and many retain their places for years, some come back to the workhouse to go out again to other employers, and scarcely any come back to remain in the house.

7. Yes, the practice does, to a small extent prevail of boys going out "to herd" in the spring, coming back for the winter months, and going out again in the following spring.

8. Yes, there are adult inmates in this workhouse who were brought up in it, some women have come back with one or sometimes more children, some legitimate, but most illegitimate, all others I think I may say from sickness and ill health.

OBSERVATION.

I would think it very advisable that children, boys and girls, whose constitution is known to be good and healthy should be forced out of the workhouse when they arrive at the age of 12 years, and when a suit-

Appendix B.
Industrial Training.

able and respectable employer offers them a situation, and that then a responsible officer of the Guardians visit each one in employment within the first month after going out, and if necessary after, and report to the Board. As a rule children kept in the workhouse after 12 years of age, according to my observation, don't "turn out" so well as if sent out about that period, or even under

JAMES NELSON, Workhouse Master.

LIMERICK.

1. The children in the boys' school receive in considerable numbers, training under the master tailor and master shoemaker, in the mending of clothes and shoes, they also assist the carpenter principally in making coffins. The children in girls' school make with the sewing machine all the clothes for the male inmates as far as the machine is suited for them, also other clothing, knitting, and their own mending They used to make their own clothes, but the School Inspector objected to their doing only coarse work to the exclusion of fine, so portion of their time is given to the usual fine work done in schools instead.

2. This is replied to in No 1.

3. No, they are taken out at an early age.

4. I send a form of agreement which must be signed by any person wanting a servant; this contains a copy of the conditions The boys are often engaged by farmers for six or nine months, never less as a rule.

5. There can be no fee given with an apprentice by the Guardians, but they generally give £1 for clothes, or the clothes Apprentices are generally taken from among the boys who have been working in the tailor's or shoemaker's shop The conditions made are such as are usual in the trade.

6. About twelve years of age. Very few remain in the schools longer. As a rule all the children remain for the term of the agreements entered into on forms referred to in Query 4.

7. No boys are allowed out except upon the terms mentioned in the printed agreements. I myself, for some years after I became clerk, used to have out to my own home daily, a boy (generally delicate) to clean shoes and go messages I got seven boys good places, but it was objected to by a Guardian, and I relinquished it.

8. There are at present in the workhouse 26 persons who were reared in the schools; of these 8 are males, and 18 females Several of these are from various causes incapacitated from working for their living

I can give no information as to how the education of workhouse children can be improved upon. They are taken out and become in this workhouse at all events self-supporting at a very early age, seldom later than twelve or thirteen years of age, according to their size and strength. Boys who go out of messages to the town are generally taken by shopkeepers and others as soon as they become acquainted with the city. I have had for the last two or three years to post all letters instead of sending the city letters by messenger, in consequence of the young boys' want of knowledge of the streets.

I have always considered that with regard to the children this workhouse can compare favourably with any institution I ever heard of. I consider that about 6,000 children must have passed through this workhouse, and, notwithstanding repeated statements to the contrary, I have never found more than about 35 grown persons at any time inmates of the workhouse who had been schoolchildren in it There are about ten or so who are lame, idiots, or crippled in some way, who are generally among the number, and the balance are persons usually temporarily out of place, and who stop for a short time for shelter, and knowing that farmers and others resort to the house for servants of their class

I have been about ten years clerk of the union, and I have a very general acquaintance among persons of various classes, and I find that most of the people who get the boys and girls out of the house once generally come again for another.

I myself have had none but boys out of this house to assist me, some certainly did not turn out well at first, but, after leaving this locality, I have reason to think they have got on very well and respectably. One of my clerks who was born and reared in this house, and an orphan from an early age passed for the excise, and got sixteenth place out of 2,600 candidates from all parts of the kingdom.

I have sent out of my office to other clerks of unions seven young boys, as far as I can recollect, who I think are all doing well.

As a rule I am informed that the only class of children who do not get on well, are children whose parents are in the house; my informants never could give a good reason for this statement, but it seems to be a fact.

I myself think that there are not a sufficient number of assistants generally in the workhouse schools, thereby throwing the girls particularly into the care of wardswomen, often of a low class It is evident that one resident teacher in the school of this workhouse cannot be always with the children, when she has to see them up and dressed in the morning, their beds made up, themselves washed, all their clothes and meals attended to, and all the various calls attended to, besides teaching, when she has only the assistance of an assistant teacher, non-resident, who attends from ten to three o'clock

C. MONCK WILSON, Clerk of Union

NEWCASTLE

1. There is no industrial training in the workhouse for children, except knitting and sewing in the female school

2. Under the supervision of the schoolmistress.

3. The guardians experience no difficulty in getting employment for the children from farmers.

4. They are generally employed by the quarter, at wages varying from ten to fifteen shillings, according to age and capability.

5. They are scarcely ever apprenticed in this union.

6. About twelve years, and they generally retain their first places.

7. They are never sent herding, except by the "quarter."

8. There are some female inmates, the cause of whose destitution is having had illegitimate children, and a few others who are disabled.

MICHAEL MOORE, Clerk of Union.

RATHKEALE.

1. Boys occasionally employed at tilling land on workhouse site, a section employed at tailoring. Girls employed at sewing and washing.

2. Master, matron, schoolmaster, and master tailor

3. They do not; there is a fair demand for them by farmers when found fit for any labour

4. The first obtained average about 15s per quarter and board; they are employed quarterly, half yearly, and yearly.

5. The board of guardians have no power to apprentice a child, but occasionally a tradesman takes a boy out of the workhouse, and arranges with some friend to keep him for about five years instructed at his trade

6. From eleven to fourteen years; as a rule they retain their first places of employment

7. No They are taken with the intention of retaining them if at all found suitable.

8. There are four, whose destitution is attributable to mental, physical, and social causes.

GENERAL OBSERVATIONS.

If guardians had the power to apprentice boys and girls to trades, and to give a moderate fee in doing so—

Appendix B
Industrial Training.

that is to orphan and deserted children—it would be found the most economical and permanently useful mode of dealing with them, and would reduce to a minimum the number and expense of those now boarded out, who, as a rule, receive no useful habit of manual or handicraft work.

MICHAEL FITZGIBBONS, Clerk of Union

BORRISOKANE.

1. The industrial training is knitting, sewing, and cleaning the workhouse for the girls, and weeding the workhouse grounds for the boys.

2. Under the supervision of the master and the schoolmistress.

3. The guardians do not experience any difficulty in getting the children into service; there is a constant demand for boys and girls

4. Wages from 7s to 12s. per quarter; usual period of service six months.

5. The children are not apprenticed.

6. The children are sent into service at ages from nine to fourteen years. They do not, as a rule, retain their first places, some because of laziness, others because the parents will not allow them.

7 They are not sent out for temporary employment.

8. There are about six adult inmates in the workhouse now who were brought up in it as children, caused by physical defects and prostitution.

CARRICK-ON-SUIR.

1. The boys in school are taught agriculture on farm, and girls are taught knitting and sewing. The boys are also taught tailoring and shoemaking when practicable.

2. Under the supervision of the respective teachers of schools.

3. No.

4. The children are sent out at wages varying from 10s per quarter upwards. The employer generally advances half the cost of outfit when necessary, to be subsequently deducted from the wages The term of service, as a rule, is for one year, with a probation of three months.

5. No

6. Twelve years and upwards, and they, as a rule, retain their first places

7. No

8. Yes, a few—one from epilepsy, and the remainder young women, with illegitimate children

GENERAL OBSERVATIONS.

With regard to the last paragraph in your letter, I may observe that in my opinion ample means are provided for the literary education of children in workhouses, but I think it desirable that facilities should be afforded orphan children to become absorbed in the general population. The matter is, however, not free from difficulty.

W. MULLINS, Clerk of Union.

CASHEL.

1 The girls are employed at scrubbing the floors, cleaning up the kitchen utensils in the officers apartments, and occasionally at washing in the laundry. They are also instructed in knitting, sewing, and making clothes. The boys are taught shoemaking, tailoring, including the use of the sewing machine, and agriculture on the workhouse farm.

2 The girls, under the supervision of the matron and female teachers The boys, under the master shoemaker, master tailor, and the schoolmaster, who is also agriculturist.

3. Generally speaking, no; though the number of applications for children has not been as numerous this year as others.

4. The wages of children vary with the ages, and range from ten to fifteen shillings per quarter. They are hired out as a rule for not less than six months; and receive clothes from the board before leaving the workhouse.

5. They are eagerly sought for by tailors and shoemakers. The custom has been to bind them for three years, the master being obliged to clothe and support his apprentice during that period, and in addition pay him £1 for the first year, and at the rate of £2 a year for the second and third years.

6. Rarely under thirteen years. They generally keep their places, or change at higher wages.

7. No.

8 There are a few, but their destitution is rather owing to some bodily defect which has prevented their earning a livelihood outside

WILLIAM PHELAN, Clerk of Union.

CLOGHEEN.

1. Boys are instructed in agriculture by working on the workhouse farm; girls in sewing, knitting, and washing

2. Under supervision of the workhouse teachers.

3. The Guardians do not experience any difficulty in getting the children into service.

4 The children are sent out on the usual wages of ten shillings per quarter.

5. Children are not apprenticed.

6. Children are sent out, on an average, at the age of twelve years.

7. Children are not sent out for short periods of service

8. There are three adults in workhouse who were brought up in it, the cause of destitution being in one case blindness, and in the other two ophthalmic.

JOS KETTLEWELL, Clerk of Union.

CLONMEL.

1. The boys—three at a time—are taught tailoring. The others able to work are employed after school hours, three days in each week, in the garden, grounds, &c., at agricultural work.

The girls are taught to sew, knit, scour, and wash. One of them, for fourteen days at a time, is employed assisting in the infirmary kitchen. There is also one employed, morning and evening—before and after school hours—in the master's kitchen, and one in the matron's kitchen

2. Under their respective head teachers.

3 None

4. Twelve to sixteen shillings per quarter, period not limited

5. None are apprenticed.

6. Twelve up to fifteen years They do. There have, however, been a few amongst them who have returned twice or thrice each to the house.

7. No.

8 There are—thirteen men and twelve women. Of the males—four from defective vision, six imbecility, one deaf and dumb, one from scrofula, one with a wife and five children

Of the women—two defective vision, one idiotic, two having illegitimate children, four sickly, two able-bodied, one in with her husband, who is blind

OBSERVATIONS.

A great fault in the training of workhouse children is their being—so to speak—constantly nursed while in the house, almost all their wants being attended to by others. It would seem desirable that they should be taught to be more self-reliant, and to do as much as possible for themselves They should be taught to cook their own food, cooking arrangements being provided in each school for this purpose. They should have their meals in their own day-rooms, and should be provided with knives, forks, &c. Boys or girls anxious to learn a trade should be apprenticed The assistant male teacher should be an intern officer and a tradesman, who should be employed after school hours in teaching the boys his own craft. The assistant female teacher should also reside in the house, and should be capable to instruct the girls in cutting out garments, and in making them up, she should also teach cooking and laundry work The adoption of this course would cause little additional expense; a spirit of emulation would be engendered between boys and girls as to cleanliness and *home* comforts; their schools would be more of a home than they now are; and when the children go out into the world, it is to be hoped they would not be found quite so helpless as it is stated some of them are found to be at present.

JOHN R. OUGHTEN, Clerk of Union.

CLONMEL.

1 As to the industrial employment of the boys:—

(a) The boys are made to do all their own necessary work, including—cleansing, washing, polishing, whitewashing, cutting hair, mending and repairing, &c

(b) Three or more boys, when there is suitable work, are taught tailoring, while every child able to use one is supplied with needles, thread and buttons, to do his own repairs—the bigger boys mending and repairing for the smaller ones.

(c) For two hours every day—except during recreation days, when the boys go to bathe, or see something of interest—they work on the farm and gardens, suitable work, according to the various ages, being provided by the master and schoolmaster, to suit the individual capacities.

2. These operations are carried on under the supervision of the head male teacher.

3. The Guardians experience no difficulty in getting the boys into service.

4. The conditions of service are generally from twelve to fifteen shillings per quarter to commence with This is very soon increased, otherwise they go where they are better paid. Two-thirds of all the boys who leave go to farming service.

5 The Board never apprentices boys, having no legal power to pay a fine, or to enter into indentures

6 As to the age children go to service, and to remaining in their places —

They are generally sent to service from twelve to fifteen years of age, and, while not in every case prepared to say what becomes of them, I speak from an experience of over twelve years, when I say they do not, as a general rule, return to the house. I recently prepared a return for the Board of all the boys that left the house—excluding "casuals"—for the previous three years, viz, 1875, 1876 and 1877, and found the following result —

Summary.—Two enlisted in the line; one in the artillery, three went to the United States, three to England, two to Dublin, three to a Protestant orphanage, and twenty-nine to farming service Of this number only six returned to the house Two went immediately again to service; two returned from causes not satisfactorily explained, and the remaining two from causes I need not specify, as no one would care to keep them in their service, being liable to injure their beds With one exception (from the cause just stated), I am happy to state *there is not a single boy* in the male school who had been at service and returned to the house

7. Boys often go out "herding," but rarely ever return

8. There are some adult boys, nearly all blind, who were reared in the house, and who are unfit for any active employment in consequence, and in the female department there are some young women whose destitution may be attributed to their being the mothers of illegitimate children

OBSERVATIONS ON THE EDUCATION OF WORKHOUSE CHILDREN.

Evil tendencies, I observe, arise principally from two causes:—1 From contact with the older inmates, both male and female 2. From the evil influence of children who come into the establishment off the streets whose parents are casuals or vagrants. The first could be best remedied by removing the boys to some part of the establishment where they would not hear the conversation of the able-bodied men or women at night. This will be accomplished should the understood recommendation of the Commissioners be carried out—of building schools apart from the present establishment No matter how rigid the classification, this would be desirable for several reasons, and has been adopted in Belfast, Cork, and the Dublin Unions, &c.

The second could only be removed by wholly excluding the children of known vagrants, and who were known to be vicious; and partially by sending them to break stones, or otherwise when over eight—children under eight being harmless

Due provision is made for the education, secular and religious, here, and the Board never refuses the necessary requisites for carrying it on.

JOHN R OUGHTEN, Clerk of Union.

NENAGH.

1. A master tailor and master shoemaker are kept constantly employed at the workhouse, and out of twenty-four boys in school twelve attend daily for three hours with those tradesmen—six from 10 A.M. to 1 P.M., who then return to school, and are replaced by six others from school, and continue there until dinner hour, three o'clock About two acres of land, growing vegetables, is attached to the workhouse, except for occasionally "weeding" the boys are not employed on it.

All the school girls—about twenty-eight—are employed two hours daily in knitting and sewing, and are taught to make their own dresses, &c. The more grown girls (twelve) attend the laundry one day in the week, and are taught to wash. Some of them are also employed in cleansing up dormitories.

2. The supervision of the boys, when at trades, is left to the master-tradesmen, at all other times, the schoolmasters The supervision of the girls—the schoolmistress, and when in laundry—the matron

3 The Guardians experience no difficulty in hiring out the grown children—the boys, generally, as farm labourers, the girls, to care young children.

4. The rate of wages varies from £4 to £2 10s a year, with maintenance, the hiring *certain* for one year—the Board generally supplying a good suit of clothes on leaving the workhouse

5. Very few instances of apprenticing; when a case occurs the Board supplys a suit of clothes. A term of five years is agreed upon—the master to maintain and clothe

6. Age from thirteen to fifteen As a rule they do About ten per cent. return to the workhouse, but temporarily, from illness, or being discharged from their employment.

7. Children are not sent out to service for a shorter period than a year.

8 There are now in this workhouse thirty-eight adult inmates, brought up in it as children—six males, thirty-two females The cause of destitution of the males being in every instance illness and deformity Of the females—twelve returned through sickness, four are blind, six, sore eyes; one lunatic; one out of employment, two with skin disease; and six, unmarried, pregnant

On inquiry I find the result of keeping the boys at trades very unsatisfactory—not more than one boy out of a daily average of twelve having, for the last three years, adopted either shoemaking or tailoring as a means of livelihood, or had been taken out by employers of that class. I believe the workshop to be a mere resort for idleness, the master-tradesmen not having (or caring to exercise) proper control over them—agricultural employment being the principal means looked forward to for their leaving the workhouse. I consider the boys would be more benefitted by an hour or two daily in charge of the schoolmaster, and instructed in the use of farming implements, the sowing of seeds, and growth of vegetables, &c.—the general complaint of employers being that when they leave the workhouse they are awkward, stupid, and know nothing of labour

The school girls are superior in manner and disposition to the boys, owing to a stricter supervision being kept over them, and less opportunity of mixing with the adult class, and kept more industriously employed They are eagerly sought after by a respectable class of farmers to care young children, and when grown become good domestic servants I regret that instances occur of some returning to the workhouse under painful circumstances, but I believe the percentage of immorality is not greater than if the girls were brought up under other circumstances than in a workhouse.

J. Houston Sheehan, Clerk of Union.

Roscrea.

1. Carpenter work, tailoring, shoemaking, farm work, household work, washing, sewing

2. Master, matron, schoolmaster, schoolmistress, carpenter, tailor, shoemaker.

3. No

4. The current wages of the district for children of like age, wages per quarter, fifteen to twenty-five shillings; period of service, unlimited.

5. No. The law does not provide for it, but an arrangement is made whereby the Relieving Officers exercise a supervision over them.

6. Ages, twelve to fifteen. Yes, where fairly treated, or until they procure better situations.

7. No.

8 One female—a cripple; another imbecile; and one other by misconduct.

J. Gray, Clerk of Union

Thurles.

1. Some of the boys are engaged at trades, and others at agricultural work on workhouse farm after school hours.

2 Tailor, shoemaker and schoolmaster

3. They do not

4. Boys generally £1, and girls 15s per quarter, and to be clothed and fed.

5 No.

6. About fourteen years As a rule I do not think that they retain their first places.

7. No.

8. There are some who remained on account of physical infirmity.

John Cooke, Clerk of Union.

Tipperary.

1 Farming, tailoring and shoemaking, and the growing girls in the female school, after school-hours, are employed in sewing, knitting, and scouring up the house

2. The agriculturist, the master-tailor, and shoemaker

3. None.

4. Two to three pounds a year.

5. Yes, occasionally, by their next of kin, the Guardians giving a few pounds for an outfit

6. From twelve years upwards

7 For no less a term than three months

8 Yes, three or four females who became loose in their morals outside, and in consequence became destitute.

W. B. Reardon, Clerk of Union.

Dungarvan.

1. For girls—making and repairing their own clothes, and knitting. For boys—agricultural labour on workhouse farm

2. Girls under schoolmistress, boys under master.

3. No.

4. Ten to fifteen shillings per quarter; period of service, quarterly.

5. No.

6. From twelve to fourteen years. As a rule it cannot be said they retain their first places.

7. No.

8. Yes. Their destitution, for the most part, is to be attributed to bodily or mental infirmity.

John J. Doyle, Clerk of Union.

Kilmacthomas.

1. The ordinary domestic training of female servants, and a little help on the workhouse farm from the boys.

2. Workhouse master and schoolmistress.

3. No.

4. Generally employed by the quarter at about 15s. or £1 per quarter.

5. No

6. From 12 to 14 or 15 years of age. As a rule they do not retain their places.

7. No.

8. No

The School is under the National Board of Education, and the Guardians are most particular in providing the best teachers I cannot suggest any improvement as regards education. I would wish to observe that from my experience for the last twenty-seven years, the longer a child remains in a workhouse the more unfitted that child becomes for any purpose whatsoever.

Wm Hunt, Clerk of Union.

Lismore.

1. There is an industrial class formed from the senior school girls. They are taught knitting, sewing, making and repairing their clothes, cooking and scouring. Boys work on the farm and in the garden No other industrial training is carried on in this workhouse

2. The works referred to are conducted under the supervision of the Matron and Schoolmistress in the case of the girls; and under the workhouse master's supervision, as regards the boys

3. The Guardians experience no difficulty in getting the children into service, once they attain the age of fourteen or fifteen years. Farmers and others wanting young servants are in the habit of coming to the workhouse and selecting such as may suit. A *healthy* child never remains in the workhouse after attaining that age.

4 Wages commence at 12s per quarter. The period of service is *for a quarter*. There is usually an advance of wages after the first quarter If the child is found to deserve it

5. Children are not apprenticed in this Union. The Poor Law does not permit Guardians to apprentice children except to the Merchant Sea Service.

6. Children are generally sent into service at about thirteen years of age. About two-thirds of them retain their first places.

7. The practice does not prevail in this Union of sending the children out for short periods of service.

8. Of the 228 inmates at present in the workhouse, there is one male and six females, adults, who were brought up in it as children The man is scrofulous and has bad eyes, two of the women have chronic sore eyes, one is in consumption, three have illegitimate children.

Maurice Healy, Clerk of Union.

WATERFORD.

SIR,—I have the honor to forward herewith the information required by the circular letter of the Poor Law Union Inquiry Commission, dated 3rd inst.

With regard to the last paragraph, I cannot pretend to speak with much authority on the subject to which it has reference, but the absence amongst workhouse children of that truthful confiding candour which characterizes the child brought under the influence of good precept and good example from the parents, is a defect which has frequently come under my observations.

The want (which indeed is not confined to workhouses) is much felt of a means of imparting *skilled practical* instructions in the various duties of a domestic servant. When on Board-days the Guardians humanely endeavour to obtain the best terms for the boy or girl going into service, the reason generally assigned to justify small wages is the inexperience of the child.

At the same time bearing in mind the stratum of society from which the workhouse child comes, and the associations and habits of the greater number of them before they enter the workhouse, coupled with the brief and uncertain periods of their residences in it, I think the success which has attended the efforts of those to whose care the children are entrusted must be considered to have been, in this Union, most satisfactory. This assertion will be borne out by the particulars which are furnished in the accompanying statements from the master of the workhouse and the schoolmistress. Both these officers have had long experience, and I have thought it well to request them to communicate their views in the hope that they may prove of interest to the Commissioners. The schoolmaster was appointed but a short time ago, and he had not been in a workhouse previously.

JOHN MACKEY, Clerk of Union.

1 & 2. The industrial training in the Workhouse at the female side consists in teaching the school children over ten years of age how to wash, cook, and scour out rooms, and their school-room and sleeping-room to keep in proper order. Their training is superintended in part by the nuns, the matron and their school-teachers.

At the male side there are always four or five boys trained to shoemaking under a paid shoemaker. About a quarter acre of the Workhouse garden is set aside for the special training of the schoolboys in gardening and rearing vegetables necessary for the use of the inmates, under the superintendence of the schoolmaster and his assistant.

3. There is not much difficulty in getting the school children to service, but at particular seasons the demand is not very great. There are now over 100 children in the schools over ten years of age, and of this number only three or four are between the ages of fourteen and fifteen years. It is generally as farm servants our children are hired out.

4. No child is hired out without being brought before the Board on Board-days, the character of the persons hiring inquired into, and, if satisfactory, the wages and hiring fixed by the Board, which generally consists in a quarterly payment of 10s. or 12s., according to the abilities of the boy or girl who may be hired out.

5. Children are not apprenticed in this Union. I think it would be highly desirable that such a privilege were extended and generally exercised by the Board of Guardians.

6. Children are never sent out until they attain the age of eleven years; as a rule they retain their first places.

7. No such practice prevails here.

8. At the male side there are three men, two aged twenty-six, and one eighteen years, respectively, one of the former was sent to a reformatory when only eleven years of age, but returned here from Cork Gaol about four years ago, where he had been committed on complaint made by the Governors of Glencree Reformatory. The second left this to go to London about four years ago, but returned here from London about six months ago. The third is delicate and in hospital.

At the female side there are at present twenty-two women who had been brought up here as children. Four of those are obliged to remain here from tender eyes and general delicacy. Seven are careless little-good-for girls who will not remain in their situations, but are continually in and out of the workhouse. Four have no parents alive, three are pert troublesome girls, and one is quiet but stupid. Of the remaining five, one has been married to a delicate good-for-nothing husband, and four are the mothers of illegitimate children, whom they are rearing up in the workhouse.

GENERAL REMARKS.

After twenty-six years' experience as workhouse master in the Waterford, Kilkenny, and Thurles Workhouses, I feel pleasure in bearing my humble testimony to the good results that have been achieved from the training available for education of children in the workhouse for the past eleven and half years. An average of at least seventy children have been sent out from this workhouse with the result that at present there are only three men and twenty-two women and girls now remaining. But gratifying as this may be, there are several wants that in my opinion require amendment. First in importance comes the moral and religious training. It is not possible for a workhouse teacher, no matter how zealous that person may be, to devote that time to this most important matter; greater moral restraint is requisite, and a more continuous supervision of the religious training is also requisite.

Next in order comes the industrial training of the children. The means available to this end are very defective, and steps should in my opinion be taken to secure competent trained supervision, so as to fit children of both sexes to have an intelligent idea of what servants would require to know either in their homes or in their industrial occupations of life.

THOMAS RYAN, Master.

CARLOW.

1. Shoemaking, tailoring and agriculture for the boys, and sewing, knitting, and washing for the girls.

2. Under paid tradesmen teachers and officers of the Union.

3. None.

4. At not less than 10s. and 12s. per quarter for first three months, and they are retained for longer periods if found suitable.

5. Children are not apprenticed.

6. Children are sent to service at twelve years of age, and, as a general rule, retain their first places.

7. No.

8. There are seven adult inmates who were brought up as children in the workhouse, who go out occasionally, three of these are labouring under bodily infirmity, four are women with illegitimate children.

The Guardians are very particular in selecting the persons to whom they allow the children to go out to service with. They must be known to some Guardian who will recommend them, or else bring a recommendation from their clergyman or other equally respectable person known to the Guardians, or some of them, before the Board will allow a child out to service. The Relieving Officers have directions from the Board to procure suitable situations for the children.

The schools of the workhouse are placed under the National Board of Education, and are conducted fairly. The Schoolmaster and Schoolmistress have been awarded results fees each year since the National School Teachers (Ireland) Act came into operation.

BALROTHERY.

SIR,—I have the honour to acknowledge the receipt of your circular of the 3rd inst. stating that the Poor Law Inquiry Commissioners are desirous of obtaining

Appendix B. Industrial Training

information with reference to the system of Industrial Training for children in the Workhouse of this Union, and requesting to be furnished with certain particulars on the subject

In reply, I beg to inform you that the boys are usually employed in weeding and assisting at agricultural work, under the supervision of the Master of the Workhouse, while the girls are taught knitting, sewing, and washing in the Laundry, under the superintendence of the Schoolmistress.

The average number of children in the Workhouse is scarcely ever more than fourteen or fifteen, and the Guardians never experience any difficulty in sending them out to service when they arrive at an age to be useful, which is, generally speaking, when they have reached eleven years. The Board enter into no conditions with employers, but they at the same time satisfy themselves that the children are likely to be well treated, and reasonably remunerated by the parties who take them out of the Workhouse, and this practice is found to work satisfactorily, as the children so sent out not only retain their first places, but scarcely ever return to the Workhouse, except in rare instances Children are not apprenticed in this union

There are four adult inmates at present in the Workhouse who were brought up in it as inmates, and the cause of their destitution is attributed in two cases to infirmity of body, one to insanity, and one to idleness or inability to earn a sufficiency to support a family, he having got married in the Workhouse (or at least took his discharge for that purpose) and now makes a practice of leaving the Workhouse for a short time at intervals, returning again after the lapse of a few days

I beg to enclose the form you sent me, into which I have entered the particulars required.

John Stack, Clerk of Union.

North Dublin Union.

1. In the male department the boys are taught shoemaking, tailoring, and carpentering, and on the farm attached to the Auxiliary Sheds, Glasnevin, they are instructed in cropping, &c., and thus many have been sent forward into the world as useful artisans, farm labourers, &c. In the female department the girls are taught knitting, needlework, and laundry work, &c., which enables them to get situations out of the Workhouse.

2. The boys learning trades are under the supervision of a master shoemaker, tailor, and carpenter, and the agricultural pursuits are performed under the directions of one of the schoolmasters who acts as agriculturist. The matron, assistant matron, and schoolmistresses superintend the industrial training of the girls

3. No. The Guardians do not experience any difficulty in getting the boys and girls situations

4 They are apprenticed to respectable parties, whose application is investigated by the Relieving Officers and the Board of Guardians before being approved of, and when sent out they get a suit of clothes, the persons to whom they are given are bound to feed and clothe them for a period of one year or more as agreed on

5 Yes, and on the above conditions

6 Generally from twelve to fifteen years of age, and in many cases they do not retain their first places.

7 No.

8 There are; their destitution being attributable to physical causes and ill health.

As regards the subject of "Education" in this Workhouse, I beg to observe that the schools are in connexion with the Board of National Education, whose Inspector visits the schools once a year, and his reports are generally of a most satisfactory nature, a large number of marks being awarded to the boys and girls in the several branches of reading, writing, arithmetic, grammar, geography, and history, and the per-centage of answering at the "Results" examinations will, I believe, contrast favourably with any other Workhouse National School in Ireland. The religious instruction is most carefully looked after by the Protestant and Roman Catholic chaplains In conclusion, I may add that some of the pupils of these schools have obtained respectable positions in life, and are useful members of society

Thos. H Atkinson, Clerk of Union.

South Dublin Union.

1 The boys are taught shoemaking, tailoring, weaving, carpentering, in the workshops of the Workhouse, and agriculture in the Workhouse garden. The girls are taught needlework, washing in the girls laundry, and the sewing machine in the machine room of the Workhouse; they are also employed by the female and married officers to assist in household duties and taught to be house servants.

2. The trades are taught to the boys by competent tradesmen elected by the Guardians, and agriculture is taught by the gardener of the institution. The girls are taught needlework by their schoolmistresses, washing by the laundress, and the sewing machine by the machinist.

3. No.

4 The usual period of service is one year and in most cases the parties taking the children out as apprentice servants agree to give them ten shillings per quarter.

5. They are apprenticed for terms from one to three years

6. Between the ages of thirteen and fifteen years. They usually leave their places after one year or eighteen months, but succeed in procuring others

7. No

8. There are, but they bear a very small proportion to the number that have succeeded in life Their destitution in some cases arises from physical defects, as scrofulous affections, sore eyes, &c.

John Byrne, Clerk of Union.

Rathdown.

1 In male department the Industrial Training is chiefly agricultural. There is a farm attached to the Workhouse where a systematic course of cropping is successfully carried out, most of the operations being performed by the school-boys who are employed on the farm four hours daily and who acquire skill and dexterity in the use of agricultural implements. The boys are also trained to make up their beds, scrub their dormitories, &c, and to be as self-reliant as circumstances will permit. Boys of proper age and otherwise suitable are taught in the Workhouse the following trades, viz., tailoring, shoemaking, and baking In female department the Industrial Training consists in teaching the girls to sew neatly; make, wash, and mend their clothes, knit their stockings, scrub and keep in order their dormitories, &c, and occasionally to weed and pick stones on land.

2 The agricultural training is conducted under the supervision of the schoolmaster, the trades-boys are under the supervision of proper tradesmen, and the matron and schoolmistress superintend the Industrial Training of the girls.

3. The Guardians experience no difficulty in getting the children into service, the demand being in excess of the supply.

4. As a rule, no conditions are imposed on persons taking children to service. No terms of wages are made, the children are to give their services in exchange for food and clothing, the Guardians giving an outfit in the first instance.

5. Children are not apprenticed in this Union

6 Children are sent to service at ages varying from eleven to fifteen years, and in many cases retain their first places for lengthened periods, the question of "wages" being very often the cause of change.

7. The practice of sending out children to temporary employment does not prevail in this Union.

8. There are but three adult inmates in this Workhouse now who were brought up in it as children, their destitution being due to physical or mental debility.

Upon the subject of "the education of children in Workhouses," I beg to tender the following observations to the Commissioners, basing my statements upon over twenty-four years' experience in this Union:—

The schools are in connexion with the Board of National Education, and the National School Inspector's reports thereon are almost invariably of a satisfactory character. A Committee of Guardians examine the schools annually in the literary subjects taught, and have always reported favourably. A fair amount of proficiency is attained in the essential branches of reading, writing, and arithmetic, by a considerable proportion of the pupils, and the per-centage of answering at the "results examinations" will contrast favourably with that attained in ordinary National schools. The religious instruction of the children is carefully attended to by the chaplains. I may add that several of the former pupils of these schools have attained respectable positions in life—two of them are at present teachers of National schools, one was an officer of this house, one is an hospital assistant, others are clerks, shop assistants, &c.

Considering the parentage of the greater portion of the children reared in the Workhouse, and other adverse circumstances, I feel bound to assert that the literary and industrial training of the Workhouse children of this Union is successfully carried out.

JOSEPH D. COPE, Clerk of Union.

ATHY.

1. The boys are employed on the farm, and the girls at household duties.

2. The schoolmaster and schoolmistress.

3. Very little difficulty.

4. About 50s per annum, quarterly, half yearly, and yearly.

5. No.

6. From twelve years of age. They very often come back to the Workhouse.

7. No.

8. There are very many females, and but few males. Some of the women have returned with illegitimate children, and the remainder are infirm. The males are nearly all infirm.

MATTHEW S. M'GRATH, Clerk of Union.

CELBRIDGE.

1. No Industrial Training beyond that of teaching the females to knit and sew by hand and machine.

2. The schoolmistress.

3. No.

4. Each child receives a suit of clothes when leaving the Workhouse. The wages are agreed upon at the Board, no fixed period of service.

5. No.

6. From twelve to fourteen years of age, and do not as a rule remain long at service.

7. No.

8. Five males. One of weak intellect, one almost blind, two remaining, whose mothers are inmates, and not disposed to let them out. One not suited for service.

NAAS.

1. Boys employed on the grounds attached to the Workhouse. Girls instructed in needlework, and some of them employed in master's kitchen.

2. Master, matron, schoolmaster, and schoolmistress.

3. No.

4. Lowest wages—10s per quarter. No limit as to period of service.

5. No.

6. From thirteen up. Boys, as a rule, remain in their first places, unless they leave them to better themselves. Girls are not very apt to remain in their first, or, in fact, in any place, more particularly if they leave mother in the Workhouse. The fact of children sent out to service leaving their mothers behind them in the Workhouse is a great inducement to both boys and girls to return thereto.

7. No.

8. There are no adult male inmates in the Workhouse who were brought up in it except a few imbeciles and those incapacitated from earning their bread by bodily infirmity. There are twelve adult women at present in the Workhouse who were brought up in it. They were forced to return to it, being the mothers of illegitimate children.

NOTE.—I have no hesitation in stating that from my experience—extending over a period of upwards of twenty-seven years—a Workhouse is the worst possible place children could be brought up in, in fact, I consider it bad for any class of inmates but the sick, old, and infirm. I have known instances of both adult men and women being much disimproved, so far as habits of industry are concerned, by even a short residence in the Workhouse.

I also feel myself bound to express my opinion on the subject of boarding out children. I do not think that, as a rule, they are sent out to the class of people from whom much benefit could be expected to accrue to them, either in a moral or industrial point of view. The people who take them out, in many cases, are only a degree removed from paupers themselves. To make the system a good one, I think children should be sent out to nurse to small respectable farmers, where they would be morally brought up, and trained to habits of industry; either that, or sent to properly conducted Industrial Schools.

G. MOLLOY, Clerk of Union.

CALLAN.

SIR,—I beg to acknowledge the receipt of your circular letter of the 3rd instant, requesting information respecting the system of industrial training for children in the workhouse of the Callan Union, and in answer to the queries in your circular I beg to state for the information of the Poor Law Inquiry Commissioners, that the female children in the workhouse of this union are taught sewing, knitting, washing, scrubbing and cleansing floors, cleaning and blackleading fireplaces, &c., under the supervision of the matron and schoolmistress.

The male children are employed whenever occasion offers at weeding, digging, &c., in the workhouse garden, after school-hours, under the supervision and instruction of the schoolmaster, and some of the boys are placed for a portion of each day in the tailor's and shoemaker's shop.

No difficulty is experienced in getting the children into service; as soon as they arrive at twelve or thirteen years of age they readily get employment, the girls principally for the minding of young children, and the boys with farmers in the country, their wages average about 13s. for the first quarter, and the guardians provide them with clothing when leaving the workhouse. They generally keep their first places about half a year (as far as I can learn), and then they look out for other places or for better wages.

A good many boys have been apprenticed out of the workhouse to shoemakers and tailors during the past ten years, the period of apprenticeship being for five years, the masters undertaking to support and clothe the apprentices during the time, and the Board of Guardians providing them with outfits of clothing on their leaving the workhouse.

Children are not sent out in this union for the kind of temporary service described in your circular (query 7).

There is only one adult at present in the workhouse

APPENDIX B.

Industrial Training.

who was brought up in it as a child—an epileptic woman, and her disease is the cause of her destitution.

With regard to the concluding paragraphs of your circular, I would beg to say that if the female children were not hired to service so young, I would like to see them instructed in simple cooking and other household duties, but as they are generally taken from the workhouse at from twelve to thirteen years of age, instruction of the kind I allude to could not be afforded them, if the giving of such instruction in workhouses were otherwise practicable.

M. MAHER, Clerk of Union.

CASTLECOMER.

1. Farm, and household work.
2. The Schoolmaster and Schoolmistress.
3. No. The demand generally exceeds the supply.
4. The guardians require that the children shall get as good wages as children of the same ages not in the workhouse, period of service, generally by the quarter.
5. The guardians are not empowered by law to apprentice children.
6. From about twelve years and upwards, and as a rule the children retain their first places.
7. No.
8. There is no adult inmate in the workhouse who was brought up in it as a child.

GENERAL OBSERVATIONS.

I think that the children brought up in workhouses should, if the workhouses are properly conducted, compare favourably with the children of the labouring classes. Nearly all the children brought up in the workhouse of this union have turned out well. The guardians are most particular as to the persons to whom they hire them out, and too much importance could not be attached to the action of Boards of Guardians in this respect. When children are hired out to persons who treat them kindly and take an interest in them, they become attached to their employers and pursue a life of industry. Where children are indiscriminately hired out to whoever may offer them employment, opposite results may reasonably be looked for.

THOMAS MAHONY, Clerk of Union.

KILKENNY.

1. Tailoring and shoemaking, knitting, sewing, &c.
2. Officers.
3. None.
4. About 10s. to 12s. per quarter; no limit.
5. No.
6. About fourteen years. Yes.
7. No.
8. Two. Having illegitimate children.

THOMASTOWN.

1. In the male department, tailoring, shoemaking, and working in the garden are partially carried on. In the female department knitting and sewing.
2. The tailor, shoemaker, schoolmaster and schoolmistress.
3. No.
4. When applied for they are hired out at various rates of wages per quarter, according to the ages and capacities of the children.
5. Boys who have had some initiatory training under the tailor and shoemaker, are sometimes apprenticed out for say three or four years to complete their knowledge of their trades. On going out the guardians provide them with a good suit of clothes, and their masters maintain and clothe them to the end of their service.
6. The children who are sent out to service are usually from twelve to fifteen years of age. As a rule they retain their first places, though there are several exceptions.
7. I cannot say the practice *prevails*, but children are sometimes hired out for such purposes and for limited periods.
8. There are a few such, who probably have not been afforded an opportunity of procuring employment, or who having had an opportunity have not been careful to retain their places. It may or may not have been the fault of some that they have returned to the workhouse.

JOHN F. MACCARTAN, Clerk of Union.

URLINGFORD.

1. Digging and weeding, &c., about one acre of land attached to the workhouse. Knitting stockings and making up clothes for the inmates.
2. Master, matron and school teachers.
3. No, not the least; in fact they are applied for before they are the proper age to go to service
4. Wages average from 15s. to £1 per quarter. Period of service is quarterly, that is three months; in some few cases the engagement is annual.
5. No.
6. They are sent when confirmed, irrespective of age, and as a rule retain their positions very satisfactorily.
7. No.
8. No.

PICK, for Clerk of Union.

EDENDERRY.

1. National.
2. Schoolmaster and schoolmistress.
3. No.
4. As may be agreed to.
5. No.
6. From nine to fifteen. They do.
7 and 8. No.

T. H. F. BOR, Clerk of Union.

PARSONSTOWN.

1. The girls are taught knitting and sewing, including the working of the sewing machine. They are also instructed in such household duties as washing, scouring, &c.

The boys work on the land attached to the Workhouse, and otherwise assist in the general work of the establishment.
2. Under that of the respective teachers.
3. No.
4. When a person applies to the Guardians for a servant, the Board, in the first place, takes care to ascertain that the child is going to a suitable place, and that he or she will be well treated and taken care of in every respect, and that the child will also be allowed to attend school, if practicable, should his or her education be backward. The Guardians do not, however, as a rule succeed in getting the employers to agree to allow the children to attend school.

The wages vary from about 10s a quarter, together with board and lodging, to £1, for grown-up boys and girls. The period of service is almost always quarterly.
5. No.
6. The age at which children are sent out to service varies from about twelve or thirteen years and upwards, and depends on the special circumstances of each case, such, for instance, as the health of the child, its education, the nature of the work to which the child will be put, and particularly the respectability of the employer, and the likelihood, or otherwise, of the child receiving kind treatment.

Unfortunately it cannot be said that, as a rule, the children retain their first places for any considerable period.
7. No; such a practice does not prevail in this Union.
8. There are a few—about eight. The cause of these persons being still in the Workhouse is due to chronic delicacy, and, in one or two cases, to immorality. Of course these persons have not remained in the Work-

house from their childhood, but were out at service (and some of them more than once), and have returned to the House.

HENRY DOOLY, Clerk of Union.

TULLAMORE.

1. The boys after school-hours are taught the system of agriculture on a farm attached to the Workhouse, and the girls are taught to knit, sew, wash, and, when necessary, to weed the crops on the Workhouse farm.

2. Under the supervision of the schoolmaster and schoolmistress.

3. No; the farmers are very anxious to get them.

4. At wages varying from 10s. to 15s. per quarter, according to age and strength of child.

5. The children in this Union are not apprenticed.

6. At from ten to fourteen years of age, and, as a rule, retain their places.

7. The practice here is to hire the children for a period of three months with parties of their own religious belief, and with the understanding that they will be properly treated; and it is found that few of them again return to the Workhouse.

8. At present there are twelve adult inmates in the Workhouse who were brought up in it as children, viz., four males and eight females.

Cause of destitution—

1 Male—Deaf and Dumb.
1 " Paralysed
2 " Imbeciles.
1 Female—Permanent Infirmity.
4 " Immorality.
3 " Imbeciles.

Total 12

With respect to the education of Workhouse children, I am of opinion that it would be a great advantage to have them trained, if possible, in an Industrial School.

JAMES M'KENNA, Clerk of Union.

BALLYMAHON.

1. That the system of Industrial Training consists in the usual household work of sewing, washing, and cooking. The boys in weeding the crops on the farm, and in keeping the yards clean.

2. The girls under the supervision of the matron and schoolmistress, and the boys under the master and porter.

3. The applications for servants are greater than the supply.

4. The wages in case of children from 10s. per quarter, and in the case of adults from 15s. upwards per quarter. The shortest period of service—six months.

5. Children are not apprenticed in this Union.

6. The children are hired out from ten years old, and sometimes under that age. Very few (if any) retain their first places.

7. The applicants for children generally state that it is for the purpose of herding they require their services.

8. At present there is only one adult in the Workhouse who was brought up in it as a child. In this case ill health is the cause, but on many previous occasions adults returned to the Workhouse because they were of so little use to their employers that they would not be retained in service; and nearly all the males that have been reared in the House have (with very few exceptions) been changing their places every three months.

WM. HEWETT.

GRANARD.

1. At present none, except a little sewing by the females.

2. The schoolmistress, chiefly.

3. No.

4. The wages for the first six or twelve months is generally low; the Guardians in most cases fix the amount before they are discharged.

5. No; there have been a few cases where mutual agreements were made between the apprentices and their employers; the Guardians were unable to pay any fee, but ordered clothing to a reasonable extent

6. Between twelve and fourteen years; as a rule they do retain their first places

7. No, the Guardians are very much opposed to such a heartless system.

8. Yes; eleven adults—ten women and one man. The latter is an idiot. Females—One blind, three are mothers of illegitimate children, two imbeciles, one, deformity; one deserted by husband, one ophthalmic case, and one scrofulous.

N.B.—I am of opinion that the moral, literary, and physical training of children should be very carefully attended to up to ten or eleven years, after which time they should be congregated into district schools, where they would be taught various trades, &c.

WM. HIGGINS

LONGFORD.

1. Tailoring, carpentry, agriculture (males); knitting, sewing, washing, &c (females).

2. Tailor, carpenter, wardmaster, and schoolmistress

3. No.

4. On an average of 12s. per quarter; for one quarter.

5. No.

6. About thirteen years of age; they retain their first engagement.

7. No.

8. There are six females in house at present; destitution attributable to want of employment and ill health.

C. COX, Clerk of Union.

ARDEE.

1. For boys—garden work. For girls—sewing, knitting, washing, and cleansing their wards

2. The master, matron, schoolmistress, and porter.

3. No.

4. By the year, at from £2 to £3 per year.

5. No.

6 At from ten to twelve; they generally change their places for better after the first or second year

7 and 8. No.

THOMAS BEATH, Clerk of Union.

DROGHEDA.

1. Tailoring, agriculture, sewing, and knitting

2. Master tailor, schoolmaster, and schoolmistress.

3. No.

4. From 10s. to 15s per quarter. A suit of clothes given to each child going to service; value £2.

5. They are. Serve five years without fee given by guardians

6. From ten to fifteen years. They do.

7. No. The guardians do not allow it.

8. Only one. Want of employment. Factories in town closed.

DUNDALK.

1. Some of the schoolboys are instructed in tailoring and shoemaking, and they are occasionally employed on the workhouse grounds, weeding, &c.; and the girls are instructed in knitting and sewing.

2. The tailoring and shoemaking under the supervision of a master-tailor and a master-shoemaker, the weeding, &c., under the schoolmaster, and the knitting and sewing under the schoolmistress.

3. Not any. The Guardians have applications nearly every week from persons desirous of hiring children out of the workhouse.

Appendix B.
Industrial Training.

4. They are hired out by the master with the consent of the Guardians, by the half-year, and quarter, at the usual rate of wages given to parties outside, viz : 24s. for the half year, or 12s. the quarter

5. Not any.

6. From about eleven to fifteen years of age, and, as a rule, they do not retain their first places.

7. It is the practice to send them out for short periods of service to herd, and nurse children.

8. There is a considerable number of adult inmates in the workhouse at present who were brought up in the workhouse. Their destitution is attributable to idle habits contracted in the workhouse, and a disinclination to work for their living outside.

I beg to observe that I have nothing to add to the above, as the industrial training in this workhouse is very limited in consequence of the children being hired out, as soon as they are able to herd or nurse as the case may be.

James Murphy, Clerk of Union.

Dunshaughlin.

[The Commissioners were unable to procure the required information from this Union in consequence of the death of the workhouse master.

Kells.

1. The boys are instructed in the baking and tailoring trades, and are occasionally employed upon the farm in weeding the crops, &c. The girls are instructed in laundry work, in sewing, knitting, and general household work.

2. Under a master baker, master tailor, schoolmaster, and schoolmistress.

3. No, the demand for servants is in excess of the supply in this locality.

4. Orphans or deserted children are not, as a rule, sent out to service under the age of fifteen. Other children, with the consent of their parents, are occasionally allowed out to service under that age. Boys are engaged at £1 10s. per half-year. Girls at 10s. per quarter.

5. No.

6. Children are sent to service (under circumstances stated in No. 4) at thirteen years of age, and they generally retain their first places.

7. No. The guardians have a decided objection to this practice.

8. Yes, two men—of whom one returned to the workhouse to learn the trade of baker, the other in a delicate state of health, and four women—two from ill-health, and two as the mothers of illegitimate children.

Nathaniel Lacy, Clerk of Union.

Navan.

1. The system of industrial training in this workhouse includes shoemaking, tailoring, and needlework.

2. Conducted under supervision of tailor, shoemaker, and schoolmistress.

3. The guardians find no difficulty in getting the children into service.

4. Rate of wages, period of service, and such like details, are arranged by the master of the workhouse. Wages ranging from 8s. to 30s. per quarter.

5. Children not apprenticed in this union.

6. Children are sent to service from the age of twelve years upwards.

7. Children not sent out for short periods of service, nor for "herding."

8. There are four adults in this workhouse at present who were brought up in it as children. Destitution attributable to weakness of mind and debility.

Geo. Lacy, Clerk of Union.

Oldcastle.

1. The girls are employed sewing and washing. The boys on the farm.

2. The girls under matrons and schoolmistresses. The boys under masters and porters.

3. Yes, owing to their lazy habits.

4. They are hired out at so much per quarter or half year.

5. Children are not apprenticed from this union.

6. Children from this union are sent to service at about the age of thirteen years, and as a rule they do not retain their places, even for the term for which they are hired out.

7. No.

8. There are six adult inmates (well able to earn a living) in this workhouse now who were brought up in it as children, and I believe that their destitution is attributable to idleness and unwillingness to work.

Thomas F. Jenkins, Clerk of Union.

Trim.

1. Boys working generally on farm from three to five, P.M. Girls at needlework and in the laundry.

2. Schoolmaster and schoolmistress.

3. No difficulty.

4. £2 to £3 a year and board; for term of twelve months.

5. No children apprenticed.

6. From fourteen or fifteen years of age.

7. Children not sent out for shorter period than twelve months.

8. Only one, who is in hospital with sore eyes.

I have to say, in answer to last paragraph of circular, that the education of the children in the workhouse is good and well attended to.

Abbeyleix.

1. I may say there is no industrial training for the children of this workhouse.

2. Any there is is carried on under the supervision of the master of the workhouse.

3. Not the least.

4. The guardians satisfy themselves that the parties applying for children are suitable persons to place them with, and the wages vary from ten shillings to fifteen shillings per quarter.

5. No.

6. Between ten and fourteen. I do not think, as a rule, they retain their first places very long.

7. No.

8. No.

The guardians do not consider it necessary to make any observation on the subject of the education of the children in the workhouse.

Donaghmore.

1 and 2. The boys are instructed in agriculture, under the supervision of the master, and the girls in sewing and household work, under the supervision of the matron and schoolmistress.

3. The guardians experience no difficulty in getting the children into service, but frequently refuse to allow them out, considering them not sufficiently old.

4. They are generally hired by the year, at from 10s. to 15s. per quarter.

5. None of the children of this union have been apprenticed by the guardians.

6. The children are not allowed out under fourteen years of age, and they generally remain in the same place until they obtain more remunerative situations.

7. The children are not sent out for short periods of service.

8. There is but one adult inmate at present in the workhouse who was brought up in it as a child; although not exactly an idiot, he is of weak mind, to which cause his destitution is attributable.

Ambrose M. Baird.

ATHLONE.

1. That the system of industrial training in this workhouse consists of, for boys—tailoring and shoemaking, and farm labour, for girls—sewing, knitting, and domestic work.

2. That this training is under the supervision of a master tailor, master shoemaker, the schoolmaster, and the master and matron.

3. That no difficulty is experienced in getting the children into service.

4. That the wages average from £2 to £3 per annum for boys, and £3 for girls; and that the hiring is usually for one quarter.

5. Children are not apprenticed by the board, but many are by their friends.

6. They are usually sent to service at twelve, and retain often for a considerable time their first places.

7. They are not employed for "herding."

8. There are a few adult inmates who were brought up in it, but they are, with one exception, idiots.

I do not know how, without a larger expenditure, the industrial training of female children in the workhouse could be more efficiently carried out, but I believe that the "boarding out" system, if judiciously carried out, would be more healthful for the children, and would more certainly absorb them in the rural population.

JOS. VAUGHAN, Clerk of Union.

DELVIN.

1. Farming for males, sewing, washing, &c., for females.

2. Master and schoolmistress and matron.

3. No difficulty, but the reverse.

4. Hired by the year, wages as good as other children outside of the same age.

5. No

6. About 11 years of age, and mostly retain their first places, or get another.

7. No.

8. Yes, we have two returned, the cause of which is sickness.

MOUNTMELLICK.

1. The boys are taught agriculture on a small scale, such as growing potatoes, turnips, mangel wurzel, onions, &c. The girls, sewing, knitting, and to make their own clothes. No trades of any kind are taught in this union.

2. Under the supervision of the schoolmaster and schoolmistress.

3. No; quite the contrary, applicants continually looking for children to take out to service.

4. Generally at from 8s to 15s. per quarter.

5. No.

6. From 11 to 14 years of age. About one half the number of children sent out to service retain their first places. Some who do not receive good treatment from their employers return to the workhouse. In some cases children have returned to the workhouse with all the appearance of having been neglected.

7. No; never for a less period than three months.

8. Very few. In fact none, except those suffering from some mental or bodily infirmity.

ROBERT GOODBODY, Clerk of Union.

MULLINGAR.

1. Girls are taught washing, sewing, spinning, knitting, and use of sewing machine. Boys—baking, tailoring, shoemaking, and farm work.

2. Under supervision of the master, matron, school teachers, and the respective tradesmen.

3. No.

4. Wages from 10s. to 20s. a quarter.

5. Boys are apprenticed without fee, the guardians merely giving outfit.

6. At fourteen years. They do.

7. No.

8. Adult inmates now in workhouse who were brought up in it, ten females—seven from general debility; three no specified cause.

DAVID HARTON, Clerk of Union.

ENNISCORTHY.

1. The boys are trained to shoemaking and tailoring, and to agricultural knowledge on the large farm connected with the place.

2. Master tailor, master shoemaker, and agriculturist.

3. None whatever. The guardians providing clothes generally to those going out.

4. Various. Children getting generally 12s. to 15s. per quarter to commence with; for twelve months certainly.

5. Yes. Often to artisans—tailors and shoemakers, &c., for four years, the board giving them a suit of clothes on leaving.

6. From twelve to fifteen. Generally they do retain their first places.

7. No.

8. There are some who were reared in it, who left and who have returned. Women with children (illegitimate) being the principal cases.

DANIEL KEOHLER, Clerk of Union.

GOREY.

1. From four to six boys are employed for 3½ hours daily with the tailor, and an equal number for same time with the shoemaker, they are occasionally employed on the farm, weeding, &c. The girls from ten to fourteen years of age are taught to sew and knit, and are occasionally employed washing and scouring boards, and making up bedrooms.

2. The boys instructed by tailor, shoemaker, and schoolmaster—the girls by schoolmistress and matron under supervision of master.

3. No.

4. The Guardians supply a suit of clothes to each child on taking its discharge, and the person hiring engages to keep it for twelve months—wages vary from 7s. 6d. per quarter.

5. No.

6. From eleven to fourteen years. They generally retain their places and as a rule do not return to the Workhouse.

7. No.

8. One girl who is almost blind.

There are a few boys anxious to get on Board training ships, and the Guardians hope to get them taken on board.

R. CREIGHTON.

NEW ROSS.

1. Boys are taught shoemaking, tailoring and agriculture.

2. Teachers of schools respectively and master tailor and shoemaker.

3. No.

4. A guarantee is signed by the person taking out the child to keep him in employment for twelve months if not sick, the Guardians supplying all outfit; wages to be paid the child by the person taking him out.

5. In general, no. One boy apprenticed to sea during the last fourteen years.

6. From twelve to fifteen years. Yes.

7. No.

8. Only one, who is now going to service. Death of parents.

Observations.—As a general rule I have found that children educated in this Workhouse without leaving, have made more progress than those who have been sent out and taught elsewhere.

GIFFORD CARR, Clerk of Union.

APPENDIX B.

Industrial Training

WEXFORD.

1. Tailoring, shoemaking, baking, horticulture and agriculture for boys; sewing, knitting, mending, washing, and cooking for girls.

2. Master, matron, schoolmaster, schoolmistresses, shoemaker, tailor, baker, and hospital cook.

3. No.

4. Generally by the year as farm and other servants at £2 10s. or £3.

5. No. Sometimes when they go to tradesmen they apprentice themselves.

6. From twelve to fifteen years. Generally they do.

7. No.

8. There are two females; laziness or idleness, arising from the interference of parents who took them from their service.

BALTINGLASS.

1. Boys are taught tailoring, shoemaking, and agricultural work on the ground; the girls, knitting and sewing.

2. Master, shoemaker, tailor, agriculturist, matron, and schoolmistress.

3. None.

4. Hired by the farmers at from 15s. to £1 per quarter.

5. None are apprenticed.

6. From ten to fourteen years of age, and as a rule they retain their places.

7. The practice is not in use in this union.

8. There are three males, one of them epileptic, one idiotic, one scrofulous; there are seven females, three epileptic, four returned with illegitimate children.

SHILLELAGH.

1. On the Workhouse farm.

2. The schoolmaster.

3. No.

4. £2 per year for twelve months.

5. No.

6. Age from twelve upwards; generally.

7. No.

8. Not as a general rule. If females, generally in the family way.

RATHDRUM.

Sir,—I beg to inform you that the Guardians of this union did not deem it expedient to take any action in favour of industrial training for children, on various grounds, and therefore no notice was taken of your communication.

I am, sir, &c., &c.,

B. MANNING, Clerk of Union.

H. A. Robinson, esq.

BALLINASLOE.

1. Boys, agriculture and tailoring; girls, household work, such as sewing, knitting, scouring, washing, &c., as far as the requirements of the house admit.

2. Workhouse master and schoolmaster, matron and schoolmistress.

3. No.

4. Wages in accordance with age and capability; period of service as long as they may be retained.

5. No.

6. From ten to fifteen. The majority, as a rule, retain their first place.

7. No.

8. Very few; delicacy of constitution.

CLIFDEN.

SIR,—In reply to your circular letter of 3rd inst. I beg to inform you, for the information of the Poor Law Union Inquiry Commissioners,

That in this Workhouse the industrial training for girls is confined to the making, repairing and washing of the clothing and bedding of the entire establishment, under the superintendence of the schoolmistress. The boys assist on the grounds in weeding and the general cultivation of about an acre of land, under the supervision of the Workhouse master.

No difficulty is felt in getting the children into service.

The wages given to the boys or girls varies from 7s. 6d. to 15s. per quarter.

There are no children apprenticed by the Guardians.

Children are eagerly sought for by the peasant class from the ages of ten to twelve years, the boys for herding, going messages and assisting in the general work of the farm; the girls for caring children and housekeeping in the absence of the family at field work.

The boys are sometimes discontented and return to the Workhouse for short periods, but, as a rule, once at service they remain so.

Children are not sent out for short periods or for temporary employment, and careful inquiry is made as to the mode of life and circumstances of persons applying for children, and a preference is given to a relative, neighbour, or one known to the child, whose wishes are always consulted.

There is no adult inmate in the Workhouse who was brought up in it as a child.

The Workhouse School of this Union is very favourably reported on by the several Inspectors and other persons who visit it. I believe it fully answers its purpose, and that any suitable industrial training can be well and efficiently carried out under the superintendence of the Workhouse master and schoolmistress.

JOHN BURKE, Clerk of Union.

GALWAY.

1. Sewing or knitting for female children; farm work for male children.

2. Workhouse master, schoolmaster, and schoolmistress.

3. No.

4. Wages and all particulars settled to the satisfaction of Guardians. Generally by the year.

5. Yes. Master to find them in food, clothes, washing, and to look after their moral welfare. In cases where practicable the Local Relieving Officer has been requested to visit them occasionally.

6. At about fourteen years. Yes.

7. No.

8. There are six adult inmates who were brought up in the Workhouse as children. Of this number two are destitute from physical infirmity; one from imbecility; one has two illegitimate children, which prevents her from getting service, and I cannot assign any reason why the other two remain in the Workhouse.

P. J. STACK, Clerk of Union.

GLENNAMADDY.

1. Male children employed at suitable occupation after school hours, cleaning yards, weeding, and picking stones on the farm; female children employed sewing, &c.

2. The industrial occupation of the male children is conducted under the supervision of the master and Workhouse porter.

The female children conducted under the supervision of the schoolmistress.

3. No.

4. Guardians having arranged with the employers quarterly or half-yearly, as the case may be, wages averaging from 12s. to 15s. per quarter.

5. Only two boys have been apprenticed in the Union for the last seven years, for a term of five years each, at the railway business. Guardians paid no fee, but clothe the boys on taking their discharge.

6. Generally between 12 and 15 years. In many cases the children again return to the Workhouse after a fortnight or so.

7. No.

8. Only one man, who occasionally takes his discharge and returns to the Workhouse (destitution attributable to the man being imbecile and lame).

EDWARD SMYTH, Clerk of Union.

GORT.

1. The few grown boys are employed after school hours on the Workhouse farm. The girls are principally employed at plain needlework and knitting, besides washing, cleaning, and making up their dormitories.

2. The boys under the master, and the girls under that of the matron and schoolmistress.

3. No.

4. The guardians are quite disposed to let the children out for any period not less than three months, and at such reasonable terms as they agree upon with the employers.

5 No.

6. From 8 years and upwards, and, as a rule, retain their first places.

7. Yes.

8. Only one, who is physically disabled.

JOHN R. SPELMAN, Clerk of Union.

LOUGHREA.

1. Boys weed, save hay, and otherwise assist in the tilling of the farm. Girls knit stockings, sew their own clothes, &c, but there are only a few grown enough to do so.

2. Boys under control of the master, and girls under supervision of the schoolmistress.

3 No; on the contrary, the demand is often greater than the supply.

4. The Guardians carefully inquire into the character, position, &c., of the employers before allowing a child out; and if not considered satisfactory application is refused.

5. No.

6 Generally not younger than 11 years of age, and, except in a few instances, they retain their places, and give satisfaction to their employers.

7. No child is hired out for a shorter period than a year in this Union, but the wages are paid by the quarter.

8. There are at present ten females—three blind, three idiots (harmless), two mothers of illegitimate children, two parents of those girls do not bear good characters, and farmers and others have an objection to hire them.

P. EGAN, Clerk of Union.

MOUNTBELLEW.

1–2. Except that the boys are occasionally employed to assist in "weeding" crops on workhouse land, and that the senior girls do a little sewing and knitting, there is no industrial training at present in the workhouse, owing to the small number of children in it, and their extreme youth.

3. The Guardians experience no difficulty in getting the children into service.

4. The conditions as to wages, period of service, &c., are arranged by the Guardians when party hiring and child are both before them The wages are regulated by the Board according to age of child, and as a certain fixed figure for the first quarter—from 7s. 6d. to 12s. 6d. —to be gradually increasing afterwards. Period of service not limited. The Guardians provide a new suit of clothes for child on going out to service. Minute of hiring, &c., recorded in minute book.

5. Children are not apprenticed in this Union.

6. Children sent to service between 11 and 15 years of age. Boys often do not retain their first places.

7 Children are not sent out for a short period of service.

8. There are seven adult females at present in the house who were brought up in it as children, and the cause of their destitution is attributable to three of them having each an illegitimate child, one being in delicate health, one blind, and two idiots.

There are no adult males who were brought up in the workhouse as children.

B. REILLY, Clerk of Union.

OUGHTERARD.

1–2. The industrial training in this house consists of the boys being taught to work in the garden under the superintendence of the master, and the girls to sew and do general house work under the superintendence of the matron and schoolmistress.

3. There is no difficulty in getting the children into service.

4. The Guardians arrange with the parties taking them for the first year.

5. There are none of the children sent out as apprentices.

6. The children are sent to service between 12 and 15 years of age, retain their places, and generally give satisfaction.

7. Children are never applied for here to go out for short periods

8. There are no adults in this house who were brought up in it as children.

J. GILLMORE, Clerk of Union.

PORTUMNA.

1. For boys, assisting in tillage operations on the Workhouse grounds. For girls, knitting, sewing, washing, ironing, and scouring down the house.

2. Boys, master and porter. Girls, schoolmistress.

3. No.

4. Children from 10 to 15 years are taken out as farm servants, at from 10s. to 15s. per quarter.

5. No.

6. (1.) From 10 to 15 years. (2.) Generally speaking, they do.

7. No.

8. No.

TUAM.

1. The system of industrial training, sewing, knitting, in regard to females. Tailoring and shoemaking in respect to males

2. The schoolmistress, a master tailor, and master shoemaker.

3. No.

4. Generally from 12s. to 16s. per quarter.

5. Children are very seldom apprenticed; not more than two or three cases have occurred within the past seven years.

6. The Guardians are very careful about sending children out to service. As a rule, they do not retain their places.

7. No.

8. There are. The cause of destitution is attributable to mental and bodily infirmity.

The industrial training of children in this Workhouse has been the cause of a large amount of good, particularly during the years immediately subsequent to those called "famine," when there were nearly 500 of each class, male and female. The greater part of the males have been instructed in tailoring, shoemaking, and baking, numbers of whom are at present doing well for themselves and their families, principally in America and also in several parts of England. The greater part of the females have left during that period as servants.

J. MORRIS, Clerk of Union

CARRICK-ON-SHANNON.

To your questions 3, 5, and 7 the answer is no.

4. The conditions enforced are six months hiring. Wages average about £3 a year, one quarter's wages to be deposited in advance.

APPENDIX B.

Industrial Training.

6. About 13 years is the average age. I cannot say they do, as a rule, retain their first places.

8. Only one, an epileptic.

On the subject of the education of children in workhouses, on which you invite my opinion, I would respectfully remark, that if the object in view be only to fit them for the lowest rank of servants and labourers I don't think the present system needs much, if any, alteration. A complaint often made to me is, that the workhouse children are better educated than those who usually employ them.

But if the object desired be, as I think it should, to improve and elevate workhouse children, then I do consider that the present system of education in workhouses should be supplemented by central schools for boys and girls, to which the good and well-conducted of both classes might be sent and educated. I would have these central schools of such a class that they would be the door of hope to the children of pauperdom, and that they would create an ambition in every boy and girl who enters a workhouse to get sent there, and for this purpose I would require a strict certificate from the chairman and officers before granting admission to these schools. As to the good conduct, &c., of the candidate, in fact, I would make admission to them a thing to be worked for and earned, and have them the very opposite, in that respect, of reformatories; for I do think the best means of improving the young is to follow the good old rule of "placing the cup of love in Benjamin's sack."

These schools, particularly the female one, could, in my opinion, be easily made centres for the supply of the better class of domestic servants, while they would open up a hundred and one ways for developing the intelligence of boys, who would otherwise sink down into discontented drudges.

The boards of guardians would, I am certain, willingly pay the cost of such institutions.

These ideas are, perhaps, too theoretic; but, even if so, you will be pleased to pardon me for submitting them to you, as I do it from a desire to promote the welfare of a class in whom I take a deep interest.

A. O'CONNOR, Clerk of Union.

MANORHAMILTON.

1. There is no complete system of industrial training. The children are educated in the programme of the National Board of Education, which includes sewing and knitting for the female children. The boys occasionally assist at farm and garden work.

2. The above industrial training, so far as it goes, is under the supervision of the schoolmistress, and for the boys under that of the master of the Workhouse.

3. They do not experience any difficulty.

4. The children are allowed out to service, if under 15 years of age, by an agreement with the Guardians as to wages for first half year, an intimation is given to the parties hiring to increase the wages after that period if the boy or girl is found suitable.

The Relieving Officer sees to their being fairly treated up to 15 years; that their wages is paid, and sufficient clothing provided.

Over 15 years the boys and girls make the best bargain they can with those seeking to employ them. In most instances they are provided with new clothing on leaving the workhouse to hire.

5. Children are not apprenticed out.

6. From 12 to 14 years of age. As a rule, they do not retain their first place. They look back to the Workhouse as a home, and feel the natural longing of youth to return there; this feeling is allowed for by the Guardians, who are kind and considerate; afterwards they remain out.

7. This practice does not prevail.

8. One male, who has but one hand. One female, who is rearing a young illegitimate child, and one female in ill health, from the effects of prostitution in early life.

REMARKS.

The Union of Manorhamilton being almost altogether rural, and no considerable town in it, the chief demand is for agricultural servants, and some knowledge of tillage, attendance on cattle, and saving of turf is required of them.

This knowledge can be gradually acquired on small wages on first hirings. Up to the age of 12 or 14 years the common school education which they receive would appear to be as much as can be fairly done in ordinary rural workhouses without an additional staff of officers, that the paucity of children may not warrant.

THOMAS CUMMINGS, Clerk of Union.

MOHILL.

1. About four boys attend the tailor, learning the business, and, with this exception, there is no other industrial training given the boys. With regard to the girls, I enclose the "girl's industrial class roll," which gives all the information I have got.

2. See industrial class roll.

3. The guardians have no difficulty in getting the children to service with the farmers round about, but there is an unwillingness upon their part from the treatment they generally receive.

4. Generally for 12 months, at wages from 10s. to 20s. per quarter.

5. Five boys were apprenticed out to tailors within the last five years, at periods from four to five years, without a fee.

6. From 12 to 16 years of age. They seldom put in their full time of service, and, as a rule, return to the Workhouse ragged and filthy.

7. No.

8. One adult male in hospital, one imbecile woman, four with illegitimate male children, and three with unbridled tongues.

THOMAS WOODWARD, Clerk of Union.

BALLINA.

1. Sewing and washing for girls, and boys occasionally employed on farm.

2. Matron, schoolmaster, and schoolmistress.

3. None, as there are many applications for them from time to time by farmers and others.

4. The Guardians, as a rule, never hire out children for shorter periods than from three to six months, and almost always with the consent of the child or its parent. The wages is fixed by the Board, and varies from 10s. to 14s. per quarter.

5. No.

6. At about fourteen years, and they do not, as a rule, retain their first places. Sometimes they return to the Workhouse, and go out again after a short period, when they are lost sight of altogether.

7. No; the Guardians do not allow the children out for short periods, and especially for such employment as "herding."

8. After careful inquiry I find there is only one such person in the House at present, who has always been in delicate health.

PATRICK M'NULTY, Clerk of Union.

BALLINROBE.

1. Girls—knitting, sewing, and making up Workhouse clothing. Boys—agricultural instruction in theory and practice, and tailoring.

2. Master, matron, schoolmaster, schoolmistress, and tailor.

3. No.

4. Boys' average wages, 15s. per quarter. Girls' average wages, 12s. per quarter.

5. No.

6. From 11 to 14 years; as a general rule, they retain their first places.

7 and 8. No.

THOMAS MAY, Clerk of Union.

BELMULLET.

1. The female children are occasionally employed in washing, sewing, and other household work. The male children receive no industrial training

2. The matron and schoolmistress supervise the work.

3. The Guardians experience much difficulty in getting the children into service.

4. Wages from 8s. to 12s. per quarter.

5. None apprenticed.

6. Hired out at from ten to fifteen years of age, and do not, as a rule, retain their places.

7. Yes.

8. No.

I may add that Belmullet Board of Guardians have adopted the petition of the Cork Board of Guardians relating to the industrial training of workhouse children.

P. M'NULTY, Clerk of Union.

CASTLEBAR.

1. Sewing, knitting, washing, scouring, cooking, and tailoring.

2. Matron and schoolmistress for the females, tailor for the males.

3. No.

4. About £2 per annum Quarterly and yearly

5. No.

6. Twelve to fifteen years of age. They do.

7. No

8. One boy, who is a cripple.

ROBERT J. NIXON, Clerk of Union

CLAREMORRIS.

1. After school hours the boys work occasionally on the farm, and the girls are usually taught knitting, sewing, and general household work.

2. Master and porter, matron and schoolmistress

3. None.

4. By the year, on an average of about £1 10s. per annum.

5 No

6. At about twelve years of age, and, as a rule, retain their first places.

7. No.

8 Yes, two males and four females; of the former, one is purblind, and the other idiotic, of the latter, two are idiotic, one very much deformed, and the fourth re-admitted on account of sickness. To those infirmities I attribute their destitution.

JAMES T. BURKE, Clerk of Union.

NEWPORT.

1. Boys working on farm, and girls sewing and knitting.

2. The master, matron, and schoolmistress.

3. Difficulty owing to very few applications being made, but, when applied for, given out to proper parties

4. Wages according to age and capabilities of the children; generally hired out by the quarter.

5 No.

6. From twelve to fourteen years of age. Do not, upon the whole, generally retain their first places.

7. No.

8. Yes, two idiotic.

SWINEFORD.

1. Sewing, knitting, darning, washing, scouring, and cooking to girls; no industrial training to boys.

2. School teacher and matron.

3. None whatever.

4. The Guardians, as a rule, agree to allow the children to service, having first made an arrangement as to wages, &c., at per quarter.

5. In a few cases the Board consented to allow some of the children to be apprenticed for periods of from three to five years.

6 Between the ages of twelve and fifteen years; there is no means at my disposal for ascertaining whether the children sent to service retain their first places or not.

7. No.

8. Nil.

BERNARD M'MANUS, Clerk of Union.

WESTPORT.

1. Boys, agriculture and tailoring; girls, sewing, sewing machine, knitting, household and laundry work

2 Schoolmaster and schoolmistress

3 None whatever, the children are much sought for as private teachers, apprentices and servants

4. From 10s. to 20s. per quarter with board and lodging, and sometimes clothing.

5. Very rarely.

6. Rarely under 15 years, and as a rule they retain their first places for a year.

7. No, scarcely ever.

8 Only one, a male aged 17 years, who had to leave service owing to an accident about a year ago

BOYLE.

1. The girls are trained in needlework, knitting, scouring, washing, and general domestic work. The boys are trained to agricultural work.

2. Girls by the schoolmistress, and boys by the schoolmaster

3. No difficulty in getting service as soon as they are strong enough

4. For six or twelve months, at from 10s. to £1 per quarter.

5. Not apprenticed.

6. From thirteen to fifteen years

7. No such practice in this Union.

8. Very few, except those that are disabled, bodily and mentally.

W. ODLUMY, Clerk of Union.

CASTLEREA.

1 & 2. Tailoring and agriculture are the only training given to boys in this workhouse, the former taught by a regular tailor, the latter by the schoolmaster.

3. The Guardians experience no difficulty in getting the children into service.

4. The average wages given is from 10s. to 12s. a quarter; children are hardly taken for more than three months at a time.

5. Children are apprenticed in this union and are bound to serve from three to five years, according to age.

6. Children are not allowed out to service until they reach the age of 12 years, and not then unless they are strong and healthy; as a rule they retain their first places.

7. Children are not sent for a shorter period of service than three months, and are not sent out herding as a rule.

8. There is only one adult inmate in the house who was brought up in it, he has been out at service for a time, when he came last into the house he had sore eyes

From my experience of workhouse training I find as a rule that children do not turn out well, they are always lazy, and prefer living in idleness to working. I think the present plan of teaching conducted in the schools here is not what it ought to be, teachers getting results fees are inclined to teach the higher branches, as they get higher results; for example, the schoolmaster here has got some of the children passed for results in algebra, and those children can hardly write or make a figure legibly.

P. SWEENY, Clerk of Union.

Appendix B

Industrial Training

ROSCOMMON.

1 For boys—agricultural work. For girls—plain needlework, knitting, washing, cooking, &c.

2. Male and female school teachers.

3. At present, no.

4. Children from eleven to fourteen. From 9s. to 12s. per three months.

5. No. If the Board could give a fee to local tradesmen, they could, with great benefit, apprentice many from time to time.

6 Boys from eleven, girls from thirteen years. Generally remain out.

7. No.

8. Yes, twelve,* viz, one blind, four nearly blind, three ill health, one from her own misconduct, one epileptic, and remaining two waiting for employment, one of the latter two being out on trial as a servant.

PATRICK MURRAY, Clerk of Union.

STROKESTOWN.

1. The industrial training, which has been attended with a good deal of success, is, for the boys practical and theoretical instruction in the cultivation of land. There is a farm attached to the Workhouse, of which about seven statute acres are under tillage, including about half an acre of garden crops. In suitable weather the boys are employed a portion of each day on the farm. The girls are made to clean down their dormitories and assist in the general cleansing of the house They are also practised in sewing and knitting and in the kneading and baking of griddle bread.

2. The training of the boys entirely devolves and is conducted by the Workhouse master, who is a professional agriculturist The training of the girls is in part under the direction of the matron and in part by the schoolmistress.

3. The Guardians never experience any difficulty in getting the children into service. Their greatest difficulty in connexion with this subject is to resist the importunities of farmers who would take out the children at too early an age

4. Employers are required to hire out the children for twelve months certain, at wages corresponding to the appearance of the children and their capacity to earn wages.

5. There has not been an apprentice for several years.

6. At twelve and thirteen, and, as a rule, they retain first places.

7. No.

8. There are seven, two of whom are imbeciles, four sick or infirm, and one who is mother of one illegitimate child, she, her mother and her maternal grandmother having been all illegitimate. Though a good portion of the infancy of this girl was spent in the House, she was constantly being taken in an out by her mother, and I am informed by the Workhouse master that he had to remove her from the school-room at the age of twelve in consequence of some observations made by her on her re-entry from the town of Elphin, of which she was a native, that showed that while out she had at that early age, through the instrumentality of her mother, acquired a carnal knowledge, a conversation on the subject of which would be calculated to corrupt the other children

At the request of the late Mr Senior, Poor Law Commissioner, I prepared an elaborate report in summer, 1861, of which I regret I have not a copy, showing the results of the training of the children brought up in the Workhouse of this Union. The earliest date of which I could obtain reliable statistics was 25th March, 1852, when there were 456 children in the House. By careful inquiry I was able to trace the history of 392 of these down to the date of my report. Of them there were but six in the Workhouse who were either sick or infirm; twenty two had attained to the position of teachers or assistant teachers of National schools; twenty had joined the army, one was a commercial traveller in Manchester, and one was assistant master of the South Dublin Union Workhouse, having passed through the various grades of wardmaster, diet clerk, and storekeeper.

The number who turned out badly was either five or eight, and in each case I was able to obtain a satisfactory reason accounting for the result altogether independent of the influence of our training In one case a boy was in prison for theft. He had been but a short time in the workhouse and his parents were notorious both as thieves and receivers of stolen property. In another case a girl had become a prostitute, she was the daughter of a prostitute, was only a year in the house, and at thirteen was taken to Manchester by her mother when her seduction was accomplished.

MICHAEL FLYNN, Clerk of Union.

DROMORE WEST.

1. Sewing and knitting

2. Matron and schoolmistress.

3. No.

4. From 10s. to 12s. per quarter.

5. No.

6 From ten to fifteen years, as a rule they do not return to the workhouse.

7. No.

8. No.

M. DOUDICAN, Clerk of Union.

SLIGO.

1. Boys trained to agriculture—girls to knitting, sewing and washing.

2. Under supervision of master, schoolmaster matron, and schoolmistress, and porter of workhouse occasionally.

3. No difficulty in getting service for children.

4 Wages generally for boys 10s. to 12s. per quarter, for girls about the same.

5. None apprenticed.

6. Children generally sent to service at from eleven to fourteen years of age, they generally with few exceptions retain their places.

7 None sent for temporary employment, period of service settled for, generally quarterly.

8. Three adult inmates (boys) at present in the workhouse, one considered simple, one partly blind, and another affected with head-disease.

I consider from information received that paupers of either sex if allowed to remain in workhouses till they are adults, do not generally become useful members of society.

I think if the female inmates were taught a regular routine of household duties beyond that presently learned in workhouses, it would be a great advantage to them when hired out to service.

N. PARKE, Clerk of Union.

TOBERCURRY.

1. Sewing and knitting.

2. Schoolmistress.

3 No.

4. By the quarter, at from 6s. to 12s. according to age

5. No.

6. At from ten to fourteen years.

7. No.

8. Only one who is at present out of service.

As a rule the children sent out from the workhouse of this union have proved themselves good members of society, not the smallest complaint, as far as I have heard, has ever been made against one of them.

JAMES DONOHOE, Clerk of Union.

* These twelve, though at present in the House, have not been continually there since they were children

Appendix B. Number of Women with Illegitimate Children in Workhouses.

No. 10. Return showing the Number of Women with Illegitimate Children in the Workhouse of each Poor Law Union, on the 30th November, 1878, and the Number of such Women who were Inmates as Children for Three Years and upwards

Union.	Number with Illegitimate children on 30th Nov. 1878.	No. in Col. 1 who were inmates as children for 3 years and upwards.
ULSTER.		
Co. Antrim		
Antrim,	20	3
Ballycastle,	10	2
Ballymoney,	13	.
Ballymena,	14	3
Belfast,	166	5
Larne,	27	3
Lisburn,	21	.
Co. Armagh		
Armagh,	29	4
Lurgan,	34	2
Co. Cavan:		
Bailieborough,	8	4
Bawnboy,	12	3
Cavan,	26	9
Cootehill,	6	1
Co. Donegal.		
Ballyshannon,	9	.
Donegal,	12	1
Dunfanaghy,	1	1
Glenties,	7	2
Inishowen,	9	.
Letterkenny,	17	.
Milford,	11	5
Stranorlar,	8	.
Co. Down		
Banbridge,	9	2
Downpatrick,	19	.
Kilkeel,	8	1
Newry,	34	5
Newtownards,	30	3
Co. Fermanagh.		
Enniskillen,	27	2
Irvinestown,	12	1
Lisnaskea,	3	1
Co. Londonderry.		
Coleraine,	13	1
Limavady,	15	1
Londonderry,	39	2
Magherafelt,	23	.
Co. Monaghan:		
Carrickmacross,	13	.
Castleblayney,	2	.
Clones,	8	1
Monaghan,	14	5
Co. Tyrone.		
Castlederg,	2	.
Clogher,	16	4
Cookstown,	5	.
Dungannon,	22	3
Gortin,	10	1
Ulster—*con.*		
Co. Tyrone—*con.*		
Omagh,	79	1
Strabane,	43	5
Total Ulster,	773	83
MUNSTER.		
Co. Clare		
Ballyvaghan,	14	2
Corrofin,	6	1
Ennis,	36	19
Ennistymon,	14	3
Killadysert,	13	6
Kilrush,	10	.
Scariff,	7	1
Tulla,	18	3
Co. Cork:		
Bandon,	17	4
Bantry,	6	2
Castletown,	2	.
Clonakilty,	12	4
Cork,	61	3
Dunmanway,	12	
Fermoy,	17	1
Kanturk,	23	.
Kinsale,	9	4
Macroom,	29	7
Mallow,	20	.
Midleton,	19	.
Millstreet,	19	.
Mitchelstown,	13	6
Skibbereen,	4	.
Skull,	8	.
Youghal,	14	3
Co. Kerry		
Cahirciveen,	5	2
Dingle,	5	1
Kenmare,	9	2
Killarney,	16	2
Listowel,	9	2
Tralee,	20	3
Co. Limerick.		
Croom,	9	4
Glin,	13	10
Kilmallock,	41	3
Limerick,	20	3
Newcastle,	21	.
Rathkeale,	10	3
Co. Tipperary.		
Borrisokane,	9	.
Carrick-on-Suir,	10	2
Cashel,	22	1
Clogheen,	14	3
Clonmel,	18	4
Nenagh,	30	10
Roscrea,	8	.
Thurles,	12	1
Tipperary,	43	5
Munster—*con.*		
Co. Waterford:		
Dungarvan,	22	5
Kilmacthomas,	11	.
Lismore,	18	4
Waterford,	45	6
Total Munster,	813	146
LEINSTER.		
Co. Carlow.		
Carlow,	35	4
Co. Dublin.		
Balrothery,	10	2
Dublin, North,	42	2
Dublin, South,	107	7
Rathdown,	39	4
Co. Kildare.		
Athy,	30	4
Celbridge,	15	1
Naas,	23	4
Co. Kilkenny		
Callan,	34	10
Castlecomer,	15	.
Kilkenny,	39	9
Thomastown,	19	4
Urlingford,	13	1
King's Co.		
Edenderry,	7	2
Parsonstown,	10	1
Tullamore,	14	1
Co. Longford		
Ballymahon,	3	.
Granard,	21	5
Longford,	11	1
Co. Louth.		
Ardee,	12	9
Drogheda,	7	1
Dundalk,	19	10
Co. Meath		
Dunshaughlin,	11	3
Kells,	18	.
Navan,	10	.
Oldcastle,	16	1
Trim,	8	1
Queen's Co.		
Abbeyleix,	14	1
Donaghmore,	5	.
Mountmellick,	21	5
Co. Westmeath.		
Athlone,	9	.
Delvin,	10	
Mullingar,	31	5
Leinster—*con.*		
Co. Wexford		
Enniscorthy,	15	1
Gorey,	12	2
New Ross,	40	2
Wexford,	37	.
Co. Wicklow		
Baltinglass,	10	3
Rathdrum,	10	2
Shillelagh,	33	5
Total Leinster,	839	117
CONNAUGHT.		
Co. Galway		
Ballinasloe,	21	3
Clifden,	8	.
Galway,	8	3
Glennamaddy,	9	.
Gort,	11	2
Loughrea,	14	2
Mount Bellew,	12	3
Oughterard,	1	.
Portumna,	6	.
Tuam,	17	.
Co. Leitrim		
Manorhamilton,	11	2
Mohill,	4	.
Co. Mayo		
Ballina,	17	4
Ballinrobe,	4	.
Belmullet,	4	.
Castlebar,	3	.
Claremorris,	1	.
Killala,	4	.
Newport,	9	.
Swineford,	4	.
Westport,	7	.
Co. Roscommon		
Boyle,	13	.
Castlerea,	11	.
Strokestown,	17	1
Roscommon,	4	1
Co. Sligo		
Dromore West,	4	.
Sligo,	34	.
Tobercurry,	7	.
Total Connaught,	272	25
Total Ireland,	2,687	369

Appendix C.

Portions of Workhouses for Harmless, &c., Lunatics.

APPENDIX C.

No. 1.—Appropriation of Portions of Workhouses for the Accommodation of Harmless and Incurable Lunatics and Imbeciles.

Copy of Minute addressed to Sir Alfred Power by the Assistant Under Secretary.

Sir Alfred Power,

His Grace has received a communication from the Poor Law Union Inquiry Commissioners in which they state that it appears to them desirable to appropriate portions of several workhouses in Ireland for the accommodation of harmless and incurable lunatics and imbeciles, and they are desirous of knowing whether the Local Government Board would object, and, if so, upon what grounds, to such appropriation.

As the lunacy requirements of the province of Ulster are at the present moment most pressing, and the Commissioners are of opinion that they could be met by the organisation of such auxiliary asylums, His Grace is desirous of ascertaining the views of the Local Government Board upon this proposal with as little delay as they can conveniently be communicated.

The Commissioners have informed His Grace that the principle of their proposal is, in all respects, similar to that which has been already before the Local Government Board in the correspondence between the Governors of the Belfast District Lunatic Asylum and the Guardians of the Ballymena Union, and that the extent to which that principle would be applied will depend upon the amount of accommodation that, without interfering with the due administration of the Poor Law, might be found to be available in the following unions:—Ballyshannon, Dunfanaghy, Letterkenny, Limavady, Magherafelt, Londonderry, Ballymena, Belfast, Banbridge, Lisburn, Armagh, Clones, Castleblayney, Cookstown, Bawnboy, Monaghan, Irvinestown, Lisnaskea, Larne, Lurgan.

H. R.

7th Nov., 1878.

Reply of Sir Alfred Power.

Mr. Robinson,

Everything will be done by the Local Government Board in this matter which His Grace may consider ought to be done.

The Imperial Exchequer has an equitable lien upon Irish workhouses, having remitted, in almost every instance,* the cost of building them; and if it is determined by the Irish Government to use any portion of the available accommodation, in order to supplement lunatic asylums, and so save expense to the country, it will be carried out by the Local Government Board to any extent which may be required, and which may be found practicable.

* See Mr. Hamilton's statement.

But I strongly recommend that further facilities be obtained from Parliament for effecting the changes, instead of attempting such a proceeding as that proposed in the case of the Belfast Asylum, in the present state of the law.

What I should desire to see, if such a course were determined upon, would be a distinct recognition by law of the proposed auxiliary asylums; power to establish them on workhouse premises conferred on the governors of the asylums, taking for that purpose what existing buildings and what land could be spared, and deriving what further expenditure might be found necessary from the county cess; the institution to be under the control of the governors, their officers, and servants.

Over so large a number of incurables as is proposed in the Belfast case there should be, in my opinion, a superior officer, to be appointed by the governors, invested with the direct management, in the same way as the medical superintendent of the parent asylum.

Whatever course, however, may be prescribed by His Grace will be at once, and I need not say scrupulously, carried out, so far as the Local Government Board is concerned.

A. P.

11th Nov., 1878.

Statement of Mr. Wm. Hamilton regarding Clonmel Workhouse.

The Guardians borrowed in the years 1851, 1852, 1854 the sum of £13,350 from parties residing in the town and neighbourhood of Clonmel, having failed to obtain a loan from the Government, who had then no funds applicable to the purpose. In the year 1859 they sold to the Commissioners of Lunatic Asylums the old House of Industry, which, on the introduction of the Poor Laws in Ireland, had been handed over to the Board of Guardians. A sum of £2,900 then borrowed from the Public Works Loan Commissioners had been expended on this house, of which sum £1,094 was repaid.

The Guardians received £2,500 for this house, which, together with a sum of £100 from the rates, was applied to reduce the debt of £13,350.

A sum of £10,750 remains due at 5 per cent., and is a charge of 1¾d. in the pound per annum on the valuation.

The Poor Law Commissioners, in a letter dated 29th April, 1866, state:—

"The case of Clonmel Union appears to be one of peculiar hardship, the Poor Law Commissioners having in the first instance converted Clonmel House of Industry into a workhouse, an arrangement which was found in the course of time to be inadequate, and when the Guardians found it necessary to build an entirely new workhouse, the time had passed by for obtaining a loan from Government, and the Guardians were obliged to borrow the money from private sources.

"It thus happened that Clonmel obtained very slight benefit from the subsequent remission of that part of the Union debts to Government which consisted of workhouse building loans."

In point of fact the interest paid by the Guardians on the building loans from the year 1851 to the present time has exceeded £15,000.

In February, 1845, the amount of Workhouse loans remitted by the Treasury was £47,268, and there was subsequently remitted, I believe, a sum of £1,323,266 16s. 0d.

W. J. Hamilton.

December 17, 1878.

Appendix C. Proposed Classification of Asylums.

No. 2.—Proposed Classification of Asylums by the Commissioners, as submitted to the Lunacy Inspectors by desire of His Grace the Lord Lieutenant with their Reports thereon.

Province.	Hospitals for Curative Treatment.	Present Accommodation.	Asylums.	Present Accommodation.	Province.	Hospitals for Curative Treatment.	Present Accommodation.	Asylums.	Present Accommodation.
Ulster,	Belfast,	420	Armagh,	250	Leinster,	Carlow,	250	Enniscorthy,	288
	Monaghan,	414	Letterkenny,	350		Richmond,	1,100	Kilkenny,	216
			Downpatrick,	300				Maryborough,	260
			Londonderry,	200				Mullingar,	400
			Omagh,	500		Total,	1,350	Total,	1,164
	Total,	834	Total,	1,500					
Munster,	Cork,	750	Killarney,	220	Connaught,	Ballinasloe,	436	Castlebar,	200
	Ennis,	260	Limerick,	500				Sligo,	230
			Clonmel,	365		Total,	436	Total,	430
			Waterford,	320					
	Total,	1,010	Total,	1,405					

Report of George W. Hatchell, Esq., M.D.

Lunatic Asylums Office, Dublin Castle.
28th November, 1878.

In compliance with the Under Secretary's minute of the 7th November, 1878, stating that "His Grace the Lord Lieutenant is desirous of receiving such observations or suggestions as I may desire to offer upon this particular proposal for classification of Asylums," I have the honour to state that, since the date of my examination before the Commissioners, I have given the matter full consideration.

From the general drift of the questions put to me by the Commissioners, I conclude that the proposed changes are these:—

1st. The selection in each province of one or more Asylums to be reserved essentially for the treatment of acute cases of insanity, or presenting features which will render very careful treatment desirable, and possibly the reception into such Provincial Asylums, of a larger proportion of private patients of the lower middle class.

2nd. The appropriation of the remaining District Asylums to the reception of cases that would not require constant treatment, or costly supervision, such Asylums being managed with a greater view to economy of public rates.

3rd. The setting apart of certain workhouses, or portions thereof, in each province for the accommodation of idiotic and harmless lunatics, who are now distributed in twos and threes, or in very small numbers in such workhouses—and the admission to these workhouses of equally harmless inmates who now overcrowd the District Asylums—such is the proposal, as I understand it from the character of the questions put to me.

I have the honour to state, for the information of His Grace the Lord Lieutenant, that upon careful reflection I have no hesitation in expressing my approval of a project such as is here sketched. Its advantages appear obvious; it would effect a very great saving of public rates by arresting the further extension of asylum buildings, it would confer a great benefit upon the middle class who are unable to place their insane friends in private asylums, but who are still willing to contribute to their support by giving a reasonable sum towards it. It would further confer a great benefit upon the lunatic poor distributed throughout the workhouses, and would render their inspection and supervision for the future a less difficult duty.

I have, however, one suggestion to submit, to which I attach considerable importance. I think it desirable that in a classification of institutions for the insane into three varieties, it would be necessary to avoid giving to any of the three classes the name of "incurable," as I remarked in my evidence, it is extremely difficult to pronounce any case of mental disease to be "incurable," and I am sure the friends of persons suffering from insanity would much dislike to hear of their being transferred to an "incurable" asylum. This objection can readily be met by, for instance, calling the first or curable class of asylums, "Provincial Hospitals" for the insane, or "Provincial Lunatic Asylums."

The second could be called as at present, by the name of the county or town of its immediate neighbourhood, such as Wexford, "the Enniscorthy," Donegal, by "the Letterkenny," &c., and the workhouse asylums the "intermediate." This is the only suggestion I have to make respecting a plan which I am quite of opinion is calculated to confer advantages upon all classes of the insane, as well as upon the ratepayers.

It will, however, require very careful supervision in its execution, and the details will also require most mature consideration.

GEORGE W. HATCHELL.

To the Under Secretary, &c.,
Dublin Castle.

Report of John Nugent, Esq., M.D., 25th November, 1878.

Being satisfied in dealing with this subject that its bearings can be best understood by taking a comprehensive view of it, I will in the first instance, concisely, and as consistently as possible with clearness, advert to the state of lunacy in England, which admits of a much larger field for observation than is presented in Ireland, while the requirements of both countries in respect to lunatic accommodation are by no means dissimilar. According to the latest authoritative records, the population of England and Wales is set down at 24,850,000, inclusive of 68,500 reputed insane; of the latter, 60,800 belong to the pauper community, and are supported out of public funds, 51,800 being located in asylums, or in poorhouses, in the proportion of 35,550 to the former, and 16,250 to the latter, the difference being maintained in borough hospitals, at home on parish allowances, in charitable institutions and the like.

This difference, as well as lunatics in private licensed houses, are eliminated from present consideration. Of the 35,500 in asylums, 2,428 only are deemed curable, or about 7 per cent., while, if individual institutions come under examination, the curables in them would occasionally dwindle down almost to zero, as

APPENDIX C.

Proposed Classification of Asylums

at Glamorgan, where there are 543 hopeless as against 34 hopeful cases, but even there additional accommodation to meet increasing applications for admission is under consideration.

To arrive at legitimate conclusions, facts, no matter whether favourable or the reverse to theory, should be borne in view, however it may be correctly assumed that in every thousand of the combined population, rich and poor, throughout the United Kingdom, three persons are mentally affected—English and Irish statistics support the proposition. It is unnecessary to enter into details which, as a rule, would be found almost alike in the various asylums of the sister country; for elucidation's sake however, and as typical of the amount and character of lunatic accommodation in England, and of the advisability felt there of its further extension, two or three of the largest, most populous, and wealthiest asylum districts may be adduced namely—the Lancashire, adjacent to Ireland, Norfolk in the east, and the Metropolitan or Middlesex. In the first-named there exists a regular hospital provision for 3,940 lunatics, exclusive of a poorhouse accommodation for 2,360 The County Justices, deeming the above insufficient, decided on increasing the amount by 600 beds through the medium of auxiliary buildings and in accordance with the desire of the Commissioners in Lunacy, that, in due proportion to an increased number of patients additional land should be annexed.

In Norfolk, owing to a similar deficiency of accommodation (it being confined to 720 beds,) the County Magistrates assembled in 1876 to meet requirements—various propositions were discussed. Three workhouses being available—one with 25 acres of land attached to it, a second with 12, the third with four—after a careful examination of each with the Government Surveyor, a committee of justices decided on purchasing for £4,300, 24 acres of land contiguous to the asylum, as a site for new buildings at an estimated cost of £28,000 for 250 inmates, "of the harmless, aged, and imbecile classes"—an arrangement, it may be parenthetically observed, which would seem not to be unfavourably regarded by some Irish Boards.

The third or Middlesex district contains three regular asylums, with an aggregate in them of 5,444 beds, independent of 600 in poorhouses; within the past two years a supplemental institution has been opened at Banstead on a farm of 100 acres, it cost £360,000 for 1,700 patients, "solely of the chronic, quiet, and harmless classes"—independent of four resident physicians and of two matrons, the general staff amounts to 114 persons. As showing, in contradistinction to the course and probabilities in physical affections, how uncertain and variable are the symptoms of mental disease, an individual, for example, placid, industrious, and amenable in the morning, becoming violent and offensive before evening, or, on the other hand, one day dangerous and difficult of control, and within the next twenty-four hours well-behaved and useful. The Commissioners, on their first inspection, while going through the wards (at the time not half occupied), saw one man consigned to a padded room for violent conduct, three women removed "for insubordination and using threatening language." On the same occasion two accidents occurred, an epileptic fractured her elbow, and a male struggling with an attendant had his arm dislocated Thus, no human foresight can anticipate their phases of insanity or its results

The cost last year in England of maintaining public asylums amounted in round numbers to about £1,200,000, including the treasury rate, in aid nearly £400,000, being £25,000 more than in the preceding twelvemonth, while of the 14,600 admissions in the same period, fully eight per cent. were cases of lunacy combined with paralysis, the most unpromising of all, but which as first admissions might come within the category of curable. In no instance, however, has the transference of insane persons, under any particular denomination, from one district to another, been adopted, or even mooted at English Boards as the means of obviating an overcrowding which is felt alike in almost each asylum.

It is unnecessary to advert in detail on poorhouse accommodation in regard to lunatics, such coming more immediately within the scope of the Local Government Board, but as pertinent to the subject the observations may be quoted of the English Commissioners, who say.—"The condition of the persons of unsound mind detained in workhouses has been fairly good. In some of the larger ones where paid attendants are employed, and attention given to diet, exercise, recreation, and cleanliness, there is little with which to find fault, our suggestions have been latterly met by two respective boards of guardians in a not unsatisfactory manner." *Mutato nomine*, a like report would be accurate in reference to the unions of this country

The number of lunatics in district asylums and poorhouses in Ireland at the close of 1877, amounted to 11,850—8,183 being under treatment in the former, of them, 1,911, or about 22 per cent. were returned as curable by the various resident physicians, as against 7 per cent. in England, the actual convalescent was limited to 362 It is proposed by the Commissioners to convert seven of the existing district asylums into hospitals for curatives alone, the aggregate accommodation in them extending to 3,577 beds; thus, *in limine*, as one of the main objects intended through the medium of this arrangement, is to secure an increased or more available provision for the insane generally, that object is frustrated by the loss of 1,666 beds, or the difference between the two figures just named—1,911 and 3,577. Hence, I am not prepared to accept the proposition that it would be either judicious as regards the insane, or economical as regards expenditure, to constitute curability as the sole basis for dividing the insane poor, although satisfied that in ordinary asylums there are many who, without the deprivation of kindly and good management, could be located in less complex and costly establishments, namely—the decrepid, the paralysed, and demented from age or otherwise, as well as congenital idiots and innoxious epileptics, comprising, on an average, perhaps 8 per cent. of the total in district institutions

A distinguished English writer, like Pinel in France, one of the greatest benefactors, both by teaching and practice, to the insane community, the late Dr. Connolly, for twenty years director of the Hanwell Asylum, would not recognise the epithet incurable beyond the confines of idiotcy. He looked on curability and improvements as convertible terms, for, in his opinion, the successful results of treatment could be equally displayed in favour of chronic patients as of those denominated curable, and as there was no definite period beyond which a recovery might not occur, he deemed it incumbent on those who deprived their fellow creatures of liberty to administer to their wants and domestic comforts, and to their improvement by occupations and quietude

Under the 1st and 2nd Geo. IV., c. 33, and subsequent Acts, 22 asylums have been erected in Ireland at, an outlay, as given in detail by the Inspectors of a million (27th Report), £240,000 for specified counties and cities, and with the specific object of harbouring the insane poor alone, belonging to such. and in which all the cost of establishment building, furniture, purchase of land, and for current maintenance were and are still levied It is then but natural to infer that Boards of Governors, and ratepayers at large would look with marked disfavour on any diminution of the benefits derivable therefrom, the very greatest of them arising from the proximity of such institutions and their facility of approach, on the outbreak of mental disorders. The question then presents itself, how would the project of having seven asylums for curative or early cases of insanity work in this country?—Premising on an average of the last three years an annual influx of 2,200 admissions into district asylums, a case or two in elucidation from each of the four provinces may be adduced as being typical of every day occurrences In all—a female after her first confinement, is stricken by puerperal mania, resident in the town of Sligo, or on a farm adjoining the asylum, to the erection and maintenance of which her family and that of her husband had been contributing since its occupation, and as an hospital inferior to none in the three Kingdoms, instead of being placed there not a mile from her dwelling, and close to her friends, she is to be transferred to Ballinasloe, a distance of 60 miles by car, an utter stranger, three days on the road, and perhaps escorted by police, who, though kindly and considerate, are not suitable companions for a delicate woman on so long a journey. If sent by railroad, before reaching her destination she will have traversed about 190 miles passing through six different counties, Sligo, Leitrim, Longford, Westmeath, Roscommon, and Galway—recovered, be it at the termination of three months, or eight months, or of any other period, or if pronounced incurable at the close of a couple of years, a return journey under all the circumstances attendant on going and coming with result, at an expense of probably £10. Now as to Ulster, a farmer, herd, or tradesman, in Donegal, Derry, Fermanagh, or Tyrone, becomes violently insane, it may quite as likely be the case of a female, the party is at once transmitted to Monaghan as dangerous, the distances varying from forty to over ninety miles, a considerable portion of which has to be travelled on cars that pass the very gates of new and well-arranged county asylums at Omagh and Letterkenny. The cost of conveyance will at least an average loss of three whole days to the escorting police, being one with another patient fully four pounds. (sic.) On recovery, return fares have to be paid, and should relapses occur, the same trouble and at a similar expense. In the province of Leinster, the Mullingar Asylum District comprises three important counties, Meath, Longford, and Westmeath, dotted over with villages and Petty Sessions Courts, at any one of which and at any time a person may be brought before the bench charged with a simple intention to commit an indictable offence, or of being dangerous, a physician called in at the moment certifies to the insanity of the individual, and that he will benefit by treatment, or it may be that a respectable ratepayer applies in due form to the Board of Governors for an asylum admission on behalf of some member of his family labouring under acute mania, in either case alike, the patient is to be remitted to the Carlow Asylum, from a distance, it may be thirty, it may be seventy miles, passing by the district institution at Mullingar, adjacent to where the parties had lived from infancy, and as a curative asylum far superior to that at Carlow.

The preceding observations hold equally applicable with reference to the Wexford, Maryborough, and Kilkenny districts.

Strong as may be admissible instances from other provinces, Munster affords still stronger, for there, be it to Cork or Ennis as curative hospitals, distances ranging from 60 to 120 miles would have to be traversed—as respects Kerry, Waterford, and Tipperary, fully one half by cars—while the utility of their own approachable asylums for early treatment would be nullified.

The Waterford district affords, perhaps, the strongest objections to the proposed arrangement. The Institution there is an object of satisfaction to the Governors and ratepayers—over £20,000 have been recently laid out on additions and improvements, much through the influence of an English Lunacy Commissioner, the Hon D. Fortescue, resident in the neighbourhood. The city, at its farthest point in a direct line, is scarcely a mile from the buildings, which, erected on a salubrious and open site, are replete with modern appliances. This asylum, the fresh admissions into which last year amounted to 56,* would become of little value when most required, viz: in the early stages of insanity, the affected, at great inconvenience and no small expense, having to be transported as it were from home, fully ninety miles, to another city, and being thus deprived of the personal sympathy and visits of their relatives become exposed to the depraving influences of their neglect, although unavoidable.

Appendix C.

Proposed Classification of Asylums.

Apart altogether from the transference of curable cases under treatment, a very important element for consideration requires special notice—2,236 incurables would need removal in accordance with the proposed scheme from the seven curable to fifteen chronic hospitals, at distances between individual establishments of from twenty four the minimum to 100 the maximum number of miles at the same time calculating that the average amount of fresh admissions for the coming two, would be proportionate to that of the past two years, nine hundred cases would have to be removed annually from their own proper receptacles to be parcelled out among the seven curative asylums—what the cost thereof might be, and how payable, it is now unnecessary to discuss. Finally, with reference to the selection of seven asylums as curative hospitals only, while fully recognising the zealous and careful investigations undertaken by the Commissioners, and their anxiety to deal with a complicated subject during a lengthened inquiry, still I cannot concur in the advisability of their choice as a whole. The asylum at Belfast is dark and gloomy, with long ill adapted corridors, the aspect is cheerless, and the airing courts confined. Nothing can be less satisfactory than the male day room provision—there exists there no suitable infirmary, no chapel, no means for indoor occupations, such as workshops, indeed the Governors themselves, within the present month, passed a resolution to sell the institution, if possible, for the purpose of erecting a new asylum in a rural locality. To the institution at Monaghan no objection whatever, either as affecting site or structural arrangement, can be made. In Ulster, on the 1st of January, there were 538 lunatics returned as curable, of whom 138 only were convalescent. As the two selected asylums contain 800 beds, a margin of 262 would, on the above data, remain unoccupied.

With regard to the province of Leinster, the Richmond or metropolitan Asylum is well circumstanced for nearly 1,100 inmates, and as a general establishment for the mentally affected. The city of Dublin, with its environs, has a population approaching to 300,000. It appears to me highly questionable whether such a population should be deprived of an institution of a mixed character, which must be the case were it devoted to reputed curables from outlying districts, as well as to its own, the latter numbering, altogether, at the commencement of this year, 348; with but fifty-five in process of recovery among them, over 700 of the existing patients, then, would have to be provided for elsewhere, and that elsewhere for one half of them is as yet to be discovered.

The Carlow Asylum is in a rather circumscribed flat situation, and enclosed by high walls, the original buildings were erected like those at Ballinasloe, Belfast, Armagh, and Derry nearly fifty years ago, and are not well adapted for the proposed object, while the new ones, judiciously planned, were intended for ordinary inmates, and as such are suited to the wants of the district comprising Carlow and Kildare—it contained 71 cases reported curable, and 138 incurable on the 1st January. Altogether I cannot but regard this asylum as much inferior, not only in domestic and special arrangements, but in openness and salubrity of position to those at Enniscorthy, Kilkenny, and Mullingar, as also at Maryborough."

With the two selections for Munster, the institutions in Cork and Clare, no fault *per se* can be found. The fact, however, that there is between them a provision for 1,000 beds, and prospective occupants for not more than 446 (according to last Parliamentary report) indicates that their would remain over 500 empty ones, in other words, that the patients who slept in them should be located somewhere else.

In Connaught three asylums only afforded an opportunity for selection. The Sligo and Castlebar—both

* See Appendix, C 3, page 221.

APPENDIX C.

Proposed Classification of Asylums.

of modern construction—and Ballinasloe, erected so far back as 1833, but since enlarged by associated dormitories and a spacious day-room for males. The old part—rather gloomy, ill-furnished, and confined in some of the lower divisions—needs considerable renovation and re-adjustment. Topographically, as will be apparent on reference to a map, none of the three are well situated for a common purpose. A radius of fifteen miles from Ballinasloe as a centre would embrace within its circle a portion of five extra provincial counties, while beyond it parishes in Galway, Sligo, Mayo, and Leitrim would be distant over sixty miles. The Castlebar asylum is very inaccessible, and if Sligo had been chosen, matters would be still more unsatisfactory, inasmuch as a circumference equal to that at Ballinasloe would not only take in baronies in three Ulster counties, but a considerable sea area. According to statistics published last April, 126 lunatics were under treatment at Ballinasloe, at the same date the total returned as curable in the three district institutions of the province amounted to 262, the convalescent among them being limited to forty. By the meditated use of that asylum 164 beds would remain untenanted, and the dispossessed occupants be largely unprovided for, owing to a want of accommodation in the other two.

Desired by His Grace the Lord Lieutenant to report on the accompanying proposition of the Commissioners of Inquiry, however diffident I may feel in dissenting from its advisability, I should be faithless to my own convictions if I did not frankly, but I trust inoffensively to others, express my opinions, and at the same time, after an experience of over thirty years, assign the reasons by which I am influenced.

JOHN NUGENT.

H. Robinson, Esq.

No. 3.—REGISTER of PATIENTS admitted to the WATERFORD DISTRICT LUNATIC ASYLUM during the year 1877.

Names and Residence	Sex	Age	Married or Single	Date of Admission	Date of Discharge	Occupation	Mental Condition on Admission	Mental Condition on Discharge or at present	Regarded as Curable	Regarded as Incurable
1. Thomas Colgan, Old Bridge Clonmel, about 75 miles	M	32	M.	Jan 8, 1877	June 8, 1878.	Farm labourer.	*Maniacal*—Violent and unmanageable, prone to destroy his own and fellow-patients clothing	*Recovered*—Intelligent and cheerful	Curable.	—
2 Betty Delaney, Ardmore, about 50 miles	F.	63	W	Jan 20, 1877.	Jan 28, 1878.	—	*Delusions*—Fancied she was pregnant. (Tried to burn her house)	*Died.*	—	Probably incurable
3 John Boland, Kilgany, about 2? miles	M	21	M.	Jan 20, 1877.	Jan 24, 1878.	Farm labourer	*Maniacal*—Dangerous, noisy, destructive, and very dirty in his habits (A very bad case)	*Recovered.*—Intelligent and cheerful.	Curable	—
4 Margaret Tobin, Patrick-street, Waterford	F.	26	M.	Feb 16, 1877.	April 1, 1877.	Tradesman's wife	*Maniacal* (Puerperal) —Violent and in a neglected state	*Recovered*	Curable.	—
5 James Lonergan, near Dungarvan, about 30 miles	M	28	S	Feb 7, 1877.	-	Labourer.	*Acutely Maniacal.*	Quiet At times rational and cheerful, and again becomes dull silent, and "absent-minded"	Probably curable	—
6 Mary Flanning, U. Workhouse, Waterford	F.	60	W	Feb 20, 1877	-	—	*Delusions*—Fancies the Union Guardians have some money of hers, and will not give it up	Generally quiet. At times becomes noisy, excitable, and destructive	—	Probably incurable.
7. Patrick Maher, Carrick U Workhouse, about 12 miles	M	50	S.	Feb. 27, 1877.	May 1, 1877.	—	*Delusions and Maniacal,* —Is very destructive to his clothing, and fancies he never eats food	*Died*	—	Probably incurable.
8 Jane Cox, Barker's street, Waterford	F	27	M	Feb. 28, 1877	Aug 18, 1877.	Clerk's wife	*Melancholia* (Puerperal) —(Avec stupeur) in a condition of stupor Did not speak for days after admission, and had to be fed	*Recovered.*	Curable.	—
9. Judith Dwyer, Newtown, Waterford	F	70	W.	March 4, 1877.	March 14, 1877.	—	*Senile Dementia*	Removed from the Asylum as unsuitable	—	Incurable.
10. Mary Kidney, Dungarvan, about 30 miles	F	28	S	March 7, 1877.	-	Servant	*Maniacal.*—Was very noisy and violent, refuses her food, weak in consequence.	Silent, but treacherous if at all annoyed, answers violently if spoken to, and keeps constantly for months past as if writing on the floor, and muttering to herself On one occasion this year (1878) refused her food requiring artificial interference.	—	Probably incurable.
11. Catherine Meehan, Castle street, Waterford.	F.	40	M	March 14, 1877.	June 21, 1878.	Pig buyer's wife	*Melancholia*—This is her second admission She came with a friend to the asylum requesting to be readmitted.	*Recovered*	Curable.	-
12. Bridget Grant, Gaol-street, Waterford	F	60	S	March 14, 1877.	-	Washerwoman	*Maniacal*—Is very excitable and noisy.	Quiet, rational, and observant, garrulous, and constantly talking of the other patients' affairs, and very free in her conversation	—	Probably incurable.
13. Martin Quinlan, Carrick U. Workhouse, about 15 miles.	M.	1?	S	April 8, 1877.	-	Labourer.	*Epileptic Idiot*—Is so since his birth Mental deficiency not extreme, is partially coherent, face much disfigured by the cicatrix of a burn Admitted by Inspector	Quiet. In much the same condition as on admission Epileptic seizures not frequent, and slight in character (petit mal) For some time past he has been employed on the farm.	-	Incurable.

No 3.—Register of Patients admitted to the Waterford District Lunatic Asylum during the year 1877—*con.*

	Name and Residence.	Sex	Age	Married or Single	Date of Admission	Date of Discharge	Occupation	Mental Condition on Admission	Mental Condition on Discharge or at Present	Regarded as Curable	Regarded as Incurable.
14	Ellen Dudley, Lismore Union Workhouse, about 40 miles.	F.	40	S	April 9, 1877	–	Servant	*Delusions.*—Fancies she is Lady Mary Dudley, and requests to be addressed as such; is a fine-looking woman, and has an optimistic expression and comportment	Perfectly quiet. Delusions fixed since admission, and no change has occurred in her manner or conduct	—	Incurable
15	John Duggan, Lismore, about 40 miles	M	34	S	April 11, 1877	–	Labourer	*Melancholia with Delusions.*—Is dull, silent and depressed; imagines his friends gave him drugged porter which drove him mad	*Recovered*	Curable	—
16	Margaret Sheehan, Lismore, about 40 miles	F.	47	S	April 14, 1877	–	Farming class	*Maniacal.*—Excitable, occasionally noisy & difficult to manage	Quiet. If annoyed becomes excited and talkative and abusive	—	Probably incurable
17.	David Hearn, Castle-st., Waterford.	M	61	M	April 17, 1877.	–	Hotel waiter.	*Melancholic.*—Is suicidal, dull, and depressed	*Recovered.*	Curable	—
18	Patrick Curran, Dungarvan U Workhouse, about 30 miles.	M.	30?	S.	April 28, 1877.	June 23, 1877.	Labourer	*Imbecile.*—Quiet, but excessively degraded in his habits, eats dirt of all kinds, is neglectful of himself, his physical condition is wretched.	Sent back to Union Workhouse as unsuitable for asylum (This patient was again sent to asylum on a magistrate's warrant and again sent back, and is now for the third time an inmate of the asylum, having become, as stated, refractory in the workhouse. He is degraded bodily and mentally, and filthy to a degree)	—	Incurable
19	James Gell, Carrig Castle, about 19 miles.	M	29	S	May 14, 1877.	–	Carpenter	*Epileptic Dementia,* with occasional post epileptic attacks of excitement, general incoherence of speech and irrationality of conduct and stupidity.	Quiet. Mental deterioration progressively increasing; for a considerable period at the end of last, and the beginning of this year, he was confined to bed from physical weakness, he has now considerably regained his strength but his limbs are tottering and irregular in their action, and he is mentally almost quite fatuous	—	Incurable
20	Patrick Hynes, U. Workhouse, Waterford	M	40	M	May 22, 1877	–	—	*Melancholic.*—At first silent, dull and depressed, subsequently became noisy, and took paroxysms of excitement characterised by loudly singing an incoherent jumble of words, and clapping his hands above his head	Generally quiet. In the mornings he very frequently takes his singing paroxysms, but when spoken to answers rationally, and seems ashamed of himself, refuses to work on the farm	—	Probably Incurable.
21.	Cornelius Keeffe, Cappoquin, about 31 miles	M	40	M.	May 28, 1877	–	Farm labourer	*Delusions.*—Fancied he possessed a large sum of money	*Recovered.*—Intelligent and cheerful	Curable	—
22.	James Power, U. Workhouse, Waterford	M	27	S	May 31, 1877	–	Pauper	*Dementia.*—Degraded mentally, filthy in his habits, at times excitable and destructive	Mental condition and habits unchanged.	—	Incurable.
23	Ellen Lynch, Colbeck-street, Waterford	F	40	S.	June 1, 1877	–	None	*Melancholic.*—Silent and depressed, disinclined to do anything and careless of her condition.	No change in her mental condition, answers questions, but her memory seems affected, she cannot recollect her previous circumstances	—	Probably Incurable
24	Patrick Curran, U Workhouse, Dungarvan, about 30 miles	M	30	S	June 2, 1877	Oct 5, 1877	Pauper	*Imbecile.*—Filthy and degraded in his habits.	Sent back to Union Workhouse as unsuitable	—	Incurable
25	Catherine M'Carthy, Ballinakill, about 2 miles	F	34	S	June 6, 1877.	–	Servant	*Maniacal.*—Violent and unmanageable, noisy and abusive.	Quieter than on admission, but treacherous and subject to paroxysms of violence and abusiveness	—	Probably Incurable
26	Johannah Murphy, City Union Workhouse.	F	54	M	June 11, 1872.	Aug 16, 1877	Servant	*Delusions.*—Is talkative and blustering, unmanageable in workhouse, quiet in asylum	*Discharged Relieved.*—Quiet, rational, and sensible	Curable.	—
27.	Alice Pollard, Ballytruckle, City Waterford	F	24	S.	June 14, 1877	Sept 19, 1877	Servant	*Melancholic* and suicidal, gloomy and silent.	*Recovered.*	Curable	—
28	Mary Brennan, Union Workhouse Waterford	F	40	S.	June 22, 1877	–	Servant	*Maniacal.*—At times noisy and excited	Quiet, and fairly rational (has no home or friends)	Probably curable.	—
29	Alice Doody, Dromore, Aglish, about 40 miles.	F	30	M	July 2, 1877	Nov 24, 1877	Small farmer's wife	*Maniacal.*—Violent and dangerous, noisy and difficult to control	*Recovered.* On the 4th August, 1877, became affected with a bad attack of typhoid fever, on recovering from which her mental condition was perfectly sound. Re-admitted August 9th, 1873, but little affected mentally	Curable.	—

No 3.—Register of Patients admitted to the Waterford District Lunatic Asylum during the year 1877—con.

No.	Name and Residence	Sex	Age	Married or Single	Date of Admission	Date of Discharge	Occupation	Mental Condition on Admission.	Mental Condition on Discharge or at Present.	Regarded as Curable	Regarded as Incurable
30	Lawrence Donoghue, Union Workhouse, Dungarvan, about 30 miles	M	45	S	July 7, 1877	Sept 17, 1878	Pauper	*Delusions* of a religious character, fancied he was a saint	Recovered Delusions passed away, quiet, rational, and inclined to occupy himself.	Curable.	—
31	Thomas Keogh, Colbeck-street, Waterford.	M	16	S	July 18, 1877.	July 18, 1877	None.	*Idiotic* —Only one day in the Asylum	Discharged by personal authority of Inspector, and sent to workhouse	—	Incurable.
32.	Geoffry Goff, Carrick U. Workhouse, about 13 miles	M.	46	M.	July 20, 1877	–	Labourer.	*Melancholia* —Suicidal, silent, gloomy, and depressed	Cut his throat while in asylum (during 1877), is now quiet, but irrational, and in poor bodily health, keeps constantly moving about	—	Probably incurable.
33	Catherine Power, Johnstown, City of Waterford.	F.	42	M	July 28, 1877.	–	None.	*Maniacal* — Restless, and talkative, and most abusive. This is her second admission	Generally quiet, but if allowed to see any male becomes noisy and abusive	—	Probably incurable.
34	Margaret Quinlan, Tramore, about 7 miles	F.	38	S	July 26, 1877	March 23, 1878	None	*Delusions* — Fancied several men wanted to marry her and that her relations prevented them. This is her second admission.	*Recovered* — Rational and intelligent, but inclined to be passionate if annoyed	Curable.	—
35	Richard Power, near Dungarvan, about 30 miles.	M	57	M	August 2, 1877	–	—	*Delusions* and depression. Fancies he is burning in his stomach, and this is persistent, with partial paralysis agitans (trembling of limbs)	Quiet, but much depressed, and constantly giving expression to the delusion that he is burning inside. The muscular trembling has not increased, but continues	—	Incurable.
36.	Thomas Cook, Peter-street, City of Waterford	M.	27	S	August 4, 1877.	–	Clerk.	*Delusions* with excitement. Fancied that his friends were wronging him in many ways	No change in his mental condition	—	Probably incurable
37.	Michael Butler, Carrickbeg, about 13 miles.	M	28	S	Aug 17, 1877	June 18, 1878	Boatman.	*Maniacal* —Noisy, and excitable	Recovered — Intelligent and cheerful	Curable	—
38	Johannah Murphy, U Workhouse, Waterford.	F	60	M	Aug 24, 1877	March 13, 1878.	Servant	But little affected mentally, difficult to manage in Workhouse, quiet here. Re-admitted in 1873	Quiet and useful	Curable.	—
39.	Mary Daly or Foley, U. Workhouse, Dungarvan, about 30 miles.	F	19	S	Aug 27, 1877.	June 24, 1878. *Dead*	None	*Maniacal* —Violent and noisy, prone to strike those around her, and destructive.	*Died.*—About a month after admission showed indications of incipient "spinal paralysis," which gradually increased until she became perfectly helpless, and the arms and legs quite rigid. Concomitantly she became affected with progressively increasing dementia, and died in a state approaching fatuity. (This was an interesting and rare case.)	—	Incurable.
40	Patrick Callaghan, Cappoquin, about 27 miles	M.	62	S.	Sept 4, 1877	Oct 19, 1878.	Country shoemaker	*Delusions* and excitable, fancied he had been a colonel in the American army, and because at times difficult to manage. This was his second admission	*Recovered* — Intelligent and cheerful, delusions had passed away	Curable.	—
41	Ellen Doran, Yellow Road, Waterford	F.	20	S	Sept 20, 1877.	-	Servant.	*Maniacal*, even to require seclusion, prone to make sudden attacks on those around her, and to take paroxysms of screaming.	Quieter, but still liable to paroxysms of screaming and violence, when she is very difficult to manage; these soon subside lasting only for a few minutes at a time	—	Probably incurable
42	Catherine Kevin, Monclogue, near Tramore, about 6 miles	F	28	S.	Sept 24, 1877	-	None	*Imbecile*, with occasional outbursts of passion, incoherence of speech and conduct	No change in her mental condition; more imbecile and weak minded	—	Incurable.
43	Bridget Moran, U Workhouse, Dungarvan, about 30 miles.	F.	24	S	Oct 5, 1877.	March 19, 1878	None	But little indications of mental derangement were observable. She was sometimes giddy, but generally quiet and useful	*Recovered.*—Mind in a perfectly normal condition	Curable	—
44.	John Maloney, Carrickbeg, about 13 miles	M.	24	S.	Oct. 10, 1877	Sept. 13, 1878.	Boatman	*Melancholia.*— Dull and stupid, silent and harmless, became more cheerful, and was employed on the farm	*Recovered* —Bright and quite rational	Curable.	—
45	Bridget Mangan, Lismore U. Workhouse, about 40 miles.	F.	65	M	Oct. 16, 1877.	March 15, 1878.	Tramp	But little indications of mental derangement were observable: suffering more from privation and exposure	*Recovered* —Sent back to Union in good health, bodily and mentally.	Curable	—

No 3.—Register of Patients admitted to the Waterford District Lunatic Asylum during the year 1877—con.

Name and Residence.	Sex.	Age.	Married or Single.	Date of Admission	Date of Discharge.	Occupation.	Mental Condition on Admission.	Mental Condition on Discharge or at Present.	Regarded as Curable.	Regarded as Incurable.
46 Catherine Quinn, Kilmacthomas, about 13 miles	F	41	M	Oct 28, 1877	March 18, 1878	Carpenter's wife	*Maniacal.*—She used to take paroxysms of excitement, followed by dulness and depression	Removed by her husband as "relieved." Re-admitted November, 1878, in much the same condition	Probably curable.	—
47 Anastasia M'Namara, Convent of Tallow, about 40 miles.	F.	55	S.	Nov 8, 1877.	—	Religious order.	*Melancholia.* — Quiet and depressed, disliked taking off her clothes, and had a low opinion of herself	Quiet, and but little affected mentally, is industrious, but still has fancies	—	Probably incurable
48 Mary Murray, U Workhouse, Dungarvan, about 30 miles.	F.	32	S	Nov. 10, 1877.	—	Servant.	*Maniacal.*—Talkative and abusive at times, and again quiet and orderly. This is her second admission	Mental condition but little altered, is occasionally noisy, and requesting to be sent home	—	Probably incurable
49. James Drohan, Kill St. Lawrence, Waterford City.	M.	20	S	Nov 14, 1877.	—	Labourer.	*Maniacal.*—Noisy and turbulent, soon became dull and stupid, and refused his food.	Quiet, but dull and incoherent, during summer of 1878 had to be fed for three months with oesophageal tube	—	Probably incurable (doubtful case).
50. Patrick Goff, near Kilmacthomas, about 11 miles	M	40	M	Nov 16, 1877	—	Small farmer.	*Demented.* — (Senile), talking to himself quite incoherently, fancied his friends were wronging him, and suspicious	Quiet, but very weak-minded and feeble physically, he is quite blind, and requires constant watching	—	Incurable.
51. John Kearns, Ballybricken, Waterford City.	M	54	M.	Nov 20, 1877.	June 12, 1878	Cattle jobber.	*Maniacal.* — Very violent, noisy, and generally turbulent	*Recovered.*—Intelligent and rational, but of a passionate disposition, and addicted to intemperance	Curable.	—
52. David Daly, Dungarvan, about 30 miles.	M	40	M.	Nov 28, 1877.	April 1–, 1878.	Labourer.	*Melancholic* with delusions, fancied his wife, whom he had recently married, took his money, soon became cheerful and industrious	*Recovered.*—Bright and rational	Curable	—
53. Patrick Hogan, near Clonmel, about 21 miles.	M	64	M	Nov. 28, 1877.	—	Labourer.	*Delusions*, which were confused one with the other, general dulness, and refusing to do any work	Mental condition but little changed, refuses to work on the farm unless he is paid wages	—	Probably incurable
54 Anne Cusack, Harb-street, Waterford.	F	26	M.	Dec. 10, 1877.	March 14, 1878	Carpenter's wife	*Maniacal* (puerperal) —Very excited, prone to take off her clothes and refuse her food, in very bad bodily health. This is her second admission—about 3½ years' interval	*Recovered.* — Mental and bodily health quite restored.	Curable	—
55 John Furan, near Dungarvan, about 30 miles.	M.	40	S.	Dec 13, 1877.	April 12, 1878	Farmer.	*Melancholic.* — Suicidally inclined (tried to burn his house), and depressed, became brighter and industrious	*Recovered.*—Bright and rational	Curable	—
56 Bridget Whelan, Yellow-road, Waterford.	F	21	S.	Dec. 26, 1877.	—	Servant.	*Imbecile.* — Took (and takes) fits of a epileptic character, when she loses consciousness and becomes partially rigid. This is her fourth admission.	Mental condition but little changed between the fits, which are of the nature of epilepsy. She is bright, intelligent, and industrious, the seizures come on without any apparent cause, and she is then incapable of any thought or action, and has to be dressed and fed, her limbs do not become cataleptically fixed	—	Probably incurable
57. Patrick Hanrahan, Abbeyside, about 30 miles.	M	17	S	Dec. 29, 1877.	Sept 14, 1878. *Died*	Labourer	*Epileptic Idiot.*—Stupid and incoherent, fits very frequent and severe	*Died.* — Mental condition deteriorated more and more, the fits continued, and he succumbed to exhaustion from a series peculiarly severe	—	Incurable

REMARKS.

1. Religious Persuasion of Patients.—With one or two exceptions, all the 57 cases were Roman Catholics
2. Original Disposition and Habits of Life of Patients.—As these have not been correctly given or known, I have omitted all reference thereto.
3. Causation of Mental Derangement.—The same remark applies to this as to the preceding
4. Classification of Mental Symptoms.—I have used the adjectival terms "maniacal," "melancholic," &c., instead of the substantive terms "mania," "melancholia," &c., as more accurately (in my opinion) expressive of forms of disorder, or rather symptoms for the time being, of a malady which is constantly varying in its character in the same individual.
5. Distance at which the Patients have resided.—The number of miles under the residence of the patient represents approximately the distance from the Asylum, this in the case of city patients not being given, as they all reside within a radius of two or three miles.

(Signed) RINGROSE ATKINS, M.D.,
Resident Medical Superintendent.

Appendix C — Lunacy.

ABSTRACT of CASES admitted to WATERFORD ASYLUM in 1877.

Distance from Cork	Name of Place	Distance from Waterford	Returned as Curable	Returned as Incurable	Distance from Cork	Name of Place.	Distance from Waterford	Returned as Curable	Returned as Incurable.
Miles.		Miles.			Miles.		Miles.		
45	Ardmore,	60	–	1	58	Kilgarry,	26	1	–
43	Ablayshis and Dungarvan,	30	5	7	54	Kilmacthomas,	15	1	1
33	Cappoquin,	37	2	–	26	Lismore and Tallow,	40	2	2
67½	Carrick-on-Suir & Carrick Beg	13	2	2	63	Tramore,	7	1	1
60	Carrick Castle,	10	–	1	70	Waterford and neighbourhood,	–	10	13
48½	Clonmel,	25	1	1					
53½	Dromore Agfish,	30	1	–		Total,	–	26	31

No. 4.—DISTRICT ASYLUMS FOR LUNATIC POOR IN IRELAND.

STATEMENT by BOARD of CONTROL of EXPENDITURE on DISTRICT LUNATIC ASYLUMS with authority of the Lord Lieutenant in Council, under Act 18 & 19 Vic., cap. 108.

Name of Asylum	When first opened: Date	When first opened: Cost, including Cost of Site	When first opened: No. of Beds	First Addition or Alteration: Date of Authority.	First Addition or Alteration: Cost of Building, &c.	First Addition or Alteration: No. of Beds
		£ s. d.			£ s. d.	
Ennis,	1868	51,316 8 6	260	—	—	—
Letterkenny,*	1866	37,887 5 3	300	27th November, 1874,	4,305 0 2	—
Downpatrick,	1869	60,377 6 5	300	—	—	—
Castlebar,†	1866	34,903 14 11	250	11th May, 1874,	—	31
Monaghan,	1869	57,662 5 5	340	—	—	—
Enniscorthy,	1868	50,008 0 6	288	—	—	—

* Detached Infirmary Buildings.
† CASTLEBAR.—The addition of thirty one beds was obtained by internal alterations made by the Board of Governors, and approved by the Board of Control on 11th May, 1874, the cost was defrayed out of current expenses by the Governors. An increase to Infirmary accommodation is in progress. Estimated cost, £4,000, approved by Orders in Council, dated 15th March, 1877, and 20th February, 1878.

STATEMENT of cost of Building and adding to seven Asylums, the original works having been carried out by the Board of Control, of which the executive members were three Commissioners of Public Works, with the authority of the Lord Lieutenant in Council, and the additions by the Board of Control as at present constituted (18 & 19 Vic., cap. 108).

Name of Asylum.	When first opened: Date	When first opened: Cost, including Cost of Site	When first opened: No. of Beds.	First Addition or Alteration: Date of Authority, Order in Council	First Addition or Alteration: Cost of Building, &c.	First Addition or Alteration: No. of Beds	Second Addition, &c.: Date of Authority, Order in Council	Second Addition, &c.: Cost of Building, &c.	Second Addition, &c.: No. of Beds
		£ s. d.			£ s. d.			£ s. d.	
Cork,*	1852	70,827 1 5	500	3rd July, 1873,	10,766 13 0	214	16th October, 1874, and 25th June, 1877,	18,000 0 0	176
Kilkenny,	1852	24,920 12 1	150	20th November, 1870,	1,476 10 3	66	—	—	–
Killarney,*	1852	28,154 8 2	250	22nd October, 1875,	10,000 0 0	100	—	—	–
Mullingar,	1855	37,716 15 9	300	23rd October, 1873,	11,250 9 11	100	—	—	–
Omagh,	1853	41,407 12 2	310	8th April, 1871,	21,200 0 0	200	—	—	–
Richmond,	1830	74,000 0 0	301	30th May, 1870,	50,733 7 4	479	—	—	–
Sligo,*	1855	30,709 6 7	250	22nd October, 1875, and 22nd March, 1878,	50,268 12 9	100	—	—	–

* Not completed.

ASYLUMS erected under the direction of the Board of Control, appointed under the Act 1 & 2 Geo. IV., c. 33. Statement of Date and Cost of original Building, and of subsequent Additions thereto.

Name of Asylum	When first opened: Date.	When first opened: Cost, including Cost of Land	When first opened: No. of Beds	First Addition or Alteration: Date of Authority, Order in Council	First Addition or Alteration: Cost of Building and additional Land	First Addition or Alteration: No. of Beds	Second Addition, &c.: Date of Authority, Order in Council	Second Addition, &c.: Cost of Building and Land	Second Addition, &c.: No. of Beds
		£ s. d.			£ s. d.			£ s. d.	
Armagh,*	1824	19,900 4 5	104	2nd September, 1864,	10,983 17 2	56	8th April, 1878,	22,700 0 0	110
Limerick,†	1827	36,630 19 1	150	—	—	240	22nd October, 1875,	14,800 0 0	110
Belfast,	1829	45,798 12 7	284	2nd July, 1837,	22,100 15 5	96	—	—	–
Londonderry,‡	1829	26,000 15 4	120	—	—	118	—	—	–
Carlow,	1832	22,553 10 4	104	10th January, 1872,	20,000 0 0	146	—	—	–
Maryborough,	1833	24,178 3 0	104	5th May, 1866,	10,908 0 0	156	—	—	–
Ballinasloe,§	1833	42,844 2 2	250	20th June, 1856,	15,818 17 8	–	20th August, 1869,	9,052 11 5	209
Waterford,‖	1835	16,848 1 0	100	24th June, 1869,	8,530 9 4	100	6th December, 1875,	14,000 0 0	100
Clonmel,¶	1834	22,323 14 5	60	29th September, 1850,	2,310 2 6	–	—	—	–
Do.,**	–	—	–	30th April, 1861,	10,849 12 10	140	16th October, 1874,	4,000 0 0	–

* Works not commenced. † Not completed, no account of cost of first increase.
‡ No account of the cost of this addition. § This increase of 209 beds was obtained at the total cost of £24,546 5s. 1d. (1856–69).
‖ Not completed. ¶ For purchase of old Workhouse. ** For purchase of additional land, and for cost of connecting tunnel.
CLONMEL.—The Inspector's report gives the accommodation at [illegible] patients.

No. 5.—INSPECTION of DISTRICT ASYLUMS, LUNATICS in WORKHOUSES, and LUNATICS at LARGE.

LIST of QUERIES addressed to the INSPECTORS of LUNATIC ASYLUMS and their REPLIES

1. For the purposes of inspection is the country divided into districts? If so, is a district left under the permanent supervision of one inspector? If not, what arrangement is made for official inspection?

For the purposes of inspection Ireland is divided into two districts, north and south They are inspected by each inspector, alternately, every three months.

2. Are the inspections of asylums made without previous notice being given to the resident medical superintendents of the inspectors' intention to make such inspection?

Yes, except for special purposes, when they visit for the object of meeting the Boards or conducting investigations, or of taking part in the discussion of local arrangements.

3. What power have the inspectors to remedy any defects in the system or in the administration which may come under their notice?

The same powers as exists with the English Lunacy Inspectors They have no immediate authority to order Boards to act on their suggestions As commissioners of control they have power under the Act to take all requisite steps which they deem advisable in the purchase of land, erection of buildings, their furniture, &c, &c. In them as trustees, conjointly with the chairman and one of the Commissioners of the Board of Works, the property of district asylums in Ireland is altogether vested

4. Are the provisions of the 24th section of the 8th & 9th Vic, cap 107, as regards the inspection of workhouses, fully carried out—if not, why not?

The inspectors cannot visit all the poorhouses in Ireland within a year. It would be physically impossible for them to embrace 163 of these institutions within the twelve month They visit them in like manner as the Lunacy Commissioners in England—from time to time—particularly those of importance, or those containing a large number of paupers mentally affected, the vast majority of whom, it may be observed, are idiots, imbeciles, or epileptics, a very few of whom, probably not three per cent., have been transferred to them from asylums

5 What knowledge have you as to the cases tabulated in Appendix B of your annual report, under the head of "Insane Persons in Workhouses?" Is your knowledge personal, or is it derived from reports from the medical officers of workhouses?

First What the inspectors know from their own observations Second They accept returns coming from duly qualified physicians of poorhouses as correct, the more so as they consider them, from experience, competent to their duties, as regards classification of the insane

6 Is the class of "lunatics at large," of which a summary by counties appears in the appendix to your annual reports, subject to any, and if so, to what inspection? If not, can you make any recommendations concerning them?

Being at large, the class referred to is not subject to any official inspection, a fact to which, in their Parliamentary reports, the inspectors have frequently and distinctly adverted The returns of the individuals in question are obtained through the Constabulary and Metropolitan Police, who include in their local reports every individual *supposed* to be mentally affected, though, in the opinion of the inspectors, a very considerable portion of them are not exactly fit objects to be deprived of their freedom, as, for example, persons subject to mild forms of epilepsy of infrequent recurrence, who are capable of performing all their social avocations again—imbeciles, considered as such simply because their mental faculties are not fully developed or properly cultured. Influenced by these circumstances, the inspectors think it would be advisable, taking a broad view of the subject, that parochial relieving officers should make returns of the supposed mentally affected in their subdistricts to the Office of Lunatic Asylums, such returns to be countersigned by the medical officers of each electoral division, giving the various types of the malady and their extent, as observed by them in individual cases

(Signed), JOHN NUGENT,
for self and colleague.

No. 6.—ADMISSION AND DISCHARGE of PATIENTS in DISTRICT ASYLUMS and the SYSTEM of SUPERVISION and INSPECTION.

LIST of QUERIES addressed to RESIDENT MEDICAL SUPERINTENDENTS and their several REPLIES.

I —ADMISSION

(a). Are the rules and regulations as laid down by Order in Council for admission of patients into the Asylum in all cases strictly adhered to?

(b) Do you consider the present mode of admission to be in any respect, and if so in what respect, defective?

(c) Are you of opinion that any change, and if so what change, is desirable in the present form or mode of admission?

(d). Can you furnish any cases, if so be good enough to do so, in illustration of your opinion?

ULSTER

ARMAGH.

(a). They are.

(b) I do not consider the present mode of admission defective; every facility is given for the early admission of patients on Form E.

(c) I cannot suggest any change as regards Form E

(d). I cannot, except as regards dangerous cases I am of opinion, and the Governors of the Asylum agree, that greater facilities might be given for the admission of "Dangerous Lunatics," viz, I myself suggest that the lunatic be brought before one justice, and that the assistance and certificate of any properly qualified medical practitioner should be sufficient—this, of course, would involve a change in the Act 30 & 31 Vic., c. cxviii.

ROBERT MACKINSTRY, M.D,
Res Med Supt

Armagh District Asylum

BELFAST.

The Privy Council Rules are in all cases adhered to in the admission of patients, and work very satisfactorily

ALEX. STEWART MERRICK, M D,
Res Med. Supt.

District Lunatic Asylum,
Belfast, 1st March, 1878.

DOWNPATRICK.

(a) Yes.

(b) I consider committals by magistrates' warrants unnecessary and objectionable Unnecessary,—the resident medical officer having the power to receive on the ordinary forms any urgent cases. Objectionable—first, as converting the lunatic into a criminal, more especially in the case of females, who are constantly

APPENDIX C — Lunacy

under the escort of the police for the greater part of a day, and, secondly, as giving too great facilities for putting people into asylums without sufficient cause; and, thirdly, as tending to frustrate justice in the future; for instance, persons suffering from delirium tremens are not subjects for a lunatic asylum, and are in all probability likely on future occasions in consequence of their habits to be tried as criminals when having been in lunatic asylums, justice is frustrated to a great extent. A clergyman was sent here on a magistrate's warrant who was bordering on delirium tremens, and who had committed an assault. He was no case for a lunatic asylum, but is now branded as a lunatic.

G. St. G. Tyner.

District Lunatic Asylum,
Downpatrick.

Letterkenny.

(a) Yes, with one exception. In the admission of cases other than dangerous lunatics, the 10th Privy Council Rule gives discretionary power to the resident medical superintendent only in exceptional cases. Taking into consideration the great distances persons have to be brought, and the almost utter want of railway communication in this district, the Board of Governors has given power to the resident medical superintendent to admit ordinary cases at whatsoever times they are presented for admission.

(b) No.

(c) No.

(d). No

Joseph Pettit, M.D.

Londonderry.

(a) The rules and regulations as laid down by order in Order in Council for admission of patients in this asylum are in all cases strictly adhered to.

(b). I do not consider the present mode to be in any way defective.

(c). I cannot suggest any change that would be desirable in the present mode or form of admission.

Monaghan.

(a). Yes

(b) Yes, defective in so far as no provision is made for the prompt admission of wandering lunatics, and of lunatics not under proper care and control.

(c) Yes. That the clause in the English Lunatic Asylums Act, 1853, 16 & 17 Vic, c. 97, be extended to Ireland.

(d). Yes. The case of William Montgomery, admitted here on 9th October, 1871. He was detained at home—a small farm house near Arvagh, county Cavan, and confined to a room, in the windows of which there was no glass, in a state of complete nudity. This patient was not under proper care and control. He was discovered in this condition by an Englishman travelling through Ireland, and who represented the case to the English Lunacy Commissioners. The Lunacy Commissioners forwarded the letter of complaint to the Inspectors of Lunatic Asylums, Ireland.

A copy of the correspondence can be supplied if required.

J. C. Robertson.

Monaghan, March 2nd, 1878.

Omagh.

(a). They are.

(b). In no respect.

(c). None.

(d). No

Edwd. J. Thompson, M.B.
Visiting Physician and Acting for Res. Med. Supt.

MUNSTER.

Clonmel.

(a). Yes, I believe so.

(b) There are four modes of admission.

1.—Magistrate's warrant. 30 and 31 V., c. 118.

2.—House form. Form E. P. C. rules.

3.—Form of application for admission of paying patients—Form H. P. C. rules.

4.—Warrant of Lord-Lieutenant.

I think the two first-mentioned modes of admission might be amended, and are defective, inasmuch as the signature of two physicians is not required to either of them as in the case of paying patients admitted under Form H. It being to my mind of as much importance to guard against the possible improper detention of a pauper as an individual in a higher social grade by taking the precaution of requiring the certificates of two independent physicians.

2.—The mode of transmission to the asylum of those committed under the Act 30 and 31 Vic, c. 118—viz., by means of an armed escort, generally handcuffed, and sometimes bound with cords, is decidedly objectionable.

(c) I think committments under the Act of Parliament quoted above might be discontinued, provided the change I recommended be adopted, viz., requiring the separate certificate of two properly qualified physicians, each physician to state the reasons *as observed by himself* for certifying to the fitness of the patients for admission.

(d). I am aware of two cases, at least, of improper committal under the Act 30 and 31 Vic, c. 118. The persons I allude to were not insane, but suffering from the effects of drink.

W. H. Garner, R.M.S.,
Clonmel.

Cork.

(a.) Yes, generally. Many cases, however try to evade the regular mode of admission, and seek admission by the resident Medical Superintendent, especially cases from the Cork Workhouse.

(b) I consider the present mode of admission by Magistrate's warrant defective to meet the case, for which such admission was intended, viz., violent and dangerous lunatics suffering from a recent and acute form of insanity; inasmuch as unless the lunatic has actually committed an indictable offence, many magistrates do not consider he comes within the meaning of the Act, and decline to issue a warrant. The magistrates should also be required to enquire into the patients pecuniary means. Cases have come under my notice, having been sent to the district asylum, who could have paid for admission to a private asylum.

(c.) I am of opinion that in the Magistrate's warrant for admission, the same engagement on the part of the patient's friends to remove the patients when certified as recovered, should be inserted as on the ordinary form of admission.

(d) I cannot just at present furnish any cases, not having any record.

J. A. Eames, M.D.,
Res. Med. Supt.

Ennis.

(a.) The rules and regulations as laid down by order in Council are always complied with.

(b.) The present mode of admission of dangerous lunatics, 10th section, 30th and 31st Vic., chap. 118—is most objectionable, as it converts the lunatic into a criminal. The ordinary form of admission (on house form) is defective, as there is no obligation on the Board or Medical Superintendent to admit. Further the rule which requires that the admission of all paying patients must be approved of by the Inspectors is most obstructive, as the Medical Superintendent has at present no power to admit such cases no matter how urgent they may be, and on his refusing to do so the friends commit the patient as a dangerous lunatic and the institution loses the benefit of the money. The rule which prohibits the Governors from receiving from paying patients more than the average cost should be rescinded, as many of this class require better diet than the ordinary run of patients, and their friends would much prefer to pay liberally for any extras that might be given them.

The present forms are also defective in not giving the qualifications of the medical man signing the certificate, also in the previous history, &c., of the patient, the latter remark applies especially to forms sent with persons committed from gaols by warrant of Lord Lieutenant, no information whatever being given in such cases except the names of patients and certifying physicians.

(*c*) The 10th sect. of the 30th and 31st Vic., chap. 118, should be repealed; the declaration of present form should be retained, but English form of admission (Schedule B, section 7, 16 & 17 Vic., chap 96), be substituted for the present form, and that sections 68, 69, and 70 of chap. 97, 16 and 17, Vic., should extend to Ireland.

Females committed as lunatics should be sent to asylums with a female in the escort.

(*d*) Application was made here in the year 1873, for the admission of Margaret Kerin, who was labouring under acute puerperal mania; her husband was in good circumstances and quite ready to pay anything reasonable for her support. I could not admit her, and as her case was most urgent she was committed as a "dangerous lunatic." She made a good recovery and was discharged after five months, but we never received one penny to our funds from her husband.

In the year 1875 an application was made for the admission of Michael Lynch, whose friends were in most comfortable circumstances, and warned by my experience in Mrs Kerin's case I admitted him as a paying patient and urgent case, and for this I was reprimanded by the Inspectors

A young woman (æt twenty-five) was, on the tenth inst., committed as a "dangerous lunatic," she was brought here from Miltown Malbay, a distance of sixteen miles in a covered car with no escort but two policemen

William Daxon,
Res Med Supt.

14th March, 1878.

Killarney.

(*a*.) The rules have of late been strictly adhered to; but there are at least six patients in the asylum who were admitted without any form, all these, save one, were re-admissions, their absence from the asylum varying from a few months to five years

(*b*) I consider the criminal warrant of a dangerous lunatic for many reasons objectionable it makes a criminal of the insane patient, and hands a nervous and diseased person whose chance of recovery may be altogether blighted by a fright, or injudicious treatment, over to the hands of the police This Act was evidently intended by the legislature to be used only in exceptional cases, but as Magistrates rarely raise a difficulty about committing, and as the lunatic is always in a measure dangerous, and liable to commit an indictable crime, this is the commonest mode of admission, 1,239 having been admitted in this way into the Irish Asylums in 1876, and only 1,030 in the ordinary or legitimate way.

This mode of admission is adopted as being the quickest and most convenient, the rules for admission under form E, which I beg to enclose, necessitating some delay. The medical certificates in both forms are too meagre, the *facts indicating insanity observed* by the *medical man* should, I think, always be inserted.

There is no power to enforce the correction of the admission form; dates and names are often incorrect.

The question as to how long a certificate is legal for, is not I think clear; seven days is the limit in England and in Irish Private Asylums, but there is no limit for the Irish District Asylums

Lunatics found "wandering at large" might be brought before the Dispensary Medical Officer, and be certified for in the ordinary way.

(*c*) It being my opinion that all insane patients should be put under treatment at the earliest possible date after developing the disease, I would think it advisable to do away with the present form of admission, and adopt instead the admission form in use in England, the declaration part of form E might be retained, so as to insure that no well-to-do person should be admitted as a pauper I do not think a Superintendent should have the power to refuse admission to a patient if the form is legally filled up Privy Council Rule XVI. "empowers the Resident Medical Superintendent in a case of *urgency* to admit the patient on his own authority stating on the face of his order the ground on which he acts," but desires that he "shall submit the case to the special consideration of the Board at its next Meeting"

(*d*) A patient was sent to this asylum some time since on a form made out two years previously; I refused him admission; he was committed by magistrates on same day as a criminal lunatic.

A female patient was sent to this asylum on a criminal warrant which had been dated three weeks before, as the case was urgent, I admitted her and had a fresh committal made out. Recently a woman was certified to be insane by a medical man, although he had not seen her for three weeks As she was violent when brought to the asylum I admitted her. In England this would not be legal.

The large majority of the medical certificates are far too meagre.

Oscar T. Woods,
Medical Superintendent,
Killarney Asylum.

Limerick.

(*a*.) Privy Council Rules XI. and XVI are strictly adhered to, so far that all patients are admitted under 30th and 31st Vic., cap 118, and under the ordinary form of application for admission, as "urgent by the physician" Scarcely any patients have been admitted by order of the Board

Rules XII and XIII have never been carried out as this asylum has always been overcrowded

(*b*) The present mode of admission is defective

1st Under the 30th and 31st Vic., cap. 118, the lunatic is converted into a criminal.

2nd The form itself is defective in information of history of patient in medical certificate, which does not state the qualifications of medical men, and does not state facts indicating insanity observed by the medical man himself

(*c*) I am of opinion that Act 30 and 31 Vic., cap. 118, sec 10, referring to dangerous lunatics, should be annulled, that the declaration of the friends on the present application should be retained, but that the remainder should be done away with, and the English form of admission, Schedule B, No 1, sec 7, 16 and 17 Vic., cap. 96 (page 342, Fry's Handbook), should be substituted in its stead.

I would also suggest that secs 67, 68, 69, and 70 of 16 and 17 Vic., cap. 97, should extend to Ireland, as at present a person may become insane, and unless he has friends or makes himself obnoxious to others, he may be left without care or treatment

(*d*) Cases have been refused admission by me and sent in the next day as dangerous lunatics

Females are constantly sent in charge of the police who have lately been confined, or are in a most depressed state, under 30 & 31 Vic.

E. Maziere Courtenay.

APPENDIX C.
Lunacy.

WATERFORD.

(*a*). The rules and regulations as laid down by Order in Council for the admission of patients are in this asylum strictly adhered to, with the view of giving the fullest effect to the intention and purposes for which asylums were erected

(*b*). The present modes of admission, as regards ordinary cases admitted by the Board of Governors and the Resident Medical Superintendent from their Homes, appear in principle to be sufficiently instructive. There are, however, certain cases sent forward from time to time from union workhouses unsuited for asylum treatment, and who may be classed as "Pauper Imbeciles," who become temporarily troublesome or refractory under some exciting cause, and who are thereupon certified as fit subjects for admission to a lunatic asylum As regards such cases some more restrictive measures would be advantageous as tending to decrease the number of individuals thus sent from union workhouses, and who, after their admission to the asylum, are in general classed as lunatics, and are subsequently looked upon as such.

(*c*). With respect to the form of admission now in use, while retaining the "declaration" existing in it, according to the Privy Council Rules, it would be well, in order to enlarge the scope and increase the definiteness of the "medical certificate," and so render it more restrictive and binding, to alter certain sections of the form so as to approximate it as nearly as practicable to that in use in the English county asylums, in which the medical certificate possesses the advantages indicated Where errors are found to have been made in the filling up and completion of the admission form some authority should exist to compel the immediate rectification of such errors, without having recourse to measures which might prove injurious to the patient Further, and in order to facilitate individuals, especially in country districts, who may become insane, being put under immediate treatment in asylums, it would be advisable, I believe, to remove the enactment (30th and 31st Vic) relating to "dangerous lunatics from the Statute book." As a widespread idea exists in certain districts that no insane person can be admitted to lunatic asylums unless some overt act has been committed, bringing him then within the terms of the enactment alluded to

(*d*). In reference to the class of cases I have adverted to as "Pauper Imbeciles," I cannot afford any illustrations from personal experience in this asylum On inquiry, however, I am informed by the Clerk of the case of a male patient admitted here on a "House Form" from the Dungarvan Union Workhouse, and who soon after his reception was found to be quite unsuited for asylum treatment, and was so certified by the medical officers, and accordingly discharged by the Board of Governors It was stated by the official who came from the workhouse to remove him from the asylum that the man was in nowise dangerous, but became troublesome, refractory, and dirty when seeking for extra diet, and it was for this reason he was sent to the asylum. Some short time after his removal he was again sent forward on a "Magistrate's Warrant" form, and having again been discharged nothing further has been heard of him since

With regard to the disadvantages which the enactment relating to "dangerous lunatics" possesses, the particulars of the following case came under my notice in the Cork Asylum, and I may, perhaps, be permitted to quote them here:—A male patient was admitted on a "Magistrate's Warrant" from the west of the county, suffering from acute melancholia, the result of the accidental death in his presence of his only son The disease had been for some time in progress, and, consequently, much valuable time had been lost. I learned soon after that the reason he had not been sent to the asylum when he first became affected was that he had committed no overt act whereby he could have been transmitted as a dangerous lunatic, and the persons in the district were unaware of any form of admission other than the "Magistrate's Warrant" I further was informed that in the end he was almost incited to do something, so that they were able to commit him on the Magistrate's Warrant.

RINGROSE ATKINS, M.D.

LEINSTER

CARLOW

(*a*) The rules and regulations, as laid down by Order in Council, and provision of Act for admission of patients are in *all* cases strictly adhered to.

(*b*). I do not consider the present mode of admission to be in any way defective.

(*c*) I doubt that any change in the present mode of admission would be advantageous

Patients are admitted in three ways, by the Governors on application; by the physicians as *urgent* cases, *provisionally*, the form being duly filled—in the latter case a special recommendation must come from the *magistrate*, clergyman, or doctor, whose names appear on the form—and the third mode is under the provision of the Act 30th & 31st Vic., c. 118

More than one-half the patients brought to the Asylum are committed as dangerous lunatics under the Act.

It has happened that the committing magistrates have not distinguished a lunatic *quiet* and *harmless* from a "dangerous lunatic" within the meaning of the Act; latterly more caution is observed.

(*d*). I have no illustrative case to offer an opinion on.

M. P. HOWLETT, R.M.S.,
Carlow.

RICHMOND.

(*a*). The rules and regulations laid down by the Order in Council are, in my opinion, strictly adhered to, subject to the following explanation:—

If the words in the 11th rule that persons (certain specified preliminaries having been gone through) shall be admissible into District Asylums after having been examined by the Resident Medical Superintendent, imply in any way that the Resident Medical Superintendent is to exercise a discretion as to the admission or non-admission of the person, dependent on the opinion he may form as to their insanity, such an examination is not made here.

The examination (invariably made here on the admission of a patient) has reference to the carrying out of the 17th, 18th, and 21st rules, but is not considered by me to authorise me in refusing admission to a person in whose case the prescribed form of application has been filled up, and the Board's Order for admission made, even though I should be of opinion myself that the person was not insane. It appears to me desirable that there should be no doubt on this point, because the power given to Boards of Governors and Resident Medical Superintendents by the 4th section of 38th and 39th Victoria., cap 67, might, in my mind, be considerably modified according to the interpretation to be given to the words referred to.

If the examination made by the Resident Medical Superintendent, after which a person in whose case the other prescribed preliminaries have been complied with, puts any responsibility on him as to the admission of the person (beyond seeing that the required forms have been complied with), and if it imposes on him a discretion as to refusing admission if he deem the person not insane, then the responsibility attached to all discretionary power attaches to the Resident Medical Superintendent, and the immunity conferred on him by the 4th section is very incomplete If on the other hand the Resident Medical Superintendent and Board of Governors, when the form of application prescribed by the 11th rule has been fulfilled, can in the words of the 4th section, take charge of, receive, and detain such patient until he shall die, or be removed, or discharged by due authority, too much power may be given to the Governors and Resident Medical Superintendent. In connexion with this point it is important to bear in mind that the opinion of the Law Advisers of the Crown has been given, that the Board of Governors may, if they think it right, refuse to give a person to his friends, though his friends may be anxious to take him out and to take charge of him.

(*b*). I consider the present mode of admission to be defective, or at least susceptible of great improvement in the following particulars:—

1. The so called ordinary form of admission, Form E of the Privy Council Rules, in my mind, is not, and does not pretend to be, an authority in the sense of a warrant for the admission or detention of a person however insane. It forms the groundwork for such a warrant and evidence of the insanity of a person and his fitness for admission, certainly for his own benefit, and presumably, perhaps, as a person, at common law, requiring restraint, but, in itself, the admission form does no more. Any legal virtue it has appears to me to arise from the 4th section of the 38th and 39th Vic., cap 67, which conferred certain power from the date of its operation and relieved from certain penalties as to the past.

2. The insane, so far as regards admission into asylums, should, I think, be dealt with by law under two aspects —

(A) Those who require to be placed under legal restraint in the interests of society, and in reference to those I would only remark that the existing statutes as regards dangerous and criminal lunatics are, in my mind, practically confounded together, as in my experience little or no heed is taken of the distinction between them. A dangerous lunatic is one who is taken under circumstances denoting a derangement of mind, and a purpose of committing some indictable offence; and a criminal lunatic is one charged with or convicted not merely of the purpose, but of the actual committing an indictable offence, but in practice in the case of a very large proportion of persons committed as dangerous lunatics, the perpetration of some indictable offence has been proved. Hence arises an important difference in the legal procedure in cases where no difference of circumstances exists and some evils appear to me to result.

(B) The second class are those whose admission to asylums is desirable in their own interests with a view to their proper care or treatment. Very great hardship arises, I think, in a very large number of such cases by the want of any provision in the Irish statutes such as exist in England, and which makes it the duty of poor law relieving officers and other officials to look after such cases and provide for their due care. The result is that in Ireland many such cases are altogether uncared for, or dealt with by magistrates and the police as dangerous or criminal lunatics, which, I think, they should not be.

I think the present mode of admission of paying patients, as prescribed by the Privy Council Rules, is objectionable, and I would suggest that considering the present nature and arrangements of district lunatic asylums in Ireland, this mode of admission should be done away with altogether. Under the 38th and 39th Vic., cap. 67, sec. 16, the cost of maintenance of patients admitted for treatment into lunatic asylums may be recovered from relatives legally liable, and this power appears to me sufficiently to meet the case of persons able to pay in whole or in part the cost of support, whether as regards the interests of such parties, or of the public who are taxed for the support of asylums.

Owing to the position of Richmond District Lunatic Asylum in the metropolitan city of Ireland (with a large number of public institutions in the district which are not local but national), cases more or less numerous are admitted and unfairly maintained at the charge either of the city of Dublin or other portions of the district.

As instances I would submit—

1. The case of a girl named M'C——, admitted from the North of Ireland as an object of charity into a charitable institution in the city and brought up there, who, having become insane, was admitted here and maintained at the expense of the county of Dublin.

2. A girl named H—— H——, who was admitted into the Deaf and Dumb Asylum at Cabra, from the county of Tipperary, and having become insane there was admitted and maintained here.

3. A boy named J—— B——, from the county of Longford, who was sent here from Glencree Reformatory, and charged to the county Wicklow.

The admission of criminal lunatics appears to me to require improvement, both as regards law and practice.

Criminal lunatics are divisible into four legal classes.

1. Persons indicted and acquitted on the ground of insanity at the time of commission of the crime: 1 and 2 Geo. IV., cap. 33, sec. 16, 8 and 9 Vic., cap. 107, sec. 26.

2. Criminals found insane at the time of their indictment 1 and 2 Geo. IV., cap. 33, sec. 17, 8 and 9 Vic., cap. 107, sec. 26.

3. Persons under sentence of imprisonment or transportation, or under warrant in default of surety to keep the peace, who are or have become insane: 1 Vic., cap. 27, sec. 11.

4. Persons committed to prison for trial for any offence who are or have become insane, or are idiots: 1 Vic. cap 27, sec. 111. Only some of the parties coming under the above four heads are sent to the Criminal Lunatic Asylum at Dundrum, and the remainder are in district lunatic asylums, under the discretion which seems to be vested in the Lord Lieutenant. I believe it is customary to send to the Central Asylum only those charged with some crime of a homicidal or very violent or aggravated nature, and that as a rule criminal lunatics, not coming under this category, are sent to and maintained in district lunatic asylums.

The principle on which the discretionary power vested in the Lord Lieutenant is exercised appears to me to be open to two objections —

1. As a local question, cases are maintained out of local rates, which ought to be maintained at the charge of the State.

2. A distinction which should be kept strongly in view is overlooked, viz.—that, as regards their insanity, criminal lunatics are divisible into two well marked classes, as laid down on the high authority of Dr. Orange, the able Resident Medical Superintendent of the Broadmoor Criminal Lunatic Asylum, viz:—

1. Those who having been charged with the commission of a criminal act, have either whilst awaiting trial or when arraigned, or when tried and found insane, been ordered to be detained during Her Majesty's pleasure, and who consist mainly of persons whose offences have been isolated criminal acts, the direct result of their insane state, and who up to the time of the outbreak of their insanity have, in many cases, led industrious and honest lives. 2. Those who, instead of being composed of persons who have committed criminal acts in the frenzy of mania, consist chiefly of those whose offences against law and order are part of their every-day life.

I think that it is not either just or proper that the ordinary patients of district lunatic asylums, whose lives have not previously exposed them to such evil influences, should be subjected to the contamination of the degraded habits and conversation of the second class of criminal lunatics. In connexion with this subject, I think that criminal lunatics of the four classes recognised, as already stated by law, should be dealt with rather with reference to the frequency of their criminal acts than to the aggravated nature of a single act.

Whether as a deterrent to others or for personal reformation by the infliction of restriction of liberty, whether in prison or in a lunatic asylum, the repetition of crime ought to be taken largely into consideration, and the restriction of liberty should be cumulative in due proportion to the cumulation of crime.

JOSEPH LALOR.

ENNISCORTHY.

(a.) The rules and regulations for the admission of patients, as laid down by order in Council, are at all times strictly observed.

(b) I consider the present modes of admission satisfactory, and in no wise defective. They appear to me to be sufficiently stringent and at the same time to afford every reasonable facility to the friends and relations of patients to obtain their admission in all suitable cases. Ample provision is also made for the immediate admission of urgent cases.

(c.) Holding the above opinion I do not suggest any change in the modes of admission.

(d) Not suggesting any changes it is unnecessary to furnish illustrations.

JOSEPH EDMUNDSON,
Res Med. Supt.

12th March, 1878.

KILKENNY.

(a) Yes.
(b), (c) No.

BARRY DELANY, M.D.,
Resident Med. Supt

MARYBOROUGH.

(a.) They are.

(b.) I believe that far too many cases are transmitted to asylums under police escorts, as dangerous lunatics, who could be admitted on the ordinary house forms, and conveyed by their friends.

(c.) Answer in query (b)

(d.) Many cases have been committed to this asylum as "Dangerous Lunatics," who were totally unsuitable to be classed as such, some of them being insane for months previously, and consequently not urgent cases, and others for the slightest cause sworn to as dangerous.

Very lately an imbecile old man was committed here for striking his wife. This old man was admitted in a very weak state and was immediately placed in bed, and though every care and attention was bestowed on him, he died within a very short period after admission.

I might mention other such cases as the above.

JOSEPH H. HATCHELL,
Resident Med. Supt.

Maryborough District Asylum,
8th March, 1878.

MULLINGAR.

(a) Yes.

I consider the mode of admission of Pay Patients into the Asylum most defective and requires immediate modification in order that they may be admitted as ordinary pauper patients.

HENRY BERKELEY, R.M.S.
Mullingar Asylum.

CONNAUGHT.

BALLINASLOE.

The rules, &c., laid down by order in Council for the admission of patients are in this asylum strictly adhered to.

Having had the experience of three District Asylums I have found the existing rules work very well.—I cannot recommend any change except that Magistrates should be more particular in satisfying themselves that patients are "*Dangerous*" within the meaning of the Act before committing them as such to asylums—Cases committed as Dangerous Lunatics, and which might have been admitted on the ordinary forms, are of daily occurrence in this district, for example:—

A female patient whose feet have been amputated.
A blind boy.
A female child, aged Eleven Years, epileptic
A boy committed as dangerous, yet stated by his Father to be "*quiet as a baby*."
Several bedridden old men and women.

R. V. FLETCHER, R.M.S.
District Asylum, Ballinasloe.

CASTLEBAR.

(a) Rules and regulations are strictly adhered to. The Governors have given me authority to admit any person appearing suitable to the asylum; in all such cases I report the matter to next meeting of Governors, and have the approval marked on Form of Admission. Persons sent in on warrant are at once admitted.

(b) Not defective in any way—except that some persons are sent to the asylum on Magistrates' warrant who might be sent in on ordinary form.

(c.) I cannot suggest any change.

(d.) No.

G. CARRE, M.D.

Castlebar Asylum,
March 5th, 1878.

SLIGO.

(a). As far as possible, but some cases, though not urgent, are admitted on the ordinary form without previous application—coming from long distances they could not be refused.

(b) 1st—Patients are often conveyed from station by the police unaccompanied by any friend who could give information as to their history.

2nd—Frequently proper modes of restraint are not used, and undue restraint is.

3rd.—Patients are often conveyed by police who could be conveyed by friends, thereby causing unnecessary expense to ratepayers which did not exist prior to the passing of the Act for the committal of dangerous lunatics to asylums. The friends in a position to convey patients or to defray the cost of their conveyance to asylums, wishing to relieve themselves of trouble, responsibility, and expense, get them conveyed by the police, finding they can do so.

4th.—Dangerous patients are often admitted on ordinary forms, and, *vice versa*, quiet people by warrant.

5th—Evidence of insanity frequently not sufficiently stated.

(c). 1st—When possible a friend should accompany the patient to the asylum to give a history of the case.

2nd.—Strict attention should be given to circular from under-secretaries to magistrates (15th July, 1874).

3rd and 4th.—When practicable friends should convey patients to asylums

5th.—Greater care should be taken to discriminate between dangerous and ordinary lunatics in accordance with circular of under-secretaries to magistrates, 10th March, 1874, or all patients might be admitted on ordinary forms with advantage, as dangerous patients are frequently kept for an undue length of time in restraint and seclusion both in their own houses and in the police barracks, it being difficult to get two magistrates together in a country place.

6th.—Greater care should be observed in stating the evidences of insanity, viz., the facts observed by the medical examiners and those communicated to him by others.

JOHN M'MUNN, M.D., R.M.S.

II.—DISCHARGE.

(a.) Are the rules and regulations as laid down by Order in Council for the discharge of patients from the Asylum in all cases strictly adhered to?

(b.) Can you suggest any improvement in the present mode of discharging patients?

ULSTER.

ARMAGH.

(a). They are.

(b). I consider the present mode an excellent one; namely,—to discharge all patients under certificate of the two medical officers, the cases before discharge to be submitted to the Governors for approval.

ROBERT MACKINSTRY, M.D.,
R. M. Supt.

Armagh District Asylum.

BELFAST.

The Privy Council Rules relative to the discharge of patients are strictly carried out.

I would suggest in the case of dangerous lunatics admitted by magistrates warrant, who have no known friends, that when they become harmless and incurable, power should be given to the Board of Governors to transfer such to the workhouse, or (much more preferable way) to an Intermediate asylum.

ALEX. STEWART MERRICK, M.D., R.M.S.

District Lunatic Asylum,
Belfast, 1st March, 1878.

DOWNPATRICK.

(a). No: I allow patients in rapidly failing bodily health to be removed by their friends.

(b) I would suggest that the discharge of patients be left entirely to the discretion of the Medical Officers.

C. ST. G. TYNTE.

LETTERKENNY.

(a). Yes, with one exception.

In cases of bodily illness where there is almost certainty of death, I have, with the consent of the Visiting and Consulting Physician, allowed the friends to take patients home, so that they might have the melancholy satisfaction of having them die at home, and this I have done without the sanction of the Board of Governors, or the Inspectors, as provided by Privy Council Rule 23. We have acted so only in cases where, on consultation, we believed the journey home could be made with safety, and where there was no suicidal tendency on the part of the patient.

(b). I am strongly of opinion that in cases such as I have stated above, discretionary powers should be given to the Resident Medical Superintendent in conjunction with the Visiting and Consulting Physician, for it is possible that a patient so discharged might die on the way home, and if an inquest was held the Resident Medical Superintendent and the Visiting and Consulting Physician might find themselves in a very awkward position with reference to Privy Council Rule 23.

JOSEPH PETIT.

LONDONDERRY.

(a) The rules and regulations as laid down by Order in Council for the discharge of patients from this asylum, are in all cases strictly adhered to.

(b). I cannot suggest any improvement in the present mode of discharging patients.

MONAGHAN.

(a). Yes.

(b). No.

J. C. ROBERTSON,
Monaghan.

2nd March, 1878.

OMAGH.

(a). Strictly.

(b). None.

EDWARD J. THOMPSON, M.B.,
Visiting Physician, acting for R.M.S.

MUNSTER.

CLONMEL.

(a.) Yes.

(b). Great difficulty is sometimes experienced in discharging patients to their friends, some being unwilling to remove them; others have no means of supporting them, while many have disappeared altogether. Perhaps it would be an improvement to have the discharge of such patients notified to the relieving officer of their district, or to some other person whose duty it might become to inquire into the circumstances of their destitution, and to see them located in the proper place for destitute persons.

R. M. S.

CORK.

(a.) Yes, so far as regards patients admitted on the ordinary house form; but, as I have stated—there being no engagement to remove the patient upon the magistrate's warrant—great difficulty is often experienced, especially as regards paupers (who have no friends) being received by the workhouse authorities.

(b) I would suggest that it should be made compulsory for the workhouse authorities to receive any pauper lunatic belonging to their district, discharged recovered from the district asylum, on receipt of a notice to that effect from the Resident Medical Superintendent.

J. A. EAMES, M.D.,
Resident Medical Superintendent.

ENNIS.

(a) Yes.

(b.) When a patient has become of sound mind, or is considered by the medical officers to be harmless and incurable, the friends of such patient should be called on to remove him or her from the asylum, and should they fail to do so within fourteen days, the Medical Superintendent should have power to send such patient to the workhouse of the Union in which such patient resided at the time of his or her admission, and it should be compulsory on Boards of Guardians to receive into their respective workhouses all such patients so sent.

The Medical Superintendent should have a discretionary power of discharging any patient, between the meetings of the Board, provided that the person applying to have such patient discharged enters into a recognizance for the peaceable behaviour or safe custody of such patient—all such discharges to be reported to the Inspectors within two days, and to the Board at their next meeting.

OBSERVATIONS.

In cases where there is a probability of death occurring within a short time, relations are often most anxious to take the patient under their own care, and as there is at present no power to discharge between the Board meetings, a month may elapse before the patient can be handed over to his or her friends, during which time the patient may either die, or become so weak as to render his removal impossible.

WILLIAM DAXON,
Resident Medical Superintendent.

14th March, 1878.

KILLARNEY.

(a) Yes.

(b) As there is often a difficulty in discharging patients who have got no friends, I think the Workhouse Authorities in the union to which they are

Appendix G. Lunacy.

chargeable should be compelled to remove them from the asylum on receiving notice.

A form of discharge to be used in all asylums might, I think, with advantage be adopted

Oscar T. Woods,
Medical Superintendent.

Limerick.

(a.) The rules and regulations are in all cases adhered to.

(b.) In Ireland no person is bound to remove a lunatic from an asylum. The friends often refuse. The Poor Law Guardians also refuse.

I would suggest that some provision similar to the enactment in 16 & 17 Vic., c. 97, sec. 80, should be introduced in Ireland.

E. Maziere Courtenay.

Waterford.

(a.) The rules and regulations laid down by Order in Council for the discharge of patients are, I am informed, strictly adhered to in this asylum.

(b.) In the case of patients whose friends during their residence in their asylum have died, leaving them destitute, with no one to receive them, or no home to go to. I am of opinion that authority should exist enabling the Medical Superintendents to send such patients on their recovery directly, to that union workhouse to which they would have been chargeable had they become destitute outside the asylum.

LEINSTER.

Carlow.

(a.) The rules and regulations as to the discharge of patients are strictly adhered to. The case is submitted to the Board of Governors at their monthly meeting. They consider the case, and the recommendation of both medical officers, and as they may see fit to order that the patient be allowed to return to his or her friends.

(b.) I cannot suggest an improvement in the present mode of discharging patients.

M. P. Howlett,
Resident Medical Superintendent.

Richmond.

(a.) The rules and regulations for the discharge of patients from this asylum are strictly adhered to in all cases; but as regards a relative or friend taking a person (committed here as a dangerous lunatic under the 30th & 31st Vic., cap. 118), under his own care and protection if he shall enter into sufficient recognizance for his or her peaceful behaviour or safe custody, according to the provision at the conclusion of the 10th Section, legal opinions received here have differed. The last legal opinion received, and which is now acted on here, is that if the recognizance has been duly entered into, the Resident Medical Superintendent should hand the lunatic over to his friends at once, without waiting for a meeting of the Board.

I believe that opinions also differ as regards the discharge of lunatics admitted here on house forms under the 11th of the Privy Council Rules. One opinion is that, on the requisition of the party on whose application the lunatic was admitted here, the person so admitted must be given over to the party making such requisition; whilst another opinion is that the discharge of such patient is discretionary with the Board of Governors. I consider that the power of a relative or friend to take out a patient admitted on a "house form" ought to be at least equal to that of a relative or friend of a party committed as a dangerous lunatic under the Act previously referred to.

Joseph Lalor.

Enniscorthy.

(a). The rules and regulations as laid down in Council for the discharge of patients from this asylum are, in every instance, strictly complied with.

(b). I consider that the present mode of discharging patients works most satisfactorily, consequently I do not suggest any change as an improvement on the present system.

Joseph Edmondson, L.K.Q.

Kilkenny.

(a.) Yes.
(b.) No.

Barry Delany, L.M.S.

Maryborough.

(a). They are.

(b) I think that on an asylum becoming overcrowded it ought not to be left optional with workhouse authorities to admit patients who have been certified by the Medical Superintendent as quiet and harmless.

Signed,
Joseph H. Hatchell,
Resident Med. Supt.

Maryborough District Asylum,
8th March, 1878.

Mullingar.

(a). Yes.
(b). No.

Hy. Berkeley, L.M.S.

Mullingar Lunatic Asylum.

CONNAUGHT.

Ballinasloe.

The rules and regulations laid down by order in Council are strictly adhered to in this asylum.

I cannot suggest any improvement in the present mode of discharging patients save in the cases of those who have no friends or relations. In such cases they should be taken into the union workhouses on the application of the governors of asylums, as it is difficulty for a discharged patient to procure employment coming direct from an asylum.

R. V. Fletcher, L.M.S.

District Asylum, Ballinasloe.

Castlebar.

(a). Strictly adhered to.
(b). No.

George Edw. Carre, M.D.

The Asylum, Castlebar,
March 5, 1878.

Sligo.

(a.) Yes.

(b.) In the intervals between meetings of Governors, in cases of urgency patients might advantageously be discharged, submitting a joint certificate from Medical Officers of Asylums to Inspectors of Lunatic Asylums, who might if they thought fit issue an order thereon for their discharge.

There should be an engagement entered into when practicable by the friends of Dangerous Lunatics, similar to that in the ordinary form of admission for their removal when recovered or considered in a fit state to be removed from the asylum.

John M'Munn, M.D., L.M.S.

III.—SUPERVISION AND INSPECTION.

With a view to efficient ADMINISTRATION in the ASYLUM and to affording protection against the improper treatment or detention of inmates, are you of opinion that the present system of VISITING and INSPECTION can be improved, or that any change or modification in the existing rules can be made with advantage.

ULSTER.

ARMAGH.

I would suggest, although the governors of the asylum do not agree with me, that a Committee of Visitors be appointed consisting of Members of the Board of Governors, whose duties would be to visit the asylum at any hour during the day, and report to the Board such improvements as might suggest themselves for the benefit of the insane.

The experience of the medical officers of the wants and requirements of the insane being pointed out and approved of would come with greater weight before the general board.

ROBT. MACKINSTRY, R.M.S.

Armagh District Asylum.

BELFAST.

The present system of visiting and inspecting the asylum is, in my opinion, most efficient, and affords every protection against either improper treatment or undue detention of the insane.

ALEX. STEWART MERRICK, M.D., R.M.S.

District Lunatic Asylum, Belfast,
1st March, 1878.

DOWNPATRICK.

The only suggestion I would make as regards the rules would be that of leaving the engaging and dismissal of servants and attendants in the hands of the Resident Medical Superintendent, subject, of course, to the approval of the Board; it tends to a higher state of discipline and gives the Resident Medical Superintendent greater authority; it has been found to work admirably in this asylum where the Governors from the first gave me that power.

G. ST. G. TYNER.

LETTERKENNY.

So far as my experience goes I consider the present system of visiting and inspecting quite sufficient protection against improper treatment or detention of inmates.

As regards any change or modification in the existing rules I have no observations to make other than those under heading (*b*.) query sheet No. II.

JOSEPH PETIT.

LONDONDERRY.

The present system, in my opinion, affords protection against improper treatment or detention of inmates. I cannot suggest any change in the present rules that could be made with advantage, or any modification of them.

MONAGHAN.

I am of opinion that the inspection of the District Asylums is amply sufficient, but at the same time I think that a change in the staff of Irish Asylums would be productive of great good, and would lead to more efficient administration in the asylum. I refer to the appointments held by the visiting physician and dispenser; both cost a large sum, and the work done is very small. If these two appointments were abolished, and an assistant medical officer be appointed instead, a better, a more constant supervision of the patients and attendants would be obtained, and there would be no increase in the expenditure.

APPENDIX G. Lunacy.

See Report of the Commissioners on Lunatic Asylums in Ireland; return to House of Commons February 1859.

J. C. ROBERTSON,
Monaghan.

2nd March, 1878.

OMAGH.

None.

Edward J. Thompson, M.D., visiting physician, acting for Resident Medical Superintendent.

MUNSTER.

CLONMEL.

I think the system of visiting and inspecting as carried on by the Inspectors—their quarterly visits—sufficient. I am of opinion that an assistant resident physician ought to be appointed to every asylum, the services of such an officer being likely to be much more advantageous than those of a visiting and consulting physician. I look on the latter office as superfluous and unnecessary in asylums provided with two resident physicians. I am of opinion, that the rules regarding matrons in their relations to the Resident Medical Superintendent, should be greatly modified, and I think that the appointment and dismissal of servants might well be entrusted to the Resident Medical Superintendent, who is held responsible for the well-being of the asylum under his charge.

W. H. GARNER, R.M.S.

CORK.

I am of opinion that the present system of visiting and inspecting is sufficient, inasmuch as the Inspectors of lunatic asylums, any governor, chaplain, or other such officer can visit any part of the Institution whenever they wish, but with a view of more efficient administration in the asylum, I am of opinion that some changes and modifications in the existing "rules" could with advantage be made. In the first place, I consider, that when the Resident Medical Superintendent is held responsible (and properly so), for the duties of the officers and attendants under him, being properly performed, he should have the selection of all to recommend to the Board as eligible for appointment, this would prevent unsuitable persons being appointed, and at the same time, give the Board of Governors the final selection; in fact, carrying out the fifty-second rule as regards the appointment of resident pupil, with all other officers, except chaplains and visiting physicians.

I also consider, that in all cases, where an officer is reported for any serious dereliction of duty, or other offence, notice of the same should be sent to the Inspectors, and that one should be present at the meeting of the Board, when such report would be considered.

I am also of opinion that it would tend to the more efficient administration in the asylum, to appoint, instead of one matron, an efficient *head* of each department, i.e., 1st. A head nurse to have charge of the bedding and clothing of the female patients, and to be responsible for the conduct of the nurses in charge of them, and for the due fulfilment of all their duties.

2nd. A head laundress to have charge of that department, and all the assistant laundresses under her care, as well as patients, and to be responsible for the clothes, bedding, &c., sent to the laundry, and for the keeping of the accounts in connexion therewith, accurately.

3rd. A housekeeper or head cook to have charge of the culinary department and all the food and extras ordered, as well as the dining hall, kitchen, scullery, &c.; also the attendants and patients in that department.

Appendix C — Lunacy

4th. A superintendent of workrooms, to have charge of all clothing to be made and repairs of same, and to be responsible that a sufficient supply is made and kept up.

These officers I would recommend to be paid liberally, and to be appointed solely on the grounds of merit, and long and efficient service in some public institution; I am aware, the Privy Council Rules provide for head-laundress, cook, &c., but not for the class I would recommend; by this means, each department would be kept separate, and too much would not be thrown on one person, who cannot efficiently exercise the supervision required.

I am also of opinion that in every asylum there should be an Assistant to the Resident Medical Superintendent, and that in asylums where there are 500 patients, there should be two assistants, and where there are 1,000 patients, three assistants.

I am also of opinion, that the Resident Medical Superintendent should have the selection of the attendants and the dismissal of same, subject to the approval of the Board.

J. A. Eames,
Resident Medical Superintendent,
Cork District Lunatic Asylum.

Ennis.

With a view to efficient administration there should be an Assistant Medical Officer in every asylum—Appointment to be made by Government—who should take the place of the Medical Superintendent in his absence. The portion of Rule xxxv. prohibiting the Medical Superintendent from being absent at the same time as the Matron should be rescinded. With reference to Rule cxi, all assistants to superior officers should discharge their duties in both male and female departments under direction of Medical Superintendent. This rule, as it stands at present, places the Assistant Medical Officer under the control of the Matron in the female department. All attendants and servants should be selected in the first instance by the Medical Superintendent, and appointed on a probation of not less than six months, or more than twelve months. These appointments to be ratified by the Governors on his recommendation. The service of attendants to reckon from their probationary appointment.—In cases of neglect of duty, &c., on the part of attendants, the Medical Superintendent should have a discretionary power of fining them instead of reporting them to the Board. Any attendant or servant objecting to be fined, to have the option of being reported to the Board. A *uniform* scale of wages for attendants should be fixed by the Government, for all Asylums in Ireland, under the 2nd sec. 30 and 31 Vic., chap 118.—Rule xvii. After word "discharge" add "or to be given to their friends if the Resident Medical Superintendent should think fit."

William Daxon,
Res Med. Supt.

14th March, 1878.

Killarney.

I believe there are few patients in Irish asylums who are improperly detained.

I am of opinion that frequent visiting by the Governors of the asylums would be of decided benefit to the patients and attendants, and would conduce much to the proper working of the asylums generally. Attendants will not care to have their patients clean and orderly at all times, and their wards as clean as possible, if the Governors and strangers do not pay visits and Governors would then see the main requirements, and be able to suggest improvements.

With regard to the "Rules," I think there are some that might with much advantage be altered. It is impossible to make a Superintendent responsible for the proper working of his asylum if he has not the selection of the servants. I consider nothing more necessary for the proper working of an asylum—no matter with what care the Governors as a body perform this duty, many inefficient and utterly worthless attendants are appointed, and nothing can possibly be more detrimental to the patients, and to the interests of the asylum generally, than the frequent changes which of necessity take place. No one can know so well as the Superintendent himself the kind of person that will make the best attendant, and that he can best mould to his own way of working. In England, in the large hospitals it is found necessary to allow the temporary house surgeons the power of engaging and discharging the servants. Unless the head of an institution has absolute authority over the staff, discipline can be but imperfectly maintained.

I think it would be to the advantage of asylums if assistant medical officers were generally appointed. A medical officer would then always be at hand in case of emergency, medical work could be performed more efficiently; case books, which are so necessary, more fully kept, and *post mortem* examinations made.

An autopsy ought to be made on every patient dying in asylum, not only that a greater insight may be gained into diseases of the nervous system, but also to ensure that the patient has received no rough treatment during his detention in the asylum.

Oscar T. Woods,
Medical Superintendent, Killarney Asylum.

Limerick.

The admission papers of all patients of every class should be forwarded to the office of Lunatic Asylums or some central authority to be examined.

The Medical Superintendent should report within three days after admission as to the mental state of every patient admitted.

A list of patients in each asylum to be kept in the office of the inspector, and brought with them when inspecting.

I would call attention to "Rules" XXXV., LXIII., LXXXIII., LXXXV., and CXI., which I think are subversive of the proper discipline of an asylum.

To the Medical Superintendent should be intrusted the appointment and dismissal of the servants, as they are the instruments in his hands for the treatment of the insane.

The appointment of assistant medical officers should be made imperative in almost all asylums, so as to insure their constant supervision by a medical man, and to allow opportunities for the study of mental disease.

I would suggest also that the practice of holding a Coroner's inquest on every case of death should extend also to asylums, as it does at present to gaols, not only for the sake of satisfying public opinion, protecting the insane, and defending asylum officials from accusation afterwards, but in order that medical officers of asylums may have the opportunity of furthering the study of mental disease by *post mortem* examinations on the bodies of patients dying in public asylums in this country.

E. Maziere Courtenay.

Waterford.

Having regard to the prevention of improper treatment and detention of inmates in Lunatic Asylums, I am of opinion that the present system of visiting and inspecting is sufficient. There are however certain "Rules" relating to the general management of asylums, which, if the above Queries includes such, might be advantageously modified or added to, *e.g.*, that relating to assistant medical officers, it would be advantageous to have one appointed on the staff in all district lunatic asylums. (2) Certain rules affecting the relations between the Resident Medical Superintendent and the matron, which may interfere with the harmonious and efficient carrying out of the purpose of the asylum ought to be modified. (3) Certain changes might be made in the rules regulating the office of consulting and visiting physicians. (4) Certain facilities should exist for the performance of post mortem examinations, where the medical officers may deem such from any cause to be advisable, any definite suggestions however for alteration or modification in the Privy Council rules could best be made after careful consideration and consultation.

RINGROSE ATKINS, M.D., R.M.S.

LEINSTER.

CARLOW.

I cannot suggest an improvement, with a view to affording further protection against improper treatment or detention of inmates, than at present exists in the inspection and visiting of district asylums.

The governors are numerous, and, as a rule, each governor, takes a special interest in patients coming from his locality.

The inspectors visit, inspect, and report, *at least*, once in every quarter.

As to the financial department, the audit is very strict, and patients' friends are admitted to visit on two days in each week.

There can be no interest on the part of officials in detaining wrongfully a patient or inmate—quite the contrary. No *profit* can accrue to anyone concerned in the government or management of a *public asylum*.

Carlow. M. P. HOWLETT, R.M.S.

RICHMOND.

The Board of Governors do not inspect or report on the asylum as required by the 1st Rule.

I consider that the number of Inspectors is too small, and I also think it would better that it should be provided by law that no person should be at the same time a Commissioner of Control and Correspondence, and an Inspector of Lunatic Asylums, as the union of the two offices in the same person appears to me undesirable.

I think that amongst the Commissioners of Control and Correspondence there should be one or more members to represent some other department or departments than the Medical and Engineering.

The system of inspection laid down for the Inspectors of Lunatic Asylums by sects. LVI. and LIX. of the the 7th George IV, cap 74; sects. XXIII. and XXIV. of the 8th and 9th Vic., cap 107, and the plan referred to at pages 8 and 9 of the 23rd report of the Inspectors of Lunatic Asylums appears to me satisfactory.

I think it would be very advantageous if the several headings set forth in this reference should be reported on by the Inspectors, as conclusions arrived at by them from their own inspection or inspections, and that their report should be made in connexion with such inspection or inspections.

JOSEPH LALOR.

ENNISCORTHY.

I am of opinion that the present system of visiting and inspection secures efficiency in asylum administration, and also affords sufficient protection to patients as regards proper treatment and detention. With respect to the latter, I cannot see what object any asylum officer, or asylum authority could have in the undue or improper detention of a pauper lunatic. I do not see that any advantage would be gained by changing or modifying the present rules in reference thereto.

JOSEPH EDMUNDSON,
12th March, 1878. Res. Med. Supt.

KILKENNY.

I am of opinion that the present system of visiting and inspecting does not require improvement, nor that any change or modification in the existing "Rules" can be made with advantage.

BARRY DELANY, M.D., R.M.S.

MARYBOROUGH.

I do not think any change necessary with regard to the present system of visiting and inspecting, but I am of opinion that it would be most desirable that in every District Asylum there should be a second Resident Medical Officer in order that a Physician should be always on the spot, a thing so desirable in asylums above all other institutions.

I think also that the rules laid down for the matron require many changes, and those for the consulting physician are very indefinite, and that they should be more clearly defined.

Signed,
JOSEPH H. HATCHELL,
Resident Med. Supt.

Maryborough District Asylum,
8th March, 1878.

MULLINGAR.

I am of opinion, founded on the experience of many years, that the system of visiting and inspection is highly satisfactory, and calculated, as it does, to counteract any irregularities or abuses that may manifest themselves. A more frequent visitation by the inspectors would be desirable.

HENRY BORGHLEY, R.M.S.

CONNAUGHT.

BALLINASLOE.

I consider improper treatment or detention almost impossible under the present system. I think, however, that the medical treatment of the insane would be forwarded by the appointment of medical assistants to the superintendents, as at present they, from their multitudinous duties, cannot give sufficient study to the individual cases.

R. V. FLETCHER, R.M.S.

District Asylum, Ballinasloe.

CASTLEBAR.

With regard to the admission, treatment, and discharge of patients, the visiting or inspection, I could not suggest any improvement.

GEORGE EDW. CARRE, M.D.,
Res. Med. Supt.

Castlebar Asylum,
March 5, 1878.

SLIGO.

I do not consider any improvement in the system and inspection necessary or any change in the rules can be made with advantage.

JOHN M'MUNN, M.D., R.M.S.

Sligo.

No. 7.—Copy of CIRCULAR inviting the OPINIONS of BOARDS of GOVERNORS of DISTRICT ASYLUMS with reference to the establishment of AUXILIARY ASYLUMS and the resolutions passed by the several BOARDS on the subject.

Poor Law Inquiry Commission,
The Four Courts,
SIR, Dublin, June 15, 1878.

I am directed by the Poor Law and Lunacy Inquiry Commissioners to request that you will take the earliest opportunity of informing the Governors of the ——— District Lunatic Asylum, that the Commissioners having been recently instructed to extend their inquiry into the condition and management of the Insane Poor in Ireland, have now under consideration a proposal to establish, in connexion with Workhouses, Auxiliary Asylums for the class of harmless and incurable lunatics. The Commissioners will be glad to receive from the Governors any information or suggestions they may desire to offer with reference to such Auxiliary Asylums, or in connexion with the general administration of the Laws relating to Lunacy in Ireland.

I am, Sir, your obedient servant,

H. A. ROBINSON, Secretary.

To the Resident Medical Superintendent of —— District Lunatic Asylum.

KILKENNY.

We, the Governors here present to-day, highly approve of the measure to establish Auxiliary Asylums for the reception of harmless and incurable lunatics.

(Signed), DARBY DELANY, M.D.,
Resident Medical Superintendent.

19th June, 1878.

ENNISCORTHY.

Having read and considered the Circular from the Poor Law Inquiry Commission, dated 15th June, 1878, we are of opinion that, considering our present accommodation, having room for 43 additional patients, allowing for each in associated dormitories 600 cubic feet, and 1,000 cubic feet for hospital patients, cell accommodation giving 700 cubic feet, it is quite unnecessary to act on the suggestions of the Commissioners as expressed in said circular.

When no pressure exists (as in our asylum) an intermediate asylum as proposed is unnecessary.

(Signed), N. N. COOKMAN, Chairman.

Board Room, June 20th, 1878.

CASTLEBAR.

Under present circumstances we disapprove of auxiliary asylums in connexion with workhouses, but if unions were amalgamated we might be of a different opinion.

(Signed), G. C. O'DONNELL.
VAL. O'C. BLAKE.

6th July, 1878.

BELFAST.

Proposed by Sir Charles Lanyon, seconded by Sir Edward Coey.

"The circular from the Poor Law Inquiry Commissioners of June 15th, having been read, resolved, that this board desire to express their great satisfaction that an inquiry such as that suggested by the circular is about being entered upon, as they have already attempted to have a scheme of this description carried out."

The board have appointed a committee to confer with the commissioners on the subject, but before taking further proceedings they would be glad to know whether there will be any local inquiry made by the Commissioners on the subject.

ALEX. STEWART MERRICK, M.D.,
Resident Medical Superintendent.

9th July, 1878.

MARYBOROUGH.

In answer to the queries of the Poor Law Inquiry Commissioners, this Board disapprove of lunatics being sent to workhouse auxiliary asylums, and consider it better to enlarge the present asylums, where there are already competent staffs, and every necessary for the comfort and management of the patients.

The Board desire to call the attention of the Commissioners to the increasing frequency of committals by magistrates of patients as dangerous lunatics, with a view to devising some means for checking the practice in cases that do not come legitimately within the Act 30 & 31 Vict., cap. 118, authorising committals of this nature.

They have reason to believe that in a considerable number of instances, patients have been committed who though lunatics were in nowise "Dangerous," but should have applied for admission to the asylum in the ordinary way.

By this means their friends escape the trouble and expense of conveying patients to the asylum, and also the responsibility of receiving and providing for them again when cured.

It is difficult to suggest a remedy, but the matter is worthy the serious attention of the Commissioners.

Differences of opinion existing as to the intentions of the Privy Council Rules for the duties of the Resident and Visiting Medical Officers of Asylums, and as there is vagueness and contradiction in the phraseology of the rules referring to those officers respectively it is considered very desirable, and calculated to secure harmony, and be to the advantage of the inmates of asylums if these rules shall be made explicit as to the cure of bodily illness as distinguished from mental disease, and with whom the responsibility of its direction rests.

JOSEPH H. HATCHELL,
Resident Medical Superintendent.

15th July, 1878.

KILLARNEY.

Resolved:—"That this Board considers that any increased asylum accommodation for harmless and incurable lunatics should be provided in connexion with the existing asylums. The Board are of opinion this would insure better care of the patients and at a much less cost than by adopting intermediate asylums.

"That the Board of Governors have been informed that the accommodation afforded by the new building here is ample for the lunatics of all classes for many years."

OSCAR T. WOODS, M.D.,
Resident Medical Superintendent.

July 12th, 1878.

ENNIS.

Resolved:—"That this Board are of opinion that if the amalgamation of unions unanimously recommended by the Guardians of the Ennis union, would be carried out, wholly or partially, one of the workhouses not required for ordinary paupers, might with advantage, be used as an auxiliary for harmless and incurable lunatics, but, that if amalgamation be not adopted, the arrangements of a portion of the existing poorhouses should be specially adapted for their reception."

J. F. VESEY FITZGERALD, Chairman.

20th July, 1878.

MULLINGAR.

We the Governors of the Mullingar District Lunatic Asylum having read and considered the letter from the Poor Law and Lunacy Commissioners of the 15th ult., inviting suggestions with reference to the establishment of auxiliary asylums for the reception of incurables, are of opinion that the establishment of such institutions would relieve the pressure on the district asylums, and thus result in the better care, relief, and treatment of the lunatic poor, and afford greater facilities for the treatment of curative cases.

JOSHUA COOPER.

8th August, 1878.

BALLINASLOE.

"That the resident physician be directed to communicate with the Poor Law and Lunacy Inquiry Commissioners, and inform them that, with every desire to reduce expenditure in the management of the insane poor in Ireland, the Governors cannot see that there would be any saving effected by instituting auxiliary asylums in Workhouses for harmless and incurable lunatics.

"With the fact before them that *all* patients require constant skilled supervision, and that a staff similar to that of this asylum would be required for them wherever located, the Governors are of opinion that it would not be for the interests of either the ratepayers or the patients to make any alteration in the present arrangements for the care of lunatics."

JOHN DARCY, Chairman.

10th Sept., 1878.

WATERFORD.

In reply to the circular of the Poor Law and Lunacy Inquiry Commission respecting the desirableness for establishing auxiliary asylums for harmless lunatics, in connexion with the Workhouses, the Board desires to state that having recently, at considerable expense, enlarged the accommodation of this asylum from 310 to 300, they do not at present see any necessity for the removal of any portion of their patients.

GEORGE J. BRISCOE,
Clerk to the Board of Governors.

14th August, 1878.

LONDONDERRY.

1. That the Board concurs in the views of the Commissioners of Poor Law and Lunacy Inquiry that it is very desirable that a classification of lunatics, maintained on the same principle of chargeability as at present, should take place with a view to the more complete division in separate asylums of the curable from the incurable patients, and to the different treatment required by the former class.

2. That in addition to the above separation the transfer of a portion of harmless incurables to a Workhouse, or part of a Workhouse, properly adapted and situated, and under the supervision of the medical superintendent of the asylum, would, without injury to the patients, obviate the further erection of large buildings at a great cost.

3. That the relative position of the asylum at Londonderry, and the advantages it possesses of easy communication, supervision, and medical assistance, fully entitle it to be the curative asylum of the future district.

4. That when relieved of its present large number of incurable patients, it may, at a moderate cost, be adapted for the treatment of curable patients, and possibly for the reception of a certain number of patients able to pay for themselves.

12th September, 1878.

MONAGHAN.

Moved by W. F. DeVesemes Kane, esq., and adopted—

1. "That considering the yearly increasing numbers of the insane throughout Great Britain, we view the proposed scheme of supplying auxiliary asylums wherever needful with approval and think the advantages would be considerable in not overcrowding the wards of the great curative establishments, nor by incongruous additions spoiling the convenience and proportion of the original buildings, while at the same time better accommodation would be secured for the insane now scattered throughout the workhouses.

2. "Also in regard to economy—we are of opinion that this will also be subserved by auxiliary asylums for incurable and otherwise suitable patients, in the first place by preventing the growth of the medium sized asylums into unwieldy establishments, the cost of which proportionally is shown by statistics to be higher than the former, and in the second place by the employment of a less expensive staff in the auxiliaries.

3. "That we recommend where practicable these auxiliary asylums should be subject to the supervision of the resident medical superintendents of the district asylums.

4. "We recommend that a more liberal scale of pensions be granted to all asylum officers either upon their being incapacitated by injury received in discharge of their duties or after stated term of service, and we suggest that the same scale should be adopted as of the English asylums."

19th September, 1878.

No. 8.—Proposed TRANSFER of HARMLESS PATIENTS from BELFAST ASYLUM to BALLYMENA WORKHOUSE.

LETTER from the UNDER SECRETARY of the LORD LIEUTENANT to the COMMISSIONERS.

14,326.

Dublin Castle, 16th August, 1878.

SIR,—I am directed by the Lord Lieutenant to transmit herewith, for the information of the Poor Law Union Inquiry Commissioners, copy of a letter from the Resident Medical Superintendent of the Belfast District Lunatic Asylum communicating a resolution adopted by the Board of Governors of that Asylum, on the 13th instant, relative to the proposal to transfer harmless patients from the asylum to Ballymena Workhouse; and I am to request that the Commissioners will favour His Grace with any information which they may be able to afford on the subject.

I am also to transmit to be laid before the Commissioners a file of papers containing former correspondence on the subject, which I am to request may be returned when no longer required.

I am, sir, your obedient servant,
(Signed), T. H. BURKE.

H. A. Robinson, Esq.,
Poor Law Union Inquiry Commission,
Four Courts.

Enclosure in Foregoing.

14,326.

Belfast District Hospital for the Insane,
14th August, 1878.

SIR,—I am directed by the Board of Governors of this Asylum, to submit for your information the subjoined resolution adopted unanimously at their meeting held 12th instant, relative to the transfer of the harmless and incurable insane inmates to the Ballymena Workhouse.

It was proposed by Sir Charles Lanyon, seconded by John Young, Esq., D.L., and unanimously adopted—

"That after hearing the Poor Law Inquiry Commissioners on "the subject of transferring a particular class of patients from this "asylum to Ballymena Workhouse in accordance with the arrange-"ments formerly discussed, and having ascertained from the Com-"missioners that they entertained a favourable opinion in reference "thereto.

"Resolved,—That this board (which has never changed its "opinion on the subject), again take such steps as may be necessary "to re-open negotiations for the carrying out of the proposed "arrangement.

"The former Committee to be re-appointed for this purpose con-"sisting of,

"Sir Thomas M'Clure,	"Lord Bishop of Down and "Connor and Dromore,
"David Taylor, Esq.,	"M. R. Dalway, Esq., M.P.
"H. H. M'Neile, Esq.,	"J. B. Houston, Esq.,
"Sir Charles Lanyon, Esq.,	"A. J. Macrory,
"John Young, Esq.,	"Viscount Templetown,
"James Cuming, Esq., M.D.,	

"A copy of this resolution to be forwarded to the Chief Secretary."

I am, &c.,
(Signed), ALEX. STEWART MERRICK, M.D.,
Resident Medical Superintendent.

The Right Honorable J. Lowther,
The Chief Secretary for Ireland,
Office, Dublin Castle.

APPENDIX C.
Lunacy

LETTER from the COMMISSIONERS to the UNDER SECRETARY of the LORD LIEUTENANT.

Four Courts, Dublin,
11th September, 1878.

SIR,—The Poor Law Inquiry Commissioners return herewith the file of papers relating to the proposed transfer of a certain number of harmless lunatics from the Belfast District Lunatic Asylum to the Ballymena Workhouse, and in accordance with the instructions conveyed in your letter of the 16th ultimo, that they should favour His Grace the Lord Lieutenant with any information they may be able to afford on the subject. Having visited the locality and carefully considered the correspondence they desire to observe with reference to the proposal that is referred to that:-

Upon the passing of the 38 & 39 Vic. c. 67, the attention of the Governors of the Belfast District Asylum was directed by Sir Thomas M'Clure, one of the governors to the 9th section of that Act, as "affording means of obviating the overcrowding of the "institution by transferring quiet and harmless cases "to some union workhouse that can afford them "accommodation at a rate of maintenance to be "mutually agreed upon." A committee of the governors of the asylum in conjunction with a committee of the Guardians of the Ballymena Union, agreed, after several conferences and much negotiation, that a certain number of harmless lunatics should be sent from the asylum to the workhouse to be there maintained upon conditions assented to by both boards, and approved of by the inspectors of lunacy.

The circumstances under which this agreement was concluded and was ultimately abandoned appear, from the file of papers to have been:—

As soon as the Governors of the Belfast Asylum and the Guardians of the Ballymena Union determined after careful consideration that it would be desirable to remove a certain number of harmless lunatics from the asylum to the workhouse, they communicated their views to the Local Government Board (October 12th, 1876), and were informed in reply (October 18th, 1876), that "the proposal as described would be a very "serious interference with the accommodation and "general arrangements of the workhouse, and one in "which as it is now presented to them, the board are "not prepared to acquiesce." The subject was again very fully reconsidered by the joint committee of governors and guardians and a carefully considered scheme and a better appropriation of accommodation agreed upon, and communicated to the Local Government Board (November 2nd, 1876). In reply the guardians were informed (November 8th, 1876), that "the board had instructed their inspector to visit the "workhouse and report to them upon the subject." Accordingly the inspector, Dr Roughan, did visit the workhouse (November 16th, 1876), and informed the guardians that he would be unable to report to the Local Government Board in compliance with their instructions "without a report from some competent "architect as to the best mode of making the pre-"mises available." A joint committee of governors and guardians again met at the workhouse, and with their architect, Mr. Lanyon, of Belfast, discussed the whole subject. The guardians communicated to the Local Government Board (December 7th, 1876), "the "estimate of Mr. Lanyon for the alterations required "to accommodate the lunatics to be transferred from "the Asylum, amounting to £452 11s." In reply the Local Government Board "suggest to the guardians "the propriety of requesting Mr. Lanyon to furnish "a detailed statement of the alterations which he "considers should be made for the accommodation of "lunatics referred to." Accordingly Mr Lanyon prepared a plan a tracing of which is annexed to this letter.

In the meantime the workhouse was visited by Dr. Roughan who met the guardians, and subsequently a joint committee of governors and guardians at the workhouse, on November 22nd. "After careful going "over the premises it was agreed on by all, that the "most suitable portion of the workhouse that could be "allocated for the lunatics without interfering with "the classification or discipline would be the two "school buildings (additional wings), used at present "as schoolrooms and dormitories for boys and girls, "which it was considered on certain alterations being "made would provide accommodation for fifty male "lunatics on one side, and fifty female lunatics on the "other side." Dr Roughan again visited the workhouse on the 29th November, 1876, "and after giving the matter the fullest consideration" (Dr. Roughan writes) :—"I have come to the conclusion that if those alterations are properly carried out, and a sufficient number of attendants provided, ample accommodation can be afforded for at least one hundred harmless lunatics without interfering with the well-being of the other inmates." Although the opinion of an official so experienced and in all respects so competent to give an opinion on such a subject needs no confirmation, we may state that after examining the workhouse and the plan of Mr Lanyon, we fully coincide with Dr Roughan.

Thus far it appears that the proposal for the removal of a certain number of harmless lunatics from the Belfast Asylum to the Workhouse of the Ballymena Union, was urgently supported by the governors and the guardians, while the apprehension expressed by the Local Government Board that "it would be a serious interference with the accommodation and general arrangements of the workhouse," is met by the deliberate opinion of the inspector that no such inconvenience need be apprehended.

The proposal was further recommended by the general approval given to it by the Inspectors of Lunacy. Writing on the 22nd of March, 1877, the Inspectors say—"If there be no legal objection to the payment of 1s. per week per head for each lunatic removed to and resident in the poorhouse at Ballymena to meet the expenses incidental to structural alterations therein. The Inspectors see no reasonable ground for objecting to the transference of certain suitable cases to the union. Thus, the Inspectors continue, "the overcrowding of the asylum would be materially obviated at present." Elsewhere the Inspectors observe:—"If the difficulty of hiring paid servants by the guardians could be got over the principle commends itself." "The guardians boarding and lodging transferred lunatics meeting all incidental expenses at a fixed sum." But as there is no "legal difficulty" about the payment of a fixed sum per head per week, to re-imburse the guardians for outlay on structural alterations, nor to the hiring of paid servants, nor indeed to any other part of the proposed arrangement, it may be assumed that it will still receive the approval of the Inspectors. Indeed upon all the details of the arrangements it appears from the correspondence that the Inspectors received full and minute information in reply to queries addressed to the Medical Superintendent by Dr. Nugent. As these replies were considered to be satisfactory, and the report of the Inspector of the Local Government Board was favourable to the proposal. The governors and guardians were taken by surprise at receiving from the Local Government Board a letter conveying their refusal, for reasons stated, to sanction the arrangement that had already almost reached completion.

The Governors of the Asylum and the Guardians of the Ballymena Union sought an interview by deputation with the Local Government Board, but failed to obtain one. They subsequently resolved to lay the facts of the case before the late Chief Secretary for Ireland, who promised that it should be inquired into, and the file of

The Commissioners find in the first place that the local authorities still desire to carry into effect the arrangement as agreed upon between them. It is true that in a minute of the 24th of October, 1877, Dr. Nugent states, in reply to a question of the Assistant Under Secretary, "An influential and large section of the governors seem unfavourable to the proposition.

On the one hand they consider that lunatics would be better treated in an asylum, and on the other that no saving would be effected in poorhouses." A statement to the same effect is published in the last Annual Report of the Inspectors, accompanied by the suggestion that the overcrowding of the Belfast Asylum should be met by the erection of another asylum for the county of Antrim. At their last meeting, which was numerously attended, the governors reappointed the committee of last year for the purpose of "taking such steps as may be necessary to re-open negotiations for carrying out the proposed arrangements." Upon the expediency of doing so, the Board of Governors state "it has never changed its opinion." This resolution was passed unanimously.

Assuming then that the Board of Governors and the Board of Guardians are still anxious to carry out the proposed arrangements at a cost of less than £500, and that the alternative is the erection, as suggested by the Inspectors of Lunacy, of a new asylum, at a cost of certainly not less than £50,000, the Commissioners venture to suggest some grounds upon which they think the Local Government Board may be moved to reconsider their refusal to sanction the proposal to appropriate a portion of the Ballymena Workhouse for the reception of a certain number of lunatics, to be transferred from the District Asylum at Belfast.

They do not think that the objection originally taken by the Local Government Board, in their letter to the guardians, that the proposal, if carried into effect, would be a serious interference with the accommodation and general arrangements of the workhouse can be sustained. Nor, indeed, does it appear to be insisted upon in the letter of April 11, subsequently addressed to the Under Secretary. The objections of the Local Government Board to the proposal are—

1st. That to provide for the reception and maintenance of harmless lunatics in the way proposed would "go far outside the provisions of the Act of Parliament, which apply only to individual cases, and seem to contemplate the dispersion of harmless lunatics among the workhouses surrounding the District Asylum."

The object of the 9th section of the Act of Parliament, and the intentions of its framer, was undoubtedly to obviate the overcrowding of, and the necessity of frequently adding to asylums, by facilitating the transfer, under certain conditions, of quiet and harmless cases to workhouses. To restrict the application of the clause to "the dispersion of individual cases among the workhouses surrounding the District Asylum" would be not simply to defeat the object of the Act but to aggravate one of the most serious evils connected with the administration of workhouses in Ireland. It would be useless, if not unreasonable, to expect Boards of Guardians to incur the necessary expense in order to make, for individual cases dispersed amongst the workhouses, such provision for proper care and supervision as the Local Government Board and the Inspectors of Lunacy would, no doubt, and very properly insist upon. And so the Act would remain as it has heretofore remained practically inoperative. It is only when a considerable number of the class of harmless lunatics are collected in one workhouse, and guardians are thus compelled to provide for their care and supervision, that their condition can be described as reasonably satisfactory. As it is in those cases in which individuals are dispersed that their condition is found to be most deplorable.

The difficulty that might arise from divided responsibility, which appears to be apprehended by the Local Government Board, might be obviated in the present case by leaving to the Ballymena Guardians the sole control and management of the establishment, subject, of course, to prescribed regulations and the periodical inspection of the Local Government Board and the Inspectors of Lunacy. Although the Local Government Board "do not know what aptitude, either the Board of Guardians, or their Medical Officer, or their Workhouse Master, or other officers may be found to possess for the successful management of wards containing 150 lunatics." Yet it may be fairly assumed that they would not be found less capable than the officers in other workhouses—as Dublin, Cork, Belfast—where although the arrangements are far less perfect than those proposed at Ballymena, the management satisfies even the requirements of the Inspectors of Lunacy. Indeed the last report upon the lunacy wards of the Ballymena Workhouse gives some earnest of the capabilities of guardians and officers. In 1875 Dr. Nugent writes—"I have inspected the lunatic wards of the Ballymena Union, in which there are, between both sexes, twenty-two inmates—idiots, epileptic, and demented. I examined each, and consider they are very humanely and carefully attended to, and daily visited by the physician. The rooms which they occupy are clean, orderly, and well ventilated, and the dietary on which they are placed, nutritious and ample." Still later in 1877 Dr. Nugent reports—"I find, as on my last visit, the insane in this poorhouse, numbering thirty, very humanely looked after in every respect. The house generally which I went through is maintained in a highly creditable manner." Without attaching too much weight to these reports as evidence of capability to manage larger institutions of the same character, the Commissioners think they may be accepted as affording reasonable grounds for confidence that, with greatly improved structural arrangements, and sufficient staff of attendants, the proposed auxiliary asylum would be found to serve the purpose for which it is designed. To say that the establishment of such wards in the Ballymena Workhouse "would go far outside the provisions of the Act of Parliament" seems to imply that an Act passed for a specific purpose must not be applied in the only way in which it is possible to give effect to it, and that the Governors of the Belfast Asylum must continue to submit to the overcrowding of their institution, or impose a very large and unnecessary burthen upon the ratepayers, although the Act was intended to obviate both difficulties, and, if carried into effect, as proposed, would do so.

By order of the Commissioners,

H. A. Robinson, Secretary.

The Under Secretary, Dublin Castle.

Appendix C — Lunacy.

No. 9.—Return of the Dates each Workhouse in Ireland was Visited by the Inspectors of Lunatics during the years ending 31st December, 1875, 1876, and 1877, showing the number of insane in the Workhouse at the period.

Unions	Year 1877		Year 1876.		Year 1875.	
	No. of Insane in Workhouse	Date of Visit	No. of Insane in Workhouse	Date of Visit	No. of Insane in Workhouse.	Date of Visit.
PROVINCE OF ULSTER.						
Co. Antrim.						
Antrim,	20	—	10	—	20	—
Ballycastle,	17	—	17	—	17	—
Ballymena,	35	18 June,	30	—	28	12 Nov.
Ballymoney,	5	—	6	—	6	—
Belfast,	210	19 June,	213	4 Dec.,	187	17 April, 12 Nov.
Larne,	30	—	30	—	32	—
Lisburn,	31	24 Nov.,	28	—	29	8 May, 29 Nov.
Co. Armagh.						
Armagh,	35	16 April,	29	7 Sept., 11 Nov.,	30	1 Jan., 28 June, 12 Oct.
Lurgan,	24	16 April,	25	14 Dec.,	26	2 Jan., 6 Sept.
Co. Cavan.						
Bailieborough,	12	—	11	—	7	—
Bawnboy,	8	—	8	—	9	—
Cavan,	21	—	19	—	23	—
Cootehill,	9	17 May,	7	—	6	—
Co. Donegal.						
Ballyshannon,	3	5 Sept.,	—	—	1	—
Donegal,	7	—	9	—	11	—
Dunfanaghy,	4	—	3	—	5	—
Glenties,	21	—	11	—	10	—
Inishowen,	34	—	39	—	33	—
Letterkenny,	2	29 May, 16 Nov.,	4	20 Sept.,	3	10 Dec.
Milford,	9	—	13	—	12	—
Stranorlar,	4	29 May, 15 Nov.,	6	—	2	—
Co. Down.						
Banbridge,	32	—	31	—	32	29 Nov.
Downpatrick,	25	25 June,	27	21 Dec.,	26	1 March.
Kilkeel,	15	—	11	—	12	—
Newry,	35	—	31	29 April, 11 Nov.	32	25 Nov.
Newtownards,	41	—	38	19 May,	46	—
Co. Fermanagh.						
Enniskillen,	17	4 Sept.,	14	—	15	—
Irvinestown,	2	—	2	—	1	—
Lisnaskea,	4	18 May,	—	—	—	—
Co. Londonderry.						
Coleraine,	16	—	19	—	16	11 Nov.
Limavady,	23	28 June,	12	—	13	—
Londonderry,	32	27 June, 29 Aug.	31	18 May, 19 Sept., 23 Nov.	33	8 June.
Magherafelt,	14	—	12	—	10	
Co. Monaghan.						
Carrickmacross,	9	—	7	—	7	18 Feb.
Castleblayney,	18	30 May,	14	14 May,	12	14 June
Clones,	3	21 Nov.,	2	12 Dec.,	—	14 June.
Monaghan,	20	18 May, 22 Nov.,	17	22 Sept.,	16	19 Nov.
Co. Tyrone.						
Castlederg,	2	—	—	—	—	—
Clogher,	12		8	22 Sept.,	9	—
Cookstown,	9	—	7	—	11	—
Dungannon,	15	31 May,	9	23 Nov.,	15	—
Gortin,	5	—	5	25 Nov.,	6	—
Omagh,	10	27 May, 28 Aug.,	9	15 Sept., 26 Nov.	10	8 Dec.
Strabane,	11	30 May, 17 Nov.,	9	21 May, 25 Nov.	10	10 Dec.

RETURN of the DATES each WORKHOUSE was VISITED by the INSPECTORS of LUNATICS during the years ending 31st December, 1875, 1876, and 1877, showing the number of Insane in the Workhouse at the period—*continued.*

UNIONS	Year 1877		Year 1876.		Year 1875	
	No. of Insane in Workhouse	Date of Visit	No. of Insane in Workhouse	Date of Visit	No. of Insane in Workhouse	Date of Visit
PROVINCE OF MUNSTER						
Co. CLARE.						
Ballyvaghan,	9	—	6	—	7	—
Corrofin,	9	—	6	—	8	—
Ennis,	45	22 June,	39	—	42	—
Ennistymon,	34	—	31	—	39	—
Killadysert,	17	—	14	—	18	—
Kilrush,	49	—	40	30 June,	44	—
Scariff,	11	—	10	—	9	—
Tulla,	25	—	24	—	18	—
Co. CORK.						
Bandon,	12	—	16	—	13	—
Bantry,	6	—	4	—	4	—
Castletown,	7	—	6	—	4	—
Clonakilty,	7	—	6	—	10	—
Cork,	131	12 June, 27 July,	142	14 June,	120	13 Jan.
Dunmanway,	1	—	1	—	1	—
Fermoy,	24	—	33	—	21	—
Kanturk,	32	—	31	—	33	—
Kinsale,	7	—	9	—	11	—
Macroom,	43	—	22	—	18	—
Mallow,	25	15 June,	24	—	18	14 Mar., 25 May, 26 Sept., 8 Nov.
Midleton,	31	—	22	—	20	—
Millstreet,	9	10 June,	10	—	7	24 May.
Mitchelstown,	6	—	6	—	6	—
Skibbereen,	7	—	7	—	6	—
Skull,	—	—	3	—	2	—
Youghal,	14	—	19	—	18	—
Co. KERRY.						
Cahersiveen,	3	—	3	—	3	—
Dingle,	3	—	3	—	3	—
Kenmare,	2	11 June,	1	—	1	—
Killarney,	15	22 Aug.,	9	1 April,	7	12 March
Listowel,	5	—	2	—	2	—
Tralee,	7	—	6	—	11	21 May.
Co. LIMERICK.						
Croom,	23	23 June.	26	7 June,	15	11 July.
Glin,	6	—	7	7 June,	4	22 June.
Kilmallock,	41	—	40	—	36	11 March
Limerick,	81	20 June, 29 Sept.	93	—	93	—
Newcastle,	14	—	10	—	11	21 June
Rathkeale,	11	—	7	5 June,	10	26 May.
Co. TIPPERARY.						
Borrisokane,	10	3 May,	5	—	6	—
Carrick-on-Suir,	24	17 Mar., 24 Aug.	30	—	29	20 May.
Cashel,	17	24 Aug.,	19	—	22	—
Clogheen,	11	—	13	—	12	—
Clonmel,	21	—	21	—	25	18 May.
Nenagh,	7	—	12	—	12	—
Roscrea,	13	4 May,	13	—	14	—
Thurles,	10	—	1	4 Aug.,	1	—
Tipperary,	34	—	31	13 June, 6 Aug.,	31	15 March, 20 May, 28 Aug.
Co. WATERFORD.						
Dungarvan,	20	—	18	—	21	—
Kilmacthomas,	12	—	9	—	12	—
Lismore,	7	—	9	—	8	—
Waterford,	92	27 June, 19 July,	61	14 July,	61	26 April

APPENDIX C. Lunacy

RETURN of the DATES each WORKHOUSE was VISITED by the INSPECTORS of LUNATICS during the years ending 31st December, 1875, 1876, and 1877, showing the number of Insane in the Workhouse at the period.—*continued.*

UNIONS	Year 1877		Year 1876.		Year 1875.	
	No. of Insane in Workhouse	Date of Visit	No. of Insane in Workhouse	Date of Visit.	No. of Insane in Workhouse.	Date of Visit
PROVINCE OF LEINSTER.						
Co. CARLOW.						
Carlow,	32	31 Aug.,	34	—	31	20 Jan.
Co. DUBLIN.						
Balrothery,	16	—	12	22 Aug., 26 Oct.,	13	—
Dublin, North,	113	—	87	—	75	—
Dublin, South,	152	—	155	—	200	—
Rathdown,	78	12 July,	97	1 Oct., 22 Aug.,	78	7 Jan., 10 April.
Co. KILDARE						
Athy,	10	—	11	5 Feb.,	13	6 April.
Celbridge,	8	—	9	29 Jan.,	10	13 Feb.
Naas,	32	15 May,	30	29 Jan., 6 Nov.,	26	13 Feb.
Co. KILKENNY.						
Callan,	15	5 Aug.,	13	—	10	25 April.
Castlecomer,	4	—	4	—	5	—
Kilkenny,	39	28 June,	43	—	40	6 March, 23 July.
Thomastown,	13	25 Feb., 27 Sept.,	11	—	14	—
Urlingford,	8	—	8	—	8	—
KING'S CO.						
Edenderry,	4	—	3	—	5	—
Parsonstown,	21	1 May,	19	—	25	—
Tullamore,	37	—	35	—	28	—
Co. LONGFORD.						
Ballymahon,	4	—	6	—	6	—
Granard,	9	—	15	—	15	—
Longford,	15	12 Nov.,	12	—	14	1 April.
Co. LOUTH.						
Ardee,	37	—	35	—	31	4 June.
Drogheda,	44	20 May,	44	14 April, 30 Sept. 28 Oct.,	50	30 March, 4 June. 26 Nov.
Dundalk,	34	17 May, 21 Nov.,	29	15 April, 14 Dec.	31	19 Feb., 6th Aug.
Co. MEATH.						
Dunshaughlin,	12	—	13	16 Nov.,	13	—
Kells,	26	—	24	22 Nov.,	20	23 Feb.
Navan,	20	—	28	14 April, 17 Nov.	24	—
Oldcastle,	13	—	13	22 Nov.,	14	22 Feb.
Trim,	17	—	20	16 Nov.,	20	—
QUEEN'S CO.						
Abbeyleix,	20	—	23	12 Aug.,	19	—
Donaghmore,	2	—	2	—	2	—
Mountmellick,	28	—	22	—	23	—
Co. WESTMEATH.						
Athlone,	16	26 Jan., 21 Aug.,	16	31 Jan.,	16	—
Delvin,	15	7 Oct.,	12	—	14	—
Mullingar,	22	9 May,	25	8 Nov.,	29	15 May, 7 Nov.
Co. WEXFORD.						
Enniscorthy,	28	24 May,	31	25 Sept.,	27	15 April.
Gorey,	20	—	16	29 Feb., 18 Nov.,	11	10 April.
New Ross,	36	—	37	9 May,	37	—
Wexford,	32	—	24	—	22	—
Co. WICKLOW.						
Baltinglass,	13	—	11	—	8	—
Rathdrum,	27	—	32	—	31	—
Shillelagh,	13	—	10	—	14	—

RETURN of the DATES each WORKHOUSE was visited by the INSPECTORS of LUNATICS during the years ending 31st December, 1875, 1876, and 1877, showing the number of Insane in the Workhouse at the period.—*continued.*

UNIONS	Year 1877.		Year 1876.		Year 1875.	
	No. of Insane in Workhouse	Date of Visit	No. of Insane in Workhouse	Date of Visit.	No. of Insane in Workhouse	Date of Visit.
PROVINCE OF CONNAUGHT.						
Co. GALWAY.						
Ballinasloe, . .	14	3 Sept., . .	16	—	13	—
Clifden, . .	7	—	8	—	4	—
Galway, . .	13	1 Feb., . .	12	10 July, . .	13	—
Glennamaddy, .	17	—	17	—	28	18 March.
Gort, . . .	3	—	3	—	3	—
Loughrea, . .	4	—	6	—	5	—
Mount Bellew, .	9	—	9	—	8	—
Oughterard, . .	9	—	8	—	6	—
Portumna, . .	—	2 May, . .	—	—	—	—
Tuam, . . .	15	—	19	—	19	—
Co. LEITRIM.						
Carrick-on-Shannon	10	—	5	—	5	30 March.
Manorhamilton, .	7	—	7	—	22	—
Mohill, . .	10	—	8	—	9	—
Co. MAYO.						
Ballina, . .	10	—	13	30 July, . .	13	—
Ballinrobe, . .	2	—	1	31 July, . .	1	—
Belmullet, . .	7	—	10	—	10	—
Castlebar, . .	13	5 Nov., . .	11	—	13	27 Dec.
Claremorris, .	12	—	13	—	16	—
Killala, . .	2	—	3	30 July, . .	3	—
Newport, . .	2	24 Aug., . .	3	—	4	—
Swineford, . .	13	—	25	—	26	—
Westport, . .	7	22 Aug., . .	5	19 July, . .	4	28 Aug.
Co. ROSCOMMON.						
Boyle, . . .	16	24 Mar., 14 June,	16	—	15	30 March.
Castlerea, . .	17	25 March, . .	18	—	24	19 March.
Roscommon, . .	27	—	26	—	34	17 March.
Strokestown, .	20	—	17	—	15	—
Co. SLIGO.						
Dromore West, .	8	—	8	—	7	—
Sligo, . . .	32	6 Sept., . .	35	16 Dec., 28 July,	34	—
Tobercurry, . .	13	—	14	—	15	—

No. 10.—ADAPTATION of Portions of UNION WORKHOUSES for the RECEPTION of a HARMLESS, QUIET, and INCURABLE CLASS of LUNATICS

ARCHITECT'S REPORT.

SIR, Dublin, September 21, 1878.

I have the honour to forward you for the Commissioners of the Poor Law Union Inquiry, a report on several buildings that I have inspected at the Union Workhouses, Ireland, agreeably to their request, with a view to consider the capabilities and the probable estimate of the capacity and cost of conversion, in case of parts of them being utilised for the reception of a harmless class of pauper lunatics.

I may mention that the Unions were originally 133 in number, the majority of the buildings of which were much on the same plan, and were completed in three or four years after their commencement in 1839-40; and that on the report and recommendation of the Boundary Commissioners, 30 more Unions were formed, making a total of 163 Workhouse Buildings. The accommodation provided in these 163 buildings, assuming them to be occupied to their fullest extent at time of extreme pressure, was for 11,500.

In the famine years, however, the additions made to the original buildings by permanent and temporary structures, such as hospitals or auxiliary buildings, including some old premises temporarily taken, the bed accommodation was increased to as many as 230,941, in December, 1853.

The reports of the architect in the annual reports of the Poor Law Commissioners explain the character of of the several Poorhouse Buildings, and the kind of additions made thereto.

The buildings inspected and proposed to be made available are, chiefly what were built in the famine years, as additions to the original Poorhouses, and include two classes, namely, those which were erected of a permanent kind as additions to the original buildings, chiefly for children or hospitals, and those which were a less costly kind of building, erected at the time as temporary or auxiliary buildings.

I may mention that the majority of the 133 buildings as originally planned, afforded great facility for their being added to, and additions have been made to almost all of them.

The buildings inspected and of which the following particulars are given, are—

1. Carrickmacross.
2. Castletown Delvin.
3. Lisburn.
4. Monaghan.
5. Newcastle.
6. Dingle.
7. Oughterard.
8. Armagh.

Appendix C.

the first, Carrickmacross, being a building, erected in the front part of what is one of the original 133 Poorhouses, on the side of the entrance building. Many of the original Unions have this kind of addition, in some cases for boys, and in some cases for girls only, and in others wing buildings for both boys and girls

Castletown Delvin is a type of one of the last 30 Unions erected on the report of the Boundary Commissioners as above mentioned. It is proposed to appropriate part of this building.

Lisburn Union is one in which the addition is rather more exceptionable than others.

Monaghan Union represents one of the buildings erected as a Fever Hospital, and a detached building alongside one of the yards of the Poorhouse, but detached like Lisburn, though in a different position, and on a different plan.

The buildings at Newcastle, Dingle, and Oughterard, represent auxiliary buildings in connexion with the other buildings belonging to the 30 Unions last formed, and were built near the same time as the permanent Poorhouse portion, these buildings are generally of a less substantial character than the others above mentioned, and were erected at very little cost per head, it is to me a surprise that they are so good at this time, the walls and roofs of most of these buildings appear in a very fair condition, and the advantage they possess over the more permanent class of structures is that they have most of them spacious yards or areas about them.

The Armagh Poorhouse represents one of the original buildings, of which it is proposed to appropriate one of the wings

Annexed is a more particular report on each of the buildings above named, with an estimate of probable cost to accompany the plans made of each. I think it right, however, to remark that I may not have sufficiently estimated for the cost of contingencies, as it is very difficult to satisfy the requirements of many of the officials who have the buildings of the kind in charge. The walls of the Poorhouse buildings were not plastered, nor were the rooms ceiled; the cost of plastering if decided on is shown by the estimates. It is also proposed to use earth closets, according to which the estimates are framed.

In describing the cubical capacity of the buildings, I should mention that the allowance by the Commissioners of Control for the new Asylum buildings erected in recent years has been 600 feet cube per dormitory space and 300 feet for day room, which, with a room 20 feet wide and 12 feet high (the usual height), gives a superficial area of 25 feet to each person for day room, and in the dormitories a bed wall space of 5 feet, which is equal to 600 cubic feet, or 900 feet cube for each person.

In the auxiliary buildings the height is generally less, and therefore the bed space—that is, the space to be allowed for each bed—will determine the amount of accommodation; to give the same cubical contents as in the new Asylum buildings it would be necessary to give more than 5 feet bed space. If this cubical content is considered more than is really necessary for the class of inmates intended to be provided for, the cubical capacity to be determined on will give the amount of accommodation, a division of the gross cubical capacity by the figures determined on will give the space required for the day and bed rooms for each inmate, the bed space requiring to be about double the day room space. The lower the ceiling the greater of course the required area for both day and bed rooms.

This data will enable the Commissioners to determine, according to their judgment, the accommodation to be obtained.

As regards cost, I may mention that the original Poorhouses cost from £8 to £15 per head, according to their size, the new wing buildings for children about £5 per head, and the auxiliary and temporary buildings a less sum.

The Lunatic Asylums in Ireland have been built at three separate periods. The first erected buildings cost upwards of £200 per head, and the later ones have varied from about £130 to £170 per head.

I may perhaps be excused by remarking that there never were any buildings erected at so low a cost as the Irish Workhouses. And in the first few years of their erection—owing to political feeling and to hostility against the Poor Law from many persons—it was a most thankless duty, their cost and construction being equally assailed.

I may mention a hundred of the large buildings were in progress at one time, and 130 built within a period of about three years; most of them have now been built for about thirty to forty-five years, show by their solidity and the state of the walls and roofs how unjust was the way in which those intrusted with the duty of building them were treated.

At the time of terminating my duties in connexion with the Poor Law, in 1855, I was not aware of a wall of any main building being one inch out of perpendicular; but such was the feeling of hostility during Sir Robert Peel's Government, that but for the progress made with buildings, it was thought the Law would have been abrogated. What the famine years would have been without them it would now be difficult to conjecture, and I cannot avoid commenting on the fact that after such a lapse of years, even the inexpensive auxiliary buildings are considered sufficient to be converted to serve as a substitute for costly lunatic asylum buildings

I am,
Yours obediently,
Geo. Wilkinson.

H. Robinson, esq.

Enclosure in Foregoing.

Carrickmacross Poorhouse

Plate I. and II.

The plan given represents the kind of building erected as permanent additions to many of the original Poorhouses and the alterations proposed to adopt them to Asylum purposes

These buildings are good substantial structures, but they require the walls to be plastered and rooms to be ceiled, and earth closets, &c.

The stairs are of wood.

Capacity, 68,000 cubic feet in wards, two single rooms.

Estimated cost is as follows:—

	£	s.	d.
Levelling gangway floors,	26	0	0
Wall plaster,	70	0	0
Ceiling,	79	0	0
Brick walls,	11	0	0
Partitions to lavatory and single rooms and four attendants rooms,	30	0	0
Lavatory—water supply and baths,	100	0	0
Ceiling joists to upper floor of third storey building and divisions of perforated boarding to trusses of roof,	30	0	0
Division yard wall,	48	0	0
Contingencies,	150	0	0
	£544	0	0

Query.—Outer boundary wall, according to extent, at 8s. per lineal foot.

Castletown Delvin Poorhouse.

Plate III. and IV.

Being one of the thirty new buildings erected on the recommendation of the Boundary Commissioners, and similar in plan to many of the new buildings.

The drawing shows the portion it has been proposed to appropriate to Asylum purposes, being part of one of the front ranges used for children, and male probationary wards.

It will be necessary to provide for the latter by a new structure, a plan of which is made on the suggestion of the Commissioners, being similar to what is now used in some of the English Poorhouses.

The part proposed to be used is part of the original

building, and is a sound, wall built structure, but the walls and rooms are not plastered or ceiled.

The stairs are of wood.

The gangway passages will require boarding, ground floors are part wood, flag, and bricks.

Water will have to be supplied from the Poorhouse by pump.

Cubical capacity is 39,000 feet.

Estimated outlay.—

	£	s.	d.
Wall plastering,	43	0	0
Ceilings,	46	0	0
Ceiling joists,	20	0	0
Divisions in trusses,	12	0	0
Gangways levelled,	14	0	0
Deal floor and joists to ground floor,	80	0	0
For work to attendants rooms and earth closets, say	40	0	0
Contingencies,	150	0	0
Wall in yard,	48	0	0
Water supply—boiler, &c., bath and lavatory,	100	0	0
Enclosure wall to front if carried out 500 feet lineal, as shown on plan,	200	0	0
Probationary building, 19,000 feet cube at 4d.	317	0	0
For two single rooms, say	20	0	0
	£1,099	0	0

LISBURN UNION.

Plate V.

Detached buildings, three stories in height, added to the original Poorhouse buildings in the position shown by the plan, including an adjoining one-storey building.

This is a substantial and spacious building, similar in construction to the original building. The staircase is of wood. It is, however, in its interior a skeleton kind of building, the object of its erection being to obtain the greatest amount of space for beds. It will require considerable outlay in sub-divisions, plastering of walls and ceilings, in making gangway floors level. The ground-floor is tiled, and has iron columns supporting the first-floor; those on upper floor being of wood, supporting the floor and centre beam of the double gabled roof.

The windows of ground floor (which is 13 ft. 6 in. high), are high up in the walls.

Cubical Capacity 51,000 feet.

The estimated cost is as follows:—

	£	s.	d.
Wall plastering,	78	0	0
Ceilings,	37	6	0
Ceiling joists,	18	0	0
Brick walls (ground-floor),	66	0	0
Partitions to upper rooms,	23	0	0
New doors,	44	0	0
Windows,	80	0	0
Fire places,	23	0	0
Shed in yard,	45	0	0
Gangways levelled,	15	0	0
Deal floors and joists to single rooms,	64	0	0
Water lavatories, &c.,	120	0	0
Yard walls (inner),	43	0	0
Contingencies,	150	0	0
	£768	6	0

Five single rooms.

MONAGHAN UNION.

Plate VI., VII., and VIII.

Fever hospital and adjoining three story building added to the original poorhouse.

The fever hospital is in excellent condition, and requires very little alteration.

The additional building which, with the fever hospital and yards are shown by plans, is a substantial building, requiring plastering to the walls and ceilings, and the gangway floors made level, and a new stone stair-case. The windows, now looking into the poorhouse yard, require removing to the outer wall.

The ground floors are part tiles and part brick floors.

Water is obtained in fever hospital by a pump in one of the yards, the additional building will have to be provided with a cistern and lead pipes from the pump.

No single rooms provided.

There are some good enclosure walls, but some additions will be required to them.

ESTIMATED COST—AUXILIARY BUILDING.

	£	s.	d.
Wall plastering,	50	0	0
Ceilings,	44	0	0
Ceiling joists to roof,	18	0	0
New ground floor,	64	0	0
Levelling gangways,	12	0	0
Altering windows,	74	0	0
New outer shed and privy,	40	0	0
New stone stair-case, and rear addition to do.,	65	0	0
Water supply,	150	0	0
New doors and windows to attendants rooms, and rear building back of stairs and partitions,	55	0	0

ALTERATIONS TO FEVER HOSPITAL.

	£	s.	d.
Stairs, boiler for hot water, &c.,	120	0	0
Contingencies,	200	0	0
Say 220 feet of enclosures and gateway,	148	0	0
	£1,048	0	0

Capacity of wards of fever hospital 30,000 cubic feet, and diningroom.

In the poorhouse building 12,000 cubic feet. No single rooms.

NEWCASTLE POORHOUSE.

Plate IX. and X.

The extensive auxiliary buildings added in the famine years to the rear portion of the original poorhouse are very much the same as the general plan followed for such structures at the time.

A plan shows the arrangement and extent; one half of the buildings was built two stories high, and one half, including the dining hall, is one story high; the latter is not required for use at the present time, and the hall is used as a coal store for an annual supply put in by yearly contract.

The buildings are substantial, and the floors appear good, except the ground floor of the unoccupied two story building, the greater part of which is an earthen floor, and such is the dining hall. The stairs are all of wood, those in the upper two story building would be unsuited for asylum patients, and a new stone staircase would be desirable.

Spouting would be required to greater part of the roofs, the windows of ground floor rooms are all one side only; many of the windows of the rear two story building and dining hall are gone, and the openings boarded up. No stone sills to any of the windows.

No water supply, it would have to be pumped from poorhouse, at present a pipe with two taps is brought to one near corner of the buildings from poorhouse.

Cubical capacity, 100,000 feet.

ESTIMATED COST.

	£	s.	d.
New floor and joists to front, range ground floor and levelling gangways in floors of rear building,	148	0	0
Tiling to dining-hall (if used as such),	75	0	0
Wall plastering,	145	0	0
Ceilings, including ceiling joists to roof of upper floors, and perforated boarding between principals,	213	0	0
Eave spouting,	53	0	0
Brick division walls,	40	0	0
46 new windows,	138	0	0
25 " doors,	56	0	0
1 flight of stone stairs,	20	0	0
Grates,	10	0	0
Lavatories, bath water supply, &c.,	200	0	0
Contingencies,	200	0	0
	£1,298	0	0

No. 6—Single rooms.

Large dining-hall.

AUXILIARY SHED BUILDINGS AT THE DINGLE POORHOUSE.

Plate XI.

These buildings consists of four ranges of one height buildings, as shown by plan, a portion of one of the

APPENDIX C.

Lunacy.

central ranges it is proposed to remove to improve the space.

Water supply will have to be obtained from the poorhouse, but it is thought practicable at a moderate cost, to get water from a spring in high ground in fields at rear of poorhouse, and carry it by a pipe.

The walls and roofs appear sound, but not equal to original buildings. The deal floors have decayed, being neglected, and will require to be new, and all the walls and ceilings will require to be plastered, many new doors and windows and steps between the several buildings, spouting required to the roofs, and drain pipes.

No stone sills to windows.

An enclosure wall will be necessary to the ground around the buildings.

Cubical capacity, 33,000 feet.

The Estimated Cost of the required Works is as follows:—

	£	s.	d.
New floor and joists,	480	0	0
Wall plaster,	104	0	0
Ceiling,	129	0	0
9in. brick walls,	189	0	0
New doors,	74	0	0
New windows,	73	0	0
8 flights of steps,	16	0	0
Spouting to roofs,	97	0	0
Drains,	80	0	0
Lavatories, earth-closets, water supply, boiler, &c.,	150	0	0
Shed building,	30	0	0
Grates, &c.,	10	0	0
Boundary wall (as on plan),	180	0	0
Gateway,	20	0	0
Contingencies,	200	0	0
	£1,801	0	0

No. 4—Single rooms.

Dining-hall, 68ft. by 16ft. by 10ft.

ARMAGH POORHOUSE.

Plate XII. and XIII.

This building which was erected for 1,000 inmates, and has had very little additions made to the original structure.

The part proposed to be applied to the use of pauper lunatics is the whole of the male wing building. To meet the requirements of the class of men now occupying it, it is proposed to apply the upper storey, which in this poorhouse is over the dining hall, as a dormitory, and making a new inner or outside staircases to the same from the yard. The present wards occupied by lunatics to be converted into a room for infirm men by removal of the division walls, as it is assumed that the lunatics will all be placed together in the wing building.

The structural character of the building is like most others, and will require wall plastering and ceilings. The ground floor has very good tiles, with boarded spaces where the beds are placed; hot and cold water can be conveniently obtained from the kitchen of the poorhouse.

It is proposed to alter the approach road, so as to give the part alongside the wing building as an airing yard for the lunatics. The field, through which the new road is proposed to be made, being the property of the guardians, and containing about four acres, would admit of being used by the patients in charge of attendants.

The sleeping space for children over school-room has the bed space only five feet one inch in width, being made for children only, and would require some structural alteration to admit of its being used for adults, but this could be done if required, in which case another stairs from yard would be required. The school-master's room can be moved out of wing into childrens' wards to allow rooms for attendants on the lunatics.

Cubical capacity, 50,000 feet.

ESTIMATED COST.

	£	s.	d.
Wall plastering,	60	0	0
Ceilings,	75	0	0
Tile paving to lavatory,	18	0	0
Levelling gangways,	17	0	0
New outer sheds and privies,	67	0	0
Water supply and earth closets,	100	0	0
2 Pairs of gates and excavation,	50	0	0
Yard walls,	100	0	0
Protecting plates,	20	0	0
Contingencies,	200	0	0
	£700	0	0

AUXILIARY BUILDINGS AT OUGHTERARD POORHOUSE.

Plate XIV.

This was one of the thirty new unions carried out on the recommendation of the Boundary Commissioners, and differs from the others in being built in connection with the auxiliary buildings at that time extensively carried out as additions to many of the original buildings.

The board-room and clerk's office are over the kitchen offices in front of the dining-hall.

There were four ranges of temporary one storey buildings, in part of which is the registration office, and the dispensary, and also the probationary ward, the latter are not used, and do not seem to be required; the dispensary and registration office and porter's-room it is proposed to retain, and to appropriate the remainder, namely, three of the four ranges to asylum purposes, one of the four having been removed.

The drawing shows the extent of the buildings, which are fairly substantial for the class of buildings, the walls are well built with dry stones, and pointed both sides with mortar, the gables have stone capping, and the chimney shafts and roof appear sound.

They all require new floors, and all the walls to be plastered, and lath and plaster ceilings to the rooms, besides the other alterations shown on plans.

Eave spouting to the roofs.

Cistern for water, to be supplied from a well on the poorhouse, which will have to be pumped into the cistern.

The dining-hall of the poorhouse and the kitchen and washhouse buildings of the poorhouse to be used for the asylum patients; the dining hall has only an earthen floor, and the fittings of kitchen offices are not good. No sills to windows.

No estimate is made for using the dining-hall.

Cubical capacity, 79,191 feet.

The Estimated Cost of the necessary Works is as follows:—

	£	s.	d.
Flooring and joists,	400	0	0
Wall plaster,	75	0	0
Ceilings,	92	0	0
Spouting,	50	0	0
New doors,	60	0	0
Windows,	60	0	0
Drains,	50	0	0
Lavatories, water supply, earth closet, and boiler,	200	0	0
Fire places,	30	0	0
Contingencies,	200	0	0
	£1,317	0	0

No. 8—Single rooms.

Carrickmacross Union

Scale for Elevations 32 feet to an Inch

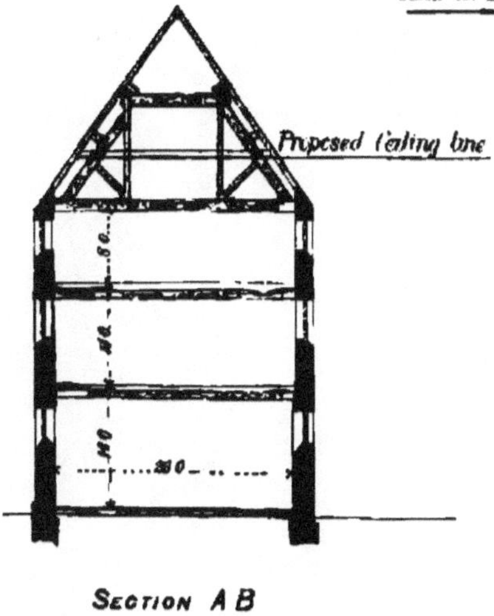

Section A B

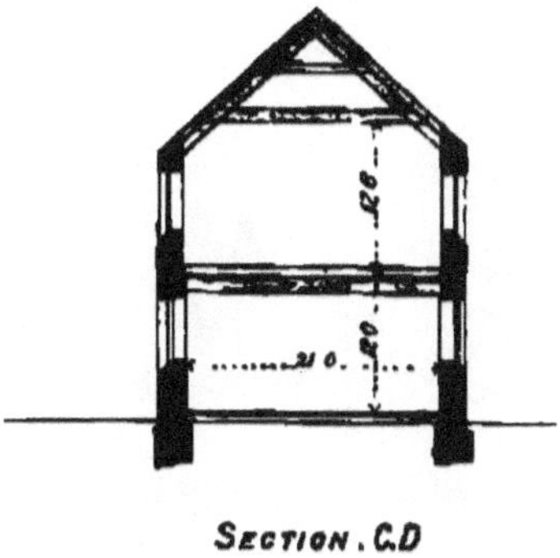

Section . C.D

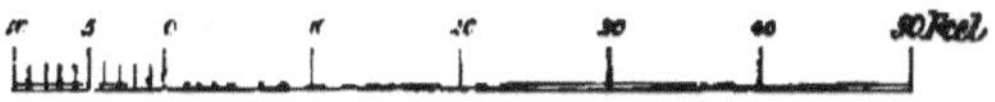

Carrickmacross Union.

Shewing Additions made to original Buildings for Children.

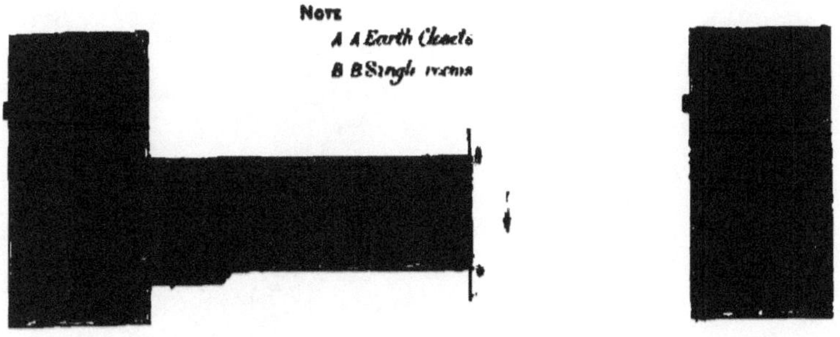

First Floor Plan

Top Floor

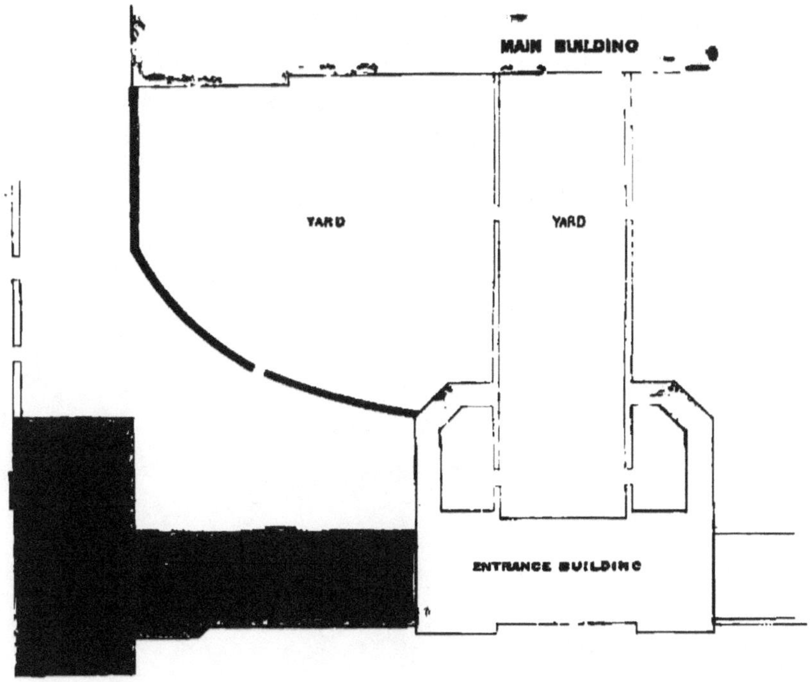

Ground Plan

the University of

CASTLETOWN DELVIN UNION

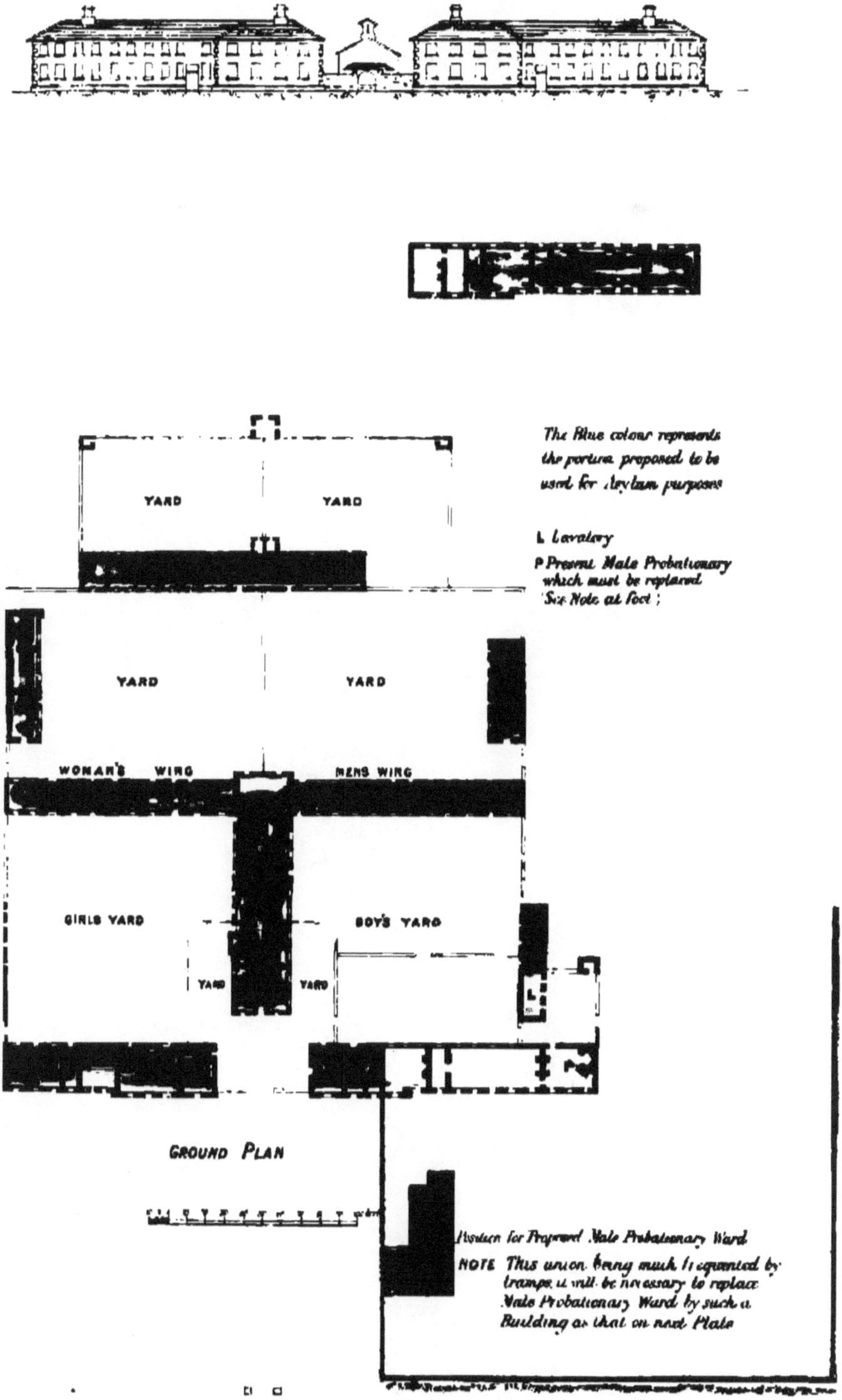

CASTLETOWN DELVIN UNION

Plan for proposed Probationary Ward for Males

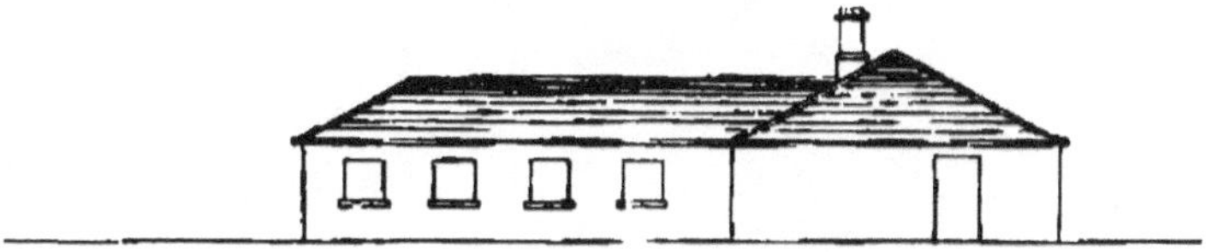

ELEVATION

SECTION

A Single Rooms
B Place for breaking Stones

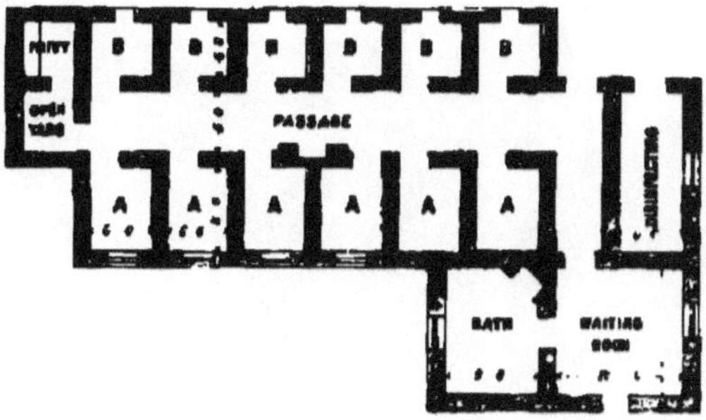

PLAN

LISBURN UNION

E.E. Earth Closets
A.A. Attendants and Stores

FIRST FLOOR PLAN
8 10 High

SECOND FLOOR PLAN
12 6 High

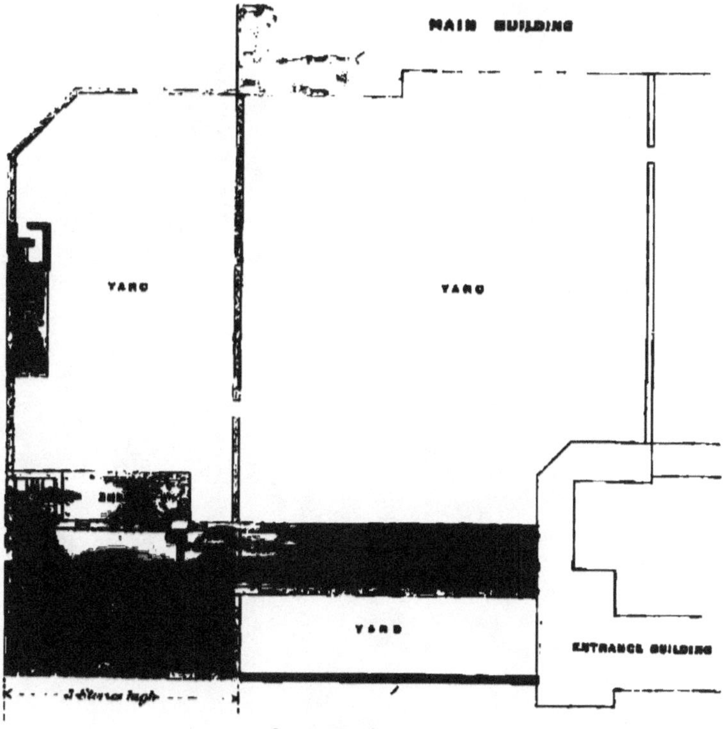

GROUND PLAN
13 6 High

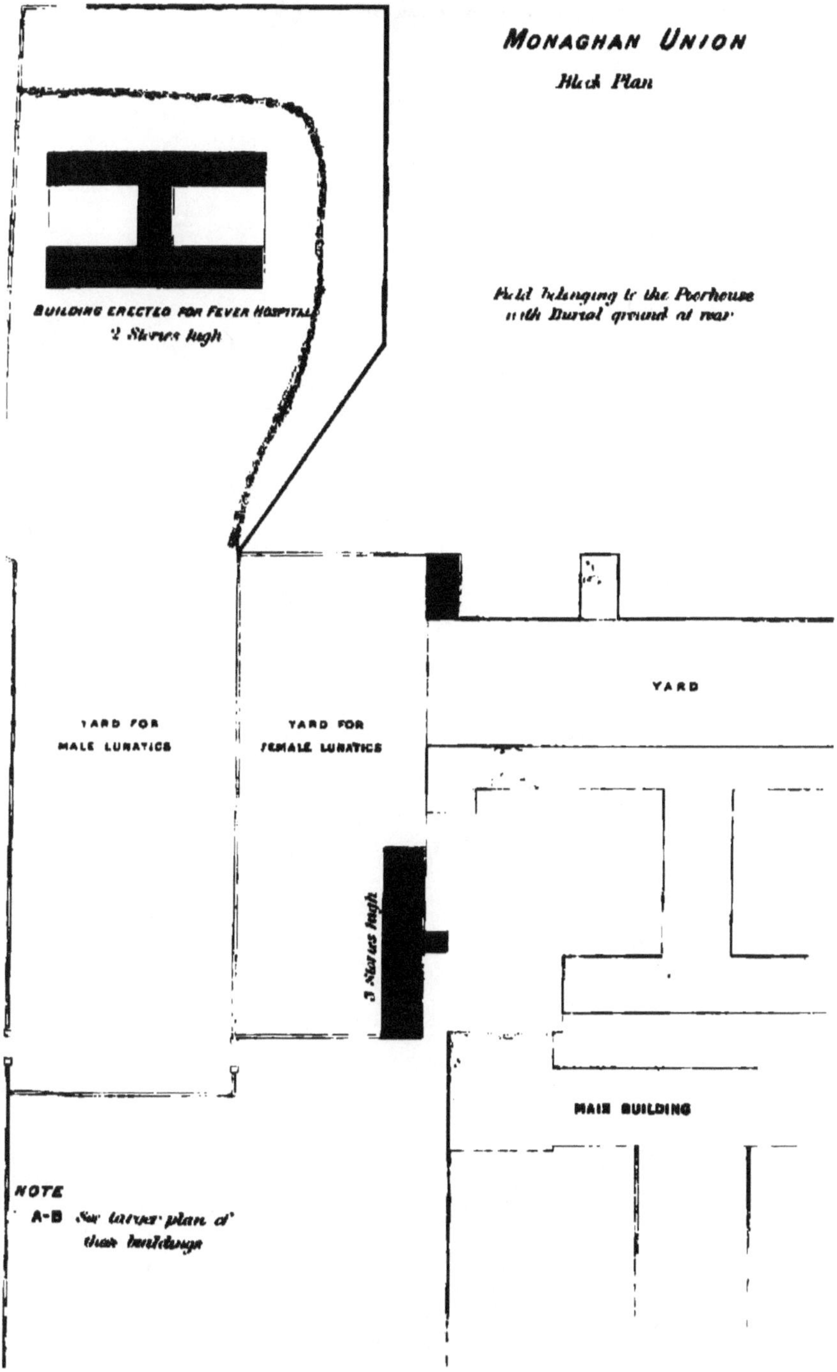
MONAGHAN UNION
Block Plan
Field belonging to the Poorhouse
with Burial ground at rear
BUILDING ERECTED FOR FEVER HOSPITAL
2 Stories high
YARD
YARD FOR
MALE LUNATICS
YARD FOR
FEMALE LUNATICS
3 Stories high
MAIN BUILDING
NOTE
A-B See larger plan of
these buildings

MONAGHAN UNION

Plan of Fever Hospital Building
Lettered A on block plan.

FRONT ELEVATION

UPPER FLOOR
11 6 High

GROUND PLAN
12 0 High

MONAGHAN UNION

Plan of Auxiliary Building lettered B on block Plan

2ND FLOOR
13 6 High

1ST FLOOR
10 6 High

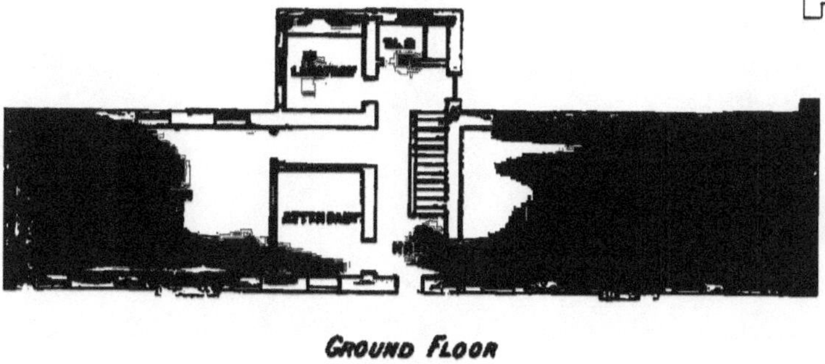

GROUND FLOOR
8 0 High

NEWCASTLE UNION

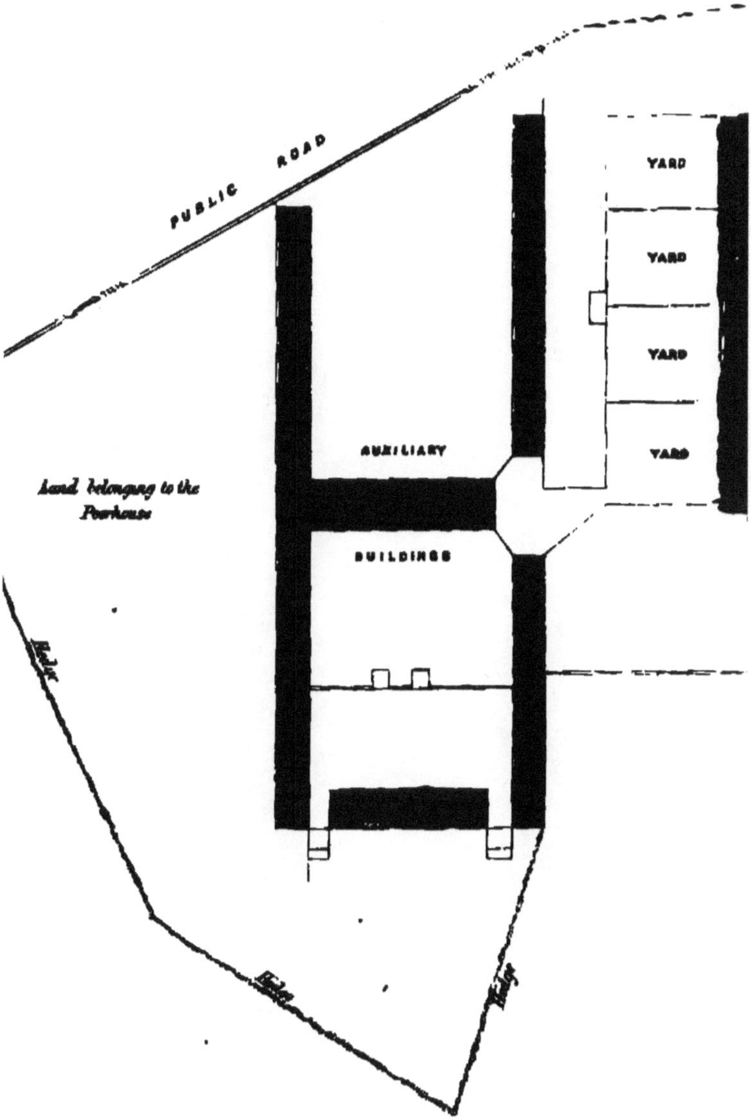

NEWCASTLE UNION

Plan of Part of the Auxiliary Buildings

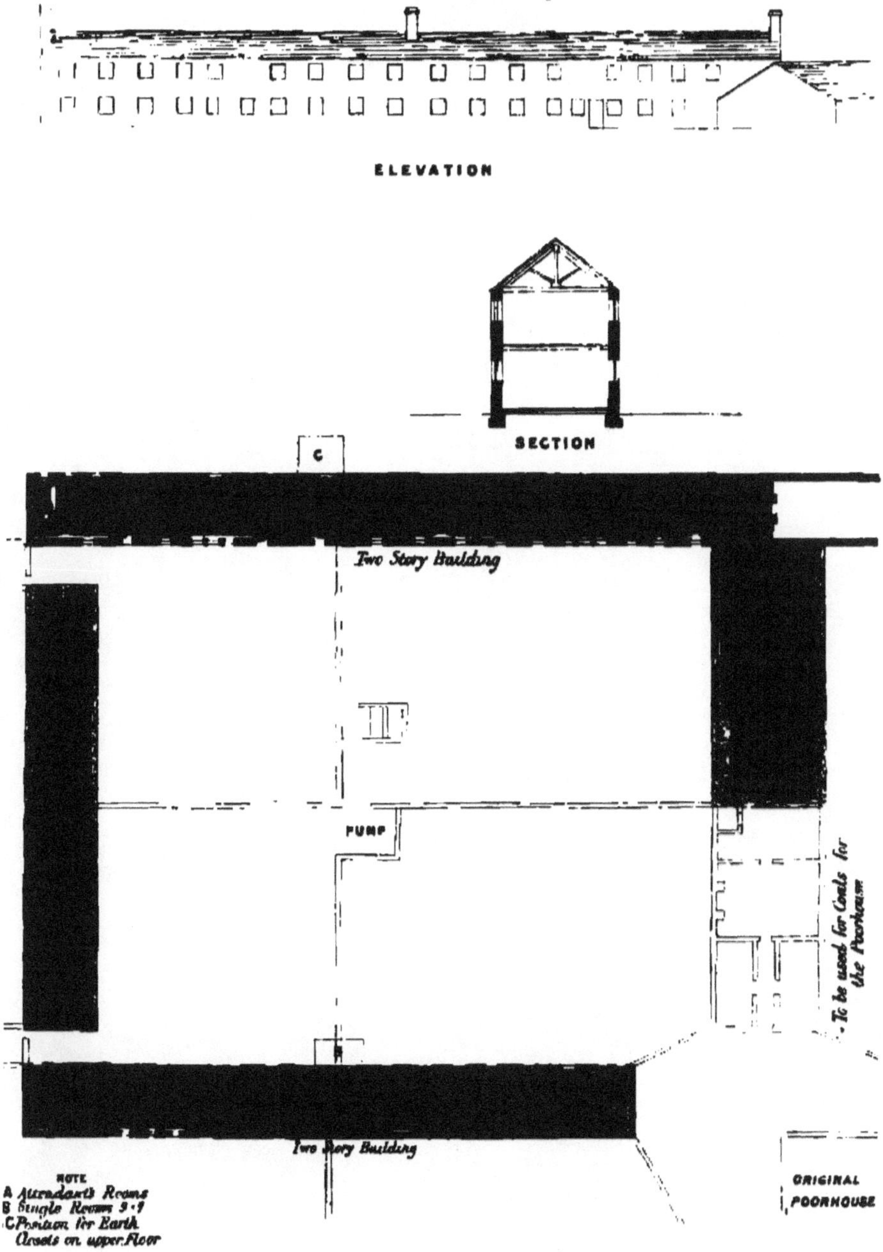

DINGLE UNION

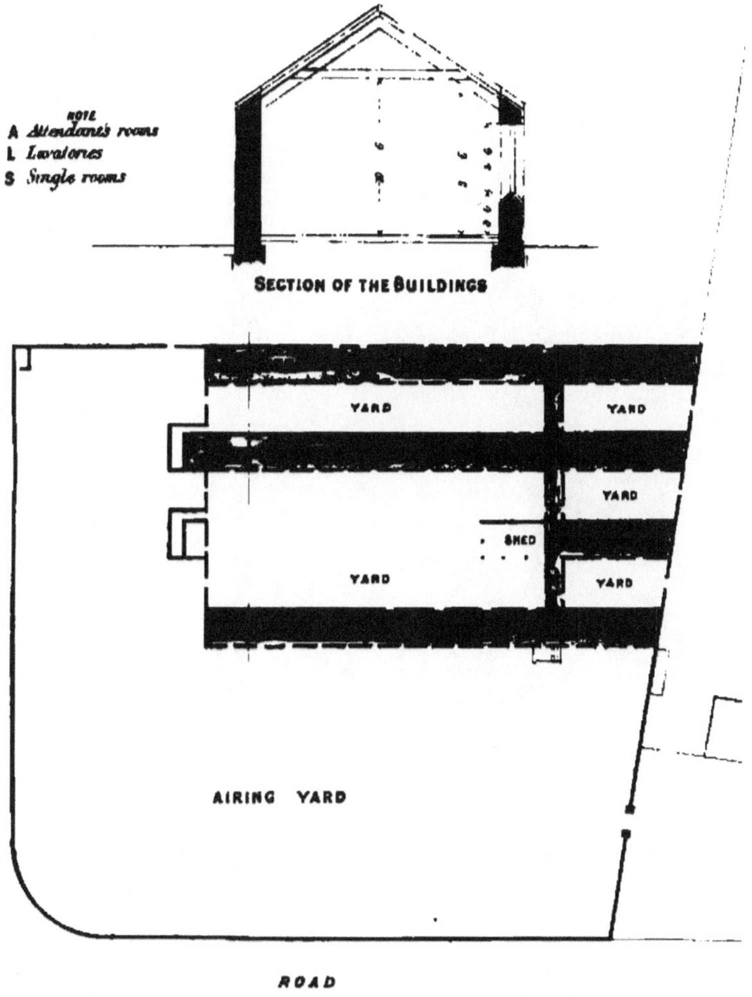

ARMAGH UNION

ELEVATION OF MAIN BUILDING

Shewing Wing A proposed to be appropriated (see plan)

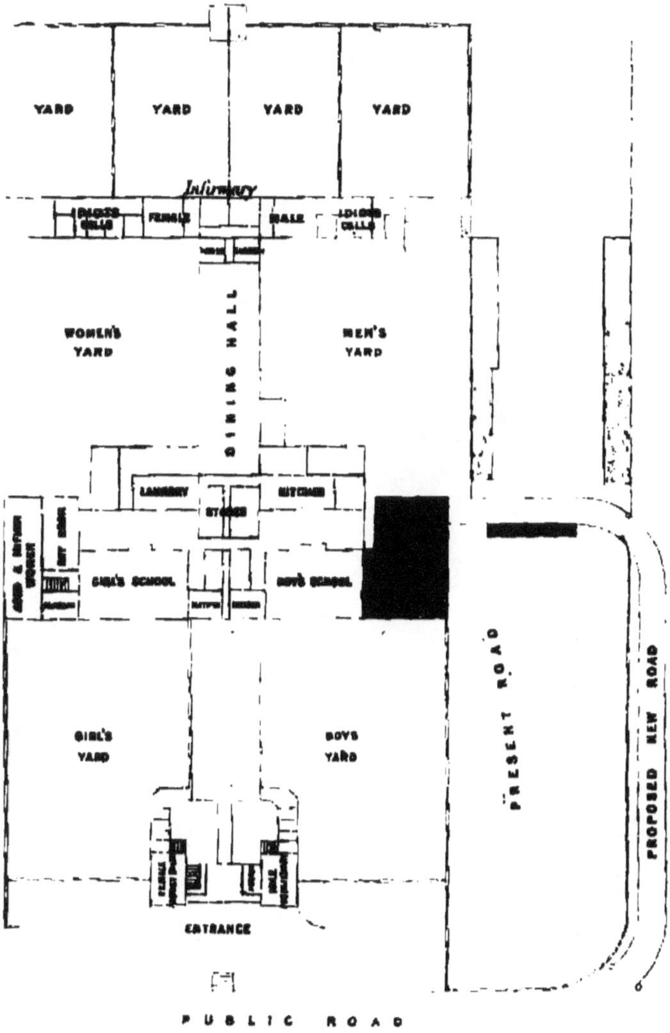

A *Wing Building proposed to be used for Lunatics.*

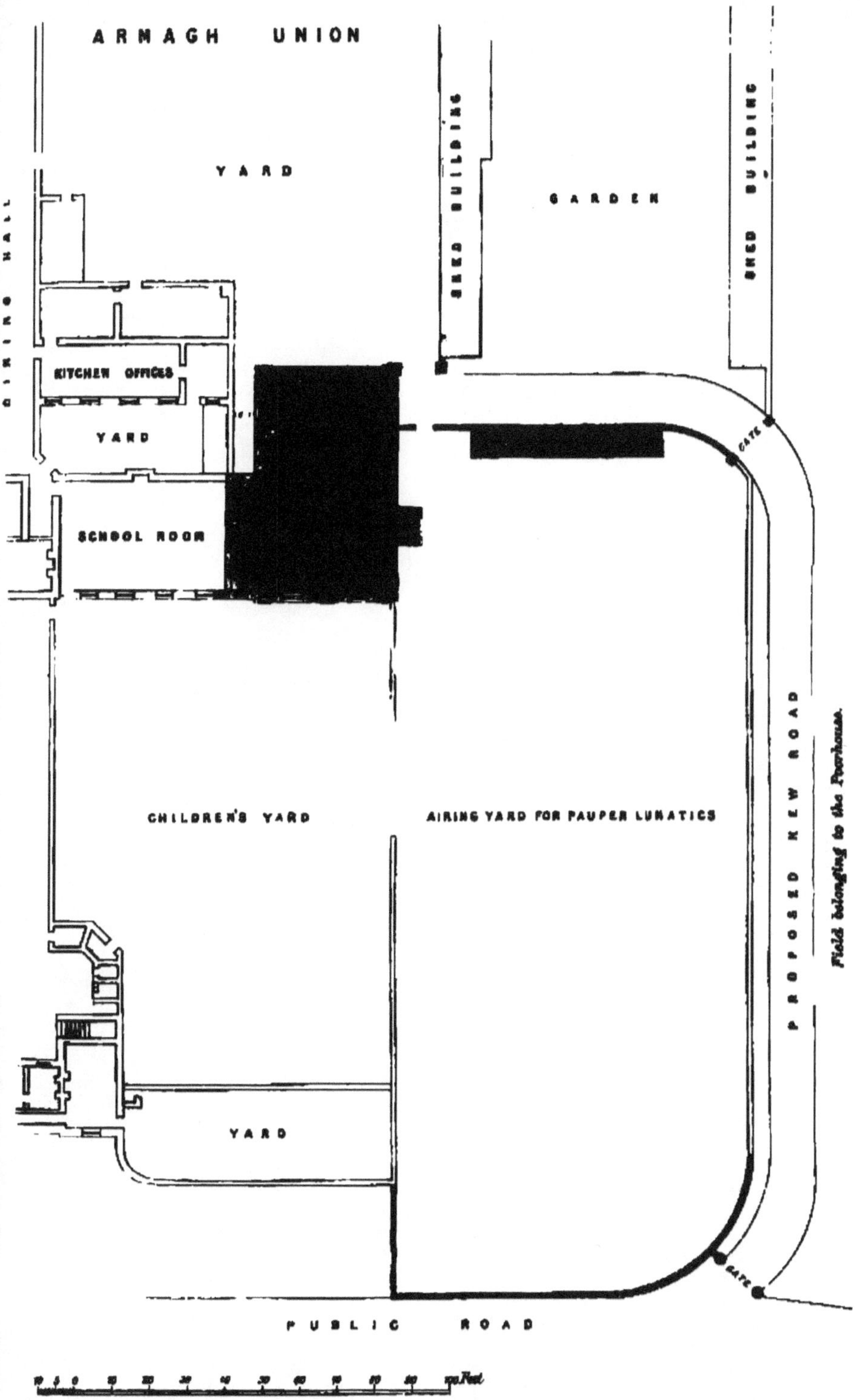

ARMAGH UNION
YARD
DINING HALL
KITCHEN OFFICES
YARD
SCHOOL ROOM
SHED BUILDING
GARDEN
SHED BUILDING
GATE
GATE
CHILDREN'S YARD
AIRING YARD FOR PAUPER LUNATICS
PROPOSED NEW ROAD
Field belonging to the Poorhouse.
YARD
PUBLIC ROAD
10 5 0 10 20 30 40 50 60 70 80 90 100 Feet

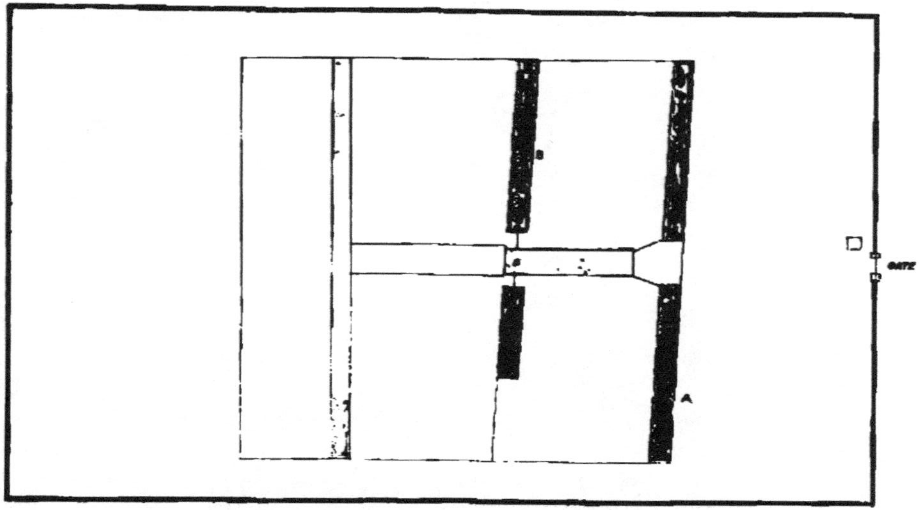

PLAN OF SITE OF POORHOUSE ENCLOSED WITH HIGH STONE WALL

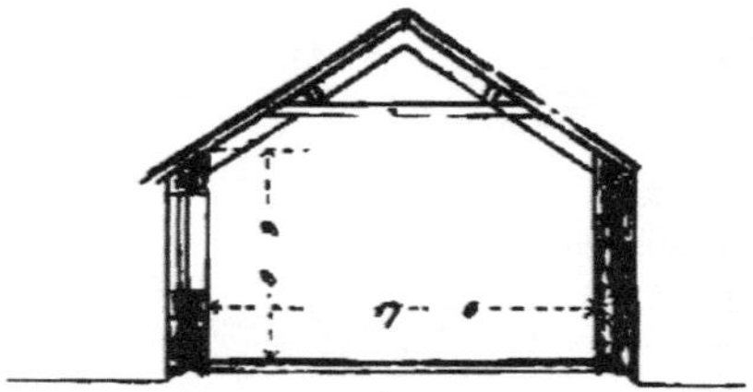

SECTION AT-B

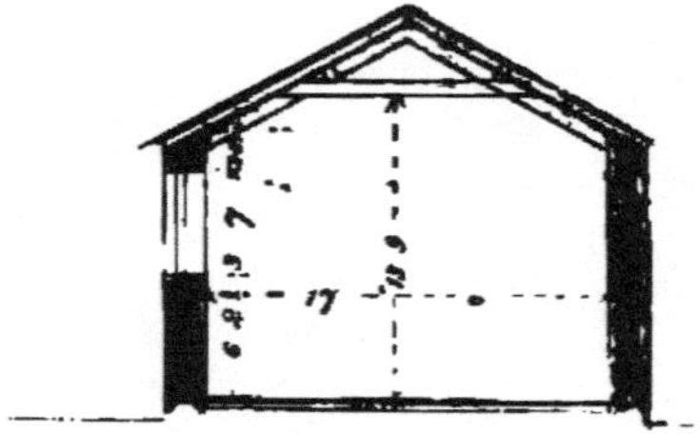

SECTION AT-A

Plate XV

Ground Plan of Oughterard Union Workhouse and Auxiliary Buildings.

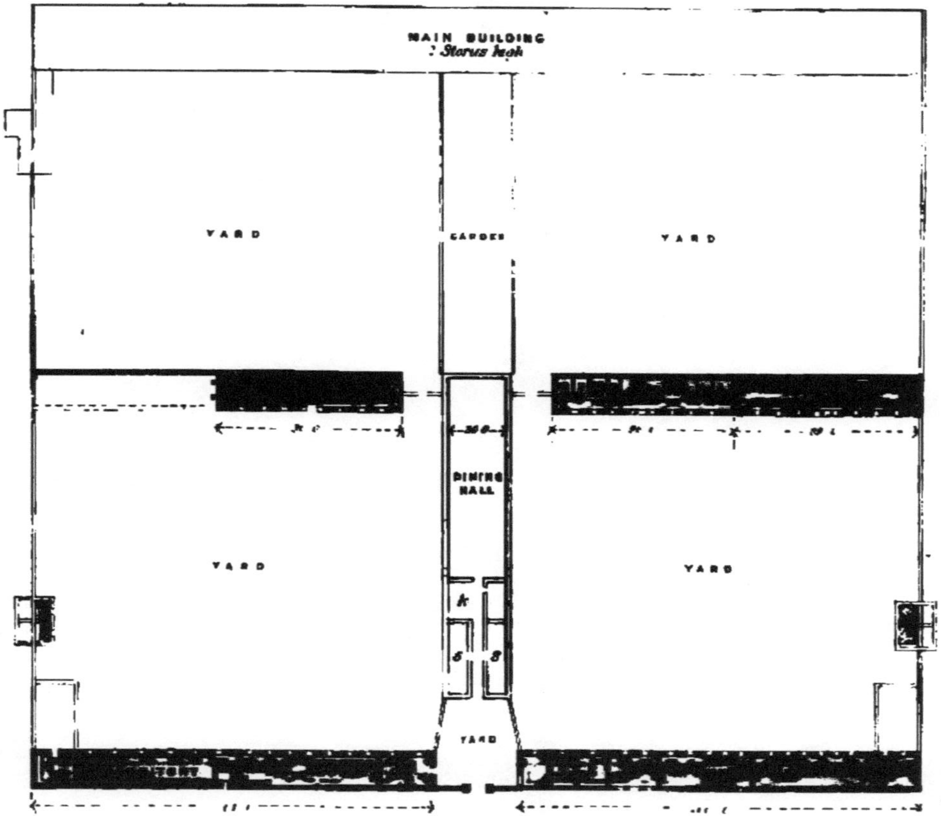

NOTE

A Attendants rooms

B Single do

L Lavatories

S Stores

K Kitchen

Buildings to be returned

C Dispensary

D Registration Office

Geo. Wilkinson
1878

No. 11.—TABLE showing Authority for admission of Patients to District Asylums, and number admitted since the year 1857.

YEARS.	Ordinary Cases admitted by the Board.			Ordinary Cases admitted as urgent by the Physicians			Dangerous Lunatics admitted by warrant of the Lord Lieutenant			Admitted from Central and other Asylums			Lunatics charged with offences admitted by warrant of the Lord Lieutenant.			Lunatics detained in default of sureties to keep the Peace by warrant of the Lord Lieutenant.			Dangerous Lunatics committed by Justices under 30 & 31 V., c. 118			Pay Patients admitted during year under P.O. rule upon terms sanctioned by Inspectors.			Total Admitted.		
	M.	F.	T.	M.	F.	T.	M.	F.	T.	M.	F.	T.	M.	F.	T.	M.	F.	T.	M.	F.	T.	M.	F.	T.	M.	F.	T.
1857	241	274	515	148	180	328	242	154	396	-	.	.	6	2	7	2	3	5	.	.	.	.	.	.	698	552	1,250
1858	230	271	501	194	176	370	222	172	394	.	.	.	20	9	29	9	.	9	.	.	.	.	.	.	664	621	1,285
1859	261	295	556	172	101	273	193	150	343	.	.	.	21	10	31	.	.	.	.	.	.	.	.	.	656	646	1,205
1860	198	263	461	220	243	463	210	161	371	.	.	.	7	8	14	1	5	6	.	.	.	.	.	.	672	678	1,310
1861	169	272	441	229	243	472	178	123	301	.	.	.	6	6	12	4	2	6	.	.	.	.	.	.	107	597	1,202
1862	204	206	410	207	167	374	241	142	283	.	.	.	28	11	39	3	.	3	.	.	.	.	.	.	625	546	1,171
1863	227	253	480	214	209	423	219	134	353	.			14	5	19	10	2	12		.	.		.		746	667	1,480
1864	176	204	380	209	262	471	260	153	347				24	8	32	4	3	7		.	.		.		619	623	1,242
1865	200	216	416	238	237	475	212	109	378		.	.	8	14	22	4	.	4		.	.	.	.		664	677	1,262
1866	247	213	460	294	431	725	232	90	400				15	7	22	6	5	11	.	.	.				920	844	1,763
1867	193	266	459	392	308	700	214	137	351			.	19	11	30	1	1	2				.		.	779	748	1,527
1868	204	183	383	290	371	662	62	68	130	142	130	272	20	7	27	3	2	5	587	392	979	.	.	.	1,234	1,194	2,428
1869	164	188	415	261	454	527	27	17	44	141	190	310	19	4	20	2	9	11	700	471	1,140	.	.	.	1,247	1,240	2,489
1870	129	142	271	241	466	540	9	3	17	17	12	20	22	5	27	7	7	17	706	436	1,142	.	.	.	1,270	1,063	2,332
1871	150	150	240	240	414	758	6	1	7	2	1	3	22	24	46	5	.	5	691	478	1,167	.	.		1,157	1,066	2,223
1872	99	118	211	297	381	758	6	2	8	3	.	3	40	20	70	3	2	5	678	444	1,119	.	.		1,167	979	2,146
1873	79	104	217	357	400	784	6	4	10	.	20	14	26	24	50	3	.	3	747	470	1,228	.	.		1,314	1,062	2,377
1874	122	141	268	347	393	746	1	2	3	2	4	6	24	10	40	2	1	3	636	465	1,100	.	-	.	1,156	958	2,104
1875	75	85	160	341	437	778	6	6	14	1	2	3	75	12	47	12	2	14	618	422	1,054	7	18	20	2,094	1,057	2,139
1876	60	117	197	387	431	794	37	6	20	4	1	5	24	16	60	8	2	10	737	467	1,224	21	24	55	1,220	1,064	2,344
1877	64	69	269	602	417	458	8	4	4	3	2	5	27	9	36	2	1	3	719	622	1,341	14	24	52	1,313	1,083	2,314

No. 12.—RETURN of PAUPER LUNATICS, CURABLE and INCURABLE, in ASYLUMS and WORKHOUSES from 1856 to 1877.

Year ending 31st December	Lunatics in Asylums. Probably Curable.			Lunatics in Asylums and Workhouses. In Asylums. Probably Incurable			In Workhouses. Probably Incurable			Total in Asylums and Workhouses probably Incurable			Total No. of Lunatics. Gross Total of Curables and Incurables in Asylums and Workhouses			Per Centage. Curables.	Incurables.
	M	F	Total	M	F	Total	M.	F.	Total	M	F	Total	M	F	Total		
1856	556	612	1,168	1,393	1,263	2,656	–	–	1,707	–	–	4,531	–	–	6,699	–	–
1857	588	599	1,187	1,281	1,368	2,669	679	1,120	1,799	2,060	2,408	4,468	2,648	3,007	5,655	20·9	79·1
1858 } 1859 }	653	622	1,275	1,434	1,281	2,615	738	1,324	2,047	2,137	2,705	4,862	2,810	3,337	6,157	20·7	79·2
1860 } 1861 } 1862 }	557	566	1,123	1,659	1,606	3,265	1,008	1,584	2,392	2,667	3,190	5,857	3,224	3,756	6,980	16·0	84·0
1863	641	573	1,214	1,798	1,660	3,458	954	1,501	2,465	2,752	3,161	5,918	3,393	3,734	7,127	17·0	83·0
1864	660	617	1,277	1,806	1,647	3,452	1,066	1,507	2,563	2,954	3,232	6,186	3,614	3,849	7,463	17·1	82·9
1865	631	551	1,213	1,836	1,795	3,622	1,100	1,686	2,783	2,996	3,258	6,256	3,679	3,869	7,568	16·0	83·9
1866	633	691	1,364	2,028	1,788	3,816	1,067	1,681	2,748	3,115	3,449	6,564	3,748	4,070	7,818	16·0	83·9
1867	612	584	1,196	2,136	1,880	4,016	1,104	1,601	2,705	3,240	3,481	6,721	3,852	4,065	7,917	15·1	84·8
1868	609	718	1,530	2,329	1,967	4,296	1,139	1,608	2,742	3,468	3,570	7,038	4,079	4,288	8,368	17·7	82·2
1869	880	754	1,634	2,559	2,170	4,693	1,177	1,780	2,907	3,698	3,900	7,569	4,559	4,664	9,199	17·6	82·3
1870	974	830	1,814	2,580	2,331	4,641	1,150	1,684	2,754	3,730	3,873	7,595	4,704	4,705	9,409	19·2	80·2
1871	1,038	659	1,917	2,782	2,843	5,075	1,178	1,741	2,914	3,908	4,064	7,889	4,963	4,973	9,806	19·3	80·6
1872	1,044	854	1,886	2,861	2,381	5,242	1,184	1,772	2,966	4,055	4,153	8,208	5,099	5,007	10,106	18·7	81·2
1873	1,080	855	1,875	2,947	2,525	5,472	1,277	1,862	3,150	4,224	4,373	8,609	5,344	5,322	10,477	17·8	82·2
1874	879	894	1,708	3,198	2,608	5,862	1,270	1,871	3,141	4,468	4,560	9,028	5,348	5,364	10,726	15·8	84·1
1875	923	846	1,769	3,219	2,753	5,972	1,275	1,904	3,179	4,494	4,657	9,151	5,417	5,503	10,920	16·1	83·8
1876	1,000	828	1,828	3,340	2,905	6,245	1,268	1,948	3,216	4,608	4,853	9,461	5,608	5,781	11,289	16·1	83·9
1877	989	922	1,911	3,404	2,868	6,272	1,265	2,104	3,379	4,673	4,972	9,644	5,661	5,894	11,555	16·5	83·4

[No. 13.

Appendix C. Inquiry.

No. 13.—Return showing the Length of Residence in Asylums of Inmates on 31st December, 1877.

District Asylums.	Probably Curable. Under 1 Year.	Over 1 and under 2	Over 2 and under 5	Over 5 and under 10	Over 10 and under 15	15 Years and upwards	Total.	Probably Incurable. Under 1 Year.	Over 1 and under 2.	Over 2 and under 5.	Over 5 and under 10.	Over 10 and under 15	15 Years and upwards.	Total
Armagh,	29	9	8	11	–	–	57	9	10	24	80	31	16	180
Ballinasloe,	49	49	38	19	–	–	150	12	1	69	89	57	58	274
Belfast,	57	21	16	6	4	4	108	41	38	88	89	24	51	331
Carlow,	28	8	13	13	3	5	70	12	12	27	44	27	29	151
Castlebar,	16	3	6	1	1	–	27	41	35	79	44	51	–	250
Clonmel,	18	13	4	–	–	–	37	59	16	62	88	65	45	335
Cork,	115	54	22	8	–	–	104	20	27	116	106	104	110	582
Down,	45	11	7	5	–	–	71	83	55	40	125	–	–	232
Ennis,	22	6	0	3	–	–	37	23	14	46	67	30	51	231
Enniscorthy,	15	1	2	–	–	–	18	21	27	57	146	–	–	251
Kilkenny,	23	19	32	17	5	9	99	14	9	91	80	14	35	150
Killarney,	13	3	1	–	–	–	16	26	33	47	56	98	66	261
Letterkenny,	24	6	6	–	–	–	36	48	35	71	54	63	–	272
Limerick,	30	6	3	1	–	–	40	33	41	67	120	56	81	397
Londonderry,	19	11	7	2	–	–	39	19	36	68	63	29	28	228
Maryborough,	31	21	6	8	1	–	67	14	24	36	43	33	30	179
Monaghan,	21	1	1	–	–	–	23	47	80	84	172	–	–	338
Mullingar,	43	31	22	9	–	–	105	53	40	46	60	40	83	337
Omagh,	72	57	29	20	4	–	182	6	48	45	56	61	109	337
Richmond,	229	63	37	8	2	–	331	37	23	193	243	62	110	687
Sligo,	39	16	22	6	–	–	85	6	14	53	60	46	58	236
Waterford,	26	16	29	6	5	–	79	13	17	54	47	26	30	187
Totals,	960	430	295	140	25	11	1,870	601	562	1,386	1,517	646	987	6,369

No. 14.—Return showing the Number of Idiots, Epileptic Imbeciles, and Lunatics, exclusive of those in Workhouses, Gaols, or Asylums, on 31st October, 1877.

Counties.	A. Lunatics. Males.	Females.	Total.	B. Idiots. Males.	Females.	Total.	C. Epileptic Imbeciles. Males.	Females.	Total.	Total of Cols. A, B, C. Males.	Females.	Total.	Religion. Protestants.	Roman Catholics.	Presbyterians.	Other Denominations.	Class of Life. Lower Class.	Middle Class.	Upper Class.
Antrim,	30	14	53	140	79	219	70	21	91	239	214	453	80	88	175	9	284	91	8
Armagh,	34	13	55	77	44	121	24	10	34	135	59	195	47	106	71	2	165	29	1
Carlow,	7	3	7	36	17	53	5	8	13	49	26	71	8	62	–	–	49	21	1
Cavan,	17	14	31	104	74	178	13	9	22	134	87	221	35	177	9	1	171	63	4
Clare,	28	17	45	84	61	145	29	19	48	161	77	238	6	222	–	–	161	64	3
Cork, E.R.,	19	21	40	94	77	171	40	27	67	153	125	268	14	253	1	–	192	69	6
Cork, W.R.,	24	18	42	108	58	164	31	20	44	144	97	241	20	223	–	1	163	81	7
Donegal,	41	43	84	139	107	246	22	24	46	279	172	345	63	277	65	2	260	75	1
Down,	14	33	47	170	121	291	36	79	65	224	179	403	84	170	144	3	273	127	3
Dublin County,	4	2	6	22	12	34	7	11	18	33	25	58	12	45	1	–	33	15	10
Dublin Metropolitan Police District,	–	1	1	57	14	71	9	2	11	66	17	83	12	65	7	1	65	17	2
Fermanagh,	19	8	27	70	44	114	9	4	13	93	59	152	60	91	–	1	102	48	1
Galway, E.R.,	8	7	15	50	54	104	13	12	25	69	74	143	6	130	–	–	98	39	1
Galway, W.R.,	7	7	14	56	34	90	23	20	43	86	61	147	3	143	–	–	124	12	2
Kerry,	7	18	25	72	62	134	19	16	35	100	96	191	7	182	–	1	148	47	2
Kildare,	6	8	14	67	23	90	17	8	25	90	36	126	12	109	1	–	95	29	6
Kilkenny,	9	15	24	64	86	142	23	25	57	96	116	212	9	203	–	–	135	51	3
King's County,	24	17	41	44	28	70	16	11	27	84	64	149	17	131	–	–	85	54	5
Leitrim,	17	28	35	51	36	87	8	13	21	78	67	145	11	131	1	–	113	31	–
Limerick,	11	11	22	103	43	155	19	14	33	133	74	211	6	209	–	–	161	40	1
Londonderry,	18	12	30	108	51	159	16	11	27	141	74	215	43	93	77	2	148	68	3
Longford,	4	6	9	41	26	67	12	7	19	57	38	95	12	82	–	–	53	42	1
Louth,	10	10	20	45	35	80	12	6	18	73	51	124	6	110	7	–	84	37	3
Mayo,	9	14	23	59	57	116	17	22	39	114	103	217	10	207	–	–	196	21	2
Meath,	15	12	27	72	76	227	20	18	38	107	76	183	2	185	–	–	145	40	–
Monaghan,	12	9	21	73	40	113	10	9	27	104	57	161	21	109	37	–	107	52	2
Queen's County,	6	5	11	40	39	79	9	11	20	63	43	106	18	94	1	–	65	48	–
Roscommon,	17	10	22	70	46	116	23	20	43	104	76	180	21	189	–	–	154	23	4
Sligo,	15	16	31	61	35	96	8	12	21	73	67	137	19	117	9	–	117	22	3
Tipperary, N.R.,	11	11	22	79	51	130	19	12	31	82	69	149	11	151	–	–	101	46	5
Tipperary, S.R.,	9	8	17	57	36	93	20	19	39	86	64	150	3	147	–	–	109	35	3
Tyrone,	26	19	45	136	74	210	34	21	55	196	125	321	63	188	70	3	195	122	2
Waterford,	3	9	12	45	28	73	17	14	30	65	52	117	5	110	–	–	74	39	4
Westmeath,	21	15	36	59	48	107	14	19	33	94	81	166	9	152	–	1	129	12	1
Wexford,	30	15	45	51	46	125	31	22	48	162	75	217	31	185	–	–	175	31	1
Wicklow,	4	4	8	35	27	62	14	11	25	52	42	94	29	68	–	–	61	50	5
Belfast Town,	4	2	5	32	22	55	19	13	32	53	40	93	31	80	93	–	79	16	–
Total,	536	451	987	2,714	1,765	4,478	879	469	1,348	3,829	2,750	6,709	903	5,323	494	35	4,727	1,512	77

No. 15.—Enlargement of the Londonderry District Lunatic Asylum.

Letter from the Under Secretary to the Commissioners.

Dublin Castle, 3rd August, 1877.

Sir,—I am directed by the Lord Lieutenant to acquaint you for the information of the Poor Law Union Inquiry Commissioners, that the question of erecting a new District Lunatic Asylum for the county of Londonderry, or of enlarging the present asylum is under the consideration of the Government, and I am to transmit to you for the perusal of the Commissioners a file of papers on the subject which I am to request you will return to this office when done with.

Before arriving at any conclusion on this subject, his Grace is desirous to learn as soon as possible whether it is probable that the inquiry of the Commissioners will result in their recommending that any workhouse in the county of Londonderry, or in the northern part of the county Antrim, can be given up, either wholly or in part, and with this view his Grace desires me to request that the Commissioners will be so good as to commence their inquiries in the above-mentioned counties, and to inform him whether it is their intention in their report to recommend the abolition, either wholly or in part, of any workhouse in the district referred to, and if so, whether such workhouse is at present suited for the purpose of a district lunatic asylum, or if it can be made suitable for the treatment of lunatic poor, and the probable cost of the necessary alterations.

I am, sir, your obedient servant,

T. H. Burke.

H. A. Robinson, esquire.

Letter from the Commissioners to the Under Secretary of the Lord Lieutenant.

Four Courts, Dublin, 5th Oct., 1877.

Sir,—With reference to your letter of the 9th August last on the subject of the overcrowded state of the Londonderry Lunatic Asylum, in which you intimate his Grace's desire to be informed whether it is the intention of the Commissioners in their report, to recommend the abolition of any union workhouse in county Londonderry, or in the northern part of county Antrim, I am now directed to acquaint you for his Grace's information that the Commissioners do not expect to be able to recommend the dissolution of any union in these counties or the removal of the pauper inmates from any workhouse. They hope, however, to be able to make recommendations in their report for utilising spare workhouse accommodation in all parts of the country, such as will materially relieve the pressure upon Londonderry and the other district asylums throughout Ireland.

I have the honour to be, sir,

Your obedient servant,

H. A. Robinson.

The Under Secretary, Dublin Castle.

No. 16.—Accommodation for Lunatics in Belfast Workhouse.

Letter from Dr. Roughan to the Commissioners.

Mountjoy Square, Dublin, July 29, 1878.

Gentlemen,—In reply to your letter of the 22nd instant, on the subject of revising the accommodation of the Belfast Union Workhouse, I beg leave to state that in my opinion it would be desirable to transfer the lunatics numbering about 200 to some more suitable place and to have the accommodation at present occupied by them added to the infirmary, and thus afford a means of relieving the overcrowded state of that department, as well as the general hospital, which at present is occupied by persons labouring under diseases of various forms, contagious and non-contagious. The accommodation in the general hospital under the revised scale, Schedule A, would be 245, while it contained according to returns obtained 333 cases in February, 1877. I may here however remark that the system of ventilation in this hospital is most perfect, and I have not heard of any evil results from overcrowding of it. In reply to the second portion of your letter I have to state that if other provision was made for the children now accommodated in a detached building, in my opinion that building might be made available for the reception of lunatics if the class now in the workhouse infirmary numbering from 200 to 250.

No separate or detached building is provided in Belfast for the reception and treatment of small pox patients, they are accommodated on the first floor in the wings of the general hospital, and are kept isolated as far as practicable from the other patients, however I think it would be most desirable that a detached building should be provided so as to prevent the possibility of the disease being communicated to patients who happen to be in hospital suffering from other diseases. Such buildings have been provided in some unions in my district as for instance Lisburn, Lurgan, Banbridge, &c. I have heard of small pox having been taken by patients labouring under ordinary medical diseases while under the same roof with small pox patients and probably communicated from them.

I have the honour to be, gentlemen,

Your obedient servant,

Geo. F. Roughan, L.C.I.

Appendix C.

Lunacy.

No. 17.—Extract of Minutes of Evidence taken before the Select Committee on Lunacy Law.

Mr John Nugent, M.D., called in and Examined.

2668. Chairman.—What position do you occupy?—I am an Inspector and Commissioner of Control in Ireland of Lunatic Asylums.

2669. How long have you been so?—Over thirty years. I have been seventeen years Commissioner of Control.

2670. Had you any experience of lunacy before that time?—Yes, I had seen a great deal of lunacy on the Continent, and I had studied it in England, attended the lunatic hospitals here.

2671. You have never yourself been the proprietor of an asylum?—Never.

2672. Nor the superintendent of one?—Never.

2673. The system in Ireland differs, I think, in some material points from that in this country?—It does as regards the construction of asylums. In England, asylums generally are built by local authorities and by local rates. I may first observe that in the year 1804 the attention of the Government was directed to the want of lunatic accommodation in Ireland, and in 1805 a Bill was introduced, but it dropped. Matters remained in abeyance until the year 1810, when there was another Committee of the House of Commons, and a grant from Parliament made for the erection of a suitable institution at Dublin capable to accommodate 200 patients, and intended as an asylum for the general insane of Ireland. It is now known as the Richmond Asylum, whereas in 1806 it was proposed to construct four provincial asylums, to contain within them 1,000 patients. Previous to 1810 there was no institution in Ireland for the reception of lunatics, excepting Swift's Hospital, which was founded by Dean Swift, and opened in the year 1745. The population of Ireland at that time was between three and four millions. To show the expansion of insanity since Dean Swift, in his will, introduced a provision that in case there could not be 140 lunatics found in Ireland to fill the asylum, some of the beds unoccupied by lunatics might be converted to other purposes, we have now about 18,600 lunatics, whose names are reported to our office in Ireland.

2674. Does Dean Swift's Asylum still exist?—It still exists unaltered and unchanged. It is in precisely the same locality, without any material additions, from the day of his death, and is principally supported by his estate.

2675. Were the other asylums to which you have alluded, built by the Government?—The manner in which the other asylums were built was as follows. In the year 1821, the 1 & 2 Geo 4 was passed, empowering the Lord Lieutenant to erect as many district asylums as he thought fit in Ireland. He directed nine to be built in addition to two then in existence, the Richmond and one in Cork; the new asylums were built by the seven Commissioners of Control, who were nominated in the Act of Parliament. For the erection of these asylums, all requisite monies were advanced primarily by the Treasury. When built, the question as to how repayments were to be made was left to the Lord Lieutenant in Council, in such proportions and at such times as he might think fit. Fourteen years for the liquidation of the advances were given, and which for the nine asylums amounted to £310,000, the repayments to be made by grand jury presentments twice each year, at spring and summer assizes, until all was recouped, the money bearing no interest. The Act of the 1 & 2 Geo. 4 practically exists now, with some alterations and amendations.

2676. What class of patients are kept in those asylums?—They are intended for the insane poor of Ireland.

2677. Before that time the insane poor wandered about the country?—Before that time there were four houses of correction or industry; one in Dublin, one in Limerick, one in Waterford, and one in Cork, in which lunatics were placed on a sort of poor roll. They were supported by voluntary grand jury presentments. There were scarcely 300 patients altogether in the four.

2678. How are those patients, who are not paupers, dealt with in Ireland?—The number of lunatics in Ireland now in public asylums is 8,073. We have now twenty-two district asylums.

2679. Are those altogether poor?—With the exception of perhaps ninety paying patients in them. We have latterly got an Act of Parliament passed, which authorises the admission of paying patients into district asylums, that is, patients who have not means to support themselves in private asylums, but whose families, from pride or feelings of self-respect, pay simply the annual cost of maintenance, so as not to be burthens on public rates. With that exception the inmates are altogether the insane poor.

2685. Who are the visitors of the asylums in Ireland?—The whole of these institutions are immediately under the inspectors. There are no recognised visitors.

2686. Who are the inspectors?—My colleague, Dr Hatchell, and I are the inspectors.

2687. Have you any visitors under you?—None whatever; we control the whole.

2688. Do you visit the whole of the asylums?—As a matter of course, we visit them four times. I am quite sure we visit some of these institutions eight and nine times in the year.

2689. But four times by statute?—Twice by statute. We visit alternately, making four times in the year, and then we go as often as we think fit.

2690. Are the justices of the peace in Ireland visitors also?—No, they have no authority to visit.

2691. In fact, there are no local authorities apparently that have any control over any of the asylums?—No.

2692. Private or public?—The Board of Governors of Public Asylums manage all the fiscal work. There are monthly meetings held in every public asylum in Ireland, and the Lord Lieutenant in each district appoints some of the gentry and nobility of the country, who become what we call the guardians or the governors of the asylum, and what in England, I believe, are called the visiting committees.

2693. They not only manage the fiscal business of the asylum, but they also visit?—They visit monthly. They do very little in the way of visiting except at the monthly meetings.

2694. At that time do they go round the asylum and see the patients?—At that time generally two or three members of the board go round the asylum while the board is sitting, and they report the result of their visit to the board, and it is entered on the proceedings of the board.

2695. In case of any misconduct, what authority takes cognisance of it?—First, there is the resident medical superintendent, and as he is manager of the institution, of course he discovers it. He has the power of suspending subordinate servants, and taking such steps as he thinks fit, under the Privy Council rules. He then reports to the governing body at the monthly meeting, and the governors' monthly meeting takes action upon it. If it is an urgent case, he writes to the inspectors between the meeting of the board, and the inspectors direct him to adopt such course as they think fit, and it is immediately acted on.

2696. Who controls him?—The resident physician in Ireland is the only officer appointed by the Lord Lieutenant; he holds office under the Lord Lieutenant, and he comes directly then under the inspectors. Of course he is subject to the control and direction of the board in everything except the medical treatment of the patients.

Admission

2701. When a person is supposed to be a lunatic, what is the process by which he is sent to an asylum?—We will first deal with the public patients. The legitimate course of admission into a public asylum is for the friends of the lunatic to make application to the board, and there is a particular form which gives the name, the residence, the locality of birth, and everything connected with the patient, his family and his parents, and then there is a certificate attached to it from a clergyman or from a magistrate, identifying the individual as being the party who is named in the application for admission, and a declaration that the party has no means sufficient to support him in a private asylum, and then there is a medical certificate of a physician certifying to the fact that the individual is insane.

2702. Of what physician?—It is immaterial. Generally a physician who has been called in, and who certifies from his own personal observation that the party is insane. That is brought before the board, and if they find that the circumstances are satisfactory, they order his admission. Unfortunately in Ireland, and it is a great mistake, we have not the same organisation with regard to the admission of pauper-patients that you have here in England, where I believe the rule is, that as soon as the physician living in the parish is made aware that there is a lunatic in it, he intimates as much to the relieving officer of the parish, or to the overseer in his absence, and then it becomes the duty of the relieving officer or overseer to intimate such to one of the magistrates, and the magistrate then takes action and has the party, if he deems fit, removed to an asylum. Now we have not the same machinery in Ireland, and the consequence is, that very often in urgent cases of insanity, if a case is presented to the resident physician, and *primâ facie*, seeing the individual who is brought, he is satisfied that the party is really insane, he is received by the physician, and the admission of the party is recognised by the board at its next meeting, that is the second mode of admission. Then there is a third mode of admission, which is the mode by which Irish asylums are principally filled, and it is this: that if a person commits, or is supposed to commit, some trivial offence, the relatives of the party go before a magistrate, and say, that this individual has shown symptoms of insanity, and that he may be violent, or that he infringed upon the law. He is then taken before a magistrate and committed to the asylum as a dangerous lunatic, and there is no subterfuge from the order of the two magistrates signing the certificate and directing admission into an asylum. The result of which is very unsatisfactory. I have constantly spoken of it, and I hope it will ultimately be rectified. The proper chargeability of the individual is not given. A person comes up from the county of Waterford, for example, to Dublin, where he commits some trivial offence, perhaps the moment he arrives in the city, being insane, is consigned at once to the Richmond Metropolitan Asylum, and so long as he remains there he is charged to the locality in which he had been taken up. That is, to the city of Dublin, were he to remain in the asylum 20 years. A lunatic from the county of Limerick goes into the county of Carlow under like circumstances; becoming chargeable to the county of Carlow. We have no law of settlement in Ireland. So far then, as the admission of lunatics into district asylums through magistrates is concerned, it is highly unsatisfactory.

2703. Can the magistrates give that order without a medical certificate?—They go through the form of having a medical certificate, and they have the power of summoning a physician to certify to the fact of the man being insane, but in the case of a stranger it is a very unsatisfactory certificate, a medical man being called to see a person for the first time, and certifying that A, B, or C is insane, without any previous knowledge of the individual or his antecedents.

2704. In fact you have three certificates for pauper lunatics?—Three modes of admission. It is the same certificate. The physician's certificate does not differ.

2705. You have three modes of admission, one by a single medical man's certificate alone?—That is presented to the board, the other is where a single medical man signs a certificate of insanity, and the patient is brought before the physician of the asylum, who, on his own authority, admits him, subject to the approval of the board at its next meeting. The third is where two magistrates sign the admission of a patient into the asylum, and that is mandatory under the Act.

2706. You appear to think neither of those satisfactory, except the first?—I think the first is the most satisfactory. There are urgent cases. The best proof I can give you of the fact is this: that I was looking over and preparing within the last fortnight the report for Parliament, and I find that the number of lunatics admitted in the ordinary or legitimate way through the board was only 197; the number admitted by resident physicians, about 798, and the number sent in by magistrates, 1,239.

2707. Do you think that under any of those forms of admission there is danger of a sane man being sent in into an asylum?—I think that very often magistrates do not exercise proper discretion, and that they send in patients that they ought not. They may be insane, but they fix them in an asylum as dangerous lunatics, when *bonâ fide* they are not dangerous lunatics, when they are simply mentally affected.

2708. What mode have you of getting patients who have recovered out of these pauper asylums?—As soon as they are recovered the cases are brought before the board, and the board order their discharge.

2709. Who brings it before the board?—The resident physician, or he writes to the inspectors, or when the inspectors are seeing the asylum, if there are patients in it whom they think fit to be discharged, they order their removal.

2733. When a patient is taken to an asylum, as you say, sometimes merely by a magistrate's order, under a certificate granted——?—He is not brought to a private asylum.

2734. Going back for a moment to the other, if a patient is detained in an asylum by a magistrate's order, after a cursory inspection by a physician, which you appear to consider unsatisfactory, how soon after that must the manager of that asylum send in a statement to the board?—As soon as the resident medical superintendent is satisfied in his own mind of the fact. We have in Ireland what does not exist in England; we have invariably attached to public asylums a visiting physician. The visiting physician is the tie, as it were, between the public and the lunatic asylums. The visiting physician goes daily; he is obliged to see every patient who is convalescent, and he sees every patient immediately on his arrival. So then there are two parties, there is the resident physician and the visiting physician, who acts as a consultant on each case, and the history of the patient is taken down, and the resident physician and the visiting physician have the management of the patient, and when they think that he is not insane, or if they think, in the first instance, there were no grounds for his admission, they notify that generally, after a fair period of probation, giving the man a full month to remain in the asylum before they decide on it.

2744. Do you know what the proportion of cures in private and public asylums is?—The proportions of cures in private asylums is, I think, greater than in public asylums; but that is very easily explained.

Overcrowding of Asylums.

2745. Will you explain it?—The reason that they are more numerous in private asylums is this, that as soon as a private patient becomes insane, the family of the patient naturally sends him away, thus taking the earliest opportunity of isolating him from causes that probably produced the insanity, and of placing him under wholesome control; whereas public asylums are

Appendix C — Lancey.

so much overcrowded in many instances as not to afford admission, and thus the disease often lurks for months, without any action being taken, so that frequently patients go into them labouring under a sort of chronic insanity.

2746. You would say the causes are early treatment and special treatment?—Decidedly. Practice is much stronger than theory. I can give you a case in point. Our Parliamentary Report is not published, but within the last fortnight I was looking over the statistics, and I found that of the number of recovered lunatics, 970, who were sent out of public institutions last year, 579 of them were patients who had been treated within three months after the attack of insanity.

2760. I think you said that there were 18,100 lunatics in Ireland?—Yes, fully.

2761. Does that number include all, pauper as well as private lunatics?—That includes all pauper lunatics; the number of lunatics in Ireland immediately under supervision is, we will say in round numbers, 8,100, in public lunatic asylums, there are 3,200 in poorhouses of all denominations mentally affected. There are 166 in the criminal asylum at Dundrum, and there are about 680 in private asylums. All those together make about 12,200. Independent of the above, we have obtained in Ireland what does not exist in England or elsewhere, a return of every idiot, imbecile, and epileptic, it is made out annually on the 31st of December. The police in Ireland are a very well-organised body, and on that date they return us the name, residence, as well as age, religion, and birthplace of every reputed idiot in their different localities, and being taken on the same occasion the same parties cannot be counted twice. It is the number of idiots, epileptics, and imbecile of every kind who are at large, that is who are not under our direct supervision. It shows the accuracy of those returns, for during the last five years there is not a variation of 400 individuals on the whole, so that we have now arrived at the fact beyond contradiction, that for about three or four successive years 18,400 may be considered at the very outside as the normal number of the mentally affected.

2762. That number includes idiots and epileptics?—Every person mentally affected, a very extraordinary fact connected with the benefits arising from lunatic treatment in Ireland, and the benefit from the poorhouses also harbouring the insane, is, that of the large number of idiots now in poorhouses, there are not more than 93 under 14 years of age, while between 14 years of age and advanced life there are 1,694, which shows the diminution of idiotcy, probably owing to the fact of wandering idiots and lunatics being sent to poorhouses in the present generation much more than they were in former times.

2763. Taking the whole 18,000, do you, as a rule, regard them as curable or incurable?—One of the reasons why the curability in pauper asylums is so much less than in public asylums is that the public asylums are filled, four-fifths of them even in this country, with chronic, hopeless, demented cases, so that there is only one-fifth of the inhabitants of public asylums who afford a chance of recovery. It is quite the reverse in private asylums where curable cases are admitted early, and where necessarily there must be a much larger number sent out cured.

2764. Do your reports contain a record of the number of recoveries?—Yes, invariably.

2765. Are there any accessible reports or statistics that would show the number resident in each house and the proportion of recoveries discharged?—Yes.

2766. Every one?—Yes.

2767. And deaths?—Yes.

2768. Have you any means of comparing the result of treatment in workhouses with the result of treatment in asylums?—No, I do not think there is, in fact, there is no treatment in poorhouses, because they have not the facilities; it would not be a fair analogy to say that the result of treatment in a poorhouse would be as good and as successful as the result of treatment in asylums where you have all the appliances which are unknown in a poorhouse. It would not be a fair analogy to contrast the patient's recovery in a poorhouse, where there are no proper facilities for treatment of early cases or curable cases, with that which obtains in an asylum where you have every facility for good treatment, air, exercise, occupation, large grounds, and due classification, which you have not in a poorhouse.

2769. Are the patients who are in poorhouses under your supervision in the same way?—Yes; but we have not the same control.

2770. In what respect?—The inspectors have the whole control and management of asylums in Ireland, and have very large authority in the management of these institutions, while the Local Government Board has the control of the poorhouses, and therefore it is a different class of people. Destitution is the test of admission into a poorhouse, and the test of admission into an asylum is want of means to support the individual in a private asylum. They are a higher class, if we can use that term, in the asylums.

2771. I understand you to say that a considerable number of pauper patients are lodged in asylums?—Yes; a considerable number of insane poor. The law draws a distinction between poor, insane poor, and paupers, the meaning of the expression insane poor, or, at least, the general acceptation of it, is an individual who has not means when affected by lunacy to seek treatment in a private asylum where he would have to pay, and it is for that class, and also for abject paupers that the asylums are built.

2772. Then the insane poor are virtually paupers?—Every one of them is a pauper so far as not having means is concerned.

2773. You have not the power of ordering the removal of an insane pauper from the workhouse to an asylum?—If I went to a poorhouse and saw a pauper in a poorhouse, and I thought he was fit to be admitted into an asylum, I have the authority directly to order the admission.

2774. Do you exercise that power frequently?—Frequently. I do not order it. I write to beg that the person be admitted, and he is admitted. I do not dictate it; I seek permission under the power of the order.

2775. You possess the power although you do not usually exercise it in that form?—No.

2797. With regard to the statistics you gave us the forty idiots under fourteen years of age, you do not ascribe all that beneficial effect to the mere treatment, do you?—No; it is hard to explain it, but there is the point.

2798. Is it not always explained in this way: you collect the idiots, you put them under workhouse restraint, and they do not multiply?—Yes, but remember these are congenital idiots. The natural inference is this, that if in a population, say of 1,000 idiots, you take them under fourteen years, and you find in the last fourteen years the number of idiots will be, say fifty, and that in the preceding fourteen years there were 300, there must be some reason to account for the difference of the number, and that, I, to a certain extent, believe to be owing to this, that those idiots are sent early into workhouses, and that the propagation of the disease is checked.

2799. They do not reproduce themselves; they do not produce offspring?—Precisely. I have known cases in Ireland of five and six members of a family, either idiotic or malformed.

2800. Mr. *Leighton*.—The system of boarding out idiots does not exist in Ireland at all, does it?—No.

2801. Are the 3,000 insane poor who are in workhouses kept in separate wards of their own?—Generally speaking they are, but as those 3,000 include epileptics and imbeciles, many of them run through the house and are usefully occupied in the poorhouse. I do not mean to say they are insane, but they are more or less mentally affected.

2802. Are there some in all the workhouses?—I think we have 163 workhouses in Ireland. In the

North Dublin Union there is the largest number, I think about 140, and in the South Dublin Union 120. Then there are some unions that go down by gradation, in which there are only perhaps two or three

2803. Do you ever send lunatics to a workhouse who do not belong to the union?—No, they would not be received

2804 You talk of the pauper asylums being overcrowded; do you mean that more are put into the asylum than the asylums accomodate, or do you mean that the asylums are built for too many?—No, the Derry Asylum, for example, was built for 140 patients, and there are 140 in it; that is what I mean by the overcrowding of asylums

2805. What is the largest number in any asylum?—One thousand and fifty; that is the Richmond Asylum

2806. What is the smallest cost of keeping a patient in a private house in Ireland?—It varies, there is an asylum called the Lucan Spa Asylum near Dublin, which is partially a Government asylum, and it is immediately under the inspectors. They bought a very large house, and the man who conducted it sought permission to make it a private asylum We allowed him to do it, and he receives patients at from £40 to £50 a year. Then in Swift's Hospital, to which I before referred, lunatics are admitted on the foundation paying £50 a year.

2087. That is charitable?—It is charitable.

2088. What is the cost in the pauper asylums?—It varies, I think the average cost would be about £24 or £25 a year.

2089. I mean in the workhouse?—I think the average cost of a pauper in a workhouse is somewhere about £9 The lunatics and the insane in workhouses are better fed, and probably their expense would be about £12.

2810. Do you consider that the system of having the lunatics in workhouses works well in Ireland?—No, I think a genuine lunatic, I am not now talking of imbeciles, but a lunatic, a person deprived of reason, and coming under the proper category of a lunatic, should be, as far as possible, treated differently from the ordinary insane that are in workhouses; I think they should be as much as possible segregated from the rest of those charitable institutions.

2811. Do you think the system of putting those selected cases in the workhouse works well in Ireland?—I am not favorable to it, we have not accommodation in the district asylums of Ireland to receive all the lunatics, therefore we are forced to send them and to keep many of them in poorhouses.

2818. I suppose the pauper patients are discharged by the Board of Governors in the same way that they are by the committees of visitors in England?—Precisely.

2819. Has the visiting physician any weight with the visitors in influencing the discharge or the detention of the patients?—When a patient is about to be discharged by the Board the system adopted is this: The report of the mental condition is signed by both the resident and the visiting physician. It is a joint certificate, you have two certificates of admission and two certificates of discharge.

2826 What class of attendants have you in asylums in Ireland?—I think the class of attendants we have in the asylums in Ireland is very good indeed. They are very well conducted, and are a very moral body. They are not, I think, so well educated as those that I saw in English asylums; but still, I think, they are a very homely, benevolent, kindly race, and being generally selected from the same class as the patients, they have a friendly feeling towards them

2827. You are alluding now to public asylums?—Yes.

2839. Are the pauper patients in public asylums in Ireland fully employed?—Very fairly; there is this distinction in which we have the advantage over England; there are very few trades in Ireland, and nearly all the patients are of the agricultural class, so that they have an opportunity of being employed upon the grounds, and they have the natural agreeability of working on land to which they have been accustomed; some of them will work and some of them will not, but they are never forced to anything.

2840 Do not you think compulsory employment would be an advantage to them?—I do not think it would, as it would irritate them, I consider the great judicious treatment of the insane to be air, exercise, occupation, fair amusement, and dietary; I rely on that as the essence of the treatment

2841. If they are kept indoors, or merely allowed to take exercise in yards as in a prison, you would not consider that a good thing?—No; I would have them as much as possible in the open air, and the more violent the more I would put them in the open air.

2842. Is that the practice in Ireland?—Yes; I think we have a good deal of open air in Ireland, but in most of the old asylums they have very restricted courtyards and very restricted grounds; that is incidental to the locality, in some of them there are sixteen or eighteen acres of ground attached.

2843. Your principle, so far as you are able to carry it out, is to give employment in the open air?—Certainly, there are very few trades in Ireland, in England you have much more than in Ireland; we are all agricultural.

2844 Is lunacy on the increase in Ireland?—No, the reason I gave for saying that was that when I have taken out the Statistical Returns for Ireland during the last four or five years, which are given with accuracy, I do not find a variation of a half or a quarter per cent. There is only a difference between this year and last year in Ireland of about 84 on the returns of the 18,000

2845. Are the statistics more carefully collected in Ireland than they were a few years ago?—I think the last 14 years we have got into that habit

2846. That would be the date of the improved supervision?—I think the supervision has been pretty uniformly the same.

2847. Do you use the police in the matter of Lunacy in Ireland in giving information? No, except in the case of the escape of a lunatic. Last year, of the 10,000 that were in Ireland, there were only four effectual escapes.

2848. Do the police report cases of detention of lunatics among poor people in a bad state in their own houses?—No, never. One of the great errors of the lunatic institutions of Ireland is this, I will take the county of Cork for example: under the Act for conveying dangerous lunatics they are always conveyed by the police, because as soon as a lunatic is pronounced dangerous, and two magistrates sign a certificate for his admission into an asylum, he is handed over to the police. I have known instances, not one instance but an everyday occurrence, of female patients being brought, to give an extreme case, from the most remote end of the county of Cork to the Cork asylum; that would be a distance of 120 miles. Fancy a female being brought up as a dangerous lunatic all that way by two policemen, the loss of time to the police, the vast expense, and the impropriety of the conveyance, not but that the police are the most respectable and well-conducted class that possibly can be, still it is an impropriety that a female should be carried that distance by the police to the lunatic asylum.

2861. Do you think that chronic incurable cases of insanity which are not dangerous could, without harm to the insane person, and with benefit to the taxpayer, be removed from the lunatic asylum to the workhouse, due precaution being taken to afford ample care and attention to the person so removed?—Yes The session before last, Sir Michael Hicks Beach brought in an Act of Parliament, and in that Act was a clause to the effect that, to obviate the overcrowding of asylums and to allow a larger vacancy for early and acute cases, and to prevent the necessity of building or adding costly additions to asylums, he proposed that boards of governors of asylums might apply to boards of guardians of poorhouses to admit these demented, quiet, and harmless cases from asylums to poorhouses, but it should be done with the sanction, on the one hand, of the Local Government Board, and the sanction, on the other hand, of the inspectors of lunatic asylums. Consequently, that was undertaken, and the inspectors of lunatic asylums having, of course, one object in view, that is the proper treatment of the lunatics so transferred, made it a *sine qua non* with the board of guardians that, before they sent any person out, they should enter into an agreement that the individual so transferred from the asylum to the poorhouse should be equally well fed, equally well apparelled, and as carefully looked after in the poorhouse as he had been in the asylum.

2862 You approve of that system?—I approve of that system so far as this, it is no great loss to the utterly demented, provided their creature comforts are as well looked after in the poorhouse as they are in the asylum. It is a small but very imperceptible gain to the ratepayers of the district, I will show you how immediately, but still it is a saving in this respect, that it obviates the necessity of making additions to the asylums, and it gives immediate facility of admission to urgent cases The proportion, I have calculated, is 6 per cent. That is the outside proportion of those who would be fit to be sent from asylums to poorhouses.

2863. You think about 6 per cent. would be the idiots, imbeciles, and harmless cases which might be sent?—Yes; 480 or 500 out of the 8,000 in lunatic asylums, might be sent to poorhouses. We make it a *sine qua non* with the Board, whether few or large, that they should be as well treated in the poorhouses as they were before. The Local Government Board object to this; it considers that the interference of the inspectors in that respect would be making the poorhouses auxiliary asylums.

2864. Has any advantage been taken of that?—I do not think there have been 60 sent. The Local Government Board has arrived at the conclusion that by so doing it would interfere with the normal discipline of the poorhouses if lunatics were sent to it, and if there was any authority exercised over poorhouses that these people should be differently treated and have paid attendants to look after them in poorhouses, which is contrary to the rule, but that it would be beneficial there is no question whatever under certain circumstances.

2882. I think the question of placing idiots in Ireland on the same footing by a rate in aid as in Scotland hardly comes within the order of reference?—I should not have referred to it, except that some Irish Members of Parliament desired that I should, inasmuch as in Scotland the idiots who are in poorhouses have the benefit of the rate in aid, and some of my friends, Members of Parliament, were speaking to me upon the subject, and were anxious that it should be adverted to.

2883. It would not benefit the idiots themselves in any way, I presume?—I think it would benefit the idiots themselves, certainly.

2884 You think they would get better treatment?—The maintenance of a pauper in a poorhouse in Ireland, a simple pauper, you may put down at about £9 a year. The maintenance of the sick, and I include amongst the sick, a certain class of the imbeciles and idiotic, may be about £12 a year; so there is a little more expense. If they get a rate in aid it is a very nice question; I think it is a moral question whether they ought to get it; but if one country gets it I do not see why another should not. The rate in aid is equivalent to £10 8s. a year, 4s a week. If a lunatic has that rate in aid in addition to a half or a third more, he must necessarily be better treated, and if he has that rate in aid he at once comes under the jurisdiction of the inspectors of lunatic asylums, because he is then recognised as part and parcel of the legitimate lunatic population of the country, that is, under the supervision of the inspectors of lunatics. At present we have merely the power of visiting poorhouses; we are bound to visit the poorhouses, and all we can do is to express our opinion whether they are kindly and properly treated, and to recommend certain improvements if there is a necessity; but we have no power to alter their dietary. We have no power to have paid attendance on them, whereas if they got a rate in aid that rate would be a *quid pro quo*, and we could demand a better treatment.

2885. If they got a rate in aid, would they be likely to send them to an asylum from the poorhouse?—No, they would be less likely to send them. The fact is, the poorhouse people would be making money by the transaction, for whilst they are in the poorhouse not receiving a rate in aid they cost £12. If they got the £10 8s. from the Government the poorhouse would be the gainer by the difference, that is to say, they would support their paupers as idiots for £1 10s. on the rates of the county.

2886. The question is whether it would be better to send these paupers, imbeciles, to the asylum?—I think myself that the legitimate place for all the mentally afflicted should be in localities solely and simply for themselves. I do not think it is a wise organization, or disorganization rather, to have lunatics mixed up with paupers in poorhouses, it interferes with the discipline of the institutions. They are under a different law, different management, and in the end it would be found cheaper, I think, to make large establishments in their districts for the reception of chronic, helpless, and demented cases, where they can be carefully looked after, maintained at a much less price, with a smaller number of attendants, and all they require is open air exercise and the common domestic comforts suited to their class; whereas the uncurable cases and the violent cases that require constant supervision as hopeless, many of them being very dangerous, require, of course, incessant watching.

2887. The question is, whether this rate in aid would induce the authorities of the poorhouses to send patients of the character you describe to the asylums?—Yes, they cannot send them to the asylums, as I mentioned before, except they are actually dangerous, because the asylum authorities have the power of refusing them.

2888 I suppose that the payments they offer now would not tempt the asylum authorities?—It is an encouragement to do it, as I mentioned yesterday. The maintenance of a lunatic in a regular institution of the insane, I am speaking now of district asylums, taking one with another, would be about £24 a year, of which £10 8s. is paid by the Treasury, leaving £13 10s. to be paid by the local rates

2889. If they got a rate in aid, they would be able to pay that more easily, would they not?—Yes.

2890. Or more, if it were desirable?—Yes.

No. 18.—Supplementary Statement to Dr. Lalor's Evidence

I will feel obliged if I am permitted to place in the hands of the Commissioners the following memoranda, in order to make clearer my views in general, but especially on the subjects referred to in queries 1942–1943, 1944, 1945, 1946, 1947, 1948, 1949, 1950, 1951, 1952, 1953, 1954, 1960, and also to afford me an opportunity of dealing with one or two parts of the subject matter of the Commissioners' inquiry, which appear to me of considerable importance, but to which I have referred, if at all, only very cursorily in my answers or reports to the Commissioners.—

First of all, I would ask them to refer to the returns and observations which I placed before them on the 17th of April last, in reply to their 4th subject of inquiry, viz., "Intermediate Asylums." In stating in those observations that a very large proportion of class A forms the most useful and industrious portion of our population, and that if they are to be removed, an increase in the paid staff will, in my mind, be necessary, I wish it to be understood that what I meant was that an increase of paid staff might be necessary if the whole of this class were removed. I think, however, that an increase of staff might be avoided if only the fully ascertained incurable and unimprovable of this class were removed, leaving in this asylum those who could not be classed as unimprovable, the fact in either case to be tested, as I shall state further on.

In remarking, also, in those observations that I trusted that none of the incurable may be removed to a smaller or less improving amount of occupation than that under which they have been placed, and without which they will be sure to deteriorate, I did not, by any means, intend to object to their removal to asylums of the general nature of Leavesden and Caterham. Such asylums might, I think, be provided chiefly, both as regards structural arrangements and those for care and maintenance, by the appropriation of some workhouses to their exclusive use, but not, in my opinion, by placing them in such numbers as 50 or 60 in workhouses in which other classes of poor would continue to be kept. In connexion with the whole question I am in favour of having all the insane poor, of all forms of insanity, who are to be supported indoors at the public expense placed in two different classes of institutions—all under one central authority. These two classes of institutions are, first, asylums for curable and improvable cases—incurable and unimprovable cases, but requiring special care, as set forth in the sub-heads of class B in return furnished April 17—uncured and unimproved, but not three years in house, and who should not therefore be stamped as incurable and unimprovable. Secondly, asylums for incurable and unimprovable cases, but quiet, harmless, and not requiring special care from any cause.

I consider that so many as are requisite of the present District Lunatic Asylums should be appropriated as asylums of the first class, and that idiots and imbeciles of all ages requiring special care, and susceptible of improvement by skilled treatment, who are not at present in asylums, should be drafted into the first class of institution, and that moral treatment by skilled educational and industrial training should be carried out in all asylums of this class. The necessary buildings and grounds for the second class of asylums might, I think, be cheaply and speedily provided almost entirely by giving up workhouses that might be diverted from their original purpose, with the addition, perhaps, in some cases, of more land.

My view is, as I have endeavoured to express it, that the insane maintained (at the public expense) as such should be kept only in two classes of institutions, such as I have indicated, and if it is assumed that there is a third or intermediate class of insane, not requiring to be dealt with as insane, but simply as paupers, I have not given that consideration to the question which would enable me to offer a competent opinion on it.

I submit tables as follows, giving the numbers approximately estimated for this and the other asylums in Ireland fit for each class of institution.

To be retained in Richmond Asylum as cases of first class:—

	Male.	Female.	Total.
Curable and improvable,	109	212	321
Incurable, but requiring special care,	156	40	196
Uncured and unimproved, but not three years in House,	45	24	69
Total,	338	324	662

To be removed to Asylums of 2nd Class uncured and unimproved, and more than three years under treatment, and, therefore, in my opinion, fit to be removed to an Asylum of 2nd Class.

Males, 148. Females, 231. Total, 379.

	Male.	Female.	Total.
Cases to be retained in this Asylum as an Institution of 1st Class for curable and improvable cases, and those requiring special care,	338	324	662
Quiet and harmless and not requiring special care, but uncured and over three years under treatment, and, therefore, considered fit to be removed to an Asylum for incurable and unimprovable cases,	146	231	379
Total,	484	555	1,038
Present accommodation of Richmond Asylum,	595	595	1,190
Deduct cases to be retained in Asylum,	338	324	662
Vacancies for curable and improvable cases that would then exist,	257	271	528
Add increased accommodation by conversion of single rooms and corridors into large rooms, &c.,	50	50	100
Total spare accommodation,	307	321	628

	Male.	Female.	Total.
Total number of Patients in District Lunatic Asylums of Ireland on 31st December, 1877,	4,393	3,790	8,183
Number in Richmond District Lunatic Asylum,	463	575	1,038
Total number of patients in District Lunatic Asylums of Ireland, exclusive of Richmond, on 31st December, 1877,	3,930	3,215	7,145

	Male.	Female.	Total.
Probable number of Patients to be retained in District Lunatic Asylums of Ireland (exclusive of Richmond) as Institutions for curable and improvable cases, and those requiring special care,	–	–	4,545
Probable number of Patients uncured and unimproved, and over three years under treatment in same Asylums and therefore considered fit to be removed to Asylums for incurable and unimprovable cases,	–	–	2,600
	–	–	7,145

	Male.	Female.	Total.
Present accommodation of all District Lunatic Asylums in Ireland, exclusive of Richmond,	3,755	3,321	7,076
Deduct cases to be retained in Asylums,	–	–	4,545
Vacancies that would then exist for Asylums of first class,	–	–	2,531
Add increased accommodation by conversion of single rooms and corridors into large rooms &c.,	–	–	1,500
Vacancies that would then exist for cases suitable for Asylums of first class,	–	–	4,031

If by the arrangements I propose, 4,031 vacancies, can be made available for curable and improvable cases, and for those requiring special care at present in district asylums, and for idiots, imbeciles, and cases of other forms of insanity, either at large or in workhouses, who have admitted claims to have some effort made for their improvement, the question arises, are there a sufficient number of those classes to fill this large number of vacancies, and if not, what is to be done with the surplus?

As to the first of these questions, my estimate of the number of cases, suitable to be retained in the District Asylums of Ireland as Institutions of the first class being 5,207, and the total accommodation available by the arrangements I propose would be 9,763, leaving 4,556 first class vacancies, and it is probable that adding together cases at present in asylums and those at large requiring to be treated in first class asylums, would fill this number of vacancies. But if there should be a balance of vacancies, I would appropriate some of the District Lunatic Asylums as second class asylums for incurable and unimprovable cases. I would leave it to the central authority to select the asylums so to be appropriated, and the same authority should, in my mind, have the selection of the workhouses to be similarly appropriated. Infact, one of the main advantages of having one central authority, and one of the strongest arguments in its favour, is the necessity of such an authority for the purpose of deciding, first, how many, and what asylums should be allocated as first class institutions, and if any remain not required as such, then to select those to serve as second class asylums, to determine the requisite number of workhouses, required to supply the deficit, and to arrange all details as to both classes of asylums.

Assuming what, I believe, must be expected, viz: that there will always be insane poor at large, some of an acute, some of a temporary, and some of a chronic nature, I think it is obvious that some skilled means should be locally provided for advising and carrying out the requirements suited to their cases. I think it should not be left to voluntary interference, or that of what may be called natural friends, to see that this advice is obtained and proper steps suitable in each case taken; but, that the relieving officer and police should have the right and the duty to interfere on the part of the public in such cases. For a large proportion of the cases, the nearest dispensary officer would be quite sufficient, and his services should be put in requisition, as in England, in the case of pauper lunatics at large.

In addition, I would have the services of the medical officers of asylums also made available for the poor, as I have seen done at the asylum of St. Anne's, in Paris, where a dispensary is held daily, at fixed hours, and advice and medicines administered by the medical officers, to all persons of the district showing symptoms of insanity, who are brought to the district asylum.

In connexion with young idiots and imbeciles, I think there are many cases for whose education and training provision might be made in schools—for waifs and strays, including such as are suitable for industrial and reformatory institutions—but who cannot be dealt with as boarders, either from the great expense involved from the expense of the boarding system or from the objections of their parents or natural guardians. Many young idiots and imbeciles might in such schools obtain education and training, not perhaps equal to that in institutions where they thus would be boarded altogether, but, having this advantage, that would be met in the best practicable manner, the requirements of many who would otherwise never get education or training of any sort. To such young idiots and imbeciles, a meal in the middle of the day might be given at the public expense, if their natural guardians would not provide it. The London School Board and some charitable societies, in London and elsewhere, have carried out such a system for classes cognate to young persons affected with idiocy and imbecility, not of an aggravated form, and this class might, I think, be educated and trained in such schools with a result advantageous on the whole to society.

JOSEPH LALOR.

DUBLIN: Printed by ALEXANDER THOM, 87 & 88 Abbey-street,
Printer to the Queen's Most Excellent Majesty.
For Her Majesty's Stationery Office.

www.ingramcontent.com/pod-product-compliance
Lightning Source LLC
Chambersburg PA
CBHW051745300426
44115CB00007B/696
* 9 7 8 3 7 4 1 1 0 4 5 0 3 *